D1383777

Contents

Preface

With *Classical Vocal Music In Print: 1995 Supplement*, Musicdata has endeavored to provide an up-to-date reference of vocal music published since 1985. The present volume includes those classical vocal listings contained in the 1986 Music-In-Print Annual Supplement plus works published since that time. The Classical Vocal 1995 Supplement updates the base volume published in 1976 and the 1985 supplement. These three volumes provide the user with the most complete listings of the in-print vocal music published throughout the world.

The three classical vocal Music-In-Print volumes are designed to meet the needs of vocal artists in search of music for use in recital, religious services, and concert stage performances. Even though "classical" appears in the title, it should be understood that all stylistic periods of music have been included. Folk songs and folk song collections have been included because of their frequent demand in recital programming. The only type of vocal music that has been excluded is that which is commonly called popular music; however, we have begun to include some popular American standards because of a growing interest in the "cross-over" repertoire.

In the process of producing this catalog, we have been confronted with problems of uniformity and consistency. For example, there may be different translations of the same title which appear to be separate works. Where possible, we have listed such works under the original title or an accepted English version of the title. Listing operatic arias has been another problematic area. Some publishers' catalogs list these works by the title of the recitative that precedes the aria, others by the aria title, and still others by the name of the opera. We have tried to list the works either by the title of the aria or by the operatic source followed by the aria title.

For the first time ever in a classical vocal catalog, we are presenting an arranger index providing access to arranged or edited music. Since the distinction that publishers make between composers and arrangers is often ill-defined, the arranger index allows the user to search for a work by arranger as well as by composer. Because the computer programs that create the arranger index were not available before 1987, we have also included in the present volume separate arranger indexes for the 1985 supplement as well as the 1976 base volume.

Music publishers have actively participated in the preparation of this volume by submitting catalogs marked with their new listings published since the appearance of the 1985 classical vocal supplement. Our work is very dependent on the cooperation of music publishers and we wish to offer our thanks to those publishers who have generously assisted us by providing accurate, up-to-date listings.

A volume such as this cannot be produced without the help and encouragement of a team of workers. Thanks to Kathe Jacoby and Joseph Pluciennik for computer help; special thanks to Noah Simon and Susan H. Simon for editorial assistance and encouragement during long hours of coding. And thanks again to Mark Resnick whose computer expertise and tireless efforts continue to make the Music-In-Print series a reality.

Philadelphia, Pennsylvania
October 1994

F. Mark Daugherty

Guide to Use

THE MUSIC-IN-PRINT SERIES

The Music-In-Print series is an ongoing effort to locate and catalog all music in print throughout the world. The intention is to cover all areas of music as rapidly as resources permit, as well as to provide a mechanism for keeping the information up to date.

Since 1973, Musicdata, Inc. has solicited catalogs and listings from music publishers throughout the world. Using the information supplied by co-operating publishers, the series lists specific editions which are available from a publisher either for sale or on a rental basis in appropriate categories. The volumes in the series are basically organized by the primary performing force, instrument or instrumental family, such as Sacred Choral Music, Organ Music or String Music.

It is often difficult to define the boundaries between the various broad areas of music covered by the volumes in the series. The definition of sacred and secular choral music varies from publisher to publisher; some major choral works are no longer listed in Orchestral Music, reflecting changing editorial practice; some solo vocal music is in Orchestral Music; etc. The user is advised to consult the preface to individual volumes for greater definition of scope. Use of more than one volume may well be necessary to locate an edition or all editions of a work.

Editorial policy is to include as much information as the publisher supplies, within the limits of practicality. An important goal of the series is to try to bring together different editions of a composition under a single title.

VOLUME FORMAT

The volumes of the Music-In-Print series have two basic formats: unified or structured. Reference to the editor's preface and the table of contents will assist in determining how a given volume is organized.

The unified volumes (e.g., Organ Music, Orchestral Music) are arranged in a single alphabetical interfiling of composers' names, titles of works and cross references. The title under a composer's name serves as the focus for major information on each composition. In the absence of a composer, the title in the main alphabet becomes the focal point for this information.

The structured volumes (e.g., String Music) are arranged by an imposed framework: instrumentation, time period, type of work or other categorization. Within each section, entries are alphabetized by composer name or, in the absence of a composer, by title. Entries will be repeated in all appropriate sections. A structured volume also contains a Composer/Title Index and, in some cases, other specialized indexes. The Composer/Title Index is a single alphabetical list of composers' names, composition titles and cross references, with a reference to the section(s) of the volume in which complete edition information will be found. The running heads on each page of the catalog enable the user to quickly find the proper section.

ENTRY TYPES

Two basic types of entries appear in the Music-In-Print series: normal and collection. A normal entry describes a single piece of music. A collection consists of any two or more associated pieces.

NORMAL ENTRY CONTENT

In order to bring together all different editions of a composition under a uniform and/or structured title, many musical form titles are translated into English (so, Konzert becomes Concerto, Fantaisie becomes Fantasy, etc.).

For each title there are two types of information: a) generic information about the composition and b) specific information pertaining to the editions which are in print. Included in the generic information category are the uniform title of the composition, a structured title for the work (e.g., Concerto No. 2 In D Minor; Cantata No. 140), a thematic catalog number or opus and number designation, the larger source from which the work was taken, and remarks.

Following the generic information about the piece is the information about the individual editions. This information includes the arranger, the published title of the edition if different from the uniform title, the language of the text (for vocal works), instrumentation required for performance, the duration of the work in minutes (') and seconds ("), a difficulty rating assigned to the edition by the publisher or editor, the format of the publication, publisher, publisher's number, and price or rental information concerning the edition.

Following is an example of a typical entry under a composer:

MOZART, WOLFGANG AMADEUS (1756-1791)
   Nozze Di Figaro, Le: Overture
      [4']
      2.2.2.2. 2.2.0.0. timp,strings
     sc,parts RICORDI-IT rental   (M1)
     "Marriage of Figaro, The: Overture"
     sc,parts BREITKOPF-W f.s.   (M2)

In this entry under the composer, Wolfgang Amadeus Mozart, the title of an excerpt, "Overture", follows the original title of the complete work, "Nozze Di Figaro, Le". It is scored for 2 flutes, 2 oboes, 2 clarinets, 2 bassoons, 2 horns, 2 trumpets, timpani and strings. Duration is approximately 4 minutes. The code RICORDI-IT indicates the publisher of the first listed edition; score and parts are offered by this publisher on rental. The sequence number (M1) marks the end of the information on this edition. The English title "Marriage Of Figaro, The: Overture" is given for the next edition which is published by BREITKOPF-W; score and parts for this edition are for sale.

The full names and addresses of all publishers or U.S. agents are given in the publisher list which follows the list of editions at the end of the book.

Following is an example of an entry with a structured title:

MOZART, WOLFGANG AMADEUS (1756-1791)
   Symphony No. 25, [excerpt]
    (Gordon, Philip) 2.1.2.1.al-
    sax. ten-sax. 2.2.1.1.timp,perc,
    strings [3'] (Menuetto, [arr.])
    PRESSER sets $7.50, and up, sc
    $1.50   (M3)

Here a structured title "Symphony No. 25," requires a different form of listing. The excerpt, "Menuetto", has been arranged by Philip Gordon for 2 flutes, oboe, 2 clarinets, bassoon, alto saxophone, tenor saxophone, 2 horns, 2 trumpets, trombone, tuba, timpani, percussion and strings. Du-

ration is three minutes. The publisher, PRESSER, offers sets of parts priced at $7.50 and up. A separate score is available for $1.50.

INSTRUMENTATION

Instrumentation is given in the customary order. When a work is scored for full orchestra, the number of wind players required is indicated by two groups of numbers—four for woodwinds (flute, oboe, clarinet, bassoon) and four for brass (horn, trumpet, trombone, tuba). Other instruments are listed by name, or abbreviated name. A number placed before a named instrument indicates the number of players. A slash is used for alternate instrumentation.

The common auxiliary wind instruments are not mentioned by most publishers. For example, 2.2.3.3. for woodwinds indicates the work is scored for two flutes, but it *may* include a piccolo part which can be played by one of the flutists. Similarly, it is possible that parts for English horn, bass clarinet and contrabassoon are provided but no additional players will be required. If the publisher does specify the auxiliary instruments required, this information is given either in parentheses (the number of players is not affected) or after a plus sign (an additional player is needed).

Example:

   2(pic).2 + opt ob.3(opt bass-clar).2 + contrabsn.
   4.2.3.0 + opt tuba.timp,2-3perc,harp,cel / pno,
   strings

This example is scored for 2 flutes and piccolo (played by one of the flutists), 2 oboes plus an optional third oboe, 3 clarinets (one may play the optional bass clarinet part), 2 bassoons plus contrabassoon (additional player required), 4 horns, 2 trumpets, 3 trombones, optional tuba, timpani, percussion (2 or 3 players), harp, celeste or piano, and strings.

The term "orch" may be substituted for a detailed listing if the publisher has not provided the instrumentation for orchestral works.

Solo instrumental parts are listed following the complete orchestration of a work.

Choral parts are given as a list of voices (e.g., SATB, TTBB, etc.). The term "cor" (and similar terms) may be substituted when the publisher has not listed the specific voices.

Solo vocal parts are given as a list of voices followed by the term "solo" or "soli." The term "solo voice(s)" is used when the publisher does not specify the voice(s). (No attempt has been made to give equivalents for scale ranges listed by publishers.)

REMARKS

The remarks are a series of codes or abbreviations giving information on the seasonal or other usage of the piece, the type of music, and the national origin and century for folk or anonymous pieces. (These codes also make it possible to retrieve, from the data base developed for the Music-In-Print series, specialized listings of music for particular seasons, types, etc.) Following this Guide to Use will be found a complete List of Abbreviations.

PRICES

Only U.S. dollar prices are given, and we can give no assurance of their accuracy. They are best used for making rough comparisons. The publishers should be consulted directly for current prices.

SEQUENCE NUMBERS

An alphanumeric number, appearing on the right margin, has been assigned to each edition represented in this catalog. These are for the purpose of easing identification and location of specific entries.

COLLECTION ENTRY CONTENT

An attempt has been made to provide the user with access to pieces contained within collections, while still keeping the work within reasonable bounds of time and space. Accordingly, the following practices have been adopted:

If the members of a collection are published separately, they are listed individually, regardless of the number of pieces involved. If the collection is only published as a whole, the members are listed only if they do not exceed six in number. For larger collections, a code is given indicating the number of pieces and whether or not the contents are listed in the publisher's catalog. For example,

CC18L indicates a collection of 18 pieces which are *listed* in the publisher's catalog
CC101U indicates a collection of 101 pieces which are *unlisted* in the publisher's catalog
CCU indicates a collection of an unknown number of pieces

Whenever the members are listed, they are also cross-referenced to the collection. For example, consider the following entry:

FIVE VOLUNTARIES, [ARR.]
    (Davies, Peter Maxwell) 3.3.2.1, 3.3.0.0.
    timp,perc,strings,cont sc,parts
    SCHOTT 10994 f.s.
    contains: Attaignant, Pierre,
        Magnificat; Clarke, Jeremiah,
        King William's March; Clarke,
        Jeremiah, Serenade; Couperin,
        Louis, Sarabande; Croft, William,
        March Tune   (F1)

Published by Schott, edition number 10994, this collection edited by Peter Maxwell Davies contains five members, which are not published separately. Under each of the members there is a cross reference saying 'see FIVE VOLUNTARIES, [ARR.]'.

Collection entries also contain many of the elements of information found in normal entries. For example, the entry shown above contains arranger, instrumentation, format of publication, publisher and publisher number.

Collections of several pieces published as a whole, but having no overall title, create another problem. In this case the complete publication information is given under the composer or title of the first piece listed, together with the comment 'contains also,' followed by titles of the other collection members.

CROSS REFERENCES

In order to provide the user with as many points of access as possible, the Music-In-Print series has been heavily cross referenced. In the unified volumes, the cross references are interfiled with the composers' names and the titles. In the structured volumes, cross references only appear in the Composer/Title Index.

Works may be located by title, with or without knowing the name of the composer. Using the first example by Mozart above, this composition may be located under either its Italian or English title in the main alphabet, as well as under the composer.

To make this possible the following cross references would exist in the main alphabet:

NOZZE DI FIGARO, LE: OVERTURE
    see Mozart, Wolfgang Amadeus

and

MARRIAGE OF FIGARO, THE: OVERTURE see
    Mozart, Wolfgang Amadeus, Nozze Di
    Figaro, Le: Overture

and in addition, the following cross reference would be found under the composer's name:

Marriage of Figaro, The: Overture
    *see Nozze Di Figaro, Le: Overture

Cross references are employed also to assist in the search for works frequently identified by popular names or subtitles, such as the "Surprise" Symphony of Haydn and the "Jupiter" Symphony of Mozart.

Numerous cross references have been made from unused and variant forms of composer names to assist the user in finding the form of name chosen for the series.

COLLECTION CROSS REFERENCES

Whenever the members of a collection are listed, they are cross referenced to the collection. In unified volumes, these are interfiled with composers' names and titles. In structured volumes, these cross references only occur in the Composer/Title Index.

Using the above example, FIVE VOLUNTARIES, [ARR.], there is a cross reference under each of the composers saying 'see FIVE VOLUNTARIES, [Arr.]'. (If a collection member lacks a composer, the cross reference will occur at the title.)

When collections are also published separately, the cross references in both directions read 'see also'. If the members are only published separately (i.e., the collection were not published as a whole) then the cross reference under the collection would read 'see' and under the members, 'see from'. Thus, 'see' and 'see also' direct the user to information concerning publication, while 'see from' provides access to the collection of which a given publication is a part.

With untitled collections, which are listed under the first composer and/or title, the cross reference 'see' under each of the other collection members directs the user to the full entry under the first member, at which point complete edition information will be found.

COMPOSER/TITLE INDEX

The Composer/Title Index is a single alphabetical listing of composer names, composition titles and cross references. This index is used to identify the location of a specific entry in a structured volume.

The actual reference is usually under the composer name, and only under a title when a work is not attributable to a person. The reference is to the chapter and/or section of the volume which contains the entry for the music sought.

For example, in String Music, IV.1 refers the user to Chapter IV, Section 1: String Quartets. Similarly, VIII refers to Chapter VIII: Music for Eight Instruments. Reference to the table of contents and the head of each page of the volume will assist the user in finding the appropriate section containing the information sought.

ARRANGER INDEX

The Arranger Index lists in alphabetical order all arrangers and editors cited in a specific volume. The arranger's or editor's name is listed in all capital letters. In the case of multiple arrangers, the arranger names appear together, separated by semi-colons. The listing under each arranger name gives the composer and title of each arranged (edited) work, in alphabetical order. If a work has no composer, it is listed by title. In the case of uniform and translated titles, the uniform titles are the ones appearing in the index.

This arrangement allows the user to look up any desired arranger or editor and then scan for the composers and titles of desired works. Once the composer and title have been determined, the work may then be looked up in the catalog itself to obtain complete bibliographic and ordering information.

MASTER INDEX

The Music-In-Print Master Index provides a single place to look in order to locate any composer or title listed in the Music-In-Print series. The Master Index eliminates all problems of knowing whether a specific piece of music is listed in a base volume, supplementary volumes, or not at all.

The Master Composer Index lists all composers found within the Music-In-Print series. Under each composer's name is a complete alphabetical listing of the titles of works by that composer to be found in the series. Next to each title is a number or series of numbers referring the user to the volume or volumes containing the specific piece. A key explaining these numbers and the volumes to which they correspond is to be found on the reverse side of the title page. Once the user has located the correct volume, it is easy to find the specific piece in the volume's alphabetical sequence. In the case of structured volumes, reference should be made to the Composer/Title Index in each volume.

The Master Title Index lists in a single alphabetical listing all titles of works within the Music-In-Print series. Each title is followed by a reference number or series of numbers, directing the user to the volume or volumes containing the specific title as explained above.

Additionally, as more supplementary volumes are added to the Music-In-Print series, certain volumes may update the Master Index in a specific area from time to time, through the publication of a specialized Master Index. In this way, the user can easily locate a piece of music within the volumes dealing with a specific area.

List of Abbreviations

The following is a general list of abbreviations developed for the Music-In-Print series. Therefore, all of the abbreviations do not necessarily occur in the present volume. Also, it should be noted that terms spelled out in full in the catalog, e.g. woodwinds, tuba, Easter, Passover, folk, Swiss, do not appear in this list.

A	alto
acap	a cappella
accomp	accompaniment
acord	accordion
Adv	Advent
Afr	African
Agnus	Agnus Dei
al-clar	alto clarinet
al-fl	alto flute
al-sax	alto saxophone
Allelu	Alleluia
AmInd	American Indian
ampl	amplified
Anh.	Anhang (supplement)
anti	antiphonal
app	appendix, appendices
arr.	arranged
Asc	Ascension
ASD	All Saints' Day
aud	audience
Austral	Australian
B	bass
Bald	Baldwin organ
Bar	baritone
bar horn	baritone horn
bar-sax	baritone saxophone
bass-clar	bass clarinet
bass-fl	bass flute
bass-sax	bass saxophone
bass-trom	bass trombone
bass-trp	bass trumpet
bds	boards
Belg	Belgian
Benton	thematic catalog of the works of Ignace Pleyel by Rita Benton
Bibl	Biblical
bk	book
Boh	Bohemian
boy cor	boys' chorus
Braz	Brazilian
Bryan	thematic catalog of the symphonies of Johann Wanhal by Paul Bryan
bsn	bassoon
BVM	Blessed Virgin Mary
BWV	Bach-Werke-Verzeichnis; thematic catalog of the works of J.S. Bach by Wolfgang Schmieder
BuxWV	Buxtehude-Werke-Verzeichnis; thematic catalog of the works of Dietrich Buxtehude by G. Kärstadt (Wiesbaden, 1974)

C&W	Country & Western
C.Landon	numbering of the keyboard sonatas of Joseph Haydn by Christa Landon
camb	cambiata
Can	Canadian
cant	cantata
Carib	Caribbean
CC	collection
CCU	collection, unlisted
CCUL	collection, partially listed
cel	celesta
Cen Am	Central American
cent	century
cf.	compare
Chin	Chinese
chord	chord organ
Circum	Circumcision
clar	clarinet
cloth	clothbound
cmplt ed	complete edition
Cnfrm	Confirmation
Commun	Communion
cong	congregation
Conn	Conn organ
cont	continuo
contrabsn	contrabassoon
copy	ed produced to order by a copy process
cor	chorus
cor pts	choral parts
cor-resp	choral response
Corpus	Corpus Christi
cradle	cradle song
cym	cymbals
D.	thematic catalog of the works of Franz Schubert by Otto Erich Deutsch
Dan	Danish
db	double bass
db-tuba	double-bass tuba
dbl cor	double chorus
Ded	Dedication
degr.	degree, 1-9 (difficulty), assigned by editor
desc	descant
diag	diagram(s)
diff	difficult

Dounias	thematic catalog of the violin concertos of Giuseppe Tartini by Minous Dounias
Doxol	Doxology
ea.	each
ECY	End of Church Year
ed	edition
educ	educational material
elec	electric
Ember	Ember Days
Eng	English
enl	enlarged
Epiph	Epiphany
eq voices	equal voices
Eur	European
evang	evangelistic
Eve	Evening
F.	thematic catalog of the instrumental works of Antonio Vivaldi by Antonio Fanna
f(f)	following
f.s.	for sale
fac ed	facsimile edition
facsim	facsimile(s)
Fest	festivals
film	music from film score
Finn	Finnish
fl	flute
Fr	French
Gd.Fri.	Good Friday
Ge.	thematic catalog of the works of Luigi Boccherini by Yves Gerard
Gen	general
Ger	German
Giegling	thematic catalog of the works of Giuseppe Torelli by Franz Giegling
girl cor	girls' chorus
glock	glockenspiel
gr. I-V	grades I-V, assigned by publisher
Greg	Gregorian chant
gtr	guitar
Gulbransen	Gulbransen organ

Hamm	Hammond organ
Harv	Harvest
Heb	Hebrew
Helm	thematic catalog of the works of C.P.E. Bach by Eugene Helm
Hill	thematic catalog of the works of F.L. Gassmann by George Hill
Hob.	thematic catalog of the works of Joseph Haydn by Anthony van Hoboken
Holywk	Holy Week
horn	French horn
hpsd	harpsichord
Hung	Hungarian
HWC	Healey Willan Catalogue
ill	illustrated, illustrations
Ind	Indian
inst	instruments
intro	introduction
ipa	instrumental parts available
ipr	instrumental parts for rent
Ir	Irish
Isr	Israeli
It	Italian
J-C	thematic catalog of the works of G.B. Sammartini by Newell Jenkins and Bathia Churgin
Jap	Japanese
Jew	Jewish
jr cor	junior chorus
Jubil	Jubilate Deo
K.	thematic catalog of the works of W.A. Mozart by Ludwig, Ritter von Köchel; thematic catalog of the works of J.J. Fux by the same author
Kaul	thematic catalog of the instrumental works of F.A. Rosetti by Oskar Kaul
kbd	keyboard
Kirkpatrick	thematic catalog of the sonatas of Domenico Scarlatti by Ralph Kirkpatrick
Kor	Korean
Krebs	thematic catalog of the works of Karl Ditters von Dittersdorf by Karl Krebs

L	listed
Landon	numbering of the keyboard trios of Joseph Haydn by H.C.R. Landon
Lat	Latin
liturg	liturgical
Longo	thematic catalog of the sonatas of Domenico Scarlatti by Alessandro Longo
Lowery	Lowery organ
Magnif	Magnificat
maj	major
man	manualiter; on the manuals alone
mand	mandolin
manuscript	manuscript (handwritten)
med	medium
mel	melody
men cor	mens' chorus
Mex	Mexican
Mez	mezzo-soprano
MIN	Musicdata Identification Number
min	minor
min sc	miniature score
mix cor	mixed chorus
Morav	Moravian
Morn	Morning
mot	motet
Neth	Netherlands
NJ	Name of Jesus
No.	number
Nor Am	North American
Norw	Norwegian
Nos.	numbers
Nunc	Nunc Dimittis
ob	oboe
oct	octavo
offer	offertory
Op.	Opus
Op. Posth.	Opus Posthumous
opt	optional, ad lib
ora	oratorio
orch	orchestra
org	organ
org man	organ, manuals only
orig	original
P., P.S.	thematic catalogs of the orchestral works of Antonio Vivaldi by Marc Pincherle
p(p)	page(s)
Palm	Palm Sunday
pap	paperbound

Paymer	thematic catalog of the works of G.B. Pergolesi by Marvin Paymer
pce, pcs	piece, pieces
Pent	Pentecost
perc	percussion
perf mat	performance material
perf sc	performance score
Perger	thematic catalog of the instrumental works of Michael Haydn by Lothar Perger
pic	piccolo
pic-trp	piccolo trumpet
pipe	pipe organ
pno	piano
pno-cond sc	piano-conducting score
pno red	piano reduction
Pol	Polish
Polynes	Polynesian
pop	popular
Port	Portuguese
pos	position
PreClass	Pre-Classical
pref	preface
Proces	processional
Psntd	Passiontide
pt, pts	part, parts
quar	quartet
quin	quintet
Quinqua	Quinquagesima
rec	recorder
Reces	recessional
Refm	Reformation
rent	for rent
repr	reprint
Req	Requiem
rev	revised, revision
Royal	royal occasion
Rum	Rumanian
Russ	Russian
RV	Ryom-Verzeichnis; thematic catalog of the works of Antonio Vivaldi by Peter Ryom
S	soprano
s.p.	separately published
Sab	Sabbath
sac	sacred
sax	saxophone
sc	score
Scot	Scottish
sec	secular

Septua	Septuagesima	trom	trombone	Wolf	thematic catalog of the symphonies of Johann Stamitz by Eugene Wolf
Sexa	Sexagesima	trp	trumpet		
show	music from musical show score	TV	music from television score	wom cor	womens' chorus
		TWV	Telemann-Werke-Verzeichnis; thematic catalog of the works of G.P. Telemann by Mencke and Ruhncke	WoO.	work without opus number; used in thematic catalogs of the works of Beethoven by Kinsky and Halm and of the works of J.N. Hummel by Dieter Zimmerscheid
So Am	South American				
sop-clar	soprano clarinet				
sop-sax	soprano saxophone				
Span	Spanish				
speak cor	speaking chorus				
spir	spiritual	U	unlisted	Wq.	thematic catalog of the works of C.P.E. Bach by Alfred Wotquenne
sr cor	senior chorus	UL	partially listed		
study sc	study score	unis	unison		
suppl	supplement	US	United States		
Swed	Swedish			Wurlitzer	Wurlitzer organ
SWV	Schütz-Werke-Verzeichnis; thematic catalog of the works of Heinrich Schütz by W. Bittinger (Kassel, 1960)			WV	Wagenseil-Verzeichnis; thematic catalog of the works of G.C. Wagenseil by Helga Scholz-Michelitsch
		vcl	violoncello		
		vibra	vibraphone		
		vla	viola		
T	tenor	vln	violin		
tamb	tambourine	voc pt	vocal part		
temp blks	temple blocks	voc sc	vocal score		
ten-sax	tenor saxophone	VOCG	Robert de Visée, Oeuvres Completes pour Guitare edited by Robert Strizich	Xmas	Christmas
Thanks	Thanksgiving			xylo	xylophone
Thomas	Thomas organ	vol(s)	volume(s)		
TI	Tárrega Index; thematic catalog of the Preludes, Studies, and Exercises of Francisco Tárrega by Mijndert Jape				
timp	timpani	Whitsun	Whitsuntide	Z.	thematic catalog of the works of Henry Purcell by Franklin Zimmerman
transl	translation	WO	without opus number; used in thematic catalog of the works of Muzio Clementi by Alan Tyson		
treb	treble				
Trin	Trinity				

A

A ARNARHOLNUM see Björnsson, Arni

A BAENUM STENDUR STULKAN VORD see Björnsson, Arni

A BIRKA-ISKOLA see Nieland, Henk

Å BRØR see Kjeldaas, Arnljot

A CAPPELLA see Ortiz, William

A CASSANDRE see Bunge, Sas

'A CHITARRA E 'O MANDULINO
med solo,pno CLASSV 1293 (A1)

A CHLORIS see Hahn, Reynaldo

A CORDOBA see Bedmar, Luis

A ESA CUMBRE see Beethoven, Ludwig van

A FRANGESA! see Costa

A GIACOMO LEOPARDI see Mascagni, Pietro

Å, GUD VELSIGNE see Kjeldaas, Arnljot

A HELENE see Bunge, Sas

Å KRIST, SOM I BRYLLAUP GJESTA see Nystedt, Knut

A KUTYA-TAR see Nieland, Henk

A LA COMPLAINTE D'AUTOMNE see Tsujii, Eisei

A LA ESPERANZA see Beethoven, Ludwig van

Å LA-LA DEG, TIRILILL see Albertsen, Per Hjort

A LA NINA see Ansink, Caroline

A LA TOURTERELLE see Bunge, Sas

Å NEI, FOR EN HIMMEL see Groven, Eivind

Å SÅ RØDBLOND see Groven, Eivind

A SEVILLA see Blanco, E.

A SOLO see Molino, Francesco

"A" STRUMMINGS see Reiner, Karel

'A SURRENTINA see Curtis, Ernesto de

A UNE DAME CRÉOLE see Aliprandi, Paul
see Regt, Hendrik de

Å, VAR EG HEIME ATT see Nystedt, Knut

A VENUS see Koumans, Rudolf

A VUCCHELLA see Tosti, Francesco Paolo

AA DEN SVALANDE VIND see Groven, Eivind

AA, KJAERE MI SIGRI see Groven, Eivind

AAGAARD-NILSEN, TORSTEIN (1964-)
Eg Er Din Ven
[Norw] SBar soli,fl,ob,trp,pno [8']
NORGE (A2)

Jacobsen Sanger
[Norw] B solo,trp in C [16'] (text
by Rolf Jacobsen) NORGE (A3)

Svart Lys
A solo,rec,vln,pno [6'] NORGE (A4)

AAN HET ROER see Broekman, Hans

AASOV AEDDAN see Groven, Eivind

ABATE, ROCCO
Nacht
SMez soli EDI-PAN EP 7223 (A5)

ABBASSA GLI OCCHI see Tosti, Francesco Paolo

ABBOTT, ALAIN (1938-)
Folie Et Mort D'Ophélie *cant
SBar soli,2.2.2.2. 2.2.2.0. perc,
timp,harp,strings [23'] (text by
Shakespeare) BILLAUDOT (A6)

ABDUCTION FROM THE SERAGLIO: ACH, ICH LIEBTE see Mozart, Wolfgang Amadeus

ABDUCTION FROM THE SERAGLIO: MARTEN ALLER ARTEN see Mozart, Wolfgang Amadeus

ABE, KOMEI (1911-)
Ogawa No Yugure
S/T solo,pno [4'] ONGAKU (A7)

ABENCERAGES: SUSPENDEZ À CES MURS see Cherubini, Luigi

ABEND see Franken, Wim see Norby, Erik

ABEND SCHWÜL, DER see Bois, Rob du

ABENDDÄMMERUNG see Roos, Robert de

ABENDEMFINDUNG see Mozart, Wolfgang Amadeus

ABENDFRIEDEN see Louis Ferdinand, Prince Of Prussia

ABENDGLOCKE see Zimmermann, Bernd Alois

ABENDLIED see Mendelssohn-Bartholdy, Felix see Norby, Erik see Schumann, Robert (Alexander)

ABENDS-SCHWÄRMEREY see Fischer, A.

ABENDSTÄNDCHEN see Louis Ferdinand, Prince Of Prussia

ABENDSTERN see Karg-Elert, Sigfrid

ABER ICH KÖNNT' VERDORBEN WERD'N see Hopp, Julius

ÅBERG, THOMAS (1952-)
Klockklang: Julsång
[Swed] solo voice,pno/org NOTERIA (A8)

ABFAHRT IN DÄMMERNDER STILLE see Selen, Reinhold

ABIDE WITH ME
(Rayner, Josephine) solo voice,pno
(easy) FENTONE (A9)

ABIKO, YOSHIRO (1951-)
Ai To Shi From The Tale Of Genji
SBar soli,clar,marimba [12'] JAPAN (A10)

ABOUT LOVE see Sommerfeldt, Öistein

ABRIL, A. GARCÍA
see GARCIA-ABRIL, ANTON

ABSCHIED see Thoroddsen, Emil

ABSCHIED DER SCHWALBEN see Kücken, Friedrich Wilhelm

ABSCHIED VON DI BERG, DER see Baumann, Alexander

ABSCHIEDSLIED DER ZUGVÖGEL see Mendelssohn-Bartholdy, Felix

ABSENCE see Bizet, Georges

ABSENT, L' see Gounod, Charles François

ABT, FRANZ (1819-1885)
Abt-Album: Ausgewählte Lieder
solo voice,pno CLASSV C008 (A11)

Children's Songs, 25
solo voice,pno CLASSV C007 (A12)

Jugend-Album Für Gesang, Op.475
solo voice,pno CLASSV C006 (A13)

Komm, Ruh An Meinem Herzen Aus
see Vier Lieder, Op. 216, Heft 1

Tritt Mein Liebchen In Dem Garten
see Vier Lieder, Op. 216, Heft 1

Über Den Sternen Ist Ruh
A solo,pno SCIEN 104 (A14)

Vier Lieder, Op. 216, Heft 1
S/T solo,pno SCIEN 105 f.s.
contains: Komm, Ruh An Meinem
Herzen Aus; Tritt Mein Liebchen
In Dem Garten (A15)

ABT-ALBUM: AUSGEWÄHLTE LIEDER see Abt, Franz

ACCENT see Bartholomée, Pierre

ACH AUS EINES ENGELS FÜHLUNG FALLE see Voortman, Roland

ACH HERR, STRAFE, MICH NICHT IN DEINEM ZORN see Meder, Johann Valentin

ACH, ICH FÜHL'S see Lyric Soprano Arias: A Master Class With Evelyn Lear, Vol. 1 see Clementi, Aldo

ACH, NENÍ see Dvorák, Antonín

ACH! SO FROMM see Flotow, Friedrich von, Martha: M'Appari Tutt' Amor

ACH WER BRINGT DIE SCHONEN TAGE see Luening, Otto

ACH WIE IST'S MÖGLICH, DASS ICH DICH LASSEN KANN
A/B solo,pno SCIEN 1755 (A16)

ACH, WIE SEHNLICH WART ICH DER ZEIT see Bach, Johann Michael

ACHALM see Bose, Hans-Jurgen Von

ACHIME see Matsumura, Teizo

ACHT ENGELMAN-LIEDEREN see Tal, Marjo

ACHT FRAGMENTE AUS BRIEFEN VON VINCENT VAN GOGH see Hummel, Bertold

ACHT GESÄNGE, OP. 5 see Zemlinsky, Alexander von

ACHT LIEBESLIEDER, OP. 83 see Dvorák, Antonín

ACHT LIEDER, OP. 57 see Sibelius, Jean

ACHT LIEDER, OP. 61 see Sibelius, Jean

ACHT LIEDER, OP. 81 see Reinecke, Carl

ACHT LIEDEREN see Borstlap, Dick

ACHT LIEDEREN see Weegenhuise, Johan

ACHT OUD HOLLANDSCHE LIEDEREN, DEEL 2 see Pijper, Willem

ACHT TIERLIEDER see Krietsch, Georg

ACIS AND GALATEA: O RUDDIER THAN THE CHERRY see Handel, George Frideric

ACK VÄRMELAND DU SKÖNA see Torstensson, Klas

ACQUAINTED WITH THE NIGHT see Gottlieb, Jack S.

AD ANNIE see Mariatti, Franco

AD BAENDAMINNI BIDJUM VER see Isolfsson, Pall

AD BAKI BLARRA HEIDA see Isolfsson, Pall

AD GANGA I DANS see Björnsson, Arni

AD SIDSUMRI see Halldorsson, Sigfus

ADAGIO SOSTENUTO see Bijvanck, Henk

ADAM, ADOLPHE-CHARLES (1803-1856)
Bravour Variationen Über Ein Thema
Von Mozart "Ah! Vous Dirai-Je,
Maman
(Westphal, Hartmut) solo voice,
orch,fl solo sc RIES (A17)

Chalet: Vallons De l'Helvétie
B solo,pno CLASSV 1546 (A18)

Postillon De Lonjumeau: Mes Amis,
Ecoutez L'histoire
T solo,pno CLASSV 0561 (A19)

ADAM LAY I-BOUNDEN see Hodkinson, Sydney P.

ADAMS, LESLIE (1932-)
Afro-American Songs *CCU
high solo/med solo,pno sc
AM.COMP.AL. $16.10 (A20)

Dunbar Songs *CCU
high solo/med solo,pno sc
AM.COMP.AL. $13.00 (A21)

Five Millay Songs
med solo,2.2.2.2. 2.0.0.0. timp,
perc,harp,strings [15']
AM.COMP.AL. (A22)

Love Memory
high solo,pno [3'] AM.COMP.AL. (A23)

Love Response
solo voice,pno [3'] AM.COMP.AL. (A24)

Wider View, The
high solo/med-high solo,pno [25']
AM.COMP.AL. (A25)

ADAMS, S. (1844-1913)
Holy City, The
med solo,pno CLASSV 1203 (A26)

Star Of Bethlehem
med solo/high solo,pno CLASSV 1179 (A27)

Thora
med solo/high solo,pno CLASSV 1213 (A28)

AIRS FROM THE SONG OF SONGS see
Isolfsson, Pall

AKAKI KONOMI see Hayakawa, Kuzuko

AKATSUMEKUSA NO HANA see Nakamura,
Yukitake

AKENU YO NI see Matsudaira, Yori-Tsune

AKERWALL, MARTIN
In Memory
see Til Minde

Til Minde
"In Memory" Mez solo,pno [10']
SAMFUNDET   (A47)

AKIAKANE see Igarashi, Tadashi

AKK, MON MIN VEI TIL KANA'AN see Med
Jesus Vil Eg Fara see Bakke, Ruth

AKOND OF SWAT, THE see Kirkwood,
Antoinette

AKSEL SCHIOETZ ANTHOLOGY OF NORDIC SOLO
SONGS, THE see Torstensson, Klas

AKSEL SCHIOETZ ANTHOLOGY OF NORDIC SOLO
SONGS, THE, VOL. 2 see Almquist,
Carl Jonas Love, Hjärtats Blomma
see Bellman, Carl Michael, Fjäriln
Vingad Syns På Haga see Karkoff,
Maurice, Ar Om Aftonen Man Bryter
Upp, Det see Linde, Bo, För Alla
Vindar see Rangström, Ture, Enda
Stunden, Den see Söderman, [Johan]
August, Flyg Ej Undan see Söderman,
[Johan] August, Mitt Älskade Lilla
Sockerskrin

AL IN DE PLANTAGE see King, Harold C.

AL PRISIONERO see Ansink, Caroline

AL TIFG'I VI see Stern, Robert Lewis

AL TORRENTE see Schubert, Franz (Peter)

ALABIEV, ALEXANDER NICHOLAEVICH
(1787-1851)
Nachtigall
see Nightingale

Nightingale
"Nachtigall" [Ger] coloratura sop,
pno CLASSV 1712   (A48)
"Usignuolo, L'" [Eng/It] coloratura
sop,pno CLASSV 1046   (A49)

Usignuolo, L'
see Nightingale

ALANDIA, EDGAR (1950-   )
Tu Avrai Delle Stelle Come Nessuno Ha
S solo,fl,ob,clar,bsn,2vln,vla,vcl
EDI-PAN EP 7240   (A50)

ALBA see Maderna, Bruno

ALBA OCCITANA see Calmel, Roger

ALBA PROVENZALE see Annovazzi,
Napoleone

ALBA SEPÀRA DALLA LUCE L'OMBRA, L' see
Tosti, Francesco Paolo

ALBANESE, GUIDO
Dolce Viaggio
solo voice,pno DE SANTIS DS 915
                             (A51)
Zumpe Zumpitte!
solo voice,pno DE SANTIS DS 986
                             (A52)

ALBASIA see Lolini, Ruggero

ALBÉNIZ, ISAAC (1860-1909)
Quatre Mélodies
med-high solo,pno CLASSV 1416 (A53)

ALBERS, BRADLEY
Martial Cadenza
male solo,bsn,perc,electronic tape
[5'] sc AM.COMP.AL. $13.00 (A54)

ALBERT, EUGÈNE FRANCIS CHARLES D'
(1864-1932)
Sieben Lieder, Op. 28
[Ger] solo voice,pno RECITAL 335
                             (A55)

ALBERT, STEPHEN JOEL (1941-1992)
Flower Of The Mountain
S solo,orch/pno pno red SCHIRM.G
50480076   (A56)

Into Eclipse
T solo,chamber orch sc SCHIRM.G
50481145   (A57)

ALBERTSEN, PER HJORT (1919-   )
À La-La Deg, Tirilill
see Sanger, Op. 2

ALBERTSEN, PER HJORT (cont'd.)

Aeveomen
see Sanger, Op. 25

Åsaseter
see Sanger, Op. 2

Blomstertid Nu Kommer, Den
[Norw] solo voice,org LYCHE (A58)

Bøndene Kommer
see Sanger, Op. 25

Der Går En Sang
see Sanger, Op. 18

Dolsi Dalom
see Sanger, Op. 36

Halling
see Sanger, Op. 18

Har Du Sett'n Øivind
see Sanger, Op. 36

Hjärtat
see Sanger, Op. 18

Høstnatt Ved Fjorden
see Sanger, Op. 18

I Såmmårhåggån
see Sanger, Op. 36

Kjelle, Kjelle Gjeta
see Sanger, Op. 36

Langt Uppi Viumdala
see Sanger, Op. 2

På Blussuvollen
see Sanger, Op. 2

Pastorale Fra Sommermesse
[Norw] Mez solo,fl,org NORK (A59)

Pling Og Pjort *duet
LYCHE 386   (A60)

Rotregla
see Sanger, Op. 36

Sanger, Op. 2
[Norw] solo voice,pno NORGE f.s.
contains: À La-La Deg, Tirilill;
Åsaseter; Langt Uppi Viumdala;
På Blussuvollen; Stev   (A61)

Sanger, Op. 18
[Norw] solo voice,pno NORGE f.s.
contains: Der Går En Sang;
Halling; Hjärtat; Høstnatt Ved
Fjorden; Syng   (A62)

Sanger, Op. 25
[Norw] solo voice,pno NORGE f.s.
contains: Aeveomen; Bøndene
Kommer; Tonen; Vårt Fedreland;
Vårvise   (A63)

Sanger, Op. 36
[Norw] solo voice,pno NORGE f.s.
contains: Dolsi Dalom; Har Du
Sett'n Øivind; I Såmmårhåggån;
Kjelle, Kjelle Gjeta; Rotregla
                             (A64)

Stev
see Sanger, Op. 2

Syng
see Sanger, Op. 18

Tonen
see Sanger, Op. 25

Vårt Fedreland
see Sanger, Op. 25

Vårvise
see Sanger, Op. 25

ALBORADA see Schubert, Franz (Peter)

ALBRECHT GOES-LIEDER see Lothar, Mark

ALBUM DE CANCONS see Sancho Marraco

ALBUM OF SONGS see Cadman, Charles
Wakefield

ALBUM OF SONGS (VOL. 1) see Chaminade,
Cécile

ALBUM OF WEDDING SONGS
("World's Favorite Series") ASHLEY
016-6   (A65)

ALBUM VERSE see Grieg, Edvard Hagerup,
Stambogsrim

ALBUM, VOL. 1 see Hirota, Ryutaro

ALBUM, VOL. 2 see Hirota, Ryutaro

ALBUM, VOL. 3 see Hirota, Ryutaro

ALCESTE: AH! MALGRÉ MOI see Gluck,
Christoph Willibald, Ritter von

ALCESTE: DIVINITÉS DU STYX see Gluck,
Christoph Willibald, Ritter von

ALCHEMISTENSPIEGEL see Einem, Gottfried
von

ALCINA: VERDI PRATI see Handel, George
Frideric

ALCYONS, LES see Massenet, Jules

ALDREI SKAL EG GLEYMA THER see
Halldorsson, Skuli

ALEKO: ALEKO'S CAVATINA see
Rachmaninoff, Sergey Vassilievich

ALEKO: ROMANCE OF THE YOUNG GYPSY see
Rachmaninoff, Sergey Vassilievich

ALELUIA see Mozart, Wolfgang Amadeus

ALEMAN, EDUARDO A.
Suenos Grises
solo voice,clar,vln,vcl,pno SEESAW
                             (A66)

ALEPH see Manoury, Philippe

ÅLESUND, OUR OWN TOWN see Knutsen,
Torbjorn, Ålesund Vår Egen By

ÅLESUND VÅR EGEN BY see Knutsen,
Torbjorn

ALF HAMBE-VISER see Åm, Magnar

ALFADIR RAEDUR see Kaldalóns, Sigvaldi
S.

ALFAMAERIN see Runolfsson, Karl Otto

ALFANO, FRANCO (1876-1954)
Risurrezione: Piangi, Si, Piangi
T solo,pno CLASSV 0925   (A67)

ALFVÉN, HUGO (1872-1960)
Saa Tag Mit Hjerte
(Gustafson, Stig) solo voice,band
GEHRMANS 6879   (A68)

Sju Dikter *Op.28
solo voice,pno LUNDQUIST 0356 (A69)

ALGRA, JOH. (1894-1973)
Ave Maria
Mez/Bar solo ZENGERINK R.383 (A70)

ALICE, A CABARET see Barab, Seymour

ALICE AT THE END see Reise, Jay

ALINDER, HAKAN (1941-   )
Bed När Mörkret Tätnar
see Två Sånger

Jag Vill Tacka Dig, O Herre
see Två Sånger

Två Sånger
solo voice,org NOTERIA 1849 f.s.
contains: Bed När Mörkret Tätnar;
Jag Vill Tacka Dig, O Herre
                             (A71)

ALIPRANDI, PAUL (1925-   )
A Une Dame Créole
S solo,2.1.2.1. 2.2.2.1. perc,harp,
pno,strings [2'] (text by
Beaudelaire) sc,pts,pno red
BILLAUDOT   (A72)

Réversibilité
S solo,2.1.2.1. 2.2.2.0. perc,harp,
strings [4'40"] (text by
Beaudelaire) sc,pts,pno red
BILLAUDOT   (A73)

ALKEMA, HENK (1944-   )
Ten Zen Songs *song cycle
med solo,pno [12'] DONEMUS   (A74)

ALL DEN STJÄRNSÅDD see Rooth, Anna-
Greta

ALL-LEBEN see Bijvanck, Henk

ALL LIVSENS LJOSGLANS SLOKNA BRATT see
Nystedt, Knut

ALL MY LIFE see Garlick, Antony

ALL NIGHT see Zahler, Noel Barry

ALL POISON THE SONG see Borodin,
Alexander Porfirievich

ALL THE FLOWERS OF THE SPRING see
Loevendie, Theo

ALL THE WORLD see Schiller, Benjie
Ellen, V'ye-Etayu

ALL THINGS PASS BY see Rachmaninoff, Sergey Vassilievich

ALL THROUGH THE NIGHT see Anonymous see Anonymous, Ar Hyd Y Nos

ALL WE NEED see Rovics, Howard

ALLA CACCIA see Vivaldi, Antonio

ALLAH see Chadwick, George Whitefield

ALLE BIRKEN GRÜNEN IN MOOR UND HEID see Giltay, Berend

ALLE JAHRE WIEDER... *CCU,Xmas
(Rist, G.; Zimbelius, L.) solo voice, gtr ZIMMER. 2624 f.s.   (A75)

ALLE MINE SKUTOR see Hol, Liv Solheim

ALLEEN see Broekman, Hans

ALLEGRO see Mesritz van Velthuysen, Anny

ALLEGRO, L': COME AND TRIP IT see Handel, George Frideric

ALLELUIA see Anderson, Beth see Mozart, Wolfgang Amadeus see Pasatieri, Thomas

ALLELUJAH see Bosco, Gilberto

ALLEN, JUDITH SHATIN
Night Blooms
S solo,pno [4'] sc AM.COMP.AL. $3.85   (A76)

Psalm No. 100
S/T solo,pno [5'] sc AM.COMP.AL. $2.35   (A77)

Wedding Song [1]
S solo,clar/English horn [5'] sc AM.COMP.AL. $2.35   (A78)

Wedding Song [2]
S solo,vla [5'] sc AM.COMP.AL. $1.95   (A79)

ALLERSEELEN see Strauss, Richard

ALLES ENDET see Wolf, Hugo

ALLES LICHT... see Cerha, Friedrich

ALLES ØYNE see Volle, Bjarne

ALLES ØYNE: 3 SONGS see Volle, Bjarne

ALLNÄCHTLICH IM TRAUME SEH ICH DICH see Mendelssohn-Bartholdy, Felix

ALLOR CH'IO DISSI: ADDIO see Handel, George Frideric

ALLTÄGLICHE, DAS see Bredemeyer, Reiner

ALMA REDEMPTORIS MATER see Biechteler, B. see Leuttner, Georg Christoph

ALMIGHTY, THE see Schubert, Franz (Peter)

ALMQUIST, CARL JONAS LOVE (1793-1866)
Hjärtats Blomma
(Josephson, J.A.) solo voice,pno EGTVED 432 f.s. from AKSEL SCHIOETZ ANTHOLOGY OF NORDIC SOLO SONGS, THE, VOL. 2   (A80)

ALNAES, EYVIND (1872-1932)
Sange, Vol. 1
[Swed] (contains op. 1, 11 & 17) RECITAL 336   (A81)

Sange, Vol. 2
[Swed] (contains op. 26 & 28) RECITAL 337   (A82)

Tre Sange, Op.26
[Norw/Ger] med solo,pno CLASSV 1396   (A83)

ALOEËTTE, VOGHEL CLEIN see Geraedts, Jaap

ALONE 2 see Haubenstock-Ramati, Roman

ALONG THE MOVING DARKNESS see Weigl, [Mrs.] Vally

ALONG THE WAY see Weigl, [Mrs.] Vally

ALONG WHAT HIGHWAYS see Bollen, Jan-Bas

ALONI, AMINADAV (1928-   )
Zeh Hayom
med solo,fl,kbd TRANSCON. 992020   (A84)

ALP MEETS HCE see Oakes, Rodney Harland

ALPENHORN, DAS see Proch, Heinrich

ALPENJÄGER, DER see Schubert, Franz (Peter)

ALRUNEN see Jensen, Ludwig Irgens

ALS ALLES STIL IS see Dekker, Dirk

ALS AUS AGYPTEN ISRAEL see Mozart, Wolfgang Amadeus

ALS DER GROSSVATER DIE GROSSMUTTER NAHM see Wustmann, Gustav

ALS UIT DEN HARTSTOCHT VAN HET AVONDROOD see Badings, Henk

ALSKANDES KLAGAN see Forsell, Jonas

ÄLSKANDES NATT, DE see Blomberg, Erik

ALTAR see Jensen, Ludwig Irgens see Volle, Bjarne

ALTDEUTSCHES BILD see Zimmermann, Bernd Alois

ALTDEUTSCHES FRÜHLINGSLIED see Mendelssohn-Bartholdy, Felix

ALTDEUTSCHES LIED see Mendelssohn-Bartholdy, Felix

ALTE HERD, DER see Keussler, Gerhard von

ALTE LIEBESLIEDER, BOOK IV see Hodkinson, Sydney P.

ALTE MEISTER DES DEUTSCHEN LIEDES (Moser) PETERS 3495   (A85)

ALTE PASSIONS- UND OSTERLIEDER AUS FÜNF JAHRHUNDERTEN *CCU
(Taubert, Karl Heinz) solo voice,kbd, opt mel inst RIES f.s.   (A86)

ALTENA, MAARTEN (1943-   )
Crossing The Water
see Three Songs

Night Dances, The
see Three Songs

Sheep In Fog
see Three Songs

Three Songs
high solo,alto fl,clar,perc,gtr, harp,vla,db DONEMUS f.s. [12'] contains: Crossing The Water; Night Dances, The; Sheep In Fog   (A87)

ALTERHAUG, BJORN (1945-   )
Seks Mutasjoner
Mez solo,S rec,A rec,T rec,org NORGE   (A88)

ALTHOUGH THE MOON see Roo, Paul de

ALTHYDUSÖNGLÖG see Einarsson, Sigfus

ALTKÖLNISCHER MEISTER see Zimmermann, Bernd Alois

ALTRA RISPOSTA see Kruse, Bjørn Howard

ALTRO È PARLAR DI MORTE see Tosti, Francesco Paolo

ALVAREZ
Partida, La: Sierras De Granada
[Span/Eng] low solo,pno CLASSV 1263   (A89)
[Span/Eng] high solo,pno CLASSV 1395   (A90)

ALVORLIGE SANGER see Dorumsgaard, Arne

ALWYN, WILLIAM (1905-   )
Invocations *song cycle
S solo,pno LENGNICK 4678   (A91)

Seascapes: Four Songs
S solo,rec/fl,pno FORSYTH   (A92)

ALYSSA see Ravel, Maurice

ÅM, MAGNAR (1952-   )
Älf Hambe-Viser
[Swed] solo voice,gtr,2vln,vla,vcl NORGE   (A93)

Effata
[Norw] STTBB soli,org NORGE   (A94)

Fjøra Som Vart Til Tusen Tonar
S solo,fl,clar,vln,vcl,pno,perc NORGE   (A95)

Fritt Fram
S solo,fl/alto fl,clar,vln,vcl,pno, perc [10'] NORGE   (A96)

Fuglane
[Norw] solo voice&opt solo voice [6'] NORGE   (A97)

ÅM, MAGNAR (cont'd.)

Songen Om Vesle Magni
[Norw] NORSK   (A98)

Vise
[Norw] solo voice,pno NORSK   (A99)

AM CHARFREITAG see Lachner, Franz

AM 1. MAI GEHN VATER UND MUTTER see Eisler, Hanns

AM FENSTER see Marx, Joseph

AM KANAL see Kölz, Ernst

AM UFER DES FLUSSES MANZANARES see Jensen, Adolf, Gesänge, Op. 21, No. 6

AMADIS: BOIS ÉPAIS see Lully, Jean-Baptiste (Lulli)

AMANT JALOUX, L': TANDIS QUE TOUT SOMMEILLE see Grétry, André Ernest Modeste

AMANTS TRAHIS, LES see Rameau, Jean-Philippe

AMARILLI, MIA BELLA see Caccini, Giulio

AMARYLLIS AT THE FOUNTAIN see Quilter, Roger

AMATO, BRUNO (1936-   )
Two Together
S solo,tuba SEESAW f.s.   (A100)

AMAVIT EUM: OFFERTORIUM see Sacchini, Antonio (Maria Gasparo Gioacchino)

AMBER BEAD, THE see Adolphe, Bruce

AMBER GLASS see Retzel, Frank

AME DES OISEAUX, L' see Massenet, Jules

ÂME ÉVAPORÉE, L' see Debussy, Claude, Romance

AMEN see Wallach, Joelle

AMERICA see Bernstein, Leonard

AMERICAN ARIAS FOR SOPRANO
S solo (CCU) SCHIRM.G 50481197 (A101)

AMERICAN ARTSONG ANTHOLOGY: VOL. 2 *CCU
high solo,pno,inst GALAXY 1.2901 f.s.   (A102)

AMERICAN DAYDREAMS see Kernis, Aaron Jay

AMERICAN FOLK SONGS FOR CHILDREN see Seeger

AMERICAN FOLK TALES AND SONGS *CC40U
(Chase, Richard) solo voice BELWIN BKD000014 $3.95   (A103)

AMERICAN NEGRO SPIRITUALS *CCU,spir
(Johnson; Johnson) solo voice DOVER BKDA 01694 $10.50   (A104)

AMERICAN SAMPLER, AN see Roosevelt, [Joseph] Willard

AMERICAN SPACE see Carl, Robert

AMERONGEN, JAN VAN (1938-   )
Arrow And The Song, The
see Thompson-Liederen

Child Musician, The
see Thompson-Liederen

Dark Night
B/Bar solo,2vln,vla,vcl [12'] DONEMUS   (A105)

Honda Trio
B/Bar solo,vln,vcl DONEMUS f.s. [14']
contains: Lotosblume, Die; Mondlicht; Stille Wasserrose, Die   (A106)

In The Mediterranean
see Thompson-Liederen

Lotosblume, Die
see Honda Trio

Mondlicht
see Honda Trio

My Soul Is Dark
see Thompson-Liederen

Stanzas For Music
see Thompson-Liederen

AMERONGEN, JAN VAN (cont'd.)

Stille Wasserrose, Die
see Honda Trio

Thompson-Liederen
B solo,pno DONEMUS f.s.
contains: Arrow And The Song,
The; Child Musician, The; In
The Mediterranean; My Soul Is
Dark; Stanzas For Music;
Travelling By Night   (A107)

Travelling By Night
see Thompson-Liederen

AMES, WILLIAM T. (1901-   )
No City
high solo,pno [5'] sc AM.COMP.AL.
$3.85   (A108)

Sanctus
ST soli,pno [8'] sc AM.COMP.AL.
$4.95   (A109)

Star Moss
high solo,pno [2'] sc AM.COMP.AL.
$3.85   (A110)

Twilight
med solo,pno [11'] sc AM.COMP.AL.
$1.60   (A111)

AMICA: SE TU AMASTI ME see Mascagni,
Pietro

AMICO FRITZ, L': NON ME RESTA see
Mascagni, Pietro

AMICO FRITZ, L': O AMORE, O BELLA LUCE
DEL CORE see Mascagni, Pietro

AMICO FRITZ, L': SON POCHI FIORI see
Mascagni, Pietro

AMMA KVAD see Halldorsson, Skuli

AMMA RAULAR I ROKKRINU see Kristinsson,
Sigursveinn D.

AMONG THY GREEN BRAES see Veeneman,
Curt

AMOR AL PRÓJIMO, EL see Beethoven,
Ludwig van

AMOR HAI VINTO see Vivaldi, Antonio

AMOR INCERT, L' see Turull, Xavier

AMOR NUEVO, VIDA NUEVA see Beethoven,
Ludwig van

AMOR OG ASNINN see Halldorsson, Sigfus

AMOR SIN DESCANSO see Schubert, Franz
(Peter)

AMOROSES, 12 CANCONS see Mestres,
Apeles

AMOUR, L' see Godard, Benjamin Louis
Paul

AMOUR! AMOUR! see Tosti, Francesco
Paolo

AMOUR DE MOI SY EST ENCLOSE, L' see
Anonymous

AMOUR ET LA MORT, L' see Theodorakis,
Mikis

AMOUR FATAL, L' see Paderewski, Ignace
Jan

AMOUR SANS AILES see Hahn, Reynaldo,
Love Without Wings

AMOURS DE HAFIZ, LES, OP. 38 see
Fairchild, Blair

AMOURS DE PIERRE DE RONSARD, LES see
Capdevielle, Pierre

AMRAM, DAVID WERNER (1930-   )
Trail Of Beauty, The
Mez solo,orch,ob solo voc sc PETERS
66704A   (A112)

AN ADELHEID see Krebs, Karl August

AN ANNA BLUME: SZENE FÜR SOPRAN, ALT
UND BARITON see Schidlowsky, Leon

AN BERTHA see Cornelius, Peter

AN DEN SCHLAF see Gerlach, Günter see
Schubert, Franz (Peter)

AN DIE EINSAMKEIT see Keussler, Gerhard
von

AN DIE ENTFERNTE see Mendelssohn-
Bartholdy, Felix

AN DIE FERNE GELIEBTE see Beethoven,
Ludwig van

AN DIE FREUNDE see Schubert, Franz
(Peter)

AN DIE LESERIN see Louis Ferdinand,
Prince Of Prussia

AN DIE MUSIK see Straesser, Joep see
Straesser, Joep

AN DIE NACHT see Bijvanck, Henk

AN DIE STERNE see Proch, Heinrich

AN EINEN HERBSTWALD see Marx, Joseph

AN FRAU MUSICA see Bodensohn, Ernst
Friedrich Wilhelm

AN MARIA see Bodensohn, Ernst Friedrich
Wilhelm

AN MEINE SEELE see Ebel, Arnold

AN MEINE ZITHER see Zumsteeg, Emilie

AN SCHWANGER KRONOS see Schubert, Franz
(Peter)

ANA DODI see Nelson, Rachelle

ANAGRAMS see Winslow, Walter

ANAKREONS GRAB see Valen, Fartein see
Wolf, Hugo

ANCESTRAL RITES OF A FORGOTTEN CULTURE
see Iglesias Rossi, Alejandro

ANCESTRAL VOICES see Anderson, T.J.

ANCHOR LINE see Beers, Jacques

AND A RECORD SHALL BE KEPT see Rich,
Richard J.

AND HE, UNDERNEATH US FLOWS, SLOWLY see
Permont, Haim

AND I JOHN see Habbestad, Kjell

AND I SAW A NEW HEAVEN AND A NEW EARTH
see Diemer, Emma Lou

AND LOOK, SHE CAME see Jordan, Sverre,
Og Se Hun Kom

AND THEN HE FLEW ON HER see Rowland,
David

AND THEN HER DOCTOR TOLD HER... see
Slonimsky, Nicolas

AND YOU SHALL BE A TRUE LOVER OF MINE
(CAMBRIC SHIRT) see Haufrecht,
Herbert

ANDERSON, ALLEN
Supra Rosa
Bar solo,bass clar,vla,vcl [4']
APNM sc $3.25, set $10.75   (A113)

ANDERSON, BETH
Alleluia *Allelu
MezT soli,2trp [3'] sc AM.COMP.AL.
$.80   (A114)

Angel, The
S solo,harp,cel,2vln,vla,vcl
[14'30"] AM.COMP.AL.   (A115)

Argument, An
female solo&male solo,tuba sc
AM.COMP.AL. $.40   (A116)

Crackers And Checkers
speaking voice [1'] sc AM.COMP.AL.
$.80   (A117)

Day, A
Mez solo,pno [1'] sc AM.COMP.AL.
$.45   (A118)

He Says He's Got
med solo,pno [2'] sc AM.COMP.AL.
$.45   (A119)

I Wish I Were Single Again
speaking voice [1'] sc AM.COMP.AL.
$.80   (A120)

If I Were A Poet
speaking voice [2'] sc AM.COMP.AL.
$1.55   (A121)

Kitchy Kitchen
speaking voice,perc [2'] sc
AM.COMP.AL. $1.60   (A122)

Knots
Mez solo,pno [4'] sc AM.COMP.AL.
$1.60   (A123)

ANDERSON, BETH (cont'd.)

Land Of Counterpane, The
T solo,pno [1'30"] AM.COMP.AL.
(A124)

Merchant's Song, The
med solo,pno [7'] sc AM.COMP.AL.
$3.85   (A125)

Music For Myself
solo voice,vibra [10'] sc
AM.COMP.AL. $.80   (A126)

My Private Beach
med solo,pno [3'] sc AM.COMP.AL.
$3.85   (A127)

Ocean Motion Mildew Mind
speaking voice,perc [2'] sc
AM.COMP.AL. $.80   (A128)

Paranoia
med solo [1'] sc AM.COMP.AL. $.40
(A129)
med solo,fl [1'] sc AM.COMP.AL.
$.45   (A130)
med solo,2fl [1'] sc AM.COMP.AL.
$1.15   (A131)

Poem To Michael, John And Allison
speaking voice [4'] sc AM.COMP.AL.
$1.55   (A132)

Postcard, A
Mez solo,pno [1'] sc AM.COMP.AL.
$.45   (A133)

She Wrote
female solo,2vln,electronic tape sc
AM.COMP.AL. $2.70   (A134)

Swatches *song cycle
S solo [5'] sc AM.COMP.AL. $3.05
(A135)

Torero Piece
2 solo voices,acap [8'] sc
AM.COMP.AL. $3.05   (A136)

Yes Sir Ree
speaking voice,perc [3'] sc
AM.COMP.AL. $.80   (A137)

ANDERSON, T.J.
Ancestral Voices
B solo,pno sc AM.COMP.AL. $6.15
(A138)

Egyptian Diary
S solo,2perc [16'15"] AM.COMP.AL.
(A139)

Songs Of Illumination
ST soli,pno [38'30"] AM.COMP.AL.
(A140)

ANDERSON, WILLIAM H.
Now The Cold Winter Days
LESLIE 1162   (A141)

ANDREAS GARTEN, DER see Mamlok, Ursula

ANDREE EXPEDITION see Argento, Dominick

ANDREWS, MARK (1875-1939)
Sea Fever
low solo SCHIRM.G ST34266   (A142)

ANDRIESSEN, HENDRIK (1892-1981)
Dageraad
see Drie Romantische Liederen

Drie Romantische Liederen
Mez solo,fl,ob,pno DONEMUS f.s.
contains: Dageraad; Manesprook;
Wolkenboot   (A143)

Fiat Domine
solo voice ZENGERINK R.136 (A144)

Magna Res Est Amor
S/T solo ZENGERINK R.135   (A145)

Manesprook
see Drie Romantische Liederen

Puisque Le Miel D'amour
see Trois Sonnets Spirituels

Tourne Un Peu Devers Moi
see Trois Sonnets Spirituels

Trois Sonnets Spirituels
S solo,org DONEMUS f.s. [8']
contains: Puisque Le Miel
D'amour; Tourne Un Peu Devers
Moi; Vie Est Une Fleur
Espineuse, La   (A146)

Twee Tantum Ergo
solo voice ZENGERINK R.354 (A147)

Vie Est Une Fleur Espineuse, La
see Trois Sonnets Spirituels

Vierge A Midi, La
med solo,org [8'] DONEMUS   (A148)

ANDRIESSEN, HENDRIK (cont'd.)

Wolkenboot
    see Drie Romantische Liederen

ANDRIESSEN, JURRIAAN (1925-   )
  Gevoelens
    see Vier Tucholsky Chansons

  Gij Wacht Wellicht
    see Vijf Nageldeuntjes

  Hoe Onsalich Was De Stonde
    see Vier Gedichten Van Revius
    see Vier Gedichten Van Revius

  How Oft When Thou, My Music, Music
      Play'st
    see Thy Black Is Fairest (3
      Shakespeare Sonnets)

  Ick Hoor De Stercke Stemme Van Mijnen
      Trouwen Vrient
    see Vier Gedichten Van Revius
    see Vier Gedichten Van Revius

  Ik Sta Geren
    see Vijf Nageldeuntjes

  Liefdespaar Bij Het Raam
    see Vier Tucholsky Chansons

  Little Love-God Lying Once Asleep,
      The
    see Thy Black Is Fairest (3
      Shakespeare Sonnets)

  Men Scheert Geen Ei
    see Vijf Nageldeuntjes

  Mij Spreekt De Blomme Eene Tale
    see Vijf Nageldeuntjes

  Mijn Lief Is Wit
    see Vier Gedichten Van Revius
    see Vier Gedichten Van Revius

  Thou Art As Tyrannous, So As Thou Art
    see Thy Black Is Fairest (3
      Shakespeare Sonnets)

  Thy Black Is Fairest (3 Shakespeare
      Sonnets)
    Bar solo,pno,2vln,vla,vcl DONEMUS
      f.s. [14']
      contains: How Oft When Thou, My
        Music, Music Play'st; Little
        Love-God Lying Once Asleep,
        The; Thou Art As Tyrannous, So
        As Thou Art   (A149)

  Tot Wederzien
    see Vijf Nageldeuntjes

  Uit
    see Vier Tucholsky Chansons

  Vier Gedichten Van Revius
    Mez solo,harp/hpsd/org/pno DONEMUS
      f.s.
      contains: Hoe Onsalich Was De
        Stonde; Ick Hoor De Stercke
        Stemme Van Mijnen Trouwen
        Vrient; Mijn Lief Is Wit; Waer
        Is U Lief   (A150)

  Vier Gedichten Van Revius
    Mez solo,harp/hpsd/org/pno DONEMUS
      f.s. [14']
      contains: Hoe Onsalich Was De
        Stonde; Ick Hoor De Stercke
        Stemme Van Mijnen Trouwen
        Vrient; Mijn Lief Is Wit; Waer
        Is U Lief   (A151)

  Vier Tucholsky Chansons
    MezT soli,fl,gtr,vcl DONEMUS f.s.
      contains: Gevoelens; Liefdespaar
        Bij Het Raam; Uit; Zij Tot Hem
                              (A152)

  Vijf Nageldeuntjes
    high solo,2vln,vla,vcl DONEMUS f.s.
      [6']
      contains: Gij Wacht Wellicht; Ik
        Sta Geren; Men Scheert Geen Ei;
        Mij Spreekt De Blomme Eene
        Tale; Tot Wederzien   (A153)

  Waer Is U Lief
    see Vier Gedichten Van Revius
    see Vier Gedichten Van Revius

  Zij Tot Hem
    see Vier Tucholsky Chansons

ANDRIESSEN, LOUIS (1939-   )
  Stijl, De
    4 female soli,3.0.0.0.5sax.
      0.4.4.0. 2perc,3pno,synthesizer,
      elec gtr,elec bass,opt db [25']
      DONEMUS f.s.   (A154)

ANDRIESSEN, WILLEM (1887-1964)
  Ave Maria
    Mez/A solo,org/pno [4'] DONEMUS
                              (A155)

ANDROMEDE ET PERSEE see Mouret, Jean
  Joseph

ANDRUM see Rehnqvist, Karin

ANGEL, THE see Anderson, Beth see
  Medtner, Nikolai Karlovich

ANGEL FARE see MacBride, David Huston

ANGELS see Balazs, Frederic

ANGEL'S SERENADE see Braga, Gaetano

ANHELO see Beethoven, Ludwig van see
  Schubert, Franz (Peter)

ANIM ZEMIROT see Gottlieb, Jack S.

ANIMA see Bodin, Lars-Gunnar

ANIMA CHRISTI see Leroux, Philippe

ANIMAL DITTIES see Plog, Anthony

ANITA see Beach, [Mrs.] H.H.A. (Amy
  Marcy Cheney)

ANKUNFT IN VENEDIG see Frid, Geza

ANNA BOLENA: AH! PAREA CHE PAR INCANTO
  see Donizetti, Gaetano

ANNA BOLENA: DEH! NON VOLER COSTRINGERE
  see Donizetti, Gaetano

ANNA HANS OLOFS see Hemberg, Eskil

ANNA LA BONNE see Israel-Meyer, Pierre

ANNABEL see Badings, Henk

ÄNNCHEN VON THARAU see Grahn, Ulf

ANNE-KARIN see Sommerfeldt, Öistein

ANNEN NATT PÅ HOSPITALET see Groven,
  Eivind

ANNES ARIE see Braein, Edvard Fliflet

ANNIE LAURIE see Scott, [Lady] John
  (Alicia Ann)

ANNONCE see Orthel, Leon

ANNOVAZZI, NAPOLEONE (1908-1984)
  Alba Provenzale
    S solo,pno BOIL B.1915   (A156)

  Dormi Fanciullo
    Mez solo,pno BOIL B.1914   (A157)

  Matinale
    solo voice,pno BOIL B.1916 (A158)

ANOKUDACCHI FANTASY see Minemura,
  Sumiko

ANONYMOUS
  Afton Water
    see Flow Gently, Sweet Afton

  All Through The Night (from Ar Hyd Y
      Nos)
    [Eng] high solo,pno CLASSV 0591
                              (A159)
    see Ar Hyd Y Nos

  Amour De Moi Sy Est Enclose, L'
    [Fr] med-high solo,pno CLASSV 1232
                              (A160)

  Ar Hyd Y Nos
    "All Through The Night" [Eng/Welsh]
      med solo,pno CLASSV 0590 (A161)

  Aria in C
    see Bella Quando Aurora

  Barbara Allan
    "It Was In And About The Mart-'Mas
      Time" med solo,pno CLASSV 1366
                              (A162)

  Barbara Ellen
    (Sharp, C.) "In Scotland I Was
      Born" Bar solo,pno CLASSV 1355
                              (A163)

  Bella Quando Aurora (Aria in C)
    (Sestak, Zdenek) S solo,org,strings
      [9'] CESKY HUD.   (A164)

  Canción De Cuna
    see Palomino, J., Canción Picaresca

  Chloris Sigh'd
    (Dolmetsch, A.) med-high solo,pno
      CLASSV 1745   (A165)

  Des Winters Als Het Reghent
    [Eng/Dutch] med-high solo,pno
      CLASSV 2099   (A166)

ANONYMOUS (cont'd.)

  Flow Gently, Sweet Afton
    "Afton Water" med solo,pno CLASSV
      0965   (A167)

  Have You Seen But A Whyte Lillie Grow
    (Dolmetsch, A.) med-high solo,pno
      CLASSV 1262   (A168)

  In Scotland I Was Born
    see Barbara Ellen

  It Was In And About The Mart-'Mas
      Time
    see Barbara Allan

  Keys Of Canterbury
    (Sharp, C.) female solo&male solo,
      pno CLASSV 1710   (A169)

  Last Rose Of Summer
    med solo,pno CLASSV 0372   (A170)

  Loch Lomond
    (Foote, Arthur) low solo,pno CLASSV
      1468   (A171)

  My Love Is Like A Red Red Rose
    high solo,pno CLASSV 1911   (A172)

  O Admirabile Veneris Idolum
    solo voice KING'S   (A173)

  Oft In The Stilly Night
    med solo,pno CLASSV 1915   (A174)

  Petite Anne, La
    (Schindler, K.) med-high solo,pno
      CLASSV 2042   (A175)

  Star Vicino
    high solo,pno CLASSV 1162   (A176)

  Stond Wel, Moder, Under Rode
    solo voice KING'S   (A177)

  Sweet Was The Song The Virgin Sang
    S/T solo,cont KING'S KM42 (A178)

  Thomas Cesus
    see Thomas Gemma Cantuarie

  Thomas Gemma Cantuarie
    "Thomas Cesus" 2countertenor,2inst
      KING'S   (A179)

ANOTHER CHOICE see Bois, Rob du

ANREDE AN DEN KRAN KARL see Eisler,
  Hanns

ANSINK, CAROLINE (1959-   )
  A La Nina
    see Al Prisionero

  Al Prisionero
    med solo,pno DONEMUS f.s.
      contains: A La Nina; Demas
        Companeros, Los; Dos Mas Dos;
        Sol De Piedra; Tramites (A180)

  Demas Companeros, Los
    see Al Prisionero

  Dos Mas Dos
    see Al Prisionero

  Sol De Piedra
    see Al Prisionero

  Tramites
    see Al Prisionero

ANSORGE, CONRAD (1862-1930)
  Fünf Lieder, Op. 17
    [Ger] (texts by Richard Dehmel)
      RECITAL 325   (A181)

ANSWER JULY see Ruiter, Wim de

ANTE LA MUERTE see Beethoven, Ludwig
  van

ANTHEIL, GEORGE (1900-1959)
  Five Songs
    BOOSEY VAB0037   (A182)

ANTHOLOGY OF ITALIAN SONG, BOOK 1 *CCU
  solo voice,pno ALFRED 3525 f.s.
                              (A183)
ANTHOLOGY OF ITALIAN SONG, BOOK 2 *CCU
  solo voice,pno ALFRED 3526 f.s.
                              (A184)
ANTHOLOGY OF ITALIAN SONGS, VOL. 1
  [It/Eng] KALMUS K 09869   (A185)

ANTHOLOGY OF ITALIAN SONGS, VOL. 2
  [It/Eng] KALMUS K 09870   (A186)

ANTHOLOGY OF SONGS *CC30U
  solo voice,pno DA CAPO 76287-0 f.s.
    contains works by: Pauline
      Duchambge, Loisa Puget, Pauline
      Viardot, Jane Vieu   (A187)

ANTINOMIA see Balassa, Sándor

ANTITHESES see Constantinides, Dinos Demetrios

ANTOLOGIA DI VOCALIZZI DI AUTORI ITALIANI CONTEMPORANEI, VOL. 1
*CCU
solo voice,pno CURCI 6539 f.s. (A188)

ANTOLOGIA DI VOCALIZZI DI AUTORI ITALIANI CONTEMPORANEI, VOL. 2
*CCU
solo voice,pno CURCI 6540 f.s. (A189)

ANTOLOGIA DI VOCALIZZI, FASCICOLO 1
*CCU
S solo,pno CURCI 7889 f.s. (A190)

ANTOLOGIA DI VOCALIZZI, FASCICOLO 2
*CCU
Mez/A solo,pno CURCI 7890 f.s. (A191)

ANTOLOGIA DI VOCALIZZI, FASCICOLO 3
*CCU
T solo,pno CURCI 7891 f.s. (A192)

ANTOLOGIA DI VOCALIZZI, FASCICOLO 4
*CCU
Bar/B solo,pno CURCI 7892 f.s. (A193)

ANTOLOGIA PIESNI I ARII STANISLAWA MONIUSZKI ORAZ PIESNI FRYDERYKA CHOPINA see Moniuszko, Stanislaw

ANTONIOU, THEODORE (1935-   )
Westwinds
[Greek/Eng] S solo,pic,perc,harp, pno,2vln,vla,vcl [12'] MARGUN MP1096 (A194)

ANTWORT see Preyer, Gottfried

ANY DREAM WILL DO see Lloyd Webber, Andrew

APHORISMEN NACH WORTEN VON RABINDRANATH TAGORE see Hukvari, Jeno

APHRODITE CANTOS see Rouse, Christopher

APOKALYPSIS see Luppi, Gian Paolo

APOLLYON, NICOLAY (1945-   )
Garden Of Delight
female solo,electronic equipment [18'20"] NORGE (A195)

Nun Komm, Der Heiden Heiland: Solocantata
[Ger] T solo,opt 3inst NORGE (A196)

Ram Of Tides
S solo,fl,ob,clar,horn,vcl, electronic equipment NORGE (A197)

APONTE-LEDEE, RAFAEL (1938-   )
Ventana Abierta
AAA soli,fl,clar,trp,pno,2perc,vln, vcl,db SEESAW f.s. (A198)

APRES UN RÊVE see Faure, Gabriel-Urbain

APRILA see Wolf-Ferrari, Ermanno, Jewels Of The Madonna: Serenade

APRILE see Tosti, Francesco Paolo

AQUILON ET ORITHIE see Rameau, Jean-Philippe

AR HYD Y NOS see Anonymous

ÄR MÄNNISKOR EN BÖRDA see Strandsjö, Göte

ÄR NÅGOT SOM, DET see Leijon, Jerker

ÄR NÅGOT SOM ÄLSKANDE HJÄRTAN VET, DET see Leijon, Jerker

ÄR OM AFTONEN MAN BRYTER UPP, DET see Karkoff, Maurice

ÄR VACKRAST, DET see Vea, Ketil

ARABIAN MELODY see Borodin, Alexander Porfirievich

ARABIC FOLK-SONG see Steinberg, Eitan

ARABY MAID, THE see Surenne, I.T.

ARASHINO, HIDEO (1935-   )
Dokoka De
Mez solo,pno [2'] ONGAKU (A199)

Naginoki Ni Yosete
Mez solo,pno [5'] ONGAKU (A200)

Niji 3 Sho
S solo,pno [6'] ONGAKU (A201)

Refrain
Mez solo,pno [4'] ONGAKU (A202)

ARASHINO, HIDEO (cont'd.)
Tarachine Part Three
ST soli,pno [37'] JAPAN (A203)

Tsuki No Kasa
S solo,pno [6'] ONGAKU (A204)

ARBEID see Kjeldaas, Arnljot

ÁRBO DEL AMOR, EL see Massana, A., Sota L'Ombreta

ARC (ARIA WITH INTERLUDES) see Hodkinson, Sydney P.

ARCADELT, JACOB (ca. 1505-1568)
Ave Maria
high solo ZENGERINK 2041 (A205)
low solo ZENGERINK 2042 (A206)

ARCHAEOLOGIST AND SPIDER see Kurokami, Yoshimitsu

ARCHITEKTUR see Koetsier, Jan

ARCO, PAOLO
Esercizi Di Stile
ST soli,pno ZERBONI 9780 (A207)

Splendid Tear, A
S solo,orch ZERBONI 9528 (A208)

ARDITA, L' see Arditi, Luigi

ARDITI, LUIGI (1822-1903)
Ardita, L'
"Magnetic Waltz" [It/Fr/Eng] A solo,pno CLASSV 1164 (A209)

Bacio, Il
high solo RICORDI-IT R32496 (A210)
solo voice,pno BOIL B.1696 (A211)
"Sulle, Sulle Labbra" S solo,pno CLASSV 0867 (A212)

Magnetic Waltz
see Ardita, L'

Sulle, Sulle Labbra
see Bacio, Il

ARDO È VER PER TE D'AMORE see Scarlatti, Alessandro

ARENSKY, ANTON STEPANOVICH (1861-1906)
But Lately In Dance I Embraced Her *Op.49,No.5
[Russ] high solo,pno CLASSV 2108 (A213)

Cradle Song *Op.70,No.3
"Lullaby" [Russ] solo voice,pno CLASSV 2107 (A214)

Don't Light The Lamp! *Op.38,No.3
[Russ] solo voice,pno CLASSV 2105 (A215)

Lullaby
see Cradle Song

Manchmal Sah Ich Von Fern *Op.38, No.6
[Russ/Ger] med solo,pno CLASSV 2115 (A216)

Schon Schwand Der Tag *Op.44,No.4
[Russ/Ger] med solo,pno CLASSV 2116 (A217)

Sechs Romanzen, Op. 44
[Russ/Ger] (not available outside U.S.A.) RECITAL 339 (A218)

Sie Schwebt' Mir Noch Kürzlich *Op.49,No.5
[Eng/Ger] high solo,pno CLASSV 0626 (A219)

Song Of The Fish *Op.27,No.1
[Russ] high solo,pno CLASSV 2104 (A220)

ÅRETS TIDER see Johansen, Bertil Palmar

ARGENTO, DOMINICK (1927-   )
Andree Expedition
BOOSEY VAB0241 (A221)

Casa Guidi
BOOSEY VAB0239 (A222)

ARGUMENT, AN see Anderson, Beth

ARIA see Johannsson, Magnus Bl.

ARIA DE LA LOCURA see Donizetti, Gaetano, Lucia Di Lammermoor: Ardo Ne Gl' Incensi

ARIA DE NATIVITATE DOMINI see Hahn, Georg Joachim Joseph

ARIA DE QUOVIS FESTO see Senkyr, Augustin, Saevit Mare Surgunt Venti

ARIA DEL TELÉFONO see Marques

ARIA DELLE CARTE see Bosco, Gilberto

ARIA OF LEVKO see Rimsky-Korsakov, Nikolai, May Night: Sleep, My Dear

ARIA OF THE WORM see Corigliano, John

ARIA PASTORITIA see Senkyr, Augustin, Huc, Huc, Pastorculi

ARIA VARIATA see Lombardo, Robert M.

ARIA VIVA see Cory, Eleanor

ARIADNE AUF NAXOS: LIEBEN see Strauss, Richard

ARIADNE AUF NAXOS: ZERBINETTA, 1ST EDITION VERSION see Strauss, Richard

ARIANNA (LAMENTO) see Lolini, Ruggero

ARIAS FROM THE CANTATAS WITH OBBLIGATO INSTRUMENTS: BASS ARIAS see Bach, Johann Sebastian

ARIAS FROM THE CANTATAS WITH OBBLIGATO INSTRUMENTS: CONTRALTO ARIAS, VOL. 1 see Bach, Johann Sebastian

ARIAS FROM THE CANTATAS WITH OBBLIGATO INSTRUMENTS: CONTRALTO ARIAS, VOL. 2 see Bach, Johann Sebastian

ARIAS FROM THE CANTATAS WITH OBBLIGATO INSTRUMENTS: CONTRALTO ARIAS, VOL. 3 see Bach, Johann Sebastian

ARIAS FROM THE CANTATAS WITH OBBLIGATO INSTRUMENTS: SOPRANO AND ALTO ARIAS (DUETS), VOL. 1 see Bach, Johann Sebastian

ARIAS FROM THE CANTATAS WITH OBBLIGATO INSTRUMENTS: SOPRANO AND ALTO ARIAS (DUETS), VOL. 2 see Bach, Johann Sebastian

ARIAS FROM THE CANTATAS WITH OBBLIGATO INSTRUMENTS: SOPRANO AND ALTO ARIAS (DUETS), VOL. 3 see Bach, Johann Sebastian

ARIAS FROM THE CANTATAS WITH OBBLIGATO INSTRUMENTS: SOPRANO ARIAS, VOL. 1 see Bach, Johann Sebastian

ARIAS FROM THE CANTATAS WITH OBBLIGATO INSTRUMENTS: SOPRANO ARIAS, VOL. 2 see Bach, Johann Sebastian

ARIAS FROM THE CANTATAS WITH OBBLIGATO INSTRUMENTS: SOPRANO ARIAS, VOL. 3 see Bach, Johann Sebastian

ARIAS FROM THE CANTATAS WITH OBBLIGATO INSTRUMENTS: TENOR ARIAS, VOL. 1 see Bach, Johann Sebastian

ARIAS FROM THE CANTATAS WITH OBBLIGATO INSTRUMENTS: TENOR ARIAS, VOL. 2 see Bach, Johann Sebastian

ARIAS FROM THE CANTATAS WITH OBBLIGATO INSTRUMENTS: TENOR ARIAS, VOL. 3 see Bach, Johann Sebastian

ARIE ANTICHE ITALIANE *CCU
(Brunelli, G.) solo voice,cont CURCI 10323 f.s. (A223)

ARIE ANTICHE, VOL. 1 *CCU
(Leiss, K.) solo voice,pno SUPRAPHON f.s. contains works by: Carissimi, Caldara, Handel, Paisiello, A. Scarlatti, Monteverdi, Gasparini, Caccini, Cimarosa, Spontini, Martini (A224)

ARIE ANTICHE, VOL. 2 *CCU
(Leiss, K.) solo voice,pno SUPRAPHON f.s. contains works by: Cesti, Bononcini, Gluck, Marcello, Traetta, Paisiello (A225)

ARIE DELL'OPERE PERDITE see Rejcha, Antonin

ARIE NELLO STILE ANTICO, 36, VOL. 1 see Donaudy, Stefano

ARIE NELLO STILE ANTICO, 36, VOL. 2 see Donaudy, Stefano

ARIE NELLO STILE ANTICO, 36, VOL. 3 see Donaudy, Stefano

ARIEL see Merryman, Marjorie

ARIEL SETTINGS see Packer, Randall

ARIEN AUS RUSSISCHEN OPERN FÜR ALT PETERS 4722 (A226)

ARIEN AUS RUSSISCHEN OPERN FÜR BASS PETERS 4725 (A227)

ARIEN AUS RUSSISCHEN OPERN FÜR SOPRAN
  PETERS 4721   (A228)

ARIEN AUS RUSSISCHEN OPERN FÜR TENOR
  PETERS 4723   (A229)

ARIETTE see Badings, Henk see Beach,
  [Mrs.] H.H.A. (Amy Marcy Cheney)
  see Ugoletti, Paolo

ARIETTE À L'ANCIENNE see Rossini,
  Gioacchino

ARIETTE DER RÖSERL see Suppe, Franz von

ARIETTE NO. 1 see Coria, Miguel Angel,
  Cancion De Belisa

ARIETTES see Badings, Henk

ARIJIGOKU see Hayakawa, Kuzuko

ARIMA, REIKO (1933-   )
  Damette Ittemo
    child solo,pno [2'] JAPAN   (A230)

  My Lovely Dutch Doll
    child solo,pno [2'] JAPAN   (A231)

  Paradise Of Cats
    child solo,pno [2'] JAPAN   (A232)

  Sakura Tsukiyo
    S solo,pno [5'] ONGAKU   (A233)

  Yasashisa Kamoshite
    child solo,pno [4'] ONGAKU   (A234)

ARIODANT: FEMME SENSIBLE, ENTENDS-TU
  see Méhul, Étienne-Nicolas

ARIOSO PER LA SCENA III see Bortolotti,
  Mauro

ARITHMÉTIQUE, L' see Gounod, Charles
  François

ARLESIANA, L': E LA SOLITA STORIA see
  Ciléa, Francesco

ARLESIANA, L': RACCONTO DEL PASTORE see
  Ciléa, Francesco

ARM EN BEVRIJD see Weegenhuise, Johan

ARMA, PAUL (PÁL) (IMRE WEISSHAUS)
  (1904-1987)
  Celui Qui Dort Et Dort *cant
    speaking voice,bsn,xylo,perc [19']
    BILLAUDOT f.s., ipr   (A235)

ARME SEELE VOR DER HIMMELSTÜR, DIE see
  Beekhuis, Hanna

ARMER, ELINOR
  Lockerbones - Airbones
    Mez solo,fl,vln,pno,perc [18']
    FALLEN LEAF sc $.15, set $55.00
                                 (A236)

ARNE, MICHAEL (1741-1786)
  Favourite Collection Of English
    Songs, Book III, A
    KING'S   (A237)

ARNE, THOMAS AUGUSTINE (1710-1778)
  Agreeable Musical Choice, The, 5
    (1753)
    sc KING'S   (A238)

  Agreeable Musical Choice, The, 7
    (1756)
    sc KING'S   (A239)

  Choice Collection Of Songs, A, 12
    (1761)
    sc KING'S   (A240)

  Collection Of Songs, A, 9 (1760)
    sc KING'S   (A241)

  Favourite Collection Of English
    Songs, A
    sc KING'S   (A242)

  Favourite Collection Of Songs, A, 14
    (1764)
    sc KING'S   (A243)

  Fear No More The Heat O' The Sun
    KING'S   (A244)

  Lass With The Delicate Air
    high solo SCHIRM.G ST14516   (A245)

  Love And Resentment *cant
    (Foster, Walter) [Eng] S solo
    RECITAL 340   (A246)

  Lover's Recantation, The *cant
    [Eng/Ger] S solo,2fl,2ob,2vln,vla,
    cont sc DEUTSCHER DV 9521   (A247)

  Lydia From Sappho, (1755, No.2)
    KING'S   (A248)

ARNE, THOMAS AUGUSTINE (cont'd.)
  Rule, Britannia
    solo voice,strings,2ob,bsn,2trp,
    timp sc,set KING'S   (A249)

  Six Cantatas
    sc KING'S   (A250)

  Soldier Tir'd Of War's Alarms
    S solo,pno ALFRED 3236   (A251)

  Soldier Tired Of War's Alarms
    S solo,pno CLASSV 0340   (A252)

  Thou Soft Flowing Avon
    Mez solo,pno CLASSV 0627   (A253)

  To Fair Fidele's Grassy Tomb
    KING'S   (A254)

  Where The Bee Sucks
    KING'S   (A255)

ARNER, GOTTHARD
  Min Vilotimma Ljuder
    solo voice,org SVERIG PROP 7883
                                 (A256)

ARNESTAD, FINN (1916-   )
  Smeden Og Bageren
    Bar solo,fl,ob,hpsd,strings [35']
    NORGE f.s.   (A257)

ARNOLD see Sønstevold, Gunnar

ARNOLD II see Sønstevold, Gunnar

ARONA, C.
  Campana De San Giusto, La
    solo voice,pno BOIL B.1717   (A258)

  Santa Lucia
    solo voice,pno BOIL B.1715   (A259)

AROUND THE CLOCK (COALITIONS III: 1983)
  see Blank, Allan

ARRIEU, CLAUDE (1903-   )
  Berger Dedans Sa Cabane, Un (from
    Chansons Du Folklore De France)
    solo voice,1.1.1.1. 0.0.0.0.
    [2'30"] BILLAUDOT   (A260)

  Ce Sont Les Filles De La Rochelle
    (from Chansons Du Folklore De
    France)
    solo voice,1.1.1.1. 1.0.0.0. perc
    [2'15"] BILLAUDOT   (A261)

  C'était La Fille D'un Roi Français
    (from Chansons Du Folklore De
    France)
    solo voice,1.1.1.1. 1.0.0.0. [2']
    BILLAUDOT   (A262)

  Derrière Chez Mon Père (from Chansons
    Du Folklore De France)
    solo voice,fl,bsn,vln,vla,vcl [3']
    BILLAUDOT   (A263)

  J'ai T'un Coquin De Frère (from
    Chansons Du Folklore De France)
    solo voice,1.1.1.1. 0.0.0.0.
    [1'10"] BILLAUDOT   (A264)

  Légende De St. Nicolas, La (from
    Chansons Du Folklore De France)
    solo voice,1.1.1.0. 0.0.0.0. 2vln,
    vla,vcl [2'40"] BILLAUDOT   (A265)

  Mois De Mai, Le (from Chansons Du
    Folklore De France)
    solo voice,2.0.0.1. 0.0.0.0.
    strings [2'50"] BILLAUDOT   (A266)

  Roi A Fait Battre Tambour, Le (from
    Chansons Du Folklore De France)
    solo voice,1.1.1.1. 0.0.0.0. perc
    [2'30"] BILLAUDOT   (A267)

  Trois Jolis Tambours (from Chansons
    Du Folklore De France)
    solo voice,1.1.1.0. 0.0.0.0. perc,
    strings [3'] BILLAUDOT   (A268)

  Y Avait Dix Filles Dans Un Pré (from
    Chansons Du Folklore De France)
    solo voice,fl,bsn,vln,vla,db
    [1'50"] BILLAUDOT   (A269)

ARROW AND THE SONG, THE see Amerongen,
  Jan van

ART IS CALLING FOR ME see Herbert,
  Victor

ART OF JOAN SUTHERLAND, THE, VOL. 1:
  FAMOUS MAD SCENES *CCU
  (Sutherland, Joan; Bonynge, Richard)
  solo voice WEINBERGER f.s.   (A270)

ART OF JOAN SUTHERLAND, THE, VOL. 2:
  EIGHTEENTH CENTURY ARIAS *CCU
  (Sutherland, Joan; Bonynge, Richard)
  solo voice WEINBERGER f.s.   (A271)

ART OF JOAN SUTHERLAND, THE, VOL. 3:
  ROMANTIC ITALIAN ARIAS *CCU
  (Sutherland, Joan; Bonynge, Richard)
  solo voice WEINBERGER f.s.   (A272)

ART OF JOAN SUTHERLAND, THE, VOL. 4:
  DONIZETTI ARIAS *CCU
  (Sutherland, Joan; Bonynge, Richard)
  solo voice WEINBERGER f.s.   (A273)

ART OF JOAN SUTHERLAND, THE, VOL. 5:
  BEL CANTO ARIAS
  (Bonynge, Richard; Sutherland, Joan)
  WEINBERGER f.s.
  contains: Bellini, Vincenzo, Norma:
    Casta Diva; Bellini, Vincenzo,
    Puritani, I: O Sento O Mio Bell'
    Angelo; Bellini, Vincenzo,
    Puritani, I: Son Vergin Vezzoza
    (Polonaise); Donizetti, Gaetano,
    Castello Di Kenilworth, Il: Par
    Che Mi Dica Ancora; Verdi,
    Giuseppe, Masnadieri, I: Lo
    Sguardo Avea Degli Angeli; Verdi,
    Giuseppe, Masnadieri, I:
    Venerabile, O Padre   (A274)

ART OF JOAN SUTHERLAND, THE, VOL. 6:
  MORE BEL CANTO ARIAS
  (Bonynge, Richard; Sutherland, Joan)
  WEINBERGER f.s.
  contains: Auber, Daniel-François-
    Esprit, Fra Diavolo: Non Temete
    Milord; Auber, Daniel-François-
    Esprit, Fra Diavolo: Or Son Sola;
    Bellini, Vincenzo, Beatrice Di
    Tenda: Ah! Se Un' Urna; Bellini,
    Vincenzo, Beatrice Di Tenda: Oh!
    Miei Fedeli!; Bellini, Vincenzo,
    Sonnambula, La: Ah! Non Credea;
    Bellini, Vincenzo, Sonnambula,
    La: Come Per Me Sereno; Rossini,
    Gioacchino, Barbiere Di Siviglia,
    Il: Una Voce Poco Fa; Rossini,
    Gioacchino, Cambiale Di
    Matrimonio, La: Come Tacer;
    Rossini, Gioacchino, Cambiale Di
    Matrimonio, La: Vorrei Spiegarvi
                                    (A275)

ART OF JOAN SUTHERLAND, THE, VOL. 7:
  VERDI ARIAS see Verdi, Giuseppe

ART OF JOAN SUTHERLAND, THE, VOL. 8:
  NINETEENTH CENTURY FRENCH ARIAS
  (Bonynge, Richard; Sutherland, Joan)
  WEINBERGER f.s.
  contains: Gounod, Charles François,
    Tribut De Zamora, Le: Guarde La
    Couronne Des Reines; Lecocq,
    Charles, Coeur Et La Main, Le:
    Bolero; Meyerbeer, Giacomo,
    Dinorah: Shadow Song; Meyerbeer,
    Giacomo, Etoile Du Nord, L':
    C'est Bien Lui; Meyerbeer,
    Giacomo, Etoile Du Nord, L':
    Veille Sur Eux Toujours;
    Meyerbeer, Giacomo, Huguenots,
    Les: O Beau Pays; Meyerbeer,
    Giacomo, Robert Le Diable: Idole
    De Ma Vie   (A276)

ART OF JOAN SUTHERLAND, THE, VOL. 9
  *CCU
  BOOSEY VAW0241   (A277)

ART OF JOAN SUTHERLAND, THE, VOL. 9:
  MASSENET ARIAS see Massenet, Jules

ART OF MODERN SINGING, THE see Menotti,
  Gian Carlo

ART OF SONGS see Hirai, Takeichiro

ART SONGS see Beyer, Emil

ART SONGS BY CONTEMPORARY TEXAS
  COMPOSERS
  SOUTHERN B368   (A278)

ART SONGS OF THREE CENTURIES
  ("World's Favorite Series") ASHLEY
  092-1   (A279)

ARTE DI JOAN SUTHERLAND, L', VOL. 1
  *CCU
  S solo,pno CURCI 10778 f.s. famous
  mad scenes   (A280)

ARTE DI JOAN SUTHERLAND, L', VOL. 2
  *CCU
  S solo,pno CURCI 10779 f.s. 18th
  century arias   (A281)

ARTE DI JOAN SUTHERLAND, L', VOL. 3
  *CCU
  S solo,pno CURCI 10780 f.s. arias of
  the Italian Romantics   (A282)

ARTE DI JOAN SUTHERLAND, L', VOL. 4
  *CCU
  S solo,pno CURCI 10781 f.s. Donizetti
  arias   (A283)

ARTE DI JOAN SUTHERLAND, L', VOL. 5
  *CCU
  S solo,pno CURCI 10782 f.s. famous

AUF, LASST UNS DEN HERREN LOBEN see
Bach, Johann Michael

AUF ZUM KAMPFE, TANKBRIGADEN see
Eisler, Hanns

AUFSCHNAITER, BENEDIKT ANTON
(1665-1742)
Kommt Beschaut Die Weisoheit
see Pastorella

Pastorella
(Ruhland, Konrad) S solo,2vln,cont
(Musik Aus Ostbayern, Heft 51)
COPPENRATH f.s. contains also:
Triosonate; Kommt Beschaut Die
Weisoheit   (A319)

Pastorella: Laufet Ihr Hirten
(Ruhland, Konrad) A solo,2vln,org
(Musik Aus Ostbayern, Heft 27)
COPPENRATH   (A320)

Triosonate
see Pastorella

AUGUN see Halldorsson, Skuli

AUGUN BLAU see Einarsson, Sigfus

AUGUN MIN OG AUGUN THIN see
Halldorsson, Skuli

AUGUN THIN see Halldorsson, Skuli

AUGUST see Baden, Conrad see Hovland,
Egil

AUGUST 27, 1986 CARSON CITY see
Lieberman, David

AUPRÈS DE TOI see Bach, Johann
Sebastian

AURA see Pezzati, Romano

AURA ONOMATOPOETICA see Erbacher,
Walther

AURE AMICHE, AH NON SPIRATE see Rejcha,
Antonin

AURE FELICE see Four Italian Melodies

AURORE see Duparc, Henri

AURORE ET CEPHALE, L' see Stuck, Jean
Baptiste

AUS ALTEN MÄRCHEN see Nyary, Thomas

AUS DEM NACHLASS DES GRAFEN C.W. see
Straesser, Joep

AUS DEM SCHI-KING, OP. 15, VOL.I: 1-9
see Sekles, Bernhard

AUS DEM SCHI-KING, OP. 15, VOL.II: 10-
18 see Sekles, Bernhard

AUS DEM TAGEBUCH see Keussler, Gerhard
von

AUS DEN KNOSPEN see Colaço Osorio-
Swaab, Reine

AUS EINEM KINDERLIEDERBUCH see Palsson,
Pall P.

AUS HELIOPOLIS see Schubert, Franz
(Peter)

AUS JIDDISCHER VOLKSPOESIE see
Shostakovich, Dmitri

AUS MEINEN GROSSEN SCHMERZEN see Nyary,
Thomas

AUS MEINEN TRÄNEN see Borodin,
Alexander Porfirievich

AUS VERGANGENER ZEIT see Isolfsson,
Pall

AUSGEWÄHLTE DEUTSCHE LIEDER MIT
BEGLEITUNG DER GUITARRE, 60 see
Seidsticker, Carl

AUSGEWÄHLTE LIEDER see Genzmer, Harald
see Lang, Max see Stockmayer, Erich

AUSGEWÄHLTE LIEDER, 30 see Schumann,
Robert (Alexander)

AUSGEWÄHLTE LIEDER 2 see Brahms,
Johannes

AUSGEWÄHLTE LIEDER (1940-1987) see
Genzmer, Harald

AUSGEWÄHLTE LIEDER AUS BAND 4-7, 52 see
Schubert, Franz (Peter)

AUSGEWÄHLTE LIEDER, HEFT 4: DIE
HOLLYWOOD ELEGIEN, SONETTE, LIEDER
see Eisler, Hanns

AUSGEWÄHLTE SINGSTÜCKE see Boieldieu,
François-Adrien

AUSTIN, JOHN
Wicked And Unfaithful Song, The
S solo,ob/English horn,bsn,
conductor [8'] sc AM.COMP.AL.
$9.15   (A321)

Writer, The
T solo,vln,vla,vcl [10'] sc
AM.COMP.AL. $8.40   (A322)

AUSTIN, LARRY (1930-   )
Canadian Coastlines
med solo,fl,rec,bsn,marimba,
electronic tape,hpsd,harp,gtr,
vln,vla,vcl,db [11'] pts
AM.COMP.AL. $14.50   (A323)

Catalogo Voce
Bar solo,electronic tape [12'] sc
AM.COMP.AL. $6.15   (A324)

Maroon Bells
S/T solo,pno,electronic tape [11']
sc AM.COMP.AL. $12.25   (A325)

AUSTRALIANA see Bank, Jacques

AUTHOR'S EPITAPH, THE see Manneke, Daan

AUTOMNE, L' see Boismortier, Joseph
Bodin de

AUTRE JOUR EN M'Y PROMENANT, L' see
Tailleferre, Germaine

AUTUMN see Bergh, Sverre, Haust see
Clarke, Henry Leland see Eggen,
Arne, Høst see Hoiby, Lee see
Maxym, R.

AUTUMN MUSIC: TWO SONGS see Chenoweth,
Gerald

AUTUMN SONG see Dydo, J. Stephen

AUTUMN SONG, THE see Groven, Eivind,
Høstsangen

AUX MARCHES DU PALAIS see Koetsier, Jan

AV LJUS ÄR DU KOMMEN: FEM SÅNGER see
Leijon, Jerker

AV "TUE BENTSØNS VISER" see Jordan,
Sverre

AVAK, THE HEALER see Hovhaness, Alan

AVALANCHE IN SPRING: SONG ALBUM see
Saito, Takanobu

AVE FORMOSISSIMA see Biggs, Hayes

AVE MARIA see Algra, Joh. see
Andriessen, Willem see Arcadelt,
Jacob see Barbiretti, Arrigo see
Barblan-Opienska, Lydia see
Cherubini, Luigi see Clemens, Henri
see Dorff, Daniel Jay see Dupre,
Marcel see Dvorák, Antonín see
Faure, Gabriel-Urbain see Franck,
Cesar see Gounod, Charles François
see Hanau, A. see Handel, George
Frideric see Heiller, Anton see
Hemmerle see Huguenin, Charles see
Jonsson, Thorarinn see Kaldalóns,
Sigvaldi S. see Luzzi, Luigi see
Mascagni, Pietro see Rossini,
Gioacchino see Saint-Yves, Bax see
Schubert, Franz (Peter) see
Schubert, Franz (Peter), Hymne An
Die Jungfrau see Soler see Walter,
Karl

AVE MARIA, OP.6 see Heydt, W.

AVE MARIA, OP.13 see Schrijvers, Jean

AVE MARIA, OP.29 see Schrijvers, Jean

AVE MARIS STELLA see Dvorák, Antonín

AVE REGINA see Biechteler, B. see
Haydn, [Johann] Michael

AVE RHEUMA see Bremer, Jetse

AVE VERUM see Mozart, Wolfgang Amadeus

AVE VERUM CORPUS see Chausson, Ernest
see Mozart, Wolfgang Amadeus

AVE VIVENS HOSTIA: HYMNE see Ett,
Kaspar

AVES QUE VENIS see Beethoven, Ludwig
van

AVNI, TZVI (1927-   )
Be In Peace
see Love Under A Different Sun

AVNI, TZVI (cont'd.)

Follow Me To The Field
see Love Under A Different Sun

In The East, On Top Of The Mountain
see Love Under A Different Sun

Love Under A Different Sun
S/Mez solo,fl,vln,vcl sc
ISR.MUS.INST. 6851 f.s.
contains: Be In Peace; Follow Me
To The Field; In The East, On
Top Of The Mountain; O Gazelle
Of Love; Woe Is Me   (A326)

Monk Observes A Skull, A
solo voice,vcl,tape recorder [8']
perf sc ISR.MUS.INST. 6922 (A327)

O Gazelle Of Love
see Love Under A Different Sun

Woe Is Me
see Love Under A Different Sun

AVOND, EEN see Weegenhuise, Johan

AVOND WINTER STRATEN see Kleppe, Joost

AVONDALE see Bush, Geoffrey

AVONDLIJK ZWIJGEN see Badings, Henk

AVONDSTER see Schouwman, Hans

AVRAN LE SERPI, O SARA see Benda, Georg
Anton (Jirí Antonín)

AVRIL see Delibes, Léo

AVRIX, MI GALARUCA see Neumann, Richard
J.

AVSHALOMOV, AARON (1894-1965)
K'e Still Ripples To Its Banks, The
S solo,pno [6'] sc AM.COMP.AL.
$3.85   (A328)

AWAKENING, THE see Torphicen, Pamela

AWAKENING OF SAPPHO, THE see Ogdon,
Wilbur L.

AWAY, AWAY see Bon, Willem Frederik

AYELET HASHAKHAR see Gideon, Miriam

AZOR AND ZEMIRA: ROSE SOFTLY BLOOMING
see Spohr, Ludwig (Louis)

AZTEKISCHE FLUITIST, DE see Bilt,
Willem van der

B

BABBITT, MILTON BYRON (1916-   )
Virginal Book, The
Mez solo,pno SMITH PUB   (B1)

BACEWICZ, GRAZYNA (1909-1969)
Piesni
"Songs" [Polish] solo voice,pno
[26'] POLSKIE   (B2)

Songs
see Piesni

BACH, CARL PHILIPP EMANUEL (1714-1788)
Frühling, Der *Wq.237
T solo,strings sc,pts KING'S   (B3)

Gellerts Geistliche Oden Und Lieder
OLMS   (B4)

BACH, JOHANN CHRISTIAN (1735-1782)
Six Canzonette, Op. 4
SS soli,cont sc KING'S   (B5)

BACH, JOHANN MICHAEL (1648-1694)
Ach, Wie Sehnlich Wart Ich Der Zeit
*cant
S solo,vln,3vla da gamba,vcl,cont
HANSSLER sc 30.621-01 f.s., pts
30.621-12, 13, 15 f.s. contains
also: Auf, Lasst Uns Den Herren
Loben (A solo,vln,3vla da gamba,
vcl,cont)   (B6)

Auf, Lasst Uns Den Herren Loben
see Ach, Wie Sehnlich Wart Ich Der
Zeit

Es Ist Ein Grosser Gewinn *cant
S solo,3vln,cont HANSSLER sc
30.620-01 f.s., pts
30.620-11, 13, 14 f.s.   (B7)

Liebster Jesu, Hör Mein Flehen
SATTB soli,2vln,2vla,cont HANSSLER
sc 30.622-01 f.s., pts
30.622-11, 15 f.s.   (B8)

BACH, JOHANN SEBASTIAN (1685-1750)
Arias From The Cantatas With
Obbligato Instruments: Bass Arias
*CC12U
[Ger] sc,pts KALMUS K 06828 f.s. (B9)

Arias From The Cantatas With
Obbligato Instruments: Contralto
Arias, Vol. 1 *sac,CC12U
[Ger] sc,pts KALMUS K 06819 f.s.
                                (B10)

Arias From The Cantatas With
Obbligato Instruments: Contralto
Arias, Vol. 2 *CC12U
[Ger] sc,pts KALMUS K 06820 f.s.
                                (B11)

Arias From The Cantatas With
Obbligato Instruments: Contralto
Arias, Vol. 3 *sac,CC6U
[Ger] sc,pts KALMUS K 06821 f.s.
                                (B12)

Arias From The Cantatas With
Obbligato Instruments: Soprano
And Alto Arias (Duets), Vol. 1
*CC3U
[Ger] sc,pts KALMUS K 06822 f.s.
                                (B13)

Arias From The Cantatas With
Obbligato Instruments: Soprano
And Alto Arias (Duets), Vol. 2
*CC4U
[Ger] sc,pts KALMUS K 06823 f.s.
                                (B14)

Arias From The Cantatas With
Obbligato Instruments: Soprano
And Alto Arias (Duets), Vol. 3
*CC4U
[Ger] sc,pts KALMUS K 06824 f.s.
                                (B15)

Arias From The Cantatas With
Obbligato Instruments: Soprano
Arias, Vol. 1 *sac,CCU
[Ger/Eng] sc,pts KALMUS K 06072
f.s.   (B16)

Arias From The Cantatas With
Obbligato Instruments: Soprano
Arias, Vol. 2 *sec,CC12U
[Ger] sc,pts KALMUS K 06817 f.s.
                                (B17)

Arias From The Cantatas With
Obbligato Instruments: Soprano
Arias, Vol. 3 *sac,CC5U
[Ger] sc,pts KALMUS K 06818 f.s.
                                (B18)

Arias From The Cantatas With
Obbligato Instruments: Tenor
Arias, Vol. 1 *CC12U
[Ger] sc,pts KALMUS K 06825 f.s.
                                (B19)

BACH, JOHANN SEBASTIAN (cont'd.)
Arias From The Cantatas With
Obbligato Instruments: Tenor
Arias, Vol. 2 *CC4U
[Ger] sc,pts KALMUS K 06826 f.s.
                                (B20)

Arias From The Cantatas With
Obbligato Instruments: Tenor
Arias, Vol. 3 *CC4U
[Ger] sc,pts KALMUS K 06827 f.s.
                                (B21)

Auprès De Toi
SCHOTT-FRER 9169   (B22)

Canconer Selecte Vol. 5 (40 Cants
Espirituals)
[Span/Ger] solo voice,pno BOIL
B.2054   (B23)

Cantata No. 51
see Jauchzet Gott In Allen Landen!

Cantata No. 54
see Widerstehe Doch Der Sunde

Cantata No. 56
see Ich Will Den Kreuzstab Gerne
Tragen

Cantata No. 57
see Selig Ist Der Mann

Cantata No. 82
see Ich Habe Genüg

Cantata No. 152
see Tritt Auf Die Glaubensbahn

Cantata No. 159
see Sehet, Wir Geh'n Hinauf Nach
Jerusalem

Cantata No. 160
see Ich Weiss, Dass Mein Erloser
Lebt

Cantata No. 170
see Vergnugte Ruh, Beliebte
Seelenlust

Cantata No. 189
see Mein Seele Ruhmt Und Preist

Cantata No. 202
see Weichet Nur, Betrube Schatten

Cantata No. 204
see Ich Bin In Mir Vergnügt

Cantata No. 209
see Was Scherz Sei Und Was Leiden

Cantata No. 210
see O Holder Tag
see O Holder Tag, Erwunscht Zeit

Cantate De La Pentecote *cant
S/T solo,pno LEDUC f.s.   (B24)

Christian, Ne'er Let Sin O'erpower
Thee
see Widerstehe Doch Der Sunde

Erbarm' Dich Mein, O Herre Gott
(Choral) *BWV 721
(Fernandez-Lavie, F.) solo voice,
vcl,gtr SCHOTTS ME 8718   (B25)

Five Chorale Preludes *CC5U
(Birtwistle, Harrison) solo voice,
clar,bass clar,basset horn sc,pts
UNIVER. UE 15559 $19.95   (B26)

Gloire A Dieu Partout Sur Terre!
see Jauchzet Gott In Allen Landen!

Herr Segne Euch, Der (from Cantata
No. 196)
TBar soli,org PETERS 6079   (B27)

Heureux Est L'Homme
see Selig Ist Der Mann

Ich Bin In Mir Vergnügt (Cantata No.
204)
S solo,strings,fl,2ob,opt bsn sc,
set KING'S   (B28)

Ich Habe Genüg (Cantata No. 82) cant
[Ger/Eng] B solo,hpsd,orch voc sc
KALMUS K 06033   (B29)

Ich Weiss, Dass Mein Erloser Lebt
(Cantata No. 160) cant
[Ger] T solo voc sc KALMUS K 09323
                                (B30)

Ich Will Den Kreuzstab Gerne Tragen
(Cantata No. 56) cant
[Ger] B solo,hpsd,org,orch voc sc
KALMUS K 06017   (B31)

J.S. Bach Duette Mit Obligat *CCU
(Adachi, Masaru) 2 solo voices,
inst,cont ONGAKU 523000 f.s.   (B32)

BACH, JOHANN SEBASTIAN (cont'd.)
Jauchzet Gott In Allen Landen!
(Cantata No. 51) cant
"Gloire A Dieu Partout Sur Terre!"
S solo,hpsd,orch voc sc KALMUS
K 09402   (B33)

Mein Seele Ruhmt Und Preist (Cantata
No. 189) cant
[Ger] T solo voc sc KALMUS K 06630
                                (B34)

Non Sa Che Sia Dolore
see Was Scherz Sei Und Was Leiden

O Holder Tag (Cantata No. 210)
S solo,strings,fl,ob,opt bsn sc,set
KING'S   (B35)

O Holder Tag, Erwunscht Zeit (Cantata
No. 210) cant
"O Jour Heureux, O Temps Beni"
[Ger/Fr] S solo voc sc KALMUS
K 06646   (B36)

O Jour Heureux, O Temps Beni
see O Holder Tag, Erwunscht Zeit

Patron, Das Macht Der Wind
S solo,pno CLASSV 0473   (B37)

Sehet, Wir Geh'n Hinauf Nach
Jerusalem (Cantata No. 159) cant
[Ger] ATB soli,hpsd,org,orch voc sc
KALMUS K 09320   (B38)

Selected Arias For Bass, Trumpet And
Piano *CCU
BREITKOPF-W EB 8535 f.s.   (B39)

Selected Songs From Schemelli's
Songbook *CCU
solo voice,gtr BREITKOPF-W EB 8557
f.s.   (B40)

Selig Ist Der Mann (Cantata No. 57)
cant
"Heureux Est L'Homme" [Ger] SB
soli,hpsd,org voc sc KALMUS
K 09404   (B41)

Tritt Auf Die Glaubensbahn (Cantata
No. 152) cant
[Ger] SB soli voc sc KALMUS K 09322
                                (B42)

Unschuld, Kleinod Reiner Seelen
[Ger] S solo,fl,ob,vln,vla sc,pts
KALMUS K 06829   (B43)

Vergnugte Ruh, Beliebte Seelenlust
(Cantata No. 170) cant
[Ger] A solo voc sc KALMUS K 09326
                                (B44)

Was Scherz Sei Und Was Leiden
(Cantata No. 209) cant
"Non Sa Che Sia Dolore" [It] S
solo,orch voc sc KALMUS K 06645
                                (B45)

Wedding Song: Go Now In Hope (from
Bist Du Bei Mir)
(Hopson, Hal H.) low solo,pno HOPE
1013   (B46)
(Hopson, Hal H.) high solo,pno HOPE
1014   (B47)

Weichet Nur, Betrube Schatten
(Cantata No. 202) cant
[Ger/Eng] S solo,org,orch voc sc
KALMUS K 06638   (B48)

Widerstehe Doch Der Sunde (Cantata
No. 54) cant
"Christian, Ne'er Let Sin O'erpower
Thee" [Ger/Eng] A solo,hpsd,orch
voc sc KALMUS K 06036   (B49)

"BACH, P.D.Q." (PETER SCHICKELE)
Shepherd On The Rocks, With A Twist
(S. 12 to 1)
bargain counter tenor and devious
instruments PRESSER 111-40111
                                (B50)

BACHELET, ALFRED (1864-1944)
Chère Nuit
med solo,pno CLASSV 0699   (B51)
high solo,pno CLASSV 0431   (B52)

BACHIANAS BRASILEIRAS NO. 5 see Villa-
Lobos, Heitor

BACIO, IL see Arditi, Luigi

BÄCK, SVEN-ERIK (1919-   )
Idealet Och Livet: Fyra Sånger För
Don Quijote Och Sancho Panza
[Swed] Bar solo,bsn,harp,2perc,
harmonium TONOS   (B53)

Tvä Kyrkovisor
[Swed] solo voice,brass quin
NORDISKA   (B54)

BACKER-GRØNDAHL, AGATHE [URSULA]
(1847-1907)
Aftnen Er Stille *Op.67,No.4
(Brevik, Tor) "Evening Is Quiet,
The" solo voice,clar,bsn,horn,
strings NORGE f.s.   (B55)

Evening Is Quiet, The
see Aftnen Er Stille

BACKER-LUNDE, JOHAN (1874-1958)
Bli Til Ett Med
see Inclusions

Butterflies
"Sommerfugler" LYCHE 58   (B56)

Compensation
"Erstatning" LYCHE 59   (B57)

Erstatning
see Compensation

Gaaet Bort
LYCHE 76   (B58)

Hie Away
"Renn Avsted" LYCHE 97   (B59)

Hinsides Haven
LYCHE 71   (B60)

Ich Liebe Dich *Op.21,No.11
[Ger] S solo,2.2.2.1. 4.2.3.1.
strings [3'] NORSK f.s.   (B61)

Inclusions
"Bli Til Ett Med" LYCHE   (B62)

Into The Night
"Ved Natt" LYCHE 98   (B63)

Kvat Havbåra Syng *Op.25
"Song Of The Sea" solo voice,4horn,
3trom,tuba,strings [4'] NORSK
f.s.   (B64)

Ottar Svarte's Song In Praise Of King
Olav
LYCHE 70   (B65)

Renn Avsted
see Hie Away

Rivulet, The *Op.39
[Eng] solo voice,strings NORSK f.s.
(B66)

Sommerfugler
see Butterflies

Song Of The Sea
see Kvat Havbåra Syng

Spanish Serenade
LYCHE 79   (B67)

Tiefe Kämmerlein, Das *Op.34
[Ger] solo voice,2horn,harp,strings
NORSK f.s.   (B68)

Unge Pikes Vals, Den
LYCHE 57   (B69)

Var Jeg Som Dugg
see Were I A Cloudlet

Ved Natt
see Into The Night

Vinternat *Op.11
"Winter Night" solo voice,4horn,
harp,strings [4'] NORSK f.s.
(B70)

Were I A Cloudlet
"Var Jeg Som Dugg" LYCHE 78 (B71)

Winter Night
see Vinternat

BACON, ERNST L. (1898-1990)
Nocturne
see Shilflied

Quiet Airs
solo voice (12 pieces with texts by
Whitman, Herrick, Dickinson,
Blake, Housman) RECITAL 2245
(B72)

Shilflied
"Nocturne" [Ger/Eng] solo voice,pno
CLASSV 1995   (B73)

Six Songs
med-low solo (texts by Dickinson,
Sandburg, Whitman) RECITAL 2243
(B74)

Songs, 50
solo voice,pno CLASSV 1990 (B75)

Songs At Parting
solo voice (8 songs; texts by
Whitman) RECITAL 2244   (B76)

Tributaries
solo voice,pno CLASSV 1991 (B77)

BAD DAY see Grieg, Edvard Hagerup, Vond
Dag

BAD MAN see Ehlen, Margriet

BADEN, CONRAD (1908-1989)
Åtte Sanger Til Tekst Av Trygve
Bjerkrheim, Op. 127
[Norw] solo voice,org NORGE (B78)

August
see Tre Sanger, Op. 121

Barcarole
[Norw] Bar solo,pno NORGE   (B79)

Besvergelse
[Norw] Bar solo,pno NORGE   (B80)

By The Vålå Lake
see På Vålåsjøen

Døden Må Vike
see Tre Salmer Til Tekst Av Svein
Ellingsen

Drag Inn
see Tre Solomotetter For Dyp Stemme
Og Orgel, Op. 123

Eders Hjerte Forferdes Ikke
see Fire Solomotetter Fra Johannes-
Evangeliet, Op. 111

Eg Er'kje Eismal
see To Stev

Eleven Songs, Op. 2
[Eng/Ger] S solo,pno NORGE (B81)

Ennu En Kort Stund
see Fire Solomotetter Fra Johannes-
Evangeliet, Op. 111

Fariseeren Og Tolderen
see Tre Solomotetter For Dyp Stemme
Og Orgel, Op. 123

Fire Bibelske Sanger, Op. 50
[Norw] S solo,org NORGE   (B82)

Fire Setrom-Sanger, Op. 15
[Norw] solo voice,pno NORGE (B83)

Fire Skjaeraasen-Sanger, Op. 98
solo voice,pno NORGE f.s.
contains: Gjenskinn; Norsk Salme;
Sang På Elva; Sinn   (B84)

Fire Solomotetter Fra Johannes-
Evangeliet, Op. 111
[Norw] solo voice,org NORGE f.s.
contains: Eders Hjerte Forferdes
Ikke; Ennu En Kort Stund; Jeg
Er Livsens Brød   (B85)

Fødd I Går
see Tre Sanger, Op. 121

Gammel Mariavise
[Norw] solo voice,pno NORSK (B86)

Gjenskinn
see Fire Skjaeraasen-Sanger, Op. 98

Herre, Kom Ditt Folk I Møte
see Tre Salmer Til Tekst Av Svein
Ellingsen

Herrens Bønn
see Tre Religiøse Sanger, Op. 127

Huldra *Op.14,No.4
[Norw] solo voice,pno NORGE (B87)

Hvert Blad Som Tiden Vender
see Tre Salmer Til Tekst Av Svein
Ellingsen

Hymnus, Op.73
[Lat] A solo,fl,ob,vla [7'] NORSK
(B88)

Ja Det Er En Fart
[Norw] solo voice,pno NORGE (B89)

Jeg Er Livsens Brød
see Fire Solomotetter Fra Johannes-
Evangeliet, Op. 111

Konn Og Gull
see To Stev

Makt, Di
see Tre Sanger, Op. 121

Nakne Hei, Den
see Tre Sanger

Ni Sanger, Op. 82
[Norw] solo voice,pno NORGE (B90)

Norsk Salme
see Fire Skjaeraasen-Sanger, Op. 98

BADEN, CONRAD (cont'd.)
På Vålåsjøen *Op.14,No.1
"By The Vålå Lake" S solo,fl,ob,
clar,2horn,strings [2'] NORGE
f.s.   (B91)
see Tre Sanger

Psalm No. 116
solo voice,org/pno NORGE f.s. (B92)

Psalm No. 119
solo voice,org/pno NORGE f.s. (B93)

Så Er Du Fri
see Tre Religiøse Sanger, Op. 127

Sang På Elva
see Fire Skjaeraasen-Sanger, Op. 98

Sinn
see Fire Skjaeraasen-Sanger, Op. 98

Søk Herren
see Tre Solomotetter For Dyp Stemme
Og Orgel, Op. 123

Takk For Den Heilage Ande
see Tre Religiøse Sanger, Op. 127

To Bibelske Sanger, Op. 104
[Norw] S solo,ob,org NORGE (B94)

To Fröding-Sanger, Op.96
[Swed] Bar solo,pno NORGE f.s.
contains: Vårfästmö, En;
Vintervisa, En   (B95)

To Stev
LYCHE 39 f.s.
contains: Eg Er'kje Eismal; Konn
Og Gull   (B96)

Tre Religiøse Sanger, Op. 127
[Norw] solo voice,pno/org NORGE
f.s.
contains: Herrens Bønn; Så Er Du
Fri; Takk For Den Heilage Ande
(B97)

Tre Salmer Til Tekst Av Svein
Ellingsen
[Norw] solo voice,org NORGE f.s.
contains: Døden Må Vike; Herre,
Kom Ditt Folk I Møte; Hvert
Blad Som Tiden Vender   (B98)

Tre Sanger
[Norw] solo voice,pno LYCHE 41 f.s.
contains: Nakne Hei, Den; På
Vålåsjøen; Veven   (B99)

Tre Sanger, Op. 121
solo voice,pno NORSK f.s.
contains: August; Fødd I Går;
Makt, Di   (B100)

Tre Solomotetter For Dyp Stemme Og
Orgel, Op. 123
[Norw] low solo,org NORGE f.s.
contains: Drag Inn; Fariseeren Og
Tolderen; Søk Herren   (B101)

Tretten Salmer Til Tekst Av Svein
Ellingsen, Op. 138
[Norw] solo voice,org NORGE (B102)

Two Songs From Edda, Op. 18
[Norw] solo voice,pno NORGE (B103)

Vårfästmö, En
see To Fröding-Sanger, Op.96

Veven
see Tre Sanger

Vintervisa, En
see To Fröding-Sanger, Op.96

BADINGS, HENK (1907-1987)
Air Sur Une Blonde
see Ariettes

Als Uit Den Hartstocht Van Het
Avondrood
see Drie Liederen Uit "Lentemaan"

Annabel
see Drie Liederen

Ariette
see Ariettes

Ariettes
high solo,pno DONEMUS f.s.
contains: Air Sur Une Blonde;
Ariette; Pastorale Pour
Jeannette; Soupirs; Vaudeville
(B104)

Avondlijk Zwijgen
see Drie Liederen

Daghet In Den Oosten, Het
see Drie Oud-Nederlandse Liederen

BADINGS, HENK (cont'd.)

Dennebosse
see Vier Liedjies Van Weemoed, Op
Suid-Afrikaanse Tekste

Doove Pijnen Sidderseinen Ver Van
Ongekende Grenzen
see Drie Liederen Uit "Lentemaan"

Drie Liederen
male solo,pno DONEMUS f.s.
contains: Annabel; Avondlijk
Zwijgen; Klein Air   (B105)

Drie Liederen Uit "Lentemaan"
A solo,fl,clar,vln,vla,vcl DONEMUS
f.s. [9']
contains: Als Uit Den Hartstocht
Van Het Avondrood; Doove Pijnen
Sidderseinen Ver Van Ongekende
Grenzen; Ik Weet Nu Zet Uw
Schoone Deemoed In Haar
Avondlijk Gebed   (B106)

Drie Oud-Nederlandse Liederen
Mez solo,fl,harp DONEMUS f.s. [8']
contains: Daghet In Den Oosten,
Het; Rijck God, Wien Sal Ick
Claghen; Viel Eens Hemels
Douwe, Het   (B107)

Du Innigkeit Im Dämmerwalt
see Sechs Lieder

Eight Songs (e.e.cummings) *CC8L
med solo,pno DONEMUS f.s.   (B108)

Ek Hoor
see Vier Liedjies Van Weemoed, Op
Suid-Afrikaanse Tekste

Frühling Ist's, Der
see Sechs Lieder

Frühlingsabend
see Fünf Lieder

Fünf Lieder
med solo,pno DONEMUS f.s.
contains: Frühlingsabend; Herbst;
Nacht; Was Aus Dir Tönt; Welt
Ist Zerbrochen, Eine   (B109)

Herbst
see Fünf Lieder

Ik Weet Nu Zet Uw Schoone Deemoed In
Haar Avondlijk Gebed
see Drie Liederen Uit "Lentemaan"

Irgendwo Will Man Ganz Ruhig Sein
see Sechs Lieder

Klein Air
see Drie Liederen

Liedjie
see Vier Liedjies Van Weemoed, Op
Suid-Afrikaanse Tekste

Meiregen, Kinderverzen *CC11L
low solo,pno DONEMUS f.s.   (B110)

Nacht
see Fünf Lieder

Pastorale Pour Jeannette
see Ariettes

Qualvoll Dieses Leise Weinen
see Sechs Lieder

Rijck God, Wien Sal Ick Claghen
see Drie Oud-Nederlandse Liederen

Schreiten Gottes Wird Zum Sturm, Das
see Sechs Lieder

Sechs Lieder
med solo,pno DONEMUS f.s.
contains: Du Innigkeit Im
Dämmerwalt; Frühling Ist's,
Der; Irgendwo Will Man Ganz
Ruhig Sein; Qualvoll Dieses
Leise Weinen; Schreiten Gottes
Wird Zum Sturm, Das; Und Es
Fällt Der Regen   (B111)

Seemeeu
see Vier Liedjies Van Weemoed, Op
Suid-Afrikaanse Tekste

Sextet III, Songs From The Tao Te
King
S solo,fl,clar,gtr,vln,db [19']
DONEMUS   (B112)

Soupirs
see Ariettes

Und Es Fällt Der Regen
see Sechs Lieder

BADINGS, HENK (cont'd.)

Vaudeville
see Ariettes

Viel Eens Hemels Douwe, Het
see Drie Oud-Nederlandse Liederen

Vier Liedjies Van Weemoed, Op Suid-
Afrikaanse Tekste
med-high solo,pno DONEMUS f.s.;
contains: Dennebosse; Ek Hoor;
Liedjie; Seemeeu   (B113)

Was Aus Dir Tönt
see Fünf Lieder

Welt Ist Zerbrochen, Eine
see Fünf Lieder

BAEKKEN see Jordan, Sverre

BAG OF THE BEE, THE see Lessard, John
Ayres

BAG OF TOOLS see Hodd, Jack Lorne

BAGGIANI, GUIDO (1932-   )
UbUng
solo voice,gong,gtr,vibra,pno EDI-
PAN EP 7367   (B114)

BAHK, JUNSANG (1938-   )
Invokation
S solo,bass clar,perc study sc
PETERS f.s.   (B115)

BAIGNE D'EAU see Massenet, Jules,
Thaïs: Duo De L'Oasis

BAILEY, BOB
I'm Walkin' (composed with Morrow,
Marvin)
med solo TRIUNE TUS 116 $1.95
(B116)

Stand
med solo TRIUNE TUS 117 $1.95
(B117)

BAILEY, MARSHALL
Three Songs *CC3U
med solo,pno sc AM.COMP.AL. $6.90
(B118)

BAILLY, JEAN GUY (1925-   )
Tombeau De Rainer Maria Rilke, Le
S solo,1.1.1.1. 2.2.2.0. 2perc,
harp,pno,strings [19'] BILLAUDOT
(B119)

BAINBRIDGE, SIMON
Landscapes And Magic Words
S solo,instrumental ensemble UNITED
MUS f.s.   (B120)

People Of The Dawn
S solo,instrumental ensemble UNITED
MUS f.s.   (B121)

BAIRD, TADEUSZ (1928-1981)
Glosy Z Oddali
[Polish] Bar solo,4.2.2.2. 4.3.3.0.
perc,2harp,strings POLSKIE f.s.
contains: Nad Wiecznym Jeziorem
Stoje, "An Einem Ewigen See
Stehe Ich"; Noc, "Nacht, Die";
W Kosciele, "In Der Kirche"
(B122)

Nad Wiecznym Jeziorem Stoje
see Glosy Z Oddali

Noc
see Glosy Z Oddali

Voices From Afar *see Glosy Z Oddali

W Kosciele
see Glosy Z Oddali

BAJITO QUISIERA see Olivella

BAKKE, RUTH (1947-   )
Akk, Mon Min Vei Til Kana'an
see Med Jesus Vil Eg Fara

Bønn
[Norw] Mez solo,gtr,org NORGE
(B123)

Enter No Silence
[Eng] A solo,pno,vcl (text by e.e.
cummings) NORGE   (B124)

Fragments D'un Homme Moderne
[Fr] Bar solo,perc,synthesizer,
electronic tape [16'] NORGE
(B125)

Hor, Alle Som Tørster
[Norw] S solo,gtr NORGE   (B126)

Jeg Ser Deg, O Guds Lam, Å Stå
see Med Jesus Vil Eg Fara

Killingdans
[Norw] S solo,fl,clar,bsn [3']
NORGE   (B127)

Krist Stod Op Af Døde
see Med Jesus Vil Eg Fara

BAKKE, RUTH (cont'd.)

Med Jesus Vil Eg Fara
solo voice,org NORGE f.s. contains
also: Akk, Mon Min Vei Til
Kana'an; Jeg Ser Deg, O Guds Lam,
Å Stå; Krist Stod Op Af Døde
(B128)

Nonsens 1
[Norw] solo voice NORGE   (B129)

Nonsens 2
[Norw] solo voice NORGE   (B130)

Nonsens 3
[Norw] solo voice NORGE   (B131)

Piken I Alvedansen
S solo,fl,vln [7'] NORGE   (B132)

Vision Blurred, A
Bar solo,vcl NORGE   (B133)

Why?
[Eng] A solo,prepared pno,vcl [5']
(text by e.e. cummings) NORGE
(B134)

BAKVENDE VERDI, DEN see Hegdal, Magne

BAL MASQUE see Poulenc, Francis

BALADA. SIROTEK (DAS WAISENKIND), OP. 5
see Dvorák, Antonín

BALADES see Mestres, Apeles

BALAKAUSKAS, OSVALDAS (1937-   )
Chopin - Hauer
[Ger] ST soli,vla,2pno, a group of
speaking, singing, clapping
actors (5), et [13'] POLSKIE
(B135)

BALAKIREV, MILY ALEXEYEVICH (1837-1910)
Barcarolle
[Russ/Ger/Fr/Eng] T solo,pno CLASSV
1063   (B136)

Brigand's Song, A
[Russ/Ger/Fr/Eng] med-high solo,pno
CLASSV 1062   (B137)

Dream, A
[Russ/Ger/Fr/Eng] T solo,pno CLASSV
0593
see Rêve, Un   (B138)

Knight, The
[Russ/Ger/Fr/Eng] med solo,pno
CLASSV 1066   (B139)

Let Me But Hear Thy Voice
[Russ/Ger/Fr/Eng] med solo,pno
CLASSV 1067   (B140)

O Come To Me
"Viens Près De Moi" [Russ/Ger/Fr/
Eng] med-high solo,pno CLASSV
1064   (B141)

Old Man's Song, The
[Russ/Ger/Fr/Eng] B solo,pno CLASSV
1065   (B142)

Prélude
[Fr/Eng] high solo,pno CLASSV 1068
(B143)

Rêve, Un
"Dream, A" [Fr/Eng] Bar solo,pno
CLASSV 1069   (B144)

Song Of Georgia, A
[Russ/Ger/Fr/Eng] T solo,pno CLASSV
1061   (B145)

Viens Près De Moi
see O Come To Me

BALASSA, SÁNDOR (1935-   )
Antinomia
S solo,clar,pno BOOSEY EMB06314
(B146)

BALAZS, FREDERIC (1920-   )
Angels
boy solo&speaking voice,1.1.1.1.
1.1.1.0. harp,pno,bass gtr,
strings without db [30']
AM.COMP.AL.   (B147)

Five Songs *CC5U
med solo,pno sc AM.COMP.AL. $14.90
(B148)

For Music
S solo,pno [8'] sc AM.COMP.AL.
$5.00   (B149)

If Only The Night Could Stand Still
Bar solo,pno [6'] AM.COMP.AL.
(B150)

BALCON, LE see Debussy, Claude

BALDVINSSON, TRYGGVI (1965-   )
Birthdaysong
high solo,pno [2'0"] ICELAND
063-011   (B151)

BALDVINSSON, TRYGGVI (cont'd.)

Folksong
solo voice,pno [1'0"] ICELAND
063-012   (B152)

BALES, RICHARD HORNER (1915-   )
Ozymandias
med solo,1.1.2.1. 2.0.0.0. strings
[5'0"] PEER   (B153)

BALFE, MICHAEL WILLIAM (1808-1870)
Bohemian Girl, The: Admiral Song,
Duet And Trio
see Could I Hush A Father's Sigh

Could I Hush A Father's Sigh
"Bohemian Girl, The: Admiral Song,
Duet And Trio" SCIEN 161   (B154)

I Dreamt That I Dwelt In Marble Halls
S solo,pno CLASSV 0383   (B155)

Trust Her Not
2 solo voices (text by Longfellow)
RECITAL 2233   (B156)

BALL, ERNEST R. (1878-1927)
Mother Machree
low solo,pno CLASSV 1886   (B157)
med solo,pno CLASSV 1885   (B158)
med-high solo,pno CLASSV 1884
                                    (B159)
high solo,pno CLASSV 1883   (B160)

BALL OF SUN see Wernick, Richard F.

BALLAD ABOUT TOSCANA, THE see Groven,
Eivind, Balladen Om Toscanaland

BALLAD ALBUM *CCU
med solo BOOSEY VAB0288 f.s.   (B161)

BALLAD BOOK OF JOHN JACOB NILES see
Niles, John Jacob

BALLAD FOR SHAHEEN see Lewis, Peter Tod

BALLAD OF ELECTED KNIGHTS see Cox,
David

BALLAD OF MR. AND MRS. DISCOBBOLOS, THE
see Orr, Buxton

BALLAD OF READING GAOL, THE see
Nielson, Lewis

BALLAD WITH EPITAPHS see Russell,
Armand King

BALLADA HAROM FALEVELRÖL see Nieland,
Henk

BALLADE DES DAMES DU TEMPS JADIS see
Franken, Wim

BALLADE DES FEMMES DE PARIS see
Franken, Wim

BALLADE DES PENDUS see Paulet, V.

BALLADE VOM NIGGER JIM see Eisler,
Hanns

BALLADE VON DEN SÄCKESCHMEISSERN see
Eisler, Hanns

BALLADE VON DER JUDENHURE MARIE SANDERS
see Eisler, Hanns

BALLADE VON DER KRÜPPELGARDE see
Eisler, Hanns

BALLADE ZUM 218 see Eisler, Hanns

BALLADEN, GESÄNGE UND LIEDER, OP. 145
see Lowe, Karl

BALLADEN, GESÄNGE UND ROMANZEN IN MUSIK
GESETZT see Kreutzer, Konradin

BALLADEN OM TOSCANALAND see Groven,
Eivind

BALLADEN, OP. 1 see Mattiesen

BALLADENBUCH see Eisler, Hanns

BALLADES, DANCES AND ECHOS see Iglesias
Rossi, Alejandro

BALLATA see Mascagni, Pietro see
Zallman, Arlene (Proctor)

BALLATA DEL BEL CAVALIERE see Buzzi-
Peccia, Arturo

BALLATELLA see Leoncavallo, Ruggiero,
Pagliacci: Qual Fiamma

BALLO IN MASCHERA, UN: ERI TU see
Verdi, Giuseppe

BALLO IN MASCHERA, UN: ERI TU CHE
MACCHIAVI see Verdi, Giuseppe

BALLO IN MASCHERA, UN: MORRÒ MA PRIMA
IN GRAZIA see Verdi, Giuseppe

BALLYNURE BALLAD, A see Hughes, Herbert

BALSATZAR, OP. 57 see Schumann, Robert
(Alexander)

BANDA, LA see Sampaoli, Luciano

BANK, JACQUES (1943-   )
Australiana
Bar solo,acord [25'] DONEMUS (B162)

Late Of The City Of Rome
Mez/T solo,4fl,pic,3alto fl,2bass
fl [20'] DONEMUS   (B163)

Taaie Winter, Een
"Tough Winter, A" solo voice,alto
fl [8'] DONEMUS   (B164)

Taaie Winter, Een, Nr. 2
"Tough Winter, A, Nr. 2" solo
voice,acord,vcl [8'] DONEMUS
                               (B165)

Tough Winter, A
see Taaie Winter, Een

Tough Winter, A, Nr. 2
see Taaie Winter, Een, Nr. 2

Very Bad Character, A
B/Bar solo,acap [7'] DONEMUS (B166)

BANKA see Matsudaira, Yori-Tsune

BÅNSULL see Olsen, Sparre see
Sommerfeldt, Öistein

BANTOCK, [SIR] GRANVILLE (1868-1946)
Five Ghazals Of Hafiz
[Eng/Ger] Bar solo RECITAL 244
                               (B167)

BANTU AND YOU, THE see Kalanzi, Benny

BÅNVISE see Olsen, Sparre

BAPTISM INVOCATION see Leifs, Jon

BAPTISMAL SONG see Macmillan, Alan

BARAB
Child's Garden Of Verse [1]
BOOSEY VAB0212   (B168)

Child's Garden Of Verse [2]
BOOSEY VAB0213   (B169)

Parodies
BOOSEY VAB0221   (B170)

BARAB, SEYMOUR (1921-   )
Alice, A Cabaret
narrator,vcl GALAXY 1.3000 $8.50
                               (B171)

BARATHON
Chansons Traditionnelles Des
Provinces De France *CCU,Fr
(Lemetre) solo voice DURAND f.s. in
4 volumes   (B172)

BARATI, GEORGE (1913-   )
Fireflies In The Garden
med solo,pno [2'] sc AM.COMP.AL.
$1.20   (B173)

Fragment From "Cities Of The
Interior"
S solo,1.1.1.1. 1.1.1.0. perc,
strings [7'] AM.COMP.AL. sc
$6.15, pts $9.95, pno red $1.95
                               (B174)

Noelani's Aria
A solo,2fl,2ob,2clar,2bsn,harp,
timp,strings [4'] sc AM.COMP.AL.
$4.60   (B175)

Once By The Pacific
B/Bar solo,pno [3'] sc AM.COMP.AL.
$1.95   (B176)

BARBARA ALLAN see Anonymous

BARBARA ELLEN see Anonymous

BARBARE see Packer, Randall

BARBAROSSA-LIEDER see Gundlach, Wilhelm

BARBER, SAMUEL (1910-1981)
Sleep Now (from Three Songs)
med solo SCHIRM.G ST38372   (B177)

Three Songs, Op. 45
high solo SCHIRM.G ED2980   (B178)
low solo SCHIRM.G ED2981   (B179)

BARBER OF SEVILLE, THE: ECCO RIDENTE
see Rossini, Gioacchino

BARBER OF SEVILLE, THE: LA CALUNNIA see
Rossini, Gioacchino

BARBER OF SEVILLE, THE: LARGO AL
FACTOTUM see Rossini, Gioacchino

BARBER OF SEVILLE, THE: UNA VOCE POCO
FA see Rossini, Gioacchino

BARBIERI DI SIVIGLIA, IL: CAVATINA DI
FIGARO see Rossini, Gioacchino

BARBIERI DI SIVIGLIA, IL: LA CALUNNIA
see Rossini, Gioacchino

BARBIERI DI SIVIGLIA, IL: UNA VOCE POCO
FA see Rossini, Gioacchino

BARBIRETTI, ARRIGO (1906-   )
Ave Maria
Mez/Bar solo ZENGERINK R.477 (B180)

BARBLAN-OPIENSKA, LYDIA
Ave Maria *BVM/Marriage
solo voice,kbd HUGUENIN EB 102
                               (B181)

BARCAROLA see Britain, Radie see
Gounod, Charles François

BARCAROLE see Baden, Conrad see
Fladmoe, Arvid see Marx, Joseph see
Schubert, Franz (Peter), Auf Dem
Wasser

BARCAROLLE see Balakirev, Mily
Alexeyevich

BARCHETA, LA see Hahn, Reynaldo

BARD OF ARMAGH, THE see Hughes, Herbert

BARE BRANCH, A see Braein, Edvard
Fliflet, Naki Grein, Ei

BAREISHO NO HANA see Miki, Minoru

BARITON-BASS-ALBUM AUS DEM REPERTOIRE
VON HANS HOTTER *CC17L
[It/Fr/Ger] DOBLINGER 08 503 f.s.
                               (B182)

BARKAN, EMANUEL J.
Ahavat Olam
solo voice,kbd TRANSCON. 991411
                               (B183)

BARKIN, ELAINE R. (1932-   )
Supple Suitor..., The
Mez solo,fl/alto fl/pic,ob,vcl,
hpsd/pno,1perc [24'] APNM sc
$11.00, pts rent   (B184)

BARN, ET see Dorumsgaard, Arne see
Fladmoe, Arvid

BARN ER FØDT I BETLEHEM, ET see Nyhus,
Rolf

BARN JESUS I EN KRYBBE LÅ see Johansen,
David Monrad

BARNEBILLEDER see Jensen, Ludwig Irgens

BARNET see Kielland, Olav see
Sønstevold, Gunnar

BARNET SOVER see Jordan, Sverre

BARONIN COLOMBINE see Bijvanck, Henk

BARRERA Y CALLEJA
Granadinas
[Span] T solo,pno CLASSV 1342 (B185)

BARRETT, RICHARD
Principia
Bar solo,pno UNITED MUS f.s. (B186)

BARRY, GERALD (1952-   )
Sweet Cork
S solo,B rec,vla da gamba,hpsd
OXFORD perf mat rent   (B187)

BARTH, FRODE (1968-   )
Onde Dronning, Den
[Norw] solo voice,gtr [2'] NORGE
                               (B188)
[Norw] Mez solo,gtr [2'] NORGE
                               (B189)
Songen Til Han Som Er Komen Igjenom
[Norw] solo voice,gtr [3'] NORGE
                               (B190)
[Norw] Mez solo,gtr [3'] NORGE
                               (B191)

BARTHELEMY, R.
Chi Se Nne Scorda Cchiù!
T solo,pno CLASSV 1057   (B192)

BARTHOLOMÉE, PIERRE (1937-   )
Accent
S/T solo,pno CBDM   (B193)
Mez solo,pno CBDM   (B194)
A/countertenor,pno CBDM   (B195)
Bar solo,pno CBDM   (B196)
B solo,pno CBDM   (B197)

BARTÓK, BÉLA (1881-1945)
Twenty Hungarian Folksongs, Vol. 1
*CCU
BOOSEY VAB0266 f.s.   (B198)

BARTÓK, BÉLA (cont'd.)

Twenty Hungarian Folksongs, Vol. 2
*CCU
BOOSEY VAB0267 f.s. (B199)

Twenty Hungarian Folksongs, Vol. 3
*CCU
BOOSEY VAB0268 f.s. (B200)

Twenty Hungarian Folksongs, Vol. 4
*CCU
BOOSEY VAB0269 f.s. (B201)

BARTOLINO DA PADOVA
Three Madrigals
(Wilkins, Nigel) 3 solo voices,opt
inst ANTICO AE9 (B202)

BARTON, HANUS
Otazka Bez Odpovedi
S solo,2.2.2.2. 4.3.3.0. timp,perc,
cel,strings [14'] CESKY HUD.
(B203)

BARTOŠ, JAN ZDENEK (1908-1981)
Detem *song cycle
S solo,pno PANTON 881 (B204)

O Honzovi
S solo,1.1.2.1. 2.2.1.0. timp,perc,
strings CESKY HUD. (B205)

Sonety O Praze
T&speaking voice,harp,strings [24']
CESKY HUD. (B206)

BASART, ROBERT (1926-1993)
Serenade
S solo,fl,clar,pno,electronic tape
[10'] FALLEN LEAF 18 accomp tape
available (B207)

BASILIO'S LAMENT see Wright, Maurice

BASTA! TI CREDO see Rejcha, Antonin

BASUN see Tveitt, Geirr

BATISTIN
see STUCK, JEAN BAPTISTE

BATTI, BATTI see Lyric Soprano Arias: A
Master Class With Evelyn Lear, Vol.
2

BATTISHILL, JONATHAN (1738-1801)
Collection Of Favourite Songs, A
(1765)
sc KING'S (B208)

BATTISTINI, M.
Eruccio
[It/Russ] med-high solo,pno CLASSV
0594 (B209)

BATTLE OF VICKSBURG, THE see Zaninelli,
Luigi

BATTLESHIP NEWSREEL see Little, David

BAUDIN, ERNESTINE VON
Kleine Blumen, Kleine Blätter *Op.9
solo voice,pno SCIEN 173 (B210)

BAUER
Honig Songs
S solo,pno PETERS 67372 (B211)

BAUER, ROSS
Four Honig Songs
S solo,pno [12'] AM.COMP.AL. (B212)

BAUMANN, ALEXANDER
Abschied Von Di Berg, Der
see 'S Is Anderscht

D' Hoamlige Liab
see Lieder, Op. 13

Da Bua In Wigl Wagl
see 'S Is Anderscht

Da Gfopti
see Lieder, Op. 13

Da Muada Ihr Wiagn G'sangl
see Lieder, Op. 13

Eifersichtigi Bua, Der
see Gebirgs-Bleameln: Sechs Lieder

Gebirgs-Bleameln: Sechs Lieder
solo voice/ solo voices,pno SCIEN
176 f.s. in Austrian dialect
contains: Eifersichtigi Bua, Der;
Hoagliche, Der; In Da Fremd; 'S
Besti Parl; Verstoss'ne, Der;
Vor Ihra Hitn (B213)

Guada Rad
see 'S Is Anderscht

Hoagliche, Der
see Gebirgs-Bleameln: Sechs Lieder

BAUMANN, ALEXANDER (cont'd.)

In Da Fremd
see Gebirgs-Bleameln: Sechs Lieder

Lieder, Op. 13
solo voice,pno SCIEN 178 f.s. in
Austrian dialect
contains: D' Hoamlige Liab; Da
Gfopti; Da Muada Ihr Wiagn
G'sangl; Nandl Ihr Almlied,
Das; 'S Hochzeit Gsangl;
Unzeitige Gsoass, Der (B214)

Nandl Ihr Almlied, Das
see Lieder, Op. 13

Pfiffige, Der
see 'S Is Anderscht

'S Besti Parl
see Gebirgs-Bleameln: Sechs Lieder

'S Hochzeit Gsangl
see Lieder, Op. 13

'S Is Anderscht
solo voice,pno (in Austrian
dialect) SCIEN 177 f.s. contains
also: Da Bua In Wigl Wagl;
Vordernbach, Almlied; Pfiffige,
Der; Guada Rad; Abschied Von Di
Berg, Der (B215)

Unzeitige Gsoass, Der
see Lieder, Op. 13

Verstoss'ne, Der
see Gebirgs-Bleameln: Sechs Lieder

Vor Ihra Hitn
see Gebirgs-Bleameln: Sechs Lieder

Vordernbach, Almlied
see 'S Is Anderscht

BAUMANN, HERBERT (1925-   )
Nasobem Und Andere, Das
T solo,rec,gtr perf sc PLUCKED STR
T 0853 $6.75 (B216)

BAVICCHI, JOHN ALEXANDER (1922-   )
Six Korean Folksongs *CC6U
S solo,pno SEESAW f.s. (B217)

To The Lighthouse
S solo,horn,pno SEESAW f.s. (B218)

Trio No. 3
S solo,vln,vcl SEESAW f.s. (B219)

BAX, [SIR] ARNOLD (1883-1953)
Celtic Lullaby, A
high solo,pno CLASSV 0637 (B220)

Celtic Song Cycle, A
high solo,pno CLASSV 1714 (B221)

Fairies, The
see Three Songs

Five Songs
solo voice,pno NOVELLO f.s.
contains: Lullaby, A; Song In The
Twilight, The; Spring Rain
(Frühlingsregen); When We Are
Lost; Youth (B222)

Golden Guendolen
see Three Songs

Lullaby, A
see Five Songs

Magnificat
see Three Songs

Song In The Twilight, The
see Five Songs

Spring Rain (Frühlingsregen)
see Five Songs

Three Songs
[Eng] RECITAL 342 f.s.
contains: Fairies, The; Golden
Guendolen; Magnificat (B223)

When We Are Lost
see Five Songs

Youth
see Five Songs

BAYLY, T. (1797-1839)
I'd Be A Butterfly
[Eng] med solo,pno CLASSV 1715
(B224)

BAZANT, JAROMÍR (1926-   )
Voice Of One's Home, The *Op.55,
song cycle
T solo,pno [12'] CZECH RADIO (B225)

BAZELON, IRWIN ALLEN (1922-   )
Four...Parts Of A World
S solo,pno PRESSER 111-40135 (B226)

BE IN PEACE see Avni, Tzvi

BE: SOLOMOTETT see Haegeland, Eilert M.

BEACH, AMY MARCY CHENEY
see BEACH, [MRS.] H.H.A.

BEACH, [MRS.] H.H.A. (AMY MARCY CHENEY)
(1867-1944)
Ah, Love, But A Day! *Op.44,No.2
high solo,pno CLASSV 0394 (B227)
low solo,pno CLASSV 0723 (B228)
SA soli,pno CLASSV 1716 (B229)
med solo,pno CLASSV 0413 (B230)

Anita *Op.41,No.1
med solo,pno CLASSV 0718 (B231)

Ariette *Op.1,No.4
med-high solo,pno CLASSV 2100
(B232)

Dearie *Op.43,No.1
med-low solo,pno CLASSV 0709 (B233)

Ecstasy *Op.19,No.2
med solo,pno CLASSV 0725 (B234)

Fairy Lullaby *Op.37,No.3
high solo,pno CLASSV 0722 (B235)

For My Love
see Je Demande À L'Oiseau

Forgotten? *Op.41,No.3
med-low solo,pno CLASSV 0720 (B236)

Go Not Too Far *Op.56,No.2
low solo,pno CLASSV 1199 (B237)

I Send My Heart Up To Thee! *Op.44,
No.3
high solo,pno CLASSV 1417 (B238)

Je Demande À L'Oiseau *Op.51,No.4
"For My Love" [Fr/Eng] low solo,pno
CLASSV 0708 (B239)

June *Op.51,No.3
[Eng/Ger] high solo,pno CLASSV 0707
(B240)
[Eng] med solo,pno,vln CLASSV 0706
(B241)

Just For This *Op.26,No.2
med-low solo,pno CLASSV 0715 (B242)

My Lassie *Op.43,No.5
high solo,pno CLASSV 0713 (B243)

My Star *Op.26,No.1
med-low solo,pno CLASSV 0714 (B244)

My Sweetheart And I *Op.21,No.3
[Eng] Mez solo,pno CLASSV 0727
(B245)
[Eng/Fr] S solo,pno CLASSV 0726
(B246)

O Mistress Mine *Op.37,No.1
high solo,pno CLASSV 0721 (B247)

O Were My Love Yon Lilac Fair
*Op.43,No.3
high solo,pno CLASSV 0711 (B248)
med solo,pno CLASSV 0712 (B249)

Scottish Cradle Song *Op.43,No.2
low solo,pno CLASSV 0710 (B250)

Silent Love *Op.51,No.1
[Ger/Eng] low solo,pno CLASSV 0704
(B251)

Songs, 23 *CC23UL
solo voice,pno DA CAPO 79717-8 f.s.
(B252)

Spring *Op.26,No.3
high solo,pno CLASSV 0716 (B253)

Thy Beauty *Op.41,No.2
med-low solo,pno CLASSV 0719 (B254)

We Three *Op.51,No.2
[Ger/Eng] high solo,pno CLASSV 0705
(B255)

Wouldn't That Be Queer *Op.26,No.4
med-low solo,pno CLASSV 0717 (B256)

Year's At The Spring, The *Op.44,
No.1
low solo,pno CLASSV 0724 (B257)
high solo,pno CLASSV 0488 (B258)

BEALE, JAMES (1924-   )
Fantomes *Op.40
B solo,clar,harp,cel,vibra,vln,vla,
vcl [35'9"] AM.COMP.AL. sc
$26.00, pts $22.20, pno red
$13.00 (B259)

BEATRICE DI TENDA: MA LA SOLA, OHIMÈ!
SON IO see Bellini, Vincenzo

BEATRIX CANZONE see Ehlen, Margriet

BEAU JOUR, UN see Bunge, Sas

BEAU SOIR see Debussy, Claude

BEAUMARCHAIS'S ARIA see Corigliano, John, Figaro Was Supposed To Return The Necklace

BEAUTIFUL BLUE DANUBE see Strauss, Johann, [Jr.]

BEAUTIFUL CHILD OF SONG see Foster, Stephen Collins

BEAUTIFUL WORLD see Sigfusson, Steingrimur

BEAUTY AND THE BEAST see Schafer, R. Murray

BEAUTY AND THE BEAST, THE see Kavasch, Deborah

BEAUTY IS BUT A PAINTED HELL see Hol, Dirk

BEAUTY IS TRUTH see Clarke, Henry Leland

BECAUSE GOING NOWHERE TAKES A LONG TIME see Bois, Rob du

BECAUSE I COULD NOT STOP FOR DEATH see Chapiro, Fania

BECERRA SCHMIDT, GUSTAVO (1925-   )
Oratorio Menor A Silvestre Revueltas De Mexico
Bar solo,clar,trp,pno/acord,vcl, gtr,perc [20'0"] PEER   (B260)

BECK, THOMAS LUDVIGSEN (1899-1963)
Ild Prøver Guld
[Norw] solo voice,pno NORGE (B261)

Wergelands Barnesanger
[Norw] solo voice,pno NORGE (B262)

BECKER, GÜNTHER (1924-   )
Fragmente Aus "Hymnen An Die Nacht"
TB&countertenor [8'] sc BREITKOPF-W BG 1383 f.s.   (B263)

Vier Gesänge *CC4U
B solo,pno BREITKOPF-W BG 1287 f.s.   (B264)

BECKER, JOHN
Four Poems From The Japanese *CC4U
S/T solo,pno sc AM.COMP.AL. $1.60   (B265)

Two Poems Of Departure *CC2U
med solo/high solo,pno sc AM.COMP.AL. $3.50   (B266)

BECKLER, STANWORTH R. (1923-   )
Songs Of Life And Love
S solo,pno SEESAW f.s.   (B267)

BECKWITH, JOHN (1927-   )
Old Meg Merillies
low solo,pno OXFORD 02.219   (B268)

BED IN SUMMER see Mourant, Walter

BED NÄR MÖRKRET TÄTNAR see Alinder, Hakan

BEDMAR, LUIS (1931-   )
A Cordoba
see Canciones Gongorinas

Canciones Gongorinas
solo voice,pno ALPUERTO 1373 f.s.
contains: A Cordoba; Hermana Marica, La; No Son Todos Ruisenores   (B269)

Hermana Marica, La
see Canciones Gongorinas

No Son Todos Ruisenores
see Canciones Gongorinas

BEECHER, KIRK
Tragic Mask, The
T solo,ob,hpsd PLUCKED STR PSSE 2027A f.s.   (B270)
T solo,mand,gtr,ob PLUCKED STR PSSE 2027 f.s.   (B271)

BEEKHUIS, HANNA (1889-1980)
Arme Seele Vor Der Himmelstür, Die *folk song
low solo,pno DONEMUS   (B272)

Chinesisches Soldatenlied
see Schi-King

Deux Flutes, Les
S solo,2fl,pno DONEMUS   (B273)

Drie Liederen
S/Mez solo,pno DONEMUS f.s.
contains: Marc Groet's Morgens De

BEEKHUIS, HANNA (cont'd.)
Dingen; Nieltje In Het Acquarium; Ze Zitten Naast Elkander   (B274)

Klage Der Garde
see Schi-King

Marc Groet's Morgens De Dingen
see Drie Liederen

Müde Soldat, Der
see Schi-King

Nachtstilte
see Vier Liederen

Nieltje In Het Acquarium
see Drie Liederen

Nocturne 1943
see Twee Liederen

Schi-King
med solo,pno DONEMUS f.s.
contains: Chinesisches Soldatenlied; Klage Der Garde; Müde Soldat, Der   (B275)

Sterbende Held, Der
see Twee Liederen

Twee Kwatrijnen
see Vier Liederen

Twee Liederen
med-low solo,pno DONEMUS f.s.
contains: Nocturne 1943, "Trommler, Der"; Sterbende Held, Der   (B276)

Uw Jonge Melodieen-Volle Vingeren
see Vier Liederen

Vier Liederen
low solo,pno DONEMUS f.s.
contains: Nachtstilte; Twee Kwatrijnen; Uw Jonge Melodieen-Volle Vingeren   (B277)

Ze Zitten Naast Elkander
see Drie Liederen

BEERMAN, BURTON (1943-   )
Cycle
S solo,org [13'] AM.COMP.AL. (B278)

Moments
S solo,pno [13'] sc AM.COMP.AL. $7.70   (B279)

Voices
S solo,db [10'] sc AM.COMP.AL. $6.90   (B280)

BEERS, JACQUES (1902-1947)
Anchor Line
see Five Negro Songs

Berceuse De Maitre Canard
see Deux Melodies Populaires Polonaises

Berceuse D'Haiti
see Trois Chansons Negres

Berceuse Presque Negre
high solo,pno DONEMUS   (B281)

Deux Melodies Populaires Polonaises
med solo,pno DONEMUS f.s.
contains: Berceuse De Maitre Canard; Paresseuse, La   (B282)

Dominus Regit Me
see Tres Psalmi

Exultare Justi In Domino
see Tres Psalmi

Five Negro Songs
DONEMUS f.s.
contains: Anchor Line (high solo, pno); Frogs, Frogs, Where Are You Going? (high solo,pno); I Am Not Going To Marry Sumpun (low solo,pno); Oh Boat, Come Back To Me (high solo,pno); Turkey Buzzard, The (high solo, pno)   (B283)

Frogs, Frogs, Where Are You Going?
see Five Negro Songs

I Am Not Going To Marry Sumpun
see Five Negro Songs

Noces Du Crocodile, Les
see Trois Chansons Negres

Oh Boat, Come Back To Me
see Five Negro Songs

BEERS, JACQUES (cont'd.)
Paresseuse, La
see Deux Melodies Populaires Polonaises

Pauv' Piti' Mamzell' Zizi
see Trois Chansons Negres

Tres Psalmi
A solo,pno DONEMUS f.s.
contains: Dominus Regit Me (Psalm No. 23); Exultare Justi In Domino (Psalm No. 33); Verba Mea Auribus (Psalm No. 5)   (B284)

Trois Chansons Negres
high solo,pno DONEMUS f.s.
contains: Berceuse D'Haiti; Noces Du Crocodile, Les; Pauv' Piti' Mamzell' Zizi   (B285)

Turkey Buzzard, The
see Five Negro Songs

Verba Mea Auribus
see Tres Psalmi

BEESON
From A Watchtower
BOOSEY VAB0302   (B286)

Nine Songs And Arias
Bar solo BOOSEY VAB0258   (B287)
S solo BOOSEY VAB0257   (B288)

BEETHOVEN, LUDWIG VAN (1770-1827)
A Esa Cumbre
see Colección De Canciones Escogidas, Cuaderno 3, Op. 98

A La Esperanza
see Colección De Canciones Escogidas, Cuaderno 4, Op. 75, No. 2

Adelaida
see Colección De Canciones Escogidas, Cuaderno 5, Op. 46

Adelaide
[Ger] med solo RECITAL 2227   (B289)
high solo,pno CLASSV 0432   (B290)

Adelaide Von Matthisson *cant
solo voice,pno SCIEN 191   (B291)

Ah! Perfido
S solo,pno CLASSV 0539   (B292)

Amor Al Prójimo, El
see Colección De Canciones Escogidas, Cuaderno 1: Seis Cantos Espirituales Op. 48

Amor Nuevo, Vida Nueva
see Colección De Canciones Escogidas, Cuaderno 4, Op. 75, No. 2

An Die Ferne Geliebte *Op.98, song cycle
"To The Distant Beloved" [Ger/Eng] high solo KALMUS K 09863   (B293)
"To The Distant Beloved" [Ger/Eng] low solo KALMUS K 09864   (B294)

Anhelo
see Colección De Canciones Escogidas, Cuaderno 2, Op. 83

Ante La Muerte
see Colección De Canciones Escogidas, Cuaderno 1: Seis Cantos Espirituales Op. 48

Aves Que Venis
see Colección De Canciones Escogidas, Cuaderno 3, Op. 98

Beso, El
see Colección De Canciones Escogidas, Cuaderno 5, Op. 46

Canción De Júbilo Y Duelo
see Colección De Canciones Escogidas, Cuaderno 4, Op. 75, No. 2

Canción De Mayo
see Colección De Canciones Escogidas, Cuaderno 5, Op. 46

Canconer Selecte Vol. 1 (25 Cancons Selectes)
[Ger/Span] BOIL B.2618   (B295)

Canto De Contrición
see Colección De Canciones Escogidas, Cuaderno 1: Seis Cantos Espirituales Op. 48

Canto De La Codorniz, El
see Colección De Canciones Escogidas, Cuaderno 2, Op. 83

BEETHOVEN, LUDWIG VAN (cont'd.)

Colección De Canciones Escogidas,
Cuaderno 1: Seis Cantos
Espirituales Op. 48
solo voice,pno BOIL B.1558 f.s.
contains: Amor Al Prójimo, El;
Ante La Muerte; Canto De
Contricción; Gloria De Dios En
El Orbe, La; Plegaria; Pobre
Divino, El (B296)

Colección De Canciones Escogidas,
Cuaderno 2, Op. 83
solo voice,pno BOIL B.1599 f.s.
contains: Anhelo; Canto De La
Codorniz, El; Delicia De La
Tristeza; Faja Florida, La
(B297)

Colección De Canciones Escogidas,
Cuaderno 3, Op. 98
solo voice,pno BOIL B.1601 f.s.
contains: A Esa Cumbre; Aves Que
Venis; De Esos Pájaros; Desde
Lo Alto De La Tierra; Feliz Nos
Da; Tonadas Que Canto, Las
(B298)

Colección De Canciones Escogidas,
Cuaderno 4, Op. 75, No. 2
solo voice,pno BOIL B.1602 f.s.
contains: A La Esperanza; Amor
Nuevo, Vida Nueva; Canción De
Júbilo Y Duelo; Hombre Leal,
El; Mignon (B299)

Colección De Canciones Escogidas,
Cuaderno 5, Op. 46
solo voice,pno BOIL B.1603 f.s.
contains: Adelaida; Beso, El;
Canción De Mayo (B300)

De Esos Pájaros
see Colección De Canciones
Escogidas, Cuaderno 3, Op. 98

Delicia De La Tristeza
see Colección De Canciones
Escogidas, Cuaderno 2, Op. 83

Desde Lo Alto De La Tierra
see Colección De Canciones
Escogidas, Cuaderno 3, Op. 98

Dve Skotske Pisne *Op.108
(Fiala, J.) solo voice,vln,vcl,pno
CESKY HUD. f.s.
contains: Hudba, Laska A Vino;
Pisen Rybaru (B301)

Faja Florida, La
see Colección De Canciones
Escogidas, Cuaderno 2, Op. 83

Feliz Nos Da
see Colección De Canciones
Escogidas, Cuaderno 3, Op. 98

Fidelio: Abscheulicher! Wo Eilst Du
Hin?
S solo,pno CLASSV 1613 (B302)

Fidelio: Gott, Welch Dunkel Hier
T solo,pno CLASSV 1514 (B303)

Gloria De Dios En El Orbe, La
see Colección De Canciones
Escogidas, Cuaderno 1: Seis
Cantos Espirituales Op. 48

Hombre Leal, El
see Colección De Canciones
Escogidas, Cuaderno 4, Op. 75,
No. 2

Hudba, Laska A Vino
see Dve Skotske Pisne

I Love You
see Ich Liebe Dich

Ich Liebe Dich
(Deis) "I Love You" high solo
SCHIRM.G ST37711 (B304)

In Questa Tomba Oscura
high solo,pno CLASSV 1718 (B305)
B solo,pno CLASSV 0577 (B306)

Mignon
see Colección De Canciones
Escogidas, Cuaderno 4, Op. 75,
No. 2

Nei Giorni Tuoi Felici
ST soli,orch/pno sc,pno red,pts
KUNZEL (B307)

Pisen Rybaru
see Dve Skotske Pisne

Plegaria
see Colección De Canciones
Escogidas, Cuaderno 1: Seis
Cantos Espirituales Op. 48

BEETHOVEN, LUDWIG VAN (cont'd.)

Pobre Divino, El
see Colección De Canciones
Escogidas, Cuaderno 1: Seis
Cantos Espirituales Op. 48

Prüfung Des Küssens
B solo,pno CLASSV 1036 (B308)

Sämtliche Lieder Und Gesänge Mit
Klavier, Band 1 *CC45L
solo voice,pno HENLE 540 f.s.
(B309)

Sämtliche Lieder Und Gesänge Mit
Klavier, Band 2 *CC38L
solo voice,pno HENLE 541 f.s.
(B310)

Songs *CCU
solo voice,pno LEA 60 $3.00 (B311)

Songs (Complete) *CC66U
[Ger/Eng] med solo KALMUS K 06081
f.s. (B312)

To The Distant Beloved
see An Die Ferne Geliebte

Tonadas Que Canto, Las
see Colección De Canciones
Escogidas, Cuaderno 3, Op. 98

Zwei Lieder Aus Goethes Egmont,
Op.84, Nos.1&2
[Ger] high solo,pno CLASSV 1719
(B313)

BEETHOVEN PÅ RINGVE see Volle, Bjarne

BEFORE IT DIES see Shut, Wasyl, Zaky
Umre

BEFORE THE DAWN see Chadwick, George
Whitefield

BEFREIT see Strauss, Richard

BEGEGNUNG see Orland, Henry

BEGIN THE SONG see Blow, John

BEGINNINGS see Zaninelli

BEHOLD see Roo, Paul de

BEHREND, SIEGFRIED (1933-1990)
Geschichte Von O-Cho-San, Die
solo voice,electronic tape,gtr
(tape - $19.00) PLUCKED STR
ZM 2120 $6.00 (B314)

Requiem Auf Hiroshima
solo voice,mand,gtr,perc perf sc
BREITKOPF-W BG 1211 f.s. (B315)

BEIDEN GRENADIERE, DIE see Schumann,
Robert (Alexander)

BEILERE see Ørbeck, Anne Marie

BEILSCHMIDT
Pastorale
PETERS 5053 (B316)

BEKAK see Nieland, Henk

BEKENTENIS see Guichelaar, Jan

BEL AGE, LE *CCU
solo voice FABER 50734 4 f.s. (B317)

BELL, LARRY
Reality Is An Activity Of The Most
August Imagination
Mez solo,pno sc AM.COMP.AL. $6.15
(B318)

BELL SONG see Delibes, Léo, Légende

BELLA MOLINERA, LA see Schubert, Franz
(Peter), Impaciencia Del Ciclo De
Canciones

BELLA QUANDO AURORA see Anonymous

BELLE, LA see Björnsson, Arni

BELLE ESCLAVE DE MAURE, LA see Regt,
Hendrik de

BELLE HÉLÉNE, LA: AU MONT IDA TROIS
DÉESSES see Offenbach, Jacques

BELLINI, VINCENZO (1801-1835)
Beatrice Di Tenda: Ma La Sola, Ohimè!
Son Io
S solo,pno CLASSV 1717 (B319)

Composizioni Da Camera Per Canto E
Pianoforte
S/Mez/T solo,pno ZEN-ON (B320)

Norma: Casta Diva
S solo,pno CLASSV 0877 (B321)

Norma: Casta Diva, Che Inargenti
S solo,pno BOIL B.1314 (B322)

BELLINI, VINCENZO (cont'd.)

Norma: Mira, O Norma
SMez soli,pno CLASSV 1153 (B323)

Puritani, I: Qui La Voce Sua Soave
S solo,pno BOIL B.1962 (B324)

Puritani, I: Son Vergin Vezzosa
S solo,pno BOIL B.1996 (B325)

Sonámbula, La: Ah! Non Crede A
Mirarti
S solo,pno BOIL B.1961 (B326)

Sonámbula, La: Care Compagni. Come
Per Me Sereno
S solo,pno BOIL B.1795 (B327)

Sonnambula: Ah! Non Credea Mirarti
S solo,pno CLASSV 0633 (B328)

Sonnambula: Prendi: L'Anel Ti Dono
ST soli,pno CLASSV 1224 (B329)

Vaga Luna Che Inargenti
med solo,pno CLASSV 1720 (B330)

BELLMAN, CARL MICHAEL (1740-1795)
Bellman Brevier, Vol. 1: 10 Songs
From "Fredmans Episteln" *CC10U
solo voice,gtr PLUCKED STR ZM 2105
$12.50 (B331)

Bellman Brevier, Vol. 2: 10 Songs
From "Fredmans Lieder" And
"Bacchi Tempel" *CC10U
solo voice,gtr PLUCKED STR ZM 2106
$12.50 (B332)

Bellman Brevier, Vol. 3: 10 Songs
From "Fredmans Episteln" And
"Fredmans Lieder" *CC10U
solo voice,gtr PLUCKED STR ZM 2311
$12.50 (B333)

Fjäriln Vingad Syns På Haga
(Josephson, J.A.) solo voice,pno
EGTVED 432 f.s. from AKSEL
SCHIOETZ ANTHOLOGY OF NORDIC SOLO
SONGS, THE, VOL. 2 (B334)

Nitton Epistlar
(Bergström, Mats; Samuelson,
Mikael) solo voice,gtr GEHRMANS
6833 (B335)

BELLMAN BREVIER, VOL. 1: 10 SONGS FROM
"FREDMANS EPISTELN" see Bellman,
Carl Michael

BELLMAN BREVIER, VOL. 2: 10 SONGS FROM
"FREDMANS LIEDER" AND "BACCHI
TEMPEL" see Bellman, Carl Michael

BELLMAN BREVIER, VOL. 3: 10 SONGS FROM
"FREDMANS EPISTELN" AND "FREDMANS
LIEDER" see Bellman, Carl Michael

BELLS, THE see Taub, Bruce J.H.

BELOUNKA HOLUBICKO see Odstrcil, Karel

BELOVED SCOTCH & IRISH SONGS
("World's Favorite Series") ASHLEY
102-2 (B336)

BELOW THE HILL see Hekster, Walter

BELTÀ CRUDELE (SANTO-MANGO) see
Rossini, Gioacchino

BELYEA, W.H.
God Is Love
LESLIE 7067 (B337)

BEMBERG, HERMAN (1859-1931)
Chant Hindou
high solo,pno CLASSV 0871 (B338)
med solo,pno CLASSV 0872 (B339)
low solo,pno CLASSV 0873 (B340)

BENAKIK NISTAR see Steinberg, Eitan

BENDA, GEORG ANTON (JIRÍ ANTONÍN)
(1722-1795)
Avran Le Serpi, O Sara
see Italske Arie, Vol. 2

Di Sdegno Tal Ora S'accende
see Italske Arie, Vol. 2

Italske Arie, Vol. 1
CESKY HUD. f.s.
contains: Mio Ben Ricordarti
(solo voice,strings,hpsd); No,
Non Vedrete Mai (solo voice,
strings,hpsd); Non Posso Che
Amara (solo voice,2fl,2horn,
hpsd,strings); Onda, Che
Mormora, L' (solo voice,2fl,
2horn,strings,hpsd); S'ella
Vuol Rendersi (solo voice,
strings,hpsd); Vo Solcando Un
Mar Crudeli (solo voice,2horn,
strings,hpsd) (B341)

BENDA, GEORG ANTON (JIRÍ ANTONÍN)
(cont'd.)

Italske Arie, Vol. 2
CESKY HUD. f.s.
contains: Avran Le Serpi, O Sara
(solo voice,ob,hpsd,strings);
Di Sdegno Tal Ora S'accende
(solo voice,2fl,hpsd,strings);
Puoi Vantar Le Tue Ritorte
(solo voice,fl,ob,2horn,hpsd,
strings,vln solo); Quel Timor
Che Mi Circonda (solo voice,
2horn,hpsd,strings); So Che
Pugnando (solo voice,2ob,2horn,
2trp,hpsd,strings); Vado Se Tu
Lo Ami (solo voice,strings,
hpsd)   (B342)

Mio Ben Ricordarti
see Italske Arie, Vol. 1

No, Non Vedrete Mai
see Italske Arie, Vol. 1

Non Posso Che Amara
see Italske Arie, Vol. 1

Onda, Che Mormora, L'
see Italske Arie, Vol. 1

Puoi Vantar Le Tue Ritorte
see Italske Arie, Vol. 2

Quel Timor Che Mi Circonda
see Italske Arie, Vol. 2

S'ella Vuol Rendersi
see Italske Arie, Vol. 1

So Che Pugnando
see Italske Arie, Vol. 2

Vado Se Tu Lo Ami
see Italske Arie, Vol. 2

Vo Solcando Un Mar Crudeli
see Italske Arie, Vol. 1

BENEATH A WEEPING WILLOW'S SHADE
(Bales, Richard) Bar solo,1.1.1.1.
2.0.0.0. triangle,harp,strings
[3'30"] PEER   (B343)

BENEDICT, [SIR] JULIUS (1804-1885)
Capinera, La
see Wren, The

Carnival Of Venice (With Concert
Variations)
coloratura sop,pno CLASSV 1121
                             (B344)
Lily Of Killarney: The Moon Has
Raised Her Lamp Above
TBar soli,pno CLASSV 1212   (B345)

Wren, The
"Capinera, La" S solo,pno,vln/fl
CLASSV 0827   (B346)

BENEDICTION see Haan, Raymond H.

BENJAMIN
Upon Silence
FABER 51251 8   (B347)

BENNETT
This Is The Garden
solo voice NOVELLO 2959 $5.50
                             (B348)
BENNETT, RICHARD RODNEY (1936-   )
Dream Songs
solo voice,pno (med diff) NOVELLO
                             (B349)
BENTON, DANIEL JOSEPH (1945-   )
Love Song
S/A solo,fl,harp SEESAW f.s. (B350)

Two Shakespeare Songs *CC2U
S solo,vln,fl,bass clar SEESAW f.s.
                             (B351)
BENVENUTO CELLINI: SEUL POUR
LUTTER...SUR LES MONTS see Berlioz,
Hector (Louis)

BEQUEST see Walker, George Theophilus

BERCEAUX, LES see Faure, Gabriel-Urbain

BERCEUSE see Bonhomme, Andree see
Brahms, Johannes, Wiegenlied see
Gretchaninov, Alexander
Tikhonovich, Slumber Song see
Massenet, Jules see Thordarson,
Sigurdur

BERCEUSE DE MAITRE CANARD see Beers,
Jacques

BERCEUSE D'HAITI see Beers, Jacques

BERCEUSE DU CHAT see Stravinsky, Igor

BERCEUSE PRESQUE NEGRE see Beers,
Jacques

BEREAVED MAID, THE see Walker, George
Theophilus

BERENHOLTZ, JIM
March To Battle
S solo,2.3.3.3. 3.3.3.1. 4perc,
strings,synthesizer [5'] sc
AM.COMP.AL. $8.45   (B352)

BERENICE see Liberda, Bruno

BERESHIT see Lagana, Ruggero

BERG, ALBAN (1885-1935)
Jugendlieder, Band 1: 1901-1904
*CC23L
(Hailey, Christopher) solo voice
UNIVER. UE 18143 f.s.   (B353)
BERG, CHRISTOPHER (1949-   )
Not Waving But Drowning
med solo,1(pic).1.1.1. 1.1.1.0.
timp,perc,harp,pno/cel,strings
[20'0"] PEER   (B354)
BERGBUINN GEKK FRAM A GNYPUBRUN see
Isolfsson, Pall

BERGE, SIGURD (1929-   )
Ho Sankar Myrull
[Norw] solo voice,pno NORGE (B355)
BERGER, ARTHUR VICTOR (1912-   )
Five Settings Of European Poets
T solo,pno [13'] APNM sc $5.75, set
$11.00   (B356)
BERGER DEDANS SA CABANE, UN see Arrieu,
Claude

BERGERAC
From France With Love
SCHIRM.G SG2707   (B357)
BERGERETTES see Weckerlin, Jean-
Baptiste-Theodore

BERGFORS, PER-GÖSTA (1929-   )
Gloria
S solo,org PROPRIUS 7912   (B358)
BERGH, SVERRE (1915-1980)
Autumn
see Haust

Bruradag
[Norw] solo voice,pno NORGE (B359)

By Oscarshall
see Ved Oscarshall

Dead Flowers
see Døde Blomar

Døde Blomar
"Dead Flowers" solo voice,1.1.2.1.
0.2.1.0. perc,strings NORGE f.s.
                             (B360)
Eg Høyrer Klang Av Klokkekor
[Norw] solo voice,pno NORGE (B361)
solo voice,pno NOTON N-9331 (B362)

Eg Vil Leva
"I Want To Live" solo voice,
1.1.2.1. 0.2.1.0. perc,strings
[2'] NORGE f.s.   (B363)

Fanden I Nøtten
"Norwegian Fairytale" narrator,
2.1.2.1. 2.2.2.0. perc,strings
NORGE f.s.   (B364)

Haust
"Autumn" narrator,1.1.2.1. 2.0.0.0.
perc,strings NORGE f.s.   (B365)

I Want To Live
see Eg Vil Leva

Norwegian Fairytale
see Fanden I Nøtten

Presten Og Klokkeren
"Priest And The Bell Ringer, The"
narrator,fl,ob,2clar,bsn,perc,
strings NORGE f.s.   (B366)

Priest And The Bell Ringer, The
see Presten Og Klokkeren

Tre Bukkene Bruse, De
narrator,1.1.2.1. 2.2.1.0. perc,
strings [5'] NORGE f.s.   (B367)

Ved Oscarshall
"By Oscarshall" 2 solo voices,
1.1.2.1. 0.2.1.0. perc,pno,
strings [4'] NORGE f.s.   (B368)

Vi Hilser Deg Hamar
solo voice,pno NOTON N-9330 (B369)

BERGMANNEN: MELODRAMA see Johnsen,
Hallvard

BERGSMA, WILLIAM LAURENCE (1921-   )
Four Songs *CC4U
med solo,clar,bsn,pno GALAXY 1.2941
$6.50   (B370)
BERGSTIMME see Roos, Robert de

BERGTEKNE, DEN see Grieg, Edvard
Hagerup

BERKELEY, MICHAEL
Songs Of Awakening Love
S solo,1.2.0.2. 2.0.0.0. strings
[26'] sc OXFORD 63.081   (B371)

Wessex Graves
solo voice,harp OXFORD 60.812 (B372)

Wild Winds
S solo,2.1.2.1. 2.1.0.0. perc,pno,
strings [12'] OXFORD   (B373)

BERKELEY CASTLE, SELECT ROLL 55: MOTETS
AND SEQUENCES
(Wathey, Andrew) 3 solo voices ANTICO
MCM3   (B374)

BERLINSKI, HERMAN (1910-   )
Adonai Roi (Psalm No. 23)
solo voice,fl TRANSCON. 991277
                             (B375)
Psalm No. 23
see Adonai Roi

BERLIOZ, HECTOR (LOUIS) (1803-1869)
Benvenuto Cellini: Seul Pour
Lutter...Sur Les Monts
T solo,pno CLASSV 1048   (B376)

Captive, La
med solo,pno,vln/vcl CLASSV 0951
                             (B377)
Damnation Of Faust: D'Amour L'Ardente
Flamme
Mez solo,pno CLASSV 1721   (B378)

Damnation Of Faust: Voici Des Roses
B solo,pno CLASSV 0631   (B379)

Didon's Monologue
see Troyens, Les: Je Vais Mourir!

Mélodies, 24
high solo,pno CLASSV C009   (B380)
low solo,pno CLASSV C010   (B381)

Mort De Cléopâtre *scena
[Ger/Eng] S solo,pno CLASSV 1418
                             (B382)
Nuits D'Ete, Les
high solo SCHIRM.G ED2780   (B383)
low solo SCHIRM.G ED2779   (B384)

Troyens, Les: Je Vais Mourir!
"Didon's Monologue" [Fr] Mez solo,
pno CLASSV 1234   (B385)

Zaïde (Boléro - 1st Version)
[Ger/Eng] S solo,pno CLASSV 1700
                             (B386)
BERMUDAS see Hoiby, Lee

BERNABEI, GIUSEPPE ANTONIO (1649-1732)
Fiera, La
(Lehrndorfer, F.) "Jahrmarkt, Der"
[Ger] SA soli,fl,strings,cont
KUNZEL GM 893   (B387)

Jahrmarkt, Der
see Fiera, La

BERNERT, HELMUT
Vier Gedichte Von Friedrich Hölderlin
*CC4U
A solo,pno BOHM f.s.   (B388)
BERNSTEIN, LEONARD (1918-1990)
America (from West Side Story)
SCHIRM.G ST44284   (B389)

Cool (from West Side Story)
SCHIRM.G ST44277   (B390)

Dream With Me
BOOSEY SGB6041   (B391)

Gee, Officer Krupke (from West Side
Story)
SCHIRM.G ST44790   (B392)

Glitter And Be Gay (from Candide)
S solo BOOSEY SGB2715   (B393)

I Feel Pretty (from West Side Story)
SCHIRM.G ST44278   (B394)

Lamentation (from Jeremiah)
BOOSEY SGB6040   (B395)

Maria (from West Side Story)
SCHIRM.G ST44279   (B396)

One Hand, One Heart (from West Side
Story)
SCHIRM.G ST44283   (B397)

BERNSTEIN, LEONARD (cont'd.)

Simple Song (from Mass)
male solo BOOSEY SGB2717 (B398)

So Pretty
BOOSEY SGB2718 (B399)

Something's Coming (from West Side Story)
SCHIRM.G ST44289 (B400)

Somewhere (from West Side Story)
SCHIRM.G ST44308 (B401)

Take Care Of This House
BOOSEY SGB2707 (B402)

Tonight (from West Side Story)
SCHIRM.G ST44282 (B403)

West Side Story Selections
solo voice,pno SCHIRM.G ED2382 (B404)

BERSTAD, RAGNHILD (1956-)
Verto
Mez solo,perc,vcl,electronic tape [15'] NORGE (B405)

BERTELIN, ALBERT
Chants Du Cobazar
[Fr] high solo,pno CLASSV 2188 (B406)

Légende De Loreley, La
high solo,pno CLASSV 2186 (B407)

BERTELSEN, MICHAEL
Seven, The
male solo,pno [15'] SAMFUNDET 243 f.s. (B408)

BERTHAS LIED IN DIE NACHT see Schubert, Franz (Peter)

BESABA see Camprubi, J.

BESARD, JEAN-BAPTISTE (1567-ca. 1625)
Airs De Court (Secolo XVI) Dal Thesaurus Harmonicus (from Thesaurus Harmonicus) CC12U
solo voice,kbd FORNI 5374 f.s. (B409)

BESCHEIDENE SCHÄFER, DER see Marx, Joseph

BESEDA-POLKA see Eisler, Hanns

BESIDES THIS MAY: 5 SONGS see Callaway, Ann

BESINNA OCH ANAMMA see Koch, Erland von

BESLY, MAURICE (1888-1945)
Three Little Fairy Songs
med solo,pno CLASSV 1137 (B410)

BESO, EL see Beethoven, Ludwig van

BEST OF VOCAL DUETS, THE *CCU
2 solo voices ALLANS $8.00 (B411)

BESTÄNDIGEN, DIE see Bijvanck, Henk

BESTEMORS-ROKKEN see Sommerfeldt, Öistein

BESTIARIUM, OP. 17 & OP. 51 see Brennan, John Wolf

BESVERGELSE see Baden, Conrad see Fladmoe, Arvid

BETSY B see Haufrecht, Herbert

BETTELLIED see Eisler, Hanns

BETWEEN HILLS AND MOUNTAINS see Millom Bakkar Og Berg

BETWEEN THE PRECIPICES OF LIFE see Christensen, Mogens, Mellem Livets Afgrunde

BEUK O'NEWCASSEL SANGS see Finnissy, Michael

BEURLE, JÜRGEN (1943-)
Diaphon
solo voice,perc sc,pts MOECK 5075 (B412)

BEVELANDER, BRIAN
Three Songs On Texts By Alice Very *CC3U
S solo,pno sc AM.COMP.AL. $6.90 (B413)

Three Songs On Texts By Hilda Morley *CC3U
Mez solo,ob,bass clar,2perc,pno sc AM.COMP.AL. $17.90 (B414)

BEWARE! (3 EARLY SONGS) see Britten, [Sir] Benjamin

BEYER, EMIL
Art Songs *CC8L
high solo,pno WILLIS 11209 f.s. (B415)

BEYERMAN-WALRAVEN, JEANNE (1878-1969)
Drie Liederen
med solo,pno DONEMUS f.s.
contains: En In Den Nacht; Ramp, De; Zijt Stil Nu (B416)

En In Den Nacht
see Drie Liederen

Mere, Trois Poemes De M. Careme
low solo,pno [9'] DONEMUS (B417)

Ramp, De
see Drie Liederen

Zijt Stil Nu
see Drie Liederen

BEYOND TIME AND SPACE see Olsen, Sparre, Gjennom Tid Og Rom

BIALOSKY, MARSHALL H. (1923-)
Three Songs *CC3U
S solo,clar SEESAW f.s. (B418)

BIANCA E FALLIERO: DELLA ROSA IL BEL VERMIGLIO see Rossini, Gioacchino

BIANCHI, LINO
Fanciulla Abbandonata, La
solo voice,pno EDI-PAN EP 7358 (B419)

BIANCHINI, RICCARDO
Di Piu Cupi Sentieri
see Tre Canti

I Have Done...
see Tre Canti

Tierra Que Era Mia, La
see Tre Canti

Tre Canti
S solo,pno EDI-PAN EP 7330 f.s.
contains: Di Piu Cupi Sentieri; I Have Done...; Tierra Que Era Mia, La (B420)

BIAS VISE see Sommerfeldt, Öistein

BIBALO, ANTONIO (1922-)
Nocturne
[Norw] solo voice,pno NORGE (B421)

Oversettelse Til Et Barn
[Norw] solo voice,pno NORGE (B422)

Reise Med Båt Uten Båt
[Norw] S solo,db NORGE (B423)

Two Intermezzi *CC2U
Bar solo,fl NORGE f.s. (B424)

BIBELSK VISEBOK, EN see Kverno, Trond

BIBLE SONGS: A SONG OF FREEDOM see Stanford, Charles Villiers

BIBLE SONGS: A SONG OF PEACE see Stanford, Charles Villiers

BIBLE SONGS, OP.113 see Stanford, Charles Villiers

BIECHTELER, B.
Alma Redemptoris Mater
see Vier Mariansche Antiphonen

Ave Regina
see Vier Mariansche Antiphonen

Regina Coeli
see Vier Mariansche Antiphonen

Salve Regina
see Vier Mariansche Antiphonen

Vier Mariansche Antiphonen
S solo,vln/ob,cont sc,pts KUNZEL GM 1147 f.s.
contains: Alma Redemptoris Mater; Ave Regina; Regina Coeli; Salve Regina (B425)

BIENVENU, LILY (1920-)
Mère
SBar soli,1.1.0.1. 1.0.0.0. perc, cel,harp,strings [19'30"] sc,pts, voc sc BILLAUDOT (B426)

BIEZEN MANDJE see Ruiter, Wim de

BIG BAND MEMORIES *CCU
solo voice HANSEN-US HANMM004 $14.95 (B427)

BIG BEN see Villa-Lobos, Heitor

BIG STEAMERS see German, [Sir] Edward (Edward German Jones)

BIGGS, HAYES
Ave Formosissima
S solo,clar,vcl [10'] AM.COMP.AL. (B428)

Northeast Reservation Lines
S solo,pno MARGUN MP1065 (B429)

Songs From Water And Stone
S solo,fl,clar,vln,vcl,pno [15'] AM.COMP.AL. (B430)

BIGGS, JOHN (1932-)
Canto Sobre La Muerte De Silvestre [Span] S solo,harp,vcl [12'] (text by Pablo Neruda) CONSORT PR CP 136 (B431)

Eccentricities
med solo,pno CONSORT PR CP 131 $8.50 (B432)

Songs Of Laughter, Love And Tears
T solo,string orch [20'] CONSORT PR CP 309 rent (B433)

BIJVANCK, HENK (1909-1969)
Adagio Sostenuto
see Vier Liederen

All-Leben
S solo,pno DONEMUS (B434)

An Die Nacht
see Vijf Liederen Voor Sopraan En Piano

Auf Herbstlichem Ast
see Vier Liederen

Baronin Colombine
see Drei Balladen
see Drei Balladen

Beständigen, Die
see Twee Liederen Voor Bariton

Drei Balladen
T solo,pno DONEMUS f.s.
contains: Baronin Colombine; Kophetua; Pierrot Pendu (B435)

Drei Balladen
B solo,pno DONEMUS f.s.
contains: Baronin Colombine; Kophetua; Pierrot Pendu (B436)

Erinnerung
see Vijf Liederen Voor Sopraan En Piano

Herz, Das
see Vier Liederen

Im Ewigen Licht
see Vier Liederen

Junge Liebe
see Twee Liederen ("Sculpturen")

Kophetua
see Drei Balladen
see Drei Balladen

Negen Liederen Voor Bariton En Piano *CC9U
Bar solo,pno DONEMUS f.s. (B437)

O Traure Nicht
see Vijf Liederen Voor Sopraan En Piano

Pierrot Pendu
see Drei Balladen
see Drei Balladen

Stille
see Vijf Liederen Voor Sopraan En Piano

Twee Liederen ("Sculpturen")
A solo,pno DONEMUS f.s.
contains: Junge Liebe; Waisenknabe (B438)

Twee Liederen Voor Bariton
Bar solo,pno DONEMUS f.s.
contains: Beständigen, Die; Wanderer Erwacht In Der Herberge (B439)

Vier Liederen
A solo,pno DONEMUS f.s.
contains: Adagio Sostenuto; Auf Herbstlichem Ast; Herz, Das; Im Ewigen Licht (B440)

Vijf Liederen Voor Sopraan En Piano
S solo,pno DONEMUS f.s.
contains: An Die Nacht; Erinnerung; O Traure Nicht; Stille; Wiegenlied (B441)

Waisenknabe
see Twee Liederen ("Sculpturen")

BIJVANCK, HENK (cont'd.)

  Wanderer Erwacht In Der Herberge
    see Twee Liederen Voor Bariton

  Wiegenlied
    see Vijf Liederen Voor Sopraan En
    Piano

BILLI
  E Canta Il Grillo
    med solo,pno CLASSV 1302   (B442)
    high solo,pno CLASSV 1301   (B443)

BILLIGE LIEDER see Kaufmann, Dieter

BILLY ASCENDS see Evett, Robert

BILT, WILLEM VAN DER (1901-)
  Aztekische Fluitist, De
    see Twee Spaanse Gedichten

  Lied (De Put Der Zuchten)
    see Twee Spaanse Gedichten

  Source Tombait Du Rocher, La
    Mez solo,pno [3'] DONEMUS   (B444)

  Twee Spaanse Gedichten
    med solo,pno DONEMUS f.s.
      contains: Aztekische Fluitist,
      De; Lied (De Put Der Zuchten)
                        (B445)

BIM BAM BUM see Kruse, Bjørn Howard

BIMBA NON PIANGERE see Mascagni,
Pietro, Lodoletta: Il Canto Dei
Fiori

BINDER, KARL
  I Hätt' A Bitt'
    solo voice,pno (in Austrian
    dialect) SCIEN 293   (B446)

BIONDINA see Gounod, Charles François

BIRCH, ROBERT FAIRFAX
  Haiku IX: Now Autumn
    solo voice,pno BIRCH   (B447)

  Haiku X: Foolish Years Of Song
    solo voice,pno (diff) BIRCH (B448)

BIRD FLEW HIGH, A see Brimberg, Jack

BIRDS, THE see Delius, Frederick see
Holt, Patricia Blomfield

BIRDS CALLING IN THE VALLEY see
Hekster, Walter

BIRDS IN SPRINGTIME see Weigl, [Mrs.]
Vally

BIRDS SONG, A see Grieg, Edvard
Hagerup, Fuglevise, En

BIRONDON see Mestres, Apeles

BIRTHDAY, A see Schmidt, Sharon Yvonne
Davis

BIRTHDAY CANTATA see Lerstad, Terje B.

BIRTHDAY GREETING, A see Shifrin,
Seymour J.

BIRTHDAYSONG see Baldvinsson, Tryggvi

BIRTWISTLE, HARRISON (1934-)
  Words Overheard
    S solo,fl,ob,bsn,strings sc UNIVER.
    UE 17982   (B449)

BISCARDI, CHESTER (1948-)
  Trusting Lightness
    S solo,pno [6'] sc AM.COMP.AL.
    $7.70   (B450)

  Turning
    S solo,vln, str trio [6'] sc
    AM.COMP.AL. $6.90   (B451)

BISCHOF, RAINER (1947-)
  Und So Sink' Ich Leise In Mich Selbst
    Hinein *Op.17, song cycle,
    Austrian
    Mez solo,vln DOBLINGER 08 829
                       (B452)

BISHOP, [SIR] HENRY (ROWLEY)
(1786-1855)
  Lo, Here The Gentle Lark
    S solo,pno,fl CLASSV 1684 (B453)

BISLEY, BRIGID
  This Land Of Water
    S solo,pno WAI-TE-ATA A4 (B454)

BIT PARTS see McLean, Edwin

BITO, YAYOI (1956-)
  Mizu No Oto
    S solo,pno [3'] JAPAN   (B455)

BITTE see Marx, Joseph

BITTER LAMENTS (LAMENT BY THE TOMB OF
OUR LORD) see Nikodemowicz,
Andrzej, Z Gorzkich Zalow (Placz Z
Grobu Chrystusa Pana)

BITTER LINE see Tal, Joseph

BITTER-SWEET see Ronsheim, John Richard

BIWA NO HANA see Yuyama, Akira

BIXIO, CESARE ANDREA
  Mamma
    high solo,pno sc PEER 60731-202
    $2.50   (B456)

BIZET, GEORGES (1838-1875)
  Absence
    "Reviens, Reviens" [Fr] high solo,
    pno CLASSV 2090   (B457)

  Adieux De L'Hotesse Arabe
    high solo,pno CLASSV 0365 (B458)
    med solo,pno CLASSV 0811 (B459)

  Agnus Dei
    [Lat/Eng] low solo,pno CLASSV 1722
                       (B460)
    [Lat] med solo,pno CLASSV 1131
                       (B461)

  Au Fond Du Temple Saint (from The
    Pearlfishers) duet
    TBar soli UNITED MUS f.s. (B462)

  Carmen: Duet "Parle-Moi"
    ST soli,pno CLASSV 0368 (B463)

  Carmen: Je Dis Que Rien
    S solo,pno CLASSV 0343   (B464)

  Carmen: La Fleur Que Tu M'avais Jetée
    "Flower Song" T solo,pno CLASSV
    0341   (B465)

  Carmen: L'Amour Est
    "Habanera" Mez solo,pno CLASSV 0433
                       (B466)

  Carmen: Les Tringles Des Sistres
    Tintaient
    [Fr/It/Eng] Mez solo,pno CLASSV
    1191   (B467)

  Carmen: Près Des Remparts De Séville
    "Seguidilla" Mez solo,pno CLASSV
    0526   (B468)

  Carmen: Votre Toast
    "Toreador Song" Bar solo,pno CLASSV
    0423   (B469)

  Cavatina De Leila (from The
    Pearlfishers)
    S solo UNITED MUS f.s.   (B470)

  Chanson Du Fou
    high solo,pno CLASSV 1723 (B471)

  Fair Maid Of Perth: Now The Shades Of
    Night
    see Jolie Fille De Perth, La:
    Serenade: A La Voix D'un Amant

  Flower Song
    see Carmen: La Fleur Que Tu M'avais
    Jetée

  Habanera
    see Carmen: L'Amour Est

  Ivan: Ouvre Ton Coeur
    high solo,pno CLASSV 0359 (B472)
    med solo,pno CLASSV 0513 (B473)

  Jolie Fille De Perth, La: Serenade: A
    La Voix D'un Amant
    "Fair Maid Of Perth: Now The Shades
    Of Night" [Eng/Fr] T solo
    RICORDI-IT LD118445   (B474)

  Jolie Fille De Perth: Echo, Viens Sur
    L'Air Embaumé
    coloratura sop,pno CLASSV 1724
                       (B475)

  Jolie Fille De Perth: Quand La Flamme
    De L'Amour
    B solo,pno CLASSV 1557   (B476)

  Ma Vie A Son Secret
    med-high solo,pno CLASSV 0812 (B477)

  Pastorale
    [Fr] high solo,pno CLASSV 0864
                       (B478)

  Pêcheurs De Pearls, Les: C'est Toi
    TB soli,pno CLASSV 0370 (B479)

  Pêcheurs De Pearls, Les: Je Crois
    Entendre
    T solo,pno CLASSV 0559   (B480)
    T solo,pno (not original key)
    CLASSV 0554   (B481)

BIZET, GEORGES (cont'd.)

  Pêcheurs De Pearls, Les: L'Orage
    S'est Calmé
    Bar solo,pno CLASSV 0950 (B482)

  Pêcheurs De Pearls, Les: Me Voilà
    Seule..Comme Autrefois
    S solo,pno CLASSV 0838   (B483)

  Pêcheurs De Pearls, Les: O Dieu
    Brahma
    S solo,pno CLASSV 0369   (B484)

  Pêcheurs De Pearls, Les: Sérénade
    T solo,pno CLASSV 0344   (B485)

  Reviens, Reviens
    see Absence

  Romance De Nadir (from The
    Pearlfishers)
    T solo UNITED MUS f.s.   (B486)

  Seguidilla
    see Carmen: Près Des Remparts De
    Séville

  Ten Songs *CC10U
    med solo FRANG $6.95   (B487)

  Toreador Song
    see Carmen: Votre Toast

  Twenty Melodies *CC20U
    KALMUS f.s. Mez/Bar solo K 06832;
    S/T solo K 06831   (B488)

BJELINSKI, BRUNO (1909-)
  Candomblé
    S solo,pno,opt perc [12'] perf sc
    BREITKOPF-W BG 1147 f.s. (B489)

BJERG, JENS
  Seks Sange
    ENGSTRÖEM 618   (B490)

BJØLLEBLOM see Ørbeck, Anne Marie

BJORK, TORGNY (1938-)
  Horisontlinje: 10 Visor
    (Sjösten, Lars) SUECIA 362 (B491)

BJÖRKLUND, STAFFAN (1944-)
  Fyra Sanger *CC4U
    Bar solo,bass clar/pno sc STIM
    PA-3274-21 f.s.   (B492)

BJØRNSONSANGER, OP. 39 see Madsen,
Trygve

BJÖRNSSON, ARNI (1905-)
  A Arnarholmn
    solo voice,pno ICELAND 001-039
                       (B493)

  A Baenum Stendur Stulkan Vord (from
    Ten Songs)
    solo voice,pno ICELAND 001-056
                       (B494)

  Ad Ganga I Dans
    solo voice,pno ICELAND 001-029
                       (B495)

  Belle, La (from Fourteen Songs)
    solo voice,pno ICELAND 001-074
                       (B496)

  Eg Hylli (from Ten Songs)
    solo voice,pno ICELAND 001-090
                       (B497)

  Ein Sit Eg Uti A Steini (from Ten
    Songs)
    solo voice,pno ICELAND 001-057
                       (B498)

  Einbuinn (from Ten Songs)
    solo voice,pno ICELAND 001-050
                       (B499)

    solo voice,pno ICELAND 001-096
                       (B500)

  Eirikur A Einum Faeti (from Fourteen
    Songs)
    solo voice,pno ICELAND 001-077
                       (B501)

  Five Songs
    S solo,pno ICELAND 001-003 (B502)

  Fjollin Bla (from Ten Songs)
    solo voice,pno ICELAND 001-049
                       (B503)

    solo voice,pno ICELAND 001-099
                       (B504)

  Fourteen Songs
    S solo,pno ICELAND 001-022 (B505)

  Fram, Fram
    solo voice,pno ICELAND 001-014
                       (B506)

  Heidathokan (from Ten Songs)
    solo voice,pno ICELAND 001-052
                       (B507)

    solo voice,pno ICELAND 001-097
                       (B508)

  Horfinn Dagur (from Ten Songs)
    solo voice,pno ICELAND 001-091
                       (B509)

    solo voice,pno ICELAND 001-048
                       (B510)

BJÖRNSSON, ARNI (cont'd.)

Hver A Ser Fegra Fodurland (from
Fourteen Songs)
solo voice,pno ICELAND 001-082
(B511)

solo voice,pno ICELAND 001-087
(B512)

Hvitu Seglin (from Fourteen Songs)
solo voice,pno ICELAND 001-076
(B513)

I Dögun (from Ten Songs)
solo voice,pno ICELAND 001-051
(B514)

solo voice,pno ICELAND 001-094
(B515)

Islands Hrafnistumenn (from Five
Songs)
solo voice,pno ICELAND 001-045
(B516)

Islendingaljod (from Three Songs)
solo voice,pno ICELAND 001-088
(B517)

Last Voyage, The
solo voice,pno ICELAND 001-042
(B518)

Leidsla (from Fourteen Songs)
solo voice,pno ICELAND 001-078
(B519)

Live With Me (from Fourteen Songs)
solo voice,pno ICELAND 001-086
(B520)

Lystu Mjer
solo voice,pno ICELAND 001-028
(B521)

Morgunn (from Fourteen Songs)
solo voice,pno ICELAND 001-083
(B522)

Nott (from Fourteen Songs)
solo voice,pno ICELAND 001-084
(B523)

Nu Er Sol (from Ten Songs)
solo voice,pno ICELAND 001-092
(B524)

Nu Er Sol Og Vor (from Fourteen
Songs)
solo voice,pno ICELAND 001-075
(B525)

Nu Faerist Ad Vigold - F.U.J. Marsinn
solo voice,pno ICELAND 001-040
(B526)

Og Andinn Mig Hreif (from Fourteen
Songs)
solo voice,pno ICELAND 001-073
(B527)

Rökkurljod (from Five Songs)
solo voice,pno ICELAND 001-041
(B528)

solo voice,pno ICELAND 001-032
(B529)

Skaldid Er Thagnad (from Fourteen
Songs)
solo voice,pno ICELAND 001-080
(B530)

Solrodin Sky (from Ten Songs)
solo voice,pno ICELAND 001-055
(B531)

solo voice,pno ICELAND 001-098
(B532)

Sönglistin
2 solo voices,pno ICELAND 001-036
(B533)

Sönglög, 10
solo voice,pno ICELAND 001-030
(B534)

Syng Frjalsa Land (from Three Songs)
solo voice,pno ICELAND 001-089
(B535)

solo voice,pno ICELAND 001-081
(B536)

Ten Songs
S solo,pno ICELAND 001-002 (B537)

Thrju Songlog
solo voice,pno ICELAND 001-034
(B538)

Thu Hryggir Mig, Gledi (from Fourteen
Songs)
solo voice,pno ICELAND 001-079
(B539)

Um Kvöld
solo voice,pno ICELAND 001-027
(B540)

Vid Dagsetur (from Ten Songs)
solo voice,pno ICELAND 001-054
(B541)

solo voice,pno ICELAND 001-093
(B542)

Vogguvisa (from Fourteen Songs)
solo voice,pno ICELAND 001-085
(B543)

When The Flowers Sleep (from Five
Songs)
solo voice,pno ICELAND 001-043
(B544)

You Ask Me To Sing (from Ten Songs)
solo voice,pno ICELAND 001-053
(B545)

solo voice,pno ICELAND 001-095
(B546)

BJÖRNSSON, RAGNAR (1926-   )
Lagaflokkur
solo voice,pno ICELAND 045-004
(B547)

BLACK DIAMONDS (I) see Horder, Mervyn

BLACK DIAMONDS (II) see Horder, Mervyn

BLACK EYES see Flothuis, Marius

BLACK HOURS see Gerber, Steven R.

BLACK IS THE COLOR see Koetsier, Jan

BLACK LAKE, THE see Shields, Alice

BLACK TEA, LAMENT FOR VIET NAM see
Violette, Andrew

BLACK WINGS see Levi, Paul Alan

BLACKBIRD, THE, VERSION I see Weigl,
[Mrs.] Vally

BLACKFORD, RICHARD
From The Song Of Songs
S solo OXFORD 345164-6 $5.00 (B548)

BLAIR FAIRCHILD
see FAIRCHILD, BLAIR

BLAKE, HOWARD (1938-   )
Snowman, The
solo voice,pno FABER FH0001 (B549)

Walking In The Air (from The Snowman)
FABER FH0001 (B550)

BLÅKLOCKA OCH KLÖVER see Rooth, Anna-
Greta

BLANCHE ET ROSE see Delibes, Léo

BLANCO, E.
A Sevilla
solo voice,pno BOIL B.0595 (B551)

BLANK, ALLAN (1925-   )
Around The Clock (Coalitions III:
1983)
S solo,fl/pic,clar/bass clar,pno
[21'] AM.COMP.AL. sc $21.30, pts
$38.80 (B552)

Cat And The Wind, The
S solo,pno [2'] sc AM.COMP.AL.
$4.60 (B553)

Coalitions
S solo,2clar,trom,pno,2perc [15']
sc AM.COMP.AL. $15.20 (B554)

Don't Let That Horse
S solo,bsn,vln SEESAW f.s. (B555)

Envoi
S solo,pno [4'30"] AM.COMP.AL.
(B556)

Four Dream Poems
S solo,clar in A,trp,pno [14']
AM.COMP.AL. (B557)

Four Yeats Songs *CC4U
med solo,pno sc AM.COMP.AL. $7.70
(B558)

I Missed His Book
SBar soli,pno,opt perc,opt trom
[4'] sc AM.COMP.AL. $7.60 (B559)

Let All The Horses Go Free
male solo,pno [5'] AM.COMP.AL.
(B560)

Music For Measure For Measure
MezMez/A soli,fl,vln,vcl,pno,gtr/
lute [10'] sc AM.COMP.AL. $10.65
(B561)

Music For Othello
MezABar soli,fl,clar,vcl/trom [8']
AM.COMP.AL. sc $5.35, pts $14.45
(B562)

Pennycandystore, The
S solo,bsn SEESAW f.s. (B563)

Recital
S solo,tuba,pno [5'] sc AM.COMP.AL.
$4.60 (B564)

Two Holy Sonnets By John Donne *CC2U
A solo,2horn/2ob,vla,harp
AM.COMP.AL. sc $8.40, pts $22.45
(B565)

V.B.Nimble, V.B.Quick
S solo,pno [3'] sc AM.COMP.AL.
$4.60 (B566)

Waiting Both
S solo,pno [3'] sc AM.COMP.AL.
$4.60 (B567)

White Dwarf
S solo,pno [5'] sc AM.COMP.AL.
$4.60 (B568)

BLANQUER, AMANDO (1935-   )
Impromptus A Maria Luisa
S solo,orch [7'] EMEC (B569)

BLASS, NOAH
Songs
solo voice,pno OR-TAV (B570)

BLAT WIR ZUR BLÜTE, DAS see Focke, Fré

BLÄTTER SIND IN GROSSER VIRWIRRUNG, DIE
see Pieper, Rene

BLÄTTERLOSEN PAPPELN STEHN SO FEIN, DIE
see Flothuis, Marius

BLAUSTEIN, SUSAN
Canzo (Due Madrigali Di Torquato
Tasso) *madrigal
S solo,fl,ob,clar,bsn,horn,trp,
trom,2vln,vla,vcl,db,pno,2perc
[11'] APNM sc $10.00, pts rent
(B571)

Espoza De Don Garcia, La
see Romansa

Moon Has Nothing To Be Sad About, The
Mez solo,fl,clar,vla,vcl,gtr,harp,
hpsd [25'] APNM sc $22.00, pts
rent (B572)

Romansa
"Espoza De Don Garcia, La" Bar
solo,pno [17'] APNM sc $8.00, set
$15.50 (B573)

Song Of Songs *cant
MezT soli,2.2.2.1. 1.1.1.0. harp,
pno,2perc,strings [23'] APNM sc
$21.00, pts rent (B574)

BLAZEK, ZDENEK (1905-1988)
Deset Pisnicek
female solo,pno PANTON 882 (B575)

BLECHTROMMELVERSE see De Lastra, Erich
Eder

BLESSED JESUS see Faure, Gabriel-
Urbain, Pie Jesu

BLEST HERO WHO IN PEACE AND WAR see
Hook, James

BLEST IS THE LOVE see Leaf, Robert

BLEU ROUGE see Furrer-Münch, Franz

BLI TIL ETT MED see Backer-Lunde,
Johan, Inclusions

BLICK AUF DEN EAST RIVER see Koetsier,
Jan

BLICKHAN, CHARLES TIMOTHY (1945-   )
Speak Softly
S solo,fl,vibra SEESAW f.s. (B576)

BLIND FLOWER GIRL'S SONG, THE see
Blockley, John

BLIND MEN see Reynolds

BLINDE GEIGER, DER see Proch, Heinrich

BLINDE KNABE, DER see Schubert, Franz
(Peter)

BLISS, [SIR] ARTHUR (DRUMMOND)
(1891-1975)
Serenade For Orchestra And Baritone
Bar solo,2.1.0.2. 2.2.1.0. timp,
perc,strings [25'] OXFORD (B577)

BLITT ER UNDIR BJORKUNUM see Isolfsson,
Pall

BLOCH, ERNEST (1880-1959)
Deux Psaumes
SCHIRM.G ST28823 f.s.
contains: Psalm No. 114; Psalm
No. 137 (B578)

Poemes D'Automme
SCHIRM.G GS13278 (B579)

Psalm No. 114
see Deux Psaumes

Psalm No. 137
see Deux Psaumes

BLOCK, STEVEN
Oh Llama De Amor Viva
Bar solo,pno [6'] AM.COMP.AL.
(B580)

Wedding Song (Bound By Affection)
[Heb] S solo,pno [6'] sc
AM.COMP.AL. $6.90 (B581)

BLOCKLEY, JOHN
Blind Flower Girl's Song, The (from
Songs Of Pompeii)
"Buy My Flowers" SCIEN 303 (B582)

Buy My Flowers
see Blind Flower Girl's Song, The

BLODEK, VILEM (WILHELM) (1834-1874)
Mlada Laska
  AS soli,2.2.2.2. 4.2.3.1. timp,
  strings [3'] CESKY HUD.   (B583)

Vstupni Arie Veruny
  A solo,2.2.2.2. 4.2.0.0. timp,
  strings [4'] CESKY HUD.   (B584)

Zpev Janka
  B solo,2.2.2.2. 4.2.0.0. timp,
  strings [3'] CESKY HUD.   (B585)

BLOEMKEN, EEN see Weegenhuise, Johan

BLOMBERG, ERIK (1922-   )
Älskandes Natt, De
  solo voice,pno STIM f.s.   (B586)

Brev Till Dig
  solo voice,pno STIM f.s.   (B587)

Ekelundiana VII
  solo voice,pno [4'] sc STIM
  PA-3276-6 f.s.   (B588)

Ekelundiana VIII
  solo voice,pno [3'] sc STIM
  PA-3274-8 f.s.   (B589)

Fötter
  solo voice,pno [10'] sc STIM
  PA-3276-23 f.s.   (B590)

Glad Och Lugn
  solo voice,pno STIM f.s.   (B591)

Lindpredikan
  solo voice,pno STIM f.s.   (B592)

Möte Vid Slutet Av
  solo voice,pno STIM f.s.   (B593)

Sådan Kärlek
  solo voice,pno/org STIM f.s. (B594)

Själen Är Blind [1]
  solo voice,pno [2'] sc STIM
  PA-3277-6 f.s.   (B595)

Själen Är Blind [2]
  solo voice,pno [2'] sc STIM
  PA-3277-5 f.s.   (B596)

Stora, Det
  solo voice,pno STIM f.s.   (B597)

BLOMDAHL, KARL-BIRGER (1916-1968)
Fyra Sånger: Ur En Doddansares Visor
  3 female soli,pno SVERIG 672 f.s.
  contains: Leken Går; Stackars;
  Stjärnorna Kvittar Det Lika;
  Träd, Ett   (B598)

Leken Går
  see Fyra Sånger: Ur En Doddansares
  Visor

Stackars
  see Fyra Sånger: Ur En Doddansares
  Visor

Stjärnorna Kvittar Det Lika
  see Fyra Sånger: Ur En Doddansares
  Visor

Träd, Ett
  see Fyra Sånger: Ur En Doddansares
  Visor

BLOMSTER FRA DEN DANSKE POESIS FLORA
see Norholm, Ib

BLOMSTERTID NU KOMMER, DEN see
Albertsen, Per Hjort

BLOSSOM-TIME see Quilter, Roger

BLOW, JOHN (1649-1708)
Ah Heav'n! What Is't I Hear?
  AT/SS soli,cont KING'S KM39 (B599)

Begin The Song
  HINRICHSEN 108   (B600)

Cantate Domino
  TT/SS soli,cont KING'S KM174 (B601)

Ode On The Death Of Purcell
  sc KING'S   (B602)

BLUE EYES OF SPRING see Tchaikovsky,
Piotr Ilyich

BLUES see Malmlöf-Forssling, Carin

BLUES FRAGMENTE see Hays

BLUMENFELD, HAROLD (1923-   )
Charioteer
  Bar solo,vla,gtr MMB X815201 (B603)

Face Cendree, La
  S solo,vcl,pno MMB X815101 (B604)

BLUMENFELD, HAROLD (cont'd.)

Rilke
  S solo,gtr MMB X815003   (B605)

Silentium
  [Russ/Eng] med solo,pno (9 poems of
  Ossip Mandelstam) MMB X814005
    (B606)

BLUMENTHAL, JACOB (JACQUES) (1829-1908)
Sechs Lieder
  [Ger/Eng] med solo RECITAL 246
    (B607)

Sieben Lieder
  [Ger/Eng] high solo RECITAL 245
    (B608)

BLUMENTHALER, V.
Escalera, La
  solo voice,fl,3sax,horn,3trp,3trom,
  pno [8'] study sc MOECK 5348
    (B609)

BLÜTEZEIT MAI see Moeskes

BOATNER, EDWARD H. (1898-   )
O What A Beautiful City
  high solo SCHIRM.G ST38856 (B610)
  med-low solo SCHIRM.G ST38855
    (B611)

BOBROWSKI-LIEDER see Katzer, Georg

BOCCHERINI, LUIGI (1743-1805)
Duetto Accademico In Mi Bem. Maggiore
  (Pais) solo voice,kbd pno red
  ZANIBON 6224   (B612)

Quindici Arie Accademiche, Fasc. 4
  (contains nos. 10 (F major), 11 (A
  major), & 12 (B-flat major)) pno
  red ZANIBON 6218   (B613)

Quindici Arie Accademiche, Fasc. 5
  (Pais) (contains nos. 13 (E major),
  14 (B-flat major), & 15 (E-flat
  major)) pno red ZANIBON 6221
    (B614)

BÖDDECKER, PHILIPP FRIEDRICH
  (1683- ?)
Natus Est Jesus
  solo voice,gtr PLUCKED STR ZM 1899
  $4.50   (B615)

BODENSEELIED see Weber

BODENSOHN, ERNST FRIEDRICH WILHELM
An Frau Musica
  see Kleines Quartett (Quintett)

An Maria
  see Kleines Quartett (Quintett)

Friede, Friede Auf Der Erde
  see Kleines Quartett (Quintett)

Heute Ist Dein Festtag
  see Kleines Quartett (Quintett)

Kammermusikalisches Tedeum
  solo voice,alto fl,B rec,fl,vln,
  vla,vcl BODENS E E 102 (B616)

Kleines Quartett (Quintett)
  opt solo voice,fl,vln,vla,vcl
  BODENS E 27 f.s.
  contains: An Frau Musica; An
  Maria; Friede, Friede Auf Der
  Erde; Heute Ist Dein Festtag
    (B617)

BODIN, LARS-GUNNAR (1935-   )
Anima
  S solo,electronic tape SUECIA 379
    (B618)

BODOROVA, SYLVIE (1954-   )
Kale Bala
  Mez solo,clar,vla,pno [10'] CESKY
  HUD.   (B619)

Struggle With The Angel
  male solo,strings [8'] CESKY HUD.
    (B620)
  male solo,strings [8'] SUPRAPHON
    (B621)

BODY, JACK
Love Sonnets Of Michelangelo
  SMez soli WAI-TE-ATA 50 (B622)

BOECKX, JEAN
Au Jardin D'enfants
  SCHOTT-FRER 8947   (B623)

Fleur Des Champs, La
  SCHOTT-FRER 8770   (B624)

BOEHMER, KONRAD (1941-   )
Je Vis - Je Meurs
  S solo,fl,perc SEESAW   (B625)

BOËLLMANN, LÉON (1862-1897)
Conte D'Amour, Op.26
  high solo,pno CLASSV 1451 (B626)

BOER, JAN DEN (1932-   )
Ochtend
  S solo,fl&vln/pno [4'] DONEMUS
    (B627)

BOGLER, BERNHARD
Lerche Morgenlied, Der *Op.31
  solo voice,pno SCIEN 305 (B628)

BOHÁC, JOSEF (1929-   )
Dest Na Bajkale
  solo voice,pno PANTON 884 (B629)

Kvetenstvi Javoru
  T solo,pno PANTON 885   (B630)

Pisne Na Indianske Motivy
  med solo,1.1.3.1. 1.2.2.0. perc,db
  [8'] CESKY HUD.   (B631)

Sonata Lirica
  S solo,vibra,strings [12'] CESKY
  HUD.   (B632)

Vokalni Poema
  4 solo voices,2.2.2.2. 2.2.0.0.
  timp,strings [18'] CESKY HUD.
    (B633)

BOHÈME, LA: CHE GELIDA MANINA see
Puccini, Giacomo

BOHÈME, LA: DA QUEL SUON SOAVEMENTE see
Leoncavallo, Ruggiero

BOHÈME, LA: DONDE LIETA see Puccini,
Giacomo

BOHÈME, LA: MARCELLO "IO NON HO" see
Leoncavallo, Ruggiero

BOHÈME, LA: MARCELLO "TESTA ADORATA"
see Leoncavallo, Ruggiero

BOHÈME, LA: MI CHIAMANO MIMI see
Puccini, Giacomo

BOHÈME, LA: QUANDO ME'N VO see Puccini,
Giacomo

BOHÈME, LA: QUANDO M'EN VÒ SOLETTA PER
LA VIA see Puccini, Giacomo

BOHÈME, LA: VECCHIA ZIMARRA see
Puccini, Giacomo

BOHEMIA see Horder, Mervyn

BOHEMIAN GIRL, THE: ADMIRAL SONG, DUET
AND TRIO see Balfe, Michael
William, Could I Hush A Father's
Sigh

BOHM, KARL (1844-1920)
Calm As The Night
  see Still Wie Die Nacht

Liebesglück Waltz, Op.224
  see Loves Ecstasy

Loves Ecstasy
  "Liebesglück Waltz, Op.224" [Eng/
  It/Ger] coloratura sop,pno CLASSV
  1726   (B634)

Still Wie Die Nacht
  "Calm As The Night" [Eng/Ger] low
  solo,pno CLASSV 1725   (B635)

BOHMISCHER KRYSTALL see Gideon, Miriam

BOIELDIEU, FRANÇOIS-ADRIEN (1775-1834)
Ausgewählte Singstücke (from Johann
Von Paris)
  solo voice,pno SCIEN 310 (B636)

Dame Blanche: Viens, Gentile Dame
  [Fr] T solo,pno CLASSV 0393 (B637)

BOIS, LES see Paladilhe, Emile

BOIS, ROB DU (1934-   )
Abend Schwül, Der
  see Drei Traurige Tänze

Another Choice
  see Words

Because Going Nowhere Takes A Long
Time
  med solo,fl,pno DONEMUS (B638)
  S solo,clar,pno DONEMUS (B639)

Choice Of 850 Words
  see Words

Delicious Lovely Sobranie
  see Songs Of Innocence

Diotima
  med solo,clar,vla,pno [9'] DONEMUS
  f.s.   (B640)

Drei Traurige Tänze
  A solo,vla DONEMUS f.s.
  contains: Abend Schwül, Der;
  Hügel Wo Wir Wandeln, Der;
  Willst Du Noch Länger (B641)

Hügel Wo Wir Wandeln, Der
  see Drei Traurige Tänze

BOIS, ROB DU (cont'd.)

Hymn To Myself
see Words

Hymn To The World-Championship Heavy-
Weight 1964
see Words

In A Morton Feldman Mood
see Words

Instrumental Scenes
see Words

My Tongue Wanders
see Songs Of Innocence

O You Are Not Working
see Songs Of Innocence

Songs Of Innocence
countertenor,T rec,db DONEMUS f.s.
[6']
contains: Delicious Lovely
Sobranie; My Tongue Wanders; O
You Are Not Working   (B642)

Willst Du Noch Länger
see Drei Traurige Tänze

Words
Mez solo,fl,pno,vcl DONEMUS f.s.
contains: Another Choice; Choice
Of 850 Words; Hymn To Myself;
Hymn To The World-Championship
Heavy-Weight 1964; In A Morton
Feldman Mood; Instrumental
Scenes   (B643)

BOISMORTIER, JOSEPH BODIN DE
(1689-1755)
Automne, L'
solo voice,fl,vln,cont BILLAUDOT
(B644)
Été, L'
solo voice,cont [15'] BILLAUDOT
(B645)
Hiver, L'
solo voice,fl,strings,cont [18']
BILLAUDOT   (B646)
Printemps, Le
solo voice,vln/fl&rec,cont [15']
BILLAUDOT   (B647)

BOITO, ARRIGO (1842-1918)
Mefistofele: Dai Campi
T solo,pno CLASSV 0548   (B648)

Mefistofele: Son Lo Spirito
B solo,pno CLASSV 0741   (B649)

BOJANAFRESKERNA see Hemberg, Eskil

BOJANAUNDRET see Hemberg, Eskil

BOKA MED SJU SEGL see Tøsse, Eilert

BOKKEN LASSON ALBUM
LYCHE 74   (B650)

BOLCOM, WILLIAM ELDEN (1938-   )
Cabaret Songs, Vol.1
med solo,pno [30'] (CC12L) MARKS
(B651)
Cabaret Songs, Vol.2
med solo,pno MARKS   (B652)

I Will Breathe A Mountain *song
cycle
med solo,pno [23'] (texts by
American women poets) MARKS
(B653)
Junction, On A Warm Afternoon, The
solo voice,pno [2'30"] MARKS (B654)

Lime Jello Marshmallow Cottage Cheese
Surprise
med solo,pno [3'] MARKS   (B655)

Mary
med solo,pno [8'] MARKS   (B656)

Morning And Evening Poems
A/T/countertenor,alto fl,harp,pno,
strings [8'] MARKS   (B657)

Open House *song cycle
T solo,pno [35'] MARKS   (B658)
T solo,1.2.1.2. 2.0.0.0. perc,kbd,
strings [35'] MARKS   (B659)

Same Thing, The
[3'] MARKS   (B660)

Songs To Dance
med solo,pno, dancer [12'] (CC11U)
MARKS   (B661)

Tears At The Happy Hour
[3'] MARKS   (B662)

Three Donald Hall Songs
med solo,fl,clar,horn,vcl,pno [11']
MARKS   (B663)

BOLCOM, WILLIAM ELDEN (cont'd.)

Three Irish Songs
med solo,fl,vln,vla,vcl,pno [7']
MARKS   (B664)

Vaslav's Song
Bar solo,pno [2'30"] MARKS (B665)

Villanelle
med solo,pno [2'30"] MARKS (B666)

BOLDEMANN, LACI (1921-1969)
Four Epitaphs, Op. 10
Mez solo,string orch GEHRMANS 6656
f.s.
contains: Mabel Osborne; Ollie
McGee; Sarah Brown; William And
Emely   (B667)

Mabel Osborne
see Four Epitaphs, Op. 10

Ollie McGee
see Four Epitaphs, Op. 10

Sarah Brown
see Four Epitaphs, Op. 10

William And Emely
see Four Epitaphs, Op. 10

BOLLEN, JAN-BAS
Along What Highways
see No Flowers For The Man-Made
Desert

I See Myself Writing
see No Flowers For The Man-Made
Desert

No Flowers For The Man-Made Desert
Bar/B solo,pno DONEMUS f.s.
contains: Along What Highways; I
See Myself Writing; There Is A
Place I Recognize; This Memory
Whirls Towards Me   (B668)

There Is A Place I Recognize
see No Flowers For The Man-Made
Desert

This Memory Whirls Towards Me
see No Flowers For The Man-Made
Desert

BOLOGNA, JACOPO DA
see JACOPO DA BOLOGNA

BOLS SONG FROM THE INCIDENTAL MUSIC TO
DRIFTEKAREN see Jensen, Ludwig
Irgens, Bols Vise Fra Driftekaren
Suite

BOLS VISE FRA DRIFTEKAREN SUITE see
Jensen, Ludwig Irgens

BON, ANDRE (1946-   )
D'un Chant Perdu
S solo,4(pic).0+ob d'amore+English
horn.4+bass clar.2+contrabsn.alto
sax.tenor sax. 4.4.3.1. pno,harp,
marimba,3perc,vln,vla,vcl,db
[15'] AMPHION A.465 f.s.   (B669)

BON, WILLEM FREDERIK (1940-1983)
Away, Away
see Songs Of A Nature

Ciel Est Par-Dessus Le Toit, Le
see Trois Poemes De Verlaine, Op.
10

Clown, Le
see Trois Poemes De Verlaine, Op.
10

In The Mountains
see Songs Of A Nature

Lune Blanche, La
see Trois Poemes De Verlaine, Op.
10

Night-Piece, A
see Songs Of A Nature

On Such A Night Of June
see Songs Of A Nature

Songs Of A Nature
Bar solo,pno DONEMUS f.s.
contains: Away, Away; In The
Mountains; Night-Piece, A; On
Such A Night Of June;
Travelling   (B670)

Travelling
see Songs Of A Nature

Trois Poemes De Verlaine, Op. 10
Mez solo,fl,pno,vcl DONEMUS f.s.
contains: Ciel Est Par-Dessus Le
Toit, Le; Clown, Le; Lune
Blanche, La   (B671)

BOND, CARRIE JACOBS (1862-1946)
Perfect Day, A
high solo,pno CLASSV 0623 (B672)

BOND, VICTORIA (1945-   )
Cornography
S solo,horn,bsn SEESAW f.s. (B673)

Margaret
S solo,fl,vln,vcl,pno SEESAW f.s.
(B674)
Mirror, Mirror
solo voice,fl,vla SEESAW   (B675)

Molly Manybloom
S solo,string quar PRESSER sc
111-40134S, pts 111-40134P (B676)

Scat 2
S solo,trp SEESAW   (B677)

Suite Aux Troubadours
S solo,lute,fl,ob,vla,vcl SEESAW
f.s.   (B678)

BØNDENE KOMMER see Albertsen, Per Hjort

BONHEUR EST CHOSE LÉGÈRE, LE see Saint-
Saëns, Camille

BONHOMME, ANDREE
Berceuse
solo voice,pno SODEN   (B679)

BONJOUR, SUZON see Delibes, Léo

BØNN see Bakke, Ruth see Gulbranson,
Eilif see Sandvold, Arild

BØNN TIL EN BOKFINK see Evensen, Bernt
Kasberg

BONONCINI, GIOVANNI (1670-1747)
Tre Cantate (composed with Bononcini,
Antonio Maria)
(Verona, G. Gentili) S/T solo,hpsd/
pno CURCI 9763   (B680)

BONONCINI, GIOVANNI MARIA (1642-1678)
Cantata Per Camera A Voce Sola, Libro
Primo *CC11U
S/B solo,cont fac ed FORNI 192 f.s.
(B681)

BOOGMAN, WILLEM
Parole, Le
S solo,pno,perc,electronic
equipment [25'] DONEMUS   (B682)

BOOK OF SONGS see Ghezzo, Dinu Dumitru

BORDSALMUR-THRIR VIKIVAKAR-STOKUR see
Jonsson, Thorarinn

BOREAS see Edmunds, John

BORIS GODUNOV: BORIS'' MONOLOGUE see
Mussorgsky, Modest Petrovich

BORIS GODUNOV: MARINA'S ARIA (ACT 3,
SCENE 1) see Mussorgsky, Modest
Petrovich

BORIS GODUNOV: PIMEN'S TALE (ACT 4,
SCENE 1) see Mussorgsky, Modest
Petrovich

BORODIEVYCH, ROMAN
Historic March (from Chernyhivs'ki
Sichovyky And Other Songs)
[Ukranian] 3 solo voices,pno DUMA
(B683)
Kiev And Other Songs
[Ukranian] solo voices,pno DUMA
(B684)

BORODIN, ALEXANDER PORFIRIEVICH
(1833-1887)
All Poison The Song
[Russ/Fr/Eng] Bar solo,pno CLASSV
0885   (B685)

Arabian Melody
[Russ/Fr/Eng] med solo,pno CLASSV
0751   (B686)

Aus Meinen Tränen
[Russ/Ger/It] med solo,pno (text by
Heinrich Heine) CLASSV 0747
(B687)
Dans Ton Pays
"Your Native Land" [Russ/Fr/Ger]
med solo,pno CLASSV 0748 (B688)

Dissonance, A
[Russ/Ger/It] med solo,pno CLASSV
2113   (B689)

Fürst Igor: Ihr Tränen
BELAIEFF 250   (B690)

Fürst Igor: Nacht
BELAIEFF 249   (B691)

Fürst Igor: Sprich, Wo Bist Du
BELAIEFF 252   (B692)

BORODIN, ALEXANDER PORFIRIEVICH
(cont'd.)

Fürst Igor: Umsonst
BELAIEFF 246   (B693)

Fürst Igor: Verwunde
BELAIEFF 247   (B694)

Fürst Igor: Wenn Ich
BELAIEFF 251   (B695)

Gernegross, Der
"Haughtiness" [Russ/Ger/It] med
solo,pno CLASSV 0749   (B696)

Haughtiness
see Gernegross, Der

Melodie Arabe
BELAIEFF 245   (B697)

Prince Igor: Cavatina Of Kontchakovna
[Russ/Ger/Fr] Mez solo,pno CLASSV
1727   (B698)

Prince Igor: Cavatina Of Vladimir
Igorevitch
[Russ/Ger/Fr/Eng] T solo,pno CLASSV
0742   (B699)

Prince Igor: Jaroslavna's Arioso
[Russ/Ger/Fr] S solo,pno CLASSV
0744   (B700)

Prince Igor: Jaroslavna's Cry
[Russ/Ger/Fr] S solo,pno CLASSV
0746   (B701)

Prince Igor: Konchak's First Aria
see Prince Igor: Verwundet...

Prince Igor: Prince Galitsky's Aria
[Russ/Fr/Ger] B solo,pno CLASSV
1223   (B702)

Prince Igor: Prince Igor's Aria
see Prince Igor: Um Sonst Nach Ruhe

Prince Igor: Um Sonst Nach Ruhe
"Prince Igor: Prince Igor's Aria"
[Russ/Ger/Fr] Bar solo,pno CLASSV
0743   (B703)

Prince Igor: Verwundet...
"Prince Igor: Konchak's First Aria"
[Russ/Ger/Fr] B solo,pno CLASSV
0745   (B704)

Princess Of The Sea
[Russ/Ger/It] Mez solo,pno CLASSV
2110   (B705)

Quatre Mélodies
[Russ/Fr/Eng] high solo,pno CLASSV
1375   (B706)

Reich Und Arm
[Russ/Ger/It] med solo,pno CLASSV
0750   (B707)

Rosenduft...Dunkler Park
[Russ/Ger/It] med solo,pno CLASSV
2111   (B708)

Sea, The
[Russ/Ger/It] high solo,pno CLASSV
2114   (B709)

Sleeping Princess, The
[Russ/Ger/It] med solo,pno CLASSV
2112   (B710)

Song Of The Dark Forest
[Russ/Ger/It] med solo,pno CLASSV
2109   (B711)

Your Native Land
see Dans Ton Pays

BOROGYIN, A.P.
see BORODIN, ALEXANDER PORFIREVICH

BORRAS DE PALAU
Papallona Argentada, La
solo voice,pno BOIL B.1052   (B712)

BORROFF, EDITH
Five Whitman Songs
T solo,pno [15'] AM.COMP.AL.   (B713)

Love And Law
TBarB soli,acap [4'] AM.COMP.AL.
(B714)

Love Song Of The Eighties
solo voice,pno [3'] AM.COMP.AL.
(B715)

BORSTLAP, DICK (1943-   )
Acht Liederen
Mez solo,pno DONEMUS   (B716)

BORTE see Grieg, Edvard Hagerup

BORTOLI, STEPHANE (1956-   )
Mein Traum
S/T solo,clar,gtr,vla [16'30"]
BILLAUDOT   (B717)

BORTOLOTTI, MAURO (1926-   )
Arioso Per La Scena III
B solo,string quar EDI-PAN EP 7241
(B718)

Breve Cantata Sacra (from La Passione
Secondo S. Matteo)
B solo,vla,vcl,pno EDI-PAN EP 7685
(B719)

Nell' Impoetico Mondo
S solo,clar,trom,horn,vln,vcl,db
EDI-PAN EP 7895   (B720)

Quattro Poesie Di Paul Eluard
S solo,clar,vcl EDI-PAN EP 721
(B721)

Room 231: Something Black
S solo,string quar EDI-PAN EP 7686
(B722)

BÖRTZ, DANIEL (1943-   )
Sinfonia No. 8
MezBar soli,3.3.4.3. 4.3.3.1. perc,
harp,strings GEHRMANS 6655 (B723)

BORUP-JORGENSEN, AXEL (1924-   )
Ende Des Herbstes, Schluszstuck
*Op.44
Mez solo,pno [7'] SAMFUNDET 324
f.s.   (B724)

BOSC ENDINS see Mestres, Apeles

BOSCO, GILBERTO (1946-   )
Allelujah
SBar soli,pno ZERBONI 9817   (B725)

Aria Delle Carte
S solo,2inst ZERBONI 9532   (B726)

Cantata
solo voice,orch ZERBONI 9420   (B727)

Serenata III
S solo,5inst ZERBONI 9455   (B728)

BOSE, HANS-JURGEN VON (1953-   )
Achalm
S solo,clar in A,bsn,horn,vln,vla,
vcl,db sc,pts SCHOTT AVV 151
(B729)

Sonnet No. 42
Bar solo,string quar SCHOTTS
AVV 129   (B730)

BOSMANS, HENRIËTTE (1895-1952)
Melodies *CC10L
med solo,pno DONEMUS f.s.   (B731)

BOSQUETA ROSSINYOLERA, LA see Mestres,
Apeles

BOSWELL SONGS see Locklair, Dan Steven

BOTEN DES HERBSTES see Korn, Peter Jona

BÖTTCHER, EBERHARD (1934-   )
Gläserne Brücke, Die
[Ger] T solo,gtr NORGE   (B732)

BOTTJE, WILL GAY (1925-   )
In A Word: 6 Songs *CC6U
S solo,pno,ob,horn,electronic tape
AM.COMP.AL. sc $9.90, pts $3.45
(B733)

Sentence Once Begun, A
S solo,2vln,vla,vcl [6']
AM.COMP.AL. sc $6.90, pts $5.40,
pno red $3.85   (B734)

BOULANGER, NADIA (1887-1979)
Four Songs
see Quatre Chants

Quatre Chants
"Four Songs" SCHIRM.G ED3217 (B735)

Songs (1901-1922)
DA CAPO ISBN 0-306-76233-1   (B736)

BOULOGNE, JOSEPH (CHEVALIER DE ST.-
GEORGES)
see SAINT-GEORGES, JOSEPH BOULOGNE DE

BOURRICOTIN see Scali

BOVE, IL see Casella, Alfredo

BOWATER, HELEN
Songs Of Mourning
T solo,string quar WAI-TE-ATA 8
(B737)

BOY, THE see Grieg, Edvard Hagerup,
Guten

BOY AND THE HIGHWAYMAN, THE see
Haufrecht, Herbert

BOYCE, WILLIAM (1711-1779)
Chaplet, The
sc KING'S   (B738)

BOYCE, WILLIAM (cont'd.)

Lyra Britannica I
sc KING'S   (B739)

BOYHOOD'S END see Tippett, [Sir]
Michael

BOYKAN, MARTIN (1931-   )
Epithalamium
Bar solo,vln,harp [10'] APNM sc
$12.00, set $24.00   (B740)

BRAAL, ANDRIES DE (1909-   )
Cantique D'Anne
see Cinq Cantiques

Cantique De La Vierge Marie
see Cinq Cantiques

Cantique De Moise
see Cinq Cantiques

Cantique De Saint Paul
see Cinq Cantiques

Cantique Du Roi David
see Cinq Cantiques

Cinq Cantiques
DONEMUS f.s. [11']
contains: Cantique D'Anne (S/Mez/
A solo,harp); Cantique De La
Vierge Marie (S/Mez/A solo,
harp); Cantique De Moise (S
solo,harp); Cantique De Saint
Paul (S solo,harp); Cantique Du
Roi David (S solo,harp) (B741)

Die Van De Liefde Zijn Gesteken
see Omtrent De Liefde

Drinkebroer Op Weg Naar Huis
see Vier Dwaze Liederen

Ghequetst Ben Ic...
see Omtrent De Liefde

Heden En Verleden In De Liefde
see Omtrent De Liefde

Ic Draghe In Minen Herte...
see Omtrent De Liefde

Nun Est Bibendum
see Omtrent De Liefde

Omnia Vincit Amor
see Omtrent De Liefde

Omtrent De Liefde
A solo,pno DONEMUS f.s.
contains: Die Van De Liefde Zijn
Gesteken; Ghequetst Ben Ic...;
Heden En Verleden In De Liefde;
Ic Draghe In Minen Herte...;
Nun Est Bibendum; Omnia Vincit
Amor   (B742)

Troost Voor Geschokte
Concertbezoekers
see Vier Dwaze Liederen

Twee Tranen
see Vier Dwaze Liederen

Vier Dwaze Liederen
S/Mez solo,pno DONEMUS f.s.
contains: Drinkebroer Op Weg Naar
Huis; Troost Voor Geschokte
Concertbezoekers; Twee Tranen;
Woedende Tiener Keurt Hemd Af
(B743)

Woedende Tiener Keurt Hemd Af
see Vier Dwaze Liederen

BRADUM KEMUR BETRI TID see Sveinsson,
Atli Heimir

BRAEIN, EDVARD FLIFLET (1924-1976)
Annes Arie (from Anne Pedersdotter)
[Norw] S solo,pno MUSIKK   (B744)

Bare Branch, A
see Naki Grein, Ei

Enno Kan Eg Gå I Mjuke Vollar
"Still I Can Walk On Soft Banks Of
Earth" solo voice,fl,ob,2clar,
bsn,2horn,strings NORGE f.s.
(B745)

Go 'Natt Da
"Good Night" S solo,fl,ob,2clar,
bsn,timp,perc,strings [3'] NORGE
f.s.   (B746)

Good Night
see Go 'Natt Da

Morgon *Op.3,No.3
"Morning" solo voice,2.1.2.1.
2.2.2.0. timp,harp,strings [3']
NORGE f.s.   (B747)

BRAEIN, EDVARD FLIFLET (cont'd.)

Morning
  see Morgon

Naki Grein, Ei *Op.3,No.1
  "Bare Branch, A" solo voice,
  1.1.2.1. 2.2.2.0. timp,perc,
  strings [3'] NORGE f.s.   (B748)

Still I Can Walk On Soft Banks Of
  Earth
  see Enno Kan Eg Gå I Mjuke Vollar

BRAGA, GAETANO (1829-1907)
  Angel's Serenade
    "O Quali Mi Risvegliano" high solo,
    pno CLASSV 0563   (B749)
    "O Quali Mi Risvegliano" med solo,
    pno,vln/fl/vcl CLASSV 0562   (B750)

  O Quali Mi Risvegliano
    see Angel's Serenade

  Reginella: Bella Del Tuo Sorriso
    T solo,pno CLASSV 1540   (B751)

  Santa Lucia (Coloratura Arr.)
    [It/Eng] coloratura sop,pno CLASSV
    1160   (B752)

BRAHMS, JOHANNES (1833-1897)
  Ausgewählte Lieder 2 *CCU
    S/T solo ZEN-ON 713912 f.s.   (B753)

  Berceuse
    see Wiegenlied

  Canción De Cuna
    [Span/Ger] solo voice,pno BOIL
    B.1899   (B754)

  Complete Songs For Voice And Piano,
    The, Vol. 1 *Op.3,Op.6,Op.7,
    Op.14,Op.19, CCU
    solo voice,pno LEA 131 $3.00 (B755)

  Complete Songs For Voice And Piano,
    The, Vol. 2 *Op.32,Op.33, CCU
    solo voice,pno LEA 132 $3.00 (B756)

  Complete Songs For Voice And Piano,
    The, Vol. 3 *Op.43,Op.46,Op.47,
    Op.48,Op.49,Op.50, CCU
    solo voice,pno LEA 133 $3.00 (B757)

  Complete Songs For Voice And Piano,
    The, Vol. 4 *Op.58,Op.59,Op.63,
    CCU
    solo voice,pno LEA 134 $3.00 (B758)

  Complete Songs For Voice And Piano,
    The, Vol. 5 *Op.69,Op.70,Op.71,
    Op.72,Op.84, CCU
    solo voice,pno LEA 135 $3.00 (B759)

  Complete Songs For Voice And Piano,
    The, Vol. 6 *Op.85,Op.86,Op.91,
    Op.94,Op.95,Op.96,Op.97, CCU
    solo voice,pno LEA 136 $3.00 (B760)

  Complete Songs For Voice And Piano,
    The, Vol. 7 *Op.105,Op.106,
    Op.107,Op.121, CCU
    solo voice,pno LEA 137 $3.00 (B761)

  Complete Songs For Voice And Piano,
    The, Vol. 8: German Folk Songs;
    Children's Folk Songs *CCU
    solo voice,pno LEA 138 $3.00 (B762)

  Four Scriptural Songs, Op. 121
    (Deis) low solo/med solo SCHIRM.G
    LB1678   (B763)

  Four Serious Songs
    (Sargent) low solo,2.2.2.2.
    4.2.3.0. timp,harp,strings [20']
    OXFORD   (B764)

  German Folk Songs *CCU
    solo voice,gtr BREITKOPF-W EB 8486
    f.s.   (B765)

  Lieder Auswahl
    high solo,pno PETERS 3925A   (B766)
    low solo,pno PETERS 3925B   (B767)

  Sérénade Inutile
    see Vergebliches Ständchen

  Serenata
    [Span] solo voice,pno BOIL B.1258
                                  (B768)

  Vain Suit, The
    see Vergebliches Ständchen

  Vergebliches Ständchen
    "Sérénade Inutile" S/T solo SCHOTT-
    FRER 9040   (B769)
    "Sérénade Inutile" Mez/Bar solo
    SCHOTT-FRER 9041   (B770)
    "Vain Suit, The" [Ger/Eng] low
    solo,pno SCIEN 322   (B771)

BRAHMS, JOHANNES (cont'd.)

  Vier Ernste Gesänge
    B solo,pno CLASSV 0981   (B772)
    high solo,pno CLASSV 1728   (B773)

  Wiegenlied *Op.49,No.4
    high solo,pno CLASSV 0558   (B774)
    low solo,pno CLASSV 0502   (B775)
    "Berceuse" S/T solo SCHOTT-FRER
    9039   (B776)
    "Berceuse" Mez/Bar solo SCHOTT-FRER
    9038   (B777)

  Zwanzig Deutsche Volkslieder
    (Rosenthal) high solo,pno PETERS
    3927A   (B778)
    (Rosenthal) low solo,pno PETERS
    3927B   (B779)

BRAMBILLA
  Cinque Ariette E Duettino
    1-2 solo voices,gtr TECLA TE043
                                  (B780)

BRANDMÜLLER, THEO (1948-   )
  Morgenstern - Abendstern
    Bar solo,2pno,perc,db,tuba [19']
    perf sc BREITKOPF-W BG 1367 f.s.
                                  (B781)

BRANDSE, WIM (1933-   )
  Drie Liederen, Op. 30
    Mez solo,PNO DONEMUS f.s. [8']
    contains: Herberg In De Lente;
    Nonnendrinklied; Si-Schy   (B782)

  Eerste Sneeuw
    see Twee Liederen

  Herberg In De Lente
    see Drie Liederen, Op. 30

  Nonnendrinklied
    see Drie Liederen, Op. 30

  Si-Schy
    see Drie Liederen, Op. 30

  Twee Liederen
    S solo,pno DONEMUS f.s.
    contains: Eerste Sneeuw;
    Zondagmorgen   (B783)

  Zondagmorgen
    see Twee Liederen

BRANSCOMBE, GENA (1881-1977)
  Lute Of Jade, A
    [Eng] low solo RECITAL 247   (B784)

  Sun Dial, The *song cycle
    [Eng] high solo RECITAL 345   (B785)

BRATLAND
  Gje Meg Handa Di, Ven (composed with
    Kleive, Kristoffer)
    solo voice,pno MUSIKK   (B786)

BRAUNE AUGEN see Grieg, Edvard Hagerup

BRAVOUR VARIATIONEN ÜBER EIN THEMA VON
  MOZART "AH! VOUS DIRAI-JE, MAMAN
  see Adam, Adolphe-Charles

BRÉBEUF see Schafer, R. Murray

BRECHT SONGS see Muldowney, Dominic

BREDEMEYER
  Gedanken
    PETERS 10330   (B787)

BREDEMEYER, REINER (1929-   )
  Alltägliche, Das *CC5U
    ST soli,orch PETERS f.s.   (B788)

  Schöne Müllerin, Die
    Bar solo,string quar,4horn
    DEUTSCHER   (B789)

  Winterreise, Die
    Bar solo,horn,pno DEUTSCHER DV 9408
                                  (B790)

BREFID HENNAR STINU see Sveinsson,
  Gunnar Reynir

BREIMO, BJØRN (1958-   )
  Song Of Love
    S solo,vcl,pno [9'] NORGE f.s.
                                  (B791)

BREMER, JETSE (1959-   )
  Ave Rheuma
    see Drie Cynische Liederen

  Drie Cynische Liederen
    med solo,pno,vln,vcl DONEMUS f.s.
    [8']
    contains: Ave Rheuma; Frits En
    Kee; Rei Van Brabantse Vrouwen
                                  (B792)

  Frits En Kee
    see Drie Cynische Liederen

  Rei Van Brabantse Vrouwen
    see Drie Cynische Liederen

BRENET, THERESE (1935-   )
  Aube Morte
    Bar solo,2.2.2.2. 4.3.3.0. 2perc,
    timp,cel,harp,strings [14']
    BILLAUDOT   (B793)

  Hommes Sur La Terre, Les
    TB soli,2.2.2.2. 2.2.2.0. 3perc,
    timp,harp,cel,strings [15'25"]
    BILLAUDOT   (B794)

  Rois Mages, Les
    BarB soli,2.2.3.2. 2.2.2.1. 2perc,
    timp,cel,strings [15'15"]
    BILLAUDOT   (B795)

  Visions Prophétiques De Cassandre,
    Les
    SB soli,2.2.3.2. 2.2.2.0. 2perc,
    timp,harp,strings [15'] BILLAUDOT
                                  (B796)

BRENNAN, JOHN WOLF
  Bestiarium, Op. 17 & Op. 51
    S/T solo PAN 300   (B797)

BRENNEND see Pröve, Bernfried

BRENTE VÅRE GÅRDER, DE see Jensen,
  Ludwig Irgens

BRESGEN, CESAR (1913-1988)
  Vier Gesänge Nach Afro-Amerikanischer
    Negerlyrik *CC4U
    Bar solo,clar,db,perc,pno sc
    BREITKOPF-W BG 543 f.s.   (B798)

  Von Waeldern Und Zigeuner
    solo voice,gtr SEESAW   (B799)

  Zwei Lieder Für Singstimme Und
    Gitarre *CC2U
    (Kanthou, E.) DOBLINGER GKM 169
    f.s.   (B800)

BREV see Haugland, Glenn Erik

BREV TILL DIG see Blomberg, Erik

BREVE CANTATA SACRA see Bortolotti,
  Mauro

BREVIK, TOR (1932-   )
  Elegi For Kammerensemble
    S solo,vla,db,2perc [7'] NORGE
                                  (B801)

  Meeting The Orchestra
    see Vi Møter Orkestret

  Vagantviser
    [Norw] Bar solo,pno NORGE   (B802)

  Vi Møter Orkestret
    "Meeting The Orchestra" narrator,
    3(pic).2.2.2. 2.2.2.0. perc,
    strings [9'] NORGE f.s.   (B803)

  Voggesong
    [Norw] solo voice,pno NORGE   (B804)

BRÉVILLE, PIERRE-ONFROY DE (1861-1949)
  Furet De Bois Joli, Le
    med solo,pno CLASSV 0762   (B805)

BRIC-A-BRAC see Horder, Mervyn

BRICIOLE, LE see Sampaoli, Luciano

BRIDGE, FRANK (1879-1941)
  Go Not, Happy Day
    high solo,pno CLASSV 1677   (B806)
    low solo,pno CLASSV 1676   (B807)

  Isobel
    high solo,pno CLASSV 1729   (B808)
    med-low solo,pno CLASSV 1731 (B809)
    med solo,pno CLASSV 1730   (B810)

  O That It Were So!
    high solo,pno CLASSV 0961   (B811)
    med solo,pno CLASSV 1043   (B812)

  Six Songs For Medium Voice And Piano
    (CC6UL) NOVELLO   (B813)

  Three Songs
    med solo,vla,pno (diff) THAMES
                                  (B814)

BRIEF, TODD
  Canteres
    S solo,4.4.5.4. 4.3.4.1. 6perc,cel,
    2harp,pno,strings [16'] sc
    AM.COMP.AL. $82.50   (B815)

  Slow Lament
    S solo,pno [18'] sc AM.COMP.AL.
    $28.30   (B816)

BRIEF ENCOUNTERS see Weigl, [Mrs.]
  Vally

BRIEF GLIMPSES... see Sims, Ezra

BRIGAND'S SONG, A see Balakirev, Mily
  Alexeyevich

BRIGHT SEAWEED REAPING see De Lio,
Thomas

BRIMBERG, JACK
Bird Flew High, A
med solo,string orch,pno [8'] sc
AM.COMP.AL. $6.15   (B817)

BRINNER EN ELD, DET see Rooth, Anna-
Greta

BRITAIN, RADIE (1908-   )
Barcarola
S solo,pno/8vcl SEESAW f.s. (B818)

BRITTEN, [SIR] BENJAMIN (1913-1976)
Beware! (3 Early Songs)
med solo FABER 50762 X   (B819)

Evening Morning Night
BOOSEY VAB0253   (B820)

Heart Of The Matter
BOOSEY VAB0300   (B821)

Journey Of The Magi
countertenor&TBar soli FABER F0438
                         (B822)

Now Sleeps The Crimson
BOOSEY VAB0254   (B823)

Opera Arias: Mezzo-Soprano *CCU
BOOSEY VAB0295 f.s.   (B824)

Opera Arias: Soprano I *CCU
BOOSEY VAB0293 f.s.   (B825)

Opera Arias: Soprano II *CCU
BOOSEY VAB0294 f.s.   (B826)

BRITTON
Tremble Thou Earth
HINRICHSEN 490   (B827)

BRIZZI, A.
Canto A Tre Voci
2 male soli&female solo,pno EDI-PAN
EP 7251   (B828)

BROADWAY REPERTOIRE: BARITONE
(CC15L) LEONARD-US 00312051 (B829)

BROADWAY REPERTOIRE: MEZZO-SOPRANO
(CC15L) LEONARD-US 00312049 (B830)

BROADWAY REPERTOIRE: SOPRANO
(CC15L) LEONARD-US 00312048 (B831)

BROADWAY REPERTOIRE: TENOR
(CC17L) LEONARD-US 00312050 (B832)

BROEKMAN, HANS (1932-   )
Aan Het Roer
see Drie Achterberg-Liederen

Alleen
see Drie A. Roland Holst-Liederen

Dit Eiland
see Vier A. Roland Holst-Liederen

Drie A. Roland Holst-Liederen
Bar solo,pno DONEMUS f.s. [9']
contains: Alleen; Nachtliedje;
Stervende, De   (B833)

Drie Achterberg-Liederen
med solo,pno DONEMUS f.s.
contains: Aan Het Roer;
Sneeuwgang; Stil Ogenblik
                         (B834)

Eens
see Vier A. Roland Holst-Liederen

Einde, Het
see Vijf Nijhoff-Liederen

Kerstliedje
see Vijf Leopold-Liederen

Mozart
see Vijf Nijhoff-Liederen

Nachtliedje
see Drie A. Roland Holst-Liederen

Nu Ik Zijn Oogen Heb Gelezen
see Vijf Leopold-Liederen

Om Mijn Oud Woonhuis
see Vijf Leopold-Liederen

Ploeger, De
see Vier A. Roland Holst-Liederen

Sneeuwgang
see Drie Achterberg-Liederen

Sonate
see Vijf Nijhoff-Liederen

Souper, Het
see Vijf Nijhoff-Liederen

BROEKMAN, HANS (cont'd.)
Stervende, De
see Drie A. Roland Holst-Liederen

Stil Ogenblik
see Drie Achterberg-Liederen

Stille Dag, Een
see Vijf Leopold-Liederen

Tempo Di Menuetto
see Vijf Nijhoff-Liederen

Vagebond, De
see Vier A. Roland Holst-Liederen

Vier A. Roland Holst-Liederen
Bar solo,pno DONEMUS f.s. [14']
contains: Dit Eiland; Eens;
Ploeger, De; Vagebond, De
                         (B835)

Vijf Leopold-Liederen
high solo,pno DONEMUS f.s. [11']
contains: Kerstliedje; Nu Ik Zijn
Oogen Heb Gelezen; Om Mijn Oud
Woonhuis; Stille Dag, Een; Zoo
Stil   (B836)

Vijf Nijhoff-Liederen
Mez solo,pno/hpsd DONEMUS f.s.
[19']
contains: Einde, Het; Mozart;
Sonate; Souper, Het; Tempo Di
Menuetto   (B837)

Zoo Stil
see Vijf Leopold-Liederen

BROGI, RENATO (1873-1924)
Lucciole, Le
med solo,pno CLASSV 1306 (B838)

Ricordo, Un
[It] high solo,pno CLASSV 2103
                         (B839)

Visione Veneziana
[It] med solo,pno CLASSV 0752
                         (B840)

BRÖLLOPSSÅNG see Sjöblom, Heimer

BROOKS, RICHARD JAMES (1942-   )
Ahab's Monologue (from Moby Dick, Act
II, Scene I)
B solo,ob,clar,vln,vla,vcl,pno [7']
AM.COMP.AL.   (B841)

Last Night I Was The Wind *song
cycle
Bar solo,wind quin AM.COMP.AL. sc
$16.75 pts $8.40   (B842)

BROOKS, WILLIAM (1943-   )
Medley
med solo,pno (text by Gertrude
Stein) SMITH PUB   (B843)

BROUWER, FONS
Casa, La
Bar solo,pno [14'] DONEMUS (B844)

BROWN
Read My Heart (composed with Childs)
solo voice LUDWIG VS-09 $1.00
                         (B845)

BROWN, FRANCIS JAMES
Cradle Song, A
Mez/Bar solo,pno [6'] AM.COMP.AL.
                         (B846)

Four Blake Songs
low solo,pno [17'] AM.COMP.AL.
                         (B847)

Four Sonnets By William Shakespeare
*CC4U
med solo,clar,pno AM.COMP.AL. sc
$13.35 pts $4.25   (B848)

Human Abstract, The
Mez/Bar solo,pno [3'30"]
AM.COMP.AL.   (B849)

In Such A Night
SBar soli,pno [8'] sc AM.COMP.AL.
$7.70   (B850)

Infant Joy
Mez/Bar solo,pno [3'] AM.COMP.AL.
                         (B851)

Lay Of Love And Death Of Cornet
Christopher Rilke, The
A solo,pno [50'] AM.COMP.AL. (B852)

Nine Songs Of Innocence, Experience
And Prophecy Of William Blake
A solo,pno [32'] AM.COMP.AL. (B853)

Prologue To "Buddha" - The Poet's
Aria
med solo,pno [12'] sc AM.COMP.AL.
$8.45   (B854)

Seven (A Cycle Of Seven Emily
Dickinson Poems) *song cycle
med solo,pno [12'] sc AM.COMP.AL.
$11.45   (B855)

BROWN, FRANCIS JAMES (cont'd.)
Three Angel Poems *CC3U
solo voice,pno sc AM.COMP.AL. $6.15
                         (B856)

Three English Folk-Songs *CC3U,folk
song
S solo,clar,pno sc AM.COMP.AL.
$8.80   (B857)

Three Samplers From The Newark Museum
med solo,pno [2'] sc AM.COMP.AL.
$5.75   (B858)

Three Songs *CC3U
med solo,pno sc AM.COMP.AL. $5.40
                         (B859)

Tiger, The
Mez/Bar solo,pno [4'] AM.COMP.AL.
                         (B860)

View From Agios Petros, Andros, The
med solo,pno [6'] sc AM.COMP.AL.
$5.00   (B861)

BROWN, JAMES
Careless Content
solo voice BANKS f.s.   (B862)

Lass For A Sailor, The
solo voice BANKS f.s.   (B863)

Nocturne, A
solo voice BANKS f.s.   (B864)

Silent Spring
solo voice BANKS f.s.   (B865)

BROWN, NEWEL KAY (1932-   )
Dejeuner Sur L'Herb
Mez solo,sax,fl,pno SEESAW (B866)

BROWN, THOMAS
Shepherd! Thy Demeanour Vary
high solo,pno CLASSV 1504 (B867)

BROZ, FRANTIŠEK (1896-1962)
Skrivanek
S solo,2.2.2.2. 2.2.1.0. timp,perc,
harp,strings [6'] CESKY HUD.
                         (B868)

BRUCH, MAX (1838-1920)
Bruch-Album: 24 Ausgewählte Lieder
[Ger/Eng] (contains op. 17, part 2
& 3; op. 33; 12 folksongs)
RECITAL 346   (B869)

BRUCH-ALBUM: 24 AUSGEWÄHLTE LIEDER see
Bruch, Max

BRUCKNER, ANTON (1824-1896)
Choralmesse
A solo,2horn,org (C maj) HÄNSSLER
sc 40.759-01 f.s., voc sc
40.759-05 f.s., pts 40.759-31, 32
f.s.   (B870)

BRUDER LIEDERLICH see Strohbach,
Siegfried

BRUID, DE see Vries Robbe, Willem de

BRUNA SEI TU MA BELLA see Riccardi,
Riccardo

BRUNALJOS see Halldorsson, Skuli

BRUNEAU, ALFRED (1857-1934)
Chansons À Danser
med-high solo,pno CLASSV 2178
                         (B871)

Lieds De France De Catulle Mendès,
Les
solo voice,pno CLASSV 2187 (B872)

BRUNNENGEPLÄTSCHER, OP. 34 see Titl,
Anton Emil

BRURADAG see Bergh, Sverre

BRUSTAD, BJARNE (1895-1978)
Berceuse
S solo,fl,2sax,2horn,harp,strings
[4'] NORGE f.s.   (B873)

Did You Cry - ?
see Grát Du - ?

Grát Du - ?
"Did You Cry - ?" solo voice,
strings [3'] NORGE f.s. (B874)

BRUSTAD, KARSTEN (1959-   )
Meditation
S solo,fl,gtr [4'] NORGE f.s. (B875)

Molnkurvor
[Swed] S solo,gtr [8'] NORGE (B876)

To Dikt
[Norw] S solo,gtr [8'] NORGE (B877)

BRYLLUP-SALME see Nyhus, Rolf

BUCCINATE IN NEOMANIA TUBA see Schütz,
Heinrich

BUCH DER BILDER, DAS see Young, Derek

BUCHANAN, DOROTHY
Mary Magdalene And The Birds
S solo,clar WAI-TE-ATA B4 (B878)

BÜCHTGER, FRITZ (1903-1978)
Chansons Irrespectueuses
S/T solo,fl,ob,strings [8'] MODERN
1194A (B879)

BUKKERITTET see Fladmoe, Arvid

BULGARIAN FOLK-SONG see Steinberg,
Eitan

BULL, EDVARD HAGERUP (1922-)
Dramatiske Sanger, Op. 53a
[Norw] S solo,pno NORGE (B880)

Gruk, Op. 53b
[Dan] S solo,pno NORGE (B881)

Guirlandes, Op. 5
[Norw/Fr] solo voice,pno NORGE
(B882)

Tre Melodies, Op. 2
S solo,pno (texts by Kumbel) NORGE
(B883)

BULLER, JOHN (1929-)
Of Three Shakespeare Sonnets
S solo,instrumental ensemble OXFORD
63.083 (B884)

Proenca
Mez solo,3.2+English horn.3.2+
contrabsn. 4.3.4.0. 4perc,harp,
strings [40'] sc OXFORD 63.079
(B885)

Two Night Pieces From "Finnegan's
Wake"
S solo,instrumental ensemble OXFORD
63.078 (B886)

BULLFROGS see May, Beth see Revueltas,
Silvestre, Ranas

BUNGE, SAS (1924-1980)
A Cassandre
see Trois Poemes De Ronsard

A Helene
see Trois Poemes De Ronsard

A La Tourterelle
see Trois Poemes De Ronsard

Adieu A Ma Soeur Helene
see Chants D'espoir

Beau Jour, Un
see Drie Poemes De Jules
Supervielle

Cant De La Verge
see Drie Spaanse Volksliederen

Chants D'espoir
med solo,pno DONEMUS f.s. [12']
contains: Adieu A Ma Soeur
Helene; Esclave, L'; Poesie Du
Soir, La (B887)

Drie Joodse Liederen
low solo,pno DONEMUS f.s. [7']
contains: Ich Habe Die Tempel
Verwaist Geseh'n; O Herr,
Erforsche Nicht Die
Unsichtbaren Wunden; Wilder
Sturm Durchbrauste Land Und
Heimat, Ein (B888)

Drie Poemes De Jules Supervielle
med solo,pno DONEMUS f.s.
contains: Beau Jour, Un; Oreilles
D'Ane; Rivieres Riaient, Les
(B889)

Drie Spaanse Volksliederen
A solo,pno DONEMUS f.s.
contains: Cant De La Verge; En
Esta Larga Ausencia; Molinillo
(B890)

En Esta Larga Ausencia
see Drie Spaanse Volksliederen

Esclave, L'
see Chants D'espoir

Four Seventeenth Century Poems
high solo,pno DONEMUS f.s. [8']
contains: Go Lovely Rose; Hag Is
Astride, The; Never Weather-
Beaten Sail; Orpheus With His
Lute (B891)

Go Lovely Rose
see Four Seventeenth Century Poems

Hag Is Astride, The
see Four Seventeenth Century Poems

Ich Habe Die Tempel Verwaist Geseh'n
see Drie Joodse Liederen

BUNGE, SAS (cont'd.)

Molinillo
see Drie Spaanse Volksliederen

Never Weather-Beaten Sail
see Four Seventeenth Century Poems

O Herr, Erforsche Nicht Die
Unsichtbaren Wunden
see Drie Joodse Liederen

Oreilles D'Ane
see Drie Poemes De Jules
Supervielle

Orpheus With His Lute
see Four Seventeenth Century Poems

Poesie Du Soir, La
see Chants D'espoir

Rivieres Riaient, Les
see Drie Poemes De Jules
Supervielle

Trois Poemes De Ronsard
med solo,pno DONEMUS f.s. [9']
contains: A Cassandre; A Helene;
A La Tourterelle (B892)

Vuurvlieg, De
A solo,pno [3'] DONEMUS (B893)

Wilder Sturm Durchbrauste Land Und
Heimat, Ein
see Drie Joodse Liederen

BURDENS see Goldberg, William

BUREN, JOHN VAN (1952-)
Five Songs From Catullus
see Fünf Gesänge Nach Catull

Fünf Gesänge Nach Catull
"Five Songs From Catullus" med
solo,fl,vibra,perc,hpsd,vcl
[25'0"] PEER (B894)

BURGAN, PATRICK (1960-)
Cristallin
2 female soli,fl,clar,horn,trp,
2perc,harp,vla,vcl,db [27']
BILLAUDOT (B895)

BURLEIGH, HENRY THACKER (1866-1949)
Five Songs Of Laurence Hope
high solo,pno CLASSV 1353 (B896)

Grey Wolf, The
med-high solo,pno CLASSV 1983
(B897)

Jean
high solo,pno CLASSV 1980 (B898)
low solo,pno CLASSV 1982 (B899)
med solo,pno CLASSV 1981 (B900)

Prayer, The
med solo,pno CLASSV 1732 (B901)

Saracen Songs (7 Songs)
high solo,pno CLASSV 0665 (B902)

BURST FORTH MY TEARS see Dowland, John

BURT, FRANCIS (1926-)
Unter Der Blanken Hacke Des Mondes
Bar solo,orch voc sc UNIVER.
UE 18416 f.s. (B903)

BUSH
Venus And Adonis
solo voice NOVELLO 2953 $5.50
(B904)

BUSH, GEOFFREY (1920-)
Avondale
see Two Stevie Smith Songs

Cat Who Went To Heaven, The
[35'] (med diff) voc sc THAMES
(B905)

Little Love Music, A *song cycle
ST soli,pno RAMSEY BR0052 (B906)

Merciless Beauty
solo voice,pno (med) NOVELLO (B907)

My Cats
see Two Stevie Smith Songs

Two Stevie Smith Songs
solo voice,pno (med) NOVELLO f.s.
contains: Avondale; My Cats
(B908)

BUSH NIGHT SONG see James, William G.

BUSH SILENCE see James, William G.

BUSSER, HENRI-PAUL (1872-1973)
Trois Rondes Et Chansons
SMez soli (not available outside
U.S.A.) RECITAL 350 (B909)

BUSTOS, M.
Canción Contra Las Violetistas
see Valledor, Jacinto, Canción
Timida

BUT LATELY IN DANCE I EMBRACED HER see
Arensky, Anton Stepanovich

BUTLER, MARTIN (1960-)
Three Emily Dickinson Songs
S solo,clar,pno OXFORD 63.080
(B910)

BUTTERCUP see Tveitt, Geirr,
Smörblomster

BUTTERFLIES see Backer-Lunde, Johan

BUTTERWORTH, GEORGE SAINTON KAYE
(1885-1916)
Eleven Housman Songs
[Eng] low solo RECITAL 248 (B911)

BUTTERWORTH, NEIL (1934-)
Letter To The World *song cycle
A solo,pno (texts by Emily
Dickinson) CHILTERN (B912)

Three Poems
solo voice,perc CHILTERN (B913)

BUTTKEWITZ, FRED
Ode An Einen Albatros
Bar solo,1.1.1.1. 2.1.1.1. timp,
perc,harp,pno,cel,strings
DEUTSCHER (B914)

BUY MY FLOWERS see Blockley, John,
Blind Flower Girl's Song, The

BUZEK, JAN (1927-)
Zpevy Stare Ciny
Mez solo,strings [15'] CESKY HUD.
(B915)

BUZZI-PECCIA, ARTURO (1854-1943)
Ballata Del Bel Cavaliere
[It/Eng] high solo,pno CLASSV 0754
(B916)

Lolita
[Eng/It] high solo,pno CLASSV 0529
(B917)
[Eng/It] med solo,pno CLASSV 0564
(B918)

Mal d'Amore
[It/Eng] high solo,pno CLASSV 0755
(B919)

Povero Pulcinella
[It/Eng] high solo,pno CLASSV 0753
(B920)

Torna Amore
[It] high solo,pno CLASSV 0845
(B921)

BY FOOTPATH AND STILE see Finzi, Gerald

BY MY SIDE see Porter

BY OSCARSHALL see Bergh, Sverre, Ved
Oscarshall

BY RONDANE see Grieg, Edvard Hagerup,
Ved Rondane

BY THE BEND OF THE RIVER see Edwards,
Sherman

BY THE BIVOUAC'S FITFUL FLAME see
Goldberg, William

BY THE ISAR see Ogdon, Wilbur L.

BY THE RIVER see Ragnarsson, Hjalmar H.

BY THE SEA see Jordan, Sverre, Ved
Havet

BY THE VÅLÅ LAKE see Baden, Conrad, På
Vålåsjøen

BYRD, WILLIAM (1543-1623)
Ye Sacred Muses
KING'S (B922)

BYRDI BETRI see Tveitt, Geirr

C

C see Lönner, Oddvar

CABARET SONGS, VOL.1 see Bolcom, William Elden

CABARET SONGS, VOL.2 see Bolcom, William Elden

CACCINI, GIULIO (1546-1618)
Amarilli, Mia Bella *madrigal
solo voice,pno BOIL B.1723   (C1)

CACERA, LA see Mestres, Apeles

CACIOPPO, CURT
To A Child Dancing In The Wind
S solo,orch [20'] APNM sc $20.00,
voc sc $6.00, pts rent   (C2)

CADENS see Heppener, Robert

CADENZA see Mannino, Franco

CADMAN, CHARLES WAKEFIELD (1881-1946)
Album Of Songs
high solo,pno CLASSV 1405   (C3)
med solo,pno CLASSV 1344   (C4)

From The Land Of The Sky-Blue Water
high solo,pno CLASSV 0584   (C5)
med solo,pno CLASSV 0585   (C6)
med-low solo,pno CLASSV 0586   (C7)

I Hear A Thrush At Eve
high solo,pno CLASSV 2092   (C8)
low solo,pno CLASSV 2094   (C9)
med solo,pno CLASSV 2093   (C10)

I Passed A Stately Cavalcade
high solo,pno CLASSV 0583   (C11)
med solo,pno CLASSV 0582   (C12)

Idyls Of The South Sea
[Eng] high solo RECITAL 249   (C13)

Sayonara, A Japanese Romance, Op. 49
high solo RECITAL 70   (C14)
low solo RECITAL 71   (C15)

CADMUS ET HERMIONE: BELLE HERMIONE
HÉLAS! see Lully, Jean-Baptiste
(Lulli)

CAGE, JOHN (1912-1992)
Composition
3 solo voices PETERS 6704   (C16)

Mesosticks Re Merce Cunningham
PETERS 6708   (C17)

Music For Voice
PETERS 67040P   (C18)

Nowth Upon Nacht
PETERS 67039   (C19)

Ryoanji
solo voice,perc,orch PETERS 66986C
(C20)

CAGED SKYLARK see Mason, Charles

CAID, LE: TAMBOUR MAJOR see Thomas, Ambroise

CAJKOVSKIJ, PETR ILJIC
see TCHAIKOVSKY, PIOTR ILYICH

CALAMITY JANE TO HER DAUGHTER see
Johnston, Benjamin Burwell (Ben)

CALDARA, ANTONIO (1670-1736)
Constanza In Amor Vince L'inganno, La
solo voice,pno BOIL B.1738   (C21)

Mirti, Faggi, Tronchi E Fronde
solo voice,pno BOIL B.1737   (C22)

Vaghe Luci È Troppo Crudo
solo voice,pno BOIL B.1758   (C23)

CALDWELL, MARY ELIZABETH (1909-   )
Christmas Triptych, A
GENTRY JG0636   (C24)

Lenten Triptych, A
GENTRY JG0705   (C25)

CALLAWAY, ANN (1949-   )
Besides This May: 5 Songs *CC5U
S solo,fl,pno sc AM.COMP.AL. $7.60
(C26)

Dream Within A Dream, A
Bar solo,pno [7'] sc AM.COMP.AL.
$7.70   (C27)

Five Songs *CC5U
S solo,perc sc AM.COMP.AL. $13.35
(C28)

CALLHOFF, HERBERT (1933-   )
Fünf Lieder *CC5U
high solo,pno BREITKOPF-W BG 1330
f.s.   (C29)

CALLIGARIS
Tre Madrigali, Op. 13
3 solo voices,org,hpsd CARISCH
22164   (C30)

CALLIGRAMMES see Giuliani, Paolo

CALLING TUNES see Kjerulf, Halfdan,
Lokkende Toner

CALM AS THE NIGHT see Bohm, Karl, Still
Wie Die Nacht

CALMEL, ROGER (1921-   )
Alba Occitana
B solo,2.2.2.2. 2.2.1.0. perc,timp,
harp,pno,strings [6'] BILLAUDOT
(C31)

CALUMNY see Kohs, Ellis Bonoff

CAMBISSA, GIORGIO (1921-   )
Veneziane
S solo,pno,chamber orch pno red
EDI-PAN EP 7255   (C32)

CAMERICA VOCAL JAZZ INCORPORATED
solo voice BELWIN CAM0034 $2.00 (C33)

CAMÍ DE LA FONT see Mestres, Apeles

CAMÍ D'ESTUDI see Mestres, Apeles

CAMINANTE, EL see Schubert, Franz
(Peter)

CAMINOS see Lopez Artiga, Angeles

CAMPANA, LA see Mestres, Apeles

CAMPANA DE SAN GIUSTO, LA see Arona, C.

CAMPANA QUE CAMINA, LA see Schumann,
Robert (Alexander)

CAMPBELL-TIPTON, LOUIS (1877-1921)
Elegy, Op.33, No.1
[Eng/Fr] high solo,pno CLASSV 1979
(C34)

Four Sea Lyrics
[Eng/Fr] high solo RECITAL 250
(C35)

Opium-Smoker, The
S solo,pno CLASSV 2217   (C36)

Rhapsodie *Op.32,No.1
[Eng/Fr] high solo,pno CLASSV 1978
(C37)

Spirit Flower, A
[Eng/Ger] high solo,pno CLASSV 1733
(C38)
[Eng/Ger] low solo,pno CLASSV 1735
(C39)
[Eng/Ger] med solo,pno CLASSV 1734
(C40)

CAMPRA, ANDRÉ (1660-1744)
Fêtes Vénitiennes, Les: Charmant
Papillon
med-high solo,pno CLASSV 0480 (C41)

CAMPRUBI, J.
Besaba
solo voice,pno BOIL B.1045   (C42)

Feriante, La
see Firaire, La

Firaire, La
"Feriante, La" solo voice,pno BOIL
B.1162   (C43)

Rie, Mujer, Rie
solo voice,pno BOIL B.1007   (C44)

CANADIAN COASTLINES see Austin, Larry

CANCION see Lopez Artiga, Angeles

CANCIÓN CONTRA LAS MADAMITAS
GORGORITADORAS see Rosales, Antonio

CANCIÓN CONTRA LAS VIOLETISTAS see
Bustos, M.

CANCIÓN DE AMOR see Llovera, J.

CANCION DE BELISA see Coria, Miguel
Angel

CANCIÓN DE CUNA see Anonymous see
Brahms, Johannes see Rausch, Carlos

CANCION DE CUNA AFRO-CUBANA see Nin-
Culmell, Joaquin

CANCIÓN DE JÚBILO Y DUELO see
Beethoven, Ludwig van

CANCIÓN DE LA GITANA HABILIDOSA see
Castell, J.

CANCIÓN DE MAYO see Beethoven, Ludwig
van

CANCIÓN PICARESCA see Palomino, J.

CANCIÓN SATÍRICA DE PRONÓSTICO see
Esteve, Pablo

CANCIÓN TIMIDA see Valledor, Jacinto

CANCIONERO DE PEDRELL see Gerhard

CANCIONERO ESCOLAR CLÁSICO
(Padro, J. Ma.) solo voice,pno
(contains works by: Beethoven,
Haydn, Mendelssohn, Mozart,
Schubert, Schumann) BOIL B.1286
(C45)

CANCIONERO MUSICAL POPULAR ESPAÑOL:
TOMO 1: EL CANTO EN LA VIDA
DOMÉSTICA
(Pedrell, Felipe) solo voice,pno BOIL
B.1595   (C46)

CANCIONERO MUSICAL POPULAR ESPAÑOL:
TOMO 2: EL CANTO EN LA VIDA PÚBLICA
(Pedrell, Felipe) solo voice,pno BOIL
B.1660   (C47)

CANCIONERO MUSICAL POPULAR ESPAÑOL:
TOMO 3: EL CANTO POPULAR Y LA
TÉCNICA DE LA ESCUELA MUSICAL
ESPAÑOLA
(Pedrell, Felipe) solo voice,pno BOIL
B.1661   (C48)

CANCIONERO MUSICAL POPULAR ESPAÑOL:
TOMO 4: EL CANTO POPULAR Y LA
TÉCNICA DE LA ESCUELA MUSICAL
ESPAÑOLA (CONTINUACIÓN)
(Pedrell, Felipe) solo voice,pno BOIL
B.1662   (C49)

CANCIONERO POPULAR VASCO see Askue, R.
Maria De

CANCIONES see Rodrigo, Joaquín

CANCIONES AMATORIAS NO.2 see Granados,
Enrique, Mañanica Era

CANCIONES AMATORIAS NO.5 see Granados,
Enrique, No Lloreis Ojuelos

CANCIONES AMATORIAS NO.7 see Granados,
Enrique, Gracia Mia

CANCIONES CLASICAS ESPAÑOLAS, VOL. 1
see Obradors, Fernando

[CANCIONES] CUADERNO 1, OP. 79 see
Schumann, Robert (Alexander)

[CANCIONES] CUADERNO 2: VIDA AMOROSA DE
UNA MUJER, OP. 42 see Schumann,
Robert (Alexander)

[CANCIONES] CUADERNO 3 see Schumann,
Robert (Alexander)

[CANCIONES] CUADERNO 4 see Schumann,
Robert (Alexander)

[CANCIONES] CUADERNO 5: EL AMOR DE UN
POETA, OP. 48 see Schumann, Robert
(Alexander)

CANCIONES DE GARCIA LORCA see Aschero,
Sergio

CANCIONES DE INFANCIA, TOMO 1 see
Schumann, Clara (Wieck)

CANCIONES DE VALLDEMOSA see Garcia-
Abril, Antón

CANCIONES ESPANOLAS see Tal, Marjo

CANCIONES ESPAÑOLAS ANTIGUAS VOL. 1
(Roma) solo voice,pno BOIL B.2125
(C50)

CANCIONES ESPAÑOLAS ANTIGUAS VOL. 2
(Roma) solo voice,pno BOIL B.2126
(C51)

CANCIONES GONGORINAS see Bedmar, Luis

CANCIONES IN POPULAR STYLE, OP. 80 see
Orrego-Salas, Juan A.

CANCIONES INFANTILES see Rodriguez
Peris, Martin Jose

CANCIONES INFANTILES, TOMO 2 see
Schumann, Clara (Wieck)

CANCÓ, LA see Mestres, Apeles

CANCÓ D'ABRIL see Mestres, Apeles

CANCÓ DE TAVERNA see Mestres, Apeles

CANCÓ DEL MAR, LA see Mestres, Apeles

CANCÓ LLUNYANA see Mestres, Apeles

CANCOES MODERNISTAS see Hartke, Stephen Paul

CANCONER SELECTE VOL. 1 (25 CANCONS SELECTES) see Beethoven, Ludwig van

CANCONER SELECTE VOL. 2 (25 CANCONS SELECTES) see Schubert, Franz (Peter)

CANCONER SELECTE VOL. 3 see Schumann, Robert (Alexander)

CANCONER SELECTE VOL. 4 see Fore

CANCONER SELECTE VOL. 5 (40 CANTS ESPIRITUALS) see Bach, Johann Sebastian

CANCONS DE BRESSOL see Pla, J. Ma.

CANCONS FESTIVES PER ALS INFANTS see Mestres, Apeles

CANCONS LIRIQUES see Massana, A.

CANÇONS PER A VEU I PIANO see Salvador, Matilde

CANDLES see Chenoweth, Gerald

CANDOMBLÉ see Bjelinski, Bruno

CANNING, THOMAS (1911-   )
Carol Of Praise, A
Mez solo,2trp,trom,bass trom,org
[6'] AM.COMP.AL.   (C52)

Little Child There Is Born, A
S solo,pno [3'] AM.COMP.AL.   (C53)

Three Songs
S solo,pno [6'25"] AM.COMP.AL.
(C54)

Two Songs
S solo,vcl,pno [3'30"] AM.COMP.AL.
(C55)

CANONIC VARIATIONS see Hegdal, Magne

CANONS, 30 see Mozart, Wolfgang Amadeus

CANT D'AMOR see Massana, A.

CANT DE LA JOVENTUT see Mestres, Apeles

CANT DE LA VERGE see Bunge, Sas

CANT DELS OCELLS, EL
(Turull, X.) solo voice,pno BOIL
B.2923   (C56)

CANTA! see Tosti, Francesco Paolo

CANTA IL MARE see De Leva, Enrico

CANTA PE' ME see Curtis, Ernesto de

CANTARE, IL GIORNO, TI SENTII: FELICE?
see Zandonai, Riccardo, Patria Lontana

CANTARES DE LOS PERDIS see Wallach, Joelle

CANTARES DE NOCHEBUENA see Falla, Manuel de see Falla, Manuel de

CANTARES: LA TIERRA PROMETIDA see Ortiz, William

CANTATA see Bosco, Gilberto see Sveinsson, Gunnar Reynir

CANTATA AL VALLE DE MEXICO see Cordero, Ernesto

CANTATA PASTORALE see Scarlatti, Alessandro

CANTATA PER CAMERA A VOCE SOLA, LIBRO PRIMO see Bononcini, Giovanni Maria

CANTATA PER IL VENERDI SANTO see Torelli, Giuseppe

CANTATA PERDIDA, UNA see Pablo, Luis de

CANTATAS FOR ALTO AND CONTINUO see Handel, George Frideric

CANTATE DE LA PENTECOTE see Bach, Johann Sebastian

CANTATE DOMINO see Blow, John see Locke

CANTATE JUBILATE see Galuppi, Baldassare

CANTATE VIRGINI see Lechler, Benedikt

CANTEMOS VOL. 1 see Schumann, Clara (Wieck)

CANTERES see Brief, Todd

CANTI DEL POPOLO AMERICANO see Noliani, C.

CANTI DELL' ANSIA E DELLA GIOIA see Prosperi, Carlo

CANTI DELL' ANSIA E DELLA GIOIA (SERIE 1) see Prosperi, Carlo

CANTI DELL' ANSIA E DELLA GIOIA (SERIE 2) see Prosperi, Carlo

CANTI DELLA SERA, I see Santoliquido, Francesco

CANTI INDULGENTI see Dall'Ongaro, Michele

CANTICLE I see Leichtling, Alan

CANTICLES OP. 56, NOS. 1-3 see Hemberg, Eskil

CANTICO DELLA VIGNA, IL see Porro, Mauro

CANTIQUE D'ANNE see Braal, Andries de

CANTIQUE DE LA VIERGE MARIE see Braal, Andries de

CANTIQUE DE MOISE see Braal, Andries de

CANTIQUE DE SAINT PAUL see Braal, Andries de

CANTIQUE DU ROI DAVID see Braal, Andries de

CANTO, IL see Coral, Giampaolo

CANTO A TRE VOCI see Brizzi, A.

CANTO DE AMOR see Massana, A., Cant D'Amor

CANTO DE CONTRICIÓN see Beethoven, Ludwig van

CANTO DE LA CODORNIZ, EL see Beethoven, Ludwig van

CANTO DE LI AUGEI, IL see Kopelent, Marek

CANTO DELLA QUAGLIA, IL see Schubert, Franz (Peter), Wachtelschlag, Der

CANTO GRATIA see Falk, Karl-Axel

CANTO III see Sampaoli, Luciano

CANTO NORDICO. VERS II see Koch, Erland von

CANTO PRIMO see Scogna, Flavio Emilio

CANTO SECONDO see Scogna, Flavio Emilio

CANTO SOBRE LA MUERTE DE SILVESTRE see Biggs, John

CANTO SPIANATO see Dresden, Sem

CANTO TERZO see Scogna, Flavio Emilio

CANTO:28 DE SEPTIEMBRE see Ortiz, William

CANTOS DE LORCA see Gabel, Gerald L.

CANTOS ESCOLARES see Mestres, Apeles

CANTUS see Sifonia, Firmino

CANZO (DUE MADRIGALI DI TORQUATO TASSO) see Blaustein, Susan

CANZONA see Lolini, Ruggero

CANZONE see Winslow, Walter

CANZONE DI DORETTA see Puccini, Giacomo, Rondine, La: Chi Il Bel Sogno

CANZONE SCORDATE, VOL. 1: TEN EARLY SPANISH SONGS (1440-1550)
(Dorumsgaard, Arne) low solo,kbd
RECITAL   (C57)

CANZONE SCORDATE, VOL. 2: TEN EARLY ITALIAN SONGS (1600-1640)
(Dorumsgaard, Arne) med solo,kbd
RECITAL   (C58)

CANZONE SCORDATE, VOL. 3: FIVE EARLY ITALIAN SONGS (1640-1700)
(Dorumsgaard, Arne) high solo,kbd
RECITAL   (C59)

CANZONE SCORDATE, VOL. 4: FIVE EARLY ITALIAN SONGS (1640-1700)
(Dorumsgaard, Arne) low solo,kbd
RECITAL   (C60)

CANZONE SCORDATE, VOL. 5: SIX EARLY ITALIAN ARIAS (1620-1750)
(Dorumsgaard, Arne) high solo,kbd
RECITAL   (C61)

CANZONE SCORDATE, VOL. 6: FIVE SCARLATTI ARIAS (1660-1725)
(Dorumsgaard, Arne) low solo,kbd
RECITAL   (C62)

CANZONE SCORDATE, VOL. 7: FIVE EARLY FRENCH SONGS (1500-1750)
(Dorumsgaard, Arne) med solo,kbd
RECITAL   (C63)

CANZONE SCORDATE, VOL. 8: FIVE ELIZABETHAN SONGS (1597-1632)
(Dorumsgaard, Arne) high solo,kbd
RECITAL   (C64)

CANZONE SCORDATE, VOL. 9: FIVE DOWLAND SONGS (1562-1626)
(Dorumsgaard, Arne) med solo,kbd
RECITAL   (C65)

CANZONE SCORDATE, VOL. 10: FIVE BELLMAN SONGS (1740-1795)
(Dorumsgaard, Arne) med solo,kbd
RECITAL   (C66)

CANZONE SCORDATE, VOL. 11: FIVE BELLMAN SONGS (1740-1795)
(Dorumsgaard, Arne) med solo,kbd
RECITAL   (C67)

CANZONE SCORDATE, VOL. 12: TEN SACRED GERMAN SONGS (1600-1700)
(Dorumsgaard, Arne) med solo,kbd
RECITAL   (C68)

CANZONE SCORDATE, VOL. 13: FIVE SACRED GERMAN SONGS (1700-1750)
(Dorumsgaard, Arne) med solo,kbd
RECITAL   (C69)

CANZONE SCORDATE, VOL. 14: FIVE J.S. BACH SONGS (1685-1750)
(Dorumsgaard, Arne) high solo,kbd
RECITAL   (C70)

CANZONE SCORDATE, VOL. 15: FIVE PH. EM. BACH SONGS (1714-1788)
(Dorumsgaard, Arne) high solo,kbd
RECITAL   (C71)

CANZONE SCORDATE, VOL. 16: NINE GERMAN SONGS (1800-1850)
(Dorumsgaard, Arne) low solo,kbd
RECITAL   (C72)

CANZONE SCORDATE, VOL. 17: SEVEN GERMAN FOLK SONGS (1750-1800)
(Dorumsgaard, Arne) low solo,kbd
RECITAL   (C73)

CANZONE SCORDATE, VOL. 18: EIGHT GERMAN FOLK SONGS (1800-1840)
(Dorumsgaard, Arne) med solo,kbd
RECITAL   (C74)

CANZONE SCORDATE, VOL. 19: FIVE FOLK SONGS FROM THE OLD WORLD
(Dorumsgaard, Arne) low solo,kbd
RECITAL   (C75)

CANZONE SCORDATE, VOL. 20: FIVE GERMAN CHRISTMAS CAROLS (1400-1850)
(Dorumsgaard, Arne) med solo,kbd
RECITAL   (C76)

CANZONE SCORDATE, VOL. 21: FIVE EARLY SECULAR ARIAS (1680-1780)
(Dorumsgaard, Arne) med solo,kbd
RECITAL   (C77)

CANZONE SCORDATE, VOL. 22: FOUR EARLY GERMAN ARIAS (1720-1760)
(Dorumsgaard, Arne) med solo,kbd
RECITAL   (C78)

CANZONE SCORDATE, VOL. 23: 22 SELECTED SONGS
(Dorumsgaard, Arne) RECITAL 425 (C79)

CANZONE VENEZIANA see Tosti, Francesco Paolo

CANZONETTA see Rossini, Gioacchino see Voormolen, Alexander Nicolas

CANZONETTA MARINA see De Leva, Enrico, Canta Il Mare

CANZONETTA SPAGNUOLA see Rossini, Gioacchino

CANZONETTAS (THREE SONGS ON ANONYMOUS TEXTS) see Meschwitz, Frieder

CANZONETTE see Loewe, Carl Gottfried

CANZONETTE A TRE VOCI see Panni, Marcello

CANZONETTE PER CAMERA A VOCE SOLA DI
   DIVERSI AUTORI *CC12U
   solo voice,cont fac ed FORNI 1255
   f.s.   (C80)

CANZONI AMOROSI see Schubert, Manfred

CANZONI DA CONCERTO OP. 72 see Nicolau,
   Dimitri

CANZONI E SCHERZI, OP. 30 see Regt,
   Hendrik de

CANZONI ELEATICHE see Renna, Enrico

CANZONI NAPOLETANE *CCU
   [It/Hung] BOOSEY EMB50261 f.s. (C81)

CAPDENAT, PHILIPPE (1934-   )
   Croce É Delizia 1985
   S solo,fl,pic,clar,bass clar,trom,
   2marimba,strings,prepared pno
   [20'] AMPHION A.420-21 f.s. (C82)

CAPDEVIELLE, PIERRE (1906-1969)
   Amours De Pierre De Ronsard, Les
   2 solo voices,fl,harp,vln,vla,vcl
   BILLAUDOT   (C83)

   Chant D'Alphesibée, Le
   S solo,fl,harp,vln,vla,vcl [10']
   sc,pts,pno red BILLAUDOT   (C84)

   Deux Apologues D'Oscar Wilde
   MezT soli,3.3.3.2. 4.3.3.1. 4perc,
   timp,cel,2harp,pno,strings [21']
   sc,pts,voc sc BILLAUDOT   (C85)

CAPINERA, LA see Benedict, [Sir]
   Julius, Wren, The

CAPLET, ANDRÉ (1878-1925)
   Ce Sable Fin Et Fuyant...
   high solo,pno CLASSV 0480   (C86)

   Viens! Une Flûte Invisible
   med solo,pno (1901 edition) CLASSV
   0763   (C87)

CAPRE, LA see Steinberg, Eitan

CAPRICORNUS, SAMUEL (1628-1665)
   Iudica Domine
   SS soli,vln,cornetto,cont NOTON
   N-9229   (C88)

CAPRISME see Metral, Pierre

CAPTIVE, LA see Berlioz, Hector (Louis)

CAPUA, EDUARDO DI
   see DI CAPUA, EDUARDO

CAPUIS, MATILDE (1913-   )
   Divagazioni
   solo voice,vcl CURCI 10198   (C89)

   Dodici Liriche
   solo voice,pno (med) BERBEN   (C90)

CAPURSO, ELISABETTA
   Quartetto Con Voce
   female solo,fl,clar,trom EDI-PAN
   EP 7684   (C91)

CARDI, MAURO
   R.I.B.E.S.
   solo voice EDI-PAN EP 7224   (C92)

CARDILLO
   Core 'Ngrato
   T solo,pno CLASSV 0555   (C93)

   Core 'Ngrato Catari Catari
   [It/Eng] solo voice RICORDI-IT
   RLD308   (C94)
   [It/Eng] med solo RICORDI-IT RLD309
                                 (C95)

CARDINAL IN MARCH see Weigl, [Mrs.]
   Vally

CARE SELVE, AURE GRATE see Handel,
   George Frideric

CARELESS CONTENT see Brown, James

CARGOL, EL see Mestres, Apeles

CARITAS see Dembski, Stephen

CARL, ROBERT
   American Space
   S solo,fl/alto fl/pic,clar,horn,
   vln,vcl,pno [12'] AM.COMP.AL. sc
   $9.95, pts $4.60   (C96)

   December 27, 1966
   S solo,fl/pic,clar,trp,perc,vln,
   vla,vcl [20'] sc AM.COMP.AL.
   $11.10   (C97)

   Distant Shore II, The
   S solo,pic,fl,horn,trp,perc,4vln,
   2vla,2vcl,db [12'] AM.COMP.AL. sc
   $10.65, pts $7.60   (C98)

CARL, ROBERT (cont'd.)
   Farewell To The Funless 80's!
   solo voice,kbd [6'] AM.COMP.AL.
                                 (C99)

   This City Makes Me Weep
   S solo,electronic tape [10'] sc
   AM.COMP.AL. $6.90   (C100)

   Two Visions
   S solo,3.2.1.1. 1.1.0.0. perc,pno,
   strings [17'] AM.COMP.AL.   (C101)

CARLSEN, PHILIP
   Fair Seed-Time
   T solo,2.2.2.2. 2.1.1.0. pno,perc,
   strings [10'] sc AM.COMP.AL.
   $31.40   (C102)

   Morning Star
   S solo,vibra [18'] sc AM.COMP.AL.
   $10.70   (C103)

   Projection
   high solo,pno [3'] sc AM.COMP.AL.
   $4.60   (C104)

   Tendril
   high male solo,clar,vln,vibra [5']
   sc AM.COMP.AL. $4.60   (C105)

   Two Little Whos
   med solo,pno [1'] sc AM.COMP.AL.
   $4.60   (C106)

   Upon Julia's Voice
   med solo,pno [2'] sc AM.COMP.AL.
   $1.60   (C107)

CARMÈ: CARMELA see De Curtis

CARMÉ!: LLI-LLI-RI-LLI-LLI-LLÁ see
   Cristofaro, A. de

CARME SECOLARE, IL see Jachino, Carlo

CARMELA see Tosti, Francesco Paolo

CARMEN: DUET "PARLE-MOI" see Bizet,
   Georges

CARMEN: JE DIS QUE RIEN see Bizet,
   Georges

CARMEN: LA FLEUR QUE TU M'AVAIS JETÉE
   see Bizet, Georges

CARMEN: L'AMOUR EST see Bizet, Georges

CARMEN: LES TRINGLES DES SISTRES
   TINTAIENT see Bizet, Georges

CARMEN: PRÈS DES REMPARTS DE SÉVILLE
   see Bizet, Georges

CARMEN: VOTRE TOAST see Bizet, Georges

CARNAVAL see Fourdrain, Felix

CARNIVAL OF VENICE (WITH CONCERT
   VARIATIONS) see Benedict, [Sir]
   Julius

CARO MIO BEN see Giordani, Giuseppe

CARO MIO BEN, CREDI MI ALMEN see
   Giordani, Tommaso

CARO MIO BENE see Giordani, Giuseppe

CAROL OF PRAISE, A see Canning, Thomas

CAROL OF THE THRUSH see Willingham,
   Lawrence

CARPENTER, JOHN ALDEN (1876-1951)
   Cock Shall Crow, The
   med solo,pno (text by Robert Louis
   Stevenson) CLASSV 1154   (C108)

   Dansons La Gigue!
   med solo,pno (text by Paul
   Verlaine) CLASSV 0993   (C109)

   Day Is No More, The
   low solo,pno CLASSV 1977 (C110)

   Don't Ceäre
   med solo,pno CLASSV 0996 (C111)

   Fog Wraiths
   med solo,pno CLASSV 1003 (C112)

   Four Chinese Tone Poems
   see Water-Colors

   Go, Lovely Rose
   med solo,pno CLASSV 0998 (C113)

   Green River, The
   med solo,pno CLASSV 0995 (C114)

   Her Voice
   med solo,pno CLASSV 1001 (C115)

CARPENTER, JOHN ALDEN (cont'd.)
   Il Pleure Dans Mon Coeur
   med solo,pno (text by Paul
   Verlaine) CLASSV 0994   (C116)

   Little Fly
   med solo,pno CLASSV 0999 (C117)

   Looking-Glass River
   med solo,pno (text by Robert Louis
   Stevenson) CLASSV 0997   (C118)

   May, The Maiden
   high solo,pno CLASSV 0992 (C119)

   Player Queen, The
   med solo,pno (text by W. B. Yeats)
   CLASSV 0991   (C120)

   Silhouettes, Les
   med solo,pno CLASSV 1000 (C121)

   To One Unknown
   med solo,pno CLASSV 1002 (C122)

   Treat Me Nice
   Bar solo,pno CLASSV 1136 (C123)

   Water-Colors
   "Four Chinese Tone Poems" [Eng] med
   solo,pno CLASSV 1674   (C124)

CARR, EDWIN
   Five Wolfskehl Songs
   Bar solo,pno WAI-TE-ATA 25 (C125)

   Songs On Poems By Dame Edith Sitwell
   *song cycle
   Mez solo,ob,pno RICORDI-IT LD556
                                (C126)

CARRERAS, F.
   Sis Cancons
   solo voice,pno BOIL B.2686 (C127)

CARTER, ANDREW
   Pancake Tuesday
   solo voice BANKS f.s.   (C128)

CARTER, ELLIOTT COOK, JR. (1908-   )
   Warble For Lilac-Time
   S solo,fl,2clar,bsn,harp,strings
   [8'0"] PEER   (C129)

CARTER, JOHN (1937-1981)
   Cantata
   S solo,2.2.2.2. 4.3.3.0. timp,perc,
   harp,strings [12'0"] PEER   (C130)

   Come With A Singing Heart (composed
   with Beall, Mary Kay) *CC10L
   med solo,pno HOPE 1053 f.s. (C131)

CARTES POSTALES see Sacre, Guy

CASA, LA see Brouwer, Fons

CASA GUIDI see Argento, Dominick

CASABLANCAS, BENET (1956-   )
   D'humanal Fragment
   Mez/A solo,string quar EMEC (C132)

   Tres Poemes Erotics
   S solo,chamber orch EMEC   (C133)

CASANOVA, ANDRÉ (1919-   )
   Cinq Mélodies
   T solo,1.1.1.1. 0.1.1.0. perc,harp,
   4vla,4vcl,2db [9'] sc,pts,voc sc
   BILLAUDOT   (C134)

CÄSAR FLAISCHLEN-ZYKLUS see Höller,
   Karl

CASE JANICE, THE: FROM A CASE RECORD
   see Germeten, Gunnar, Tilfellet
   Janice: Fra En Sykejournal

CASELLA, ALFREDO (1883-1947)
   Bove, Il
   see Due Canti

   Due Canti
   med solo,pno CLASSV 0839 f.s.
   contains: Bove, Il; Pianto Antico
                                (C135)

   Pianto Antico
   see Due Canti

CASSILS, CRAIG
   Child Of The Universe
   solo voice,pno SOMERSET SP 816
                                (C136)

CASTELL, J.
   Canción De La Gitana Habilidosa
   (Subira, Jose) solo voice,pno BOIL
   B.1026 f.s. contains also: Muson,
   L., Seguidilla Dolorosa De Una
   Enamorada; Esteve, Pablo, Canción
   Satírica De Pronóstico   (C137)

CASTELNUOVO-TEDESCO, MARIO (1895-1968)
Vogelweide
Bar solo,gtr/pno BERBEN (C138)

CASTERBRIDGE FAIR see Downes, Andrew

CASTILLON, ALEXIS DE (1838-1873)
Six Poesies D'Armand Silvestre
[Fr] RECITAL 251 (C139)

CAT AND THE WIND, THE see Blank, Allan

CAT WHO WENT TO HEAVEN, THE see Bush, Geoffrey

CATALANI, ALFREDO (1854-1893)
Edmea: In Qual T'aggiri Immacolata Stella
T solo,pno CLASSV 0917 (C140)

Loreley: Amor, Celeste
S solo,pno CLASSV 0574 (C141)

Loreley: Ove Son? Che Fu?
T solo,pno CLASSV 0879 (C142)

Wally, La: Ebben? Ne Andrò Lontana
S solo,pno CLASSV 0391 (C143)

Wally, La: Nè Ma Dunque
S solo,pno CLASSV 0575 (C144)

Wally, La: Un Giorno Sciolte Le Sue Vele
S solo,pno CLASSV 1513 (C145)

CATALOGO VOCE see Austin, Larry

CATALYSIS NO.3 see Shimoyama, Hifumi

CATHEDRAL OF THE INCARNATION see Stearns, Peter Pindar

CATTLE CALL AND SUMMER NIGHT see Storbekken, Egil, Lokketrall Og Somar-Natt

CAUSE US, O LORD OUR GOD see Kalmanoff, Martin

CAVALLERIA RUSTICANA: AVE MARIA see Mascagni, Pietro

CAVALLERIA RUSTICANA: BRINDISI see Mascagni, Pietro

CAVALLERIA RUSTICANA: IL CAVALLO SCALPITA see Mascagni, Pietro

CAVALLERIA RUSTICANA: O LOLA BIANCA see Mascagni, Pietro

CAVALLERIA RUSTICANA: STORNELLO DI LOLA see Mascagni, Pietro

CAVALLERIA RUSTICANA: VOI LO SAPETE see Mascagni, Pietro

CAVATINA DE LEILA see Bizet, Georges

CE QUE DISENT LES CLOCHES see Massenet, Jules

CE SABLE FIN ET FUYANT... see Caplet, André

CE SONT LES FILLES DE LA ROCHELLE see Arrieu, Claude

CECCONI, MONIC (1936-)
Muse Qui Est La Grâce, La
SBar soli,2.2.3.2. 2.2.2.1. 2perc, timp,cel,harp,strings [15']
BILLAUDOT (C146)

CEELY, ROBERT PAIGE (1930-)
Lullaby
S solo,trom [5'] sc AM.COMP.AL. $5.40 (C147)

CELEBRATION OF DEAD LADIES see Sims, Ezra

CELEBRI ARIE DI OPERE (VOL.1) SOPRANO
(CC12L) RICORDI-IT R127532 (C148)

CELEBRI ARIE DI OPERE (VOL.2) SOPRANO
(CC12L) RICORDI-IT R127533 (C149)

CELEBRI ARIE DI OPERE (VOL.3) MEZZO-SOPRANO
(CC12L) RICORDI-IT R127534 (C150)

CELEBRI ARIE DI OPERE (VOL.4) TENOR
(CC12L) RICORDI-IT R127535 (C151)

CELEBRI ARIE DI OPERE (VOL.5) BARITONE
(CC12L) RICORDI-IT R127536 (C152)

CELEBRI ARIE DI OPERE (VOL.6) BASS
(CC12L) RICORDI-IT R127537 (C153)

CELI see Finnissy, Michael

CELTIC LULLABY, A see Bax, [Sir] Arnold

CELTIC SONG CYCLE, A see Bax, [Sir] Arnold

CELUI QUI DORT ET DORT see Arma, Paul (Pál) (Imre Weisshaus)

CENDRE ROUGE, LA see Saint-Saëns, Camille

CENDRILLON: AH! QUE MES...RESTE AU FOYER, PETIT GRILLON see Massenet, Jules

CENDRILLON: AH! QUE MES SOEURS SONT HEUREUSES! see Massenet, Jules

CENERENTOLA, LA: NACQUI ALL' AFFANNO...NON PIÙ MESTA see Rossini, Gioacchino

CENERENTOLA: UN SEGRETO D'IMPORTANZE see Rossini, Gioacchino

CENT CANCONS, LES: CANCONS PER A INFANTS see Mestres, Apeles

CENT CANCONS, LES, PRIMERA SERIE (QUADERN PRIMER) see Mestres, Apeles

CENT CANCONS, LES, PRIMERA SERIE (QUADERN SEGON) see Mestres, Apeles

CENT CANCONS, LES, PRIMERA SERIE (QUADERN TERCER) see Mestres, Apeles

CENT CANCONS, LES, SEGONA SERIE (QUADERN PRIMER) see Mestres, Apeles

CENT CANCONS, LES, SEGONA SERIE (QUADERN SEGON) see Mestres, Apeles

CENT CANCONS, LES, SEGONA SERIE (QUADERN TERCER) see Mestres, Apeles

CENTENIUM see Vaage, Knut

CERCA DE TI see Schumann, Robert (Alexander)

CERCA DEL AMADO see Schubert, Franz (Peter)

CEREMUGA, JOSEF (1930-)
Laska K Milemu *song cycle
S/T solo,3.2.2.2. 3.2.3.1. timp, perc,harp,strings [15'] PANTON (C154)
solo voice,pno PANTON 887 (C155)

CERFS EN RUT, LES see King, Harold C.

CERHA, FRIEDRICH (1926-)
Alles Licht...
T solo,vla DOBLINGER 08 833 (C156)

Fünf Geistliche Gesänge
low solo DOBLINGER 08 662 (C157)

Letzte Art Chansons, Eine
solo voice,pno,db,perc UNIVER. UE 19462K (C158)

Relazioni Fragili
S/Mez solo,fl,bass clar,trp,perc, harp,cel,hpsd,vln,vla,vcl [24'] MODERN 932 (C159)

CERNOHORSKY, BOHUSLAV MATĚJ (1684-1742)
Regina Coeli
[Lat] S solo,vcl,org CESKY HUD. (C160)

CESARINI, C.P.
Gelosia, La: Filli Nol Niego
solo voice,pno BOIL B.1726 (C161)

CEST ANELET QUI J'AI OU DOY see Tal, Marjo

C'EST L'HISTOIRE see Auber, Daniel-François-Esprit, Manon Lescaut: L'Éclat De Rire

C'ETAIT ANNE DE BRETAGNE see Nigg, Serge

C'ÉTAIT LA FILLE D'UN ROI FRANÇAIS see Arrieu, Claude

CHABRIER, [ALEXIS-] EMMANUEL (1841-1894)
España: A Séville
[Fr] Mez solo,pno CLASSV 1358 (C162)
[Fr] high solo,pno CLASSV 1737 (C163)
Île Heureuse, L'
[Fr] high solo,pno CLASSV 1738 (C164)

CHABRIER, [ALEXIS-] EMMANUEL (cont'd.)

Invitation Au Voyage, L'
[Fr] solo voice,pno,opt bsn RECITAL 421 (C165)
med-high solo,pno,bsn CLASSV 1147 (C166)

CHACOUNNE, -A SONG, -OOOH see Gross, Robert Arthur

CHADWICK, GEORGE WHITEFIELD (1854-1931)
Allah
high solo,pno CLASSV 0336 (C167)

Before The Dawn
med solo,pno CLASSV 1420 (C168)
high solo,pno CLASSV 1422 (C169)

Danza, The
med solo,pno CLASSV 1421 (C170)
high solo,pno CLASSV 1419 (C171)

Du Bist Wie Eine Blume *Op.11,No.3
med solo,pno CLASSV 1424 (C172)
high solo,pno CLASSV 1423 (C173)

Song Album (15 Songs)
S/T solo,pno CLASSV 1988 (C174)

Song Album (17 Songs)
A/Bar solo,pno CLASSV 1976 (C175)

CHAIKOVSKII, PETR IL'ICH see TCHAIKOVSKY, PIOTR ILYICH

CHALET: VALLONS DE L'HELVÉTIE see Adam, Adolphe-Charles

CHALLENGE see Weigl, [Mrs.] Vally

CHAMBER CANTATA ON CHINESE POEMS see Sims, Ezra

CHAMBER MUSIC NO. 2 see Rosenman, Leonard

CHAMBER SETTING NO. 1 see Pollock, Robert Emil

CHAMBER SETTING NO. 2 see Pollock, Robert Emil

CHAMBER SETTING WITH VOICE see Pleskow, Raoul

CHAMBERLIN, ROBERT (1950-)
Psalmus
high solo,pno MMB X814006 (C176)

CHAMBRE BLANCHE, LA see Grovlez, Gabriel (Marie)

CHAMINADE, CÉCILE (1857-1944)
Album Of Songs (Vol. 1)
DA CAPO ISBN 0-306-76245-5 (C177)

Mélodies, 20, Vol.1
med solo,pno CLASSV C011 (C178)

Mélodies, 20, Vol.2
med solo,pno CLASSV C012 (C179)

Mélodies, 20, Vol.3
med solo,pno CLASSV C013 (C180)

CHAMPION, THE see Heilner, Irwin

CHANCE, NANCY LAIRD (1931-)
Darksong
S solo,chamber group SEESAW f.s. (C181)

Edensong
S solo,fl,clar,vcl,harp,perc SEESAW f.s. (C182)

Three Poems
S solo,fl,English horn,vcl SEESAW f.s. (C183)

CHANGEMENT DE DECOR see Samama, Leo

CHANLER, THEODORE WARD (1902-1961)
Eight Epitaphs
BOOSEY VAB0035 (C184)

Lamb, The
med solo AMP AMP194561 (C185)

CHANSON À BOIRE DU VIEUX TEMPS see Saint-Saëns, Camille

CHANSON ARABE see Godard, Benjamin Louis Paul

CHANSON-BOUTIQUE, BAND 2 see Schmitz, Manfred

CHANSON D'AMOUR see Faure, Gabriel-Urbain see Liberda, Bruno

CHANSON D'AUTOMNE see Haxton, Kenneth see Orthel, Leon

CHANSON DE CHIQUITA, LA see Devries, Ivan

CHANSON DE CROISADE, AVEC LEURS
     MÉLODIES, LES *CCU
     (Bedier, Joseph; Aubry, Pierre) solo
     voice SLATKINE f.s.   (C186)

CHANSON DE DEUX SAINTS, LA see Kef,
     Kees

CHANSON DE FLORIAN see Godard, Benjamin
     Louis Paul

CHANSON DE FOL see Hubeau, Jean

CHANSON DE LA CIGALE, LA see Lecocq,
     Charles

CHANSON DE LA GLU see Gounod, Charles
     François

CHANSON DE LA GRENOUILLERE see Forsyth,
     Josephine

CHANSON DE L'ADIEU see Tosti, Francesco
     Paolo

CHANSON DE LE VENT see Maruyama,
     Kazunori

CHANSON DE L'INFANTE see Viardot-
     Garcia, Pauline

CHANSON DE L'OISELEUR see Delibes, Léo

CHANSON DE MA MIE, LA (5 MÉLODIES) see
     Puget, Paul-Charles-Marie

CHANSON DES BOIS see Chopin, Frédéric,
     Minute Waltz

CHANSON DES PRES, LA see Godard,
     Benjamin Louis Paul

CHANSON D'EVE, LA see Faure, Gabriel-
     Urbain

CHANSON DU BÉBÉ, LA see Rossini,
     Gioacchino

CHANSON DU COEUR BRISÉ see Moya, H.,
     Song Of Songs

CHANSON DU FOU see Bizet, Georges

CHANSON DU PETIT CORDNNIER see Forsyth,
     Josephine

CHANSON ESPAGÑOLE see Delibes, Léo,
     Filles De Cadix, Les

CHANSON HEBRAIQUE see Rimsky-Korsakov,
     Nikolai

CHANSON PERPÉTUELLE see Chausson,
     Ernest

CHANSON TRISTE (FIRST VERSION) see
     Duparc, Henri

CHANSONETTE see Shut, Wasyl

CHANSONNIER FRANCOIS, LE *CCU
     solo voice SLATKINE f.s.   (C187)

CHANSONS II SUR TEXTES FRANÇAIS see
     Songs II To French Texts

CHANSONS III SUR TEXTES FRANÇAIS see
     Songs III To French Texts

CHANSONS IV SUR TEXTES ANGLAIS see
     Songs IV To English Texts

CHANSONS À DANSER see Bruneau, Alfred

CHANSONS AU VILLAGE see Metral, Pierre

CHANSONS BRUNES ET BLONDES (7 MÉLODIES)
     see Puget, Paul-Charles-Marie

CHANSONS CANADIENNES *CC24U
     (Willan, Healey; Barbeau, Marius)
     [Eng/Fr] solo voice,kbd HARRIS f.s.
                                        (C188)

CHANSONS DE MARJOLIE see Dubois,
     Theodore

CHANSONS DE TOILE, LES see Zink, Michel

CHANSONS DES BOIS D'AMARANTHE see
     Massenet, Jules

CHANSONS DU FOLKLORE DE FRANCE see
     Nigg, Serge, Au Pont De Mirobel see
     Nigg, Serge, C'etait Anne De
     Bretagne see Nigg, Serge, De Bon
     Matin Se Leve see Nigg, Serge,
     Grande D'Auvergne see Nigg, Serge,
     Rossignolet Du Bois, Rossignolet
     Sauvage see Tailleferre, Germaine,
     Autre Jour En M'y Promenant, L' see
     Tailleferre, Germaine, En Revenant
     De Nantes see Tailleferre,
     Germaine, Jean De La Réole see
     Tailleferre, Germaine, Mon Père
     Toujours Me Crie see Tailleferre,
     Germaine, Nocture-Fox see

Tailleferre, Germaine, Pernette Se
     Lève, La

CHANSONS DU VALET DE COEUR see Hüe,
     Georges-Adolphe

CHANSONS GRISES see Hahn, Reynaldo

CHANSONS INTIMES see Engel, Carl

CHANSONS IRRESPECTUEUSES see Büchtger,
     Fritz

CHANSONS LÉGÈRES VOL. 2 see Nadaud, G.

CHANSONS LES PLUS COURTES..., LES see
     Tal, Marjo

CHANSONS LIBERTINES DE CLAUDE DE
     CHOUVIGNY, LES see Chouvigny,
     Claude de

CHANSONS POPULAIRES DES PROVINCES
     BELGES, TOME 2
     (Closson) SCHOTT-FRER 8879   (C189)

CHANSONS POPULAIRES DES XVE ET XVIE
     SIÈCLES *CCU
     (Gerold, Théodore) solo voice
     SLATKINE f.s.   (C190)

CHANSONS PRINTANIERES see Hüe, Georges-
     Adolphe

CHANSONS TRADITIONNELLES DES PROVINCES
     DE FRANCE see Barathon

CHANSONS TRISTES see Moret, Ernest

CHANT D'ALPHESIBÉE, LE see Capdevielle,
     Pierre

CHANT D'AMOUR, CHANT DE MORT DE TROILUS
     see Aubin, Tony

CHANT DE CEUX QUI S'EN VONT SUR MER see
     Saint-Saëns, Camille

CHANT DE LA MÈRE see Opienski, Henryk

CHANT DE L'ALMÉE see Delibes, Léo

CHANT FUNEBRE, OP.5, NO.4 see
     Gretchaninov, Alexander
     Tikhonovich, Epicedium

CHANT HINDOU see Bemberg, Herman

CHANTONS NOEL see Zurfluh, Eliane

CHANTS D'AMOUR ORIENTAUX see Pouget,
     Leo

CHANTS D'ESPOIR see Bunge, Sas

CHANTS DU COBAZAR see Bertelin, Albert

CHANTS DU DESIR, 4 SONNETS DE LOUISE
     LABE see Escher, Rudolf George

CHAPIRO, FANIA (1926-   )
     Because I Could Not Stop For Death
        see Three Songs Of Death

     I Died For Beauty
        see Three Songs Of Death

     Last Night That She Lived..., The
        see Three Songs Of Death

     Three Songs Of Death
        S/Mez solo,pno DONEMUS f.s. [8'],
        texts by Emily Dickinson
        contains: Because I Could Not
        Stop For Death; I Died For
        Beauty; Last Night That She
        Lived..., The   (C191)

CHAPLET, THE see Boyce, William

CHARACTERS FROM SHAKESPEARE see Saudek,
     Vojtech

CHARIOTEER see Blumenfeld, Harold

CHARITÉ see Faure, Jean-Baptiste

CHARITY
     (Moore, Dorothy Rudd) SS soli,pno
     [3'] sc AM.COMP.AL. $1.55   (C192)

CHARLES, ERNEST (1895-   )
     Songs Of Ernest Charles *CC19L
     SCHIRM.G f.s. high solo 50481361;
        low solo 50481362   (C193)

CHARLES VI: HUMBLE FILLE DES CHAMPS see
     Halévy, Jacques

CHASALOW, ERIC
     Furies, The
        S solo,electronic tape [14'] (tape
        - $15.00) sc APNM $7.25   (C194)

CHASALOW, ERIC (cont'd.)

     Triptych
        S solo,pno [6'] APNM sc $5.50, set
        $10.50   (C195)

CHAT, LE see Regt, Hendrik de

CHAULIEU, CHARLES
     Giascun Lo Dice
        solo voice,pno SCIEN 361   (C196)

CHAUSSON, ERNEST (1855-1899)
     Ave Verum Corpus *Op.3
        S/T solo,pno LEDUC f.s.   (C197)
        [Lat] med solo,pno CLASSV 1739
                                     (C198)

     Chanson Perpétuelle *Op.37
        [Fr] med-high solo,pno CLASSV 1701
                                     (C199)

     Colibri, Le *Op.2,No.7
        med solo,pno CLASSV 1148   (C200)

     Nuit, La *Op.11,No.1
        [Fr] high solo&med solo,pno CLASSV
        1740   (C201)

     Oraison
        [Fr] med-high solo,pno CLASSV 1741
                                     (C202)

     Serres Chaudes, Op. 24 *song cycle
        [Fr] med solo (poems of Maurice
        Maeterlinck) RECITAL 88   (C203)

     Songs, 33 *CC33U
        [Fr] KALMUS K 09889 f.s.   (C204)

     Trois Lieder, Op.27
        med solo,pno CLASSV 1140   (C205)

     Vingt Melodies
        med solo/high solo SALABERT
        50481187   (C206)

CHAUVES-SOURIS, LES see Delafosse, L.

CHE NULLA SIA DISSOLTO see Razzi,
     Fausto

CHEMIN, LE see Kef, Kees

CHEN, QIGANG (1951-   )
     Poème Lyrique
        solo voice,1.1.1.0. 1.0.0.0. perc,
        harp,2vln,vla,vcl,db [15']
        BILLAUDOT   (C207)

     Poème Lyrique II
        solo voice,1.1.1.0. 0.0.0.0. perc,
        harp,mand,gtr,vln,vla,vcl,db
        [15'] BILLAUDOT   (C208)

CHENOWETH, GERALD
     Autumn Music: Two Songs *CC2U
        A solo,fl,ob,clar,bsn,horn,timp,
        pno,vln,vla,vcl AM.COMP.AL. sc
        $11.10, pts $13.35   (C209)

     Candles
        S solo,clar,harp,perc,vln,vla,vcl,
        conductor [20'] AM.COMP.AL. sc
        $14.50, pts $19.90   (C210)

CHÈRE NUIT see Bachelet, Alfred

CHÉRUBIN: CES VERS SONT FAITS POUR MOI
     see Massenet, Jules

CHERUBIN: LORSQUE VOUS N'AUREZ RIEN A
     FAIRE see Massenet, Jules

CHERUBINI, LUIGI (1760-1842)
     Abencerages: Suspendez À Ces Murs
        T solo,pno CLASSV 0353   (C211)

     Ave Maria
        [Lat/Eng] high solo RICORDI-IT
        R50499   (C212)
        [Ger/Lat] high solo,pno,vln/vcl
        (optional duet) CLASSV 0905
                                     (C213)

     Medea: Dei Tuoi Figli La Madre
        [It] S solo,pno CLASSV 1742 (C214)

CHEVAL MORT, LE see Eisma, Will

CHEVALIER DE SAINT-GEORGES
     see SAINT-GEORGES, JOSEPH BOULOGNE DE

CHEVEAUX DE BOIS see Kef, Kees

CHEVREFEUILLE, LA see Sauguet, Henri

CHI SE NNE SCORDA CCHIÙ! see
     Barthelemy, R.

CHI VUOLE INNAMORARSI see Scarlatti,
     Alessandro

CHIEKO-SHO see Nakajima, Hal

CHIHIRO TOMO see Matsudaira, Yori-Tsune

CHIISANA HANA see Yuyama, Akira

CHIKURIN HOKO see Murakami, Taro

CHILCOT, THOMAS (ca. 1700-1766)
Choir Awake, The
S solo,strings,2ob,opt bsn,2trp,
timp sc,pts KING'S   (C215)

Orpheus With His Lute
S solo,fl,2vln,vcl/db sc,pts KING'S
(C216)

Twelve English Songs (C.1744)
sc KING'S   (C217)

CHILD, PETER B. (1953-   )
Heracliti Reliquae
S solo,fl/pic,ob,clar,vln,vcl [10']
APNM sc $6.50, pts rent   (C218)

CHILD MUSICIAN, THE see Amerongen, Jan
van

CHILD OF GOD see Four Traditional
American Songs

CHILD OF THE UNIVERSE see Cassils,
Craig

CHILDHOOD FABLES see Fine

CHILDREN CRY FOR CASTORIA! see
Slonimsky, Nicolas

CHILDREN OF EDEN THEME SONG see
Schwartz

CHILDREN OF LOVE see Schwab, Sigi

CHILDREN'S LAND see Nagaba, Naoki

CHILDREN'S SONGS, 25 see Abt, Franz

CHILDREN'S SONGS see MacBride, David
Huston

CHILDREN'S SONGS ON RUSSIAN AND
UKRAINIAN MELODIES see Tchaikovsky,
Piotr Ilyich

CHILDS, EDWIN T.
Lord, Be Our Wedding Guest
high solo AMSI V-12   (C219)

CHILD'S GARDEN OF VERSE [1] see Barab

CHILD'S GARDEN OF VERSE [2] see Barab

CHIMÄRE see Meijering, Cord

CHINESISCHES SOLDATENLIED see Beekhuis,
Hanna

CHINI, ANDRE (1945-   )
Omniphobie
Mez solo,2wind quin,db SUECIA 375
(C220)

CHINOISERIE see Falla, Manuel de

CHLORIS SIGH'D see Anonymous

CHOCOLATE SOLDIER: MY HERO see Straus,
Oscar

CHOHINA 2 see Reibel, Guy

CHOICE COLLECTION OF SONGS, A, 12
(1761) see Arne, Thomas Augustine

CHOICE OF 850 WORDS see Bois, Rob du

CHOIR AWAKE, THE see Chilcot, Thomas

CHOIX ET ARRANGEMENTS POUR 2 VOIX ET
PIANO DE MÉLODIES CÉLÈBRES DE
SCHUMANN (SCÈNES CHAMPÊTRES)
(Nauwelaers) 2 solo voices,pno
SCHOTT-FRER 8628   (C221)

CHOIX ET ARRANGEMENTS POUR 2 VOIX ET
PIANO DE MÉLODIES CÉLÈBRES DE
STRAUSS (GAZOUILLIS DE PRINTEMPS)
(Nauwelaers) 2 solo voices,pno
SCHOTT-FRER 8292   (C222)

CHOIX TERRESTRE see King, Harold C.

CHOPIN, FRÉDÉRIC (1810-1849)
Chanson Des Bois
see Minute Waltz

Lamento
see Mensajero, El

Mensajero, El
solo voice,pno BOIL B.0719 f.s.
contains also: Voto De Doncella;
Lamento   (C223)

Minute Waltz *Op.64
(Philipp) "Chanson Des Bois"
coloratura sop CLASSV 2214 (C224)

Tristesse (from Etude Op.10, No.3 in
E)
[Russ/Ger/Fr] high solo,pno CLASSV
2069   (C225)

CHOPIN, FRÉDÉRIC (cont'd.)

Voto De Doncella
see Mensajero, El

CHOPIN - HAUER see Balakauskas,
Osvaldas

CHOPIN WALTZ see Marx, Joseph

CHORAL see Holter, Iver

CHORALIA
(Wuytack, Jos) SCHOTT-FRER 9283
(C226)

CHORALMESSE see Bruckner, Anton

CHOSEN see Owens

CHOUVIGNY, CLAUDE DE
Chansons Libertines De Claude De
Chouvigny, Les *CCU
(Lachevre, Frédéric) solo voice
SLATKINE f.s.   (C227)

CHRIST COMPLAINS see Jordan, Sverre,
Christus Klagt

CHRIST IS RISEN see Rachmaninoff,
Sergey Vassilievich

CHRIST MY REFUGE see Warren, Betsy

CHRISTBAUM see Marx, Joseph

CHRISTE REDEMPTOR see Galuppi,
Baldassare

CHRISTENSEN, BERNHARD
O Be Joyful In The Lord
solo voice,org [6'] SAMFUNDET
(C228)

Two Psalms Of David
solo voice,org [13'] SAMFUNDET
(C229)

CHRISTENSEN, MOGENS
Between The Precipices Of Life
see Mellem Livets Afgrunde

Mellem Livets Afgrunde
"Between The Precipices Of Life" S
solo,gtr,perc [4'] SAMFUNDET
(C230)

Trae
"Tree" SS soli,2fl,clar,trp,2perc,
pno,2vln,vcl,4db [14'] SAMFUNDET
(C231)

Tree
see Trae

CHRISTIAN MORGENSTERN, HEFT I see
Lothar, Mark

CHRISTIAN MORGENSTERN, HEFT II see
Lothar, Mark

CHRISTIAN, NE'ER LET SIN O'ERPOWER THEE
see Bach, Johann Sebastian,
Widerstehe Doch Der Sunde

CHRISTIANSEN, HENNING (1932-   )
To Play To Day *Op.25
2 male soli&female solo,2.2.2.1.
2.2.2.1. perc,pno,strings [40']
sc,pts SAMFUNDET 249 rent (C232)

CHRISTKINDLEINS WIEGENLIED see Glaeser,
Franz

CHRISTMAS ANGELS see Rippentrop, Denice

CHRISTMAS GUITAR SONGBOOK, THE *CC49U,
Xmas
(Statford, Elaine) solo voice,gtr
(easy) UNIVERSE 491-00353 $6.95
(C233)

CHRISTMAS MORN see Warren, Betsy

CHRISTMAS SOLOIST, THE *CC10UL
(Althouse) ALFRED med-high solo,pno
3385 f.s.; med-low solo,pno 3386
f.s.   (C234)

CHRISTMAS SONG ALBUM VOL. 2 see
Citkowitz, Israel

CHRISTMAS TREE, THE see Lake

CHRISTMAS TRIPTYCH, A see Caldwell,
Mary Elizabeth

CHRISTUS KLAGT see Jordan, Sverre

CHTEL BYSEM NAPSAT TI PSANI see Pauer,
Jiri

CHURCH ARIA FOR SOPRANO AND ORGAN,
OP.26, NO.2 see Kvandal, Johan, O
Domine Deus

CHVALOZPEVY MIRU see Slezak, Pavel

CIAIKOVSKI, PIETRO
see TCHAIKOVSKY, PIOTR ILYICH

CIARLANTINI, PAOLA
Au Retour
S solo,gtr,vcl EDI-PAN EP 7783
(C235)

CICLO DE CANCIONES LLORENS TORRES see
Ortiz, William

CID, LE see Massenet, Jules

CID, LE: O SOUVERAIN, Ô JUGE, O PÈRE
see Massenet, Jules

CID, LE: PLEUREZ, PLEUREZ see Massenet,
Jules

CID, LE: PLEUREZ, PLEUREZ MES YEUX see
Massenet, Jules

CID, LE: PLUS DE TOURMENTS see
Massenet, Jules

CIEL EST PAR-DESSUS LE TOIT, LE see
Bon, Willem Frederik

CIEL EST TRÉS BAS, LE see Paderewski,
Ignace Jan

CILÉA, FRANCESCO (1866-1950)
Adriana Lecouvreur: Ecco Il Monologo
[It] Bar solo,pno CLASSV 1252
(C236)
Arlesiana, L': E La Solita Storia
T solo,pno (original key) CLASSV
1668   (C237)
T solo,pno (semi-tone down) CLASSV
1455   (C238)
T solo,pno (whole tone down) CLASSV
1456   (C239)

Arlesiana, L': Racconto Del Pastore
"Come Due Tizzi Accesi" Bar solo,
pno CLASSV 0959   (C240)

Come Due Tizzi Accesi
see Arlesiana, L': Racconto Del
Pastore

CILENSEK, JOHANN (1913-   )
Liebeslieder
PETERS 5097   (C241)

CIMARA, PIETRO (1887-1967)
Stelle Chiare
[It] Mez solo,pno CLASSV 2176
(C242)
Stornello
high solo,pno CLASSV 0808   (C243)
med solo,pno CLASSV 0339   (C244)

Tornan Le Stelle
med solo,pno CLASSV 1127   (C245)

CIMAROSA, DOMENICO (1749-1801)
Matrimonio Segreto: Perdonate, Signor
Mio
S solo,pno CLASSV 1744   (C246)

Matrimonio Segreto: Pria Che Spunti
T solo,pno CLASSV 1743   (C247)

CINCO CANCIONES DE AMOR see Michans,
Carlos

CINCO CANCIONES NEGRAS see
Montsalvatge, Xavier

CINCO INVOCACIONES AL CRUCIFICADO see
Montsalvatge, Xavier

CINCO POEMAS see Ponjee, Ted

CINQ CANTIQUES see Braal, Andries de

CINQ LIEDER see Lalo, Edouard

CINQ-MARS: NUIT RESPLENDISSANTE see
Gounod, Charles François

CINQ MÉLODIES see Casanova, André see
Sporck, Georges

CINQ MELODIES, OP. 16 see Rhene-Baton
(René Baton)

CINQ MÉLODIES, OP.58 see Faure,
Gabriel-Urbain

CINQ POEMES DE FRANCOIS VILLON see
Franken, Wim

CINQ POEMS DE CHARLES BAUDELAIRE see
Debussy, Claude

CINQ RONDEAUX DE CHARLES D'ORLEANS see
Devries, Ivan

CINQUANTES MÉLODIES FRANÇAISES
(Panzera) SCHOTT-FRER 9181   (C248)

CINQUE ARIETTE E DUETTINO see Brambilla

CINQUE CANTI DELL' ARS NOVA see Lupi, Roberto

CINQUE CANTI TROVADORICI see Lupi, Roberto

CINQUE LIEDER - CINQUE POESIE see Mannino, Franco

CINQUE LIRICHE see Pizzetti, Ildebrando

CIRCUMFLEXIONS ON MALLARME see Gilbert, Janet

CIRCUS, THE see Reif, Paul

CIRIBIRIBIN see Pestalozza, A.

CITKOWITZ, ISRAEL (1909-1974)
    Christmas Song Album Vol. 2 *CCU
        BOOSEY VAB0218 f.s.   (C249)

    Five Songs
        BOOSEY VAB0242   (C250)

CITY OF SAND IN A LABYRINTH see Kanno, Yoshihiro

CIVIL WAR SONGBOOK, THE *CC37U
    (Crawford, Richard) solo voice BELWIN
    BKD001622 $6.00   (C251)

CLAIR DE LUNE see Debussy, Claude

CLAIR-OBSCUR see Sacre, Guy

CLARKE, HENRY LELAND (1907-   )
    Autumn
        med solo,pno [2'] sc AM.COMP.AL.
        $.80   (C252)

    Beauty Is Truth
        med solo,pno [2'] sc AM.COMP.AL.
        $1.60   (C253)

    December
        med solo,pno [2'] sc AM.COMP.AL.
        $.80   (C254)

    Do And Live
        med solo,pno [1'] sc AM.COMP.AL.
        $1.60   (C255)

    Let Me Go
        med solo,pno [3'] sc AM.COMP.AL.
        $1.95   (C256)

    Listen To Me
        med solo,pno [2'] sc AM.COMP.AL.
        $1.60   (C257)

    One Step Forward And Two Steps Back
        med solo,pno [3'] sc AM.COMP.AL.
        $1.60   (C258)

    Opposites
        med solo,vla/vcl [5'] sc
        AM.COMP.AL. $3.10   (C259)

    Plowshares
        med solo,pno [2'] sc AM.COMP.AL.
        $.80   (C260)

    Pray For Peace
        med solo,pno [2'] sc AM.COMP.AL.
        $1.60   (C261)

    Revelation Is Not Sealed
        SB soli,kbd [3'] sc AM.COMP.AL.
        $3.05   (C262)

    Soleil Ni La Mort, Le
        med solo,pno [1'] sc AM.COMP.AL.
        $.45   (C263)

    This Partridge
        med solo,pno [4'] sc AM.COMP.AL.
        $3.10   (C264)

    Three Numbers From The Early Twenties
        med solo,pno [4'] sc AM.COMP.AL.
        $1.95   (C265)

    Twentieth Century
        SBar soli,pno [2'] sc AM.COMP.AL.
        $1.90   (C266)

    Winter Is A Cold Thing
        med solo,pno [3'] sc AM.COMP.AL.
        $.80   (C267)

CLASSIC SONGS *CCU
    (Taylor) ALFRED high solo,pno 3542
    f.s.; low solo,pno 3543 f.s.   (C268)

CLASSICAL CAROLS
    (Walters, Richard) low solo,pno,opt
        inst (CC10L) LEONARD-US 00747025
                                         (C269)
    (Walters, Richard) high solo,pno,opt
        inst (CC10L) LEONARD-US 00747024
                                         (C270)
CLASSICAL SINGER'S CHRISTMAS ALBUM, THE
    low solo,pno (CC13L, INCLUDES
    RECORDED ACCOMPANIMENTS) LEONARD-US
    00747021   (C271)

high solo,pno (CC13L, INCLUDES
    RECORDED ACCOMPANIMENTS) LEONARD-US
    00747022   (C272)

CLAUSEN, RENE
    Greatest Of These Is Love, The
        med solo,org FOSTER MF 2047M   (C273)
        high solo,org FOSTER MF 2047H
                                         (C274)
CLAVELITOS see Valverde, Joaquin

CLAY, FRÉDÉRIC (1838-1889)
    I'll Sing Thee Songs Of Araby
        med solo,pno CLASSV 1257   (C275)

CLAYTON
    Cree Songs To The Newborn
        S solo,chamber group PETERS 66845
                                         (C276)
CLEAN AS GOLD IS YOUR HEART see
    Knutsen, Torbjorn, Gullrent Er Ditt
    Hjerte

CLEFTA PRIGIONE, IL see Pizzetti,
    Ildebrando

CLEMENGIS LA DOULOUREUSE IMAGE, DE see
    Saint-Georges, Joseph Boulogne de,
    Duo From "Ernestine"

CLEMENS, HENRI
    Ave Maria
        solo voice ZENGERINK R.317A   (C277)

    Lied Voor Een Priesterfeest
        Mez/Bar solo,kbd ZENGERINK R.332
                                         (C278)
CLEMENTI, ALDO (1925-   )
    Ach Ich Fühl's
        solo voice,15inst ZERBONI 9457
                                         (C279)
    Otto Frammenti
        S&countertenor,3inst ZERBONI 8485
                                         (C280)
CLEMENZA DI TITO: NON PIÙ DI FIORI see
    Mozart, Wolfgang Amadeus

CLEOPATRA, PART I: LONGING FOR ANTHONY
    see Stewart, Robert

CLEOPATRA, PART IV: A DREAM see
    Stewart, Robert

CLEOPATRA, PART V: THE DEATH OF
    CLEOPATRA see Stewart, Robert

CLÉRAMBAULT, LOUIS-NICOLAS (1676-1749)
    Léandre Et Héro
        S solo, early music ensemble
        [17'20"] sc,pts,voc sc BILLAUDOT
                                         (C281)
    Orphée
        Bar solo,fl,vln,cont [17'] voc sc,
        pts BILLAUDOT   (C282)
CLIFF'S EDGE, THE (SONGS OF A
    PSYCHOTIC) see Garwood, Margaret

CLIMBING FOR TREE FROGS see Lombardo,
    Robert M.

CLIMBING FOR TREE FROGS: FOUR LOVE
    SONGS see Lombardo, Robert M.

CLIMBING HIGHER AND HIGHER see
    Straesser, Joep

CLOCHE, LA: SEULE EN TA SOMBRE TOUR see
    Saint-Saëns, Camille

CLOCHES DU SOIR, LE see Franck, Cesar

CLOÎTRE HAUT, LE see Paderewski, Ignace
    Jan

CLOSTRE, ADRIENNE (1921-   )
    Sie Waren So Schön Und Herrlich
        A solo,1.2.1.1. 2.2.1.0. 3perc,timp
        [15'] (alternate version: voice
        and solo violin) sc,pts,voc sc
        BILLAUDOT   (C283)
CLOTHS OF HEAVEN, THE see Dunhill,
    Thomas Frederick see Elwyn-Edwards,
    Dilys

CLOUD OF UNKNOWING, THE see Primosch,
    James

CLOUDS: FIVE SONGS see Riley, Dennis

CLOUGH-LEIGHTER, HENRY (1874-1956)
    Love-Garden, A *Op.22, song cycle
        [Eng] high solo (poetry by Charles
        Hanson Towne) RECITAL 252   (C284)

    My Lover, He Comes On The Skee
        S solo,pno CLASSV 2218   (C285)

CLOWN, LE see Bon, Willem Frederik

CLOWNEN see Koch, Erland von

COALITIONS see Blank, Allan

COATES, ROBERT
    Aere Vaere Gud
        see Tre Hymner I Advent

    Sjå Lyset Er Tent
        see Tre Hymner I Advent

    Tre Hymner I Advent
        solo voice,org NOTON N-9362 f.s.
        contains: Aere Vaere Gud; Sjå
        Lyset Er Tent; Vi Vender Oss
        Til Herren   (C286)

    Vi Vender Oss Til Herren
        see Tre Hymner I Advent

COCK SHALL CROW, THE see Carpenter,
    John Alden

CODA see Tal, Marjo

CODA (THE WIND) see Sevriens, Jean

COEDES
    Poème De Mai
        med-high solo,pno CLASSV 2184
                                         (C287)
COEDES, A.
    Jour Ou Sylvain M'a Parlé!, Le
        S/T solo,pno SCIEN 379   (C288)

COEUR DE HIALMAR, LE see Lutz, H.

COHEN, EDWARD (1940-   )
    Elegy
        S solo,fl,ob,clar,vln,vla,vcl [16']
        APNM sc $11.25, pts rent   (C289)

    Portrait No. 2
        Mez solo,vla,vcl,org [6'] APNM sc
        $6.50, set $19.00   (C290)

    Ruin, The
        S solo,vln,pno [15'] APNM sc $7.75,
        set $22.00   (C291)

    Stone And Earth
        Mez solo,string orch [8'] APNM sc
        $6.50, pts rent   (C292)

    Three Songs [1] *CC3U
        SMez soli,vln,vcl APNM sc $5.00,
        set $18.50   (C293)

    Three Songs [2] *CC3U
        S solo,clar,vla,vcl APNM sc $6.00,
        set $15.00   (C294)

COHEN, FRED
    Three For Emily
        S solo,fl/pic,clar,horn,vln,vla,
        vcl,pno,perc [15'] AM.COMP.AL.
                                         (C295)
COLAÇO OSORIO-SWAAB, REINE (1889-1971)
    Aus Den Knospen
        see Sänge Eines Fahrenden
        Spielmanns

    Heisst Es Viel
        see Sänge Eines Fahrenden
        Spielmanns

    Sänge Eines Fahrenden Spielmanns
        med solo,pno DONEMUS f.s.
        contains: Aus Den Knospen; Heisst
        Es Viel; So Ich Traurig Bin;
        Worte Trügen, Worte Fliehen
                                         (C296)
    So Ich Traurig Bin
        see Sänge Eines Fahrenden
        Spielmanns

    Worte Trügen, Worte Fliehen
        see Sänge Eines Fahrenden
        Spielmanns

COLDING-JORGENSEN, HENRIK (1944-   )
    Enfance II
        Mez solo,bass clar [4'] SAMFUNDET
                                         (C297)
    Fire Albertsange *CC4U
        A solo SAMFUNDET 322 f.s.   (C298)

    Late Idyl
        see Senidyl

    Nunc Est
        Mez solo,clar,org [18'] SAMFUNDET
                                         (C299)
    Senidyl
        "Late Idyl" Bar solo,vln,pno [5']
        sc,pts SAMFUNDET f.s.   (C300)

    Two Songs By Keats
        S solo,gtr [7'] SAMFUNDET   (C301)

COLECCIÓN DE CANCIONES ESCOGIDAS,
    CUADERNO 1: SEIS CANTOS
    ESPIRITUALES OP. 48 see Beethoven,
    Ludwig van

COLECCIÓN DE CANCIONES ESCOGIDAS,
    CUADERNO 2, OP. 83 see Beethoven,
    Ludwig van

COLECCIÓN DE CANCIONES ESCOGIDAS, CUADERNO 3, OP. 98 see Beethoven, Ludwig van

COLECCIÓN DE CANCIONES ESCOGIDAS, CUADERNO 4, OP. 75, NO. 2 see Beethoven, Ludwig van

COLECCIÓN DE CANCIONES ESCOGIDAS, CUADERNO 5, OP. 46 see Beethoven, Ludwig van

COLIBRI, LE see Chausson, Ernest

COLLECTED POEMS see Thomson, Virgil Garnett

COLLECTED SONGS
(Adler) SOUTHERN B465   (C302)

COLLECTED SONGS, VOL. 1 see Faure, Gabriel-Urbain see Vaughan Williams, Ralph

COLLECTED SONGS, VOL. 2 see Faure, Gabriel-Urbain see Vaughan Williams, Ralph

COLLECTED SONGS, VOL. 3 see Faure, Gabriel-Urbain see Vaughan Williams, Ralph

COLLECTION OF FAVOURITE SONGS, A (1765) see Battishill, Jonathan

COLLECTION OF NEW SONGS AND BALLADS SUNG AT VAUXHALL, A see Worgan

COLLECTION OF SONGS, A, 9 (1760) see Arne, Thomas Augustine

COLLECTION OF SONGS, A see Kijima, Kiyohiko

COLLECTION OF SONGS, A see Shibata, Minao

COLLET, HENRI (1885-1951)
Sept Chansons Populaires De Burgos *Op.80
"Siete Canciones Populares De Burgos" solo voice,pno LEDUC HE 29262   (C303)

Siete Canciones Populares De Burgos see Sept Chansons Populaires De Burgos

COLLINE'S ARIA see Puccini, Giacomo, Bohème, La: Vecchia Zimarra

COLLOQUE SENTIMENTAL see Orland, Henry

COLOMBA, LA
(Schindler) med solo,pno CLASSV 1307   (C304)

COLOMBES, LES see Falla, Manuel de

COLONIAL HERITAGE see Verrall, John Weedon

COLONNE D'ALBA see Radulescu, Horatio

COLOR SCHEME see Rodgers, Lou

COLORI see Razzi, Fausto

COLORS WHERE THE MOON NEVER COULD see Lennon, John Anthony

COMBATTIMENTO DI TANCREDI E CLORINDA see Monteverdi, Claudio

COMBINAZIONI III see Lewis, Robert Hall

COME see Haxton, Kenneth

COME AWAY DEATH see Wordsworth, William

COME AWAY: FIVE SONGS see Sims, Ezra

COME CLOSER, MY HORSE see Permont, Haim

COME DUE TIZZI ACCESI see Ciléa, Francesco, Arlesiana, L': Racconto Del Pastore

COME! I LOVE YOU ONLY see Straus, Oscar, Chocolate Soldier: My Hero

COME, LOVE see Griffes, Charles Tomlinson

COME MY BELOVED see Gottlieb, Jack S.

COME NOW, MY DARLING see Corigliano, John

COME, ON THIS WEDDING DAY see Hustad, Donald Paul

COME SUNDAY see Ellington, Edward Kennedy (Duke)

COME WITH A SINGING HEART see Carter, John

COMME UNE PÂLE FLEUR see Thomas, Ambroise, Hamlet: Arioso

COMMENCEMENT DU PRINTEMPS, LE see Matsudaira, Yori-Tsune

COMMENT, DISAIENT-ILS see Liszt, Franz

COMMUNION HYMN see Warren, Betsy

CÓMO DIBUJAR UN NIÑO see Rodriguez Peris, Martin Jose

CÓMO DIBUJAR UNA BRUJA see Rodriguez Peris, Martin Jose

COMO NACE EL AMOR see Schumann, Clara (Wieck)

COMPENSATION see Backer-Lunde, Johan

COMPLAINTE DE LA SEINE see Weill

COMPLETE ALBUM see Taki, Rentaro

COMPLETE AVE MARIA *CC2L
solo voice,pno/org LEONARD-US f.s. includes 16 versions of the Ave Marias by Schubert and Bach-Gounod   (C305)

COMPLETE BOOK OF WEDDING MUSIC *CCU
solo voice HANSEN-US HAND304 $6.95   (C306)

COMPLETE LORD'S PRAYER FOR EVERY BUSY ACCOMPANIST, THE see Malotte, Albert Hay

COMPLETE PUBLISHED SONGS OF LOUIS MOREAU GOTTSCHALK (WITH A SELECTION OF OTHER SONGS ON MID-NINETEENTH CENTURY AMERICA) see Gottschalk, Louis Moreau

COMPLETE SONGS FOR VOICE AND PIANO, THE, VOL. 1 see Brahms, Johannes

COMPLETE SONGS FOR VOICE AND PIANO, THE, VOL. 2 see Brahms, Johannes

COMPLETE SONGS FOR VOICE AND PIANO, THE, VOL. 3 see Brahms, Johannes

COMPLETE SONGS FOR VOICE AND PIANO, THE, VOL. 4 see Brahms, Johannes

COMPLETE SONGS FOR VOICE AND PIANO, THE, VOL. 5 see Brahms, Johannes

COMPLETE SONGS FOR VOICE AND PIANO, THE, VOL. 6 see Brahms, Johannes

COMPLETE SONGS FOR VOICE AND PIANO, THE, VOL. 7 see Brahms, Johannes

COMPLETE SONGS FOR VOICE AND PIANO, THE, VOL. 8: GERMAN FOLK SONGS; CHILDREN'S FOLK SONGS see Brahms, Johannes

COMPLETE SONGS OF ALMA MAHLER, THE see Mahler, Alma

COMPLETE SONGS VOL. 1 see Tosti, Francesco Paolo

COMPLETE SONGS, VOL. 1 see Schumann, Clara (Wieck)

COMPLETE SONGS, VOL. 2 see Schumann, Clara (Wieck)

COMPLIMENTS OF THE SEASON see Roe, Betty

COMPOSITION see Cage, John

COMPOSITION 9 see Rimmer, John

COMPOSIZIONI DA CAMERA PER CANTO E PIANOFORTE see Bellini, Vincenzo

COMPOSIZIONI DA CAMERA PER CANTO E PIANOFORTE 2 see Tosti, Francesco Paolo

COMPROMIS see Franken, Wim

COMRADES OF MINE see James, William G.

COMTE ORY: EN PROIE À LA TRISTESSE see Rossini, Gioacchino

COMTE ORY: QUE LES DESTINS PROSPÈRES see Rossini, Gioacchino

COMTE ORY: VEILLER SANS CESSE see Rossini, Gioacchino

CON EL VITO see Folklore Andalusia

CON SORDINO see Marx, Joseph

CONCERT ARIA see Winslow, Walter

CONCERT PIECE 1 see Steiner, Gitta Hana

CONCERT PIECE 2 see Steiner, Gitta Hana

CONCERTO FOR TWO SOPRANOS AND ORCHESTRA see Norby, Erik

CONCERTO SACRO NO.5, FOR BASS, CHORUS AND ORCHESTRA see Fuga, Sandro

CONCERTOS SACRED see Schütz, Heinrich

CONCLUSION see Parchman, Gen Louis

CONFESSIONS OF GOLIARDS see Pehrson, Joseph Ralph

CONFIDÈNCIA see Mestres, Apeles

CONFITEBOR III see Monteverdi, Claudio

CONFUSA, SMARRITA see Pergolesi, Giovanni Battista

CONFUSION BREATHS... see Le Siege, Annette

CONSIDER THE LILIES OF THE FIELD see Hoffman

CONSOLATION I see Lachenmann, Helmut Friedrich

CONSOLATION II see Lachenmann, Helmut Friedrich

CONSOLATIONS, LES see Lachenmann, Helmut Friedrich

CONSOLATIONS OF SCHOLARSHIP, THE see Weir, Judith

CONSTANCY see Foote, Arthur see Mourant, Walter

CONSTANT LOVER, THE see Wordsworth, William

CONSTANTINIDES, DINOS DEMETRIOS (1929-   )
Antitheses
T&speaking voice,chamber group SEESAW f.s.   (C307)

Four Songs By Sappho
solo voice,pno SEESAW   (C308)

Reflections
S solo,ob&ob d'amore&English horn/ 3clar SEESAW   (C309)

CONSTANZA IN AMOR VINCE L'INGANNO, LA see Caldara, Antonio

CONTAGION, LA see Semenoff, Ivan

CONTE D'AMOUR, OP.26 see Boëllmann, Léon

CONTEMPLATED BY A PORTRAIT OF A DIVINE see Glanert, Detlev

CONTEMPLATION see Godard, Benjamin Louis Paul

CONTEMPLATION UPON FLOWERS see Hoddinott, Alun

CONTEMPORARY AMERICAN SONGS *CCU
(Taylor) ALFRED high solo,pno 3544 f.s.; low solo,pno 3545 f.s.   (C310)

CONTEMPORARY CHRISTIAN CLASSICS, VOL. 2 *CCU
(Sewell, Gregg) solo voice,kbd LAUREL PP 113 $6.95   (C311)

CONTRECOUP see De Lio, Thomas

CONVALESCENT see Horder, Mervyn

COOKE, ARNOLD (1906-   )
Nocturnes
S solo,horn,pno OXFORD 63.061   (C312)

COOL see Bernstein, Leonard

COPLAND, AARON (1900-1990)
Four Early Songs
BOOSEY VAB0245   (C313)

Old Poem
med solo BOOSEY SGB2708   (C314)

COPPELIA: WALTZ-SONG see Delibes, Léo

COQ D'OR, LE: HYMN TO THE SUN see Rimsky-Korsakov, Nikolai

COQUARD, ARTHUR (1846-1910)
Mélodies, 12
solo voice,pno CLASSV C014   (C315)

COQUILLAGES see Sourisse, Brigitte

COR, LE see Flegier, Ange

CORAL, GIAMPAOLO (1944-   )
Canto, Il
S solo,vcl CURCI 10727   (C316)

CORBETT, W.
Lost Is My Love
sc KING'S   (C317)

CORDERO, ERNESTO (1946-   )
Cantata Al Valle De Mexico
solo voice,fl,gtr,vcl SCHOTTS
ME 8745   (C318)
solo voice,fl,gtr,vcl SCHOTTS
ME 8746   (C319)

CORDS see Wallach, Joelle

CORE 'NGRATO see Cardillo

CORE 'NGRATO CATARI CATARI see Cardillo

CORGHI, AZIO (1937-   )
Lumina Solis
solo voice,3inst ZERBONI 9605
(C320)

CORIA, MIGUEL ANGEL (1937-   )
Ariette No. 1
see Cancion De Belisa

Cancion De Belisa
"Ariette No. 1" S solo,orch [2'45"]
EMEC   (C321)

CORIGLIANO, JOHN (1938-   )
Aria Of The Worm (from The Ghosts Of
Versailles)
T solo SCHIRM.G 50481809   (C322)

As Summer Brings A Wistful Breeze
(from The Ghosts Of Versailles)
SS soli SCHIRM.G 50481811   (C323)

Beaumarchais's Aria
see Figaro Was Supposed To Return
The Necklace

Come Now, My Darling (from The Ghosts
Of Versailles)
SSMezBar soli SCHIRM.G 50481812
(C324)

Figaro Was Supposed To Return The
Necklace (from The Ghosts Of
Versailles)
"Beaumarchais's Aria" Bar solo
SCHIRM.G 50481813   (C325)

Figaro's Aria
see They Wish They Could Kill Me

Foggy Dew, The
see Three Irish Folksong Settings

Marie Antoinette's Aria
see They Are Always With Me

O God Of Love (from The Ghosts Of
Versailles)
SSSMezTT soli SCHIRM.G 50481814
(C326)

Petit Fours
SCHIRM.G ED3269   (C327)

Poem In October
SCHIRM.G ED2967   (C328)

Salley Gardens, The
see Three Irish Folksong Settings

Samira's Aria (from The Ghosts Of
Versailles)
Mez solo SCHIRM.G 50481815   (C329)

She Moved Through The Fair
see Three Irish Folksong Settings

They Are Always With Me (from The
Ghosts Of Versailles)
"Marie Antoinette's Aria" S solo
SCHIRM.G 50481816   (C330)

They Wish They Could Kill Me (from
The Ghosts Of Versailles)
"Figaro's Aria" Bar solo SCHIRM.G
50481810   (C331)

Three Irish Folksong Settings
T solo,fl SCHIRM.G 50481666 f.s.
contains: Foggy Dew, The; Salley
Gardens, The; She Moved Through
The Fair   (C332)

CORINTHIANS I: 13 see Rebel, Meeuwis

CORMORANT DAM see Hekster, Walter

CORNELIUS, PETER (1824-1874)
An Bertha *song cycle
low solo,pno (not original key)
CLASSV 0794   (C333)
high solo,pno CLASSV 0793   (C334)

CORNELIUS, PETER (cont'd.)
Holdes Bild
low solo,pno KAHNT 1821   (C335)

Kehr Ich Heim
med solo,pno KAHNT 2538C   (C336)

Lust Am Rhein
med solo,pno KAHNT 2538A   (C337)

Mit Hellem Klang
med solo,pno KAHNT 2538B   (C338)

Neun Geistliche Lieder, Op.2
see Vater Unser

Rheinische Lieder (Vier Lieder)
high solo,pno CLASSV 0791   (C339)
low solo,pno CLASSV 0792   (C340)

Tod Des Verräthers, Der
TBarB soli,pno SCHUBERTH,J   (C341)

Ton, Ein
med solo,pno CLASSV 0354   (C342)

Trauer Und Trost (Sechs Lieder)
*Op.3
high solo,pno CLASSV 0790   (C343)

Vater Unser
"Neun Geistliche Lieder, Op.2" high
solo,pno CLASSV 0789   (C344)

CORNOGRAPHY see Bond, Victoria

CORONA see Rice, Thomas N.

CORONACH; A KADDISH
Mez solo,English horn, chanter (diff)
PRESSER 111-40110   (C345)

CORRIDORS see Moryl, Richard

CORRIS WINTER see Freudenthal, Otto

CORSARO: MEDORA'S ARIA see Verdi,
Giuseppe

CORY, ELEANOR (1943-   )
Aria Viva
T solo,fl,ob,English horn,bsn,gtr
[9'] AM.COMP.AL. sc $10.65, pts
$13.70   (C346)

Surroundings
Mez solo,pno [15'] APNM sc $6.50,
set $12.50   (C347)

COSE BELLE, LE see Zandonai, Riccardo,
Serenata, La

COSÌ FAN TUTTE: COME SCOGLIO see
Mozart, Wolfgang Amadeus

COSÌ FAN TUTTE: É AMORE UN LADRONCELLO
see Mozart, Wolfgang Amadeus

COSÌ FAN TUTTE: SMANIE IMPLACABILE see
Mozart, Wolfgang Amadeus

COSÌ FAN TUTTE: TRADITO! SCHERNITO! see
Mozart, Wolfgang Amadeus

COSÌ FAN TUTTE: UN' AURA AMOROSA see
Mozart, Wolfgang Amadeus

COSMOS DONNED LANE, THE see Osawa,
Kazuko

COSSONI, CARLO DONATI (? -1700)
Libro Primo Delle Canzonette Amorose
A Voce Sola *CC20U
solo voice,cont fac ed FORNI 2452
f.s.   (C348)

COSTA
A Frangesa!
med solo,pno CLASSV 1300   (C349)
high solo,pno CLASSV 1313   (C350)

Era De Maggio
T solo,pno CLASSV 1362   (C351)

Oje Carulì
med-low solo,pno CLASSV 1310   (C352)

COSTELLAZIONE DI ARIANNA see Zangelmi,
Piero Luigi

COSTINESCU, GHEORGHE
Jubilus
S solo,trp,perc [10'] AM.COMP.AL.
(C353)

COTTRAU, TEODORO (1827-1879)
Addio A Napoli
med solo,pno CLASSV 1058   (C354)

COULD I HUSH A FATHER'S SIGH see Balfe,
Michael William

COULD MAN BE DRUNK FOREVER see Heilner,
Irwin

COUNT UGOLINO see Willingham, Lawrence

COUNTRY GOSPEL CLASSICS *CCU
solo voice TRIUNE MTB 103 $7.95
(C355)

COUNTRY OF THE CAMISARDS, THE see
Homer, Sidney

COUP DE DES, UN see Grahn, Ulf

COUPLET BERICHON DU XVIE see Jolivet,
Andre

COURT LADY, A see Straesser, Joep

COURTSHIP OF THE YONGLY BONGLY BO see
Thomson, Virgil Garnett

COVERED WAGON see Hirai, Kozaburoy

COW, THE see Mourant, Walter

COWLES, DARLEEN
Like Strangers
S solo,fl/pic,clar,horn,2perc,cel,
harp,vln,vla,db [17'] sc
AM.COMP.AL. $16.90   (C356)

COX, DAVID (1916-   )
Ballad Of Elected Knights
T solo,pno,perc SEESAW   (C357)

COYNER, LOU (1931-   )
Normal Madness, A
S solo,harp,vcl,pno,db, amp. hpschd
[12'] sc AM.COMP.AL. $6.15 (C358)

CRACKERS AND CHECKERS see Anderson,
Beth

CRADLE HYMN see MacDowell, Edward
Alexander

CRADLE SONG see Arensky, Anton
Stepanovich see Janson, Alfred,
Vuggesang see Jordan, Sverre,
Vuggevise: Og Drengen Ligger På
Moders Skjød see Knutsen, Torbjorn,
Vuggesang

CRADLE SONG, A see Brown, Francis James

CRADLE SONG 1915 see Kreisler, Fritz

CRADLE SONG OF YEREMOUSHKA see
Mussorgsky, Modest Petrovich

CRADLESONG see Van de Vate, Nancy Hayes

CRAW AND THE PITCHER, THE see Kavasch,
Deborah

CREATE IN ME A CLEAN HEART, O GOD see
Diemer, Emma Lou

CREATION, THE: WITH VERDURE CLAD see
Haydn, [Franz] Joseph

CREATIVE SOLOIST, THE see Jones,
Marjorie

CREATURE see Tsukatani, Akihiro

CREATURE TO CREATURE see Gideon, Miriam

CREDO see Kittelsen, Guttorm

CREE SONGS TO THE NEWBORN see Clayton

CREPUSCULE see D'orsay, M.L. see
Massenet, Jules

CRESSWELL, LYELL
Six Poems By Amy Lowell
Mez solo,pno WAI-TE-ATA 23   (C359)

CRESTON, PAUL (1906-1985)
Dance Variations, Op. 30
solo voice,pno pno red SCHIRM.G
ED3328   (C360)

CRICKET, THE see Goldberg, William

CRIPPLE CREEK see Four Traditional
American Songs

CRISEYDE see Montague, Stephen

CRIST, BAINBRIDGE (1883-1969)
Into A Ship, Dreaming
high solo,pno (text by Walter de la
Mare) CLASSV 1974   (C361)

Mistletoe
med solo,pno (text by Walter de la
Mare) CLASSV 1973   (C362)

O Come Hither!
coloratura sop,pno CLASSV 1975
(C363)

CRISTALLIN see Burgan, Patrick

CRISTOFARO, A. DE
Carmé!: Lli-Lli-Ri-Lli-Lli-Llá
SBar soli,pno CLASSV 1298 (C364)

CROAL, GEORGE
Queen Of The Village, The
SCIEN 395 (C365)

CROCE E DELIZIA 1985 see Capdenat,
Philippe

CROCKETT, DONALD (1951-)
Ecstatic Songs 1
T solo,pno MMB X814010 (C366)

Lyrikos
T solo,2(alto fl).2.2(bass clar).2.
2.2.1.0. 2harp,strings [21'0"]
PEER (C367)

Occhi Dell'Alma Mia
high solo,gtr MMB S815001 (C368)

Pensive Traveller, The
high solo,pno (6 songs on poems by
Henry David Thoreau) MMB S814001 (C369)

CROQUIS D'ORIENT, SET 1 see Hüe,
Georges-Adolphe

CROQUIS D'ORIENT, SET 2 see Hüe,
Georges-Adolphe

CROSSE, GORDON (1937-)
Verses In Memoriam David Munrow
countertenor,rec,vcl,hpsd OXFORD
perf mat rent (C370)

Wake Again, A
2countertenor,2rec,vcl,hpsd OXFORD
perf mat rent (C371)

CROSSING THE BAR see Gerschefski, Edwin
see Stanford, Charles Villiers

CROSSING THE WATER see Altena, Maarten

CROTTY, GERARD
Verses
S solo,clar WAI-TE-ATA 60 (C372)

CRUDELE ACERBA see Kerstens, Huub

CRUDELI, MATTHIAS
Salve Regina
(Ruhland, Konrad) S solo,opt bass
inst,org solo (Musik Aus
Ostbayern, Heft 18) COPPENRATH (C373)

CRUFT, ADRIAN (1921-1987)
Into God's Kingdom, Op. 80 *song
cycle
Bar solo,pno/strings&harp [14']
JOAD (C374)

Mine Own Sweet Jewel *Op.19
med-high solo,pno/string quar [3']
JOAD (C375)

Songs Of Good Counsel, Op. 73
Mez solo,pno [20'] JOAD (C376)

Two Canadian Poems, Op. 56
med solo,string quar/string orch/
pno [7'30"] JOAD (C377)

Two Nursery Rhymes, Op. 23
med solo,string quar/string orch/
pno [2'] JOAD (C378)

Two Songs Of Quiet, Op. 12
S/Mez solo,vln [5'] JOAD (C379)
A solo,vla [5'] JOAD (C380)

CTYRI MALA HLASOVA CVICENI see Klusák,
Jan

CTYRI PISNE see Haas, Pavel

CUARTO COMPOSICIONES see Puig, G.

CUARTO DE LOS NIÑOS, EL see Mussorgsky,
Modest Petrovich

CUATRO CANCIONES DE IBN GABIROL see
Pablo, Luis de

CUATRO CANCIONES POPULARES ESPANOLAS
see Martínez Chumilla, Manuel

CUATRO CANCIONES SOBRE POESIAS DE
FEDERICO GARCIA LORCA see
Lauridsen, Morten Johannes

CUBA SI see Truhlar, Jan

CUCKOO SONG see Quilter, Roger

CUCU see Rodriguez Peris, Martin Jose

CUERPO DE MUJER see Michans, Carlos

CUI, CÉSAR ANTONOVICH (1835-1918)
Ici Bas *Op.54,No.5
[Fr/Russ] med-high solo,pno (text
by Prudhomme) CLASSV 1359 (C381)

Statue At Czarskoe-Selo, The
[Russ] high solo,pno CLASSV 1220 (C382)
[Russ/Ger/Fr] med solo,pno CLASSV
1221 (C383)

Vier Sonette, Op. 48
[Ger/Polish/Russ] high solo RECITAL
253 (C384)

CUMMERBUND, THE see Kirkwood,
Antoinette

CUN QUELL' ÖGLIADA see Flothuis, Marius

CUPID, TURN THY BOW see Mourant, Walter

CURRITE POPULI see Monteverdi, Claudio

CURSCHMANN, KARL FRDR
Kleine Hans, Der
A/Bar solo,pno SCIEN 397 (C385)
S solo,pno SCIEN 398 (C386)

CURTIS, ERNESTO DE
'A Surrentina
high solo,pno CLASSV 1292 (C387)

Canta Pe' Me
high solo,pno CLASSV 1297 (C388)

Senza Nisciuno
T solo,pno CLASSV 0646 (C389)

Torna A Surriento
high solo,pno CLASSV 1317 (C390)

Tu, Ca Nun Chiagne!
high solo,pno CLASSV 1318 (C391)

Voce 'E Notte
high solo,pno CLASSV 1315 (C392)
med solo,pno CLASSV 1308 (C393)

CUSHENDALL, OP. 118 see Stanford,
Charles Villiers

CUVILLIER, CHARLES (1877-1955)
Vingt Mélodies, Vol. 1
solo voice,pno CLASSV C015 (C394)

CYCLE see Beerman, Burton

CYCLE OF FOUR RELIGIOUS SONGS, A see
Tcimpidis, David

CYCLE OF NOVELTIES see Parchman, Gen
Louis

CYCLE OF SONGS FROM TENNYSON'S MAUD see
Somervell, Arthur

CYCLUS I see Ehlen, Margriet

CYKLUS PISNI see Aim, Vojtech Borivoj

CYNTHIAS REVELLS: THREE SONGS see
Parris, Robert

CYTHÈRE see Poldowski, [Lady] Dean Paul

CZERNOHORSKY, BOHUSLAV MATÊJ
see CERNOHÓRSKY, BOHUSLAV MATÊJ

D

D' HOAMLIGE LIAB see Baumann, Alexander

DA BUA IN WIGL WAGL see Baumann,
Alexander

DA COLOMBO A BROADWAY see Mannino,
Franco

DÅ EG VAR EIN LITEN GUT see Karlsen,
Kjell Mørk

DA GFOPTI see Baumann, Alexander

DA HIMMEL see Holzel, Gustav

DA ICH EIN KIND see Gretscher

DA ICH VOR IHR AUF EWIG SCHIED see
Pieper, Rene

DA LACHEN JA DIE HÜHNER see Maasz,
Gerhard

DA LIEG ICH UNTER DEN BÄUMEN see
Mendelssohn-Bartholdy, Felix

DA MUADA IHR WIAGN G'SANGL see Baumann,
Alexander

DA PATER see King, Harold C.

DA UHU SCHAUD ME SO DRAURECH AU see
Schwertsik, Kurt

DABROWSKI, FLORIAN (1913-)
Expectations
see Oczekiwania

Oczekiwania
"Expectations" [Polish] S solo,pno
POLSKIE (D1)

DADDY AND ME see Perkins

DAG see Evensen, Bernt Kasberg

DAG ER PÅ HIMLEN KOMIN see Eggen, Arne

DÄGÄ DÄGÄ see Wallin, Peter

DAGEN VAKNAR see Kielland, Olav

DAGERAAD see Andriessen, Hendrik

DAGHET IN DEN OOSTEN, HET see Badings,
Henk

DAGURINN KEMUR see Isolfsson, Pall

DAHL, VIVIAN
At Dusk
see I Skumringen

Dreamer, The
see Drømmeren

Drømmeren *song cycle
"Dreamer, The" A solo,pno SAMFUNDET
f.s. (D2)

I Skumringen
"At Dusk" A solo,pno SAMFUNDET f.s. (D3)

Nattetimen *song cycle
"Night Hour, The" A solo,pno
SÄMFUNDET f.s. (D4)

Night Hour, The
see Nattetimen

Sange Er Våben
"Songs Are Weapon" T solo,pno
SAMFUNDET f.s. (D5)

Sange Til Årstiderne
"Songs To The Seasons" T solo,pno
SAMFUNDET f.s. (D6)

Songs Are Weapon
see Sange Er Våben

Songs To The Seasons
see Sange Til Årstiderne

DALBY, MARTIN (1942-)
Wanderer Song Cycle
Mez solo,pno RICORDI-IT LD560 (D7)

DALCROZE, JACQUES
see JAQUES-DALCROZE, ÉMILE

DALE, SJUR
I Himmelen
see Tre Koraler

No Timen Er Komen
see Tre Koraler

DALE, SJUR (cont'd.)

Nu La Oss Takke Gud
see Tre Koraler

Tre Koraler
(Volle, Bjarne) solo voice,org
NOTON N-9020-G f.s.
contains: I Himmelen; No Timen Er
Komen; Nu La Oss Takke Gud (D8)

DALE DE BETÚN see Planas, A.

DALENDE DAG, EN STAKKET STUND, EN see
Nystedt, Knut

DALLESANDRO, GERALD
Mrs. Santa Claus
solo voice LUDWIG VS-10 $1.50 (D9)

DALL'ONGARO, MICHELE
Canti Indulgenti
S solo,fl,clar,horn,pno,2vln,vla,
vcl EDI-PAN EP 7394   (D10)

Vita Mia
S solo,vln,vcl,pno EDI-PAN EP 7336
(D11)

DALVISUR see Thorarinsson, Leifur

DAMAIS, EMILE (1906-   )
O Nuit
S/T solo,2.3.2.2.soprano sax.alto
sax. 2.3.2.1. timp,perc,opt Ondes
Martenot [10'] BILLAUDOT sc,pts
rent, voc sc f.s.   (D12)

DAME BLANCHE: VIENS, GENTILE DAME see
Boieldieu, François-Adrien

DAME SEULE see Orthel, Leon

DAMETTE ITTEMO see Arima, Reiko

DÄMMERUNG see Koetsier, Jan

DAMNATION OF FAUST: D'AMOUR L'ARDENTE
FLAMME see Berlioz, Hector (Louis)

DAMNATION OF FAUST: VOICI DES ROSES see
Berlioz, Hector (Louis)

DAMOISELLE ÉLUE see Debussy, Claude

DAMROSCH, LEOPOLD (1832-1885)
Fünf Lieder, Op.5
high solo,pno CLASSV 0757   (D13)

DAMROSCH, W.
Danny Deever
Bar solo,pno (text by Kipling)
CLASSV 0756   (D14)

DANCE see Plagge, Wolfgang see
Thorkelsdottir, Mist

DANCE MASTER, THE see Wolpe, Stefan,
La-Menatzeach Al Ha-Mecholot

DANCE OF THE KIDS see Grieg, Edvard
Hagerup, Killingdans

DANCE VARIATIONS, OP. 30 see Creston,
Paul

DANDY JIM OF CAROLINE see Russel, Henry

DANIELSEN, RAGNAR (1917-1976)
November
[Norw] solo voice,pno NORK (D15)

DANIELSSON, HARRY (1905-   )
Dolce Far Niente
solo voice,pno STIM f.s.   (D16)

Jag Diktar För Ingen
solo voice,pno STIM f.s.   (D17)

Melodi
(Kjellberg, Olle) solo voice,orch
STIM f.s.   (D18)

Pilen - Skrivet På Vandring En Tidig
Vårdag
solo voice,orch STIM sc PA-3272-19
f.s., pts KL-33272-8 f.s.   (D19)

Sigurd Jorsalafar
B solo,pno STIM f.s.   (D20)

Vaggvisa
solo voice,pno [2'] sc STIM
PA-3272-2 f.s.   (D21)

Valsen Från Förr
solo voice,pno [2'] sc STIM
PA-3272-3 f.s.   (D22)

Vocalise
solo voice,pno [2'] sc STIM
PA-3272-2 f.s.   (D23)

DANK see Louis Ferdinand, Prince Of
Prussia

DANNY BOY
(Violette, Andrew) med solo,pno [3']
sc AM.COMP.AL. $.80   (D24)

DANNY DEEVER see Damrosch, W.

DANO TIORE see Hvoslef, Ketil

DANS DER KRISTALLEN, DE see Kersters,
Willem

DANS LA FORÊT see Paderewski, Ignace
Jan

DANS LE SANG see Glazunov, Alexander
Konstantinovich

DANS LES COINS BLEUS see Saint-Saëns,
Camille

DANS L'ÉTÉ see Hahn, Reynaldo

DANS TON PAYS see Borodin, Alexander
Porfirievich

DANSK MESSE see Kongsted,Ole

DANSONS LA GIGUE! see Carpenter, John
Alden see Szulc, Josef Zygmunt

DANZA, LA see Rossini, Gioacchino

DANZA, THE see Chadwick, George
Whitefield

DAPPLE GREY see Jeffreys, John

DÄR LIGGER SVERIGE see Hemberg, Eskil

DARASSE, XAVIER (1934-1992)
Messe Pour Montserrat
4 solo voices,2pno SALABERT f.s.
(D25)

DARDANUS: JOURS HEUREUX see Sacchini,
Antonio (Maria Gasparo Gioacchino)

DARDANUS: MONSTRE AFFREUX see Rameau,
Jean-Philippe

DAREST THOU NOW O SOUL see Valen,
Fartein

DARGOMYZHSKY, ALEXANDER SERGEYEVICH
(1813-1869)
I Love Him Still
[Russ] Mez solo,pno CLASSV 2117
(D26)

Rusalka: Cavatina Act III
[Russ] T solo,pno CLASSV 0645 (D27)

DARK LADY, THE see Stefansson, Finnur
Torfi

DARK NIGHT see Amerongen, Jan van

DARKHARBOR see Moss, Lawrence Kenneth

DARKSONG see Chance, Nancy Laird

DAS IST DORT, WO DIE LETZTEN HÜTTEN
SIND see Franken, Wim

DAS SIND TRIUMPFE UNSRER ZEIT see
Schild, Th. F.

DASS SIE HÜR GEWESEN see Schubert,
Franz (Peter)

D'ASTORGA, EMANUELE
see ASTORGA, EMANUELE D'

DAUDS-MANNS-SUNDID see Gudmundsson,
Björgvin

DAUGHERTY
I Love Thee Lord
solo voice SOUTHERN $2.50   (D28)

I Never Knew Jesus
solo voice SOUTHERN $2.50   (D29)

DAVID, FÉLICIEN-CÉSAR (1810-1876)
Herculanum: Je Crois Au Dieu
B solo,pno CLASSV 1555   (D30)

Lalla Roukh: Si Vous Ne Savez Plus
Charmer
[Fr] S solo,pno CLASSV 1709 (D31)

Perle Du Brésil, La: Charmant Oiseau
Mez solo,pno CLASSV 1707   (D32)
S solo,pno CLASSV 0380   (D33)

Vingt Cinq, Vol.2
solo voice,pno CLASSV C019 (D34)

Vingt Mélodies
solo voice,pno CLASSV C018 (D35)

DAVID, THOMAS CHRISTIAN (1925-   )
Drei Goethe-Lieder
Bar solo,pno DOBLINGER 08 670 (D36)
S solo,pno DOBLINGER 08 671 (D37)

DAVID 112 see Sigurbjörnsson, Thorkell

DAVID'S 42. PSALM see Koppel, Herman
David

DAVIDS NIMM see Rehnqvist, Karin

DAVIDSON, CHARLES STUART (1929-   )
Yihyu L'ratzon
solo voice,kbd TRANSCON. 991312
(D38)

DAVIDSSON, ELIAS (1941-   )
Flottinn
Bar solo,pno ICELAND 039-015 (D39)

Hoxi Stikkfri
Bar solo,pno ICELAND 039-008 (D40)

Remuneration, The
solo voice,pno [6'0"] ICELAND
039-014   (D41)

DAVIES, EILUNED
There Is No Rose
S solo,pno BARDIC BE0322   (D42)

DAVIS, SHARON
see SCHMIDT, SHARON YVONNE DAVIS

DAWN, OP. 46, NO. 6 see Tchaikovsky,
Piotr Ilyich

DAWSON, WILLIAM LEVI (1898-1990)
Out In The Fields
high solo,pno,opt orch/band KJOS
TH130 f.s., ipr   (D43)
med solo,pno,opt orch/band KJOS
TM130 f.s., ipr   (D44)

Rugged Yank, The
high solo,pno KJOS TH132   (D45)
low solo,pno KJOS TL132   (D46)

Talk About A Child That Do Love Jesus
high solo FITZSIMONS F0110 (D47)
low solo FITZSIMONS F0111   (D48)

There Is A Balm In Gilead
high solo,pno KJOS TH105   (D49)
low solo,pno KJOS TL105   (D50)

DAY, A see Anderson, Beth

DAY IS BRIGHTENING see Eggen, Arne, Dag
Er På Himlen Komin

DAY IS GONE, THE see Glière, Reinhold
Moritzovich

DAY IS NO MORE, THE see Carpenter, John
Alden

DAY OF A CHILD see Dillard, Donald E.

DAY OF CALM SEA see Smolanoff, Michael
Louis

DAY OF LOVE see Pasatieri, Thomas

DAY ONE see Maxym, R.

DAYDREAM see Schelle, Michael

DAYS AND NIGHTS see Erickson, Robert

DE AMORE ET MORTE: SEVEN SONGS see
Silsbee, Ann

DE BLASIO, ANTONIO
Ode
S solo,fl,pno EDI-PAN EP 7235 (D51)

DE BON MATIN SE LEVE see Nigg, Serge

DE_CRESCENZO
Tarantella Sincera
T solo,pno CLASSV 1135   (D52)

Uocchie Celeste
T solo,pno CLASSV 1139   (D53)

DE CURTIS
Carmè: Carmela
high solo,pno CLASSV 1296   (D54)
med-high solo,pno CLASSV 0622 (D55)

DE CURTIS, ERNESTO
see CURTIS, ERNESTO DE

DE ESOS PÁJAROS see Beethoven, Ludwig
van

DE FILIPPIS, C.
Don't Make A Fool Of Me
see Due Arie

Due Arie
solo voice,pno CURCI 9672 f.s.
contains: Don't Make A Fool Of
Me, "Che Mai Sara Di Me";
Laughing At Me   (D56)

Laughing At Me
see Due Arie

DE GOEDE, NICHOLAAS
Julbön
see Marias Tröstesång

Marias Tröstesång
"Julbön" solo voice SVERIG
PROP 7914   (D57)

DE GRANDIS, RENATO (1927-   )
Salterio Popolare I
solo voice,pno SEESAW   (D58)

Salterio Popolare II
solo voice,pno SEESAW   (D59)

DE IMMACULATA CONCEPTIONE see
Stradella, Alessandro

DE KOVEN, (HENRY LOUIS) REGINALD
(1859-1920)
Oh Promise Me
high solo SCHIRM.G ST7550   (D60)
low solo SCHIRM.G ST41318   (D61)

DE LA HABANA HA VENIDO UN BARCO see
Lopez De Saa, Emilio

DE LA SOIREE PASSEE see Stuppner,
Hubert

DE LASTRA, ERICH EDER (1933-   )
Blechtrommelverse
[Ger] S solo,pno [8'] REIMERS
101072   (D62)

Hymnus An Eine Anonyme Gottheit
solo voice,vla REIMERS 101071 (D63)

DE L'AUBE see Vermeulen, Matthijs

DE LEVA, ENRICO (1867-1955)
Canta Il Mare
"Canzonetta Marina" med solo,pno
CLASSV 1295   (D64)

Canzonetta Marina
see Canta Il Mare

DE LIO, THOMAS
At Briggflatts Meetinghouse
S solo,pno SMITH PUB   (D65)

Bright Seaweed Reaping
S solo,3clar,pno,2perc SMITH PUB (D66)

Contrecoup
S solo,fl,pno,perc SMITH PUB   (D67)

Granite, And
S solo,pno,2perc,ob,3clar SMITH PUB
                               (D68)

DE MIDI see Vermeulen, Matthijs

DE PABLO, LUIS
see PABLO, LUIS DE

DE PONTE, NIEL
Mort Du Roi Renaud, La
solo voice,fl,English horn,harp,
vln,vla,vcl BILLAUDOT   (D69)

DE PROFUNDIS see Gaathaug, Morten see
Jastrzebska, Anna see Lerstad,
Terje B. see Nielson, Lewis see
Orthel, Leon

DEAD FLOWERS see Bergh, Sverre, Døde
Blomar

DEAD PIGEONS ARE FALLING AROUND ME see
Sweeden, Hans Van, Dode Duiven
Vallen Om Mij Heen

DEAR FRIEND see Tal, Marjo

DEAR FRIEND, DON'T YOU SEE see Tal,
Marjo

DEAREST NAME see Verdi, Giuseppe,
Rigoletto: Caro Nome

DEARIE see Beach, [Mrs.] H.H.A. (Amy
Marcy Cheney)

DEATH FUGUE see Kernis, Aaron Jay

DEATH OF GOLIATH, THE see Downes,
Andrew

DEATH OF LOVE: MONO DRAMA see Kurachi,
Tatsuya

DEATH-WORDS FROM CHEROKEE see
Hutchison, (David) Warner

DEBUSSY, CLAUDE (1862-1918)
Âme Évaporée, L'
see Romance

Balcon, Le
see Cinq Poems De Charles
Baudelaire

Beau Soir
med solo,pno CLASSV 0846   (D70)
high solo,pno CLASSV 0439   (D71)

DEBUSSY, CLAUDE (cont'd.)
Cinq Poems De Charles Baudelaire
[Fr] solo voice,pno POLSKIE f.s.
contains: Balcon, Le; Harmonie Du
Soir; Jeu D'eau, Le; Mort Des
Amants, Le; Recueillement (D72)

Clair De Lune
high solo,pno CLASSV 0625   (D73)

Damoiselle Élue
"Je Voudrais Qu'il Fût Déjà Près De
Moi" S solo,pno CLASSV 1260   (D74)

Enfant Prodigue, L': Azaël
see Enfant Prodigue, L': Ces Airs

Enfant Prodigue, L': Ces Airs
"Enfant Prodigue, L': Azaël" med
solo,pno CLASSV 0668   (D75)
"Enfant Prodigue, L': Azaël" T
solo,pno CLASSV 0878   (D76)

Enfant Prodigue, L': L'Année
Mez solo,pno (lower key) CLASSV
0669   (D77)

Enfant Prodigue, L': Récit. Et Air De
Lia
S solo,pno CLASSV 0399   (D78)

Frühe Lieder *CCU
(Zimmermann, Reiner) solo voice,pno
PETERS f.s.   (D79)

Fünf Lieder Auf Gedichte Von Paul
Bourget *CC5U
(Zimmermann, Reiner) solo voice,pno
PETERS f.s.   (D80)

Harmonie Du Soir
see Cinq Poems De Charles
Baudelaire

Je Voudrais Qu'il Fût Déjà Près De
Moi
see Damoiselle Élue

Jeu D'eau, Le
see Cinq Poems De Charles
Baudelaire

Mort Des Amants, Le
see Cinq Poems De Charles
Baudelaire

Pelléas: Les Cheveux (Act 3)
Bar solo,pno CLASSV 0667   (D81)

Recueillement
see Cinq Poems De Charles
Baudelaire

Romance
"Âme Évaporée, L'" [Fr/Eng] high
solo,pno CLASSV 1746   (D82)

Trois Ballades De Francois Villon
solo voice,3.2+English horn.2.2+
contrabsn. 4.2.0.0. harp,strings
[14'] KALMUS A6312 sc $17.00, pts
$20.00   (D83)

Trois Chansons De Bilitis *CC3U
(Zimmermann, Reiner) solo voice,pno
PETERS f.s.   (D84)

DECEMBER see Clarke, Henry Leland see
Sveinsson, Atli Heimir

DECEMBER 27, 1966 see Carl, Robert

DECOUST, MICHEL (1936-   )
Quais
solo voice,harp [35'] SALABERT
EAS18371 f.s.   (D85)

DEDEN, OTTO (1925-   )
Hofsuite
Bar solo,fl,2vla,vcl,perc,pno [15']
DONEMUS f.s.   (D86)

DEDICATION CANTATA see Hilliard, John

DEDICATORIA see Schumann, Robert
(Alexander)

DEEP IN THY SHADE see Handel, George
Frideric, Serse: Ombra Mai Fu
(Largo)

DEEP SONG see MacBride, David Huston

DEFESCH, WILLIAM
see FESCH, WILLEM DE

DEFOTIS, WILLIAM
Against That Time
S&opt Mez soli,2(pic).1+English
horn.3(bass clar).3(contrabsn).
4.3.3.1. 3perc,cel,harp,strings
[20'] sc AM.COMP.AL. $31.40 (D87)

DEFOTIS, WILLIAM (cont'd.)
e.e. cummings bagatelles
Mez solo,pno, one performer only
[10'] AM.COMP.AL.   (D88)

DEGEN, JOHANNES (1910-   )
Vingar I Skymningen *Op.70
S/T solo,string quar/string orch
STIM f.s.   (D89)

DEH TORNA MIO BENE: VARIATIONS see
Proch, Heinrich

DEH VIENI, NON TARDAR see Lyric Soprano
Arias: A Master Class With Evelyn
Lear, Vol. 2

DEI CANTI DI LINGUAGGIO see Giuffre,
Gaetano

DEIN ANGESICHT see Weegenhuise, Johan

DEIN BIN ICH see Mozart, Wolfgang
Amadeus

DEIN BLICK see Marx, Joseph

DEIN ENTZÜCKEND HELLES LACHEN see
Glière, Reinhold Moritzovich

DÉJANIRE: EPITHALAME see Saint-Saëns,
Camille

DEJEUNER SUR L'HERB see Brown, Newel
Kay

D'EKJE GREIT see Taubo, Lillian Gulowna

DEKKER, DIRK (1945-   )
Als Alles Stil Is
see Drie Liederen

Drie Liederen
Mez solo,woodwind quin,pno,vln,vla,
vcl,db DONEMUS f.s. [12']
contains: Als Alles Stil Is;
Oorverdovend Samenleven; Rivier
Onder De Grond   (D90)

Oorverdovend Samenleven
see Drie Liederen

Rivier Onder De Grond
see Drie Liederen

DEKOVEN, REGINALD
see DE KOVEN, (HENRY LOUIS) REGINALD

DEL CABELLO MÁS SUTIL see Obradors,
Fernando

DEL DITT BROD MED SULTEN BROR see
Nystedt, Knut

DEL RIEGO
Homing
low solo,pno CLASSV 1751   (D91)
med solo,pno CLASSV 1750   (D92)
high solo,pno CLASSV 1749   (D93)

DELAFOSSE, L.
Chauves-Souris, Les
[Fr] high solo (not available
outside U.S.A.) RECITAL 351 (D94)

DELAGE, MAURICE (1879-1961)
Quatre Poemes Hindous
[Fr] high solo,orch (not available
outside U.S.A.) sc,pts RECITAL
352   (D95)
[Fr] RECITAL 327   (D96)
Mez solo,pno CLASSV 0758   (D97)

DELDEN, LEX VAN (1919-1988)
Galathea *Op.99
S/T solo,pno [3'] DONEMUS   (D98)
high solo,pno [3'] DONEMUS   (D99)

Goede Burgers, De
see Vier Liederen Uit Kaf, Op. 5b

Ik Snak Naar Warmte
see Vier Liederen Uit Kaf, Op. 5b

Ruikt Naar Bier, Het
see Vier Liederen Uit Kaf, Op. 5b

Tusschen God En De Menschen
see Vier Liederen Uit Kaf, Op. 5b

Vier Liederen Uit Kaf, Op. 5b
B solo,pno DONEMUS f.s. [3']
contains: Goede Burgers, De; Ik
Snak Naar Warmte; Ruikt Naar
Bier, Het; Tusschen God En De
Menschen   (D100)

DELFT, MARC VAN (1958-   )
Symphonisch Gedicht (De Legende Van
Het Solsche Gat *Op.9
speaking voice,3.3.3.3. 4.3.3.1.
8perc,harp,pno/cel,strings [25']
DONEMUS f.s.   (D101)

DELIBES, LÉO (1836-1891)
Avril
high solo,pno CLASSV 0674   (D102)

Bell Song
see Légende

Blanche Et Rose
S solo,pno CLASSV 0681   (D103)

Bonjour, Suzon
high solo,pno CLASSV 0429   (D104)
med solo,pno CLASSV 0670   (D105)

Chanson De L'Oiseleur
T solo,pno CLASSV 0678   (D106)

Chanson Espagñole
see Filles De Cadix, Les

Chant De L'Almée
S solo,pno CLASSV 0680   (D107)

Coppelia: Waltz-Song
S solo,pno CLASSV 1028   (D108)

Départ
T solo,pno CLASSV 0675   (D109)

Églogue
"Viens! Une Flûte Invisible" med-
high solo,pno CLASSV 0671   (D110)

Filles De Cadix, Les
"Chanson Espagñole" S solo,pno
CLASSV 0676   (D111)

Flower Duet
see Sous Le Dôme Épais

Heure Du Soir
T solo,pno CLASSV 0677   (D112)

Lakmé: Fantaisie Aux Divins
T solo,pno CLASSV 0371   (D113)

Lakmé: Indian Bell Song
S solo,pno CLASSV 0345   (D114)

Lakmé: Tu M'as Donné Le Plus Doux
Rêve
[Fr] S solo,pno CLASSV 1747 (D115)

Lakmé: Viens, Mallika
SA soli,pno CLASSV 0448   (D116)

Légende (from Lakmé)
"Bell Song" [Eng/Fr] S solo UNITED
MUS f.s.   (D117)

Mélodies, 17, Vol.2
solo voice,pno CLASSV C017   (D118)

Myrto
Mez solo,pno CLASSV 0673   (D119)

O Mer, Ouvre-Toi (Arioso)
Mez solo,pno CLASSV 0684   (D120)

Peine d'Amour
T solo,pno CLASSV 0683   (D121)

Que L'Heure Est Donc Brève
T solo,pno CLASSV 0672   (D122)

Quinze Mélodies Et Deux Choeur
solo voice,pno CLASSV C016   (D123)

Regrets
med-high solo,pno CLASSV 0679
(D124)

Roi L'a Dit, Le: Ah! Quelle Offense
[Ger/Fr] coloratura sop,pno CLASSV
0913   (D125)

Roi L'a Dit, Le: De Ja Les
Hirondelles
[Fr/Eng] 2 solo voices RECITAL 2232
(D126)

Rossignol, Le: Ariette
Mez solo,pno CLASSV 0682   (D127)

Sous Le Dôme Épais (from Lakmé) duet
"Flower Duet" [Fr] SS soli UNITED
MUS f.s.   (D128)

Viens! Une Flûte Invisible
see Églogue

DELICIA DE LA TRISTEZA see Beethoven,
Ludwig van

DELICIOUS LOVELY SOBRANIE see Bois, Rob
du

DELILAH see Marsh, Roger

DELIUS, FREDERICK (1862-1934)
Birds, The
see Four Songs For Voice And
Orchestra

Four Posthumous Songs
solo voice,pno UNIVER. UE17428
(D129)

DELIUS, FREDERICK (cont'd.)

Four Songs For Voice And Orchestra
solo voice,2.2.2.2. 4.2.0.0. timp,
harp,strings OXFORD perf mat rent
contains: Birds, The; Let
Springtime Come; Summer
Landscape; Twilight Fancies
(D130)

Let Springtime Come
see Four Songs For Voice And
Orchestra

Nineteen Songs
solo voice (CC19U) OXFORD 60.202
(D131)

Sixteen Songs
solo voice,pno BOOSEY DCE0018B
(D132)

Summer Landscape
see Four Songs For Voice And
Orchestra

Twilight Fancies
see Four Songs For Voice And
Orchestra

DELIVER US see Tcimpidis, David

DELL' OFFESE A VENDICARMI see Zipoli,
Domenico

DELL'ACQUA, EVA (1866-1930)
J'ai Vu Passer L'Hirondelle
see Villanelle

Villanelle
SCHOTT-FRER 4031B   (D133)
"J'ai Vu Passer L'Hirondelle" [Fr/
Eng] high solo,pno CLASSV 1748
(D134)

DELLINGS DURUM see Tveitt, Geirr

DELNOOZ, HENRI (1942-   )
Drie Kinderliederen, Uit De
"Svendborger Gedichte"
Bar solo,vcl DONEMUS f.s. [7']
contains: Pflaumenbaum, Der;
Schneider Von Ulm, Der; Vom
Kind, Das Sich Nicht Waschen
Wollte   (D135)

Pflaumenbaum, Der
see Drie Kinderliederen, Uit De
"Svendborger Gedichte"

Schneider Von Ulm, Der
see Drie Kinderliederen, Uit De
"Svendborger Gedichte"

Vom Kind, Das Sich Nicht Waschen
Wollte
see Drie Kinderliederen, Uit De
"Svendborger Gedichte"

DEM GENIUS DES AUGENBLICKS see Marx,
Joseph

DEMARE, L.
Matabu
solo voice,pno BOIL B.1057   (D136)

DEMAS COMPANEROS, LOS see Ansink,
Caroline

DEMBSKI, STEPHEN (1949-   )
Adult Epigram
S solo,gtr [2'] sc AM.COMP.AL. $.80
(D137)

Caritas
SATB soli,acap [4'] sc AM.COMP.AL.
$2.30   (D138)

Flower Given To My Daughter, A
S solo,harp [6'] sc AM.COMP.AL.
$1.60   (D139)

Of Mere Being
S solo,pno [10'] sc AM.COMP.AL.
$4.60   (D140)

Simples *CC3U
S solo,pno sc AM.COMP.AL. $6.90
(D141)

DEMON see Rubinstein, Anton

DEN FARENDE SVEND see Runolfsson, Karl
Otto

DEN HOLDEN ANBLICK SOLL ICH MEIDEN see
Kreutzer, Konradin, Libussa:
Duettino

DENIQUE APERTOS BACCUS AMAT COLLES see
Rendine, Sergio

DENK ES, O SEELE see Valen, Fartein

DENKER, DER see Marx, Joseph

DENKMAL AN DER GRENZE DES FRUCHTLANDES
see Manassen, Alex

DENNEBOSSE see Badings, Henk

DENSE see Hekster, Walter

DENZA, LUIGI (1846-1922)
Addio!
med solo,pno CLASSV 0599   (D142)

Echange, L'
[Fr] med-high solo,pno CLASSV 0843
(D143)

Fuggimi!
med-low solo,pno CLASSV 0600 (D144)

Hirondelle!
[It] med solo,pno CLASSV 0595
(D145)

If
see Se

Non M'ami Più!
low solo,pno CLASSV 1159   (D146)
med solo,pno CLASSV 1251   (D147)

Non T'amo Più!
[It] high solo,pno CLASSV 1425
(D148)

Occhi Di Fata
[It] med solo,pno CLASSV 0501
(D149)
[It] high solo,pno CLASSV 1752
(D150)

Occhi Turchini
[It] high solo CLASSV 1753   (D151)

Or Che Notte
high solo&med solo,pno CLASSV 0851
(D152)

Se
"If" [It/Eng] high solo,pno CLASSV
0601   (D153)
"If" [It/Eng] low solo,pno CLASSV
1229   (D154)
"If" [It/Eng] med solo,pno CLASSV
1228   (D155)

Si Tu M'aimais!
[It/Eng] high solo,pno CLASSV 0602
(D156)
[It/Eng] med solo,pno CLASSV 0603
(D157)

Si Vous L'aviez Compris!
high solo,pno,vln/vcl CLASSV 0596
(D158)
low solo,pno,vln/vcl CLASSV 0597
(D159)

Telefono, Lo
T solo,pno CLASSV 1054   (D160)

Torna!
T solo,pno CLASSV 0985   (D161)
T solo,pno,vln/vcl CLASSV 0986
(D162)

Tu!
high solo,pno CLASSV 0598   (D163)

Vieni!
[It] high solo,pno CLASSV 0933
(D164)
[It] med-high solo,pno CLASSV 1754
(D165)

DÉPART see Delibes, Léo

DEPRAZ, RAYMOND (1915-   )
Feu Roi, Le
A solo,pno,trp,6perc [18']
BILLAUDOT   (D166)

Poursuivant, Le
countertenor,1.0.1.1. 1.1.1.0.
timp,cel,vln,vla,db [15']
BILLAUDOT   (D167)

...DER DIE GESÄNGE ZERSCHLUG see
Ruzicka, Peter

DER GÅR EN SANG see Albertsen, Per
Hjort

DER GRANENE SUSER see Taubo, Lillian
Gulowna

DER LIGGER ET LAND see Nordraak, Rikard

DER SYNGER INGEN FUGLE see Jordan,
Sverre

DER VIDDEVINDEN BUR see Saeverud,
Tormod

DERETTER SÅ JEG see Maehlum, Svein

DERNIER RENDEZ-VOUS, LE see Sevriens,
Jean

DERNIERE LUMIERE, LA see Giraud

DERNIÈRE VALSE, LA see Hahn, Reynaldo

DERRIÈRE CHEZ MON PÈRE see Arrieu,
Claude

DERTELE SATER, DE see Ketting, Piet

DES HAFIS LIEBESLIEDER, OP. 24 see
Szymanowski, Karol

DES HIMMELS DUNKLERER BRUDER see Schmidt, Christfried

DES ILES see Tveitt, Geirr

DES KNABEN WUNDERHORN I see Mahler, Gustav

DES KNABEN WUNDERHORN II see Mahler, Gustav

DES KNABEN WUNDERHORN: NINE SONGS see Mahler, Gustav

DES LEVRES NOCTURNES see Regteren Altena, Lucas van

DES PREZ, JOSQUIN (ca. 1440-1521)
  Huit Chansons
    (Ravier, C.) solo voice,rec, krummhorn, viol, hurdy-gurdy
    BILLAUDOT   (D168)

DES WINTERS ALS HET REGHENT see Anonymous

DESCENT, THE see Pollock, Robert Emil

DESDE LO ALTO DE LA TIERRA see Beethoven, Ludwig van

DESDICHADO, EL see Saint-Saëns, Camille

DESERT PLACES see Gerber, Steven R.

DESERTED see MacDowell, Edward Alexander

DÉSERTEUR, LE: ADIEU, CHÈRE LOUISE see Monsigny, Pierre-Alexandre

DESET PISNICEK see Blazek, Zdenek

DESET POETICKYCH DUET NA SLOVA V. NEZVALA see Eben, Petr

DESIRE see Glinka, Mikhail Ivanovich see Rubinstein, Anton

DÉSOLATION DE WERTHER see Massenet, Jules, Werther: J'Aurais Sur Ma Poitrino

DESPRES, JOSQUIN
  see DÉS PREZ, JOSQUIN

DESSAU, PAUL (1894-1979)
  Friede
    PETERS 5160   (D169)

  Lieder Aus Dem "Dreistrophen-Kalender, 27, Heft 1: Neun Lieder Für Hohen Sopran, Bariton Und Klavier *CC9U
    SBar soli,pno DEUTSCHER DV 9008 f.s.   (D170)

  Lieder Aus Dem "Dreistrophen-Kalender, 27, Heft 2: Neun Lieder Für Sopran, Bass Und Klavier *CC9U
    SB soli,pno DEUTSCHER DV 9009 f.s.
                                 (D171)

  Lieder Aus Dem "Dreistrophen-Kalender", 27, Heft 3: Neun Lieder Für Alt, Tenor Und Klavier *CC9U
    AT soli,pno DEUTSCHER DV 9010 f.s.
                                 (D172)

  Sieben Schwestern
    PETERS G 1541   (D173)

DESSAUER, JOSEF
  Lockung
    A/Bar solo,pno (text by Eichendorff) SCIEN 423   (D174)

DESSIN D'UN MAITRE INCONNU see Orthel, Leon, Martyre, Une

DEST NA BAJKALE see Bohác, Josef

DESTINY see Rachmaninoff, Sergey Vassilievich

DESTNIK Z PICCADILLY see Hanuš, Jan

DETEM see Bartoš, Jan Zdenek

DETTE ER TIMEN see Gjerstrom, Bjorn G.

DEUR IN LOOD, EEN see Slangen, John

DEUTSCHE VOLKSLIEDER (1. UND 2. FOLGE) see Kochan

DEUTSCHE VOLKSLIEDER *CCU
  (Kochan, Günter) solo voice,pno
    PETERS f.s.   (D175)

DEUX APOLOGUES D'OSCAR WILDE see Capdevielle, Pierre

DEUX AVARES, LES: PLUS DE DÉPIT, PLUS DE TRISTESSE see Grétry, André Ernest Modeste

DEUX CHANSONS POPULAIRES CUBAINES see Nin-Culmell, Joaquin

DEUX FLUTES, LES see Beekhuis, Hanna

DEUX GRENADIERS, LES see Wagner, Richard

DEUX MELODIES POPULAIRES POLONAISES see Beers, Jacques

DEUX PIGIONS, LES see Gounod, Charles François

DEUX POEMES see Mul, Jan

DEUX POÉSIES DE K. BALMONT see Stravinsky, Igor

DEUX PSAUMES see Bloch, Ernest

DEUX PSAUMES ET TROIS CHANSONS see Huygens, Constantin

DEUX RONDEAUX, PRIS DANS LE RECUEIL "TENDRE ET DANGEREUX" see Tal, Marjo

DEUXIEME CANTATE see Martin, Frederick

DEVCIC, NATKO (1914-)
  Konzert
    T solo,2perc,marimba/vibra,Ondes Martenot,4vln,4vla [16'] sc
    BREITKOPF-W BG 815 f.s.   (D176)

DEVOTION TO THE SMALL see Powell, Kit

DEVRIES, IVAN (1909-)
  Chanson De Chiquita, La
    girl solo,2gtr,2perc [3'] BILLAUDOT
                                 (D177)

  Cinq Rondeaux De Charles D'Orleans
    solo voice,fl,ob,English horn,trp, 3vla,2vcl,db,2harp [11']
    BILLAUDOT   (D178)

DEWY, DEWY DENS OF YARROW, THE see Haufrecht, Herbert

DEYR FE, DEYR FRENDAR see Tveitt, Geirr

D'HUMANAL FRAGMENT see Casablancas, Benet

DI CAPUA, EDUARDO (1864-1917)
  I' Te Vurria Vasà!
    [Fr] med-high solo,pno CLASSV 1304
                                 (D179)

  Maria, Marì
    med solo,pno CLASSV 1055   (D180)

  O Sole Mio
    [It/Eng] high solo,pno CLASSV 0944
                                 (D181)

    [It/Eng] low solo,pno CLASSV 1653
                                 (D182)

    [It/Eng] med solo,pno CLASSV 1311
                                 (D183)

DI PIU CUPI SENTIERI see Bianchini, Riccardo

DI SDEGNO TAL ORA S'ACCENDE see Benda, Georg Anton (Jiří Antonín)

DI TE!... see Tirindelli, Pier Adolfo

DIABELLI, ANTON (1781-1858)
  Philomele *CCUL
    solo voice,pno SCIEN 442 f.s.
    contains works by: Rossini, Weber, Bellini, Donizetti, and others   (D184)

  Philomele, Eine Sammlung *CCUL
    solo voice,gtr SCIEN 443 f.s.
    contains works by: Rossini, Donizetti, and others   (D185)

DIABLE DANS LA NUIT, LE see Hubeau, Jean

DIAGONAL LINE see Shimazu, Takehito

DIALOG, EIN see King, Harold C., Dialogue, A

DIALOGUE, A see King, Harold C.

DIALOGUES AND ENTERTAINMENTS see Kraft, William

DIALOGUES OF LOVERS see Lombardo, Robert M.

DIAMOND, DAVID (1915-)
  Don't Cry
    high solo,pno SCHIRM.G 50488489
                                 (D186)

  Hebrew Melodies
    med solo,pno sc PEER 60582-213
    $7.00   (D187)

DIAPHON see Beurle, Jürgen

DIAVOLO IN GIARDINO, IL see Mannino, Franco

DICHTERLIEBE, OP. 48 see Schumann, Robert (Alexander)

DICITE: PUSILLANIMES CONFORTAMINI, OP. 17 see Schlee, Thomas Daniel

DICKERSON, ROGER DONALD (1934-)
  New Orleans Concerto
    S solo,3(pic).3(English horn).3(bass clar).2. 4.3.3.1. timp,perc,strings,pno solo [25']
    PEER   (D188)

DID YOU CRY - ? see Brustad, Bjarne, Grät Du - ?

DIDONE ABBANDONATA: NON HA RAGIONE, INGRATO see Sarri, Domenico

DIDON'S MONOLOGUE see Berlioz, Hector (Louis), Troyens, Les: Je Vais Mourir!

DIE DEN MUND AUFHATTEN see Eisler, Hanns

DIE HARDEKENS see Visser, Peter

DIE VAN DE LIEFDE ZIJN GESTEKEN see Braal, Andries de

DIEMER, EMMA LOU (1927-)
  And I Saw A New Heaven And A New Earth
    med-high solo,trp,org/pno [6'45"]
    ARSIS   (D189)

  Create In Me A Clean Heart, O God
    med solo,org/pno [3'35"] ARSIS
                                 (D190)

  I Will Sing Of Your Steadfast Love
    high solo,org [4'25"] ARSIS (D191)

  Lute Songs On Renaissance
    S/T solo,pno SEESAW   (D192)

  Who Can Find A Virtuous Woman?
    med-high solo,org/pno [4'35"] ARSIS
                                 (D193)

DIEPENBROCK, ALPHONS (1862-1921)
  Poilus De L'Argonne, Les
    med solo,pno ALSBACH   (D194)

  Vin De La Revanche, Le
    med solo,pno ALSBACH   (D195)

DIES ILLAE see Madsen, Trygve

DIES IRAE see Masseus, Jan

DIEU VOUS GARD' see Warren, Betsy

DIG RÖRDE ALDRIG MÖRKRET see Jeppsson, Kerstin

DIGTERENS GRAVSKRIFT OVER SIG SELV see Karlsen, Kjell Mørk

DIJK, L. VAN
  Levend Water: Vijf Nieuwe Geestelijke Liederen
    ZENGERINK R.556   (D196)

DILLARD, DONALD E.
  Day Of A Child *song cycle
    T solo,wind quin [22'] (med diff)
    sc,pts DANE SV301   (D197)

  Face Of Beauty, The
    med-high solo/med-low solo,pno (med easy) DANE SV302   (D198)

  Go Down, Moses
    med-low solo,pno (med easy) DANE SV303   (D199)

  God-Child, The
    med-low solo/med-high solo,org (med easy) DANE SV304   (D200)

  Godly Woman, The
    med-high solo,org (med easy) DANE SV305   (D201)

  Lord's Prayer, The
    high solo&high solo,org (med easy) DANE SV306   (D202)

  Nails
    high solo,org (med diff) DANE SV307
                                 (D203)

  O Crucified Christ
    high solo,pno/org (med diff) DANE SV308   (D204)

  Peace Of Christ, The
    med-high solo,org (med easy) DANE SV309   (D205)

  Quiet Grandeur
    high solo,pno,2horn (med diff) DANE SV310   (D206)

DILLARD, DONALD E. (cont'd.)

Soliloquy Of A Silhouette *song
    cycle
    high solo,pno (med diff) DANE SV311
                                    (D207)

Testimony
    high solo,2vln,vla,2vcl,db (diff)
    sc,pts DANE SV213   (D208)

DILLON
Evening Rain
    PETERS 7246   (D209)

Roaring Flame
    PETERS 7249   (D210)

Time Lag Zero
    PETERS 7295   (D211)

Who Do You Love
    PETERS 7245   (D212)

DIMITRI: PÂLES ÉTOILES see Joncieres,
    Victorin de

DIN VEG see Fladmoe, Arvid

D'INDY, VINCENT
    see INDY, VINCENT D'

DING DONG BELL see Jeffreys, John

DINGEDING-VISAN see Wahlberg, Rune

DINORAH: OMBRA LEGGERA see Meyerbeer,
    Giacomo

DINORAH (PARDON DE PLOËRMEL): AH! MON
    REMORDS TE VENGE see Meyerbeer,
    Giacomo

DINORAH (PARDON DE PLOËRMEL): LE JOUR
    EST LEVÉ see Meyerbeer, Giacomo

DINORAH (PARDON DE PLOËRMEL): OMBRE
    LÉGÈRE see Meyerbeer, Giacomo

DIOMEDE see Walton, [Sir] William
    (Turner)

DIOTIMA see Bois, Rob du

DIRRIWACHTER, WIM (1937-   )
    Afvaart
        see Drie Liederen

    Drie Liederen
        Bar solo,pno DONEMUS f.s. [8']
        contains: Afvaart; Mist; Samen
                                    (D213)
    Mist
        see Drie Liederen

    Samen
        see Drie Liederen

DIRTY WORK see Nelson, Havelock

DISCOURS see Haubenstock-Ramati, Roman

DISILLUSIONMENT AT 10 O'CLOCK see
    Wyner, Yehudi

DISPA, ROBERT (1929-   )
    Door Onze Handen
        see Ode Aan Het Kind

    Gebed
        see Ode Aan Het Kind

    Kleine Mensen
        see Ode Aan Het Kind

    Ode Aan Het Kind
        B solo,fl,perc,2vln,vla,vcl,db
        DONEMUS f.s. [25']
        contains: Door Onze Handen;
        Gebed; Kleine Mensen; Wegwerp
        Kinderen   (D214)

    Wegwerp Kinderen
        see Ode Aan Het Kind

DISSONANCE, A see Borodin, Alexander
    Porfirievich

DISTANT PLACE, A see Leniado-Chira,
    Joseph

DISTANT SHORE II, THE see Carl, Robert

DIT EILAND see Broekman, Hans

DITIRAMBO see Rossi, D.

DITTERSDORF, KARL DITTERS VON
    (1739-1799)
    Aria No. 10
        see Rosalie

    Rosalie (Aria No. 10) (from Doktor
    Und Apotheker)
        solo voice,strings,hpsd [4'] CESKY
        HUD.   (D215)

DITTRICH, PAUL-HEINZ (1930-   )
    Vier Lieder *CC4U
        high solo,pno PETERS f.s.   (D216)

DITTY, A see Foote, Arthur

DIVAGAZIONI see Capuis, Matilde

DIVOKY CHMEL see Podést, Ludvík

DIVORNE, ANDRE
    Oraison Dominicale, L' *Commun
        solo voice,kbd HUGUENIN EB 121
                                    (D217)

DIWAN see Ruyneman, Daniel

DIX CHANSONS ENFANTINES see Grovlez,
    Gabriel (Marie)

DIX MÉLODIES see Saint-Saëns, Camille

DIX POESIES see Strohl, Rita

DIXON, HUGH
    Five Shakespeare Songs
        Mez solo,pno WAI-TE-ATA 15   (D218)

DJUPT TILL VILA PÅ EN STJÄRNA see
    Freudenthal, Otto

DO AND LIVE see Clarke, Henry Leland

DO, L'ENFANT DO... see Escher, Rudolf
    George

DO NOT GO, MY LOVE see Hageman, Richard

DO NOT LET ME DIE see Selmer, Johan
    Peter, La Meg Ei Dø

DOBRÚ NOC see Dvorák, Antonín

DOCE CANCIONES see Moretti see Puig, G.

DOCE MADRIGALS see Mestres, Apeles

DØD MANN RIDER see Madsen, Trygve

DØDE, DE see Fladmoe, Arvid

DØDE BLOMAR see Bergh, Sverre

DODE DUIVEN VALLEN OM MIJ HEEN see
    Sweeden, Hans Van

DØDE FUGLER see Lunde, Ivar

DØDEN MÅ VIKE see Baden, Conrad

DODICI LIRICHE see Capuis, Matilde

DOE, THE see Hoiby, Lee

DOGS see Heilner, Irwin

DOGYO NININ see Munakata, Kazu

DÖHL, FRIEDHELM (1936-   )
    Fragment "Sybille"
        Bar solo,fl,vla,vcl,pno [10']
        BREITKÖPF-W f.s.   (D219)

    Medea
        S solo,1.0.1.0. 0.1.1.0. 2perc,pno,
        vcl,db [17'] BREITKÖPF-W f.s.
                                    (D220)

DOHNÁNYI, ERNST VON (1877-1960)
    Im Lebenslenz, Op. 16
        [Ger/Eng] (6 poems by W.C. Gomoll)
        RECITAL 328   (D221)

    Sechs Gedichte, Op. 14
        (Heindl, Victor) low solo DOBLINGER
        08 664   (D222)
        (Heindl, Victor) high solo
        DOBLINGER 08 665   (D223)

DOI, YOSHIYUKI (1944-   )
    Mafuyu No Katami Ni
        Mez solo,pno [8'] JAPAN   (D224)

    Shoto
        S solo,pno [8'] JAPAN   (D225)

DÖKKA ROS, HIN see Halldorsson, Skuli

DOKOKA DE see Arashino, Hideo

DOLÇ CAUTIVERI see Massana, A.

DOLCE FAR NIENTE see Danielsson, Harry

DOLCE VIAGGIO see Albanese, Guido

DOLOR see Aird, Donald

DOLSI DALOM see Albertsen, Per Hjort

DOMANDA E RISPOSTE see Mortari,
    Virgilio

DOMINUS REGIT ME see Beers, Jacques

DON CARLO: DORMIRÒ SOL NEL MANTO MIO
    REGAL see Verdi, Giuseppe

DON CARLO: FONTAINEBLEAU! see Verdi,
    Giuseppe

DON CARLO: O DON FATALE see Verdi,
    Giuseppe

DON CARLO: PER ME GIUNTO see Verdi,
    Giuseppe

DON GIOVANNI: BATTI BATTI see Mozart,
    Wolfgang Amadeus

DON GIOVANNI: BATTI, BATTI O BEL
    MASETTO see Mozart, Wolfgang
    Amadeus

DON GIOVANNI: CRUDELE!...NON MI DIR see
    Mozart, Wolfgang Amadeus

DON GIOVANNI: DALLA SUA PACE see
    Mozart, Wolfgang Amadeus

DON GIOVANNI: DEH VIENI ALLA FINESTRA
    see Mozart, Wolfgang Amadeus

DON GIOVANNI: IL MIO TESORO see Mozart,
    Wolfgang Amadeus

DON GIOVANNI: MADAMINA! IL CATALOGO see
    Mozart, Wolfgang Amadeus

DON GIOVANNI: MADAMINA! IL CATALOGO È
    QUESTO see Mozart, Wolfgang Amadeus

DON GIOVANNI: NON MI DIR see Mozart,
    Wolfgang Amadeus

DON GIOVANNI: VEDRAI, CARINO, SE SEI
    BUONINO see Mozart, Wolfgang
    Amadeus

DON JUAN'S SERENADE see Tchaikovsky,
    Piotr Ilyich

DON PASQUALE: BELLA SICCOME UN ANGELO
    see Donizetti, Gaetano

DON PASQUALE: COM' È GENTIL see
    Donizetti, Gaetano

DON PASQUALE: SO ANCH'IO LA VIRTÙ
    MAGICA see Donizetti, Gaetano

DON SEBASTIANO: DESERTO IN TERRA see
    Donizetti, Gaetano

DON SEBASTIANO: O LISBONA, ALFIN TI
    MIRO see Donizetti, Gaetano

DON SEBASTIANO: TERRA ADORATA see
    Donizetti, Gaetano

DONA D'AIGUA, LA see Mestres, Apeles

DONA NOBIS PACEM see Friedman, Stanley

DONALDSON, WALTER (1893-1947)
    Whoopee
        solo voice SCHIRM.G 50251820 (D226)

DONAUDY, STEFANO (1879-1925)
    Arie Nello Stile Antico, 36, Vol. 1
    *CC12U
        [It] solo voice RICORDI-IT R117220
                                    (D227)
    Arie Nello Stile Antico, 36, Vol. 2
    *CC12U
        [It] solo voice RICORDI-IT R117223
                                    (D228)
    Arie Nello Stile Antico, 36, Vol. 3
    *CC12U
        [It] solo voice RICORDI-IT R118842
                                    (D229)

DONDE LIETA see Puccini, Giacomo

DONIZETTI, GAETANO (1797-1848)
    Anna Bolena: Ah! Parea Che Par
    Incanto
        Mez solo,pno CLASSV 1582   (D230)

    Anna Bolena: Deh! Non Voler
    Costringere
        Mez solo,pno CLASSV 1583   (D231)

    Aria De La Locura
        see Lucia Di Lammermoor: Ardo Ne
        Gl' Incensi

    Don Pasquale: Bella Siccome Un Angelo
        Bar solo,pno CLASSV 1275   (D232)

    Don Pasquale: Com' È Gentil
        T solo,pno CLASSV 0549   (D233)

    Don Pasquale: So Anch'io La Virtù
    Magica
        S solo,pno CLASSV 0955   (D234)

    Don Sebastiano: Deserto In Terra
        [It/Eng] T solo,pno CLASSV 1214
                                    (D235)
    Don Sebastiano: O Lisbona, Alfin Ti
    Miro
        Bar solo,pno CLASSV 1227   (D236)

DONIZETTI, GAETANO (cont'd.)

Don Sebastiano: Terra Adorata
  Mez solo,pno CLASSV 1587   (D237)

Duca D'Alba, Il: Angelo Casto E Bel
  T solo,pno CLASSV 0962   (D238)

Elisir D'Amour: Una Furtiva Lagrima
  T solo,pno BOIL B.1623   (D239)

Elizir D'Amore, L': Una Furtiva
  Lagrima
  T solo,pno CLASSV 0589   (D240)

Favorita, La: A Tanto Amor
  B solo,pno CLASSV 1552   (D241)

Favorita, La: O Mio Fernando
  Mez solo,pno CLASSV 1589   (D242)
  S/Mez solo,pno BOIL B.1872   (D243)

Favorita, La: Spirito Gentil
  T solo,pno CLASSV 1124   (D244)

Favorita, La: Spiritto Gentil
  T solo,pno BOIL B.1607   (D245)

Favorita, La: Una Vergine
  T solo,pno BOIL B.1606   (D246)

Favorita, La: Una Vergine, Un Angel
  Di Dio
  T solo,pno CLASSV 0927   (D247)

Favorita, La: Vien, Leonora
  Bar solo,pno CLASSV 0587   (D248)

Favorite, La: Pour Tant D'amour
  [Fr] B solo RECITAL 2231   (D249)

Figlia Del Reggimento, La: Convien
  Partir
  [It] S solo,pno CLASSV 1168   (D250)
  S solo,pno BOIL B.1690   (D251)

Fille Du Regiment: Chacun Le Sait
  [Fr] S solo,pno CLASSV 0446   (D252)

Fille Du Regiment: Il Faut Partir
  [Fr] S solo,pno (not original key)
    CLASSV 1373   (D253)
  [Fr] S solo,pno (original key)
    CLASSV 1374   (D254)

Linda Di Chamounix: Se Tanto In Ira
  Agli Uomini
  T solo,pno CLASSV 1757   (D255)

Lucia Di Lammermoor: Ardo Ne Gl'
  Incensi
  "Aria De La Locura" S solo,pno BOIL
    B.1913   (D256)

Lucia Di Lammermoor: Cruda, Funesta
  Smania
  Bar solo,pno CLASSV 1640   (D257)

Lucia Di Lammermoor: Mad Scene
  S solo,pno CLASSV 0503   (D258)

Lucia Di Lammermoor: Regnava Nel
  Silenzio
  S solo,pno BOIL B.1900   (D259)

Lucia Di Lammermoor: Tu Che A Dio
  Spiegasti
  T solo,pno BOIL B.1987   (D260)

Lucrezia Borgia: Com' È Bello (With
  Cabaletta)
  S solo,pno CLASSV 0392   (D261)

Lucrezia Borgia: Il Segreto
  Mez solo,pno CLASSV 0630   (D262)

Lucrezia Borgia: Vieni! La Mia
  Vendetta
  B solo,pno CLASSV 1559   (D263)

Maria Di Rohan: Ah! Forse, ...Alma
  Soave E Cara
  [It/Ger] T solo,pno CLASSV 1758
                                (D264)

Maria Di Rohan: Per Non Istare In
  Ozio
  Mez solo,pno CLASSV 1593   (D265)

Maria Di Rudenz: Ah! Non Avea Più
  Lagrime
  Bar solo,pno CLASSV 1642   (D266)

Poliuto: Di Tua Beltade Immagine
  Bar solo,pno CLASSV 0588   (D267)

Poliuto: D'un' Alma Troppo Fervida
  T solo,pno CLASSV 0924   (D268)

Rataplan, The (from La Figlia Del
  Reggimento)
  (Glover, C.W.) SCIEN 465   (D269)

Song Of The Regiment, The (from La
  Figlia Del Reggimento)
  S solo,pno SCIEN 464   (D270)

DONIZETTI, GAETANO (cont'd.)

Zingara, La
  [It/Eng] med solo,pno CLASSV 0909
                                (D271)
  [It/Eng] S solo,pno CLASSV 0863
                                (D272)

DONNE, DONNE, CHI VI CREDE see Rejcha,
  Antonin

DONNE L'AMORE (MAYER) see Four Italian
  Melodies

DONS DE IACQUET A ISABEAU, LES see
  Koumans, Rudolf

DON'T CEÄRE see Carpenter, John Alden

DON'T CRY see Diamond, David

DON'T LET THAT HORSE see Blank, Allan

DON'T LIGHT THE LAMP! see Arensky,
  Anton Stepanovich

DON'T MAKE A FOOL OF ME see De
  Filippis, C.

DONZELLA MALALTA, LA see Mestres,
  Apeles

DOODENMARSCH see King, Harold C.

DOODLOPENDE WEG see Veldhuis, Jacob ter

DOOR DE BOMEN STAART see Ruiter, Wim de

DOOR ONZE HANDEN see Dispa, Robert

DOOR STANDING OPEN, THE see Wallach,
  Joelle

DOOVE PIJNEN SIDDERSEINEN VER VAN
  ONGEKENDE GRENZEN see Badings, Henk

DOPISY PSANE MAJEM see Kubik, Ladislav

DOPPELBAUER, JOSEF FRIEDRICH
  (1918-1989)
  Drei Geistliche Gesänge Nach Alten
  Texten *CC3U
  med solo,org DOBLINGER 08 873 f.s.
                                (D273)

DØRA GÅR OPP see Sønstevold, Gunnar

DORET, GUSTAVE (1866-1943)
  Airs Et Chansons Couleur Du Temps
  med solo,pno CLASSV C020   (D274)

DORFF, DANIEL JAY (1956-   )
  Ave Maria
  [Lat] Mez solo,pno/org (med easy)
    PRESSER 111-40104 $2.50   (D275)
  [Lat] Mez solo,fl,ob,2clar,glock
    (med easy) PRESSER 111-40104P
    $7.50   (D276)

DORIA see Gerber, Steven R.

DORMI FANCIULLO see Annovazzi,
  Napoleone

DORMI JESU DULCISSIME see Esterhazy,
  [Prince] Pal

D'ORSAY, M.L.
  Crepuscule
  solo voice,pno BOIL B.0908   (D277)

  Nuit Bleu
  solo voice,pno BOIL B.0909   (D278)

DORUMSGAARD, ARNE (1921-   )
  Alvorlige Sanger
  [Norw] solo voice,pno NORGE f.s.
    contains: Barn, Et; I Ormegil;
    Salme   (D279)

  Barn, Et
  see Alvorlige Sanger

  Fire Sanger Med Orkester *Op.17
  [Swed] solo voice,2.2(English
    horn).2.2. 4.2.3.0. perc,harp,
    strings NORGE f.s.
    contains: Göm Mig, Göm Mig;
    Jorden Är Människans Hem; Var
    Inte Rädd För Mörkret; Var
    Stilla, Hjärta   (D280)

  Göm Mig, Göm Mig
  see Fire Sanger Med Orkester

  I Ormegil
  see Alvorlige Sanger

  Jorden Är Människans Hem
  see Fire Sanger Med Orkester

  Salme
  see Alvorlige Sanger

  Var Inte Rädd För Mörket
  see Fire Sanger Med Orkester

DORUMSGAARD, ARNE (cont'd.)

  Var Stilla, Hjärta
  see Fire Sanger Med Orkester

DOS MAS DOS see Ansink, Caroline

DOS POEMAS DE JUAN LARREA see Pablo,
  Luis de

DOSHCHYK see Shut, Wasyl

DOUBT see Glinka, Mikhail Ivanovich

DOUW, ANDRE (1951-   )
  Herrick Songs
  B/Bar solo,2vln,vla,vcl DONEMUS
    f.s. [16']
    contains: Lilly In A Christal,
    The; On Himselfe; To Musique,
    To Becalme His Fever; Upon The
    Troublesome Times; Women
    Uselesse - An Hymne To Love
                                (D281)

  Lilly In A Christal, The
  see Herrick Songs

  On Himselfe
  see Herrick Songs

  To Musique, To Becalme His Fever
  see Herrick Songs

  Upon The Troublesome Times
  see Herrick Songs

  Women Uselesse - An Hymne To Love
  see Herrick Songs

DOUZE MELODIES see Roussel, Albert
  (Charles Paul)

DOUZE MÉLODIES (1ER RECUEIL) see
  Jaques-Dalcroze, Émile

DOUZE MÉLODIES, OP. 22 see Paderewski,
  Ignace Jan

DOWLAND
  English Lute Songs
  solo voice,gtr/lute (CC12U) TECLA
    TE038   (D282)

DOWLAND, JOHN (1562-1626)
  Burst Forth My Tears
  S solo,lute sc KING'S   (D283)

  Fine Knacks For Ladies
  high solo,pno CLASSV 1759   (D284)

DOWN BY THE SALLY GARDENS see Hughes,
  Herbert

DOWNES, ANDREW (1950-   )
  Casterbridge Fair *Op.1, song cycle
  Mez/Bar solo,pno [11'] (texts by
    Thomas Hardy) LYNWD   (D285)

  Death Of Goliath, The *Op.17, cant
  SMezBar/SBar&countertenor,pno [20']
    LYNWD   (D286)

  Dreamland *Op.42
  S solo,soprano sax,pno [20'] (text
    by Edgar Allen Poe) LYNWD   (D287)

  Lost Love *Op.15, song cycle
  S solo,T rec/fl,vla da gamba/vcl,
    hpsd/pno [15'] (texts by Thomas
    Hardy) LYNWD   (D288)

  Old Love's Domain *Op.29, song cycle
  T solo,pno [21'] (texts by Thomas
    Hardy) LYNWD   (D289)

  Songs From Spoon River *Op.39, song
  cycle
  Mez solo,pno [22'] (texts by Edgar
    Lee Masters) LYNWD   (D290)

DOWNSTREAM see Kennaway, Lamont

DOWNTOWN BLUES FOR UPTOWN see Gottlieb,
  Jack S.

DOZEN DUETS FOR EVERYONE, EVERYWHERE, A
  *CC12U
  (Van Camp, Leonard) med solo&med
    solo,pno LAUDA LA0128B accomp tape
    available   (D291)

DRAG INN see Baden, Conrad

DRAGONFLIES, OP. 53 see Rimsky-
  Korsakov, Nikolai

DRAGONFLY AND THE ANT, THE see
  Shostakovich, Dmitri

DRAGSTRA, WILLEM
  Vier Herbstlieder
  solo voice,pno (texts by Rainer
    Maria Rilke) SODEN   (D292)

DRAKEFORD, RICHARD
Three Nonsense Songs *CC3U
Bar solo NOVELLO 25 2730 f.s.
(D293)

DRAMATISKE SANGER, OP. 53A see Bull,
Edvard Hagerup

DRÄNGEN IST IN MEINEM HERZEN, EIN see
Marx, Joseph

DRAUM see Kverndokk, Gisle

DRAUMALANDID see Einarsson, Sigfus

DRAUMSJON see Isolfsson, Pall

DREAM, A see Balakirev, Mily
Alexeyevich see Balakirev, Mily
Alexeyevich, Rêve, Un see Grieg,
Edvard Hagerup

DREAM, THE see Shut, Wasyl, Son

DREAM DIALOGUE see Steiner, Gitta Hana

DREAM ISLAND see Tsukatani, Akihiro

DREAM KEEPER, THE see Raphling, Sam

DREAM OF CHRISTOPHENE, THE see Rouse,
Christopher

DREAM OF THE MORNING SKY see Kernis,
Aaron Jay

DREAM SONGS see Bennett, Richard Rodney

DREAM WITH ME see Bernstein, Leonard

DREAM WITHIN A DREAM, A see Callaway,
Ann see Loeffler, Charles Martin
see Lovendusky, James

DREAMER, THE see Dahl, Vivian,
Drømmeren

DREAMLAND see Downes, Andrew

DREAMS see Parris, Robert

DREAMS ALONE: SIX SONGS see Golub,
Peter

DREAMS, YELLOW LIONS see Harris, Ross

DREAMSONG see Halldorsson, Skuli

DREI ABENDLIEDER see Gerlach, Günter

DREI BALLADEN see Bijvanck, Henk

DREI BALLADEN see Bijvanck, Henk

DREI BALLADEN, OP. 129 see Lowe, Karl

DREI CHINESISCHE LIEDER see Verhaar,
Ary

DREI DUETTE FÜR ZWEI SOPRAN-STIMMEN see
Kücken, Friedrich Wilhelm

DREI FRAUENLIEDER, OP. 5 see Thuille,
Ludwig (Wilhelm Andreas Maria)

DREI GEDICHTE IM VOLKSTON, OP. 26 see
Moszkowski, Moritz

DREI GEDICHTE VON HANS MAGNUS
ENZENSBERGER see Lechner, Konrad

DREI GEISHA LIEDER see Verhaar, Ary

DREI GEISTLICHE GESÄNGE NACH ALTEN
TEXTEN see Doppelbauer, Josef
Friedrich

DREI GEISTLICHE KONZERTE ZUR
WEIHNACHTSZEIT see Loth, Urban

DREI GEISTLICHE LIEDER see Zimmermann,
Bernd Alois

DREI GEISTLICHE LIEDER see Lohmann,
Heinz

DREI GESÄNGE see Lichey, Reinhold

DREI GESÄNGE, OP. 84 see Mendelssohn-
Bartholdy, Felix

DREI GOETHE-LIEDER see David, Thomas
Christian

DREI HYMNEN VON WALT WHITMAN see
Hindemith, Paul

DREI KINDERLIEDER see Eisler, Hanns

DREI KIRCHENARIEN FÜR SOPRAN see
Galuppi, Baldassare

DREI KLEINE GEISTLICHE KONZERTE see
Schütz, Heinrich

DREI LAUB AUF EINER LINDEN see Simon,
Hermann

DREI LIEDER see Metsk, Juro see
Mizokami, Hideo see Nobre, Marlos
see Orland, Henry see Prado, Ameida
see Schlemm, Gustav Adolf see
Steuermann, Edward

DREI LIEDER see Giltay, Berend

DREI LIEDER see Zimmerman, S.A.

DREI LIEDER AUF GEDICHTE VON JANOS
PILINSZKY see Kurtag, György

DREI LIEDER DES THURMWÄCHTERS LYNCEUS
see Loewe, Carl Gottfried

DREI LIEDER NACH GEDICHTEN VON ARNOLD
KRIEGER see Korn, Peter Jona, Boten
Des Herbstes

DREI LIEDER, OP. 1 see Lowenstamm,
Franz Jos.

DREI LIEDER, OP. 3 see Riedel, Hermann

DREI LIEDER, OP. 10 see Schlick, E.

DREI LIEDER, OP. 12 see Medtner,
Nikolai Karlovich

DREI LIEDER ÜBER DEN SCHNEE see Henze,
Hans Werner

DREI NACHTSTÜCKE see Muller-Hornbach,
Gerhard

DREI NEUGRIECHISCHE GEDICHTE, OP. 50
see Dvořák, Antonín

DREI PERSISCHE LIEDER see Ruyneman,
Daniel

DREI PINTOS, DIE: EIN MÄDCHEN VERLOREN
see Weber, Carl Maria von

DREI ROMANTISCHE LIEDER see Roos,
Robert de

DREI SCHUBERT-LIEDER (NACH GEDICHTEN
VON GOETHE) see Schubert, Franz
(Peter)

DREI SONETTE MICHELANGELOS, OP. 5 see
Schelb, Josef

DREI SONGS see Lason, Aleksander

DREI SPATZEN, DIE see Lothar, Mark

DREI TRAURIGE TÄNZE see Bois, Rob du

DREI VAGANTEN LIEDER see Verhaar, Ary

DREI VOLKSLIEDER see Weegenhuise, Johan

DREI WEIHNACHTSLIEDER see Humperdinck,
Engelbert

DREI ZIGEUNER see Liszt, Franz

DREI ZWEISTIMMIGE LIEDER, OP. 77 see
Mendelssohn-Bartholdy, Felix

DREIZEHN LIEDER, OP. 2 see Zemlinsky,
Alexander von

DRESDEN, SEM (1881-1957)
Canto Spianato
see Four Vocalises

Fiorette
see Four Vocalises

Four Vocalises
Mez solo,fl,clar,bsn,perc,pno,vln,
vla DONEMUS f.s. [10']
contains: Canto Spianato;
Fiorette; Portamento; Staccato
(D294)

Portamento
see Four Vocalises

Staccato
see Four Vocalises

DRESSEL, ERWIN (1909-   )
Tierlieder Op. 39
solo voice,pno RIES   (D295)

DREW, JAMES M. (1929-   )
Lute In The Attic
solo voice,gong,vcl,clar,fl PRESSER
111-40118   (D296)

Songs Of Death And Bluelight Dancing
solo voice,pno PRESSER 111-40129
(D297)

DREY THRAENEN, DIE see Zimmerman, S.A.

DRICK, OP. 30, NO. 2 see Jordan, Sverre

DRIE A. ROLAND HOLST-LIEDEREN see
Broekman, Hans

DRIE ACHTERBERG-LIEDEREN see Broekman,
Hans

DRIE ARABESKEN see Maessen, Antoon

DRIE CYNISCHE LIEDEREN see Bremer,
Jetse

DRIE JOODSE LIEDEREN see Bunge, Sas

DRIE KERSTLIEDEREN see Visser, Peter

DRIE KINDERLIEDEREN, UIT DE
"SVENDBORGER GEDICHTE" see Delnooz,
Henri

DRIE KLEINE LIEDEREN see Ehlen,
Margriet

DRIE LIEDER VOOR ALT EN PIANO see
Mengelberg, Karel

DRIE LIEDEREN see Badings, Henk

DRIE LIEDEREN see Beekhuis, Hanna

DRIE LIEDEREN see Beyerman-Walraven,
Jeanne

DRIE LIEDEREN see Dirriwachter, Wim

DRIE LIEDEREN see Koetsier, Jan

DRIE LIEDEREN see Mesritz van
Velthuysen, Anny

DRIE LIEDEREN see Vliet, Henk van der

DRIE LIEDEREN see Vries Robbe, Willem
de

DRIE LIEDEREN see Dekker, Dirk

DRIE LIEDEREN, OP. 30 see Brandse, Wim

DRIE LIEDEREN, OP. 55 see Orthel, Leon

DRIE LIEDEREN OP TEKSTEN VAN MARTIN
BOOT see Ehlen, Margriet

DRIE LIEDEREN UIT "LENTEMAAN" see
Badings, Henk

DRIE LUCEBERT LIEDEREN see Voorn, Joop

DRIE MEILIEDEREN see Maessen, Antoon

DRIE MIDDELEEUWSE LIEDEREN see
Weegenhuise, Johan

DRIE NACHTLIEDEREN see Mulder, Herman

DRIE OUD-NEDERLANDSE LIEDEREN see
Badings, Henk

DRIE POEMES DE JULES SUPERVIELLE see
Bunge, Sas

DRIE ROMANTISCHE LIEDEREN see
Andriessen, Hendrik

DRIE SHAKESPEARE-LIEDEREN, UIT
"DRIEKONINGENAVOND" see Frid, Geza

DRIE SPAANSE VOLKSLIEDEREN see Bunge,
Sas

DRIE VROMAN LIEDEREN see Voorn, Joop

DRIGO, RICCARDO (1846-1930)
Venetian Serenade
[Eng/It] med-high solo,pno CLASSV
0876   (D298)

DRING, MADELEINE
Four Night Songs
S solo,pno CAMBRIA CP504 $6.25
contains: Frosty Night; Holding
The Night; Separation; Through
The Centuries   (D299)

Frosty Night
see Four Night Songs

Holding The Night
see Four Night Songs

Separation
see Four Night Songs

Through The Centuries
see Four Night Songs

DRINKEBROER OP WEG NAAR HUIS see Braal,
Andries de

DRINKING-SONG see Mascagni, Pietro,
Cavalleria Rusticana: Brindisi see
Verdi, Giuseppe, Traviata, La:
Brindisi (Libiam Ne Lieti)

DRÖM see Ehlen, Margriet

DRØMMEREN see Dahl, Vivian

DRONNING BERTILLAS VUGGEVISE see
Jordan, Sverre

DRONNINGENS KLAGE OG BØNN see Simonsen,
Melvin

DROOM see Voorn, Joop

DRUCKMAN, JACOB RAPHAEL (1928-   )
Nor Spell
Mez solo,English horn BOOSEY
VAB02787   (D300)

DRUM-TAPS: THREE PATRIOTIC POEMS see
Gerber, Steven R.

DRUMS OF WAR, THE see Weigl, [Mrs.]
Vally

DRUMTAPS see Moss, Lawrence Kenneth

DRYKKJUVISA see Halldorsson, Skuli

DU BIST DIE RUH see Schubert, Franz
(Peter)

DU BIST EIN FALTBUCH UND EIN FLÜGEL see
Evensen, Bernt Kasberg

DU BIST WIE EINE BLUME see Chadwick,
George Whitefield see Weegenhuise,
Johan

DU BLANC LE JOUR SON ESPACE see
Fenelon, Philippe

DU BOIS, ROB
see BOIS, ROB DU

DU CLAIR AU SOMBRE see Nigg, Serge

DU DAG MED RO OG KVILE see Nystedt,
Knut

DU FRAGST, WARUM ICH LIEBE? see Riedel,
Hermann

DU GIR see Fongaard, Bjørn

DU INNIGKEIT IM DÄMMERWALT see Badings,
Henk

DU LIEBST MICH NICHT see Schubert,
Franz (Peter)

DU SKA ITTE TRØ I GRASET see Nystedt,
Knut see Volle, Bjarne

DU SOIR see Vermeulen, Matthijs

DU SOM TENDRA SOL OG STJERNE see Egge,
Klaus

DU STRIDER TRØYT see Johnsen, Hallvard

DU SUNDAGSKVELD see Johnsen, Hallvard

DU VESLE BEKK PÅ VILLAN MO see Jordan,
Sverre

DU VISE MÄNNEN see Jordan, Sverre

DU WUNDERHOLDE MAID see Kücken,
Friedrich Wilhelm

DUALIS: LIEDERBUCH NACH TEXTEN VON
PABLO NERUDA UND FERNANDO PESSAO
see Schaathun, Asbjørn

DUBOIS, THEODORE (1837-1924)
Chansons De Marjolie
[Fr] high solo RECITAL 254   (D301)

Six Melodies
[Fr] high solo RECITAL 255   (D302)

DUCA D'ALBA, IL: ANGELO CASTO E BEL see
Donizetti, Gaetano

DUCKWEED POOL see Hekster, Walter

DUCLOS, PIERRE (1929-1974)
Religieuse Portugaise, La
S solo,1.1.1.1. 1.1.1.0. 2perc,
timp,gtr,harp,cel,pno,strings
[60'] BILLAUDOT   (D303)

DUE ARIE see Milella, Donato see
Tutino, Marco

DUE ARIE see De Filippis, C.

DUE CANTI see Hazon, Roberto

DUE CANTI see Casella, Alfredo

DUE CANTI ANTICHI see Tutino, Marco

DUE FOSCARI, I: CABALETTA DI JACOPO see
Verdi, Giuseppe

DUE FOSCARI: DAL PIÙ REMOTO ESILIO see
Verdi, Giuseppe

DUE RIME D'AMORE see Hazon, Roberto

DUE TARLI, I: IL TARLO DELLA VECCHIA
BIBLIOTECA see Zandonai, Riccardo

DUE VOCALIZZI see Gelalian, Boghos

DUEL see Miyoshi, Akira

DUERMETE, NINO see Rodrigo, Joaquín

DUET FOR A DUCK AND A CANARY see
Revueltas, Silvestre, Duo Para Pato
Y Canario

DUET IN E-FLAT see Ryba, Jan Jakub
Simon, Duetto In Mi-Flat

DUET "RAISE THE GLASS", A see
Kobayashi, Arata

DUETS see Hegdal, Magne

DUETTE, OP. 15 see Holstein, Jean-Paul

DUETTO ACCADEMICO IN MI BEM. MAGGIORE
see Boccherini, Luigi

DUETTO E INTERMEZZO see Kurachi,
Tatsuya

DUETTO IN MI-FLAT see Ryba, Jan Jakub
Simon

DUFAY, GUILLAUME (ca. 1400-1474)
Huit Chansons
(Ravier, C.) solo voice,rec,
krummhorn, viol, hurdy-gurdy
BILLAUDOT   (D304)

DUFT VON LICHT, EIN see Schmidt, Lorenz

DUKE
Songs, Vol. 1
high solo,pno SOUTHERN B347   (D305)

Songs, Vol. 2
med solo,pno SOUTHERN B348   (D306)

Songs, Vol. 3
med solo&high solo,pno SOUTHERN
B365   (D307)

Three Songs For High Voice (composed
with Nickson)
solo voice,pno SOUTHERN V078 (D308)

Three Songs For Tenor (composed with
Nickson)
solo voice,pno SOUTHERN V077 (D309)

Two Songs For Baritone (composed with
Nickson)
Bar solo,pno SOUTHERN V079   (D310)

Wild Swans
solo voice,pno SOUTHERN V072 (D311)

DUKE, JOHN WOODS (1899-1984)
Songs Of John Duke *CCUL
SCHIRM.G f.s. high solo,pno
50488485; low solo,pno 50488486
                              (D312)

DULCE CAUTIVERIO see Massana, A., Dolç
Cautiveri

DULCES CANTILENAE see Novak

DUMA see Kálik, Vaclav

DUMA PRO SAVU TCHALOHO see Shut, Wasyl

D'UN CHANT PERDU see Bon, Andre

D'UN COEUR QUI T'AIME see Gounod,
Charles François

D'UN VANNEUR DE BLE AUX VENTS see
Koumans, Rudolf

DUNA see McGill, Josephine

DUNBAR SONGS see Adams, Leslie

DUNCAN, CHESTER
Funeral Blues
LESLIE   (D313)

Longing
S solo LESLIE 7069   (D314)

DÜNEN LICHSTRAHL II see Koetsier, Jan

DUNHILL, THOMAS FREDERICK (1877-1946)
Cloths Of Heaven, The
high solo,pno (text by Yeats)
CLASSV 0738   (D315)
med solo,pno (text by Yeats) CLASSV
0737   (D316)

DUNKLE NACHT DER SEELE, DIE see Valen,
Fartein, Noche Oscura Del Alme, La

DUO see MacBride, David Huston

DUO FROM "ERNESTINE" see Saint-Georges,
Joseph Boulogne de

DUO PARA PATO Y CANARIO see Revueltas,
Silvestre

DUO PER SOPRANO E VIOLINO see
Mortensen, Finn

DUPARC, HENRI (1848-1933)
Au Pays Où Se Fait La Guerre
Mez solo,pno CLASSV 0395   (D317)

Aurore
solo voice,4gtr (available in high,
medium, or low voice) JELLO
FGV101   (D318)

Chanson Triste (First Version)
high solo,pno CLASSV 1666   (D319)

Extase
solo voice,4gtr (available in high,
medium, or low voice) JELLO
FGV100   (D320)

Fuite, La
ST soli,pno CLASSV 0409   (D321)

Galop
"Galop, Le" Bar solo,pno CLASSV
0407   (D322)

Galop, Le
see Galop

Romance De Mignon
S solo,pno CLASSV 0405   (D323)

Sérénade
"Si J'étais" Bar solo,pno CLASSV
0401   (D324)

Si J'étais
see Sérénade

DUPONT, AUGUSTE (1827-1890)
Poeme D'amour, Op. 54
[Fr] med-high solo RECITAL 256
                              (D325)

DUPONT, GABRIEL (1878-1914)
Poemes D'Automne
[Fr] med-high solo RECITAL 257
                              (D326)

DUPRE, MARCEL (1886-1971)
Ave Maria *Op.9,No.2
solo voice LEDUC f.s.   (D327)

DURCH DIE GARTEN see Weegenhuise, Johan

DURCH EINSAMKEITEN see Marx, Joseph

DURCH WINTER GEHT see Freudenthal, Otto

DUTACQ, AMEDEE (1852- ?)
Six Rondels
[Fr] high solo (not available
outside U.S.A.) RECITAL 354
                              (D328)

DVE PISNE see Martinu, Bohuslav (Jan)
see Saudek, Vojtech

DVE ROZMARNE BALADY see Gregor, Cestmír

DVE SKOTSKE PISNE see Beethoven, Ludwig
van

DVORÁCEK, JIRÍ (1928-   )
Prstynek Z Travy
[Czech/Ger] S solo,pno PANTON 889
                              (D329)

Take Mnou Zije Amerika!
[Czech/Ger/Eng] female solo&male
solo,trp,pno PANTON 97   (D330)

DVORÁK, ANTONÍN (1841-1904)
Ach, Není
see Four Songs, Op. 73

Acht Liebeslieder, Op. 83
[Czech/Ger/Eng] RECITAL 323   (D331)

Ave Maria
see Vier Geistliche Stücke Für
Einzelstimme Und Orgel

Ave Maris Stella
see Vier Geistliche Stücke Für
Einzelstimme Und Orgel

Balada. Sirotek (Das Waisenkind), Op.
5
[Czech/Ger] RECITAL 312   (D332)

Dobrú Noc
see Four Songs, Op. 73

Drei Neugriechische Gedichte, Op. 50
[Czech/Ger] RECITAL 319   (D333)
[Ger/Czech] med solo,pno CLASSV
1398   (D334)

DVORÁK, ANTONÍN (cont'd.)

Ej
see Four Songs, Op. 73

Four Songs, Op. 73
med-high solo,pno CLASSV 1225 f.s.
contains: Ach, Není; Dobrú Noc;
Ej; Zalo Dievca (D335)

God Is My Shepherd *Op.99,No.4
[Eng] med-high solo,pno CLASSV 1250
(D336)

Hymnus Ad Laudes In Festo S.S.
Trinitatis
see Vier Geistliche Stücke Für
Einzelstimme Und Orgel

Klänge Aus Mähren, Op. 32
[Ger/Eng] SA soli RECITAL 318 (D337)

O Sanctissima
see Vier Geistliche Stücke Für
Einzelstimme Und Orgel

Rusalka: Arie Des Wassermanns
[Ger/Czech] B solo,pno CLASSV 0765
(D338)

Rusalka's Song To The Moon
[Ger/Czech] S solo,pno CLASSV 0333
(D339)

Vecerni Pisne, Op. 31
[Czech] RECITAL 317 (D340)

Vier Duette, Op. 20
[Ger/Eng] ST soli RECITAL 316 f.s.
contains also: Vier Duette, Op.
38 (2 solo voices) (D341)

Vier Duette, Op. 38
see Vier Duette, Op. 20

Vier Geistliche Stücke Für
Einzelstimme Und Orgel
CARUS 40.769 f.s.
contains: Ave Maria (Mez/Bar
solo,org); Ave Maris Stella
(Mez/Bar solo,org); Hymnus Ad
Laudes In Festo S.S. Trinitatis
(Mez/Bar solo,org); O
Sanctissima (ABar soli,org)
(D342)

Vier Lieder, Op. 2
[Czech/Ger] RECITAL 310 (D343)

Vier Lieder, Op. 3
[Ger] RECITAL 311 (D344)

Vier Lieder, Op. 6
[Ger/Eng] RECITAL 313 (D345)

Vier Lieder, Op. 7
[Ger/Eng] RECITAL 314 (D346)

Vier Lieder, Op. 9
[Ger] RECITAL 315 (D347)

Vier Lieder, Op. 73
[Czech/Ger/Eng] RECITAL 321 (D348)

Vier Lieder, Op. 82
[Ger/Eng] RECITAL 322 (D349)
[Ger/Eng/Czech] low solo,pno CLASSV
0766 (D350)

Zalo Dievca
see Four Songs, Op. 73

Zehn Biblische Lieder, Op. 99
[Czech/Ger/Eng] RECITAL 324 (D351)

[Sieben] Zigeunermelodien, Op. 55
[Czech/Ger/Eng] RECITAL 320 (D352)

DYDO, J. STEPHEN (1948-   )
Autumn Song
S solo,fl,vln,gtr [6'] APNM sc
$4.75, set $16.75 (D353)

Solomon Songs, Book *CCU
S solo,fl,bsn,vln,vcl,pno sc
AM.COMP.AL. $16.90 (D354)

Summer Song
S solo,fl,bsn,vln,vcl [3'] APNM sc
$3.50, set $14.50 (D355)

Winter Song
S solo,fl,mand,vcl,bsn [9'] APNM sc
$6.75, pts rent (D356)

DYGG SKAL SAL see Helgason, Hallgrimur

DYING, DYING IN THE NIGHT! see Samuel,
Gerhard

E

E CANTA IL GRILLO see Billi

E.E. CUMMINGS BAGATELLES see DeFotis,
William

E LA VITA see Verdi, Giuseppe

E L'UCCELLINO... see Puccini, Giacomo

E MORTO PULCINELLA! see Tosti,
Francesco Paolo

E NATALE CANTIAMO INSIEME *CCU
(Lucia, I.) solo voice,pno CURCI
10752 f.s. (E1)

E NON SEI MAI TORNATO see Mannino,
Franco

E POI... see Fedele, Ivan

EACH MAN see Tautenhahn, Gunther

EAGER SPRING see Somers-Cocks, John

EARLY EASTER MORNING see Weigl, Karl

EARLY ON ONE WINTRY COOL DAY: ARIOSO
see Sibelius, Jean

EARLY PUCCINI FOR SOPRANO: FIVE ARIAS
FROM LE VILLI AND EDGAR see
Puccini, Giacomo

EARLY SONGS see Orff, Carl

EARTH see Strand, Ragnvald, Jord

EARTH AND THE ROSE, THE see Pieper,
Rene

EARTH IS SO LOVELY, THE see Van de
Vate, Nancy Hayes

EARTH MANUAL - 1976 see Van Nostrand,
Burr

EAST, JAMES H.
God Made You Gentle
solo voice,pno (med easy) DANE
WOC1004 (E2)

EASTER see Tomasson, Jonas

EASTER: A SONG CYCLE see Wienhorst,
Richard

EASTER SONGBOOK *CCU
solo voice HANSEN-US HAN0389 $5.95
(E3)

EASTER-WINGS see Ronsheim, John Richard

EBEL, ARNOLD (1883-1963)
An Meine Seele
Bar solo,orch KISTNER sc f.s., pno
red f.s., pts rent (E4)

EBEN, PETR (1929-   )
Deset Poetickych Duet Na Slova V.
Nezvala
PANTON 891 (E5)

ECCENTRICITIES see Biggs, John

ECCO IL PETTO see Marcello

ECHANGE, L' see Denza, Luigi

ECHO see Somers-Cocks, John

ECHO OF AN ECHO see Thommessen, Olav
Anton

ECHO'S SONGS see Hagen, Daron

ECKERT, MICHAEL
Sea-Changes
Mez solo,2fl,2clar,horn,trp,harp,
cel/pno,vln,vla,vcl,perc [15']
AM.COMP.AL. sc $23.00, pts $53.60
(E6)
Three Poems Of Emily Dickinson *CC3U
S solo,fl,clar,bsn,horn,pno/cel,
vln,vla,vcl AM.COMP.AL. sc
$19.00, pts $12.95 (E7)
Three Songs From The Chinese *CC3U
Bar solo,pno sc AM.COMP.AL. $7.70
(E8)

ECO see Jarrell, Michael

ECSTASY see Beach, [Mrs.] H.H.A. (Amy
Marcy Cheney)

ECSTATIC SONGS 1 see Crockett, Donald

ED E SUBITO SERA... see Schmidt,
Christfried

EDEN-ROSE, THE see Foote, Arthur

EDENSONG see Chance, Nancy Laird

EDER, HELMUT (1916-   )
Eine Rose Überwältigt Alles, Die
*Op.88,No.1
T solo,pno DOBLINGER 08 661 (E9)

EDERKI see Pablo, Luis de

EDERS HJERTE FORFERDES IKKE see Baden,
Conrad

EDGING OUT see Schudel, Thomas

EDITH PIAF SONG COLLECTION
solo voice,pno (CC10L) SALABERT
50481348 (E10)

EDMEA: IN QUAL T'AGGIRI IMMACOLATA
STELLA see Catalani, Alfredo

EDMUNDS, JOHN (1913-   )
Boreas
solo voice,pno CLASSV 1994 (E11)

Faucon, The
solo voice,pno CLASSV 1992 (E12)

Hesperides
solo voice,pno CLASSV 1993 (E13)

EDWARDS
Lullaby From "Harriet Tubman"
high solo WILLIS 10954 $1.25 (E14)

Psalm No. 67
Bar solo WILLIS 10621 $1.25 (E15)

EDWARDS, GEORGE (1943-   )
Leaden Echo And The Golden Echo, The
SMezA soli,fl,pic,ob,clar,bass
clar,bsn,horn,2vln,vla,vcl [14']
sc AM.COMP.AL. $27.40 (E16)

Mirth But Open'd, A
S solo,pno [19'] sc AM.COMP.AL.
$16.50 (E17)

Three Hopkins Songs *CC3U
SS soli,2pno APNM sc $5.50, set
$21.00 (E18)

Wild Air
A solo,4rec [2'] AM.COMP.AL. sc
$5.00, pts $5.00 (E19)

EDWARDS, LEO
God Be Merciful Unto Us
see Psalm No. 67

Lullaby (from Harriet Tubman)
high solo,pno WILLIS 10954 (E20)

Psalm No. 67
"God Be Merciful Unto Us" Bar solo,
pno/org WILLIS 10621 (E21)

EDWARDS, SHERMAN (1919-1981)
By The Bend Of The River
low solo SCHIRM.G ST33500 (E22)

Into The Night
high solo SCHIRM.G ST37357 (E23)
med solo SCHIRM.G ST38491 (E24)
low solo SCHIRM.G ST38490 (E25)

Momma Look Sharp (from 1776)
SCHIRM.G 50453930 (E26)

1776 Vocal Selections
SCHIRM.G 50453960 (E27)

EENS see Broekman, Hans

EENZAAM STERVEN see Orthel, Leon

EENZAME NACHT see Weegenhuise, Johan

EERSTE CORINTHE: 13 see Rebel, Meeuwis,
Corinthians I: 13

EERSTE LENTEDAG see Roosendael, Jan
Rokus van

EERSTE SNEEUW see Brandse, Wim

EERSTE VREUGD, DIE see Maessen, Antoon

EF ENGILL EG VAERI see Helgason,
Hallgrimur

EFFATA see Åm, Magnar

EFFET DE NEIGE see Poldowski, [Lady]
Dean Paul

EFTERSOMMER see Jordan, Sverre

EFTESTOL, SVERRE (1952-   )
Sanctus-Agnus Dei
S solo,trp,org MUSIKK (E28)
[Lat] S solo,org,trp/fl [4'30"]
NORGE (E29)

EFTIRMALI AEVINTYRIS (FINALE) see
Sveinsson, Atli Heimir

EG ER DIN VEN see Aagaard-Nilsens,
Torstein

EG ER GULL OG GERSEMI see Sveinsson,
Atli Heimir

EG ER MYRKRID see Sveinsson, Gunnar
Reynir

EG ER NARSISSA... see Isolfsson, Pall

EG ER'KJE EISMAL see Baden, Conrad

EG HEV EI JENTE see Ørbeck, Anne Marie

EG HEV FUNNE MIN FLØYNE LOKKAR ATT I
MITT SVARMRUS, OP. 35B see
Søderlind, Ragnar

EG HEV FUNNE MIN FLØYSNE LOKKAR ATT I
MITT SVARMERUS see Søderlind,
Ragnar

EG HEV TVETTA HAORET MJUKT see Tveitt,
Geirr

EG HEYRI YKKUR KVAKA see Isolfsson,
Pall

EG HØYRER KLANG AV KLOKKEKOR see Bergh,
Sverre

EG HYLLI see Björnsson, Arni

EG KOM I GARD MINN see Isolfsson, Pall

EG KVEIKI A KERTUM MINUM see Isolfsson,
Pall

EG SER LANGT MEIR see Støyva, Njål
Gunnar

EG SØKJER DEG TIDLEG see Nystedt, Knut

EG STRØYER MINE SONGAR UT see Vaage,
Knut

EG SYNG UM THIG see Kaldalóns, Sigvaldi
S.

EG TARV IKKJE LJOSE Å KVEJKJE see
Sinding, Christian

EG UNDRAST see Olsen, Sparre

EG VIL KENNA THER OSKARAD see
Sveinsson, Atli Heimir

EG VIL LEVA see Bergh, Sverre

ÉGALITÉ see Hanson, Sten

EGGE, KLAUS (1906-1979)
Du Som Tendra Sol Og Stjerne
see Tre Hovden - Salmer

Fagert Er Landet
see Tre Hovden - Salmer

Fjell-Norig: Symfonisk Høgsong
*Op.15
"Montaineous Norway: Symphonic
Thanksgiving" solo voice,
2.2.2(bass clar).2. 2.2.0.0.
timp,perc,strings [9'] NORGE f.s.
(E30)

Grønland, Op. 2
[Norw] solo voice,pno NORSK (E31)

Montaineous Norway: Symphonic
Thanksgiving
see Fjell-Norig: Symfonisk Høgsong

Pa Kne Framfor Gud
see Tre Hovden - Salmer

Til Kongen
LYCHE 89 (E32)
[Norw] solo voice,pno LYCHE (E33)

Tre Hovden - Salmer
solo voice,pno LYCHE 907 f.s.
contains: Du Som Tendra Sol Og
Stjerne; Fagert Er Landet; Pa
Kne Framfor Gud (E34)

EGGEN, ARNE (1881-1955)
Aere Det Evige Foraar I Livet
"Eternal Spring" solo voice,
2.1.2.2. 3.2.3.0. timp,strings
[3'] NORGE f.s. (E35)

Autumn
see Høst

Dag Er På Himlen Komin (from King
Olav)
"Day Is Brightening" solo voice,
2.2.2.2. 4.3.4.0. timp,perc,harp,
strings NORGE f.s. (E36)

EGGEN, ARNE (cont'd.)

Day Is Brightening
see Dag Er På Himlen Komin

Eternal Spring
see Aere Det Evige Foraar I Livet

Gulnar Lauvet, Det
"Yellow Leaves" solo voice,strings
[3'] NORGE f.s. (E37)

Hald Ut, Hjarte
"My Weary Heart" solo voice,
2.1.2.2. 3.1.2.0. timp,harp,
strings [6'] NORGE f.s. (E38)

Ho Mor Faer Lofotfolket Sitt Heim
"Return Of The Lofoten People, The"
solo voice,strings [3'] NORGE
f.s. (E39)

Høst
"Autumn" solo voice,strings [1']
NORGE f.s. (E40)

Ikke Enhver, Som Siger Til Mig
(Psalm)
solo voice,2.2.2.2. 4.3.4.0. timp,
strings [3'] NORGE f.s. (E41)

Little Bird, A
see Og Det Var Litin Småfugl

Min Miders Arvesølv (from Olav
Liljekrans)
"My Mother's Silver" S solo,
2.2.2.2. 4.2.3.1. timp,harp,
strings [2'] NORGE f.s. (E42)

My Mother's Silver
see Min Miders Arvesølv

My Weary Heart
see Hald Ut, Hjarte

No Sprette Lauvet
"Spring Tide" T solo,2.2(English
horn).2.2. 4.2.3.1. timp,harp,
strings [3'] NORGE f.s. (E43)

Og Det Var Litin Småfugl
"Little Bird, A" solo voice,2ob,
harp,strings [3'] NORGE f.s.
(E44)

Olavs Fortelling (from Olav
Liljekrans)
"Olav's Story" T solo,2.2(English
horn).2.2. 4.2.1.0. cel,harp,
strings NORGE f.s. (E45)

Olavs Monolog Og Arie (from Olav
Liljekrans)
"Olav's Monologue And Aria" T solo,
2.2(English horn).2(bass clar).2.
4.2.3.1. timp,perc,harp,strings
NORGE f.s. (E46)

Olav's Monologue And Aria
see Olavs Monolog Og Arie

Olav's Story
see Olavs Fortelling

Out, Out, That Is Norsemen's Yearning
see Ut, Ja Ut, Det Var Nordmanns
Traa

Psalm
see Ikke Enhver, Som Siger Til Mig

Return Of The Lofoten People, The
see Ho Mor Faer Lofotfolket Sitt
Heim

Sleep Little Child Jesus
see Sov Barn Jesus Lille

Snjo
"Snow" solo voice,strings [3']
NORGE f.s. (E47)

Snow
see Snjo

Solfager
"Sunfair" solo voice,2.1.2.2.
2.0.0.0. timp,harp,strings [3']
NORGE f.s. (E48)

Sov Barn Jesus Lille
"Sleep Little Child Jesus" solo
voice,2clar,2bsn,strings [4'] pno
red NORGE f.s. (E49)

Sparrow, The
see Sporven

Sporven
"Sparrow, The" solo voice,2fl,
2clar,perc,strings [3'] NORGE
f.s. (E50)

Spring Tide
see No Sprette Lauvet

EGGEN, ARNE (cont'd.)

Sunfair
see Solfager

Til En Gammel Kirke
"To An Old Church" solo voice,clar,
strings [3'] pno red NORGE f.s.
(E51)

To An Old Church
see Til En Gammel Kirke

Ut, Ja Ut, Det Var Nordmanns Traa
"Out, Out, That Is Norsemen's
Yearning" solo voice,2clar,bsn,
2horn,timp,strings [3'] NORGE
f.s. (E52)

Yellow Leaves
see Gulnar Lauvet, Det

EGILSSON, ÁRNI (1939-)
Heimatgedanken
Mez solo,pno ICELAND 068-002 (E53)

EGLI NON...NON SO LE TETRE see Verdi,
Giuseppe, Corsaro: Medora's Aria

ÉGLOGUE see Delibes, Léo

EGO FLOS CAMPI see Monteverdi, Claudio

EGYPTIAN DIARY see Anderson, T.J.

EHLEN, MARGRIET (1943-)
Bad Man
see Drie Liederen Op Teksten Van
Martin Boot

Beatrix Canzone
see Drie Liederen Op Teksten Van
Martin Boot

Cyclus I
med solo,pno DONEMUS f.s. [10']
contains: Goud En Gebladerde
Vissen; Lupinen; Media Vita;
Mimosa; Recycling (E54)

Drie Kleine Liederen
solo voice,fl [3'] SODEN (E55)

Drie Liederen Op Teksten Van Martin
Boot
med solo,pno DONEMUS f.s. [5']
contains: Bad Man; Beatrix
Canzone; Maan Hangt In Glazen
Bellen, De (E56)

Dröm
solo voice,fl [3'20"] SODEN (E57)

Eurydice *song cycle
solo voice,3fl,alto fl [12'] SODEN
(E58)

Goud En Gebladerde Vissen
see Cyclus I

Ik Ben Gehuwd, Ailacen
see Wijfken, Staat Oppe

Kleine Reisepoetik
see Palimpseste

Kleine Reispoetica
see Palimpsesten

Lupinen
see Cyclus I

Maan Hangt In Glazen Bellen, De
see Drie Liederen Op Teksten Van
Martin Boot

Media Vita
see Cyclus I

Meer Van Ohrid
see Palimpsesten

Mijn Alderliefste Lief
see Wijfken, Staat Oppe

Mimosa
see Cyclus I

O Dood, Hoe Bitter Is Uw Gedinken
see Wijfken, Staat Oppe

Ohrid, Der See
see Palimpseste

Palimpsest
see Palimpseste
see Palimpsesten

Palimpseste
med solo,pno DONEMUS f.s. [6']
contains: Kleine Reisepoetik;
Ohrid, Der See; Palimpsest;
Schnee Oder Asche (E59)

Palimpsesten
Mez solo,pno DONEMUS f.s. [6']
contains: Kleine Reispoetica;
Meer Van Ohrid; Palimpsest;

EHLEN, MARGRIET (cont'd.)

Sneeuw Of As   (E60)

Recycling
see Cyclus I

Schnee Oder Asche
see Palimpseste

Sneeuw Of As
see Palimpsesten

Wijfken, Staat Oppe
S solo,fl DONEMUS f.s. [17']
contains: Ik Ben Gehuwd, Ailacen;
Mijn Alderliefste Lief; O Dood,
Hoe Bitter Is Uw Gedinken (E61)

EICHENDORFF-LIEDER, VOL. 1 see Wolf, Hugo

EICHENDORFF-LIEDER, VOL. 2 see Wolf, Hugo

EIERTANZ, DER see Kunad, Rainer

EIFERSICHTIGI BUA, DER see Baumann, Alexander

EIGHT AMERICAN INDIAN CHILDREN'S POEMS see Udow, Michael William

EIGHT BLAKE SONGS see Farquhar, David

EIGHT EPITAPHS see Chanler, Theodore Ward

EIGHT GREAT BAROQUE ARIAS
(Gavall, John) solo voice,gtr
(contains works by: Bach, Caldara,
Erlebach, Giordani, Gluck, Handel,
Paisiello, & A. Scarlatti) RICORDI-
IT LD660   (E62)

EIGHT OPERATIC ARIAS FOR THE SOPRANO VOICE see Mozart, Wolfgang Amadeus

EIGHT POEMS, OP. 24 see Medtner, Nikolai Karlovich

EIGHT SONGS see Olivero, Betty, Juego De Siempre

EIGHT SONGS (E.E.CUMMINGS) see Badings, Henk

EIGHT SONGS, OP. 47 (REV. ED. OF 1906) see MacDowell, Edward Alexander

EIGHT SONGS, OP. 47 (REV. ED. OF 1908) see MacDowell, Edward Alexander

EIGHT SONGS TO POEMS BY SIGBJØRN OBSTFELDER see Madsen, Trygve

EIGHT VARIANT VERSIONS FROM "LE NOZZE DI FIGARO" see Mozart, Wolfgang Amadeus

EIGHTEEN ETUDES VOCALISES see Mindlin, Adolfo

EIGNIR KARLS see Sveinsson, Atli Heimir

EILSEN, STEINAR
Er Ikke Hjertet Som Banker Det Er
Sjelen Som Banker På Hjertet,
Det: Seks Sanger
[Norw] Mez/Bar solo,clar,perc
[16'30"] NORGE   (E63)

Er Ikke Hjertet Som Banker Det Er
Sjelen Som Banker På Hjertet,
Det: Six Songs
Mez/Bar solo,clar,perc [16'30"]
NORGE   (E64)

EIN SIT EG UTI A STEINI see Björnsson, Arni

EINARSSON, SIGFUS (1877-1939)
Althydusönglög
solo voice,harmonium ICELAND
044-008   (E65)

Augun Blau
(Thorarinsson, Jon) solo voice,
1.1.1.1. 1.1.0.0. perc/timp,
strings ICELAND 044-031   (E66)

Draumalandid
(Thorarinsson, Jon) solo voice,
1.2.1.1. 1.1.0.0. timp,strings
ICELAND 044-033   (E67)

Four Songs
solo voice,1.1.1.1. 1.1.0.0. timp,
harp,strings ICELAND 044-900   (E68)
solo voice,pno ICELAND 044-013   (E69)

Gigjan
(Thorarinsson, Jon) solo voice,
1.1.1.1. 1.1.0.0. timp,harp,
strings ICELAND 044-030   (E70)

EINARSSON, SIGFUS (cont'd.)

Islandsdaetur
solo voice,pno ICELAND 044-029   (E71)

Sofnar Loa
solo voice,1.1.1.1. 1.1.0.0. timp,
harp,strings ICELAND 044-032   (E72)

Songs, 22
solo voice,pno ICELAND 044-014   (E73)

EINBUINN see Björnsson, Arni

EIND VAN DE DAG, HET see Orthel, Leon

EINDE, HET see Broekman, Hans see Orthel, Leon

EINE ROSE ÜBERWÄLTIGT ALLES, DIE see Eder, Helmut

EINEM, GOTTFRIED VON (1918-)
Alchemistenspiegel *Op.90
solo voice,0.0.2.2. 2.0.1.0. timp,
perc,strings study sc DOBLINGER
STP 652   (E74)

Känguruh Im Schnee, Ein
see Prinzessin Traurigkeit

Lebenstanz *Op.69, song cycle
med solo,pno [12'] BOTE f.s.   (E75)

Prinzessin Traurigkeit *Op.100
"Känguruh Im Schnee, Ein" MezBar
soli,pno DOBLINGER 08 675   (E76)

Schatten Der Rose *Op.95, song cycle
med solo,pno DOBLINGER 08 672 (E77)

Vier Tierlieder *Op.96
DOBLINGER 08 674   (E78)

Zwölf Tag- Und Nachtlieder, Op. 73
*CC12U
med solo,pno LIENAU RL 1568 f.s.   (E79)

EINEN AUGENBLICK SICH FINDEN see Riedel, Hermann

EINERLEI see Pezzati, Romano

EINFACHE LIEDER, OP. 9 see Korngold, Erich Wolfgang

EINKAMAL see Halldorsson, Skuli

EINLEG see Olsen, Sparre

EINLEITUNG UND FÜNF GALGENLIEDER see Ágústsson, Herbert Hriberschek

EINMANA see Johannsson, Magnus Bl.

EINS OG LJOSSINS SKAERA SKRUDA see Kaldalóns, Sigvaldi S.

EINSAM see Hekster, Walter

EINSAM MANN see Kjellsby, Erling

EINSAME, DER see Grieg, Edvard Hagerup, Bergtekne, Den see Strauss, Richard

EINSIEDLER, DER see Lohmann, Heinz

EINSLEG see Olsen, Sparre

EINST TRÄUMTEN WIR see Focke, Fré

EIRIKSDOTTIR, KAROLINA (1951-)
Land Possessed By Poems
Bar solo,pno [15'15"] ICELAND
037-020   (E80)

Ljodnamuland
[Icelandic] Bar solo,pno [15']
REIMERS 101149   (E81)

Six Poems From The Japanese
Mez solo,fl,vcl [4'50"] ICELAND
037-001   (E82)

EIRIKUR A EINUM FAETI see Björnsson, Arni

EISHET CHAYIL see Gideon, Miriam, Woman Of Valor, A

EISLER, HANNS (1898-1962)
Am 1. Mai Gehn Vater Und Mutter
solo voice,1.2.1. 2.1.0.0. perc,
strings DEUTSCHER   (E83)

Anrede An Den Kran Karl
see Balladenbuch

Auf Zum Kampfe, Tankbrigaden
"Lied Der Tankisten" solo voice,
pic,clar,tenor sax,horn,trp,trom,
perc,acord,gtr,db DEUTSCHER (E84)

Ausgewählte Lieder, Heft 4: Die
Hollywood Elegien, Sonette,
Lieder *CCU

EISLER, HANNS (cont'd.)

DEUTSCHER DV 9084 f.s.   (E85)

Ballade Vom Nigger Jim
see Balladenbuch

Ballade Von Den Säckeschmeissern
solo voice,alto sax,tenor sax,trp,
trom,perc,banjo,pno DEUTSCHER   (E86)

Ballade Von Der Judenhure Marie
Sanders
solo voice,fl,clar,bsn,pno,db
DEUTSCHER   (E87)

Ballade Von Der Krüppelgarde
see Balladenbuch

Ballade Zum 218
see Balladenbuch

Balladenbuch *Op.18
solo voice,pno UNIVER. UE 3742 f.s.
contains: Anrede An Den Kran
Karl; Ballade Vom Nigger Jim;
Ballade Von Der Krüppelgarde;
Ballade Zum 218; Lied Vom
Trockenbrot; Song Von Angebot
Und Nachfrage   (E88)

Beseda-Polka
solo voice,fl,2clar,horn,trp,trom,
tuba,perc,gtr,pno,db DEUTSCHER   (E89)

Bettellied
solo voice,vln,vcl DEUTSCHER (E90)

Die Den Mund Aufhatten
solo voice,2clar,vla,vcl DEUTSCHER   (E91)

Drei Kinderlieder
solo voice,vln,horn DEUTSCHER (E92)
solo voice,vla DEUTSCHER (E93)

Friedenslied
solo voice,clar,banjo,pno,db
DEUTSCHER   (E94)

Grabrede Für Einen Genossen, Der An
Die Wand Gestellt Wurde
solo voice,fl,horn,clar,trp,banjo,
db,perc,pno DEUTSCHER   (E95)

Hast Am Feldrain Geblüht
solo voice,clar,horn,acord,db
DEUTSCHER   (E96)

Heimliche Aufmarsch, Der
solo voice,3clar,alto sax,tenor
sax,2trp,trom,tuba,banjo,pno,
2vcl,db DEUTSCHER   (E97)

Hymne Auf Die UdSSR
solo voice,ob,clar,bsn,strings
DEUTSCHER   (E98)

Im Gefängnis Zu Singen
Bar solo,fl,clar,horn,trp,perc,
banjo,pno,db DEUTSCHER   (E99)

In Unserm Land
see Nein

Läuse-Lied
solo voice,2clar,2bsn,2horn,trp,
timp,perc,strings DEUTSCHER   (E100)

Lied Der Tankisten
see Auf Zum Kampfe, Tankbrigaden

Lied Eines Freudenmädchens (from Die
Rundköpfe Und Die Spitzköpfe)
solo voice,trp,alto sax,tenor sax,
banjo,perc,pno,db DEUTSCHER   (E101)

Lied Über Die Gerechtigkeit
MezBar soli,fl,clar,bsn,horn,trp,
perc,pno,db DEUTSCHER   (E102)

Lied Vom Kriegerischen Lehrer, Das
solo voice,fl,ob,clar,bsn,horn,trp,
perc,pno,vcl,db DEUTSCHER (E103)

Lied Vom SA-Mann
solo voice,alto sax,trp,trom,perc,
banjo,pno DEUTSCHER   (E104)

Lied Vom Trockenbrot
see Balladenbuch

Lied Von Der Belebenden Wirkung Des
Geldes (from Die Rundköpfe Und
Die Spitzköpfe)
solo voice,fl,4clar,alto sax,tenor
sax,2trp,trom,perc,pno DEUTSCHER   (E105)

Lieder Für Eine Singstimme Und
Klavier *CCU
solo voice,pno DEUTSCHER DV 4869
f.s.   (E106)

Lob Des Kommunismus (from Die Mutter)
solo voice,fl,clar,horn,trp,perc,
pno,banjo,db DEUTSCHER   (E107)

EISLER, HANNS (cont'd.)

Lob Des Lernens (from Die Mutter)
solo voice,fl,clar,horn,trp,perc,
banjo,pno,db DEUTSCHER (E108)

Marsch Des Fünfte Regiments
solo voice,fl,clar,bsn,tenor sax,
trp,horn,perc,trom,db DEUTSCHER
(E109)

Nein *cant
"In Unserm Land" solo voice,string
quar DEUTSCHER (E110)

Neue Deutsche Volkslieder *CCU
DEUTSCHER DV 9086 f.s. (E111)

Neue Deutsche Volkslieder, Chansons,
Kinder- Und Jugendlieder *CCU
DEUTSCHER DV 4868 f.s. (E112)

Neun Balladen Aus Dem Lehrstück "Die
Mutter" *CC9U
solo voice,trp,trom,perc,pno
DEUTSCHER f.s. sc DV 1354A, pts
DV 1354B (E113)

O Fallada, Da Du Hangest
solo voice,fl,ob,clar,bsn,horn,trp,
drums,pno,db DEUTSCHER (E114)

Ohne Kapitalisten Geht Es Besser
solo voice,clar,alto sax,trp,trom,
gtr,perc,pno,db DEUTSCHER (E115)

Präludium
S solo,3.2.3.2. 4.0.0.0. perc,
strings DEUTSCHER (E116)

Räuber Und Sein Knecht, Der
solo voice,fl,clar,bsn,horn,trp,
trom,elec gtr,pno,vcl,db
DEUTSCHER (E117)

Regimenter Gehn
Bar solo,2.2.2.2. 4.4.0.0. timp,
perc,pno,strings DEUTSCHER (E118)

Resolution
solo voice,fl,ob,clar,bsn,horn,trp,
trom,gtr,perc,acord,pno,vcl,db
DEUTSCHER (E119)

Sei Uns Gegrüsst, Du Weihnachtsbaum
"Weihnachtslied" solo voice,fl,
clar,hpsd,gtr,db DEUTSCHER (E120)

Sieh, Da Steht Das Erholungsheim
see Wohltätigkeit

Song Von Angebot Und Nachfrage
see Balladenbuch

Spaziergänge, Die
solo voice,fl,ob,clar,bsn,horn,trp,
trom,banjo,perc,acord,pno,vcl,db
DEUTSCHER (E121)

Teppichweber Von Kujan-Bulak, Die
*cant
S solo,1.1.2.2. 3.1.0.0. timp,perc,
strings sc DEUTSCHER DV 1079
(E122)

"Vielleicht"-Lied, Das
solo voice,fl,4clar,alto sax,tenor
sax,2trp,trom,perc,pno DEUTSCHER
(E123)

Weihnachtslied
see Sei Uns Gegrüsst, Du
Weihnachtsbaum

Wie Die Krähe (from Die Mutter)
solo voice,fl,clar,horn,trp,perc,
banjo,pno,db DEUTSCHER (E124)

Wilhelm Hat Ein Schloss
solo voice,fl,ob,clar,bsn,horn,trp,
pno,vcl,db DEUTSCHER (E125)

Wohltätigkeit
"Sieh, Da Steht Das Erholungsheim"
solo voice,2clar,alto sax,2trp,
trom,perc,banjo,pno,db DEUTSCHER
(E126)

EISMA, WILL (1929-)
Cheval Mort, Le
Mez solo,bass clar,perc,pno,
2synthesizer,electronic tape
[18'] DONEMUS (E127)

EJ see Dvořák, Antonín

EK HOOR see Badings, Henk

EKELUNDIANA VII see Blomberg, Erik

EKELUNDIANA VIII see Blomberg, Erik

EKLUND, HANS (1927-)
I Gräshoppstakt Och Snigelfart
solo voice,pno STIM (E128)

EKTE - UEKTE see Kjeldaas, Arnljot

ELDSLOGAN see Ørbeck, Anne Marie

ELECTION CAMPAIGN SPEECH FOR PRESIDENCY
OF THE US OF CHINAMERICA see
Weidberg, Ron

ELECTRIC SILENCE see Udow, Michael
William

ELEGI see Knutsen, Torbjorn see Lie,
Harald

ELEGI FOR KAMMERENSEMBLE see Brevik,
Tor

ELEGIA see Glinka, Mikhail Ivanovich

ELEGIA DE UN SOLDADO VIVO see Ponjee,
Ted

ELEGIA ETERNA see Granados, Enrique

ELEGIA OP. 44 see Procaccini, Teresa

ÉLÉGIE see Massenet, Jules see Rossini,
Gioacchino, Au Chevet D'un Mourant

ELEGIE NA ODCHODNOU see Raichl,
Miroslav

ELEGIE - NACH RILKE see Sims, Ezra

ELEGY see Lilburn, Douglas

ELEGY, OP.33, NO.1 see Campbell-Tipton,
Louis

ELEVEN BALLATE see Perugia, Niccolo da

ELEVEN HOUSMAN SONGS see Butterworth,
George Sainton Kaye

ELEVEN SONGS FROM A SHROPSHIRE LAD see
Leichtling, Alan

ELEVEN SONGS, OP. 2 see Baden, Conrad

ELFE, DIE see Marx, Joseph

ELFENLIED see Wolf, Hugo

ELFENREIGEN see Lothar, Mark

ELGAR, [SIR] EDWARD (WILLIAM)
(1857-1934)
Five Scenes From "The Spanish Lady"
(Young, Percy M.) solo voice
NOVELLO f.s. (E129)

Four Songs From "The Fringes Of The
Fleet"
med solo,pno (texts by Kipling)
CLASSV 1760 (E130)
low solo,pno (texts by Kipling)
CLASSV 1761 (E131)

Land Of Hope And Glory
high solo,pno CLASSV 0916 (E132)
med solo,pno CLASSV 0579 (E133)
low solo,pno CLASSV 0912 (E134)

Thirteen Songs, Vol. 1
solo voice,pno (CCU, med diff)
NOVELLO (E135)

Thirteen Songs, Vol. 2
solo voice,pno (CCU, med diff)
NOVELLO (E136)

Where Corals Lie *Op.37,No.4 (from
Sea Pictures)
solo voice,pno FENTONE (E137)
med solo,pno CLASSV 1190 (E138)

ELGARØY, JAN (1930-)
Fem Religiøse Folketoner Fra Valdres
[Norw] solo voice,org MUSIKK (E139)

Fem Salmetoner
[Norw] solo voice,pno MUSIKK (E140)

Fem Sanger Til Tekster Av Hauge Og
Hovden
[Norw] solo voice,pno MUSIKK f.s.
contains: Guds Omsorg; I Eit Evig
Sekund; Krossens Lidingstre;
Vakraste Blomen, Den; Vårt
Ansvar (E141)

Fire Advent-Salmer
[Norw] solo voice,pno MUSIKK (E142)
[Norw] MUSIKK (E143)

Fjortan Folkeviser Fra Østfold
solo voice,pno MUSIKK (E144)

Guds Omsorg
see Fem Sanger Til Tekster Av Hauge
Og Hovden

I Eit Evig Sekund
see Fem Sanger Til Tekster Av Hauge
Og Hovden

ELGARØY, JAN (cont'd.)

Krossens Lidingstre
see Fem Sanger Til Tekster Av Hauge
Og Hovden

Tre Folkeviser Fra Ostfold
solo voice,pno MUSIKK (E145)

Vakraste Blomen, Den
see Fem Sanger Til Tekster Av Hauge
Og Hovden

Vårt Ansvar
see Fem Sanger Til Tekster Av Hauge
Og Hovden

Ved Nådens Brønn
[Norw] solo voice,org/pno MUSIKK
(E146)
Ved Nådens Brønn: 9 Sanger Til Tekst
Av Sverre Therkeldsen
[Norw] MUSIKK (E147)

ELI SJURSDOTTER SYNG ÅT FRIEREN see
Tveitt, Geirr

ELIJAH: HEAR YE, ISRAEL! see
Mendelssohn-Bartholdy, Felix

ELIJAH: IF WITH ALL YOUR HEARTS see
Mendelssohn-Bartholdy, Felix

ELIJAH: IT IS ENOUGH see Mendelssohn-
Bartholdy, Felix

ELIJAH: LORD GOD OF ABRAHAM see
Mendelssohn-Bartholdy, Felix

ELISCU, ROBERT (1944-)
Man Of Madras, The
solo voice,org,rec,perc,gtr,db,
rauschpfeiffen [7'] MODERN 2125
(E148)

ELISIR D'AMORE: UNA FURTIVA LAGRIMA see
Donizetti, Gaetano

ELIZIR D'AMORE, L': UNA FURTIVA LAGRIMA
see Donizetti, Gaetano

ELLE A FUI see Lyric Soprano Arias: A
Master Class With Evelyn Lear, Vol.
1

ELLE MARCHE D'UN PAS DISTRAIT see
Paderewski, Ignace Jan

ELLENS ZWEITER GESANG see Schubert,
Franz (Peter)

ELLINGTON, EDWARD KENNEDY (DUKE)
(1899-1974)
Come Sunday (from Black, Brown, And
Beige)
low solo,pno SCHIRM.G 50488482
(E149)

ELLIOTT, MARJORIE REEVE (1890-)
God Gave Us Love
FITZSIMONS H0999 (E150)

ELMEHED, RUNE (1925-)
Herren Är Min Herde
solo voice,vcl,org/pno NOTERIA 1868
(E151)

ELOGIUM see Razzi, Fausto

ELS FRARES ENCANTATS see Mestres,
Apeles

ELS TRES ENAMORATS see Mestres, Apeles

ELSK see Grieg, Edvard Hagerup

ELVIRA ANIMA MIA see Vivaldi, Antonio

ELWYN-EDWARDS, DILYS
Cloths Of Heaven, The
solo voice,pno [3'] ROBERTON 1068
(E152)

EMBARQUES-VOUS! see Godard, Benjamin
Louis Paul

EMBARQUEZ-VOUS! see Godard, Benjamin
Louis Paul

EMBLA see Ragnarsson, Hjalmar H.

EMERGENCY SONGS see Lubetsky, Ronald

EMILY DICKINSON SONGS see Walker,
George Theophilus

EMILY DICKINSON SONGS see Walker,
George Theophilus

EMILY DICKINSON SONGS (FOR SOPRANO AND
PIANO) see Glickman, Sylvia

ÉMIR DE BENGADOR, L' see Franck, Cesar

EMMER, HUIB (1951-)
Rags Of Time, The
Bar solo,fl,clar,perc,mand,gtr,
harp,vln,db [12'] DONEMUS (E153)

EMPRESS IWA NO HIME see Straesser, Joep

EMPRESS SAIMEI see Straesser, Joep

EMPTY CUP, THE see Haxton, Kenneth

EN ESTA LARGA AUSENCIA see Bunge, Sas

EN IN DEN NACHT see Beyerman-Walraven, Jeanne

EN LA TUMBA DE ANSELMO see Schubert, Franz (Peter)

EN PRIÈRE see Faure, Gabriel-Urbain

EN REVENANT DE NANTES see Tailleferre, Germaine

EN SOURDINE see Szulc, Josef Zygmunt see Tal, Marjo

EN TI LOS RIOS CANTAN see Michans, Carlos

ÉNAMOURÉE, L' see Hahn, Reynaldo

ENBAN NO GOGATSU see Tanaka, Satoshi

ENCHANTMENT, THE see Mourant, Walter

ENCHU see Sugiura, Masayoshi

ENDA STUNDEN, DEN see Rangström, Ture

ENDE AM HERBST see Norby, Erik

ENDE DES HERBSTES, SCHLUSZSTUCK see Borup-Jorgensen, Axel

ENDENICH see Matthews, William

ENDRECA see Mestres, Apeles

ENDURFUNDIR see Stefansson, Fjölnir

ENEA NEL LAZIO: DEH! SE IN OZIO see Righini, Vincenzo

ENESCO, GEORGES (ENESCU) (1881-1955)
    Sept Chansons De Clément Marot, Op.15
    [Fr] med solo,pno CLASSV 1333
        (E154)

ENFANCE II see Colding-Jorgensen, Henrik

ENFANT PRODIGUE, L': AZAËL see Debussy, Claude, Enfant Prodigue, L': Ces Airs

ENFANT PRODIGUE, L': CES AIRS see Debussy, Claude

ENFANT PRODIGUE, L': L'ANNÉE see Debussy, Claude

ENFANT PRODIGUE, L': RÉCIT. ET AIR DE LIA see Debussy, Claude

ENFANT, SI J'ÉTAIS ROI see Liszt, Franz

ENFANTS-POETES see Smit Sibinga, Theo H.

ENGEL, CARL (1883-1944)
    Chansons Intimes
    [Fr/Eng] high solo RECITAL 258
        (E155)

ENGEL, DIE see Flothuis, Marius

ENGEL DAALDE NEDER, EEN see Geraedts, Jaap

ENGEL GOTTES KÜNDEN see Mozart, Franz Xaver Wolfgang

ENGINN THYDIR, HEL, THITT HELGILETUR see Isolfsson, Pall

ENGLE, DAVID
    Night Song
    "Silent, Silent Night" S solo,pno
    (text by William Blake) WILLIS
    11330   (E156)

    Silent, Silent Night
    see Night Song

ENGLISH LUTE SONGS see Dowland

[FOUR] ENGLISH LYRICS (FIRST SET) see Parry, [Sir] Charles Hubert Hastings

[FIVE] ENGLISH LYRICS (SECOND SET) see Parry, [Sir] Charles Hubert Hastings

[SIX] ENGLISH LYRICS (THIRD SET) see Parry, [Sir] Charles Hubert Hastings

[SIX] ENGLISH LYRICS (FOURTH SET) see Parry, [Sir] Charles Hubert Hastings

[SEVEN] ENGLISH LYRICS (FIFTH SET) see Parry, [Sir] Charles Hubert Hastings

[SIX] ENGLISH LYRICS (SIXTH SET) see Parry, [Sir] Charles Hubert Hastings

[SIX] ENGLISH LYRICS (SEVENTH SET) see Parry, [Sir] Charles Hubert Hastings

[SIX] ENGLISH LYRICS (EIGHTH SET) see Parry, [Sir] Charles Hubert Hastings

[SEVEN] ENGLISH LYRICS (NINTH SET) see Parry, [Sir] Charles Hubert Hastings

ENGLISH ROMANTIC SONGS AND BALLADS *CC17UL
    solo voice,gtr TECLA TE041 f.s.
        (E157)

ENID'S SONG FROM IDYLS OF THE KING see Homer, Sidney

ENKHUIZEN see King, Harold C.

ENLOE, NEIL
    Statue Of Liberty, The
    solo voice HARRIS,R RHS0705 $2.25
        (E158)

ENN A KULDASKOM see Sveinsson, Atli Heimir

ENN SYNGUR VORNOTTIN see Runolfsson, Karl Otto

ENNEMIE, L' see Paderewski, Ignace Jan

ENNO KAN EG GÅ I MJUKE VOLLAR see Braein, Edvard Fliflet

ENNTHA SKIN SOL see Helgason, Hallgrimur

ENNU EN KORT STUND see Baden, Conrad

ENTELECHIAE see Helmschrott, Robert M.

ENTER NO SILENCE see Bakke, Ruth

ENTREAT ME NOT see Gounod, Charles François, Song Of Ruth

ENTREAT ME NOT TO LEAVE YOU see Roff, Joseph

ENTSÜHNTE OREST, DER see Schubert, Franz (Peter)

ENVOI see Blank, Allan see Manneke, Daan

EPICEDIUM see Gretchaninov, Alexander Tikhonovich see Mimaroglu, Ilhan Kamaleddin

EPILOGUE see Flothuis, Marius

EPIPHANIA see Nilsson, Torsten

EPIPHANIAS see Wolf, Hugo

EPISODIOS ANIMALS see Prado, Ameida

EPITAPHE ET VERSET see Franken, Wim

EPITHALAMION see Lessard, John Ayres

EPITHALAMIUM see Boykan, Martin

EPITHALAMIUM BREVIS see Ultan, Lloyd

ER DEN DRAUMEN, DET see Søderlind, Ragnar

ER DU TRETT, ER DU BESVAERET see Nistad, Hans Ihlen

ER GODT Å VAERA ELSKA, DET see Taubo, Lillian Gulowna

ER IKKE HJERTET SOM BANKER DET ER SJELEN SOM BANKER PÅ HJERTET, DET: SEKS SANGER see Eilsen, Steinar

ER IKKE HJERTET SOM BANKER DET ER SJELEN SOM BANKER PÅ HJERTET, DET: SIX SONGS see Eilsen, Steinar

ER IST AUFERSTANDEN see Evensen, Bernt Kasberg

ER IST'S see Wolf, Hugo

ER NØDIG, DETTE ENE, ETT see Nyhus, Rolf

ERA DE MAGGIO see Costa

ERBACHER, WALTHER
    Aura Onomatopoetica *Op.8
    16 solo voices [12'] voc sc
    BREITKOPF-W BG 832 f.s.   (E159)

ERBARM' DICH MEIN, O HERRE GOTT (CHORAL) see Bach, Johann Sebastian

ERDENGANG see Weyrauch, Johannes

ERDLEN, HERMANN (1893-1972)
    Wiegenlied
    solo voice,pno SEESAW   (E160)

ERDMANN, DIETRICH (1917-   )
    Gesänge Des Abschieds *CCU
    high solo,fl,pno BREITKOPF-W
    BG 1365 f.s.   (E161)

ERFÜLLUNG DER ZEITEN see Weiss, Manfred

ERICKSON, ROBERT (1917-   )
    Days And Nights
    see Two Songs

    Idea Of Order At Key West, The
    S solo,fl,clar,trp,vla,vcl SMITH
    PUB   (E162)

    Seasonal
    see Two Songs

    Three Contralto Songs
    A solo,pno SMITH PUB   (E163)

    Two Songs
    S solo,clar,vla,pno SMITH PUB f.s.
    contains: Days And Nights;
    Seasonal   (E164)

ERINNERUNG see Bijvanck, Henk see Marx, Joseph

ERINNERUNG AN HOLLAND see Perdeck, Rudolf, Herinnering Aan Holland

ERIT GLORIA DOMINI see Jeffreys

ERKENNTNIS, DIE see Fongaard, Bjørn

ERLA see Kaldalóns, Sigvaldi S.

ERLKÖNIG see Schubert, Franz (Peter)

ERLUSTEF see Sveinsson, Atli Heimir

ERNANI: ERNANI INVOLAMI see Verdi, Giuseppe

ERNANI: INFELICE... E TUO CREDEVI see Verdi, Giuseppe

ERNST, HEINRICH WILHELM (1814-1865)
    Fünf Lieder
    [Ger] high solo RECITAL 259   (E165)

ERÖD, I.
    Vier Gesänge, Op. 44
    low solo DOBLINGER 08 660   (E166)

EROGENOUS ZONES, OR NEGLECTED PARTS see Lombardo, Robert M.

EROS REMINISCED: FOUR SONGS see Yannay, Yehuda

EROTIKON see Novak, Vitezslav, Sechs Lieder, Op. 46 see Terzakis, Dimitri

ERSTATNING see Backer-Lunde, Johan, Compensation

ERSTE HILFE see Straesser, Joep

ERSTE STUNDE see Norby, Erik

ERSTER VERLUST see Mendelssohn-Bartholdy, Felix see Schubert, Franz (Peter)

ERSTES LEID see Govers, Klaas

ERUCCIO see Battistini, M.

ES BIRGT DIE NACHTIGALL see Handel, George Frideric

ES ELLA! see Schumann, Robert (Alexander)

ES GEHT MIR GUT see Hanson, Sten

ES GIBT EIN LIED see Louis Ferdinand, Prince Of Prussia

ES IST EIN GROSSER GEWINN see Bach, Johann Michael

ES IST NACHT see Flothuis, Marius

ES IST VORBEI see Franz, Carl, When Love Has Gone

ES LA MANANA LLENA see Michans, Carlos

ES LÄUFT DER FRÜHLINGSWIND DURCH KAHLE ALLEEN see Flothuis, Marius

ES LAUSCHTE DAS LAUB SO DUNKELGRÜN see Mendelssohn-Bartholdy, Felix

ES RAGT IN'S MEER DER RUNENSTEIN see Hornstein, Robert Von

ES WAR EINMAL see Helgason, Hallgrimur

ES WAR IM HERBST see Koetsier, Jan

ES WEISS UND RÄTH ES DOCH KEINER see Mendelssohn-Bartholdy, Felix

ES WERDE LICHT see Mattiesen

ESA EINAI see Steinberg, Ben

ESCALERA, LA see Blumenthaler, V.

ESCHER, RUDOLF GEORGE (1912-1980)
Chants Du Desir, 4 Sonnets De Louise Labe
Mez solo,pno DONEMUS f.s. [15']
contains: Je Vis, Je Meurs; On Voit Mourir; Tant Que Mes Yeux; Tout Aussitot (E167)

Do, L'Enfant Do...
see Trois Poemes De Tristan Corbiere

Je Vis, Je Meurs
see Chants Du Desir, 4 Sonnets De Louise Labe

On Voit Mourir
see Chants Du Desir, 4 Sonnets De Louise Labe

Petit Mort Pour Rire
see Trois Poemes De Tristan Corbiere

Rondel
see Trois Poemes De Tristan Corbiere

Tant Que Mes Yeux
see Chants Du Desir, 4 Sonnets De Louise Labe

Tout Aussitot
see Chants Du Desir, 4 Sonnets De Louise Labe

Trois Poemes De Tristan Corbiere
S solo,pno DONEMUS f.s. [13'];
contains: Do, L'Enfant Do...; Petit Mort Pour Rire; Rondel (E168)

Vie Du Sieur De Dalibray, La *song cycle
T solo,pno [27'] DONEMUS (E169)

ESCLARMONDE: D'UNE LONGUE TORPEUR see Massenet, Jules

ESCLARMONDE: ROLAND!...COMME CE NOM ME TROUBLE see Massenet, Jules

ESCLAVE, L' see Bunge, Sas

ESERCIZI DI STILE see Arco, Paolo

ESORCISMI see Laneri, Roberto

ESPACE SONORE see Gartenlaub, Odette

ESPAÑA: A SÉVILLE see Chabrier, [Alexis-] Emmanuel

ESPECIALLY FOR VOCALISTS, BOOK II *CCU
(Lyon) solo voice SONOS S075 $5.95 (E170)

ESPIGA I LA ROSELLA, L' see Mestres, Apeles

ESPINAS see Massana, A., Espines

ESPINES see Massana, A.

ESPOSITO
Ass-Enzio
S solo,clar,pno CARISCH 22154 (E171)

ESPOZA DE DON GARCIA, LA see Blaustein, Susan, Romansa

ESTERHAZY, [PRINCE] PAL (1635-1713)
Dormi Jesu Dulcissime
(Ruhland, Konrad) SS soli,2rec, 2vln,cont (Coppenraths Kleine Reihe, Heft 5) COPPENRATH f.s.
contains also: Nil Canitur Iucundius (S solo,2rec,2vln,cont) (E172)

Nil Canitur Iucundius
see Dormi Jesu Dulcissime

ESTEVE, PABLO (? -1794)
Canción Satírica De Pronóstico
see Castell, J., Canción De La Gitana Habilidosa

ESTRELLA DEL ANOCHECER, LA see Schumann, Robert (Alexander)

ET INCARNATUS EST see Galuppi, Baldassare see Mozart, Wolfgang Amadeus

ET L'AUBE ROUVRE LE POING see Wissmer, Pierre

ÉTÉ, L' see Boismortier, Joseph Bodin de

ETERNAL, THE see Korngold, Erich Wolfgang, Unvergaenglichkeit see Korngold, Erich Wolfgang, Unvergänglichkeit

ETERNAL PRISONER, THE see Menotti, Gian Carlo

ETERNAL SPRING see Eggen, Arne, Aere Det Evige Foraar I Livet

ETHIOPIA SALUTING THE COLORS see Wood, Charles

ETHOS GAMMA I see Terzakis, Dimitri

ETHOS GAMMA II see Terzakis, Dimitri

ÉTIENNE MARCEL: O BEAUX RÊVES ÉVANOUIS see Saint-Saëns, Camille

ETOILE DU NORD, L': O JOURS HEUREUX see Meyerbeer, Giacomo

ETT, KASPAR (1788-1847)
Ave Vivens Hostia: Hymne
(Hochstein, Wolfgang) solo voice, fl,org COPPENRATH (E173)

ETTER EI FROSTNATT see Ørbeck, Anne Marie

EUGENE ONEGIN: GREMIN'S ARIA see Tchaikovsky, Piotr Ilyich

EUGENE ONEGIN: LENSKI'S ARIA see Tchaikovsky, Piotr Ilyich

EURYANTHE: GLÖCKLEIN IM TALE! see Weber, Carl Maria von

EURYANTHE: UNTER BLÜHNDEN MANDELBÄUMEN see Weber, Carl Maria von

EURYANTHE: WO BERG' ICH MICH? see Weber, Carl Maria von

EURYDICE see Ehlen, Margriet

EVANGELIMANN, DER: SELIG SIND, DIE VERFOLGUNG LEIDEN see Kienzl, Wilhelm

EVANGELISCHES-MUSIKALISCHES LIEDER-BUCH see Telemann, Georg Philipp

EVEN KJERRINGDALT see Sommerfeldt, Öistein

EVEN-OR, MARY (1939-1989)
Time
[Eng] solo voice,pno [8'] (text from Ecclesiastes) perf sc ISR.MUS.INST. 6859 (E174)

EVENING see Goldberg, William see Hoiby, Lee

EVENING, THE see Sinding, Christian, Kvelden

EVENING ATMOSPHERE see Kjerulf, Halfdan, Aftenstemning

EVENING IS QUIET, THE see Backer-Grøndahl, Agathe [Ursula], Aftnen Er Stille

EVENING MORNING NIGHT see Britten, [Sir] Benjamin

EVENING, OP. 46, NO. 1 see Tchaikovsky, Piotr Ilyich

EVENING PRAYER see Gudmundsson, Björgvin

EVENING RAIN see Dillon

EVENING SONG see Hadley, Henry (Kimball)

EVENING STAR see Winslow, Walter

EVENSEN, BERNT KASBERG (1944-   )
Bønn Til En Bokfink *Op.35
[Norw] Bar solo,fl,vla,harp,perc [22'] (text by Aasmund Brynhildsen) NORGE (E175)

Dag
see Tre Dikt Av Sigbjørn Obstfelder

Du Bist Ein Faltbuch Und Ein Flügel
[Ger] solo voice,fl,gtr NORGE (E176)

Er Ist Auferstanden
[Ger] solo voice,pno NORGE (E177)

Herbsttag
[Ger] solo voice,pno (text by Rainer Maria Rilke) NORGE (E178)

Hymne
see Tre Dikt Av Sigbjørn Obstfelder

Intermission
[Eng] solo voice,org NORGE (E179)

Kan Speilet Tale?
see Tri Sanger Til Dikt Av Sigbjørn Obstfelder, Op. 4

Mariposa De Luz
[Span] S solo,2gtr NORGE (E180)

Naki Grein, Ei
solo voice,vla,pno NORGE f.s. (E181)

Nocturne
see Tre Dikt Av Sigbjørn Obstfelder

Råe Bergveggen
[Norw] solo voice,vla,pno NORGE (E182)

Rosen
see Tri Sanger Til Dikt Av Sigbjørn Obstfelder, Op. 4

Salme
see Tri Sanger Til Dikt Av Sigbjørn Obstfelder, Op. 4

Sjette Dag, Den
[Norw] solo voice,ob,org NORGE (E183)

Skrinet Med Det Rare I
solo voice,vln,Orff inst NORGE (E184)

Stabat Mater
[Lat] solo voice,fl,ob,clar,timp, pno,vln,vcl NORGE (E185)

To Johanna: Asleep After Our Battle For You
[Eng] solo voice,harp NORGE (E186)

Torii
[Ger] solo voice,pno [14'] NORGE (E187)

Tre Dikt Av Sigbjørn Obstfelder
[Norw] Bar solo,org NORGE f.s.
contains: Dag; Hymne; Nocturne (E188)

Tri Sanger Til Dikt Av Sigbjørn Obstfelder, Op. 4
solo voice,pno NORGE f.s.
contains: Kan Speilet Tale?; Rosen; Salme (E189)

EVENSEN, KRISTIAN (1953-   )
Kyrie
Bar solo,string quar [18'] NORGE f.s. (E190)

Rings Of Saturn, The
[Eng] S solo,ob,vcl,pno [9'] NORGE (E191)

Three Poems By Basho
[Eng] S solo,clar,pno [7'] NORGE (E192)

Vocalise For Two Sopranos And Ensemble
SS soli,pic,fl,clar,bass clar,3gtr, pno,db [7'] NORGE f.s. (E193)

EVERY ONE SANG see Somers-Cocks, John

EVERY SMALL STEP see Nordal, Jon

EVETT, ROBERT (1922-1975)
Billy Ascends (Symphony No. 2)
Bar solo,2.3.3.3. 4.3.3.1. cel, timp,perc,strings [14']
AM.COMP.AL. sc $26.75, pno red $10.70 (E194)

Symphony No. 2
see Billy Ascends

EVOLUTION see Weigl, [Mrs.] Vally

EV'RY TIME I FEEL DE SPIRIT see Walker, George Theophilus

EWIG, SO SPRICHT DIE SEELE see Handel, George Frideric

EXECUTION, L'
Bar solo,pno (diff) DURAND   (E195)

EXERCISES FOR GYDLI see Kapr, Jan

EXERCISES FOR TRAINING THE VOICE see
Myer, Edmund J.

EXPECTATIONS see Dabrowski, Florian,
Oczekiwania

EXPOSITION OF A PICTURE see Oliver,
Stephen

EXPRESSIONS LYRIQUES see Massenet,
Jules

EXSULTATE JUBILATE see Mozart, Wolfgang
Amadeus

EXSULTATE JUBILATE, K.165 see Mozart,
Wolfgang Amadeus

EXTASE see Duparc, Henri

EXTRASENSORY CONCEPTIONS II see Hanson,
Sten

EXULTA FILIA see Monteverdi, Claudio

EXULTARE JUSTI IN DOMINO see Beers,
Jacques

EXULTATE, JUBILATE see Mozart, Wolfgang
Amadeus

EXULTENT FILIA SION see Monteverdi,
Claudio

EYSER, EBERHARD (1932-   )
Vid Havet
[Swed] solo voice,pno TONOS   (E196)

EZRA POUND'S CANTO CXVI see Tipei,
Sever

F

FA FRET! see Mestres, Apeles

FABLER OG BARNERIM see Jensen, Ludwig
Irgens

FABRICIUS, JACOB
Three Songs *CC3U
Mez solo,org SAMFUNDET f.s.   (F1)

FACE CENDREE, LA see Blumenfeld, Harold

FACE OF BEAUTY, THE see Dillard, Donald
E.

FACETTEN see Roosendael, Jan Rokus van

FÅGELDRÖM, EN see Sandström, Jan

FÅGELPOESI see Lidström, John

FAGERT ER LANDET see Egge, Klaus see
Johnsen, Hallvard

"FAGRA VEROLD" see Kentish, Oliver see
Masson, Askell

FAIR CHILD OF MINE see Williams, David
H.

FAIR MAID OF PERTH: NOW THE SHADES OF
NIGHT see Bizet, Georges, Jolie
Fille De Perth, La: Serenade: A La
Voix D'un Amant

FAIR PROVENCE see Verdi, Giuseppe,
Traviata, La: Di Provenza

FAIR SEED-TIME see Carlsen, Philip

FAIR SUMMER DROOPS see Rowland, David

FAIRCHILD, BLAIR (1877-1933)
Amours De Hafiz, Les, Op. 38
[Fr] RECITAL 329   (F2)

Ten Songs
[Eng] med solo RECITAL 260   (F3)

FAIRIES, THE see Bax, [Sir] Arnold

FAIRY BOY, THE see Lover, Samuel

FAIRY LULLABY see Beach, [Mrs.] H.H.A.
(Amy Marcy Cheney)

FAIRY'S VOYAGE, THE see Lightfoot,
Miss, Make Ready! Make Ready! My
Nautilus Bark

FAJA FLORIDA, LA see Beethoven, Ludwig
van

FALCON FLEW, THE see Malek, Jan

FALK, KARL-AXEL (1958-   )
Canto Gratia
S solo [4'] NORGE   (F4)

FALL see Kreutz, Robert Edward

FALLA, MANUEL DE (1876-1946)
Cantares De Nochebuena *CC9U
solo voice,gtr SCHOTT EMF1001 f.s.
                            (F5)
Cantares De Nochebuena
solo voice,gtr SCHOTTS EMF 1002
                            (F6)
Chinoiserie
see Trois Mélodies

Colombes, Les
see Trois Mélodies

Séguidille
see Trois Mélodies

Seven Spanish Folksongs
[Span/Fr/Eng] high solo AMP
50234660   (F7)
[Span/Fr/Eng] med solo AMP 50234830
                            (F8)
Trois Mélodies
[Fr] high solo,pno CLASSV 1271 f.s.
contains: Chinoiserie; Colombes,
Les; Séguidille   (F9)

Vida Breve, La: Air De Salud
Mez solo,pno CLASSV 0922   (F10)

FALLEN IS BABYLON THE GREAT, HALLELUJAH
see Lockwood, Normand

FALLEN IS THY THRONE, OH ISRAEL see
Stevenson, John

FALLING ASLEEP IN AN ORCHARD see
Flothuis, Marius

FALLING LEAVES see Ragnarsson, Hjalmar
H.

FALLING OF THE LEAVES, THE see Parke,
Dorothy

FALSE THOUGH SHE BE see Mourant, Walter

FALSTAFF: E SOGNO? O REALTÀ? see Verdi,
Giuseppe

FALSTAFF: QUAND' ERO PAGGIO see Verdi,
Giuseppe

FALSTAFF: SUL FIL D'UN SOFFIO ETESIO
see Verdi, Giuseppe

FALTUS, L.
Marijanek Starobyly
female solo,pno PANTON 893   (F11)

FAMOUS NEGRO SPIRITUALS
(Dorumsgard) med solo (CCU) LYCHE 136
                            (F12)
FAMOUS SACRED SONGS *CCU
solo voice ALLANS $6.00   (F13)

FANCIULLA ABBANDONATA, LA see Bianchi,
Lino

FANCIULLA DEL WEST, LA: CH'ELLA MI
CREDA see Puccini, Giacomo

FANCIULLA DEL WEST: CH' ELLA MI CREDA
see Puccini, Giacomo

FANCY see Roosendael, Jan Rokus van

FANDEN I NØTTEN see Bergh, Sverre

FANFARE AND ARIA see Lombardo, Robert
M.

FANINN see Sveinbjörnsson, Sveinbjörn

FANTOCHES see Poldowski, [Lady] Dean
Paul

FANTOMES see Beale, James

FANTOOM see Hekster, Walter

FAREWELL! BUT, WHENEVER YOU WELCOME THE
HOUR see Stevenson, John

FAREWELL TO THE FARM see Mourant,
Walter

FAREWELL TO THE FUNLESS 80'S! see Carl,
Robert

FARFALETTA S'AGGIRA AL LUME, LA see
Vivaldi, Antonio

FARFALLA DELLA PRIMAVERA, LA see
Hirose, Ryohei

FARFALLETTA S'AGGIRA ALLUME CANTATA, LA
see Vivaldi, Antonio

FARISEEREN OG TOLDEREN see Baden,
Conrad

FARQUHAR, DAVID (1928-   )
Eight Blake Songs
Mez/Bar solo,pno WAI-TE-ATA 67
                            (F14)
Six Songs Of Women
S solo,pno WAI-TE-ATA 71   (F15)

Three Cilla McQueen Songs
Mez/Bar solo,pno perf sc,study sc
WAI-TE-ATA 74   (F16)

FARSAELDA FRON ORGANUM II see Helgason,
Hallgrimur

FARWELL, ARTHUR (1872-1952)
Mädchenlieder
"Vier Lieder, Op.2" [Ger/Eng] med
solo,pno CLASSV 1688   (F17)

Three Indian Songs, Op.32
[Eng] med solo,pno CLASSV 1687
                            (F18)
Vier Lieder, Op.2
see Mädchenlieder

FATHER OF HEAVEN see Verdi, Giuseppe,
Forza Del Destino, La: Pace, Pace
Mio Dio

FATHER O'FLYNN see Stanford, Charles
Villiers

FATTIG ER MITT LIV see Sommerfeldt,
Oistein

FAUCON, THE see Edmunds, John

FAUNA see Olan, David

FAURE, GABRIEL-URBAIN (1845-1924)
Adieu
see Poème D'un Jour, Op.21

Apres Un Rêve
med solo,pno CLASSV 0472   (F19)
high solo,pno CLASSV 0364   (F20)

Ave Maria *Op.67,No.2
S/T solo,pno/org LEDUC f.s.   (F21)

Berceaux, Les
med solo,pno CLASSV 1762   (F22)

Blessed Jesus
see Pie Jesu

Chanson D'Amour
solo voice,2gtr (available in high,
medium, or low voice) JELLO
TGV100   (F23)

Chanson D'Eve, La
[Fr] KALMUS K 09883   (F24)

Cinq Mélodies, Op.58
[Fr] med solo,pno (texts by
Verlaine) CLASSV 1331   (F25)

Collected Songs, Vol. 1
S/T solo,pno (cc201) MARKS 00008272
                              (F26)
Mez/Bar solo,pno (cc201) MARKS
00008249   (F27)

Collected Songs, Vol. 2
S/T solo,pno (cc201) MARKS 00008253
                              (F28)
Mez/Bar solo,pno (cc201) MARKS
00008252   (F29)

Collected Songs, Vol. 3
S/T solo,pno (cc201) MARKS 00008251
                              (F30)
Mez/Bar solo,pno (cc201) MARKS
00008250   (F31)

En Prière
Mez solo,pno LEDUC f.s.   (F32)
solo voice,2gtr (available in high,
medium, or low voice) JELLO
TGV101   (F33)

Il Est Né, Le Divin Enfant
S solo,org LEDUC f.s.   (F34)

Noël *Op.43,No.1
S/Mez solo,pno LEDUC f.s.   (F35)

O Salutaris
S/Mez solo,pno/org LEDUC f.s. (F36)

Pavane, Op. 50
SA soli RECITAL 2225   (F37)

Pie Jesu (from Requiem)
"Blessed Jesus" low solo,kbd
FITZSIMONS F0112   (F38)
"Blessed Jesus" high solo,kbd
FITZSIMONS F0101   (F39)

Pie Jesus
S/Mez solo,pno LEDUC f.s.   (F40)

Pleurs D'Or
MezBar soli,pno CLASSV 0760   (F41)
ST soli,pno CLASSV 0759   (F42)

Poème D'un Jour, Op.21
[Fr/Eng] med solo,pno CLASSV 1698
f.s.
contains: Adieu; Recontre;
Toujours   (F43)

Puisqu'ici-Bas Toute Âme
SS/ST soli,pno CLASSV 0761   (F44)

Recontre
see Poème D'un Jour, Op.21

Ses Melodies Oeuvres Completes 1
solo voice,pno ZEN-ON 713701 (F45)

Tarentelle: Aux Cieux La Lune
[Fr] SS/ST soli,pno CLASSV 1426
                              (F46)
Toujours
see Poème D'un Jour, Op.21

FAURE, JEAN-BAPTISTE (1830-1914)
Charité
[Fr/Eng] med-high solo,pno CLASSV
1763   (F47)

Mélodies, 20, Vol.2
high solo,pno CLASSV C022   (F48)

Mélodies, 20, Vol.3
high solo,pno CLASSV C023   (F49)

Mélodies, 25, Vol.1
med-high solo,pno CLASSV C021 (F50)

FAUST: AVANT DE QUITTER see Gounod,
Charles François

FAUST: FAITES LUI see Gounod, Charles
François

FAUST: JEWEL SONG see Gounod, Charles
François

FAUST: SALUT! DEMEURE CHASTE see
Gounod, Charles François

FAUST: SI LE BONHEUR À SOURIRE see
Gounod, Charles François

FAUST: VOUS QUI FAITES L'ENDORMIE see
Gounod, Charles François

FAVORITA, LA: A TANTO AMOR see
Donizetti, Gaetano

FAVORITA, LA: O MIO FERNANDO see
Donizetti, Gaetano

FAVORITA, LA: SPIRITO GENTIL see
Donizetti, Gaetano

FAVORITA, LA: SPIRITTO GENTIL see
Donizetti, Gaetano

FAVORITA, LA: UNA VERGINE see
Donizetti, Gaetano

FAVORITA, LA: UNA VERGINE, UN ANGEL DI
DIO see Donizetti, Gaetano

FAVORITA, LA: VIEN, LEONORA see
Donizetti, Gaetano

FAVORITE, LA: POUR TANT D'AMOUR see
Donizetti, Gaetano

FAVORITE FRENCH ART SONGS
high solo,pno (CC12U) LEONARD-US
00312035 accomp tape available
                              (F51)
low solo,pno (CC12U) LEONARD-US
00312036 accomp tape available
                              (F52)

FAVORITE GERMAN ART SONGS
high solo,pno (CC11U) LEONARD-US
00312033 accomp tape available
                              (F53)
low solo,pno (CC11U) LEONARD-US
00312034 accomp tape available
                              (F54)

FAVORITE OPERA ARIAS *CCU
(Varga) BOOSEY EMB02429 f.s. (F55)

FAVORITE SONGS, 24 see Schubert, Franz
(Peter)

FAVORITE SONGS OF THE NINETIES *CC98U
(Fremont, Robert A.) solo voice
BELWIN BKD000340 $12.95   (F56)

FAVOURITE COLLECTION OF ENGLISH SONGS,
A see Arne, Thomas Augustine

FAVOURITE COLLECTION OF ENGLISH SONGS,
BOOK III, A see Arne, Michael

FAVOURITE COLLECTION OF SONGS, A, 14
(1764) see Arne, Thomas Augustine

FEAR NO MORE THE HEAT O' THE SUN see
Arne, Thomas Augustine

FEBERDIGTE see Jordan, Sverre

FEDAK, ALFRED V.
You Are The Chosen Of The Lord
*Marriage
med solo AMSI V-10   (F57)

FEDELE, IVAN
E Poi...
S solo,12inst ZERBONI 9145   (F58)

FÉE AUX ROSES, LA: EN DORMANT C'EST À
MOI see Halévy, Jacques

FEED MY SHEEP see Warren, Betsy

FEIGIN, JOEL
Paradiso Terrestre, Il
S solo,pno [5'] AM.COMP.AL.   (F59)

FELDERHOF, JAN (1907-   )
Sonnet: Things Of The Distance
med solo,pno [5'] DONEMUS   (F60)

FELICITAT see Mestres, Apeles

FELIX, VÁCLAV (1928-   )
Nad Postylkou
[Czech/Ger] S solo,pno PANTON 894
                              (F61)
Symfonie
female solo,orch PANTON 1042 (F62)

FELIZ NOS DA see Beethoven, Ludwig van

FEM GAMMELTESTAMENTLIGE BØNNER, OP.45
see Karlsen, Kjell Mørk

FEM JOHANNES-SANGER see Ugland, Johan
Varen

FEM RELIGIØSE FOLKETONER FRA
RØROSDISTRIKTET see Nyhus, Rolf

FEM RELIGIØSE FOLKETONER FRA VALDRES
see Elgarøy, Jan

FEM SALMETONER see Elgarøy, Jan

FEM SANGER, OP. 12 see Kjeldaas,
Arnljot

FEM SANGER, OP. 34 see Hovland, Egil

FEM SANGER TIL DIKT AV TARJEI VESAAS
see Sønstevold, Gunnar

FEM SANGER TIL TEKST AV JAN MAGNUS
BRUHEIM, OP. 86 see Karlsen, Kjell
Mørk

FEM SANGER TIL TEKSTER AV HAUGE OG
HOVDEN see Elgarøy, Jan

FEM SONGAR see Grov, Magne

FEM VUGGESANGER see Karlsen, Kjell Mørk

FEM VUGGEVISER, OP. 42, NO. 2 see
Karlsen, Kjell Mørk

FENELON, PHILIPPE (1952-   )
Du Blanc Le Jour Son Espace
Bar solo,fl,pic,alto fl,ob,English
horn,clar,bass clar,horn,trp in
C,trom,tuba,pno,cel,org [19']
AMPHION A.462-63 f.s.   (F63)

FENESTA CHE LUCIVE!
high solo,pno CLASSV 1667   (F64)
med solo,pno CLASSV 1303   (F65)

FENNIMORE, JOSEPH WILLIAM (1940-   )
Infant Joy
med-high solo,pno (text by William
Blake) CLASSV 0733   (F66)

Inscape
med-high solo,pno (texts by G.
Manley Hopkins) CLASSV 0983   (F67)

Mary Weeps For Her Child
med-high solo,pno CLASSV 0731 (F68)

My Heart
med-high solo,pno (text by Sappho)
CLASSV 0735   (F69)

Now Death Has Shut Your Eyes
med-high solo,pno CLASSV 0734 (F70)

Snow Grew Out Of The Sky Last Night,
The
med-high solo,pno CLASSV 0732 (F71)

Winter Love
med solo,pno CLASSV 0730   (F72)

FENSTERSCHEIBE, DIE see Schumann,
Robert (Alexander)

FERDALOK see Halldorsson, Skuli

FERDAMANN see Kielland, Olav

FERDAVISUR see Palsson, Helgi

FERIANTE, LA see Camprubi, J., Firaire,
La

FERMA E L'ANTICA VOCE see Lasagna,
Marco

FERN HILL see Lyne, Peter

FERNANDERE, F.
Minuetto En Alabanza De La Música
Seria
see Galvan, Ventura, Seguidilla Del
Oficial Cortejante

FERNANDEZ, LUIS SANCHEZ
Siete Canciones *CC7U
solo voice PILES 1209-X f.s. (F73)

FERRARI
Sei Canzonette
solo voice,gtr TECLA TE042   (F74)

FERRATA, GIUSEPPE (1865-1928)
Seven Lyric Melodies, Op. 21
[Eng] RECITAL 261   (F75)

FESCH, WILLEM DE (1687-1761)
Songs In The Tempest, The (C.1746)
sc KING'S   (F76)

FESTA DE RATES, LA see Mestres, Apeles

FÊTES VÉNITIENNES, LES: CHARMANT
PAPILLON see Campra, André

FEU ROI, LE see Depraz, Raymond

FEUERANBETER, DER see Verhaar, Ary

FEUILLES TOMBENT, LES see Hahn,
Reynaldo, Dernière Valse, La

FEVER POEMS see Jordan, Sverre,
Feberdigte

FIALA, PETR (1943-   )
Poselstvi
see Symphony No. 3

Symphony No. 3
"Poselstvi" Bar solo,2.2.2.2.
4.5.3.1. perc,pno,strings [22']
CESKY HUD.   (F77)

FIAT DOMINE see Andriessen, Hendrik

FICHTENBAUM STEHT EINSAM, EIN see Marx,
Joseph

FIDDLER OF DOONEY see Kauder, Hugo

FIDELIO: ABSCHEULICHER! WO EILST DU
HIN? see Beethoven, Ludwig van

FIDELIO: GOTT, WELCH DUNKEL HIER see
Beethoven, Ludwig van

FIELD, COREY
Three Lullabies
solo voice,pno (med diff) HELICON
EA00693   (F78)

FIELD BELOVED see Rachmaninoff, Sergey
Vassilievich, O, Du Wogendes Feld

FIELDS OF WONDER see Owens, Robert

FIERA, LA see Bernabei, Giuseppe
Antonio

FIERCE FLAMES ARE RAGING see Verdi,
Giuseppe, Trovatore, Il: Stride La
Vampa!

FIFTEEN LIEDER see Kauder, Hugo

FIFTEEN MOTETS FOR SOLO VOICE AND
CONTINUO see Philips, Peter

FIFTEEN RUSSIAN SONGS AND ROMANCES
*CC15U
(Malukoff, A.) [Ger/Russ] PLUCKED STR
ZM 1321 $6.00   (F79)

FIFTEEN SCOTTISH, WELSH AND IRISH
FOLKSONGS see Haydn, [Franz] Joseph

FIFTEEN SONGS AND AIRS FOR CONTRALTO OR
BARITONE FROM THE OPERAS AND
MASQUES see Purcell, Henry

FIFTEEN SONGS AND AIRS FOR SOPRANO OR
TENOR FROM THE OPERAS AND THE ODES
see Purcell, Henry

FIFTY-FIVE SONGS see Schumann, Robert
(Alexander)

FIGARO WAS SUPPOSED TO RETURN THE
NECKLACE see Corigliano, John

FIGARO'S ARIA see Corigliano, John,
They Wish They Could Kill Me

FIGLIA DEL REGGIMENTO, LA: CONVIEN
PARTIR see Donizetti, Gaetano

FIGLIUOL PRODIGO, IL: PACE, GRAN DIO
see Ponchielli, Amilcare

FIGURINE see Regteren Altena, Lucas van

FIKENTREET UTEN FRUKT see Hovland, Egil

FILL THE BUMPER FAIR!
(Stanford) med solo,pno CLASSV 2096
(F80)

FILLE AUX FLEURS, LA see Thommessen,
Reidar

FILLE DU REGIMENT: CHACUN LE SAIT see
Donizetti, Gaetano

FILLE DU REGIMENT: IL FAUT PARTIR see
Donizetti, Gaetano

FILLE QUI CHANTE, LA see Philippe,
Pierre

FILLES DE CADIX, LES see Delibes, Léo

FILLES DU ROI D'ESPAGNE, LES see
Vermeulen, Matthijs

FIMM NUMER I ISLENSKUM THJODBUNINGUM
see Sveinsson, Gunnar Reynir

FIMM POSTLUDIUR see Sveinsson, Gunnar
Reynir

FIMM SMALOG see Fridriksson, Rikhardur
H.

FIMM SÖNGLÖG see Ágústsson, Herbert
Hriberschek see Thordarson,
Sigurdur

FIN DE LA JORNEE, LA see Vuursteen,
Frans

FINA KISA see Sveinsson, Atli Heimir

FINALE see Mesritz van Velthuysen, Anny

FINE
Childhood Fables
BOOSEY FIN0017   (F81)

Mutability
BOOSEY FIN0016   (F82)

FINE, VIVIAN (1913-   )
Great Wall Of China
solo voice,pno PRESSER 144-40104
(F83)

FINE KNACKS FOR LADIES see Dowland,
John

FINGRAMAL see Sveinsson, Atli Heimir

FINK
As My Heart Was
Bar solo,gtr SOUTHERN ST400   (F84)

Three Devotional Miniatures
S solo,gtr SOUTHERN V091   (F85)

FINK, SIEGFRIED
Tangents
solo voice,gtr PLUCKED STR ZM 1970
$6.50   (F86)

FINLAND see Jordan, Sverre

FINNES EN DYREBAR ROSE, DET see
Hovland, Egil

FINNISSY, MICHAEL (1946-   )
Beuk O'Newcassel Sangs
S solo,pno OXFORD 63.084   (F87)

Celi
SS soli,chamber group UNITED MUS
f.s.   (F88)

Unknown Ground
Bar solo,3pno OXFORD 61.019   (F89)

FINNS ETT HEM LÅNGT BORTOM SORGENS
HEMLAND, DET see Janácek, Bedrich

FINNS ETT SVAR FÖR DIG, DET see Mostad,
Jon

FINZI, GERALD (1901-1956)
By Footpath And Stile
Bar solo BOOSEY VAB0220   (F90)

FIOR DI GIAGGI see Mascagni, Pietro,
Cavalleria Rusticana: Stornello Di
Lola

FIORETTE see Dresden, Sem

FIPS see Lothar, Mark

FIRAIRE, LA see Camprubi, J.

FIRE ADVENT-SALMER see Elgaröy, Jan

FIRE ALBERTSANGE see Colding-Jorgensen,
Henrik

FIRE AUKRUST-SALMAR, OP.4 see Olsen,
Sparre

FIRE BIBELSKE SANGER, OP. 50 see Baden,
Conrad

FIRE, FIRE, FIRE... see Hol, Dirk

FIRE FOLKETONER OM DET KRISTNE HÅP
*CC4U
(Tøsse, Eilert) S solo,org NORGE f.s.
(F91)

FIRE FOLKETONER OM DET KRISTNE HÅP see
Tøsse, Eilert

FIRE NORDMØRSKE RELIGIØSE FOLKETONER
see Kverno, Trond

FIRE SALMETONER see Nystedt, Knut

FIRE SANGE MED KLAVER, OP. 33 see
Jordan, Sverre

FIRE SANGE, OP. 15 see Jordan, Sverre

FIRE SANGE TIL TEKST AV TORVALD TU'S
"STRENGJER SOM SYNG" see Jordan,
Sverre

FIRE SANGER see Indrehus, Per

FIRE SANGER MED ORKESTER see
Dorumsgaard, Arne

FIRE SANGER. OP. 41 see Jordan, Sverre

FIRE SANGER TIL TEKST AV GUNVOR HOFMO
see Killengreen, Christian

FIRE SETROM-SANGER, OP. 15 see Baden,
Conrad

FIRE SKJAERAASEN-SANGER, OP. 98 see
Baden, Conrad

FIRE SOLOMOTETTER FRA JOHANNES-
EVANGELIET, OP. 111 see Baden,
Conrad

FIRE SOLRENNINGSDIKT, OP. 2 see Olsen,
Sparre

FIRE SONGAR, OP. 29 see Søderlind,
Ragnar

FIRE TOSSERIER see Hall, Pauline

FIREFLIES IN THE GARDEN see Barati,
George

FIRSOVA, ELENA (1950-   )
Three Poems Of Osip Mandelstam
*Op.23
[Russ/Eng] S solo,pno SCHIRM.G
50481557   (F92)

FIRST BOOK OF BARITONE (BASS) SOLOS,
THE
(Boytim) Bar/B solo,pno (CC35L)
SCHIRM.G 50481176   (F93)

FIRST BOOK OF MEZZO-SOPRANO (ALTO)
SOLOS, THE
(Boytim) Mez/A solo,pno (CC34L)
SCHIRM.G 50481174   (F94)

FIRST BOOK OF SOPRANO SOLOS, THE
(Boytim) S solo,pno (CC34L) SCHIRM.G
50481173   (F95)

FIRST BOOK OF TENOR SOLOS, THE
(Boytim) T solo,pno (CC34L) SCHIRM.G
50481175   (F96)

FIRST KISS see Sibelius, Jean, Första
Kyssen, Den

FIRST LAY OF GUDRUN, THE see
Strindberg, Henrik, Första Kvädet
Om Gudrun, Det

FIRST MEETING, THE see Grieg, Edvard
Hagerup, Første Møde, Det

FIRST MEETING'S DELIGHT, THE see Grieg,
Edvard Hagerup, Første Møtes Sødme,
Det

FIRST SNOW, THE see Itoh, Mikio

FIRST STRATUM OF EMPYREAN see Rouse,
Christopher

FISCHBACH, KLAUS (1935-   )
Treues Vorwärtswandern
med solo,horn,pno BOHM f.s.   (F97)

FISCHER, A.
Abends-Schwärmerey
see Sechs Lieder

Hoffnung
see Sechs Lieder

Klage Der Schaeferin
see Sechs Lieder

Mädchen Aus Der Fremde, Das
see Sechs Lieder

Musik, Die
see Sechs Lieder

Nannys Nachruf An Philidor
see Sechs Lieder

Sechs Lieder
solo voice,pno SCIEN 542 f.s.
contains: Abends-Schwärmerey;
Hoffnung; Klage Der Schaeferin;
Mädchen Aus Der Fremde, Das;
Musik, Die; Nannys Nachruf An
Philidor   (F98)

FISCHER, EDUARD (1930-   )
Tiche Pisne *song cycle
S solo,pno,string orch [18'] CESKY
HUD.   (F99)

FISCHER, IRWIN (1903-1977)
Friendship
med solo,pno [4'] sc AM.COMP.AL.
$1.15   (F100)

In Transitu
see Now Sweeping Down The Years

Now Sweeping Down The Years
"In Transitu" med solo/high solo,
pno [4'] sc AM.COMP.AL. $1.90

FISCHER, IRWIN (cont'd.)

Sea-Bird, The (F101)
med solo,3.2.2.2. 4.2.3.1. timp,
cym,strings [3'] sc AM.COMP.AL.
$4.60 (F102)

That Which Is *sac
med solo,pno/org [2'] sc
AM.COMP.AL. $1.20 (F103)

There Shall Be No Sorrow
med solo,pno [4'] sc AM.COMP.AL.
$.80 (F104)

FISCHER, DER see Schubert, Franz
(Peter)

FISCHERMÄDCHEN, DAS see Proch, Heinrich

FISHER, ALFRED (1942-)
Night Elegy
Mez solo,vln,vla,vcl,hpsd,cel
SEESAW (F105)

Remembrance
see Zakhor

Two Last Words
S/T solo,pno SEESAW (F106)

Zakhor
"Remembrance" Mez/B solo,pno SEESAW
(F107)
FISHERGIRL IN DESPAIR, THE see Selmer,
Johan Peter, Fiskerjenten Fortvilet

FISHES AND POET'S HANDS see Reif, Paul

FISKAREN see Lundin, Dag

FISKERENS AFTENSANG see Jensen, Ludwig
Irgens

FISKERJENTEN FORTVILET see Selmer,
Johan Peter

FISKIRODUR see Sveinsson, Atli Heimir

FITZSIMONS, H.T.
Love And Arithmetic
FITZSIMONS F0104 (F108)

FIUME, ORAZIO (1908-)
Tamburo Di Panno, Il
solo voice,pno pno red CURCI 7653
(F109)
FIVE ADVERTISING SONGS see Slonimsky,
Nicolas

FIVE AMERICAN FOLKSONGS see Maw

FIVE AMERICAN GOSPEL SONGS see
Zaninelli

FIVE AMERICAN LYRICS see Hoekman,
Timothy

FIVE AMERICAN REVIVAL SONGS see
Zaninelli

FIVE ANGLO-NORMAN MOTETS
(Everist, Mark) 3 solo voices ANTICO
AE24 (F110)

FIVE BALLADES FOR THE HOUSE OF FOIX
(Lefferts, Peter) solo voices ANTICO
AE27 (F111)

FIVE BLACK SONGS see Montsalvatge,
Xavier, Cinco Canciones Negras

FIVE BROWN SONGS see Pluister, Simon

FIVE CHORALE PRELUDES see Bach, Johann
Sebastian

FIVE EARLY SONGS see Mahler, Gustav

FIVE-FOLD AMEN see Wallach, Joelle

FIVE FOLK SONGS, VOL. 2 see Zaninelli

FIVE GHAZALS OF HAFIZ see Bantock,
[Sir] Granville

FIVE GOETHE SONGS see Suben, Joel Eric

FIVE INVOCATIONS TO THE CRUCIFIED ONE
see Montsalvatge, Xavier, Cinco
Invocaciones Al Crucificado

FIVE LITTLE SONGS see Hahn, Reynaldo

FIVE LYRICS see Reuland, Jacques

FIVE MADRIGALS AND A CACCIA see
Perugia, Niccolo da

FIVE MILLAY SONGS see Adams, Leslie

FIVE MYSTICAL SONGS see Vaughan
Williams, Ralph

FIVE NEGRO SONGS see Beers, Jacques

FIVE NEGRO SPIRITUALS see Suben, Joel
Eric

FIVE NORWEGIAN FOLK TUNES, OP.35, NO.2
see Karlsen, Kjell Mørk

FIVE ORCHESTRAL SONGS see Karchin,
Louis S.

FIVE POEMS BY ROBERT HERRICK see
Lessard, John Ayres

FIVE POEMS OF JAMES JOYCE see
Planchart, Alejandro

FIVE POEMS OF WALLACE STEVENS see
Shearer, Allen

FIVE QUATRAINS FROM THE RUBÁIYÁT OF
OMAR KHAYYAM see Rogers, James
Henderson

FIVE ROMANCES see Shostakovich, Dmitri,
Satires (Pictures Of The Past) Op.
109

FIVE ROMANCES, OP. 42 see Koreshchenko,
Arseny

FIVE ROMANTIC SONGS see Hervig, Richard
B.

FIVE SCENES FROM "THE SPANISH LADY" see
Elgar, [Sir] Edward (William)

FIVE SETTINGS OF EUROPEAN POETS see
Berger, Arthur Victor

FIVE SHAKESPEARE SONGS see Dixon, Hugh

FIVE SHORT ARIAS see Scarlatti,
Alessandro

FIVE SONGS see Antheil, George see
Björnsson, Arni see Citkowitz,
Israel see Glinka, Mikhail
Ivanovich see Kristinsson,
Sigursveinn D. see Kristjánsson,
Oddgeir see Mozart, Wolfgang
Amadeus see Satoh, Shin see Seeger
see Stefansson, Fjölnir

FIVE SONGS see Balazs, Frederic

FIVE SONGS see Meneely-Kyder, Sarah

FIVE SONGS see Meneely-Kyder, Sarah

FIVE SONGS see Sims, Ezra

FIVE SONGS see Weigl, Karl

FIVE SONGS see Woollen, Russell

FIVE SONGS see Callaway, Ann

FIVE SONGS see Kreiger, Arthur V.

FIVE SONGS see Weigl, Karl

FIVE SONGS see Yannay, Yehuda

FIVE SONGS see Menotti, Gian Carlo

FIVE SONGS see Bax, [Sir] Arnold

FIVE SONGS see Koch, Frederick

FIVE SONGS see Shifrin, Seymour J.

FIVE SONGS see Shifrin, Seymour J.

FIVE SONGS BY POEM OF JUKICHI YAGI see
Kurokami, Yoshimitsu

FIVE SONGS (EMILY DICKINSON) see
Ruiter, Wim de

FIVE SONGS FROM CATULLUS see Buren,
John van, Fünf Gesänge Nach Catull

FIVE SONGS FROM WILLIAM BLAKE see
Thomson, Virgil Garnett

FIVE SONGS: "NOHARA UTA" see Kawasaki,
Etsuo

FIVE SONGS OF LAURENCE HOPE see
Burleigh, Henry Thacker

FIVE SONGS OF ROBERT FROST see
Wigglesworth, Frank

FIVE SONGS ON CHILDREN'S POEMS see
Rhodes, Phillip

FIVE SONGS ON ENGLISH POEMS see
Manneke, Daan

FIVE SONGS ON POEMS BY WENDY COPE see
Man, Roderik De

FIVE SONGS ON POEMS OF HESSE see Jaffe

FIVE SONGS, OP. 11 & 12 see MacDowell,
Edward Alexander

FIVE SONGS, OP. 15 see Madsen, Trygve

FIVE SONGS, OP.26 see Grieg, Edvard
Hagerup

FIVE SONGS, OP.60 see Grieg, Edvard
Hagerup

FIVE SONGS, OP.69 see Grieg, Edvard
Hagerup

FIVE SONGS, OP.70 see Grieg, Edvard
Hagerup

FIVE SONNETS, OP. 36 see Reizenstein,
Franz

FIVE SPIRITUALS AND WORK SONGS see
Meneely-Kyder, Sarah

FIVE TENOR SOLOS FROM THE OPERA "LORD
BYRON" see Thomson, Virgil Garnett

FIVE VOCAL GEMS FOR BASS
HLH ANT103 f.s.
contains: Bach, Johann Sebastian,
Coffee Cantata: Hat Man Nicht Mit
Seinen Kindern; Handel, George
Frideric, Ezio: Nasce Al Bosco;
Pachelbel, Carl Theodorus,
Magnificat In C: Deposuit
Potentes; Sullivan, [Sir] Arthur
Seymour, I Would I Were A King;
Wagner, Richard, Tannhäuser: O Du
Mein Holder Abendstern (F112)

FIVE VOCAL GEMS FOR MEZZO-SOPRANO AND
ALTO
HLH ANT101 f.s.
contains: Bach, Johann Sebastian,
St. John Passion: Es Ist
Vollbracht; Handel, George
Frideric, Samson: Return, Return,
O God Of Host; Monteverdi,
Claudio, Incoronazione Di Poppea,
L': Ottavia's Lament; Pachelbel,
Carl Theodorus, Magnificat In C:
Et Misericordia; Saint-Saëns,
Camille, Christmas Oratorio:
Expectans Expectavi Dominum
(F113)

FIVE VOCAL GEMS FOR SOPRANO
HLH ANT100 f.s.
contains: Haydn, [Franz] Joseph,
Small Organ Mass: Benedictus;
Mozart, Wolfgang Amadeus,
Vesperae Solennes De Confessore:
Laudate Dominum; Purcell, Henry,
Dido And Aeneas: Pursue Thy
Conquest, Love; Strauss, Johann,
[Jr.], Fledermaus, Die: Csárdás;
Sullivan, [Sir] Arthur Seymour,
Ivanhoe: O Awful Death (F114)

FIVE VOCAL GEMS FOR TENOR
HLH ANT102 f.s.
contains: Bach, Johann Sebastian,
Kirchenkantate 68: Mein Gläubiges
Herze, Frohlocke; Handel, George
Frideric, Atalanta: Care Selve;
Handel, George Frideric, Chandos
Anthem No. 4: The Waves Of The
Sea; Pachelbel, Carl Theodorus,
Magnificat In C: Esurientes;
Puccini, Giacomo, Messa Di
Gloria: Gratias, Agimus Tibi
(F115)
FIVE WELSH FOLK SONGS *CC5U,folk song,
Welsh
(Roberts, Trevor) solo voice BANKS
f.s. (F116)

FIVE WHITMAN SONGS see Borroff, Edith

FIVE WOLFSKEHL SONGS see Carr, Edwin

FJALLID EINA see Kaldalóns, Sigvaldi S.

FJALLID EINBUI see Isolfsson, Pall

FJÄRILN VINGAD SYNS PÅ HAGA see
Bellman, Carl Michael

FJELL-LENGT see Kielland, Olav

FJELL-NOREG see Olsen, Sparre

FJELL-NORIG see Olsen, Sparre

FJELL-NORIG: SYMFONISK HØGSONG see
Egge, Klaus

FJELL-SUITE see Storbekken, Egil

FJELLVIND see Groven, Eivind

FJÖGUR SÖNGLÖG see Ágústsson, Herbert
Hriberschek see Halldorsson, Sigfus
see Helgason, Hallgrimur see
Isolfsson, Pall see Runolfsson,
Karl Otto

FJOGUR THJODLOG see Helgason, Hallgrimur

FJOLLIN BLA see Björnsson, Arni

FJØRA SOM VART TIL TUSEN TONAR see Åm, Magnar

FJORD TRIO, EIN see Haugland, Glenn Erik

FJORTAN FOLKEVISER FRA ØSTFOLD see Elgarøy, Jan

FJORTEN MELODIER FRA BRORSONS SVANESANG see Lindeman, Ludvig Mathias

FLADMOE, ARVID (1915-   )
　Barcarole
　　[Norw] Bar solo,pno NORGE   (F117)
　　[Norw] Bar solo,2vln,vla,vcl NORGE
　　　　　　　　　　　　　　　　(F118)
　Barn, Et
　　[Norw] solo voice,pno NORGE (F119)
　Besvergelse
　　[Norw] solo voice,pno NORGE (F120)
　　[Norw] Bar solo,pno NORGE   (F121)
　　[Norw] Bar solo,2vln,vla,vcl NORGE
　　　　　　　　　　　　　　　　(F122)
　Bukkerittet
　　"Reindeer Ride, The" MezBar soli,
　　2.2.2.2. 2.2.2.1. timp,perc,
　　strings NORGE f.s.   (F123)
　Din Veg
　　see Tre Sanger
　Døde, De
　　see Tre Sanger
　Frigjort
　　see Tre Sanger
　Kannarhaugane
　　[Norw] solo voice,pno NORGE f.s.
　　　　　　　　　　　　　　　　(F124)
　På Kannarhaugene
　　see Tre Sange
　Reindeer Ride, The
　　see Bukkerittet
　Ride Båtkvelvet
　　see Tre Sange
　Sanger Om Døden
　　[Norw] S solo,vln,vla,vcl NORGE
　　　　　　　　　　　　　　　　(F125)
　Svana Eld
　　see Tre Sange
　Svana Eld Fra "På Kannarhaugenë
　　[Norw] solo voice,2vln,vla,vcl
　　NORGE   (F126)
　Three Songs *CC3U
　　S solo,vln,vla,vcl NORGE f.s.
　　　　　　　　　　　　　　　　(F127)
　Tre Sange *Op.11
　　Bar solo,2(pic).2.2.2. 0.3.0.0.
　　timp,perc,cel,strings NORGE f.s.
　　contains: På Kannarhaugene; Ride
　　　Båtkvelvet; Svana Eld   (F128)
　Tre Sanger
　　[Norw] S solo,vln,vla,vcl NORGE
　　f.s.
　　contains: Din Veg; Døde, De;
　　　Frigjort   (F129)

FLAHERTY, THOMAS (1950-   )
　Asylum Piece
　　Mez solo,clar,vln,vla,vcl,pno [8']
　　sc AM.COMP.AL. $10.70   (F130)

FLAME AND SHADOW see Murray, Bain

FLANAGAN, WILLIAM (1926-1969)
　Weeping Pleiades, The
　　Bar solo,fl,clar,pno,strings,vln
　　solo [13'0"] PEER   (F131)

FLAXEN HEADED COW BOY, A see Shield, William

FLEDERMAUS, DIE: MEIN HERR MARQUIS see Strauss, Johann, [Jr.]

FLEGIER, ANGE (1846-1927)
　Cor, Le
　　B solo,pno CLASSV 0449   (F132)

FLENDER, REINHARD DAVID (1953-   )
　Pirkei Tehillim
　　"Three Hebrew Psalms" med solo,
　　2.2.2.2. 3.2.0.1. timp,2perc,
　　marimba,harp,strings [20'0"] PEER
　　　　　　　　　　　　　　　　(F133)
　Three Hebrew Psalms
　　see Pirkei Tehillim

FLEUR DES CHAMPS, LA see Boeckx, Jean

FLEURETTE see Puget, Louise

FLEURS DORMENT, LES see Gounod, Charles François, Par Une Belle Nuit!

FLEURS DU MAL, LES see Gretchaninov, Alexander Tikhonovich

FLEURS PARISIENNES see Lecocq, Charles

FLEXICA see Perder, Kjell

FLICKAN GÅR I MÖRKAN SKOG see Freudenthal, Otto

FLIEGENDE HOLLÄNDER: TRAFT IHR DAS SCHIFF see Wagner, Richard

FLOATING POINT see Nordensten, Frank Tveor

FLOATING POINT, OP.78A see Nordensten, Frank Tveor

FLØITESTUBB see Sommerfeldt, Öistein

FLOODS OF SPRING see Rachmaninoff, Sergey Vassilievich

FLOR DE AMOR see Mayoral, R.

FLORAL DANCE, THE see Moss, Katie

FLORENTZ, JEAN-LOUIS
　Vocalise
　　med solo LEDUC AL 27115   (F134)

FLOTHUIS, MARIUS (1914-   )
　Black Eyes
　　see Four Trifles, Op. 33
　Blätterlosen Pappeln Stehn So Fein,
　　Die
　　see Vorfrühling, Op. 15
　Cun Quell' Ögliada
　　see Quatter Miniaturas Rumantschas,
　　Op. 68
　Engel, Die
　　see November, Op. 90
　Epilogue
　　see Negro Lament, Op. 49
　Es Ist Nacht
　　see Vier Morgenstern Liederen, Op.
　　3
　Es Läuft Der Frühlingswind Durch
　　Kahle Alleen
　　see Vorfrühling, Op. 15
　Falling Asleep In An Orchard
　　see Four Trifles, Op. 33
　Four Trifles, Op. 33
　　DONEMUS high solo,pno f.s.; low
　　solo,pno f.s.
　　contains: Black Eyes; Falling
　　　Asleep In An Orchard; Look,
　　　The; Seal-Woman, The   (F135)
　Fragment
　　see November, Op. 90
　Harlem Night Song
　　see Negro Lament, Op. 49
　Härte Schwand
　　see Vorfrühling, Op. 15
　Hy Droech Onse Smerten
　　see Twee Sonnetten, Op. 10
　I Chatscha Di
　　see Quatter Miniaturas Rumantschas,
　　Op. 68
　Lied
　　see Twee Liederen, Op. 15
　Look, The
　　see Four Trifles, Op. 33
　Morgen War Von Dir Erfüllt, Der
　　see Vier Morgenstern Liederen, Op.
　　3
　Negro Lament, Op. 49
　　A solo,alto sax,pno DONEMUS f.s.
　　[13']
　　contains: Epilogue; Harlem Night
　　　Song; Proem; Roland Hayes
　　　Beaten (Georgia 1942); Troubled
　　　Woman; White Ones, The   (F136)
　November, Op. 90
　　Mez solo,pno DONEMUS f.s. [12']
　　contains: Engel, Die; Fragment;
　　　Windmühle   (F137)
　O Nacht
　　see Vier Morgenstern Liederen, Op.
　　3

FLOTHUIS, MARIUS (cont'd.)
　Plövgia
　　see Quatter Miniaturas Rumantschas,
　　Op. 68
　Proem
　　see Negro Lament, Op. 49
　Quatter Miniaturas Rumantschas, Op.
　　68
　　S solo,fl DONEMUS f.s. [6']
　　contains: Cun Quell' Ögliada; I
　　　Chatscha Di; Plövgia; Uniun
　　　　　　　　　　　　　　　　(F138)
　Rebel, Mijn Hart
　　see Twee Sonnetten, Op. 10
　Roland Hayes Beaten (Georgia 1942)
　　see Negro Lament, Op. 49
　Rondel *Op.15a
　　S solo,pno [6'] DONEMUS   (F139)
　　see Twee Liederen, Op. 15
　Seal-Woman, The
　　see Four Trifles, Op. 33
　Troubled Woman
　　see Negro Lament, Op. 49
　Twee Liederen, Op. 15
　　S/Mez solo,fl,ob d'amore,clar,bsn,
　　horn,db DONEMUS f.s. [4']
　　contains: Lied; Rondel   (F140)
　Twee Sonnetten, Op. 10
　　med solo,pno DONEMUS f.s. [5']
　　contains: Hy Droech Onse Smerten;
　　　Rebel, Mijn Hart   (F141)
　Uniun
　　see Quatter Miniaturas Rumantschas,
　　Op. 68
　Vier Morgenstern Liederen, Op. 3
　　S solo,pno DONEMUS f.s. [8']
　　contains: Es Ist Nacht; Morgen
　　　War Von Dir Erfüllt, Der; O
　　　Nacht; Wasserfall Bei Nacht
　　　　　　　　　　　　　　　　(F142)
　Vorfrühling, Op. 15
　　Mez solo,pno DONEMUS f.s. [6']
　　contains: Blätterlosen Pappeln
　　　Stehn So Fein, Die; Es Läuft
　　　Der Frühlingswind Durch Kahle
　　　Alleen; Härte Schwand   (F143)
　Wasserfall Bei Nacht
　　see Vier Morgenstern Liederen, Op.
　　3
　White Ones, The
　　see Negro Lament, Op. 49
　Windmühle
　　see November, Op. 90

FLOTOW, FRIEDRICH VON (1812-1883)
　Ach! So Fromm
　　see Martha: M'Appari Tutt' Amor
　Air Des Larmes
　　[Fr/Ger] S/T solo SCHOTT-FRER 9004
　　　　　　　　　　　　　　　　(F144)
　Marta: M'Appari Tutt' Amour
　　T solo,pno BOIL B.1702   (F145)
　Marta: M'appari Tutt'amor
　　"Soft And Pure, Like A Dream" T
　　solo RICORDI-IT LD359   (F146)
　Martha: Lasst Mich Euch Fragen
　　B solo,pno CLASSV 1563   (F147)
　Martha: M'Appari Tutt' Amor
　　"Ach! So Fromm" [It/Ger/Eng] T
　　solo,pno CLASSV 1326   (F148)
　Romance De La Rose
　　SCHOTT-FRER 9010   (F149)
　Soft And Pure, Like A Dream
　　see Marta: M'appari Tutt'amor

FLOTTINN see Davidsson, Elias

FLOW GENTLY, SWEET AFTON see Mermaid & Two Other Water Songs, The see Anonymous

FLOWER DUET see Delibes, Léo, Sous Le Dôme Épais

FLOWER GIVEN TO MY DAUGHTER, A see Dembski, Stephen

FLOWER HAWTHORN, A see Nakada, Kazutsugu

FLOWER OF THE MOUNTAIN see Albert, Stephen Joel

FLOWER SONG see Bizet, Georges, Carmen: La Fleur Que Tu M'avais Jetée

FLOWER THAT GROWS UPON THE THORN, THE
see Loder, Edwin James

FLUGSURR see Ørbeck, Anne Marie

FLUT UND SCHWAMM see Goorissen, Jan

FLUVIA, A.
Tinc Enveja Del Matí
solo voice,pno BOIL B.0790 (F150)

Vostre Riure
solo voice,pno BOIL B.0791 (F151)

FLY, THE see Kirkwood, Antoinette

FLY AND I, THE see Pluister, Simon

FLYG EJ UNDAN see Söderman, [Johan]
August

FLYING EAGLE see Jordan, Sverre,
Flyvende Ørn

FLYKTINGAR VÅRA SYSKON see Österberg,
Sven

FLYSKREKK! see Germeten, Gunnar

FLYVENDE ØRN see Jordan, Sverre

FOCKE, FRÉ (1910-   )
Blat Wir Zur Blüte, Das
see Übergänge 1. Folge

Einst Träumten Wir
see Übergänge 1. Folge

Ich Fühle Deine Schönheit
see Übergänge 1. Folge

Ich Habe Das Gefäss Meines Herzens
see Übergänge 1. Folge

Lösche Die Lampe
see Übergänge 1. Folge

Nacht Ist Es
see Übergänge 2. Folge

Übergänge 1. Folge
Mez solo,pno DONEMUS f.s. [3']
contains: Blat Wir Zur Blüte,
Das; Einst Träumten Wir; Ich
Fühle Deine Schönheit; Ich Habe
Das Gefäss Meines Herzens;
Lösche Die Lampe (F152)

Übergänge 2. Folge
med solo,fl,pno DONEMUS f.s. [5']
contains: Nacht Ist Es; Weiss
Schlagen Die Wellen; Wie Im
Traum Liegt Der Morgen; Wilde,
Steile Brandung; Wissend Würzte
Es Den Anfang (F153)

Übergänge 3. Folge *CC7L
med solo,ob,pno DONEMUS f.s. (F154)

Übergänge, 11 Lieder Nach Japanischen
Gedichte *CC11U
Mez solo,pno DONEMUS f.s. [8']
(F155)

Weiss Schlagen Die Wellen
see Übergänge 2. Folge

Wendungen, 17 Gedichte Von W. Focke
*CC17U
S solo,pno DONEMUS f.s. [15']
(F156)

Wie Im Traum Liegt Der Morgen
see Übergänge 2. Folge

Wilde, Steile Brandung
see Übergänge 2. Folge

Wissend Würzte Es Den Anfang
see Übergänge 2. Folge

FØDD I GÅR see Baden, Conrad

FØDD I GÅR: THREE SONGS TO HALDIS MOREN
VESAAS TEXTS see Volle, Bjarne

FOG see Heilner, Irwin see Weigl,
[Mrs.] Vally

FOG WRAITHS see Carpenter, John Alden

FOGGY DEW, THE see Corigliano, John

FOLIE ET MORT D'OPHÉLIE see Abbott,
Alain see Louvier, Alain

FOLK, ETT, OP. 22 see Stenhammar,
Wilhelm

FOLK SOM VANDRER I MØRKET, DET see
Holter, Stig Wernø

FOLK SONGS FOR SOLO SINGERS *CC11UL
(Althouse) ALFRED med-high solo,pno
4952 accomp tape available; med-low
solo 4953 accomp tape available
(F157)

FOLK SONGS SING ALONG
("World's Favorite Series") ASHLEY
011-5 (F158)

FOLKETONE FRA IVELAND see Haegeland,
Eilert M.

FOLKEVISE see Ørbeck, Anne Marie

FOLKLORE ANDALUSIA *Span
(Haus, Karl) S/Mez/T solo,perc,
guitar ensemble VOGT f.s.
contains: Adiós, Malaga; Con El
Vito; Paño, El; Tres Morillas;
Viva Sevilla (F159)

FOLKSONG see Baldvinsson, Tryggvi

FOLKSONG TRANSFORMATIONS *CCU
(Parker, Alice) solo voice GALAXY
1.3052 $4.50 (F160)

FOLKSONGS see Young, Douglas

FOLKSONGS, 40
(Filippov; Rimsky-Korsakov) KALMUS
K 05285 (F161)

FOLLOW ME TO THE FIELD see Avni, Tzvi

FOMENKO, MYKOLA (1895-1961)
Willow, The
[Ukranian] S solo,pno DUMA (F162)

FONGAARD, BJØRN (1919-1981)
Du Gir
see Seks Sanger, Op. 149, Nos. 1-6

Erkenntnis, Die *Op.137
[Ger] S solo,vln,perc [15'] NORGE
(F163)

Fra Salomos Ordsprog
[Norw] S solo,pno NORGE (F164)

Kappen
see Seks Sanger, Op. 149, Nos. 1-6

Month Of Love, The
see Øyeblikksbilder, Op. 146, No. 3

Nyttår Ved Havet *Op.13
[Norw] solo voice,pno,gtr,vln NORGE
(F165)

Øyeblikksbilder, Op. 146, No. 3
"Month Of Love, The" [Norw] S solo,
pno NORGE (F166)

Seks Sanger, Op. 149, Nos. 1-6
[Norw] Bar solo,pno NORGE f.s.
contains: Du Gir; Kappen;
Skumring; Tankens Vinge; Til
Den Lille Fugl; Tør Jeg (F167)

Sextet
[Norw] S solo,vln,bsn,harp,hpsd,
vibra [10'] NORGE (F168)

Skumring
see Seks Sanger, Op. 149, Nos. 1-6

Tankens Vinge
see Seks Sanger, Op. 149, Nos. 1-6

Til Den Lille Fugl
see Seks Sanger, Op. 149, Nos. 1-6

Tør Jeg
see Seks Sanger, Op. 149, Nos. 1-6

Vinternatt, Op.12
[Norw] solo voice,pno,gtr,vln NORGE
(F169)

FONTENAILLES, H. DE
Obstination
high solo,pno CLASSV 0533 (F170)

FONTYN, JACQUELINE (1930-   )
Ku Soko
high solo,kbd PEER 61764-202 (F171)
solo voice,pno (diff) PEER (F172)

FOOTE, ARTHUR (1853-1937)
Ashes Of Roses *Op.51,No.4
low solo,pno CLASSV 1464 (F173)

Constancy *Op.55,No.1
low solo,pno CLASSV 1968 (F174)

Ditty, A *Op.26,No.8
"My True Love Hath My Heart" med-
high solo,pno CLASSV 1467 (F175)
"My True Love Hath My Heart" low
solo,pno CLASSV 1466 (F176)

Eden-Rose, The
high solo,pno CLASSV 1465 (F177)

I'm Wearing Awa' To The Land O' The
Leal *Op.13,No.2
med solo,pno CLASSV 1462 (F178)

Irish Folk-Song, An
[Eng] low solo,pno CLASSV 1969
(F179)

FOOTE, ARTHUR (cont'd.)

It Was A Lover And His Lass *Op.10,
No.1
med-high solo,pno CLASSV 1469
(F180)

Lilac Time
high solo,pno CLASSV 1971 (F181)
med solo,pno CLASSV 1972 (F182)

My True Love Hath My Heart
see Ditty, A

O Swallow, Swallow Flying South
high solo,pno (text by Tennyson)
CLASSV 1457 (F183)

On The Way To Kew
low solo,pno CLASSV 1459 (F184)

Persian Song From The Rubáiyát Of
Omar Khayyám *Op.40
med solo,pno CLASSV 1970 (F185)

Rose And The Gardener, The *Op.51,
No.1
low solo,pno CLASSV 1463 (F186)

Song Of The Forge
med solo,pno CLASSV 1460 (F187)

Songs By Arthur Foote, Op.26
solo voice,pno CLASSV 1989 (F188)

To Blossoms *Op.26,No.6
med-high solo,pno (text by Robert
Herrick) CLASSV 1461 (F189)

When Icicles Hang By The Wall
B solo,pno CLASSV 1458 (F190)

FÖR ALLA VINDAR see Linde, Bo

FØR DET SNER see Vea, Ketil

FOR HAVET see Vaage, Knut

FOR LENNY, AT 70 see Schat, Peter

FOR MUSIC see Balazs, Frederic

FOR MY LOVE see Beach, [Mrs.] H.H.A.
(Amy Marcy Cheney), Je Demande À
L'Oiseau

FOR MY MOTHER see Malotte, Albert Hay

FORÅR FARVER JORDEN GRØNN, ET see
Lunde, Ivar

FORD, RONALD (1959-   )
Four Songs On Texts Of Dylan Thomas
S solo,pno DONEMUS f.s. [15']
contains: I Have Longed To Move
Away; Should Lanterns Shine;
Twenty-Four Years; Was There A
Time (F191)

I Have Longed To Move Away
see Four Songs On Texts Of Dylan
Thomas

Should Lanterns Shine
see Four Songs On Texts Of Dylan
Thomas

Twenty-Four Years
see Four Songs On Texts Of Dylan
Thomas

Was There A Time
see Four Songs On Texts Of Dylan
Thomas

FORD'S MONOLOGUE see Verdi, Giuseppe,
Falstaff: E Sogno? O Realtà?

FORE
Canconer Selecte Vol. 4
[Span/Ger] solo voice,pno BOIL
B.2151 (F192)

FORESTRY see Thwaites, Penelope

FOREWORD TO MY WORKS, OP. 123 see
Shostakovich, Dmitri

FORGOTTEN? see Beach, [Mrs.] H.H.A.
(Amy Marcy Cheney)

FORKEIKUR AD "SKUGGA-SVEINI" see
Runolfsson, Karl Otto

FÖRKLARING see Gjerstrom, Bjorn G.

FORLATT see Torjussen, Trygve

FORMS IN CHANGE see Paccione, Paul

FORSBERG, ROLAND (1939-   )
Jungfru Marias Lovsång *Op.140,No.1
Mez solo,org STIM f.s. (F193)

Skall Stenarna Ropa
[Swed] solo voice,pno/org WESSMAN
(F194)

FORSELL, JONAS (1957-   )
Alskandes Klagan
[Swed] solo voice,perc [4'30"]
REIMERS 101197   (F195)

Honsskit
solo voice,pno REIMERS 101193
                        (F196)

Pask 1968
[Swed] solo voice,perc [1'40"]
REIMERS 101196   (F197)
[Swed] solo voice,perc REIMERS from
TRE SANGER UR VARIATIONER EFTER
W. B. YEATS   (F198)

Tiden Och En Flicka
[Swed] solo voice,perc [4'30"]
REIMERS 101198   (F199)
[Swed] solo voice,perc REIMERS from
TRE SANGER UR VARIATIONER EFTER
W. B. YEATS   (F200)

Tre Sånger Ur Variationer Efter W. B.
Yeats
see Pask 1968
see Tiden Och En Flicka

FÖRSTA KVÄDET OM GUDRUN, DET see
Strindberg, Henrik

FÖRSTA KYSSEN, DEN see Sibelius, Jean

FØRSTE MØDE, DET see Grieg, Edvard
Hagerup

FØRSTE MØTES SØDME, DET see Grieg,
Edvard Hagerup

FØRSTE SOMMERFUGL, DEN see Nordheim,
Arne

FORSYTH, JOSEPHINE (1889-1940)
Adieu De La Mariee
see Three Metis Songs

Chanson De La Grenouillere
see Three Metis Songs

Chanson Du Petit Cordnnier
see Three Metis Songs

Three Metis Songs
med solo,pno SCHIRM.G 50481051 f.s.
contains: Adieu De La Mariee;
Chanson De La Grenouillere;
Chanson Du Petit Cordnnier
                        (F201)

FORT JUNIPER SONGS see Jaffe, Stephen

FORTROLLA SKOG see Tveitt, Geirr

FORTUNETELLER ON THE SLOPE see Morita,
Shin-Ichi

FORZA DEL DESTINO, LA: MADRE, PIETOSA
VERGINE see Verdi, Giuseppe

FORZA DEL DESTINO, LA: PACE, PACE see
Verdi, Giuseppe

FORZA DEL DESTINO, LA: PACE, PACE MIO
DIO see Verdi, Giuseppe

FORZA DI AMARE, LA see Nicolai, Bruno

FOSCA: QUALE ORRIBILE PECCATO see
Gomes, Antônio Carlos

FOSTER, DAN
There's A Reason
solo voice HARRIS,R RHS0707 $2.00
                        (F202)

FOSTER, STEPHEN COLLINS (1826-1864)
Ah! May The Red Rose Live Alway
med solo,pno CLASSV 1340   (F203)

Beautiful Child Of Song
med solo,pno (2 versions) CLASSV
1341   (F204)

Happy Hours At Home
med-high solo,pno CLASSV 1765
                        (F205)

Stephen Foster Songbook
("World's Favorite Series") ASHLEY
083-2   (F206)

Three Songs By Stephen Foster
(Zaninelli) high solo SHAWNEE 0077
                        (F207)

Why, No One To Love?
med solo,pno CLASSV 1764   (F208)

FÖTTER see Blomberg, Erik

FOUNTAIN MINGLES WITH THE RIVER, THE
see Gounod, Charles François

FOUR see Thomas, Andrew

FOUR AMERICAN WOMEN POETS see Haxton,
Kenneth

FOUR AND TWENTY TAILORS see Jeffreys,
John

FOUR BLAKE SONGS see Brown, Francis
James

FOUR CATALONIAN SONGS see Rodrigo,
Joaquín

FOUR CHILDREN'S SONGS see Ikebe, Shin-
Ichiro

FOUR CHINESE LOVE POEMS see Wood,
Joseph

FOUR CHINESE TONE POEMS see Carpenter,
John Alden, Water-Colors

FOUR CHRISTMAS SONGS see
Sigurbjörnsson, Thorkell

FOUR DICKINSON SONGS see Hoiby, Lee

FOUR DREAM POEMS see Blank, Allan

FOUR DUCKS ON A POND see Needham,
Alicia Adelaide

FOUR EARLY SONGS see Copland, Aaron

FOUR EPITAPHS, OP. 10 see Boldemann,
Laci

FOUR FAMOUS AVE MARIA see Quatre
Célèbres Ave Maria

FOUR GERMAN SONGS see Mamlok, Ursula

FOUR HAIKU SETTINGS see Ator, James
Donald

FOUR HAIKU SONGS see Smolanoff, Michael
Louis

FOUR HEINE LIEDER see Noland, Gary

FOUR HONIG SONGS see Bauer, Ross

FOUR INDIAN LOVE SONGS see Woodforde-
Finden, Amy

FOUR ITALIAN MELODIES
(Challoner, Neville Butler) solo
voice,pno SCIEN 360 f.s.
contains: Aure Felice; Donne
L'Amore (Mayer); Fra Tante
Angoscie (Caraffa); Tu Vedrai
(Bellini)   (F209)

FOUR LAST SONGS see Vaughan Williams,
Ralph

FOUR LATE POEMS & AN EPIGRAM see
Knussen, Oliver

FOUR LORCA SONGS see Lauridsen, Morten
Johannes, Cuatro Canciones Sobre
Poesias De Federico Garcia Lorca

FOUR LOVE SONGS see Mulholland, James

FOUR LYRIC SONGS see Uzaki, Koichi

FOUR MEDIAEVAL LYRICS see Tremain,
Ronald

FOUR NIGHT SONGS see Dring, Madeleine

FOUR...PARTS OF A WORLD see Bazelon,
Irwin Allen

FOUR POEMS ABOUT CLOUD VALLEY, THE
ESTATE OF HUANG-FU-YUAN see
Hekster, Walter

FOUR POEMS (FROM A CHILD'S GARDEN OF
VERSES) see Wayne, Harry

FOUR POEMS FROM AFTONLAND see Sanders,
Noel

FOUR POEMS FROM THE JAPANESE see
Becker, John

FOUR POEMS OF SHOVE see Vaughan
Williams, Ralph

FOUR POEMS ON THE PLEASURES OF THE
COUNTRY see Hekster, Walter

FOUR POSTHUMOUS SONGS see Delius,
Frederick

FOUR PSALMS, OP. 22 see Nystedt, Knut,
Tru Og Saeledrust

FOUR RELIGIOUS SONGS FROM C.U.L. ADD.
MS 5943
(Rastall, Richard) 2-3 solo voices
ANTICO AE18   (F210)

FOUR ROMANCES, OP. 2 see Rimsky-
Korsakov, Nikolai

FOUR ROMANCES, OP. 3 see Rimsky-
Korsakov, Nikolai

FOUR ROMANCES, OP. 4 see Rimsky-
Korsakov, Nikolai

FOUR ROMANCES, OP. 7 see Rimsky-
Korsakov, Nikolai

FOUR ROMANCES, OP. 26 see Rimsky-
Korsakov, Nikolai

FOUR ROMANCES, OP. 27 see Rimsky-
Korsakov, Nikolai

FOUR ROMANCES, OP. 39 see Rimsky-
Korsakov, Nikolai

FOUR ROMANCES, OP. 40 see Rimsky-
Korsakov, Nikolai

FOUR ROMANCES, OP. 41 see Rimsky-
Korsakov, Nikolai

FOUR ROMANCES, OP. 42 see Rimsky-
Korsakov, Nikolai

FOUR ROMANCES, OP. 55 see Rimsky-
Korsakov, Nikolai

FOUR SACRED SONGS see Warren, Betsy

FOUR SCRIPTURAL SONGS, OP. 121 see
Brahms, Johannes

FOUR SEA LYRICS see Campbell-Tipton,
Louis

FOUR SEPHARDI SONGS
(Knapp, Alexander) med solo,pno
TRANSCON. 991330 f.s.
contains: Mama, Yo No Tengo Visto;
Mi Padre Era De Francia; Nani,
Nani; Yo M'enamori D'un Aire
                        (F211)

FOUR SERIOUS SONGS see Brahms, Johannes

FOUR SETTINGS OF IRISH COUNTRY SONGS
see Tal, Marjo

FOUR SETTINGS OF W.C. WILLIAMS see
Kreiger, Arthur V.

FOUR SEVENTEENTH CENTURY POEMS see
Bunge, Sas

FOUR SHAKESPEARE SONNETS see Norby,
Erik

FOUR SOMBER SONGS see Van de Vate,
Nancy Hayes

FOUR SONGS see Boulanger, Nadia, Quatre
Chants see Einarsson, Sigfus see
Nelson, David see Sigurbjörnsson,
Thorkell see Stutschevsky, Joachim
see Tal, Marjo

FOUR SONGS [1] see Roosevelt, [Joseph]
Willard

FOUR SONGS [2] see Roosevelt, [Joseph]
Willard

FOUR SONGS see Lockwood, Normand

FOUR SONGS see Tillis, Frederick C.

FOUR SONGS see Wright, Maurice

FOUR SONGS see Lockwood, Normand

FOUR SONGS see Ruiter, Wim de

FOUR SONGS see Ruiter, Wim de

FOUR SONGS see Bergsma, William
Laurence

FOUR SONGS see Schubert, Franz (Peter)

FOUR SONGS see Steiner, Gitta Hana

FOUR SONGS see Steuermann, Edward

FOUR SONGS BY SAPPHO see
Constantinides, Dinos Demetrios

FOUR SONGS ("DES KNABEN WUNDERHORN")
see Weigl, Karl

FOUR SONGS FOR SOLO VOICE AND WOODWIND
see Warren, Betsy

FOUR SONGS FOR VOICE AND ORCHESTRA see
Delius, Frederick

FOUR SONGS FROM "THE FRINGES OF THE
FLEET" see Elgar, [Sir] Edward
(William)

FOUR SONGS FROM "THE GOLDEN GATE" see
Isolfsson, Pall

FOUR SONGS OF DEPARTURE see Zahler,
Noel Barry

FOUR SONGS OF MIRZA SCHAFFY, OP. 2 see
Quilter, Roger

FOUR SONGS OF SAPPHO see Yavelow,
Christopher Johnson

FOUR SONGS OF THE SEA see Quilter,
Roger

FOUR SONGS ON POEMS BY THOMAS CAMPION
see Hol, Dirk

FOUR SONGS ON TEXTS OF DYLAN THOMAS see
Ford, Ronald

FOUR SONGS, OP. 6 see Madsen, Trygve

FOUR SONGS, OP.7 see Gretchaninov,
Alexander Tikhonovich

FOUR SONGS, OP. 14 see Quilter, Roger

FOUR SONGS, OP. 19 see Madsen, Trygve

FOUR SONGS, OP.20 see Gretchaninov,
Alexander Tikhonovich

FOUR SONGS, OP.21 see Grieg, Edvard
Hagerup

FOUR SONGS, OP. 68 see Kadosa, Pal

FOUR SONGS, OP. 73 see Dvořák, Antonín

FOUR SONGS TO ICELANDIC POEMS see
Ragnarsson, Hjalmar H.

FOUR SONGS TO POEMS BY CLAES GILL see
Rammo, Peeter

FOUR SONGS TO POEMS BY KARIN BOYE see
Støyva, Njål Gunnar

FOUR SONGS TO WORDS BY MADELINE CHASE
see Ross, Colin Archibald Campbell

FOUR SONNETS BY WILLIAM SHAKESPEARE see
Brown, Francis James

FOUR SONNETS FROM THE PORTUGUESE see
Parmentier, F. Gordon

FOUR TONADILLAS: BY THGE INN'S GATE
(Surinach, Carlos; Subira, Jose)
"Four Tonadillas: Una Mesonera Y Un
Arriero" SBar soli,1(pic).1.0.1.
1.1.0.0. timp,perc,4mand/hpsd/pno,
strings [12'0"] PEER   (F212)

FOUR TONADILLAS: EL MAJO Y LA MAJA see
Four Tonadillas: Lovers' Quarrels

FOUR TONADILLAS: LA MAJA LIMONERA see
Four Tonadillas: The Lemon Girl

FOUR TONADILLAS: LOS CIEGOS FINGIDOS
see Four Tonadillas: The Beggars

FOUR TONADILLAS: LOVERS' QUARRELS
(Surinach, Carlos; Subira, Jose)
"Four Tonadillas: El Majo Y La
Maja" ST soli,1(pic).1.1.1.
1.1.0.0. timp,perc,hpsd/pno,strings
[28'0"] PEER   (F213)

FOUR TONADILLAS: THE BEGGARS
(Surinach, Carlos; Subira, Jose)
"Four Tonadillas: Los Ciegos
Fingidos" SMezBar soli,1.1.1.1.
1.0.0.0. timp,hpsd/pno,strings
[16'0"] PEER   (F214)

FOUR TONADILLAS: THE LEMON GIRL
(Surinach, Carlos; Subira, Jose)
"Four Tonadillas: La Maja Limonera"
ST soli,1(pic).1.1.1. 1.1.0.0.
timp,perc,4mand/hpsd/pno,strings
[16'0"] PEER   (F215)

FOUR TONADILLAS: UNA MESONERA Y UN
ARRIERO see Four Tonadillas: By
Thge Inn's Gate

FOUR TRADITIONAL AMERICAN SONGS
(Moores, M.) med solo,pno RAMSEY
BR0031 f.s.
contains: Child Of God; Cripple
Creek; Red, Rosey Bush; Single
Girl   (F216)

FOUR TRIFLES, OP. 33 see Flothuis,
Marius

FOUR VOCALISES see Shore, Clare

FOUR VOCALISES see Dresden, Sem

FOUR WALT WHITMAN SONGS see Weill, Kurt

FOUR WEDDING SOLOS see McConnell, Doug

FOUR YEATS SONGS see Blank, Allan

FOURDRAIN, FELIX (1880-1923)
Carnaval
high solo,pno CLASSV 0764   (F217)

Papillon, Le
high solo,pno CLASSV 1661   (F218)

FOURTEEN SONGS see Björnsson, Arni see
Mahler, Gustav

FOWLER, JENNIFER (1939-   )
Voice Of The Shades
S solo,ob/clar,vln,2trp fac ed
UNIVER. UE 29200 f.s.   (F219)

FOX, FREDERICK ALFRED (FRED)
(1931-   )
Time Excursions
S&narrator,fl,clar,vln,vla,vcl,pno,
2perc SEESAW   (F220)

FRA DIAVOLO: QUEL BONHEUR JE RESPIRE
see Auber, Daniel-François-Esprit

FRA DIAVOLO: QUELL' UOM DAL FIERO
ASPETTO see Auber, Daniel-François-
Esprit

FRA "JONSOKNATT" see Ørbeck, Anne Marie

FRA MONTE PINCIO see Grieg, Edvard
Hagerup

FRA "MUNKEN VENDT" see Marcussen, Kjell

FRÅ O.M. SANDVIKS
"GUDBRANDSDALSMUSIKKEN" see Grov,
Magne

FRA SALOMOS ORDSPROG see Fongaard,
Bjørn

FRA TANTE ANGOSCIE (CARAFFA) see Four
Italian Melodies

FRA TANTE PENE see Handel, George
Frideric

FRAGE UND ANTWORT see Marx, Joseph

FRAGEN EINES ENGAGIERTEN DICHTERS see
Straesser, Joep

FRAGEN UND DIE ANTWORTEN, DIE see
Straesser, Joep

FRAGMENT see Flothuis, Marius

FRAGMENT FROM "CITIES OF THE INTERIOR"
see Barati, George

FRAGMENT "SYBILLE" see Döhl, Friedhelm

FRAGMENTE AUS "HYMNEN AN DIE NACHT" see
Becker, Günther

FRAGMENTE EINER KLEISTHYMNE see Medek,
Tilo

FRAGMENTER see Hojsgaard, Erik

FRAGMENTER, OP. 13 see Strömholm, Folke

FRAGMENTS see Hojsgaard, Erik,
Fragmenter

FRAGMENTS D'UN HOMME MODERNE see Bakke,
Ruth

FRAGMENTS FROM ANTIQUITY see Wyner,
Yehudi

FRAGMENTS FROM HIPPONAX see Wood,
Joseph

FRAGMENTS FROM THE CANTOS OF EZRA POUND
see Lessard, John Ayres

FRAM, FRAM see Björnsson, Arni

FRAMENCO see Nakamura, Yukitake

FRAMMENTI DI EROS see Morricone, Ennio

FRAMMENTO see Razzi, Fausto

FRAMMENTO 2 see Razzi, Fausto

FRÅN DUNKLA SILVERSKYAR NER see
Hallnäs, Lars

FRÅN TRIESTES KUST see Lidström, John

FRANCAIX, JEAN (1912-   )
Grenouilles, Les
see Trois Duos

Oiseaux, Les
see Trois Duos

Priere De Sulpicia
see Trois Duos

Trois Duos
SS soli,string quar SCHOTT ME 8557
f.s.

FRANCAIX, JEAN (cont'd.)

contains: Grenouilles, Les;
Oiseaux, Les; Priere De
Sulpicia   (F221)

FRANCHETTI, ALBERTO (1860-1942)
Germania: No, Non Chiuder Gli Occhi
Vaghi
[It/Eng] T solo,pno CLASSV 1215
(F222)

FRANCK
Geistliche Lieder
KAHNT 7578   (F223)

Seek Thou This Soul Of Mine
(Zaninelli) high solo SHAWNEE 5088
(F224)

FRANCK, CESAR (1822-1890)
Aimer
high solo,pno CLASSV 0647   (F225)

Ave Maria
S/T solo SCHOTT-FRER 8938   (F226)
Mez/Bar solo SCHOTT-FRER 8939
(F227)

Cloches Du Soir, Le
high solo,pno CLASSV 0648   (F228)

Émir De Bengador, L'
med-high solo,pno CLASSV 0653
(F229)

Lied
high solo,pno CLASSV 0650   (F230)

Ninon
high solo,pno CLASSV 0651   (F231)

O Bread Of Life
see Panis Angelicus

O Lord Most Holy
see Panis Angelicus

O Salutaris
S/T solo,org LEDUC f.s.   (F232)

Panis Angelicus
T/S solo (A maj) SCHOTT-FRER 8926
(F233)
Bar/Mez solo (G maj) SCHOTT-FRER
8927   (F234)
"O Bread Of Life" [Eng/Lat] low
solo,pno CLASSV 1767   (F235)
"O Lord Most Holy" [Eng/Lat] high
solo,org CLASSV 1766   (F236)

Passez! Passez Toujours!
med solo,pno CLASSV 0654   (F237)

Rédemption, 1er Air De l'Archange
S solo,pno HEUGEL f.s.   (F238)

Rédemption, 2e Air De l'Archange
S solo,pno HEUGEL f.s.   (F239)

Robin Gray
med-high solo,pno CLASSV 0655
(F240)

Souvenance
high solo,pno CLASSV 0652   (F241)

Sylphe, Le
med solo,pno,vcl CLASSV 0656 (F242)

Tantum Ergo
S solo,pno LEDUC f.s.   (F243)

Vase Brisé, Le
med solo,pno CLASSV 0649   (F244)

FRANCO, CESARE
see FRANCK, CESAR

FRANCO, JOHAN (1908-   )
Little Lamb
S solo,gtr [5'] sc AM.COMP.AL. $.80
(F245)

Shroud Of Turin, The
med solo,pno [7'] sc AM.COMP.AL.
$3.50   (F246)

Word Came Forth, The
med solo,pno [5'] sc AM.COMP.AL.
$1.95   (F247)

FRANCOIS SOLAIRE see Lerstad, Terje B.

FRANDSEN, JOHN (1956-   )
Seven Silly Songs
Mez solo,gtr [12'] REIMERS 101145
(F248)

Songs Of Innocence
S/T solo,gtr [12'] SAMFUNDET (F249)

FRANKEN, WIM (1922-   )
Abend
see Zes Rilke-Liederen

Ballade Des Dames Du Temps Jadis
see Cinq Poemes De Francois Villon

Ballade Des Femmes De Paris
see Cinq Poemes De Francois Villon

FRANKEN, WIM (cont'd.)

Cinq Poemes De Francois Villon
    T solo,pno DONEMUS f.s. [13']
    contains: Ballade Des Dames Du
    Temps Jadis; Ballade Des Femmes
    De Paris; Epitaphe Et Verset;
    Question Au Clerc Du Quichet;
    Rondeau A La Mort   (F250)

Compromis
    see Zes Slauerhoff-Liederen

Das Ist Dort, Wo Die Letzten Hütten
    Sind
    see Zes Rilke-Liederen

Epitaphe Et Verset
    see Cinq Poemes De Francois Villon

Herbst
    see Zes Rilke-Liederen

Herbsttag
    see Zes Rilke-Liederen

Huivering
    see Zes Slauerhoff-Liederen

Ik Zal Ook Eens Komen
    see Zes Slauerhoff-Liederen

In Mijn Leven...
    see Zes Slauerhoff-Liederen

Question Au Clerc Du Quichet
    see Cinq Poemes De Francois Villon

Rondeau A La Mort
    see Cinq Poemes De Francois Villon

Schwan, Der
    see Zes Rilke-Liederen

Voor De Verre Prinses
    see Zes Slauerhoff-Liederen

Waar Zal Ik Wezen...
    see Zes Slauerhoff-Liederen

Zes Rilke-Liederen
    low solo,pno DONEMUS f.s. [12']
    contains: Abend; Das Ist Dort, Wo
    Die Letzten Hütten Sind;
    Herbst; Herbsttag; Schwan, Der;
    Zum Einschlafen Zu Sagen (F251)

Zes Slauerhoff-Liederen
    med solo,pno DONEMUS f.s. [9']
    contains: Compromis; Huivering;
    Ik Zal Ook Eens Komen; In Mijn
    Leven...; Voor De Verre
    Prinses; Waar Zal Ik Wezen...
                              (F252)

Zum Einschlafen Zu Sagen
    see Zes Rilke-Liederen

FRANZ, CARL
Es Ist Vorbei
    see When Love Has Gone

When Love Has Gone
    "Es Ist Vorbei" [Eng/Ger] ST/SB
    soli RICORDI-IT LD332   (F253)

FRANZ LISZT: COMPLETE WORKS FOR ORGAN
VOLUME 9, WORKS FOR VOICE(S) AND
ORGAN see Liszt, Franz

FRANZSON, BJÖRN (1906-1974)
Tiu Lög
    solo voice,pno ICELAND 043-001
                              (F254)
FRAUEN KOMPONIEREN *CC25U
    (Rieger, Eva; Walter, Käte) solo
    voice,pno SCHOTT ED 7810 (F255)

FRAUENLIEBE see Loewe, Carl Gottfried

FRAUENLIEBE UND LEBEN see Schumann,
Robert (Alexander)

FRAUENLIEBE UND LEBEN, OP. 42 see
Schumann, Robert (Alexander)

FRAUENTANZ see Weill, Kurt

FRED see Groven, Eivind

FREDERICKX, H.
Gloria-Lied: Gods Woord En Wijsheid
    solo voice,kbd ZENGERINK R.554
                              (F256)
FREDSBØNN see Kjeldaas, Arnljot

FREEDOM see Ghezzo, Dinu Dumitru

FREISCHÜTZ, DER: DURCH DIE WÄLDER see
Weber, Carl Maria von

FREISCHÜTZ, DER: SCHWEIG'! DAMIT DICH
NIEMAND WARNT see Weber, Carl Maria
von

FREISCHÜTZ, DER: UND OB DIE WOLKE SIE
VERHÜLLE see Weber, Carl Maria von

FREISCHÜTZ, DER: WIE NAHTE; LEISE,
LEISE see Weber, Carl Maria von

FREMDE OIGN see Suben, Joel Eric

FREMMEDE FUGLEN, DEN see Lunde, Ivar

FRENCH ART SONGS
    ("World's Favorite Series") ASHLEY
    082-4   (F257)

FRENCH CHILD CALLING HER DOG, A see
Heilner, Irwin

FRENCH LYRIC LAIS
    (Buckley, Ann) ANTICO AE31 (F258)

FREUDENTHAL, OTTO (1934-   )
Att Åldras
    solo voice,pno STIM   (F259)

Corris Winter
    [Eng] S solo,clar,pno TONOS (F260)

Djupt Till Vila På En Stjärna
    [Swed] solo voice,pno TONOS (F261)

Durch Winter Geht
    [Ger] solo voice,fl,pno TONOS
                              (F262)
Flickan Går I Mörkan Skog
    see Två Folkliga Sånger

Hej Gamla Gube
    [Swed] solo voice,pno TONOS (F263)

Septembermond 1-2 *song cycle
    [Ger] S solo,pno TONOS   (F264)

Två Folkliga Sånger
    solo voice,pno STIM f.s.
    contains: Flickan Går I Mörkan
    Skog; Vintervisa   (F265)

Vintervisa
    see Två Folkliga Sånger

Wir Wandelten *song cycle
    S solo,pno TONOS   (F266)

FREUND see Wolf, Hugo

FREUNDIN, ICH KOMM MIT DER ZITHER see
Mozart, Wolfgang Amadeus

FREYSCHÜTZE, DER: LEISE, LEISE, FROMME
WEISE see Weber, Carl Maria von

FREYWILLIGES VERSINKEN see Schubert,
Franz (Peter)

FRIBERG, TOMAS
Tre Månader
    [Swed] A solo,harp,wind quin TONOS
                              (F267)
FRICKER, PETER RACINE (1920-1990)
Gryphius Songs
    high solo,pno MMB S814002 f.s., ipr
                              (F268)
Two Songs For Baritone And Piano
    MMB X814002   (F269)

FRID, GEZA (1904-   )
Ankunft In Venedig
    see Venedig, Op. 83

Drie Shakespeare-Liederen, Uit
    "Driekoningenavond"
    Bar solo,harp/pno DONEMUS f.s. [8']
    contains: Kom Nader, Dood; O
    Meisje Mijn; Slotlied   (F270)

Gondel
    see Venedig, Op. 83

Jenseits Des St. Gotthard
    see Venedig, Op. 83

Kom Nader, Dood
    see Drie Shakespeare-Liederen, Uit
    "Driekoningenavond"

Kreuzgang Von Santo Stefano, Der
    see Venedig, Op. 83

O Meisje Mijn
    see Drie Shakespeare-Liederen, Uit
    "Driekoningenavond"

Padua
    see Venedig, Op. 83

Slotlied
    see Drie Shakespeare-Liederen, Uit
    "Driekoningenavond"

Venedig, Op. 83 *song cycle
    Bar solo,pno DONEMUS f.s. [12']
    contains: Ankunft In Venedig;
    Gondel; Jenseits Des St.
    Gotthard; Kreuzgang Von Santo
    Stefano, Der; Padua   (F271)

FRIDRIKSSON, RIKHARDUR H. (1960-   )
Fimm Smalog
    solo voice,harp ICELAND 059-010
                              (F272)
Vögguvisa
    solo voice,pno ICELAND 059-008
                              (F273)
FRIEDE see Dessau, Paul

FRIEDE, FRIEDE AUF DER ERDE see
Bodensohn, Ernst Friedrich Wilhelm

FRIEDENSLIED see Eisler, Hanns

FRIEDMAN, STANLEY
Dona Nobis Pacem
    Mez solo,trp,pno SEESAW f.s. (F274)

Moravian Cantata
    S solo,8trom SEESAW   (F275)
    S solo,3trp,3horn,4trom,2tuba
    SEESAW   (F276)

FRIENDSHIP see Fischer, Irwin

FRIGJORT see Fladmoe, Arvid

FRISSELL
Soprano Voice
    S solo BRANDEN 1388-1 $10.00 (F277)

Tenor Voice
    T solo BRANDEN 1387-3 $10.00 (F278)

FRITS EN KEE see Bremer, Jetse

FRITT FRAM see Åm, Magnar

FROEHLICHE WIEDERSCHEIN see Haydn,
[Johann] Michael

FROGS, FROGS, WHERE ARE YOU GOING? see
Beers, Jacques

FRÖHLICHE MUSIKUS see Mattiesen

FRÖHLICHE WEIHNACHT see Winter

FROM A COMPOSER'S LETTER AND ITS REPLY
see Lunde, Ivar

FROM A DISTANT PLANET see Marez Oyens,
Tera de

FROM A WATCHTOWER see Beeson

FROM AN OLD GARDEN: SIX SONGS, OP. 26
see MacDowell, Edward Alexander

FROM COCOON FORTH see Glickman, Sylvia

FROM FRANCE WITH LOVE see Bergerac

FROM GITANJALI see Sohal, Naresh

FROM KATHLEEN RAINE'S POETRY, OP. 55
see Sommerfeldt, Öistein

FROM MONTE PINCIO see Grieg, Edvard
Hagerup, Fra Monte Pincio

FROM "NOTES TO NINE LOVERS" see
Meneely-Kyder, Sarah

FROM OLD JAPAN see Salter, Mary Turner

FROM THE ANALECTS see Johnson, A. Paul

FROM THE BAT POET see Thomas, Andrew

FROM "THE BLACK RIDERS" see Haxton,
Kenneth

FROM THE BOOK OF PICTURES see
Lindenfeld, Harris Nelson

FROM THE BOOK OF SONGS see Vandor, Ivan

FROM THE BOOK OF THEL: THRENODY see
Aston, Peter G.

FROM THE CHINESE RESTAURANT see
Straesser, Joep

FROM THE LAND OF THE SKY-BLUE WATER see
Cadman, Charles Wakefield

FROM THE ORIENT see Smolanoff, Michael
Louis

FROM THE SONG OF SONGS see Blackford,
Richard

FROM "THREE CABARET SONGS" see
MacBride, David Huston

FROM WILLIAM BLAKE'S POETRY see
Sommerfeldt, Öistein

FROMM-MICHAELS, ILSE (1888-   )
Fünf Lieder Op. 9 Nach Texten Aus
    "Des Knaben Wunderhorn"
    solo voice,pno RIES 60012 (F279)

FROMM-MICHAELS, ILSE (cont'd.)

Vier Winzige Wunderhornlieder Op. 9b
solo voice,pno RIES 60013   (F280)

FROMMEL, GERHARD (1906-   )
Lieder 1-6, Op. 2 Aus "Der Siebente
Ring"
low solo,instrumental ensemble/pno
pno red RIES 60011   (F281)

FROSTED WINDOW: VARIATIONS ON WHITE see
Lombardo, Robert M.

FROSTY NIGHT see Dring, Madeleine

FROTTOLE ALLA CORTE MANTOVANA see
Tromboncino, Bartolomeo

FRÜHE BUND, DER see Haydn, [Johann]
Michael

FRÜHE KAFKA-TEXTE see Zechlin, Ruth

FRÜHE LIEDER see Debussy, Claude

FRÜHLING, DER see Bach, Carl Philipp
Emanuel

FRÜHLING IST'S, DER see Badings, Henk

FRÜHLINGS ENDE see Hekster, Walter

FRÜHLINGSABEND see Badings, Henk

FRÜHLINGSGLOCKEN see Schumann, Robert
(Alexander)

FRÜHLINGSLIED see Mendelssohn-
Bartholdy, Felix see Morthenson,
Jan W.

FRÜHLINGSMOND see Malmlöf-Forssling,
Carin

FRÜHLINGSNACHT see Hekster, Walter

FRÜHLINGSSTIMMEN see Strauss, Johann,
[Jr.]

FRÜHLUNGSWIND, EIN see Straesser, Joep

FUEGOS, LOS see Pablo, Luis de

FUGA, SANDRO (1906-   )
Concerto Sacro No.5, For Bass, Chorus
And Orchestra
B solo,pno pno red CURCI 10391
(F282)

FUGGIMI! see Denza, Luigi

FUGLANE see Åm, Magnar

FUGLEVISE, EN see Grieg, Edvard Hagerup

FÜHLT MEINE SEELE see Wolf, Hugo

FUITE, LA see Duparc, Henri

FUJIWARA, MICHIYO
Haha Ga Hana Yori Chiriisogi
solo voice,pno [5'] JAPAN   (F283)

Kobo
solo voice,pno [4'] JAPAN   (F284)

Kokuu
solo voice,pno [3'] JAPAN   (F285)

Ofukuhagaki
solo voice,pno [2'] JAPAN   (F286)

Utaimasho
solo voice,pno [2'] JAPAN   (F287)

Yurikamome
solo voice,pno [4'] JAPAN   (F288)

FUKUDA, AKIRA (1956-   )
Hara Tamiki No Shi Ni Yoru Kakyokushu
S/T solo,pno [30'] JAPAN   (F289)

FUKUI, TETSUO (1931-   )
Tradition Of Mt. Kumotori
Mez/Bar solo [5'] ONGAKU   (F290)

Warabe Uta
S solo [5'] ONGAKU   (F291)

FUKUSHIMA, YUJIRO (1932-   )
Songs For Loving Myself
S solo,pno [12'] JAPAN   (F292)

FULL CIRCLE see Sydeman, William J.

FULL FATHOM FIVE see Oliver, Harold

FULLY CLOTHED see Rice, Thomas N.

FUNERAL BLUES see Duncan, Chester

FUNERAL SONG AND LAMENT see Rudbeck,
Olof, Sorg- Och Klagesång

FÜNF ALTE WEIHNACHTSLIEDER *Op.32,
CC5U
(Hallwachs, Karl) solo voice RIES
f.s.   (F293)

FÜNF DIALOGE see Schramowski, Hebert

FÜNF GEDICHTE DER KÖNIGIN MARIA STUART
see Schumann, Robert (Alexander)

FÜNF GEISTLICHE GESÄNGE see Cerha,
Friedrich

FÜNF GESÄNGE DER SCHIRIN see Muller-
Hornbach, Gerhard

FÜNF GESÄNGE NACH CATULL see Buren,
John van

FÜNF ISLANDISCHE LIEDER see Helgason,
Hallgrimur

FÜNF JAPANISCHE GEDICHTE see Pieper,
Rene

FÜNF LIEBESLIEDER see Ragwitz, Erhard

FÜNF LIEBESLIEDER, OP. 16 see
Vanderstucken, Frank

FÜNF LIEDER see Ernst, Heinrich Wilhelm
see Mittler, Franz see Wetzler,
Hermann Hans

FÜNF LIEDER see Callhoff, Herbert

FÜNF LIEDER see Badings, Henk

FÜNF LIEDER see Schubert, Franz (Peter)

FÜNF LIEDER AUF GEDICHTE VON PAUL
BOURGET see Debussy, Claude

FÜNF LIEDER "KAZE" see Mizokami, Hideo

FÜNF LIEDER NACH FRIEDRICH HÖLDERLIN
see Wolpe, Stefan

FÜNF LIEDER NACH GEDICHTEN VON JOSEPH
VON EICHENDORFF see Hummel, Bertold

FÜNF LIEDER, OP. 4 see Schreker, Franz
see Thuille, Ludwig (Wilhelm
Andreas Maria)

FÜNF LIEDER, OP.5 see Damrosch, Leopold

FÜNF LIEDER, OP. 7 see Zemlinsky,
Alexander von

FÜNF LIEDER OP. 9 NACH TEXTEN AUS "DES
KNABEN WUNDERHORN" see Fromm-
Michaels, Ilse

FÜNF LIEDER, OP. 17 see Ansorge, Conrad

FÜNF LIEDER, OP. 28 see Stöhr, Richard

FÜNF LIEDER, OP. 40 see Schumann,
Robert (Alexander)

FÜNF LIEDER, OP. A-4 see Manen, Joan

FÜNF NEUE KINDERLIEDER see Reger, Max

FÜNF NEUE KINDERLIEDER see Reger, Max

FÜNF VOLKSLIEDER see Krek, Uros

FUNNY DEATH see Little, David

FUNNY FELLOW, A see Head, Michael
(Dewar)

FUNNY YOU SHOULD SING THAT...THE SONGS
OF JEREMY NICHOLAS see Nicholas,
Jeremy

FURET DE BOIS JOLI, LE see Bréville,
Pierre-Onfroy de

FURIES, THE see Chasalow, Eric

FURRER-MÜNCH, FRANZ (1924-   )
Bleu Rouge
S solo,ob,clar,vcl [12'30"] MODERN
1844   (F294)

Zeit Zu Singen
solo voice,db,perc [12'] MODERN
2121   (F295)

FÜRST IGOR: IHR TRÄNEN see Borodin,
Alexander Porfirievich

FÜRST IGOR: NACHT see Borodin,
Alexander Porfirievich

FÜRST IGOR: SPRICH, WO BIST DU see
Borodin, Alexander Porfirievich

FÜRST IGOR: UMSONST see Borodin,
Alexander Porfirievich

FÜRST IGOR: VERWUNDE see Borodin,
Alexander Porfirievich

FÜRST IGOR: WENN ICH see Borodin,
Alexander Porfirievich

FUSSREISE see Wolf, Hugo

FUTILITY see Heilner, Irwin see Pieper,
Rene

FUYU NO HAE see Miki, Minoru

FYLGD see Kristinsson, Sigursveinn D.

FYRA SANGER see Björklund, Staffan

FYRA SÅNGER TILL DIKTER AV GABRIELA
MISTRAL see Rooth, Anna-Greta

FYRA SÅNGER: UR EN DODDANSARES VISOR
see Blomdahl, Karl-Birger

FYRA STAGNELIUSSÅNGER see Winter, Tomas

FYRR THIN GAEDIR FYSILIG see Isolfsson,
Pall

FYRSTA VISA JONASAR see Halldorsson,
Skuli

FYRSTE SONGEN, DEN see Kielland, Olav

G

G. SCHIRMER OPERA ANTHOLOGY: ARIAS FOR
    BARITONE
    (Larsen, Robert L.) (CC24L) SCHIRM.G
    50481100   (G1)

G. SCHIRMER OPERA ANTHOLOGY: ARIAS FOR
    BASS
    (Larsen, Robert L.) (CC22L) SCHIRM.G
    50481101   (G2)

G. SCHIRMER OPERA ANTHOLOGY: ARIAS FOR
    MEZZO-SOPRANO
    (Larsen, Robert L.) (CC30L) SCHIRM.G
    50481098   (G3)

G. SCHIRMER OPERA ANTHOLOGY: ARIAS FOR
    SOPRANO
    (Larsen, Robert L.) (CC31L) SCHIRM.G
    50481097   (G4)

G. SCHIRMER OPERA ANTHOLOGY: ARIAS FOR
    TENOR
    (Larsen, Robert L.) (CC34L) SCHIRM.G
    50481099   (G5)

GAAET BORT see Backer-Lunde, Johan

GAATHAUG, MORTEN (1955-   )
    De Profundis *Op.20
    [Span] S solo,2.2.2.2. 4.2.3.1.
    timp,3perc,harp,pno,strings [10']
    NORGE f.s.   (G6)

    Six Songs, Op. 33
    see Vinden Ser Aldri På Veiviseren

    Vinden Ser Aldri På Veiviseren
    "Six Songs, Op. 33" [Norw] solo
    voice,pno NORGE   (G7)

GABEL, GERALD L. (1950-   )
    Cantos De Lorca
    B solo,pno SEESAW   (G8)

    Songs And Epitaphs
    S solo,fl,harp,cel,2perc SEESAW
                                            (G9)

GABUS, MONIQUE (1926-   )
    Two Vocalises *CC2U
    med solo,pno PRESSER 511-00864
    $6.50   (G10)

GACELA DEL AMOR IMPREVISTO see Rouse,
    Christopher

GAGNLØYSA see Kielland, Olav

GAKKTU HAEGT see Sveinsson, Atli Heimir

GALANTE, CARLO
    Ai! Laurie Lambar
    solo voice,3inst ZERBONI 9902 (G11)

    Our Share Of Night
    solo voice,6inst ZERBONI 9919 (G12)

    Serenata
    S solo,orch ZERBONI 9401   (G13)

    Songs Of Innocence
    solo voice,pno ZERBONI 9571   (G14)

GALATHEA see Delden, Lex van

GALGENLIEDER see Kölz, Ernst see
    Kropfreiter, Augustinus Franz

GALLOP, THE see Sveinbjörnsson,
    Sveinbjörn

GALLOWS TREE, THE see Tal, Marjo

GALOP see Duparc, Henri

GALOP, LE see Duparc, Henri, Galop

GALUPPI, BALDASSARE (1706-1785)
    Cantate Jubilate
    T solo,2horn,strings KUNZEL GM 1174
                                            (G15)

    Christe Redemptor
    see Drei Kirchenarien Für Sopran

    Drei Kirchenarien Für Sopran
    KUNZEL GM 1173 f.s.
    contains: Christe Redemptor (S
        solo,strings); Pastores Mecum
        Omnes Venite Adoremus (S solo,
        strings); Veni Creator Spiritus
        (S solo,2rec,strings)   (G16)

    Et Incarnatus Est
    SS soli,2vln,vcl,org KUNZEL GM 867
                                            (G17)
    Pastores Mecum Omnes Venite Adoremus
    see Drei Kirchenarien Für Sopran

GALUPPI, BALDASSARE (cont'd.)

    Regina Coeli
    S solo,string orch KUNZEL GM 1116
                                            (G18)

    Veni Creator Spiritus
    see Drei Kirchenarien Für Sopran

GALVAN, VENTURA (fl. 1762-1772)
    Seguidilla Del Oficial Cortejante
    (Subira, Jose) solo voice,pno BOIL
    B.1027 f.s. contains also:
    Fernandere, F., Minuetto En
    Alabanza De La Música Seria;
    Rosales, Antonio, Canción Contra
    Las Madamitas Gorgoritadoras
                                            (G19)

GALWAY KINNELL SONGS see Tsontakis,
    George

GAMBS
    Lullaby
    HINRICHSEN 203   (G20)

GAMLE, DEN see Jensen, Ludwig Irgens

GAMLE GRENDI see Johnsen, Hallvard

GAMMEL BERGSTUE, EN see Tveitt, Geirr

GAMMEL MARIAVISE see Baden, Conrad

GAMMEL VISE, EN see Jordan, Sverre

GANCHOFF, MOSHE
    Magein Avot
    med solo,kbd TRANSCON. 992026 (G21)

GANYMED see Wolf, Hugo

GÅR DU PÅ GATEN EN DAG see Volle,
    Bjarne, Alles Øyne

GARCIA-ABRÍL, ANTÓN (1933-   )
    Canciones De Valldemosa
    solo voice,pno ALPUERTO 1484   (G22)

GARCIA MORANTE, MANUEL (1937-   )
    Siete Canciones
    solo voice,gtr EMEC   (G23)

GARDEN OF DELIGHT see Apollyon, Nicolay

GARDEN OF LOVE, THE see Holten, Bo

GARDEN OF THE HEART, THE see Schafer,
    R. Murray

GARDHELG see Madsen, Trygve

GARDNER, JOHN
    It's This Island
    B solo,2.2.2.2. 4.0.3.1. harp,
    strings [6'] OXFORD   (G24)

GARLANDS AND FLOWERS see Heilner, Irwin

GARLICK, ANTONY (1927-   )
    All My Life
    Mez solo,pno SEESAW   (G25)

    Psalm No. 23
    T solo,pno SEESAW f.s.   (G26)

    Rubaiyat Song Cycle
    solo voice,pno SEESAW   (G27)

    Two Songs
    B solo,pno SEESAW   (G28)

GARNI see Janssen, Guus

GARTENLAUB, ODETTE
    Espace Sonore
    SA soli,1.0.1.1.soprano sax.alto
    sax. 0.1.1.1. perc,pno/cel,harp,
    db [6'30"] BILLAUDOT   (G29)

GÄRTNER see Wolf, Hugo

GÄRTNER, DER see Schumann, Robert
    (Alexander)

GARWOOD, MARGARET (1927-   )
    Cliff's Edge, The (Songs Of A
    Psychotic)
    S solo,pno HILD 09103B   (G30)

    Six Japanese Songs, For Soprano,
    Clarinet And Piano
    sc,pts HILD 09103A   (G31)

GAST, DER see Marx, Joseph

GASTALDON, STANISLAS (1861-1939)
    Musica Proibita
    [Eng/It] high solo,pno CLASSV 0450
                                            (G32)
    [Eng/It] med-high solo,pno CLASSV
    0474   (G33)

GATTIR ADLAR see Tveitt, Geirr

GAUBERT, PHILIPPE (1879-1941)
    Au Jardin De L'infante
    [Fr] high solo RECITAL 422   (G34)

    Heures D'Apres-Midi, Les
    [Fr] high solo RECITAL 355   (G35)

GAUSSIN, ALLAIN (1943-   )
    Voix De La Memoire, Les
    S solo [10'] SALABERT EAS18361 f.s.
                                            (G36)

GAZZA LADRA, LA: DI PIACER MI BALZA IL
    COR see Rossini, Gioacchino

GEBED see Dispa, Robert

GEBET see Louis Ferdinand, Prince Of
    Prussia see Marx, Joseph see Wolf,
    Hugo

GEBET DES AMFORTAS see Wagner, Richard,
    Parsifal: Mein Vater

GEBETH, DAS see Preyer, Gottfried

GEBHARD, A.M.
    Salve Regina
    (Kirchberger, A.) S/T solo,strings,
    fl solo pno red KUNZEL GM 254
                                            (G37)

GEBIRGS-BLEAMELN: SECHS LIEDER see
    Baumann, Alexander

GEDANKEN see Bredemeyer

GEDANKEN DER LIEBE see Hrasky, Rainer

GEDICHTE see Shostakovich, Dmitri

GEDICHTE VON GOETHE, OP. 6 see Valen,
    Fartein

GEDICHTE VON JOHANN WOLFGANG VON
    GOETHE, HEFT 1 see Wolf, Hugo

GEDICHTE VON JOHANN WOLFGANG VON
    GOETHE, HEFT 2 see Wolf, Hugo

GEDICHTE VON JOHANN WOLFGANG VON
    GOETHE, HEFT 3 see Wolf, Hugo

GEDICHTE VON JOHANN WOLFGANG VON
    GOETHE, HEFT 4 see Wolf, Hugo

GEDICHTE VON JOHANN WOLFGANG VON
    GOETHE, HEFT 5 see Wolf, Hugo

GEDICHTE VON JOHANN WOLFGANG VON
    GOETHE, HEFT 6 see Wolf, Hugo

GEDICHTE VON JOHANN WOLFGANG VON
    GOETHE, HEFT 7 see Wolf, Hugo

GEDICHTE VON JOHANN WOLFGANG VON
    GOETHE, HEFT 8 see Wolf, Hugo

GEE, OFFICER KRUPKE see Bernstein,
    Leonard

GEELEN, MATHIEU (1933-   )
    Ozeane In Zerstreuung
    see Sechs Wasserlieder

    Runde Erde
    see Sechs Wasserlieder

    Sechs Wasserlieder
    high solo,elec org DONEMUS f.s.
    [12']
    contains: Ozeane In Zerstreuung;
        Runde Erde; Sinkt Sie; Was Hat
        Uns Dazu Bewogen; Wassertiefe;
        Wassertropfen   (G38)

    Sinkt Sie
    see Sechs Wasserlieder

    Was Hat Uns Dazu Bewogen
    see Sechs Wasserlieder

    Wassertiefe
    see Sechs Wasserlieder

    Wassertropfen
    see Sechs Wasserlieder

GEFÄHRTIN see Keussler, Gerhard von

GEFANGEN see Suppe, Franz von

GEFORS, HANS (1952-   )
    Höst
    see Sånger Om Förtröstan, Op. 3

    Moln
    see Sånger Om Förtröstan, Op. 3

    Om Förtröstan
    see Sånger Om Förtröstan, Op. 3

    Sånger Om Förtröstan, Op. 3
    B/A solo,gtr SUECIA 390 f.s.
    contains: Höst; Moln; Om
        Förtröstan; Vilket Främmande
        Spel   (G39)

GEFORS, HANS (cont'd.)

Sånger Om Glädje *Op.8
S solo,clar,vcl STIM   (G40)

Vilket Främmande Spel
see Sånger Om Förtröstan, Op. 3

GEHEIMNES see Schubert, Franz (Peter)

GEHOORD GEDICHT see Ruiter, Wim de

GEISSLER, FRITZ (1921-1984)
Symphony No. 11
A solo,3.3.3.3. 6.4.4.1. timp,
4perc,harp,cel,pno,strings [20']
DEUTSCHER   (G41)

GEISTHARDT, HANS-JOACHIM (1925-   )
Lieder Für Tenor
PETERS 10379   (G42)

GEISTLICHE GESÄNGE see Loewe, Carl
Gottfried

GEISTLICHE LIEDER see Franck see Medek,
Tilo

GELALIAN, BOGHOS (1927-   )
Due Vocalizzi
solo voice,pno CURCI 8977   (G43)

GELLERTS GEISTLICHE ODEN UND LIEDER see
Bach, Carl Philipp Emanuel

GELOSIA, LA: FILLI NOL NIEGO see
Cesarini, C.P.

GEME L'ONDA CHE PARTE DEL FONTE see
Vivaldi, Antonio

GEMROT, JIRI (1957-   )
Pet Lyrickych Pisni
[Czech/Ger] solo voice,pno PANTON
145   (G45)

GENERAL NO ES MALO, ES EMOCIONADITO, EL
see Zuidam, Rob

GENERATION OF LEAVES, A see Nielson,
Lewis

GENEVIEVE DE BRABANT see Satie, Erik

GENTIL COUCOU
(Divito) (CCU, children's songs)
SCHOTT-FRER 9285   (G46)

GENTLE JESUS, MEEK AND MILD see Hodd,
Jack Lorne

GENTLE LADY see Mozart, Wolfgang
Amadeus, Don Giovanni: Madamina! Il
Catalogo

GENZMER, HARALD (1909-   )
Ausgewählte Lieder
S solo,pno RIES 60018   (G47)

Ausgewählte Lieder (1940-1987)
Bar solo,pno RIES 60017   (G48)

GERAEDTS, JAAP (1924-   )
Aloeëtte, Voghel Clein
SSA/TTB soli ZENGERINK V.380   (G49)

Engel Daalde Neder, Een
see Vier Kinderliedjes

Heilige Franciscus
see Vier Kinderliedjes

In Den Hemel Daar Is Het Goed Woonen
see Vier Kinderliedjes

O, Jezuskind Teer
see Vier Kinderliedjes

Vier Kinderliedjes
S solo,pno DONEMUS f.s. [5']
contains: Engel Daalde Neder,
Een; Heilige Franciscus; In Den
Hemel Daar Is Het Goed Woonen;
O, Jezuskind Teer   (G50)

GERBER, STEVEN R. (1948-   )
After The Funeral
Bar solo,vln,vla,vcl [9'] APNM sc
$5.75, set $14.75   (G51)

Black Hours
S solo,pno [16'] APNM sc $5.75, set
$11.00   (G52)

Desert Places *CC5U
med solo,pno sc AM.COMP.AL. $7.70
(G53)

Doria
S solo,pno [10'] APNM sc $4.75, set
$9.25   (G54)

GERBER, STEVEN R. (cont'd.)

Drum-Taps: Three Patriotic Poems
*CC3U
S solo,pno sc AM.COMP.AL. $7.70
(G55)

Harmonium
S solo,2.2.2.2. 4.2.2.0. harp,cel/
pno,timp,perc,strings [20'] sc
AM.COMP.AL. $21.30   (G56)

"My Papa's Waltz" And Other Songs
S solo,pno [7'] APNM sc $4.75, set
$9.25   (G57)

Sestina: Altaforte
Bar solo,pno [4'] APNM sc $3.50,
set $5.50   (G58)

Songs From "The Wild Swans At Coole"
*CCU
S/T solo,pno sc AM.COMP.AL. $11.10
(G59)

Two Lyrics *CC3U
S solo,vln,vla,vcl APNM sc $3.75,
set $14.00   (G60)

Words For Music Perhaps
S solo,2vln [16'] AM.COMP.AL. sc
$10.30, pts $24.10   (G61)

GERHARD
Cancionero De Pedrell
BOOSEY VAB0290   (G62)

GERLACH, GÜNTER (1928-   )
An Den Schlaf
see Drei Abendlieder

Drei Abendlieder
S solo,clar,org ERES 2652 f.s.
contains: An Den Schlaf; Schnelle
Tag Ist Hin, Der; Tag Mit
Seinem Lichte, Der   (G63)

Schnelle Tag Ist Hin, Der
see Drei Abendlieder

Tag Mit Seinem Lichte, Der
see Drei Abendlieder

GERMAN, [SIR] EDWARD (EDWARD GERMAN
JONES) (1862-1936)
Big Steamers
low solo,pno (text by Kipling)
CLASSV 1768   (G64)
med solo,pno (text by Kipling)
CLASSV 1769   (G65)

Rolling Down To Rio
med solo,pno (text by Kipling)
CLASSV 1157   (G66)
low solo,pno (text by Kipling)
CLASSV 1156   (G67)

GERMAN FOLK SONGS see Brahms, Johannes

GERMAN FOR AMERICANS see Reif, Paul

GERMAN SONGBOOK *CCU
solo voice HANSEN-US HANO393 $5.95
(G68)

GERMANIA: NO, NON CHIUDER GLI OCCHI
VAGHI see Franchetti, Alberto

GERMETEN, GUNNAR (1947-   )
Case Janice, The: From A Case Record
see Tilfellet Janice: Fra En
Sykejournal

Flyskrekk!
[Norw] S solo,ob,clar,bsn,horn [5']
NORGE   (G69)

Katedral For Kjaerleik I Eit
Nøtteskal, Ein
[Norw] Bar solo,clar,vln,acord,db,
actor [15'] NORGE   (G70)

Krølltango - Et Kaféverk...
[Norw] solo voice,vln,pno,acord,db,
opt gtr [6'] NORGE   (G71)

Skarve Engel I Brutalias Land, En
[Norw] S solo,pno NORGE   (G72)

Tilfellet Janice: Fra En Sykejournal
"Case Janice, The: From A Case
Record" S solo,3.2.3.2.sax.
4.2.3.1. timp,perc,strings [8']
NORGE f.s.   (G73)

Vuggevise Til Kotick
[Norw] solo voice,pno NORGE   (G74)

GERNEGROSS, DER see Borodin, Alexander
Porfirievich

GERSCHEFSKI, EDWIN (1909-   )
Crossing The Bar
low solo,pno [5'] sc AM.COMP.AL.
$4.60   (G75)

Prayer Of St. Francis Of Assisi
*Op.61,No.2
med solo,pno [6'] sc AM.COMP.AL.

GERSCHEFSKI, EDWIN (cont'd.)

$2.70   (G76)

Three Variations *Op.74
med solo,pno [10'] sc AM.COMP.AL.
$5.00   (G77)

GERSTER, OTTMAR (1897-1969)
Lieder
PETERS 5162   (G78)

GESANG DER FRAUEN AN DEN DICHTER see
Orthel, Leon

GESANG DES LEBENS see Marx, Joseph

GESANG EINER GEFANGENEN AMSEL see
Kofron, Petr

GESANG WEYLAS see Wolf, Hugo

GESÄNGE see Riedel, Auguste

GESÄNGE see Riedel, Auguste

GESÄNGE see Wetz, Richard

GESÄNGE AUS WILHELM MEISTER VON GÖTHE
see Schubert, Franz (Peter)

GESÄNGE, BAND 1 see Matthus, Siegfried

GESÄNGE, BAND 2 see Matthus, Siegfried

GESÄNGE DER SCHIRIN see Muller-
Hornbach, Gerhard

GESÄNGE DES ABSCHIEDS see Erdmann,
Dietrich

GESÄNGE FÜR KIRCHLICHE ANLÄSSE
low solo,org/pno KUNZEL GM 912A (G79)

GESÄNGE FÜR KIRCHLICHE UND WELTLICHE
ANLÄSSE
med solo,org/pno KUNZEL GM 912B (G80)

GESÄNGE, OP. 21, NO. 6 see Jensen,
Adolf

GESÄNGE, OP. 89, NO. 2 see
Herzogenberg, Heinrich von

GESÄNGE, OP. 89, NO. 3 see
Herzogenberg, Heinrich von

GESÄNGE UND LIEDER FÜR EINE UND ZWEI
SINGSTIMMEN see Hackel, Anton

GESÄNGE ZUR LEIER see Wagner-Regeny,
Rudolf

GESCHICHTE VON O-CHO-SAN, DIE see
Behrend, Siegfried

GESPENSTER see Huber, Nicolaus A.

GESTÖRTE STÄNDCHEN, DAS see Mozart,
Wolfgang Amadeus

GESTURES IN THE FACE see Jacobs,
Kenneth

GET HENCE FOULE GRIEFE see Jenni,
Donald Martin see Lessard, John
Ayres

GETROOSTE DOOD, DE see Regt, Hendrik de

GETTY, GORDON
Hostess' Aria (from Plump Jack, Scene
4)
(med diff) PRESSER   (G81)

My Lord, The Man I Know (from Plump
Jack, Scene 1)
(med diff) PRESSER   (G82)

White Election, The *song cycle
S solo,pno [60'] (med) PRESSER
491-00356 $17.50   (G83)

GEVOELENS see Andriessen, Jurriaan

GEZANG TZU ISRAEL, A see Hans, Edith

GEZEL, DE see Masseus, Jan

GEZIELTES SPIELZEUG see Straesser, Joep

GHEQUETST BEN IC... see Braal, Andries
de

GHEZZO, DINU DUMITRU (1941-   )
Book Of Songs
S solo,fl,harp,electronic tape
SEESAW   (G84)

Freedom
S solo,clar,trp,perc,electronic
tape SEESAW   (G85)

Two Prayers
S solo,electronic tape,opt pno
SEESAW   (G86)

GHIRLANDE DE BLOIS, LA see Togni,
Camillo

GHOST OF AMSTERDAM, THE see Heilner,
Irwin

GHOSTFIRES see Lennon, John Anthony

GIANI LUPORINI, GAETANO (1936-   )
Pantomima
2 solo voices,instrumental ensemble
EDI-PAN EP 7441   (G87)

Scena Di Una Seduzione
solo voice,orch EDI-PAN EP 7765
                                (G88)

GIANNI SCHICCHI: O MIO BABBINO CARO see
Puccini, Giacomo

GIANOTTI, ROBERTO
Perch'io
male solo,clar,vcl,pno EDI-PAN
EP 7243   (G89)

GIASCUN LO DICE see Chaulieu, Charles

GIB LICHT MEINEN AUGEN see Zimmermann,
Udo

GIBBA see Sveinsson, Atli Heimir

GIBBS, CECIL ARMSTRONG (1889-1960)
Ten Songs
(CC10U) NOVELLO   (G90)
NOVELLO   (G91)

GIBSON, ROBERT (1950-   )
Vier Lieder Für Sopran Und Klavier
S solo,pno (text by Denise
Levertov) FEJA MME 11   (G92)

GIDEON, MIRIAM (1906-   )
Ayelet Hashakhar *Heb
"Morning Star" med solo,pno [8'] sc
AM.COMP.AL. $.80   (G93)

Bohmischer Krystall
high solo,fl,clar,vln,vcl,pno [3']
AM.COMP.AL.   (G94)

Creature To Creature
solo voice,fl,harp sc BOELKE-BOM
$12.50   (G95)

Eishet Chayil
see Woman Of Valor, A

Lockung
high solo,pno [2'] sc AM.COMP.AL.
$1.95   (G96)

Morning Star
see Ayelet Hashakhar

She Weeps Over Rahoon
high solo,pno [2'] AM.COMP.AL.
                                (G97)

Too-Late Born, The
high solo,pno [3'18"] AM.COMP.AL.
                                (G98)

Vergiftet Sind Meine Lieder
high solo,pno [2'] sc AM.COMP.AL.
$.80   (G99)

Voices From Elysium
high solo,fl,clar,vln,vcl,pno [12']
AM.COMP.AL. sc $11.45, pts rent (G100)

Wing'd Hour
high solo,fl,ob,vibra,vln,vcl sc
PETERS 67031 $12.50   (G101)

Woman Of Valor, A *song cycle,Heb
"Eishet Chayil" med solo,pno [5']
sc AM.COMP.AL. $3.85   (G102)

GIFT GOES ON, THE see Harris, Ronald S.

GIGJAN see Einarsson, Sigfus

GIJ WACHT WELLICHT see Andriessen,
Jurriaan

GIKK DU GJENNOM SKOGEN, KJAERE see
Taubo, Lillian Gulowna, Lyrisk
Romanse

GILBERT, JANET
Circumflexions On Mallarme
S solo [3'] sc AM.COMP.AL. $1.55
                                (G103)

Orange Book, The
S solo,sax,electronic tape [17'] sc
AM.COMP.AL. f.s.   (G104)

Paisaje Con Dos Tumbas Y Un Perro
Asirio
S solo,electronic tape [10'] sc
AM.COMP.AL. $3.85   (G105)

GILLET, BRUNO (1936-   )
Solfeggio
ST soli,pno ZERBONI 8347   (G106)

GILLYFLOWER see Groven, Eivind, Til Min
Gyllenlakk

GILTAY, BEREND (1910-1975)
Alle Birken Grünen In Moor Und Heid
see Drei Lieder

Drei Lieder
A solo,2vln,vla,vcl DONEMUS f.s.
[10']
contains: Alle Birken Grünen In
Moor Und Heid; Im Flammenden
Morgenrot; Was Frag' Ich Nach
Den Menschen   (G107)

Im Flammenden Morgenrot
see Drei Lieder

Was Frag' Ich Nach Den Menschen
see Drei Lieder

GINASTERA, ALBERTO (1916-1983)
Horas De Una Estancia, Las
solo voice,pno (med) PEER   (G108)

GING HEUT' MORGENS UBERS FELD see
Mahler, Gustav

GINGA see Hayakawa, Kuzuko

GIOCONDA, LA: AH! PESCATOR see
Ponchielli, Amilcare

GIOCONDA, LA: CIELO E MAR! see
Ponchielli, Amilcare

GIOCONDA, LA: OMBRE DI MIA PROSAPIA see
Ponchielli, Amilcare

GIOCONDA, LA: SUICIDIO see Ponchielli,
Amilcare

GIOCONDA, LA: VOCE DI DONNA see
Ponchielli, Amilcare

GIORDANI, GIUSEPPE (ca. 1753-1798)
Caro Mio Ben
med solo,pno CLASSV 0557   (G109)
[It/Ger] high solo,pno CLASSV 1686
                                (G110)

Caro Mio Bene
solo voice,pno BOIL B.1230   (G111)

GIORDANI, TOMMASO (1730-1806)
Caro Mio Ben, Credi Mi Almen
SSA/TTB soli ZENGERINK V.227   (G112)

GIORDANO, UMBERTO (1867-1948)
Siberia: Orride Steppe!
T solo,pno CLASSV 0929   (G113)

GIRAUD
Derniere Lumiere, La
S solo,8inst [11'] SALABERT
EAS18240P f.s.   (G114)

GIRL I LEFT BEHIND ME, THE see Mourant,
Walter

GIRL OF THE GOLDEN WEST, THE: LET HER
BELIEVE see Puccini, Giacomo,
Fanciulla Del West, La: Ch'ella Mi
Creda

GIRLS WERE MADE TO HUG AND KISS see
Lehar, Franz

GISARO see Kukiyama, Naoshi

GISLINGE, FREDERIK
Sorcerer In Bakkeby, The
see Troldmanden I Bakkeby

Troldmanden I Bakkeby
"Sorcerer In Bakkeby, The" speaking
voice,2.2.2.2. 4.2.2.1. 2perc,
harp,strings [30'] sc,pts
SAMFUNDET f.s.   (G115)

GITA IN GONDOLA, LA see Rossini,
Gioacchino

GITANJALI see Schafer, R. Murray

GIUFFRE, GAETANO (1918-   )
Dei Canti Di Linguaggio
Mez solo,pno SEESAW   (G116)

Interlocutions
S/T solo,English horn SEESAW   (G117)

GIULIANI, MAURO (1781-1829)
Sechs Kavatinen, Op. 39
solo voice,gtr PETERS 8525   (G118)

GIULIANI, PAOLO
Calligrammes
A solo,ob,clar,bsn,pno,vln EDI-PAN
EP 7640   (G119)

GIULIANI, VITTORIO
Pace!
ST soli,pno CURCI 10837   (G120)

GIULIETTA ET ROMEO: AH! SE TU DORMI see
Vaccai, Nicola

GIURAMENTO, IL: BELLA, ADORATA
INCOGNITA see Mercadante, G.
Saverio

GIURAMENTO, IL: S'IO L'AMAVA!
SCIAGURATA! see Mercadante, G.
Saverio

GIVE ME A KISS see Halldorsson, Skuli

GIVE ME A SONG see Nakada, Yoshinao

GIVE YOUR HEARTS see Glans, Fredrik

GJE MEG HANDA DI, VEN see Bratland

GJENNOM DØDSSKYGGENS DAL see Nystedt,
Knut

GJENNOM TID OG ROM see Olsen, Sparre

GJENSKINN see Baden, Conrad

GJENTA see Karlsen, Kjell Mørk see
Olsen, Sparre

GJENTEBRILUR see Ørbeck, Anne Marie

GJERSTROM, BJORN G. (1939-   )
Dette Er Timen *Op.26
[Norw] solo voice,pno NORGE   (G121)

Förklaring *Op.26
[Norw] solo voice,pno NORGE   (G122)

Landskap Med Sne *Op.26
[Norw] solo voice,pno NORGE   (G123)

Nyttår Ved Havet *Op.13
[Norw] solo voice,pno,gtr,vln NORGE
                                (G124)

Vinternatt *Op.12
[Norw] solo voice,pno,gtr,vln NORGE
                                (G125)

GLAD OCH LUGN see Blomberg, Erik

GLAESER, FRANZ
Christkindleins Wiegenlied
KAHNT 8457   (G126)

Menagerie In Krähwinkel, Die: Duetto
2 solo voices,pno SCIEN 592   (G127)

GLANERT, DETLEV (1960-   )
Contemplated By A Portrait Of A
Divine *Op.26
S solo,bass clar,pno,vla,vcl,db
BOTE   (G128)

GLANS, FREDRIK (1966-   )
Give Your Hearts
[Eng] solo voice,clar [3'15"] (text
by Kahlil Gibran) NORGE   (G129)

GLANTZ, YEHUDA LEIB
Songs For Voice And Piano *CCU
solo voice,pno TRANSCON. f.s.   (G130)

GLASER, DAVID
Morning Star
S solo,fl,ob,bsn,pno,vln,vla,vcl
[10'] APNM sc $4.75, pts rent
                                (G131)

GLASER, WERNER WOLF (1910-   )
Sulamith: Romantische Szene
S solo,pno STIM   (G132)

GLÄSERNE BRÜCKE, DIE see Böttcher,
Eberhard

GLASS, PHILIP (1937-   )
Habeve Song
S solo,clar,bsn [8'] DUNV   (G133)

Hymn To The Sun (from Akhnaten)
countertenor,2.2.2.2. 2.2.2+bass
trom.1. strings DUNV   (G134)

GLAUS, D.
Zerstreute Wege
solo voice sc HUG GH 11332 f.s.
                                (G135)

GLAZUNOV, ALEXANDER KONSTANTINOVICH
(1865-1936)
Dans Le Sang
see Two Melodies, Op.27

Pourquoi Donc
see Two Melodies, Op.27

Romance De Nina: Le Bal Masqué
[Russ/Fr] Mez solo,pno CLASSV 1176
                                (G136)

Rossignol, Le
[Russ/Eng/Fr] med-high solo,pno
CLASSV 2129   (G137)

Six Songs, Op.60
[Russ/Eng/Fr] high solo,pno CLASSV
2130   (G138)

GLAZUNOV, ALEXANDER KONSTANTINOVICH
  (cont'd.)

  Two Melodies, Op.27
    med solo,pno CLASSV 1175 f.s.
      contains: Dans Le Sang; Pourquoi
      Donc   (G139)

GLEDE see Strömholm, Folke

GLEDER see Knutsen, Torbjorn

GLICKMAN, SYLVIA (1932-   )
  After Great Pain
    see Emily Dickinson Songs (For
    Soprano And Piano)

  Emily Dickinson Songs (For Soprano
    And Piano)
    S solo,pno HILD 09104 f.s.
      contains: After Great Pain; From
      Cocoon Forth; It Will Be Summer
                                    (G140)
  From Cocoon Forth
    see Emily Dickinson Songs (For
    Soprano And Piano)

  It Will Be Summer
    see Emily Dickinson Songs (For
    Soprano And Piano)

GLIÈRE, REINHOLD MORITZOVICH
  (1875-1956)
  Day Is Gone, The *Op.10,No.3
    [Russ/Ger/Fr/Eng] med solo,pno
    CLASSV 2124   (G141)

  Dein Entzückend Helles Lachen
    *Op.23,No.2
    [Russ/Ger] high solo,pno CLASSV
    2121   (G142)

  Lieblich Sang Die Holde Nachtigall
    *Op.36,No.1
    [Russ/Ger] high solo,pno CLASSV
    2118   (G143)

  Sei Dir Endlich Des Lenztrugs Bewusst
    *Op.28,No.6
    [Russ/Ger] high solo,pno CLASSV
    2122   (G144)

  Wie Michs Bangt *Op.52,No.6
    [Russ/Ger] high solo,pno CLASSV
    2119   (G145)

  Wie Zauberisch Glüh'n *Op.52,No.3
    [Russ/Ger] high solo,pno CLASSV
    2123   (G146)

GLINKA, MIKHAIL IVANOVICH (1804-1857)
  Desire
    [Russ] high solo,pno CLASSV 2127
                                    (G147)
  Doubt
    [Russ/Ger] high solo,pno CLASSV
    0767   (G148)
    [Russ/Ger] low solo,pno,vcl CLASSV
    0565   (G149)

  Elegia
    [Russ/Polish] ST soli,pno CLASSV
    1239   (G150)

  Five Songs
    [Russ] solo voice,pno CLASSV 2128
                                    (G151)
  Gretchen Am Spinnrade
    [Russ/Fr/Ger/Eng] S solo,pno CLASSV
    0775   (G152)

  Hope Of Israel, The
    [Russ/Fr/Ger/Eng] high solo,pno
    CLASSV 0776   (G153)

  How Sweet By Thy Side
    [Russ/Fr/Ger/Eng] T solo,pno CLASSV
    0773   (G154)

  I Recall The Wonderful Moment
    [Russ] med solo,pno CLASSV 2125
                                    (G155)
  If I That Voice But Hear
    [Russ/Fr/Ger/Eng] T solo,pno CLASSV
    0774   (G156)

  Life For The Tsar, A: Orphan's Song
    (#1)
    [Russ/Fr/Ger/Eng] Mez solo,pno
    CLASSV 1414   (G157)

  Life For The Tsar, A: Soussanine's
    Aria
    [Russ/Fr/Ger/Eng] B solo,pno CLASSV
    0936   (G158)

  Midnight Review
    [Russ] low solo,pno CLASSV 1051
                                    (G159)
  Nay, Ask No Further Songs Of Love
    [Russ/Fr/Ger/Eng] high solo,pno
    CLASSV 0772   (G160)

  Oh, What Grief Is Mine
    [Russ/Fr/Ger/Eng] S solo,pno CLASSV
    0768   (G161)

GLINKA, MIKHAIL IVANOVICH (cont'd.)

  Ruslan And Ludmilla: Cavatina Of
    Ludmilla
    [Russ] S solo,pno CLASSV 1770
                                    (G162)
  Sleep, My Angel, Slumber Mild
    [Russ/Fr/Ger/Eng] S solo,pno CLASSV
    0771   (G163)

  Traveller's Song
    [Russ] med-low solo,pno CLASSV 2126
                                    (G164)
  Uncle
    [Russ/Fr/Ger/Eng] T solo,pno CLASSV
    0770   (G165)

  Why Thy Sorrow, Why Thy Weeping?
    [Russ/Fr/Ger/Eng] T solo,pno CLASSV
    0769   (G166)

GLINSKY, ALBERT
  Twilight Serenade
    Mez solo,pno [14'] sc AM.COMP.AL.
    $14.50   (G167)

GLITTER AND BE GAY see Bernstein,
  Leonard

GLOBOKAR, VINKO (1934-   )
  Jenseits Der Sicherheit
    PETERS 8588   (G168)

  Miserere
    S&speaking voice&speaking voice,
    1actor, 1translator, jazz trio
    and orchestra [50'] AMPHION f.s.
                                    (G169)
  Realites
    SATBarB soli,electronic tape, film,
    projector [30'] AMPHION f.s.
                                    (G170)
  Sternbild Der Grenze
    ABar&SATBarB soli,orch, marionettes
    [50'] AMPHION f.s.   (G171)

GLÖCKLEIN, DAS see Schlick, E.

GLOIRE A DIEU PARTOUT SUR TERRE! see
  Bach, Johann Sebastian, Jauchzet
  Gott In Allen Landen!

GLORIA DE DIOS EN EL ORBE, LA see
  Beethoven, Ludwig van

GLORIA IN EXCELSIS see Haegeland,
  Eilert M.

GLORIA IN EXCELSIS DEO, OP.21 see
  Haegeland, Eilert M.

GLORIA-LIED: GODS WOORD EN WIJSHEID see
  Frederickx, H.

GLOSELUND see Kvam, Oddvar S.

GLOSY Z ODDALI see Baird, Tadeusz

GLUCK, CHRISTOPH WILLIBALD, RITTER VON
  (1714-1787)
  Alceste: Ah! Malgré Moi
    S solo,pno CLASSV 1606   (G172)

  Alceste: Divinités Du Styx
    Mez solo,pno CLASSV 0418   (G173)
    S solo,pno CLASSV 0426   (G174)
    A solo,pno CLASSV 1773   (G175)

  Iphigénie En Tauride: De Noirs
    Pressentiments
    B solo,pno CLASSV 1556   (G176)

  O Del Mio Dolce Ardor
    [It/Eng] high solo,pno CLASSV 1772
                                    (G177)
  Orfeo: Che Faro
    A solo,pno CLASSV 0520   (G178)
    Mez solo,pno CLASSV 0521   (G179)
    high solo,pno CLASSV 1771   (G180)

  Orfeo: Che Faró Senza Euridice
    A solo,pno BOIL B.1817   (G181)

  Orfeo Ed Euridice: Che Farò
    Mez solo,strings sc,set,pts KING'S
                                    (G182)
  Orfeo Ed Euridice: Che Faro Senza
    Euridice?
    "What Is Life To Me?" A solo
    RICORDI-IT LD114719   (G183)

  Semiramide Riconosciuta: Vieni, Che
    Poi Sereno
    [It] med-high solo,pno CLASSV
    1290   (G184)

  Trionfo Di Cecilia, Il: Ah Ritorna
    Etá Del Oro
    solo voice,pno BOIL B.1747   (G185)

  What Is Life To Me?
    see Orfeo Ed Euridice: Che Faro
    Senza Euridice?

GLÜCK AUF! GUDS FRED! see Nyhus, Rolf

GNOSTIC FRAGMENTS: A MUSICAL
  RECONSTRUCTION see Thommessen, Olav
  Anton

GO DOWN, MOSES see Dillard, Donald E.

GO FORGET ME see Knight, Joseph Phillip

GO LOVELY ROSE see Bunge, Sas see
  Carpenter, John Alden

GO 'NATT DA see Braein, Edvard Fliflet

GO NOT, HAPPY DAY see Bridge, Frank

GO NOT TOO FAR see Beach, [Mrs.] H.H.A.
  (Amy Marcy Cheney)

GO WHERE THE WATER GLIDETH GENTLY EVER
  see Mourant, Walter

GOD BE MERCIFUL UNTO US see Edwards,
  Leo, Psalm No. 67

GOD BLESS NORWAY see Olsen, Sparre, Gud
  Signe Norigs Land

GOD-CHILD, THE see Dillard, Donald E.

GOD GAVE US LOVE see Elliott, Marjorie
  Reeve

GOD, HURRAH! see Wetzler, Robert

GOD IS LOVE see Belyea, W.H.

GOD IS MY SHEPHERD see Dvorák, Antonín

GOD IS OUR SONG see Lovelace

GOD, LIEF see Zagwijn, Henri

GOD MADE YOU GENTLE see East, James H.

GOD MAKES DUCKS see Mollicone, Henry

GOD NATT see Olsen, Sparre

GOD-SONG see Swayne, Giles

GOD, THAT MADEST ALL THINGS see
  Wigglesworth, Frank

GODARD, BENJAMIN LOUIS PAUL (1849-1895)
  Amour, L'
    solo voice,pno CLASSV 0783   (G186)

  Chanson Arabe
    med solo,pno CLASSV 0777   (G187)

  Chanson De Florian
    high solo,pno CLASSV 0778   (G188)
    med solo,pno CLASSV 0779   (G189)

  Chanson Des Pres, La
    high solo,pno CLASSV 0782   (G190)

  Contemplation
    high solo,pno CLASSV 0780   (G191)

  Embarques-Vous!
    T/Bar solo,pno CLASSV 0781   (G192)

  Embarquez-Vous!
    Mez/Bar solo,pno SCIEN 598   (G193)

  Jocelyn: Lullaby
    T solo,pno,vln CLASSV 0617   (G194)
    see Jocelyn: Oh! No T'éveille Pas

  Jocelyn: Oh! No T'éveille Pas
    "Jocelyn: Lullaby" T solo,pno
    CLASSV 1531   (G195)

  Te Souviens-Tu
    solo voice,pno CLASSV 0784   (G196)

  Viens! Une Flûte Invisible
    high solo,pno CLASSV 0785   (G197)

GODE GJERNINGER, DE see Olsen, Sparre

GODFREY, DANIEL (1949-   )
  Two Wedding Airs *CC2U
    S solo,A rec sc AM.COMP.AL. $4.60
                                    (G198)
GODLY WOMAN, THE see Dillard, Donald E.

GODØY, ROLF INGE (1952-   )
  Poem By Hölderlin, A
    [Ger] S solo,clar/bass clar,bsn,
    trp,trom,vln,db,perc NORGE (G199)

GOD'S GRANDEUR see Hopkins

GOEDE BURGERS, DE see Delden, Lex van

GOETHE-LIEDER, VOL. 2 see Wolf, Hugo

GOETHE-LIEDER, VOL. 3 see Wolf, Hugo

GOETHE NIGHTSONGS see Sanders, Noel

GOETZ, HERMANN (1840-1876)
Sechs Lieder, Op. 12
[Ger/Eng] high solo RECITAL 357
(G200)

GOEYVAERTS, KAREL (1923-1993)
Voix Du Verseau, Les
S solo,fl,clar,vln,vcl,pno CBDM
(G201)

GOLD AND GREEN see Sveinbjörnsson,
Sveinbjörn

GOLDBERG, WILLIAM
Burdens
low solo/med solo,pno (poem by
Harold Siegelbaum) CORMORANT
(G202)

By The Bivouac's Fitful Flame
see Two Whitman Songs

Cricket, The
SS soli,pno CORMORANT   (G203)

Evening
SS/SMez soli,pno (text by Sappho)
CORMORANT   (G204)

I Sing Of A Maiden
med solo,pno CORMORANT 5-100-3
$2.75   (G205)

Look Down Fair Moon
see Two Whitman Songs

Outing, An
med solo,pno (poem by Harold
Siegelbaum) CORMORANT   (G206)

Two Whitman Songs
med solo/high solo,pno CORMORANT
f.s.
contains: By The Bivouac's Fitful
Flame; Look Down Fair Moon
(G207)

GOLDEN GUENDOLEN see Bax, [Sir] Arnold

GOLDMAN, MAURICE (1910-   )
I Am My Beloved's
high solo,kbd TRANSCON. 991231
(G208)
med solo,kbd TRANSCON. 991232
(G209)

GOLDMARK, KARL (1830-1915)
Heimchen Am Herd, Das: Ein Geheimnis
Wundersüss
[Ger] S solo,pno CLASSV 1238 (G210)

Queen Of Sheba: Blick Empor Zu Jenen
Räumen
[Ger] Bar solo,pno CLASSV 1774
(G211)

Queen Of Sheba: Magische Töne
T solo,pno CLASSV 0445   (G212)

GOLTERMANN, GEORG (1824-1898)
Wo Wohnt Der Liebe Gott?
solo voice,pno SCIEN 602   (G213)

GOLUB, PETER
Dreams Alone: Six Songs *CC6U
S solo,fl,ob,clar,vcl,harp
AM.COMP.AL. sc $11.45, pts $37.50
(G214)

Three Songs *CC3U
S solo,fl,harp sc AM.COMP.AL. $7.70
(G215)

GÖM MIG, GÖM MIG see Dorumsgaard, Arne

GOMES, ANTÔNIO CARLOS (1836-1896)
Fosca: Quale Orribile Peccato
S solo,pno CLASSV 1657   (G216)

Guarany, Il: C'era Una Volta Un
Principe
S solo,pno CLASSV 0888   (G217)

Guarany, Il: Polacca: Gentile Di
Cuore
S solo,pno CLASSV 0889   (G218)

Guarany, Il: Senza Tetto, Senza Cuna
Bar solo,pno CLASSV 1635   (G219)

Salvator Rosa: Forma Sublime, Eterea
T solo,pno CLASSV 1542   (G220)

Salvator Rosa: Mia Piccirella
S solo,pno (D flat maj) CLASSV 0658
(G221)
S solo,pno (E flat maj) CLASSV 1775
(G222)

Schiavo, Lo: Quando Nascesti Tu
T solo,pno CLASSV 0832   (G223)

GONDAI, ATSUHIKO (1965-   )
Psalm No. 137
Mez solo,harp,perc,electronic tape
[15'] JAPAN   (G224)

Zero Hour
Mez solo,clar,db,perc [17'] JAPAN
(G225)

GONDEL see Frid, Geza

GONG, EIN see Søderlind, Ragnar

GOOD-BYE!! DRAGONFLIES see Nakada,
Kazutsugu

GOOD DEEDS, THE see Olsen, Sparre, Gode
Gjerninger, De

GOOD NEWS AMERICA, GOD LOVES YOU see
Kasha, Al

GOOD NIGHT see Braein, Edvard Fliflet,
Go 'Natt Da see Sigfusson,
Steingrimur

GOODBYE see Tosti, Francesco Paolo

GOORISSEN, JAN
Flut Und Schwamm
female solo,cym,3winds SODEN (G226)

Niño, El
S&2 speaking voices SODEN   (G227)

Where - Wer
S solo,string quar SODEN   (G228)

GORGHEGGI E SOLFEGGI (VOCALISES) see
Rossini, Gioacchino

GOSPEL FAVOURITES *gospel
(Bell, A. Craig) solo voice CRAMER
$2.50
contains: Joshua Fight De Battle Ob
Jericho; Swing Low, Sweet
Chariot; Were You There? (G229)

GOTES D'AIGUA, LES see Mestres, Apeles

GOTTLIEB, JACK S. (1930-   )
Acquainted With The Night
solo voice,kbd TRANSCON. 983048
(G230)

Anim Zemirot
solo voice,kbd TRANSCON. 983027
(G231)

Come My Beloved
solo voice,kbd TRANSCON. 983051
(G232)

Downtown Blues For Uptown
BOOSEY VAB0250   (G233)

Haiku Souvenirs
BOOSEY VAB0082   (G234)

Hoofprints
S solo BOOSEY VAB0249   (G235)

I Think Continually
BOOSEY VAB0255   (G236)

It Is Evening
solo voice,kbd TRANSCON. 983035
(G237)

Kedusha
solo voice,kbd TRANSCON. 983033
(G238)

Light And Splendour
BOOSEY SGB5982   (G239)
BOOSEY VAB0256   (G240)

Mah Tovu
solo voice,kbd TRANSCON. 983025
(G241)

Shachar Avakeshcha
solo voice,kbd TRANSCON. 983026
(G242)

Songs Of Loneliness *CCU
BOOSEY VAB0252 f.s.   (G243)

Tefilot Sheva
solo voice,kbd TRANSCON. 983038
(G244)

Two Blues For Female And Clarinet
BOOSEY VAB0251   (G245)

Ve-Ahavta
solo voice,kbd TRANSCON. 983031
(G246)

GOTTSCHALK, LOUIS MOREAU (1829-1869)
Complete Published Songs Of Louis
Moreau Gottschalk (With A
Selection Of Other Songs On Mid-
Nineteenth Century America)
(Jackson, Richard) MARGUN MM106
(G247)

GOUD EN GEBLADERDE VISSEN see Ehlen,
Margriet

GOUNOD, CHARLES FRANÇOIS (1818-1893)
Absent, L'
high solo,pno CLASSV 0786   (G248)
med solo,pno CLASSV 1141   (G249)

Air De Bijou
see Faust: Jewel Song

Arithmétique, L'
[Fr] 2 med soli,pno CLASSV 1781
(G250)

Au Printemps
med-high solo,pno CLASSV 0874
(G251)

Aubade
"Aube Nait, L'" [Fr] med solo,pno
CLASSV 1776   (G252)

GOUNOD, CHARLES FRANÇOIS (cont'd.)

Aube Nait, L'
see Aubade

Ave Maria
med solo,pno CURCI 4277   (G253)
S/T solo,pno CURCI 5954   (G254)
Mez/Bar solo,pno CURCI 5950 (G255)
[Fr/Lat/Ger] S/T solo SCHOTT-FRER
8995   (G256)
[Fr/Lat/Ger] A/Bar solo SCHOTT-FRER
8997   (G257)
[Eng/Fr] low solo,pno (C maj)
CLASSV 1517   (G258)
med-low solo,pno (D maj) CLASSV
1348   (G259)
[Lat/Eng] med solo,harmonium/org,
vln/vcl (E flat maj) CLASSV 1662
(G260)
med solo,pno (F maj) CLASSV 0468
(G261)
high solo,pno (G maj) CLASSV 0469
(G262)
[Lat] solo voice,pno BOIL B.0352
(G263)

Barcarola
[It/Fr] SBar soli,pno CLASSV 0821
(G264)

Biondina *song cycle
[Fr/It] med-high solo,pno CLASSV
1332   (G265)

Chanson De La Glu
S solo,pno CLASSV 0566   (G266)

Cinq-Mars: Nuit Resplendissante
Mez solo,pno CLASSV 1585   (G267)

Deux Pigions, Les
high solo,pno CLASSV 0787   (G268)

D'un Coeur Qui T'Aime
[Fr] SA soli,pno CLASSV 1783 (G269)

Entreat Me Not
see Song Of Ruth

Faust: Avant De Quitter
Bar solo,pno (D flat maj) CLASSV
0402   (G270)
Bar solo,pno (E flat maj) CLASSV
0535   (G271)

Faust: Faites Lui
"Siebel's Aria" Mez solo,pno CLASSV
0347   (G272)

Faust: Jewel Song
"Air De Bijou" S solo,pno CLASSV
0352   (G273)

Faust: Salut! Demeure Chaste
T solo,pno CLASSV 0456   (G274)

Faust: Si Le Bonheur À Sourire
Mez solo,pno CLASSV 1588   (G275)

Faust: Vous Qui Faites L'Endormie
B solo,pno CLASSV 1551   (G276)

Fleurs Dorment, Les
see Par Une Belle Nuit!

Fountain Mingles With The River, The
[Eng] med solo,pno CLASSV 1210
(G277)

Hymne A Sainte Cécile
solo voice,pno/harp LEDUC f.s.
(G278)

Jesus Of Nazareth
[Eng/Fr] B solo,pno CLASSV 1780
(G279)
[Eng/Fr] Bar solo,pno CLASSV 1779
(G280)
[Eng/Fr] med solo,pno CLASSV 1778
(G281)
[Eng/Fr] high solo,pno CLASSV 1702
(G282)

Ma Belle Amie Est Morte
med-high solo,pno CLASSV 0810
(G283)

Medjé
high solo,pno CLASSV 0463   (G284)

Mireille: Anges Du Paradis
T solo,pno CLASSV 0464   (G285)

Mireille: Chanson Du Berger
Mez solo,pno CLASSV 0884   (G286)

Mireille: Le Jour Se Lève
Mez solo,pno CLASSV 0641   (G287)

Mireille: Mon Coeur Ne Peut Se
Changer
S solo,pno CLASSV 1618   (G288)

Mireille: O Légère Hirondelle
S solo,pno CLASSV 0470   (G289)

Neue Lieder
Mez solo,pno SCIEN 617   (G290)

GOUNOD, CHARLES FRANÇOIS (cont'd.)

Par Une Belle Nuit!
"Fleurs Dorment, Les" SA soli,pno
CLASSV 0820 (G291)

Philémon Et Baucis: Ah! Si Je
Redevenais
S solo,pno CLASSV 1621 (G292)

Philémon Et Baucis: Au Bruit Des
Lourds
B solo,pno CLASSV 1572 (G293)

Philémon Et Baucis: Que Les Songes
Heureux
B solo,pno CLASSV 1573 (G294)

Polyeucte: Nymphes Attentives
T solo,pno CLASSV 1538 (G295)

Polyeucte: Source Délicieuse
T solo,pno CLASSV 1539 (G296)

Prière
high solo,pno CLASSV 0788 (G297)

Quand Tu Chantes
see Sérénade

Quanti Mai!
med solo,pno CLASSV 0553 (G298)

Quatre-Vingts (80) In 2 Vols.
med solo,pno CLASSV C026 (G299)

Quinze Duos
MezBar soli,pno CLASSV C035 (G300)

Quinze Mélodies
med solo,pno CLASSV 0567 (G301)

Quinze Mélodies Enfantines
solo voice,pno CLASSV C034 (G302)

Reine De Saba: Inspirez-Moi
T solo,pno CLASSV 1541 (G303)

Reine De Saba: Plus Grand Dans Son
Obscurité
S solo,pno CLASSV 1622 (G304)

Reine De Saba: Sous Les Pieds D'une
Femme
B solo,pno CLASSV 1574 (G305)

Romeo Et Juliette: Ah, Je Veux Vivre
S solo,pno CLASSV 0357 (G306)
coloratura sop,pno CLASSV 1782
(G307)

Romeo Et Juliette: Ah! Lèvetoi,
Soleil!
T solo,pno (B maj, original key)
CLASSV 1343 (G308)
T solo,pno (B flat maj) CLASSV 0943
(G309)

Sapho: Héro, Sur La Tour Solitaire
Mez solo,pno CLASSV 0698 (G310)

Sapho: O Jours Heureux
T solo,pno CLASSV 1543 (G311)

Sapho: O Ma Lyre Immortelle
Mez solo,pno (semi-tone lower)
CLASSV 1603 (G312)
Mez solo,pno (original key) CLASSV
0817 (G313)

Sérénade
"Quand Tu Chantes" [Fr] high solo,
pno CLASSV 1274 (G314)
"Quand Tu Chantes" [Fr] high solo,
pno,vln CLASSV 0547 (G315)

Siebel's Aria
see Faust: Faites Lui

Song Of Ruth
"Entreat Me Not" [Eng] S solo,pno
CLASSV 0532 (G316)

There Is A Green Hill Far Away
med-high solo,pno CLASSV 0578
(G317)

Vingt Mélodies, Vol.1
high solo,pno CLASSV C030 (G318)
med solo,pno CLASSV C032 (G319)
low solo,pno CLASSV C027 (G320)

Vingt Mélodies, Vol.2
high solo,pno CLASSV C033 (G321)
med solo,pno CLASSV C031 (G322)
low solo,pno CLASSV C028 (G323)

Vingt Mélodies, Vol.3
low solo,pno CLASSV C029 (G324)

GOVERS, KLAAS
Erstes Leid
see Korte Verhalen Van Franz Kafka

Hungerkünstler, Ein
solo voice,inst [70'] DONEMUS
(G325)

GOVERS, KLAAS (cont'd.)

Korte Verhalen Van Franz Kafka
T/countertenor,instrumental
ensemble DONEMUS f.s. [35']
contains: Erstes Leid;
Kübelreiter, Der; Nachts; Vor
Dem Gesetz (G326)

Kübelreiter, Der
see Korte Verhalen Van Franz Kafka

Landarzt, Ein
high solo,pno/3inst [45'] DONEMUS
(G327)

Nachts
see Korte Verhalen Van Franz Kafka

Vor Dem Gesetz
see Korte Verhalen Van Franz Kafka

GOYESCAS: LA MAJA Y EL RUISEÑOR see
Granados, Enrique

GØYM MEG MOR see Tveitt, Geirr

GRABMAL EINES JUNGEN MÄDCHENS see
Norby, Erik

GRABNER, HERMANN (1886-1969)
Lieder Und Gesänge
KAHNT 8628 (G328)

Zwiegespräch
solo voice,org,vla KAHNT 8613
(G329)

GRABREDE FÜR EINEN GENOSSEN, DER AN DIE
WAND GESTELLT WURDE see Eisler,
Hanns

GRACIA MIA see Granados, Enrique

GRADUS AD PARNASSUM see Yttrehus, Rolv

GRÁFICO DE LA PETENERA see Oltra

GRAHAM, P.
Z Plani A Pralesu
male solo,perc PANTON 98 (G330)

GRAHN, ULF (1942-   )
Ännchen Von Tharau
see Three German Folksongs

Coup De Des, Un
S solo,fl,clar,perc,vln,vcl,pno NGL
(G331)

Loreley, Die
see Three German Folksongs

Mond Ist Aufgegangen, Der
see Three German Folksongs

Thorn, A
[Eng] solo voice,pno TONOS (G332)

Three German Folksongs
[Ger] S solo,pno,vln&vcl/fl&bsn NGL
f.s.
contains: Ännchen Von Tharau;
Loreley, Die; Mond Ist
Aufgegangen, Der (G333)

GRAINGER, ELLA
Love At First Sight
solo voice,pno BARDIC BE0091 (G334)

GRAINGER, PERCY ALDRIDGE (1882-1961)
In Bristol Town
(Gibbs, Alan) med solo,pno BARDIC
BE0251 (G335)

Leezie Lindsay (from Songs Of The
North (No. 8))
med solo,pno BARDIC BE0027 (G336)

Thirteen Folksongs
solo voice,pno (cc131) SCHIRM.G
ED3744 (G337)

Thirteen Folksongs, Vol.1
solo voice,pno (CCU, med diff)
NOVELLO (G338)

Thirteen Folksongs, Vol.2
solo voice,pno (CCU, med diff)
NOVELLO (G339)

GRAN RAÏM, EL see Mestres, Apeles

GRANADA see Lara, Agustin

GRANADINAS see Barrera Y Calleja

GRANADOS, ENRIQUE (1867-1916)
Canciones Amatorias No.2
see Mañanica Era

Canciones Amatorias No.5
see No Lloreis Ojuelos

Canciones Amatorias No.7
see Gracia Mia

GRANADOS, ENRIQUE (cont'd.)

Elegia Eterna
[Span] high solo,pno CLASSV 0819
(G340)

Goyescas: La Maja Y El Ruiseñor
[Span/Eng] high solo,pno CLASSV
0964 (G341)

Gracia Mia
"Canciones Amatorias No.7" [Span/
Eng] high solo,pno CLASSV 1431
(G342)

Maja Dolorosa, La
[Span] Mez solo,pno CLASSV 0990
(G343)

Mañanica Era
"Canciones Amatorias No.2" [Span/
Eng] med-high solo,pno CLASSV
1432 (G344)

No Lloreis Ojuelos
"Canciones Amatorias No.5" [Span/
Eng] Mez solo,pno CLASSV 1433
(G345)

GRAND' ARIA DI SCENA see Ugoletti,
Paolo

GRAND DUO CONCERTANT see Raxach,
Enrique

GRAND YACHT DESPAIR, LE see
Petitgirard, Alain

GRANDE CHRONIQUE BERLINOISE see
Pousseur, Henri

GRANDE D'AUVERGNE see Nigg, Serge

GRANDE DUCHESSE, LA: VOICI LE SABRE DO
MON PÈRE see Offenbach, Jacques

GRANDI, ALESSANDRO (? -1630)
O Quam Tu Pulchra Es
S/T solo,cont KING'S KM71 (G346)

GRANDIS, RENATO see
see DE GRANDIS, RENATO

GRANDS OISEAUX BLANCS see Viardot-
Garcia, Pauline

GRANDS VENTS VENUS D'OUTREMER, LES see
Ravel, Maurice

GRANITE, AND see De Lio, Thomas

GRAPHIQUES see Keller, Ginette

GRÅT DU - ? see Brustad, Bjarne

GRATIAS AGIMUS: A SONG FOR PEACE see
Thommessen, Olav Anton

GRATITTLINGURINN see Halldorsson, Skuli

GRAVEDIGGERS see Lindenfeld, Harris
Nelson

GRAVESTONES AT HANCOCK, N.H. see
Slonimsky, Nicolas

GRAVSKRIFT see Karlsen, Kjell Mørk

GRAY, G.
I Have A Little Heart
solo voice,pno/harp SCIEN 623
(G347)

GREAT SPACES see Koch, Frederick

GREAT SPRING, A see Torjussen, Trygve,
Veldig Forår, Et

GREAT WALL OF CHINA see Fine, Vivian

GREAT YOU ARE see Shut, Wasyl, Velyka
Ty

GREATEST OF ALL TIME STANDARDS
solo voice,pno ("World's Favorite
Series") ASHLEY 072-7 (G348)

GREATEST OF THESE IS LOVE, THE see
Clausen, Rene

GREECE see Selmer, Johan Peter,
Grekenland

GREEK SONGBOOK *CCU
solo voice HANSEN-US HANO402 $6.95
(G349)

GREEN RIVER, THE see Carpenter, John
Alden

GREENBURG, LAURA (1942-   )
Hidalgo, Un
Bar solo,marimba,tom-tom,vcl
[5'15"] AM.COMP.AL. (G350)

Spanish Songs
S solo,pno [9'] AM.COMP.AL. (G351)

GREENSLEEVES
(Stickles) SCHIRM.G ST44213 (G352)
see Vaughan Williams, Ralph

GREESON
Three Poems By Stephen Crane *CC3U
high solo,gtr WILLIS 10825 $1.50
(G353)

GREGOR, CESTMÍR (1926-)
Dve Rozmarne Balady
S solo,pno PANTON 897 (G354)

GREKENLAND see Selmer, Johan Peter

GRENEN GUNGAR see Koch, Erland von

GRENERS TYNGDE see Mortensen, Finn

GRENERS TYNGDE, OP. 33 see Mortensen, Finn

GRENOUILLES, LES see Francaix, Jean

GRETCHANINOV, ALEXANDER TIKHONOVICH (1864-1956)
Berceuse
see Slumber Song

Chant Funebre, Op.5, No.4
see Epicedium

Epicedium
"Chant Funebre, Op.5, No.4" [Russ/Fr/Ger] high solo,pno CLASSV 1078 (G355)
Fleurs Du Mal, Les
"Hymne, Op.48, No1" [Fr/Russ] high solo,pno CLASSV 1106 (G356)
Four Songs, Op.7
[Russ/Fr/Ger] high solo,pno CLASSV 2133 (G357)
Four Songs, Op.20
[Russ/Fr/Ger] med solo,pno CLASSV 2131 (G358)
Hymne, Op.48, No1
see Fleurs Du Mal, Les

Il S'est Tu Le Charmant Rossignol *Op.20,No.2
[Eng/Fr] high solo,pno CLASSV 1784 (G359)
[Eng/Fr] med solo,pno CLASSV 1074 (G360)
Jadis Tu M'as Aimé! *Op.7,No.1
[Russ/Fr/Ger] high solo,pno CLASSV 1071 (G361)
Larmes, Les *Op.7,No.2
[Russ/Fr/Ger] high solo,pno CLASSV 1072 (G362)
My Native Land *Op.1,No.4
[Russ/Fr/Ger] high solo,pno CLASSV 2132 (G363)
Night Voices *Op.1,No.1
[Russ/Fr/Ger] med solo,pno CLASSV 1110 (G364)
Nuit, La *Op.5,No.2
[Russ/Fr/Ger] high solo,pno CLASSV 1076 (G365)
Pourquoi Se Fanent Tes Feuilles? *Op.5,No.3
[Russ/Fr/Ger] med-high solo,pno CLASSV 1077 (G366)
Schneeflöckchen *Op.47,No.1
[Russ/Ger] med solo,pno CLASSV 1107 (G367)
Slumber Song *Op.1,No.5
"Berceuse" [Eng/Fr] S solo,pno CLASSV 1108 (G368)
"Berceuse" [Eng/Fr] Mez solo,pno CLASSV 1109 (G369)
Soir *Op.20,No.1
[Russ/Fr/Ger] med solo,pno CLASSV 1073 (G370)
Triste Est Le Steppe *Op.5,No.1
[Russ/Fr/Ger] med-high solo,pno CLASSV 1075 (G371)

GRETCHEN AM SPINNRADE see Glinka, Mikhail Ivanovich

GRETCHENS BITTE see Schubert, Franz (Peter)

GRÉTRY, ANDRÉ ERNEST MODESTE (1741-1813)
Amant Jaloux, L': Tandis Que Tout Sommeille
T solo,pno CLASSV 1524 (G372)

Deux Avares, Les: Plus De Dépit, Plus De Tristesse
S solo,pno CLASSV 1609 (G373)

Let The Sultan Saladin
SCIEN 626 (G374)

Oh! Richard
SCIEN 627 (G375)

GRÉTRY, ANDRÉ ERNEST MODESTE (cont'd.)
Où Peut-On Être Mieux
SCHOTT-FRER 7073 (G376)

Richard Coeur De Lion: O Richard, Ô Mon Roi!
Bar solo,pno CLASSV 1646 (G377)

Zémire Et Azor: Du Moment Qu'on Aime
T solo,pno CLASSV 1545 (G378)

Zémire Et Azor: La Fauvette
S solo,pno,fl CLASSV 0642 (G379)

GRETSCHER
Da Ich Ein Kind
high solo,pno KAHNT 4842A (G380)
low solo,pno KAHNT 4842B (G381)

GREY WOLF, THE see Burleigh, Henry Thacker

GRIEG, EDVARD HAGERUP (1843-1907)
Album Verse
see Stambogsrim

Bad Day
see Vond Dag

Bergtekne, Den *Op.32
"Einsame, Der" Bar solo,2horn, strings [6'] PETERS f.s. (G382)

Birds Song, A
see Fuglevise, En

Borte *Op.70,No.3
(Vea, Ketil) [Dan] Mez solo, 2.1.1.1. 1.1.1.0. timp,strings NORGE f.s. (G383)

Boy, The
see Guten

Braune Augen
low solo,pno PETERS 467M (G384)

By Rondane
see Ved Rondane

Dance Of The Kids
see Killingdans

Dream, A
[Ger/Eng] med solo,pno CLASSV 1386 (G385)
[Ger/Eng] high solo,pno CLASSV 1385 (G386)

Einsame, Der
see Bergtekne, Den

Elsk *Op.67,No.5
(Olsen, C.G.Sparre) "Love" Mez solo,2.2.2.2. 0.0.0.0. strings NORSK f.s. (G387)

First Meeting, The
see Første Møde, Det

First Meeting's Delight, The
see Første Møtes Sødme, Det

Five Songs, Op.26
med-high solo,pno CLASSV 1799 (G388)
Five Songs, Op.60
med-high solo,pno CLASSV 1806 (G389)
Five Songs, Op.69
med-high solo,pno CLASSV 1809 (G390)
Five Songs, Op.70
med solo,pno CLASSV 1810 (G391)

Første Møde, Det *Op.21,No.2
(Olsen, Carl Gustav Sparre) "First Meeting, The" [Norw/Ger] solo voice,strings [4'] PETERS f.s. (G392)
Første Møtes Sødme, Det *Op.21,No.1
(Olsen, C.G.Sparre) "First Meeting's Delight, The" S solo, 1.1.2.1. 2.0.0.0. strings NORSK f.s. (G393)

Four Songs, Op.21
high solo,pno CLASSV 1795 (G394)

Fra Monte Pincio *Op.39,No.1
"From Monte Pincio" S solo,2.0.2.2. 2.0.0.0. perc,harp,strings [5'] PETERS f.s. (G395)

From Monte Pincio
see Fra Monte Pincio

Fuglevise, En *Op.25,No.6
(Brevik, Tor) "Birds Song, A" solo voice,2fl,2clar,2horn,strings NORGE f.s. (G396)

Guten *Op.33,No.1
(Gunstrom, E.G.) "Boy, The" solo voice,strings [3'] NORSK f.s. (G397)

GRIEG, EDVARD HAGERUP (cont'd.)
Hoffnung
high solo,pno PETERS 2456A (G398)

I Travelled In A Lovely Summer Evening
see Jeg Reiste En Deilig Sommerkveld

Ich Liebe Dich
[Ger/Eng] low solo,pno CLASSV 1394 (G399)
[Ger/Eng] med solo,pno CLASSV 1393 (G400)
[Ger/Eng] high solo,pno CLASSV 1392 (G401)

It Sings
see Syng, Det

Jeg Reiste En Deilig Sommerkveld *Op.26
(Olsen, C.G.Sparre) "I Travelled In A Lovely Summer Evening" [Dan] S solo,strings NORSK f.s. (G402)

Killingdans *Op.6,No.6
(Olsen, C.G.Sparre) "Dance Of The Kids" Mez solo,1.1.2.1. 0.0.0.0. strings NORSK f.s. (G403)

Last Spring
see Våren

Love
see Elsk

Lys Nat *Op.25,No.5
(Vea, Ketil) Mez solo,2.1.1.1. 1.1.1.0. timp,strings NORGE f.s. (G404)

Margrete's Cradle Song
see Margrete's Vuggesang

Margrete's Vuggesang *Op.15,No.1
(Brevik, Tor) "Margrete's Cradle Song" solo voice,strings NORGE f.s. (G405)

Med En Primula Veris *Op.26,No.4
(Brevik, Tor) "With A Primula Veris" solo voice,2clar,2bsn, horn,strings NORGE f.s. (G406)

Mit Einer Primula Veris
[Ger/Eng] Mez solo,pno CLASSV 1389 (G407)

Odalisken Synger: Nu Synker Solen I Asiens Dale
med-high solo,pno CLASSV 1800 (G408)

Posthumous Songs Book 1
med-high solo,pno CLASSV 1811 (G409)

Posthumous Songs Book 2
med-high solo,pno CLASSV 1812 (G410)

Prinsessen: Prinsessen Sad Høyt I Sit
med-high solo,pno CLASSV 1801 (G411)

Rejseminder Fra Fjeld Og Fjord *Op.44
med-high solo,pno CLASSV 1813 (G412)

Selected Songs For High Voice *CC36U
[Eng/Ger] KALMUS f.s. (G413)

Selected Songs For Low Voice *CC36U
[Eng/Ger] KALMUS f.s. (G414)

Six Elegiac Songs, Op.59
med solo,pno CLASSV 1805 (G415)

Six Songs, Op.25
med-high solo,pno CLASSV 1798 (G416)

Six Songs, Op.39
med-high solo,pno CLASSV 1804 (G417)

Solvejg's Cradle Song
[Ger/Eng] Mez solo,pno CLASSV 1388 (G418)
[Ger/Eng] S solo,pno CLASSV 1387 (G419)

Solvejg's Song
[Ger/Eng] Mez solo,pno CLASSV 1390 (G420)
[Ger/Eng] S solo,pno CLASSV 1383 (G421)

Songs, Op.18, Book 1
med solo,pno CLASSV 1793 (G422)

Songs, Op.18, Book 2
med solo,pno CLASSV 1794 (G423)

Songs, Op.33, Book 1
med-high solo,pno CLASSV 1802 (G424)

Songs, Op.33, Book 2
med-high solo,pno CLASSV 1803 (G425)

Songs, Op.67, Book 1
med-high solo,pno CLASSV 1807 (G426)

GRIEG, EDVARD HAGERUP (cont'd.)

Songs, Op.67, Book 2
  med-high solo,pno CLASSV 1808
                                    (G427)

Stambogsrim *Op.25,No.3
  (Brevik, Tor) "Album Verse" solo
  voice,horn,strings NORGE f.s.
                                    (G428)

Swan, A
  [Ger/Eng] low solo,pno CLASSV 1391
                                    (G429)
  [Ger/Eng] high solo,pno CLASSV 1384
                                    (G430)

Syng, Det *Op.67
  (Olsen, C.G.Sparre) "It Sings" Mez
  solo,2(pic).1.2.1. 2.1.1.0. pno,
  strings NORSK f.s.   (G431)

Three Songs From Peer Gynt, Op.23
  solo voice,pno (2 songs for s, 1
  song for bar) CLASSV 1797 (G432)

Ti Songar (Ten Songs) *Op.33, CC10L
  (Söderlind, Ragnar) Bar solo,
  2.2(English horn).2.2(contrabsn).
  4.2.3.1. timp,perc,harp,strings
  NORGE f.s.   (G433)

Til Norge *Op.58,No.2
  (Vea, Ketil) Mez solo,2.1.1.1.
  1.1.1.0. timp,strings NORGE f.s.
                                    (G434)

Two Songs, Op.22
  T solo,pno CLASSV 1796   (G435)

Våren *Op.33,No.2
  "Last Spring" solo voice,strings
  [4'] PETERS f.s.   (G436)

Ved Rondane *Op.33,No.9
  (Halvorsen, J.) "By Rondane" S
  solo,2.2.2.2. 4.0.0.0. strings
  NORSK f.s.   (G437)

Vier Lieder, Op.2
  [Ger] A solo,pno CLASSV 1041 (G438)

Vond Dag *Op.67
  (Olsen, C.G.Sparre) "Bad Day" Mez
  solo,strings NORSK f.s.   (G439)

With A Primula Veris
  see Med En Primula Veris

GRIESBACH, KARL-RUDI (1916-   )
  Lieder
  PETERS 5173, 5372   (G440)

GRIFFES, CHARLES TOMLINSON (1884-1920)
  Auf Dem Teich, Dem Regungslosen
  [Ger/Eng] low solo,pno CLASSV 1430
                                    (G441)

Auf Geheimem Waldespfade
  [Ger/Eng] high solo,pno CLASSV 1255
                                    (G442)
  [Ger/Eng] low solo,pno CLASSV 1428
                                    (G443)
  [Ger/Eng] med solo,pno CLASSV 1427
                                    (G444)

Come, Love
  see Two Rondels, Op.4

Nachtlied
  [Ger/Eng] high solo,pno PETERS
  66940   (G445)

Seven Songs *CC7U
  med-high solo,pno PETERS 66937
  $15.00   (G446)

Six Songs *CC6U
  med solo,pno PETERS 66938 $12.50
                                    (G447)

Song Of The Dagger
  T solo,pno PETERS 66939   (G448)

Songs Of Charles Griffes, Vol. 1
  *CC9L
  high solo,pno SCHIRM.G 50488509
  f.s.   (G449)

Songs Of Charles Griffes, Vol. 2
  *CC12L
  med solo,pno SCHIRM.G 50488510 f.s.
                                    (G450)

This Book Of Hours
  see Two Rondels, Op.4

Träumende See, Der
  [Ger/Eng] med-high solo,pno CLASSV
  1429   (G451)

Two Rondels, Op.4
  S solo,pno CLASSV 0970 f.s.
  contains: Come, Love; This Book
  Of Hours   (G452)

Zwei Könige Sassen Auf Orkadal
  low solo,pno CLASSV 0447 (G453)

GRÍMSDÓTTIR, BÁRA (1960-   )
  As It Goes
  Mez solo,pno ICELAND 072-006 (G454)

GRIMSEYJARKARLINN see Sveinsson, Atli
  Heimir

GRINDE, NILS (1927-   )
  Tvo Kristelige Sanger
  [Norw] solo voice,pno MUSIKK (G455)

GRISELIDIS: DES LARMES BRULENT MA
  PAUPIERE see Massenet, Jules

GRISELIDIS: JE SUIS L'OISEAU see
  Massenet, Jules

GRISEY, GERARD (1946-   )
  Initiation
  solo voice,trom,db AMPHION
  R.2387-88 f.s.   (G456)

GRONDAHL, AGATHE (URSULA) BACKER
  see BACKER-GRONDAHL, AGATHE (URSULA)

GRONDAHL, SISSEL MARGRETHE (1960-   )
  Scherzo Of Seasons, Op.7
  [Norw] S solo,vcl NORGE   (G457)

GRØNLAND, OP. 2 see Egge, Klaus

GROSS, ROBERT ARTHUR (1914-   )
  Chacounne, -A Song, -Oooh
  S solo,vln [5'] sc AM.COMP.AL.
  $1.95   (G458)

GROSSE BÜNDNIS see Keussler, Gerhard
  von

GROTE KEEL OM MEE TE DRINKEN, 'N see
  Meijering, Chiel

GROTE ZOMER..., DE see Guichelaar, Jan

GROV, MAGNE (1938-   )
  Fem Songar
  [Norw] solo voice,pno NORGE f.s.
  contains: Kveld I Køvadalen;
  Lyset; Naki Grein, Ei; Or
  Livsens Bok; Vårvise   (G459)

Frå O.M. Sandviks
  "Gudbrandsdalsmusikken"
  [Norw] solo voice,pno NORGE (G460)

Kveld I Køvadalen
  see Fem Songar

Lyset
  see Fem Songar

Naki Grein, Ei
  see Fem Songar

Or Hovs Hallar
  [Norw] solo voice,pno NORGE (G461)

Or Livsens Bok
  see Fem Songar

Vårvise
  see Fem Songar

GROVEN, EIVIND (1901-1977)
  Å Nei, For En Himmel
  [Norw] solo voice,pno NORGE (G462)

Å Så Rødblond *Op.9,No.1
  "Oh, So Sandy" solo voice,2.1.2.2.
  4.1.0.0. harp,strings [2'] NORGE
  f.s.   (G463)

Aa Den Svalande Vind
  [Norw] solo voice,pno GROVEN (G464)

Aa, Kjaere Mi Sigri
  [Norw] solo voice,pno NORGE (G465)

Aasov Aeddan
  [Norw] solo voice,pno NORGE (G466)

Annen Natt På Hospitalet
  [Norw/Ger] solo voice,pno NORSK
                                    (G467)

Astri, Mi Astri
  [Norw] solo voice,pno NORGE (G468)

Autumn Song, The
  see Høstsangen

Ballad About Toscana, The
  see Balladen Om Toscanaland

Balladen Om Toscanaland *Op.8
  "Ballad About Toscana, The" solo
  voice,2(pic).2.2.2. 4.2.2.0.
  timp,perc,harp,strings [6'] NORGE
  f.s.   (G469)

Fjellvind *Op.10
  "Mountain Wind" solo voice,
  3(pic).2.2.2. 0.0.0.0. strings
  [2'] GROVEN f.s.   (G470)
  see Tvo Songar

Fred
  "Peace" solo voice,3(pic).2.2.2.
  3.2.3.0. timp,strings [5'] NORGE
  f.s.   (G471)

GROVEN, EIVIND (cont'd.)

Gillyflower
  see Til Min Gyllenlakk

Heath, The
  see Moen

Høstsangen *Op.35
  "Autumn Song, The" solo voice,
  2.2.2.2. 4.1.0.1. strings [4']
  GROVEN f.s.   (G472)

In The Evening
  see Om Kvelden

In The Hospital At Night
  see På Hospitalet Om Natten

Kun Øieblikket
  [Norw] solo voice,pno NORGE (G473)

Moderens Korstegn *Op.13,No.1
  "Mother's Sign Of The Cross, The" S
  solo,fl,clar,strings [3'] NORGE
  f.s.   (G474)

Moen
  [Norw] solo voice,pno NORSK (G475)
  "Heath, The" S solo,1.0.1.2.
  1.1.0.0. timp,strings [3'] NORGE
  f.s.   (G476)

Mother's Sign Of The Cross, The
  see Moderens Korstegn

Mountain Wind
  see Fjellvind

Nesland Church, The
  see Neslandskyrkja

Neslandskyrkja *Op.11
  "Nesland Church, The" S solo,fl,
  2clar,2bsn,strings [3'] NORGE
  f.s.   (G477)
  see Tvo Songar

Oh, So Sandy
  see Å Så Rødblond

Om Kvelden *Op.60
  "In The Evening" S solo,fl,strings
  [5'] GROVEN f.s.   (G478)

På Hospitalet Om Natten *Op.13,No.2
  "In The Hospital At Night" S solo,
  fl,pic,clar,harp,strings [3']
  NORGE f.s.   (G479)

Peace
  see Fred

Praeriekonens Bånsull
  [Norw] solo voice,harp NORGE (G480)

Prayer Of Veronica, The
  see Veronicas Bøn

Så Høy En Himmel
  [Norw] solo voice,pno NORGE (G481)

Sanger Til Tekster Fra Hans E. Kincks
  Drama "Driftekaren"
  [Norw] solo voice,pno GROVEN (G482)

Serenade Av "Venetianerne"
  [Norw] solo voice,pno NORGE (G483)

Sommerfuglen
  [Norw] solo voice,pno NORGE (G484)

Til Min Gyllenlakk *Op.22
  "Gillyflower" solo voice,2fl,clar,
  horn,harp,strings [3'] NORGE f.s.
                                    (G485)

Tvo Songar
  [Norw] solo voice,pno NORSK f.s.
  contains: Fjellvind;
  Neslandskyrkja   (G486)

Våren Kommer
  [Norw] solo voice,pno NORGE (G487)

Veronicas Bøn *Op.7
  "Prayer Of Veronica, The" S solo,
  1.1.2.2. 1.0.0.0. timp,strings
  [4'] NORGE f.s.   (G488)

GROVLEZ, GABRIEL (MARIE) (1879-1944)
  Chambre Blanche, La
  solo voice,pno CLASSV 2215 (G489)

Dix Chansons Enfantines
  [Fr/Eng] med solo RECITAL 262
                                    (G490)

Guitares Et Mandolines
  [Fr] high solo,pno CLASSV 2204
                                    (G491)

Trois Melodies
  [Fr] med solo (not available
  outside U.S.A.) RECITAL 358
                                    (G492)

Trois Mélodies Sur Des Poèmes De Jean
  Dominique
  [Fr] med solo,pno CLASSV 1786

GROVLEZ, GABRIEL (MARIE) (cont'd.)
(G493)
GRUK, OP. 53B see Bull, Edvard Hagerup

GRUNDAR DOMA, HVERGI HANN see
Isolfsson, Pall

GRUPPE AUS DEM TARTARUS see Valen,
Fartein

GRUPPE AUS DEM TARTURUS see Schubert,
Franz (Peter)

GRUSS see Mendelssohn-Bartholdy, Felix

GRYPHIUS SONGS see Fricker, Peter
Racine

GUADA RAD see Baumann, Alexander

GUARANY, IL: C'ERA UNA VOLTA UN
PRINCIPE see Gomes, Antônio Carlos

GUARANY, IL: POLACCA: GENTILE DI CUORE
see Gomes, Antônio Carlos

GUARANY, IL: SENZA TETTO, SENZA CUNA
see Gomes, Antônio Carlos

GUARDA QUI CHE LO VEDRAI see Haydn,
[Franz] Joseph

GUD SIGNE NORIGS LAND see Olsen, Sparre

GUDELUNDER I PORTAASSKOGEN see Tveitt,
Geirr

GUDMUNDSSON, BJÖRGVIN (1891-1961)
Dauds-Manns-Sundid
solo voice,pno ICELAND 032-006
(G494)
Evening Prayer
solo voice,pno ICELAND 032-004
(G495)
Nu Haustar A Heidum
TB soli,pno ICELAND 032-021 (G496)

Serenade
solo voice,pno (text by Percy B.
Shelley) ICELAND 032-007 (G497)

Sextiu Og Sex Einsöngslög
solo voice,pno ICELAND 032-026
(G498)
Tonhendur 1. Hefti
solo voice&opt solo voice,pno
ICELAND 032-012 (G499)
Tonhendur, Nytt Safn 1. Hefti
solo voice,pno ICELAND 032-013
(G500)
Tonhendur, Nytt Safn 2. Hefti
solo voice,pno ICELAND 032-014
(G501)
2 solo voices,pno ICELAND 032-014
(G502)
Two Songs
solo voice,pno ICELAND 032-011
(G503)
Vogguvisa Hollu (from Fjalla-
Eyvindur)
solo voice,pno ICELAND 032-005
(G504)
GUDS HJERTE see Madsen, Trygve

GUDS IDAG see Strandsjö, Göte

GUDS OMSORG see Elgaröy, Jan

GUDS PORT see Thoresen, Lasse

GUDSMODERN see Ørbeck, Anne Marie

GUERRERO, FRANCISCO (1528-1599)
Vada
SS soli,9inst ZERBONI 9183 (G505)

GUEST, THE see Rovics, Howard

GUGLIELMO RATCLIFF SPARTITO see
Mascagni, Pietro

GUGLIELMO TELL: O MUTO ASIL DEL PIANTO
see Rossini, Gioacchino

GUGLIELMO TELL: RESTA IMMOBILE see
Rossini, Gioacchino

GUGLIELMO TELL: SELVA OPACA see
Rossini, Gioacchino

GUICHELAAR, JAN
Bekentenis
see Zes Liederen

Grote Zomer..., De
see Zes Liederen

Herfsttij...
see Zes Liederen

Ierse Nacht
see Zes Liederen

GUICHELAAR, JAN (cont'd.)
Julinacht
see Zes Liederen

Signaal, Het
see Zes Liederen

Zes Liederen
S solo,pno DONEMUS f.s. [13']
contains: Bekentenis; Grote
Zomer..., De; Herfsttij...;
Ierse Nacht; Julinacht;
Signaal, Het (G506)

GUILLAUME TELL: SOIS IMMOBILE see
Rossini, Gioacchino

GUIRLANDES, OP. 5 see Bull, Edvard
Hagerup

GUITARES ET MANDOLINES see Grovlez,
Gabriel (Marie) see Saint-Saëns,
Camille

GUITARRE see Moszkowski, Moritz

GULBRANSON, EILIF (1897-1958)
Bønn
"Prayer" S solo,strings [2'] NORGE
f.s. (G507)

Kristkyrkja
LYCHE 50 (G508)

Prayer
see Bønn

GULDSKYEN see Jensen, Ludwig Irgens

GULLGRAVERVISE FRÅ STRILELANDET see
Tveitt, Geirr

GULLRENT ER DITT HJERTE see Knutsen,
Torbjorn

GULNAR LAUVET, DET see Eggen, Arne

GUMBERT
Mein Lied, Op. 108
low solo SCIEN 635 (G509)

GUNDLACH, WILHELM
Barbarossa-Lieder
see Heldenlieder Der Deutschen
Kaiserzeit

Heldenlieder Der Deutschen Kaiserzeit
SCIEN 638 f.s.
contains: Barbarossa-Lieder;
Hrotsvith Von Gandersheim:
Ottolied; Sang Vom
Sachsenkrieg, Der (G510)

Hrotsvith Von Gandersheim: Ottolied
see Heldenlieder Der Deutschen
Kaiserzeit

Sang Vom Sachsenkrieg, Der
see Heldenlieder Der Deutschen
Kaiserzeit

GUPTA, ROLF (1967-   )
Haiku: An Intimate Trio Based On
Haiku Texts
[Eng] Bar solo,trom,vcl NORGE
(G511)
GURO IS RIDING TO MATINS see Guro Rid
Til Ottesong

GURO RID TIL OTTESONG *folk song
(Groven, Eiving) "Guro Is Riding To
Matins" solo voice,ob,clar,bsn,
strings GROVEN f.s. (G512)

GURRELIEDER: NUN SAG ICH see
Schoenberg, Arnold

GURRELIEDER: SO TANZEN see Schoenberg,
Arnold

GÜRSCHING, ALBRECHT (1934-   )
Nachtigallentränen
"Tears Of The Nightingale" S solo,
2.2.2.2. 4.2.3.0. strings [14'0"]
PEER (G513)

Tears Of The Nightingale
see Nachtigallentränen

GUSTAV MAHLER: SELECTED SONGS see
Mahler, Gustav

GUTE-NACHT-LIED ODER BERCEUSE see
Liberda, Bruno

GUTEN see Grieg, Edvard Hagerup

GUTTORMSEN, GUTTORM (1950-   )
Terje Vigen
[Norw] B solo,2.2.2.2. 4.2.3.1.
timp,perc,cel,harp,strings [35']
(text by Henrik Ibsen) NORGE
(G514)

GUY-ROPARTZ, JOSEPH
see ROPARTZ, JOSEPH GUY (MARIE)

H

HA A VILAG RIGO LENNE see Nieland, Henk

HA-AZINU see Suben, Joel Eric

HA DA VENIR! see Tosti, Francesco Paolo

HAAN, RAYMOND H.
Benediction
low solo/med solo AMSI V-9 $1.00
(H1)
med solo/low solo,kbd,opt fl/ob/vln
AMSI V-9
(H2)

HAAS, PAVEL (1899-1944)
Ctyri Pisne
B/Bar solo,pno PANTON 146   (H3)

Vier Lieder Nach Chinesischer Poesie
[Czech/Ger/Eng] B/Bar/A solo,pno
BOTE
(H4)

HABANERA see Bizet, Georges, Carmen:
L'Amour Est

HABBESTAD, KJELL (1955-   )
And I John
[Eng] Bar solo,org [15'] NORGE (H5)

Illuxit, Op. 23
Bar solo,trp,org [10'] NORGE   (H6)

Lament: An Orchestral Song
S solo,3(pic).3(English
horn).3(bass clar).3(contrabsn).
4.3.3.1. timp,perc,cel,harp,pno,
strings [13'] NORGE f.s.   (H7)

Tre Høgsongar *CC3U
female solo,string quar,vibra,
congas NORGE f.s.   (H8)

HABEVE SONG see Glass, Philip

HABIT OF PERFECTION, THE see Winham,
Godfrey

HACHIMURA, YOSHIO (1938-1985)
One Hour At Every One Breath
ST soli,fl,clar,sax,perc ONGAKU
492571 f.s.   (H9)

Sigarami
S solo,fl,vln,pno ONGAKU 492575
f.s.   (H10)

HACIA EL COMIENZO see Lavista, Mario

HACKEL, ANTON
Gesänge Und Lieder Für Eine Und Zwei
Singstimmen
solo voice/2 solo voices,pno SCIEN
644   (H11)

HACKENSÖLLNER, L.
Linde, Die
solo voice,pno SCIEN 645   (H12)

HAD A HORSE, A FINER NO ONE EVER SAW
see Korbay, Francis Alexander

HADLEY, HENRY (KIMBALL) (1871-1937)
Evening Song *Op.53,No.3
high solo,pno CLASSV 1963   (H13)
med solo,pno CLASSV 1964   (H14)

I Heard A Maid With Her Guitar
*Op.44,No.3
high solo,pno CLASSV 1966   (H15)

Il Pleut Des Pétales De Fleurs
[Fr/Eng] high solo,pno CLASSV 1785
(H16)
[Fr/Eng] med solo,pno CLASSV 1965
(H17)
Stille, Träumende Frühlingsnacht
*Op.42,No.1
[Ger/Eng] med solo,pno CLASSV 1967
(H18)

HAEC AURORA GRATIOSA see Lokaj, Jakub

HAEC EST REGINA VIRGINUM see Handel,
George Frideric

HAECCEITY-HESSE see Kitzke, Jerome P.

HAEGELAND, EILERT M. (1951-   )
Be: Solomotett
[Norw] S/T solo,pno/org NORGE (H19)

Folketone Fra Iveland
"O Hvilket Herlig Bytte" [Norw]
solo voice,org [4'30"] NORGE
(H20)

Gloria In Excelsis
solo voice,org,trp NOTON N-9124
(H21)

Gloria In Excelsis Deo, Op.21
[Lat] S solo,trp,org [5'15"] NORGE
(H22)

HAEGELAND, EILERT M. (cont'd.)

Herre, Skynd Deg Å Hjelpe Meg (Motet,
Op. 20)
[Norw] A solo,org [6'] NORGE (H23)

Lauvsongaren
Mez solo,pno [2'50"] NORGE   (H24)

Motet, Op. 20
see Herre, Skynd Deg Å Hjelpe Meg

O Hvilket Herlig Bytte
see Folketone Fra Iveland

Psalm No. 40, Op. 6
see Salme 40, Op.6

Salme 40, Op.6 (Psalm No. 40, Op. 6)
[Norw] S solo,org [4'] NORGE (H25)

Six Songs, Op. 24
[Norw] A/Bar solo,pno NOTON N-9267
(H26)
Tre Salmetoner
solo voice,org,ob NOTON N-9235
(H27)

HAFIS-LIEDER see Streicher, Theodore

HAFRSFJORD see Sommerfeldt, Öistein

HAFVETS SOMMAR (10 SANGE) see
Rangström, Ture

HAG IS ASTRIDE, THE see Bunge, Sas

HAGEMAN, RICHARD (1882-1966)
Do Not Go, My Love
low solo,pno CLASSV 1787   (H28)

May Night
[Eng] high solo,pno CLASSV 2088
(H29)
HAGEN, DARON
Echo's Songs
high solo,pno (med diff, contains
11 settings of poems by William
Blake, Sara Teasdale, Edgar Allen
Poe, Ben Johnson, Gertrude Stein,
Carl Sandburg, Kenneth Rexroth,
Walt Whitman, Anonymous, and e.e.
cummings) SCHIRM.EC 4425   (H30)

Love Songs *song cycle
high solo,pno (med diff) SCHIRM.EC
4426   (H31)

HAGERER, FRANZ SALES IGNAZ (1700-1768)
Salve Regina
(Ruhland, Konrad) S solo,org,vln
solo (Musik Aus Ostbayern, Heft
53) COPPENRATH   (H32)

HAGERTY, MARK
How To Live, What To Do: And Songs On
Poems Of Wallace Stevens
T solo,vln,vcl,pno [25'] APNM sc
$6.50, set $19.50   (H33)

HAGERUP BULL, EDVARD
see BULL, EDVARD HAGERUP

HAGI, KYOKO (1956-   )
Kaze Ga Omote De Yondeiru
SBar soli,pno [16'] JAPAN   (H34)

HAHA GA HANA YORI CHIRIISOGI see
Fujiwara, Michiyo

HAHN, GEORG JOACHIM JOSEPH (1712-1772)
Aria De Nativitate Domini *Op.5,No.7
(Biba, Otto) "Jetzt Auf Erden
Woll't Fröhlich Werden" S solo,
vln,cont (Süddeutsche
Weihnachtsmusik, Band 5)
COPPENRATH   (H35)

Jetzt Auf Erden Woll't Fröhlich
Werden
see Aria De Nativitate Domini

HAHN, REYNALDO (1875-1947)
A Chloris
med-high solo,pno CLASSV 1380 (H36)

Air, L' (from Rondels (#4))
[Fr] high solo,pno CLASSV 1377
(H37)
Amour Sans Ailes
see Love Without Wings

Au Pays Musulman
[Fr] med solo,pno CLASSV 1402 (H38)

Barcheta, La
[Fr] high solo,pno CLASSV 1788
(H39)
Chansons Grises
[Fr] med solo,pno (text by
Verlaine) CLASSV 1330   (H40)

Dans L'Été
[Fr] med-high solo,pno CLASSV 1376
(H41)

HAHN, REYNALDO (cont'd.)

Dernière Valse, La
"Feuilles Tombent, Les" [Fr] high
solo,pno CLASSV 1669   (H42)

Énamourée, L'
med solo,pno CLASSV 2097   (H43)

Feuilles Tombent, Les
see Dernière Valse, La

Five Little Songs
[Eng/Fr] med-high solo,pno (texts
by Robert Louis Stevenson) CLASSV
1790   (H44)

Heure Exquise, L'
low solo,pno CLASSV 0507   (H45)
med solo,pno CLASSV 0514   (H46)

Incrédule, L'
[Fr] med solo,pno (text by
Verlaine) CLASSV 1791   (H47)

Love Without Wings
"Amour Sans Ailes" [Eng/Fr] med
solo,pno CLASSV 1689   (H48)

Printemps, Le (from Rondels (#3))
[Fr] high solo,pno CLASSV 1789
(H49)
Rêverie
[Fr] med solo,pno (text by V. Hugo)
CLASSV 1694   (H50)

Rondels, Vol.1
[Fr] solo voice,pno CLASSV 1378
(H51)
Rondels, Vol.2
[Fr] solo voice,pno CLASSV 1379
(H52)
Rossignol Des Lilas, Le
[Fr] high solo,pno CLASSV 1351
(H53)
Si Mes Vers Avaient Des Ailes
low solo,pno CLASSV 0854   (H54)
med solo,pno CLASSV 0855   (H55)
high solo,pno CLASSV 0477   (H56)

Venezia
med solo LEDUC HE 20678   (H57)

HAIKANSONA see Ator, James Donald

HAIKU see Hegaard, Lars

HAIKU: AN INTIMATE TRIO BASED ON HAIKU
TEXTS see Gupta, Rolf

HAIKU IX: NOW AUTUMN see Birch, Robert
Fairfax

HAIKU SOUVENIRS see Gottlieb, Jack S.

HAIKU X: FOOLISH YEARS OF SONG see
Birch, Robert Fairfax

HALA, V.
Lidice Varuji
solo voice,pno PANTON 898   (H58)

HALD UT, HJARTE see Eggen, Arne

HALÉVY, JACQUES (1799-1862)
Charles VI: Humble Fille Des Champs
Mez solo,pno CLASSV 1584   (H59)

Fée Aux Roses, La: En Dormant C'est À
Moi
S solo,pno CLASSV 1612   (H60)

Juive, La: Il Va Venir
S solo,pno CLASSV 1617   (H61)

Juive, La: Rachel, Quand Du Seigneur
T solo,pno CLASSV 1193   (H62)

Juive, La: Si La Rigueur
B solo,pno CLASSV 1558   (H63)

Reine De Chypre: Le Gondolier Dans Sa
Pauvre Nacelle
Mez solo,pno CLASSV 1598   (H64)

HALKA: GDYBY RANNEM SLONKIEM see
Moniuszko, Stanislaw

HALKA'S ARIA see Moniuszko, Stanislaw,
Halka: Gdyby Rannem Slonkiem

HALL, JEFFREY (1941-   )
Vogelschau
Mez solo,pno [9'] APNM sc $4.50,
set $8.75   (H65)

HALL, PAULINE (1890-1969)
Fire Tosserier
[Dan] S solo,clar,bsn,trp,horn [9']
NORGE   (H66)

Nachtwandler
"Night Wanderer" [Ger] SSTTBB soli,
2(pic).2.2.2. 2.2.0.0. timp,perc,
strings NORGE f.s.   (H67)

HALL, PAULINE (cont'd.)

Night Wanderer
  see Nachtwandler

Ørneland
  see To Sanger, Op. 4

Rondeau
  [Norw] solo voice,pno NORGE   (H68)

Svend Herlufsens Ord
  see To Sanger, Op. 4

Tagelied
  solo voice,3(pic).2.2.2. 3.0.0.0.
  cel,harp,strings NORGE f.s.   (H69)

To Sanger, Op. 4
  solo voice,pno NORSK f.s.
    contains: Ørneland; Svend
    Herlufsens Ord   (H70)

To Unge Elskende
  solo voice,2(pic).2.2.2(contrabsn).
  4.2.3.1. timp,perc,harp,cel,
  strings NORGE f.s.   (H71)

HALL, THEODORA G.
  Holy, Holy Is Thy Name (composed with
  Williams, Harriet H.) *CC12U,
  gospel
  med solo,kbd (easy) PARACLETE
  PPM08311 $4.95   (H72)

HALLDORSSON, SIGFUS (1920-   )
  Ad Sidsumri
    solo voice,pno ICELAND 047-028 (H73)

  Amor Og Asninn
    solo voice,pno ICELAND 047-015
                                 (H74)

  Fjögur Sönglög
    solo voice,pno ICELAND 047-013
                                 (H75)

  Hvers Vegna?
    solo voice,pno ICELAND 047-016
                                 (H76)

  I Graenum Mo
    solo voice,pno ICELAND 047-019
                                 (H77)

  Islenzkt Astarljod
    (Billich, Carl) solo voice,pno
    ICELAND 047-020   (H78)

  Jatning
    solo voice,pno ICELAND 047-009
                                 (H79)

  Litla Flugan
    (Billich, Carl) solo voice,pno
    ICELAND 047-008   (H80)

  1993
    solo voice,pno ICELAND 047-027
                                 (H81)

  Sex Songlog
    solo voice,pno ICELAND 047-005
                                 (H82)

  Sjo Songlog
    solo voice,pno ICELAND 047-014
                                 (H83)

  Skjott Hefur Sol Brugdid Sumri
    solo voice,pno ICELAND 047-023
                                 (H84)

  Songs
    solo voice,pno ICELAND 047-004
                                 (H85)

  Sumarauki
    solo voice,pno ICELAND 047-022
                                 (H86)

  Sumarkvedja Til Islenzkra Barna
    solo voice,pno ICELAND 047-021
                                 (H87)

  Tiu Songlog
    solo voice,pno ICELAND 047-010
                                 (H88)

  Tondeleyo
    solo voice,pno ICELAND 047-007
                                 (H89)

  Tvo Visnalog
    solo voice,pno ICELAND 047-012
                                 (H90)

  Vegir Liggja Til Allra Atta & Litill
  Fugl
    solo voice,pno ICELAND 047-006
                                 (H91)

HALLDORSSON, SKULI (1914-   )
  Aeskan Min
    solo voice,pno ICELAND 023-123
                                 (H92)
    solo voice,pno ICELAND 023-048
                                 (H93)

  Afmaeliskvedja
    solo voice,pno ICELAND 023-045
                                 (H94)

  Aldrei Skal Eg Gleyma Ther
    solo voice,pno ICELAND 023-089
                                 (H95)

  Amma Kvad
    solo voice,pno ICELAND 023-090
                                 (H96)

  Augun
    solo voice,pno ICELAND 023-091
                                 (H97)

HALLDORSSON, SKULI (cont'd.)

  Augun Min Og Augun Thin
    solo voice,pno ICELAND 023-092
                                 (H98)

  Augun Thin
    solo voice,pno ICELAND 023-036
                                 (H99)

  Brunaljos
    solo voice,pno ICELAND 023-088
                                 (H100)

  Dökka Ros, Hin
    solo voice,pno ICELAND 023-097
                                 (H101)

  Dreamsong
    solo voice,pno ICELAND 023-093
                                 (H102)

  Drykkjuvisa
    solo voice,pno ICELAND 023-094
                                 (H103)

  Einkamal
    solo voice,pno ICELAND 023-085
                                 (H104)
    solo voice,pno [4'35"] ICELAND
    023-028   (H105)

  Ferdalok
    solo voice,pno [6'15"] ICELAND
    023-034   (H106)
    solo voice,pno ICELAND 023-086
                                 (H107)

  Fyrsta Visa Jonasar
    solo voice,pno ICELAND 023-095
                                 (H108)

  Give Me A Kiss
    S solo,pno ICELAND 023-056 (H109)

  Gratittlingurinn
    solo voice,pno ICELAND 023-096
                                 (H110)

  Harpa
    solo voice,pno ICELAND 023-051
                                 (H111)

  Haustkvold
    solo voice,pno ICELAND 023-044
                                 (H112)

  Heimthra
    solo voice,pno ICELAND 023-083
                                 (H113)
    solo voice,pno ICELAND 023-042
                                 (H114)

  Hve Rosirnar Ilma
    solo voice,pno [5'0"] ICELAND
    023-029   (H115)

  I Landsyn
    solo voice,pno ICELAND 023-098
                                 (H116)

  Illgresi
    solo voice,pno ICELAND 023-050
                                 (H117)

  Kvedja
    solo voice,pno ICELAND 023-099
                                 (H118)

  Kvoldkyrrd
    1-2 solo voices,pno ICELAND 023-040
                                 (H119)

  Linda
    solo voice,pno [2'0"] ICELAND
    023-007   (H120)

  Litill Fugl
    solo voice,pno ICELAND 023-047
                                 (H121)
    solo voice,pno ICELAND 023-100
                                 (H122)

  Mamma
    solo voice,pno ICELAND 023-046
                                 (H123)

  Mansongur
    solo voice,pno ICELAND 023-043
                                 (H124)
    solo voice,pno ICELAND 023-101
                                 (H125)

  Meyjan Min Hin Vaena
    solo voice,pno ICELAND 023-102
                                 (H126)

  Modir Min & Fylgdarlaun
    solo voice,pno ICELAND 023-038
                                 (H127)

  Morning
    S solo,pno ICELAND 023-032 (H128)
    solo voice,pno ICELAND 023-103
                                 (H129)

  My Mother
    solo voice,pno ICELAND 023-104
                                 (H130)

  O, Ad Eg Ynni Ther Ad Nyju
    solo voice,pno ICELAND 023-105
                                 (H131)

  Rökkurljod Theodoru
    solo voice,pno ICELAND 023-106
                                 (H132)

  Saeunn And The Poet
    solo voice,pno (text by Heinrich
    Heine) ICELAND 023-111   (H133)

  Seven Songs
    solo voice,pno ICELAND 023-037
                                 (H134)

  Sidasti Valsinn
    solo voice,pno ICELAND 023-084
                                 (H135)

  Skilnadur
    solo voice,pno ICELAND 023-055
                                 (H136)

HALLDORSSON, SKULI (cont'd.)

  Soknudur
    solo voice,pno ICELAND 023-112
                                 (H137)

  Solsetursljod
    solo voice,pno ICELAND 023-109
                                 (H138)

  Songlog
    solo voice,pno ICELAND 023-008
                                 (H139)

  Songs
    solo voice,pno ICELAND 023-013
                                 (H140)
    solo voice,pno ICELAND 023-035
                                 (H141)
    solo voice,pno ICELAND 023-023
                                 (H142)
    solo voice,pno (text by Jón
    Thoroddsen) ICELAND 023-016 (H143)

  Songs I
    solo voice,pno ICELAND 023-900
                                 (H144)

  Songverk 2
    solo voice,pno ICELAND 023-901
                                 (H145)

  Sonurinn Kvedur
    solo voice,pno ICELAND 023-107
                                 (H146)

  Sortnar Thu Sky
    solo voice,pno ICELAND 023-108
                                 (H147)

  Stökur
    solo voice,pno ICELAND 023-110
                                 (H148)

  Sudraeni Blaer, Hinn
    solo voice,pno ICELAND 023-041
                                 (H149)
    solo voice,pno ICELAND 023-087
                                 (H150)

  Thad Er Leikur Ad Laera
    solo voice,pno ICELAND 023-119
                                 (H151)

  Thad Kom Songfugl Ad Sunnan
    solo voice,pno ICELAND 023-120
                                 (H152)

  Thegar Their Jordudu Jongeir
    solo voice,pno ICELAND 023-121
                                 (H153)

  Their Fundu Hann
    solo voice,pno ICELAND 023-122
                                 (H154)

  Theodora
    solo voice,pno ICELAND 023-113
                                 (H155)

  Three Songs
    solo voice,pno ICELAND 023-039
                                 (H156)

  Thrir Valsar
    solo voice,pno ICELAND 023-022
                                 (H157)

  Til Elskunnar
    solo voice,pno ICELAND 023-114
                                 (H158)

  Til Rosarinnar
    solo voice,pno ICELAND 023-115
                                 (H159)

  Vedurvisur
    solo voice,pno ICELAND 023-116
                                 (H160)

  Vid Svala Lind
    solo voice,pno ICELAND 023-117
                                 (H161)

  Volvankvad
    solo voice,pno ICELAND 023-118
                                 (H162)

  Vor
    solo voice,pno ICELAND 023-049
                                 (H163)

HALLELUJA see Hummel, Ferdinand see
  Krieger, Johann

HALLIN, MARGARETA
  Starke, Den
    [Swed] SS soli,clar TONOS   (H164)

HALLING see Albertsen, Per Hjort

HALLNÄS, EYVIND (1937-   )
  Kort Tid, En
    solo voice,org NOTERIA 2669 (H165)

  När Gud I Himlen Lekte
    solo voice,org NOTERIA 2670 (H166)

HALLNÄS, LARS (1950-   )
  Från Dunkla Silverskyar Ner
    [Swed] solo voice,pno TONOS (H167)

HALMRAST, TOR (1951-   )
  Pièce Fausse
    [Norw] S solo,fl,2vln,vla,vcl NORGE
                                 (H168)

  Pièce Faussen
    [Norw] S solo,pno NORGE   (H169)

HALVORSEN, JOHAN (1864-1935)
  Sangen Om Iver Huitfeldt
    "Song Of Iver Huitfeldt, The" solo
    voice,2.2.2.2. 4.2.3.1. timp,
    perc,strings NORSK f.s.   (H170)

  Song Of Iver Huitfeldt, The
    see Sangen Om Iver Huitfeldt

HAMARSANGEN see Waaler, Fredrikke

HAMBRAEUS, BENGT (1928-)
Loitsu: (Incantation)
S solo,pno CAN.MUS.CENT. (H171)

HAMELLE
Voici Noël, O Douce Nuit
Mez/MezMez soli,pno voc sc LEDUC
f.s. (H172)

HAMILTON, IAIN (1922-)
Cantata No. 1
T solo,pno PRESSER 111-40130 (H173)

Now And Then
S solo,fl,vla,harp PRESSER
141-40036 (H174)

Songs Of Summer
high solo,clar,vcl,pno PRESSER
411-41061P (H175)

Spirit Of Delight
SBar soli,pno PRESSER 111-40127
(H176)

HAMLET: ARIOSO see Thomas, Ambroise

HAMLET: DRINKING SONG see Thomas,
Ambroise

HAMLET: OPHELIA'S MAD SCENE see Thomas,
Ambroise

HAMRABORGIN see Kaldalóns, Sigvaldi S.

HAN SAR see Kromer, Philip

HANAU, A.
Ave Maria
high solo ZENGERINK R.28 (H177)
low solo ZENGERINK R.29 (H178)

HANDEL, GEORGE FRIDERIC (1685-1759)
Acis And Galatea: O Ruddier Than The
Cherry
(Prout) B solo RECITAL 2229 (H179)

Ah Mio Cor Schernito Sei
solo voice,pno BOIL B.1706 (H180)

Alcina: Verdi Prati
Mez solo,pno CLASSV 1581 (H181)

Allegro, L': Come And Trip It
(Carmichael, Mary) med solo,pno
CLASSV 1194 (H182)

Allor Ch'io Dissi: Addio
see Ten Solo Cantatas, Vol. 1

Ave Maria
see O Salutaris

Cantatas For Alto And Continuo
(Harris) OXFORD (H183)

Care Selve, Aure Grate
see Ten Solo Cantatas, Vol. 2

Deep In Thy Shade
see Serse: Ombra Mai Fu (Largo)

Es Birgt Die Nachtigall (from
Deidamia)
S solo,strings,cont DEUTSCHER (H184)

Ewig, So Spricht Die Seele (from
Poros)
SB soli,strings,cont DEUTSCHER
(H185)

Fra Tante Pene
see Ten Solo Cantatas, Vol. 2

Haec Est Regina Virginum *HWV235
solo voice,pno BREITKOPF-W pno red
EB 8422, sc PB 5149, pts OB 5149
(H186)
Handel Opera Repertory, The *CC6U
Mez solo STAINER 3.3223 $9.50 (H187)

Italienische Duette No. 4: Allzu
Grausam
SA soli PETERS G 1634 (H188)

Italienische Duette No. 7: Geh,
Hoffnung
SS soli PETERS G 1637 (H189)

Italienische Duette No. 8: Immer Muss
Ich Nach Euch Schauen
SA soli PETERS G 1558 (H190)

Italienische Duette No. 12: Soviel
Pfeile Hast Verschossen
SA soli PETERS G 1551 (H191)

Italienische Duette No. 13:
Schmachtend, Flehend
SA soli PETERS G 1562 (H192)

Italienische Duette No. 14: Willst Du
Die Lieb'
SA soli PETERS G 1554 (H193)

HANDEL, GEORGE FRIDERIC (cont'd.)
Italienische Duette No. 17: Nein, Ich
Will
SA soli PETERS G 1553 (H194)

Italienische Duette No. 19: Wie
Leichtes Laub
SA soli PETERS G 1552 (H195)

Italienische Duette No. 20: Ach, Hier
Im Irdischen Leben
SS soli PETERS G 1528 (H196)

Jeptha: Waft Her Angels
[Eng] med solo,pno CLASSV 1818
(H197)

Lungi Dal Mio Bel Numbe
solo voice,pno ALFRED 3233 (H198)

Manca Pur Quanto Sai
see Ten Solo Cantatas, Vol. 2

Nice, Che Fa? Che Pensa?
see Ten Solo Cantatas, Vol. 1

Notre Père
solo voice,pno LEDUC f.s. (H199)

O Salutaris
S/Mez/T solo,org/harmonium LEDUC
f.s. contains also: Ave Maria
(H200)
Occhi Miei, Che Faceste?
see Ten Solo Cantatas, Vol. 1

Opera Arias
(Watanabe, K.; Misawa, T.) ZEN-ON
713201 (H201)

Parti, L'idolo Mio
solo voice,pno ALFRED 3234 (H202)

Pensieroso, Il: Sweetbird
S solo,pno CLASSV 0465 (H203)

Quando Sperasti, O Core
see Ten Solo Cantatas, Vol. 1

Quel Fior Che All'alba Ride
see Ten Solo Cantatas, Vol. 2

Récitatif Et Air Du Messie
S/T solo,pno LEDUC f.s. (H204)

Rings Schallen Schon Trompeten (from
Ezio)
Bar/B solo,2ob,bsn,strings,cont
DEUTSCHER (H205)

Salve Regina, HWV 241
solo voice,pno BREITKOPF-W pno red
EB 8537, sc PB 5186, pts OB 5186
(H206)
Samson: Let The Bright Seraphim
S solo,pno CLASSV 0375 (H207)
S solo,org CLASSV 1815 (H208)

Sarai Contenta Un Di
see Ten Solo Cantatas, Vol. 1

Se Per Fatal Destino
see Ten Solo Cantatas, Vol. 2

Semele: Hence, Hence, Iris, Hence
Away
[Eng/Ger] Mez solo,pno CLASSV 1681
(H209)
Semele: Where'er You Walk
high solo,pno CLASSV 0915 (H210)
low solo,pno CLASSV 0914 (H211)
med solo,pno CLASSV 1231 (H212)

Serenata
(Zimmerman) "There In Blissful
Shades" SMezB soli,2vln,cont
OXFORD 64.015 (H213)

Serse: Ombra Mai Fu
med solo,pno (E flat maj) CLASSV
0487 (H214)
med solo,pno (F maj) CLASSV 1817
(H215)
high solo,pno CLASSV 0486 (H216)

Serse: Ombra Mai Fu (Largo)
"Deep In Thy Shade" Mez solo
RICORDI-IT LD 299 (H217)

Silete Venti *HWV242
solo voice,strings,2ob,bsn sc,set
KING'S (H218)

Songs And Cantatas
(Burrows, Donald) S solo,cont
OXFORD 68.237 (H219)

Ten Solo Cantatas, Vol. 1
(Jones) S solo,cont FABER F0843
f.s.
contains: Allor Ch'io Dissi:
Addio; Nice, Che Fa? Che
Pensa?; Occhi Miei, Che
Faceste?; Quando Sperasti, O
Core; Sarai Contenta Un Di
(H220)

HANDEL, GEORGE FRIDERIC (cont'd.)
Ten Solo Cantatas, Vol. 2
(Jones) S solo,cont FABER F0897
f.s.
contains: Care Selve, Aure Grate;
Fra Tante Pene; Manca Pur
Quanto Sai; Quel Fior Che
All'alba Ride; Se Per Fatal
Destino (H221)

There In Blissful Shade: Serenata
(Zimmerman) SMezB soli,2vln,ob,cont
OXFORD 356994-9 $24.00 (H222)

There In Blissful Shades
see Serenata

Three Ornamented Arias
(Dean) solo voice,2ob,strings
[17'30"] OXFORD (H223)

HANDEL OPERA REPERTORY, THE see Handel,
George Frideric

HANDS see Johannsson, Magnus Bl.

HANDSOME NELL see Reuland, Jacques

HANNA see Isolfsson, Pall

HANS, EDITH
Gezang Tzu Israel, A
[Yiddish] solo voice,pno OR-TAV
(H224)
Ver Bistu Mentsh?
[Yiddish] solo voice,pno OR-TAV
(H225)

HANS HEILING: AN JENEM TAG see
Marschner, Heinrich (August)

HÄNSEL UND GRETEL: EVENING PRAYER see
Humperdinck, Engelbert

HANSON, STEN (1936-)
Auf Dem Land
see Wienerlieder

Égalité
S solo STIM (H226)

Es Geht Mir Gut
see Wienerlieder

Extrasensory Conceptions II
S solo,5perc,electronic equipment
STIM (H227)

Hosi
see Wienerlieder

Ich Bin So Froh
see Wienerlieder

Puppen, Die
see Wienerlieder

Wenn Die Sterne
see Wienerlieder

Wienerlieder
female solo&3 speaking voices,
electronic tape,pno STIM perf mat
rent
contains: Auf Dem Land; Es Geht
Mir Gut; Hosi; Ich Bin So Froh;
Puppen, Die; Wenn Die Sterne
(H228)
Zwei Geistliche Lieder
[Ger] solo voice,pno TONOS (H229)

HANTISE D'AMOUR see Szulc, Josef
Zygmunt

HANUŠ, JAN (1915-)
Destnik Z Piccadilly
B solo,3.3.3.2. 4.3.3.1. timp,perc,
vibra,harp,cel,strings [26']
CESKY HUD. (H230)

HAPPY HOURS AT HOME see Foster, Stephen
Collins

HAR DOMMEDAG FUNNET STED? see Waring,
Rob

HAR DU SETT'N ØIVIND see Albertsen, Per
Hjort

HARA TAMIKI NO SHI NI YORU KAKYOKUSHU
see Fukuda, Akira

HARBINGER see Lunde, Ivar

HARBISON, JOHN (1938-)
Mirabai Songs
S/Mez solo,pno/chamber group [17']
AMP 50480104 f.s., ipr (H231)

Mottetti Di Montale
AMP 50480303 (H232)

HARDARSON, ÁRNI (1956-)
Three Songs
S solo,pno ICELAND 066-001   (H233)

HARLEM NIGHT SONG see Flothuis, Marius

HARMONI, EN see Madsen, Trygve

HARMONIE DU SOIR see Debussy, Claude

HARMONIUM see Gerber, Steven R.

HARMONIZATIONS (LUTHER CHORALES) see
Violette, Andrew

HARP, THE see Roosendael, Jan Rokus van

HARP OF FIRE, THE see Roosendael, Jan
Rokus van see Roosendael, Jan Rokus
van

HARPA see Halldorsson, Skuli

HARPER, EDWARD JAMES (1941-)
Homage To Thomas Hardy
Bar solo,2.2.2.2. 2.2.0.0. tubular
bells,strings [27'] OXFORD (H234)

Seven Poems By e.e. cummings
S solo,2.2.2.2. 4.2.3.1. 3perc,
harp,pno/cel,strings [23'] OXFORD
(H235)

HARPESPELAREN see Olsen, Sparre

HARRINGTON, FRANK J. (1963-)
Where Poppies Blow! *song cycle
Bar solo,pno [20'] LYNWD   (H236)

HARRIS, DONALD (1931-)
Mains, Les
[Fr] Mez solo,pno [5'] (diff)
PRESSER 111-40105   (H237)

Pierrot Lieder
S solo,instrumental ensemble MARGUN
MP3051   (H238)

HARRIS, MATTHEW
In Just Spring
med solo,pno [11'] AM.COMP.AL.
(H239)

Sno (I. Of Impressions)
Mez solo,fl,clar,vla,db,harp,pno,
2perc [5'] sc AM.COMP.AL. $10.30
(H240)

HARRIS, RONALD S. (1941-)
Gift Goes On, The (composed with
Cloninger, Claire)
solo voice HARRIS,R RHS0303 $2.00
(H241)
In This Very Room - The Collected
Songs Of Ron Harris *CCU
solo voice folio HARRIS,R RHV0601
$12.95   (H242)
You're Bringing Out The Very Best In
Me (composed with Williamson,
Jan)
solo voice HARRIS,R RHS0307 $2.00
(H243)

HARRIS, ROSS
Dreams, Yellow Lions
Bar solo,vln,vcl,sax,flügelhorn,
bass clar WAI-TE-ATA 83 (H244)

HARRISON, A.F.
In The Gloaming
low solo,pno CLASSV 1820   (H245)
med solo,pno CLASSV 1819   (H246)

HARRISON, LOU (1917-)
Symphony No. 4
Bar solo,3(pic).3(English
horn).3(bass clar).3(contrabsn).
4.3.3.1. 4perc,cel,prepared pno,
harp,strings [45'0"] PEER (H247)

HÄRTE SCHWAND see Flothuis, Marius

HARTKE, STEPHEN PAUL (1952-)
Cancoes Modernistas
S solo,pno/clar&bass clar&vla MMB
X814001 f.s., ipr
contains: No Meio Do Caminho, "In
The Middle Of The Road";
Tristeza No Ceu, "Sadness In
Heaven"   (H248)

Iglesia Abandonada
S solo,vln MMB S815002   (H249)

No Meio Do Caminho
see Cancoes Modernistas

Tristeza No Ceu
see Cancoes Modernistas

HARTMANN, CHRISTIAN (1910-)
Hunter, The
see Jegeren

Jegeren
"Hunter, The" solo voice,2fl,ob,
2clar,bsn,strings NORGE f.s.
(H250)

HARTMANN, LUDWIG
Sechs Lieder *Op.13, CC6U
solo voice,pno sc KISTNER f.s.
(H251)

HARU WA AKEBONO see Matsumoto, Hinoharu

HARVEY
Lullaby For The Unsleeping
solo voice FABER 51003 5   (H252)

Song Offerings
FABER 50980 0   (H253)

HASHIRAMOTO, MASARU (1956-)
Missing Piece, The
S solo,clar,vln,pno [11'] JAPAN
(H254)

HASKALAH
med solo/high solo,orch [15']
TRANSCON. 970199 rent   (H255)

HASQUENOPH, PIERRE (1922-1982)
Quatre Poesies
S solo,2.2.2.2. 2.2.1.0. perc,timp,
cel,pno,strings BILLAUDOT (H256)

HASSE, JOHANN ADOLPH (1699-1783)
Miserere
ATB/TTB soli (F maj) HÄNSSLER
40.807 f.s. contains also:
Mozart, Wolfgang Amadeus,
Miserere (ATB/TTB soli) (A min)
(H257)

HAST AM FELDRAIN GEBLÜHT see Eisler,
Hanns

HAT DICH DIE LIEBE BERÜHRT see Marx,
Joseph

HATIDASONGUR see Ragnarsson, Hjalmar H.

HATIDASONGVAR SJOMANNADAGSINS see
Thoroddsen, Emil

HATSLIL BAGAI see Stutschevsky, Joachim

HATTORI, KAZUHIKO (1944-)
Aru Mono
S solo,fl,vla,pno [6'] JAPAN (H258)

Three Poems
S solo,fl,vla,pno [13'] JAPAN
(H259)

HATZIS, CHRISTOS
Kleidocymbalon I
any instruments or voices SEESAW
(H260)

HAUBENSTOCK-RAMATI, ROMAN (1919-)
Alone 2
solo voice [10'-15'] ARIAD 80033
(H261)
Discours
solo voice,gtr [10'-15'] ARIAD
80034   (H262)
Kreise
solo voice,perc [15'] ARIAD 80037
(H263)
Sonnambula, La
solo voice,opt gtr [10'-15'] ARIAD
80036   (H264)

HAUFRECHT, HERBERT (1909-)
And You Shall Be A True Lover Of Mine
(Cambric Shirt)
med solo,pno [5'] sc AM.COMP.AL.
$3.10   (H265)
Betsy B
med solo,pno [5'] sc AM.COMP.AL.
$3.10   (H266)
Boy And The Highwayman, The
med solo,pno [5'] sc AM.COMP.AL.
$6.15   (H267)
Dewy, Dewy Dens Of Yarrow, The
med solo,pno [5'] sc AM.COMP.AL.
$2.35   (H268)
He Has Gone To Sea
med solo,pno [3'] sc AM.COMP.AL.
$2.35   (H269)
I Walked The Road Again
med solo,pno [4'] sc AM.COMP.AL.
$1.60   (H270)
Lullaby
Mez solo,pno [3'] sc AM.COMP.AL.
$.80   (H271)
Missy Mouse And Mister Frog
med solo,pno [33'] sc AM.COMP.AL.
$1.60   (H272)
Mountain Moods
solo voice,fl,pno [7'] AM.COMP.AL.
(H273)
Shanty Lad, The
med solo,pno [3'] sc AM.COMP.AL.
$1.60   (H274)

HAUGBUAR see Isolfsson, Pall

HAUGHTINESS see Borodin, Alexander
Porfirievich, Gernegross, Der

HAUGLAND, GLENN ERIK (1961-)
Brev
[Norw] solo voice,electronic tape
NORGE   (H275)
Fjord Trio, Ein
[Norw] A solo,pno,db NORGE   (H276)
Hymne Se Nomme, L'
S/T solo,2rec/2fl,2gtr,vla,vcl,hpsd
NORGE f.s.   (H277)
So Ro Rull: Ein Reise-Rondo
solo voice,horn NORGE   (H278)
Som Sang, En
solo voice NORGE   (H279)

HAUGTUSSA see Taubo, Lillian Gulowna

HAUKSSON, THORSTEINN (1948-)
Psychomachia
S solo,vcl ICELAND 041-009 (H280)
[Lat] S solo,vcl [8'30"] REIMERS
101146   (H281)
Webby In The Woodland
S solo,pno [2'30"] ICELAND 041-008
(H282)

HAUPTMANN
Trauungslied
KAHNT 5281   (H283)

HAUSMUSIK see Wagner-Regeny, Rudolf

HAUST see Bergh, Sverre see Kielland,
Olav see Sveinsson, Atli Heimir

HAUSTKVOLD see Halldorsson, Skuli

HAUSTVISA see Johnsen, Hallvard

HÅVAMÅL see Tveitt, Geirr

HAVE YOU SEEN BUT A WHYTE LILLIE GROW
see Anonymous

HAVETS VISA see Nystroem, Gösta

HAWK, THE see Haxton, Kenneth

HAWLEY, CHARLES BEACH (1858-1915)
Three Songs
S solo,vln,pno SEESAW   (H284)

HAXTON, KENNETH
Chanson d'Automne
high solo,pno [3'] sc AM.COMP.AL.
$1.60   (H285)
Come
high solo,pno [3'] sc AM.COMP.AL.
$1.60   (H286)
Empty Cup, The
high solo,pno [2'] sc AM.COMP.AL.
$1.60   (H287)
Four American Women Poets
high solo,pno [12'15"] AM.COMP.AL.
(H288)
From "The Black Riders"
high solo,pno [5'] AM.COMP.AL.
(H289)
Hawk, The
high solo,pno [3'] sc AM.COMP.AL.
$4.25   (H290)
Human Dignity
high solo,pno [2'] sc AM.COMP.AL.
$1.60   (H291)
In My Craft Or Sullen Art
high solo,pno [4'] AM.COMP.AL.
(H292)
Infant Sorrow
high solo,pno [2'] sc AM.COMP.AL.
$1.60   (H293)
Life XCVI
high solo,pno [2'] sc AM.COMP.AL.
$1.60   (H294)
Little Boy Lost, Interlude, Little
Boy Found
high solo,pno [8'] sc AM.COMP.AL.
$5.75   (H295)
Love XXXIII
high solo,pno [2'] sc AM.COMP.AL.
$1.60   (H296)
Lullaby
high solo,pno [3'] sc AM.COMP.AL.
$1.60   (H297)
Mad Song
high solo,pno [3'] sc AM.COMP.AL.
$4.25   (H298)
Mermaid, The
high solo,pno [3'] sc AM.COMP.AL.
$1.60   (H299)

HAXTON, KENNETH (cont'd.)

Mothers And Children
S solo,ob,vcl,pno [15'] AM.COMP.AL.
sc $22.20, pts $5.75   (H300)

Music I Heard With You
high solo,pno sc AM.COMP.AL. $4.25
(H301)

Narcissus
high solo,pno [3'] sc AM.COMP.AL.
$1.60   (H302)

Night, The
high solo,pno [3'] sc AM.COMP.AL.
$1.60   (H303)

Old Men Admiring Themselves In The
Water, The
high solo,pno [2'] sc AM.COMP.AL.
$1.60   (H304)

Orpheus
high solo,pno/hpsd [4'] sc
AM.COMP.AL. $1.60   (H305)

Psalm No. 121
high solo,pno [4'] sc AM.COMP.AL.
$4.25   (H306)

Ring, The
med solo,pno [2'] AM.COMP.AL.
(H307)

Sick Rose, The
high solo,pno [3'] sc AM.COMP.AL.
$1.60   (H308)

Snare, The
high solo,pno [3'] sc AM.COMP.AL.
$1.60   (H309)

So Proud She Was To Die
high solo/med solo,pno [3']
AM.COMP.AL.   (H310)

Sound And The Fury, The
A solo,3.2(English horn).2(bass
clar).2. 4.3.3.1. timp,perc,pno,
strings [30'] AM.COMP.AL. (H311)

Sylphe, Le
high solo,pno [3'] sc AM.COMP.AL.
$1.60   (H312)

Tell All The Truth
high solo,pno [4'] sc AM.COMP.AL.
$4.25   (H313)

Times Are Nightfall, The
high solo,pno [2'] sc AM.COMP.AL.
$1.60   (H314)

To A Child Dancing In The Wind
high solo,pno [4'] sc AM.COMP.AL.
$4.25   (H315)

Unloved To His Beloved, The
high solo,pno [3'] sc AM.COMP.AL.
$4.25   (H316)

When The Hand Of Spring
high solo,pno [4'] sc AM.COMP.AL.
$4.25   (H317)

Widow's Lament In Springtime, The
med solo,pno [4'] AM.COMP.AL.
(H318)

Witchcraft By A Picture
high solo,pno [2'] sc AM.COMP.AL.
$4.25   (H319)

Year After Year
high solo,pno [2'] sc AM.COMP.AL.
$1.60   (H320)

HAYAKAWA, KUZUKO (1944-   )
Akaki Konomi
B solo,pno [3'] ONGAKU   (H321)

Arijigoku
A solo,pno [5'] JAPAN   (H322)

Atarashiki Toshi No Hajime Ni
TB soli,pno [5'] ONGAKU   (H323)

Ginga
T solo,pno [7'] ONGAKU   (H324)

Hi
A solo,pno [5'] JAPAN   (H325)

Ike No Hotori Naru Take
Bar solo,pno [4'] ONGAKU   (H326)

Junrei
Bar solo,pno [3'] ONGAKU   (H327)

Kodoku
B solo,pno [4'] ONGAKU   (H328)

London Dayori
Mez solo,pno [4'] ONGAKU   (H329)

Momijiba
T solo,pno [4'] ONGAKU   (H330)

HAYAKAWA, KUZUKO (cont'd.)

Nemu No Hana
Bar solo,pno [5'] ONGAKU   (H331)

Take
A solo,pno [4'] JAPAN   (H332)

Yukikemuri
T solo,pno [6'] ONGAKU   (H333)

Yuzutsu O Mite
T solo,pno [3'] ONGAKU   (H334)

HAYASHI, HIKARU (1931-   )
Hosuke No Hiyoko
S solo,pno [15'] JAPAN   (H335)

Sky
S solo,fl ONGAKU 492643 f.s.   (H336)

HAYDN, [FRANZ] JOSEPH (1732-1809)
Creation, The: With Verdure Clad
high solo,pno CLASSV 0489   (H337)

Fifteen Scottish, Welsh And Irish
Folksongs *CC15U
(Jones, David Wyn) high solo,vln,
vcl,pno sc,pts UNIV.CR P66317
f.s.   (H338)

Guarda Qui Che Lo Vedrai
see Zwei Duette

Orfeo: Del Mio Core
S solo,pno CLASSV 1620   (H339)

Orfeo: Il Pensier Sta Negli Oggetti
Bar solo,pno CLASSV 1643   (H340)

Sacred And Secular Songs *CC50U
med solo KALMUS K 06842 f.s. (H341)

Saper Vorrei Se M'ami
see Zwei Duette

She Never Told Her Love
low solo,pno CLASSV 0556   (H342)
med solo,pno CLASSV 0490   (H343)

Zwei Duette *Hob.XXVa:1-2
ST soli,pno HENLE 538 f.s.
contains: Guarda Qui Che Lo
Vedrai; Saper Vorrei Se M'ami
(H344)

Zwei Pastorellen
(Biba, Otto) S solo,2vln,vla,cont,
opt 2horn (Süddeutsche
Weihnachtsmusik, Band 6)
COPPENRATH   (H345)

HAYDN, [JOHANN] MICHAEL (1737-1806)
Ave Regina
B solo,strings,vla solo KUNZEL
GM 30   (H346)

Froehliche Wiederschein
BOOSEY EMB07000   (H347)

Frühe Bund, Der
see Vier Lieder

Heiligste Nacht!
see Zwei Weihnachtslieder

Seligkeit Der Liebe, Die
see Vier Lieder

Vergänglichkeit, Die
see Vier Lieder

Verlassene Mutter Am Strome, Die
see Vier Lieder

Vier Lieder
high solo,pno CLASSV 1038 f.s.
contains: Frühe Bund, Der;
Seligkeit Der Liebe, Die;
Vergänglichkeit, Die;
Verlassene Mutter Am Strome,
Die   (H348)

Wie Trostreich Ist Uns Adamskindern
see Zwei Weihnachtslieder

Wir Beten Dich Unendlich Wesen
SA soli,strings,cont KUNZEL GM 207
(H349)

Zwei Weihnachtslieder
(Biba, Otto) SA soli,2horn,cont
COPPENRATH f.s. Süddeutsche
Weihnachtsmusik, Band 2
contains: Heiligste Nacht!; Wie
Trostreich Ist Uns Adamskindern
(H350)

HAYFORD
Majesty
(Keesecker) solo voice,pno PRESSER
491-00364   (H351)

HAYS
Blues Fragmente
PETERS 66913   (H352)

HAZON, ROBERTO (1930-   )
Due Canti (from Cancionero Espanol)
solo voice,pno CURCI 9804   (H353)

Due Rime D'amore
solo voice,pno CURCI 9805   (H354)

HAZZARD, PETER PEABODY (1949-   )
Massage
SAB soli,fl,clar,flügelhorn,sax,
trom,perc SEESAW f.s.   (H355)

HE HAS GONE TO SEA see Haufrecht,
Herbert

HE IS MY REDEEMER see Schofield, Joe

HE SAYS HE'S GOT see Anderson, Beth

HE TOOK ALL FROM ME see Rachmaninoff,
Sergey Vassilievich

HEAD, MICHAEL (DEWAR) (1900-1976)
Funny Fellow, A
BOOSEY SGB2607F   (H356)

Song Album, Vol. 1 *CCU
BOOSEY VAB0226 f.s.   (H357)

Song Album, Vol. 2: Roma *CCU
BOOSEY VAB0227 f.s.   (H358)

Song Album, Vol. 3
(CCU) BOOSEY VAB0228 f.s.   (H359)

HEAR US, LORD see Tcimpidis, David

HEART OF THE MATTER see Britten, [Sir]
Benjamin

HEART ON THE WALL see Owens, Robert

HEART WORSHIPS, THE see Holst, Gustav

HEATH, THE see Groven, Eivind, Moen

HEAVEN-HAVEN see Manneke, Daan

HEAVENLY AIDA see Verdi, Giuseppe,
Aida: Celeste Aida

HEAVENLY SACRED SONGS
("World's Favorite Series") ASHLEY
144   (H360)

HEAVIEST SORROW AND GRIEF, THE see
Sinding, Christian, Tyngste Sorg Og
Møda, Den

HEBEND DIE BLICKE VOM BUCH see
Voortman, Roland

HEBREW MELODIES see Diamond, David

HEBREW MOURNER, THE
SCIEN 680   (H361)

HEBREW SONG see Mussorgsky, Modest
Petrovich

HEDEN EN VERLEDEN IN DE LIEFDE see
Braal, Andries de

HEERSER see Ruiter, Wim de

HEGAARD, LARS
Haiku
S solo,vln,pno [16'] SAMFUNDET
(H362)

HEGDAL, MAGNE (1944-   )
Air: Til En Gotisk Katedral
[Norw] S solo,pno,marimba/timp
[12'] NORGE   (H363)

Bakvende Verdi, Den
[Norw] Mez solo,pno [21'] NORGE
(H364)

Canonic Variations
solo voice,pno NORGE   (H365)

Duets
S solo,pno,vln/vcl,fl/clar,perc,
opt additional insts. [21'] NORGE
f.s.   (H366)

Hendelser
[Norw] S&speaking voice,fl,clar,
vln,vcl,pno,perc [30'] NORGE
(H367)

Komposisjon: Nattlandskap
singing female flutist & cellist
[18'] NORGE   (H368)

Sequentia: Labyrintische Form Nach
Texten Von Isolde Loock
[Ger] Mez/A solo,A rec,perc [11']
NORGE   (H369)

Zärtliche Ode, Eine
[Ger] solo voice,pno NORGE   (H370)

HEIDASVANURINN see Helgason, Hallgrimur

HEIDATHOKAN see Björnsson, Arni

HEIDBLAA FJOLAN MIN FRIDA see Jonsson, Thorarinn

HEIDENRÖSLEIN see Schubert, Franz (Peter)

HEIDIN HA see Kaldalóns, Sigvaldi S.

"HEIDLOAR-KVAEDI" see Johannsson, Magnus Bl.

HEILAGKVEDI, OP. 13 see Johnsen, Hallvard

HEILIGE FRANCISCUS see Geraedts, Jaap

HEILIGSTE NACHT! see Haydn, [Johann] Michael

HEILLER, ANTON (1923-1979)
  Ave Maria
    S solo,vln,vla sc,pts DOBLINGER
    08 874   (H371)

HEILNER, IRWIN (1908-   )
  Champion, The
    med solo,pno [1'] sc AM.COMP.AL.
    $1.95   (H372)

  Could Man Be Drunk Forever
    med solo,gtr [2'] sc AM.COMP.AL.
    $1.60   (H373)

  Dogs
    med solo,pno [2'] sc AM.COMP.AL.
    $1.95   (H374)

  Fog
    med solo,pno [1'] sc AM.COMP.AL.
    $.55   (H375)

  French Child Calling Her Dog, A
    S solo [1'] sc AM.COMP.AL. $.25   (H376)

  Futility
    med solo,pno [1'] sc AM.COMP.AL.
    $1.95   (H377)

  Garlands And Flowers
    high solo,pno [4'] sc AM.COMP.AL.
    $3.85   (H378)

  Ghost Of Amsterdam, The
    med solo,alto sax/tenor sax [10']
    sc AM.COMP.AL. $4.60   (H379)

  Herd Boy, The
    ST soli,pno [2'] sc AM.COMP.AL.
    $1.90   (H380)

  Hey There *round
    3 solo voices,acap [3'] sc
    AM.COMP.AL. $.80   (H381)

  House In Granada, The
    high solo,lute,vla da gamba,rec,
    cornettos [4'] sc AM.COMP.AL.
    $4.25   (H382)

  I Shall Not Care
    med solo,gtr [3'] sc AM.COMP.AL.
    $1.60   (H383)

  If We Die
    med solo,gtr [1'] sc AM.COMP.AL.
    $1.20   (H384)

  Illinois Farmer
    med solo,pno [2'] sc AM.COMP.AL.
    $1.20   (H385)

  In Yalta
    med solo,gtr [5'] sc AM.COMP.AL.
    $3.10   (H386)

  Isaac Woodard
    med solo,pno [1'] sc AM.COMP.AL.
    $1.95   (H387)

  Little Girl Practicing, A
    high solo,pno [11'] sc AM.COMP.AL.
    $1.20   (H388)

  Love Songs *CCU
    Bar solo,vcl sc AM.COMP.AL. $7.70   (H389)

  Modern Youth
    med solo,pno [1'] sc AM.COMP.AL.
    $1.95   (H390)

  Moonlight
    S solo [1'] sc AM.COMP.AL. $.25   (H391)

  My Poems Are Full Of Poison
    med solo,gtr [1'] sc AM.COMP.AL.
    $.45   (H392)

  Poem
    med solo,pno [2'] sc AM.COMP.AL.
    $1.20   (H393)

  Psalm No. 23
    med solo,pno [2'] sc AM.COMP.AL.
    $3.85   (H394)

HEILNER, IRWIN (cont'd.)

  Santy Isn't Santa Claus
    med solo,pno [1'] sc AM.COMP.AL.
    $1.95   (H395)

  Southern Mammy Sings
    med solo,pno [1'] sc AM.COMP.AL.
    $.45   (H396)

  Stars Have Not Dealt Me The Worst
    They Could, The
    med solo,gtr [1'] sc AM.COMP.AL.
    $1.60   (H397)

  Teardrop Millionaire, The
    med solo,pno [1'] sc AM.COMP.AL.
    $1.20   (H398)

  To His Wife
    ST soli,pno [3'] sc AM.COMP.AL.
    $2.70   (H399)

  To The Guitarists
    high solo,gtr [2'] sc AM.COMP.AL.
    $1.20   (H400)

  Traveler, The
    med solo,pno [3'] sc AM.COMP.AL.
    $1.60   (H401)
    med solo,2.2.2.2. 2.0.0.0. harp,
    perc,strings [3'] pno red
    AM.COMP.AL. $1.60   (H402)

  Vernal Equinox
    high solo,pno [1'] sc AM.COMP.AL.
    $1.95   (H403)

  Why The Soup Tastes Like The Daily
    News
    med solo,gtr [1'] sc AM.COMP.AL.
    $1.20   (H404)

HEIM see Kielland, Olav

HEIMA see Kristjánsson, Oddgeir

HEIMATGEDANKEN see Egilsson, Árni

HEIMCHEN AM HERD, DAS: EIN GEHEIMNIS
  WUNDERSÜSS see Goldmark, Karl

HEIME see Ludt, Finn

HEIME, VESLEMØY VED ROKKEN see Taubo,
  Lillian Gulowna

HEIMERL, CHR.
  Mein Kind, Wir Waren Kinder
    solo voice,pno BOHM f.s.   (H405)

HEIMGANG see Mattiesen

HEIMIR see Isolfsson, Pall see
  Kaldalóns, Sigvaldi S.

HEIMLICHE AUFMARSCH, DER see Eisler,
  Hanns

HEIMLICHKEIT see Lowe, Karl

HEIMTHRA see Halldorsson, Skuli see
  Helgason, Hallgrimur see Isolfsson,
  Pall see Runolfsson, Karl Otto

HEIMWEH see Wolf, Hugo

HEINZELMÄNNCHEN, DIE see Loewe, Carl
  Gottfried

HEISST ES VIEL see Colaço Osorio-Swaab,
  Reine

HEJ GAMLA GUBE see Freudenthal, Otto

HEKSTER, WALTER (1937-   )
  Below The Hill
    see Four Poems On The Pleasures Of
    The Country

  Birds Calling In The Valley
    see Four Poems About Cloud Valley,
    The Estate Of Huang-Fu-Yuan

  Cormorant Dam
    see Four Poems About Cloud Valley,
    The Estate Of Huang-Fu-Yuan

  Dense
    see Four Poems On The Pleasures Of
    The Country

  Duckweed Pool
    see Four Poems About Cloud Valley,
    The Estate Of Huang-Fu-Yuan

  Einsam
    see Songs From The Japanese

  Fantoom
    see Vier Achterberg Liederen

  Four Poems About Cloud Valley, The
    Estate Of Huang-Fu-Yuan
    Bar solo,pno DONEMUS f.s. [6']
    contains: Birds Calling In The

HEKSTER, WALTER (cont'd.)

    Valley; Cormorant Dam; Duckweed
    Pool; Lotus Flower Bank   (H406)

  Four Poems On The Pleasures Of The
    Country
    S solo,pno DONEMUS f.s. [7']
    contains: Below The Hill; Dense;
    Peach Flowers; Picking Water
    Chestnuts   (H407)

  Frühlings Ende
    see Songs From The Japanese

  Frühlingsnacht
    see Songs Of All Seasons

  Herbstlied
    see Songs Of All Seasons

  Improvisation An Einem Wintertag
    see Songs Of All Seasons

  Japanese Settings
    solo voice,fl,vcl,perc,gtr [9']
    DONEMUS f.s.   (H408)

  Lotus Flower Bank
    see Four Poems About Cloud Valley,
    The Estate Of Huang-Fu-Yuan

  Morgenglocke, Die
    see Songs From The Japanese

  Morgenmist
    see Vier Achterberg Liederen

  Nacht
    see Vier Achterberg Liederen

  Peach Flowers
    see Four Poems On The Pleasures Of
    The Country

  Picking Water Chestnuts
    see Four Poems On The Pleasures Of
    The Country

  Sommerliche Freuden Auf Dem Lande
    see Songs Of All Seasons

  Songs From The Japanese
    med solo,clar,pno DONEMUS f.s. [8']
    contains: Einsam; Frühlings Ende;
    Morgenglocke, Die; Trübeslied;
    Weide Im Wind, Die   (H409)

  Songs Of All Seasons
    S solo,fl&alto fl&pic,perc,harp,db
    DONEMUS f.s. [12']
    contains: Frühlingsnacht;
    Herbstlied; Improvisation An
    Einem Wintertag; Sommerliche
    Freuden Auf Dem Lande   (H410)

  Trübeslied
    see Songs From The Japanese

  Verloren
    see Vier Achterberg Liederen

  Vier Achterberg Liederen
    Bar solo,bass clar,perc,harp,vla
    DONEMUS f.s. [9']
    contains: Fantoom; Morgenmist;
    Nacht; Verloren   (H411)

  Weide Im Wind, Die
    see Songs From The Japanese

HELDENLIEDER DER DEUTSCHEN KAISERZEIT
  see Gundlach, Wilhelm

HELGASON, HALLGRIMUR (1914-   )
  Dygg Skal Sal
    solo voice,pno ICELAND 007-018
                               (H412)

  Ef Engill Eg Vaeri
    solo voice,pno ICELAND 007-023
                               (H413)

  Enntha Skin Sol
    solo voice,pno ICELAND 007-053
                               (H414)

  Es War Einmal
    solo voice,pno ICELAND 007-062
                               (H415)

  Farsaelda Fron Organum II
    (Helgason, Hallgrímur) solo voice,
    pno (45 Icelandic songs) ICELAND
    007-900   (H416)

  Fjögur Sönglög
    solo voice,pno ICELAND 007-039
                               (H417)

  Fjogur Thjodlog
    solo voice,pno ICELAND 007-038
                               (H418)

  Fünf Islandische Lieder
    solo voice,pno ICELAND 007-067
                               (H419)

  Heidasvanurinn
    solo voice,pno ICELAND 007-063
                               (H420)

HELGASON, HALLGRIMUR (cont'd.)

Heimthra
solo voice,pno ICELAND 007-071
(H421)

Herbstabend
solo voice,pno ICELAND 007-055
(H422)

Islands Hrafnistumenn
solo voice,pno ICELAND 007-015
(H423)

Laub
solo voice,pno ICELAND 007-061
(H424)

Leidin Long
solo voice,pno ICELAND 007-066
(H425)

Ljos
solo voice,pno ICELAND 007-068
(H426)

Loan I Monum
solo voice,pno ICELAND 007-051
(H427)

Mariuvisa
solo voice,pno ICELAND 007-017
(H428)

Meistari Himna
solo voice,pno ICELAND 007-019
(H429)

Midnight
solo voice,pno ICELAND 007-052
(H430)

Nu Afhjupast Ljosin
solo voice,pno ICELAND 007-020
(H431)

Rodd Volvu
solo voice,pno ICELAND 007-069
(H432)

Senn
solo voice,pno ICELAND 007-065
(H433)

Siglum A Saeinn
solo voice,pno ICELAND 007-042
(H434)

Smalastulkan
solo voice,pno ICELAND 007-016
(H435)

Systurnar Godu
solo voice,pno ICELAND 007-064
(H436)

Thratefli
solo voice,pno ICELAND 007-070
(H437)

Thu Blafjalla Geimur
solo voice,pno ICELAND 007-050
(H438)

Vetrarsolhvorf
solo voice,pno ICELAND 007-021
(H439)

Vitaslagur
solo voice,pno ICELAND 007-022
(H440)

Winterrast
solo voice,pno ICELAND 007-060
(H441)

HELLERMANN, WILLIAM (1939-   )
Poem For Soprano And Four Instruments
[8'] AM.COMP.AL. sc $9.15, pts
$26.00 (H442)

HELLIGE BIRGITTAS SALME, DEN see
Jensen, Ludwig Irgens

HELLSTENIUS, HENRIK (1963-   )
Kall Meg En Krakk
[Norw/Swed] S solo,fl,vln,vla,pno
NORGE (H443)

Noe Der
[Norw] S solo,fl NORGE (H444)

HELMSCHROTT, ROBERT M. (1938-   )
Entelechiae (Sinfonia No. 2)
S solo,2(pic).2(English
horn).2(bass clar).2. 4.2.3.1.
timp,perc,harp,pno,strings [24']
ORLANDO f.s. (H445)

Influentiae (Sinfonia No. 1)
speaking voice,2(pic).2(English
horn).2(bass clar).2. 4.3.3.1.
timp,perc,harp,pno,strings
[16'30"] ORLANDO f.s. (H446)

Sinfonia No. 1
see Influentiae

Sinfonia No. 2
see Entelechiae

HEM OF HIS GARMENT, THE see Pryce,
Linda

HEMBERG, ESKIL (1938-   )
Anna Hans Olofs
see Tre Sånger

Bojanafreskerna
see Canticles Op. 56, Nos. 1-3

Bojanaundret
see Canticles Op. 56, Nos. 1-3

Canticles Op. 56, Nos. 1-3
STB soli,ob,harp,perc NORDISKA
10646 f.s.

HEMBERG, ESKIL (cont'd.)

contains: Bojanafreskerna;
Bojanaundret; 1981 (H447)

Där Ligger Sverige
see Tre Sånger

1981
see Canticles Op. 56, Nos. 1-3

Psalmodikon
see Tre Sånger

Three Selected Poems, Op. 79
S solo,pno STIM (H448)

Tre Sånger *Op.70
solo voice,pno STIM f.s.
contains: Anna Hans Olofs; Där
Ligger Sverige; Psalmodikon
(H449)

HEMMA see Strandsjö, Göte

HEMMERLE
Ave Maria
S solo,pno HEUGEL f.s. (H450)

HEN OVER JORDEN ET PILGRIMSTOG see
Nystedt, Knut

HENDELSER see Hegdal, Magne

HENGEVELD, GERARD (1910-   )
Liederen *CC8L
med solo,pno DONEMUS f.s. (H451)

HENRY VIII: QUI DONC COMMANDE QUAND IL
AIME see Saint-Saëns, Camille

HENSEL, FANNY MENDELSSOHN (1805-1847)
Lieder Für Gesang Und Klavier *Op.1,
Op.7, CCU
[Ger] S solo,pno BOTE f.s. reprint
of the original edition of 1946
(H452)

Selected Songs, Vol. 2 *CCU
BREITKOPF-W EB 8596 f.s. (H453)

HENZE, HANS WERNER (1926-   )
Drei Lieder Über Den Schnee
SBar soli,clar,bass clar,horn,bsn,
2vln,vla,vcl,db sc,pts SCHOTTS
ED 7729 (H454)

Whispers From Heavenly Death
high solo,8inst/pno pno red SCHOTTS
ED 7881 (H455)

HEPPENER, ROBERT (1925-   )
Cadens
Mez solo,fl,clar,perc,pno,vln,db
[19'] DONEMUS (H456)

Memento, A Dramatic Scene
S solo,fl,clar,bass clar,mand,
marimba,gtr,harp,vcl,db [20']
DONEMUS f.s. (H457)

Tussen Bomen
Bar solo,pno [20'] DONEMUS f.s.
(H458)

HER ER DET LAND see Johnsen, Hallvard

HER GROR DET GYLNE KORN see Olsen,
Sparre

HER VIL EG KVILE see Nystedt, Knut

HER VOICE see Carpenter, John Alden

HERACLITI RELIQUAE see Child, Peter B.

HERALDS see Smolanoff, Michael Louis

HERBEI, O IHR GLÄUBIGEN see Adeste
Fideles

HERBERG IN DE LENTE see Brandse, Wim

HERBERT, VICTOR (1859-1924)
Art Is Calling For Me
"I Want To Be A Prima Donna" S
solo,pno CLASSV 1294 (H459)

I Want To Be A Prima Donna
see Art Is Calling For Me

If I Were On The Stage
S solo,pno CLASSV 0358 (H460)

Natoma: I List The Trill In Golden
Throat
S solo,pno CLASSV 1822 (H461)

Neapolitan Love Song
see T'Amo!

T'Amo!
"Neapolitan Love Song" [Eng/It] Bar
solo,pno CLASSV 1489 (H462)
"Neapolitan Love Song" [Eng/It] T
solo,pno CLASSV 1814 (H463)

HERBERT-CAESARI, EDGARD
Love He Must Or Flatter Me
see Three Songs

There Is A Garden In Her Face
see Three Songs

Three Songs
solo voice RICORDI-IT LD566 f.s.
contains: Love He Must Or Flatter
Me; There Is A Garden In Her
Face; Was It A Dream? (H464)

Was It A Dream?
see Three Songs

HERBERT HOWELLS SONG ALBUM see Howells,
Herbert Norman

HERBST see Badings, Henk see Franken,
Wim see Marx, Joseph see Norby,
Erik see Orthel, Leon see Visser,
Peter

HERBSTABEND see Helgason, Hallgrimur

HERBSTGANG see Jordan, Sverre

HERBSTGESANG see Jordan, Sverre

HERBSTLIED see Hekster, Walter see
Mendelssohn-Bartholdy, Felix see
Schillings, Max von see Szalonek,
Witold

HERBSTSTURM see Malmlöf-Forssling,
Carin

HERBSTTAG see Evensen, Bernt Kasberg
see Franken, Wim

HERBSTZEITLOSE see Marx, Joseph

HERCULANUM: JE CROIS AU DIEU see David,
Félicien-César

HERD BOY, THE see Heilner, Irwin

HERE GROWS THE GOLDEN GRAIN see Olsen,
Sparre, Her Gror Det Gylne Korn

HERE PEACEFULLY LIES THE ONCE HAPPY
FATHER see Slonimsky, Nicolas

HERE'S TO THY HEALTH see Reuland,
Jacques

HERFST DER MUZIEK see Voorn, Joop

HERFST, OP. 87 see Orthel, Leon

HERFSTTIJ... see Guichelaar, Jan

HERFSTWEER see Orthel, Leon

HERINNERING AAN HOLLAND see King,
Harold C. see Perdeck, Rudolf

HERITAGE OF TWENTIETH CENTURY BRITISH
SONG, VOL. 1 *CCU
BOOSEY VAB0091A f.s. (H465)

HERITAGE OF TWENTIETH CENTURY BRITISH
SONG, VOL. 2 *CCU
BOOSEY VAB0091B f.s. (H466)

HERITAGE OF TWENTIETH CENTURY BRITISH
SONG, VOL. 3 *CCU
BOOSEY VAB0092A f.s. (H467)

HERITAGE OF TWENTIETH CENTURY BRITISH
SONG, VOL. 4 *CCU
BOOSEY VAB0092B f.s. (H468)

HERMANA MARICA, LA see Bedmar, Luis

HÉRODIADE: DORS, Ô CITÉ PERVERSE! see
Massenet, Jules

HÉRODIADE: HÉRODE! NE ME REFUSE PAS!
see Massenet, Jules

HÉRODIADE: IL EST DOUX see Massenet,
Jules

HÉRODIADE: NE ME REFUSE PAS! see
Massenet, Jules

HÉRODIADE: NE POUVANT RÉPRIMER see
Massenet, Jules

HÉRODIADE: PHANUEL'S ARIA see Massenet,
Jules, Hérodiade: Dors, Ô Cité
Perverse!

HÉRODIADE: SALOMÉ-HEROD see Massenet,
Jules

HÉRODIADE: SALOMÉ, SALOMÉ see Massenet,
Jules

HÉRODIADE: VISION FUGITIVE see
Massenet, Jules

HEROLD, LOUIS-JOSEPH-FERDINAND
    (1791-1833)
    Lied
      see Neuestes Theater-Journal

    Neuestes Theater-Journal (from Zampa)
      solo voice,pno SCIEN 1215 f.s.
      contains: Lied, "Mag Die Welle
        Mich Schwingen"; Romanze,
        "Nicht Bestimmt, Um Zu Trauern"
                                        (H469)

    Romanze
      see Neuestes Theater-Journal

HERR LÖFFEL UND FRAU GABEL see Lothar,
    Mark

HERR OLUF see Loewe, Carl Gottfried

HERR SEGNE EUCH, DER see Bach, Johann
    Sebastian

HERRE, DET STORMER I MITT SINN see
    Karlsen, Kjell Mørk

HERRE, HERRE, DU HAR KALLA see Jordan,
    Sverre

HERRE, KOM DITT FOLK I MØTE see Baden,
    Conrad

HERRE, REKK UT DIN ALLMEKTIGE HAND see
    Nystedt, Knut

HERRE, SKYND DEG Å HJELPE MEG see
    Haegeland, Eilert M.

HERRE, TIL HIMMELEN REKKER DIN
    MISKUNNHET see Nyhus, Rolf

HERREN ÄR MIN HERDE see Elmehed, Rune

HERREN ER BLITT KONGE see Volle, Bjarne

HERREN SKALL AVTORKA TÅRARNA FRÅN ALLA
    ANSIKTEN see Lidström, John

HERRENS BØNN see Baden, Conrad

HERRICK SONGS see Douw, Andre

HERRMANN, W.
    Wenn Weihnacht Ist *CC35U
      solo voice,pno BRATFISCH G.B.3091
      f.s.   (H470)

HERSCHEPPING see Vries Robbe, Willem de

HERSTORY I see Vercoe, Elizabeth

HERSTORY III: JEHANNE DE LORRAINE see
    Vercoe, Elizabeth

HERTEL, THOMAS (1951-   )
    Ode Y Memento
      Mez solo,2.2.2.2. 3.3.3.0. timp,
      perc,harp,pno,strings,vcl solo
      [15'] DEUTSCHER   (H471)

HERVIG, RICHARD B. (1917-   )
    Five Romantic Songs
      AMP AMP7959-3   (H472)

HERZ, DAS see Bijvanck, Henk

HERZ, HENRI (1803-1888)
    'Tis Sad To Part
      SCIEN 700   (H473)

HERZ VOLLER LIEB, DAS see Schild, Th.
    F.

HERZELEID see Schumann, Robert
    (Alexander)

HERZLICH LIEB HAB ICH DICH see Schütz,
    Heinrich

HERZOGENBERG, ELISABETH VON
    Volks-Kinderlieder
      solo voice,pno SCIEN 704   (H474)

HERZOGENBERG, HEINRICH VON (1843-1900)
    Gesänge, Op. 89, No. 2
      PETERS 3702B   (H475)

    Gesänge, Op. 89, No. 3
      PETERS 3702C   (H476)

HESELTINE, PHILIP ("PETER WARLOCK")
    (1894-1930)
    Songs 1918-1919
      solo voice,pno NOVELLO   (H477)

    Songs 1911-1917
      solo voice,pno NOVELLO   (H478)

    Songs 1920-1922
      solo voice,pno NOVELLO   (H479)

    Songs 1922-1923
      solo voice,pno NOVELLO   (H480)

HESPERIDES see Edmunds, John

HESS, W.
    Im Flügelschlag Der Zeit *Op.85,
      song cycle
      med solo,pno KUNZEL GM 856   (H481)

    Kindermärchen, Ein *Op.34
      med solo,fl,pno KUNZEL GM 117
                                        (H482)

    Klang Der Stile, Op.91
      see Meditation, Op.90

    Meditation, Op.90
      med solo,pno (2 song cycles) KUNZEL
      GM 965 f.s. contains also: Klang
      Der Stile, Op.91   (H483)

    Nach Dem Hinschiede Der Gattin
      *Op.84
      med solo,pno KUNZEL GM 855   (H484)

    Summermaie *Op.35
      solo voice,pno KUNZEL GM 713   (H485)

HEUBERGER, RICHARD (1850-1914)
    Opernball, Der: Im Chambre Séparée
      [Ger] med-low solo,pno CLASSV 1151
                                        (H486)
      [Ger] high solo,pno CLASSV 1150
                                        (H487)

HEURE DU SOIR see Delibes, Léo

HEURE ESPAGNOLE, L': GONZALVE'S ARIA
    see Ravel, Maurice

HEURE ESPAGNOLE, L': OH! LA PITOYABLE
    AVENTURE! see Ravel, Maurice

HEURE EXQUISE, L' see Hahn, Reynaldo

HEURE VÉCUE see Massenet, Jules

HEURES D'APRES-MIDI, LES see Gaubert,
    Philippe

HEUREUX EST L'HOMME see Bach, Johann
    Sebastian, Selig Ist Der Mann

HEUSSI
    Trauungslied
      KAHNT 5170   (H488)

HEUTE IST DEIN FESTTAG see Bodensohn,
    Ernst Friedrich Wilhelm

HEY! FOR THE FACTOTUM see Rossini,
    Gioacchino, Barber Of Seville, The:
    Largo Al Factotum

HEY NONNY NO see Walker, George
    Theophilus

HEY THERE see Heilner, Irwin

HEYDT, W.
    Ave Maria, Op.6
      Mez/Bar solo ZENGERINK R.120 (H489)

HEYR, THAD ER UNNUSTI MINN... see
    Isolfsson, Pall

HI see Hayakawa, Kuzuko

HIDALGO, DER see Schumann, Robert
    (Alexander)

HIDALGO, UN see Greenburg, Laura

HIDE ME MOTHER see Tveitt, Geirr, Gøym
    Meg Mor

HIE AWAY see Backer-Lunde, Johan

HIER LIEGT VOR DEINER MAJESTÄT see
    Jungbauer, Coelestin

HIGH SERIOUSNESS see Kirkwood,
    Antoinette

HILDRING I SPEIL, OP. 48 see
    Sommerfeldt, Öistein

HILLEMACHER, PAUL (1852-1933)
    Solitudes, 15
      solo voice,pno CLASSV C024   (H490)

    Vingt Mélodies Vol.2
      high solo,pno CLASSV C025   (H491)

HILLIARD, JOHN
    Dedication Cantata *cant
      high solo,clar,vcl pno [16'] sc
      AM.COMP.AL. $12.20   (H492)

    Three Trees
      med solo,pno [9'] sc AM.COMP.AL.
      $5.00   (H493)

HIMITSU see Kosuge, Yasuo

HIMMLISCHE LIEDER see Schop, Johann

HINDEMITH, PAUL (1895-1963)
    Drei Hymnen Von Walt Whitman *Op.14,
      CC3U
      Bar solo,pno SCHOTTS ED 7117 f.s.
                                        (H494)

HIN'NI see Richards, Stephen

HINOHARA, HIDEHIKO (1964-   )
    Vecchia Del Sonno, La *song cycle
      S solo,instrumental ensemble [30']
      JAPAN   (H495)

HINSIDES HAVEN see Backer-Lunde, Johan

HINZTA KVEDJAN see Kaldalóns, Sigvaldi
    S.

HIPPOLYTE ET ARICIE: ROSSIGNOLS
    AMOUREUX see Rameau, Jean-Philippe

HIRAI, KOZABUROY (1910-   )
    Covered Wagon
      solo voice,pno [1'] ONGAKU   (H496)

    Nihon No Hana - 39 Songs Of Japanese
      Flowers *CCU
      solo voice ONGAKU 525810 f.s.
                                        (H497)

    Shakukei
      S/T solo,pno [3'] ONGAKU   (H498)

HIRAI, TAKEICHIRO (1937-   )
    Art Of Songs *CCU
      solo voice ONGAKU 525850 f.s.
                                        (H499)

    Sakuraso
      Mez solo,pno [5'] ONGAKU   (H500)

HIRONDELLE! see Denza, Luigi

HIROSE, RYOHEI (1930-   )
    Farfalla Della Primavera, La
      coloratura sop,pno/fl&strings [6']
      JAPAN   (H501)

HIROTA, RYUTARO
    Album, Vol. 1 *CCU
      (Hirota, Yuriko) solo voice ONGAKU
      525901 f.s.   (H502)

    Album, Vol. 2 *CCU
      (Hirota, Yuriko) solo voice ONGAKU
      525902 f.s.   (H503)

    Album, Vol. 3 *CCU
      (Hirota, Yuriko) solo voice ONGAKU
      525903 f.s.   (H504)

HIRT AUF DEM FELSEN, DER see Schubert,
    Franz (Peter)

HIRTENLIED see Mendelssohn-Bartholdy,
    Felix see Meyerbeer, Giacomo

HIS ROAD see Roosendael, Jan Rokus van

HISTORIC MARCH see Borodievych, Roman

HISTORIE MEHO SRDCE see Jelinek,
    Stanislav

HIVER, L' see Boismortier, Joseph Bodin
    de

HJA LYGNRI MODU see Runolfsson, Karl
    Otto

HJARDIR DAT VITU see Tveitt, Geirr

HJARTAD GRAETUR see Isolfsson, Pall

HJÄRTAT see Albertsen, Per Hjort see
    Vea, Ketil

HJÄRTATS BLOMMA see Almquist, Carl
    Jonas Love

HJÄRTATS SPRÅK see Leijon, Jerker

HLAS NEJSLADSI see Jirák, Karel
    Boleslav

HLAVACEK, LIBOR (1928-   )
    Poema O Ceskomoravske Vysocine
      Bar solo,2.2.2.2. 2.2.0.0. timp,
      strings [13'] CESKY HUD.   (H505)

HLEDAM TE, KRASO see Vacek, Miloš

HO MOR FAER LOFOTFOLKET SITT HEIM see
    Eggen, Arne

HO SANKAR MYRULL see Berge, Sigurd

HOAGLICHE, DER see Baumann, Alexander

HOBSON, BRUCE (1943-   )
    Portraits
      B solo,pno [10'] APNM sc $5.75, set
      $11.00   (H506)

HOCHSOMMERNACHT see Marx, Joseph

HODD, JACK LORNE
    Bag Of Tools
      LESLIE 7068   (H507)

    Gentle Jesus, Meek And Mild
      solo voice,pno LESLIE 7066 f.s.
                                        (H508)

HODDINOTT, ALUN (1929-   )
    Contemplation Upon Flowers
        solo voice,2.1.2.1. 2.1.0.0. perc,
        strings [15'] voc sc OXFORD
        63.074   (H509)

HODIE CHRISTUS NATUS EST see Valentini,
    Giovanni

HODKINSON, SYDNEY P. (1934-   )
    Adam Lay I-Bounden
        Mez solo,English horn [5']
        AM.COMP.AL.   (H510)

    Alte Liebeslieder, Book IV *CC6U
        med solo,ob,vcl,pno,opt perc
        AM.COMP.AL. sc $27.15, pts $17.65
                                            (H511)
    ARC (Aria With Interludes)
        S solo,fl/pic,pno,2perc [14'] sc
        AM.COMP.AL. $18.25   (H512)

    Roethke-Lieder, Book 1 *CC6U
        S/T solo,pno sc AM.COMP.AL. $11.45
                                            (H513)
    Roethke Lieder, Book 2 *CCU
        S/T solo,fl/pic,hpsd/pno
        AM.COMP.AL. sc $16.90, pts $38.30
                                            (H514)
    Roethke Lieder, Book 3 *CCU
        S/T solo,fl/alto fl,pic,hpsd/pno
        AM.COMP.AL. sc $13.35, pts $4.60
                                            (H515)

HOE DUIZENDVOUDIG see Mulder, Herman

HOE ONSALICH WAS DE STONDE see
    Andriessen, Jurriaan

HOEKMAN, TIMOTHY
    Five American Lyrics
        [Eng] high solo RECITAL 423 (H516)

    Seven Housman Songs
        [Eng] high solo RECITAL 263 (H517)
        [Eng] med solo RECITAL 264   (H518)

HOELLER, KARL
    see HÖLLER, KARL

HOFFMAN
    Consider The Lilies Of The Field
        solo voice SONOS S081 $2.50 (H519)

HOFFMANN VON FALLERSLEBEN, HEINRICH
    AUGUST
    Kinderlieder, 43
        (Schletterer, Hans Michel) SCIEN
        714   (H520)

    Neue Kinderlieder, 50
        (Richter, Ernst) SCIEN 715   (H521)

HOFFNUNG see Fischer, A. see Grieg,
    Edvard Hagerup

HOFSUITE see Deden, Otto

HOHE UFER, DAS see Koetsier, Jan

HOIBY, LEE (1926-   )
    Autumn
        see Songs For Leontyne

    Bermudas
        2 solo voices SCHIRM.G 50481542
                                     (H522)
    Doe, The
        see Songs For Leontyne

    Evening
        see Songs For Leontyne

    Four Dickinson Songs
        high solo,pno PEER   (H523)

    In The Wand Of The Wind
        see Songs For Leontyne

    Lady Of The Harbor
        SCHIRM.G ST48818   (H524)

    Serpent, The
        med solo,2(pic).1.1(bass clar).1.
        0.0.0.1. perc,harp,strings [4'0"]
        PEER   (H525)
        see Songs For Leontyne

    Songs For Leontyne
        high solo,pno sc PEER 61242-212
        $10.00
        contains: Autumn; Doe, The;
            Evening; In The Wand Of The
            Wind; Serpent, The; Winter Song
                                     (H526)
    Thirteen Songs
        solo voice,pno SCHIRM.G ED3758
                                     (H527)
    Winter Song
        see Songs For Leontyne

HOJSGAARD, ERIK (1954-   )
    Fragmenter
        "Fragments" S solo,vln,gtr [12']
        SAMFUNDET 341   (H528)

HOJSGAARD, ERIK (cont'd.)
    Fragments
        see Fragmenter

HOL, DIRK
    Beauty Is But A Painted Hell
        see Four Songs On Poems By Thomas
        Campion

    Fire, Fire, Fire...
        see Four Songs On Poems By Thomas
        Campion

    Four Songs On Poems By Thomas Campion
        med solo,gtr DONEMUS f.s. [16']
        contains: Beauty Is But A Painted
            Hell; Fire, Fire, Fire...; Now
            Winter Nights Enlarge; O Sweet
            Delight   (H529)

    Now Winter Nights Enlarge
        see Four Songs On Poems By Thomas
        Campion

    O Sweet Delight
        see Four Songs On Poems By Thomas
        Campion

HOL, LIV SOLHEIM
    Alle Mine Skutor
        S solo,pno NOTON N-9227   (H530)

HOL, RICHARD (1825-1904)
    O Cor, Voluptas Coelitum
        B solo ZENGERINK R.34   (H531)

    O Quam Suavis
        Bar solo ZENGERINK R.36   (H532)

    O Sacrum Convivium
        T solo ZENGERINK R.35   (H533)

HOLD, TREVOR
    Something Rich And Strange
        high solo,pno RAMSEY BR0142 (H534)

HOLD OUT YOUR LIGHT see McLin, Lena J.

HOLDES BILD see Cornelius, Peter

HOLDING THE NIGHT see Dring, Madeleine

HOLIEST VOW, THE see Williams, David H.

HOLL, R.
    Nachtgesänge
        med solo DOBLINGER 08 669   (H535)

HOLLAND see King, Harold C. see Vries
    Robbe, Willem de see Weegenhuise,
    Johan

HÖLLER, KARL (1907-   )
    Cäsar Flaischlen-Zyklus *song cycle
        med solo,pno HIEBER MH 1018 f.s.
                                     (H536)

HOLLFELDER, WALDRAM (1924-   )
    Kleine Viechereien
        solo voice,pno SEESAW   (H537)

HOLLYWOOD ELEGIES see Noland, Gary

HOLM, KRISTIN (1965-   )
    Lorelei: Et Tysk Folkeeventyr
        [Norw] S&narrator,pno,harp,perc,
        electronic tape [3'30"] (German
        fairytale) NORGE   (H538)

    Lossna
        [Swed] S solo,pno,horn,gtr [8']
        NORGE   (H539)

    Nattergalen Og Rosen *Op.9
        [Norw] solo voice,vcl,pno,
        electronic tape, slides NORGE
                                     (H540)
HOLM, MOGENS WINKEL (1936-   )
    Prison Music III
        SSS soli,3ob,harp [8'] sc,pts
        SAMFUNDET   (H541)

    Prison Music IV
        SSS soli,3ob,harp [8'] sc,pts
        SAMFUNDET   (H542)

    Songs For Soprano And 3 Chamber
        Ensembles
        see Syster, Min Syster

    Syster, Min Syster
        "Songs For Soprano And 3 Chamber
        Ensembles" S solo,fl,contrabsn,
        trp,pno,vln sc,pts SAMFUNDET
                                     (H543)
        "Songs For Soprano And 3 Chamber
        Ensembles" S solo,clar,cornet,
        bass trom,vibra,vcl sc,pts
        SAMFUNDET   (H544)
        "Songs For Soprano And 3 Chamber
        Ensembles" S solo,ob,trom,harp,
        vcl,db sc,pts SAMFUNDET   (H545)

HOLMQUIST, NILS-GUSTAF
    Lyrisk Cykel: 5 Sånger
        [Swed] S solo,gtr TONOS   (H546)

HOLOFERNES see Matthus, Siegfried

HOLST, GUSTAV (1874-1934)
    Heart Worships, The
        med solo,pno CLASSV 0869   (H547)

HOLSTEIN, JEAN-PAUL (1939-   )
    Duette, Op. 15
        2 solo voices,pno PETERS 3539
                                     (H548)
HOLT, PATRICIA BLOMFIELD (1910-   )
    Birds, The
        LESLIE 7070   (H549)

HOLTEN, BO (1948-   )
    Garden Of Love, The
        S solo,English horn,clar,strings
        [9'] sc,pts SAMFUNDET f.s. (H550)

HOLTER, IVER (1850-1941)
    Choral
        [Dan] Bar solo,strings NORGE f.s.
                                     (H551)
HOLTER, STIG WERNØ (1953-   )
    Folk Som Vandrer I Mørket, Det
        "Solomotett, Op. 3, No. 4" [Norw]
        solo voice,org [1'40"] NORGE
                                     (H552)
    Hosea 6 *Op.3,No.6
        [Norw] solo voice,org [3'] NORGE
                                     (H553)
    How Blest *Op.10
        [Eng] S solo,fl,gtr,vcl NORSK
                                     (H554)
    Jeg Takker Deg: Dåpsmotett, Op.22
        S solo,fl,org [2'40"] NORGE (H555)

    Jesaja 53 *Op.3,No.1
        [Norw] Mez solo,org [3'30"] NORGE
                                     (H556)
    Solomotett, Op. 3, No. 4
        see Folk Som Vandrer I Mørket, Det

HOLY CITY, THE see Adams, S.

HOLY, HOLY IS THY NAME see Hall,
    Theodora G.

HOLY THURSDAY see Teed, Roy

HOLZEL, GUSTAV
    Da Himmel *Op.9
        solo voice,pno SCIEN 727   (H557)

    Mir Hat À Mal Vom Teufel Trämt
        solo voice,pno SCIEN 728   (H558)

HOMAGE TO THOMAS HARDY see Harper,
    Edward James

HOMBRE LEAL, EL see Beethoven, Ludwig
    van

HOMBRE PEQUEÑITO see Lopez Artiga,
    Angeles

HOME SONGBOOK, AN ANTHOLOGY OF SONGS
    see Moniuszko, Stanislaw, Spiewnik
    Domowy, Antologia Piesni

HOMECOMING, THE: AN AUTUMN GATHERING
    see Nuernberger, L. Dean

HOMER, SIDNEY (1864-1953)
    Country Of The Camisards, The
        high solo,pno (text by Robert Louis
        Stevenson) CLASSV 1473   (H559)
        low solo,pno (text by Robert Louis
        Stevenson) CLASSV 1478   (H560)

    Enid's Song From Idyls Of The King
        med solo,pno (text by Tennyson)
        CLASSV 1487   (H561)

    Infant Sorrow *Op.26,No.2
        low solo,pno (text by William
        Blake) CLASSV 1492   (H562)

    Last Leaf, The *Op.14,No.1
        low solo,pno (text by Oliver W.
        Holmes) CLASSV 1491   (H563)

    Michael Robartes Bids His Beloved Be
        At Peace
        high solo,pno (text by Yeats)
        CLASSV 1474   (H564)
        low solo,pno (text by Yeats) CLASSV
        1479   (H565)

    Pirate Story: A Child's Garden Of
        Verses
        low solo,pno (text by Robert Louis
        Stevenson) CLASSV 1987   (H566)

    Requiem "From Underwoods" *Op.15,
        No.2
        high solo,pno (text by Robert Louis
        Stevenson) CLASSV 1485   (H567)
        low solo,pno (text by Robert Louis
        Stevenson) CLASSV 1486   (H568)

HOMER, SIDNEY (cont'd.)

Seventeen Lyrics From Sing-Song, Book
1 *Op.19
low solo,pno (texts by Rossetti)
CLASSV 1483 (H569)

Seventeen Lyrics From Sing-Song, Book
2
low solo,pno (texts by Rossetti)
CLASSV 1484 (H570)

Sheep And Lambs
high solo CLASSV 1475 (H571)
low solo,pno CLASSV 1480 (H572)

Sick Rose, The *Op.26,No.1
high solo,pno (text by William
Blake) CLASSV 1476 (H573)
low solo,pno (text by William
Blake) CLASSV 1481 (H574)

Sing Me A Song Of A Lad That Is Gone
low solo,pno (text by Robert Louis
Stevenson) CLASSV 1488 (H575)

Unforgotten, The
high solo,pno (text by Robert Louis
Stevenson) CLASSV 1477 (H576)
low solo,pno (text by Robert Louis
Stevenson) CLASSV 1482 (H577)

Woman's Last Word, A *Op.12,No.2
low solo,pno (text by Robert
Browning) CLASSV 1493 (H578)

HOMESICKNESS see Kentish, Oliver see
Stefansson, Finnur Torfi

HOMING see Del Riego

HOMMAGE A JACQUES PREVERT see Tal,
Marjo

HOMMAGE A JOHANN SEBASTIAN BACH see
Turkat, Michael

HOMMES SUR LA TERRE, LES see Brenet,
Therese

HOMO VIATOR AND OTHER SACRED SONGS see
Pallasz, Edward, Homo Viator I Inne
Sakralne Piosenki

HOMO VIATOR I INNE SAKRALNE PIOSENKI
see Pallasz, Edward

HONDA TRIO see Amerongen, Jan van

HONEGGER, ARTHUR (1892-1955)
Melodies Et Chansons
solo voice,pno (CC36U) SALABERT
50488445 (H579)

Three Psalms (34, 140, 238)
SALABERT 50404590 (H580)

HONGAARSE LIEDERN I see Nieland, Henk

HONGAARSE LIEDERN II see Nieland, Henk

HONIG SONGS see Bauer

HONOKA NI HITOTSU see Nakada, Yoshinao

HONSSKIT see Forsell, Jonas

HOOFPRINTS see Gottlieb, Jack S.

HOOK, JAMES (1746-1827)
Blest Hero Who In Peace And War
S solo,2vln,vcl sc,pts KING'S
(H581)

Lass Of Richmond Hill, The
S/T solo,strings,2fl,opt bsn,2horn,
kbd KING'S (H582)

HOOTENANNY SING ALONG
("World's Favorite Series") ASHLEY
027-1 (H583)

HOPE OF ISRAEL, THE see Glinka, Mikhail
Ivanovich

HOPKINS
God's Grandeur
(Whear) solo voice LUDWIG VS-08
$2.50 (H584)

HOPKINS, FRANKLIN
Seven Selected Songs
[Eng] high solo RECITAL 265 (H585)

HOPKINSON, FRANCIS (1737-1791)
Six Songs
(Milligan) high solo RECITAL 2246
(H586)
(Milligan) low solo RECITAL 2247
(H587)

HOPP, JULIUS
Aber Ich Könnt' Verdorben Werd'n
SCIEN 730 (H588)

HOR, ALLE SOM TØRSTER see Bakke, Ruth

HOR D'OEUVRES see Walker, Gwyneth

HORAS DE UNA ESTANCIA, LAS see
Ginastera, Alberto

HORDER, MERVYN (1910-   )
Black Diamonds (I)
med-high solo,pno BARDIC BE0092
f.s.
contains: Bohemia; My Own True
Love; Unfortunate Coincidence
(H589)

Black Diamonds (II)
med-high solo,pno BARDIC f.s.
contains: Bric-A-Brac;
Convalescent; Wail (H590)

Bohemia
see Black Diamonds (I)

Bric-A-Brac
see Black Diamonds (II)

Convalescent
see Black Diamonds (II)

My Own True Love
see Black Diamonds (I)

Unfortunate Coincidence
see Black Diamonds (I)

Wail
see Black Diamonds (II)

HORFI EG UR HAFI see Palsson, Helgi

HORFINN DAGUR see Björnsson, Arni

HORISONTLINJE: 10 VISOR see Bjork,
Torgny

HORKY, KAREL (1909-1988)
Tri Pisne
solo voice,pno PANTON 899 (H591)

HORNSTEIN, ROBERT VON
Es Ragt In's Meer Der Runenstein
solo voice,pno (text by Heinrich
Heine) SCIEN 732 (H592)

HORVIT, MICHAEL M. (1932-   )
How Like A Dream It Was
see Yom Kippur Afternoon Service

I Have Taken An Oath
see Yom Kippur Afternoon Service

Ochila La'eil
see Yom Kippur Afternoon Service

Prophecy Of Amos
S solo,org SOUTHERN V087 (H593)

Silence
see Yom Kippur Afternoon Service

Three Faces Of Love
solo voice,pno SOUTHERN V085 (H594)

Three Sonnets Of William Shakespeare
S solo,clar,pno RECITAL 123 (H595)

Yom Kippur Afternoon Service
solo voice,org TRANSCON. 992011
f.s.
contains: How Like A Dream It
Was; I Have Taken An Oath;
Ochila La'eil; Silence (H596)

HOSEA 6 see Holter, Stig Wernø

HOSHI WA SUBARU see Matsumoto, Hinoharu

HOSI see Hanson, Sten

HOSOKAWA, TOSHIO (1955-   )
Renka I
[Eng/Jap] S solo,gtr SCHOTTS
SJ 1066 (H597)

HOSSZU AZ UTCA see Nieland, Henk

HØST see Eggen, Arne see Gefors, Hans

HØST VED RUGELSJØEN see Tveitt, Geirr

HOSTESS' ARIA see Getty, Gordon

HÖSTLJUS see Lundin, Dag

HØSTNATT VED FJORDEN see Albertsen, Per
Hjort

HØSTSANGEN see Groven, Eivind

HOSUKE NO HIYOKO see Hayashi, Hikaru

HOTELS see Tal, Marjo

HOUSE IN GRANADA, THE see Heilner,
Irwin

HOVHANESS, ALAN (1911-   )
Avak, The Healer
S solo,trp,string orch [20'0"] PEER
(H598)

HOVLAND, EGIL (1924-   )
Atte Sanger, Op. 2
[Norw] solo voice,pno NORGE (H599)

August *Op.34,No.4
solo voice,2clar,2bsn,horn,strings
NORGE f.s. (H600)
see Fem Sanger, Op. 34

Cantata No. 1 for Solo Voice, Op. 27
[Norw] B solo,org NORSK (H601)

Fem Sanger, Op. 34
solo voice,pno NORGE f.s.
contains: August; Jeg Vil Hjem;
Juli; November; Voggesong Til
Siri (H602)

Fikentreet Uten Frukt
[Norw] solo voice,org NORSK (H603)

Finnes En Dyrebar Rose, Det
[Norw] S solo,vln,pno NORGE (H604)

Hva Gagner Det Et Menneske
solo voice,org LYCHE 915 (H605)

I Want To Go Home
see Jeg Vil Hjem

Jeg Vil Hjem *Op.34,No.6
"I Want To Go Home" solo voice,cel,
strings NORGE f.s. (H606)
see Fem Sanger, Op. 34

Juli
see Fem Sanger, Op. 34

Lilja
narrator,3.3.2.2. 2.1.1.0. perc,
pno,strings [16'] NORGE f.s.
(H607)

Liturgisk Musikk
[Norw] solo voice,org NORGE (H608)

Most Beautiful Rose, The
see Vakreste Rosen, Den

November
see Fem Sanger, Op. 34

Rorate *Op.55
SSSSS soli,fl,ob,org,perc,strings,
electronic tape [24'] NORSK f.s.
(H609)

Saelaste På Jord, Det
[Norw] NORSK (H610)

Song Of Songs, The *Op.42
S solo,vln,pno,perc NORSK (H611)

Spurven
LYCHE 523 (H612)

Vakreste Rosen, Den *Op.71
"Most Beautiful Rose, The" SSSS&
narrator,1(pic).2(English
horn).1.0. 1.1.0.0. org,pno/cel,
strings [19'] NORGE f.s. (H613)

Voggesong Til Siri
see Fem Sanger, Op. 34

HOW BLESSED TO KNOW see Powell

HOW BLEST see Holter, Stig Wernø

HOW CAN I SLEEP? see Walton, [Sir]
William (Turner)

HOW CAN THE TREE BUT WITHER? see
Vaughan Williams, Ralph

HOW DO I LOVE THEE see Kieran

HOW LIKE A DREAM IT WAS see Horvit,
Michael M.

HOW? MY HEART ACHES! see Rachmaninoff,
Sergey Vassilievich

HOW OFT WHEN THOU, MY MUSIC, MUSIC
PLAY'ST see Andriessen, Jurriaan

HOW SWEET BY THY SIDE see Glinka,
Mikhail Ivanovich

HOW TO LIVE. WHAT TO DO: AND SONGS ON
POEMS OF WALLACE STEVENS see
Hagerty, Mark

HOW WILL THEY KNOW? see Sleeth, Natalie
Wakeley

HOWE, HUBERT S. (1942-   )
Six Songs Based On Unknown Texts
S solo,pno [13'] AM.COMP.AL. (H614)

HVERS VEGNA? see Halldorsson, Sigfus

HVERT BLAD SOM TIDEN VENDER see Baden, Conrad

HVILE I SKOVEN see Kjerulf, Halfdan

HVITI TRUDURINN see Tomasson, Jonas

HVITU SEGLIN see Björnsson, Arni

HVORFOR SAA DU PAA MIG see Jordan, Sverre

HVOSLEF, KETIL (1939)
    Dano Tiore
        S solo,vln,vla,vcl,hpsd NORGE
                                                (H675)
    Kvartoni
        S solo,rec,gtr,pno [10'] NORSK
                                                (H676)
HY DROECH ONSE SMERTEN see Flothuis, Marius

HYMN see Strand, Ragnvald, Hymne

HYMN SOLOS FOR ALL SEASONS *CC10UL
    (Cutter) ALFRED med-high solo 4873
    accomp tape available; med-low solo
    4874 accomp tape available   (H677)

HYMN TO MYSELF see Bois, Rob du

HYMN TO THE SUN see Glass, Philip

HYMN TO THE WORLD-CHAMPIONSHIP HEAVY-
    WEIGHT 1964 see Bois, Rob du

HYMNE see Evensen, Bernt Kasberg see
    Strand, Ragnvald

HYMNE A SAINT ANDRE see Jolivet, Andre

HYMNE A SAINTE CÉCILE see Gounod,
    Charles François

HYMNE AN DIE JUNGFRAU see Schubert,
    Franz (Peter)

HYMNE AUF DIE UDSSR see Eisler, Hanns

HYMNE, OP.48, NO1 see Gretchaninov,
    Alexander Tikhonovich, Fleurs Du
    Mal, Les

HYMNE SE NOMME, L' see Haugland, Glenn
    Erik

HYMNS TO THE HOLY TRINITY see Lawes,
    Henry

HYMNUS AD LAUDES IN FESTO S.S.
    TRINITATIS see Dvorák, Antonín

HYMNUS AN EINE ANONYME GOTTHEIT see De
    Lastra, Erich Eder

HYMNUS, OP.73 see Baden, Conrad

I

I AM MY BELOVED'S see Goldman, Maurice

I AM NOT GOING TO MARRY SUMPUN see
    Beers, Jacques

I AM PROUD TO BE AN AMERICAN see
    Malotte, Albert Hay

I AM SO BIG see Sigurbjörnsson,
    Thorkell

I AM THINE, O LORD see Walz, Adam

I AM TITANIA see Thomas, Ambroise

I AUGUST see Jordan, Sverre

I BERGET see Ørbeck, Anne Marie

I BJØRKESKOGEN KLOKKEN FIRE MORGEN see
    Tveitt, Geirr

I BLODET HANS BLØMDE see Jensen, Ludwig
    Irgens

I CAME TO HER see Rachmaninoff, Sergey
    Vassilievich

I CANNOT WASH YOUR SMOKE see Marez
    Oyens, Tera de

I CHATSCHA DI see Flothuis, Marius

I CHOOSE APRIL see Selmer, Johan Peter,
    Jeg Velger Meg April

I DAG ER NADENS TID see Nystedt, Knut

I DARE NOT ASK A KISS see Noland, Gary

I DENNE JORD see Olsen, Sparre

I DID NOT BREAK THE FLOWER see Shut,
    Wasyl, Ne Lamala Tsvitu

I DIED FOR BEAUTY see Chapiro, Fania

I DITT ÖGA see Levin, Stefan

I DÖGUN see Björnsson, Arni

I DON'T KNOW WHAT YOU ARE THINKING see
    Revueltas, Silvestre, No Se Por Que
    Piensas Tu

I DREAM OF MEADOWS AND OTHER SONGS TO
    POEMS OF YAR SLAVUTYCH see Wolff,
    Joachim

I DREAMT THAT I DWELT IN MARBLE HALLS
    see Balfe, Michael William

I EIT EVIG SEKUND see Elgarøy, Jan

I EN HOFPOETS NAVN see Karlsen, Kjell
    Mørk

I FEEL PRETTY see Bernstein, Leonard

I GOT A HOME IN THAT ROCK
    (Bonds, Margaret) solo voice,pno (med
    easy) MERCURY   (I1)

I GOT A LETTER FROM JESUS see Walker,
    George Theophilus

I GRAENUM MO see Halldorsson, Sigfus

I GRÄSHOPPSTAKT OCH SNIGELFART see
    Eklund, Hans

I GUDS FRIDI see Palsson, Pall P.

I HARMANNA HELGILUNDUM see Isolfsson,
    Pall

I HÄTT' A BITT' see Binder, Karl

I HAVE A LITTLE HEART see Gray, G.

I HAVE COME TO GREET YOU see Rimsky-
    Korsakov, Nikolai

I HAVE DONE... see Bianchini, Riccardo

I HAVE FOUND MY HANDSOME LOVER BACK see
    Søderlind, Ragnar, Eg Hev Funne Min
    Fløysne Lokkar Att I Mitt Svarmerus

I HAVE LONGED TO MOVE AWAY see Ford,
    Ronald

I HAVE NO LIFE BUT THIS see Walker,
    George Theophilus

I HAVE RETURNED see Marez Oyens, Tera
    de

I HAVE TAKEN AN OATH see Horvit,
    Michael M.

I HEAR A THRUSH AT EVE see Cadman,
    Charles Wakefield

I HEAR CASTANETS see Ise, Chizuko

I HEAR YOU CALLING ME see Marshall, C.

I HEARD A MAID WITH HER GUITAR see
    Hadley, Henry (Kimball)

I HIMMELEN see Dale, Sjur

I HVILU MINNI UM NOTT see Isolfsson,
    Pall

I ISTIDA see Tveitt, Geirr

I KIRKJUGARDI see Sveinsson, Gunnar
    Reynir

I KNOW THE LORD'S LAID HIS HANDS ON ME
    see McLin, Lena J.

I KVELDSDIMMA see Ørbeck, Anne Marie

I KYRKJA see Taubo, Lillian Gulowna

I LANDSYN see Halldorsson, Skuli

I LIGHT MY CANDLES see Johannsson,
    Magnus Bl.

I LIKE... see Itoh, Mikio

I LOVE HIM STILL see Dargomyzhsky,
    Alexander Sergeyevich

I LOVE LITTLE KITTY see Jeffreys, John

I LOVE MY LADY see Zonn, Paul

I LOVE THEE LORD see Daugherty

I LOVE YOU see Beethoven, Ludwig van,
    Ich Liebe Dich

I LUNDI LJODS OG HLJOMA see Thordarson,
    Sigurdur

I MISSED HIS BOOK see Blank, Allan

I MOAN see Lerstad, Terje B.

I NEVER KNEW JESUS see Daugherty

I ÖGAT see Lindsjo, Inga

I ORMEGIL see Dorumsgaard, Arne

I PASSED A STATELY CAVALCADE see
    Cadman, Charles Wakefield

I RECALL THE WONDERFUL MOMENT see
    Glinka, Mikhail Ivanovich

I RÖRELSE see Wallgren, Jan

I SÅMMÅRHÅGGÅN see Albertsen, Per Hjort

I SAW A MAN see As, Cees van

I SAW A SUMMER BANQUETING HOUSE see
    Rowland, David

I SAW TWO BIRDS see Weigl, [Mrs.] Vally

I SEE MYSELF WRITING see Bollen, Jan-
    Bas

I SEND MY HEART UP TO THEE! see Beach,
    [Mrs.] H.H.A. (Amy Marcy Cheney)

I SHALL NOT CARE see Heilner, Irwin

I SING OF A MAIDEN see Goldberg,
    William

I SING THE WIND AROUND see O'Leary,
    Jane

I SKUMRINGEN see Dahl, Vivian

I SPEAK FOR THE EARTH see Walker,
    Gwyneth

I TALLKOTTSRIKET see Koch, Erland von
    see Koch, Erland von

I' TE VURRIA VASÀ! see Di Capua,
    Eduardo

I THINK CONTINUALLY see Gottlieb, Jack
    S.

I TOO see Wernick, Richard F.

I TRAVELLED IN A LOVELY SUMMER EVENING
    see Grieg, Edvard Hagerup, Jeg
    Reiste En Deilig Sommerkveld

I TVERÅSAL-HYTTA see Kielland, Olav

I VAAGELIDANN see Johansen, David Monrad

I VILLE HEID see Olsen, Sparre

I VILLE HEIDI see Olsen, Sparre

I WAITED FOR THE LORD see Mendelssohn-Bartholdy, Felix

I WALKED THE ROAD AGAIN see Haufrecht, Herbert

I WANT TO BE A PRIMA DONNA see Herbert, Victor, Art Is Calling For Me

I WANT TO GO HOME see Hovland, Egil, Jeg Vil Hjem

I WANT TO LIVE see Bergh, Sverre, Eg Vil Leva

I WENT TO HEAVEN see Walker, George Theophilus

I WILL BREATHE A MOUNTAIN see Bolcom, William Elden

I WILL GIVE MY LOVE AN APPLE
  (Vaughan Williams, Ralph) solo voice, pno NOVELLO 16 1133 f.s.   (I2)

I WILL GIVE YOU SHEPHERDS see Ultan, Lloyd

I WILL RETURN see Shut, Wasyl, Ja Pryjidu

I WILL SING OF YOUR STEADFAST LOVE see Diemer, Emma Lou

I WISH I WERE SINGLE AGAIN see Anderson, Beth

IBERISCHES STÄNDCHEN see Suppe, Franz von

IBSEN SONGS, OP. 35A see Plagge, Wolfgang

IC DRAGHE IN MINEN HERTE... see Braal, Andries de

IC SEG ADIEU see Weegenhuise, Johan

ICE FLOWERS see Jordan, Sverre, Isblomar

ICELAND see Sveinbjörnsson, Sveinbjörn

ICELANDIC FOLK SONGS see Sveinbjörnsson, Sveinbjörn see Vidar, Jorunn

ICH BIN DIE SEEL' IM ALL see Soler, J.

ICH BIN IN MIR VERGNÜGT see Bach, Johann Sebastian

ICH BIN SO FROH see Hanson, Sten

ICH FÜHLE DEINE SCHÖNHEIT see Focke, Fré

ICH HAB' EINE GLUHEND MESSER IN EINEM BRUST see Mahler, Gustav

ICH HABE DAS GEFÄSS MEINES HERZENS see Focke, Fré

ICH HABE DIE TEMPEL VERWAIST GESEH'N see Bunge, Sas

ICH HABE GENÜG see Bach, Johann Sebastian

ICH HÖR EIN VÖGLEIN LOCKEN see Mendelssohn-Bartholdy, Felix

ICH LIEBE DICH see Backer-Lunde, Johan see Beethoven, Ludwig van see Grieg, Edvard Hagerup

ICH LIEGE DIR ZU FÜSSEN see Pijper, Willem

ICH MÖCHT AN ALLE FENSTER SCHLEICHEN see Lambort, Carl R. Von

ICH SINGE DIR MIT HERZ UND MUND see Lohmann, Heinz

ICH WEISS, DASS MEIN ERLOSER LEBT see Bach, Johann Sebastian

ICH WILL DEN KREUZSTAB GERNE TRAGEN see Bach, Johann Sebastian

ICH WOLLT' MEINE LIEB' ERGÖSSE SICH ALL' IN EIN EINZIG WORT see Mendelssohn-Bartholdy, Felix

ICHIBA, KOSUKE (1910-   )
  Pappus Of A Dandelion, The
    Mez solo,pno [5'] ONGAKU   (I3)

ICI BAS see Cui, César Antonovich

ICI LES TENDRES OISEAUX see Saint-Saëns, Camille, Pastorale

ICK HOOR DE STERCKE STEMME VAN MIJNEN TROUWEN VRIENT see Andriessen, Jurriaan

I'D BE A BUTTERFLY see Bayly, T.

I'D LIKE IN A SINGLE WORD see Tchaikovsky, Piotr Ilyich

I'D ROCK MY OWN SWEET CHILDIE see Stanford, Charles Villiers, Irish Lullaby, An

IDDANE HERMUND
  (Tveit, Sigvald) solo voice NORSK NMO 9526 f.s.   (I4)

IDEA OF ORDER AT KEY WEST, THE see Erickson, Robert

IDEALE see Tosti, Francesco Paolo

IDEALET OCH LIVET: FYRA SÅNGER FÖR DON QUIJOTE OCH SANCHO PANZA see Bäck, Sven-Erik

IDEE ARMONICHE, OP. 13 see Legrenzi, Giovanni

IDLE GIFT, THE see Menotti, Gian Carlo

IDOLO CINESE, L' see Paisiello, Giovanni

IDYLL see Rangström, Ture, Enda Stunden, Den

IDYLS OF THE SOUTH SEA see Cadman, Charles Wakefield

IERSE NACHT see Guichelaar, Jan

IF see Denza, Luigi, Se

IF I COULD BE THE WIND see Ise, Chizuko

IF I COULD GIVE YOU ALL I HAVE see McLin, Lena J.

IF I THAT VOICE BUT HEAR see Glinka, Mikhail Ivanovich

IF I WERE A POET see Anderson, Beth

IF I WERE ON THE STAGE see Herbert, Victor

IF MUSIC BE THE FOOD see Purcell, Henry

IF ONLY see Marez Oyens, Tera de see Marez Oyens, Tera de

IF ONLY THE NIGHT COULD STAND STILL see Balazs, Frederic

IF POYSENOUS MINERALS
  B solo,horn,trom/bass trom,vla,vcl,db [6'] (parts for each are for rent) sc APNM $3.75 from SONNETS FROM JOHN DONNE   (I5)

IF WE DIE see Heilner, Irwin

IF YOU ONLY KNEW see Shut, Wasyl, Jakby Ty Znav

IGARASHI, TADASHI (1918-   )
  Akiakane
    S solo,pno [5'] ONGAKU   (I6)

  Kaze No Nake
    S solo,pno [3'] JAPAN   (I7)

  Portulaca, A
    S solo,pno [3'] JAPAN   (I8)

  White Camellia
    Mez solo,pno [4'] ONGAKU   (I9)

IGLESIA ABANDONADA see Hartke, Stephen Paul

IGLESIAS ROSSI, ALEJANDRO (1960-   )
  Ancestral Rites Of A Forgotten Culture
    Mez solo,perc [20'] study sc MOECK 5290   (I10)

  Ballades, Dances And Echos
    S solo,rec,fl,hpsd,vla [28'] study sc MOECK 5327   (I11)

IHR BLAUEN AUGEN, GUTE NACHT! see Müller, Adolf

IK BEN GEHUWD, AILACEN see Ehlen, Margriet

IK DROOM VAN BERGEN see Zagwijn, Henri

IK HEB U LIEF see Mulder, Herman

IK SCHRIJF U THANS see Mulder, Herman

IK SNAK NAAR WARMTE see Delden, Lex van

IK STA GEREN see Andriessen, Jurriaan

IK WEET NU ZET UW SCHOONE DEEMOED IN HAAR AVONDLIJK GEBED see Badings, Henk

IK WORD ZO DONKER see Samama, Leo

IK ZAL OOK EENS KOMEN see Franken, Wim

IKE NO HOTORI NARU TAKE see Hayakawa, Kuzuko

IKEBE, SHIN-ICHIRO (1943-   )
  Four Children's Songs
    S solo,pno [15'] JAPAN   (I12)

  Two Songs
    S solo,pno [10'] JAPAN   (I13)

IKEDA, SATORU (1961-   )
  Story Of A Salesman, The
    SBar soli,pno [40'] JAPAN   (I14)

IKENOUCHI, TOMOJIRO (1906-   )
  Yuya
    S solo,orch ONGAKU 490201 sc f.s., pts rent   (I15)

IKKE ENHVER, SOM SIGER TIL MIG see Eggen, Arne

IL EST GRAND TEMPS see Scelsi, Giacinto

IL EST NÉ, LE DIVIN ENFANT see Faure, Gabriel-Urbain

IL FAUT NOUS AIMER see Hubeau, Jean

IL FAUT TRAVAILLER... see Tal, Marjo

IL ME TARDE QUE LUNDI VIENGNE see Tal, Marjo

IL PLEURE DANS MON COEUR see Carpenter, John Alden

IL PLEUT see Saariaho, Kaija

IL PLEUT DES PÉTALES DE FLEURS see Hadley, Henry (Kimball)

IL PLEUT DOUCEMENT SUR LA VILLE see Regt, Hendrik de

IL S'EST TU LE CHARMANT ROSSIGNOL see Gretchaninov, Alexander Tikhonovich

ILD PRØVER GULD see Beck, Thomas Ludvigsen

ÎLE HEUREUSE, L' see Chabrier, [Alexis-] Emmanuel

I'LL SING THEE SONGS OF ARABY see Clay, Frédéric

I'LL TELL YOU HOW THE SUN ROSE see Taesch, R.

ILLGRESI see Halldorsson, Skuli

ILLINOIS FARMER see Heilner, Irwin

ILLUXIT, OP. 23 see Habbestad, Kjell

ILS ONT TUÉ TROIS PETITES FILLES see Schmitt, Florent

I'M A SOLDIER IN THE ARMY OF THE LORD see McLin, Lena J.

IM DORFE DIE GASSE ENTLANG see Riedel, Hermann

IM DUNKEL see Weigl, Karl

IM EWIGEN LICHT see Bijvanck, Henk

IM FLAMMENDEN MORGENROT see Giltay, Berend

IM FLÜGELSCHLAG DER ZEIT see Hess, W.

IM FRÜHLING see Marx, Joseph see Schubert, Franz (Peter)

IM GEFÄNGNIS ZU SINGEN see Eisler, Hanns

IM KAHN see Vidar, Jorunn

IM LEBENSLENZ, OP. 16 see Dohnányi, Ernst von

IM MAIEN see Marx, Joseph

I'M OFF TO CHEZ MAXIME see Lehar, Franz

IM TREIBHAUS see Wagner, Richard

I'M WALKIN' see Bailey, Bob

I'M WEARING AWA' TO THE LAND O' THE LEAL see Foote, Arthur

IM WUNDERSCHÖNEN MONAT MAI see Lowenstamm, Franz Jos.

IMAGES, A WINTER'S CALENDAR see Ogdon, Wilbur L.

IMAGES III (MY FELLOW AMERICANS see Tanenbaum, Elias

IMAGINARY NO "THE FIVE-COLOURED CORD" see Tanaka, Terumichi

IMAGINATIONS NO. 2 see Nasveld, Robert

IMMORTALITE see Massenet, Jules

IMPACIENCIA DEL CICLO DE CANCIONES see Schubert, Franz (Peter)

IMPATIENCE see Schubert, Franz (Peter), Ungeduld

IMPRESSION IV see Reimann, Aribert

IMPROMPTUS A MARIA LUISA see Blanquer, Amando

IMPROVISATION AN EINEM WINTERTAG see Hekster, Walter

IN A MORTON FELDMAN MOOD see Bois, Rob du

IN A WORD: 6 SONGS see Bottje, Will Gay

IN BRISTOL TOWN see Grainger, Percy Aldridge

IN DA FREMD see Baumann, Alexander

IN DANZIG see Louis Ferdinand, Prince Of Prussia

IN DEM SCHATTEN see Wolf, Hugo

IN DEN HEMEL DAAR IS HET GOED WOONEN see Geraedts, Jaap

IN DIE FERNE see Kletke, H.

IN DIE PASCHAE: PSALM see Lechner, Konrad

IN DIESEM WETTER see Mahler, Gustav

IN DORMITURIO see King, Harold C.

IN DROOMOMHELZINGEN see Mulder, Herman

IN EINEM WIENER CAFE　*CC18L
DOBLINGER 89 152 f.s.　　　　　(I16)

IN EV'RY FLOWER see Wellock, Richard

IN GEDEMPTEN TOON, OP. 110 see Mulder, Herman

IN GRATO JUBILO see Pinkham, Daniel

IN HEAVENLY LOVE ABIDING see Macmillan, Alan

IN JUST SPRING see Harris, Matthew

IN MEMORIAM J.H. see Leifs, Jon

IN MEMORY see Akerwall, Martin, Til Minde

IN MEMORY OF A FAILED VIRTUOSO see Vidar, Jorunn

IN MIJN LEVEN... see Franken, Wim

IN MY CRAFT OR SULLEN ART see Haxton, Kenneth

IN MY TIME see MacDermott, Galt

IN QUESTA TOMBA OSCURA see Beethoven, Ludwig van

IN SCOTLAND I WAS BORN see Anonymous, Barbara Ellen

IN SHADOW see Silverman, Faye-Ellen

IN SLEEPLESS NIGHTS see Stutschevsky, Joachim

IN SPRING - FOUR ROMANCES, OP. 43 see Rimsky-Korsakov, Nikolai

IN SUCH A NIGHT see Brown, Francis James

IN SUMMER WHEN THE SUN IS HIGH see Johannsson, Magnus Bl.

IN TEERE SCHADUW see Mulder, Herman

IN TERRA PAX, PAX HOMINIBUS see Hrasky, Rainer

IN THE EAST, ON TOP OF THE MOUNTAIN see Avni, Tzvi

IN THE EVENING see Groven, Eivind, Om Kvelden

IN THE GARDEN NEAR THE RIVER, OP. 46, NO. 4 see Tchaikovsky, Piotr Ilyich

IN THE GLOAMING see Harrison, A.F.

IN THE HOSPITAL AT NIGHT see Groven, Eivind, På Hospitalet Om Natten

IN THE MEDITERRANEAN see Amerongen, Jan van

IN THE MOOD OF THE WIND see Nakagawa, Toshio

IN THE MOUNTAINS see Bon, Willem Frederik

IN THE SILENCE see Le Siege, Annette

IN THE SILENCE OF THE NIGHT see Rachmaninoff, Sergey Vassilievich

IN THE SOUL OF EACH OF US see Rachmaninoff, Sergey Vassilievich

IN THE SPRING see Vaughan Williams, Ralph

IN THE WAND OF THE WIND see Hoiby, Lee

IN THIS VERY ROOM - THE COLLECTED SONGS OF RON HARRIS see Harris, Ronald S.

IN THOSE SOFT SILKEN CURTAINS see Puccini, Giacomo, Manon Lescaut: In Quelle Trine Morbide

IN TIME OF DAFFODILS see Malipiero, Riccardo

IN TRANSITU see Fischer, Irwin, Now Sweeping Down The Years

IN UNSERM LAND see Eisler, Hanns, Nein

IN VERNALIS TEMPORIS see Sveinbjörnsson, Sveinbjörn

IN WINTER IN MY ROOM see Ruiter, Wim de

IN YALTA see Heilner, Irwin

INAURA, SHIRABE (1951-　　)
Kuma No Kaze
S solo,vln,euphonium,pno [15']
JAPAN　　　　　　　　　　　　(I17)

INCLUSIONS see Backer-Lunde, Johan

INCORONAZIONE DI POPPEA, L': PUR TI MIRO see Monteverdi, Claudio

INCRÉDULE, L' see Hahn, Reynaldo

INDARNO CERCA LA TORTORELLA see Vivaldi, Antonio

INDES GALANTES, LES: BRILLANT SOLEIL see Rameau, Jean-Philippe

INDIA, SIGISMONDO D' (ca. 1582- ?)
Musiche De Cantar Solo, Le　*CCU
(Mompellio, Federico) solo voice
MONTEVERDI f.s. vol. IV of
"Monumenta"　　　　　　　　(I18)

INDIAN BOYHOOD see Larson, Martin

INDREHUS, PER
Fire Sanger (composed with Dale)
solo voice,gtr MUSIKK　　　(I19)

INDY, VINCENT D' (1851-1931)
Madrigal
"Qui Jamais Fut De Plus Charmant
Visage" low solo,pno CLASSV 1755
　　　　　　　　　　　　　　(I20)
"Qui Jamais Fut De Plus Charmant
Visage" med solo,pno CLASSV 1756
　　　　　　　　　　　　　　(I21)
Qui Jamais Fut De Plus Charmant
Visage
see Madrigal

INEDITI PER TENORE see Verdi, Giuseppe

INFANT CRYING, AN see Smith, Larry

INFANT JOY see Brown, Francis James see Fennimore, Joseph William

INFANT SORROW see Haxton, Kenneth see Homer, Sidney

INFANTA MARÍA, L' see Morera, Enrique

INFINITY see Karlins, M. William

INFLUENTIAE see Helmschrott, Robert M.

INGALO see Runolfsson, Karl Otto

INGENUITAT see Mestres, Apeles

INITIATION see Grisey, Gerard

INNO A DIANA see Puccini, Giacomo

INNO DELLA CROCE ROSSA ITALIANA GIOVANILE see Montanari, A.

INNO DI MAMELI see Novaro, M.

INNOCENCE IN IRON see Rydberg, Bo

INNOCENTIUM CARMINA see Lamb, Hubert Weldon

INNSKRIFTER, OP. 31 see Plagge, Wolfgang

INSCAPE see Fennimore, Joseph William

INSELN see Koetsier, Jan

INSIDE THIS CLAY JUG see Rovics, Howard

INSONNIA, OP. 34 see Veldhuis, Jacob ter

INSPIRATION see Wiernik, Adam

INSTRUMENTAL SCENES see Bois, Rob du

INTERCOLLEGIATE SONGBOOK　*CCU
solo voice HANSEN-US HANM564 $6.95
　　　　　　　　　　　　　(I22)

INTERLOCUTIONS see Giuffre, Gaetano

INTERLUDE see Steinberg, Eitan

INTERLUDIUM see Lachenmann, Helmut Friedrich

INTERMEDIO: LYRIC BALLET see Wyner, Yehudi

INTERMEZZO see Sønstevold, Gunnar

INTERMISSION see Evensen, Bernt Kasberg

INTET ÄR FÖRGÄVES see Jeppsson, Kerstin

INTIMISMOS see Lopez Artiga, Angeles

INTO A SHIP, DREAMING see Crist, Bainbridge

INTO ECLIPSE see Albert, Stephen Joel

INTO GOD'S KINGDOM, OP. 80 see Cruft, Adrian

INTO THE NIGHT see Backer-Lunde, Johan see Edwards, Sherman

INTRODUCTORY SONGBOOK (from The Songbook Series) CC17L,educ
solo voice,kbd (very easy) HARRIS
f.s.　　　　　　　　　　　(I23)

INUNDATIONS II ("WILLOW") see Montague, Stephen

INVANO! see Tosti, Francesco Paolo

INVENCIONS see Mestres-Quadreny, Josep Maria

INVICTUS see Huhn, Bruno

INVIOLATA see Schrijvers, Jean

INVITATION AU VOYAGE, L' see Chabrier, [Alexis-] Emmanuel

INVITO, L' see Rossini, Gioacchino

INVOCATION see Stutschevsky, Joachim

INVOCATION À LA MUSE see Leoncavallo, Ruggiero

INVOCATIONS see Alwyn, William

INVOKATION see Bahk, Junsang

INWOOD, MARY (1928-　　)
Verses From Song Of Songs
S solo,fl SEESAW　　　　　(I24)

IO LA VIDI see Verdi, Giuseppe

IO SON ZITELLA see Perti, Giacomo Antonio

IO VOGLIO AMARTI! see Tosti, Francesco Paolo

IPHIGÉNIE EN TAURIDE: DE NOIRS PRESSENTIMENTS see Gluck, Christoph Willibald, Ritter von

IRELAND, JOHN (1879-1962)
Sea Fever
  B solo,pno CLASSV 1825   (I25)
  Bar solo,pno CLASSV 0891   (I26)

IRGENDWO WILL MAN GANZ RUHIG SEIN see Badings, Henk

IRIS: APRI LA TUA FINESTRA see Mascagni, Pietro

IRIS: UN DÌ, ERO PICCINA see Mascagni, Pietro

IRISH FOLK-SONG, AN see Foote, Arthur

IRISH IDYLL, AN see Stanford, Charles Villiers

IRISH LOVE SONG, OP. 22 see Lang, Margaret Ruthven

IRISH LULLABY, AN see Stanford, Charles Villiers

IRISH MAGIC
  med solo,kbd PEER 61770-213   (I27)
  (O'Brien; Docker) solo voice,pno (med easy, contains 10 popular Irish folksongs) PEER   (I28)

IRISH MELODIES OF T. MOORE, OP.60 (Stanford, C.V.) solo voice,pno CLASSV 2199   (I29)

IRISH SONGBOOK *CCU
solo voice HANSEN-US HANO392 $5.95   (I30)

IRISH SONGS AND BALLADS, 30 (Stanford, C. Villiers) solo voice, pno CLASSV 2198   (I31)

ISAAC WOODARD see Heilner, Irwin

ISAACSON, MICHAEL NEIL (1946-)
N'shamah Shenatata Bi
  med solo,kbd TRANSCON. 992022 (I32)

Seasons In Time, Vol. 1: Solo Songs For The Jewish Family Life Cycle
solo voice,kbd TRANSCON. 991310   (I33)
Seasons In Time, Vol. 2: Duets For Holiday And Life Cycle
2 solo voices,kbd TRANSCON. 991314   (I34)

ISABEAU: O POPOLO DI VILI...E PASSERÀ LA VIVA see Mascagni, Pietro

ISABEAU: QUESTO MIO BIANCO MANTO see Mascagni, Pietro

ISABEAU: TU CH'ODI LO MIO GRIDO see Mascagni, Pietro

ISBLOMAR see Jordan, Sverre

ISE, CHIZUKO (1925-)
I Hear Castanets
  solo voice,pno [7'] JAPAN   (I35)

If I Could Be The Wind
  solo voice,pno [3'] JAPAN   (I36)

Mama's Sugar Cube Sweet
  solo voice,pno [3'] JAPAN   (I37)

ISGANGSVAER see Nystedt, Knut

ISHIKETA, MAREO (1916-)
Symphonic Revelation
  S solo,orch [40'] ZEN-ON perf mat rent   (I38)

Thousand Voices In Thousand Hearts
solo voice,chamber orch ONGAKU 490332   (I39)

ISLAND see Jonsson, Thorarinn

ISLAND IN THE SKERRIES see Tveitt, Geirr, Skjaergaardsø

ISLANDS HRAFNISTUMENN see Björnsson, Arni see Helgason, Hallgrimur

ISLANDSDAETUR see Einarsson, Sigfus

ISLANDSMOEN, SIGURD (1881-1965)
Stridsmand
  Bar solo,1.1.2.1. 2.2.2.0. timp, strings NORGE f.s.   (I40)

ISLE, THE see Torphicen, Pamela

ISLENDINGALJOD see Björnsson, Arni

ISLENZKT ASTARLJOD see Halldorsson, Sigfus

ISLYS see Kruse, Bjørn Howard

ISOBEL see Bridge, Frank

ISOLDE see Marx, Joseph

ISOLFSSON, PALL (1893-1974)
Ad Baendaminni Bidjum Ver
  solo voice,pno ICELAND 019-090   (I41)

Ad Baki Blarra Heida
  solo voice,pno ICELAND 019-057   (I42)

Airs From The Song Of Songs
  solo voice,pno ICELAND 019-007   (I43)

Aus Vergangener Zeit
  solo voice,pno ICELAND 019-062   (I44)

Bergbuinn Gekk Fram A Gnypubrun
  solo voice,pno (text by H. Ibsen) ICELAND 019-065   (I45)

Blitt Er Undir Bjorkunum
  solo voice,pno ICELAND 019-041   (I46)

Dagurinn Kemur
  solo voice,pno ICELAND 019-058   (I47)

Draumsjon
  solo voice,pno ICELAND 019-088   (I48)

Eg Er Narsissa...
  solo voice,pno (Bible text) ICELAND 019-049   (I49)

Eg Heyri Ykkur Kvaka
  solo voice,pno ICELAND 019-079   (I50)

Eg Kom I Gard Minn
  solo voice,pno (Bible text) ICELAND 019-050   (I51)

Eg Kveiki A Kertum Minum
  solo voice,pno ICELAND 019-074   (I52)

Enginn Thydir, Hel, Thitt Helgiletur
  solo voice,pno ICELAND 019-092   (I53)

Fjallid Einbui
  solo voice,pno ICELAND 019-054   (I54)

Fjogur Songlog
  solo voice,pno ICELAND 019-018   (I55)

Four Songs From "The Golden Gate"
  solo voice,pno ICELAND 019-001   (I56)

Fyrr Thin Gaedir Fysilig
  solo voice,pno ICELAND 019-066   (I57)

Grundar Doma, Hvergi Hann
  solo voice,pno ICELAND 019-072   (I58)

Hanna
  solo voice,pno ICELAND 019-086   (I59)

Haugbuar
  solo voice,pno ICELAND 019-085   (I60)

Heimir
  solo voice,pno ICELAND 019-046   (I61)
  solo voice,pno ICELAND 019-091   (I62)

Heimthra
  solo voice,pno ICELAND 019-059   (I63)

Heyr, Thad Er Unnusti Minn...
  solo voice,pno (Bible text) ICELAND 019-048   (I64)
  solo voice,pno (Bible text) ICELAND 019-068   (I65)

Hjartad Graetur
  solo voice,pno ICELAND 019-093   (I66)

Hrosshar I Strengjum
  solo voice,pno ICELAND 019-040   (I67)

Hvad Er Thad, Sem Kemur Ur Heidinni?
  solo voice,pno (Bible text) ICELAND 019-053   (I68)

I Harmanna Helgilundum
  solo voice,pno ICELAND 019-075   (I69)

I Hvilu Minni Um Nott
  solo voice,pno ICELAND 019-052   (I70)

Jarpur Skeidar Fljotur, Frar
  solo voice,pno ICELAND 019-070   (I71)

Jolasalmur
  solo voice,pno ICELAND 019-022   (I72)
  solo voice,pno ICELAND 019-073   (I73)

Kossavisur
  solo voice,pno ICELAND 019-055   (I74)

ISOLFSSON, PALL (cont'd.)
Litla Kvaedid Um Litlu Hjonin
  solo voice,pno ICELAND 019-076   (I75)

Mariuvers
  solo voice,pno ICELAND 019-042   (I76)

Meer Erglanzte, Das
  solo voice,pno ICELAND 019-061   (I77)

Minningaland
  solo voice,pno ICELAND 019-032   (I78)

Mitt Nafn Er Lif
  solo voice,pno ICELAND 019-084   (I79)

Nu Lokar Dagur Ljosri Bra
  solo voice,pno ICELAND 019-077   (I80)

Psalm, Ein
  solo voice,pno ICELAND 019-064   (I81)

Reikult Er Rotlaust Thangid
  solo voice,pno ICELAND 019-089   (I82)

Salmur
  solo voice,pno ICELAND 019-067   (I83)

Saud Thid Hana Systur Mina
  solo voice,pno ICELAND 019-015   (I84)
  solo voice,pno ICELAND 019-043   (I85)

Sjo Songlog
  solo voice,pno ICELAND 019-005   (I86)

Smidurinn
  solo voice,pno ICELAND 019-034   (I87)

Snati Og Oli
  solo voice,pno ICELAND 019-078   (I88)

Soknudur
  solo voice,pno ICELAND 019-044   (I89)

Songljod I
  solo voice,pno ICELAND 019-026   (I90)

Songsdottir Sat I Dyrri Höll
  solo voice,pno ICELAND 019-069   (I91)

Songur Blau Nunnanna
  solo voice,pno ICELAND 019-071   (I92)

Songur Volvunnar
  solo voice,pno ICELAND 019-047   (I93)

Sumar
  solo voice,pno ICELAND 019-045   (I94)

Svort Er Eg...
  solo voice,pno ICELAND 019-051   (I95)

Thid Sjaist Aldrei Framar
  solo voice,pno ICELAND 019-056   (I96)

Ur Utsae Risa Islandsfjoll
  solo voice,pno ICELAND 019-060   (I97)

Veizlusöngur Rotary
  solo voice,pno ICELAND 019-087   (I98)

Vist Ertu, Jesu, Kongur Klar *hymn
  T solo,org ICELAND 019-023   (I99)

Wiegenlied
  solo voice,pno ICELAND 019-063   (I100)

ISRAEL-MEYER, PIERRE (1933-1979)
Anna La Bonne
  "Mädchen Anna, Das" A solo,2perc, pno/harmonium,strings [11'] BILLAUDOT   (I101)

Mädchen Anna, Das
see Anna La Bonne

IST EINER... see Visser, Peter

IST SCHMERZ, SOBALD AN EINE NEUE SCHICHT see Voortman, Roland

IT BURNS see Kingsley, Gershon Gary

IT HAPPENS see Niehaus, Manfred

IT IS BEST NOT TO BE BORN see Vogel, Roger Craig

IT IS EVENING see Gottlieb, Jack S.

IT IS TIME see Rachmaninoff, Sergey Vassilievich

IT SINGS see Grieg, Edvard Hagerup, Syng, Det

IT WAS A LOVER AND HIS LASS see Foote, Arthur

IT WAS IN AND ABOUT THE MART-'MAS TIME see Anonymous, Barbara Allan

IT WAS THOU THE DESTROYER see Verdi,
   Giuseppe, Ballo In Maschera, Un:
   Eri Tu Che Macchiavi

IT WILL BE SUMMER see Glickman, Sylvia

ITACA, OP. 25 see Nicolau, Dimitri

ITALIAN ARIAS FOR HIGH VOICE AND
   ORCHESTRA see Rejcha, Antonin

ITALIAN ART SONGS OF THE ROMANTIC ERA
   *CCU
   (Chiti) ALFRED med-high solo,pno 4954
   f.s.; med-low solo,pno 4955 f.s.
                                      (I102)

ITALIAN MUSIC - SONGS & DANCES
   ("World's Favorite Series") ASHLEY
   043-3   (I103)

ITALIAN SONGBOOK see Wolf, Hugo,
   Italienisches Liederbuch

ITALIAN SONGBOOK *CCU
   solo voice HANSEN-US HAN0392 $5.95
                                      (I104)

ITALIAN SONGS AND ARIAS, 26 *CC26U
   (Paton) ALFRED med-high solo 3402
   accomp tape available; med-low solo
   3403 accomp tape available   (I105)

ITALIAN SONGS AND ARIAS, 28 *CC28U
   med-low solo ALFRED 3552 f.s. (I106)

ITALIAN SONGS & ARIAS: 17TH & 18TH
   CENTURIES
   ("World's Favorite Series") ASHLEY
   129-4   (I107)

ITALIANA IN ALGERI, L': CRUDA SORTE!
   AMOR TIRANNO! see Rossini,
   Gioacchino

ITALIENISCHE DUETTE NO. 4: ALLZU
   GRAUSAM see Handel, George Frideric

ITALIENISCHE DUETTE NO. 7: GEH,
   HOFFNUNG see Handel, George
   Frideric

ITALIENISCHE DUETTE NO. 8: IMMER MUSS
   ICH NACH EUCH SCHAUEN see Handel,
   George Frideric

ITALIENISCHE DUETTE NO. 12: SOVIEL
   PFEILE HAST VERSCHOSSEN see Handel,
   George Frideric

ITALIENISCHE DUETTE NO. 13:
   SCHMACHTEND, FLEHEND see Handel,
   George Frideric

ITALIENISCHE DUETTE NO. 14: WILLST DU
   DIE LIEB' see Handel, George
   Frideric

ITALIENISCHE DUETTE NO. 17: NEIN, ICH
   WILL see Handel, George Frideric

ITALIENISCHE DUETTE NO. 19: WIE
   LEICHTES LAUB see Handel, George
   Frideric

ITALIENISCHE DUETTE NO. 20: ACH, HIER
   IM IRDISCHEN LEBEN see Handel,
   George Frideric

ITALIENISCHES LIEDERBUCH see Wolf, Hugo

ITALIENISCHES LIEDERBUCH AUSWAHL see
   Wolf, Hugo

ITALIENISCHES LIEDERBUCH VOL. 1 see
   Marx, Joseph see Wolf, Hugo

ITALIENISCHES LIEDERBUCH VOL. 2 see
   Marx, Joseph see Wolf, Hugo

ITALSKE ARIE, VOL. 1 see Benda, Georg
   Anton (Jiří Antonín)

ITALSKE ARIE, VOL. 2 see Benda, Georg
   Anton (Jiří Antonín)

ITHACA see Sønstevold, Maj

ITOH, HIROYUKI (1963-   )
   Lecture On Nothing
   2 solo voices [3'] JAPAN   (I108)

ITOH, MIKIO (1942-   )
   First Snow, The
   solo voice,pno [2'] JAPAN   (I109)

   I Like...
   solo voice,pno [2'] JAPAN   (I110)

   Under The Wisteria Trellis
   solo voice,pno [2'] JAPAN   (I111)

ITOH, OHSUKE (1911-   )
   Nagare-Toro
   solo voice,pno [3'] JAPAN   (I112)

ITOH, OHSUKE (cont'd.)

   Okaasan!
   solo voice,pno [3'] JAPAN   (I113)

   Sayonara Dakko
   solo voice,pno [2'] JAPAN   (I114)

   Skip Dance
   solo voice,pno [2'] KAWAI   (I115)

   Suitcho
   solo voice,pno [3'] JAPAN   (I116)

IT'S THIS ISLAND see Gardner, John

IT'S WONDERFUL TO BE AN AMERICAN see
   Tobin, John

ITSUKA YUHI NO see Sasaki, Shigeru

ITSUMADEMO see Takami, Toshio

IUDICA DOMINE see Capricornus, Samuel

IVAN: OUVRE TON COEUR see Bizet,
   Georges

IVES, CHARLES (1874-1954)
   Lincoln The Great Commoner
   med solo,pno sc PEER 60693-203
   $2.50   (I117)

   One Hundred Fourteen Songs *CC114U
   solo voice,pno sc PEER 60867-211
                                 (I118)
   Sunrise
   (Kirkpatrick) solo voice,vln,pno
   PETERS 66663   (I119)

IX POEMAS ZEN see Ortiz, William

J

J.S. BACH DUETTE MIT OBLIGAT see Bach,
   Johann Sebastian

JA DET ER EN FART see Baden, Conrad

JA PRYJIDU see Shut, Wasyl

JA VISST GÖR DET ONT see Kruse, Bjørn
   Howard

JABBERWOCKY see Levi, Paul Alan

JACHINO, CARLO (1889-1971)
   Carme Secolare, Il
   (Mancuso, U.) solo voice,pno CURCI
   1408   (J1)

JACKSON, FRANCIS ALAN (1917-   )
   Tree At My Window
   solo voice BANKS f.s.   (J2)

JACOBS, KENNETH
   Gestures In The Face
   S solo,pno/electronic tape SEESAW
                                 (J3)

JACOBS-BOND, CARRIE MINETTA
   see BOND, CARRIE MINETTA JACOBS

JACOBSEN, ODD-ARNE (1947-   )
   Vocalise
   Mez solo,gtr NORGE   (J4)

JACOBSEN SANGER see Aagaard-Nilsen,
   Torstein

JACOBSSON, JOHN (1835-1909)
   Ur Min Portfölj
   solo voice,pno GEHRMANS 6249 (J5)

JACOPO DA BOLOGNA
   Three Madrigals
   (Wilkins, Nigel) 3 solo voices
   ANTICO AE5   (J6)

JADASSOHN, SOLOMON (1831-1902)
   Terzette
   3 solo voices,pno PETERS 2262 (J7)

JADIS TU M'AS AIMÉ! see Gretchaninov,
   Alexander Tikhonovich

JAFFE
   Five Songs On Poems Of Hesse
   solo voice,pno SOUTHERN V083 (J8)

JAFFE, STEPHEN (1954-   )
   Fort Juniper Songs
   SMez soli,pno PRESSER 141-40032
                                 (J9)

JAG DIKTAR FÖR INGEN see Danielsson,
   Harry

JAG KYSSER DIN OSYNLIGA ROS see
   Malmlöf-Forssling, Carin

JAG ÖNSKAR JAG ÄGDE ROSOR see Sjöblom,
   Heimer

JAG SKA SKAPA ETT NYTT ORD see
   Lidström, John

JAG VÄNTAR MÅNEN see Nystroem, Gösta

JAG VILL TACKA DIG, O HERRE see
   Alinder, Hakan

JAGATARA-BUMI see Nakajima, Hal

JAGDLIED see Mendelssohn-Bartholdy,
   Felix

JÄGER, DER see Zimmerman, S.A.

JÄGER UND SEINE MUTTER, DER see
   Schlick, E.

JAHRMARKT, DER see Bernabei, Giuseppe
   Antonio, Fiera, La

J'AI PEUR D'UN BAISER see Szulc, Josef
   Zygmunt

J'AI PLEURÉ EN RÊVE see Hüe, Georges-
   Adolphe

J'AI T'UN COQUIN DE FRÈRE see Arrieu,
   Claude

J'AI VU PASSER L'HIRONDELLE see
   Dell'Acqua, Eva, Villanelle

JAK MILE, ROZKOSNE see Ryba, Jan Jakub
   Simon

JAKA KRASA VIDRODZHENNIA KRAINY see
   Shut, Wasyl

JAKBY TY ZNAV see Shut, Wasyl

JAMES, MARION
 see PRICE, MARION JAMES

JAMES, WILLIAM G.
 Bush Night Song
  see Six Australian Bush Songs

 Bush Silence
  see Six Australian Bush Songs

 Comrades Of Mine
  see Six Australian Bush Songs

 King Billy's Song
  see Six Australian Bush Songs

 Land Of Who Knows Where!, The
  see Six Australian Bush Songs

 Six Australian Bush Songs
  RICORDI-IT LD118896 f.s.
   contains: Bush Night Song; Bush
   Silence; Comrades Of Mine; King
   Billy's Song; Land Of Who Knows
   Where!, The; Stockriders Song,
   The   (J10)

 Stockriders Song, The
  see Six Australian Bush Songs

JAMES JOYCE'S CHAMBER MUSIC: THE LOST
 SONG SETTINGS see Palmer, Geoffrey
 Molyneux

JANÁCEK, BEDRICH (1920-   )
 Finns Ett Hem Långt Bortom Sorgens
  Hemland, Det
  see Mot Fridens Land (Tre Sånger)

 Mot Fridens Land (Tre Sånger)
  solo voice,org/pno NOTERIA 1862
  f.s.
   contains: Finns Ett Hem Långt
   Bortom Sorgens Hemland, Det; O
   Livets Gud, Vi Tackar Dig;
   Tänds Ett Ljus, Det   (J11)

 O Livets Gud, Vi Tackar Dig
  see Mot Fridens Land (Tre Sånger)

 Tänds Ett Ljus, Det
  see Mot Fridens Land (Tre Sånger)

 Tio Små Andliga Sånger
  solo voice,org/pno NOTERIA 1864
                                (J12)

JANE GREY see Sinding, Christian

JANSON, ALFRED (1937-   )
 Cradle Song
  see Vuggesang

 Vuggesang
  "Cradle Song" S solo,48strings [7']
  NORGE f.s.   (J13)

JANSSEN, GUUS (1951-   )
 Garni
  Bar solo,fl,clar,perc,harp,gtr,
  mand,pno,vln,vla,db [1'] DONEMUS
                                (J14)

JANSSON, JOHANNES (1950-   )
 Nimbus
  Bar solo,orch STIM f.s.   (J15)

JAPANESE FAN [1] see Mourant, Walter

JAPANESE FAN [2] see Mourant, Walter

JAPANESE FOLK SONGS *CCU
 (Ishii, Kan) solo voice ONGAKU 524300
 f.s.   (J16)

JAPANESE SETTINGS see Hekster, Walter

JAPANISCHES REGENLIED see Marx, Joseph

JAPANSKT LJOD see Runolfsson, Karl Otto

JAPONSKY ROK see Vicar, Jan

JAQUES-DALCROZE, ÉMILE (1865-1950)
 Douze Mélodies (1er Recueil)
  med solo,pno CLASSV 1450   (J17)

JARDIM DO AMOR E PAIXAO see Prado,
 Ameida

JARPUR SKEIDAR FLJOTUR, FRAR see
 Isolfsson, Pall

JARRAMA I see Kruse, Bjørn Howard

JARRAMA II see Kruse, Bjørn Howard

JARRELL, MICHAEL (1958-   )
 Eco
  solo voice,pno (diff) LEMOINE (J18)

 Trace-Ecart
  SA soli,3perc,fl,ob&English horn,
  clar&bass clar,bsn&contrabsn,trp
  in C,2horn,bass trom,harp,pno&
  cel&elec org,vln,vla,vcl,db

JARRELL, MICHAEL (cont'd.)

  (diff) LEMOINE   (J19)

JASMINE DOOR, THE see Scott, [Lady]
 John (Alicia Ann)

JASPER TERRACE, THE see Speight, John
 A.

JASTRZEBSKA, ANNA (1950-   )
 De Profundis
  [Norw] S solo,vcl [14'] REIMERS
   101147   (J20)
  S solo,vcl REIMERS   (J21)

JATNING see Halldorsson, Sigfus

JAUBERT, MAURICE (1900-1940)
 Jeanne D'Arc
  S solo,3.3.3.3. 0.2.2.1. 3perc,
  timp,harp,pno,strings without db
  [26'40"] BILLAUDOT   (J22)

JAUCHZET GOTT IN ALLEN LANDEN! see
 Bach, Johann Sebastian

JAVA DE LA FEMME, LA see Milhaud,
 Darius

JE BRULE, DIT-ELLE UN JOUR A UN
 CAMARADE see Leroux, Philippe

JE DEMANDE À L'OISEAU see Beach, [Mrs.]
 H.H.A. (Amy Marcy Cheney)

JE NE T'AIME PAS see Weill

JE VIS - JE MEURS see Boehmer, Konrad
 see Escher, Rudolf George

JE VOUDRAIS QU'IL FÛT DÉJÀ PRÈS DE MOI
 see Debussy, Claude, Damoiselle
 Élue

JEAN see Burleigh, Henry Thacker

JEAN DE LA RÉOLE see Tailleferre,
 Germaine

JEANNE D'ARC see Jaubert, Maurice see
 Riondy, Lucien

JEANNE D'ARC: ADIEU FORETS see
 Tchaikovsky, Piotr Ilyich

JEDEM DAS SEINE see Preyer, Gottfried

JEFFREYS
 Erit Gloria Domini
  SS/TT soli,cont KING'S KM32 (J23)

JEFFREYS, JOHN
 Dapple Grey
  see When I Was Young, Part 3

 Ding Dong Bell
  see When I Was Young, Part 2

 Four And Twenty Tailors
  see When I Was Young, Part 3

 Goosey Goosey Gander
  see When I Was Young, Part 2

 Humpty Dumpty
  see When I Was Young, Part 3

 I Love Little Kitty
  see When I Was Young, Part 2

 Matthew Mark Luke And John
  see When I Was Young, Part 2

 Old Mother Hubbard
  see When I Was Young, Part 3

 Second Book Of Songs *CCU
  solo voice,pno (easy/med) ROBERTON
  491-00350 $22.00   (J24)

 Third And Last Book Of Songs
  solo voice,pno (contains 31 songs)
  ROBERTON 1537   (J25)

 This Little Pig
  see When I Was Young, Part 2

 Tjere Was A Crooked Man
  see When I Was Young, Part 2

 To Bed, To Bed
  see When I Was Young, Part 3

 Tom The Piper's Son
  see When I Was Young, Part 3

 When I Was Young
  T solo,pno ROBERTON 491-00351 $3.25
                                (J26)

 When I Was Young, Part 2
  S/T solo,pno ROBERTON 1538 f.s.
   contains: Ding Dong Bell; Goosey
   Goosey Gander; I Love Little
   Kitty; Matthew Mark Luke And
   John; This Little Pig; Tjere

JEFFREYS, JOHN (cont'd.)

  Was A Crooked Man   (J27)

  When I Was Young, Part 3
   S/T solo,pno ROBERTON 1539 f.s.
    contains: Dapple Grey; Four And
    Twenty Tailors; Humpty Dumpty;
    Old Mother Hubbard; To Bed, To
    Bed; Tom The Piper's Son   (J28)

JEG BEILED' EN GANG TIL EN PIGE see
 Volle, Bjarne, Kjaerlighedsvise, En

JEG DRØMTE see Jordan, Sverre

JEG ER LIVSENS BRØD see Baden, Conrad

JEG GÅR OMKRING see Lunde, Ivar

JEG GIKK MEG VILL I SKOGENE see Nyhus,
 Rolf

JEG LØFTER MINE ØYNE see Nyhus, Rolf

JEG LØFTER MINE ØYNE TIL FJELLENE see
 Nyhus, Rolf

JEG LØFTER OPP TIL GUD MIN SANG see
 Kverndokk, Gisle

JEG REISTE EN DEILIG SOMMERKVELD see
 Grieg, Edvard Hagerup

JEG SER see Moland, Eirik

JEG SER DEG, O GUDS LAM, Å STÅ see Med
 Jesus Vil Eg Fara see Bakke, Ruth

JEG SYNS JEG SELV MÅ STRÅLE see Plau,
 Arild

JEG TAKKER DEG: DÅPSMOTETT, OP.22 see
 Holter, Stig Wernø

JEG VELGER MEG APRIL see Selmer, Johan
 Peter

JEG VET AT JEG FÅR ALDRI SE see Taubo,
 Lillian Gulowna

JEG VIL HJEM see Hovland, Egil

JEGEREN see Hartmann, Christian

JELINEK, STANISLAV (1945-   )
 Historie Meho Srdce
  Bar solo,1.0.1.0. 0.0.0.0. perc,
  pno,strings [19'] CESKY HUD.
                                (J29)

JENNEFELT, THOMAS (1954-   )
 Längs Radien
  SMezTBar soli,orch STIM f.s. (J30)

JENNI, DONALD MARTIN (1937-   )
 Get Hence Foule Griefe
  T solo,harp [5'] sc AM.COMP.AL.
  $3.85   (J31)

JENSEITS DER SICHERHEIT see Globokar,
 Vinko

JENSEITS DES ST. GOTTHARD see Frid,
 Geza

JENSEN, ADOLF (1837-1879)
 Am Ufer Des Flusses Manzanares
  see Gesänge, Op. 21, No. 6

 Gesänge, Op. 21, No. 6
  "Am Ufer Des Flusses Manzanares"
  SCIEN 766   (J32)

 Sieben Lieder Von Robert Burns
  *Op.49
  [Ger] high solo RECITAL 269   (J33)

 Zwölf Gesänge Von Paul Heyse
  med solo,pno CLASSV 2216   (J34)

JENSEN, LUDWIG IRGENS (1894-1969)
 Alrunen
  [Norw] solo voice,pno NORGE   (J35)

 Altar
  [Eng] solo voice,strings [3'] NORGE
  f.s.   (J36)

 Barnebilleder
  [Norw] solo voice,pno NORSK   (J37)

 Bols Song From The Incidental Music
  To Driftekaren
  see Bols Vise Fra Driftekaren Suite

 Bols Vise Fra Driftekaren Suite
  "Bols Song From The Incidental
  Music To Driftekaren" solo voice,
  1.1.1.1. 2.0.0.0. harp,cel,
  strings [3'] NORSK   (J38)

 Brente Våre Gårder, De
  [Norw] solo voice,pno NORSK   (J39)

JENSEN, LUDWIG IRGENS (cont'd.)

Fabler Og Barnerim
[Norw] solo voice,pno NORSK   (J40)

Fiskerens Aftensang
[Norw] solo voice,pno NORSK   (J41)

Gamle, Den
[Swed] solo voice,pno NORSK   (J42)

Guldskyen
[Norw] solo voice,pno NORGE   (J43)

Hellige Birgittas Salme, Den
[Norw] solo voice,pno NORGE   (J44)

I Blodet Hans Blømde
[Norw] solo voice,pno NORGE   (J45)

Landevei
[Norw] solo voice,pno NORGE   (J46)

Leaning On The Fence
see Lutad Mot Gärdet

Lutad Mot Gärdet
"Leaning On The Fence" [Swed] solo
voice,2.1.1.1. 2.0.0.0. cel,
strings [3'] NORGE f.s.   (J47)

Mädchen Auf Der Brücke, Das
[Ger] solo voice,pno NORGE   (J48)

Meer Erstrahlt, Das
[Ger] solo voice,pno (text by
Heinrich Heine) NORGE   (J49)

Nimm Mich Auf, Uralte Nacht
[Ger] solo voice,pno (text by
Heinrich Heine) NORGE   (J50)

Qu'as Tu Fait?
[Fr] solo voice,pno (text by Paul
Verlaine) NORGE   (J51)

Rosenstaden
[Swed] solo voice,pno NORGE   (J52)

Til Kongen
[Norw] solo voice,pno NORSK   (J53)

To Fabler
[Norw] solo voice,pno NORGE   (J54)

Vårbekken
[Ger] solo voice,pno NORGE   (J55)

JENSEN, WALTHER G.
Two Songs, Op. 45
Mez/A solo,pno [14'] SAMFUNDET
(J56)

JENTZSCH, WILFRIED (1941-   )
Quattro Sonetti Per Tenore E
Orchestra
T solo,1.1.1.1. 2.2.1.1. harp,pno,
strings [15'] DEUTSCHER   (J57)

JEPPSSON, KERSTIN (1948-   )
Dig Rörde Aldrig Mörkret
see Tre Sånger Om Livet I Romantisk
Stil

Intet Är Förgäves
see Tre Sånger Om Livet I Romantisk
Stil

När Du Sluter Mina Ögon
see Tre Sånger Om Livet I Romantisk
Stil

Tre Sånger Om Livet I Romantisk Stil
S/T solo,pno/org SUECIA 409 f.s.
contains: Dig Rörde Aldrig
Mörkret; Intet Är Förgäves; När
Du Sluter Mina Ögon   (J58)

JEPTHA: WAFT HER ANGELS see Handel,
George Frideric

JEREMIA-WORD see Nystedt, Knut

JEREMIAS BEKJENNELSER see Ødegaard,
Henrik

JESAJA 53 see Holter, Stig Wernø

JESU DULCIS MEMORIA see Schrijvers,
Jean

JESU SYV ORD PÅ KORSET see Karlsen,
Kjell Mørk

JESU, WIJS EN WONDERMACHTIG see Meima,
Herman

JESUS, DIN SØTE FORENING see Nyhus,
Rolf

JESUS IS NU EEN KINDEKIJN see
Weegenhuise, Johan

JESUS MY LOVE MY JOY see Telfer, Nancy

JESUS OF NAZARETH see Gounod, Charles
François

JESUS, VÅR HERRE see Okkenhaug, Ingrid
Buran

JETZT AUF ERDEN WOLL'T FRÖHLICH WERDEN
see Hahn, Georg Joachim Joseph,
Aria De Nativitate Domini

JEU DE LA SOLSTICE see Tveitt, Geirr,
Jonsokspel

JEU D'EAU, LE see Debussy, Claude

JEUNE PÂTRE, UN see Paderewski, Ignace
Jan

JEWELS OF THE MADONNA: BACIO DI LAMA
see Wolf-Ferrari, Ermanno

JEWELS OF THE MADONNA: E NDRINGHETE,
NDRANGHETE see Wolf-Ferrari,
Ermanno

JEWELS OF THE MADONNA: SERENADE see
Wolf-Ferrari, Ermanno

JEWISH SONGBOOK   *CCU
solo voice HANSEN-US HANO390 $5.95
(J59)

JIEDNA see Vea, Ketil

JIHOCESKE LETO see Stepka, Karel Vaclav

JIRÁK, KAREL BOLESLAV (1891-1972)
Hlas Nejsladsi *song cycle
med solo,3.2.2.2. 4.2.0.0. timp,
harp,strings CESKY HUD.   (J60)

Tri Zpevy Domova
med solo,2.3.3.0. 4.2.0.0. timp,
perc,harp,cel,strings [12'] CÉSKY
HUD.   (J61)

JIRASEK, IVO (1920-   )
Portret Zeny
S solo,fl,bass clar,vibra,pno
PANTON 912   (J62)

JOBS KLAGAN see Sjöblom, Heimer

JOCELYN: LULLABY see Godard, Benjamin
Louis Paul see Godard, Benjamin
Louis Paul, Jocelyn: Oh! No
T'eveille Pas

JOCELYN: OH! NO T'ÉVEILLE PAS see
Godard, Benjamin Louis Paul

JOHANNSSON, MAGNUS BL. (1925-   )
Air
S solo,pno ICELAND 018-015   (J63)

Aria
solo voice,pno ICELAND 018-025
(J64)

Einmana
solo voice,pno ICELAND 018-013
(J65)

Hands
solo voice,pno ICELAND 018-012
(J66)

"Heidloar-Kvaedi"
solo voice,pno ICELAND 018-017
(J67)

I Light My Candles
solo voice,org ICELAND 018-010
(J68)

In Summer When The Sun Is High
solo voice,pno ICELAND 018-014
(J69)

Na-No-Mani
solo voice&opt solo voice,pno
[3'0"] ICELAND 018-024   (J70)

Rakki
solo voice,pno ICELAND 018-016
(J71)

JOHANSEN, BERTIL PALMAR (1954-   )
Årets Tider
[Norw] Mez/Bar solo,pno [11'30"]
NORGE   (J72)

JOHANSEN, DAVID MONRAD (1888-1974)
Barn Jesus I En Krybbe Lå
[Norw] solo voice,pno NORSK   (J73)

I Vaagelidann *Op.6,No.7
solo voice,1.1.1.2. 2.0.0.0.
strings [4'] MUSIKK f.s.   (J74)

Mor Syng Og Andre Dikt Av Idar
Handgard *Op.1
[Norw] solo voice,pno NORSK   (J75)

Nocturne
[Norw] solo voice,pno MUSIKK   (J76)

Svend Herulfsens Ord *Op.2,No.1
"Words Of Svend Herulfsen, The"
solo voice,1.1.2.1. 2.2.2.0.
timp,perc,harp,strings NORGE f.s.
(J77)

JOHANSEN, DAVID MONRAD (cont'd.)
Words Of Svend Herulfsen, The
see Svend Herulfsens Ord

JOHANSSON, ROGER
Näcken
Bar solo,org NOTERIA 1863   (J78)

JOHN MCCORMACK SONG ALBUM *CCU
BOOSEY VAB0229 f.s.   (J79)

JOHNSEN, HALLVARD (1916-   )
Bergmannen: Melodrama *Op.81
"Miner, The" narrator.
4(2pic).3(English
horn).2.3(contrabsn). 4.3.2.1.
timp,perc,strings NORGE f.s.
(J80)

Du Strider Trøyt
see Heilagkvedi, Op. 13

Du Sundagskveld
see Seks Sanger, Op. 9

Fagert Er Landet
see Heilagkvedi, Op. 13

Gamle Grendi
see Seks Sanger, Op. 9

Haustvisa
see Seks Sanger, Op. 9

Heilagkvedi, Op. 13
[Norw] solo voice,pno NORSK f.s.
contains: Du Strider Trøyt;
Fagert Er Landet; Høyr Kor
Kyrkjeklokka Lokkar; Soli Hev
Sitt Same Lag   (J81)

Her Er Det Land
see Seks Sanger, Op. 9

Høyr Kor Kyrkjeklokka Lokkar
see Heilagkvedi, Op. 13

Kjaeringi Med Kjelken
see Seks Sanger, Op. 9

Miner, The
see Bergmannen: Melodrama

Seks Sanger, Op. 9
[Norw] solo voice,pno NORGE f.s.
contains: Du Sundagskveld; Gamle
Grendi; Haustvisa; Her Er Det
Land; Kjaeringi Med Kjelken;
Vårdag   (J82)

Soli Hev Sitt Same Lag
see Heilagkvedi, Op. 13

Ti Salmer, Op.78
[Norw] solo voice,org NORGE   (J83)

Vårdag
see Seks Sanger, Op. 9

JOHNSON, A. PAUL (1955-   )
From The Analects
S solo,fl,pno [15'] AM.COMP.AL. sc
$8.80, pts $3.10   (J84)

Peter's Denial
STB soli,org [6'] sc AM.COMP.AL.
$6.15   (J85)

Seeing You Leave
S solo,pno sc AM.COMP.AL. $4.60
(J86)

Stranger, The
S solo,pno sc AM.COMP.AL. $1.95
(J87)

Two Early Songs *CC2U
S solo,pno sc AM.COMP.AL. $6.15
(J88)

JOHNSON, GEIR (1953-   )
Talking - Singing
[Eng] solo voice (text by e.e.
cummings) NORGE   (J89)

JOHNSON, NOEL
Noddy Song Book
RICORDI-IT LD361   (J90)

JOHNSTON, BENJAMIN BURWELL (BEN)
(1926-   )
Calamity Jane To Her Daughter
S solo,vln,kbd,org,drums SMITH PUB
(J91)

Somewhere I Have Never Traveled
T solo,pno (text by e.e. cummings)
SMITH PUB   (J92)

JOLAS, BETSY (1926-   )
Plupart Du Temps II
T solo,tenor sax,vcl LEDUC   (J93)

JOLASALMUR see Isolfsson, Pall

JOLIE FILLE DE PERTH, LA: SERENADE: A
LA VOIX D'UN AMANT see Bizet,
Georges

JOLIE FILLE DE PERTH: ECHO, VIENS SUR
L'AIR EMBAUMÉ see Bizet, Georges

JOLIE FILLE DE PERTH: QUAND LA FLAMME
DE L'AMOUR see Bizet, Georges

JOLIVET, ANDRE (1905-1974)
  Couplet Berichon Du XVIe
    see Quatre Melodies Sur Des Poesies
    Anciennes

  Hymne A Saint Andre
    [Lat] solo voice,org [5'] BILLAUDOT
                                        (J94)

  Lay Ou Plutost Rondeau De F. Villon
    see Quatre Melodies Sur Des Poesies
    Anciennes

  Paroles De Marie A Son Fils XIII
    see Quatre Melodies Sur Des Poesies
    Anciennes

  Poemes Pour L'enfant
    S/Mez solo,1.1.1.1. 0.1.0.0. pno,
    harp,2vln,vla,vcl [22'] BILLAUDOT
                                        (J95)

  Quatre Melodies Sur Des Poesies
  Anciennes
    S/Mez solo,1.1.2.1. 0.2.2.0. 2perc,
    pno,string quin BILLAUDOT f.s.
    contains: Couplet Berichon Du
      XVIe; Lay Ou Plutost Rondeau De
      F. Villon; Paroles De Marie A
      Son Fils XIII; Rondel De F.
      Villon   (J96)

  Rondel De F. Villon
    see Quatre Melodies Sur Des Poesies
    Anciennes

  Trois Chants Des Hommes
    Bar solo,3.3.3.3. 4.3.3.1. 3perc,
    timp,2harp,pno,strings [30']
    BILLAUDOT   (J97)

  Trois Poemes
    solo voice,string quar,pno (diff)
    BILLAUDOT   (J98)

JOMFRU MARIAS TÅREGRAS see Madsen,
Trygve

JOMMELLI, NICCOLO (1714-1774)
  Sieben Kleine Kirchenkompositionen
    various solo voices & continuo
    KUNZEL GM 1223   (J99)

  Zwei Veni Sponsa Christi
    S solo,strings,cont KUNZEL GM 1214
                                        (J100)

JONAH see Warren, Betsy

JONCIERES, VICTORIN DE (1839-1903)
  Dimitri: Pâles Étoiles
    S solo,pno CLASSV 1610   (J101)

  Sardanapale: Le Front Dans La
  Poussière
    B solo,pno CLASSV 1577   (J102)

JONE: O JONE! O DI QUEST' ANIMA see
Petrella, Errico

JONES, MARJORIE
  Creative Soloist, The
    GENTRY JG0680   (J103)

JONGLEUR DE NOTRE DAME, LE: LEGENDE DE
LA SAUGE see Massenet, Jules

JONSOK see Kjeldaas, Arnljot

JONSOKNATT see Tveitt, Geirr

JONSOKSPEL see Tveitt, Geirr

JONSSON, THORARINN (1900-1974)
  Ave Maria
    S solo,pno ICELAND 034-006 (J104)

  Bordsalmur-Thrir Vikivakar-Stokur
    solo voice,pno ICELAND 034-004
                                        (J105)

  Heidblaa Fjolan Min Frida
    solo voice,pno ICELAND 034-009
                                        (J106)

  Island
    SA soli ICELAND 034-027   (J107)

  Nordur Vid Heimskaut
    solo voice ICELAND 034-031 (J108)

  Pastorale
    solo voice,pno ICELAND 034-012
                                        (J109)

  Überglückliche, Der
    solo voice ICELAND 034-030 (J110)

JORD see Strand, Ragnvald

JORDAN, SVERRE (1889-1972)
  And Look, She Came
    see Og Se Hun Kom

JORDAN, SVERRE (cont'd.)

  Av "Tue Bentsøns Viser" *Op.44
    "Tue Bentsons Songs" T solo,
    3(pic).2.2.2. 4.2.2.0. timp,perc,
    2harp,cel,strings [10']   (J111)

  Baekken
    see Seks Poesier, Op. 18

  Barnet Sover
    see Tva Sanger, Op. 54

  By The Sea
    see Ved Havet

  Christ Complains
    see Christus Klagt

  Christus Klagt *Op.7,No.1
    "Christ Complains" [Ger] T/Bar
    solo,2.2.2.2. 2.0.0.0. strings
    [4'] NORGE f.s.   (J112)

  Cradle Song
    see Vuggevise: Og Drengen Ligger På
    Moders Skjød

  Der Synger Ingen Fugle *Op.33,No.3
    "There Are No Birds Singing" S/T
    solo,2.2.2.1. 2.0.0.0. strings
    [2'] NORGE f.s.   (J113)
    see Fire Sange Med Klaver, Op. 33

  Drick, Op. 30, No. 2
    [Swed] solo voice,pno NORSK (J114)

  Dronning Bertillas Vuggevise
    see Seks Poesier, Op. 18

  Du Vesle Bekk På Villan Mo
    see Sanger For En Mellomstemme
    Piano

  Du Vise Männen
    see Seks Sange, Op. 21

  Eftersommer *Op.73,No.4
    "Late Summer" solo voice,2.2.2.2.
    2.2.0.0. harp,strings [3'] NORGE
    f.s.   (J115)

  Feberdigte *Op.13
    "Fever Poems" narrator,
    3(pic).2.2.2. 2.2.2.1. timp,perc,
    harp,strings [20'] NORGE f.s.
                                        (J116)

  Fever Poems
    see Feberdigte

  Finland
    see Sange, Op. 5

  Fire Sange Med Klaver, Op. 33
    [Norw] solo voice,pno NORSK f.s.
    contains: Der Synger Ingen Fugle;
      Landskab; Pil Og Bue; Under
      Haender, Et   (J117)

  Fire Sange, Op. 15
    [Norw/Ger] solo voice,pno NORSK
                                        (J118)

  Fire Sange Til Tekst Av Torvald Tu's
    "Strengjer Som Syng" *Op.27
    solo voice,pno NORSK   (J119)

  Fire Sanger, Op. 41
    [Norw] solo voice,pno NORSK f.s.
    contains: Gammel Vise, En; Syng
      Mine Strengjer; Tårar; Uår
                                        (J120)

  Flying Eagle
    see Flyvende Ørn

  Flyvende Ørn *Op.11,No.1
    "Flying Eagle" [Dan] solo voice,
    3.2.2.3. 4.2.3.0. timp,perc,harp,
    strings NORGE f.s.   (J121)

  Gammel Vise, En *Op.41,No.4
    "Old Tune, An" solo voice,2.2.2.2.
    2.0.0.0. harp,strings [3'] NORGE
    f.s.   (J122)
    see Fire Sanger, Op. 41

  Herbstgang *Op.5,No.5
    [Ger] T solo,2.2.2.2. 2.0.0.0.
    harp,strings [3'] HANSEN-DEN f.s.
                                        (J123)

  Herbstgesang
    see Sange, Op. 5

  Herre, Herre, Du Har Kalla
    see Sanger For En Mellomstemme
    Piano

  Hvorfor Saa Du Paa Mig
    see Seks Sange, Op. 21

  I August
    see Seks Poesier, Op. 18

  Ice Flowers
    see Isblomar

JORDAN, SVERRE (cont'd.)

  Isblomar *Op.27,No.1
    "Ice Flowers" solo voice,2.2.2.2.
    2.0.0.0. strings [3'] NORGE f.s.
                                        (J124)

  Jeg Drømte
    see Two Sange Med Orkester

  Jutta Comes To Folkungarna
    see Jutta Kommer Til Folkungarna

  Jutta Kommer Til Folkungarna *Op.18,
    No.3
    "Jutta Comes To Folkungarna" [Swed]
    S solo,1.1.2.1. 2.0.0.0. harp,
    strings [2'] NORGE f.s.   (J125)
    see Seks Poesier, Op. 18

  Kindesgebet *Op.69,No.2
    [Ger] S solo,2fl,bsn,2horn,harp,
    strings [2'] NORGE f.s.   (J126)

  Kjaerlighetssang: Hører Du Mitt
    *Op.11,No.3
    "Love Song" solo voice,2.1.2.1.
    2.2.2.0. timp,strings [2'] NORGE
    f.s.   (J127)

  Landscape
    see Landskab

  Landskab
    "Landscape" Mez/Bar solo,2.1.2.1.
    2.0.0.0. harp,strings [2'] NORGE
    f.s.   (J128)
    see Fire Sange Med Klaver, Op. 33

  Late Summer
    see Eftersommer

  Love Song
    see Kjaerlighetssang: Hører Du Mitt

  Morgen
    see Seks Sange, Op. 21
    see Two Sange Med Orkester

  Nu Er Stunden Rikast
    see Seks Sange, Op. 21

  Og Se Hun Kom *Op.2,No.5
    "And Look, She Came" [Dan/Ger] S/T
    solo,fl,glock,strings [2']
    HANSEN-DEN f.s.   (J129)

  Og Sig Mig, Hvorfor Du Vil Fare
    see Seks Poesier, Op. 18

  Old Tune, An
    see Gammel Vise, En

  Pil Og Bue
    see Fire Sange Med Klaver, Op. 33

  Sange, Op. 5
    [Dan/Ger] HANSEN-DEN f.s.
    contains: Finland; Herbstgesang;
      Ved Søbredden   (J130)

  Sanger For En Mellomstemme Piano
    [Norw/Ger] solo voice,pno NORSK
    f.s.
    contains: Du Vesle Bekk På Villan
      Mo; Herre, Herre, Du Har Kalla
                                        (J131)

  Seks Poesier, Op. 18
    solo voice,pno NORSK f.s.
    contains: Baekken; Dronning
      Bertillas Vuggevise; I August;
      Jutta Kommer Til Folkungarna;
      Og Sig Mig, Hvorfor Du Vil
      Fare; Søvnen   (J132)

  Seks Sange, Op. 21
    [Norw/Swed/Dan] solo voice,pno
    NORSK f.s.
    contains: Du Vise Männen; Hvorfor
      Saa Du Paa Mig; Morgen; Nu Er
      Stunden Rikast; Ung Aslaug;
      Vårvisa   (J133)

  Seks Sange Til Klaver, Op. 23
    [Norw/Ger] NORSK   (J134)

  Sing My Chords
    see Syng Mine Strengjer

  Søvnen
    see Seks Poesier, Op. 18

  Spring Song
    see Vårvisa

  Syng Mine Strengjer *Op.41,No.3
    "Sing My Chords" solo voice,
    2.2.2.2. 2.2.0.0. harp,strings
    [2'] NORGE f.s.   (J135)
    see Fire Sanger. Op. 41

  Tårar
    see Fire Sanger. Op. 41

  There Are No Birds Singing
    see Der Synger Ingen Fugle

JORDAN, SVERRE (cont'd.)

Thirteen Years
    see Tretton År

Til Et Barn *Op.30,No.1
    [Norw] solo voice,pno NORGE (J136)

Tretton År *Op.54,No.1
    "Thirteen Years" [Swed] S solo,fl,
    clar,harp,cel,strings [2'] NORGE
    f.s.   (J137)
    see Tva Sanger, Op. 54

Tue Bentsons Songs
    see Av "Tue Bentsøns Viser"

Tva Sanger, Op. 54
    [Swed] solo voice,pno NORSK f.s.
    contains: Barnet Sover; Tretton
    År   (J138)

Two Sange Med Orkester
    [Norw/Dan/Ger] solo voice,2.2.2.2.
    2.0.0.0. harp,strings NORSK f.s.
    contains: Jeg Drømte, Op.15,No.1;
    Morgen, Op.21,No.1   (J139)

Uår
    see Fire Sanger. Op. 41

Under Haender, Et
    see Fire Sange Med Klaver, Op. 33

Ung Aaslaug *Op.21,No.2
    "Young Aaslaug" S solo,2.2.2.2.
    2.2.1.0. timp,perc,harp,strings
    [4'] NORGE f.s.   (J140)

Ung Aslaug
    see Seks Sange, Op. 21

Vårvisa *Op.21,No.4
    "Spring Song" [Swed/Ger] solo
    voice,2.2.2.2. 2.2.2.0. timp,
    harp,strings [3'] NORGE f.s.   (J141)
    see Seks Sange, Op. 21

Ved Havet *Op.73,No.1
    "By The Sea" [Dan] S/T solo,
    2.2.2.2. 4.2.3.0. timp,perc,
    strings [2'] NORGE f.s.   (J142)

Ved Søbredden
    see Sange, Op. 5

Vuggevise: Og Drengen Ligger På
    Moders Skjød *Op.2,No.1
    "Cradle Song" solo voice,1.1.2.1.
    2.0.0.0. strings [2'] NORGE f.s. (J143)

Young Aaslaug
    see Ung Aaslaug

JORDEN ÄR MÄNNISKANS HEM see
    Dorumsgaard, Arne

JORDENS ORO VIKER see Karlsen, Kjell
    Mørk

JOSEPH EN ÉGYPTE: CHAMPS PATERNELS see
    Méhul, Étienne-Nicolas

JOSHUA FIGHT DE BATTLE OB JERICHO see
    Gospel Favourites

JOSQUIN
    see DES PREZ, JOSQUIN

JOUR OU SYLVAIN M'A PARLÉ!, LE see
    Coedes, A.

JOURNEY OF THE MAGI see Britten, [Sir]
    Benjamin

JOURNEY TOWARD OBLIVION see Silverman,
    Faye-Ellen

JOVEN EN EL TOZAL, EL see Schubert,
    Franz (Peter)

JUBILATE DEO see Schütz, Heinrich

JUBILUS see Costinescu, Gheorghe

JUEGO DE SIEMPRE see Olivero, Betty

JUFFERTJE IN HET GROEN, HET see Orthel,
    Leon

JUGEND-ALBUM FÜR GESANG, OP.475 see
    Abt, Franz

JUGEND UND ALTER see Marx, Joseph

JUGENDLIEDER, BAND 1: 1901-1904 see
    Berg, Alban

JUGENDLIEDERKREIS see Weegenhuise,
    Johan

JUIVE, LA: IL VA VENIR see Halévy,
    Jacques

JUIVE, LA: RACHEL, QUAND DU SEIGNEUR
    see Halévy, Jacques

JUIVE, LA: SI LA RIGUEUR see Halévy,
    Jacques

JUL see Okkenhaug, Ingrid Buran

JULBÖN see De Goede, Nicholaas, Marias
    Tröstesång

JULESANG see Kvam, Oddvar S. see Olsen,
    Sparre see Strand, Tor

JULI see Hovland, Egil

JULINACHT see Guichelaar, Jan

JUMP BACK see Sargon

JUMPING RAINDROP, THE see Stutschevsky,
    Joachim

JUNCTION, ON A WARM AFTERNOON, THE see
    Bolcom, William Elden

JUNE see Beach, [Mrs.] H.H.A. (Amy
    Marcy Cheney) see Quilter, Roger

JUNG, HELGE (1943-   )
    ...Von Goethe *Op.35
    T solo,wind quin,pno DEUTSCHER   (J144)

JUNG DIETHELM see Sinding, Christian

JUNGBAUER, COELESTIN (1747-1823)
    Hier Liegt Vor Deiner Majestät
    (Ruhland, Konrad) S solo,org (Musik
    Aus Ostbayern, Heft 24)
    COPPENRATH   (J145)

JUNGE LIEBE see Bijvanck, Henk

JUNGER DICHTER DENKT AN DIE GELIEBTE,
    EIN see Marx, Joseph

JUNGFRU MARIAS LOVSÅNG see Forsberg,
    Roland

JUNREI see Hayakawa, Kuzuko

JUST A LITTLE RAIN see Walker, Gwyneth

JUST FOR THIS see Beach, [Mrs.] H.H.A.
    (Amy Marcy Cheney)

JUTTA COMES TO FOLKUNGARNA see Jordan,
    Sverre, Jutta Kommer Til
    Folkungarna

JUTTA KOMMER TIL FOLKUNGARNA see
    Jordan, Sverre

JYO-SHI see Kobata, Ikuo

K

KAARES SANG see Nordraak, Rikard

KABELÁC, MILOSLAV (1908-1977)
    Ohlasy Dalav
    A solo,pno PANTON 99   (K1)

KADDISH see Stein, Leon

KADOSA, PAL (1903-1983)
    Four Songs, Op. 68
    BOOSEY EMB06572   (K2)

KAFKA-FRAGMENTE, OP. 24 see Kurtag,
    György

KAGEL, MAURICIO (1931-   )
    Tango Aleman
    solo voice,vln,acord,pno PETERS
    8412   (K3)

KAGURAUTA see Mikami, Jiro

KAHRS, SVEN LYDER (1959-   )
    Two Poems
    [Eng] Mez solo,vln [5'] NORGE (K4)

KALACH, JIRI (1934-   )
    Tise
    A solo,string orch [20'] CESKY HUD.
                                       (K5)

KALANZI, BENNY (1938-   )
    Bantu And You, The *Afr
    KUNZEL GM 3   (K6)

KALDALÓNS, SIGVALDI S. (1881-1946)
    Adfangadagskvold Jola
    solo voice,pno ICELAND 071-018 (K7)

    Alfadir Raedur
    solo voice,pno ICELAND 071-007 (K8)

    Ave Maria (from Dansinn I Hruna)
    solo voice,pno ICELAND 071-004 (K9)

    Eg Syng Um Thig
    solo voice,pno ICELAND 071-037
                                       (K10)

    Eins Og Ljossins Skaera Skruda
    solo voice,pno ICELAND 071-012
                                       (K11)

    Erla
    solo voice,pno ICELAND 071-025
                                       (K12)

    Fjallid Eina
    solo voice,pno ICELAND 071-035
                                       (K13)

    Hamraborgin
    solo voice,pno ICELAND 071-033
                                       (K14)

    Heidin Ha
    solo voice,pno ICELAND 071-034
                                       (K15)

    Heimir
    (Thorarinsson, Jón) solo voice,
    1.1.1.1. 1.1.0.0. timp,perc,harp,
    strings ICELAND 071-009   (K16)

    Hinzta Kvedjan
    solo voice,pno ICELAND 071-005
                                       (K17)

    Hreidrid Mitt
    solo voice,pno ICELAND 071-023
                                       (K18)

    Huldur
    solo voice,pno ICELAND 071-032
                                       (K19)

    Hun Kysti Mig
    solo voice,pno ICELAND 071-017
                                       (K20)

    Kossavisur
    solo voice,pno ICELAND 071-021
                                       (K21)

    Leitin
    solo voice,pno ICELAND 071-013
                                       (K22)

    Ljuflingar
    solo voice,pno (12 songs) ICELAND
    071-902   (K23)

    Med Solskinsfana Ur Suduratt
    solo voice,pno ICELAND 071-036
                                       (K24)

    Moon, The
    solo voice,pno ICELAND 071-003
                                       (K25)

    Mutter Mochte Schlafen
    solo voice,pno ICELAND 071-024
                                       (K26)

    Regn Um Nott
    solo voice,pno ICELAND 071-016
                                       (K27)

    Sangsvanen
    solo voice,pno ICELAND 071-026
                                       (K28)

    Six Songs
    solo voice,pno ICELAND 071-904
                                       (K29)

KALDALÓNS, SIGVALDI S. (cont'd.)

Sofdu, Unga Astin Min
solo voice,pno ICELAND 071-006
(K30)

Solardagur
solo voice,pno ICELAND 071-014
(K31)

Three Songs
solo voice,pno ICELAND 071-900
(K32)

(Thorarinsson, Jón) solo voice,
2.2.1.2. 2.2.0.0. perc,harp,
strings ICELAND 071-901 (K33)

Thu Eina Hjartans Yndid Mitt
(Thorarinsson, Jón) solo voice,
2.2.1.2. 2.2.0.0. harp,strings
ICELAND 071-011 (K34)

Til Naeturinnar
solo voice,pno ICELAND 071-015
(K35)

Vald
solo voice,pno ICELAND 071-020
(K36)

Vid Sundid
(Thorarinsson, Jón) solo voice,
1.1.1.1. 1.1.0.0. perc,harp,
strings ICELAND 071-010 (K37)

Vorsins Fridur, Vorsins Thra
solo voice,pno ICELAND 071-022
(K38)

Vorvindur
solo voice,pno ICELAND 071-019
(K39)

KALE BALA see Bodorova, Sylvie

KÁLIK, VACLAV (1891-1951)
Duma
Bar solo,2.2.2.2. 4.0.0.0. timp,
harp,strings CESKY HUD. (K40)

KALINOWE DWORY see Szymanowski, Karol

KALL MEG EN KRAKK see Hellstenius,
Henrik

KALMANOFF, MARTIN (1920-)
Cause Us, O Lord Our God
med solo,kbd TRANSCON. 991102 (K41)

KALYPSO see Konietzny, Heinrich

KAMMERMUSIK II see Schmidt,
Christfried, Ed E Subito Sera...

KAMMERMUSIKALISCHES TEDEUM see
Bodensohn, Ernst Friedrich Wilhelm

KAN SPEILET TALE? see Evensen, Bernt
Kasberg

KANEKO, ATSUO (1936-)
Paesaggio I
S solo,fl,vibra,pno ONGAKU 490831
f.s. (K42)

KÄNGURUH IM SCHNEE, EIN see Einem,
Gottfried von, Prinzessin
Traurigkeit

KANNARHAUGANE see Fladmoe, Arvid

KANNO, YOSHIHIRO (1953-)
City Of Sand In A Labyrinth
S solo,pno,synthesizer,2perc [15']
ONGAKU (K43)

KANTATE ÜBER DIE WELTZEIT see Pfiffner,
Ernst

KANTATE VON DEN BEIDEN see Matthus,
Siegfried

KANTORENBUCH - KLEINAUSGABE *CCU
solo voice CHRIS 52171 f.s. (K44)

KANTORENBUCH ZUM GOTTESLOB *CCU
(Nordhues, Paul; Wagner, Alois) solo
voice CHRIS 52170 f.s. (K45)

KAPELLE, DIE see Zumsteeg, Emilie

KAPPEN see Fongaard, Bjørn

KAPR, JAN (1914-1988)
Exercises For Gydli
S solo,fl,harp [9'] SUPRAPHON (K46)

Lanzhotska
see Symphony No. 10

Musica Per Mila
S solo,chamber orch [7'] GENERAL
(K47)
S solo,harp [7'] GENERAL (K48)

Symphony No. 10
"Lanzhotska" MezT soli,3.3.2.2.
4.3.3.1. timp,perc,2harp,gtr,
strings [50'] CESKY HUD. (K49)

KAPR, JAN (cont'd.)

Vendanges *song cycle
SBar soli,pno [15'] GENERAL (K50)

KARABITO NO see Matsudaira, Yori-Tsune

KARCHIN, LOUIS S. (1951-)
Five Orchestral Songs *CC5U
S solo,2+pic.2.2(bass clar).2+
contrabsn. 4.2.2.1. 4perc,strings
sc AM.COMP.AL. $36.35 (K51)

Songs Of John Keats *CCU
S solo,fl,clar,vln,vcl,perc,pno
AM.COMP.AL. sc $14.50, pts $15.75
(K52)

Songs Of John Keats *CCU
S solo,2.2.2.3. 1.1.0.0. 2perc,
harp,strings sc AM.COMP.AL.
$42.45 (K53)

KARFREITAGSKANTATE see Torelli,
Giuseppe, Cantata Per Il Venerdi
Santo

KARG-ELERT, SIGFRID (1877-1933)
Abendstern *Op.98,No.1
S solo,org CHILTERN (K54)

Sphärenmusik *Op.66,No.2 (from Vom
Himmel Hoch) Xmas
S solo,vln,org CHILTERN (K55)

Zehn Epigramme, Op. 56
[Ger] med-high solo RECITAL 270
(K56)

KARINS MANSDOTTERS LULLABY FOR KING
ERIC XIV see Sveinsson, Atli Heimir

KARINS SÅNGER see Wallgren, Jan

KARKOFF, MAURICE (1927-)
Är Om Aftonen Man Bryter Upp, Det
*Op.10,No.5
solo voice,pno EGTVED MF 432 from
AKSEL SCHIOETZ ANTHOLOGY OF
NORDIC SOLO SONGS, THE, VOL. 2
(K57)

Tio Japanska Romanser *Op.45
solo voice,pno MUSIKAL. (K58)

Tyst Mitt Hjärta *Op.64a
low solo STIM (K59)

KARKOSCHKA, ERHARD (1923-)
Salve Regina
high solo,org [10'] ARIAD 82005
(K60)

Versuch Für Alle
audience,4 solo voices&4 solo
voices,23inst [20'] BREITKOPF-W
BG 795 f.s. (K61)

KARLINS, M. WILLIAM (1932-)
Infinity
female solo,ob d'amore,clar,vla
[10'] AM.COMP.AL. sc $6.90, pts
$7.25 (K62)

Returning The Scroll To The Ark
Bar solo,org [4'] sc AM.COMP.AL.
$1.60 (K63)

KARLOWICZ, MIECZYSLAW (1876-1909)
Six Songs, Op. 1
[Polish/Ger] high solo,pno CLASSV
1370 (K64)

KARLSEN, KJELL MØRK (1947-)
Adventssalme
see Seks Salmetoner, Op. 5, No. 2
see Seks Salmetoner Til Tekster Av
Erling Dittmann, Op.5,No.2

Cantata, Op. 4
see Nu Beder Vi Den Hellige Ånd

Då Eg Var Ein Liten Gut
see Seks Barnerim Fra
Gudbrandsdalen

Digterens Gravskrift Over Sig Selv
see Seks Sanger, Op. 3

Fem Gammeltestamentlige Bønner, Op.45
[Norw] solo voice,org NORSK (K65)

Fem Sanger Til Tekst Av Jan Magnus
Bruheim, Op. 86
[Norw] Bar solo,pno NORGE (K66)

Fem Vuggesanger
S solo,pno NOTON N-9293 (K67)

Fem Vuggeviser, Op. 42, No. 2
[Norw] solo voice,pno [11'] NORGE
(K68)

Five Norwegian Folk Tunes, Op.35,
No.2
[Norw] solo voice,rec NORSK (K69)

Gjenta
see Seks Barnerim Fra
Gudbrandsdalen

KARLSEN, KJELL MØRK (cont'd.)

Gravskrift
see Seks Sanger, Op. 3

Herre, Det Stormer I Mitt Sinn
see Seks Salmetoner Til Tekster Av
Erling Dittmann, Op.5, No.2

I En Hofpoets Navn
see Seks Sanger, Op. 3

Jesu Syv Ord På Korset
SA soli,pno NOTON N-9292 (K70)

Jordens Oro Viker *Op.31
[Swed] A solo,T rec,hpsd NORGE
(K71)
solo voice,pno,T rec/fl NOTON
N-9347 (K72)

Kierlighed Og Smørrebrød
see Seks Sanger, Op. 3

Kor Langt Vil Du Reisa
see Seks Barnerim Fra
Gudbrandsdalen

Kors Og Lilje *Op.34
[Norw] S solo,fl,pno NORGE (K73)

Kvar Skal Fuglane Fljuga
see Seks Barnerim Fra
Gudbrandsdalen

Lokk
see Seks Barnerim Fra
Gudbrandsdalen

Missa Brevis, Op.10, No.1
[Lat] Mez/A solo,fl,hpsd NORGE
(K74)
[Lat] A/Mez solo,fl,hpsd NORSK
(K75)

Nu Beder Vi Den Hellige Ånd (Cantata,
Op. 4)
[Norw/Ger] solo voice,rec,org [12']
NORSK (K76)

Nunc Dimittis
SA soli,pno/org,fl NOTON N-9308
(K77)

Nyaarsvers
see Seks Sanger, Op. 3

Olsoksalme
see Seks Salmetoner, Op. 5, No. 2
see Seks Salmetoner Til Tekster Av
Erling Dittmann, Op.5,No.2

Om Kjaerlighet, Op. 77
S/T solo,pno NORGE (K78)

Ordet
see Seks Salmetoner, Op. 5, No. 2
see Seks Salmetoner Til Tekster Av
Erling Dittmann, Op.5,No.2

Salme For Dagen, En
see Seks Salmetoner Til Tekster Av
Erling Dittmann, Op.5,No.2

Salme For Dagen-Herre, Det Stormer I
Mitt Sinn, En
see Seks Salmetoner, Op. 5, No. 2

Salve Regina, Op. 19, No. 3a
[Lat] S solo,org NORGE (K79)

Sanctus, Op. 33
Bar solo,trom,org [8'] NORSK (K80)

Seks Barnerim Fra Gudbrandsdalen
solo voice,pno NOTON N-8938 f.s.
contains: Då Eg Var Ein Liten
Gut; Gjenta; Kor Langt Vil Du
Reisa; Kvar Skal Fuglane
Fljuga; Lokk; Vesle Blå Bukken
(K81)

Seks Salmetoner, Op. 5, No. 2
low solo,org NOTON N-8909-A f.s.
contains: Adventssalme;
Olsoksalme; Ordet; Salme For
Dagen-Herre, Det Stormer I Mitt
Sinn, En; Tilgi Meg, Jesus
(K82)

Seks Salmetoner, Op. 5, No. 2
high solo,org NOTON N-8909-L (K83)

Seks Salmetoner Til Tekster Av Erling
Dittmann, Op.5, No.2
[Norw] solo voice,pno/org NOTON
f.s.
contains: Adventssalme; Herre,
Det Stormer I Mitt Sinn;
Olsoksalme; Ordet; Salme For
Dagen, En; Tilgi, Meg Jesus
(K84)

Seks Sanger, Op. 3
NOTON f.s. high solo,pno N-8908A;
low solo,pno N-8908L
contains: Digterens Gravskrift
Over Sig Selv; Gravskrift; I En
Hofpoets Navn; Kierlighed Og
Smørrebrød; Nyaarsvers;
Serenade (K85)

KARLSEN, KJELL MØRK (cont'd.)

Seks Sanger Til Tekst Av Johan Herman
  Wessel, Op. 3
  [Norw] S solo,pno NOTON   (K86)

Serenade
  see Seks Sanger, Op. 3

Ti Salmetoner, Op.5, No.1
  [Norw] solo voice,org NORGE   (K87)

Tilgi Meg, Jesus
  see Seks Salmetoner, Op. 5, No. 2
  see Seks Salmetoner Til Tekster Av
  Erling Dittmann, Op.5, No.2

To Solomotetter
  S solo,org NOTON N-9296   (K88)

Tolv Barnerim Fra Jaeren *Op.50
  [Norw] Mez solo,wind quin NORGE
                                   (K89)

Tri Julesekvenser, Op. 53
  [Norw] S solo,fl,org [10'] NORGE
                                   (K90)

Two Solo Motets For Soprano And
  Organ, Op. 19, Nos. 1&2
  [6'] NOTON N-9296   (K91)

Vesle Blå Bukken
  see Seks Barnerim Fra
  Gudbrandsdalen

KARPMAN, LAURA (1959-   )
  On My Wedding Day
    high solo,pno/chamber group MMB
    X814008 f.s., ipr from STANZAS
    FOR MUSIC   (K92)

  So We'll Go No More A-Roving
    high solo,pno/chamber group MMB
    X814009 f.s., ipr from STANZAS
    FOR MUSIC   (K93)

  Song Pictures - Five Songs Based On
    Native American Poetry
    S solo,synthesizer sc MMB X811002
    accomp tape available   (K94)

  Stanzas For Music
    S solo,fl,English horn,bass clar,
    hpsd,marimba,vln,vla,db [8']
    AM.COMP.AL. sc $17.65, pts $24.10
                                   (K95)
    high solo,pno/chamber group MMB
    X814007 f.s., ipr from STANZAS
    FOR MUSIC   (K96)
    see On My Wedding Day
    see So We'll Go No More A-Roving
    see Stanzas For Music

KASCHUBISCHES WEIHNACHTSLIED see
  Taubert, Karl Heinz

KASEKI see Ozaki, Toshiyuki

KASHA, AL (1937-   )
  Good News America, God Loves You
    (composed with Day, Ken;
    Hirschhorn, Joel)
    solo voice BROADMAN 4120-11 $1.95
                                   (K97)

KASSANDRA see Nielson, Lewis

KASTRUP LUFTHAVN see Thorarinsson,
  Leifur

KATABAMI see Nakada, Yoshinao

KATAKURI NO HANA see Nakada, Yoshinao

KATALANISCHES LIEDERBUCH *CCU
  (Rovenstrunck, Bernhard) solo voice,
  gtr PLUCKED STR T 0602 $24.75 (K98)

KATEDRAL FOR KJAERLEIK I EIT NØTTESKAL,
  EIN see Germeten, Gunnar

KATSURA see Matsudaira, Yori-Tsune

KATTEN OG MÅNEN see Sommerfeldt,
  Øistein

KATZER, GEORG (1935-   )
  Bobrowski-Lieder
    Mez solo,pic/alto fl,pno PETERS
    5667   (K99)

  Lieder Nach Leising
    med solo,fl,clar,vcl,perc,pno
    DEUTSCHER DV 9407   (K100)

KAUDER, HUGO (1888-1972)
  Fiddler Of Dooney
    solo voice,vln SEESAW f.s.   (K101)

  Fifteen Lieder
    solo voice,pno SEESAW   (K102)

  Song Of Deirdre
    solo voice,fl,harp SEESAW f.s.
                                   (K103)

  Two Songs *CC2U
    solo voice,horn,harp SEESAW f.s.
                                   (K104)

KAUFMANN, DIETER (1941-   )
  Billige Lieder
    [Ger] solo voice&speaking voice,
    chamber orch,electronic tape
    [30'] sc REIMERS 101139   (K105)

  Meine Welt - Ich Sehe Keine Andere
    [Ger] Bar solo,band,electronic tape
    [8'] sc REIMERS 101101   (K106)

KAUN, HUGO (1863-1932)
  Sechs Lieder, Op. 46
    [Ger] high solo RECITAL 362   (K107)

KAVASCH, DEBORAH
  Beauty And The Beast, The
    [Eng] S solo,db,vcl [4'] sc REIMERS
    101122   (K108)

  Craw And The Pitcher, The
    [Eng] S solo REIMERS 101121   (K109)

  Tortoise And The Hare, The
    [Eng] S solo,bass clar [4'] REIMERS
    101120   (K110)

KAWARAJI TO see Matsudaira, Yori-Tsune

KAWASAKI, ETSUO (1959-   )
  Five Songs: "Nohara Uta"
    S solo,pno [18'] JAPAN   (K111)

KAZDODENNI MALE PISNE see Podéšt,
  Ludvík

KAZE GA OMOTE DE YONDEIRU see Hagi,
  Kyoko

KAZE NO NAKE see Igarashi, Tadashi

KAZEMATTEN, DE see Ruiter, Wim de

KDE DOMOV MUJ? see Skroup, František

KDYZ ZASLA CESTA see Kvech, Otomar

K'E STILL RIPPLES TO ITS BANKS, THE see
  Avshalomov, Aaron

KEDUSHA see Gottlieb, Jack S.

KEEP GOING, BY GEORGE see Tanenbaum,
  Elias

KEF, KEES (1894-1961)
  Chanson De Deux Saints, La
    see Quatre Chansons

  Chemin, Le
    see Quatre Chansons

  Cheveaux De Bois
    see Quatre Chansons

  Quatre Chansons
    med solo,pno DONEMUS f.s.
      contains: Chanson De Deux Saints,
      La; Chemin, Le; Cheveaux De
      Bois; Spleen Pour Rire (K112)

  Spleen Pour Rire
    see Quatre Chansons

KEHR ICH HEIM see Cornelius, Peter

KEIZER, HENK (1948-   )
  Luid Dan De Tijd *CC11L
    A solo,pno DONEMUS f.s.   (K113)

  Michel Le Roux
    see Pour Toi Mon Amour

  Pour Toi Mon Amour
    med solo,alto fl,clar,pno,vla
    DONEMUS f.s. [10']
      contains: Michel Le Roux; Sonnet;
      Voeu D'une Dame A Venus (K114)

  Sonnet
    see Pour Toi Mon Amour

  Voeu D'une Dame A Venus
    see Pour Toi Mon Amour

KELLER, GINETTE (1925-   )
  Graphiques
    S solo,fl,clar,horn,perc,pno,vln,
    vla,vcl [14'] BILLAUDOT   (K115)

KELLY, ROBERT T. (1916-   )
  Patterns *cant
    S solo,1.1.1.1. 1.1.1.0. perc,
    strings [15'] sc AM.COMP.AL. sc
    $16.75, pno red $12.20   (K116)

  Rural Songs *Op.58, CCU
    S solo,2.2.2.2. 2.0.0.0. timp,perc,
    strings AM.COMP.AL. sc $25.85,
    pno red $11.40   (K117)

KENBEA, OP. 241 see Kimura, Masanobu

KENNAWAY, LAMONT
  Downstream
    HINRICHSEN 418   (K118)

KENNEDY-FRASER, MARJORY (1857-1930)
  Land Of Heart's Desire
    [Eng] high solo,pno CLASSV 1827
                                   (K119)

KENNST DU DAS LAND see Meneely-Kyder,
  Sarah

KENTISH, OLIVER (1954-   )
  "Fagra Verold"
    solo voice,pno [8'0"] ICELAND
    069-010   (K120)

  Homesickness
    Bar solo,pno [3'0"] ICELAND 069-009
                                   (K121)

KERN, JEROME (1885-1945)
  Man And His Music In Story, Picture
    And Song, The
    solo voice BELWIN CL21017 $7.95
                                   (K122)

KERNIS, AARON JAY (1960-   )
  American Daydreams
    Mez solo,fl,clar,trp,horn,perc,
    harp,strings [18'] sc AM.COMP.AL.
    $31.05   (K123)

  Death Fugue
    B solo,perc,db [11'] sc AM.COMP.AL.
    $12.25   (K124)

  Dream Of The Morning Sky
    S solo,3(pic).3(English
    horn).3(bass clar).3(contrabsn).
    4.3.2(bass trom).1. 4-5perc,pno/
    cel,harp,strings [24'] sc
    AM.COMP.AL. $37.85   (K125)

  Six Fragments Of Gertrude Stein
    S solo,fl/alto fl/pic [6'] sc
    AM.COMP.AL. $4.25   (K126)

KERRY DANCE, THE see Molloy, James
  Lyman

KERSTENS, HENK (1947-   )
  Stille Weg, De
    MezB soli,vln,pno [8'] DONEMUS f.s.
                                   (K127)

KERSTENS, HUUB (1947-   )
  Crudele Acerba
    SMezATB soli [4'] DONEMUS f.s.
                                   (K128)

KERSTERS, WILLEM (1929-   )
  Dans Der Kristallen, De *Op.80
    med solo CBDM   (K129)

KERSTLIEDJE see Broekman, Hans see
  King, Harold C.

KETIL see Tveitt, Geirr

KETTING, PIET (1905-1984)
  Dertele Sater, De
    see Minnedeuntjes

  Koridon
    see Minnedeuntjes

  Little Love-God, The
    see Three Sonnets

  Minnedeuntjes
    med solo,pno DONEMUS f.s. [5']
      contains: Dertele Sater, De;
      Koridon   (K130)

  Music To Hear
    see Three Sonnets

  Since I Left You
    see Three Sonnets

  Three Sonnets
    med solo/low solo,pno DONEMUS f.s.
      contains: Little Love-God, The;
      Music To Hear; Since I Left You
                                   (K131)

KEULEN, GEERT VAN (1943-   )
  Nightpiece
    see Trieste

  On The Beach At Fontana
    see Trieste

  Trieste
    S solo,fl,clar,vibra,mand,gtr,harp,
    vln,db DONEMUS f.s. [15']
      contains: Nightpiece; On The
      Beach At Fontana; Watching The
      Needleboats At San Sabba (K132)

  Watching The Needleboats At San Sabba
    see Trieste

KEUSSLER, GERHARD VON (1874-1949)
  Alte Herd, Der
    PETERS 3804B   (K133)

  An Die Einsamkeit
    PETERS 3804D   (K134)

KEUSSLER, GERHARD VON (cont'd.)

Aus Dem Tagebuch
PETERS 3802A   (K135)

Gefährtin
PETERS 3803A   (K136)

Grosse Bündnis
PETERS 3803B   (K137)

Lied Von Der Liebe
PETERS 3804A   (K138)

Nachtklänge
PETERS 3804C   (K139)

Rhapsodie
PETERS 3801B   (K140)

Von Der Sühne
PETERS 3802B   (K141)

KEVÄTTEILTÄ see Nummi, Seppo

KEYS OF CANTERBURY see Anonymous

KHOVANSHCHINA: SHAKLOVITY see
Mussorgsky, Modest Petrovich

KI NO KANE see Miki, Minoru

KI NO YONI see Shibuya, Takucho

KIELLAND, OLAV (1901-   )
Barnet
[Norw] solo voice,pno NORGE (K142)

Dagen Vaknar
see Mot Blåsnøhøgdom

Ferdamann
see Seks Sivle-Songar

Fjell-Lengt
see Mot Blåsnøhøgdom

Fyrste Songen, Den
see Seks Sivle-Songar

Gagnløysa
[Norw] solo voice,pno NORGE (K143)

Haust
see Seks Sivle-Songar

Heim
see Seks Sivle-Songar

I Tveråsal-Hytta
see Mot Blåsnøhøgdom

Litet Stev Til Mor, Eit
[Norw] solo voice,pno NORGE (K144)

Mot Blåsnøhøgdom *Op.14
high solo,2(pic).2.2.2. 4.2.0.0.
timp,harp,strings NORGE f.s.
contains: Dagen Vaknar; Fjell-
Lengt; I Tveråsal-Hytta (K145)

Salme
[Norw] solo voice,pno NORGE (K146)

Sanger Av Eichendorff
[Ger] Bar solo,pno NORGE   (K147)

Sanger Av Obstfelder
[Norw] solo voice,pno [10'30"]
NORGE   (K148)

Seks Sivle-Songar *Op.17
solo voice,2.2.3(bass clar).2.
4.2.0.0. timp,perc,harp,strings
NORGE f.s.
contains: Ferdamann; Fyrste
Songen, Den; Haust; Heim; Te
Kjaerasten Min; Til Telemork
                             (K149)
Stundom Ingen Um Elsken Veit
[Norw] solo voice,pno [3'] NORGE
                             (K150)

Te Kjaerasten Min
see Seks Sivle-Songar

Til Telemork
see Seks Sivle-Songar

To Salmer, Op. 6
[Norw] solo voice,pno NORGE (K151)
[Norw] solo voice,org NORGE (K152)

Tri Visur I Vå Og Von, Op. 29
[Norw] solo voice,pno NORGE (K153)

Vaaren, Op. 30
[Norw] solo voice,pno [5'10"] NORGE
                             (K154)
KIENZL, WILHELM (1857-1941)
Evangelimann, Der: Selig Sind, Die
Verfolgung Leiden
[Ger] T solo,pno CLASSV 1828 (K155)

Liebesfrühling, Op. 11 *song cycle
[Ger] high solo (texts by Friedrich
Rückert) RECITAL 271   (K156)

KIERAN
How Do I Love Thee
low solo WILLIS 10870 $.95 (K157)

KIERLIGHED OG SMØRREBRØD see Karlsen,
Kjell Mørk

KIEV AND OTHER SONGS see Borodievych,
Roman

KIJIMA, KIYOHIKO (1917-   )
Collection Of Songs, A *CCU
solo voice ONGAKU 624550 f.s.
                             (K158)
KIKUCHI, MASAHARU (1938-   )
Yama No Kareha
solo voice,pno [5'] JAPAN   (K159)

KILLENGREEN, CHRISTIAN (1954-   )
Fire Sanger Til Tekst Av Gunvor Hofmo
[Norw] solo voice,pno NORGE (K160)

Retrospekt
[Swed] A solo,ob,vcl,pno [7'] NORGE
                             (K161)
Spring Night
see Vårkveld

Vårkveld
"Spring Night" [Norw] solo voice,
pno NORGE f.s.   (K162)

KILLINGDANS see Bakke, Ruth see Grieg,
Edvard Hagerup

KILPINEN, YRJÖ (1892-1959)
Twenty-Seven Songs, Vol. 1 *Op.48,
CCU
med solo,pno sc PEER 61533-213
$4.00   (K163)

Twenty-Seven Songs, Vol. 2 *Op.49,
CCU
med solo,pno sc PEER 61534-213
$4.00   (K164)

Twenty-Seven Songs, Vol. 3 *Op.50,
CCU
med solo,pno sc PEER 61535-213
$4.00   (K165)

Twenty-Seven Songs, Vol. 4 *Op.51a,
CCU
med solo,pno sc PEER 61536-213
$4.00   (K166)

Twenty-Seven Songs, Vol. 5 *Op.51b,
CCU
med solo,pno sc PEER 61537-213
$4.00   (K167)

KIM, EARL (1920-   )
Three Poems In French
S solo,string quar PRESSER pts
141-40034P, sc 141-40034S (K168)

KIMURA, MASANOBU (1941-   )
Kenbea, Op. 241
T solo,pno [5'] JAPAN   (K169)

KINA-REIS see Tveitt, Geirr

KIND see Mengelberg, Karel

KIND, DAS see Orthel, Leon

KIND EN KRAAI see Schat, Peter

KIND NOCH KEGEL see Schat, Peter, Kind
En Kraai

KINDERLIEDER see Reimann, Aribert

KINDERLIEDER, 43 see Hoffmann Von
Fallersleben, Heinrich August

KINDERLIEDERFOLGE see Simon

KINDERMÄRCHEN, EIN see Hess, W.

KINDERTOTENLIEDER see Mahler, Gustav
see Mahler, Gustav

KINDESGEBET see Jordan, Sverre

KINDNESS TO HORSES see Tal, Marjo

KINDSCHER, LUDWIG (1836-1903)
Lieder Mönch
KAHNT 4344   (K170)

KINERET see Leniado-Chira, Joseph

KING, HAROLD C. (1895-1984)
Al In De Plantage
see Lof Van Nederland, Vol. 4

Cerfs En Rut, Les
see Trois Chansons D'Amour Et Une
Epigramme

Choix Terrestre
see Vergers, Vol. 1

KING, HAROLD C. (cont'd.)

Da Pater
see Tres Orationes (Three Prayers)

Dialog, Ein
see Dialogue, A

Dialogue, A
"Dialog, Ein" Bar solo,bsn/vcl,pno
[9'] DONEMUS   (K171)

Doodenmarsch
see Lof Van Nederland, Vol. 2

Enkhuizen
see Lof Van Nederland, Vol. 3

Herinnering Aan Holland
see Lof Van Nederland, Vol. 3

Holland
see Lof Van Nederland, Vol. 2

In Dormiturio
see Tres Orationes (Three Prayers)

Kerstliedje
see Lof Van Nederland, Vol. 4

Lof Van Nederland, Vol. 1
med solo,pno DONEMUS f.s. [11']
contains: Psalm No. 69; Psalm No.
121; Psalm No. 137   (K172)

Lof Van Nederland, Vol. 2
med solo,pno DONEMUS f.s. [10']
contains: Doodenmarsch; Holland;
Luctor Et Emergo   (K173)

Lof Van Nederland, Vol. 3
med solo,pno DONEMUS f.s. [10']
contains: Enkhuizen; Herinnering
Aan Holland; Vecht, De   (K174)

Lof Van Nederland, Vol. 4
med solo,pno DONEMUS f.s. [11']
contains: Al In De Plantage;
Kerstliedje; Matrozenlied (K175)

Lof Van Nederland, Vol. 5
med solo,pno DONEMUS f.s. [10']
contains: Najaarslied;
Schutsluis, De; Silhouetten
                          (K176)
Luctor Et Emergo
see Lof Van Nederland, Vol. 2

Matrozenlied
see Lof Van Nederland, Vol. 4

Mes Vers Fuiraient
see Trois Chansons D'Amour Et Une
Epigramme

Mignonne
see Trois Chansons D'Amour Et Une
Epigramme

Najaarslied
see Lof Van Nederland, Vol. 5

Oratio D. Alcuini In Nocte
see Tres Orationes (Three Prayers)

Paume (Vergers VII)
see Vergers, Vol. 1

Psalm No. 69
see Lof Van Nederland, Vol. 1

Psalm No. 121
see Lof Van Nederland, Vol. 1

Psalm No. 137
see Lof Van Nederland, Vol. 1

Schutsluis, De
see Lof Van Nederland, Vol. 5

Silhouetten
see Lof Van Nederland, Vol. 5

Tres Orationes (Three Prayers)
Bar solo,T rec,lute DONEMUS f.s.
[11']
contains: Da Pater; In
Dormiturio; Oratio D. Alcuini
In Nocte   (K177)

Trois Chansons D'Amour Et Une
Epigramme
med solo,S rec/T rec DONEMUS f.s.
[11']
contains: Cerfs En Rut, Les; Mes
Vers Fuiraient; Mignonne; Viens
                          (K178)
Vecht, De
see Lof Van Nederland, Vol. 3

Vergers VII
see Vergers, Vol. 1

Vergers VIII
see Vergers, Vol. 1

KING, HAROLD C. (cont'd.)

Vergers IX
  see Vergers, Vol. 1

Vergers XII
  see Vergers, Vol. 3

Vergers XVI
  see Vergers, Vol. 3

Vergers XVIII
  see Vergers, Vol. 2

Vergers XXIV
  see Vergers, Vol. 3

Vergers XXVII
  see Vergers, Vol. 4

Vergers XXVIII (LA DEESSE)
  see Vergers, Vol. 2

Vergers XXXII
  see Vergers, Vol. 2

Vergers XXXIII
  see Vergers, Vol. 4

Vergers XXXVI
  see Vergers, Vol. 4

Vergers XL
  see Vergers, Vol. 2

Vergers LVI (La Dormeuse)
  see Vergers, Vol. 4

Vergers, Vol. 1
  S solo,pno DONEMUS f.s. [8']
  contains: Choix Terrestre; Paume
  (Vergers VII); Vergers VII;
  Vergers VIII; Vergers IX (K179)

Vergers, Vol. 2
  S solo,pno DONEMUS f.s. [8']
  contains: Vergers XVIII; Vergers
  XXVIII (LA DEESSE); Vergers
  XXXII; Vergers XL   (K180)

Vergers, Vol. 3
  S solo,pno DONEMUS f.s. [5']
  contains: Vergers XII; Vergers
  XVI; Vergers XXIV   (K181)

Vergers, Vol. 4
  S solo,pno DONEMUS f.s. [7']
  contains: Vergers XXVII; Vergers
  XXXIII; Vergers XXXVI; Vergers
  LVI (La Dormeuse) (K182)

Viens
  see Trois Chansons D'Amour Et Une
  Epigramme

KING, REGINALD (1904-)
  Plantation Mood
  solo voice,pno BARDIC BE0308 (K183)

KING BILLY'S SONG see James, William G.

KING SVERRE see Sveinbjörnsson,
  Sveinbjörn

KINGDOM BY THE SEA, A see Somervell,
  Arthur

KINGSLEY, GERSHON GARY (1925-)
  It Burns
  see Three Songs From The Ghetto

Last Butterfly, The
  see Three Songs From The Ghetto

Lullaby At Ponar
  see Three Songs From The Ghetto

Three Songs From The Ghetto
  solo voice,kbd TRANSCON. 991356
  f.s.
  contains: It Burns; Last
  Butterfly, The; Lullaby At
  Ponar   (K184)

KINT IS ONS GHEBOORN, EEN see Visser,
  Peter

KIRCHNER, LEON (1919-)
  Twilight Stood, The
  AMP AMP7939   (K185)

KIRK
  Old Man Of The Isles
  solo voice,pno SOUTHERN V076 (K186)

KIRK, WHEATLEY
  My Home! My Home Is There
  SCIEN 816   (K187)

KIRKWOOD, ANTOINETTE
  Akond Of Swat, The
  ST soli,pno BARDIC BE0275 (K188)
  ST soli,gtr BARDIC BE0275A (K189)

KIRKWOOD, ANTOINETTE (cont'd.)

Cummerbund, The
  ST soli,pno BARDIC BE0276 (K190)
  ST soli,gtr BARDIC BE0276A (K191)

Fly, The
  med solo,pno BARDIC BE0270 (K192)

High Seriousness
  solo voice,pno BARDIC BE0274 (K193)

Krönung
  high solo,pno BARDIC BE0281 (K194)
  high solo,strings BARDIC BE0281A
    (K195)

Must She Go?
  solo voice,pno BARDIC BE0271 (K196)

Oyster Catcher's Song, The
  high solo,pno BARDIC BE0273 (K197)

Remembrance
  med solo,pno BARDIC BE0279 (K198)

Schiffbrüchige, Der
  high solo,pno BARDIC BE0280 (K199)
  high solo,strings BARDIC BE0280A
    (K200)

Snowflake
  med solo,pno BARDIC BE0277 (K201)

Song Of The Fisherman Of Cacru
  med solo,pno BARDIC BE0272 (K202)

Visit To The Killing Fields
  med solo,pno BARDIC BE0278 (K203)

KISA MIN see Sveinsson, Atli Heimir

KISSED BY SUN see Stefansson, Finnur
  Torfi

KITCHY KITCHEN see Anderson, Beth

KITTELSEN, GUTTORM (1951-)
  Credo
  [Lat] solo voice,sax,trp,trom,kbd,
  elec gtr,elec bass,perc [25']
  NORGE   (K204)

KITTY MY LOVE, WILL YOU MARRY ME? see
  Hughes, Herbert

KITZKE, JEROME P.
  Haecceity-Hesse
  S solo,fl,clar,vln,vcl,pno,vibra,
  3perc [18'] sc AM.COMP.AL. $49.40
    (K205)

171st Chorus
  med solo,db sc AM.COMP.AL. $6.55
    (K206)

Two Dreams
  Bar solo,bass clar [5'30"]
  AM.COMP.AL.   (K207)

KJAERINGI MED KJELKEN see Johnsen,
  Hallvard

KJAERLIGHEDSVISE, EN see Volle, Bjarne

KJAERLIGHETSSANG: HØRER DU MITT see
  Jordan, Sverre

KJELDAAS, ARNLJOT (1916-)
  Å Brør
  [Norw] S/T solo,2vln,vla,vcl [2']
  NORGE   (K208)

Å, Gud Velsigne
  see Tre Hovden-Sanger

Arbeid
  see Tre Hovden-Sanger

Ekte - Uekte
  [Norw] solo voice,pno [1'] NORGE
    (K209)

Fem Sanger, Op. 12
  [Norw] solo voice,pno NORGE (K210)

Fredsbønn
  [Norw] solo voice,pno [3'] NORGE
    (K211)

Jonsok
  [Norw] solo voice,pno [2'] NORGE
    (K212)

Kveldsvers
  see Tre Hovden-Sanger

Op, Hvis Herrens Egen Røst
  [Norw] solo voice,pno [1'] NORGE
    (K213)

Pers Vuggevise
  [Norw] solo voice,pno [2'] NORGE
    (K214)

Syv Sanger, Op. 3
  solo voice,pno NORGE   (K215)

Syv Sanger, Op. 18
  [Norw] S/T solo,pno NORGE (K216)

Syv Wildenvey Sanger, Op. 24
  [Norw] solo voice,pno NORGE (K217)

KJELDAAS, ARNLJOT (cont'd.)

Tårene
  [Norw] solo voice,pno [2'] NORGE
    (K218)

To Sanger, Op. 9
  [Norw] solo voice,pno MUSIKK (K219)

To Sanger, Op. 30
  [Norw] solo voice,pno NORGE (K220)

Tre Hovden-Sanger
  [Norw] solo voice,pno LYCHE f.s.
  contains: Å, Gud Velsigne;
  Arbeid; Kveldsvers   (K221)

Tre Sanger, Op. 21
  [Norw] B solo,pno NORGE (K222)

Tre Sanger, Op. 29
  [Norw] solo voice,pno NORGE (K223)

KJELL see Sommerfeldt, Öistein

KJELLE, KJELLE GJETA see Albertsen, Per
  Hjort

KJELLSBY, ERLING (1901-1976)
  Einsam Mann
  "Lonesome Man" solo voice,2.2.2.2.
  4.1.3.0. timp,perc,harp,strings
  [3'] NORGE f.s.   (K224)

Lonesome Man
  see Einsam Mann

KJERULF, HALFDAN (1815-1868)
  Aftenstemning *Op.11,No.4
  (Brevik, Tor) "Evening Atmosphere"
  solo voice,strings NORGE f.s.
    (K225)

At The Mountain
  see På Fjellet

Calling Tunes
  see Lokkende Toner

Evening Atmosphere
  see Aftenstemning

Hvile I Skoven *Op.5,No.3
  (Olsen, C.G.Sparre) "Rest In The
  Forest" S solo,1.1.2.1. 0.0.0.0.
  strings NORSK f.s.   (K226)

Lokkende Toner *Op.3,No.6
  (Olsen, C.G.Sparre) "Calling Tunes"
  S solo,fl,ob,clar,strings NORSK
  f.s.   (K227)

På Fjellet *Op.6,No.4
  (Olsen, C.G.Sparre) "At The
  Mountain" solo voice,1.1.1.0.
  0.1.0.0. pno,strings NORSK f.s.
    (K228)

Princess, The
  see Prinsessen: Aftenstemning

Prinsessen: Aftenstemning *Op.14,
  No.1
  (Olsen, C.G.Sparre) "Princess, The"
  S solo,1.1.2.0. 0.0.0.0. strings
  NORSK f.s.   (K229)

Rest In The Forest
  see Hvile I Skoven

Signpost Sings, The
  see Veiviseren Synger

Veiviseren Synger *Op.6,No.1
  (Olsen, C.G.Sparre) "Signpost
  Sings, The" solo voice,1.1.2.0.
  0.0.0.0. strings NORSK f.s.
    (K230)

Venevil *Op.6,No.6
  (Brevik, Tor) solo voice,2clar,
  2horn,strings NORGE f.s. (K231)

KLAGE DER GARDE see Beekhuis, Hanna

KLAGE DER SCHAEFERIN see Fischer, A.

KLAGE DES HIOB, DIE see Kühnl, Claus

KLALLAM SONG see Rovics, Howard

KLANG DER STILE, OP.91 see Hess, W.

KLÄNGE AUS MÄHREN, OP. 32 see Dvorák,
  Antonín

KLASSIKER DES DEUTSCHEN LIEDES, BAND 1
  med solo,pno PETERS 4578A (K232)
  low solo,pno PETERS 4575A (K233)

KLASSIKER DES DEUTSCHEN LIEDES, BAND 2
  med solo,pno PETERS 4578B (K234)
  low solo,pno PETERS 4575B (K235)

KLEIBERG, STÅLE (1958-)
  Lyssmeden
  S solo,ob,pno NORGE f.s. (K236)

KLEIBERG, STÅLE (cont'd.)

Three Shakespeare Sonnets
[Eng] solo voice,pno NORGE (K237)

Two Poems By Montale
[It] S solo,fl,pno NORGE (K238)

KLEIDOCYMBALON I see Hatzis, Christos

KLEIN, LEONARD
Man With The Blue Guitar, The
solo voice,vln,vcl,pno [13'] APNM
sc $5.75, set $11.75 (K239)

KLEIN, RICHARD RUDOLF (1921-)
Männlein In Der Gans, Das
(Tappert, Johannes) solo voice,gtr
(texts by Friedrich Rückert) VOGT
VF 409 (K240)

Zwölf Songs Nach Alten Jiddischen
Weisen
Bar solo,pno RIES 60025 (K241)

KLEIN AIR see Badings, Henk

KLEIN DRIELUIK, OP. 77 see Orthel, Leon

KLEINE BLUMEN, KLEINE BLÄTTER see
Baudin, Ernestine Von

KLEINE GESCHICHTE see Siebert, F.

KLEINE HANS, DER see Curschmann, Karl
Frdr

KLEINE MENSEN see Dispa, Robert

KLEINE REISEPOETIK see Ehlen, Margriet

KLEINE REISPOETICA see Ehlen, Margriet

KLEINE VIECHEREIEN see Hollfelder,
Waldram

KLEINES ABENDLIED see Louis Ferdinand,
Prince Of Prussia

KLEINES QUARTETT (QUINTETT) see
Bodensohn, Ernst Friedrich Wilhelm

KLEPPE, JOOST
Avond Winter Straten
see Winter

Landschap
see Winter

Vorst
see Winter

Winter
S solo,clar,pno,vln,vcl DONEMUS
f.s. [12']
contains: Avond Winter Straten;
Landschap; Vorst; Winter (K242)

Winter
see Winter

KLERK, ALBERT DE (1917-)
Priere Pour La Paix
B solo,pno/org [5'] DONEMUS (K243)
Bar solo,pno/org [5'] DONEMUS
(K244)

Twee Psalmen (121 En 133)
high solo,pno/org [8'] DONEMUS
(K245)

Vocalise
high solo,pno [4'] DONEMUS (K246)

KLETKE, H.
In Die Ferne
solo voice,pno SCIEN 820 (K247)

KLINGE, KLINGE, MEIN PANDERO see
Rubinstein, Anton

KLOCKKLANG: JULSÅNG see Åberg, Thomas

KLOPSTOCK-ODE see Kunad, Rainer

KLUSÁK, JAN (1934-)
Ctyri Mala Hlasova Cviceni
solo voice,winds PANTON 1051 (K248)

KLUSAK, VLADIMIR (1916-)
Slovacke Pisne
solo voice,pno PANTON 914 (K249)

KNABE, DER see Orthel, Leon see Visser,
Peter

KNIFE, THE see Selmer, Johan Peter,
Tollekniven

KNIGHT, JOSEPH PHILLIP
Go Forget Me
SCIEN 826 (K250)

KNIGHT, THE see Balakirev, Mily
Alexeyevich

KNOTS see Anderson, Beth

KNOWEST THOU see Thomas, Ambroise

KNUSSEN, OLIVER (1952-)
Four Late Poems & An Epigram
solo voice FABER 51096 5 (K251)

Ocean De Terre
sc FABER 50583 X (K252)

Winnie The Pooh
FABER 50885 5 (K253)

KNUTSEN, TORBJORN (1904-1987)
Ålesund, Our Own Town
see Ålesund Vår Egen By

Ålesund Vår Egen By
"Ålesund, Our Own Town" solo voice,
1.1.1.1. 0.1.1.0. pno,strings
NORGE f.s. (K254)
"Ålesund, Our Own Town" solo voice,
2.2.2.3. 4.3.3.1. timp,strings
NORGE f.s. (K255)

Clean As Gold Is Your Heart
see Gullrent Er Ditt Hjerte

Cradle Song
see Vuggesang

Elegi
LYCHE 30 (K256)
[Norw] solo voice,pno LYCHE (K257)

Gleder
LYCHE 36 (K258)
[Norw] solo voice,pno LYCHE (K259)

Gullrent Er Ditt Hjerte
"Clean As Gold Is Your Heart" solo
voice,2.1.1.1. 2.2.1.0. timp,
harp,strings NORGE f.s. (K260)

Out From The Wide World
see Ute Fra Verden Den Vide

Sang I Skumring
"Song In The Twilight" solo voice,
2.1.1.2. 2.2.1.0. timp,pno/harp,
strings NORGE f.s. (K261)

Song In The Twilight
see Sang I Skumring

Togni
LYCHE 37 (K262)

Ute Fra Verden Den Vide
LYCHE 103 (K263)
"Out From The Wide World" solo
voice,strings [3'] NORGE f.s.
(K264)

Vuggesang
"Cradle Song" solo voice,2.1.1.1.
2.2.1.0. timp,harp/pno,cel,
strings NORGE f.s. (K265)

KNUTSON, GEIR
Lille Norge
solo voice,pno NORSK NMO 10251
(K266)

KOALA see Sourisse, Brigitte

KOBATA, IKUO (1951-)
Jyo-Shi
Bar/Mez solo,pno [7'] JAPAN (K267)

KOBAYASHI, ARATA (1929-)
Duet "Raise The Glass", A
SBar soli,pno [5'] ONGAKU (K268)

Motto (With One's Whole Heart) And
Shiguseigan
S solo,fl,2vln,vla,vcl,gtr,hpsd
[3'] JAPAN (K269)

Song "The Hope", A
S/T solo,pno [4'] ONGAKU (K270)

KOBO see Fujiwara, Michiyo

KOCH
Terzette
female solo&female solo&female solo
KAHNT 8276 (K271)

Weihnachtslied
KAHNT 5987 (K272)

KOCH, ERLAND VON (1910-)
Besinna Och Anamma
see I Tallkottsriket

Canto Nordico. Vers II
Mez solo,pno GEHRMANS (K273)

Clownen
see I Tallkottsriket

Grenen Gungar
see I Tallkottsriket

KOCH, ERLAND VON (cont'd.)

I Tallkottsriket
solo voice,pno sc STIM PA-3275-10
f.s.
contains: Besinna Och Anamma;
Clownen; Grenen Gungar; I
Tallkottsriket; Lyckan (K274)

I Tallkottsriket
see I Tallkottsriket

Lyckan
see I Tallkottsriket

Två Malungsmelodier
(Lindberg, Nils) solo voice,org
GEHRMANS (K275)

KOCH, FREDERICK (1924-)
Five Songs *CC5U
med solo,prepared pno SEESAW f.s.
(K276)

Great Spaces
S solo,pno SEESAW f.s. (K277)

Monadnock Cadenzas
solo voice,instrumental ensemble
SEESAW f.s. (K278)

String Quartet 2
S solo,string quar SEESAW f.s.
(K279)

Trio Of Praise
med solo,vln,pno SEESAW f.s. (K280)

KOCH, FRIEDRICH E. (1862-1927)
Triptych
Mez solo,fl,clar,pno SEESAW (K281)

KOCHAN
Deutsche Volkslieder (1. Und 2.
Folge)
PETERS 4906A (K282)

Volkslieder, Op. 11b
PETERS 4906 (K283)

KODOKU see Hayakawa, Kuzuko

KOECHLIN, CHARLES (1867-1950)
Moisson Prochaine
med solo,pno CLASSV 1695 (K284)

Neuf Rondels, Series 3, Part 1
[Fr] high solo (rondels 1-5)
RECITAL 142 (K285)

Neuf Rondels, Series 3, Part 2
[Fr] solo voice, opt wom cor
(rondels 6-9) RECITAL 143 (K286)

Quatorze Plusieurs Melodies, Vol. 1:
Nos. 1-7
[Fr] RECITAL 138 (K287)

Quatorze Plusieurs Melodies, Vol. 2:
Nos. 8-14
[Fr] RECITAL 139 (K288)

Rondels (1er Série)
high solo,pno CLASSV 1453 (K289)

Rondels (2e Série)
high solo,pno CLASSV 1452 (K290)

Sept Rondels, Series 2
[Fr] high solo (6 rondels for 1
voice; 1 rondel for T+D or T+Z)
RECITAL 141 (K291)

Sheherazade, Teil 1 *Op.56
T solo,pno SCHOTTS ME 8593 (K292)

Sheherazade, Teil 2 *Op.84
Bar solo,pno SCHOTTS ME 8594 (K293)

Thé, Le
[Fr] low solo,pno CLASSV 1254
(K294)

KOEKOEK see Weegenhuise, Johan

KOENIG, FRANZ
Morgenstern-Lieder
solo voice,pno SEESAW (K295)

Schlichte Lieder
solo voice,pno SEESAW (K296)

KOERING, RENE (1940-)
Lecture Trois De Mahler
S&speaking voice,string orch
BILLAUDOT (K297)

Mahler: A. De Mahler
SA soli,1.1.1.0. 2.1.1.0. 2perc,
pno,strings [15'] sc,pts,pno red
BILLAUDOT perf mat rent (K298)

Mahler: Aria De R. De Mahler
S solo,vcl,string quar BILLAUDOT
(K299)

Mahler: R. De Mahler
S solo,3.3.3.3. 6.4.3.1. 4perc,
timp,2harp,2pno,strings,vcl solo
[20'] BILLAUDOT (K300)

KOERU KAGE NI see Miyoshi, Akira

KOETSIER, JAN (1911-   )
   Architektur
     see Vor Bildern Lyonel Feiningers,
     12 Lieder, Heft 2

   Aux Marches Du Palais
     see Trois Chansons, Aus "Strategen
     Der Liebe"

   Black Is The Color
     see Trois Chansons, Aus "Strategen
     Der Liebe"

   Blick Auf Den East River
     see Vor Bildern Lyonel Feiningers,
     12 Lieder, Heft 2

   Dämmerung
     see Vor Bildern Lyonel Feiningers,
     12 Lieder, Heft 2

   Drie Liederen
     high solo,pno DONEMUS f.s. [8']
      contains: Mijn Lieveken Open Je
      Deurken En Lach; Wat Beweegt
      Daar Snel; Zangrig Blaast Een
      Knaap De Fluit   (K301)

   Dünen Lichstrahl II
     see Vor Bildern Lyonel Feiningers,
     12 Lieder, Heft 1

   Es War Im Herbst
     see Trois Chansons, Aus "Strategen
     Der Liebe"

   Hohe Ufer, Das
     see Vor Bildern Lyonel Feiningers,
     12 Lieder, Heft 2

   Inseln
     see Vor Bildern Lyonel Feiningers,
     12 Lieder, Heft 1

   Lehnstedt
     see Vor Bildern Lyonel Feiningers,
     12 Lieder, Heft 1

   Mijn Lieveken Open Je Deurken En Lach
     see Drie Liederen

   Mondgespinst
     see Vor Bildern Lyonel Feiningers,
     12 Lieder, Heft 2

   Rauchschrift
     see Vor Bildern Lyonel Feiningers,
     12 Lieder, Heft 2

   Regamündung
     see Vor Bildern Lyonel Feiningers,
     12 Lieder, Heft 1

   Regentag Am Strand
     see Vor Bildern Lyonel Feiningers,
     12 Lieder, Heft 1

   Strasse In Treptow An Der Rega
     see Vor Bildern Lyonel Feiningers,
     12 Lieder, Heft 1

   Three Songs Of Ellen, Op. 106
     Mez solo,org [15'] DONEMUS   (K302)

   Trois Chansons, Aus "Strategen Der
     Liebe"
     T solo,pno DONEMUS f.s. [4']
      contains: Aux Marches Du Palais;
      Black Is The Color; Es War Im
      Herbst   (K303)

   Vor Bildern Lyonel Feiningers, 12
     Lieder, Heft 1
     med solo,pno DONEMUS f.s.
      contains: Dünen Lichstrahl II;
      Inseln; Lehnstedt; Regamündung;
      Regentag Am Strand; Strasse In
      Treptow An Der Rega   (K304)

   Vor Bildern Lyonel Feiningers, 12
     Lieder, Heft 2
     med solo,pno DONEMUS f.s.
      contains: Architektur; Blick Auf
      Den East River; Dämmerung; Hohe
      Ufer, Das; Mondgespinst;
      Rauchschrift   (K305)

   Wat Beweegt Daar Snel
     see Drie Liederen

   Zangrig Blaast Een Knaap De Fluit
     see Drie Liederen

KOFFLER, JOSEF (1896-1943)
   Cantata
     see Milosc

   Milosc (Cantata)
     [Polish/Ger] solo voices,clar,vla,
     vcl POLSKIE   (K306)

KOFRON, PETR (1955-   )
   Gesang Einer Gefangenen Amsel
     S solo,3.3.3.3. 4.2.2.1. timp,
     strings [5'] CESKY HUD.   (K307)

KOGARASHI NO see Matsudaira, Yori-Tsune

KOHOUTEK, CTIRAD (1929-   )
   Zrozeni Cloveka
     ST soli,2.2.2.2. 2.2.0.0. timp,
     perc,pno,strings [18'] CESKY HUD.
                           (K308)

KOHS, ELLIS BONOFF (1916-   )
   Calumny
     Bar solo,fl,horn,vcl,2timp [4'] sc
     AM.COMP.AL. $6.90   (K309)

KOKOROTTE FUSHIGI see Yuyama, Akira

KOKUU see Fujiwara, Michiyo

KOLUMBINE see Marx, Joseph

KÖLZ, ERNST (1929-   )
   Am Kanal
     DOBLINGER 08 656   (K310)

   Galgenlieder
     DOBLINGER 08 657   (K311)

KOM BLIDA TID, MED BARNSINS FRID see
   Palsson, Helgi

KOM ETT BREV, DET see Ohlsson, Sven-
   Olof

KOM NADER, DOOD see Frid, Geza

KOMDU see Sveinsson, Atli Heimir

KOMM! DU SCHÖNES FISCHERMÄDCHEN see
   Meyerbeer, Giacomo

KOMM, RUH AN MEINEM HERZEN AUS see Abt,
   Franz

KOMM, UND SENKE DIE UMFLORTEN see
   Schubert, Franz (Peter), An Den
   Schlaf

KOMMT BESCHAUT DIE WEISOHEIT see
   Aufschnaiter, Benedikt Anton

KOMT TROMPETTEN see Purcell, Henry,
   Sound The Trumpet

KONGSTED,OLE
   Dansk Messe
     cantor,org ENGSTROEM 565   (K312)

   Otte Steensen-Sange
     ENGSTROEM 580   (K313)

KONIETZNY, HEINRICH
   Kalypso
     A solo,gtr PLUCKED STR T 649 $11.50
                           (K314)

KÖNIG VON MÜNSTER, DER see Orthel, Leon

KÖNIG VON THULE, DER see Schubert,
   Franz (Peter)

KONISHI, NAGAKO (1945-   )
   Vase For Lamentation
     SS soli,gtr,pno [10'] JAPAN (K315)

KONN OG GULL see Baden, Conrad

KONSERT FOR FLØYTE SOLO, RESITASJON OG
   KAMMERORKESTER see Vea, Ketil

KONT, PAUL (1920-   )
   Zehn Lieder Nach Gedichten Von Joseph
     Von Eichendorff *CC10U
     DOBLINGER 08 659 f.s.   (K316)

KONZERT see Devcic, Natko

KONZERTARIE FÜR ALT UND ORCHESTRA,
   K.255 see Mozart, Wolfgang Amadeus,
   Ombra Felice

KOOITJE see Ruiter, Wim de

KOOP, OL.
   Op Een Priesterfeest
     Mez/Bar solo ZENGERINK D.130 (K317)

KOPELENT, MAREK (1932-   )
   Agnus Dei
     S solo,1.0.1.0. 0.0.1.0. perc,pno,
     vln,vla,vcl [16'] (Breitkopf &
     Haertel (Wiesbaden) for all
     countries except Czech) CESKY
     HUD.   (K318)

   Canto De Li Augei, Il
     S solo,2.2.2.2. 1.2.1.0. perc,harp,
     strings [14'] CESKY HUD.   (K319)
     S solo,2(pic).2(English horn).2.2.
     1.2.1.0. 4perc,harp,strings [14']
     BREITKOPF-W f.s.   (K320)

KOPHETUA see Bijvanck, Henk

KOPPEL, HERMAN DAVID (1908-   )
   David's 42. Psalm
     "Som Hjorten Skriger Efter Rindende
     Vand, Op.68" S solo,pno SAMFUNDET
                           (K321)

   Som Hjorten Skriger Efter Rindende
     Vand, Op.68
     see David's 42. Psalm

   To Bibelske Sange *Op.59, CC2U
     S solo,2.2.2.2. 2.2.0.0. timp,cel,
     harp,strings sc,pts SAMFUNDET
     f.s.   (K322)

KOPRIVA, JAN JACHYM (1734-1792)
   Benedictus (from Mass In D)
     (Sestak, Zdenek) S solo,org,strings
     [6'] CESKY HUD.   (K323)

KOPRIVA, KAREL BLAZEJ (1756-1785)
   Ah, Cordi Trito
     (Sestak, Zdenek) [Lat] S solo,
     0.2.0.0. 2.0.0.0. org,strings
     [6'] CESKY HUD.   (K324)

   Aria in B flat
     see Siste Ultricem Dexteram

   Qui Tollis
     (Sestak, Zdenek) [Lat] A solo,
     0.2.0.0. 2.0.0.0. org,strings
     [4'] CESKY HUD.   (K325)

   Quod Pia Voce Cano
     (Sestak, Zdenek) [Lat] B solo,
     0.2.0.0. 2.0.0.0. org,strings
     [7'] CESKY HUD.   (K326)

   Siste Ultricem Dexteram (Aria in B
     flat)
     (Sestak, Zdenek) [Lat] S solo,
     0.2.0.0. 2.0.0.0. org,strings
     CESKY HUD.   (K327)

KOPYLOV, ALEXANDER ALEXANDROVICH
   (1854-1911)
   Three Songs, Op. 28
     [Russ] solo voice,pno CLASSV 2106
                           (K328)

KOR LANGT VIL DU REISA see Karlsen,
   Kjell Mørk

KORBAY, FRANCIS ALEXANDER (1846-1913)
   Had A Horse, A Finer No One Ever Saw
     [Eng/Ger] low solo,pno CLASSV 2196
                           (K329)

KORESHCHENKO, ARSENY (1870-1921)
   Five Romances, Op. 42
     [Russ] high solo (not available
     outside U.S.A.) RECITAL 364
                           (K330)

KORIDON see Ketting, Piet

KORN, PETER JONA (1922-   )
   Boten Des Herbstes *Op.47
     "Drei Lieder Nach Gedichten Von
     Arnold Krieger" high solo,pno
     SCHUBERTH,J   (K331)

   Drei Lieder Nach Gedichten Von Arnold
     Krieger
     see Boten Des Herbstes

   Two Nocturnes On Poems By Shelley
     *Op.20
     "Zwei Nachtlieder Nach Shelley"
     [Eng/Ger] S solo,clar in A,harp/
     pno SCHUBERTH,J   (K332)

   Zwei Nachtlieder Nach Shelley
     see Two Nocturnes On Poems By
     Shelley

KORNGOLD, ERICH WOLFGANG (1897-1957)
   Einfache Lieder, Op. 9
     [Ger] med solo,pno CLASSV 1660
                           (K333)

   Eternal, The
     see Unvergaenglichkeit
     see Unvergänglichkeit

   Unvergaenglichkeit
     "Eternal, The" solo voice,pno
     SCHOTT ST07751   (K334)

   Unvergänglichkeit
     "Eternal, The" solo voice,pno
     SCHOTTS ED 7751   (K335)

KORS OG LILJE see Karlsen, Kjell Mørk

KÖRSBÄRSBLOMMOR: 5 KORTA JAPANSKA
   KÄRLEKSDIKT see Söderlind, Ragnar

KORT TID, EN see Hallnäs, Eyvind

KORTE, KARL (1928-   )
   Whistling Wind
     Mez solo,electronic tape SEESAW
     f.s.   (K336)

KORTE VERHALEN VAN FRANZ KAFKA see
   Govers, Klaas

KORTKAMP, JOHANN (1643-1721)
Uns Ist Ein Kind Geboren
SSB soli,2vln,cont HÄNSSLER sc
10.361-01 f.s., pts 10.361.11-13
f.s.   (K337)

KOSMISCHE ZEICHEN see Wolschina,
Reinhard

KOSSAVISUR see Isolfsson, Pall see
Kaldalóns, Sigvaldi S.

KOSTEL, ARNOST
Vandrovali Hudci
[Czech/Ger] Mez solo,clar,vla,pno
PANTON 916   (K338)

KOSUGE, YASUO (1940-   )
Himitsu
S solo [5'] ONGAKU   (K339)

Shio Ga Hiku Youni
S solo [5'] ONGAKU   (K340)

KOUMANS, RUDOLF (1929-   )
A Venus
see Trois Voeuz Rustiques

Dons De Iacquet A Isabeau, Les
see Trois Voeuz Rustiques

D'un Vanneur De Ble Aux Vents
see Trois Voeuz Rustiques

Trois Voeuz Rustiques
S solo,clar,pno DONEMUS f.s. [8']
contains: A Venus; Dons De
Iacquet A Isabeau, Les; D'un
Vanneur De Ble Aux Vents   (K341)

KOUNADIS, ARGHYRIS (1924-   )
Nachtigall, Die
S solo,10db [15'] BREITKOPF-W f.s.
                                  (K342)

KOUZELNE NOCI see Martinu, Bohuslav
(Jan)

KOVEN, REGINALD DE
see DE KOVEN, (HENRY LOUIS) REGINALD

KOYAMA, KIYOSHIGE (1914-   )
Song Album *CCU
solo voice ONGAKU 524720 f.s.
                                  (K343)

KRAFT, LEO ABRAHAM (1922-   )
Spring In The Harbor
S solo,fl,vcl,pno SEESAW   (K344)

KRAFT, WILLIAM (1923-   )
Dialogues And Entertainments
S solo,4(pic).4(English
horn).4(bass
clar).4(contrabsn).4sax. 8.4.4.2.
db,timp,6perc [15'] NEW MUSIC
WEST rent   (K345)

Settings From Pierrot Lunaire
S solo,fl&pic,clar&bass clar,vln/
vla,vcl,pno,perc [28'] NEW MUSIC
WEST   (K346)

Silent Boughs
S solo,string orch [17'15"] pno red
NEW MUSIC WEST   (K347)

Sublime And The Beautiful, The
T solo,fl,clar,perc,pno,vln,vcl
[15'10"] study sc NEW MUSIC WEST
                                  (K348)

KRALL, JOHANN
Pater Noster
"Vater Unser" solo voice,vln,vla,
vcl,db,org SCIEN 846   (K349)

Vater Unser
S/T solo,org/harmonica SCIEN 847
                                  (K350)
see Pater Noster

KRANICHSTEINER KAMMERKANTATE see
Maderna, Bruno

KRAUSE-GRAUMNITZ, HEINZ (1911-1979)
Lieder
PETERS 5328   (K351)

KRCEK, JAROSLAV (1939-   )
Maiestas Carolina *song cycle
solo voice,2.1.0.1. 0.0.0.0. harp,
cimbalom,strings [23'] CESKY HUD.
                                  (K352)

KREBS, JOACHIM (1952-   )
Traumkraut
ABar soli,2(pic,alto fl).1(English
horn).1(bass clar).1+contrabsn.
2.0.0.0. 2perc,2vln,2vcl [23'0"]
PEER   (K353)

KREBS, KARL AUGUST
An Adelheid
see Lieder Für Eine Singstimme Mit
Begleit. D. Guitarre

Lieder Für Eine Singstimme Mit
Begleit. D. Guitarre
solo voice,gtr SCIEN 855 f.s.

KREBS, KARL AUGUST (cont'd.)

contains: An Adelheid; Nichts
Schöneres; Sehnsucht   (K354)

Nichts Schöneres
see Lieder Für Eine Singstimme Mit
Begleit. D. Guitarre

Sehnsucht
see Lieder Für Eine Singstimme Mit
Begleit. D. Guitarre

KREIGER, ARTHUR V. (1945-   )
Five Songs *CC5U
S solo,fl,clar,vln AM.COMP.AL. sc
$10.70, pts $33.70   (K355)

Four Settings Of W.C. Williams *CC4U
Mez/S solo,vla,pno APNM sc $4.00,
set $11.50   (K356)

KREISE see Haubenstock-Ramati, Roman

KREISLER, FRITZ (1875-1962)
Cradle Song 1915 (from Caprice
Viennois by Kreisler)
[Eng] S solo,pno CLASSV 1829 (K357)

KREK, UROS (1922-   )
Fünf Volkslieder *CC5U
high solo,pno BREITKOPF-W BG 573
f.s.   (K358)

KREUTZ, ROBERT EDWARD (1922-   )
Fall
high solo,pno/org WILLIS 11310
                                 (K359)

KREUTZER, KONRADIN (1780-1849)
Balladen, Gesänge Und Romanzen In
Musik Gesetzt
solo voice,pno SCIEN 862   (K360)

Den Holden Anblick Soll Ich Meiden
see Libussa: Duettino

Libussa: Duettino *Op.48,No.3
"Den Holden Anblick Soll Ich
Meiden" solo voice,pno SCIEN 861
                                 (K361)

KREUZGANG VON SANTO STEFANO, DER see
Frid, Geza

KREUZIGUNG see Orthel, Leon

KRIEBAUM, FRANZ
Medium, Das
solo voice,pno SCIEN 867 from
WIENER COUPLETS FÜR PIANOFORTE
UND GESANG   (K362)

Wiener Couplets Für Pianoforte Und
Gesang
see Medium, Das

KRIEGER, ARMANDO (1940-   )
Piedra Negra
S solo,wind quin,perc,pno,strings
SEESAW   (K363)

Radiante America
ST soli,1.1.1.1. 2.2.2.0. 3perc,
harp,pno,strings SEESAW   (K364)

KRIEGER, JOHANN (1651-1735)
Halleluja
see Weihnachtliches Konzert, 2
Barock-Arien

Weihnachtliches Konzert, 2 Barock-
Arien (composed with Krieger,
Johann Philipp)
RIES 60026 f.s.
contains: Halleluja; Weynacht-
Andacht   (K365)

Weynacht-Andacht
see Weihnachtliches Konzert, 2
Barock-Arien

KRIEGSGEFANGEN see Medek, Tilo

KRIESBERG, MATTHIAS (1953-   )
Not From This Anger
T solo,fl,vln,vla,db,pno,3perc
[10'] sc AM.COMP.AL. $23.00
                                 (K366)

KRIETSCH, GEORG (1904-1969)
Acht Tierlieder
solo voice,pno SEESAW   (K367)

KRIST STOD OP AF DØDE see Med Jesus Vil
Eg Fara see Bakke, Ruth

KRISTINSSON, SIGURSVEINN D. (1911-1990)
Amma Raular I Rokkrinu
solo voice,pno ICELAND 021-020
                                 (K368)

Five Songs
Bar solo,strings ICELAND 021-013
                                 (K369)

Fylgd
solo voice,pno ICELAND 021-016
                                 (K370)

KRISTINSSON, SIGURSVEINN D. (cont'd.)

Lagnaetti
solo voice,pno [2'0"] ICELAND
021-010   (K371)

Songs
solo voice,pno ICELAND 021-011
                                 (K372)

KRISTJÁNSSON, ODDGEIR (1911-1966)
Agustnott
solo voice,pno ICELAND 025-003
                                 (K373)

Five Songs
solo voice,pno ICELAND 025-005
                                 (K374)

Heima
solo voice,pno ICELAND 025-004
                                 (K375)

Songs, 26
solo voice,pno ICELAND 025-002
                                 (K376)

KRISTKYRKJA see Gulbranson, Eilif

KRISTUS, DU ER ALT MITT HAP see
Nystedt, Knut

KRISTUS ER VERDENS LYS see Nyhus, Rolf

KROEGER, KARL (1932-   )
Tres Psalmi Davidis
S solo,bass trom [15'] AM.COMP.AL.
                                 (K377)

KROL, BERNHARD (1920-   )
Nachtigall, Die *Op.77
Mez solo,fl,pno SCHUBERTH,J   (K378)

KRØLLTANGO - ET KAFÉVERK... see
Germeten, Gunnar

KROMER, PHILIP
Han Sar
LYCHE 14   (K379)

KRÖNUNG see Kirkwood, Antoinette

KROPFREITER, AUGUSTINUS FRANZ
(1936-   )
Galgenlieder
med solo DOBLINGER 08 668   (K380)

KROSSENS LIDINGSTRE see Elgaröy, Jan

KROTAD I SAND see Sveinsson, Atli
Heimir

KRUG
Weihnachtsalbum
KAHNT 8001   (K381)

KRUSE, BJØRN HOWARD (1946-   )
Altra Risposta
[It] Mez solo,pno [7'] NORGE   (K382)

Bim Bam Bum
[Ger] S solo,pno,perc [7'] NORGE
                                 (K383)

Islys
[Norw] S solo,gtr NORGE   (K384)

Ja Visst Gör Det Ont
"Yes, It Certainly Hurts" [Swed] A
solo,1.1.1.1. 3.0.0.0. perc,
strings [8'] NORGE f.s.   (K385)

Jarrama I
[Swed] Bar solo,2perc NORGE   (K386)

Jarrama II
[Swed] B solo,perc REIMERS 101150
                                 (K387)
[Swed] Bar solo,perc REIMERS (K388)

Lys
S solo,fl,clar,vln,vcl,pno,perc
[1'] NORGE   (K389)

Metal
solo voice,2(2pic).2.2.2.
4.3(piccolo trp).3.1. perc,timp,
harp,tenor sax jazztrio -
pno, bass, drums [10'] NORGE f.s.
                                 (K390)

Synergo
SMez soli,vln,gtr,pno/acord NORGE
                                 (K391)

Women
[Eng] S solo,fl,pno [7'] NORGE
                                 (K392)

Yes, It Certainly Hurts
see Ja Visst Gör Det Ont

KRZANOWSKI, ANDRZEJ (1951-1990)
Audycja VI
"Sixth Programme" [Polish] S solo,
2vln,vla,vcl [23'] sc POLSKIE
f.s.   (K393)

Relief IV
S solo,tubular bells [8'] POLSKIE
                                 (K394)

Sixth Programme
see Audycja VI

KU SOKO see Fontyn, Jacqueline

KÜBELREITER, DER see Govers, Klaas

KUBICKA, MIROSLAV (1951-)
Pisne Citove A Zertovne
S solo,2.1.2.2. 2.1.1.0. harp,xylo,
vibra,strings [13'] CESKY HUD.
(K395)

KUBIK, LADISLAV
Dopisy Psane Majem
solo voice,pno PANTON 920 (K396)

Narek Bojovnikovy Zeny
S solo,vla,bass clar,pno,perc
PANTON 921 (K397)

Slova
Mez solo,2.2.2.2. 2.0.0.0. timp,
strings [14'] CESKY HUD. (K398)

KUBO, MAYAKO (1947-)
Masago-Lieder
Mez solo,chamber group ARIAD 92017
(K399)

KUCHARZ, LAWRENCE
1973 #2
solo voice,fl/pic,clar/bass clar,
trp,tuba,timp,vln,vla,vcl [16']
AM.COMP.AL. (K400)

KÜCKEN, FRIEDRICH WILHELM (1810-1882)
Abschied Der Schwalben
SS soli,pno SCIEN 874 from DREI
DUETTE FÜR ZWEI SOPRAN-STIMMEN
(K401)

Drei Duette Für Zwei Sopran-Stimmen
see Abschied Der Schwalben

Du Wunderholde Maid
see Lieder Mit Begleitung D.
Guitarre

Lieder Mit Begleitung D. Guitarre
solo voice,gtr SCIEN 876 f.s.
contains: Du Wunderholde Maid;
Mädchen Von Juda, Das (K402)

Mädchen Von Juda, Das
see Lieder Mit Begleitung D.
Guitarre

Wo Still Ein Herz Von Liebe Glüht
solo voice,pno SCIEN 875 (K403)

KUCKUCK RUFT, DER see Marx, Joseph

KÜHL IST DIE BRISE see Pieper, Rene

KÜHNL, CLAUS (1957-)
Klage Des Hiob, Die *CC5U
narrator,org,pno perf sc BREITKOPF-
W KM 2186 f.s. (K404)

KUIPER, KLAUS (1956-)
Lover Complayneth The Unkindness Of
His Love, The
see Two Wyatt Songs

Renouncing Of Love, A
see Two Wyatt Songs

Two Wyatt Songs
S solo,fl,pno,vcl DONEMUS f.s.
[12']
contains: Lover Complayneth The
Unkindness Of His Love, The;
Renouncing Of Love, A (K405)

KUKIYAMA, NAOSHI (1958-)
Gisaro
solo voice,fl,clar,pno [12'] JAPAN
(K406)

KULOKK see Taubo, Lillian Gulowna

KUMA NO KAZE see Inaura, Shirabe

KUN ØIEBLIKKET see Groven, Eivind

KUNAD, RAINER (1936-)
Eiertanz, Der
(Hübner, Wilhelm) solo voice,7inst,
7 puppets, conductor pno red
PETERS f.s. (K407)

Klopstock-Ode
(Stephan, K.D.) "Losreissung" Bar
solo,2.2.2.2. 3.2.3.0. timp,
2perc,strings [20'] voc sc
DEUTSCHER DV 6130 (K408)

Losreissung
see Klopstock-Ode

KUNIEDA, HARUE (1958-)
Lead, Lied, Read, Reed
SS soli,2clar,pno,perc [12'] JAPAN
(K409)

Serenade
S solo,harp [10'] JAPAN (K410)

KUNTZ, MICHAEL (1915-1992)
Psalm No. 62
see Sehnsucht Nach Gott

KUNTZ, MICHAEL (cont'd.)
Sehnsucht Nach Gott (Psalm No. 62)
Bar solo,org COPPENRATH (K411)

KURACHI, TATSUYA (1962-)
Death Of Love: Mono Drama
S solo,vln,vla,vcl,pno,2perc [10']
JAPAN (K412)

Duetto E Intermezzo
ST soli,2synthesizer [9'] JAPAN
(K413)

KUROKAMI, YOSHIMITSU (1933-)
Archaeologist And Spider
solo voice,pno [10'] JAPAN (K414)

Five Songs By Poem Of Jukichi Yagi
solo voice,pno [10'] JAPAN (K415)

Little Sheep, Early Spring
solo voice,pno [8'] JAPAN (K416)

Trumpet Of Pale-Blue Color
solo voice,pno [4'] ZEN-ON (K417)

Window Float In Lake
solo voice,pno [8'] ZEN-ON (K418)

KURTAG, GYÖRGY (1926-)
Drei Lieder Auf Gedichte Von Janos
Pilinszky *Op.11a
solo voice,pno UNIVER. UE 18999
(K419)

Kafka-Fragmente, Op. 24
BOOSEY EMB13505 (K420)

Remembrance Noise
BOOSEY EMB07940 (K421)

Scenes From A Novel
BOOSEY EMB12661 (K422)

KUSAGAWA, KEI
Song Album *CCU
solo voice ONGAKU 524600 f.s.
(K423)

KUSAZUKIYO NO KOTOBA see Okajima,
Masaoki

KVA VAR DET? see Olsen, Sparre

KVAM, ODDVAR S. (1927-)
Afterwards Everything Is Too Late
see Att Döda Ett Barn

Att Döda Ett Barn *Op.44
"Afterwards Everything Is Too Late"
[Swed] narrator,3.3.3.3. 4.3.2.1.
timp,perc,strings [21'] NORGE
f.s. (K424)

Gloselund *Op.56b
solo voice,2.2.2.2(contrabsn).
2.2.2.1. timp,perc,strings [20']
NORGE f.s. (K425)

Julesang
[Norw] solo voice,pno MUSIKK (K426)

Today's News: From A Newspaper 1979
*Op.54
[Norw/Eng/Ger/Fr] solo voice,fl,
clar,vln,vcl,perc,pno/cel [18']
MUSIKK (K427)

Tre Nis Petersen-Sange *Op.69,No.1
[Dan] S/T solo,horn,gtr,perc,pno
NORGE (K428)

KVAMME, SIGMUND
Ljosnar Det Aldri
LYCHE 45 (K429)

KVANDAL, JOHAN (1919-)
Church Aria For Soprano And Organ,
Op.26, No.2
see O Domine Deus

Norske Stevtoner *Op.40
[Norw] solo voice,pno MUSIKK (K430)

O Domine Deus
"Church Aria For Soprano And Organ,
Op. 26, No.2" [Lat] S solo,org
[4'] NORSK (K431)

Solokantate No. 1 *Op.10
S/T solo,3(pic).2.2.2. 4.2.0.0.
timp,perc,strings [8'] NORGE f.s.
(K432)

Syv Sanger, Op. 4
[Norw] solo voice,pno NORGE (K433)

Three Christmas Psalms
[Norw] solo voice,pno NORSK (K434)

Three Solo Cantatas
solo voice,org/pno (CC3U) NORSK
NMO 10031 (K435)
[Norw] solo voice,pno/org (texts
from The Bible) NORGE (K436)
[Norw] solo voice,org NORSK (K437)

KVANDAL, JOHAN (cont'd.)
To Fröding-Sanger: Min Stjärnas
Songer
[Swed] S/T solo,pno NORSK (K438)

To Religiøse Sanger
[Norw] solo voice,pno/org NORSK
(K439)

KVAR SKAL FUGLANE FLJUGA see Karlsen,
Kjell Mørk

KVARTONI see Hvoslef, Ketil

KVAT HAVBÅRA SYNG see Backer-Lunde,
Johan

KVECH, OTOMAR (1950-)
Kdyz Zasla Cesta *song cycle
S solo,pno PANTON 924 (K440)

V Krajine Vzpominani
solo voice,string orch [14'] CESKY
HUD. (K441)
solo voice,pno PANTON 925 (K442)

KVEDJA see Halldorsson, Skuli

KVELD I KØVADALEN see Grov, Magne

KVELDAR see Ørbeck, Anne Marie

KVELDEN see Sinding, Christian

KVELDING-SETER see Sommerfeldt, Öistein

KVELDSSONG see Olsen, Sparre

KVELDSSONG - KVILE see Olsen, Sparre

KVELDSVERS see Kjeldaas, Arnljot

KVEN VIL VENTE PÅ EIN TAPAR see
Sønstevold, Gunnar

KVENDELAGNAD see Olsen, Sparre

KVERNDOKK, GISLE (1967-)
Draum
[Norw] Bar solo,hpsd/pno NORGE
(K443)

Jeg Løfter Opp Til Gud Min Sang
[Norw] Mez solo,vcl NORGE (K444)

Refleks
[Norw] solo voice,pno NORGE (K445)

Sanger Til Dikt Av Liv Holtskog
[Norw] solo voice,pno NORGE (K446)

Skirmish
3 high soli,ob,gtr,perc,pno NORGE
(K447)

Speglar Me Oss Av
[Norw] A solo,fl,clar,vcl,pno,perc
NORGE (K448)

KVERNO, TROND (1945-)
Bibelsk Visebok, En
[Norw] solo voice,gtr,fl NORSK
(K449)

Fire Nordmørske Religiøse Folketoner
[Norw] solo voice,org NORSK (K450)

Motet, Op. 8, No. 1
see Salige Er De Døde

Salige Er De Døde (Motet, Op. 8, No.
1)
[Norw] S/T solo,org NORSK (K451)

KVETENSTVI JAVORU see Bohác, Josef

KVETOMLUVA see Sluka, Luboš

KVI TRALAR DET IKKJE LENGER I SKOGEN
see Olsen, Sparre

KVILE see Olsen, Sparre

KVIN KANTOJ see Schipper, Dirk

KVINNAN OCH SOMMAREN see Rooth, Anna-
Greta

KVITSYMRE see Sommerfeldt, Öistein

KVOLDKYRRD see Halldorsson, Skuli

L

LA KAPELO see Schipper, Dirk

LA MEG EI DØ see Selmer, Johan Peter

LA-MENATZEACH AL HA-MECHOLOT see Wolpe, Stefan

LA MONTAINE, JOHN (1920-   )
Songs Of The Rose Of Sharon *Op.6, CC7L
S solo,pno/orch BROUDE BR. pno red f.s., study sc CCSSS BB 24, sc, pts (L1)

LA OSS TELLE VÅRE DAGER see Nyhus, Rolf

LA TOMBELLE, FERNAND DE (1854-1928)
Vieilles Chanteries
[Fr] RECITAL 299 (L2)

LAAT NU UITSLAAN M'N WILD VERLANGEN see Zagwijn, Henri

LAATSTE WOORD, HET see Röntgen, Johannes

LAC, LE see Niedermeyer, Louis

LACHEN UND WEINEN see Schubert, Franz (Peter)

LACHENDE HERZ, DAS see Ragwitz, Erhard

LACHENMANN, HELMUT FRIEDRICH
(1935-   )
Consolation I
12 solo voices,4perc [12'30"] sc BREITKOPF-W BG 766 f.s. (L3)
see Consolations, Les

Consolation II
16 solo voices [6'30"] voc sc BREITKOPF-W BG 767 f.s. (L4)
see Consolations, Les

Consolations, Les
SSSSAAAATTTTBBBB soli,4(pic).3.3+ bass clar.3+contrabsn. 4.3.3.1. 6perc,2harp,2pno,strings BREITKOPF-W f.s.
contains: Consolation I; Consolation II; Interludium; Postludium; Präludium (L5)

Interludium
see Consolations, Les

Postludium
see Consolations, Les

Präludium
see Consolations, Les

LACHNER
Songs By Lachner *CCU
solo voice,pno ALFRED 3547 f.s. (L6)

LACHNER, FRANZ (1803-1890)
Am Charfreitag
see Zwei Geistliche Gesaenge

Morgengesang Von Klopstock
see Zwei Geistliche Gesaenge

Sänger Am Rhein, Der
solo voice,pno SCIEN 893 (L7)

Zwei Geistliche Gesaenge
solo voice,org/pno SCIEN 894 f.s.
contains: Am Charfreitag; Morgengesang Von Klopstock (L8)

LACRIME D'ERMINIA, LE see Marini, Biagio

LADINO SONGS OF LOVE AND SUFFERING see Adolphe, Bruce

LADY BEWITCHER see Lason, Aleksander

LADY LAZARUS see Runswick, Daryl

LADY OF THE HARBOR see Hoiby, Lee

LAER MEG see Olsen, Sparre

LAGAFLOKKUR see Björnsson, Ragnar

LAGANA, RUGGERO (1956-   )
Bereshit
S solo,5inst ZERBONI 9057 (L9)

Leolam
solo voice,pno ZERBONI 9150 (L10)

Tambourin
solo voice,vln,hpsd,db,org ZERBONI 9324 (L11)

LAGNAETTI see Kristinsson, Sigursveinn D.

LAGO ERLAF, EL see Schubert, Franz (Peter)

LAJTHA, LASZLO (1891-1963)
Motet, Op. 8
[Fr/Hung/Ger] solo voice LEDUC f.s. (L12)

LAKE
Christmas Tree, The
SCHIRM.G ED2747 (L13)

LAKE, THE see Willingham, Lawrence

LAKMÉ: FANTAISIE AUX DIVINS see Delibes, Léo

LAKMÉ: INDIAN BELL SONG see Delibes, Léo

LAKMÉ: TU M'AS DONNÉ LE PLUS DOUX RÊVE see Delibes, Léo

LAKMÉ: VIENS, MALLIKA see Delibes, Léo

LALLA ROUKH: SI VOUS NE SAVEZ PLUS CHARMER see David, Félicien-César

LALO, EDOUARD (1823-1892)
Au Fond A Des Halliers
MezBar soli,pno CLASSV 0822 (L14)

Aubade (from Le Roi d'Ys)
T/Bar solo,pno UNITED MUS f.s. (L15)

Cinq Lieder
[Fr] high solo,pno CLASSV 1397 (L16)

Melodies
(Fauquet, Joel-Marie) solo voice, pno LEDUC (L17)

Roi d'Ys, Le: Vainement
T solo,pno (A maj, original key) CLASSV 0813 (L18)
T solo,pno (A flat maj) CLASSV 0421 (L19)

Songs For Voice And Piano *CCU
[Fr] KALMUS K 09885 f.s. (L20)

LAMAN, WIM (1946-   )
Midas' Tomb
med solo,2vln,vla,vcl,electronic tape [19'] DONEMUS (L21)

LAMB, HUBERT WELDON (1900-   )
Innocentium Carmina
Bar solo,wind quin NEW VALLEY 168 $15.00 (L22)

LAMB, THE see Chanler, Theodore Ward see Mourant, Walter see Whear, Paul William

LAMBORT, CARL R. VON
Ich Möcht An Alle Fenster Schleichen
solo voice,pno SCIEN 898 from LIEDER UND GESÄNGE (L23)

Lieder Und Gesänge
see Ich Möcht An Alle Fenster Schleichen

LAMENT see Maros, Rudolf, Sirato see Walker, George Theophilus

LAMENT: AN ORCHESTRAL SONG see Habbestad, Kjell

LAMENT OF TASSO see Selmer, Johan Peter, Tassos Klage

LAMENT OF THE MARTYRS, THE see Wright, Maurice

LAMENTACIÓN DEL PASTOR see Schubert, Franz (Peter)

LAMENTACJA (RYTHM DO PANA JEZUSA UKRZYZOWANEGO PATRZAC NA FIGURE MEKI PANSKIEJ) see Nikodemowicz, Andrzej

LAMENTACJA (RYTHM DO PANA JEZUSA UKRZYZOWANEGO PATRZAC NA FIGURE MEKI PANSKIEJ) - VERSION 2 see Nikodemowicz, Andrzej

LAMENTATION see Bernstein, Leonard

LAMENTATION (RHYTHM TO THE CRUCIFIED JESUS CHRIST WHILE CONTEMPLATING AN IMAGE OF THE PASSION) see Nikodemowicz, Andrzej, Lamentacja (Rythm Do Pana Jezusa Ukrzyzowanego Patrzac Na Figure Meki Panskiej)

LAMENTATION (RHYTHM TO THE CRUCIFIED JESUS CHRIST WHILE CONTEMPLATING AN IMAGE OF THE PASSION) - VERSION 2 see Nikodemowicz, Andrzej, Lamentacja (Rythm Do Pana Jezusa Ukrzyzowanego Patrzac Na Figure Meki Panskiej) - Version 2

LAMENTO see Chopin, Frédéric

LAMENTO DI DONA BLANCA DE BIVAR, IL see Lauricella, Sergio

LAMENTS FOR HEKTOR see Merryman, Marjorie

LAMPLIGHTER, THE see Mourant, Walter

LAND OF COUNTERPANE, THE see Anderson, Beth see Mourant, Walter

LAND OF HEART'S DESIRE see Kennedy-Fraser, Marjory

LAND OF HOPE AND GLORY see Elgar, [Sir] Edward (William)

LAND OF NOD, THE see Mourant, Walter

LAND OF WHO KNOWS WHERE!, THE see James, William G.

LAND POSSESSED BY POEMS see Eiriksdottir, Karolina

LANDARZT, EIN see Govers, Klaas

LANDEVEI see Jensen, Ludwig Irgens

LÄNDLICH - SITTLICH see Suppe, Franz von

LANDORMY, PAUL (CHARLES-RENE)
(1869-1943)
Trois Mélodies
[Fr] med solo,pno CLASSV 2189 (L24)

LANDSCAPE see Jordan, Sverre, Landskab

LANDSCAPES AND MAGIC WORDS see Bainbridge, Simon

LANDSCHAP see Kleppe, Joost see Vries Robbe, Willem de

LANDSKAB see Jordan, Sverre

LANDSKAP MED SNE see Gjerstrom, Bjorn G.

LANDUNG, DIE see Warren, Betsy

LANE-WILSON, HENRY
see WILSON, HENRY LANE

LANERI, ROBERTO (1945-   )
Esorcismi
solo voice,clar,trom,vla,perc SEESAW f.s. (L25)

LANG, JOSEPHINE (1815-1880)
Selected Songs
DA CAPO ISBN 0-306-76097-5 (L26)

LANG, MARGARET RUTHVEN (1867-1972)
Irish Love Song, Op. 22
low solo,pno CLASSV 1986 (L27)
med-high solo,pno CLASSV 1985 (L28)
high solo,pno CLASSV 1984 (L29)

LANG, MAX (1917-   )
Ausgewahlte Lieder
solo voice,pno SEESAW (L30)

LANGELEIKEN see Tveitt, Geirr

LANGERT, JULES
Three Emily Dickinson Songs *CC3U
solo voice,pno sc FALLEN LEAF $12.00 (L31)

LÄNGS RADIEN see Jennefelt, Thomas

LANGT INN PÅ VILLE HEI see Tøsse, Eilert

LANGT OPPI HØGAN DALAR see Olsen, Sparre

LANGT UPPI VIUMDALA see Albertsen, Per Hjort

LANIER SONGS see Turok, Paul Harris

LANZA, SERGIO
Trittico Dell' Immaginario
female solo,fl,vln EDI-PAN EP 7677 (L32)

LANZHOTSKA see Kapr, Jan, Symphony No. 10

LARA, AGUSTIN (1900-1970)
Granada
med solo,pno (C maj) sc PEER 60542-203 $2.50 (L33)
(Diaz, H.) med solo,orch (C maj) set PEER 60538-248 $15.00 (L34)

LARMES, LES see Gretchaninov, Alexander Tikhonovich

LARSON, MARTIN (1967-)
　　Indian Boyhood
　　　　see Six Songs On Poems By Spike
　　　　　Milligan

　　Love Song
　　　　see Six Songs On Poems By Spike
　　　　　Milligan

　　Manic Depression
　　　　see Six Songs On Poems By Spike
　　　　　Milligan

　　New Rose, The
　　　　see Six Songs On Poems By Spike
　　　　　Milligan

　　Opus I
　　　　see Six Songs On Poems By Spike
　　　　　Milligan

　　Sång För Röst Och Orgel
　　　　[Swed] solo voice,org TONOS　(L35)

　　Six Songs On Poems By Spike Milligan
　　　　S solo,pno TONOS f.s.
　　　　　contains: Indian Boyhood; Love
　　　　　Song; Manic Depression; New
　　　　　Rose, The; Opus I; To Robert
　　　　　Graves　　　　　　　　(L36)

　　[The]Met Al Pond
　　　　[Swed] S solo,ob,pno TONOS　(L37)

　　To Robert Graves
　　　　see Six Songs On Poems By Spike
　　　　　Milligan

LARSSON, LARS-ERIK (1908-1986)
　　Ut Mot Udden
　　　　solo voice,pno GEHRMANS 6614　(L38)

LASAGNA, MARCO
　　Ferma E L'antica Voce
　　　　female solo,pno EDI-PAN EP 688
　　　　　　　　　　　　　　　　　(L39)

LASCIATA...GIOVINEZZA... see Lolini,
　　Ruggero

LASCIATI AMAR see Leoncavallo, Ruggiero

LASERNA, BLAS DE (1751-1816)
　　Seguidillas Majas
　　　　see Palomino, J., Canción Picaresca

LASKA K MILEMU see Ceremuga, Josef

LASON, ALEKSANDER (1951-)
　　Drei Songs
　　　　Mez solo,ob,vln,vcl,pno SEESAW
　　　　　　　　　　　　　　　　(L40)

　　Lady Bewitcher
　　　　see Trzy Piesni Do Slow Kazimiery
　　　　　Illakowiczowny

　　Licho
　　　　see Trzy Piesni Do Slow Kazimiery
　　　　　Illakowiczowny

　　Skarga Stworu
　　　　see Trzy Piesni Do Slow Kazimiery
　　　　　Illakowiczowny

　　Three Songs To Words By Kazimiera
　　　　Illakowicz　*see Trzy Piesni Do
　　　　Slow Kazimiery Illakowiczowny

　　Trzy Piesni Do Slow Kazimiery
　　　　Illakowiczowny
　　　　[Polish] A solo,ob,vln,vcl,pno
　　　　POLSKIE f.s.
　　　　　contains: Lady Bewitcher; Licho,
　　　　　"Evil Spirit"; Skarga Stworu,
　　　　　"Creature's Complaint";
　　　　　Urocznica　　　　　　(L41)

　　Urocznica
　　　　see Trzy Piesni Do Slow Kazimiery
　　　　　Illakowiczowny

LASS FOR A SAILOR, THE see Brown, James

LASS OF RICHMOND HILL, THE see Hook,
　　James

LASS WITH THE DELICATE AIR see Arne,
　　Thomas Augustine

LASSEN, EDUARD (1830-1904)
　　Song Album (Acht Lieder)
　　　　[Ger/Eng] high solo RECITAL 272
　　　　　　　　　　　　　　　　(L42)

LAST BUTTERFLY, THE see Kingsley,
　　Gershon Gary

LAST DANCE see Runolfsson, Karl Otto

LAST LEAF, THE see Homer, Sidney

LAST LETTERS FROM STALINGRAD see
　　Tanenbaum, Elias

LAST NIGHT I WAS THE WIND see Brooks,
　　Richard James

LAST NIGHT THAT SHE LIVED..., THE see
　　Chapiro, Fania

LAST ROSE OF SUMMER see Anonymous

LAST SPRING see Grieg, Edvard Hagerup,
　　Våren

LAST VOYAGE, THE see Björnsson, Arni

LATE IDYL see Colding-Jorgensen,
　　Henrik, Senidyl

LATE OF THE CITY OF ROME see Bank,
　　Jacques

LATE SUMMER see Jordan, Sverre,
　　Eftersommer

LATEINISCHE LIEDER DER ALTEN UND
　　MITTELALTEN KIRCHE
　　　　(Clemen, O.) solo voice,kbd SCIEN 376
　　　　　　　　　　　　　　　　(L43)

LAUB see Helgason, Hallgrimur

LAUD TO THE NATIVITY see Respighi,
　　Ottorino

LAUDATE DOMINUM see Monteverdi, Claudio
　　see Mozart, Wolfgang Amadeus

LAUDI see Stout, Alan

LAUER, ELIZABETH
　　Song Cycle
　　　　Mez solo,clar/fl,vcl,pno [8']
　　　　AM.COMP.AL.　　　　　(L44)

LAUGHING AT ME see De Filippis, C.

LAURA (ELEGIES INTIMES) see Mestres,
　　Apeles

LAURENTIUS VON SCHNÜFFIS (JOHANN
　　MARTIN) (1633-1702)
　　Mirantische Maul-Trummel
　　　　OLMS　　　　　　　　　(L45)

LAURICELLA, SERGIO
　　Lamento Di Dona Blanca De Bivar, Il
　　　　S&speaking voice,strings EDI-PAN
　　　　EP 7879　　　　　　　(L46)

LAURIDSEN, MORTEN JOHANNES (1943-)
　　Cuatro Canciones Sobre Poesias De
　　　　Federico Garcia Lorca
　　　　"Four Lorca Songs" high solo,clar,
　　　　vcl,pno [10'0"] PEER　(L47)

　　Four Lorca Songs
　　　　see Cuatro Canciones Sobre Poesias
　　　　　De Federico Garcia Lorca

　　Winter Come
　　　　high solo,pno PEER　　(L48)

LAUSCHE MEINEN TÖNEN see Suppe, Franz
　　von, Iberisches Ständchen

LÄUSE-LIED see Eisler, Hanns

LAUTE, DIE see Norby, Erik

LAUTE-SPIELENDER ENGEL see Lothar, Mark

LAUTENDE STILLE - LARMENDER TAG see
　　Rovenstrunck, Bernhard

LAUTERBACH, LORENZ (1906-)
　　Meiner Mutter
　　　　solo voice,pno BOHM f.s.　(L49)

LAUVSONGAREN see Haegeland, Eilert M.

LAVISTA, MARIO (1943-)
　　Hacia El Comienzo
　　　　"Toward The Beginning" med solo,
　　　　2.2+English horn.2+bass clar.2.
　　　　4.2.2.0. harp,strings [9'0"] PEER
　　　　　　　　　　　　　　　　(L50)

　　Toward The Beginning
　　　　see Hacia El Comienzo

LAVMAELT see Madsen, Trygve

LAWES, HENRY (1596-1662)
　　Hymns To The Holy Trinity
　　　　(Beechey) med solo,cont OXFORD
　　　　62.233　　　　　　　(L51)

LAY OF LOVE AND DEATH OF CORNET
　　CHRISTOPHER RILKE, THE see Brown,
　　Francis James

LAY OU PLUTOST RONDEAU DE F. VILLON see
　　Jolivet, Andre

LAZY ANDY ANT see Wolpe, Stefan

LAZZARI, SILVIO (1857-1944)
　　Trois Chansons De Sheherazade
　　　　[Fr/Eng] high solo RECITAL 273
　　　　　　　　　　　　　　　　(L52)

LE BARON, ANNE (1953-)
　　Sea And The Honeycomb, The
　　　　Mez solo,fl/pic,clar/bass clar,pno,
　　　　2perc [7'] AM.COMP.AL. sc $12.95,
　　　　pts $27.40　　　　　(L53)

LE FANU, NICOLA
　　see LEFANU, NICOLA

LE SIEGE, ANNETTE
　　Confusion Breaths...
　　　　S solo,electronic tape,vla,perc,pno
　　　　SEESAW　　　　　　　(L54)

　　In The Silence
　　　　S solo,alto fl,vibra,pno SEESAW
　　　　　　　　　　　　　　　　(L55)

　　Night Songs
　　　　S/T solo,pno SEESAW　　(L56)

　　Ordinary Things
　　　　solo voice,fl,sax,vibra,vcl,pno
　　　　SEESAW f.s.　　　　　(L57)

　　Outside The Frame
　　　　solo voice,vibra,pno SEESAW f.s.
　　　　　　　　　　　　　　　　(L58)

LEAD, LIED, READ, REED see Kunieda,
　　Harue

LEADEN ECHO AND THE GOLDEN ECHO, THE
　　see Edwards, George

LEAF, ROBERT
　　Blest Is The Love　*Marriage
　　　　AMSI V-15　　　　　(L59)

LÉANDRE ET HÉRO see Clérambault, Louis-
　　Nicolas

LEANING ON THE FENCE see Jensen, Ludwig
　　Irgens, Lutad Mot Gärdet

LEAVINGS see Silsbee, Ann

LEBENSTANZ see Einem, Gottfried von

LECHLER, BENEDIKT (1594-1659)
　　Cantate Virgini
　　　　(Fürlinger, Wolfgang) SS soli,2vln,
　　　　cont (Coppenraths Kleine Reihe,
　　　　Heft 7) COPPENRATH　(L60)

LECHNER, KONRAD (1911-1989)
　　Drei Gedichte Von Hans Magnus
　　　　Enzensberger
　　　　solo voice,fl [6'] study sc MOECK
　　　　5219　　　　　　　　(L61)

　　In Die Paschae: Psalm
　　　　high solo [5'] BREITKOPF-W BG 1235
　　　　f.s.　　　　　　　　(L62)

　　Verkündigung, Monumentum Veit Stoss
　　　　S solo,3brass,3strings,kbd,perc
　　　　BREITKOPF-W f.s.　　　(L63)

LECOCQ, CHARLES (1832-1918)
　　Chanson De La Cigale, La
　　　　S solo,pno CLASSV 2213　(L64)

　　Fleurs Parisiennes
　　　　[Fr] high solo RECITAL 274　(L65)

　　Suzette Et Suzon
　　　　med solo,pno CLASSV 1035　(L66)

LECTURE ON NOTHING see Itoh, Hiroyuki

LECTURE TROIS DE MAHLER see Koering,
　　Rene

LEERLING, DE see Masseus, Jan

LEEUW, TON DE (1926-)
　　Vocalise
　　　　A/solo voice DONEMUS　　(L67)

LEEZIE LINDSAY see Grainger, Percy
　　Aldridge

LEFANU, NICOLA (1947-)
　　Penny For A Song, A　*song cycle
　　　　S solo,pno (diff) NOVELLO　(L68)

LEFT BEHIND see Torjussen, Trygve,
　　Forlatt

LEGEND OF KINERET, THE see Leniado-
　　Chira, Joseph

LÉGENDE see Delibes, Léo see Linjama,
　　Jyrki

LÉGENDE DE LORELEY, LA see Bertelin,
　　Albert

LÉGENDE DE ST. NICOLAS, LA see Arrieu,
　　Claude

LÉGENDE DU BAISER, LA see Massenet,
　　Jules

LEGG IKKJE DITT LIV I MI HAND see
　　Søderlind, Ragnar

LEGRENZI, GIOVANNI (1626-1690)
Idee Armoniche, Op. 13
sc KING'S (L69)

O Dilectissime Jesu
S solo,2vln,vcl,org KING'S L8 (L70)

O Mirandum Mysterium
A solo,2vln,org KING'S L5 (L71)

LEGUERNEY, JACQUES (1897-   )
Poemes De La Pleiade #1
S/T solo,pno SALABERT SEAS18846
(L72)

Poemes De La Pleiade #2
S/T solo,pno SALABERT SEAS18847
(L73)

LEHAR, FRANZ (1870-1948)
Girls Were Made To Hug And Kiss (from
Paganini)
[Eng] pno red GLOCKEN GL00168 (L74)

I'm Off To Chez Maxime (from The
Merry Widow)
[Eng] pno red GLOCKEN GL00166 (L75)

Love, Live Forever (from Paganini)
[Eng] pno red GLOCKEN GL00167 (L76)

Lustige Witwe, Die: Vilja-Lied
[Ger] S solo,pno CLASSV 1697 (L77)

Oh Maiden, My Maiden (from Frederica)
[Eng] pno red GLOCKEN GL00170 (L78)

On My Lips Every Kiss Is Like Wine
(from Giuditta)
[Eng] pno red GLOCKEN GL00169 (L79)

Vilia (from The Merry Widow)
[Eng] pno red GLOCKEN GL00165 (L80)

You Are My Heart's Delight (from The
Land Of Smiles)
[Eng] pno red GLOCKEN GL00171 (L81)

LEHMANN
When Love Is Kind
[Eng] high solo,pno CLASSV 1334
(L82)
[Eng] low solo,pno CLASSV 1335
(L83)

LEHMANN, HANS ULRICH (1937-   )
Tantris
S solo,fl,vcl BREITKOPF-W BG 1311
f.s. (L84)

LEHMANN, LIZA (1862-1918)
Ah Moon Of My Delight
high solo,pno CLASSV 0398 (L85)
med solo,pno CLASSV 0638 (L86)

No Candle Was There And No Fire
high solo,pno CLASSV 0835 (L87)
med solo,pno CLASSV 0836 (L88)

There Are Faires At The Bottom Of Our
Garden
med-high solo,pno CLASSV 1830 (L89)
high solo,pno CLASSV 1831 (L90)

LEHNSTEDT see Koetsier, Jan

LEICHTLING, ALAN (1947-   )
Canticle I
S solo,fl SEESAW f.s. (L91)

Eleven Songs From A Shropshire Lad
Bar solo,chamber group SEESAW f.s.
(L92)
Psalm No. 37
A solo,chamber group SEESAW f.s.
(L93)
Rubaiyat Fragments
B solo,clar,horn,pno SEESAW f.s.
(L94)
Songs In Winter
S solo,pno SEESAW f.s. (L95)

Three Songs Of Emily Dickinson *CC3U
B solo,vcl SEESAW f.s. (L96)

Trial And Death
solo voice,clar,fl,harp SEESAW f.s.
(L97)
Two Proverbs *CC2U
A solo,3clar SEESAW f.s. (L98)

LEID MEG, GUD, OVER BYLGJANDE HAV see
Nystedt, Knut

LEIDENSGESCHICHTE NACH JOHANNES see
Rohr, Heinrich

LEIDENSGESCHICHTE NACH LUKAS see Rohr,
Heinrich

LEIDIN LONG see Helgason, Hallgrimur

LEIDSLA see Björnsson, Arni

LEIFS, JON (1899-1968)
Baptism Invocation
Bar solo,pno [4'30"] ICELAND
033-035 (L99)

LEIFS, JON (cont'd.)

In Memoriam J.H.
Mez/Bar solo,pno ICELAND 033-038
(L100)

Lord's Prayer, The
S/T solo,org ICELAND 033-044 (L101)

Love Songs From The Edda
T solo,pno ICELAND 033-048 (L102)

Songs To The Saga Symphony
T solo,pno ICELAND 033-040 (L103)

Three Ancient Songs
solo voice,pno ICELAND 033-039
(L104)

Three Edda Songs
S/T solo,pno ICELAND 033-045 (L105)

Three Saga Songs
T solo,pno ICELAND 033-036 (L106)

Three Songs
solo voice,pno ICELAND 033-037
(L107)

Torrek
solo voice,pno ICELAND 033-041
(L108)

Two Songs
solo voice,pno ICELAND 033-046
(L109)
solo voice,pno ICELAND 033-042
(L110)

LEIJON, JERKER
Är Något Som, Det
solo voice,pno/org WESSMAN 9108
f.s.
contains: Är Något Som Älskande
Hjärtan Vet, Det; Maria,
Jungfru Maria; Maria
Synderskans Bön; Skönaste Jag
Vet Är Din Vidöppna Famn, Det;
Visst Måste Det Vara Nå't
Särskilt Där (L111)

Är Något Som Älskande Hjärtan Vet,
Det
see Är Något Som, Det

Av Ljus Är Du Kommen: Fem Sånger
solo voice,pno/org GEHRMANS 6553
(L112)
Hjärtats Språk
solo voice,pno/org GEHRMANS 6569
(L113)
Maria, Jungfru Maria
see Är Något Som, Det

Maria Synderskans Bön
see Är Något Som, Det

Skönaste Jag Vet Är Din Vidöppna
Famn, Det
see Är Något Som, Det

Visst Måste Det Vara Nå't Särskilt
Där
see Är Något Som, Det

LEISE FLEHEN see Schubert, Franz
(Peter), Serenade

LEISNER, DAVID
Outdoor Shadows *CC5U
high solo,gtr (med) PRESSER
141-40018 $7.50 (L114)

LEITIN see Kaldalóns, Sigvaldi S.

LEKEN GÅR see Blomdahl, Karl-Birger

LEKETØY see Sønstevold, Gunnar

LEKEU, GUILLAUME (1870-1894)
Nocturne
see Trois Poèmes

Pavots, Les
[Fr] med-high solo,pno CLASSV 1368
(L115)
Ronde
see Trois Poèmes

Sur Une Tombe
see Trois Poèmes

Trois Poèmes
[Fr] high solo,pno CLASSV 1367 f.s.
contains: Nocturne; Ronde; Sur
Une Tombe (L116)

LENIADO-CHIRA, JOSEPH
Distant Place, A
see Legend Of Kineret, The

Kineret
see Legend Of Kineret, The

Legend Of Kineret, The
narrator,fl,strings TRANSCON.
970168 rent
contains: Distant Place, A;
Kineret; Night Music; Pavanne
(L117)

LENIADO-CHIRA, JOSEPH (cont'd.)

Night Music
see Legend Of Kineret, The

Pavanne
see Legend Of Kineret, The

LENKET TIL DIN TYNGDE see Ødegaard,
Henrik

LENNON, JOHN ANTHONY (1950-   )
Colors Where The Moon Never Could
S solo,cel,perc,vln,vla,vcl [7']
AM.COMP.AL. sc $13.00, pts $9.95
(L118)

Ghostfires
Mez solo,perc,fl,gtr,harp [16']
AM.COMP.AL. (L119)

LENTEN TRIPTYCH, A see Caldwell, Mary
Elizabeth

LENZFAHRT see Marx, Joseph

LEO, LEONARDO (ORTENSIO SALVATORE DE)
(1694-1744)
Morte Di Abele, La: Dunque Si Sforza
low solo,pno CLASSV 0900 (L120)

Olimpiade: Io Vado...De Pensa Ad
Aristea
solo voice,pno BOIL B.1748 (L121)

LEOLAM see Lagana, Ruggero

LEON, TANIA JUSTINA (1944-   )
Pueblo Mulato
S solo,ob,gtr,perc,pno,db [10'0"]
PEER (L122)

LEONCAVALLO, RUGGIERO (1858-1919)
Ballatella
see Pagliacci: Qual Fiamma

Bohème, La: Da Quel Suon Soavemente
Mez solo,pno CLASSV 0691 (L123)

Bohème, La: Marcello "Io Non Ho"
T solo,pno CLASSV 0694 (L124)

Bohème, La: Marcello "Testa Adorata"
T solo,pno CLASSV 0931 (L125)

Invocation À La Muse
med solo,pno CLASSV 0689 (L126)

Lasciati Amar
T solo,pno CLASSV 0657 (L127)

Mattinata
low solo,pno (B flat maj) CLASSV
1327 (L128)
med-low solo,pno (C maj) CLASSV
0481 (L129)
med-high solo,pno (D maj) CLASSV
0692 (L130)
[It] med-high solo,pno (D flat maj)
CLASSV 1832 (L131)
high solo,pno (E maj) CLASSV 0387
(L132)
[It] high solo,pno (E flat maj)
CLASSV 1833 (L133)

Pagliacci: O Columbina
"Serenade" T solo,pno CLASSV 0460
(L134)

Pagliacci: Prologue "Si Può?"
[It/Eng] B solo,pno (lower key)
CLASSV 1272 (L135)
[It/Eng] Bar solo,pno (original
key) CLASSV 0693 (L136)

Pagliacci: Qual Fiamma
"Ballatella" S solo,pno CLASSV 0639
(L137)

Pagliacci: Vesti La Giubba
[It/Eng] T solo,pno (D min) CLASSV
1834 (L138)
T solo,pno CLASSV 0696 (L139)

Serenade
see Pagliacci: O Columbina

Sérénade Francaise
high solo,pno CLASSV 0690 (L140)
med-high solo,pno,vln CLASSV 0804
(L141)
Sérénade Napolitain
med-high solo,pno CLASSV 0805
(L142)
med-high solo,pno,vln CLASSV 0806
(L143)
Zaza: Buona Zazà
Bar solo,pno CLASSV 0695 (L144)

Zaza: Non Odi?
S solo,pno CLASSV 0906 (L145)

Zaza: O Mio Piccolo Tavolo
T solo,pno CLASSV 0907 (L146)

Zaza: Zaza Piccola Zingara
Bar solo,pno CLASSV 0403 (L147)

LEOPARDI CANTI see Lybbert, Donald

LERCHE MORGENLIED, DER see Bogler,
Bernhard

LEROUX, PHILIPPE (1959-   )
Anima Christi
SATB soli (diff) BILLAUDOT   (L148)

Je Brule, Dit-Elle Un Jour A Un
Camarade
S solo,acap (diff) BILLAUDOT (L149)

Veni Sancte
3S (diff) BILLAUDOT   (L150)

LERSTAD, TERJE B. (1955-   )
Birthday Cantata *Op.177
SATTTTB soli [9'] NORGE f.s. (L151)

De Profundis (Psalm No. 130) Op.139
A solo,clar,electronic tape,strings
[12'] NORGE f.s.   (L152)

Francois Solaire *Op.176a
ST/SBar soli,pic,fl,alto fl,clar,
alto clar in E flat,contrabass
clar,vln/vla,db,pno [106'] NORGE
f.s.   (L153)
[Fr] ST/SBar soli,pno [106'] NORGE
f.s.   (L154)

I Moan *Op.152
[Eng] Mez solo,vla da gamba [7']
(text by Shakespeare) NORGE
(L155)

Psalm No. 130
see De Profundis

Sonata Di Spazzatura *Op.179b
"Sonata For Various Instruments"
Mez/Bar solo,rec,clar,pno [11']
NORGE   (L156)
"Sonate For Diverse Instrumenter"
Mez/Bar solo,rec,clar,pno [11']
NORGE   (L157)

Sonata For Various Instruments
see Sonata Di Spazzatura

Sonate For Diverse Instrumenter
see Sonata Di Spazzatura

Til Elise Merete *Op.190b
solo voice [2'30"] NORGE   (L158)

LESSARD, JOHN AYRES (1920-   )
Bag Of The Bee, The
low solo,pno [2'] sc AM.COMP.AL.
$1.20   (L159)

Epithalamion
high solo/med solo,pno [4'] sc
AM.COMP.AL. $6.15   (L160)

Five Poems By Robert Herrick *CC5U
Mez solo,vln,pno AM.COMP.AL. sc
$11.45, pts $4.60   (L161)

Fragments From The Cantos Of Ezra
Pound
Bar solo,fl,2horn,2trp,trom,vln,
vla,vcl [24'] AM.COMP.AL. sc
$16.10, pts $32.20   (L162)

Get Hence Foule Griefe
med solo,pno [2'] sc AM.COMP.AL.
$1.95   (L163)

Mother Goose
low solo,pno [3'] sc AM.COMP.AL.
$4.25   (L164)

Pond In A Bowl, The (5 Songs)
S solo,pno,perc [17'] AM.COMP.AL.
(L165)

Stars Hill Valley
S solo,pno [6'] sc AM.COMP.AL.
$6.90   (L166)

Three Songs For St. Cecilia's Day
*CC3U
med solo,pno sc AM.COMP.AL. $7.70
(L167)

Twelve Mother Goose Songs *CC12U
med solo,pno sc AM.COMP.AL. $10.70
(L168)

Twelve Mother Goose Songs *CC12U
med solo,pno,str trio AM.COMP.AL. sc
$11.45, pts $17.65   (L169)

LET ALL THE HORSES GO FREE see Blank,
Allan

LET GOD ARISE see Rogers, Bernard,
Psalm No. 68

LET IT BE FORGOTTEN see Lybbert, Donald

LET ME BUT HEAR THY VOICE see
Balakirev, Mily Alexeyevich

LET ME GO see Clarke, Henry Leland

LET SPRINGTIME COME see Delius,
Frederick

LET THE BRIGHT SERAPHIM see Lyric
Soprano Arias: A Master Class With
Evelyn Lear, Vol. 1

LET THE DREADFUL ENGINES see Purcell,
Henry

LET THE SULTAN SALADIN see Grétry,
André Ernest Modeste

LETELA TUDY LABUTE see Raichl, Miroslav

LET'S HAVE AN ENGLISH SONG see Zpivame
Anglicky

LETTER SCENE see Offenbach, Jacques,
Périchole, La: O Mon Cher Amant

LETTER TO A FRIEND'S LONELINESS see Van
de Vate, Nancy Hayes

LETTER TO THE WORLD see Butterworth,
Neil

LETTERA A RAINER MARIA RILKE see Ricci,
Paolo

LETTERS FROM HELSINKI see Malan, J. de
Vos

LETTERS FROM ITALY HILL see Phillips,
Burrill

LETTRE, LA see Aubert, Louis-Francois-
Marie

LETZTE ART CHANSONS, EINE see Cerha,
Friedrich

LETZTER GRUSS see Levi

LEUCHTENDE TAGE see Marx, Joseph

LEUTTNER, GEORG CHRISTOPH (1625-1703)
Alma Redemptoris Mater
(Ruhland, Konrad) S solo,string
quin,cont (Musica Practica, Heft
7) COPPENRATH   (L170)

LEVADE, CHARLES (GASTON) (1869-1948)
Mélodies Et Poëmes, 23, Vol. 1
solo voice,pno CLASSV C038 (L171)

LEVEN EN DOOD see Roosendael, Jan Rokus
van

LEVEND WATER: VIJF NIEUWE GEESTELIJKE
LIEDEREN see Dijk, L. Van

LEVI
Letzter Gruss
low solo,pno PETERS 3571B   (L172)

LEVI, PAUL ALAN (1941-   )
Black Wings
S solo,pno [30'] sc AM.COMP.AL.
$38.65   (L173)

Jabberwocky
Bar solo,pno [5'] sc AM.COMP.AL.
$5.00   (L174)

This Much I Know
S solo,pno [3'] sc AM.COMP.AL.
$3.85   (L175)

Truth, The
S solo,vcl solo,fl,clar,bsn,hpsd,
pno,2vln,vla,vcl [11']
AM.COMP.AL. sc $18.40, pts $88.75
(L176)

LEVIN, STEFAN
I Ditt Öga
S solo,fl,gtr TONOS   (L177)

LEVY, FRANK EZRA (1930-   )
Specks Of Light
S solo,fl,horn,strings,harp SEESAW
f.s.   (L178)

LEWIN, FRANK (1925-   )
Variations On Greek Themes
Mez solo,fl,vla,harp,pno [26']
AM.COMP.AL. sc $27.55, pts $44.75
(L179)

LEWIS, PETER TOD (1932-1982)
Ballad For Shaheen
med solo,pno [6'] sc AM.COMP.AL.
$5.40   (L180)

LEWIS, ROBERT HALL (1926-   )
Combinazioni III
narrator,ob/English horn,1perc
[12'] (diff) PRESSER 114-40386
$15.00   (L181)

Duo No. 5
S solo,pno DOBLINGER 08 673 (L182)

LEWKOVITCH, BERNHARD (1927-   )
Ten Strings
Bar solo,pno ENGSTROEM 597 (L183)

LIBERDA, BRUNO (1953-   )
Berenice
S solo,db [9'] ARIAD 79027 (L184)

Chanson D'Amour
female solo [5'-8'] ARIAD   (L185)

Gute-Nacht-Lied Oder Berceuse
female solo,vcl,electronic tape
[15'-20'] ARIAD   (L186)

LIBOU PISNICKU SVEMU JEZISKU see Ryba,
Jan Jakub Simon

LIBRO PRIMO DELLE CANZONETTE AMOROSE A
VOCE SOLA see Cossoni, Carlo Donati

LICHEY, REINHOLD
Drei Gesänge *Op.70, CC3U
solo voice,org KISTNER f.s. (L187)

Vaterunser *Op.71
solo voice,org KISTNER f.s. (L188)

LICHO see Lason, Aleksander

LICHT DES MONDES, DAS see Meijering,
Cord

LICHT VAN BINNEN see Regt, Hendrik de

LIDHOLM, INGVAR (1921-   )
Stamp Music I
S solo,tam-tam NORDISKA 10392
(L189)

LIDICE VARUJI see Hala, V.

LIDOVA NOKTURNA see Schreiber, Josef

LIDSTRÖM, JOHN (1957-   )
Cantata, Op. 9
see Herren Skall Avtorka Tårarna
Från Alla Ansikten

Fågelpoesi *Op.11,No.1-5
[Swed] S/T solo,pno TONOS   (L190)

Från Triestes Kust *Op.10,No.1
S solo,fl,bsn,vln,pno TONOS (L191)

Herren Skall Avtorka Tårarna Från
Alla Ansikten (Cantata, Op. 9)
[Swed] SBar soli,vln,vcl,vibra,pno
TONOS   (L192)

Jag Ska Skapa Ett Nytt Ord *Op.10,
No.2
[Swed] S solo,2ob,2clar,2bsn TONOS
(L193)

Storas Klocka, Det *Op.10,No.3
Bar solo,fl,perc,cel,vcl TONOS
(L194)

LIE, HARALD (1902-1942)
Auf Dunkler Schwingen
see Skinnvengbrev

Elegi *Op.3
Bar solo,2.2(English horn).3(bass
clar).2. 4.2.0.0. harp,strings
[9'] NORGE f.s.   (L195)

Skinnvengbrev *Op.6
"Auf Dunkler Schwingen" [Norw/Ger]
S solo,2.2(English horn).2.2.
4.0.0.0. timp,perc,harp,strings
[5'] NORGE f.s.   (L196)

LIE, SIGURD (1871-1904)
Tvo Sange (Two Songs) *CC2U
(Halvorsen, J.) solo voice,strings
NORSK f.s.   (L197)

LIEBENDE SCHREIBT, DIE see Mendelssohn-
Bartholdy, Felix

LIEBENDEN, DIE see Straesser, Joep

LIEBER AUGUSTIN see Three Celebrated
Waltzes

LIEBERMAN, DAVID
August 27, 1986 Carson City
A solo,2clar,sax,trom,perc,pno,2vcl
[16'] AM.COMP.AL.   (L198)

LIEBERMAN, GLENN
Metamorphosis
S solo,trp,vibra,pno,gtr,harp [14']
AM.COMP.AL. sc $19.00, pts $18.25
(L199)

Songs I Said
S solo,fl/pic,clar/bass clar,vln,
vcl,pno,perc [16'] sc AM.COMP.AL.
$16.90   (L200)

Wedding Song: An Apache Prayer
S solo,pno [4'] sc AM.COMP.AL.
$1.20   (L201)

LIEBES- UND EROTISCHE VOLKSLIEDER
(Molkenbur) PETERS 10299   (L202)

LIEBESFRÜHLING, OP. 11 see Kienzl,
Wilhelm

LIEBESGLÜCK WALTZ, OP.224 see Bohm,
Karl, Loves Ecstasy

LIEBESLIEDER see Cilensek, Johann see
Schultheiss, Ulrich

LIEBESLIEDER, OP. 9 see Mattiesen

LIEBLICH SANG DIE HOLDE NACHTIGALL see
Glière, Reinhold Moritzovich

LIEBLINGSPLÄTZCHEN see Mendelssohn-
Bartholdy, Felix

LIEBSTER JESU, HÖR MEIN FLEHEN see
Bach, Johann Michael

LIED see Flothuis, Marius see Franck,
Cesar see Herold, Louis-Joseph-
Ferdinand see Marx, Joseph see
Richter, Nico see Solbiati,
Alessandro see Zimmerman, S.A.

LIED AUS RUG BLAS see Mendelssohn-
Bartholdy, Felix

LIED (DE PUT DER ZUCHTEN) see Bilt,
Willem van der

LIED DER SONNE see Lothar, Mark

LIED DER TANKISTEN see Eisler, Hanns,
Auf Zum Kampfe, Tankbrigaden

LIED EINES FREUDENMÄDCHENS see Eisler,
Hanns

LIED EINES MÄDCHENS see Marx, Joseph

LIED EINES SCHIFFERS AN DIE DIOSKUREN
see Schubert, Franz (Peter)

LIED IN DER FERNE see Zumsteeg, Emilie

LIED TEDESCO, IL, VOL. 1 *CCU
(Battaglia, E.) S/T solo,pno CURCI
10919 f.s.   (L203)

LIED TEDESCO, IL, VOL. 2 *CCU
(Battaglia, E.) Mez/Bar solo,pno
CURCI 10920 f.s.   (L204)

LIED TEDESCO, IL, VOL. 3 *CCU
(Battaglia, E.) A/B solo,pno CURCI
10921 f.s.   (L205)

LIED ÜBER DIE GERECHTIGKEIT see Eisler,
Hanns

LIED VOM KRIEGERISCHEN LEHRER, DAS see
Eisler, Hanns

LIED VOM SA-MANN see Eisler, Hanns

LIED VOM TROCKENBROT see Eisler, Hanns

LIED VON DER BELEBENDEN WIRKUNG DES
GELDES see Eisler, Hanns

LIED VON DER ERDE, DAS see Mahler,
Gustav

LIED VON DER LIEBE see Keussler,
Gerhard von

LIED VON MEER see Norby, Erik

LIED VOOR EEN PRIESTERFEEST see
Clemens, Henri

LIED ZUR TRAUUNG see Hummel, Bertold

LIEDEKIJN see Visser, Peter

LIEDER see Gerster, Ottmar see
Griesbach, Karl-Rudi see Krause-
Graumnitz, Heinz see Meyer see
Petzold, Rudolf

LIEDER, 101 see Roelli, H.

LIEDER 1-6, OP. 2 AUS "DER SIEBENTE
RING" see Frommel, Gerhard

LIEDER see Wagner-Regeny, Rudolf

LIEDER ALBUM see Volkmar, Andrae

LIEDER ALBUM FÜR DIE JUGEND, OP. 79 see
Schumann, Robert (Alexander)

LIEDER AND ROMANCES see Offenbach,
Jacques

LIEDER AUS ASIEN, OP. 11 see Verhaar,
Ary

LIEDER AUS DEM "DREISTROPHEN-KALENDER,
27, HEFT 1: NEUN LIEDER FÜR HOHEN
SOPRAN, BARITON UND KLAVIER see

Dessau, Paul

LIEDER AUS DEM "DREISTROPHEN-KALENDER,
27, HEFT 2: NEUN LIEDER FÜR SOPRAN,
BASS UND KLAVIER see Dessau, Paul

LIEDER AUS DEM "DREISTROPHEN-KALENDER",
27, HEFT 3: NEUN LIEDER FÜR ALT,
TENOR UND KLAVIER see Dessau, Paul

LIEDER AUS DER JUGENDZEIT see Wolf,
Hugo

LIEDER AUS DES KNABEN WUNDERHORN, 30,
VOL. 1, NOS. 1-10 see Streicher,
Theodore

LIEDER AUS DES KNABEN WUNDERHORN, 30,
VOL. 2, NOS. 11-20 see Streicher,
Theodore

LIEDER AUS DES KNABEN WUNDERHORN, 30,
VOL. 3, NOS. 21-30 see Streicher,
Theodore

LIEDER AUS LETZTER ZEIT see Mahler,
Gustav

LIEDER AUSWAHL see Brahms, Johannes

LIEDER, BAND 1 see Liszt, Franz see
Meyerbeer, Giacomo

LIEDER, BAND 1 see Louis Ferdinand,
Prince Of Prussia

LIEDER, BAND 2 see Liszt, Franz

LIEDER, BAND 2 see Louis Ferdinand,
Prince Of Prussia

LIEDER, BAND 3 see Liszt, Franz

LIEDER, BAND 3 see Louis Ferdinand,
Prince Of Prussia

LIEDER, BAND 4 see Louis Ferdinand,
Prince Of Prussia

LIEDER, BAND 5 see Louis Ferdinand,
Prince Of Prussia

LIEDER, BAND 6 see Louis Ferdinand,
Prince Of Prussia

LIEDER DER VOLKER, VOL. 1 *CCU
(Behrend, Siegfried) solo voice,gtr
PLUCKED STR ZM 1398 $5.25   (L206)

LIEDER DER VOLKER, VOL. 2 *CCU
(Behrend, Siegfried) solo voice,gtr
PLUCKED STR ZM 1709 $5.25   (L207)

LIEDER DER VOLKER, VOL. 3 *CCU
(Behrend, Siegfried) solo voice,gtr
PLUCKED STR ZM 1745 $5.25   (L208)

LIEDER DER VOLKER, VOL. 4 *CCU
(Behrend, Siegfried) solo voice,gtr
PLUCKED STR ZM 1784 $5.25   (L209)

LIEDER DER VOLKER, VOL. 5 *CCU
(Behrend, Siegfried) solo voice,gtr
PLUCKED STR ZM 1785 $5.25   (L210)

LIEDER EINES FAHRENDEN GESELLEN see
Mahler, Gustav see Mahler, Gustav

LIEDER EINES MALERS MIT RANDZEICHNUNGEN
SEINER FREUNDE see Reinick, Robert

LIEDER FÜR EINE SINGSTIMME MIT BEGLEIT.
D. GUITARRE see Krebs, Karl August

LIEDER FÜR EINE SINGSTIMME UND KLAVIER
see Eisler, Hanns

LIEDER FÜR GESANG UND KLAVIER see
Hensel, Fanny Mendelssohn

LIEDER FÜR TENOR see Geisthardt, Hans-
Joachim

LIEDER MIT BEGLEITUNG D. GUITARRE see
Kücken, Friedrich Wilhelm

LIEDER MIT BEGLEITUNG D. PIANOFORTE see
Lindblad, Adolf Fredrik

LIEDER MÖNCH see Kindscher, Ludwig

LIEDER NACH FONTANE see Wagner-Regeny,
Rudolf

LIEDER NACH LEISING see Katzer, Georg

LIEDER NACH TEXTEN VON RELLSTAB, HEINE
UND SEIDL see Schubert, Franz
(Peter)

LIEDER (NEUAUSGABE), BAND 1 see
Schubert, Franz (Peter)

LIEDER (NEUAUSGABE), BAND 2 see
Schubert, Franz (Peter)

LIEDER (NEUAUSGABE), BAND 3 see
Schubert, Franz (Peter)

LIEDER (NEUAUSGABE), BAND 4 see
Schubert, Franz (Peter)

LIEDER, OP. 2 see Mattiesen

LIEDER, OP. 3 see Mattiesen

LIEDER, OP. 11 see Mattiesen

LIEDER, OP. 12 see Mattiesen

LIEDER, OP. 13 see Baumann, Alexander

LIEDER UND GESÄNGE see Grabner, Hermann

LIEDER UND GESÄNGE see Lambort, Carl R.
Von

LIEDER UND GESÄNGE MIT BEGLEITUNG D.
PIANOFORTE see Mendelssohn-
Bartholdy, Felix

LIEDER UND GESANGE, PART 2, OP. 51 see
Schumann, Robert (Alexander)

LIEDER UND GESANGE, PART 3, OP. 77 see
Schumann, Robert (Alexander)

LIEDER UND GESÄNGE, VOL. 1 see
Vanderstucken, Frank

LIEDER UND GESÄNGE, VOL. 2 see
Vanderstucken, Frank

LIEDER UND ROMANZEN see Audefroi Le
Bastard

LIEDER, VOL. 1 see Shimizu, Osamu

LIEDER, VOL. 2 see Shimizu, Osamu

LIEDER ZU GEDICHTEN VON TAGORE see
Sønstevold, Gunnar

LIEDER ZUR FESTLICHEN ZEIT see Taubert,
Karl Heinz

LIEDEREN see Hengeveld, Gerard

LIEDEREN OP ZUID-AFRIKAANSE TEKST see
Wijdeveld, Wolfgang

LIEDERKRANZ FÜR BASS, OP. 145 see
Loewe, Carl Gottfried

LIEDERKREIS, OP. 39 see Schumann,
Robert (Alexander)

LIEDERZYKLUS BEPPINO see Wilbrandt,
Jürgen

LIEDJE see Weegenhuise, Johan

LIEDJIE see Badings, Henk

LIEDS DE FRANCE DE CATULLE MENDÈS, LES
see Bruneau, Alfred

LIEFDESPAAR BIJ HET RAAM see
Andriessen, Jurriaan

LIER, BERTUS VAN (1906-1972)
Vrijheid
high solo,pno/org [6'] DONEMUS
(L211)

LIFE FOR THE TSAR, A: ORPHAN'S SONG
(#1) see Glinka, Mikhail Ivanovich

LIFE FOR THE TSAR, A: SOUSSANINE'S ARIA
see Glinka, Mikhail Ivanovich

LIFE STUDY see Sollberger, Harvey

LIFE XCVI see Haxton, Kenneth

LIGHT see As, Cees van see Norholm, Ib,
Lys

LIGHT AND SPLENDOUR see Gottlieb, Jack
S.

LIGHTFOOT, MISS
Fairy's Voyage, The
see Make Ready! Make Ready! My
Nautilus Bark

Make Ready! Make Ready! My Nautilus
Bark
"Fairy's Voyage, The" SCIEN 947
(L212)

LIGNELSE, EN see Taubo, Lillian Gulowna

LIKE A LILAC see Sveinbjörnsson,
Sveinbjörn

LIKE BLOSSOM DEW see Rachmaninoff,
Sergey Vassilievich

LIKE STRANGERS see Cowles, Darleen

LILAC TIME see Foote, Arthur

LILACS see Rachmaninoff, Sergey
Vassilievich

LILBURN, DOUGLAS (1915-   )
Elegy
Bar solo,pno WAI-TE-ATA 93   (L213)

Sings Harry
T solo,gtr WAI-TE-ATA 44   (L214)

Three Songs
Bar solo,vla WAI-TE-ATA 100 (L215)
solo voice,pno WAI-TE-ATA 101
(L216)

LILJA see Hovland, Egil see
Sigurbjörnsson, Thorkell

LILJA, BERNHARD (1895-   )
Liten Visa, En
solo voice,pno STIM f.s.   (L217)

Vårvisa
solo voice,pno STIM f.s.   (L218)

Visan Om Kossan Och Flugan
solo voice,pno STIM f.s.   (L219)

LILLE NORGE see Knutson, Geir

LILLY IN A CHRISTAL, THE see Douw,
Andre

LILY OF KILLARNEY: THE MOON HAS RAISED
HER LAMP ABOVE see Benedict, [Sir]
Julius

LIME JELLO MARSHMALLOW COTTAGE CHEESE
SURPRISE see Bolcom, William Elden

LINA: TU CHE VOLASTI see Ponchielli,
Amilcare

LINCOLN THE GREAT COMMONER see Ives,
Charles

LINDA see Halldorsson, Skuli

LINDA DI CHAMOUNIX: SE TANTO IN IRA
AGLI UOMINI see Donizetti, Gaetano

LINDBLAD, ADOLF FREDRIK (1801-1878)
Lieder Mit Begleitung D. Pianoforte
SCIEN 950   (L220)

Sånger Och Visor Vid Pianoforte
(Linder, Kerstin) (contains 23
pieces) GEHRMANS 6532   (L221)

LINDE, BO (1933-1970)
För Alla Vindar
solo voice,pno EGTVED 432 from
AKSEL SCHIØETZ ANTHOLOGY OF
NORDIC SOLO SONGS, THE, VOL. 2
(L222)

Tio Naiva Sånger *Op.20
Mez solo,pno SUECIA 302   (L223)

LINDE, DIE see Hackensöllner, L.

LINDEMAN, LUDVIG MATHIAS (1812-1887)
Fjorten Melodier Fra Brorsons
Svanesang *CC14U
LYCHE 507 f.s.   (L224)

LINDEN LEA see Vaughan Williams, Ralph

LINDENBAUM see Schubert, Franz (Peter)

LINDENFELD, HARRIS NELSON (1945-   )
From The Book Of Pictures
[Ger] S solo,fl,clar,perc,vln,vla,
vcl,pno [17'] AM.COMP.AL. sc
$24.45, pts $39.05   (L225)

Gravediggers
S solo,fl,pno,perc [6'] sc
AM.COMP.AL. $11.70   (L226)

Three Dickinson Songs *CC3U
S solo,clar in E flat,pno
AM.COMP.AL. sc $7.70, pts $10.30
(L227)

Three Songs After Rilke *CC3U
S solo,fl,clar,horn,vcl,perc,pno,
conductor sc AM.COMP.AL. $24.90
(L228)

Two Poems Of Robert Hedin *CC2U
S solo,clar,pno sc AM.COMP.AL.
$1.90   (L229)

LINDGREN, OLOF (1934-   )
Sex Sånger Till Texter Av Emil
Hagström
[Swed] Bar solo,orch TONOS   (L230)

LINDGREN, PÄR (1952-   )
Shadowes That In Darknesse Dwell
S solo,chamber orch,pno SUECIA 341
(L231)

LINDPREDIKAN see Blomberg, Erik

LINDSJO, INGA (1922-   )
I Ögat
solo voice,2rec STIM   (L232)

LINDWALL, CHRISTER
Twang
S solo,bass clar,pno TONOS   (L233)

LINES see Sifonia, Firmino

LINJAMA, JYRKI
Legende
[Ger] S solo,fl REIMERS 101142
(L234)

LINKE, NORBERT (1933-   )
...Und Nahm Gestalt An
28 solo voices [6'] voc sc
BREITKOPF-W BG 600 f.s.   (L235)

Was Sterblich War...
28 solo voices [10'] voc sc
BREITKOPF-W BG 744 f.s.   (L236)

LINLEY, GEORGE (1798-1865)
Night Before The Bridal, The
SCIEN 954   (L237)

Swiss Girl, The
solo voice,pno SCIEN 953   (L238)

LION YAWNS, THE see Nystedt, Knut,
Løven Gjesper

LIPTAK, DAVID (1949-   )
Pulse Music
Mez solo,fl,vla [5'] sc AM.COMP.AL.
$5.40   (L239)

Seven Songs *CC7U
med solo,pno sc AM.COMP.AL. $12.65
(L240)

LIRICHE SU VERLAINE see Maderna, Bruno

LISTEN...! see Tenney, James C.

LISTEN TO ME see Clarke, Henry Leland

LISZT, FRANZ (1811-1886)
Comment, Disaient-Ils
[Ger/Fr] high solo,pno (1st
version) CLASSV 1835   (L241)

Drei Zigeuner
[Eng/Ger] low solo,pno CLASSV 1192
(L242)

Enfant, Si J'étais Roi
[Ger/Eng] high solo,pno (1st
version) CLASSV 1836   (L243)

Franz Liszt: Complete Works For Organ
Volume 9, Works For Voice(S) And
Organ *CC13L
(Haselboeck, Martin) UNIVER.
UE17891   (L244)

Lieder, Band 1
(D'Albert) high solo,pno KAHNT
1000A   (L245)
(D'Albert) med solo,pno KAHNT 1000B
(L246)
(D'Albert) low solo,pno KAHNT 1000C
(L247)

Lieder, Band 2
(D'Albert) high solo,pno KAHNT
1100A   (L248)
(D'Albert) med solo,pno KAHNT 1100B
(L249)
(D'Albert) low solo,pno KAHNT 1100C
(L250)

Lieder, Band 3
(D'Albert) high solo,pno KAHNT
1200A   (L251)
(D'Albert) med solo,pno KAHNT 1200B
(L252)
(D'Albert) low solo,pno KAHNT 1200C
(L253)

Oh! Quand Je Dors
high solo,pno CLASSV 0458   (L254)
med solo,pno CLASSV 0815   (L255)

Psalm No. 23
high solo,org KAHNT 2387   (L256)

S'il Est Un Charmant Gazon (1st
Version)
[Fr/Ger] high solo,pno CLASSV 1841
(L257)

S'il Est Un Charmant Gazon (2nd
Version)
[Fr] med-high solo,pno CLASSV 1837
(L258)

Songs, Vol. 1
[Ger/Fr] high solo KALMUS K 09375
(L259)

Songs, Vol. 1 *CCU
BOOSEY EMB03346 f.s.   (L260)

Songs, Vol. 2
[It/Ger] high solo KALMUS K 09376
(L261)

Songs, Vol. 2 *CCU
BOOSEY EMB03347 f.s.   (L262)

Songs, Vol. 3 *CCU
BOOSEY EMB03348 f.s.   (L263)

Songs, Vol. 4 *CCU
BOOSEY EMB04005 f.s.   (L264)

LISZT, FRANZ (cont'd.)

Songs, Vol. 5
[Ger] high solo KALMUS K 09379
(L265)

Songs, Vol. 5 *CCU
BOOSEY EMB04006 f.s.   (L266)

Songs, Vol. 6 *CCU
BOOSEY EMB04007 f.s.   (L267)

Tre Sonetti Di Petrarca (1st Version)
T solo,pno CLASSV 0824   (L268)

Tre Sonetti Di Petrarca (2nd Version)
Bar solo,pno CLASSV 0823   (L269)

Zwanzig Ausgewählte Lieder
(D'Albert) high solo,pno PETERS
8590A   (L270)
(D'Albert) high solo,pno KAHNT
1300A   (L271)
(D'Albert) med solo,pno KAHNT 1300B
(L272)
(D'Albert) low solo,pno KAHNT 1300C
(L273)

LITA JENTE, EI see Taubo, Lillian
Gulowna

LITANIES DE LA BEAUTÉ see Puget, Paul-
Charles-Marie

LITEN VISA, EN see Lilja, Bernhard

LITEN VISE, EN see Volle, Bjarne

LITET STEV TIL MOR, EIT see Kielland,
Olav

LITILL FUGL see Halldorsson, Skuli

LITLA FLUGAN see Halldorsson, Sigfus

LITLA KVAEDID UM LITLU HJONIN see
Isolfsson, Pall

LITO see Shut, Wasyl

LITTLE, DAVID (1952-   )
Battleship Newsreel
see Reality Sandwiches

Funny Death
see Reality Sandwiches

On Burrough's Work
see Reality Sandwiches

Reality Sandwiches
T solo,pno DONEMUS f.s. [17']
contains: Battleship Newsreel;
Funny Death; On Burrough's
Work; Sakyamuni Coming Out From
The Mountain   (L274)

Sakyamuni Coming Out From The
Mountain
see Reality Sandwiches

LITTLE BIRD, A see Eggen, Arne, Og Det
Var Litin Småfugl

LITTLE BIRD AND STARS, A see Asaoka,
Makiko

LITTLE BOY LOST, INTERLUDE, LITTLE BOY
FOUND see Haxton, Kenneth

LITTLE CHILD THERE IS BORN, A see
Canning, Thomas

LITTLE DAMOZEL see Novello

LITTLE FLY see Carpenter, John Alden

LITTLE GIRL PRACTICING, A see Heilner,
Irwin

LITTLE JESUS, SWEETLY SLEEP see
Sowerby, Leo

LITTLE LAMB see Franco, Johan

LITTLE LOVE-GOD, THE see Ketting, Piet

LITTLE LOVE-GOD LYING ONCE ASLEEP, THE
see Andriessen, Jurriaan

LITTLE LOVE MUSIC, A see Bush, Geoffrey

LITTLE SHEEP, EARLY SPRING see
Kurokami, Yoshimitsu

LITTLE SONGS FOR LITTLE VALLY see
Weigl, [Mrs.] Vally

LITTLE VAGABOND, THE see Luening, Otto

LITURGIE DES DÉFUNTS see Meyer

LITURGISK MUSIKK see Hovland, Egil

LIVE WITH ME see Björnsson, Arni

LIVRO BRAZILEIRO I see Prado, Ameida

LIVRO BRAZILEIRO II see Prado, Ameida

LJODAKORN see Sveinsson, Atli Heimir

LJODNAMULAND see Eiriksdottir, Karolina

LJOS see Helgason, Hallgrimur

LJOSNAR DET ALDRI see Kvamme, Sigmund

LJUFLINGAR see Kaldalóns, Sigvaldi S.

LJUVT KLOKKENE KIMER FRÅ HIMELRIK see
Madsen, Trygve

LLOVERA, J.
Canción De Amor
solo voice,pno BOIL B.0648 (L275)

Tus Ojos
solo voice,pno BOIL B.0649 (L276)

LLOYD WEBBER, ANDREW (1949-)
Any Dream Will Do (from Joseph And
The Amazing Technicolor
Dreamcoat)
NOVELLO 170288 (L277)

LO, HERE THE GENTLE LARK see Bishop,
[Sir] Henry (Rowley)

LOAN I MONUM see Helgason, Hallgrimur

LOB DER THRÄNEN see Schubert, Franz
(Peter)

LOB DES FRÜHLINGS see Marx, Joseph

LOB DES KOMMUNISMUS see Eisler, Hanns

LOB DES LEIDENS see Strauss, Richard

LOB DES LERNENS see Eisler, Hanns

LOB DES SISYPHUS see Meier, Burkhard

LOCH LOMOND see Anonymous

LOCKE
Cantate Domino
SS/TT soli,cont KING'S KM37 (L278)

O Domine Jesu Christe
SS/TT soli,cont KING'S KM38 (L279)

LOCKERBONES - AIRBONES see Armer,
Elinor

LOCKLAIR, DAN STEVEN (1949-)
Boswell Songs
high solo,pno KERBY 50481265 (L280)

Portraits [1]
S solo,pno KERBY 50481267 (L281)

Portraits [2]
S solo,pno KERBY 50481257 (L282)

LOCKUNG see Dessauer, Josef see Gideon,
Miriam

LOCKWOOD, NORMAND (1906-)
Fallen Is Babylon The Great,
Hallelujah
Mez solo,pno [17'] sc AM.COMP.AL.
$13.00 (L283)

Four Songs *song cycle
S solo,pno [12'] sc AM.COMP.AL.
$7.70 (L284)

Four Songs *song cycle
S solo,vln,org [12'] sc AM.COMP.AL.
$9.15 (L285)

To Margarita Debayle
S solo,pno [12'] sc AM.COMP.AL.
$9.15 (L286)

LODER, EDWIN JAMES
Flower That Grows Upon The Thorn, The
SCIEN 977 (L287)

LODOLETTA: IL CANTO DEI FIORI see
Mascagni, Pietro

LODOLETTA: IL RIMPIANTO DI FLAMMEN see
Mascagni, Pietro

LOEFFLER, CHARLES MARTIN (1861-1935)
Dream Within A Dream, A
med solo,pno (text by Edgar A. Poe)
CLASSV 1654 (L288)

Quatre Poems, Op. 5
med solo,vla CLASSV 0568 (L289)

LOEVENDIE, THEO (1930-)
All The Flowers Of The Spring
MezT soli,pno [4'] DONEMUS f.s.
(L290)

As Fast As Thou Shalt Wane (from
Naima)
S solo,pno [2'] DONEMUS (L291)

LOEVENDIE, THEO (cont'd.)

see Two Songs From The Opera Naima
see Two Songs, From The Opera Naima

Man Of Life Upright, The
see Two Songs From The Opera Naima
see Two Songs, From The Opera Naima

Nachtegaal In Echternach, Een
S/Mez solo,pno [4'] DONEMUS (L292)

Two Songs From The Opera Naima
Mez solo,fl,bass clar,perc,mand,
gtr,harp,vln,db DONEMUS f.s. [6']
contains: As Fast As Thou Shalt
Wane; Man Of Life Upright, The
(L293)

Two Songs, From The Opera Naima
Mez solo,pno DONEMUS f.s. [6']
contains: As Fast As Thou Shalt
Wane; Man Of Life Upright, The
(L294)

LOEWE, CARL GOTTFRIED (1796-1869)
Canzonette
"War Schöne Als Der Schönste Tag"
high solo,pno CLASSV 0572 (L295)

Drei Lieder Des Thurmwächters Lynceus
med-high solo,pno (text by Goethe)
CLASSV 0571 (L296)

Frauenliebe *song cycle
A solo,pno CLASSV 0736 (L297)

Geistliche Gesänge *CC25L
(Hirschberg, Leopold) med solo,pno/
org BRATFISCH f.s. (L298)

Heinzelmännchen, Die *Op.83
[Ger] B solo,pno CLASSV 2101 (L299)

Herr Oluf *Op.2,No.2
B solo,pno (lower in d) CLASSV 1839
(L300)

Liederkranz Für Bass, Op. 145
[Ger] B solo RECITAL 2239 (L301)

Meeresleuchten *Op.145,No.1
B solo,pno CLASSV 1838 (L302)

Meine Ruh' Ist Hin
A solo,pno (text by Goethe) CLASSV
1052 (L303)

Papagei, Der
high solo,pno (text by Rückert)
CLASSV 0467 (L304)

Scene Aus Faust: Ach Neige, Du
Schmerzenreiche
Mez solo,pno (text by Goethe)
CLASSV (L305)

Verliebte Schäferin Scapine, Die
Mez solo,pno (text by Goethe)
CLASSV 1050 (L306)

Wandrers Nachtlied: Der Du Von Dem
Himmel Bist
med-high solo,pno (text by Goethe)
CLASSV 0569 (L307)

Wandrers Nachtlied: Über Allen
Gipfeln Ist Ruh
med-high solo,pno (text by Goethe)
CLASSV 1053 (L308)

War Schöne Als Der Schönste Tag
see Canzonette

Wenn Der Blüthen Frühlingsregen
med-high solo,pno (text by Goethe)
CLASSV 1049 (L309)

LOEWE, KARL
see LOEWE, CARL GOTTFRIED

LOF VAN NEDERLAND, VOL. 1 see King,
Harold C.

LOF VAN NEDERLAND, VOL. 2 see King,
Harold C.

LOF VAN NEDERLAND, VOL. 3 see King,
Harold C.

LOF VAN NEDERLAND, VOL. 4 see King,
Harold C.

LOF VAN NEDERLAND, VOL. 5 see King,
Harold C.

LOGORATO IL TEMPO see Sampaoli, Luciano

LOHENGRIN: ELSA'S DREAM see Wagner,
Richard

LOHENGRIN: IN FERNEM LAND see Wagner,
Richard

LOHMANN, HEINZ
Drei Geistliche Lieder
S solo,clar,org ERES 2653 f.s.
contains: Einsiedler, Der; Ich
Singe Dir Mit Herz Und Mund;

LOHMANN, HEINZ (cont'd.)

Zufriedenheit, Die (L310)

Einsiedler, Der
see Drei Geistliche Lieder

Ich Singe Dir Mit Herz Und Mund
see Drei Geistliche Lieder

Zufriedenheit, Die
see Drei Geistliche Lieder

LOITSU: (INCANTATION) see Hambraeus,
Bengt

LOKAJ, JAKUB (1752- ?)
Haec Aurora Gratiosa
(Sestak, Zdenek) [Lat] S solo,
0.2.0.0. 2.0.0.0. org,strings
[5'] CESKY HUD. (L311)

LOKK see Karlsen, Kjell Mørk

LOKKENDE TONER see Kjerulf, Halfdan

LOKKETRALL OG SOMAR-NATT see
Storbekken, Egil

LOLA, OP. 116 see Saint-Saëns, Camille

LOLINI, RUGGERO (1932-)
Albasia
Bar solo,fl,ob,bsn,pno EDI-PAN
EP 7733 (L312)

Arianna (Lamento)
solo voice,vln,clar,pno EDI-PAN
EP 7444 (L313)

Asheham
solo voice,wind quin EDI-PAN
EP 7244 (L314)

Canzona
solo voice,gtr,pno,opt hpsd&cel
EDI-PAN EP 7452 (L315)

Lasciata...Giovinezza... (from Emily
D)
S solo,pno EDI-PAN EP 643 (L316)

Oh Nacht!...
solo voice,clar EDI-PAN EP 7447
(L317)

Ora Che E Venuta La Notte (from
Requiem Dei Poveri)
S solo,pno EDI-PAN EP 626 (L318)

Passi Che Conosco E Temo (from Emily
D)
S solo,pno,vcl EDI-PAN EP 644
(L319)

Tavor
S solo,sax,pno EDI-PAN EP 7203
(L320)

...Tra Foglie
solo voice EDI-PAN EP7375 (L321)

LOLITA see Buzzi-Peccia, Arturo

LOMBARDI, DANIELE
Orphee
S solo,pno EDI-PAN EP 7827 (L322)

LOMBARDI, I: LA MIA LETIZIA INFONDERE
see Verdi, Giuseppe

LOMBARDI, I: SALVE MARIA see Verdi,
Giuseppe

LOMBARDO, ROBERT M. (1932-)
Aria Variata
S solo,string orch [11']
AM.COMP.AL. (L323)

Climbing For Tree Frogs
S solo,pno/hpsd [9'] sc AM.COMP.AL.
$7.70 (L324)

Climbing For Tree Frogs: Four Love
Songs *CC4U
S solo,fl,ob,clar,marimba,harp,vla,
db AM.COMP.AL. sc $15.30, pts
$6.55 (L325)

Dialogues Of Lovers
SBar soli,fl,ob,clar,trom,pno,perc,
vln,vla,vcl [12'] AM.COMP.AL. sc
$22.80, pts $43.35 (L326)

Erogenous Zones, Or Neglected Parts
S solo,pic/fl/alto fl,perc [9'] sc
AM.COMP.AL. $6.90 (L327)

Fanfare And Aria
S solo,vcl,2perc [2'] sc
AM.COMP.AL. $3.50 (L328)

Frosted Window: Variations On White
S solo,bsn,vla,perc [9']
AM.COMP.AL. sc $5.40, pts $3.10
(L329)

Songs To Kandinsky
S solo,clar/bass clar,vla [11'] sc
AM.COMP.AL. $9.15 (L330)

LONDON DAYORI see Hayakawa, Kuzuko

LONELINESS see Rachmaninoff, Sergey Vassilievich

LONELY see Olsen, Sparre, Einsleg

LONESOME MAN see Kjellsby, Erling, Einsam Mann

LONESOME WOMAN, THE see Prosperi, Maurizio

LONG AGO IN ALCALA see Messager, Andre

LONGEST WAIT, THE see Menotti, Gian Carlo

LONGING see Duncan, Chester

LONGING FOR THE EMPEROR (INTERVALS III) see Straesser, Joep

LONGING FOR THE EMPEROR (INTERVALS III), SECOND & EXTENDED VERSION see Straesser, Joep

LÖNNER, ODDVAR (1954-   )
    C
    [Ger] T solo,pno [5'] (text from
        The Bible: Epistle to the Romans)
        NORGE   (L331)

    Missa Prolationum
        S solo,vln,vla,2vcl,db,pno,
        wienerhorn [20'] NORGE   (L332)

LONTANANZA see Savina, Carlo

LOOK, THE see Flothuis, Marius

LOOK DOWN FAIR MOON see Goldberg, William

LOOKING BACK AT FADED CHANDELIERS see Rosenman, Leonard

LOOKING-GLASS RIVER see Carpenter, John Alden

LOOR A MARGARITA see Massana, A.

LOPEZ ARTIGA, ANGELES
    Caminos *CC7L
        solo voice PILES 1211-P f.s. (L333)

    Cancion
        see Intimismos

    Hombre Pequeñito
        see Intimismos

    Intimismos
        solo voice PILES 1210-P f.s.
        contains: Cancion; Hombre
        Pequeñito; Mujer De Barro;
        Pensamiento Raro   (L334)

    Mujer De Barro
        see Intimismos

    Pensamiento Raro
        see Intimismos

LOPEZ DE SAA, EMILIO
    De La Habana Ha Venido Un Barco
        solo voice,pno BOIL B.2834 (L335)

LORD, BE OUR WEDDING GUEST see Childs, Edwin T.

LORD IS MY SHEPHERD, THE see Matthews, Thomas

LORD'S PRAYER, THE see Dillard, Donald E. see Leifs, Jon see Lybbert, Donald

LORELEI: ET TYSK FOLKEEVENTYR see Holm, Kristin

LORELEI: FAVORITE PIECES OF YUMIKO SAMEZIMA
    (Deutsch, H.) (CCU) ONGAKU 522310
                                (L336)

LORELEY see Silcher, Friedrich

LORELEY, DIE see Grahn, Ulf

LORELEY: AMOR, CELESTE see Catalani, Alfredo

LORELEY: OVE SON? CHE FU? see Catalani, Alfredo

LORNA'S SONG see Ross, Colin Archibald Campbell

LORTZING, (GUSTAV) ALBERT (1801-1851)
    Waffenschmied, Der: Er Schläft - Er
        Ist So Gut
        [Ger] S solo,pno CLASSV 1181 (L337)

LÖSCHE DIE LAMPE see Focke, Fré

LOSREISSUNG see Kunad, Rainer, Klopstock-Ode

LOSSNA see Holm, Kristin

LOST CHORD see Sullivan, [Sir] Arthur Seymour

LOST IS MY LOVE see Corbett, W.

LOST LOVE see Downes, Andrew

LOTH, URBAN (1580-1636)
    Drei Geistliche Konzerte Zur
        Weihnachtszeit
        (Ruhland, Konrad) SS/TT soli,cont
        (Musik Aus Ostbayern, Heft 14)
        COPPENRATH   (L338)

LOTHAR, MARK (1902-1985)
    Albrecht Goes-Lieder *Op.61
        solo voice RIES f.s.
        contains: Laute-Spielender Engel;
        Rose Des Abendlandes; Schritte,
        Die; Unendlichkeit   (L339)

    Christian Morgenstern, Heft I
        solo voice RIES f.s.
        contains: Elfenreigen; Fips; Herr
        Löffel Und Frau Gabel;
        Traumliedchen   (L340)

    Christian Morgenstern, Heft II
        solo voice RIES f.s.
        contains: Drei Spatzen, Die; Lied
        Der Sonne; Weihnachtsbäumlein,
        Das; Winternacht   (L341)

    Drei Spatzen, Die
        see Christian Morgenstern, Heft II

    Elfenreigen
        see Christian Morgenstern, Heft I

    Fips
        see Christian Morgenstern, Heft I

    Herr Löffel Und Frau Gabel
        see Christian Morgenstern, Heft I

    Laute-Spielender Engel
        see Albrecht Goes-Lieder

    Lied Der Sonne
        see Christian Morgenstern, Heft II

    Rose Des Abendlandes
        see Albrecht Goes-Lieder

    Schritte, Die
        see Albrecht Goes-Lieder

    Traumliedchen
        see Christian Morgenstern, Heft I

    Unendlichkeit
        see Albrecht Goes-Lieder

    Weihnachtsbäumlein, Das
        see Christian Morgenstern, Heft II

    Winternacht
        see Christian Morgenstern, Heft II

    Zwei Lieder Des Mephisto Op. 39
        solo voice,pno RIES 60035   (L342)

LOTOSBLUME, DIE see Amerongen, Jan van
    see Schumann, Robert (Alexander)

LOTUS FLOWER BANK see Hekster, Walter

LOUIS FERDINAND, PRINCE OF PRUSSIA
    (1907-1994)
    Abendfrieden
        see Lieder, Band 3

    Abendständchen
        see Lieder, Band 3

    An Die Leserin
        see Lieder, Band 2

    Dank
        see Lieder, Band 1

    Es Gibt Ein Lied
        see Lieder, Band 6

    Gebet
        see Lieder, Band 1

    In Danzig
        see Lieder, Band 3

    Kleines Abendlied
        see Lieder, Band 1

    Lieder, Band 1
        high solo,pno HEINRICH. 766 f.s.
        contains: Dank; Gebet; Kleines
        Abendlied; Musikantengruss;
        Vorgefühl; Wiegenlied   (L343)

LOUIS FERDINAND, PRINCE OF PRUSSIA
    (cont'd.)
    Lieder, Band 2
        high solo,pno HEINRICH. 614 f.s.
        contains: An Die Leserin;
        Russisches Volkslied; Tote
        Spricht, Der; Woher Ich Komme
                                    (L344)

    Lieder, Band 3
        low solo,pno HEINRICH. 877 f.s.
        contains: Abendfrieden;
        Abendständchen; In Danzig;
        Meeressehnsucht; Russische
        Romanze; Treue; Währende, Das
                                    (L345)

    Lieder, Band 4 *CC11L
        high solo,pno HEINRICH. 959 f.s.
                                    (L346)

    Lieder, Band 5 *CC12L
        high solo,pno HEINRICH. 1844 f.s.
                                    (L347)

    Lieder, Band 6
        high solo,pno HEINRICH. 2035 f.s.
        contains: Es Gibt Ein Lied;
        Morgensonne; Mutterjubel;
        Phantasie   (L348)

    Meeressehnsucht
        see Lieder, Band 3

    Morgensonne
        see Lieder, Band 6

    Musikantengruss
        see Lieder, Band 1

    Mutterjubel
        see Lieder, Band 6

    Phantasie
        see Lieder, Band 6

    Russische Romanze
        see Lieder, Band 3

    Russisches Volkslied
        see Lieder, Band 2

    Tote Spricht, Der
        see Lieder, Band 2

    Treue
        see Lieder, Band 3

    Vorgefühl
        see Lieder, Band 1

    Währende, Das
        see Lieder, Band 3

    Wiegenlied
        see Lieder, Band 1

    Woher Ich Komme
        see Lieder, Band 2

LOUR I AKRI see Thordarson, Sigurdur

LOUVIER, ALAIN (1945-   )
    Folie Et Mort D'Ophelie *cant
        SBar soli,2.2.2.2. 2.2.2.0. perc,
        timp,strings [20'] BILLAUDOT
                                    (L349)

LOVA HERREN MIN SJÄL see Sköld, Bengt-Göran

LOVANO, MAGUY
    Sourdre
        BarB soli,vla,ob,horn,pno, 1dancer,
        2mimes BILLAUDOT   (L350)

LOVE see Grieg, Edvard Hagerup, Elsk
    see Warren, Betsy

LOVE AND ARITHMETIC see Fitzsimons, H.T.

LOVE AND LAW see Borroff, Edith

LOVE AND MUSIC see Puccini, Giacomo, Tosca: Vissi D'Arte

LOVE AND PITY see Orland, Henry

LOVE AND RESENTMENT see Arne, Thomas Augustine

LOVE AT FIRST SIGHT see Grainger, Ella

LOVE-GARDEN, A see Clough-Leighter, Henry

LOVE HE MUST OR FLATTER ME see Herbert-Caesari, Edgard

LOVE IN THE ASYLUM see Plante, Daniel

LOVE IS CRUEL see Nelson, Havelock

LOVE, LIVE FOREVER see Lehar, Franz

LOVE, LOVE, LOVE see Mourant, Walter

LOVE ME LITTLE, LOVE ME LONG see Mourant, Walter

LOVE MEMORY see Adams, Leslie

LOVE RESPONSE see Adams, Leslie

LOVE SONG see Benton, Daniel Joseph see Jordan, Sverre, Kjaerlighetssang: Hører Du Mitt see Larson, Martin see Stutschevsky, Joachim

LOVE SONG OF THE EIGHTIES see Borroff, Edith

LOVE SONGS see Hagen, Daron

LOVE SONGS see Heilner, Irwin

LOVE SONGS FROM THE EDDA see Leifs, Jon

LOVE SONNETS OF MICHELANGELO see Body, Jack

LOVE UNDER A DIFFERENT SUN see Avni, Tzvi

LOVE WITHOUT WINGS see Hahn, Reynaldo

LOVE XXXIII see Haxton, Kenneth

LOVELACE
God Is Our Song
med solo SHAWNEE 5081   (L351)

LOVELACE, AUSTIN COLE (1919-   )
Wedding Benediction
SCHIRM.G ST41917   (L352)

LOVELY ROSE, IN MEMPHIS, TENNESSEE, A see Slonimsky, Nicolas

LØVEN GJESPER see Nystedt, Knut

LOVENDUSKY, JAMES
Dream Within A Dream, A
S solo,vcl [5'] AM.COMP.AL. sc
$5.40, pts $.80   (L353)

LOVER, SAMUEL
Fairy Boy, The
SCIEN 985   (L354)

LOVER COMPLAYNETH THE UNKINDNESS OF HIS LOVE, THE see Kuiper, Klaus

LOVER'S LAMENT, THE see Sveinbjörnsson, Sveinbjörn

LOVER'S RECANTATION, THE see Arne, Thomas Augustine

LOVES ECSTASY see Bohm, Karl

LØVETANN see Sommerfeldt, Öistein

LOVSANG see Nystedt, Knut

LOWE, KARL
Balladen, Gesänge Und Lieder, Op. 145
see Heimlichkeit

Drei Balladen, Op. 129
see Nöck, Der

Heimlichkeit
med solo,pno SCIEN 986 from
BALLADEN, GESÄNGE UND LIEDER, OP.
145   (L355)

Nöck, Der
solo voice,pno SCIEN 987 from DREI
BALLADEN, OP. 129   (L356)

LOWENSTAMM, FRANZ JOS.
Drei Lieder, Op. 1
S/T solo,pno SCIEN 989 f.s.
contains: Im Wunderschönen Monat
Mai; Mein Herzthu Dich Auf;
Nach Dem Abschiede   (L357)

Im Wunderschönen Monat Mai
see Drei Lieder, Op. 1

Mein Herzthu Dich Auf
see Drei Lieder, Op. 1

Nach Dem Abschiede
see Drei Lieder, Op. 1

LOWLANDS (SHANTY) see Mermaid & Two Other Water Songs, The

LUBETSKY, RONALD
Emergency Songs *CCU
T solo,fl,clar/bass clar,horn,cel,
perc,vln,vla,vcl AM.COMP.AL. sc
$16.90, pts $8.45, pno red $6.90
                              (L358)
Sonnet Cycle
med-high solo,alto fl/pic,ob,clar
in E flat,2perc,pno,harp,vcl
[25'] AM.COMP.AL. sc $18.40, pts
$54.75   (L359)

LUCCIOLE, LE see Brogi, Renato

LUCENT FLOWERS see Thome, Diane

LUCHT, EEN see Ruiter, Wim de

LUCIA DI LAMMERMOOR: ARDO NE GL' INCENSI see Donizetti, Gaetano

LUCIA DI LAMMERMOOR: CRUDA, FUNESTA SMANIA see Donizetti, Gaetano

LUCIA DI LAMMERMOOR: MAD SCENE see Donizetti, Gaetano

LUCIA DI LAMMERMOOR: REGNAVA NEL SILENZIO see Donizetti, Gaetano

LUCIA DI LAMMERMOOR: TU CHE A DIO SPIEGASTI see Donizetti, Gaetano

LUCREZIA BORGIA: COM' È BELLO (WITH CABALETTA) see Donizetti, Gaetano

LUCREZIA BORGIA: IL SEGRETO see Donizetti, Gaetano

LUCREZIA BORGIA: VIENI! LA MIA VENDETTA see Donizetti, Gaetano

LUCTOR ET EMERGO see King, Harold C.

LUDT, FINN (1918-   )
Atte Sanger Til Tekster Fra
"Himmelvarden" Av Olav Aukrust
[Norw] NORSK   (L360)

Heime
[Norw] solo voice,pno NORSK (L361)

Rosa
[Norw] solo voice,pno NORSK (L362)

Vårvise
[Norw] solo voice,pno LYCHE 234
                              (L363)

LUEDEKE, RAYMOND (1944-   )
Pictures From Brueghel
MezBar soli,fl,ob,clar,bsn,horn
[15'] sc AM.COMP.AL. $17.50
                              (L364)
Whispers Of Heavenly Death
SS soli,pno [5'] sc AM.COMP.AL.
$8.40   (L365)

LUENING, OTTO (1900-   )
Ach Wer Bringt Die Schonen Tage
S solo,fl,pno [5'] AM.COMP.AL.
                              (L366)
Little Vagabond, The
med solo,pno [3'] sc AM.COMP.AL.
$2.35   (L367)
Noon Silence
med solo,pno [2'] sc AM.COMP.AL.
$.80   (L368)
Silent, Silent Night
med solo,pno [1'] sc AM.COMP.AL.
$.80   (L369)
Three Songs For Soprano And Small
Orchestra
S solo,2.2.2.1. 2.0.0.0. bells,
harp,strings,vcl solo [6']
AM.COMP.AL.   (L370)
S solo,pno [6'] AM.COMP.AL.   (L371)
Venilia
med solo,pno [22'] sc AM.COMP.AL.
$1.20   (L372)

LUID DAN DE TIJD see Keizer, Henk

LUKAS, ZDENEK (1928-   )
Zasadit Strom *song cycle
B solo,string orch [14'] CESKY HUD.
                              (L373)

LULLABY
(Moore, Dorothy Rudd) SS soli,pno
[4'] sc AM.COMP.AL. $1.90   (L374)
see Arensky, Anton Stepanovich,
Cradle Song see Ceely, Robert Paige
see Edwards, Leo see Gambs see
Haufrecht, Herbert see Haxton,
Kenneth see Olsen, Sparre, Bånsull
see Stutschevsky, Joachim see
Tveitt, Geirr, Voggesong

LULLABY, A see Bax, [Sir] Arnold

LULLABY AT PONAR see Kingsley, Gershon Gary

LULLABY FOR BEN, A see Miller, Edward

LULLABY FOR DAISY PAULINE see Oliveros, Pauline

LULLABY FOR THE UNSLEEPING see Harvey

LULLABY FROM "HARRIET TUBMAN" see Edwards

LULLABY IN COME AWAY, THE see Sims, Ezra

LULLABY OF THE NATIVITY, A see Young, Douglas

LULLABYE see Olsen, Sparre, Voggsong

LULLY, JEAN-BAPTISTE (LULLI)
(1632-1687)
Amadis: Bois Épais
T solo,pno CLASSV 1134   (L375)
Bar solo,pno CLASSV 0455   (L376)

Cadmus Et Hermione: Belle Hermione
Hélas!
[Fr] Bar solo,pno CLASSV 1372
                              (L377)
O Dulcissime Domine
(Sanvoisin, M.) 3S,org,cont [4'30"]
BILLAUDOT   (L378)
Recueil D'airs Divers De Lully
(Verschaeve; Berstel) high solo,pno
(med diff) LEMOINE   (L379)
Regina Coeli
(Sanvoisin, M.) SMez soli,org,cont
[4'] BILLAUDOT   (L380)

LUME see Luppi, Gian Paolo

LUMINA SOLIS see Corghi, Azio

LUNA D'ESTATE see Tosti, Francesco Paolo

LUNAR POSSESSION MANUAL - 1973, A WINTER CEREMONIAL see Van Nostrand, Burr

LUND, SIGNE (1868-1950)
Selfdependence *Op.54
[Eng] solo voice,2.2.2.2. 4.2.3.0.
timp,perc,harp,strings NORGE f.s.
                              (L381)
LUNDBORG, (CHARLES) ERIK (1948-   )
Seafarer, The
B solo,pno [9'] sc AM.COMP.AL.
$9.15   (L382)
Spring And Fall
S solo,vla,triangle [7']
AM.COMP.AL.   (L383)

LUNDE, IVAR (1944-   )
Døde Fugler
see Seks Norske Dikt, Op. 40

Forår Farver Jorden Grønn, Et
see Seks Norske Dikt, Op. 40

Fremmede Fuglen, Den
see Seks Norske Dikt, Op. 40

From A Composer's Letter And Its
Reply
see Three Songs, Op. 63

Harbinger *Op.86
[Eng] solo voice,pno NORGE f.s.
                              (L384)
Jeg Går Omkring
see Seks Norske Dikt, Op. 40

November
see Seks Norske Dikt, Op. 40

Prayer
see Three Songs, Op. 63

Seks Norske Dikt, Op. 40
[Norw] S solo,pno NORGE f.s.
contains: Døde Fugler; Forår
Farver Jorden Grønn, Et;
Fremmede Fuglen, Den; Jeg Går
Omkring; November; Trolldom
                              (L385)
Success
see Three Songs, Op. 63

Three Songs, Op. 63
[Eng] med solo,pno NORGE f.s.
contains: From A Composer's
Letter And Its Reply; Prayer;
Success   (L386)
Trolldom
see Seks Norske Dikt, Op. 40

LUNDE, JOHAN BACKER
see BACKER-LUNDE, JOHAN

LUNDIN, DAG (1943-   )
Fiskaren
see Två Sånger

Höstljus
see Två Sånger

Två Sånger
solo voice,pno TONOS f.s.
contains: Fiskaren; Höstljus
                              (L387)

LUNE BLANCHE, LA see Bon, Willem
Frederik see Szulc, Josef Zygmunt

LUNE EST VENUE, LA see Smit Sibinga,
Theo H.

LUNE FROIDE see Paderewski, Ignace Jan

LUNE OFFENSEE, LA see Regt, Hendrik de

LUNGI DAL CARO BENE see Sarti, Giuseppe
see Secchi, A.

LUNGI DAL MIO BEL NUMBE see Handel,
George Frideric

LUOGHI DA ARES see Salvadori, Luca

LUPI, ROBERTO (1908-1971)
Cinque Canti Dell' Ars Nova
DE SANTIS DS 1118   (L388)

Cinque Canti Trovadorici
solo voice,pno DE SANTIS DS 1117
(L389)

LUPINEN see Ehlen, Margriet

LUPPI, GIAN PAOLO
Apokalypsis
S solo,fl,clar,vln,vla,vcl,db EDI-
PAN EP 7852   (L390)

Lume
S solo,vln,vla,vcl,db,cel EDI-PAN
EP 7518   (L391)

LUST AM RHEIN see Cornelius, Peter

LUSTIGE WITWE, DIE: VILJA-LIED see
Lehar, Franz

LUSTIGEN WEIBER VON WINDSOR: ALS
BÜBLEIN KLEIN see Nicolai, Otto

LUSTIGEN WEIBER VON WINDSOR: HORCH, DIE
LERCHE see Nicolai, Otto

LUTAD MOT GÄRDET see Jensen, Ludwig
Irgens

LUTE IN THE ATTIC see Drew, James M.

LUTE OF JADE, A see Branscombe, Gena

LUTE SONG, THE see MacBride, David
Huston

LUTE SONGS ON RENAISSANCE see Diemer,
Emma Lou

LUTZ, H.
Coeur De Hialmar, Le
solo voice,orch voc sc CLASSV 2183
(L392)

LUZZI, LUIGI (1828-1876)
Ave Maria
low solo,pno CLASSV 0870   (L393)
high solo,pno CLASSV 1454 (L394)

LYBBERT, DONALD (1923-   )
Leopardi Canti
S solo,fl,vla,bass clar [15']
AM.COMP.AL. sc $15.30, pts $13.00
(L395)

Let It Be Forgotten
high solo,pno [3'] sc AM.COMP.AL.
$1.95   (L396)

Lord's Prayer, The
high solo,pno [2'] sc AM.COMP.AL.
$1.60   (L397)

Octagon
S solo,fl,bass clar,vln,vcl,db,pno,
perc [28'] AM.COMP.AL. sc $38.30,
pts $56.60   (L398)

LYCKAN see Koch, Erland von

LYDIA see Slonimsky, Nicolas

LYDIA FROM SAPPHO, (1755, NO.2) see
Arne, Thomas Augustine

LYELL, MARGARET (1910-   )
Sweet Pastorale
med solo,fl,pno BARDIC BE0157
(L399)

LYNE, PETER (1946-   )
Fern Hill
S solo,fl,bsn,pno/cel/marimba,vln,
vla,vcl,perc SUECIA 374   (L400)

Remember
S solo,clar,vcl,marimba,perc [5']
sc STIM PA-3275-7 f.s.   (L401)

LYRA BRITANNICA I see Boyce, William

LYRE, FIDELE O MON AMIE see Rejcha,
Antonin

LYRIC AND LAMENT see Pleskow, Raoul

LYRIC SOPRANO ARIAS: A MASTER CLASS
WITH EVELYN LEAR, VOL. 1
SCHIRM.G 50481368 f.s. includes
cassette with recorded piano
accompaniments
contains: Ach, Ich Fühl's; Elle A
Fui; Let The Bright Seraphim; Mi
Chiamano Mimi; Vedrai Carino
(L402)

LYRIC SOPRANO ARIAS: A MASTER CLASS
WITH EVELYN LEAR, VOL. 2
SCHIRM.G 50481369 f.s. includes
cassette with recorded piano
accompaniments
contains: Ah! Je Veux Vivre; Batti,
Batti; Deh Vieni, Non Tardar; O
Wär Ich Schon; Quando Men Vo
(L403)

LYRICAL INTERVAL see Weisgall, Hugo

LYRIKOS see Crockett, Donald

LYRISK CYKEL: 5 SÅNGER see Holmquist,
Nils-Gustaf

LYRISK ROMANSE see Taubo, Lillian
Gulowna

LYRO, TY LASKO, MA DRUZKO STALA see
Rejcha, Antonin, Lyre, Fidele O Mon
Amie

LYS see Kruse, Bjørn Howard see
Norholm, Ib

LYS NAT see Grieg, Edvard Hagerup

LYSE DAG FORGANGEN ER, DEN see Nystedt,
Knut

LYSET see Grov, Magne

LYSSMEDEN see Kleiberg, Ståle

LYSSNA see Rooth, Anna-Greta

LYST see Shut, Wasyl

LYSTU MJER see Björnsson, Arni

M

MA BELLE AMIE EST MORTE see Gounod,
Charles François

MA LASKO VZACNA see Rejcha, Antonin,
Aure Amiche, Ah Non Spirate

MA VIE A SON SECRET see Bizet, Georges

MAAN see Voorn, Joop

MAAN HANGT IN GLAZEN BELLEN, DE see
Ehlen, Margriet

MAANLICHT see Schouwman, Hans

MAASZ, GERHARD (1906-1984)
Da Lachen Ja Die Hühner (composed
with Schortemeier, Dirk)
speaking voice&opt solo voice,
2.1.2.1. 1.2.1.0. perc,strings
[24'] RIES   (M1)

MABEL OSBORNE see Boldemann, Laci

MAC VOICES see Matsudaira, Yori-Aki

MACBETH: AH, LA PATERNA MANO see Verdi,
Giuseppe

MACBETH: COME DAL CIEL PRECIPITA see
Verdi, Giuseppe

MACBETH: PIETÀ, RISPETTO, ONORE see
Verdi, Giuseppe

MACBRIDE, DAVID HUSTON (1951-   )
Angel Fare
SS soli,pno,db,bsn,vibra,alto sax,
trp,perc,bass clar,trom,marimba,
conductor [13'] AM.COMP.AL. sc
$23.00, pts $19.15   (M2)

Children's Songs *CCU
SS soli,pno,3perc sc AM.COMP.AL.
$38.00   (M3)

Deep Song
S&narrator,pno,string quar [16']
AM.COMP.AL.   (M4)

Duo
2 solo voices,vla,bsn,pno,elec pno/
org,perc [9'] AM.COMP.AL. sc
$7.70, pts $11.45   (M5)

From "Three Cabaret Songs"
S solo,2alto sax,tenor sax,baritone
sax,4trp,4trom,gtr,pno,db,drums
[7'] AM.COMP.AL.   (M6)

Lute Song, The
S solo,fl,pno/harp [5'] sc
AM.COMP.AL. $3.85   (M7)

Poet In New York [1]
T solo,2vln,vla,vcl [12'] sc
AM.COMP.AL. $8.40   (M8)

Poet In New York [2]
T solo,2vla,2gtr [12'] AM.COMP.AL.
sc $7.70, pts $9.15   (M9)

S.F., Three Songs *CC3U
S solo,pno sc AM.COMP.AL. $7.25
(M10)

Three Poems Of Ai Qing *CC3U
S solo,vln/vla,db,pno,perc
AM.COMP.AL. sc $11.95, pts $24.10
(M11)

To..., Three Songs *CC3U
S solo,pno,perc sc AM.COMP.AL.
$9.60   (M12)

Whole Sheet Of Solitude, A
med solo,pno/harp [3'] sc
AM.COMP.AL. $1.20   (M13)

World Is Our Home, The
ST&narrator,vln,harp,pno [12']
AM.COMP.AL.   (M14)

MCCARTNEY, [JOHN] PAUL (1942-   )
World You're Coming Into, The (from
Liverpool Oratorio) (composed
with Davis, Carl)
solo voice,pno FABER 50481585 (M15)

MCCONNELL, DOUG
Four Wedding Solos *CC4U,Marriage
solo voice AUG-FOR 3-8501 $3.95
(M16)

MACDERMOTT, GALT (1928-   )
In My Time *gospel
solo voice,pno,gtr (easy) PRESSER
(M17)

MCDONALD, HARL (1899-1955)
Three Songs
solo voice,pno PRESSER 161-00069
(M18)

MACDOWELL, EDWARD ALEXANDER (1861-1908)
Cradle Hymn *Op.33,No.2
med solo,pno CLASSV 1503 (M19)

Deserted
see Two Old Songs, Op. 9

Eight Songs, Op. 47 (Rev. Ed. Of
1906)
[Eng/Ger] med solo,pno CLASSV 1498
(M20)

Eight Songs, Op. 47 (Rev. Ed. Of
1908)
[Eng/Ger] low solo,pno CLASSV 1840
(M21)

Five Songs, Op. 11 & 12
[Ger/Eng] med-high solo,pno CLASSV
1499 (M22)

From An Old Garden: Six Songs, Op. 26
med solo,pno CLASSV 1495 (M23)

Sea, The *Op.47,No.7
[Eng/Ger] low solo,pno CLASSV 1497
(M24)
[Eng/Ger] med-high solo,pno CLASSV
1496 (M25)

Six Love Songs, Op. 40
med-high solo,pno CLASSV 1501 (M26)

Slumber Song
see Two Old Songs, Op. 9

Thy Beaming Eyes *Op.40,No.3
med solo,pno CLASSV 1502 (M27)

Two Old Songs, Op. 9
med solo,pno CLASSV 1500 f.s.
contains: Deserted; Slumber Song
(M28)

MCGILL, JOSEPHINE (1877-1919)
Duna
low solo,pno CLASSV 1898 (M29)
med-low solo,pno CLASSV 1897 (M30)
med solo,pno CLASSV 1896 (M31)

MÁCHA, OTMAR (1922-)
Moravske Lidove Pisne
3 female soli,pno PANTON 926 (M32)

MACHI NI see Watanabe, Kenji

MACKEY, STEVEN (1956-)
Two Dances From William Carlos
Williams
Mez solo,pno [7'] sc AM.COMP.AL.
$7.70 (M33)

MCLEAN, EDWIN
Bit Parts
4 female soli,4trom [12'] sc
AM.COMP.AL. $12.20 (M34)

MCLIN, LENA J. (1928-)
Hold Out Your Light
solo voice,pno KJOS GV1 (M35)

I Know The Lord's Laid His Hands On
Me
solo voice,pno KJOS GV2 (M36)

If I Could Give You All I Have
solo voice,pno KJOS GV5 (M37)

I'm A Soldier In The Army Of The Lord
solo voice,pno KJOS GV3 (M38)

My Love
solo voice,pno KJOS GV9 (M39)

Wait Till I Put On My Crown
solo voice,pno KJOS GV4 (M40)

MACMILLAN, ALAN
Baptismal Song
med solo,pno/org (easy) PARACLETE
PPM08222 $2.00 (M41)

In Heavenly Love Abiding
med-high solo,org/pno,opt vln (med)
PARACLETE PPM08221 $3.00 (M42)

Take Me, Jesus, To Thy Breast
med-high solo,pno/org (easy)
PARACLETE PPM08223 $2.00 (M43)

Wedding Prayer, A
high solo,org,opt fl/opt vln (med)
PARACLETE PPM08224 $3.50 (M44)

Wedding Song
med-low solo,pno/org (med diff)
PARACLETE PPM08303 $3.50 (M45)

MACMURROUGH, DERMOT
Macushla
med-high solo,pno CLASSV 1843 (M46)
high solo,pno CLASSV 1842 (M47)
med solo,pno CLASSV 1844 (M48)

MCTEE, CINDY (1953-)
Psalm 142: Threnody
med solo,org MMB X814003 (M49)

MACUSHLA see Macmurrough, Dermot

MAD SONG see Haxton, Kenneth see
Willingham, Lawrence

MADAMA BUTTERFLY: UN BEL DI VEDREMO see
Puccini, Giacomo

MADAME BUTTERFLY: UN BEL DI VEDREMO see
Puccini, Giacomo

MÄDCHEN, DAS see Schubert, Franz
(Peter)

MÄDCHEN ANNA, DAS see Israel-Meyer,
Pierre, Anna La Bonne

MÄDCHEN AUF DER BRÜCKE, DAS see Jensen,
Ludwig Irgens

MÄDCHEN AUS DER FREMDE, DAS see
Fischer, A.

MÄDCHEN VON JUDA, DAS see Kücken,
Friedrich Wilhelm

MÄDCHENLIEDER see Farwell, Arthur see
Schwaen, Kurt

MADELEINE AU DÉSERT, LA see Reyer,
Louis Étienne Ernest

MADERNA, BRUNO (1920-1973)
Alba
A solo,string orch ZERBONI 8992
(M50)

Kranichsteiner Kammerkantate
SB soli,orch ZERBONI 8995 (M51)

Liriche Su Verlaine
solo voice,pno ZERBONI 8991 (M52)

MADRE AL FIGLIO LONTANO, LA see
Pizzetti, Ildebrando

MADRIGAL see Indy, Vincent d' see
Mestres, Apeles see Niikura, Ken

MADRIGALI see Adolphe, Bruce

MADRIGALI DELL' ESTATE see Stachowski,
Marek

MADSEN, TRYGVE (1940-)
Bjørnsonsanger, Op. 39
[Norw] S solo,pno NORGE (M53)

Dies Illae
see Five Songs, Op. 15

Død Mann Rider
see Four Songs, Op. 6

Eight Songs To Poems By Sigbjørn
Obstfelder *Op.9
[Norw] solo voice,pno NORGE (M54)

Five Songs, Op. 15
[Norw] solo voice,pno NORGE f.s.
contains: Dies Illae; Guds
Hjerte; Lavmaelt; Morgen, Kan
Jeg Ta Deg Inn Til Meg; Pavane
(M55)

Four Songs, Op. 6
[Norw] solo voice,pno NORGE f.s.
contains: Død Mann Rider;
Harmoni, En; Nattergalens Sang;
Sangen Om Et Slott (M56)

Four Songs, Op. 19
[Norw] solo voice,pno NORGE f.s.
contains: Regn I Demring; Snart;
Søyle I Chartres, En; Tett Bak
Din Fot (M57)

Gardhelg
see Tri Maria-Kvede, Op. 29

Guds Hjerte
see Five Songs, Op. 15

Harmoni, En
see Four Songs, Op. 6

Jomfru Marias Tåregras
see Tri Maria-Kvede, Op. 29

Lavmaelt
see Five Songs, Op. 15

Ljuvt Klokkene Kimer Frå Himelrik
see Tri Maria-Kvede, Op. 29

Morgen, Kan Jeg Ta Deg Inn Til Meg
see Five Songs, Op. 15

Nattergalens Sang
see Four Songs, Op. 6

...Och Icke De Smaa At Foragte
[Norw] S solo,fl,org NORGE (M58)

MADSEN, TRYGVE (cont'd.)

Pavane
see Five Songs, Op. 15

Regn I Demring
see Four Songs, Op. 19

Sangen Om Et Slott
see Four Songs, Op. 6

Snart
see Four Songs, Op. 19

Songs, Op. 14
[Norw] solo voice,pno NORGE (M59)

Songs To German Texts, Op. 12
[Ger] solo voice,pno (texts by
Richard Schankal & Eduard Mörike)
NORGE (M60)

Søyle I Chartres, En
see Four Songs, Op. 19

Tett Bak Din Fot
see Four Songs, Op. 19

Tre Sanger, Op. 3
solo voice,pno MUSIKK (M61)

Tri Maria-Kvede, Op. 29
[Norw] solo voice,pno NORGE f.s.
contains: Gardhelg; Jomfru Marias
Tåregras; Ljuvt Klokkene Kimer
Frå Himelrik (M62)

MADUR HEFUR NU see Sveinsson, Gunnar
Reynir

MAEHLUM, SVEIN (1943-)
Deretter Så Jeg
"Solomotett For Allehelgensdag"
[Norw] solo voice,org NORGE (M63)

Si Til Sions Datter
solo voice,org [4'] NORGE (M64)

Solomotett For Allehelgensdag
see Deretter Så Jeg

MAESSEN, ANTOON (1919-)
Drie Arabesken
S solo,pno DONEMUS f.s. [9']
contains: Onweer; Ster Sprong Op,
Een; Stilte Is In De Natuur,
Een (M65)

Drie Meiliederen
S solo,fl,pno DONEMUS f.s. [7']
contains: Eerste Vreugd, Die; Mei
Plezant, Die; Schoon Lieveken
(M66)

Eerste Vreugd, Die
see Drie Meiliederen

Mei Plezant, Die
see Drie Meiliederen

Onweer
see Drie Arabesken

Schoon Lieveken
see Drie Meiliederen

Ster Sprong Op, Een
see Drie Arabesken

Stilte Is In De Natuur, Een
see Drie Arabesken

MAESTRO DI MUSICA: BELLA MIA see
Pergolesi, Giovanni Battista

MAFUYU NO KATAMI NI see Doi, Yoshiyuki

MAGABUNDA see Schwantner, Joseph

MAGEIN AVOT see Ganchoff, Moshe

MAGNA RES EST AMOR see Andriessen,
Hendrik

MAGNETIC WALTZ see Arditi, Luigi,
Ardita, L'

MAGNIFICAT see Bax, [Sir] Arnold

MAH TOVU see Gottlieb, Jack S.

MAHLER, ALMA
Complete Songs Of Alma Mahler, The
*CCU
med solo,pno UNIVER. UE 18016
$14.95 (M67)

MAHLER, GUSTAV (1860-1911)
Des Knaben Wunderhorn I
solo voice ONGAKU 481219 f.s. (M68)

Des Knaben Wunderhorn II
solo voice ONGAKU 481220 f.s. (M69)

Des Knaben Wunderhorn: Nine Songs
*CC9U
EUR.AM.MUS. high solo,pno ST07740

MAHLER, GUSTAV (cont'd.)

   f.s.; low solo,pno ST07741 f.s.
                       (M70)

Five Early Songs
   (Berio, Luciano) male solo,orch
   study sc UNIVER. UE18651   (M71)

Fourteen Songs
   [Ger] high solo (includes 9 from
   Des Knaben Wunderhorn) KALMUS
   K 06840   (M72)
   [Ger] low solo (includes 9 from Des
   Knaben Wunderhorn) KALMUS K 06841
                       (M73)

Ging Heut' Morgens Ubers Feld
   see Lieder Eines Fahrenden Gesellen

Gustav Mahler: Selected Songs *CCU
   solo voice,pno SCHOTT ST07534 f.s.
                       (M74)

Ich Hab' Eine Gluhend Messer In Einem
   Brust
   see Lieder Eines Fahrenden Gesellen

In Diesem Wetter
   see Kindertotenlieder

Kindertotenlieder
   [Ger] solo voice,3.3.3.3. 4.0.0.0.
   perc,harp,cel,strings POLSKIE
   f.s.
     contains: In Diesem Wetter; Nun
     Seh' Ich Wohl, Warum So Dunkle
     Flammen; Nun Will Die Sonn' So
     Hell Aufgehn; Oft Denkt' Ich
     Sie Sind Nur Ausgegangen!; Wenn
     Die Mutterlein   (M75)

Kindertotenlieder *song cycle
   solo voice ONGAKU 481252 f.s.(M76)
   [Ger/Fr] med solo,pno KAHNT 6339
                       (M77)

Lied Von Der Erde, Das *song cycle
   solo voice ONGAKU 481217 f.s.(M78)
   (Hefling, Stephan E.) high solo&med
   solo,pno UNIVER. UE 13937   (M79)

Lieder Aus Letzter Zeit
   [Ger/Eng] high solo,pno KAHNT 7613
                       (M80)
   [Ger/Eng] med solo,pno KAHNT 7614
                       (M81)
   [Ger/Eng] low solo,pno KAHNT 7615
                       (M82)

Lieder Eines Fahrenden Gesellen
   (Hansen, M.) [Ger] solo voice,
   3.3.3.2. 4.2.3.0. perc,strings
   POLSKIE f.s.
     contains: Ging Heut' Morgens
     Ubers Feld; Ich Hab' Eine
     Gluhend Messer In Einem Brust;
     Wenn Mein Schatz Hochzeit
     Macht; Zwei Blauen Augen, Die
                     (M83)

Lieder Eines Fahrenden Gesellen
   *song cycle
   (Hansen, Mathias) solo voice,orch
   pno red PETERS f.s.   (M84)

Neun Lieder Und Gesänge (from Des
   Knaben Wunderhorn)
   low solo,pno SCHOTTS ED 7741 (M85)
   high solo,pno SCHOTTS ED 7740 (M86)

Nun Seh' Ich Wohl, Warum So Dunkle
   Flammen
   see Kindertotenlieder

Nun Will Die Sonn' So Hell Aufgehn
   see Kindertotenlieder

Oft Denkt' Ich Sie Sind Nur
   Ausgegangen!
   see Kindertotenlieder

Sechs Frühe Lieder
   (Berio, Luciano) solo voice,orch
   UNIVER. UE 18307   (M87)

Sieben Lieder *CC7U
   solo voice ONGAKU 481253 f.s. (M88)

Tamboursg'sell, Der
   high solo,5brass WESTERN WIM273
                       (M89)

Wenn Die Mutterlein
   see Kindertotenlieder

Wenn Mein Schatz Hochzeit Macht
   see Lieder Eines Fahrenden Gesellen

Wir Genessen Die Himmlischen Freuden
   (from Symphony No. 4)
   [Ger] S solo KALMUS K 03689 (M90)

Zwei Blauen Augen, Die
   see Lieder Eines Fahrenden Gesellen

MAHLER: A. DE MAHLER see Koering, Rene

MAHLER: ARIA DE R. DE MAHLER see
   Koering, Rene

MAHLER: R. DE MAHLER see Koering, Rene

MAIENBLÜTEN see Marx, Joseph

MAIESTAS CAROLINA see Krcek, Jaroslav

MAIGLÖCKCHEN UND DIE BLÜMELEIN see
   Mendelssohn-Bartholdy, Felix

MAINS, LES see Harris, Donald see
   Massenet, Jules

MAISTJARNAN see Asgeirsson, Jon

MAÎTRE WOLFRAM: LES LARMES see Reyer,
   Louis Étienne Ernest

MAJA DOLOROSA, LA see Granados, Enrique

MAJESTY see Hayford

MAKE READY! MAKE READY! MY NAUNTILUS
   BARK see Lightfoot, Miss

MAKE THIS A DAY OF PEPSODENT! see
   Slonimsky, Nicolas

MAKT, DI see Baden, Conrad

MAL D'AMORE see Buzzi-Peccia, Arturo

MALAN, J. DE VOS
   Letters From Helsinki
     solo voice,instrumental ensemble
     SEESAW f.s.   (M91)

MALEDICTION see Sydeman, William J.

MALEK, JAN (1938-   )
   Falcon Flew, The
     Bar solo,fl,ob,vcl,pno [12'] CESKY
     HUD.   (M92)

MALINCHE see Pablo, Luis de

MALIPIERO, GIAN FRANCESCO (1882-1973)
   Sonetti Delle Fate, I: 6 Liriche
     [It] S solo,pno CLASSV 2102 (M93)

MALIPIERO, RICCARDO (1914-   )
   In Time Of Daffodils
     SBar soli,orch pno red ZERBONI 6341
                     (M94)

   Voicequintet
     S solo,string quar ZERBONI 9887
                     (M95)

MALMFURU see Olsen, Sparre

MALMLÖF-FORSSLING, CARIN (1916-   )
   Blues
     see Tre Upplevelser

   Frühlingsmond
     see Vollmond: Drei Japanische
     Haiku-Gedichte

   Herbststurm
     see Vollmond: Drei Japanische
     Haiku-Gedichte

   Jag Kysser Din Osynliga Ros
     see Tre Upplevelser

   Neujahr
     see Vollmond: Drei Japanische
     Haiku-Gedichte

   Sorg
     see Tre Upplevelser

   Tre Upplevelser
     S solo,fl STIM f.s.
      contains: Blues; Jag Kysser Din
      Osynliga Ros; Sorg   (M96)

   Vollmond: Drei Japanische Haiku-
     Gedichte
     S solo,pno SUECIA 373 f.s.
      contains: Frühlingsmond;
      Herbststurm; Neujahr   (M97)

MALOTTE, ALBERT HAY (1895-1964)
   Complete Lord's Prayer For Every Busy
     Accompanist, The
     (12 versions) SCHIRM.G 50481088
                     (M98)

   For My Mother
     med solo SCHIRM.G ST38565   (M99)

   I Am Proud To Be An American
     solo voice,pno SCHIRM.G 50481510
                    (M100)

MALVEN see Strauss, Richard

M'AMA...NON M'AMA see Mascagni, Pietro

MAMA, YO NO TENGO VISTO see Four
   Sephardi Songs

MAMAMIMAMO THE WIZARD see Morita, Shin-
   Ichi

MAMANGAKIS, NIKOS (1929-   )
   Sprachsymbole
     SB soli,fl,English horn,horn,trp,
     tuba,glock,vibra,xylo,3perc,vln,
     vla,vcl [25'] MODERN 1131 (M101)

MAMA'S SUGAR CUBE SWEET see Ise,
   Chizuko

MAMI see Shut, Wasyl

MAMIYA, MICHIO (1929-   )
   Postage Stamp *song cycle
     solo voice,vln,krummhorn/rec,lute
     [12'] JAPAN   (M102)

   Serenade II
     solo voice,vln,pno ZEN-ON 899450
                    (M103)

MAMLOK, URSULA (1928-   )
   Andreas Garten, Der
     Mez solo,fl&pic&alto fl,harp sc
     PETERS 67224   (M104)

   Four German Songs *CC4U
     S solo,pno sc AM.COMP.AL. $7.70
                    (M105)

MAMMA see Bixio, Cesare Andrea see
   Halldorsson, Skuli

MAMMA MIA CHE VO' SAPÈ see Nutile

MAN, RODERIK DE
   At 3 A.M.
     see Five Songs On Poems By Wendy
     Cope

   Five Songs On Poems By Wendy Cope
     Mez solo,pno DONEMUS f.s. [8']
      contains: At 3 A.M.; Prelude;
      Some People; Spring Onions;
      Summer Villanelle   (M106)

   Prelude
     see Five Songs On Poems By Wendy
     Cope

   Some People
     see Five Songs On Poems By Wendy
     Cope

   Spring Onions
     see Five Songs On Poems By Wendy
     Cope

   Summer Villanelle
     see Five Songs On Poems By Wendy
     Cope

MAN AND HIS MUSIC IN STORY, PICTURE AND
   SONG, THE see Kern, Jerome

MAN OF LIFE UPRIGHT, THE see Loevendie,
   Theo

MAN OF MADRAS, THE see Eliscu, Robert

MAN WHO WANTS TO EAT, A see Straesser,
   Joep

MAN WITH THE BLUE GUITAR, THE see
   Klein, Leonard

MAÑANICA ERA see Granados, Enrique

MANANTIAL, EL see Pablo, Luis de

MANASSEN, ALEX (1950-   )
   Denkmal An Der Grenze Des
     Fruchtlandes
     S solo,pic,ob,clar,bsn,horn,pno,
     vln,vla,vcl [3'] DONEMUS (M107)

   Moordunkel
     S solo,bass clar,vibra/synthesizer,
     acord [14'] DONEMUS   (M108)

MANAZASHI see Nakamura, Yukitake

MANCA PUR QUANTO SAI see Handel, George
   Frideric

MANCHMAL SAH ICH VON FERN see Arensky,
   Anton Stepanovich

MANDANICI, MARCELLA
   Senza Testo
     solo voice EDI-PAN EP 7474 (M109)

MANDOLINE see Szulc, Josef Zygmunt

MANELLA MIA! see Valente

MANEN, JOAN (1883-1971)
   Fünf Lieder, Op. A-4
     [Ger] high solo RECITAL 275 (M110)

   Vier Lieder, Op. A-10
     [Ger] high solo RECITAL 276 (M111)

MANEN, WILLEM VAN (1940-   )
   Mikrotoop
     SSAA soli,2.0.1.0.4sax. 1.4.3.0.
     4perc,2elec pno,4elec bass [13']
     DONEMUS f.s.   (M112)

MANESPROOK see Andriessen, Hendrik

MANIC DEPRESSION see Larson, Martin

MANNEKE, DAAN (1939-   )
   Author's Epitaph, The
      see Five Songs On English Poems

   Envoi
      see Five Songs On English Poems

   Five Songs On English Poems
      low solo,hpsd/pno/org DONEMUS f.s.
      [12']
         contains: Author's Epitaph, The;
         Envoi; Heaven-Haven; Silence;
         World A Hunting Is, The   (M113)

   Heaven-Haven
      see Five Songs On English Poems

   Sept Poemes *CC7L
      med solo,pno/org/hpsd DONEMUS f.s.
                                      (M114)

   Silence
      see Five Songs On English Poems

   World A Hunting Is, The
      see Five Songs On English Poems

   Zeven Vocalises *CC7U
      med solo,pno/org/hpsd DONEMUS f.s.
                                      (M115)

MÄNNER HABN'S GUT, DIE see Müller,
   Adolf

MÄNNERLIEDER see Schubert, Franz
   (Peter)

MANNEY, CHARLES FONTEYN (1872-1951)
   Shropshire Lad, A *song cycle
      [Eng] med solo (texts by A.E.
      Housman) RECITAL 277   (M116)

MANNINO, FRANCO (1924-   )
   Cadenza
      S solo CURCI 9807   (M117)

   Cinque Lieder - Cinque Poesie *CC5U
      solo voice,pno CURCI 10953 f.s.
                                  (M118)

   Da Colombo A Broadway
      (Bentivegna, Massimo) solo voice,
      trp,pno CURCI 10938   (M119)

   Diavolo In Giardino, Il
      solo voice,pno CURCI 7866   (M120)

   E Non Sei Mai Tornato
      S solo,pno CURCI 10824   (M121)

MÄNNLEIN IN DER GANS, DAS see Klein,
   Richard Rudolf

MANNUCCI, ANDREA
   Verra La Morte E Avra I Tuoi Occhi
      S solo,10inst ZERBONI 9966 (M122)

MANON: AH! FUYEZ, DOUCE IMAGE see
   Massenet, Jules

MANON: INSTANT CHARMANT see Massenet,
   Jules, Manon: Le Rêve

MANON: JE MARCHE...OBÉISSONS see
   Massenet, Jules

MANON: JE SUIS...ENCOR see Massenet,
   Jules

MANON: LE RÊVE see Massenet, Jules

MANON LESCAUT: DONNA NON VIDI MAI see
   Puccini, Giacomo

MANON LESCAUT: IN QUELLE TRINE MORBIDE
   see Puccini, Giacomo

MANON LESCAUT: L'ÉCLAT DE RIRE see
   Auber, Daniel-François-Esprit

MANON LESCAUT: SULLA VETTA TU DEL MONTE
   (MADRIGALE) see Puccini, Giacomo

MANON LESCAUT: TRA VOI, BELLE, BRUNE
   see Puccini, Giacomo

MANON, OP. 21 see Svoboda, Jiri

MANOS AMIGAS see Rausch, Carlos

MANOURY, PHILIPPE
   Aleph
      SATB soli, orch in 4 groups [65']
      AMPHION A.470.71 f.s.   (M123)

MANSONGUR see Halldorsson, Skuli see
   Olafsson, Kjartan

MANY KINDS OF YES see Orr, Buxton

MAOMETTO: "SORGETE": IN SÌ BEL GIORNO.
   DUCE DI TANTI EROI see Rossini,
   Gioacchino

MAR EN CALMA - PRIMER DESENGAÑO see
   Schubert, Franz (Peter)

MARC GROET'S MORGENS DE DINGEN see
   Beekhuis, Hanna

MARCELLO
   Ecco Il Petto
      SA soli,pno BOIL B.1749   (M124)

MARCELLO, BENEDETTO (1686-1739)
   Salmo Quarantesimosecundo
      B solo,pno,org,strings DURAND
      C.3546 rent   (M125)

   Salmo Quarantesimosesto
      S solo,pno,org,strings DURAND
      C.3547 rent   (M126)

   Salmo Vigesimoprimo
      A solo,harp,pno,org,strings DURAND
      C.3543 rent   (M127)

MARCH TO BATTLE see Berenholtz, Jim

MARCO VISCONTI: RONDINELLA PELLEGRINA
   see Petrella, Errico

MARCUSSEN, KJELL (1952-   )
   Fra "Munken Vendt"
      T solo,pno [8'] NORGE   (M128)

   Utsyn: Fem Tableauer Fra Arne Garborg
      [Norw] T solo,fl,vla,vcl,pno,perc
      [30'] NORGE   (M129)

MARECHIARE see Tosti, Francesco Paolo

MAREZ OYENS, TERA DE (1932-   )
   From A Distant Planet
      Bar solo,pno [13'] DONEMUS   (M130)

   I Cannot Wash Your Smoke
      see If Only

   I Have Returned
      see If Only

   If Only
      S solo,fl,2perc,pno DONEMUS f.s.
      [16']
         contains: I Cannot Wash Your
         Smoke; I Have Returned; If
         Only; Riding On Wind; We Walk
         The Earth Together   (M131)

   If Only
      see If Only

   Recurring Thoughts Of A Haunted
      Traveller
      S solo,soprano sax,alto sax,tenor
      sax,baritone sax [11'] DONEMUS
                                   (M132)

   Riding On Wind
      see If Only

   Ryoanji Temple
      A solo,ob,vln,vla,vcl [6'] DONEMUS
                                   (M133)

   Shadow Of A Prayer
      female solo,fl,pno [12'] DONEMUS
                                   (M134)

   Vignettes
      S solo,fl,perc,pno [12'] DONEMUS
                                   (M135)

   We Walk The Earth Together
      see If Only

MARGARET see Bond, Victoria

MARGARITA DEBAYLE, A see Violette,
   Andrew

MARGARITA EN LA RUECA see Schubert,
   Franz (Peter)

MARGRETE'S CRADLE SONG see Grieg,
   Edvard Hagerup, Margrete's
   Vuggesang

MARGRETE'S VUGGESANG see Grieg, Edvard
   Hagerup

MARIA see As, Cees van see Bernstein,
   Leonard see Toebosch, Louis

MARIA DI ROHAN: AH! FORSE, ...ALMA
   SOAVE E CARA see Donizetti, Gaetano

MARIA DI ROHAN: PER NON ISTARE IN OZIO
   see Donizetti, Gaetano

MARIA DI RUDENZ: AH! NON AVEA PIÙ
   LAGRIME see Donizetti, Gaetano

MARIA, JUNGFRU MARIA see Leijon, Jerker

MARIA, MARÌ see Di Capua, Eduardo

MARIA STUART, OP. 172 see Raff, Joseph
   Joachim

MARIA SYNDERSKANS BÖN see Leijon,
   Jerker

MARIAS TRÖSTESÅNG see De Goede,
   Nicholaas

MARIATTI, FRANCO
   Ad Annie
      solo voice,harp CURCI 9983   (M136)

MARIE ANTOINETTE'S ARIA see Corigliano,
   John, They Are Always With Me

MARIE-MAGDELEINE: O MES SOEURS see
   Massenet, Jules

MARIENLIED see Marx, Joseph

MARIJANEK STAROBYLY see Faltus, L.

MARINI, BIAGIO (ca. 1595-1665)
   Lacrime D'Erminia, Le
      solo voice,cont fac ed FORNI 1273
                                   (M137)

MARIPOSA see Schumann, Robert
   (Alexander)

MARIPOSA DE LUZ see Evensen, Bernt
   Kasberg

MARITS VISOR see Peterson-Berger,
   (Olof) Wilhelm

MARIUVERS see Isolfsson, Pall

MARIUVISA see Helgason, Hallgrimur

MARKS, JAMES
   Three Songs
      [Eng] high solo (texts by e.e.
      cummings) RECITAL 424   (M138)

MAROON BELLS see Austin, Larry

MAROS, RUDOLF (1917-1982)
   Lament
      see Sirato

   Sirato
      "Lament" med solo,1(alto fl).1.1.1.
      0.0.0.0. harp,perc,strings [7'0"]
      PEER 61121-245   (M139)

MÂROUF: A TRAVERS LE DÉSERT see Rabaud,
   Henri

MÂROUF: IL EST DES MUSULMANS see
   Rabaud, Henri

MARQUES
   Aria Del Teléfono
      solo voice,pno BOIL B.1575   (M140)

   Primavera-Estju
      "Printemps-Été" solo voice,pno BOIL
      B.1155   (M141)

   Printemps-Été
      see Primavera-Estiu

MARSCH DES FÜNFTE REGIMENTS see Eisler,
   Hanns

MARSCHNER, HEINRICH (AUGUST)
   (1795-1861)
   Hans Heiling: An Jenem Tag
      Bar solo,pno CLASSV 1637   (M142)

MARSH, ROGER (1949-   )
   Delilah
      female solo,clar in A NOVELLO f.s.
                                   (M143)

MARSHALL, C.
   I Hear You Calling Me
      high solo,pno CLASSV 1511   (M144)

MARSMAN-CYLUS, OP. 20 see Masseus, Jan

MARTA: M'APPARI TUTT' AMOUR see Flotow,
   Friedrich von

MARTA: M'APPARI TUTT'AMOR see Flotow,
   Friedrich von

MARTHA: LASST MICH EUCH FRAGEN see
   Flotow, Friedrich von

MARTHA: M'APPARI TUTT' AMOR see Flotow,
   Friedrich von

MARTHINSEN, NIELS (1963-   )
   War Songs
      [Eng] B solo,perc [12'] (texts by
      Walt Whitman and Stephan Crane)
      REIMERS 101151   (M145)

MARTIAL CADENZA see Albers, Bradley

MARTIN, FREDERICK (1958-   )
   Cantata No. 2, Op. 20
      see Deuxieme Cantate

   Cantata No. 3
      solo voice,bass fl,bass clar,horn,
      bass trom,elec gtr,harp,pno,perc,
      vcl,db [14'] BILLAUDOT   (M146)

MARTIN, FREDERICK (cont'd.)

Deuxieme Cantate (Cantata No. 2, Op. 20)
countertenor,alto fl,clar,vln,vcl, pno [10'] BILLAUDOT   (M147)

MARTÍN Y SOLER, VICENT (1754-1806)
Sis Cançons Italianes *CC6U
(Domènech, Josep) solo voice PILES 118-V f.s.   (M148)

MARTINEZ CHUMILLA, MANUEL (1902-   )
Cuatro Canciones Populares Espanolas solo voice,pno ALPUERTO 1465 (M149)

MARTINI, GIOVANNI
see MARTINI, JEAN PAUL EGIDE

MARTINI, JEAN PAUL EGIDE
(SCHWARZENDORF) (1741-1816)
Piacer D'Amor
solo voice,pno BOIL B.1814   (M150)

Plaisir D'Amour
low solo,pno CLASSV 0508   (M151)
high solo,pno CLASSV 0509   (M152)

MARTINON, JEAN (1910-1976)
Ode Au Soleil Né De La Mort
solo voice,3.3.3.3. 4.3.3.1. timp, perc,cel,2harp,strings [12'50'] BILLAUDOT sc,pts rent, voc sc rent   (M153)

MARTINU, BOHUSLAV (JAN) (1890-1959)
Dve Pisne
[Czech/Fr] solo voice,pno PANTON 928   (M154)

Kouzelne Noci
S solo,4.3.2.2. 2.2.0.0. perc,harp, cel,strings [16'] PANTON (M155)
S solo,4.3.2.2. 2.2.0.0. perc,harp, cel,strings [16'] BÄREN. (M156)
[Czech/Ger] S solo,orch PANTON 1055   (M157)

Nipponari
S solo,4fl,English horn,triangle, tam-tam,harp,cel,pno,strings [24'] PANTON   (M158)

MARTYRE, UNE see Orthel, Leon

MARUYAMA, KAZUNORI (1959-   )
Chanson De Le Vent
solo voice,orch [3'] JAPAN   (M159)

Soiree, Il Tombe De La Neige
A solo,orch [9'] JAPAN   (M160)

MARX, JOSEPH (1882-1964)
Am Fenster
med solo,pno CLASSV 1143   (M161)

An Einen Herbstwald
med solo,pno CLASSV 1444   (M162)

Barcarole
high solo,pno CLASSV 1014   (M163)

Bescheidene Schäfer, Der
high solo,pno CLASSV 1023   (M164)

Bitte
med solo,pno (text by Hermann Hesse) CLASSV 1010   (M165)

Chopin Waltz
med solo,pno CLASSV 0632   (M166)

Christbaum
high solo,pno CLASSV 1846   (M167)

Con Sordino
T solo,pno (text by Hermann Hesse) CLASSV 1847   (M168)

Dein Blick
high solo,pno CLASSV 1848   (M169)

Dem Genius Des Augenblicks
[Ger] med solo,pno CLASSV 1449   (M170)

Denker, Der
med solo,pno CLASSV 1142   (M171)

Drängen Ist In Meinem Herzen, Ein
high solo,pno CLASSV 1852   (M172)

Durch Einsamkeiten
med solo,vla CLASSV 1851   (M173)

Elfe, Die
high solo,pno (text by Eichendorff) CLASSV 1850   (M174)

Erinnerung
high solo,pno (text by Eichendorff) CLASSV 1018   (M175)

Fichtenbaum Steht Einsam, Ein
med solo,pno (text by Heinrich Heine) CLASSV 1438   (M176)

MARX, JOSEPH (cont'd.)

Frage Und Antwort
S solo,pno (text by A. Rückert) CLASSV 1009   (M177)

Gast, Der
med solo,pno CLASSV 1441   (M178)

Gebet
med solo,pno CLASSV 1448   (M179)

Gesang Des Lebens
med-high solo,pno CLASSV 1853   (M180)

Hat Dich Die Liebe Berührt
high solo,pno CLASSV 1024   (M181)

Herbst
med solo,pno CLASSV 1854   (M182)

Herbstzeitlose
med solo,pno CLASSV 1015   (M183)

Hochsommernacht
high solo,pno CLASSV 1855   (M184)

Im Frühling
T solo,pno CLASSV 1856   (M185)

Im Maien
high solo,pno CLASSV 1020   (M186)

Isolde
Mez solo,pno CLASSV 1857   (M187)

Italienisches Liederbuch Vol. 1
med solo,pno CLASSV 1345   (M188)

Italienisches Liederbuch Vol. 2
med solo,pno CLASSV 1346   (M189)

Japanisches Regenlied
med solo,pno CLASSV 1149   (M190)

Jugend Und Alter
high solo,pno (text by Walt Whitman) CLASSV 1016   (M191)
med solo,pno (text by Walt Whitman) CLASSV 1012   (M192)

Junger Dichter Denkt An Die Geliebte, Ein
med solo,pno CLASSV 1013   (M193)

Kolumbine
med solo,pno CLASSV 1439   (M194)

Kuckuck Ruft, Der
high solo,pno CLASSV 1849   (M195)

Lenzfahrt
T solo,pno CLASSV 1858   (M196)

Leuchtende Tage
med solo,pno CLASSV 1859   (M197)

Lied
[Ger] T solo,pno CLASSV 1437 (M198)

Lied Eines Mädchens
Mez solo,pno CLASSV 1860   (M199)

Lob Des Frühlings
high solo,pno CLASSV 1446   (M200)

Maienblüten
high solo,pno CLASSV 1025   (M201)

Marienlied
high solo,pno CLASSV 1008   (M202)

Nachtgebet
T solo,pno CLASSV 1861   (M203)

Neugriechisches Mädchenlied
high solo,pno CLASSV 1011   (M204)

Nocturne
high solo,pno CLASSV 1022   (M205)

O Süsser Tod
med solo,pno CLASSV 1440   (M206)

Pan Trauert Um Syrinx
high solo,pno,fl CLASSV 1862 (M207)

Peregrina V.
T solo,pno (text by Eduard Mörike) CLASSV 1863   (M208)

Piemontesisches Volkslied
high solo,pno CLASSV 1864   (M209)

Pierrot Dandy
high solo,pno CLASSV 1865   (M210)

Rauch, Der
med solo,pno CLASSV 1443   (M211)

Regen
med solo,pno (text by P. Verlaine) CLASSV 1442   (M212)

MARX, JOSEPH (cont'd.)

Sankta Maria
high solo,pno CLASSV 1866   (M213)

Schlafend Trägt Man Mich In Mein Heimatland
med-high solo,pno CLASSV 1867   (M214)

Schönheit
T solo,pno CLASSV 1868   (M215)

Selige Nacht
med solo,pno CLASSV 0960   (M216)

Septembermorgen
med solo,pno (text by Eduard Mörike) CLASSV 1005   (M217)

Serenata
high solo,pno CLASSV 1869   (M218)

Sommerlied
high solo,pno CLASSV 1021   (M219)

Songs Of Joseph Marx [1]
high solo,pno (cc171, includes companion cassette of distinguished recorded performances) SCHIRM.G 00747027   (M220)

Songs Of Joseph Marx [2]
med solo,pno (cc161, includes companion cassette of distinguished recorded performances) SCHIRM.G 00747026   (M221)

Sonnenland
med solo,pno CLASSV 1445   (M222)

Ton, Der
med solo,pno CLASSV 1004   (M223)

Toskanischer Frühling
med-high solo,pno CLASSV 1870   (M224)

Traumgekrönt
high solo,pno (text by Rainer Maria Rilke) CLASSV 1871   (M225)

Und Gestern Hat Er Mir Rosen Gebracht
high solo,pno CLASSV 1027   (M226)

Venetianisches Wiegenlied
high solo,pno CLASSV 1019   (M227)
low solo,pno CLASSV 1133   (M228)

Vergessen
med solo,pno CLASSV 1872   (M229)

Violine, Die
med solo,pno CLASSV 1447   (M230)

Waldseligkeit
high solo,pno (text by Richard Dehmel) CLASSV 1026   (M231)

Wanderers Nachtlied
med solo,pno (text by Goethe) CLASSV 1406   (M232)

Wanderliedchen
high solo,pno CLASSV 1873   (M233)

Warnung
S solo,pno CLASSV 1874   (M234)

Wie Einst
med solo,pno CLASSV 1007   (M235)

Windräder
med solo,pno CLASSV 1006   (M236)

Zigeuner
high solo,pno CLASSV 1017   (M237)

MARY see Bolcom, William Elden

MARY MAGDALENE AND THE BIRDS see Buchanan, Dorothy

MARY WEEPS FOR HER CHILD see Fennimore, Joseph William

MARY WORE THREE LINKS OF CHAIN see Walker, George Theophilus

MASAGO-LIEDER see Kubo, Mayako

MASARYK, J.
Narodni Pisne
[Czech/Russ/Eng/Ger] solo voice,pno PANTON 100   (M238)

MASCAGNI, PIETRO (1863-1945)
A Giacomo Leopardi
solo voice,pno/orch pno red CURCI 10079   (M239)

Ah! Ritrovarla
see Lodoletta: Il Rimpianto Di Flammen

Amica: Se Tu Amasti Me
Bar solo,pno CLASSV 0935   (M240)

MASCAGNI, PIETRO (cont'd.)

Amico Fritz, L': Non Me Resta
   S solo,pno CLASSV 1881   (M241)

Amico Fritz, L': O Amore, O Bella
   Luce Del Core
   T solo,pno CLASSV 0920   (M242)

Amico Fritz, L': Son Pochi Fiori
   [It] S solo,pno CLASSV 1285 (M243)

Ave Maria (from Cavalleria Rusticana:
   Intermezzo)
   S/T solo,pno HEUGEL f.s.   (M244)
   [Lat/Eng] low solo RECITAL 2236
                                (M245)
   [Lat/Eng] med solo RECITAL 2235
                                (M246)
Ballata
   TS soli,pno CURCI 10080   (M247)

Bimba Non Piangere
   see Lodoletta: Il Canto Dei Fiori

Cavalleria Rusticana: Ave Maria (from
   Intermezzo)
   high solo,pno,vln CLASSV 1876 (M248)

Cavalleria Rusticana: Brindisi
   "Drinking-Song" [It/Eng] T solo,pno
   CLASSV 1875   (M249)

Cavalleria Rusticana: Il Cavallo
   Scalpita
   Bar solo,pno CLASSV 1030   (M250)

Cavalleria Rusticana: O Lola Bianca
   T solo,pno CLASSV 0921   (M251)

Cavalleria Rusticana: Stornello Di
   Lola
   "Fior Di Giaggi" Mez solo,pno
   CLASSV 1877   (M252)

Cavalleria Rusticana: Voi Lo Sapete
   S solo,pno CLASSV 0382   (M253)

Drinking-Song
   see Cavalleria Rusticana: Brindisi

Fior Di Giaggi
   see Cavalleria Rusticana: Stornello
   Di Lola

Guglielmo Ratcliff Spartito
   solo voice,pno SONZOGNO 880 f.s.
                                (M254)
Iris: Apri La Tua Finestra
   T solo,pno CLASSV 0895   (M255)

Iris: Un Dì, Ero Piccina
   S solo,pno CLASSV 0576   (M256)

Isabeau: O Popolo Di Vili...E Passerà
   La Viva
   T solo,pno CLASSV 0948   (M257)

Isabeau: Questo Mio Bianco Manto
   S solo,pno CLASSV 0934   (M258)

Isabeau: Tu Ch'odi Lo Mio Grido
   T solo,pno CLASSV 0949   (M259)

Lodoletta: Il Canto Dei Fiori
   "Bimba Non Piangere" T solo,pno
   CLASSV 1879   (M260)

Lodoletta: Il Rimpianto Di Flammen
   "Ah! Ritrovarla" T solo,pno CLASSV
   1878   (M261)

M'ama...Non M'ama
   T solo,pno CLASSV 1880   (M262)

Nerone
   solo voice,pno pno red CURCI 10461
                                (M263)
Peace To (from Cavalleria Rusticana:
   Intermezzo)
   [Eng] med-high solo RECITAL 2234
                                (M264)
Serenata: Come Col Capo Sotto L'ala
   Bianca
   T solo,pno CLASSV 0828   (M265)

Serenata Di Lorenzo Stecchetti
   med solo SONZOGNO 2960 f.s. (M266)

Silvano: S'è Spento Il Sol
   T solo,pno CLASSV 0919   (M267)

Six Songs
   med solo,pno CLASSV 1284   (M268)

Spes Ultima
   high solo,pno CLASSV 0898   (M269)

MASNADIERI, I: TU DEL MIO CARLO see
   Verdi, Giuseppe

MASON, CHARLES
   Caged Skylark
   S solo,electronic tape [5'50"]
   AM.COMP.AL.   (M270)

MASS IN SALT AIR see Pollock, Robert
   Emil

MASSAGE see Hazzard, Peter Peabody

MASSANA, A.
   Árbo Del Amor, El
   see Sota L'Ombreta

Cancons Liriques
   solo voice,pno BOIL B.2697   (M271)

Cant D'Amor (from Idilios Y Cantos
   Misticos)
   "Canto De Amor" solo voice,pno BOIL
   B.0801   (M272)

Canto De Amor
   see Cant D'Amor

Dolç Cautiveri (from Idilios Y Cantos
   Misticos)
   "Dulce Cautiverio" solo voice,pno
   BOIL B.0799   (M273)

Dulce Cautiverio
   see Dolç Cautiveri

Espinas
   see Espines

Espines (from Idilios Y Cantos
   Misticos)
   "Espinas" solo voice,pno BOIL
   B.0797   (M274)

Loor A Margarita
   solo voice,org/harmonium BOIL
   B.2698   (M275)

Rosalía (from Idilios Y Cantos
   Misticos)
   solo voice,pno BOIL B.0796   (M276)

Si Yo Robara Al Ruiseñor
   see Sijo Tingués Del Rossinyol

Sijo Tingués Del Rossinyol (from
   Idilios Y Cantos Misticos)
   "Si Yo Robara Al Ruiseñor" solo
   voice,pno BOIL B.0798   (M277)

Sospirs (from Idilios Y Cantos
   Misticos)
   "Suspiros" solo voice,pno BOIL
   B.0802   (M278)

Sota L'Ombreta (from Idilios Y Cantos
   Misticos)
   "Árbo Del Amor, El" solo voice,pno
   BOIL B.0800   (M279)

Suspiros
   see Sospirs

MASSÉ, VICTOR (1822-1884)
   Premières Mélodies (3 Cycles)
   solo voice,pno CLASSV C040   (M280)

Vingt Mélodies
   solo voice,pno CLASSV C039   (M281)

MASSENET, JULES (1842-1912)
   Alcyons, Les
   see Mélodies, Vol.1

Ame Des Oiseaux, L'
   see Mélodies, Vol.2

Art Of Joan Sutherland, The, Vol. 9:
   Massenet Arias
   (Bonynge, Richard; Sutherland,
   Joan) WEINBERGER f.s.
   contains: Cendrillon: Ah! Que Mes
   Soeurs Sont Heureuses!;
   Cherubin: Lorsque Vous N'aurez
   Rien A Faire; Cid, Le: Pleurez,
   Pleurez Mes Yeux; Esclarmonde:
   D'une Longue Torpeur;
   Griselidis: Des Larmes Brulent
   Ma Paupiere; Herodiade: Il Est
   Doux; Marie-Magdeleine: O Mes
   Soeurs; Roi De Lahore, Le: J'ai
   Fui La Chambre Nuptiale!; Roi
   De Lahore, Le: Que Les Douleurs
   De La Terre; Vierge, La:
   L'extase De La Vierge   (M282)

Baigne D'eau
   see Thaïs: Duo De L'Oasis

Berceuse
   see Mélodies, Vol.1

Ce Que Disent Les Cloches
   see Mélodies, Vol.2

Cendrillon: Ah! Que Mes...Reste Au
   Foyer, Petit Grillon
   S solo,pno CLASSV 1888   (M283)

Cendrillon: Ah! Que Mes Soeurs Sont
   Heureuses!
   see Art Of Joan Sutherland, The,
   Vol. 9: Massenet Arias

MASSENET, JULES (cont'd.)

Chansons Des Bois D'Amaranthe
   [Fr] 1-4 solo voices,pno CLASSV
   1382   (M284)

Chérubin: Ces Vers Sont Faits Pour
   Moi
   Mez solo,pno CLASSV 1887   (M285)

Cherubin: Lorsque Vous N'aurez Rien A
   Faire
   see Art Of Joan Sutherland, The,
   Vol. 9: Massenet Arias

Cid, Le
   med solo,pno CLASSV 1892   (M286)

Cid, Le: O Souverain, Ô Juge, O Père
   T solo,pno CLASSV 0342   (M287)

Cid, Le: Pleurez, Pleurez
   S solo,pno CLASSV 0348   (M288)
   Mez solo,pno CLASSV 1893   (M289)

Cid, Le: Pleurez, Pleurez Mes Yeux
   see Art Of Joan Sutherland, The,
   Vol. 9: Massenet Arias

Cid, Le: Plus De Tourments
   S solo,pno CLASSV 1607   (M290)

Crépuscule
   med solo,pno CLASSV 0859   (M291)

Désolation De Werther
   see Werther: J'Aurais Sur Ma
   Poitrino

Élégie
   high solo,pno,vln/vcl/fl CLASSV
   0546   (M292)
   med solo,pno,vln/vcl/fl CLASSV 1128
                                (M293)
   low solo,pno CLASSV 1889   (M294)
   med solo,pno CLASSV 0848   (M295)
   high solo,pno CLASSV 0475   (M296)

Esclarmonde: D'une Longue Torpeur
   see Art Of Joan Sutherland, The,
   Vol. 9: Massenet Arias

Esclarmonde: Roland!...Comme Ce Nom
   Me Trouble
   S solo,pno CLASSV 1155   (M297)

Expressions Lyriques
   [Fr] high solo RECITAL 278 (M298)

Griselidis: Des Larmes Brulent Ma
   Paupiere
   see Art Of Joan Sutherland, The,
   Vol. 9: Massenet Arias

Griselidis: Je Suis L'Oiseau
   T solo,pno CLASSV 1890   (M299)

Hérodiade: Dors, Ô Cité Perverse!
   "Hérodiade: Phanuel's Aria" B solo,
   pno CLASSV 1291   (M300)

Hérodiade: Hérode! Ne Me Refuse Pas!
   Mez solo,pno CLASSV 1125   (M301)

Hérodiade: Il Est Doux
   S solo,pno CLASSV 0396   (M302)
   see Art Of Joan Sutherland, The,
   Vol. 9: Massenet Arias

Hérodiade: Ne Me Refuse Pas!
   Mez solo,pno CLASSV 0880   (M303)

Hérodiade: Ne Pouvant Réprimer
   T solo,pno CLASSV 0971   (M304)

Hérodiade: Phanuel's Aria
   see Hérodiade: Dors, Ô Cité
   Perverse!

Hérodiade: Salomé-Herod
   SBar soli,pno CLASSV 0615   (M305)

Hérodiade: Salomé, Salomé
   Bar solo,pno CLASSV 1639   (M306)

Hérodiade: Vision Fugitive
   Bar solo,pno CLASSV 0406   (M307)

Heure Vécue
   see Mélodies, Vol. 3

Immortalite *canon
   2 solo voices BARDIC BE0093 (M308)

Jongleur De Notre Dame, Le: Legende
   De La Sauge
   [Fr/Eng] Bar solo RECITAL 2237
                                (M309)
Légende Du Baiser, La
   high solo,pno CLASSV 1280 from
   TROIS POÈMES CHASTES   (M310)

Mains, Les
   see Mélodies, Vol.2

MASSENET, JULES (cont'd.)

Manon: Ah! Fuyez, Douce Image
  [Fr] T solo,pno CLASSV 1167   (M311)

Manon: Instant Charmant
  see Manon: Le Rêve

Manon: Je Marche...Obéissons
  S solo,pno CLASSV 0397   (M312)

Manon: Je Suis...Encor (from Manon's
  Entrance, Act I)
  S solo,pno CLASSV 1845   (M313)

Manon: Le Rêve
  "Manon: Instant Charmant" T solo,
  pno CLASSV 1894   (M314)

Marie-Magdeleine: O Mes Soeurs
  see Art Of Joan Sutherland, The,
  Vol. 9: Massenet Arias

Mélodie Des Baisers, La
  med solo,pno CLASSV 1882   (M315)
  high solo,pno CLASSV 1891   (M316)

Mélodies, Vol.1
  (Moody, Nell; Moody, John) [Fr/Eng]
  med solo,pno UNITED MUS f.s.
  contains: Alcyons, Les; Berceuse;
  Mort De La Cigale, La; Nuit
  d'Espagne; Soleil Couchant;
  Sonnet   (M317)

Mélodies, Vol.2
  (Moody, Nell; Moody, John) [Fr/Eng]
  med solo,pno UNITED MUS f.s.
  contains: Ame Des Oiseaux, L'; Ce
  Que Disent Les Cloches; Mains,
  Les; Rondel De La Belle Au
  Bois; Soir De Rêve; Voix
  Suprême   (M318)

Mélodies, Vol. 3
  (Moody, Nell; Moody, John) [Fr/Eng]
  med solo,pno UNITED MUS f.s.
  contains: Heure Vécue; Mousmé!;
  Pleuvait, Il; Plus Vite;
  Rivière, La; Voix De Femmes (M319)

Mort De La Cigale, La
  see Mélodies, Vol.1

Mousmé!
  see Mélodies, Vol. 3

Nuit D'Espagne
  high solo,pno CLASSV 0853   (M320)
  see Mélodies, Vol.1

Oh! Si Les Fleurs Avaient Des Yeux
  [Fr/Eng] med solo,pno CLASSV 1218
                             (M321)
  [Fr/Eng] high solo,pno CLASSV 1217
                             (M322)

Ouvre Tes Yeux Bleus
  med solo,pno CLASSV 0862   (M323)
  high solo,pno CLASSV 0847   (M324)

Pauv' Petit, Le
  high solo,pno CLASSV 1278 from
  TROIS POÈMES CHASTES   (M325)

Pensée D'Automne
  med solo,pno CLASSV 0868   (M326)

Pleuvait, Il
  see Mélodies, Vol. 3

Plus Vite
  see Mélodies, Vol. 3

Poëme D'Amour
  [Fr] med-high solo,pno (5 mélodies
  & 1 duet) CLASSV 1360   (M327)

Poëme D'Avril
  [Fr] T solo,pno CLASSV 1323 (M328)

Poëme D'Hiver
  [Fr] high solo,pno CLASSV 1322
                             (M329)

Poëme D'Octobre
  [Fr] med solo,pno CLASSV 1320
                             (M330)

Poëme Du Souvenir
  Bar solo,pno CLASSV 1325   (M331)

Poëme D'un Soir
  [Fr] med solo,pno CLASSV 1321
                             (M332)

Poëme Pastoral
  med-high solo,pno CLASSV 1324
                             (M333)

Printemps Dernier
  med solo,pno CLASSV 0875   (M334)

Quel L'Heure Est Donc Brève
  med solo,pno CLASSV 0860   (M335)
  low solo,pno CLASSV 0861   (M336)

Rivière, La
  see Mélodies, Vol. 3

MASSENET, JULES (cont'd.)

Roi De Lahore, Le: J'ai Fui La
  Chambre Nuptiale!
  see Art Of Joan Sutherland, The,
  Vol. 9: Massenet Arias

Roi De Lahore, Le: Que Les Douleurs
  De La Terre
  see Art Of Joan Sutherland, The,
  Vol. 9: Massenet Arias

Roi De Lahore: Ferme Les Yeux
  Mez solo,pno CLASSV 1600   (M337)

Roi De Lahore: Promesse De Mon Avenir
  Bar solo,pno CLASSV 1648   (M338)

Rondel De La Belle Au Bois
  see Mélodies, Vol.2

Sais-Tu, Le
  med solo,pno CLASSV 0844   (M339)

Sapho: Ah! Qu'il Est Loin Mon Pays
  T solo,pno CLASSV 0947   (M340)

Sapho: Je T'ai Tenue Entre Mes Bras
  T solo,pno CLASSV 0946   (M341)

Serenade De Zanetto
  see Sérénade Du Passant

Sérénade Du Passant
  "Serenade De Zanetto" high solo,pno
  CLASSV 0858   (M342)

Sevillana (from Don César De Basan:
  Interlude)
  [Fr] coloratura sop,pno CLASSV 1283
                             (M343)

Si Tu Veux, Mignonne
  high solo,pno CLASSV 0857   (M344)

Soir De Rêve
  see Mélodies, Vol.2

Soleil Couchant
  see Mélodies, Vol.1

Sonnet
  see Mélodies, Vol.1

Thaïs: Ah! Je Suis Fatigué...Dis-Moi
  Que Je Suis Belle
  S solo,pno CLASSV 1282   (M345)

Thaïs: Duo De L'Oasis
  "Baigne D'eau" SBar soli,pno CLASSV
  0422   (M346)

Trois Poèmes Chastes
  see Légende Du Baiser, La
  see Pauv' Petit, Le
  see Vers Béthléem

Vers Béthléem
  high solo,pno CLASSV 1279 from
  TROIS POÈMES CHASTES   (M347)

Vierge, La: L'extase De La Vierge
  see Art Of Joan Sutherland, The,
  Vol. 9: Massenet Arias

Vingt Mélodies Vol. 1
  high solo,pno CLASSV C042   (M348)
  med solo,pno CLASSV C041   (M349)

Vingt Mélodies Vol. 2
  med solo,pno CLASSV C043   (M350)

Vingt Mélodies Vol. 3
  med solo,pno CLASSV C044   (M351)

Vingt Mélodies Vol. 5
  med solo,pno CLASSV C045   (M352)

Vingt Mélodies Vol. 6
  high solo,pno CLASSV C046   (M353)

Voix De Femmes
  see Mélodies, Vol. 3

Voix Suprême
  see Mélodies, Vol.2

Werther: J'Aurais Sur Ma Poitrine
  "Désolation De Werther" T solo,pno
  CLASSV 1237   (M354)

MASSEUS, JAN (1913-   )
  Dies Irae
  see Marsman-Cylus, Op. 20

Gezel, De
  see Triptyque Maconnique, Op. 57

Leerling, De
  see Triptyque Maconnique, Op. 57

Marsman-Cylus, Op. 20
  A solo,pno DONEMUS f.s. [11]
  contains: Dies Irae; Paradise
  Regained; Polderland   (M355)

MASSEUS, JAN (cont'd.)

Meester, De
  see Triptyque Maconnique, Op. 57

My Kingdom
  see My Kingdom, Op. 47a

My Kingdom, Op. 47a
  med solo,pno DONEMUS f.s. [8']
  contains: My Kingdom; Rain;
  Singing; Where Go The Boats?;
  Windy Nights   (M356)

Paradise Regained
  see Marsman-Cylus, Op. 20

Polderland
  see Marsman-Cylus, Op. 20

Rain
  see My Kingdom, Op. 47a

Singing
  see My Kingdom, Op. 47a

Triptyque Maconnique, Op. 57
  B solo,fl,org DONEMUS f.s. [12']
  contains: Gezel, De; Leerling,
  De; Meester, De   (M357)

Where Go The Boats?
  see My Kingdom, Op. 47a

Windy Nights
  see My Kingdom, Op. 47a

MASSON, ASKELL (1953-   )
  Fagra Verold
  solo voice,pno ICELAND 003-060
                             (M358)

MASSUMOTO, KIKUKO (1937-   )
  Three Songs From Medieval Japan
  (Bertagnolio, L.; Fujisaki, I.)
  (CCU) ONGAKU 526060   (M359)

MASTERS OF SONG, VOL. 1 *CCU
  BOOSEY EMB01751 f.s.   (M360)

MASTERS OF SONG, VOL. 2 *CCU
  BOOSEY EMB02110 f.s.   (M361)

MASTERS OF SONG, VOL. 3 *CCU
  BOOSEY EMB02262 f.s.   (M362)

MASTERS OF SONG, VOL. 4 *CCU
  BOOSEY EMB02909 f.s.   (M363)

MASTERS OF SONG, VOL. 5 *CCU
  BOOSEY EMB03118 f.s.   (M364)

MASTERS OF SONG, VOL. 6 *CCU
  BOOSEY EMB03602 f.s.   (M365)

MASTERS OF SONG, VOL. 7A *CCU
  BOOSEY EMB04470 f.s.   (M366)

MASTERS OF SONG, VOL. 7B *CCU
  BOOSEY EMB04471 f.s.   (M367)

MASTERS OF SONG, VOL. 7C *CCU
  BOOSEY EMB04472 f.s.   (M368)

MATABU see Demare, L.

MATER DOLOROSA see Sigurbjörnsson,
  Thorkell

MATHIAS, WILLIAM (1934-1992)
  Songs Of William Blake
  Mez solo,instrumental ensemble fac
  ed OXFORD 61.804   (M369)

MATINALE see Annovazzi, Napoleone

MATOUSEK, LUKAS (1943-   )
  Tartuff's Punishment
  SMez soli,fl,bass clar [4'] CESKY
  HUD.   (M370)

MATRIMONIO SEGRETO: PERDONATE, SIGNOR
  MIO see Cimarosa, Domenico

MATRIMONIO SEGRETO: PRIA CHE SPUNTI see
  Cimarosa, Domenico

MATROZENLIED see King, Harold C.

MATSUDAIRA, YORI-AKI (1931-   )
  Mac Voices
  solo voice,electronic equipment,
  electronic tape [60'] JAPAN
                             (M371)

  Semiology For John Dowland
  S solo,electronic tape [15'] JAPAN
                             (M372)

MATSUDAIRA, YORI-TSUNE (1907-   )
  Akenu Yo Ni
  S solo,koto [5'] JAPAN   (M373)

  Banka
  S solo,prepared pno [5'] JAPAN
                             (M374)

  Chihiro Tomo
  S solo,fl [5'] JAPAN   (M375)

MATSUDAIRA, YORI-TSUNE (cont'd.)

Commencement Du Printemps, Le
solo voice,inst ONGAKU rent   (M376)

Karabito No
S solo, sho [5'] JAPAN   (M377)

Katsura
solo voice,fl,harp,gtr,perc ONGAKU
rent   (M378)

Kawaraji To
S solo,cel/pno, koto [5'] JAPAN
(M379)

Kogarashi No
S solo,clar [5'] JAPAN   (M380)

Oborozukiyo Ni
S solo [5'] JAPAN   (M381)

Okata No
S solo [5'] JAPAN   (M382)

Okutomiru
S solo,2alto fl [5'] JAPAN   (M383)

Poeme Du Juillet
S solo,pno [5'] JAPAN   (M384)

Requiem
S solo,fl&alto fl,ob&English horn,
clar,bsn,sax,harp,pno,6vln [5']
JAPAN   (M385)

Sode Nururu
S solo,fl, sho [5'] JAPAN   (M386)

Uranaku Mo
S solo,fl [5'] JAPAN   (M387)

Yogatari Ni (Dit Du Genji)
S solo, sho [5'] JAPAN   (M388)

MATSUMOTO, HINOHARU (1945-   )
Haru Wa Akebono
solo voice, koto [16'] JAPAN (M389)

Hoshi Wa Subaru
S solo,fl,perc, koto [15'] JAPAN
(M390)

Oiseau D'Autrefois, L'
solo voice,electronic equipment,
koto [16'] JAPAN   (M391)

MATSUMURA, TEIZO (1929-   )
Achime
S solo,fl,ob,clar,alto sax,bsn,
horn,trp,trom,perc,pno,vcl,db
ONGAKU rent   (M392)

MATTEI, TITO (1841-1914)
Non È Ver
med solo,pno CLASSV 0852   (M393)
high solo,pno CLASSV 1895   (M394)

MATTHEW MARK LUKE AND JOHN see
Jeffreys, John

MATTHEWS, COLIN (1946-   )
Strugnell's Haiku
solo voice FABER 51173 2   (M395)

MATTHEWS, THOMAS (1915-   )
Lord Is My Shepherd, The
high solo,org FITZSIMONS F0103
(M396)
low solo,org FITZSIMONS F0113
(M397)

MATTHEWS, WILLIAM (1950-   )
Endenich
S solo [8'] sc AM.COMP.AL. $1.55
(M398)

Music From Cold Mountain
S solo,3string quin, conductor
[19'] sc AM.COMP.AL. $20.70
(M399)

Paysage
S solo,fl,clar,vcl,perc,pno [10']
AM.COMP.AL. sc $9.95, pts $7.25
(M400)

MATTHUS, SIEGFRIED (1934-   )
Gesänge, Band 1
PETERS 5343   (M401)

Gesänge, Band 2
PETERS 5343A   (M402)

Holofernes
Bar solo,3.3.3.3. 4.3.4.1. timp,
4perc,elec bass,harp,pno&cel,
strings [20'] sc DEUTSCHER
DV 1128   (M403)

Kantate Von Den Beiden
SBar&speaking voice,3.3.3.2.
1.0.0.0. timp,perc,harp,cel,pno,
strings [15'] DEUTSCHER   (M404)

Nachtlieder
Bar solo,string quar,harp DEUTSCHER
(M405)

Wem Ich Zu Gefallen Suche *CCU
TBar/TB soli,pno DEUTSCHER DV 9048
f.s.   (M406)

MATTIESEN
Balladen, Op. 1
PETERS 3500   (M407)

Es Werde Licht
PETERS 3851   (M408)

Fröhliche Musikus
PETERS 3850   (M409)

Heimgang
high solo,pno PETERS 3887A   (M410)
low solo,pno PETERS 3887B   (M411)

Liebeslieder, Op. 9
PETERS 3734A   (M412)

Lieder, Op. 2
PETERS 3501B   (M413)

Lieder, Op. 3
PETERS 3502B   (M414)

Lieder, Op. 11
PETERS 3736A   (M415)

Lieder, Op. 12
PETERS 3736B   (M416)

Vom Schmerz *Op.14
PETERS 3738   (M417)

MATTINATA see Leoncavallo, Ruggiero

MAUD see Somervell, Arthur

MAUSFALLENSPRÜCHLEIN see Wolf, Hugo

MAW
Five American Folksongs
solo voice FABER 51191 0   (M418)

MAXIMS OF SAINT TERESA see Pike, Lionel

MAXWELTON BRAES ARE BONNY see Scott,
[Lady] John (Alicia Ann), Annie
Laurie

MAXYM, R.
Autumn
see Recollections (Six Songs For
Soprano And Orchestra)
see Recollections (Six Songs For
Soprano And Piano)

Day One
see Recollections (Six Songs For
Soprano And Orchestra)
see Recollections (Six Songs For
Soprano And Piano)

Maya No. 3
see Recollections (Six Songs For
Soprano And Orchestra)
see Recollections (Six Songs For
Soprano And Piano)

Meditation
see Recollections (Six Songs For
Soprano And Orchestra)
see Recollections (Six Songs For
Soprano And Piano)

Objective Knowledge
see Recollections (Six Songs For
Soprano And Orchestra)
see Recollections (Six Songs For
Soprano And Piano)

Recollections (Six Songs For Soprano
And Orchestra)
ZINNEB ZI 60 f.s.
contains: Autumn; Day One; Maya
No. 3; Meditation; Objective
Knowledge; Winter   (M419)

Recollections (Six Songs For Soprano
And Piano)
ZINNEB ZI 59 f.s.
contains: Autumn; Day One; Maya
No. 3; Meditation; Objective
Knowledge; Winter   (M420)

Winter
see Recollections (Six Songs For
Soprano And Orchestra)
see Recollections (Six Songs For
Soprano And Piano)

MAY, BETH
Bullfrogs
Bar solo,alto sax,vcl (diff) sc,pts
DANE WOC1006   (M421)

MAY LAURELS CROWN THY BROW see Verdi,
Giuseppe, Aida: Ritorna Vincitor

MAY NIGHT see Hageman, Richard

MAY NIGHT: SLEEP, MY DEAR see Rimsky-
Korsakov, Nikolai

MAY OF DISCUS see Tanaka, Satoshi see
Tanaka, Satoshi, Enban No Gogatsu

MAY SONG IT FLOURISH see Roosevelt,
[Joseph] Willard

MAY, THE MAIDEN see Carpenter, John
Alden

MAYA NO. 3 see Maxym, R.

MAYORAL, R.
Flor De Amor
solo voice,pno BOIL B.0679   (M422)

MAZELLIER, JULES (1879-1959)
Six Melodies
[Fr] RECITAL 330   (M423)

MAZEPA: MAZEPA'S ARIOSO see
Tchaikovsky, Piotr Ilyich

ME PISNE see Seidel, Jan

ME VOICI DANS see Thomas, Ambroise,
Mignon: Frederick's Gavotte

MED EN PRIMULA VERIS see Grieg, Edvard
Hagerup

MED JESUS VIL EG FARA
(Bakke, Ruth) solo voice,org NORGE
f.s. contains also: Akk, Mon Min
Vei Til Kana'an; Jeg Ser Deg, O
Guds Lam, Å Stå; Krist Stod Op Af
Døde   (M424)
see Bakke, Ruth

MED RØDE ROSER see Nyhus, Rolf

MED SOLSKINSFANA UR SUDURATT see
Kaldalóns, Sigvaldi S.

MEDEA see Döhl, Friedhelm

MEDEA: CHI M'ARRESTA see Mercadante, G.
Saverio

MEDEA: DEI TUOI FIGLI LA MADRE see
Cherubini, Luigi

MEDEK, TILO (1940-   )
Fragmente Einer Kleisthymne
T solo,wind quin,pno [17'] MOECK
study sc 5262A, voc pt 5262B
(M425)

Geistliche Lieder
med solo,org [15'] (CC6U) MOECK
5297   (M426)
high solo,org [15'] (CC6U) MOECK
5297A   (M427)

Kriegsgefangen
T solo,wind quin,pno,drums [10']
study sc MOECK 5397   (M428)

MEDEMA
More Songs For The Turning
(2 book set) SHAWNEE 5092   (M429)

Songs For The Turning
SHAWNEE 5087   (M430)

MEDEMA, KENNETH PETER (1943-   )
Words Of Praise
solo voice HARRIS,R RHS0304 $2.00
(M431)

MEDER, JOHANN VALENTIN (1649-1719)
Ach Herr, Strafe, Mich Nicht In
Deinem Zorn
S solo,2vln,vcl,cont HÄNSSLER sc
10.363-01 f.s., pts
10, 363-11, 13 f.s.   (M432)

MEDIA VITA see Ehlen, Margriet

MEDIEVAL DIPTYCH see Rawsthorne, Alan

MEDINA, EMILIO
'Nnammurato Senza Ammore
see Serenatella

Serenatella
"'Nnammurato Senza Ammore" high
solo,pno CLASSV 1316   (M433)

MEDITATION see Maxym, R.

MEDITATION, OP.90 see Hess, W.

MEDIUM, DAS see Kriebaum, Franz

MEDJÉ see Gounod, Charles François

MEDLEY see Brooks, William

MEDTNER, NIKOLAI KARLOVICH (1880-1951)
Angel, The *Op.1a
[Ger/Russ] med-high solo,pno CLASSV
2141   (M434)

Drei Lieder, Op. 12
[Ger/Russ] solo voice,pno (text by
Heinrich Heine) CLASSV 2192
(M435)

Eight Poems, Op. 24
[Russ/Eng] solo voice,pno CLASSV
2142   (M436)

MEDTNER, NIKOLAI KARLOVICH (cont'd.)

Neun Lieder, Op. 6
[Russ/Ger] high solo,pno (text by
Goethe) CLASSV 2191   (M437)

Rose, The *Op.29,No.6
[Russ/Ger] med-low solo,pno CLASSV
2138   (M438)

Sechs Gedichte Von Goethe, Op. 18
[Ger/Russ] solo voice,pno CLASSV
2140   (M439)

Seven Poems Of Pushkin, Op. 29
[Russ/Eng] (not available outside
U.S.A.) RECITAL 372   (M440)

Seven Songs, Op. 28
[Ger/Russ] solo voice,pno CLASSV
2195   (M441)

Singer, The *Op.29,No.2
[Russ/Ger] med-high solo,pno CLASSV
2137   (M442)

Six Songs, Op. 3
[Russ/Ger] high solo,pno CLASSV
2190   (M443)

Two Songs, Op. 13
[Russ/Ger] high solo,pno CLASSV
2193   (M444)

Waves...Thoughts... *Op.24,No.3
[Russ/Ger] high solo,pno CLASSV
2135   (M445)

Whispering Nature *Op.24,No.7
[Russ/Ger] med solo,pno CLASSV 2136
                           (M446)

Willow Tree, The *Op.24,No.2
[Russ/Ger] high solo,pno CLASSV
2134   (M447)

Zwei Gedichte Von Nietzsche *Op.19a
[Ger/Russ] solo voice,pno CLASSV
2139   (M448)

Zwölf Lieder Von Goethe, Op. 15
[Ger/Russ] high solo,pno CLASSV
2194   (M449)

MEER ERGLANZTE, DAS see Isolfsson, Pall

MEER ERSTRAHLT, DAS see Jensen, Ludwig
Irgens

MEER VAN OHRID see Ehlen, Margriet

MEERESLEUCHTEN see Loewe, Carl
Gottfried

MEERESSEHNSUCHT see Louis Ferdinand,
Prince Of Prussia

MEESTER, DE see Masseus, Jan

MEETING THE ORCHESTRA see Brevik, Tor,
Vi Møter Orkestret

MEFANO, PAUL (1937-   )
Que L'Oiseau Se Dechire En Sables
S solo,clar in A,perc LEDUC
HE 33666   (M450)

MEFISTOFELE: DAI CAMPI see Boito,
Arrigo

MEFISTOFELE: SON LO SPIRITO see Boito,
Arrigo

MÉHUL, ÉTIENNE-NICOLAS (1763-1817)
Ariodant: Femme Sensible, Entends-Tu
Bar solo,pno CLASSV 1627   (M451)

Joseph En Égypte: Champs Paternels
T solo,pno CLASSV 0349   (M452)

MEI PLEZANT, DIE see Maessen, Antoon

MEIER, BURKHARD
Lob Des Sisyphus *song cycle
low solo,pno DEUTSCHER DV 9047
                           (M453)

MEIJERING, CHIEL (1954-   )
Grote Keel Om Mee Te Drinken, 'N
Mez solo,alto sax,perc,pno [11']
DONEMUS   (M454)

MEIJERING, CORD (1955-   )
Chimäre
Mez solo,fl,clar,horn,vla,vcl,gtr,
perc [32'] MOECK 5392   (M455)

Licht Des Mondes, Das
Mez solo,2(pic).2(English
horn).4.3. 4.3.3.1. harp,pno,
timp,perc,strings [26'] study sc
MOECK 5336   (M456)

November
S/Mez solo,gtr [11'] MOECK 5382
                           (M457)

MEIJERING, CORD (cont'd.)

Rotfärbung Des Flusses
Mez solo,clar,vcl,pno [30'5"] MOECK
5447   (M458)

Zwei Lorca-Lieder
S/Mez solo,pno [6'30"] MOECK 5402
                           (M459)
MEIMA, HERMAN (1905-   )
Jesu, Wijs En Wondermachtig
med solo,org [2'] DONEMUS (M460)

Psalm No. 130
Bar/B solo,org [3'] DONEMUS (M461)

Verkündigung
med solo,org [3'] DONEMUS (M462)

MEIN HERR MARQUIS see Strauss, Johann,
[Jr.]

MEIN HERZTHU DICH AUF see Lowenstamm,
Franz Jos.

MEIN KIND, WIR WAREN KINDER see
Heimerl, Chr.

MEIN LIED, OP. 108 see Gumbert

MEIN SEELE RUHMT UND PREIST see Bach,
Johann Sebastian

MEIN TRAUM see Bortoli, Stephane

MEINE LIEDER, MEINE SÄNGE see Weber,
Carl Maria von

MEINE ROSE see Schumann, Robert
(Alexander)

MEINE RUH' IST HIN see Loewe, Carl
Gottfried

MEINE WELT - ICH SEHE KEINE ANDERE see
Kaufmann, Dieter

MEINER MUTTER see Lauterbach, Lorenz

MEIREGEN, KINDERVERZEN see Badings,
Henk

MEISTARI HIMNA see Helgason, Hallgrimur

MEISTERSINGER VON NÜRNBERG, DIE: AM
STILLEN HERD see Wagner, Richard

MEISTERSINGER VON NÜRNBERG, DIE:
MORGENLICH LEUCHTEND see Wagner,
Richard

MEISTERSINGER VON NÜRNBERG, DIE: NUN
HÖRT UND VERSTEHT see Wagner,
Richard

MEISTERSINGER VON NÜRNBERG, DIE: WAHN!
WAHN! see Wagner, Richard

MEISTERSINGER VON NÜRNBERG, DIE:
WALTHER'S PRIZE-SONG see Wagner,
Richard

MEISTERSINGER VON NÜRNBERG, DIE: WAS
DUFTET DOCH DER FLIEDER see Wagner,
Richard

MEJOR TINTA, LA see Violette, Andrew

MELBY, JOHN B. (1941-   )
Men That Are Falling, The
S solo,pno,electronic tape [11'] sc
AM.COMP.AL. $10.70, perf mat rent
                           (M463)
MELLEM LIVETS AFGRUNDE see Christensen,
Mogens

MELODI see Danielsson, Harry

MELODIE see Rubinstein, Anton

MELODIE AM ABEND see Pütz, Eduard

MELODIE ARABE see Borodin, Alexander
Porfirievich

MÉLODIE DES BAISERS, LA see Massenet,
Jules

MELODIE ITALIANE 1 DALL' OTTOCENTO AL
NOVECENTO see Wagner, Richard

MELODIE ITALIANE 2 DALL' OTTOCENTO AL
NOVECENTO see Wagner, Richard

MELODIE ITALIANE PER CANTO E PIANOFORTE
see Rossini, Gioacchino

MELODIES see Lalo, Edouard see
Niedermeyer, Louis

MÉLODIES, 12 see Coquard, Arthur

MÉLODIES, 17, VOL.2 see Delibes, Léo

MÉLODIES, 20, VOL.1 see Chaminade,
Cécile see Moret, Ernest

MÉLODIES, 20, VOL.2 see Chaminade,
Cécile see Faure, Jean-Baptiste

MÉLODIES, 20, VOL.3 see Chaminade,
Cécile see Faure, Jean-Baptiste

MÉLODIES, 22 see Vaucorbeil, Auguste-
Emmanuel

MÉLODIES, 24 see Berlioz, Hector
(Louis)

MÉLODIES, 25, VOL.1 see Faure, Jean-
Baptiste

MELODIES see Bosmans, Henriëtte

MELODIES ET CHANSONS see Honegger,
Arthur see Milhaud, Darius see
Mompou, Federico see Poulenc,
Francis see Satie, Erik

MÉLODIES ET POËMES, 23, VOL. 1 see
Levade, Charles (Gaston)

MÉLODIES PERSANES see Rubinstein,
Anton, Twelve Persian Songs, Op. 34
see Saint-Saëns, Camille

MÉLODIES POSTHUMES see Ravel, Maurice

MÉLODIES, VOL.1 see Massenet, Jules see
Moor, Emanuel

MÉLODIES, VOL.2 see Massenet, Jules see
Paladilhe, Emile see Reber,
Napoleon-Henri

MÉLODIES, VOL. 3 see Massenet, Jules
see Paladilhe, Emile

MELOPEE see Regt, Hendrik de

MELOPOEIA see Tipei, Sever

MEME SI JE VOYAIS see Scelsi, Giacinto

MEMENTO, A DRAMATIC SCENE see Heppener,
Robert

MEMMON see Schubert, Franz (Peter)

MEMNON see Schubert, Franz (Peter)

MEMORARE see Schrijvers, Jean

MEMORIES OF THE TYROL [1] see Weigl,
[Mrs.] Vally

MEMORIES OF THE TYROL [2] see Weigl,
[Mrs.] Vally

MEN SCHEERT GEEN EI see Andriessen,
Jurriaan

MEN THAT ARE FALLING, THE see Melby,
John B.

MENAGERIE IN KRÄHWINKEL, DIE: DUETTO
see Glaeser, Franz

MENDELSSOHN, FANNY
see HENSEL, FANNY MENDELSSOHN

MENDELSSOHN: 24 SONGS see Mendelssohn-
Bartholdy, Felix

MENDELSSOHN-BARTHOLDY, FELIX
(1809-1847)
Abendlied
"Wenn Ich Auf Dem Lager Liege" 2
solo voices,pno SCIEN 1046 (M464)

Abschiedslied Der Zugvögel
see Sechs Zweistimmige Lieder, Op.
63

Aehrenfeld, Das
see Drei Zweistimmige Lieder, Op.
77

Allnächtlich Im Traume Seh Ich Dich
see Sechs Gesänge, Op. 86

Altdeutsches Frühlingslied
see Sechs Gesänge, Op. 86

Altdeutsches Lied
see Sechs Lieder, Op. 57

An Die Entfernte
see Sechs Lieder, Op. 71

Auf Die Wanderschaft
see Sechs Lieder, Op. 71

Auf Flügeln Des Gesanges
see Sechs Gesänge, Op. 34

Da Lieg Ich Unter Den Bäumen
see Drei Gesänge, Op. 84

MENDELSSOHN-BARTHOLDY, FELIX (cont'd.)

Drei Gesänge, Op. 84
    low solo,pno SCIEN 1051 f.s.
    contains: Da Lieg Ich Unter Den
        Bäumen; Herbstlied; Jagdlied
                                        (M465)
Drei Zweistimmige Lieder, Op. 77
    2 solo voices,pno SCIEN 1052 f.s.
    contains: Aehrenfeld, Das; Lied
        Aus Rug Blas; Sonntagsmorgen
                                        (M466)
Elijah: Hear Ye, Israel!
    S solo,pno CLASSV 0537   (M467)
Elijah: If With All Your Hearts
    T solo,pno CLASSV 1132   (M468)
Elijah: It Is Enough
    Bar solo,pno CLASSV 0842   (M469)
Elijah: Lord God Of Abraham
    [Eng] Bar solo,pno CLASSV 1665
                                   (M470)
Erster Verlust
    see Sechs Gesänge, Op. 99
Es Lauschte Das Laub So Dunkelgrün
    see Sechs Gesänge, Op. 86
Es Weiss Und Räth Es Doch Keiner
    see Sechs Gesänge, Op. 99
Frühlingslied
    see Sechs Gesänge, Op. 34
    see Sechs Lieder, Op. 71
Gruss
    solo voice,pno SCIEN 1056 from
    LIEDER UND GESÄNGE MIT BEGLEITUNG
        D. PIANOFORTE   (M471)
    see Sechs Zweistimmige Lieder, Op.
        63
Herbstlied
    see Drei Gesänge, Op. 84
    see Sechs Zweistimmige Lieder, Op.
        63
Hirtenlied
    see Sechs Lieder, Op. 57
I Waited For The Lord
    [Eng/Ger] SA soli,pno CLASSV 0978
                                   (M472)
Ich Hör Ein Vöglein Locken
    see Zwei Gesänge
Ich Wollt' Meine Lieb' Ergösse Sich
    All' In Ein Einzig Wort
    see Sechs Zweistimmige Lieder, Op.
        63
Jagdlied
    see Drei Gesänge, Op. 84
Liebende Schreibt, Die
    see Sechs Gesänge, Op. 86
Lieblingsplätzchen
    see Sechs Gesänge, Op. 99
Lied Aus Rug Blas
    see Drei Zweistimmige Lieder, Op.
        77
Lieder Und Gesänge Mit Begleitung D.
    Pianoforte
    see Gruss
Maiglöckchen Und Die Blümelein
    see Sechs Zweistimmige Lieder, Op.
        63
Mendelssohn: 24 Songs (composed with
    Hensel, Fanny Mendelssohn)
    *CC24U
    (Paton) ALFRED high solo,pno 3387
        f.s.; med solo,pno 3388 f.s.
                                   (M473)
Minnelied
    see Sechs Gesänge, Op. 34
Mond, Der
    see Sechs Gesänge, Op. 86
Morgenlied
    see Sechs Gesänge, Op. 86
Nachtlied
    see Sechs Lieder, Op. 71
O For The Wings Of A Dove
    [Eng/Ger] A solo,pno (solo only)
        CLASSV 1249   (M474)
    [Eng/Ger] S solo,pno (solo only)
        CLASSV 1248   (M475)
O Jugend, O Schöne Rosenzeit
    see Sechs Lieder, Op. 57
On Wings Of Song
    (Moore, Dorothy Rudd) SS soli,pno
        [3'] sc AM.COMP.AL. $1.55 (M476)

MENDELSSOHN-BARTHOLDY, FELIX (cont'd.)

Reiselied
    see Sechs Gesänge, Op. 34
Saint Paul: But The Lord Is Mindful
    Of His Own
    A solo,pno CLASSV 0977   (M477)
Saint Paul: O God, Have Mercy
    [Eng] B solo,pno CLASSV 1247   (M478)
Sämtliche Lieder
    (Friedlaender) high solo,pno PETERS
        1774A   (M479)
    (Friedlaender) med solo,pno PETERS
        1774B   (M480)
    (Friedlaender) low solo,pno PETERS
        1774C   (M481)
Schifflein, Das
    see Sechs Gesänge, Op. 99
Schilflied
    see Sechs Lieder, Op. 71
Sechs Gesänge, Op. 34
    solo voice,pno SCIEN 1061 f.s.
    contains: Auf Flügeln Des
        Gesanges; Frühlingslied;
        Minnelied; Reiselied;
        Sonntagslied; Suleika   (M482)
Sechs Gesänge, Op. 86
    solo voice,pno SCIEN 1062 f.s.
    contains: Allnächtlich Im Traume
        Seh Ich Dich; Altdeutsches
        Frühlingslied; Es Lauschte Das
        Laub So Dunkelgrün; Liebende
        Schreibt, Die; Mond, Der;
        Morgenlied   (M483)
Sechs Gesänge, Op. 99
    solo voice,pno SCIEN 1063 f.s.
    contains: Erster Verlust; Es
        Weiss Und Räth Es Doch Keiner;
        Lieblingsplätzchen; Schifflein,
        Das; Sterne Schau'n In Stiller
        Nacht, Die; Wenn Sich Zwei
        Herzen Scheiden   (M484)
Sechs Lieder *CC6U
    S/T solo,2.2.2.2. 2.0.0.0. timp,
    2perc,harp,strings DEUTSCHER
                                   (M485)
Sechs Lieder, Op. 57
    solo voice,pno SCIEN 1064 f.s.
    contains: Altdeutsches Lied;
        Hirtenlied; O Jugend, O Schöne
        Rosenzeit; Suleika;
        Venetianisches Gondellied;
        Wanderlied   (M486)
Sechs Lieder, Op. 71
    solo voice,pno SCIEN 1065 f.s.
    contains: An Die Entfernte; Auf
        Die Wanderschaft;
        Frühlingslied; Nachtlied;
        Schilflied; Tröstung   (M487)
Sechs Schottische Nationallieder
    *CC6U
    [Ger/Eng] DEUTSCHER DV 9080 f.s.
                                   (M488)
Sechs Zweistimmige Lieder, Op. 63
    solo voice,pno SCIEN 1068 f.s.
    contains: Abschiedslied Der
        Zugvögel; Gruss; Herbstlied;
        Ich Wollt' Meine Lieb' Ergösse
        Sich All' In Ein Einzig Wort;
        Maiglöckchen Und Die Blümelein;
        Volkslied   (M489)
Sixteen Selected Songs
    [Ger/Eng] solo voice,pno (cc161)
        SCHIRM.G LB1645   (M490)
Songs, 79 *CC79U
    [Ger] KALMUS f.s. high solo
        K 09886; med solo K 09887; low
        solo K 09888   (M491)
Sonntagslied
    see Sechs Gesänge, Op. 34
Sonntagsmorgen
    see Drei Zweistimmige Lieder, Op.
        77
Sterne Schau'n In Stiller Nacht, Die
    see Sechs Gesänge, Op. 99
Suleika
    see Sechs Gesänge, Op. 34
    see Sechs Lieder, Op. 57
Suleika Und Hatem
    ST soli,pno SCIEN 1069   (M492)
Todeslied Der Bojaren
    see Zwei Gesänge
Tröstung
    see Sechs Lieder, Op. 71

MENDELSSOHN-BARTHOLDY, FELIX (cont'd.)

Venetianisches Gondellied
    see Sechs Lieder, Op. 57
Venezianisches Gondellied *Op.57,
    No.5
    high solo,pno CLASSV 0620   (M493)
Volkslied
    see Sechs Zweistimmige Lieder, Op.
        63
Wanderlied
    see Sechs Lieder, Op. 57
Wenn Ich Auf Dem Lager Liege
    see Abendlied
Wenn Sich Zwei Herzen Scheiden
    see Sechs Gesänge, Op. 99
Zwei Gesänge
    solo voice,pno SCIEN 1071 f.s.
    contains: Ich Hör Ein Vöglein
        Locken; Todeslied Der Bojaren
                                   (M494)
Zwölf Gesänge, Op. 8
    solo voice,pno SCIEN 1072   (M495)

MENEELY-KYDER, SARAH
    Five Songs *CC5U
        S solo,pno sc AM.COMP.AL. $4.25
                                   (M496)
    Five Songs *CC5U
        B solo,pno sc AM.COMP.AL. $4.25
                                   (M497)
    Five Spirituals And Work Songs *CC5U
        B solo,pno sc AM.COMP.AL. $9.95
                                   (M498)
    From "Notes To Nine Lovers"
        S solo,fl,pno [10'] AM.COMP.AL.
                                   (M499)
    Kennst Du Das Land
        S solo,pno [2'] sc AM.COMP.AL.
        $1.95   (M500)
    Narsissus Monologue
        T solo,fl,rec,pic,ob,clar,bass
        clar,contrabsn,horn,trp,trom,
        perc,harp,cel,vla,vcl [10'] sc
        AM.COMP.AL. $15.75   (M501)
    Psalm No. 13
        S solo,pno [3'] sc AM.COMP.AL.
        $3.85   (M502)
    Sweethearts
        female solo,perc [10'] sc
        AM.COMP.AL. $4.60   (M503)
    Weep, The Mighty Typhoons
        Mez solo,pno [14'] sc AM.COMP.AL.
        $8.05   (M504)

MENGELBERG, KAREL (1902-1984)
    Drie Lieder Voor Alt En Piano
        A solo,pno DONEMUS f.s. [5']
        contains: Kind; Moeder; Toekomst
                                   (M505)
    Kind
        see Drie Lieder Voor Alt En Piano
    Moeder
        see Drie Lieder Voor Alt En Piano
    Toekomst
        see Drie Lieder Voor Alt En Piano

MENOTTI, GIAN CARLO (1911-   )
    Art Of Modern Singing, The
        solo voice BELWIN CAM0120 $12.95
                                   (M506)
    Eternal Prisoner, The
        see Five Songs
    Five Songs
        solo voice,pno SCHIRM.G 50480034
        f.s.
        contains: Eternal Prisoner, The;
            Idle Gift, The; Longest Wait,
            The; My Ghost; Swing, The
                                   (M507)
    Idle Gift, The
        see Five Songs
    Longest Wait, The
        see Five Songs
    My Ghost
        see Five Songs
    Nocturne
        S solo,harp,string quar/string orch
        sc,pts SCHIRM.G 50480037   (M508)
    Swing, The
        see Five Songs

MENSAJERO, EL see Chopin, Frédéric

MENSAJES DEL EVANGELIO see Peinado,
    Angel

MERCADANTE, G. SAVERIO (1795-1870)
Giuramento, Il: Bella, Adorata
Incognita
T solo,pno CLASSV 1592   (M509)

Giuramento, Il: S'io L'Amava!
Sciagurata!
ST soli,pno CLASSV 1267   (M510)

Medea: Chi M'Arresta
Mez solo,pno CLASSV 1594   (M511)

MERCHANT'S SONG, THE see Anderson, Beth

MERCILESS BEAUTY see Bush, Geoffrey

MÈRE see Bienvenu, Lily

MERE, TROIS POEMES DE M. CAREME see
Beyerman-Walraven, Jeanne

MERMAID, THE see Mermaid & Two Other
Water Songs, The see Haxton,
Kenneth

MERMAID & TWO OTHER WATER SONGS, THE
(Vignoles, Roger) solo voice,pno
THAMES 978302 f.s.
contains: Flow Gently, Sweet Afton;
Lowlands (Shanty); Mermaid, The
(M512)
MERRIE ENGLISH LOVE SONGS see Schmidt,
Sharon Yvonne Davis

MERRYMAN, MARJORIE
Ariel
S solo,clar,vcl,1perc [8'] APNM sc
$4.75, set $18.50   (M513)

Laments For Hektor
SSA soli,fl,clar,horn,pno,1perc,
vln,vcl [14'] APNM sc $9.00, pts
rent   (M514)

Three Songs From Antigone *CC3U
Mez solo,pno APNM sc $4.75, set
$9.00   (M515)

MES RÊVES DE JEUNE FILLE see Puget,
Louise

MES VERS FUIRAIENT see King, Harold C.

MESCHWITZ, FRIEDER (1936-1983)
Canzonettas (Three Songs On Anonymous
Texts)
med solo,pno (med) PEER   (M516)

Recuerdo *song cycle
med solo,pno (med diff) PEER (M517)

Shadow Of The Blues: Four Poems By
Langston Hughes
med solo,pno (med diff) PEER (M518)

MESE see Nieland, Henk

MESOSTICKS RE MERCE CUNNINGHAM see
Cage, John

MESRITZ VAN VELTHUYSEN, ANNY
(1897-1965)
Allegro
see Drie Liederen

Drie Liederen
A solo,pno DONEMUS f.s. [5']
contains: Allegro; Finale;
Scherzo   (M519)

Finale
see Drie Liederen

Scherzo
see Drie Liederen

MESSAGER, ANDRE (1853-1929)
Long Ago In Alcala
med-high solo,pno CLASSV 0856
(M520)
low solo,pno CLASSV 1152   (M521)

Neige Rose
high solo,pno CLASSV 1899   (M522)

MESSE POUR MONTSERRAT see Darasse,
Xavier

MESTRES, APELES
Amoroses, 12 Cancons
solo voice,pno BOIL B.0854   (M523)

Balades
solo voice,pno BOIL B.0868   (M524)

Birondon
see Cent Cancons, Les, Primera
Serie (Quadern Tercer)

Bosc Endins
see Cent Cancons, Les, Segona Serie
(Quadern Primer)

Bosqueta Rossinyolera, La
see Cent Cancons, Les, Primera
Serie (Quadern Primer)

MESTRES, APELES (cont'd.)

Cacera, La
see Cancons Festives Per Als
Infants

Camí De La Font
see Cent Cancons, Les, Primera
Serie (Quadern Segon)

Camí D'Estudi
see Cancons Festives Per Als
Infants

Campana, La
see Cancons Festives Per Als
Infants

Cancó, La
see Cent Cancons, Les, Segona Serie
(Quadern Primer)

Cancó D'Abril
see Cent Cancons, Les, Primera
Serie (Quadern Tercer)

Cancó De Taverna
see Cent Cancons, Les, Primera
Serie (Quadern Primer)

Cancó Del Mar, La
see Cent Cancons, Les, Segona Serie
(Quadern Tercer)

Cancó Llunyana
see Cent Cancons, Les, Segona Serie
(Quadern Tercer)

Cancons Festives Per Als Infants
solo voice,pno BOIL B.0862 f.s.
contains: Cacera, La; Camí
D'Estudi; Campana, La; Cargol,
El; Fa Fret!; Festa De Rates,
La   (M525)

Cant De La Joventut
see Cent Cancons, Les, Segona Serie
(Quadern Tercer)

Cantos Escolares
solo voice,pno BOIL B.0783A   (M526)

Cargol, El
see Cancons Festives Per Als
Infants

Cent Cancons, Les: Cancons Per A
Infants *CC12L
solo voice,pno BOIL B.0783 f.s.
(M527)
Cent Cancons, Les, Primera Serie
(Quadern Primer)
solo voice,pno BOIL B.0738 f.s.
contains: Bosqueta Rossinyolera,
La; Cancó De Taverna;
Felicitat; Gotes D'Aigua, Les;
Minuet; Non-Non De La Morta, La
(M528)
Cent Cancons, Les, Primera Serie
(Quadern Segon)
solo voice,pno BOIL B.0754 f.s.
contains: Camí De La Font;
Endreca; Madrigal; Non-Non Dels
Blats, La; Poll I La Pussa, El;
Rossinyol, El   (M529)

Cent Cancons, Les, Primera Serie
(Quadern Tercer)
solo voice,pno BOIL B.0763 f.s.
contains: Birondon; Cancó
D'Abril; Dona D'Aigua, La; Els
Frares Encantats; Moli, El;
Vella, La   (M530)

Cent Cancons, Les, Segona Serie
(Quadern Primer)
solo voice,pno BOIL B.0774 f.s.
contains: Bosc Endins; Cancó, La;
Ingenuitat; Pastoral De Vano;
Potentat, El (Cancó Del Camí);
Son-Soneta, La   (M531)

Cent Cancons, Les, Segona Serie
(Quadern Segon)
solo voice,pno BOIL B.0794 f.s.
contains: Donzella Malalta, La;
Espiga I La Rosella, L'; Gran
Raïm, El; Misteri; Toc
D'Oració; Vianant, El   (M532)

Cent Cancons, Les, Segona Serie
(Quadern Tercer)
solo voice,pno BOIL B.0814 f.s.
contains: Cancó Del Mar, La;
Cancó Llunyana; Cant De La
Joventut; Confidència; Els Tres
Enamorats; Roses De Maig   (M533)

Confidència
see Cent Cancons, Les, Segona Serie
(Quadern Tercer)

Doce Madrigals
solo voice,pno BOIL B.0845   (M534)

MESTRES, APELES (cont'd.)

Dona D'Aigua, La
see Cent Cancons, Les, Primera
Serie (Quadern Tercer)

Donzella Malalta, La
see Cent Cancons, Les, Segona Serie
(Quadern Segon)

Els Frares Encantats
see Cent Cancons, Les, Primera
Serie (Quadern Tercer)

Els Tres Enamorats
see Cent Cancons, Les, Segona Serie
(Quadern Tercer)

Endreca
see Cent Cancons, Les, Primera
Serie (Quadern Segon)

Espiga I La Rosella, L'
see Cent Cancons, Les, Segona Serie
(Quadern Segon)

Fa Fret!
see Cancons Festives Per Als
Infants

Felicitat
see Cent Cancons, Les, Primera
Serie (Quadern Primer)

Festa De Rates, La
see Cancons Festives Per Als
Infants

Gotes D'Aigua, Les
see Cent Cancons, Les, Primera
Serie (Quadern Primer)

Gran Raïm, El
see Cent Cancons, Les, Segona Serie
(Quadern Segon)

Ingenuitat
see Cent Cancons, Les, Segona Serie
(Quadern Primer)

Laura (Elegies Intimes)
solo voice,pno BOIL B.2115   (M535)

Madrigal
see Cent Cancons, Les, Primera
Serie (Quadern Segon)

Minuet
see Cent Cancons, Les, Primera
Serie (Quadern Primer)

Misteri
see Cent Cancons, Les, Segona Serie
(Quadern Segon)

Moli, El
see Cent Cancons, Les, Primera
Serie (Quadern Tercer)

Muñeca, La
solo voice,pno BOIL B.0783B   (M536)

Non-Non De La Morta, La
see Cent Cancons, Les, Primera
Serie (Quadern Primer)

Non-Non Dels Blats, La
see Cent Cancons, Les, Primera
Serie (Quadern Segon)

Nous Madrigals
solo voice,pno BOIL B.0848   (M537)

Noves Cancons Per Infants
solo voice,pno BOIL B.1108   (M538)

Pastoral De Vano
see Cent Cancons, Les, Segona Serie
(Quadern Primer)

Poll I La Pussa, El
see Cent Cancons, Les, Primera
Serie (Quadern Segon)

Potentat, El (Cancó Del Camí)
see Cent Cancons, Les, Segona Serie
(Quadern Primer)

Roses De Maig
see Cent Cancons, Les, Segona Serie
(Quadern Tercer)

Rossinyol, El
see Cent Cancons, Les, Primera
Serie (Quadern Segon)

Son-Soneta, La
see Cent Cancons, Les, Segona Serie
(Quadern Primer)

Toc D'Oració
see Cent Cancons, Les, Segona Serie
(Quadern Segon)

MESTRES, APELES (cont'd.)

Vella, La
see Cent Cancons, Les, Primera
Serie (Quadern Tercer)

Vianant, El
see Cent Cancons, Les, Segona Serie
(Quadern Segon)

MESTRES-QUADRENY, JOSEP MARIA
(1929-   )
Invencions
SS soli,trp,elec gtr SEESAW f.s.
(M539)

Musica Per A Anna
S solo,string quar [10'] MOECK 5066
(M540)

Poemma
S solo,pno SEESAW f.s.   (M541)

METAL see Kruse, Bjørn Howard

METAMORFOSE see Sommerfeldt, Öistein

METAMORPHOSIS see Lieberman, Glenn

METRAL, PIERRE (1936-   )
Caprisme
S solo,gtr/hpsd,3perc SEESAW (M542)

Chansons Au Village
S/B solo,pno,clar,trp,horn,trom,
perc SEESAW   (M543)

Notte, La
S solo,pno/fl&vln&harp&db&perc
SEESAW   (M544)

METSK, JURO
Drei Lieder
"Tri Spewy" med solo,pno DEUTSCHER
DV 9057   (M545)

Tri Spewy
see Drei Lieder

MEYER
Lieder
PETERS 5084, 5323   (M546)

Liturgie Des Défunts
solo voice,org (in 2 volumes) LEDUC
f.s.   (M547)

Nun Steuermann
solo voice,strings PETERS 5369
(M548)

Ordinaire De La Messe
solo voice,org LEDUC f.s.   (M549)

MEYERBEER, GIACOMO (1791-1864)
Africaine, L': Adamastor, Roi Des
Vagues Profondes
Bar solo,pno CLASSV 1625   (M550)

Africaine, L': Adieu, Mon Doux Rivage
[Fr] S solo,pno CLASSV 1523 (M551)

Africaine, L': Fille Des Rois
Bar solo,pno CLASSV 1626   (M552)

Africaine, L': O Paradis
[Fr] T solo,pno CLASSV 0500 (M553)

Africaine, L': Sur Mes Genoux
"Air Du Sommeil" S solo,pno CLASSV
1900   (M554)

Africana, L': All, Erta, Marinar
[It] Bar solo,pno CLASSV 0910
(M555)

Africana, L': Figlio Del Sol, Mio
Dolce Amor
[It] S solo,pno CLASSV 0957 (M556)

Africana, L': O Paradiso
T solo,pno BOIL B.1605   (M557)
"Oh! Land Entrancing" T solo
RICORDI-IT LD118449   (M558)

Air Du Sommeil
see Africaine, L': Sur Mes Genoux

Dinorah: Ombra Leggera
S solo,pno BOIL B.1909   (M559)

Dinorah (Pardon De Ploërmel): Ah! Mon
Remords Te Venge
Bar solo,pno CLASSV 1644   (M560)

Dinorah (Pardon De Ploërmel): Le Jour
Est Levé
B solo,pno CLASSV 1571   (M561)

Dinorah (Pardon De Ploërmel): Ombre
Légère
"Shadowsong" coloratura sop,pno
CLASSV 0404   (M562)

Etoile Du Nord, L': O Jours Heureux
B solo,pno CLASSV 1550   (M563)

Hirtenlied
high solo,pno,clar CLASSV 1226
(M564)

MEYERBEER, GIACOMO (cont'd.)

Huguenots: Nobles Seigneurs
"Huguenots: Pages' Aria" Mez solo,
pno CLASSV 0337   (M565)
"Huguenots: Pages' Aria" A solo,pno
CLASSV 1146   (M566)

Huguenots: Non, Non, Non, Non
[Fr/It] Mez solo,pno CLASSV 1184
(M567)

Huguenots: O Beau Pays
coloratura sop,pno CLASSV 0892
(M568)

Huguenots: Pages' Aria
see Huguenots: Nobles Seigneurs

Huguenots: Piff, Paff
B solo,pno CLASSV 0412   (M569)

Huguenots: Plus Blanche Que La
Blanche Hermine
T solo,pno CLASSV 1530   (M570)

Komm! Du Schönes Fischermädchen
[Fr] Bar solo,pno CLASSV 1901 (M571)

Lieder, Band 1
(Zimmermann) PETERS 9783A   (M572)

Nein!
SCIEN 1083   (M573)

Oh! Land Entrancing
see Africana, L': O Paradiso

Poète Mourant, Le
[Fr] med solo,pno CLASSV 1902
(M574)

Prophète: Ah! Mon Fils!
Mez solo,pno CLASSV 1596   (M575)

Prophète: Donnez! Donnez!
Mez solo,pno CLASSV 1597   (M576)

Robert Le Diable: Nonnes Qui Reposez
(Invocation)
B solo,pno CLASSV 1576   (M577)

Robert Le Diable: Robert, Toi Que
S solo,pno CLASSV 0482   (M578)

Shadowsong
see Dinorah (Pardon De Ploërmel):
Ombre Légère

MEYERS, RANDALL
Sometimes Taste Sour
[Eng] S solo,fl,ob,clar,bsn NORGE
(M579)

Zen Songs For Guitar And Voice
[Eng] NORGE   (M580)

MEYJAN MIN HIN VAENA see Halldorsson,
Skuli

MEZZA NOTTE see Tchaikovsky, Piotr
Ilyich

M'HA PRESO ALLA SUA RAGNA see Paradies,
Pietro Domenico (Paradisi)

MI AMAS LA ROZOJN see Schipper, Dirk

MI CHIAMANO MIMI see Lyric Soprano
Arias: A Master Class With Evelyn
Lear, Vol. 1 see Puccini, Giacomo

MI PADRE ERA DE FRANCIA see Four
Sephardi Songs

MI VOLNEK? see Nieland, Henk

MIA SPOSA SARÀ LA MIA BANDIERA see
Rotoli

MICA, FRANTISEK VACLAV (1694-1744)
O Puvodu Jaromeric
SBar soli,hpsd,strings [12'] CESKY
HUD.   (M581)

MICHAEL ROBARTES BIDS HIS BELOVED BE AT
PEACE see Homer, Sidney

MICHALICKA, JAN
Pastorella In G
see Pastorelle Boemiche

Pastorelle Boemiche
"Pastorella In G" S solo,fl,2horn,
2vln,vcl CESKY HUD.   (M582)

MICHANS, CARLOS (1950-   )
Ah Tu Voz Misteriosa
see Cinco Canciones De Amor

Ah Vastedad De Pinos
see Cinco Canciones De Amor

Cinco Canciones De Amor
Bar solo,pno DONEMUS f.s. [13']
contains: Ah Tu Voz Misteriosa;
Ah Vastedad De Pinos; Cuerpo De
Mujer; En Ti Los Rios Cantan;
Es La Manana Llena   (M583)

MICHANS, CARLOS (cont'd.)

Cuerpo De Mujer
see Cinco Canciones De Amor

En Ti Los Rios Cantan
see Cinco Canciones De Amor

Es La Manana Llena
see Cinco Canciones De Amor

MICHEL LE ROUX see Keizer, Henk

MICHELANGELO LIEDER see Wolf, Hugo

MID-SUMMER NIGHT see Tveitt, Geirr,
Jonsoknatt

MIDAS' TOMB see Laman, Wim

MIDNIGHT see Helgason, Hallgrimur

MIDNIGHT REVIEW see Glinka, Mikhail
Ivanovich

MIDSUMMER NIGHT see Thommessen, Reidar

MIDTSOMMERSANG see Sommerfeldt, Öistein

MIGNON see Beethoven, Ludwig van see
Valen, Fartein

MIGNON (1) see Wolf, Hugo

MIGNON: CONNAIS-TU LE PAYS? see Thomas,
Ambroise

MIGNON: DE SON COEUR J'AI CALMÉ LA
FIÈVRE see Thomas, Ambroise

MIGNON: ELLE NE CROYAIT PAS see Thomas,
Ambroise

MIGNON: FREDERICK'S GAVOTTE see Thomas,
Ambroise

MIGNON IN MUSIK see Orosz, Francis

MIGNON: JE SUIS TITANIA see Thomas,
Ambroise

MIGNON: LÉGÈRES HIRONDELLES see Thomas,
Ambroise

MIGNON: ROMANZE see Thomas, Ambroise

MIGNONNE see King, Harold C.

MIJ SPREEKT DE BLOMME EENE TALE see
Andriessen, Jurriaan

MIJN ALDERLIEFSTE LIEF see Ehlen,
Margriet

MIJN LIEF IS WIT see Andriessen,
Jurriaan

MIJN LIEVEKEN OPEN JE DEURKEN EN LACH
see Koetsier, Jan

MIKAMI, JIRO (1961-   )
Kagurauta
Bar solo,pno [10'] JAPAN   (M584)

MIKI, MINORU (1930-   )
Bareisho No Hana
S solo,pno [5'] JAPAN   (M585)

Fuyu No Hae
S solo,pno [5'] JAPAN   (M586)

Ki No Kane
S solo, Japanes instrument ensemble
[33'] JAPAN   (M587)

MIKROTOOP see Manen, Willem van

MILELLA, DONATO
Due Arie (from Una Storia D'altri
Tempi)
S solo,pno CURCI 9910   (M588)

MILHAUD, DARIUS (1892-1974)
Java De La Femme, La
solo voice,pno SALABERT RD7548 f.s.
(M589)

Melodies Et Chansons
solo voice,pno (cc281) SALABERT
50481566   (M590)

MILI SYNACKOVE, POJD'TE K BETLEMU see
Ryba, Jan Jakub Simon

MILLER, EDWARD
Lullaby For Ben, A
female solo,marimba [4'] sc
AM.COMP.AL. $5.75   (M591)

MILLER, EDWARD JAY (1930-   )
Ninnananna: A Lullaby For Ben
female solo,2harp [7'] sc
AM.COMP.AL. $9.15   (M592)

MILLER, FRANZ R. (1926-   )
Ständchen Für Einen Verleger: "Ho,
    Mich Trägt Die Welle"
    T solo,pno BOHM f.s.   (M593)

MILLOM BAKKAR OG BERG
    (Groven, Eiving) "Between Hills And
    Mountains." solo voice,1.1.1.1.
    2.2.2.0. timp,strings GROVEN f.s.
                                  (M594)

MILNER, CH.
    Sefardic Songs And Ballads (composed
    with Storm, P.)
    med solo,acap (contains 97 songs in
    Ladino and Dutch) ALBERSEN AZ 4
                                  (M595)

MILOSC see Koffler, Josef

MIMAROGLU, ILHAN KAMALEDDIN (1926-)
    Epicedium
    A solo,vln,vcl,clar,pno SEESAW f.s.
                                  (M596)

MIMI'S FAREWELL see Puccini, Giacomo,
    Donde Lieta

MIMOSA see Ehlen, Margriet

MIN MIDERS ARVESØLV see Eggen, Arne

MIN VERDEN see Thommessen, Reidar

MIN VILOTIMMA LJUDER see Arner,
    Gotthard

MINAMI, SATOSHI (1955-   )
    Uta No Kage Yori *Op.13
    solo voice,harp,vln,vcl,pno [20']
    JAPAN 8607   (M597)

MINCIACCHI, DIEGO
    Some Of The Colours You Like
    solo voice,gtr,fl,vla,pno,2perc,
    hpsd EDI-PAN EP 7414   (M598)

MINDLIN, ADOLFO
    Eighteen Etudes Vocalises
    (med) ZURFLUH   (M599)

MINE IS A CRUEL GOD see Verdi,
    Giuseppe, Otello: Credo In Un Dio
    Crudel

MINE OWN SWEET JEWEL see Cruft, Adrian

MINEMURA, SUMIKO (1941-   )
    Anokudacchi Fantasy
    T solo,vcl,pno [15'] JAPAN   (M600)

    Sazanka In A Garden
    Mez solo,pno [13'] JAPAN   (M601)

MINER, THE see Johnsen, Hallvard,
    Bergmannen: Melodrama

MINIATUREN, CAHIER 4 (SOLFEGGIO) see
    Tal, Marjo

MINIATUREN, CAHIER IV see Tal, Marjo

MINNEDEUNTJES see Ketting, Piet

MINNELIED see Mendelssohn-Bartholdy,
    Felix

MINNELIEDER see Schafer, R. Murray

MINNI PRENTLISTARINNAR see
    Thorarinsson, Jón

MINNINGALAND see Isolfsson, Pall

MINSTREL BOY, THE (from The Moreen)
    [Eng] med-high solo,pno CLASSV 2095
                                  (M602)
    (Fisher) [Eng] med solo,pno CLASSV
    2098   (M603)

MINUET see Mestres, Apeles

MINUETTO EN ALABANZA DE LA MÚSICA SERIA
    see Fernandere, F.

MINUTE WALTZ see Chopin, Frédéric

MINUTOVE PISNICKY see Hurník, Ilja

MIO BEN RICORDARTI see Benda, Georg
    Anton (Jirí Antonín)

MIR HAT À MAL VOM TEUFEL TRÄMT see
    Holzel, Gustav

MIRABAI SONGS see Harbison, John

MIRAGE AND INCANTATIONS see Tanenbaum,
    Elias

MIRAGES see Silsbee, Ann

MIRANTISCHE MAUL-TRUMMEL see Laurentius
    Von Schnüffis (Johann Martin)

MIREILLE: ANGES DU PARADIS see Gounod,
    Charles François

MIREILLE: CHANSON DU BERGER see Gounod,
    Charles François

MIREILLE: LE JOUR SE LÈVE see Gounod,
    Charles François

MIREILLE: MON COEUR NE PEUT SE CHANGER
    see Gounod, Charles François

MIREILLE: O LÉGÈRE HIRONDELLE see
    Gounod, Charles François

MIRIGLIANO, ROSARIO (1950-   )
    Quando
    solo voice,alto fl,trom,vcl,perc
    EDI-PAN EP 7382   (M604)

MIRROR, MIRROR see Bond, Victoria

MIRTH BUT OPEN'D, A see Edwards, George

MIRTI, FAGGI, TRONCHI E FRONDE see
    Caldara, Antonio

MISADVENTURES OF STRUWWELPETER, THE see
    Schelle, Michael

MISERABLES, LES *CCU
    solo voice,pno FABER F0950 f.s.
                                  (M605)

MISERERE see Globokar, Vinko see Hasse,
    Johann Adolph see Mozart, Wolfgang
    Amadeus

MISSA BREVIS, OP.10, NO.1 see Karlsen,
    Kjell Mørk

MISSA PROLATIONUM see Lönner, Oddvar

MISSING PIECE, THE see Hashiramoto,
    Masaru

MRS. SANTA CLAUS see Dallesandro,
    Gerald

MISSY MOUSE AND MISTER FROG see
    Haufrecht, Herbert

MIST see Dirriwachter, Wim

MISTERI see Mestres, Apeles

MISTERIO see Schubert, Franz (Peter)

MISTICA see Tirindelli, Pier Adolfo

MISTLETOE see Crist, Bainbridge

MIT EINER PRIMULA VERIS see Grieg,
    Edvard Hagerup

MIT HELLEM KLANG see Cornelius, Peter

MITT ÄLSKADE LILLA SOCKERSKRIN see
    Söderman, [Johan] August

MITT FRÖDING-DIARIUM VÄRMLAND 25 JULI -
    6 AUGUSTI 1972 see Simai, Pavol

MITT HJERTE see Plau, Arild

MITT NAFN ER LIF see Isolfsson, Pall

MITTERNACHTLIEDER see Rouse,
    Christopher

MITTLER, FRANZ
    Fünf Lieder
    [Ger] high solo RECITAL 279   (M606)

MIYAHARA, TEIJI
    Song Album *CCU
    solo voice ONGAKU 526200 f.s.
                                  (M607)

MIYOSHI, AKIRA (1933-   )
    Duel
    S solo,2(pic).2.2.2. 2.2.3.0.
    4perc,pno/cel,harp,strings ONGAKU
    rent   (M608)

    Koeru Kage Ni
    S solo,pno [14'] JAPAN   (M609)

MIZOKAMI, HIDEO (1936-   )
    Drei Lieder
    solo voice,pno JAPAN   (M610)

    Fünf Lieder "Kaze"
    S solo,pno JAPAN   (M611)

MIZU NO OTO see Bito, Yayoi

MIZUIRO NO BERU see Takami, Toshio

MLADA LASKA see Blodek, Vilem (Wilhelm)

MODERENS KORSTEGN see Groven, Eivind

MODERN SOPRANO OPERATIC ALBUM
    (CC32L) RICORDI-IT R133628   (M612)

MODERN TENOR OPERATIC ALBUM
    (CC35L) RICORDI-IT R133159   (M613)

MODERN YOUTH see Heilner, Irwin

MODERNE SLAVEN see Orthel, Leon

MODIR MIN & FYLGDARLAUN see
    Halldorsson, Skuli

MOEDER see Mengelberg, Karel

MOEN see Groven, Eivind

MOERIKE-LIEDER IN TWO VOLUMES, VOL. 1
    see Wolf, Hugo

MOERIKE-LIEDER IN TWO VOLUMES, VOL. 2
    see Wolf, Hugo

MOERIKE-LIEDER, VOL. 1 see Wolf, Hugo

MOERIKE-LIEDER, VOL. 2 see Wolf, Hugo

MOERIKE-LIEDER, VOL. 3 see Wolf, Hugo

MOERIKE-LIEDER, VOL. 4 see Wolf, Hugo

MOERIKE-LIEDER, VOL. 5 see Wolf, Hugo

MOESKES
    Blütezeit Mai
    KAHNT 5553   (M614)

MOIS DE MAI, LE see Arrieu, Claude

MOISSON PROCHAINE see Koechlin, Charles

MOLAND, EIRIK (1959-   )
    Jeg Ser
    [Norw] S solo,fl,clar,vcl NORGE
                                  (M615)

    Some Nightmare Music
    [Norw] Bar solo,1(pic).1.1(bass
    clar).1. 0.0.2.0. timp,perc,
    3strings [6'] NORGE   (M616)

MOLI, EL see Mestres, Apeles

MOLINILLO see Bunge, Sas

MOLINO, FRANCESCO (1775-1847)
    A Solo
    [It] S solo,string quar CARISCH
    22110   (M617)

    Suite Di Frammenti Da "Il Cavalier
    Selvatico"
    S solo,ob,vcl CARISCH 22111   (M618)

MOLLICONE, HENRY (1946-   )
    God Makes Ducks
    S solo,pno [5'] sc AM.COMP.AL.
    $7.70   (M619)

MOLLOY, JAMES LYMAN (1837-1909)
    Kerry Dance, The
    low solo,pno CLASSV 1903   (M620)

MOLLY BRANNIGAN see Stanford, Charles
    Villiers

MOLLY MANYBLOOM see Bond, Victoria

MOLN see Gefors, Hans

MOLNKURVOR see Brustad, Karsten

MOMENTS see Beerman, Burton

MOMIJIBA see Hayakawa, Kuzuko

MOMMA LOOK SHARP see Edwards, Sherman

MOMPOU, FEDERICO (1893-1987)
    Melodies Et Chansons
    solo voice,pno (cc221) SALABERT
    50488478   (M621)

MON PÈRE TOUJOURS ME CRIE see
    Tailleferre, Germaine

MONADNOCK CADENZAS see Koch, Frederick

MOND, DER see Mendelssohn-Bartholdy,
    Felix

MOND IST AUFGEGANGEN, DER see Grahn,
    Ulf

MONDGESPINST see Koetsier, Jan

MONDLICHT see Amerongen, Jan van

MONDNACHT, DIE see Schubert, Franz
    (Peter)

MONIUSZKO, STANISLAW (1819-1872)
    Antologia Piesni I Arii Stanislawa
    Moniuszki Oraz Piesni Fryderyka
    Chopina (composed with Chopin,
    Frédéric)
    (Foltyn, M.; Rudzinski, W.)
    "Stanislaw Moniuszko - Selected
    Songs And Arias, Fryderyk Chopin
    - Selected Songs From Opus 74"
    [Polish/It/Fr/Ger/Russ] solo
    voice,pno POLSKIE   (M622)

MONIUSZKO, STANISLAW (cont'd.)

Halka: Gdyby Rannem Slonkiem
"Halka's Aria" [Polish] S solo,pno
CLASSV 1269   (M623)

Halka's Aria
see Halka: Gdyby Rannem Slonkiem

Home Songbook, An Anthology Of Songs
see Spiewnik Domowy, Antologia
Piesni

Spiewnik Domowy, Antologia Piesni
(Nowaczyk, E.) "Home Songbook, An
Anthology Of Songs" [Polish] solo
voice,pno POLSKIE   (M624)

Stanislaw Moniuszko - Selected Songs
And Arias, Fryderyk Chopin -
Selected Songs From Opus 74
see Antologia Piesni I Arii
Stanislawa Moniuszki Oraz Piesni
Fryderyka Chopina

MONK OBSERVES A SKULL, A see Avni, Tzvi

MONOCHROME see Terashima, Naohiko

MONOLOG JULIE see Zahradník, Zdenek

MONOLOG JULIE II see Zahradník, Zdenek

MONRAD JOHANSEN, DAVID
see JOHANSEN, DAVID MONRAD

MONRO, GEORGE (1680-1731)
My Lovely Celia
(Wilson, H. Lane) med solo,pno
CLASSV 1656   (M625)
(Wilson, H. Lane) high solo,pno
CLASSV 1655   (M626)

MONRO, J.
Oh! Cold Was The Climate
SCIEN 1105   (M627)

MONSIGNY, PIERRE-ALEXANDRE (1729-1817)
Déserteur, Le: Adieu, Chère Louise
Bar solo,pno CLASSV 1630 (M628)

Roi Et Le Fermier, Le: I Regardait
Mon Bouquet
S solo,pno CLASSV 1623   (M629)

MONTAGUE, STEPHEN (1943-   )
Criseyde
female solo,electronic tape,
ocarina [20'] MODERN 1822 (M630)

Inundations II ("Willow")
S solo,pno,electronic tape MODERN
1806   (M631)

Tigida Pipa
4 amplified voices (SATB) UNITED
MUS f.s.   (M632)

MONTAINEOUS NORWAY: SYMPHONIC
THANKSGIVING see Egge, Klaus,
Fjell-Norig: Symfonisk Høgsong

MONTANARI, A.
Inno Della Croce Rossa Italiana
Giovanile
solo voice,pno CURCI 9986 (M633)

MONTEVERDI, CLAUDIO (ca. 1567-1643)
Combattimento Di Tancredi E Clorinda
sc,pts KING'S   (M634)

Confitebor III
S solo,strings sc KING'S (M635)

Currite Populi
T/S solo,cont KING'S KM68 (M636)

Ego Flos Campi
A/T solo,cont KING'S KM50 (M637)

Exulta Filia
S solo,cont KING'S   (M638)

Exultent Filia Sion
S solo,cont KING'S KM163 (M639)

Incoronazione Di Poppea, L': Pur Ti
Miro
SS soli,cont KING'S KM4   (M640)

Laudate Dominum
S/T solo,cont KING'S KM35 (M641)

O Quam Pulchra Es
T/S solo,cont KING'S KM47 (M642)

Tempro La Cetra
T solo,strings KING'S   (M643)

Ut Queant Laxis
SS soli,2vln,cont sc,set KING'S
                          (M644)

Zefiro Torna
TT/SS soli,cont KING'S KM36 (M645)

MONTH OF LOVE, THE see Fongaard, Bjørn,
Øyeblikksbilder, Op. 146, No. 3

MONTSALVATGE, XAVIER (1912-   )
Cinco Canciones Negras
"Five Black Songs" med solo,
2.2.3.2. 2.2.2.0. timp,pno/cel,
harp,strings [13'0"] PEER (M646)

Cinco Invocaciones Al Crucificado
"Five Invocations To The Crucified
One" S solo,3fl,timp,perc,harp,
pno,cel,db [23'30"] PEER (M647)

Five Black Songs
see Cinco Canciones Negras

Five Invocations To The Crucified One
see Cinco Invocaciones Al
Crucificado

MOON, THE see Kaldalóns, Sigvaldi S.

MOON AND THE YEW TREE, THE see Packer,
Randall

MOON HAS NOTHING TO BE SAD ABOUT, THE
see Blaustein, Susan

MOONLIGHT see Heilner, Irwin

MOOR, EMANUEL (1863-1931)
Mélodies, Vol. 1
[Fr] med solo,pno CLASSV 2212
                          (M648)

Songs, Vol. 4
med solo,pno CLASSV 2211 (M649)

MOORDUNKEL see Manassen, Alex

MOORE, DOROTHY RUDD
see RUDD-MOORE, DOROTHY

MOR SYNG OG ANDRE DIKT AV IDAR HANDGARD
see Johansen, David Monrad

MORALISCHE KANTATEN see Telemann, Georg
Philipp

"MORALITETER" ELLER "MÅSKE ER DER MANGE
KILOMETER TIL DEN NAERMESTE
EDDERKOP" see Norholm, Ib

"MORALITIES" OR "MAYBE IT'S MANY
KILOMETRES TO THE NEAREST SPIDER"
see Norholm, Ib, "Moraliteter"
Eller "Måske Er Der Mange Kilometer
Til Den Naermeste Edderkop"

MORAVIAN CANTATA see Friedman, Stanley

MORAVSKE LIDOVE PISNE see Mácha, Otmar

MORE SONGS FOR THE TURNING see Medema

MORE SONGS OF AUTUMN see Wigglesworth,
Frank

MOREAU, H.
Six Fables De La Fontaine
high solo,pno CLASSV 2179 (M650)

MORERA, ENRIQUE (1865-1942)
Infanta Maria, L'
solo voice,pno BOIL B.0619 (M651)

Serventa Bonica, La
solo voice,pno BOIL B.0642 (M652)

MORET, ERNEST (1871-1949)
Chansons Tristes
[Fr] high solo (not available
outside U.S.A.) RECITAL 375
                          (M653)

Mélodies, 20, Vol. 1
solo voice,pno CLASSV C048 (M654)

Poème Du Silence (1st Set)
[Fr] med-high solo,pno CLASSV 2209
                          (M655)

Poème Du Silence (2nd Set)
[Fr] med-high solo,pno CLASSV 2210
                          (M656)

MORETTI
Doce Canciones *song cycle
[Span] solo voice,gtr TECLA TE007
                          (M657)

MORGEN see Jordan, Sverre see Olsen,
Sparre see Strauss, Richard

MORGEN, EN see Ødegaard, Henrik

MORGEN, KAN JEG TA DEG INN TIL MEG see
Madsen, Trygve

MORGEN WAR VON DIR ERFÜLLT, DER see
Flothuis, Marius

MORGENFREUDE see Zumsteeg, Emilie

MORGENGESANG VON KLOPSTOCK see Lachner,
Franz

MORGENGLOCKE, DIE see Hekster, Walter

MORGENLIED see Mendelssohn-Bartholdy,
Felix see Schubert, Franz (Peter)

MORGENLIJK VERWACHTEN see Weegenhuise,
Johan

MORGENMIST see Hekster, Walter

MORGENSONNE see Louis Ferdinand, Prince
Of Prussia

MORGENSTERN - ABENDSTERN see
Brandmüller, Theo

MORGENSTERN-LIEDER see Koenig, Franz

MORGON see Braein, Edvard Fliflet see
Støyva, Njål Gunnar

MORGON MELLAN FJÄLLEN see Wahlberg,
Rune

MORGUNN see Björnsson, Arni

MORI, FRANK
Soldier's Bridal, The
SCIEN 1112   (M658)

MORI, JUNKO (1948-   )
Nanohana To Watashi
S solo,pno [40'] ONGAKU   (M659)

MORI, KONATE (1950-   )
Songs "For People Who Are Children At
Heart"
S solo,pno [15'] JAPAN   (M660)

White Autumn, A: Song Cycle
S solo,pno [60'] JAPAN   (M661)

MORITA, SHIN-ICHI (1948-   )
Fortuneteller On The Slope
Bar solo,perc,synthesizer [7']
JAPAN   (M662)

Mamamimamo The Wizard
Bar solo,perc,synthesizer [8']
JAPAN   (M663)

To The Fabled Princess
Bar solo,perc,synthesizer [8']
JAPAN   (M664)

War Song Of The Kingdom Of Star, A
Bar solo,perc,synthesizer [12']
JAPAN   (M665)

MORIWAKI, KENZO
Song Album *CCU
solo voice ONGAKU 526300 f.s.
                          (M666)

MØRKE NATT FORGANGEN ER, DEN see
Tveitt, Geirr

MØRKET OMKRING OSS see Okkenhaug,
Ingrid Buran

MORN, MORN see Sommerfeldt, Öistein

MORNING see Braein, Edvard Fliflet,
Morgon see Halldorsson, Skuli see
Stefansson, Finnur Torfi

MORNING AND EVENING POEMS see Bolcom,
William Elden

MORNING STAR see Carlsen, Philip see
Gideon, Miriam, Ayelet Hashakhar
see Glaser, David

MORRICONE, ENNIO (1928-   )
Frammenti Di Eros
S solo,pno,orch ZERBONI 9830 (M667)

MORT DE CLÉOPÂTRE see Berlioz, Hector
(Louis)

MORT DE LA CIGALE, LA see Massenet,
Jules

MORT DES AMANTS, LE see Debussy, Claude

MORT D'HERCULE, LA see Regt, Hendrik de

MORT D'OPHÉLIE, LA see Saint-Saëns,
Camille

MORT DU ROI RENAUD, LA see De Ponte,
Niel

MORTARI, VIRGILIO (1902-   )
Domanda E Risposte
SBar soli,string quar ZERBONI 9349
                          (M668)

MORTE DI ABELE, LA: DUNQUE SI SFORZA
see Leo, Leonardo (Ortensio
Salvatore de)

MORTENSEN, FINN (1922-   )
Duo, Op. 8
see Duo Per Soprano E Violino

Duo Per Soprano E Violino (Duo, Op.
8)
S solo,vln [8'] NORGE   (M669)

MORTENSEN, FINN (cont'd.)

Greners Tyngde
"Three Songs To Poems By Paal
Brekke" S solo,pno NORSK NMO 9561
(M670)

Greners Tyngde, Op. 33
[Norw] S solo,pno [6'] NORGE (M671)

Three Songs To Poems By Paal Brekke
see Greners Tyngde

MORTHENSON, JAN W. (1940-   )
Frühlingslied
[Ger] S solo,bass clar,pno (text by
Heinrich Heine) sc REIMERS 101132
(M672)

MORYL, RICHARD (1929-   )
Corridors
med solo,perc,electronic tape [7']
sc AM.COMP.AL. rent   (M673)

MOSCA, LUCA (1957-   )
Trenta Novellette
solo voice,pno,orch ZERBONI 9738
(M674)

solo voice,pno ZERBONI 9728 (M675)

MOSS, KATIE
Floral Dance, The
high solo,pno CLASSV 1905   (M676)

MOSS, LAWRENCE KENNETH (1927-   )
Darkharbor
solo voice,electronic tape SEESAW
(M677)

Drumtaps
B solo,pno SEESAW   (M678)

Somewhere Inside Me...
S solo,fl,gtr SEESAW   (M679)

Three Rilke Songs *CC3U
A solo,pno SEESAW f.s.   (M680)

MOST BEAUTIFUL ROSE, THE see Hovland,
Egil, Vakreste Rosen, Den

MOSTAD, JON (1942-   )
Finns Ett Svar För Dig, Det
[Swed] Mez/Bar solo,pno [8'] NORGE
(M681)

To Tekster Fra Spårvagnslektyr Av
Johanna Schwarz
[Swed] Bar/Mez solo,pno NORGE
(M682)

[Swed] S/T solo,pno NORGE   (M683)

MOSZKOWSKI, MORITZ (1854-1925)
Drei Gedichte Im Volkston, Op. 26
[Ger/Eng] med solo,pno CLASSV 1404
(M684)

Guitarre
(Szulc) [Ger/Fr] high solo,pno
CLASSV 1403   (M685)

Springtime Of Love
"Waltz Song, Op. 34, No. 1 [arr.]"
high solo,pno CLASSV 1904   (M686)

Waltz Song, Op. 34, No. 1 [arr.]
see Springtime Of Love

MOT BLÅSNØHØGDOM see Kielland, Olav

MOT DAG see Olsen, Sparre

MOT EN VERDEN AV LYS: TO STEIN MEHREN-
SANGER, OP. 34A see Sommerfeldt,
Oistein

MOT FRIDENS LAND (TRE SÅNGER) see
Janácek, Bedrich

MØTE see Taubo, Lillian Gulowna

MÖTE VID SLUTET AV see Blomberg, Erik

MOTET D' ADONIS see Suzuki, Teruaki

MOTHER GOOSE see Lessard, John Ayres

MOTHER MACHREE see Ball, Ernest R.

MOTHERS AND CHILDREN see Haxton,
Kenneth

MOTHER'S EVENING PRAYER see Warren,
Betsy

MOTHER'S SIGN OF THE CROSS, THE see
Groven, Eivind, Moderens Korstegn

MOTTETTI DI MONTALE see Harbison, John

MOTTO (WITH ONE'S WHOLE HEART) AND
SHIGUSEIGAN see Kobayashi, Arata

MOUNTAIN MOODS see Haufrecht, Herbert

MOUNTAIN NORWAY see Olsen, Sparre,
Fjell-Noreg

MOUNTAIN WIND see Groven, Eivind,
Fjellvind

MOURANT, WALTER (1910-   )
At The Sea-Side
med solo,pno [2'] sc AM.COMP.AL.
$.80   (M687)

Bed In Summer
med solo,pno [2'] sc AM.COMP.AL.
$1.20   (M688)

Constancy
med solo,pno [2'] sc AM.COMP.AL.
$.80   (M689)

Cow, The
med solo,pno [1'] sc AM.COMP.AL.
$.80   (M690)

Cupid, Turn Thy Bow
high solo,pno [2'] sc AM.COMP.AL.
$1.20   (M691)

Enchantment, The
med solo,pno [1'] sc AM.COMP.AL.
$.80   (M692)

False Though She Be
med solo,pno [1'] sc AM.COMP.AL.
$.80   (M693)

Farewell To The Farm
solo voice,pno [2'] AM.COMP.AL.
(M694)

Girl I Left Behind Me, The
med solo,pno [3'] sc AM.COMP.AL.
$1.60   (M695)

Go Where The Water Glideth Gently
Ever
med solo,harp [4'] sc AM.COMP.AL.
$2.35   (M696)

Japanese Fan [1]
med solo,pno [2'] sc AM.COMP.AL.
$1.20   (M697)

Japanese Fan [2]
med solo,harp [2'] sc AM.COMP.AL.
$1.20   (M698)

Lamb, The
S solo,pno [3'] sc AM.COMP.AL.
$1.60   (M699)

Lamplighter, The
med solo,pno [2'] sc AM.COMP.AL.
$1.20   (M700)

Land Of Counterpane, The
med solo,pno [2'] sc AM.COMP.AL.
$1.60   (M701)

Land Of Nod, The
med solo,pno [3'] sc AM.COMP.AL.
$1.60   (M702)

Love, Love, Love
S solo,harp [3'] sc AM.COMP.AL.
$1.60   (M703)

Love Me Little, Love Me Long
med solo,pno [2'] sc AM.COMP.AL.
$.80   (M704)

My Bed Is A Boat
med solo,pno [2'] sc AM.COMP.AL.
$1.60   (M705)

Oh, If Thou Wilt Not Give Thine Heart
med solo,harp [2'] sc AM.COMP.AL.
$1.20   (M706)

Oh, Say Not Woman's Heart Is Bought
S solo,harp [2'] sc AM.COMP.AL.
$1.20   (M707)

Oh, When I Was In Love With You
med solo,harp [2'] sc AM.COMP.AL.
$.80   (M708)

On The Eve Of His Execution
Bar solo,pno [7'] sc AM.COMP.AL.
$3.10   (M709)

Piper, The
med solo,harp [2'] sc AM.COMP.AL.
$1.20   (M710)
med solo,pno [2'] sc AM.COMP.AL.
$1.20   (M711)

Primrose, The
S solo,harp [2'] sc AM.COMP.AL.
$1.20   (M712)

Rain
med solo,pno [1'] sc AM.COMP.AL.
$.80   (M713)

Singing
med solo,pno [1'] sc AM.COMP.AL.
$.80   (M714)

Swing, The
med solo,pno [1'] sc AM.COMP.AL.
$1.20   (M715)

MOURANT, WALTER (cont'd.)

This Way To Winter
med solo,pno [2'] sc AM.COMP.AL.
$1.20   (M716)

Time To Rise
med solo,pno [1'] sc AM.COMP.AL.
$.45   (M717)

Two Songs *CC2U
med solo,harp sc AM.COMP.AL. $3.85
(M718)

Where Go The Boats?
med solo,pno [3'] sc AM.COMP.AL.
$1.20   (M719)

Why?
med solo,pno [4'] sc AM.COMP.AL.
$2.70   (M720)

Why Should I Blush To Own I Love?
S solo,harp [3'] sc AM.COMP.AL.
$1.20   (M721)

Windy Nights
med solo,pno [1'] sc AM.COMP.AL.
$1.20   (M722)

MOURET, JEAN JOSEPH (1682-1738)
Andromede Et Persee *cant
(Blanchard, R.) S solo,strings,cont
[15'] BILLAUDOT   (M723)

Regina Coeli
(Durand, H.A.) S solo,vla da gamba,
pno,strings [10'] DURAND C.3397
rent   (M724)

Venite Exultemus
(Durand, H.A.) S solo,cont,pno,
strings [7'] DURAND C.3409 rent
(M725)

MOURNING MADRIGALS see Wallach, Joelle

MOUSMÉ! see Massenet, Jules

MOUSSORGSKY, MODEST PETROVITCH
see MUSSORGSKY, MODEST PETROVICH

MOWINCKEL, JOHAN LUDVIG (1895-1940)
Three Billy-Goats Gruse, The
see Tre Bukkene Bruse, De

Tre Bukkene Bruse, De
"Three Billy-Goats Gruse, The"
narrator,2.1.2.2. 2.2.1.0. perc,
strings NORGE f.s.   (M726)

MOYA, H.
Chanson Du Coeur Brisé
see Song Of Songs

Song Of Songs
"Chanson Du Coeur Brisé" med-low
solo,pno CLASSV 1202   (M727)
"Chanson Du Coeur Brisé" med solo,
pno CLASSV 1240   (M728)

MOYLAN, WILLIAM (1956-   )
Now, The
Mez solo,horn,pno SEESAW   (M729)

MOZART see Broekman, Hans

MOZART, FRANZ XAVER WOLFGANG
(1791-1844)
Engel Gottes Künden
(Biba, Otto) SS soli,fl,string quar
(Süddeutsche Weihnachtsmusik,
Band 19) COPPENRATH   (M730)

MOZART, WOLFGANG AMADEUS (1756-1791)
Abduction From The Seraglio: Ach, Ich
Liebte
S solo,pno CLASSV 0958   (M731)

Abduction From The Seraglio: Marten
Aller Arten
coloratura sop,pno CLASSV 1165
(M732)

Abendempfindung
high solo,pno CLASSV 0887   (M733)
low solo,pno CLASSV 0498   (M734)

Agnus Dei
solo voice,pno LEDUC f.s.   (M735)

Ah! Vous Diraije, Maman: Variations
(Adam) coloratura sop,pno,fl CLASSV
1711   (M736)

Air De Don Juan (from Don Giovanni)
[It/Fr/Ger] SCHOTT-FRER 9012 (M737)

Air De Zerline (from Don Giovanni)
[It/Fr/Ger] SCHOTT-FRER 9001 (M738)

Aleluia
solo voice,pno BOIL B.1472 (M739)

Alleluia (from Exultate Jubilate)
S/T solo SCHOTT-FRER 8936   (M740)
Mez/Bar solo SCHOTT-FRER 8952
(M741)

MOZART, WOLFGANG AMADEUS (cont'd.)

Als Aus Agypten Israel
see Zwei Deutsche Kirchenlieder,
K.343

Ave Verum
S solo,pno/org LEDUC f.s.   (M742)

Ave Verum Corpus
solo voice ZENGERINK G.230   (M743)

Canons, 30 *CC30U
BOOSEY EMB12084 f.s.   (M744)

Clemenza Di Tito: Non Più Di Fiori
S solo,pno CLASSV 1608   (M745)

Così Fan Tutte: Come Scoglio
S solo,pno CLASSV 0538   (M746)

Così Fan Tutte: É Amore Un
Ladroncello
Mez solo,pno CLASSV 0484   (M747)

Così Fan Tutte: Smanie Implacabile
Mez solo,pno CLASSV 0483   (M748)

Così Fan Tutte: Tradito! Schernito!
T solo,pno CLASSV 0527   (M749)

Così Fan Tutte: Un' Aura Amorosa
T solo,pno CLASSV 0505   (M750)

Dein Bin Ich *K.208 (from Il Re
Pastore)
S solo,vln,pno ERES 2015   (M751)

Don Giovanni: Batti Batti
S solo,pno CLASSV 0459   (M752)

Don Giovanni: Batti, Batti O Bel
Masetto
S solo,pno BOIL B.2045   (M753)

Don Giovanni: Crudele!...Non Mi Dir
S solo,pno CLASSV 1908   (M754)

Don Giovanni: Dalla Sua Pace
T solo,pno CLASSV 0536   (M755)

Don Giovanni: Deh Vieni Alla Finestra
Bar solo,pno CLASSV 1632   (M756)

Don Giovanni: Il Mio Tesoro
T solo,pno CLASSV 0367   (M757)

Don Giovanni: Madamina! Il Catalogo
"Gentle Lady" Bar solo RICORDI-IT
LD321   (M758)

Don Giovanni: Madamina! Il Catalogo È
Questo
B solo,pno CLASSV 1549   (M759)

Don Giovanni: Non Mi Dir
S solo,pno BOIL B.1836   (M760)

Don Giovanni: Vedrai, Carino, Se Sei
Buonino
S solo,pno BOIL B.2044   (M761)

Eight Operatic Arias For The Soprano
Voice
(Steber, Eleanor; Beatie) (CC8L)
SCHIRM.G 50489866   (M762)

Eight Variant Versions From "Le Nozze
Di Figaro"
(Tyson, Alan) OXFORD 60.016   (M763)

Et Incarnatus Est (from Mass In C
Minor, K. 417a)
[Lat] S solo,pno CLASSV 1704   (M764)

Exsultate Jubilate *K.165
solo voice,pno BREITKOPF-W pno red
EB 5232, sc PB 5229, pts OB 5229
                                (M765)

Exsultate Jubilate, K.165
[Lat] S solo KALMUS K 06332   (M766)

Exultate, Jubilate
(Maunder) S solo,2ob,2horn,strings
OXFORD sc 345594-3, voc sc
345593-5   (M767)
(Maunder, Richard) S solo,orch/pno
OXFORD sc 63.112, pno red 63.113
                                (M768)

Five Songs
solo voice,gtr BREITKOPF-W EB 8543
                                (M769)

Freundin, Ich Komm Mit Der Zither
see Terzette Für 2 Tenöre, Bass Und
Klavier

Gentle Lady
see Don Giovanni: Madamina! Il
Catalogo

Gestörte Ständchen, Das
see Terzette Für 2 Tenöre, Bass Und
Klavier

MOZART, WOLFGANG AMADEUS (cont'd.)

Konzertarie Für Alt Und Orchestra,
K.255
see Ombra Felice

Laudate Dominum (from Vesperae
Solennes, K. 339)
S solo,pno,vln CLASSV 1907   (M770)
(Case, John) "O Praise The Lord"
solo voice,pno (med) NOVELLO
                                (M771)

Miserere
see Hasse, Johann Adolph, Miserere

Mozart: 12 Songs *CC12U
(Paton) ALFRED high solo,pno 3389
f.s.; med solo,pno 3390 f.s.
                                (M772)

Mozart Arias For Baritone & Bass
(Walters, Richard; Larsen, Robert
L.) (CC10L, includes recorded
accompaniments) SCHIRM.G 00742019
                                (M773)

Mozart Arias For Mezzo-Soprano
(Walters, Richard; Larsen, Robert
L.) (CC10L, includes recorded
accompaniments) SCHIRM.G 00742020
                                (M774)

Mozart Arias For Soprano
(Walters, Richard; Larsen, Robert
L.) (CC10L, includes recorded
accompaniments) SCHIRM.G 00742019
                                (M775)

Mozart Arias For Tenor
(Walters, Richard; Larsen, Robert
L.) (CC10L, includes recorded
accompaniments) SCHIRM.G 00742018
                                (M776)

Mozart Arien Der Maria Stader
[Ger/It] S solo,pno UNIVER.
UE 12152   (M777)

Nacht Ist Finster, Die
see Terzette Für 2 Tenöre, Bass Und
Klavier

Non, Non (Berceuse)
solo voice,pno BOIL B.1786   (M778)

Nozze Di Figaro, Le: Deh Vieni Non
Tardar
S solo,pno CLASSV 0417   (M779)

Nozze Di Figaro, Le: Dove Sono
S solo,pno CLASSV 0457   (M780)

Nozze Di Figaro, Le: Non Più Andrai
B solo,pno CLASSV 1130   (M781)
"So, Sir Page" B solo RICORDI-IT
LD307   (M782)

Nozze Di Figaro, Le: Non So Più Cosa
Son
Mez solo,pno CLASSV 1129   (M783)
Mez solo,pno BOIL B.1812   (M784)

Nozze Di Figaro, Le: Porgi Amor
S solo,pno CLASSV 0471   (M785)
S solo,pno BOIL B.1837   (M786)

Nozze Di Figaro, Le: Se Vuol Ballare
B solo,pno CLASSV 1569   (M787)

Nozze Di Figaro, Le: Sull' Aria
SS soli,pno CLASSV 0427   (M788)

Nozze Di Figaro, Le: Vedrò Mentr' Io
Sospiro
[Ger/It] Bar solo,pno CLASSV 0940
                                (M789)

Nozze Di Figaro, Le: Voi Che Sapete
Mez solo,pno CLASSV 0506   (M790)
Mez solo,pno BOIL B.1604   (M791)
"Ye Who Have Duly Learnt" Mez solo
RICORDI-IT LD114728   (M792)

O Gotteslamm
see Zwei Deutsche Kirchenlieder,
K.343

O Praise The Lord
see Laudate Dominum

Oeuvres Complettes, Heft 5: 30
Gesänge
solo voice,pno SCIEN 1123   (M793)

Ombra Felice
"Konzertarie Für Alt Und Orchestra,
K.255" A solo,orch KUNZEL EKB 13P
                                (M794)

Per Pietà, Non Ricercate
T solo,pno CLASSV 0528   (M795)

Quando Miro Quel Bel Ciglio
solo voice,pno BOIL B.1705   (M796)

Re Pastore, Il: L'Amerò
(Lauterbach) S solo,pno,vln CLASSV
0499   (M797)

Schon Lacht Der Holde Frühling
*K.518
(David, Th. Chr.) S solo,0.0.2.2.
2.0.0.0. strings DOBLINGER sc,set

MOZART, WOLFGANG AMADEUS (cont'd.)

DM 1164, pno red DM 1164A   (M798)

So, Sir Page
see Nozze Di Figaro, Le: Non Più
Andrai

Solfeggi *K.393
(Swarowsky, Hans) solo voice
UNIVER. UE 12656 f.s.   (M799)

Songs
[Eng/Ger] med-high solo (contains
35 songs) KALMUS K 06322   (M800)

Songs For Voice And Piano
(complete urtext edition) LEA 59
                                (M801)

Stille, Stille! Leise Still!
see Terzette Für 2 Tenöre, Bass Und
Klavier

Terzette Für 2 Tenöre, Bass Und
Klavier
(Pilss, Karl) DOBLINGER 55 209 f.s.
contains: Freundin, Ich Komm Mit
Der Zither; Gestörte Ständchen,
Das; Nacht Ist Finster, Die;
Stille, Stille! Leise Still!;
Verewigt Glüht Hier Herz Und
Sinn   (M802)

Twenty-One Songs
(Hamburger, Paul) solo voice,pno
OXFORD 68.238   (M803)

Veilchen, Das
low solo,pno CLASSV 0886   (M804)

Verewigt Glüht Hier Herz Und Sinn
see Terzette Für 2 Tenöre, Bass Und
Klavier

Ye Who Have Duly Learnt
see Nozze Di Figaro, Le: Voi Che
Sapete

Zauberflöte: Ach! Ich Fühl's
S solo,pno CLASSV 0381   (M805)

Zauberflöte: Der Hölle Rache
coloratura sop,pno CLASSV 0334
                                (M806)

Zauberflöte: Dies Bildnis
T solo,pno CLASSV 0945   (M807)

Zauberflöte: In Diesen Heilgen
B solo,pno CLASSV 0400   (M808)

Zauberflöte: O Isis Und Osiris
[Eng/It/Ger] B solo,pno CLASSV 1166
                                (M809)

Zauberflöte: O Zittre Nicht
coloratura sop,pno CLASSV 0335
                                (M810)

Zwei Deutsche Kirchenlieder, K.343
(Biba, Otto) solo voice,org
COPPENRATH f.s. Kirchenmusik der
Wiener Klassik, Band 6
contains: Als Aus Agypten Israel;
O Gotteslamm   (M811)

MOZART, WOLFGANG AMADEUS (SON)
see MOZART, FRANZ XAVER WOLFGANG

MOZART: 12 SONGS see Mozart, Wolfgang
Amadeus

MOZART ARIAS FOR BARITONE & BASS see
Mozart, Wolfgang Amadeus

MOZART ARIAS FOR MEZZO-SOPRANO see
Mozart, Wolfgang Amadeus

MOZART ARIAS FOR SOPRANO see Mozart,
Wolfgang Amadeus

MOZART ARIAS FOR TENOR see Mozart,
Wolfgang Amadeus

MOZART ARIEN DER MARIA STADER see
Mozart, Wolfgang Amadeus

MOZARTIAN CONSTRAINT see Wright,
Maurice

MUCI, ITALO RUGGERO
Quattro Frammenti Da Lirici Greci
[It] S solo,pno pno red PRESSER
                                (M812)

MÜDE SOLDAT, DER see Beekhuis, Hanna

MUERTE Y LA DONCELLA, LA see Schubert,
Franz (Peter)

MUETTE DE PORTICI: DU PAUVRE SEUL AMI
see Auber, Daniel-François-Esprit

MUJER DE BARRO see Lopez Artiga,
Angeles

MUL, JAN (1911-1971)
  Deux Poemes
    med solo,pno BROEKMANS f.s.
      contains: Ode Du Premier Jour De
        Mai; Villanelle   (M813)

  Ode Du Premier Jour De Mai
    see Deux Poemes

  Villanelle
    see Deux Poemes

MULDER, HERMAN (1894-   )
  Drie Nachtliederen
    low solo,pno DONEMUS f.s.
      contains: Ik Heb U Lief; Ik
        Schrijf U Thans; Vleermuis
        Zwingt, De   (M814)

  Hoe Duizendvoudig
    see In Gedempten Toon, Op. 110

  Ik Heb U Lief
    see Drie Nachtliederen

  Ik Schrijf U Thans
    see Drie Nachtliederen

  In Droomomhelzingen
    see In Gedempten Toon, Op. 110

  In Gedempten Toon, Op. 110 *song
    cycle
    S solo,pno DONEMUS f.s.
      contains: Hoe Duizendvoudig; In
        Droomomhelzingen; In Teere
        Schaduw; Stille Dag, Een; Uw
        Handen; Wiegeland Hoofd   (M815)

  In Teere Schaduw
    see In Gedempten Toon, Op. 110

  Stille Dag, Een
    see In Gedempten Toon, Op. 110

  Uw Handen
    see In Gedempten Toon, Op. 110

  Vleermuis Zwingt, De
    see Drie Nachtliederen

  Wiegeland Hoofd
    see In Gedempten Toon, Op. 110

MULDOWNEY, DOMINIC (1952-   )
  Brecht Songs
    solo voice FABER 51276 3   (M816)

MULHOLLAND, JAMES   *CC4U
  Four Love Songs   *CC4U
    S solo,vcl,pno ALFRED 3231 f.s.
        (M817)

MÜLLER, ADOLF (1839-1901)
  Ihr Blauen Augen, Gute Nacht!   *Op.27
    solo voice,pno SCIEN 1191   (M818)

  Männer Habn's Gut, Die
    SCIEN 1192   (M819)

  Mütterchen An Die Kirchenthür, Das
    solo voice,pno SCIEN 1193   (M820)

  Retter, Der   *Op.26
    solo voice,pno SCIEN 1194   (M821)

MULLER, C.F.
  Souvenir De Salzbrunn Et Warmbrunn
    *Op.29
    solo voice,pno SCIEN 1196   (M822)

MULLER-HORNBACH, GERHARD (1951-   )
  Drei Nachtstücke   *CC3U
    Bar solo,vcl,horn,pno perf sc
      BREITKOPF-W KM 2226 f.s.   (M823)

  Fünf Gesänge Der Schirin   *CC5U
    S solo,gtr perf sc BREITKOPF-W
      EB 9004 f.s.   (M824)

  Gesänge Der Schirin
    S solo,vla d'amore,21strings [20']
      BREITKOPF-W f.s. pts EB 9019,
      study sc PB 5163   (M825)

MÜLLER-MEDEK, TILO
  see MEDEK, TILO

MÜLLER-ZÜRICH, PAUL (1898-   )
  Psalmenmusik
    S solo,strings pno red KUNZEL
      GM 982   (M826)

MUNAKATA, KAZU (1928-   )
  Dogyo Ninin
    Bar solo,pno [6'] ONGAKU   (M827)

  Price, The
    Mez solo,pno [3'] ONGAKU   (M828)

MUNASTERIO see Napoli, Jacopo

MÜNCH, FRANZ FURRER
  see FURRER-MÜNCH, FRANZ

MUÑECA, LA see Mestres, Apeles

MUNRO
  My Lovely Celia
    BOOSEY SGB0385A   (M829)

MURAKAMI, TARO (1910-   )
  Chikurin Hoko
    Bar solo,pno [3'] ONGAKU   (M830)

MURRAY, BAIN (1926-   )
  Flame And Shadow   *song cycle
    S solo,pno LUDWIG VS-06 $5.00   (M831)

MUSE QUI EST LA GRÂCE, LA see Cecconi,
  Monic

MUSETTA'S WALTZ see Puccini, Giacomo,
  Bohème, La: Quando Me'n Vo

MUSETTA'S WALTZ SONG see Puccini,
  Giacomo, Quando M'en Vo

MUSETTE, LA see Rameau, Jean-Philippe

MUSIC BRINGS SLEEP see Stoker, Richard

MUSIC CALLETH see Olthuis, Kees

MUSIC FOR AN EXPERIMENTAL LAB ENSEMBLE,
  NO. 2 see Tillis, Frederick C.

MUSIC FOR MEASURE FOR MEASURE see
  Blank, Allan

MUSIC FOR MYSELF see Anderson, Beth

MUSIC FOR OTHELLO see Blank, Allan

MUSIC FOR VOICE see Cage, John

MUSIC FROM COLD MOUNTAIN see Matthews,
  William

MUSIC I HEARD WITH YOU see Haxton,
  Kenneth

MUSIC TO HEAR see Ketting, Piet

MUSICA PER A ANNA see Mestres-Quadreny,
  Josep Maria

MUSICA PER MILA see Kapr, Jan

MUSICA PROIBITA see Gastaldon,
  Stanislas

MUSICAL WIFE, THE see Parry, Jun

MUSICHE DE CANTAR SOLO, LE see India,
  Sigismondo d'

MUSICHE VOCALI ITALIANE DE CAMERA:
  OPERISTI 1
    (Bertagnolio, L.; Fujisaki, I.) (CCU)
      ONGAKU 523810   (M832)

MUSICHE VOCALI ITALIANE DE CAMERA:
  OPERISTI 2
    (Bertagnolio, L.; Fujisaki, I.) (CCU)
      ONGAKU 523820   (M833)

MUSICHE VOCALI ITALIANE DE CAMERA:
  RESPIGHI see Respighi, Ottorino

MUSICHE VOCALI ITALIANE DE CAMERA:
  TOSTI 1 see Tosti, Francesco Paolo

MUSICHE VOCALI ITALIANE DE CAMERA:
  TOSTI 2 see Tosti, Francesco Paolo

MUSICIAN'S PRAYER see Rice, Thomas N.

MUSIK see Sigurbjörnsson, Thorkell

MUSIK, DIE see Fischer, A.

MUSIKANT see Wolf, Hugo

MUSIKANTENGRUSS see Louis Ferdinand,
  Prince Of Prussia

MUSIKK FOR STJERNER, OP. 51 see
  Søderlind, Ragnar

MUSON, L.
  Seguidilla Dolorosa De Una Enamorada
    see Castell, J., Canción De La
      Gitana Habilidosa

MUSSORGSKY, MODEST PETROVICH
  (1839-1881)
  Boris Godunov: Boris' Monologue
    (Lamm) [Russ/Ger] Bar solo,pno
      CLASSV 2147   (M834)

  Boris Godunov: Marina's Aria (Act 3,
    Scene 1)
    [Russ/Fr] Mez solo,pno CLASSV 2144
        (M835)

  Boris Godunov: Pimen's Tale (Act 4,
    Scene 1)
    (Lamm) Bar solo,pno CLASSV 2145
        (M836)

MUSSORGSKY, MODEST PETROVICH (cont'd.)
  Cradle Song Of Yeremoushka
    [Russ/Ger/Eng] med-low solo,pno
      CLASSV 2148   (M837)

  Cuarto De Los Niños, El
    solo voice,pno BOIL B.1246   (M838)

  Hebrew Song
    [Russ/Eng/Ger] med-high solo,pno
      CLASSV 2143   (M839)

  Khovanshchina: Shaklovity
    [Russ/Ger] Bar solo,pno CLASSV 2146
        (M840)

  Song Of The Flea
    B solo,pno CLASSV 0454   (M841)

  Songs And Dances Of Death
    (Aho, Kalevi) B solo,orch FAZER
      perf mat rent   (M842)

  Sorochintsy Fair: Dream Of The Young
    [Russ/Fr] T solo,pno CLASSV 1909
        (M843)

  Sorochintsy Fair: Parasha's Revery
    And Dance
    [Russ] S solo,pno CLASSV 0938   (M844)

MUST SHE GO? see Kirkwood, Antoinette

MUSTO, JOHN
  Quiet Songs
    high solo,kbd PEER 61704-212 (M845)

MUTABILITY see Fine

MUTTER ERDE, DIE see Schubert, Franz
  (Peter)

MUTTER MOCHTE SCHLAFEN see Kaldalóns,
  Sigvaldi S.

MÜTTERCHEN AN DIE KIRCHENTHÜR, DAS see
  Müller, Adolf

MUTTERJUBEL see Louis Ferdinand, Prince
  Of Prussia

MUZA see Shut, Wasyl

MY BED IS A BOAT see Mourant, Walter

MY BLESSING FALL see Tchaikovsky, Piotr
  Ilyich, Pilgrim' Song

MY CATS see Bush, Geoffrey

MY DINOSAUR see Pluister, Simon

MY EYEBROWS ARE NOT BUSHY see Schwartz,
  Francis

MY GENIUS see Tchaikovsky, Piotr Ilyich

MY GHOST see Menotti, Gian Carlo

MY GOD, WHY HAST THOU FORSAKEN ME? see
  Noland, Gary

MY HEART see Fennimore, Joseph William

MY HOME! MY HOME IS THERE see Kirk,
  Wheatley

MY KINGDOM see Masseus, Jan

MY KINGDOM, OP. 47A see Masseus, Jan

MY LASSIE see Beach, [Mrs.] H.H.A. (Amy
  Marcy Cheney)

MY LORD, THE MAN I KNOW see Getty,
  Gordon

MY LORD, WHAT A MOURNING
  (Dawson, William) high solo
    FITZSIMONS F0105   (M846)
  (Dawson, William) low solo FITZSIMONS
    F0106   (M847)

MY LOVE see McLin, Lena J.

MY LOVE IS A TANGO see Schwab, Sigi

MY LOVE IS LIKE A RED RED ROSE see
  Anonymous

MY LOVELY CELIA see Monro, George see
  Munro

MY LOVELY DUTCH DOLL see Arima, Reiko

MY LOVER, HE COMES ON THE SKEE see
  Clough-Leighter, Henry

MY LOVE'S AN ARBUTUS see Stanford,
  Charles Villiers

MY MOTHER see Halldorsson, Skuli

MY MOTHER'S HOME see Nakada, Kazutsugu

MY MOTHER'S SILVER see Eggen, Arne, Min Miders Arvesølv

MY NATIVE LAND see Gretchaninov, Alexander Tikhonovich

MY OWN TRUE LOVE see Horder, Mervyn

"MY PAPA'S WALTZ" AND OTHER SONGS see Gerber, Steven R.

MY POEMS ARE FULL OF POISON see Heilner, Irwin

MY PRIVATE BEACH see Anderson, Beth

MY SOUL IS DARK see Amerongen, Jan van

MY STAR see Beach, [Mrs.] H.H.A. (Amy Marcy Cheney)

MY SWEETHEART AND I see Beach, [Mrs.] H.H.A. (Amy Marcy Cheney)

MY TONGUE WANDERS see Bois, Rob du

MY TREASURE see Nakada, Yoshinao

MY TRUE LOVE HATH MY HEART see Foote, Arthur, Ditty, A

MY WEARY HEART see Eggen, Arne, Hald Ut, Hjarte

MY WHOLE LIFE I HAVE EATEN see Straesser, Joep

MYER, EDMUND J. (1846-1932)
    Exercises For Training The Voice
        RECITAL 280   (M848)

MYGATT, LOUISE
    Through The Edge
        S solo,clar,vln,2perc,pno [15']
        APNM sc $10.50, pts rent   (M849)

MYRTO see Delibes, Léo

MYSLIVECZEK, JOSEPH (1737-1781)
    Notturno No. 2
        SS soli,2clar,2horn,strings CESKY
        HUD.   (M850)

    Quod Est In Igne Calor
        [Lat] solo voice,2ob,bsn,2horn,org,
        strings [10'] CESKY HUD.   (M851)

MYSTERIES see As, Cees van

MYSTERIES, OP. 2 see As, Cees van

MYTHEN, OP. 25 see Schumann, Robert (Alexander)

N

NA-NO-MANI see Johannsson, Magnus Bl.

NA PROTIGENIM see Steinberg, Eitan

NA ROZLOUCENOU see Skroup, František

NAASEN, NILS (1960-)
    Sonnet 60
        [Eng] S solo,pno (text by
        Shakespeare) NORGE   (N1)

NABUCCO: PREGHIERA DI FENENA see Verdi, Giuseppe

NABUCCO: TU SUL LABBRO DE VEGGENTI see Verdi, Giuseppe

NACH DEM ABSCHIEDE see Lowenstamm, Franz Jos.

NACH DEM HINSCHIEDE DER GATTIN see Hess, W.

NACH HAUSE GEH'N WIR NICHT see Reckmann, J.

NACHGELASSENE MUSIKALISCHE DICHTUNGEN see Schubert, Franz (Peter)

NACHGELASSENE WERKE, FOLGE 1: LIEDER MIT KLAVIERBEGLEITUNG see Wolf, Hugo

NACHLESE see Strauss, Richard

NACHT see Abate, Rocco see Badings, Henk see Hekster, Walter see Pijper, Willem

NACHT, DIE see Schubert, Franz (Peter)

NACHT DER FRÜHLINGSWENDE, DIE see Visser, Peter

NACHT IST ES see Focke, Fré

NACHT IST FINSTER, DIE see Mozart, Wolfgang Amadeus

NACHT-STILTE see Weegenhuise, Johan

NACHT UND TRÄUME see Schubert, Franz (Peter)

NACHTEGAAL IN ECHTERNACH, EEN see Loevendie, Theo

NACHTEGALEN, DE see Orthel, Leon

NACHTGEBET see Marx, Joseph

NACHTGESÄNGE see Holl, R. see Schubert, Manfred see Thiele, Siegfried

NACHTIGALL see Alabiev, Alexander Nicholaevich, Nightingale

NACHTIGALL, DIE see Kounadis, Arghyris see Krol, Bernhard

NACHTIGALL SINGT ÜBERALL, DIE see Schubert, Franz (Peter), Seufzer

NACHTIGALLENTRÄNEN see Gürsching, Albrecht

NACHTKLÄNGE see Keussler, Gerhard von

NACHTLIED see Griffes, Charles Tomlinson see Mendelssohn-Bartholdy, Felix

NACHTLIEDER see Matthus, Siegfried

NACHTLIEDJE see Broekman, Hans

NACHTS see Govers, Klaas

NACHTSTILTE see Beekhuis, Hanna

NACHTSTUNDE, BIN ICH OHNE ANGST see Voortman, Roland

NACHTWANDLER see Hall, Pauline

NÄCKEN see Johansson, Roger

NAD POSTYLKOU see Felix, Václav

NAD WIECZNYM JEZIOREM STOJE see Baird, Tadeusz

NADAUD, G.
    Chansons Légères Vol. 2
        solo voice,pno CLASSV C049   (N2)

NADELSON, ANDREW
    Three Villenalles *CC3U
        S solo,pno APNM sc $6.75, set
        $13.00   (N3)

NAERE TING, DE see Ørbeck, Anne Marie

NAETURLAG see Sigurbjornsson, Hrodmar Ingi

NAGABA, NAOKI (1935-)
    Children's Land
        solo voice,pno [14'] JAPAN   (N4)

NAGARE-TORO see Itoh, Ohsuke

NAGINOKI NI YOSETE see Arashino, Hideo

NAGUÈRE see Paderewski, Ignace Jan

NÄHE DES GELIEBTEN see Schubert, Franz (Peter)

NAHUA SONGS see Winslow, Walter

NAILS see Dillard, Donald E.

NAJAARSLIED see King, Harold C.

NAKADA, KAZUTSUGU (1921-)
    Flower Hawthorn, A
        Bar solo,pno [4'] ONGAKU   (N5)

    Good-Bye!! Dragonflies
        Bar solo,pno [2'] JAPAN   (N6)

    My Mother's Home
        Bar solo,pno [4'] ONGAKU   (N7)

    Sleepy Chipmunk, A
        T solo,pno [2'] JAPAN   (N8)

NAKADA, YOSHINAO (1923-)
    Give Me A Song
        solo voice,pno [5'] JAPAN   (N9)

    Honoka Ni Hitotsu
        solo voice,pno [3'] JAPAN   (N10)

    Katabami
        solo voice,pno [3'] JAPAN   (N11)

    Katakuri No Hana
        solo voice,pno [2'] JAPAN   (N12)

    My Treasure
        solo voice,pno [2'] JAPAN   (N13)

    Popular Song Album *CCU
        solo voice ONGAKU 525300 f.s. (N14)

    Reijinso
        solo voice,pno [4'] JAPAN   (N15)

    Season Of Violet
        solo voice,pno [3'] JAPAN   (N16)

    Shadow
        solo voice,pno [3'] JAPAN   (N17)

    Watching The Moon
        solo voice,pno [4'] JAPAN   (N18)

NAKAGAWA, TOSHIO (1958-)
    In The Mood Of The Wind
        S solo,fl,harp JAPAN   (N19)

NAKAJIMA, HAL (1942-)
    Chieko-Sho
        S/T solo, koto, shakuhachi [18']
        JAPAN   (N20)

    Jagatara-Bumi
        S solo, 17-gen, shakuhachi [20']
        ZEN-ON   (N21)

    Shiroi Manjushage
        Mez solo, koto, shakuhachi [9']
        ZEN-ON   (N22)

NAKAMURA, YUKITAKE (1944-)
    Akatsumekusa No Hana
        Mez solo,pno [3'] JAPAN   (N23)

    Framenco
        T solo,pno [4'] ONGAKU   (N24)

    Manazashi
        S solo,pno [3'] JAPAN   (N25)

    Sardana Hiroba
        Bar solo,pno [6'] ONGAKU   (N26)

NAKI GREIN, EI see Braein, Edvard Fliflet see Evensen, Bernt Kasberg see Grov, Magne

NAKNE HEI, DEN see Baden, Conrad

NANDL IHR ALMLIED, DAS see Baumann, Alexander

NANI, NANI see Four Sephardi Songs

NIELAND, HENK (cont'd.)

Bekak
see Hongaarse Liedern I

Ha A Vilag Rigo Lenne
see Hongaarse Liedern II

Hongaarse Liedern I
S solo,pno DONEMUS f.s. [10']
contains: A Birka-Iskola; A
Kutya-Tar; Bekak; Hosszu Az
Utca; Mi Volnek?; Pletykazo
Asszonyok (N63)

Hongaarse Liedern II
S solo,pno DONEMUS f.s. [20']
contains: Ballada Harom
Falevelröl; Ha A Vilag Rigo
Lenne; Mese; Para; Tancnota;
Tul, Tul (N64)

Hosszu Az Utca
see Hongaarse Liedern I

Mese
see Hongaarse Liedern II

Mi Volnek?
see Hongaarse Liedern I

Para
see Hongaarse Liedern II

Pletykazo Asszonyok
see Hongaarse Liedern I

Tancnota
see Hongaarse Liedern II

Tul, Tul
see Hongaarse Liedern II

NIELSEN, SVEND (1937-   )
Ascent To Akseki
see Opstigning Mod Akseki

Opstigning Mod Akseki
"Ascent To Akseki" S solo,vln/
vibra,gtr [8'] sc,pts SAMFUNDET
(N65)

Sonnets Of Time
S solo,fl,vln,gtr,vcl [14']
SAMFUNDET (N66)

NIELSEN, TAGE (1929-   )
Ritual
Mez solo,fl,perc,pno [5'] SAMFUNDET
(N67)

NIELSEN, THORVALD
Udsigt Fra Fløien
solo voice,pno NOTON N-9142-A (N68)

NIELSON, LEWIS
Ballad Of Reading Gaol, The
Mez/A solo,fl,clar,2bsn,trom,3perc,
pno,vla,2vcl [19'] AM.COMP.AL. sc
$26.75, pts $32.95 (N69)

De Profundis
[Lat] S solo,string quar [10']
AM.COMP.AL. sc $9.15, pts $5.70
(N70)

Generation Of Leaves, A
[Greek] Mez solo,2.0(English
horn).1.0. 1.2.0(bass trom).0.
2perc,strings [14'] sc
AM.COMP.AL. $23.00 (N71)

Kassandra
Mez solo,vln,perc,pno [12'] sc
AM.COMP.AL. $7.70 (N72)

World Inside, A: Five Songs *CC5U
B solo,pno,1perc sc AM.COMP.AL.
$16.75 (N73)

NIELTJE IN HET ACQUARIUM see Beekhuis,
Hanna

NIGG, SERGE (1924-   )
Au Pont De Mirobel
T solo,ob,vln,vla,vcl,harp
BILLAUDOT from CHANSONS DU
FOLKLORE DE FRANCE (N74)

C'etait Anne De Bretagne
solo voice,fl,ob,clar,bsn BILLAUDOT
from CHANSONS DU FOLKLORE DE
FRANCE (N75)

De Bon Matin Se Leve
ST soli,2vln,vla,vcl,harp BILLAUDOT
from CHANSONS DU FOLKLORE DE
FRANCE (N76)

Du Clair Au Sombre *song cycle
S solo,pno (diff) BILLAUDOT (N77)
S solo,1.1.1.1. 2.1.1.0. 2perc,
timp,harp,cel,strings [20'25"]
pno red,sc,pts BILLAUDOT f.s.
perf mat rent (N78)

Grande D'Auvergne
solo voice,fl,ob,bsn,vln,vla,vcl
BILLAUDOT from CHANSONS DU

NIGG, SERGE (cont'd.)

FOLKLORE DE FRANCE (N79)

Rossignolet Du Bois, Rossignolet
Sauvage
S/T solo,fl,harp BILLAUDOT from
CHANSONS DU FOLKLORE DE FRANCE
(N80)

NIGHT, THE see Haxton, Kenneth

NIGHT BEFORE THE BRIDAL, THE see
Linley, George

NIGHT BLOOMS see Allen, Judith Shatin

NIGHT DANCES, THE see Altena, Maarten

NIGHT ELEGY see Fisher, Alfred

NIGHT HOUR, THE see Dahl, Vivian,
Nattetimen

NIGHT IN THE ROYAL ONTARIO MUSEUM, A
see Van de Vate, Nancy Hayes

NIGHT MUSIC see Leniado-Chira, Joseph

NIGHT-PIECE, A see Bon, Willem Frederik

NIGHT SONG see Engle, David

NIGHT SONGS see Adolphe, Bruce see Le
Siege, Annette

NIGHT VOICES see Gretchaninov,
Alexander Tikhonovich

NIGHT WANDERER see Hall, Pauline,
Nachtwandler

NIGHT WATCH see Wright, Maurice

NIGHT, YOU AREN'T HERE see Schneider,
Gary M.

NIGHTFALL IN THE MOUNTAINS see Weigl,
[Mrs.] Vally

NIGHTINGALE see Alabiev, Alexander
Nicholaevich

NIGHTINGALE, THE (HARLAN COUNTY,
KENTUCKY)
(Brockway, H.) [Eng] med solo,pno
CLASSV 1675 (N81)

NIGHTINGALE AND THE ROSE see Saint-
Saëns, Camille

NIGHTPIECE see Keulen, Geert van

NIHON NO HANA - 39 SONGS OF JAPANESE
FLOWERS see Hirai, Kozaburoy

NIIKURA, KEN (1951-   )
Madrigal
6 female soli,2perc [12'] JAPAN
8904 (N82)

Three Songs
Bar solo,pno [14'] JAPAN (N83)

NIJI 3 SHO see Arashino, Hideo

NIKODEMOWICZ, ANDRZEJ (1925-   )
Bitter Laments (Lament By The Tomb Of
Our Lord)
see Z Gorzkich Zalow (Placz Z Grobu
Chrystusa Pana)

Lamentacja (Rythm Do Pana Jezusa
Ukrzyzowanego Patrzac Na Figure
Meki Panskiej)
"Lamentation (Rhythm To The
Crucified Jesus Christ While
Contemplating An Image Of The
Passion)" S solo,2clar,bsn [6']
(Old Polish) POLSKIE (N84)

Lamentacja (Rythm Do Pana Jezusa
Ukrzyzowanego Patrzac Na Figure
Meki Panskiej) - Version 2
"Lamentation (Rhythm To The
Crucified Jesus Christ While
Contemplating An Image Of The
Passion) - Version 2" S solo,
2clar,bsn,vcl [12'] (Old Polish)
POLSKIE (N85)

Lamentation (Rhythm To The Crucified
Jesus Christ While Contemplating
An Image Of The Passion)
see Lamentacja (Rythm Do Pana
Jezusa Ukrzyzowanego Patrzac Na
Figure Meki Panskiej)

Lamentation (Rhythm To The Crucified
Jesus Christ While Contemplating
An Image Of The Passion) -
Version 2
see Lamentacja (Rythm Do Pana
Jezusa Ukrzyzowanego Patrzac Na
Figure Meki Panskiej) - Version 2

NIKODEMOWICZ, ANDRZEJ (cont'd.)

Z Gorzkich Zalow (Placz Z Grobu
Chrystusa Pana)
"Bitter Laments (Lament By The Tomb
Of Our Lord)" [Polish] Bar solo,
chamber orch [11'30"] POLSKIE
(N86)

"Bitter Laments (Lament By The Tomb
Of Our Lord)" [Polish] Bar solo,
string orch [11'30"] POLSKIE
(N87)

NIL CANITUR IUCUNDIUS see Esterhazy,
[Prince] Pal

NILES, JOHN JACOB (1892-1980)
Ballad Book Of John Jacob Niles *CCU
solo voice DOVER BKDO 00070 $7.95
(N88)

Songs Of John Jacob Niles, The
low solo,pno (CC24L) SCHIRM.G
50481653 (N89)

NILSSON, ANDERS (1954-   )
Aria
S solo,org STIM f.s. (N90)

Reflections
[Eng] S solo,fl&alto fl,clar,2vln,
vla,vcl [10'] sc REIMERS 101098
(N91)

Reflections: Three Songs
S solo,fl&alto fl,clar,string quar
REIMERS 98 (N92)

NILSSON, TORSTEN (1920-   )
Epiphania
[Lat] T solo,2perc,org (diff)
REIMERS (N93)

NIMBUS see Jansson, Johannes

NIMM MICH AUF, URALTE NACHT see Jensen,
Ludwig Irgens

NIN-CULMELL, JOAQUIN (1908-   )
Cancion De Cuna Afro-Cubana
solo voice,pno ESCHIG 8781 from
DEUX CHANSONS POPULAIRES CUBAINES
(N94)

Deux Chansons Populaires Cubaines
see Cancion De Cuna Afro-Cubana
see Nina De Guatemala, La

Nina De Guatemala, La
solo voice,pno ESCHIG 8782 from
DEUX CHANSONS POPULAIRES CUBAINES
(N95)

Si Ves Un Monte De Espumas
solo voice,pno ESCHIG 8783 (N96)

NINA DE GUATEMALA, LA see Nin-Culmell,
Joaquin

NINE SONGS see Sigurbjörnsson, Thorkell

NINE SONGS AND ARIAS see Beeson

NINE SONGS FOR VOICE AND PIANO see
Stutschevsky, Joachim

NINE SONGS OF INNOCENCE, EXPERIENCE AND
PROPHECY OF WILLIAM BLAKE see
Brown, Francis James

1981 see Hemberg, Eskil

1993 see Halldorsson, Sigfus see
Thorarinsson, Leifur

1973 #2 see Kucharz, Lawrence

NINETEEN SONGS see Delius, Frederick

NINETEEN SONGS FROM "FOLK SONGS OF
EUROPE" *CC19U
(Holst, I.; Karpeles, Maud) solo
voice,pno NOVELLO 49 0383 f.s.
(N97)

NIÑEZ, LA, VOL. 2 see Schumann, Clara
(Wieck)

NINNANANNA: A LULLABY FOR BEN see
Miller, Edward Jay

NIÑO, EL see Goorissen, Jan

NINON see Franck, Cesar

NIPPONARI see Martinu, Bohuslav (Jan)

NIRVANA... see Hunfeld, Xander see
Torjussen, Trygve

NISTAD, HANS IHLEN
Er Du Trett, Er Du Besvaeret
LYCHE 203 (N98)

NITTON EPISTLAR see Bellman, Carl
Michael

NIXE BINSEFUSS see Wolf, Hugo

NIZZA, JE PUIS SANS PEINE see Rossini,
Gioacchino, Canzonetta

'NNAMMURATO SENZA AMMORE see Medina, Emilio, Serenatella

NO CANDLE WAS THERE AND NO FIRE see Lehmann, Liza

NO CITY see Ames, William T.

NO ER DAGEN RUNNEN see Nystedt, Knut

NO ER MIN HUG STILL see Søderlind, Ragnar

NO FLOWERS FOR THE MAN-MADE DESERT see Bollen, Jan-Bas

NO LLOREIS OJUELOS see Granados, Enrique

NO MEIO DO CAMINHO see Hartke, Stephen Paul

NO MORE SHINY NOSE! see Slonimsky, Nicolas

NO, NON VEDRETE MAI see Benda, Georg Anton (Jirí Antonín)

NO PROPHET I see Rachmaninoff, Sergey Vassilievich

NO-RAI see Polin, Claire

NO SE POR QUE PIENSAS TU see Revueltas, Silvestre

NO SKAL DU LEVA see Nystedt, Knut

NO SON TODOS RUISENORES see Bedmar, Luis

NO SPRETTE LAUVET see Eggen, Arne

NO TIMEN ER KOMEN see Dale, Sjur

NOBLE, THOMAS TERTIUS (1867-1953)
    O Sweet Content
        solo voice BANKS f.s.   (N99)

NOBRE, MARLOS (1939-   )
    Drei Lieder
        solo voice,pno SEESAW   (N100)

    Trovas
        solo voice,pno SEESAW   (N101)

NOC see Baird, Tadeusz

NOC PRED KRASNYM DNEM see Zenkl, Michal

NOCES DU CROCODILE, LES see Beers, Jacques

NOCHE, UNE see Neumann, Richard J.

NOCHE DE LUNA see Schumann, Robert (Alexander)

NOCHE DE PRIMAVERA see Schumann, Robert (Alexander)

NOCHE OSCURA DEL ALME, LA see Valen, Fartein

NÖCK, DER see Lowe, Karl

NOCTURE-FOX see Tailleferre, Germaine

NOCTURNE see Bacon, Ernst L., Shilflied
    see Bibalo, Antonio see Évensen,
    Bernt Kasberg see Johansen, David
    Monrad see Lekeu, Guillaume see
    Marx, Joseph see Menotti, Gian
    Carlo see Sigurbjornsson, Hrodmar
    Ingi see Yuyama, Akira

NOCTURNE, A see Brown, James

NOCTURNE 1943 see Beekhuis, Hanna

NOCTURNE (DES CANTILÈNES) see
    Poldowski, [Lady] Dean Paul

NOCTURNES see Cooke, Arnold

NOCTURNO DEL CAZADOR see Schubert, Franz (Peter)

NODDY SONG BOOK see Johnson, Noel

NOE DER see Hellstenius, Henrik

NOËL see Faure, Gabriel-Urbain

NOELANI'S ARIA see Barati, George

NOEN MÅ VÅKE
    [Norw] solo voice,pno NORSK   (N102)

NOISELESS PATIENT SPIDER, A see Yannay, Yehuda

NOLAND, GARY (1957-   )
    Four Heine Lieder *Op.19
        S solo,pno FREEPUB FP22   (N103)

    Hollywood Elegies *Op.2
        S solo,pno (texts by Bertolt
        Brecht) FREEPUB FP4   (N104)

    I Dare Not Ask A Kiss *Op.7
        med solo,hpsd (text by Robert
        Herrick) FREEPUB FP3   (N105)

    My God, Why Hast Thou Forsaken Me?
        *Op.9
        SA/TB soli FREEPUB FP6   (N106)

NOLIANI, C.
    Canti Del Popolo Americano *CCU
        solo voice,pno CARISCH 20937 f.s.
                                      (N107)

NON CREDO see Widor, Charles-Marie

NON È VER see Mattei, Tito

NON M'AMI PIÙ! see Denza, Luigi

NON, NON (BERCEUSE) see Mozart, Wolfgang Amadeus

NON-NON DE LA MORTA, LA see Mestres, Apeles

NON-NON DELS BLATS, LA see Mestres, Apeles

NON POSSO CHE AMARA see Benda, Georg Anton (Jirí Antonín)

NON SA CHE SIA DOLORE see Bach, Johann Sebastian, Was Scherz Sei Und Was Leiden

NON T'AMO PIÙ! see Denza, Luigi

NONE BUT THE LONELY HEART see Tchaikovsky, Piotr Ilyich

NONE BUT THE WEARY HEART see Tchaikovsky, Piotr Ilyich

NONE SHALL SLEEP see Puccini, Giacomo, Turandot: Nessun Dorma

NONNENDRINKLIED see Brandse, Wim

NONSENS 1 see Bakke, Ruth

NONSENS 2 see Bakke, Ruth

NONSENS 3 see Bakke, Ruth

NOON SILENCE see Luening, Otto

NOR SPELL see Druckman, Jacob Raphael

NORAH O'NEALE see Hughes, Herbert

NORBY, ERIK (1936-   )
    Abend
        see Sechs Herbstlieder

    Abendlied
        see Sechs Herbstlieder

    Concerto For Two Sopranos And
        Orchestra
        SS soli,3.3.3.3. 4.3.3.1. timp,
        3perc,harp,elec pno,strings [20']
        SAMFUNDET   (N108)

    Ende Am Herbst
        see Sechs Herbstlieder

    Erste Stunde
        see Sechs Herbstlieder

    Four Shakespeare Sonnets
        Mez solo,fl,vla,vcl [10'] SAMFUNDET
                                      (N109)

    Grabmal Eines Jungen Mädchens
        see To Rilke Sange

    Herbst
        see Sechs Herbstlieder

    Laute, Die
        see Sechs Herbstlieder

    Lied Von Meer
        see To Rilke Sange

    Rilke Lieder
        Mez solo,3.3.3.3. 4.3.3.1. timp,
        harp,cel,pno,strings [20']
        SAMFUNDET   (N110)

    Sechs Herbstlieder
        solo voice,fl,gtr ENGSTROEM f.s.
        contains: Abend; Abendlied; Ende
        Am Herbst; Erste Stunde;
        Herbst; Laute, Die   (N111)

    Three Shakespeare Sonnets
        S solo,ob,db,pno,string quar
        SAMFUNDET   (N112)

NORBY, ERIK (cont'd.)

    To Rilke Sange
        solo voice ENGSTROEM ES.547 f.s.
        contains: Grabmal Eines Jungen
        Mädchens; Lied Von Meer   (N113)

NORDAL, JON (1926-   )
    Every Small Step
        solo voice,pno ICELAND 012-018
                                      (N114)

NORDENSTEN, FRANK TVEOR (1955-   )
    Floating Point *Op.78
        [Eng] S solo,fl/alto fl,clar,elec
        gtr,pno,vln,vcl [15'] (texts by
        Oscar Wilde and William Blake)
        AAP   (N115)

    Floating Point, Op.78a
        [Eng] S solo,pno,vln,horn (version
        for reduced ensemble) AAP   (N116)

NORDHEIM, ARNE (1931-   )
    Første Sommerfugl, Den
        [Norw] S solo,harp [4'50"] NORGE
                                      (N117)

    Tempora Noctis
        [Lat] SMez soli,2(pic).2(English
        horn).2(bass clar).2(contrabsn).
        1.1.1.1. electronic tape,timp,
        perc,harp,pno,cel,strings [39']
        HANSEN-DEN f.s.   (N118)

    Tre Voci For Soprano Og
        Kammerensemble
        [It] S solo,fl/pic,clar/bass clar,
        vln,vcl,perc,pno HANSEN-DEN
                                      (N119)

NORDLANDET see Vea, Ketil

NORDOFF, PAUL (1909-1977)
    Prayers From The Ark
        solo voice,opt inst PRESSER
        412-41070 f.s.   (N120)

NORDRAAK, RIKARD (1842-1866)
    Der Ligger Et Land
        (Olsen, C.G.Sparre) "There Lies A
        Country" solo voice,1.1.1.0.
        0.1.1.0. strings NORSK f.s.
                                      (N121)

    Kaares Sang
        (Halvorsen, J.) "Song Of Kaare,
        The" solo voice,3(pic).2.2.2.
        4.2.1.0. timp,strings NORSK f.s.
                                      (N122)

    Song Of Kaare, The
        see Kaares Sang

    Taylors Sang
        (Brevik, Tor) solo voice,1.0.2.2.
        2.2.0.0. timp,strings NORGE f.s.
                                      (N123)
        (Olsen, C.G.Sparre) "Taylor's Song"
        solo voice,fl,ob,clar,strings
        NORSK f.s.   (N124)

    Taylor's Song
        see Taylors Sang

    There Lies A Country
        see Der Ligger Et Land

    Tonen *Op.2,No.1
        (Olsen, C.G.Sparre) "Tune, The"
        solo voice,fl,ob,clar,strings
        NORSK f.s.   (N125)

    Tune, The
        see Tonen

NORDUR see Thordarson, Sigurdur

NORDUR VID HEIMSKAUT see Jonsson, Thorarinn

NORGE MITT LAND see Nystedt, Knut

NORHOLM, IB (1931-   )
    Blomster Fra Den Danske Poesis Flora
        *Op.36
        ENGSTROEM 562   (N126)

    Light
        see Lys

    Lys *Op.78
        "Light" S solo,fl,harp,perc,vcl sc,
        pts SAMFUNDET f.s.   (N127)

    "Moraliteter" Eller "Måske Er Der
        Mange Kilometer Til Den Naermeste
        Edderkop" (Symphony No. 6, Op.
        85)
        ""Moralities" Or "Maybe It's Many
        Kilometres To The Nearest
        Spider"" MezBar&2 speaking
        voices,2.2.2.2. 4.3.3.1. timp,4-
        5perc,cel,strings [34'] sc,pts
        SAMFUNDET f.s.   (N128)

    "Moralities" Or "Maybe It's Many
        Kilometres To The Nearest Spider"
        see "Moraliteter" Eller "Måske Er
        Der Mange Kilometer Til Den
        Naermeste Edderkop"

NORHOLM, IB (cont'd.)

Six Songs *Op.64, CC6U
S solo,pno SAMFUNDET f.s.   (N129)

Songs, Op. 64
see Three Songs, Op. 54

Still Life
see Stilleliv

Stilleliv *Op.45
"Still Life" S solo,gtr,perc [15']
sc,pts SAMFUNDET f.s.   (N130)

Symphony No. 6, Op. 85
see "Moraliteter" Eller "Måske Er
Der Mange Kilometer Til Den
Naermeste Edderkop"

Three Songs, Op. 54
A solo,pno SAMFUNDET f.s. contains
also: Songs, Op. 64 (S solo,pno);
Three Songs, Op. 75 (Mez solo,
pno)   (N131)

Three Songs, Op. 75
see Three Songs, Op. 54

NORMA: CASTA DIVA see Bellini, Vincenzo

NORMA: CASTA DIVA, CHE INARGENTI see
Bellini, Vincenzo

NORMA: MIRA, O NORMA see Bellini,
Vincenzo

NORMAL MADNESS, A see Coyner, Lou

NORSK KJAERLEIKSSONG see Olsen, Sparre

NORSK SALME see Baden, Conrad

NORSKE FOLKEVISUR FRA GUDBRANDSDALEN
see Olsen, Sparre

NORSKE STEVTONER see Kvandal, Johan

NORTH LABRADOR see Pieper, Rene

NORTHEAST RESERVATION LINES see Biggs,
Hayes

NORWAY MY COUNTRY see Nystedt, Knut,
Norge Mitt Land

NORWEGIAN FAIRYTALE see Bergh, Sverre,
Fanden I Nøtten

NOT EARTH ALONE see Weigl, [Mrs.] Vally

NOT FROM THIS ANGER see Kriesberg,
Matthias

NOT TWO, BUT ONE see Nelson, Ronald A.

NOT WAVING BUT DROWNING see Berg,
Christopher

NOT YET see Torphicen, Pamela

NOTRE PÈRE see Handel, George Frideric

NOTT see Björnsson, Arni

NOTTE, LA see Metral, Pierre

NOTTE ILLUMINATA, LA see Perti, Giacomo
Antonio

NØTTELITEN AND NINE OTHER TUNES FOR
CHILDREN AND ADULTS see Øian, Johan

NOTTIN ER TIL THESS AD GRATA I see
Sveinsson, Gunnar Reynir

NOTTURNI see Ugoletti, Paolo

NOTTURNO see Schnabel, Artur

NOTTURNO A DUE VOCI see Rossini,
Gioacchino, Regata Veneziana, La:
Voga, O Tonio

NOTTURNO, OP. 59 see Schouwman, Hans

NOUS MADRIGALS see Mestres, Apeles

NOVAK
Dulces Cantilenae
[Lat] S solo,vcl PANTON 933   (N132)

NOVAK, VITEZSLAV (1870-1949)
Erotikon
see Sechs Lieder, Op. 46

Sechs Lieder, Op. 46
"Erotikon" [Ger/Czech] high solo
(not available outside U.S.A.)
RECITAL 378   (N133)

Zigeunerlieder, Op. 14 *song cycle
[Czech/Ger/Eng] med solo (texts by
Adolf Heyduk) RECITAL 282   (N134)

NOVARO, M.
Inno Di Mameli
med solo,pno CLASSV 1305   (N135)

NOVELLO
Little Damozel
[Eng] BOOSEY SGB0189E   (N136)

NOVEMBER see Danielsen, Ragnar see
Hovland, Egil see Lunde, Ivar see
Meijering, Cord see Roosendael, Jan
Rokus van

NOVEMBER, OP. 90 see Flothuis, Marius

NOVEMBRE see Tremisot, Edouard

NOVES CANCONS PER INFANTS see Mestres,
Apeles

NOW, THE see Moylan, William

NOW AND THEN see Hamilton, Iain

NOW DEATH HAS SHUT YOUR EYES see
Fennimore, Joseph William

NOW IS THE MONTH OF MAYING see
Sveinbjörnsson, Sveinbjörn

NOW SLEEPS THE CRIMSON see Britten,
[Sir] Benjamin

NOW SWEEPING DOWN THE YEARS see
Fischer, Irwin

NOW THE COLD WINTER DAYS see Anderson,
William H.

NOW WINTER NIGHTS ENLARGE see Hol, Dirk

NOWAK, LIONEL (1911-   )
Summer Is Away
low solo,fl,clar,bsn,vcl,pno [20']
sc AM.COMP.AL. $12.50   (N137)

NOWTH UPON NACHT see Cage, John

NOZZE DI FIGARO, LE: DEH VIENI NON
TARDAR see Mozart, Wolfgang Amadeus

NOZZE DI FIGARO, LE: DOVE SONO see
Mozart, Wolfgang Amadeus

NOZZE DI FIGARO, LE: NON PIÙ ANDRAI see
Mozart, Wolfgang Amadeus

NOZZE DI FIGARO, LE: NON SO PIÙ COSA
SON see Mozart, Wolfgang Amadeus

NOZZE DI FIGARO, LE: PORGI AMOR see
Mozart, Wolfgang Amadeus

NOZZE DI FIGARO, LE: SE VUOL BALLARE
see Mozart, Wolfgang Amadeus

NOZZE DI FIGARO, LE: SULL' ARIA see
Mozart, Wolfgang Amadeus

NOZZE DI FIGARO, LE: VEDRÒ MENTR' IO
SOSPIRO see Mozart, Wolfgang
Amadeus

NOZZE DI FIGARO, LE: VOI CHE SAPETE see
Mozart, Wolfgang Amadeus

N'SHAMAH SHENATATA BI see Isaacson,
Michael Neil

NU AFHJUPAST LJOSIN see Helgason,
Hallgrimur

NU BEDER VI DEN HELLIGE ÅND see
Karlsen, Kjell Mørk

NU ER SOL see Björnsson, Arni

NU ER SOL OG VOR see Björnsson, Arni

NU ER STUNDEN RIKAST see Jordan, Sverre

NU FAERIST AD VIGOLD - F.U.J. MARSINN
see Björnsson, Arni

NU HAUSTAR A HEIDUM see Gudmundsson,
Björgvin

NU IK ZIJN OOGEN HEB GELEZEN see
Broekman, Hans

NU LA OSS TAKKE GUD see Dale, Sjur

NU LOKAR DAGUR LJOSRI BRA see
Isolfsson, Pall

NUAGES, LES see Sourisse, Brigitte

NUERNBERGER, L. DEAN
Homecoming, The: An Autumn Gathering
TBar soli, 15 early and modern
instruments [12'] APNM sc $6.00,
pts rent   (N138)

NUESTRAS CANCIONES VOL. 1 see Schumann,
Clara (Wieck)

NUESTRAS CANCIONES VOL. 2 see Schumann,
Clara (Wieck)

NUEVA COLECCIÓN DE CANCIONES INFANTILES
VOL. 1 see Schumann, Clara (Wieck)

NUEVA COLLECIÓN DE CANCIONES INFANTILES
VOL. 2 see Schumann, Clara (Wieck)

NUIT, LA see Chausson, Ernest see
Gretchaninov, Alexander Tikhonovich

NUIT BLEU see D'orsay, M.L.

NUIT D'ESPAGNE see Massenet, Jules

NUIT PERSANES see Saint-Saëns, Camille

NUITS D'ETE, LES see Berlioz, Hector
(Louis)

NUMI, NUMI see Stern, Robert Lewis

NUMMI, SEPPO
Kevätteiltä
"On Spring Roads" solo voice FAZER
F.M. 06958-3 f.s.   (N139)

On Spring Roads
see Kevätteiltä

NUN ERST see Voortman, Roland

NUN EST BIBENDUM see Braal, Andries de

NUN KOMM, DER HEIDEN HEILAND:
SOLOCANTATA see Apollyon, Nicolay

NUN SEH' ICH WOHL, WARUM SO DUNKLE
FLAMMEN see Mahler, Gustav

NUN STEUERMANN see Meyer

NUN WANDRE MARIA see Wolf, Hugo

NUN WILL DIE SONN' SO HELL AUFGEHN see
Mahler, Gustav

NUNC DIMITTIS see Karlsen, Kjell Mørk

NUNC EST see Colding-Jorgensen, Henrik
see Zanolini, Bruno

NUR, WER DIE SEHNSUCHT KENNT see
Tchaikovsky, Piotr Ilyich

NUTILE
Mamma Mia Che Vo' Sapè
high solo,pno CLASSV 0987   (N140)

NYAARSVERS see Karlsen, Kjell Mørk

NYARY, THOMAS
Aus Alten Märchen
see Zwei Gesänge, Op. 1

Aus Meinen Grossen Schmerzen
see Zwei Gesänge, Op. 1

Zwei Gesänge, Op. 1
T solo,pno SCIEN 1223 f.s.
contains: Aus Alten Märchen; Aus
Meinen Grossen Schmerzen (N141)

NYE SALMER see Plaetner, Jørgen

NYHUS, ROLF (1938-   )
Barn Er Født I Betlehem, Et
see Fem Religiøse Folketoner Fra
Rørosdistriktet

Bryllup-Salme
solo voice,pno/org MUSIKK 2455
(N142)

Er Nødig, Dette Ene, Ett
see Fem Religiøse Folketoner Fra
Rørosdistriktet

Fem Religiøse Folketoner Fra
Rørosdistriktet
solo voice,org NOTON N-9130 f.s.
contains: Barn Er Født I
Betlehem, Et; Er Nødig, Dette
Ene, Ett; Jesus, Din Søte
Forening; O Du Min Immanuel;
Yndigste Rose, Den   (N143)

Glück Auf! Guds Fred!
solo voice,org NOTON N-9004 (N144)

Herre, Til Himmelen Rekker Din
Miskunnhet
see To Bibelske Sanger

Jeg Gikk Meg Vill I Skogene
see To Sanger

Jeg Løfter Mine Øyne (Psalm No. 121)
solo voice,org,2fl NOTON N-8943
(N145)

Jeg Løfter Mine Øyne Til Fjellene
(Psalm No. 121)
[Norw] Mez solo,2fl,org NORGE
(N146)

NYHUS, ROLF (cont'd.)

Jesus, Din Søte Forening
see Fem Religiøse Folketoner Fra
Rørosdistriktet

Kristus Er Verdens Lys
[Norw] solo voice,org MUSIKK (N147)

La Oss Telle Våre Dager
see To Bibelske Sanger

Med Røde Roser
see To Sanger

O Du Min Immanuel
see Fem Religiøse Folketoner Fra
Rørosdistriktet

Psalm No. 121
see Jeg Løfter Mine Øyne
see Jeg Løfter Mine Øyne Til
Fjellene

To Adventsalmer
[Norw] solo voice,pno NORGE (N148)
low solo,org NOTON N-9211-L (N149)
high solo,org NOTON N-9211-A (N150)

To Bibelske Sanger
NOTON f.s. high solo,org N-8941-A;
low solo,org N-8941-L
contains: Herre, Til Himmelen
Rekker Din Miskunnhet; La Oss
Telle Våre Dager (N151)

To Sanger
[Norw] solo voice,pno NORGE (N152)

To Sanger
solo voice,pno NOTON N-9002 f.s.
contains: Jeg Gikk Meg Vill I
Skogene; Med Røde Roser (N153)

Tre Kveldssalmer
[Norw] solo voice,fl,org MUSIKK
(N154)

Yndigste Rose, Den
see Fem Religiøse Folketoner Fra
Rørosdistriktet

NYSTEDT, KNUT (1915-　　)
Å Krist, Som I Bryllaup Gjesta
[Norw] solo voice,org LYCHE (N155)

Å, Var Eg Heime Att
see Setrom-Songar, Op. 12

All Livsens Ljosglans Slokna Bratt
see Fire Salmetoner

Åtte Salmetoner
[Norw] solo voice,org LYCHE 637
(N156)
Dalende Dag, En Stakket Stund, En
see Seks Salmetoner

Del Ditt Brod Med Sulten Bror
see Seks Salmetoner

Du Dag Med Ro Og Kvile
see Seks Salmetoner

Du Ska Itte Trø I Graset
[Norw] solo voice,pno LYCHE 288
(N157)
Eg Søkjer Deg Tidleg
[Norw] solo voice,org NORSK (N158)

Fire Salmetoner
solo voice,org LYCHE 991 f.s.
contains: All Livsens Ljosglans
Slokna Bratt; Herre, Rekk Ut
Din Allmektige Hand; Leid Meg,
Gud, Over Bylgjande Hav;
Lovsang (N159)

Four Psalms, Op. 22
see Tru Og Saeledrust

Gjennom Dødsskyggens Dal　*Op.42,No.2
[Norw] solo voice,pno LYCHE 321
(N160)
Hen Over Jorden Et Pilgrimstog
see Seks Salmetoner

Her Vil Eg Kvile
see Setrom-Songar, Op. 12

Herre, Rekk Ut Din Allmektige Hand
see Fire Salmetoner

I Dag Er Nadens Tid
see Tre Religiose Folketoner, Op.
34

Isgangsvaer　*Op.31
"Thaw" solo voice,strings [3']
NORSK f.s. (N161)

Jeremia-Word
[Norw/Eng] solo voice,pno NORGE
(N162)
[Norw] solo voice,pno (text from
The Bible: Jeremiah 17:7-8) NORGE
(N163)

NYSTEDT, KNUT (cont'd.)

Kristus, Du Er Alt Mitt Hap
see Seks Salmetoner

Leid Meg, Gud, Over Bylgjande Hav
see Fire Salmetoner

Lion Yawns, The
see Løven Gjesper

Løven Gjesper　*Op.38,No.3
"Lion Yawns, The" solo voice,
2.2.2.2. 4.2.2.0. perc,strings
[2'] NORSK f.s. (N164)

Lovsang
see Fire Salmetoner

Lyse Dag Forgangen Er, Den
see Tre Religiose Folketoner, Op.
34

Natt
see Setrom-Songar, Op. 12

No Er Dagen Runnen
see Setrom-Songar, Op. 12

No Skal Du Leva
[Norw] S solo,pno [1'30"] NORGE
(N165)
Norge Mitt Land　*Op.15
"Norway My Country" Bar solo,
2.2.2.2. 2.2.2.0. timp,perc,
strings [15'] NORSK f.s. (N166)

Norway My Country
see Norge Mitt Land

O Jesus Kristus Var Herre Kjaer
see Seks Salmetoner

Ordet　*Op.42,No.1
[Norw] solo voice,pno LYCHE 320
(N167)
Se Solens Skjonne Prakt
see Tre Religiose Folketoner, Op.
34

Seks Salmetoner
solo voice,org LYCHE 615 f.s.
contains: Dalende Dag, En Stakket
Stund, En; Del Ditt Brod Med
Sulten Bror; Du Dag Med Ro Og
Kvile; Hen Over Jorden Et
Pilgrimstog; Kristus, Du Er Alt
Mitt Hap; O Jesus Kristus Var
Herre Kjaer (N168)

Seks Sonetter, Op. 38
[Norw] solo voice,pno NORSK (N169)

Setrom-Songar, Op. 12
[Norw] solo voice,pno NORSK f.s.
contains: Å, Var Eg Heime Att;
Her Vil Eg Kvile; Natt; No Er
Dagen Runnen; Soldag I Fjellet
(N170)
Soldag I Fjellet　*Op.12,No.3
"Sunny Day In The Mountaians" solo
voice,1.1.1.1. 2.0.0.0. strings
[3'] NORSK f.s. (N171)
see Setrom-Songar, Op. 12

Stjerne Klar, En
[Norw] solo voice,pno,opt fl&vln
NORSK NMO 10415 (N172)

Sunny Day In The Mountaians
see Soldag I Fjellet

Tenebrae Factae Sunt
[Lat] Bar/B solo,org NORSK (N173)

Thaw
see Isgangsvaer

To Motetter
[Norw] solo voice,org LYCHE 524
(N174)
Tre Religiose Folketoner, Op. 34
LYCHE 259 f.s.
contains: I Dag Er Nadens Tid;
Lyse Dag Forgangen Er, Den; Se
Solens Skjonne Prakt (N175)

Tru Og Saeledrust
"Four Psalms, Op. 22" [Norw] solo
voice,pno NORGE (N176)

NYSTROEM, GÖSTA (1890-1966)
Havets Visa (from The Aksel Schioetz
Anthology Of Nordic Solo Songs,
Vol.2)
solo voice,pno EGTVED 432 f.s.
contains also: Jag Väntar Månen
(N177)
Jag Väntar Månen
see Havets Visa

NYTTÅR I NORGE see Sinding, Christian

NYTTÅR VED HAVET see Fongaard, Bjørn
see Gjerstrom, Bjorn G.

O

O, AD EG YNNI THER AD NYJU see
Halldorsson, Skuli

O ADMIRABILE VENERIS IDOLUM see
Anonymous

O, ALTIJD DAT MOE-E VERLANGEN see
Zagwijn, Henri

O ALTITUDO see Stout, Alan

O BE JOYFUL IN THE LORD see
Christensen, Bernhard

O BREAD OF LIFE see Franck, Cesar,
Panis Angelicus

O CANADA
(Le Lacheur) solo voice,kbd HARRIS
(O1)

O CESSATE DI PIAGARMI see Scarlatti,
Alessandro

O COME HITHER! see Crist, Bainbridge

O COME TO ME see Balakirev, Mily
Alexeyevich

O COR, VOLUPTAS COELITUM see Hol,
Richard

O CRUCIFIED CHRIST see Dillard, Donald
E.

O DEL MIO DOLCE ARDOR see Gluck,
Christoph Willibald, Ritter von

O DILECTISSIME JESU see Legrenzi,
Giovanni

O DIOTIMA see Prosperi, Carlo

O DIVES see Rosenmüller, Johann

O DOMINE DEUS see Kvandal, Johan

O DOMINE JESU CHRISTE see Locke

O DOOD, HOE BITTER IS UW GEDINKEN see
Ehlen, Margriet

O DU MIN IMMANUEL see Nyhus, Rolf

O, DU SOM ER VÅRT LIV OG LYS see
Thoresen, Lasse

O, DU WOGENDES FELD see Rachmaninoff,
Sergey Vassilievich

O DULCISSIME DOMINE see Lully, Jean-
Baptiste (Lulli)

O FALLADA, DA DU HANGEST see Eisler,
Hanns

O FATAL GIFT see Verdi, Giuseppe, Don
Carlo: O Don Fatale

O FOR THE WINGS OF A DOVE see
Mendelssohn-Bartholdy, Felix

O GAZELLE OF LOVE see Avni, Tzvi

O GOD OF LOVE see Corigliano, John

O GOTTESLAMM see Mozart, Wolfgang
Amadeus

O, GUD VORS LANDS see Sveinbjörnsson,
Sveinbjörn

O HERR, ERFORSCHE NICHT DIE
UNSICHTBAREN WUNDEN see Bunge, Sas

O HOLDER TAG see Bach, Johann Sebastian

O HOLDER TAG, ERWUNSCHT ZEIT see Bach,
Johann Sebastian

O HONZOVI see Bartoš, Jan Zdenek

O HVILKET HERLIG BYTTE see Haegeland,
Eilert M., Folketone Fra Iveland

O, JAK BAHATO see Shut, Wasyl

O, JAK PLESA VE MNE SRDICKO see Ryba,
Jan Jakub Simon

O JESU NOMEN DULCE see Schütz, Heinrich

O JESUS KRISTUS VAR HERRE KJAER see
Nystedt, Knut

O, JEZUSKIND TEER see Geraedts, Jaap

O JOUR HEUREUX, O TEMPS BENI see Bach,
Johann Sebastian, O Holder Tag,
Erwunscht Zeit

O JUGEND, O SCHÖNE ROSENZEIT see
    Mendelssohn-Bartholdy, Felix

O KOMM, GELIEBTE see Ruyneman, Daniel

O LIVETS GUD, VI TACKAR DIG see
    Janácek, Bedrich

O LORD MOST HOLY see Franck, Cesar,
    Panis Angelicus

O LOVE THAT WILT NOT LET ME GO *CC7L
    (Smith, Michael W.; Kaiser, Kurt)
    solo voice sc BROADMAN 4525-19
    $8.95, accomp tape available   (02)

O MARENARIELLO
    med-high solo,pno CLASSV 1059   (03)

O MEISJE MIJN see Frid, Geza

O MER, OUVRE-TOI (ARIOSO) see Delibes,
    Léo

O MIRANDUM MYSTERIUM see Legrenzi,
    Giovanni

O MISERICORDISSIME JESU see Schütz,
    Heinrich

O MISTRESS MINE see Beach, [Mrs.]
    H.H.A. (Amy Marcy Cheney) see
    Willan, Healey

O NACHT see Flothuis, Marius

O NUIT see Damais, Emile

O PRAISE THE LORD see Mozart, Wolfgang
    Amadeus, Laudate Dominum

O PRIMAVERA see Tirindelli, Pier Adolfo

O PURE AND TENDER STAR OF EVE see
    Wagner, Richard

O PUVODU JAROMERIC see Mica, Frantisek
    Vaclav

O QUALI MI RISVEGLIANO see Braga,
    Gaetano, Angel's Serenade

O QUAM CARAE ET QUAM BEATAE SILVAE see
    Sacchini, Antonio (Maria Gasparo
    Gioacchino)

O QUAM PULCHRA ES see Monteverdi,
    Claudio

O QUAM SUAVIS see Hol, Richard

O QUAM TU PULCHRA ES see Grandi,
    Alessandro

O SACRUM CONVIVIUM see Hol, Richard

O SALIGHET STOR see Tøsse, Eilert

O SALUTARIS see Faure, Gabriel-Urbain
    see Franck, Cesar see Handel,
    George Frideric see Widor, Charles-
    Marie

O SANCTISSIMA see Dvořák, Antonín

O SANCTISSIMA: 10 CHRISTMAS SONGS FROM
    ITALY, ENGLAND, SPAIN AND FRANCE
    see Ragossnig, K.

O SOLE MIO see Di Capua, Eduardo

O SÜSSER TOD see Marx, Joseph

O SWALLOW, SWALLOW FLYING SOUTH see
    Foote, Arthur

O SWEET CONTENT see Noble, Thomas
    Tertius

O SWEET DELIGHT see Hol, Dirk

O TANNENBAUM see Tre Celebri Canti Di
    Natale

O THAT IT WERE SO! see Bridge, Frank

O THOU BILLOWY HARVEST see
    Rachmaninoff, Sergey Vassilievich

O TRAURE NICHT see Bijvanck, Henk

O TRISTE ÉTAIT MON AME see Schmitt,
    Florent

O TUNEFUL VOICE see Roberts, Timothy

O VIN, DISSIPE LA TRISTESSE see Thomas,
    Ambroise, Hamlet: Drinking Song

O WÄR ICH SCHON see Lyric Soprano
    Arias: A Master Class With Evelyn
    Lear, Vol. 2

O WEEP NO MORE, LIU see Puccini,
    Giacomo, Turandot: Non Piangere,
    Liu

O WERE MY LOVE YON LILAC FAIR see
    Beach, [Mrs.] H.H.A. (Amy Marcy
    Cheney)

O WHAT A BEAUTIFUL CITY see Boatner,
    Edward H.

O YOU ARE NOT WORKING see Bois, Rob du

O YOU WHO OFTEN see Reif, Paul

OAK, THE see Sevriens, Jean

OAKES, RODNEY HARLAND (1937-   )
    ALP Meets HCE
        S solo,clar,electronic tape SEESAW
                                         (04)

OB ICH DICH LIEBE see Rosenweig,
    Wilhelm

OB SIE WOHL KOMMEN WIRD see Preyer,
    Gottfried

OBERON: ARABIENS EINSAM KIND see Weber,
    Carl Maria von

OBERON: OCEAN! DU UNGEHEUER! see Weber,
    Carl Maria von

OBJECTIVE KNOWLEDGE see Maxym, R.

OBOROZUKIYO NI see Matsudaira, Yori-
    Tsune

OBRADORS, FERNANDO
    Canciones Clasicas Españolas, Vol. 1
        [Span] high solo,pno CLASSV 1699
                                         (05)

    Del Cabello Más Sutil
        med-high solo,pno CLASSV 1914   (06)

OBSTINATION see Fontenailles, H. de

OCCHI DELL'ALMA MIA see Crockett,
    Donald

OCCHI DI FATA see Denza, Luigi

OCCHI MIEI, CHE FACESTE? see Handel,
    George Frideric

OCCHI TURCHINI see Denza, Luigi

OCEAN DE TERRE see Knussen, Oliver

OCEAN MOTION MILDEW MIND see Anderson,
    Beth

...OCH ICKE DE SMAA AT FORAGTE see
    Madsen, Trygve

OCHILA LA-EL see Suben, Joel Eric

OCHILA LA'EIL see Horvit, Michael M.

OCHTEND see Boer, Jan den

OCTAGON see Lybbert, Donald

OCZEKIWANIA see Dabrowski, Florian

ODALISKEN SYNGER: NU SYNKER SOLEN I
    ASIENS DALE see Grieg, Edvard
    Hagerup

ODE see De Blasio, Antonio see Otten,
    Ludwig

ODE AAN HET KIND see Dispa, Robert

ODE AN EINEN ALBATROS see Buttkewitz,
    Fred

ODE AU SOLEIL NÉ DE LA MORT see
    Martinon, Jean

ODE DU PREMIER JOUR DE MAI see Mul, Jan

ODE ON THE DEATH OF PURCELL see Blow,
    John

ODE Y MEMENTO see Hertel, Thomas

ØDEGAARD, HENRIK (1955-   )
    Jeremias Bekjennelser
        [Norw] Bar solo,org NORGE   (07)

    Lenket Til Din Tyngde
        see Tre Dikt Av Hans Børli

    Morgen, En
        see Tre Dikt Av Hans Børli

    Når Timen Slår
        see Tre Dikt Av Hans Børli

    Proprium Missae Nativitatis
        [Lat] Bar solo,string quar [25']
        NORGE   (08)

    Tre Dikt Av Hans Børli
        [Norw] Bar solo,pno NORGE f.s.
        contains: Lenket Til Din Tyngde;
        Morgen, En; Når Timen Slår   (09)

ODEN I see Witzenmann, Wolfgang

ODEN III see Witzenmann, Wolfgang

ODEN V see Witzenmann, Wolfgang

ODSTRCIL, KAREL (1930-   )
    Belounka Holubicko
        S solo,2.1.2.1. 2.2.1.0. timp,perc,
        strings [14'] CESKY HUD.   (010)

OELSCHLEGEL, ALFRED
    Schelm Von Bergen, Der: Balduin-
    Marsch
        solo voice,pno SCIEN 1246   (011)

OESTERREICHISCHE VOLKSLIEDER MIT IHREN
    SINGEWEISEN see Ziska, Franz

OEUVRES COMPLETTES, HEFT 5: 30 GESÄNGE
    see Mozart, Wolfgang Amadeus

OF HONEY AND VINEGAR see Wallach,
    Joelle

OF LOVE AND DEATH see Thorarinsson, Jón

OF MERE BEING see Dembski, Stephen

OF ROME, PARTING AND SPRING see
    Pleskow, Raoul

OF THREE SHAKESPEARE SONNETS see
    Buller, John

OFFENBACH, JACQUES (1819-1880)
    Belle Héléne, La: Au Mont Ida Trois
    Déesses
        T solo,pno CLASSV 1256   (012)

    Grande Duchesse, La: Voici Le Sabre
    Do Mon Père
        Mez solo,pno CLASSV 1126   (013)

    Letter Scene
        see Périchole, La: O Mon Cher Amant

    Lieder And Romances *CCU
        (Smola, Emmerich) [Fr/Ger] med
        solo,pno BOTE f.s.   (014)

    Oiseaux, Les
        see Tales Of Hoffmann: Doll Song

    Perichole, La: Ah! Que Les Hommes
    Sont Betes
        S solo RECITAL 2241   (015)

    Périchole, La: Ah! Quel Diner
        "Tipsy Song" S solo,pno CLASSV 0807
                                      (016)

    Périchole, La: O Mon Cher Amant
        "Letter Scene" S solo,pno CLASSV
        0865   (017)

    Perichole, La: Tu N'es Pas Beau
        S solo RECITAL 2240   (018)

    Tales Of Hoffmann: Belle Nuit
        SA soli,pno CLASSV 0540   (019)

    Tales Of Hoffmann: Chanson De
    Kleinzach
        T solo,pno CLASSV 0963   (020)

    Tales Of Hoffmann: Dans Les Rôles
    D'Amoureux
        B solo,pno CLASSV 0840   (021)

    Tales Of Hoffmann: Doll Song
        "Oiseaux, Les" coloratura sop,pno
        CLASSV 0355   (022)

    Tales Of Hoffmann: Elle A Fui, La
    Tourterelle!
        coloratura sop,pno CLASSV 0956 (023)

    Tipsy Song
        see Périchole, La: Ah! Quel Diner

    Voyage Dans La Lune: Monde Charmant
        [Fr] S solo,pno CLASSV 2220 (024)

OFFRETS TIMME see Agopov, Vladimir

OFT DENKT' ICH SIE SIND NUR
    AUSGEGANGEN! see Mahler, Gustav

OFT IN THE STILLY NIGHT see Anonymous

OFUKUHAGAKI see Fujiwara, Michiyo

OFVITINN see Sveinsson, Atli Heimir

OG ANDINN MIG HREIF see Björnsson, Arni

OG DET VAR LITIN SMÅFUGL see Eggen,
    Arne

OG SE HUN KOM see Jordan, Sverre

OG SIG MIG, HVORFOR DU VIL FARE see
    Jordan, Sverre

OGAWA NO YUGURE see Abe, Komei

OGDON, WILBUR L. (1921-   )
    Awakening Of Sappho, The
        SSBarB soli,harp,pno,perc,vla,db,
        tubular bells, alto kalimba [30']
        APNM sc $12.75, pts rent   (025)

    By The Isar
        SA soli,fl,db [7'] APNM sc $3.75,
        pts $10.75   (026)

    Images, A Winter's Calendar
        S solo,fl,clar,trp/ob,pno,perc
        [10'] APNM sc $5.75, pts rent
        (027)

    Summer Images And Reflections
        S solo,fl,clar,trp,pno/perc [10']
        APNM sc $5.25, pts rent   (028)

    Three Songs *CC3U
        Bar solo,pno APNM sc $3.75, set
        $7.25   (029)

    Tombeau De Jean Cocteau, Un
        S solo,pno [8'] APNM sc $4.50, set
        $8.75   (030)

    Tombeau De Jean Cocteau III, Un
        S&narrator,ob/clar,pno,electronic
        tape, slides [12'] APNM sc $6.50,
        pts rent   (031)

    Two Ketchwa Songs *CC2U
        S solo,pno APNM sc $3.75, set $7.25
        (032)

OH BOAT, COME BACK TO ME see Beers,
    Jacques

OH! COLD WAS THE CLIMATE see Monro, J.

OH, GOD COME DOWN see Reuland, Jacques

OH! HEART OF MINE see Rachmaninoff,
    Sergey Vassilievich, Loneliness

OH, I ENTREAT THEE see Puccini,
    Giacomo, Turandot: Signore, Ascolta

OH, IF THOU WILT NOT GIVE THINE HEART
    see Mourant, Walter

OH! LAND ENTRANCING see Meyerbeer,
    Giacomo, Africana, L': O Paradiso

OH LLAMA DE AMOR VIVA see Block, Steven

OH LORD OF MYSTERIES see Weigl, [Mrs.]
    Vally

OH, LOVE DOTH MAKE THE DAY see Weigl,
    [Mrs.] Vally

OH MAIDEN, MY MAIDEN see Lehar, Franz

OH, MY BELOVED FATHER see Puccini,
    Giacomo, Gianni Schicchi: O Mio
    Babbino Caro

OH NACHT!... see Lolini, Ruggero

OH PROMISE ME see De Koven, (Henry
    Louis) Reginald

OH! QUAND JE DORS see Liszt, Franz

OH! RICHARD see Grétry, André Ernest
    Modeste

OH, SAY NOT WOMAN'S HEART IS BOUGHT see
    Mourant, Walter

OH! SI LES FLEURS AVAIENT DES YEUX see
    Massenet, Jules

OH, SO SANDY see Groven, Eivind, Å Så
    Rødblond

OH STAY see Rachmaninoff, Sergey
    Vassilievich

OH! STEER MY BARK TO ERIN'S ISLE see
    Nelson, Sidney

OH, WHAT GRIEF IS MINE see Glinka,
    Mikhail Ivanovich

OH, WHEN I WAS IN LOVE WITH YOU see
    Mourant, Walter

OHLASY DALAV see Kabelác, Miloslav

OHLSSON, SVEN-OLOF
    Kom Ett Brev, Det
        solo voice,pno NOTERIA 1870   (033)

OHNE KAPITALISTEN GEHT ES BESSER see
    Eisler, Hanns

OHRID, DER SEE see Ehlen, Margriet

ØIAN, JOHAN
    Nøtteliten And Nine Other Tunes For
        Children And Adults *CC10U
        (Hartmann) solo voice,pno NORSK
        NMO 9570 f.s.   (034)

OISEAU D'AUTREFOIS, L' see Matsumoto,
    Hinoharu

OISEAUX, LES see Francaix, Jean see
    Offenbach, Jacques, Tales Of
    Hoffmann: Doll Song

OJE CARULÌ see Costa

OJOS NEGROS see Salina

OJOS NUNCA TAN AMADOS see Rausch,
    Carlos

OKAASAN! see Itoh, Ohsuke

OKAJIMA, MASAOKI (1945-   )
    Kusazukiyo No Kotoba
        S solo,fl,pno [11'] JAPAN   (035)

OKATA NO see Matsudaira, Yori-Tsune

OKIYAMA, CHIKAKO (1944-   )
    Venice Sanka
        T/S solo,pno [4'] ONGAKU   (036)

OKKENHAUG, INGRID BURAN
    Jesus, Vår Herre
        see Tre Hovden-Salmar

    Jul
        see Tre Hovden-Salmar

    Mørket Omkring Oss
        see To Salmer

    Strå Sonings Ord
        see Tre Hovden-Salmar

    To Salmer
        solo voice,pno NOTON N-9318 f.s.
        contains: Mørket Omkring Oss; Vi
            Står Med Tomme Hender   (037)

    Tre Hovden-Salmar
        (Albertsen, Per Hjort) solo voice,
        pno NOTON N-9317 f.s.
        contains: Jesus, Vår Herre; Jul;
            Strå Sonings Ord   (038)

    Vi Står Med Tomme Hender
        see To Salmer

OKKENHAUG, PAUL (1908-1975)
    To Tormod-Stev (Two Norwegian Folk
        Songs) *CC2U
        solo voice,2.2.2.2. 4.2.1.0. timp,
        strings NORGE f.s.   (039)

OKUNAI-SAMA see Oyama, Junko

OKUTOMIRU see Matsudaira, Yori-Tsune

OLAFSSON, KJARTAN (1958-   )
    Mansongur
        S solo,pno [2'0"] ICELAND 049-012
        (040)

OLAN, DAVID
    After Great Pain
        S solo,electronic tape [10']
        AM.COMP.AL.   (041)

    Fauna
        S solo,db [8'] sc AM.COMP.AL.
        $13.35   (042)

    Three Poems Of Kenneth Rexroth
        S solo,clar/bass clar [7'] sc
        AM.COMP.AL. $5.00   (043)

OLAV KYRRE see Tveitt, Geirr

OLAVS FORTELLING see Eggen, Arne

OLAVS MONOLOG OG ARIE see Eggen, Arne

OLAV'S MONOLOGUE AND ARIA see Eggen,
    Arne, Olavs Monolog Og Arie

OLAV'S STORY see Eggen, Arne, Olavs
    Fortelling

OLD CHRISTMAS SONG, AN see Vidar,
    Jorunn

OLD EUROPEAN SONGS
    (Fromm) SOUTHERN B454   (044)

OLD HUNGARIAN SONGS, VOL. 2 *CCU
    solo voice,gtr BOOSEY EMB08864 f.s.
    (045)

OLD HUNGARIAN SONGS, VOL. 3 *CCU
    (Benk) solo voice,gtr BOOSEY EMB12429
    f.s.   (046)

OLD LOVE'S DOMAIN see Downes, Andrew

OLD MAN OF THE ISLES see Kirk

OLD MAN'S SONG, THE see Balakirev, Mily
    Alexeyevich

OLD MEG MERRILLIES see Beckwith, John

OLD MEN ADMIRING THEMSELVES IN THE
    WATER, THE see Haxton, Kenneth

OLD MOTHER HUBBARD see Jeffreys, John

OLD POEM see Copland, Aaron

OLD POEM, AN see Sigurbjörnsson,
    Thorkell

OLD SONG see Thorarinsson, Leifur

OLD SPANISH SONGS AND ROMANCES, VOL. 1
    *CCU
    solo voice,gtr BREITKOPF-W EB 8487
    f.s.   (047)

OLD SPANISH SONGS AND ROMANCES, VOL. 2
    *CCU
    solo voice,gtr BREITKOPF-W EB 8488
    f.s.   (048)

OLD SPANISH SONGS AND ROMANCES, VOL. 3
    *CCU
    solo voice,gtr BREITKOPF-W EB 8489
    f.s.   (049)

OLD TUNE, AN see Jordan, Sverre, Gammel
    Vise, En

O'LEARY, JANE (1946-   )
    I Sing The Wind Around
        S solo,fl,clar [2'] APNM sc $3.00,
        set $5.50   (050)

    Poem From A Three Year Old
        S solo,fl,clar [7'] APNM sc $3.75,
        set $6.75   (051)

    Prisoner, The
        Bar solo,horn,pno [3'] APNM sc
        $4.50, set $13.00   (052)

    Three Voices: Lightning, Peace, Grass
        S solo,ob,pno [9'] APNM sc $5.75,
        set $16.75   (053)

OLIMPIADE: IO VADO...DE PENSA AD
    ARISTEA see Leo, Leonardo (Ortensio
    Salvatore de)

OLIMPIADE: NÉ GIORNI TUOI FELICI see
    Pergolesi, Giovanni Battista

OLIVELLA
    Bajito Quisiera
        solo voice,pno BOIL B.1855   (054)

OLIVER, HAROLD (1942-   )
    Full Fathom Five
        S solo,fl/alto fl/pic,clar/basset
        horn,clar/bass clar,vln/vla,pno
        [17'] APNM sc $9.50, pts rent
        (055)

    Winter Settings
        high solo,pno [6'] APNM sc $3.50,
        set $6.75   (056)

OLIVER, STEPHEN (1950-1992)
    Exposition Of A Picture
        TBar soli,string quar NOVELLO f.s.
        (057)

OLIVERO, BETTY (1954-   )
    Eight Songs
        see Juego De Siempre

    Juego De Siempre
        "Eight Songs" female solo,fl,clar,
        harp,perc,vln,vla,vcl [29']
        ISR.MUS.INST. 6920R   (058)

OLIVEROS, PAULINE (1932-   )
    Lullaby For Daisy Pauline
        SMITH PUB   (059)

ÖLL BÖRN SOFA see Sveinsson, Atli
    Heimir

OLLIE MCGEE see Boldemann, Laci

OLSEN, OTTO
    Solefaldssang *Op.60
        "Song By The Sunset" solo voice,
        1.0.1.0. 0.1.1.0. perc,pno,
        harmonium,strings [4'] HANSEN-DEN
        f.s.   (060)

    Song By The Sunset
        see Solefaldssang

OLSEN, SPARRE (1903-1984)
    Bånsull *Op.3,No.2
        "Lullaby" solo voice,1.1.1.1.
        1.1.1.0. strings NORGE f.s.   (061)
        see Tri Aukrust-Songar, Op. 3

    Bånvise
        see Tre Sanger, Op. 26

    Beyond Time And Space
        see Gjennom Tid Og Rom

    Eg Undrast
        see Tre Sanger
        see Vill Guri

OLSEN, SPARRE (cont'd.)

Einleg
see Fire Solrenningsdikt, Op. 2

Einsleg *Op.11,No.3
"Lonely" solo voice,strings [3']
NORGE f.s. (062)

Fire Aukrust-Salmar, Op.4
solo voice,pno NORSK f.s.
contains: Harpespelaren; Laer
Meg; Morgen; Mot Dag (063)

Fire Solrenningsdikt, Op. 2
[Norw] solo voice,pno NORSK f.s.
contains: Einleg; Kvendelagnad;
Saele; Svik (064)

Fjell-Noreg *Op.3,No.1
"Mountain Norway" solo voice,
strings NORGE f.s. (065)

Fjell-Norig
see Tri Aukrust-Songar, Op. 3

Gjennom Tid Og Rom *Op.52,No.2
"Beyond Time And Space" solo voice,
2.2.2.2. 2.2.2.0. strings NORGE
f.s. (066)

Gjenta
see Tre Sanger
see Vill Guri

God Bless Norway
see Gud Signe Norigs Land

God Natt
see Tre Sanger, Op. 26

Gode Gjerninger, De *Op.52,No.9
"Good Deeds, The" solo voice,
2.2.2.2. 2.2.2.0. strings NORGE
f.s. (067)

Good Deeds, The
see Gode Gjerninger, De

Gud Signe Norigs Land
"God Bless Norway" solo voice,
1.1.2.1. 0.2.1.0. pno,strings
[2'] NORGE f.s. (068)

Harpespelaren
see Fire Aukrust-Salmar, Op.4

Her Gror Det Gylne Korn *Op.52,No.8
"Here Grows The Golden Grain" solo
voice,2.2.2.2. 2.2.2.0. strings
NORGE f.s. (069)

Here Grows The Golden Grain
see Her Gror Det Gylne Korn

I Denne Jord
[Norw] solo voice,pno NORSK (070)
[Norw] solo voice,org NORSK (071)

I Ville Heid
[Norw] solo voice,pno NORSK f.s.
contains: I Ville Heidi; Langt
Oppi Høgan Dalar; Som Vind På
Heidi (072)

I Ville Heidi
see I Ville Heid

Julesang
[Norw] solo voice,pno NORSK (073)

Kva Var Det?
see Tre Kjaerleikssongar, Op. 36
see Tri Kjaerleikssongar

Kveldssong
see To Sanger

Kveldssong - Kvile
[Norw] solo voice,pno LYCHE (074)
[Norw] solo voice,org LYCHE (075)

Kvendelagnad
see Fire Solrenningsdikt, Op. 2

Kvi Tralar Det Ikkje Lenger I Skogen
*Op.1,No.2
"Where Is The Song In The Forest"
solo voice,2.2.2.2. 0.1.1.1.
harp/pno,strings [3'] NORGE f.s.
(076)

Kvile
see To Sanger

Laer Meg
see Fire Aukrust-Salmar, Op.4

Langt Oppi Høgan Dalar
see I Ville Heid

Lonely
see Einsleg

Lullaby
see Bånsull

OLSEN, SPARRE (cont'd.)

Lullabye
see Voggsong

Malmfuru
solo voice,1.1.2.1. 0.1.1.0. timp,
pno,strings [2'] NORGE f.s. (077)

Morgen
see Fire Aukrust-Salmar, Op.4

Mot Dag
see Fire Aukrust-Salmar, Op.4

Mountain Norway
see Fjell-Noreg

Navigare Necesse Est *Op.52,No.16
solo voice,2.2.2.2. 2.2.2.0.
strings NORGE f.s. (078)

Norsk Kjaerleikssong
see Tre Kjaerleikssongar, Op. 36
see Tri Kjaerleikssongar

Norske Folkevisur Fra Gudbrandsdalen
[Norw/Eng] solo voice,pno NORSK
(079)

Saele
see Fire Solrenningsdikt, Op. 2

Såg Du Mitt Land
[Norw] solo voice,pno (text by
Halvor Floden) NORSK (080)

Seven Songs To Poems By Inge Krokann
see Sju Krokann-Songar

Sju Krokann-Songar *Op.28
"Seven Songs To Poems By Inge
Krokann" solo voice,2.2.2.2.
2.1.1.0. timp,strings [13']
MUSIKK f.s. (081)

So Lang Ei Tid
"Such A Long Time" solo voice,
1.1.2.1. 0.2.1.0. perc,pno,
strings [4'] NORGE f.s. (082)

Som Vind På Heidi
see I Ville Heid

Such A Long Time
see So Lang Ei Tid

Sunni Syng
see Tre Kjaerleikssongar, Op. 36
see Tri Kjaerleikssongar

Svik
see Fire Solrenningsdikt, Op. 2

Til Bergmannen
[Norw] solo voice,pno (text by
Anders Hovden) NORSK (083)

Til Min Gyllenlakk
see Tre Sanger, Op. 26

To Sanger
LYCHE 818 f.s.
contains: Kveldssong; Kvile (084)

Tre Kjaerleikssongar, Op. 36
[Norw] solo voice,pno NORSK f.s.
contains: Kva Var Det?; Norsk
Kjaerleikssong; Sunni Syng
(085)

Tre Sanger
LYCHE 603 f.s.
contains: Eg Undrast; Gjenta;
Vill-Guri (086)

Tre Sanger, Op. 26
[Norw] solo voice,pno MUSIKK f.s.
contains: Bånvise; God Natt; Til
Min Gyllenlakk (087)

Tri Aukrust-Songar, Op. 3
[Norw] solo voice,pno NORSK f.s.
contains: Bånsull; Fjell-Norig;
Vårblå Himmel I Mars (088)

Tri Kjaerleikssongar *Op.36
S solo,fl,ob,2clar,bsn,harp/pno,
strings NORGE f.s.
contains: Kva Var Det?; Norsk
Kjaerleikssong; Sunni Syng
(089)

Tvo Edda Kvad *Op.8, CC2U
[Norw] S solo,2.2.2.2. 1.1.0.0.
timp,strings NORSK f.s. (090)

Vårblå Himmel I Mars
see Tri Aukrust-Songar, Op. 3

Vill Guri
LYCHE f.s. contains also: Eg
Undrast; Gjenta (091)
see Tre Sanger

Voggsong *Op.1,No.1
"Lullabye" solo voice,2.1.2.0.
0.2.2.1. strings NORGE f.s. (092)

OLSEN, SPARRE (cont'd.)

Where Is The Song In The Forest
see Kvi Tralar Det Ikkje Lenger I
Skogen

OLSOKSALME see Karlsen, Kjell Mørk

OLTHUIS, KEES (1940-)
Music Calleth
Mez solo,ob,clar,bsn,vln,vla,vcl
[21'] DONEMUS (093)

OLTRA
Gráfico De La Petenera
solo voice,pno BOIL B.2679 (094)

OM FÖRTRÖSTAN see Gefors, Hans

OM KJAERLIGHET, OP. 77 see Karlsen,
Kjell Mørk

OM KVELDEN see Groven, Eivind

OM MIJN OUD WOONHUIS see Broekman, Hans

OMBRA FELICE see Mozart, Wolfgang
Amadeus

OMNIA VINCIT AMOR see Braal, Andries de

OMNIPHOBIE see Chini, Andre

OMOKAGE TO YOBARERU ONNA-OMOTE NI see
Oyama, Junko

OMTRENT DE LIEFDE see Braal, Andries de

ON BEGLIETT see Pablo, Luis de

ON BURROUGH'S WORK see Little, David

ON GEORGIAN HILLS see Rimsky-Korsakov,
Nikolai

ON HIMSELFE see Douw, Andre

ON MY LIPS EVERY KISS IS LIKE WINE see
Lehar, Franz

ON MY WEDDING DAY see Karpman, Laura

ON NE PASSE PAS see Vermeulen, Matthijs

ON SPRING ROADS see Nummi, Seppo,
Kevätteiltä

ON SUCH A NIGHT OF JUNE see Bon, Willem
Frederik

ON THE BEACH AT FONTANA see Keulen,
Geert van

ON THE EVE OF HIS EXECUTION see
Mourant, Walter

ON THE PROBLEMS OF THE HOUR see
Pluister, Simon

ON THE ROAD TO MANDALAY see Speaks,
Oley

ON THE WAY TO KEW see Foote, Arthur

ON THIS MOST VOLUPTUOUS NIGHT: FIVE
SONGS see Wyner, Yehudi

ON THREE OLD ENGLISH RHYMES see
Pleskow, Raoul

ON TWO ANCIENT TEXTS see Pleskow, Raoul

ON VOIT MOURIR see Escher, Rudolf
George

ON WINGS OF SONG see Mendelssohn-
Bartholdy, Felix

ONCE BY THE PACIFIC see Barati, George

ONDA, CHE MORMORA, L' see Benda, Georg
Anton (Jirí Antonín)

ONDE DRONNING, DEN see Barth, Frode

ONDERGANG VAN TENOCHTITLAN, DE see
Zelm, Jan van

ONE see Retzel, Frank

ONE FINE DAY see Puccini, Giacomo,
Madama Butterfly: Un Bel Di Vedremo

ONE HAND, ONE HEART see Bernstein,
Leonard

ONE HOUR AT EVERY ONE BREATH see
Hachimura, Yoshio

ONE HUNDRED FOURTEEN SONGS see Ives,
Charles

171ST CHORUS see Kitzke, Jerome P.

ONE STEP FORWARD AND TWO STEPS BACK see
Clarke, Henry Leland

ONLY THE COLD BARE MOON see Silsbee,
Ann

ONLY THE MOON REMEMBERS see Weigl,
[Mrs.] Vally

ONS GHENAKET see Weegenhuise, Johan

ONWEER see Maessen, Antoon

ONZE MELODIES see Pierne, Gabriel

OOK VANDAAG WEER see Ruiter, Wim de

OORVERDOVEND SAMENLEVEN see Dekker,
Dirk

OP EEN PRIESTERFEEST see Koop, Ol. see
Schaik, Johan Ant. Stephanus Van

OP, HVIS HERRENS EGEN RØST see
Kjeldaas, Arnljot

OPEN HOUSE see Bolcom, William Elden

OPERA AMERICAN STYLE: ARIAS FOR SOPRANO
(Walters, Richard) (CC11L) LEONARD-US
00660180   (095)

OPERA ARIAS see Handel, George Frideric

OPERA ARIAS: MEZZO-SOPRANO see Britten,
[Sir] Benjamin

OPERA ARIAS: SOPRANO I see Britten,
[Sir] Benjamin

OPERA ARIAS: SOPRANO II see Britten,
[Sir] Benjamin

OPERA EVENINGS, VOL. 1 (SOPRANO &
MEZZO-SOPRANO) *CCU
BOOSEY EMB03383 f.s.   (096)

OPERA EVENINGS, VOL. 2 (TENOR) *CCU
BOOSEY EMB03384 f.s.   (097)

OPERA EVENINGS, VOL. 3 (BARITONE &
BASS) *CCU
BOOSEY EMB03385 f.s.   (098)

OPERATIC ALBUM: BARITONE
RICORDI-IT LD110414 f.s.
   contains: Mozart, Wolfgang Amadeus,
   Don Giovanni: Deh Vieni Alla
   Finestra; Ponchielli, Amilcare,
   Gioconda, La: Pescator, Affonde
   Lesca; Rossini, Gioacchino,
   Barber Of Seville, The: Largo Al
   Factotum; Verdi, Giuseppe, Ballo
   In Maschera, Un: Eri Tu; Verdi,
   Giuseppe, Falstaff: Quand'ero
   Paggio; Wagner, Richard,
   Tannhäuser: O Du Mein Holder
   Abendstern   (099)

OPERATIC ALBUM: BASS
RICORDI-IT LD110415 f.s.
   contains: Bellini, Vincenzo,
   Sonnambula, La: Vi Ravviso;
   Gounod, Charles François, Faust:
   Le Veau D'or; Gounod, Charles
   François, Faust: Vous Qui Faites
   L'endormie; Halévy, Jacques,
   Juive, La: Si La Rigueur;
   Puccini, Giacomo, Boheme, La:
   Vecchia Zimarra; Verdi, Giuseppe,
   Don Carlos: Ella Giammai M'amo
                                   (0100)

OPERATIC ALBUM: CONTRALTO
RICORDI-IT LD110412 f.s.
   contains: Donizetti, Gaetano,
   Lucrezia Borgia: Il Segreto;
   Gluck, Christoph Willibald,
   Ritter von, Orfeo E Euridice: Che
   Faro Senza Euridice?; Gluck,
   Christoph Willibald, Ritter von,
   Paris And Helen: O Del Mio Dolce
   Ce Ardor; Handel, George
   Frideric, Rinaldo: Lascia Ch'io
   Pianga; Ponchielli, Amilcare,
   Gioconda, La: Voce Di Donna;
   Verdi, Giuseppe, Ballo In
   Maschera, Un: Re Dell'abisso
                                   (0101)

OPERATIC ALBUM: MEZZO-SOPRANO VOL. 1
RICORDI-IT LD110411 f.s.
   contains: Donizetti, Gaetano,
   Favorita, La: O Mio Fernando;
   Gounod, Charles François, Faust:
   Faites Lui Mes Aveux; Meyerbeer,
   Giacomo, Prophete, Le: Ah Mon
   Fils; Ponchielli, Amilcare,
   Gioconda, La: Stella Del Marinar;
   Puccini, Giacomo, Manon Lescaut:
   Sulla Vetta Tu Del Monte; Verdi,
   Giuseppe, Trovatore, Il: Stride
   La Vampa   (0102)

OPERATIC ALBUM: MEZZO-SOPRANO VOL. 2
RICORDI-IT LD112553 f.s.
   contains: Donizetti, Gaetano, Don
   Sebastiano: Terra Adorata;

Gounod, Charles François, Faust:
   Si Le Bonheur; Handel, George
   Frideric, Julius Caesar: Piangero
   Mio Sorte; Mozart, Wolfgang
   Amadeus, Nozze Di Figaro, Le: Voi
   Che Sapete; Verdi, Giuseppe,
   Trovatore, Il: Condotta Ell'era;
   Weber, Carl Maria von,
   Freischütz, Der: Kommt Ein
   Schlanker Bursch   (0103)

OPERATIC ALBUM: SOPRANO
RICORDI-IT LD110410 f.s.
   contains: Mascagni, Pietro, Iris:
   Un Di Ero Piccina; Mozart,
   Wolfgang Amadeus, Magic Flute,
   The: Ah! Lo So; Puccini, Giacomo,
   Tosca: Vissi d'Arte; Verdi,
   Giuseppe, Ballo In Maschera, Un:
   Saper Vorreste; Verdi, Giuseppe,
   Rigoletto: Caro Nome; Wagner,
   Richard, Lohengrin: Einsam In
   Trüben Tagen (Elsa's Dream)
                                   (0104)

OPERATIC ALBUM: TENOR VOL. 1
RICORDI-IT LD110413 f.s.
   contains: Donizetti, Gaetano,
   Elisir D'amore, L': Una Furtiva
   Lagrima; Gounod, Charles
   François, Faust: Salut, Demeure;
   Puccini, Giacomo, Boheme, La: Che
   Gelida Manina; Verdi, Giuseppe,
   Aida: Celeste Aida; Verdi,
   Giuseppe, Rigoletto: Questa O
   Quella; Wagner, Richard,
   Lohengrin: In Fernem Land   (0105)

OPERATIC ALBUM: TENOR VOL. 2
RICORDI-IT LD112554 f.s.
   contains: Donizetti, Gaetano, Don
   Pasquale: Com'e Gentil; Flotow,
   Friedrich von, Martha: M'appari
   Tutt'amor; Mascagni, Pietro,
   Iris: Apri Tua La Finestra;
   Puccini, Giacomo, Tosca: E
   Lucevan Le Stelle; Verdi,
   Giuseppe, Rigoletto: La Donna E
   Mobile; Wagner, Richard,
   Lohengrin: Mein Lieber Schwann
                                   (0106)

OPERATIC AND CHAMBER ENSEMBLES
(Righini; Penhorwood) SOUTHERN B489
                                   (0107)

OPERATIC DUETS (SOPRANO & MEZZO-
SOPRANO) *CCU
BOOSEY EMB13116 f.s.   (0108)

OPERN ARIEN FÜR SOPRAN, BAND 1
S solo,pno PETERS 9995A   (0109)

OPERN ARIEN FÜR SOPRAN, BAND 2
S solo,pno PETERS 9995B   (0110)

OPERN ARIEN FÜR SOPRAN, BAND 3
S solo,pno PETERS 9995C   (0111)

OPERNBALL, DER: IM CHAMBRE SÉPARÉE see
Heuberger, Richard

OPERNDUETTE FÜR 2 FRAUENSTIMMEN, BAND 1
(Martienssen) PETERS 3839A   (0112)

OPERNDUETTE FÜR 2 FRAUENSTIMMEN, BAND 2
(Martienssen) PETERS 3839B   (0113)

OPIENSKI, HENRYK (1870-1942)
Chant De La Mère
   solo voice,kbd HUGUENIN EB 112A
                                   (0114)

OPIUM-SMOKER, THE see Campbell-Tipton,
Louis

OPPO, FRANK (1935-   )
Silenzio
   A solo,ob,vln,vla,vcl EDI-PAN
   EP 7247   (0115)

OPPOSITES see Clarke, Henry Leland

OPSTIGNING MOD AKSEKI see Nielsen,
Svend

OPUS I see Larson, Martin

OR CHE NOTTE see Denza, Luigi

OR HOVS HALLAR see Grov, Magne

OR LIVSENS BOK see Grov, Magne

ORA CHE E VENUTA LA NOTTE see Lolini,
Ruggero

ORACLE II see Wernick, Richard F.

ORAEFI see Runolfsson, Karl Otto

ORAISON see Chausson, Ernest

ORAISON DOMINICALE, L' see Divorne,
Andre

ORANGE BOOK, THE see Gilbert, Janet

ORANGE-COLORED FLOWER see Asaoka,
Makiko

ORATIO D. ALCUINI IN NOCTE see King,
Harold C.

ORATORIO MENOR A SILVESTRE REVUELTAS DE
MEXICO see Becerra Schmidt, Gustavo

ØRBECK, ANNE MARIE (1911-   )
Beilere
   see Tre Sanger

Bjølleblom
   [Norw] solo voice,pno NORGE (0116)

Eg Hev Ei Jente
   see Tre Sanger (1954-55)

Eldslogan
   see Tre Sanger

Etter Ei Frostnatt
   see To Sanger

Flugsurr
   [Swed] solo voice,pno NORGE (0117)

Folkevise
   [Norw] solo voice,pno NORGE (0118)

Fra "Jonsoknatt"
   [Norw] solo voice,pno NORGE (0119)

Gjentebrilur
   see Tre Sanger

Gudsmodern
   [Swed] solo voice,pno NORGE (0120)

Hver Dag Er En Sjelden Gave
   [Norw] solo voice,pno NORGE (0121)

I Berget
   [Norw] solo voice,pno NORGE (0122)

I Kveldsdimma
   see To Sanger

Kveldar
   [Norw] solo voice,pno NORGE (0123)

Naere Ting, De
   [Norw] solo voice,pno NORGE (0124)

Salme Om Kunsten
   [Norw] solo voice,pno NORGE (0125)

Sne
   [Norw] solo voice,pno NORGE (0126)

So Rodde Dei Fjordan
   "Then They Rowed On The Fjord" solo
   voice,2.2.0.2. 2.0.0.0. perc,
   harp,strings [3'] NORGE f.s.
                                   (0127)
   see Tre Sanger (1954-55)

Sommergåte
   [Norw] solo voice,pno NORGE (0128)

Staresong
   [Norw] solo voice,pno NORGE (0129)

Then They Rowed On The Fjord
   see So Rodde Dei Fjordan

To Sanger
   solo voice,pno LYCHE 146 f.s.
   contains: Etter Ei Frostnatt; I
   Kveldsdimma   (0130)

Tre Sanger
   solo voice,pno NORSK f.s.
   contains: Beilere; Eldslogan;
   Gjentebrilur   (0131)

Tre Sanger (1954-55)
   [Norw] solo voice,pno NORGE f.s.
   contains: Eg Hev Ei Jente; So
   Rodde Dei Fjordan; Vill Guri
                                   (0132)

Vaggsong
   [Swed] solo voice,pno NORGE (0133)

Vill Guri
   see Tre Sanger (1954-55)

ORBON, JULIAN (1925-   )
Three Songs Of The King
   see Tres Cantigas Del Rey

Tres Cantigas Del Rey
   "Three Songs Of The King" S solo,
   hpsd,perc,2vln,vla,vcl [10'0"]
   PEER   (0134)

ORDET see Karlsen, Kjell Mørk see
Nystedt, Knut

ORDINAIRE DE LA MESSE see Meyer

ORDINARY THINGS see Le Siege, Annette

OREILLES D'ANE see Bunge, Sas

OREST AUF TAURIS see Schubert, Franz
(Peter)

ORFEO: CHE FARO see Gluck, Christoph
Willibald, Ritter von

ORFEO: CHE FARÒ SENZA EURIDICE see
Gluck, Christoph Willibald, Ritter
von

ORFEO: DEL MIO CORE see Haydn, [Franz]
Joseph

ORFEO ED EURIDICE: CHE FARÒ see Gluck,
Christoph Willibald, Ritter von

ORFEO ED EURIDICE: CHE FARO SENZA
EURIDICE? see Gluck, Christoph
Willibald, Ritter von

ORFEO: IL PENSIER STA NEGLI OGGETTI see
Haydn, [Franz] Joseph

ORFF, CARL (1895-1982)
Early Songs *CC14U
solo voice,pno SCHOTT STO7024
$12.95   (0135)

ORGIA, L' see Rossini, Gioacchino

ORIGINAL SIN, THE see Proctor, Simon

ORLAND, HENRY (1918-   )
Begegnung
solo voice,pno SEESAW f.s.   (0136)

Colloque Sentimental
S/T solo,pno SEESAW f.s.   (0137)

Drei Lieder
solo voice,pno SEESAW f.s.   (0138)

Elegy
high solo,pno SEESAW f.s.   (0139)

Love And Pity
S solo,clar,vla SEESAW f.s. (0140)

Reve
solo voice,pno SEESAW f.s.   (0141)

Six Occasional Songs *CC6U
solo voice,pno SEESAW f.s.   (0142)

Two Ballads *CC2U
low solo,pno SEESAW f.s.   (0143)

ORMVISA see Wiren, Dag Ivar

ØRNELAND see Hall, Pauline

OROSZ, FRANCIS
Mignon In Musik
solo voice,pno SCIEN 1251   (0144)

OROYSON NOSTRE-DAME, L' see Slothouwer,
Jochem

ORPHÉE see Clérambault, Louis-Nicolas
see Lombardi, Daniele

ORPHELINE DU TYROL, L' see Rossini,
Gioacchino

ORPHEUS see Haxton, Kenneth

ORPHEUS TIMES LIGHT see Serebrier, Jose

ORPHEUS WITH HIS LUTE see Bunge, Sas
see Chilcot, Thomas see Sullivan,
[Sir] Arthur Seymour see Vaughan
Williams, Ralph

ORR, BUXTON
Ballad Of Mr. And Mrs. Discobbolos,
The
T solo,pno KUNZEL GM 213   (0145)

Many Kinds Of Yes *song cycle
SA soli,pno KUNZEL GM 214   (0146)

ORREGO-SALAS, JUAN A. (1919-   )
Canciones In Popular Style, Op. 80
S solo,gtr MMB X815001   (0147)

Psalms, Op. 74
Bar solo,pno (text from Psalms 5,
24, 25, 33, 143) MMB X814004
(0148)

ORTHEL, LEON (1905-1985)
Adieu, Clown
see Vier Liederen, Op. 64

Annonce
see Vijf Liederen, Op. 94

Chanson D'Automne
see Herfst, Op. 87

Dame Seule
see Vijf Liederen, Op. 94

ORTHEL, LEON (cont'd.)
De Profundis
see Vier Liederen, Op. 64

Dessin D'un Maitre Inconnu
see Martyre, Une

Drie Liederen, Op. 55
med solo,pno DONEMUS f.s. [10']
contains: Gesang Der Frauen An
Den Dichter; Pieta; Wenn Die
Uhren So Nah   (0149)

Eenzaam Sterven
see Vier Liederen, Op. 86

Eind Van De Dag, Het
see Vier Liedjes, Op. 75

Einde, Het
see Vier Liedjes, Op. 75

Gesang Der Frauen An Den Dichter
see Drie Liederen, Op. 55

Herbst
see Herfst, Op. 87

Herfst, Op. 87
S solo,pno DONEMUS f.s. [5']
contains: Chanson D'Automne;
Herbst   (0150)

Herfstweer
see Klein Drieluik, Op. 77

Juffertje In Het Groen, Het
see Vier Liederen, Op. 64

Kind, Das
see Twee Liederen, Op. 53

Klein Drieluik, Op. 77
Bar solo,pno DONEMUS f.s. [4']
contains: Herfstweer; Moderne
Slaven; Recept   (0151)

Knabe, Der
see Twee Liederen, Op. 54

König Von Münster, Der
see Twee Liederen, Op. 53

Kreuzigung
see Twee Liederen, Op. 54

Martyre, Une *Op.71
"Dessin D'un Maitre Inconnu" high
solo,pno [11'] DONEMUS   (0152)

Moderne Slaven
see Klein Drieluik, Op. 77

Nachtegalen, De
see Vier Liedjes, Op. 75

Pharao's Minne
see Vier Liederen, Op. 86

Pieta
see Drie Liederen, Op. 55

Recept
see Klein Drieluik, Op. 77

Rondeau
see Vier Liedjes, Op. 75

Schlangenbeschwörung
see Twee Liederen, Op. 56

Twee Liederen, Op. 53
S solo,pno DONEMUS f.s. [3']
contains: Kind, Das; König Von
Münster, Der   (0153)

Twee Liederen, Op. 54
Bar solo,pno DONEMUS f.s. [4']
contains: Knabe, Der; Kreuzigung
(0154)

Twee Liederen, Op. 56
B/Bar solo,pno DONEMUS f.s. [5']
contains: Schlangenbeschwörung;
Versuchung, Die   (0155)

Vagebond, De
see Vijf Liederen, Op. 94

Versuchung, Die
see Twee Liederen, Op. 56

Vier Liederen, Op. 64
high solo,pno/clar DONEMUS f.s.
[8']
contains: Adieu, Clown; De
Profundis; Juffertje In Het
Groen, Het   (0156)

Vier Liederen, Op. 86
S solo,pno DONEMUS f.s. [10']
contains: Eenzaam Sterven;
Pharao's Minne; Voor Tineke;
Waterleelie, De   (0157)

ORTHEL, LEON (cont'd.)
Vier Liedjes, Op. 75
Bar solo,pno DONEMUS f.s. [4']
contains: Eind Van De Dag, Het;
Einde, Het; Nachtegalen, De;
Rondeau   (0158)

Vijf Liederen, Op. 94
Bar solo,pno DONEMUS f.s. [6']
contains: Annonce; Dame Seule;
Vagebond, De; Voor De Verre
Prinses; Voorpost, De   (0159)

Voor De Verre Prinses
see Vijf Liederen, Op. 94

Voor Tineke
see Vier Liederen, Op. 86

Voorpost, De
see Vijf Liederen, Op. 94

Waterleelie, De
see Vier Liederen, Op. 86

Wenn Die Uhren So Nah
see Drie Liederen, Op. 55

ORTIZ, WILLIAM
A Cappella
3 male soli&female solo,acap [5']
sc AM.COMP.AL. $1.55   (0160)

Cantares: La Tierra Prometida
SBar soli,ob,horn,vla,perc,pno
[15'] sc AM.COMP.AL. $11.40
(0161)

Canto:28 De Septiembre
S solo,pno [7'] sc AM.COMP.AL.
$3.85   (0162)

Ciclo De Canciones Llorens Torres
T solo,pno [7'] sc AM.COMP.AL.
$7.70   (0163)

Ix Poemas Zen
[Span] ST soli,fl,gtr [15']
AM.COMP.AL. sc $15.20, pts $50.95
(0164)

Pero Aun, Mas Te Quiero
T/S solo,pno [6'] sc AM.COMP.AL.
$3.85   (0165)

Three Songs From El Barrio *CC3U
Bar solo,pno sc AM.COMP.AL. $3.50
(0166)

OSAWA, KAZUKO (1926-   )
Cosmos Donned Lane, The
Mez solo,pno [4'] ONGAKU   (0167)

Time, Stay Awhile
Mez solo,pno [4'] ONGAKU   (0168)

OSORIO SWAAB, REINE COLAÇO
see COLAÇO OSORIO-SWAAB, REINE

OSSUARIUM see Ruiter, Wim de

ÖSTERBERG, SVEN (1933-   )
Flyktingar Våra Syskon
solo voice,pno NOTERIA 1873 (0169)

Tonernas Rike
solo voice,pno NOTERIA 1866 (0170)

ØSTERN, PER HROAR
Ni Ti Kykelipi
[Norw] solo voice,pno MUSIKK (0171)

OT IDU JA SLOBODOIU see Shut, Wasyl

OTAZKA BEZ ODPOVEDI see Barton, Hanus

OTELLO: AVE MARIA see Verdi, Giuseppe

OTELLO: CREDO IN UN DIO CRUDEL see
Verdi, Giuseppe

OTELLO: SALCE see Verdi, Giuseppe

OTHELLO: WILLOW SONG see Rossini,
Gioacchino

OTHER HEARTS see Weigl, [Mrs.] Vally

OTHER SUMMERS see Weigl, [Mrs.] Vally

OTO, HANA see Suzuki, Hideaki

OTTAR SVARTE'S SONG IN PRAISE OF KING
OLAV see Backer-Lunde, Johan

OTTE STEENSEN-SANGE see Kongsted,Ole

OTTEN, LUDWIG (1924-   )
Ode
S solo,3trom,bass trom [7'] DONEMUS
(0172)

Pavane-Galliarde
see Weerklank

Wandellied
see Weerklank

OTTEN, LUDWIG (cont'd.)

Weerklank
S solo,3trom,bass trom DONEMUS f.s.
[9']
contains: Pavane-Galliarde;
Wandellied   (O173)

OTTO FRAMMENTI see Clementi, Aldo

OÙ PEUT-ON ÊTRE MIEUX see Grétry, André
Ernest Modeste

OUD HOLLANDSCHE MINNELIEDEREN see
Pijper, Willem

OUR LOVE IS PRECIOUS see Young

OUR SHARE OF NIGHT see Galante, Carlo

OUT FROM THE WIDE WORLD see Knutsen,
Torbjørn, Ute Fra Verden Den Vide

OUT IN THE FIELDS see Dawson, William
Levi

OUT OF "TAME XENIAS" see Reiner, Karel

OUT OF THE WHIRLWIND (VICTIMS AND
SURVIVORS OF THE HOLOCAUST) see
Adolphe, Bruce

OUT, OUT, THAT IS NORSEMEN'S YEARNING
see Eggen, Arne, Ut, Ja Ut, Det Var
Nordmanns Traa

OUTDOOR SHADOWS see Leisner, David

OUTING, AN see Goldberg, William

OUTING TO THE MOUNTAINS see Saudek,
Vojtech

OUTSIDE THE FRAME see Le Siege, Annette

OUVRE TES YEUX BLEUS see Massenet,
Jules

OVER DEN EENZAMEN VIJVER see Pijper,
Willem

OVER HET GRAS see Weegenhuise, Johan

ÖVERGE MIG ALDRIG see Rooth, Anna-Greta

OVERSETTELSE TIL ET BARN see Bibalo,
Antonio

OVERTOCHT, DE see Regt, Hendrik de

OWENS
Chosen
med solo,pno SHAWNEE 5084   (O174)

OWENS, ROBERT (1925-   )
Fields Of Wonder *CC11U
T solo,strings ORLANDO f.s. (O175)

Heart On The Wall *CC5U
S solo,1.1.2.1. 3.3.0.0. strings
ORLANDO f.s.   (O176)

OWL, THE see Revueltas, Silvestre,
Tecolote, El

OWL AND THE PUSSYCAT see Somers, Harry
Stewart

OY, NA HORI ZHYTO see Shut, Wasyl

OYAMA, JUNKO (1954-   )
Okunai-Sama (from Legends Of Tono)
S/T solo,pno [3'] JAPAN   (O177)

Omokage To Yobareru Onna-Omote Ni
T/S solo,pno, shino, nokan [10']
JAPAN   (O178)

Two Pieces On The Fantasy In An Old
Capital
T/S solo,perc,pno, shino, nokan
[16'] JAPAN   (O179)

ØYEBLIKKSBILDER, OP. 146, NO. 3 see
Fongaard, Bjørn

OYENS, TERA DE MARZ
see MAREZ OYENS, TERA DE

OYSTER CATCHER'S SONG, THE see
Kirkwood, Antoinette

OZAKI, TOSHIYUKI (1946-   )
Kaseki
S solo,pno, shakuhachi [16'] JAPAN
                             (O180)

OZEANE IN ZERSTREUUNG see Geelen,
Mathieu

OZYMANDIAS see Bales, Richard Horner

P

PÅ BLUSSUVOLLEN see Albertsen, Per
Hjort

PÅ BOTNEN AV ALT see Søderlind, Ragnar

PÅ FJELLET see Kjerulf, Halfdan

PÅ HAUKELI ALLE INNE see Tveitt, Geirr

PÅ HOSPITALET OM NATTEN see Groven,
Eivind

PÅ KANNARHAUGENE see Fladmoe, Arvid

PA KNE FRAMFOR GUD see Egge, Klaus

PÅ VÅLÅSJØEN see Baden, Conrad

PAA HVAELVET see Tveitt, Geirr

PABLO, LUIS DE (1930-   )
Cantata Perdida, Una
solo voice,2inst ZERBONI 8930 (P1)

Cuatro Canciones De Ibn Gabirol
Bar solo,4inst ZERBONI 9511   (P2)

Dos Poemas De Juan Larrea
S solo,10inst ZERBONI 9609   (P3)

Ederki
S solo,2inst ZERBONI 8441   (P4)

Fuegos, Los
S solo,11inst ZERBONI 9613   (P5)

Malinche
solo voice,pno ZERBONI 9590   (P6)

Manantial, El
S solo,6inst ZERBONI 9085   (P7)

On Begliett
solo voice,trom ZERBONI 9620 (P8)

Surcar Vemos
S solo ZERBONI 9587   (P9)

Visto De Cerca
3 male soli ZERBONI 7912   (P10)

PACCIONE, PAUL (1952-   )
Forms In Change
S solo,fl,alto fl,clar,trp,trom,
tuba,vln,vla,db,pno [10']
AM.COMP.AL. sc $12.25, pts $16.90
                             (P11)

PACE! see Giuliani, Vittorio

PACKER, RANDALL
Ariel Settings
T solo,2vln,vla,vcl [10']
AM.COMP.AL. sc $7.60, pts $3.80
                             (P12)

Barbare
T solo,ob,2perc,harp,pno [15'] sc
AM.COMP.AL. $7.70   (P13)

Moon And The Yew Tree, The
Mez solo,alto fl,vla,pno [10']
AM.COMP.AL. sc $10.30, pts $11.10
                             (P14)

Phrases
high solo,pno [22'] sc AM.COMP.AL.
$9.15   (P15)

PADEREWSKI, IGNACE JAN (1860-1941)
Amour Fatal, L' *Op.22,No.11
[Fr] med solo,pno CLASSV 1100 (P16)

Ciel Est Trés Bas, Le *Op.22,No.3
[Fr] med solo,pno CLASSV 1092 (P17)

Cloître Haut, Le *Op.22,No.7
[Fr] med solo,pno CLASSV 1096 (P18)

Dans La Forêt *Op.22,No.1
[Fr] med solo,pno CLASSV 1090 (P19)

Douze Mélodies, Op. 22
med solo,pno CLASSV 1692   (P20)

Elle Marche D'un Pas Distrait
*Op.22,No.6
[Fr] med solo,pno CLASSV 1095 (P21)

Ennemie, L' *Op.22,No.12
[Fr] med solo,pno CLASSV 1101 (P22)

Jeune Pâtre, Un *Op.22,No.5
[Fr] med solo,pno CLASSV 1094 (P23)

Lune Froide *Op.22,No.9
[Fr] med solo,pno CLASSV 1098 (P24)

Naguère *Op.22,No.4
[Fr] med solo,pno CLASSV 1093 (P25)

PADEREWSKI, IGNACE JAN (cont'd.)

Querelleuse *Op.22,No.10
[Fr] med solo,pno CLASSV 1099 (P26)

Ton Coeur Est D'Or Pur *Op.22,No.2
[Fr] med solo,pno CLASSV 1091 (P27)

Viduité *Op.22,No.8
[Fr] med solo,pno CLASSV 1097 (P28)

PADUA see Frid, Geza

PAESAGGIO I see Kaneko, Atsuo

PAESIELLO, GIOVANNI (1741-1816)
Quando Lo Stral Spezzai
SS soli,pno BOIL B.1763   (P29)

PAGES FROM A SUMMER JOURNAL see
Steiner, Gitta Hana

PAGLIACCI: O COLUMBINA see Leoncavallo,
Ruggiero

PAGLIACCI: PROLOGUE "SI PUÒ?" see
Leoncavallo, Ruggiero

PAGLIACCI: QUAL FIAMMA see Leoncavallo,
Ruggiero

PAGLIACCI: VESTI LA GIUBBA see
Leoncavallo, Ruggiero

PAIR OF SANDALS, A see Stutschevsky,
Joachim

PAISAJE CON DOS TUMBAS Y UN PERRO
ASIRIO see Gilbert, Janet

PAISIELLO, GIOVANNI (1740-1816)
Idolo Cinese, L'
(Tintori, G.) solo voice,pno CURCI
10623   (P30)

PAJARITO, EL see Rodriguez Peris,
Martin Jose

PALADILHE, EMILE (1844-1926)
Bois, Les
med-high solo,pno CLASSV 1916 (P31)

Mélodies, Vol. 2
solo voice,pno CLASSV C050   (P32)

Mélodies, Vol. 3
solo voice,pno CLASSV C051   (P33)

Psyché
high solo,pno CLASSV 0495   (P34)
med-high solo,pno CLASSV 0494 (P35)

PÁLENÍCEK, JOSEF (1914-1991)
Quetzal Coatl
ABar soli,4.3.3.3. 4.3.3.1. timp,
perc,xylo,vibra,harp,cel,pno,
marimba,strings [34'] CESKY HUD.
                             (P36)

PALESTER, ROMAN (1907-   )
Three Poems By Czeslaw Milosz
see Trzy Wiersze Czeslawa Milosza

Trzy Wiersze Czeslawa Milosza
"Three Poems By Czeslaw Milosz"
[Polish/Eng] S solo,harp,pno,cel,
4vln,3vla,2vcl [14'-15'] sc,pno
red POLSKIE   (P37)

PALIMPSEST see Ehlen, Margriet

PALIMPSESTE see Ehlen, Margriet

PALIMPSESTEN see Ehlen, Margriet

PALINURUS see Winslow, Walter

PALLASZ, EDWARD (1936-   )
Homo Viator And Other Sacred Songs
see Homo Viator I Inne Sakralne
Piosenki

Homo Viator I Inne Sakralne Piosenki
"Homo Viator And Other Sacred
Songs" [Polish] solo voice,pno
POLSKIE   (P38)

PALMER, GEOFFREY MOLYNUEX (1882-1957)
James Joyce's Chamber Music: The Lost
Song Settings
(Russel, Myra Teicher) INDIANA
0-253-34994-X   (P39)

PALOMINO, J.
Canción Picaresca
(Subira, Jose) solo voice,pno BOIL
B.1174 f.s. contains also:
Anonymous, Canción De Cuna;
Laserna, Blas de, Seguidillas
Majas   (P40)

PALSSON, HELGI (1899-1964)
Ferdavisur
solo voice,pno ICELAND 008-005
                             (P41)

PALSSON, HELGI (cont'd.)

Horfi Eg Ur Hafi
solo voice,pno ICELAND 008-009
(P42)

Hreidrid Mitt
solo voice,pno ICELAND 008-010
(P43)

Kom Blida Tid, Med Barnsins Frid
solo voice,pno ICELAND 008-012
(P44)

Söngur I Regni
solo voice,pno ICELAND 008-011
(P45)

Vorblaer
solo voice,pno ICELAND 008-007
(P46)

PALSSON, PALL P. (1928-   )
Aus Einem Kinderliederbuch
S solo,horn ICELAND 020-059   (P47)

I Guds Fridi
S solo,horn ICELAND 020-058   (P48)

Three Love Songs
solo voice,pno [6'20"] ICELAND
020-030   (P49)

Ut
solo voice,pno ICELAND 020-063
(P50)

PAN TRAUERT UM SYRINX see Marx, Joseph

PANCAKE TUESDAY see Carter, Andrew

PANCHO VILLA see Zuidam, Rob

PANIS ANGELICUS see Franck, Cesar

PANKEY
Volkslieder Neger
PETERS 5208   (P51)

PANNI, MARCELLO (1940-   )
Canzonette A Tre Voci
S solo,fl/clar,vcl/vla/vcl EDI-PAN
EP 7236   (P52)

Petit Septuor
solo voice,clar,trp,trom,perc,vln,
gtr EDI-PAN EP 7207   (P53)

Tre Haiku
S solo,fl,alto fl,clar,soprano clar
in E flat,vln,gtr EDI-PAN EP 7315
(P54)

PAÑO, EL see Folklore Andalusia

PANOFKA, HEINRICH (1807-1887)
Tarantella
coloratura sop,pno CLASSV 0969
(P55)

PANTOMIMA see Giani Luporini, Gaetano

PAPAGEI, DER see Loewe, Carl Gottfried

PAPALLONA ARGENTADA, LA see Borras De
Palau

PAPILLON, LE see Fourdrain, Felix

PAPPUS OF A DANDELION, THE see Ichiba,
Kosuke

PAR UNE BELLE NUIT! see Gounod, Charles
François

PARA see Nieland, Henk

PARA MI LA GUERRA EMPEZO CUANDO NACI
see Zuidam, Rob

PARADIES, PIETRO DOMENICO (PARADISI)
(1707-1791)
M'ha Preso Alla Sua Ragna
solo voice,pno BOIL B.1704   (P56)

PARADISE OF CATS see Arima, Reiko

PARADISE REGAINED see Masseus, Jan

PARADISO TERRESTRE, IL see Feigin, Joel

PARANOIA see Anderson, Beth

PARAY, PAUL (1886-1979)
Trois Mélodies
high solo,pno CLASSV 1472   (P57)

PARCHMAN, GEN LOUIS (1929-   )
Conclusion
S solo,orch SEESAW f.s.   (P58)

Cycle Of Novelties
S solo,pno SEESAW f.s.   (P59)

PARESSEUSE, LA see Beers, Jacques

PARISOTTI
Se Tu M'ami
solo voice,pno CLASSV 0624   (P60)

PARK, JAMES
Quiet Goodbyes: Two Songs *CC2U
med solo,pno sc AM.COMP.AL. $3.85
(P61)

Schuyler's "Song"
Mez solo,pno [4'30"] AM.COMP.AL.
(P62)

PARKE, DOROTHY
Falling Of The Leaves, The
solo voice,pno [2'30"] (med diff)
ROBERTON 1050   (P63)

Wish, The
solo voice,pno [2'] ROBERTON 1069
(P64)

PARKER, HORATIO WILLIAM (1863-1919)
Seven Songs, Op. 70
high solo (poems of Brian Hooker)
RECITAL 194   (P65)
low solo (poems of Brian Hooker)
RECITAL 195   (P66)

PARKYNS, B.
Portrait, Le
med-high solo,pno CLASSV 1919 (P67)

PARLA L'AVI, CANCÓ see Sole, Ll. Ma.

PARLA! "NON MI GUARDAR COSÍ" see Tosti,
Francesco Paolo

PARMENTIER, F. GORDON
Four Sonnets From The Portuguese
*CC4U
S/T solo,2.2.2.0. 2.2.2.0. timp,
harp,perc,strings sc AM.COMP.AL.
rent   (P68)

PARODIES see Barab

PAROLE, LE see Boogman, Willem

PAROLES DE MARIE A SON FILS XIII see
Jolivet, Andre

PARRIS, ROBERT (1924-   )
Cynthias Revells: Three Songs *CC3U
B solo,pno sc AM.COMP.AL. $5.40
(P69)

Dreams
S solo,fl,ob,vcl,db,pno,cel,4perc
[13'] APNM sc $11.25, pts rent
(P70)

Synthias Revells: Three Songs *CC3U
Bar solo,gtr sc AM.COMP.AL. $7.70
(P71)

Three Love Songs *CC3U
B solo,pno sc AM.COMP.AL. $5.40
(P72)

PARRY, [SIR] CHARLES HUBERT HASTINGS
(1848-1918)
[Four] English Lyrics (First Set)
RECITAL 301   (P73)

[Five] English Lyrics (Second Set)
RECITAL 302   (P74)

[Six] English Lyrics (Third Set)
RECITAL 303   (P75)

[Six] English Lyrics (Fourth Set)
RECITAL 304   (P76)

[Seven] English Lyrics (Fifth Set)
RECITAL 305   (P77)

[Six] English Lyrics (Sixth Set)
RECITAL 306   (P78)

[Six] English Lyrics (Seventh Set)
RECITAL 307   (P79)

[Six] English Lyrics (Eighth Set)
RECITAL 308   (P80)

[Seven] English Lyrics (Ninth Set)
RECITAL 309   (P81)

PARRY, JUN
Musical Wife, The
SCIEN 1268   (P82)

PARSIFAL: MEIN VATER see Wagner,
Richard

PÄRT, ARVO (1935-   )
Stabat Mater
SAT soli,vln,vla,vcl UNIVER. sc
UE 19053, pts UE 19053 A-D (P83)

PARTENZA, LA see Rossini, Gioacchino

PARTI, L'IDOLO MIO see Handel, George
Frideric

PARTIDA, LA: SIERRAS DE GRANADA see
Alvarez

PARTY IS OVER, THE see Sigfusson,
Steingrimur

PAS D'ARMES DU ROI JEAN, LE see Saint-
Saëns, Camille

PAS VU CA see Tal, Marjo

PASATIERI, THOMAS (1945-   )
Alleluia *Xmas
solo voice,pno/harp/orch (med)
PRESSER 111-40131   (P84)

Day Of Love *song cycle
SCHIRM.G ED3076   (P85)

Sieben Lehmannlieder
solo voice,pno (diff) PRESSER
411-41091   (P86)

Three Sonnets From The Portuguese
SCHIRM.G ED3431   (P87)

Windsongs
S solo,pno (cc81) SCHIRM.G 50488937
(P88)

PASK 1968 see Forsell, Jonas

PASQUALI
Twelve English Songs (1750)
sc KING'S   (P89)

PASSAGE see Tisne, Antoine

PASSAGES see Rinehart, John see
Zwilich, Ellen Taaffe

PASSEGGIATA see Pizzetti, Ildebrando

PASSEZ! PASSEZ TOUJOURS! see Franck,
Cesar

PASSI CHE CONOSCO E TEMO see Lolini,
Ruggero

PASSIO JESU CHRISTI see Soler, Josep

PASSION NACH MATTHÄUS see Quack, Erhard

PASSION SPENT, OP. 46, NO. 5 see
Tchaikovsky, Piotr Ilyich

PASTORAL DE VANO see Mestres, Apeles

PASTORAL SYMPHONY, A see Rawsthorne,
Alan

PASTORALE see Beilschmidt see Bizet,
Georges see Jonsson, Thorarinn see
Saint-Saëns, Camille

PASTORALE FRA SOMMERMESSE see
Albertsen, Per Hjort

PASTORALE POUR JEANNETTE see Badings,
Henk

PASTORALE (VOCALISE) see Stravinsky,
Igor

PASTORELLA see Aufschnaiter, Benedikt
Anton

PASTORELLA, LA see Schubert, Franz
(Peter)

PASTORELLA, LA: ODIA LA see Rossini,
Gioacchino

PASTORELLA AL PRATO, LA see Schubert,
Franz (Peter), Pastorella, La

PASTORELLA DELLE ALPI, LA see Rossini,
Gioacchino

PASTORELLA IN G see Michalicka, Jan,
Pastorelle Boemiche

PASTORELLA: LAUFET IHR HIRTEN see
Aufschnaiter, Benedikt Anton

PASTORELLE BOEMICHE see Michalicka, Jan

PASTORES MECUM OMNES VENITE ADOREMUS
see Galuppi, Baldassare

PASTORI, I see Pizzetti, Ildebrando

PATER NOSTER see Krall, Johann see
Vranken, Alph.

PATHOLOGIE see Vliet, Henk van der

PATIENCE see Straesser, Joep

PATRIA LONTANA see Zandonai, Riccardo

PATRON, DAS MACHT DER WIND see Bach,
Johann Sebastian

PATTERNS see Kelly, Robert T.

PAUER, JIRÍ (1919-   )
Chtel Bysem Napsat Ti Psani
male solo,2.2.3.2. 2.2.2.1. timp,
perc,xylo,harp,strings [16']
CESKY HUD.   (P90)

Pisen O Lasce
male solo,2.2.2.2. 2.0.0.0. perc,
harp,cel,strings [14'] CESKY HUD.
(P91)

PAULET, V.
Ballade Des Pendus
solo voice,clar in A,string quar,
pno [16'] BILLAUDOT   (P92)

PAUME (VERGERS VII) see King, Harold C.

PAUV' PETIT, LE see Massenet, Jules

PAUV' PITI' MAMZELL' ZIZI see Beers,
Jacques

PAUVRE PIERROT see Sourisse, Brigitte

PAVANE see Madsen, Trygve

PAVANE-GALLIARDE see Otten, Ludwig

PAVANE, OP. 50 see Faure, Gabriel-
Urbain

PAVANNE see Leniado-Chira, Joseph

PAVOTS, LES see Lekeu, Guillaume

PAYSAGE see Matthews, William

PEACE see Groven, Eivind, Fred see
Schoonenbeek, Kees

PEACE, MY HEART see Weigl, [Mrs.] Vally

PEACE OF CHRIST, THE see Dillard,
Donald E.

PEACE TO see Mascagni, Pietro

PEACH FLOWERS see Hekster, Walter

PECCHÉ?
high solo,pno CLASSV 1312   (P93)
med solo,pno CLASSV 1906   (P94)

PÊCHEUR DE CREVETTES see Sourisse,
Brigitte

PÊCHEURS DE PEARLS, LES: C'EST TOI see
Bizet, Georges

PÊCHEURS DE PEARLS, LES: JE CROIS
ENTENDRE see Bizet, Georges

PÊCHEURS DE PEARLS, LES: L'ORAGE S'EST
CALMÉ see Bizet, Georges

PÊCHEURS DE PEARLS, LES: ME VOILÀ
SEULE..COMME AUTREFOIS see Bizet,
Georges

PÊCHEURS DE PEARLS, LES: O DIEU BRAHMA
see Bizet, Georges

PÊCHEURS DE PEARLS, LES: SÉRÉNADE see
Bizet, Georges

PEHRSON, JOSEPH RALPH (1950-   )
Confessions Of Goliards
T solo,fl,vln,vcl SEESAW   (P95)

PEINADO, ANGEL
Mensajes Del Evangelio
solo voice,org ALPUERTO 1685 (P96)

PEINE D'AMOUR see Delibes, Léo

PELLÉAS: LES CHEVEUX (ACT 3) see
Debussy, Claude

PENNY FOR A SONG, A see LeFanu, Nicola

PENNYCANDYSTORE, THE see Blank, Allan

PENSAMIENTO RARO see Lopez Artiga,
Angeles

PENSÉE D'AUTOMNE see Massenet, Jules

PENSIEROSO, IL: SWEETBIRD see Handel,
George Frideric

PENSIVE TRAVELLER, THE see Crockett,
Donald

PEOPLE OF THE DAWN see Bainbridge,
Simon

PER PIETÀ, NON RICERCATE see Mozart,
Wolfgang Amadeus

PERCH'IO see Gianotti, Roberto

PERDECK, RUDOLF (1925-   )
Erinnerung An Holland
see Herinnering Aan Holland

Herinnering Aan Holland
"Erinnerung An Holland" low solo,
pno [4'] DONEMUS   (P97)

PERDER, KJELL (1954-   )
Flexica
5 solo voices,orch [12'] sc STIM
PA-3273-20 f.s.   (P98)

PEREGRINA V. see Marx, Joseph

PERERA
Sleep Now
BOOSEY VAB0301   (P99)

PERFECT DAY, A see Bond, Carrie Jacobs

PERGOLESI, GIOVANNI BATTISTA
(1710-1736)
Confusa, Smarrita
[It/Ger] Mez solo,pno CLASSV 1920
                            (P100)

Maestro Di Musica: Bella Mia
B solo,pno CLASSV 1562   (P101)

Olimpiade: Né Giorni Tuoi Felici
BOIL B.1764   (P102)

Salve Regina
A solo,strings KUNZEL 10093A (P103)

Se Tu M'ami
solo voice,pno BOIL B.1722 (P104)

Siciliana
A solo,pno SCIEN 1273   (P105)

Stabat Mater
SA soli,string orch KUNZEL 10173A
                            (P106)
(Rosler, G.) [Lat] SA soli,string
orch,cont pno red POLSKIE   (P107)

Tre Giorni Son Che Nina
solo voice,pno BOIL B.1703 (P108)
A solo SCIEN 1275   (P109)

PERICHOLE, LA: AH! QUE LES HOMMES SONT
BETES see Offenbach, Jacques

PÉRICHOLE, LA: AH! QUEL DINER see
Offenbach, Jacques

PÉRICHOLE, LA: O MON CHER AMANT see
Offenbach, Jacques

PERICHOLE, LA: TU N'ES PAS BEAU see
Offenbach, Jacques

PERKINS
Daddy And Me
solo voice,pno SOUTHERN V075 (P110)

PERLE, GEORGE (1915-   )
Two Rilke Songs *CC2U
solo voice,pno sc BOELKE-BOM $8.00
                            (P111)

PERLE DU BRÉSIL, LA: CHARMANT OISEAU
see David, Félicien-César

PERLONGO, DANIEL JAMES (1942-   )
Six Songs *CC6U
S solo,pno sc AM.COMP.AL. $6.90
                            (P112)

PERMONT, HAIM (1950-   )
And He, Underneath Us Flows, Slowly
see Return To The South, A

Come Closer, My Horse
see Return To The South, A

Return To The South, A
Mez/A solo,pno pno red
ISR.MUS.INST. 6872B f.s.
contains: And He, Underneath Us
Flows, Slowly; Come Closer, My
Horse; We Came To The Sand
                            (P113)

We Came To The Sand
see Return To The South, A

PERNETTE SE LÈVE, LA see Tailleferre,
Germaine

PERO AUN, MAS TE QUIERO see Ortiz,
William

PERS VUGGEVISE see Kjeldaas, Arnljot

PERSIAN SONG FROM THE RUBÁIYÁT OF OMAR
KHAYYÁM see Foote, Arthur

PERSUASIONS see Wilson, Richard
(Edward)

PERTI, GIACOMO ANTONIO (1661-1756)
Io Son Zitella
S solo,pno BOIL B.1727   (P114)

Notte Illuminata, La *cant
B solo,strings fac ed FORNI 496
                            (P115)

PERUGIA, NICCOLO DA
Eleven Ballate
(Kelly, Stephen) 2 solo voices
ANTICO AE26   (P116)

Five Madrigals And A Caccia
(Kelly, Stephen) 2-3 solo voices
ANTICO AE28   (P117)

PESCADOR, EL see Schubert, Franz
(Peter)

PESSARD, EMILE-LOUIS-FORTUNE
(1843-1917)
Six Melodies
[Fr] med solo RECITAL 283   (P118)

Vingt Mélodies
high solo,pno CLASSV C059   (P119)

PESTALOZZA, A. (1851-1934)
Ciribiribin
female solo&male solo,pno CLASSV
1299   (P120)

PET LYRICKYCH PISNI see Gemrot, Jiri

PETER'S DENIAL see Johnson, A. Paul

PETERSON-BERGER, (OLOF) WILHELM
(1867-1942)
Marits Visor *Op.12
(Sköld, Sven) solo voice,2.1.2.2.
1.0.0.0. strings,pno LUNDQUIST
3005   (P121)

Tre Sånger, Op. 3
high solo,pno CLASSV 0941   (P122)

Ur Fridolins Visor
solo voice,pno LUNDQUIST 0531
                            (P123)

PETIT, JEAN ARMAND (1886-1973)
Reves Et Realites
solo voice,2.2.2.2. 4.3.2.1. perc,
strings [17'] pno red,sc,pts
BILLAUDOT   (P124)

PETIT FOURS see Corigliano, John

PETIT GARCON, LE see Smit Sibinga, Theo
H.

PETIT JEU see Souris, Andre

PETIT MORT POUR RIRE see Escher, Rudolf
George

PETIT POISSON ROUGE, UN see Smit
Sibinga, Theo H.

PETIT SEPTUOR see Panni, Marcello

PETITE ANNE, LA see Anonymous

PETITE FLEUR, LA see Smit Sibinga, Theo
H.

PETITGIRARD, ALAIN (1940-   )
Grand Yacht Despair, Le *cant
BarB soli,2.2.2.2. 2.2.2.1. 3perc,
timp,harp,cel,strings BILLAUDOT
                            (P125)

PETITS POËMES JAPONAIS see
Santoliquido, Francesco

PETRELLA, ERRICO (1813-1877)
Jone: O Jone! O Di Quest' Anima
T solo,pno CLASSV 2011   (P126)

Marco Visconti: Rondinella Pellegrina
A solo,pno CLASSV 0939   (P127)

PETRZELKA, VILÉM (1889-1967)
Zivly *Op.7, song cycle
Bar solo,3.3.3.3. 4.3.3.1. timp,
perc,harp,strings [12'] CESKY
HUD.   (P128)

PETZOLD, RUDOLF (1908-   )
Lieder
KAHNT 5650   (P129)

PEYTON, MALCOLM C. (1932-   )
Songs From Walt Whitman *CCU
S/Mez solo,pno,vln APNM sc $7.50,
set $15.00   (P130)

PEZZATI, ROMANO (1939-   )
Aura
solo voice,rec,gtr,orch ZERBONI
9337   (P131)

Einerlei
S solo,7inst ZERBONI 8826   (P132)

Recordare III
SATB soli,9inst ZERBONI 8539 (P133)

PFAUTSCH, LLOYD ALVIN (1921-   )
Six Songs
low solo LAWSON 4-52582   (P134)
high solo LAWSON 4-52583   (P135)

Solos For The Church Soloist
low solo,pno LAWSON 4-877   (P136)

PFIFFIGE, DER see Baumann, Alexander

PFIFFNER, ERNST (1910-   )
Kantate Über Die Weltzeit
Bar solo,perc,pno PAN f.s. (P137)

PFISTER
Saisons Du Coeur, Les
solo voice,pno,vln CLASSV 2185
                            (P138)

PFITZNER, HANS (1869-1949)
Sonst *Op.15,No.4
high solo,pno (text by Eichendorff)
CLASSV 0740   (P139)
med-low solo,pno (text by
Eichendorff) CLASSV 0816   (P140)

PFLAUMENBAUM, DER see Delnooz, Henri

PHANTASIE see Louis Ferdinand, Prince
Of Prussia

PHARAO'S MINNE see Orthel, Leon

PHILÉMON ET BAUCIS: AH! SI JE
REDEVENAIS see Gounod, Charles
François

PHILÉMON ET BAUCIS: AU BRUIT DES LOURDS
see Gounod, Charles François

PHILÉMON ET BAUCIS: QUE LES SONGES
HEUREUX see Gounod, Charles
François

PHILIPPE, PIERRE
Fille Qui Chante, La
S solo,2.2.2.2. 2.0.0.0. perc,pno,
strings [1'45"] pno red,sc,pts
BILLAUDOT   (P141)

PHILIPS, PETER (1561-1628)
Fifteen Motets For Solo Voice And
Continuo
(Pike, Lionel) solo voice,cont
ANTICO AB1   (P142)

PHILLIPS, BURRILL (1907-1988)
Letters From Italy Hill
S solo,fl,clar,string quar,pno
[21'] sc,pts FALLEN LEAF $30.00
                               (P143)

Song In A Winter Night
med solo,pno [6'] sc FALLEN LEAF
$12.00   (P144)

PHILLIPS, JOHN C. (1921-   )
Young Jesus Sweit
high solo,acap RAMSEY BR0008 (P145)

PHILOCTET see Schubert, Franz (Peter)

PHILOMELE see Diabelli, Anton

PHILOMELE, EINE SAMMLUNG see Diabelli,
Anton

PHILOSOPHES RÊVEURS see Saint-Saëns,
Camille, Chanson À Boire Du Vieux
Temps

PHILOSOPHIE DER LIEBE see Selmer, Johan
Peter

PHOENIX, THE see Pickard, John

PHRASES see Packer, Randall

PIACER D'AMOR see Martini, Jean Paul
Egide (Schwarzendorf)

PIANTO ANTICO see Casella, Alfredo

PIANTO DELLE PIE DONNE, IL see
Sammartini, Giovanni Battista

PICCOLA CANTATA DEL VENERDI SANTO see
Napoli, Jacopo

PICCOLO OMAGGIO A DALLAPICCOLA see
Vescovo, Italo

PICKARD, JOHN
Phoenix, The
S solo,pno BARDIC BE0316   (P146)

PICKING WATER CHESTNUTS see Hekster,
Walter

PICTURES FROM BRUEGHEL see Luedeke,
Raymond

PIE JESU see Faure, Gabriel-Urbain see
Smeets, Leo

PIE JESUS see Faure, Gabriel-Urbain

PIÈCE EN FORME DE HABANERA see Ravel,
Maurice

PIÈCE FAUSSE see Halmrast, Tor

PIÈCE FAUSSEN see Halmrast, Tor

PIEDRA NEGRA see Krieger, Armando

PIEMONTESISCHES VOLKSLIED see Marx,
Joseph

PIEPER, RENE (1955-   )
Auf Ein Wenig Wasser
see Fünf Japanische Gedichte

Blätter Sind In Grosser Virwirrung,
Die
see Fünf Japanische Gedichte

PIEPER, RENE (cont'd.)

Da Ich Vor Ihr Auf Ewig Schied
see Fünf Japanische Gedichte

Earth And The Rose, The
S solo,woodwind quin,pno,vln,vla,
vcl,db DONEMUS f.s. [9']
contains: Futility; North
Labrador; Sea Rose   (P147)

Fünf Japanische Gedichte
S solo,fl,bass clar,4perc,2vln,vla,
2vcl DONEMUS f.s. [12']
contains: Auf Ein Wenig Wasser;
Blätter Sind In Grosser
Virwirrung, Die; Da Ich Vor Ihr
Auf Ewig Schied; Kühl Ist Die
Brise; Sieh, Den Herbst   (P148)

Futility
see Earth And The Rose, The

Kühl Ist Die Brise
see Fünf Japanische Gedichte

North Labrador
see Earth And The Rose, The

Sea Rose
see Earth And The Rose, The

Sieh, Den Herbst
see Fünf Japanische Gedichte

PIERNE, GABRIEL (1863-1937)
Onze Melodies
[Fr] high solo RECITAL 284   (P149)

PIERROT DANDY see Marx, Joseph

PIERROT LIEDER see Harris, Donald

PIERROT PENDU see Bijvanck, Henk

PIESNE NASICH PRIATEL'OV
3 solo voices,acord PANTON 854 (P150)

PIESNI see Bacewicz, Grazyna see
Szymanowski, Karol

PIETA see Orthel, Leon see Søderlind,
Ragnar

PIJPER, WILLEM (1894-1947)
Acht Oud Hollandsche Liederen, Deel 2
*CC8L
med solo,pno DONEMUS f.s.   (P151)

Ich Liege Dir Zu Füssen
see Vier Liederen Uit 1912-'13

Nacht
see Vier Liederen Uit 1912-'13

Oud Hollandsche Minneliederen *CC9L
med solo,pno DONEMUS f.s.   (P152)

Over Den Eenzamen Vijver
see Vier Liederen Uit 1912-'13

Spinnerin, Die
see Vier Liederen Uit 1912-'13

Vier Liederen Uit 1912-'13
high solo,pno DONEMUS f.s.
contains: Ich Liege Dir Zu
Füssen; Nacht; Over Den
Eenzamen Vijver; Spinnerin, Die
                               (P153)

PIKE, LIONEL (1939-   )
Maxims Of Saint Teresa *song cycle
S solo,pno [40'] LYNWD   (P154)

Pilgrim Way, The *song cycle
Mez solo,pno [40'] LYNWD   (P155)

PIKEN I ALVEDANSEN see Bakke, Ruth

PIKET, FREDERICK (1903-1974)
T'filah
med solo,kbd TRANSCON. 981227
                               (P156)

This Is My God
high solo,kbd TRANSCON. 981228
                               (P157)

PIL OG BUE see Jordan, Sverre

PILEN - SKRIVET PÅ VANDRING EN TIDIG
VÅRDAG see Danielsson, Harry

PILGRIM' SONG see Tchaikovsky, Piotr
Ilyich

PILGRIM UND DER ALPENJÄGER, DER see
Schubert, Franz (Peter)

PILGRIM WAY, THE see Pike, Lionel

PINCK, LOUIS
Zwölf Lothringer Volkslieder (from
Verklingenden Weisen)
med solo,pno SCIEN 1280   (P158)

PINES SONGS see Asia, Daniel

PINKHAM, DANIEL (1923-   )
In Grato Jubilo
S solo,fl,ob,clar,bsn,horn,3trp,
2trom,db [33'] sc AM.COMP.AL.
rent   (P159)

PINNOCHIO see Vea, Ketil

PIPER, THE see Mourant, Walter

PIQUE DAME: HERMAN'S ARIOSO see
Tchaikovsky, Piotr Ilyich

PIQUE DAME: HERMAN'S CONFESSION see
Tchaikovsky, Piotr Ilyich

PIQUE DAME: LISA'S ARIA see
Tchaikovsky, Piotr Ilyich

PIQUE DAME: PAULINE'S ROMANCE see
Tchaikovsky, Piotr Ilyich

PIQUE DAME: PRINCE YELETSKY'S ARIA (ACT
2) see Tchaikovsky, Piotr Ilyich

PIRATE DREAMS (LULLABY) see Huerter,
Charles

PIRATE STORY: A CHILD'S GARDEN OF
VERSES see Homer, Sidney

PIRATES OF PENZANCE see Sullivan, [Sir]
Arthur Seymour

PIRATES OF PENZANCE: POOR WANDERING ONE
see Sullivan, [Sir] Arthur Seymour

PIRKEI TEHILLIM see Flender, Reinhard
David

PISEN O LASCE see Pauer, Jirí

PISEN RYBARU see Beethoven, Ludwig van

PISK, PAUL AMADEUS (1893-1990)
Three Songs *CC3U
S solo,string quar AM.COMP.AL. sc
$6.85, pts $11.40   (P160)

PISNE see Hruška, J.

PISNE CITOVE A ZERTOVNE see Kubicka,
Miroslav

PISNE NA INDIANSKE MOTIVY see Bohác,
Josef

PISNIA see Shut, Wasyl

PISNIA PRO POLTAVU see Shut, Wasyl

PISNICKY K SITI see Vackár, Dalibor
Cyril

PISNICKY O LASCE see Hula, Zdenek

PISNICKY O LASCE 2 see Hula, Zdenek

PITCHIPOI, THE CHILDEN OF DRANCY see
Ultan, Lloyd

...PIU SOPRA LE STELLE... see Solbiati,
Alessandro

PIZZETTI, ILDEBRANDO (1880-1968)
Cinque Liriche
see Clefta Prigione, Il
see Madre Al Figlio Lontano, La
see Passeggiata
see Pastori, I
see San Basilio

Clefta Prigione, Il
[It] med solo,pno CLASSV 1434 from
CINQUE LIRICHE   (P161)

Madre Al Figlio Lontano, La
[It] high solo,pno CLASSV 1921 from
CINQUE LIRICHE   (P162)

Passeggiata
[It] high solo,pno CLASSV 1435 from
CINQUE LIRICHE   (P163)

Pastori, I
[It] high solo,pno CLASSV 1436 from
CINQUE LIRICHE   (P164)

San Basilio
[It] high solo,pno CLASSV 1922 from
CINQUE LIRICHE   (P165)

PLA, J. MA.
Cancons De Bressol
solo voice,pno BOIL B.2665 (P166)

PLA, M.
Seguidillas Religiosas
see Valledor, Jacinto, Canción
Timida

PLACE FOR MARY TO LIE, A see Reilly,
Dadee

PLACIDO DOMINGO'S VIENNA, CITY OF MY
  DREAMS *CCU
  GLOCKEN GL00140 f.s.   (P167)

PLAETNER, JØRGEN (1930-   )
  New Hymns
    see Nye Salmer

  Nye Salmer
    "New Hymns" solo voice,pno
    SAMFUNDET   (P168)

PLAGGE, WOLFGANG (1960-   )
  Dance *Op.62
    solo voice,tamb,vln,vla,trp NORGE
                                        (P169)
    solo voice,vln,vla,trp,tamb [2']
    NORGE   (P170)

  Ibsen Songs, Op. 35a
    [Norw] Bar solo,pno (texts by
      Henrik Ibsen) NORGE   (P171)

  Innskrifter, Op. 31
    [Norw] [10'] (text by O. Aukrust)
    NORGE   (P172)

  Psalm No. 12 *Op.40
    [Lat] S&speaking voice,vln,acord,
      org [15'] NORGE   (P173)

  Sólarljód: Solsanger Fra Norrøn
      Middelalder *Op.68
    [Norw] solo voice,pno [24'] NORGE
                                        (P174)
  Sólarljöö *Op.68
    "Solsanger Fra Norrøn Middelalder"
    S solo,pno [24'] (text by Ivar
      Orgland) NORGE   (P175)

  Solsanger Fra Norrøn Middelalder
    see Sólarljöö

  Vesaas-Sanger, Op. 35b
    [Norw] Bar solo,pno (text by Tarjei
      Vesaas) NORGE   (P176)

PLAISIR D'AMOUR see Martini, Jean Paul
  Egide (Schwarzendorf)

PLAISIRS DU CHANT, VOL. 1, LES *CCU
  (Bonnardot) med solo (easy) LEMOINE
  f.s.   (P177)

PLAISIRS DU CHANT, VOL. 2, LES *CCU
  (Bonnardot) med solo (easy) LEMOINE
  f.s.   (P178)

PLANAS, A.
  Dale De Betún
    solo voice,pno BOIL B.0895 (P179)

PLANCHART, ALEJANDRO (1935-   )
  Five Poems Of James Joyce
    high solo,pno MMB S814003   (P180)

PLANT A TREE see Sveinsson, Atli Heimir

PLANTATION MOOD see King, Reginald

PLANTE, DANIEL
  Love In The Asylum
    S solo,fl/alto fl,ob d'amore,cel,
      hpsd,3harp,3perc,2vla,vcl [7']
      APNM sc $15.00, voc sc $4.00, pts
      rent   (P181)

  Three Lullabies *CC3U
    Bar solo,pno APNM sc $4.50, set
    $8.75   (P182)

  Two Songs *CC2U
    Bar solo,alto fl/clar,lute,gtr/harp
    APNM sc $4.00, set $11.50   (P183)

PLATE, ANTON (1950-   )
  Sting, The
    S solo,2clar,horn,trp,perc,tape
      recorder,pno,strings without vcl
      [15'] MOECK 5332   (P184)

PLAU, ARILD (1920-   )
  Jeg Syns Jeg Selv Må Stråle
    [Norw] solo voice,pno NORGE (P185)
    [Norw] solo voice,pno (text by
      Vilhelm Krag) NORGE   (P186)

  Mitt Hjerte
    [Norw] solo voice,pno NORGE (P187)
    [Norw] solo voice,pno (text by Jens
      Bjørneboe) NORGE   (P188)

PLAYER QUEEN, THE see Carpenter, John
  Alden

PLAYTHINGS OF THE WIND see Weigl,
  [Mrs.] Vally

PLEGARIA see Beethoven, Ludwig van

PLESKOW, RAOUL (1931-   )
  Chamber Setting With Voice
    solo voice,fl,vln,vcl [10']
    AM.COMP.AL.   (P189)

PLESKOW, RAOUL (cont'd.)
  Lyric And Lament
    T solo,pno [6'] sc AM.COMP.AL.
    $4.25   (P190)

  Of Rome, Parting And Spring
    S solo,fl,vcl,pno,vibra/clar/vln
      [10'] AM.COMP.AL. sc $10.70, pts
      $11.10   (P191)

  On Three Old English Rhymes
    med solo,pno [6'] sc AM.COMP.AL.
    $5.40   (P192)
    med solo,fl,clar,vcl,pno [6']
      AM.COMP.AL. sc $9.15, pts $13.80,
      pno red $5.40   (P193)

  On Two Ancient Texts
    S solo,fl,clar,vcl,pno [10']
      AM.COMP.AL. sc $9.15, pts $23.00
                                        (P194)

  Psalm Setting
    med solo,pno [3'] sc AM.COMP.AL.
    $4.60   (P195)

  Six Brief Verses
    SS soli,pno [8'] sc AM.COMP.AL.
    $11.40   (P196)

  Three Early Songs
    S solo,pno [6'] AM.COMP.AL. (P197)

  Villanelle, Dirge And Song
    high solo,pno [10'] sc AM.COMP.AL.
    $10.70   (P198)
    high solo,3.2.2.2. 2.2.0.0. pno,
      strings [10'] sc AM.COMP.AL.
      $25.10   (P199)

PLETYKAZO ASSZONYOK see Nieland, Henk

PLEURS D'OR see Faure, Gabriel-Urbain

PLEUVAIT, IL see Massenet, Jules

PLEYEL, IGNACE JOSEPH (1757-1831)
  Twelve Elegant Ballads (1750)
    sc KING'S   (P200)

PLING OG PJORT see Albertsen, Per Hjort

PLOEGER, DE see Broekman, Hans

PLOG, ANTHONY (1947-   )
  Animal Ditties
    narrator,2trp,pno BRASS PRESS
    715643 $8.00   (P201)

PLOUGHMAN'S LIFE, THE see Reuland,
  Jacques

PLÖVGIA see Flothuis, Marius

PLOWSHARES see Clarke, Henry Leland

PLOYHAR, JAMES D., EDITOR
  Testimonials To Liberty
    narrator,inst (gr. III) BELWIN
    BD 00750 $50.00   (P202)

PLUISTER, SIMON (1913-   )
  Five Brown Songs
    S solo,fl,alto sax,pno DONEMUS f.s.
      [11']
    contains: Fly And I, The; My
      Dinosaur; On The Problems Of
      The Hour; Song Within, The;
      Winter's Rose, A   (P203)

  Fly And I, The
    see Five Brown Songs

  My Dinosaur
    see Five Brown Songs

  On The Problems Of The Hour
    see Five Brown Songs

  Song Within, The
    see Five Brown Songs

  Winter's Rose, A
    see Five Brown Songs

PLUPART DU TEMPS II see Jolas, Betsy

PLUS VITE see Massenet, Jules

PLUVO see Schipper, Dirk

PLYSTREVISE see Taubo, Lillian Gulowna

POBRE DIVINO, EL see Beethoven, Ludwig
  van

PODÉŠT, LUDVÍK (1921-1968)
  Divoky Chmel
    Bar solo,pno PANTON 936   (P204)

  Kazdodenni Male Pisne *song cycle
    solo voice,pno PANTON 937   (P205)

POEM see Heilner, Irwin see Sveinsson,
  Atli Heimir

POEM BY HÖLDERLIN, A see Godøy, Rolf
  Inge

POEM FOR SOPRANO AND FOUR INSTRUMENTS
  see Hellermann, William

POEM FROM A THREE YEAR OLD see O'Leary,
  Jane

POEM IN OCTOBER see Corigliano, John

POEM RECITED IN THE NIGHT see Shibata,
  Minao

POEM TO MICHAEL, JOHN AND ALLISON see
  Anderson, Beth

POEMA see Ponjee, Ted

POEMA DE ESPERANZA see Ponjee, Ted

POEMA O CESKOMORAVSKE VYSOCINE see
  Hlavacek, Libor

POÈME D'AMOUR see Massenet, Jules

POEME D'AMOUR, OP. 54 see Dupont,
  Auguste

POÈME D'AVRIL see Massenet, Jules

POÈME DE MAI see Coedes

POÈME D'HIVER see Massenet, Jules

POEME DISCONTINU see Regteren Altena,
  Lucas van

POÈME D'OCTOBRE see Massenet, Jules

POEME DU JUILLET see Matsudaira, Yori-
  Tsune

POÈME DU REGRET see Hüe, Georges-
  Adolphe

POÈME DU SILENCE (1ST SET) see Moret,
  Ernest

POÈME DU SILENCE (2ND SET) see Moret,
  Ernest

POÈME DU SOUVENIR see Massenet, Jules

POÈME D'UN JOUR, OP.21 see Faure,
  Gabriel-Urbain

POÈME D'UN SOIR see Massenet, Jules

POÈME LYRIQUE see Chen, Qigang

POÈME LYRIQUE II see Chen, Qigang

POÈME PASTORAL see Massenet, Jules

POEMES D'AUTOMNE see Bloch, Ernest

POEMES D'AUTOMNE see Dupont, Gabriel

POEMES DE LA PLEIADE #1 see Leguerney,
  Jacques

POEMES DE LA PLEIADE #2 see Leguerney,
  Jacques

POEMES POUR L'ENFANT
  S solo,woodwinds,trp,harp,pno,strings
    (diff) BILLAUDOT   (P206)
  see Jolivet, Andre

POEMMA see Mestres-Quadreny, Josep
  Maria

POEMS FROM THE JAPANESE II see Stout,
  Alan

POESIA A MI PATRIA see Ponjee, Ted

POESIE DU SOIR, LA see Bunge, Sas

POET, THE see Tal, Marjo

POET IN NEW YORK [1] see MacBride,
  David Huston

POET IN NEW YORK [2] see MacBride,
  David Huston

POETA, DE see Radulescu, Michael

POÈTE MOURANT, LE see Meyerbeer,
  Giacomo

POILUS DE L'ARGONNE, LES see
  Diepenbrock, Alphons

POISON TREE, A see Wernick, Richard F.

POLDERLAND see Masseus, Jan

POLDOWSKI, [LADY] DEAN PAUL (1880-1932)
  Attente, L'
    [Fr] med solo,pno (text by
      Verlaine) CLASSV 1926   (P207)

POLDOWSKI, [LADY] DEAN PAUL (cont'd.)

Cythère
[Fr] med solo,pno (text by
Verlaine) CLASSV 1923 (P208)

Effet De Neige
[Fr] med solo,pno (text by
Verlaine) CLASSV 1924 (P209)

Fantoches
[Fr] med solo,pno (text by
Verlaine) CLASSV 1925 (P210)

Nocturne (Des Cantilènes)
[Fr] high solo,pno CLASSV 1927 (P211)

Spleen
[Fr] med solo,pno (text by
Verlaine) CLASSV 1928 (P212)

POLE STAR see Slothouwer, Jochem

POLIN, CLAIRE (1926-)
No-Rai
S solo,fl,db SEESAW f.s. (P213)

POLISH SONGBOOK *CCU
solo voice HANSEN-US HANO397 $5.95 (P214)

POLITISCHE LIEDER
PETERS 5301 (P215)

POLIUTO: DI TUA BELTADE IMMAGINE see
Donizetti, Gaetano

POLIUTO: D'UN' ALMA TROPPO FERVIDA see
Donizetti, Gaetano

POLL I LA PUSSA, EL see Mestres, Apeles

POLLOCK, ROBERT EMIL (1946-)
Chamber Setting No. 1
Bar solo,ob,clar,bsn,vln,vla,vcl
[8'] APNM sc $5.00, pts $3.50,
voc sc $3.50 (P216)

Chamber Setting No. 2
narrator,5perc [20'] APNM sc
$11.25, pts rent (P217)

Descent, The
S solo,fl,pno [5'] APNM sc $5.50,
set $14.25 (P218)

Mass In Salt Air
S solo,pno [4'] APNM sc $3.75, set
$7.25 (P219)

Small Song
S solo,pno [2'] APNM sc $3.25, set
$6.25 (P220)

Song
S solo,fl,clar [2'] APNM sc $3.50,
set $9.25 (P221)

Song Cycle *song cycle
S solo,pno [16'] APNM sc $8.75, set
$17.00 (P222)

Three Knots
S solo,pno [8'] APNM sc $5.50, set
$10.50 (P223)

Tumbling Hair
A solo,alto fl,bass clar,pno [2']
APNM sc $3.25, set $11.50 (P224)

POLOLÁNÍK, ZDENEK (1935-)
Proglas
S solo,horn,perc,hpsd,strings [17']
CESKY HUD. (P225)

POLYEUCTE: NYMPHES ATTENTIVES see
Gounod, Charles François

POLYEUCTE: SOURCE DÉLICIEUSE see
Gounod, Charles François

POLYMETRES: SIX LIEDER SUR DES POÊMES
DE JEAN-PAUL see Sauguet, Henri

POMES PENYEACH see Rebel, Meeuwis

POMMIERS, LES see Sourisse, Brigitte

PONCHIELLI, AMILCARE (1834-1886)
Ah! Suicide
see Gioconda, La: Suicidio

Figliuol Prodigo, Il: Pace, Gran Dio
T solo,pno CLASSV 0926 (P226)

Gioconda, La: Ah! Pescator
Bar solo,pno CLASSV 1634 (P227)

Gioconda, La: Cielo E Mar!
T solo,pno CLASSV 1529 (P228)

Gioconda, La: Ombre Di Mia Prosapia
B solo,pno CLASSV 1554 (P229)

Gioconda, La: Suicidio
S solo,pno CLASSV 0461 (P230)
"Ah! Suicide" S solo RICORDI-IT

PONCHIELLI, AMILCARE (cont'd.)

LD117330 (P231)

Gioconda, La: Voce Di Donna
Mez solo,pno CLASSV 1590 (P232)

Lina: Tu Che Volasti
T solo,pno CLASSV 0918 (P233)

POND IN A BOWL, THE (5 SONGS) see
Lessard, John Ayres

PONJEE, TED (1953-)
Cinco Poemas
S solo,3clar,bass clar DONEMUS f.s.
[17']
contains: Elegia De Un Soldado
Vivo; Poema; Poema De
Esperanza; Poesia A Mi Patria;
Zorzal, El (P234)

Elegia De Un Soldado Vivo
see Cinco Poemas

Poema
see Cinco Poemas

Poema De Esperanza
see Cinco Poemas

Poesia A Mi Patria
see Cinco Poemas

Zorzal, El
see Cinco Poemas

POPE, CONRAD (1951-)
...Through The Silence
S solo,pno [16'] APNM sc $11.75,
set $23.00 (P235)

Wanderers Nachtlied
S solo,clar,pno [3'] APNM sc $3.00,
set $8.50 (P236)

POPULAR BALLADS FOR CLASSICAL SINGERS
(Walters, Richard) high solo,pno
(CC10L) LEONARD-US 00660204 accomp
tape available (P237)
(Walters, Richard) low solo,pno
(CC10L) LEONARD-US 00660205 accomp
tape available (P238)

POPULAR NURSERY RHYMES *CCU
solo voice ALLANS $5.50 (P239)

POPULAR SONG ALBUM see Nakada, Yoshinao

POPULAR SONGS OF NINETEENTH-CENTURY
AMERICA *CC64U
(Jackson, Richard) solo voice BELWIN
BKD001518 $9.95 (P240)

PORRO, MAURO
Cantico Della Vigna, Il
S solo,fl,ob,clar,bsn,horn,2vln,
vla,vcl,db EDI-PAN EP 7789 (P241)

PORTAMENTO see Dresden, Sem

PORTER
By My Side *Marriage
solo voice,kbd,opt gtr GIA G-3357 (P242)

PORTO, NINO
Stella Polare
solo voice,pno EDI-PAN EP 7305 (P243)

PORTRAIT, LE see Parkyns, B.

PORTRAIT NO. 2 see Cohen, Edward

PORTRAITS see Hobson, Bruce

PORTRAITS [1] see Locklair, Dan Steven

PORTRAITS [2] see Locklair, Dan Steven

PORTRET ZENY see Jirasek, Ivo

PORTULACA, A see Igarashi, Tadashi

POSELSTVI see Fiala, Petr, Symphony No.
3

POSTAGE STAMP see Mamiya, Michio

POSTCARD, A see Anderson, Beth

POSTHUMOUS SONGS BOOK 1 see Grieg,
Edvard Hagerup

POSTHUMOUS SONGS BOOK 2 see Grieg,
Edvard Hagerup

POSTILLON DE LONJUMEAU: MES AMIS,
ECOUTEZ L'HISTOIRE see Adam,
Adolphe-Charles

POSTLUDIUM see Lachenmann, Helmut
Friedrich

POTENTAT, EL (CANCÓ DEL CAMÍ) see
Mestres, Apeles

POUGET, LEO
Chants D'Amour Orientaux
[Fr] high solo,pno CLASSV 2182 (P244)

POULENC, FRANCIS (1899-1963)
Bal Masque *sec,cant
Bar/Mez solo,chamber orch/pno pno
red SALABERT 50405160 (P245)

Huit Chansons Polonaises
[Polish/Fr] (CC8L) SALABERT
50413090 (P246)

Melodies Et Chansons
solo voice,pno (CCU) SALABERT (P247)

POUR TOI MON AMOUR see Keizer, Henk

POUR UN BAISER! see Tosti, Francesco
Paolo

POURQUOI? see Tchaikovsky, Piotr Ilyich

POURQUOI DONC see Glazunov, Alexander
Konstantinovich

POURQUOI RESTER SEULETTE see Saint-
Saëns, Camille

POURQUOI SE FANENT TES FEUILLES? see
Gretchaninov, Alexander Tikhonovich

POURSUIVANT, LE see Depraz, Raymond

POUSSEUR, HENRI (1929-)
Grande Chronique Berlinoise
Bar solo,5inst ZERBONI 8279 (P248)

Sur Le Qui-Vive
female solo,5inst ZERBONI 9561 (P249)

Tales And Songs From The Bible Of
Hell
ZERBONI 8689 (P250)

POVERO PULCINELLA see Buzzi-Peccia,
Arturo

POWELL
How Blessed To Know
med solo SHAWNEE 5082 (P251)

POWELL, KIT
Devotion To The Small
solo voice,perc WAI-TE-ATA 107 (P252)

POWERS, ANTHONY (1953-)
Souvenirs Du Voyage
S solo,pno OXFORD 63.082 (P253)

Venexiana I
2T,2vln,vcl,hpsd OXFORD perf mat
rent (P254)

PRADO, AMEIDA
Drei Lieder
solo voice,pno SEESAW (P255)

Episodios Animals
solo voice SEESAW (P256)

Jardim Do Amor E Paixao
B solo,pno SEESAW (P257)

Livro Brazileiro I
B solo,pno SEESAW (P258)

Livro Brazileiro II
S solo,pno SEESAW (P259)

Triptico Celeste
S solo,pno SEESAW (P260)

PRAERIEKONENS BÅNSULL see Groven,
Eivind

PRAISE YE THE LORD see Presser, William
Henry

PRAJUNA-PARAMITA see S(C)Enshu, Jiro

PRÄLUDIUM see Eisler, Hanns see
Lachenmann, Helmut Friedrich

PRAY FOR PEACE see Clarke, Henry Leland

PRAYER see Gulbranson, Eilif, Bønn see
Lunde, Ivar see Ronsheim, John
Richard see Sveinsson, Atli Heimir

PRAYER, THE see Burleigh, Henry Thacker

PRAYER OF ST. FRANCIS OF ASSISI see
Gerschefski, Edwin

PRAYER OF VERONICA, THE see Groven,
Eivind, Veronicas Bøn

PRAYERS FROM THE ARK see Nordoff, Paul

PRAZSKA DOMOVNI ZNAMENI see Tausinger,
Jan

PRÉLUDE see Balakirev, Mily Alexeyevich
see Man, Roderik De

PRELUDE AND FOUR SCENES see Rosenman, Leonard

PRELUDIUM see Renosto, Paolo

PREMIÈRES MÉLODIES (3 CYCLES) see Massé, Victor

PRESSER, WILLIAM HENRY (1916-   )
Praise Ye The Lord
S solo,horn,pno (med) TENUTO (P261)

PRESTEN OG KLOKKEREN see Bergh, Sverre

PRETTY CREATURE, THE see Storace, Stephen

PREYER, GOTTFRIED
Antwort
solo voice,pno SCIEN 1297   (P262)

Gebeth, Das
solo voice,pno SCIEN 1298   (P263)

Jedem Das Seine
SCIEN 1299 f.s. contains also: Ob
Sie Wohl Kommen Wird   (P264)

Ob Sie Wohl Kommen Wird
see Jedem Das Seine

PRICE, MARION JAMES (1913-   )
Thou May'st Love
SCIEN 761   (P265)

PRICE, THE see Munakata, Kazu

PRIÈRE see Gounod, Charles François see
Huguenin, Charles, Ave Maria

PRIERE DANS L'ARCHE see Yannatos, James D.

PRIERE DE SULPICIA see Francaix, Jean

PRIERE POUR LA PAIX see Klerk, Albert de

PRIERES DANS L'ARCHE see Yannatos, James D.

PRIEST AND THE BELL RINGER, THE see
Bergh, Sverre, Presten Og Klokkeren

PRIMAVERA-ESTIU see Marques

PRIMOSCH, JAMES (1956-   )
Cloud Of Unknowing, The
S solo,chamber orch MARGUN MP6074 (P266)

Three Sacred Songs
solo voice,pno (med) MERION
441-41021   (P267)

Weil Alles Unsagbar Ist
solo voice,fl,vln,vcl,pno PRESSER
pts 141-40025P, sc 141-40025S (P268)

PRIMROSE, THE see Mourant, Walter

PRINCE IGOR: CAVATINA OF KONTCHAKOVNA
see Borodin, Alexander Porfirievich

PRINCE IGOR: CAVATINA OF VLADIMIR
IGOREVITCH see Borodin, Alexander
Porfirievich

PRINCE IGOR: JAROSLAVNA'S ARIOSO see
Borodin, Alexander Porfirievich

PRINCE IGOR: JAROSLAVNA'S CRY see
Borodin, Alexander Porfirievich

PRINCE IGOR: KONCHAK'S FIRST ARIA see
Borodin, Alexander Porfirievich,
Prince Igor: Verwundet...

PRINCE IGOR: PRINCE GALITSKY'S ARIA see
Borodin, Alexander Porfirievich

PRINCE IGOR: PRINCE IGOR'S ARIA see
Borodin, Alexander Porfirievich,
Prince Igor: Um Sonst Nach Ruhe

PRINCE IGOR: UM SONST NACH RUHE see
Borodin, Alexander Porfirievich

PRINCE IGOR: VERWUNDET... see Borodin,
Alexander Porfirievich

PRINCESS, THE see Kjerulf, Halfdan,
Prinsessen: Aftenstemning

PRINCESS NIU see Straesser, Joep

PRINCESS OF THE SEA see Borodin,
Alexander Porfirievich

PRINCESS OKU see Straesser, Joep

PRINCIPIA see Barrett, Richard

PRINSESSEN: AFTENSTEMNING see Kjerulf,
Halfdan

PRINSESSEN: PRINSESSEN SAD HØYT I SIT
see Grieg, Edvard Hagerup

PRINTEMPS, LE see Boismortier, Joseph
Bodin du see Hahn, Reynaldo

PRINTEMPS DERNIER see Massenet, Jules

PRINTEMPS-ÉTÉ see Marques, Primavera-
Estiu

PRINZESSIN TRAURIGKEIT see Einem,
Gottfried von

PRISON MUSIC III see Holm, Mogens
Winkel

PRISON MUSIC IV see Holm, Mogens Winkel

PRISONER, THE see O'Leary, Jane

PRIVATE MATTER see Sigfusson,
Steingrimur

PROCACCINI, TERESA (1934-   )
Elegia Op. 44
Mez solo,fl,pno EDI-PAN EP 7237
(P269)

PROCH, HEINRICH (1809-1878)
Alpenhorn, Das
solo voice,pno,opt horn/vcl SCIEN
1301   (P270)

An Die Sterne
solo voice,pno,opt vcl SCIEN 1302
(P271)

Blinde Geiger, Der
solo voice,vln SCIEN 1303   (P272)

Deh Torna Mio Bene: Variations
coloratura sop,pno CLASSV 0440
(P273)

Fischermädchen, Das
solo voice,pno SCIEN 1304   (P274)

Theme and Variations for Solo Voice
and Orchestra
solo voice,2.2.2.2. 2.2.3.0. perc,
timp [5'20"] BILLAUDOT set ipr,
voc sc f.s.   (P275)

Theme Celebre Avec Variation (from
The Barber Of Seville)
S solo,2.2.2.2. 2.2.3.0. perc,timp,
strings [5'20"] pno red,pts
BILLAUDOT   (P276)

Wanderer, Der *Op.10
solo voice,pno SCIEN 1307   (P277)

PROCTOR, SIMON
Original Sin, The
S solo, serpent CHILTERN   (P278)

PRODIGAL PLANET see Schmidt, Sharon
Yvonne Davis

PROEM see Flothuis, Marius

PROENCA see Buller, John

PROGLAS see Pololáník, Zdenek

PROJECTION see Carlsen, Philip

PROKOFIEV, SERGE (1891-1953)
Seven Mass Songs For Voice And Piano,
Op. 79
see Works For Voice And Piano, Vol.
3

Seven Mass Songs For Voice And Piano,
Op. 89, No. 2
see Works For Voice And Piano, Vol.
3

Three Children's Songs *Op.68
[Russ] solo voice,pno CLASSV 2174
(P279)
Three Children's Songs, Op. 68
see Works For Voice And Piano, Vol.
3

Three Romances, Op. 73
see Works For Voice And Piano, Vol.
3

Works For Voice And Piano, Vol. 3
KALMUS K 05020 f.s.
contains: Seven Mass Songs For
Voice And Piano, Op. 79; Seven
Mass Songs For Voice And Piano,
Op. 89, No. 2; Three Children's
Songs, Op. 68; Three Romances,
Op. 73   (P280)

PROLOGO see Sifonia, Firmino

PROLOGUE TO "BUDDHA" - THE POET'S ARIA
see Brown, Francis James

PROMESSA, LA see Rossini, Gioacchino

PROMISE, THE see Stutschevsky, Joachim

PROPHECY OF AMOS see Horvit, Michael M.

PROPHÈTE: AH! MON FILS! see Meyerbeer,
Giacomo

PROPHÈTE: DONNEZ! DONNEZ! see
Meyerbeer, Giacomo

PROPRIUM MISSAE NATIVITATIS see
Ødegaard, Henrik

PROSIT BEI TAG UND NACHT see Tober-
Vogt, Elke

PROSPERI, CARLO (1921-   )
Canti Dell' Ansia E Della Gioia
solo voice,pno ZERBONI 9865 (P281)

Canti Dell' Ansia E Della Gioia
(Serie 1)
ST soli,9inst ZERBONI 8832   (P282)

Canti Dell' Ansia E Della Gioia
(Serie 2)
ST soli,9inst ZERBONI 9264   (P283)

O Diotima
S solo,3inst ZERBONI 8896   (P284)

PROSPERI, MAURIZIO
Lonesome Woman, The
Mez solo,pno EDI-PAN EP 7790 (P285)

PROTESTSONGS see Visser, Peter

PROULX, RICHARD (1937-   )
Wedding Song From Colossians
solo voice,kbd GIA G-3784   (P286)

PRÖVE, BERNFRIED (1963-   )
Brennend
Mez solo,3(pic).3.3.3(contrabsn).
4.3.3.1. timp,3perc,cel,pno,
strings [20'] MODERN 2256 f.s.
(P287)

Zeitrisse
S solo,fl,gtr,vln,vla,vcl [7'-10']
MODERN 2258 f.s.   (P288)

PRSTYNEK Z TRAVY see Dvorácek, Jirí

PRÜFUNG DES KÜSSENS see Beethoven,
Ludwig van

PRYCE, LINDA
Hem Of His Garment, The
solo voice,pno,gtr (easy) FENTONE
(P289)

PRYJSHLA see Shut, Wasyl

PSALM see Eggen, Arne, Ikke Enhver, Som
Siger Til Mig see Torjussen,
Trygve, Salme

PSALM, EIN see Isolfsson, Pall

PSALM: FOR A FEASTDAY see Smolanoff,
Michael Louis

PSALM NO. 12 see Plagge, Wolfgang

PSALM NO. 13 see Meneely-Kyder, Sarah

PSALM NO. 23 see Berlinski, Herman,
Adonai Roi see Garlick, Antony see
Heilner, Irwin see Liszt, Franz see
Sullivan

PSALM NO. 30 see Asia, Daniel

PSALM NO. 37 see Leichtling, Alan

PSALM NO. 40, OP. 6 see Haegeland,
Eilert M., Salme 40, Op.6

PSALM NO. 62 see Kuntz, Michael,
Sehnsucht Nach Gott

PSALM NO. 67 see Edwards see Edwards,
Leo

PSALM NO. 68 see Rogers, Bernard

PSALM NO. 100 see Allen, Judith Shatin

PSALM NO. 116 see Baden, Conrad

PSALM NO. 119 see Baden, Conrad

PSALM NO. 121 see Haxton, Kenneth see
Nyhus, Rolf, Jeg Løfter Mine Øyne
see Nyhus, Rolf, Jeg Løfter Mine
Øyne Til Fjellene see Warren, Betsy

PSALM NO. 126 see Stanford, Charles
Villiers, Bible Songs: A Song Of
Freedom

PSALM NO. 130 see Lerstad, Terje B., De
Profundis see Meima, Herman

PSALM NO. 137 see Gondai, Atsuhiko

PSALM NO. 139 see Scrivener, Joseph

PSALM NO. 148 see Volkonsky, Andrei

PSALM 142: THRENODY see McTee, Cindy

PSALM SETTING see Pleskow, Raoul

PSALMENMUSIK see Müller-Zürich, Paul

PSALMODIKON see Hemberg, Eskil

PSALMS, OP. 74 see Orrego-Salas, Juan A.

PSALMUS see Chamberlin, Robert

PSYCHÉ see Paladilhe, Emile

PSYCHOMACHIA see Hauksson, Thorsteinn

PUCCINI, GIACOMO (1858-1924)
Bohème, La: Che Gelida Manina
  T solo,pno (C maj) CLASSV 2000
  (P290)
  T solo,pno (D flat maj) CLASSV 1999
  (P291)
  T solo,pno BOIL B.2621   (P292)
  "Your Tiny Hand Is Frozen" T solo
  (in 3 keys:D flat maj (LD112615);
  C maj (LD112616); B flat maj
  (LD119015)) RICORDI-IT   (P293)

Bohème, La: Donde Lieta
  S solo,pno CLASSV 2001   (P294)

Bohème, La: Mi Chiamano Mimi
  S solo,pno (D maj) CLASSV 2002
  (P295)
  S solo,pno BOIL B.2619   (P296)

Bohème, La: Quando Me'n Vo
  "Musetta's Waltz" S solo,pno (E
  maj) CLASSV 1996   (P297)
  "Musetta's Waltz" S solo,pno (E
  flat maj) CLASSV 1997   (P298)

Bohème, La: Quando M'en Vò Soletta
  Per La Via
  S solo,pno BOIL B.2620   (P299)

Bohème, La: Vecchia Zimarra
  B solo,pno BOIL B.2622   (P300)
  "Colline's Aria" B solo,pno CLASSV
  1998   (P301)

Canzone Di Doretta
  see Rondine, La: Chi Il Bel Sogno

Colline's Aria
  see Bohème, La: Vecchia Zimarra

Donde Lieta
  "Mimi's Farewell" S solo RICORDI-IT
  LD114087   (P302)

E L'Uccellino...
  med solo,pno CLASSV 0908   (P303)

Early Puccini For Soprano: Five Arias
  From Le Villi and Edgar
  LEONARD-US 00747028   (P304)

Fanciulla Del West, La: Ch'ella Mi
  Creda
  "Girl Of The Golden West, The: Let
  Her Believe" T solo RICORDI-IT
  LD121157   (P305)

Fanciulla Del West, La: Ch' Ella Mi Creda
  T solo,pno (G flat maj) CLASSV 2006
  (P306)

Gianni Schicchi: O Mio Babbino Caro
  "Oh, My Beloved Father" S solo (in
  2 keys: A flat maj (LD120667); F
  maj (LD120669)) RICORDI-IT (P307)

Girl Of The Golden West, The: Let Her
  Believe
  see Fanciulla Del West, La: Ch'ella
  Mi Creda

In Those Soft Silken Curtains
  see Manon Lescaut: In Quelle Trine
  Morbide

Inno A Diana
  high solo,pno CLASSV 0942 (P308)
  (Spada) solo voice,pno (med) BSE
  (P309)

Love And Music
  see Tosca: Vissi D'Arte

Madama Butterfly: Un Bel Di Vedremo
  "One Fine Day" S solo (in 3 keys: G
  flat maj (LD112625); F maj
  (LD115750); E flat maj
  (LD114115)) RICORDI-IT   (P310)

Madama Butterfly: Un Bel Di Vedremo
  S solo,pno BOIL B.2626   (P311)

Manon Lescaut: Donna Non Vidi Mai
  T solo,pno CLASSV 0634   (P312)
  "Never Did I Behold" T solo
  RICORDI-IT LD97541   (P313)

PUCCINI, GIACOMO (cont'd.)

Manon Lescaut: In Quelle Trine
  Morbide
  "In Those Soft Silken Curtains" S
  solo RICORDI-IT LD97542   (P314)

Manon Lescaut: Sulla Vetta Tu Del
  Monte (Madrigale)
  Mez solo,pno CLASSV 2007   (P315)

Manon Lescaut: Tra Voi, Belle, Brune
  T solo,pno CLASSV 2005   (P316)

Mi Chiamano Mimi
  "They Call Me Mimi" S solo (in 3
  keys:D maj (LD112617); C maj
  (LD112618); B flat maj
  (LD119016)) RICORDI-IT   (P317)

Mimi's Farewell
  see Donde Lieta

Musetta's Waltz
  see Bohème, La: Quando Me'n Vo

Musetta's Waltz Song
  see Quando M'en Vo

Never Did I Behold
  see Manon Lescaut: Donna Non Vidi
  Mai

None Shall Sleep
  see Turandot: Nessun Dorma

O Weep No More, Liu
  see Turandot: Non Piangere, Liu

Oh, I Entreat Thee
  see Turandot: Signore, Ascolta

Oh, My Beloved Father
  see Gianni Schicchi: O Mio Babbino
  Caro

One Fine Day
  see Madama Butterfly: Un Bel Di
  Vedremo

Puccini: Arias For Soprano
  (CC7L, includes recorded piano
  accompaniments) RICORDI-IT
  R134624   (P318)

Quando M'en Vo
  "Musetta's Waltz Song" S solo (in 3
  keys:E maj (LD112619); E flat maj
  (LD112161); D maj (LD112620))
  RICORDI-IT   (P319)

Rondine, La: Chi Il Bel Sogno
  "Canzone Di Doretta" S solo,pno
  CLASSV 1917   (P320)

Rondine, La: Dimmi Che Vuoi Seguirmi
  T solo,pno CLASSV 2004   (P321)

Rondine, La: Two Arias
  "Two Arias From La Rondine" S solo
  LEONARD-US 00747027   (P322)

Songs For Voice And Piano
  (Kaye, Michael) solo voice,pno
  OXFORD 96.801   (P323)

Strange Harmony
  see Tosca: Recondita Armonia

They Call Me Mimi
  see Mi Chiamano Mimi

Thou Who With Ice
  see Turandot: Tu Che Di Gel

Tosca: E Lucevan Le Stelle
  T solo,pno (B flat min, semi-tone
  lower) CLASSV 1287   (P324)
  T solo,pno (A min, whole-tone
  lower) CLASSV 2003   (P325)
  T solo,pno BOIL B.2625   (P326)
  "When The Stars Were Brightly
  Shining" T solo (in 2 keys: B min
  (LD112623); A min (LD119018))
  RICORDI-IT   (P327)

Tosca: Non La Sospiri
  "Tosca's Love Idyll" S solo
  RICORDI-IT LD118867   (P328)

Tosca: Recondita Armonia
  T solo,pno (F maj, original) CLASSV
  2008   (P329)
  T solo,pno (E maj, semi-tone lower)
  CLASSV 2009   (P330)
  T solo,pno (E flat maj, whole-tone
  lower) CLASSV 2010   (P331)
  T solo,pno BOIL B.2624   (P332)
  "Strange Harmony" T solo (in 2
  keys: F maj (LD112621); E flat
  maj (LD324)) RICORDI-IT   (P333)

Tosca: Vissi D'Arte
  S solo,pno BOIL B.2623   (P334)
  "Love And Music" S solo (in 2 keys:
  E maj (LD112622); D maj

PUCCINI, GIACOMO (cont'd.)

  (LD119017)) RICORDI-IT   (P335)

Tosca's Love Idyll
  see Tosca: Non La Sospiri

Turandot: Nessun Dorma
  "None Shall Sleep" T solo (in 2
  keys: G maj (LD120755); F maj
  (LD330)) RICORDI-IT   (P336)

Turandot: Non Piangere, Liu
  "O Weep No More, Liu" T solo
  RICORDI-IT LD121032   (P337)

Turandot: Signore, Ascolta
  "Oh, I Entreat Thee" S solo
  RICORDI-IT LD120751   (P338)

Turandot: Tu Che Di Gel
  "Thou Who With Ice" S solo RICORDI-
  IT LD120757   (P339)

Two Arias From La Rondine
  see Rondine, La: Two Arias

Unknown Puccini, The *CCU
  (Kaye, Michael) solo voice OXFORD
  385745-6 $47.50   (P340)

Villi, Le: Anima Santa Della Figlia
  Mia
  [It] Bar solo,pno CLASSV 1512
  (P341)

Villi, Le: Se Come Voi Piccina
  [It] S solo,pno CLASSV 1277 (P342)
  "Were I But Like These" S solo
  RICORDI-IT LD574   (P343)

Villi, Le: Torna Ai Felici Dì
  T solo,pno CLASSV 1516   (P344)

Were I But Like These
  see Villi, Le: Se Come Voi Piccina

When The Stars Were Brightly Shining
  see Tosca: E Lucevan Le Stelle

Your Tiny Hand Is Frozen
  see Bohème, La: Che Gelida Manina

PUCCINI: ARIAS FOR SOPRANO see Puccini,
Giacomo

PUEBLO MULATO see Leon, Tania Justina

PUGET, LOUISE
Fleurette
  SCIEN 1317   (P345)

Mes Rêves De Jeune Fille
  SCIEN 1318   (P346)

PUGET, PAUL-CHARLES-MARIE (1848-1917)
Chanson De Ma Mie, La (5 Mélodies)
  [Fr] high solo,pno CLASSV 2180
  (P347)

Chansons Brunes Et Blondes (7
  Mélodies)
  [Fr] solo voice,pno CLASSV 2177
  (P348)

Litanies De La Beauté
  [Fr] med-high solo,pno CLASSV 2181
  (P349)

PUIG, G.
Cuarto Composiciones
  solo voice,pno BOIL B.2680 (P350)

Doce Canciones
  solo voice,pno BOIL B.2674 (P351)

PUISQUE LE MIEL D'AMOUR see Andriessen,
Hendrik

PUISQU'ICI-BAS TOUTE ÂME see Faure,
Gabriel-Urbain

PUKSÅNGER - LOCKROP see Rehnqvist,
Karin

PULSE MUSIC see Liptak, David

PUOI VANTAR LE TUE RITORTE see Benda,
Georg Anton (Jiri Antonín)

PUPPEN, DIE see Hanson, Sten

PURCELL, HENRY (1658 or 59-1695)
Fifteen Songs And Airs For Contralto
  Or Baritone From The Operas And
  Masques *CC15U
  [Eng] KALMUS K 06850 f.s. (P352)

Fifteen Songs And Airs For Soprano Or
  Tenor From The Operas And The
  Odes *CC15U
  [Eng] KALMUS K 06851 f.s. (P353)

If Music Be The Food
  (Moore, Dorothy Rudd) SS soli,pno
  [5'] sc AM.COMP.AL. $1.90 (P354)

Komt Trompetten
  see Sound The Trumpet

PURCELL, HENRY (cont'd.)

Let The Dreadful Engines
(Britten, Benjamin) FABER 51285 2
                                              (P355)
Six Songs From "Orpheus Brittanicus"
*CC6U
[Eng] high solo/Bar solo KALMUS
K 06852 f.s.   (P356)

Sound The Trumpet
"Komt Trompetten" SA/TB soli
ZENGERINK V.136   (P357)

PURITANI, I: QUI LA VOCE SUA SOAVE see
Bellini, Vincenzo

PURITANI, I: SON VERGIN VEZZOSA see
Bellini, Vincenzo

PUSSY CAT DUETS see Warren, Betsy

PÜTZ, EDUARD (1911-   )
Melodie Am Abend
solo voice,pno SEESAW   (P358)

Requiem Im Park
Mez solo,ob,clar,bsn,horn,vcl,pno,
perc SEESAW   (P359)

When We Dead Awaken
S solo,fl,gtr,pno,db,2perc SEESAW
                                              (P360)

PYGMALION see Zur, Menachem

Q

QUACK, ERHARD (1904-   )
Passion Nach Matthäus
3 solo voices CHRIS 50526 f.s. (Q1)

QUAIS see Decoust, Michel

QUALVOLL DIESES LEISE WEINEN see
Badings, Henk

QUAND TU CHANTES see Gounod, Charles
François, Sérénade

QUANDO see Mirigliano, Rosario

QUANDO LO STRAL SPEZZAI see Paesiello,
Giovanni

QUANDO MEN VO see Lyric Soprano Arias:
A Master Class With Evelyn Lear,
Vol. 2 see Puccini, Giacomo

QUANDO MIRO QUEL BEL CIGLIO see Mozart,
Wolfgang Amadeus

QUANDO SORGE LA LUNA see Tosti,
Francesco Paolo, Marechiare

QUANDO SPERASTI, O CORE see Handel,
George Frideric

QUANTI MAI! see Gounod, Charles
François

QUARTA SINFONIA OP. 70 see Nicolau,
Dimitri

QUARTETTO CON VOCE see Capurso,
Elisabetta

QU'AS TU FAIT? see Jensen, Ludwig
Irgens

QUATORZE PLUSIEURS MELODIES, VOL. 1:
NOS. 1-7 see Koechlin, Charles

QUATORZE PLUSIEURS MELODIES, VOL. 2:
NOS. 8-14 see Koechlin, Charles

QUATRE CÉLÈBRES AVE MARIA
"Four Famous Ave Maria" S/T solo,pno
(contains works by: Cherubini,
Franck, Schubert & Gounod) SCHOTT-
FRER 9419   (Q2)

QUATRE CHANSONS see Kef, Kees

QUATRE CHANSONS DE PAUL FORT see
Hubeau, Jean

QUATRE CHANTS see Boulanger, Nadia

QUATRE MÉLODIES see Albéniz, Isaac see
Borodin, Alexander Porfirievich

QUATRE MELODIES SUR DES POESIES
ANCIENNES see Jolivet, Andre

QUATRE POÈMES D'APRÈS L'INTERMEZZO DE
HENRI HEINE see Ropartz, Joseph Guy
(Marie)

QUATRE POEMES HINDOUS see Delage,
Maurice

QUATRE POEMS, OP. 5 see Loeffler,
Charles Martin

QUATRE POESIES see Hasquenoph, Pierre

QUATRE RONDELS MELANCOLIQUES see
Vuillemin, Louis

QUATRE-VINGTS (80) IN 2 VOLS. see
Gounod, Charles François

QUATTER MINIATURAS RUMANTSCHAS, OP. 68
see Flothuis, Marius

QUATTRO CANTI OP. 27 see Nicolau,
Dimitri

QUATTRO FRAMMENTI DA LIRICI GRECI see
Muci, Italo Ruggero

QUATTRO MELODIE, OP. 35 see Sgambati,
Giovanni

QUATTRO ODI DI ORAZIO see Nicolai,
Bruno

QUATTRO POESIE DI PAUL ELUARD see
Bortolotti, Mauro

QUATTRO RISPETTI, OP. 12 see Wolf-
Ferrari, Ermanno

QUATTRO SONETTI PER TENORE E ORCHESTRA
see Jentzsch, Wilfried

QUATTUOR DIALOGI see Sklenicka, Karel

QUE L'HEURE EST DONC BRÈVE see Delibes,
Léo

QUE L'OISEAU SE DECHIRE EN SABLES see
Mefano, Paul

QUEEN OF SHEBA: BLICK EMPOR ZU JENEN
RÄUMEN see Goldmark, Karl

QUEEN OF SHEBA: MAGISCHE TÖNE see
Goldmark, Karl

QUEEN OF THE VILLAGE, THE see Croal,
George

QUEER CORNERED CAP see Schudel, Thomas

QUEL FIOR CHE ALL'ALBA RIDE see Handel,
George Frideric

QUEL L'HEURE EST DONC BRÈVE see
Massenet, Jules

QUEL TIMOR CHE MI CIRCONDA see Benda,
Georg Anton (Jirí Antonín)

QUERELLEUSE see Paderewski, Ignace Jan

QUEROL, MIGUEL (1912-   )
Tonos Humanos Del Siglo XVII
solo voice,pno ALPUERTO 1284   (Q3)

QUESTION AU CLERC DU QUICHET see
Franken, Wim

QUETZAL COATL see Pálenícek, Josef

QUI JAMAIS FUT DE PLUS CHARMANT VISAGE
see Indy, Vincent d', Madrigal

QUI TOLLIS see Kopriva, Karel Blazej

QUIET AIRS see Bacon, Ernst L.

QUIET GOODBYES: TWO SONGS see Park,
James

QUIET GRANDEUR see Dillard, Donald E.

QUIET SONGS see Musto, John

QUILTER, ROGER (1877-1953)
Amaryllis At The Fountain
med solo,pno CLASSV 0686   (Q4)

Blossom-Time *Op.15,No.3
med-high solo,pno CLASSV 2014 (Q5)

Cuckoo Song *Op.15,No.1
high solo,pno CLASSV 2013   (Q6)

Four Songs Of Mirza Schaffy, Op. 2
[Ger/Eng] med-high solo,pno CLASSV
0688   (Q7)

Four Songs Of The Sea
high solo/low solo,pno FORSYTH (Q8)

Four Songs, Op. 14
high solo,pno CLASSV 0664   (Q9)
low solo,pno CLASSV 0663   (Q10)

June
low solo,pno CLASSV 0739   (Q11)

Seven Elizabethan Lyrics, Op. 12
[Eng] high solo KALMUS K 09957
                                (Q12)
[Eng] low solo KALMUS K 09958 (Q13)
low solo,pno CLASSV 1703   (Q14)

Slumber Song (from Where The Rainbow
Ends)
med solo,pno CLASSV 2015   (Q15)

Three Songs From Op. 18 (To Wine &
Beauty)
Bar solo,pno CLASSV 0687   (Q16)

Three Songs Of The Sea, Op. 1
high solo,pno CLASSV 0662   (Q17)
low solo,pno CLASSV 0661   (Q18)

Three Songs Of William Blake, Op. 20
high solo,pno CLASSV 2012   (Q19)

To Julia
med solo BOOSEY VAB0289   (Q20)

To Julia (Six Lyrics Of R. Herrick)
T solo,pno CLASSV 0543   (Q21)
Bar solo,pno CLASSV 0544   (Q22)

QUINDICI ARIE ACCADEMICHE, FASC. 4 see
Boccherini, Luigi

QUINDICI ARIE ACCADEMICHE, FASC. 5 see
Boccherini, Luigi

QUINTET WITH VOICE see Wolpe, Stefan

QUINZE DUOS see Gounod, Charles
François

QUINZE MÉLODIES see Gounod, Charles
François

QUINZE MÉLODIES ENFANTINES see Gounod,
Charles François

QUINZE MÉLODIES ET DEUX CHOEUR see
Delibes, Léo

QUOD EST IN IGNE CALOR see Mysliveczek,
Joseph

QUOD PIA VOCE CANO see Kopriva, Karel
Blazej

R

R.I.B.E.S. see Cardi, Mauro

RABAUD, HENRI (1873-1949)
Mârouf: A Travers Le Désert
[Fr] T solo,pno CLASSV 2016   (R1)

Mârouf: Il Est Des Musulmans
[Fr] T solo,pno CLASSV 2017   (R2)

RABINOWITCH, ALEXANDRE
Requiem Pour Une Maree Noire
S solo,pno,perc [18'] ARIAD 80023
(R3)
RACCOLTA DI BRANI CLASSICI PER PICCOLI
CORI *CCU
(Comolli, N.) solo voice,pno CURCI
10412 f.s.   (R4)

RACCOLTA DI CANTATE PER VOCI E BASSO
CONTINUO *CC24U
solo voice,cont fac ed FORNI 723 f.s.
(R5)
RACHMANINOFF, SERGEY VASSILIEVICH
(1873-1943)
Again I Am Alone *Op.26,No.9
[Russ/Ger] low solo,pno CLASSV 2164
(R6)
[Russ/Ger] med solo,pno CLASSV 2165
(R7)
Aleko: Aleko's Cavatina
[Russ] Bar solo,pno CLASSV 0643
(R8)
Aleko: Romance Of The Young Gypsy
[Russ] T solo,pno CLASSV 0644 (R9)

All Things Pass By *Op.26,No.15
[Russ/Ger] high solo,pno CLASSV
2167   (R10)

Christ Is Risen *Op.26,No.6
[Russ/Ger] CLASSV 2162   (R11)

Destiny *Op.21,No.1
[Russ] high solo,pno CLASSV 2156
(R12)
Field Beloved
see O, Du Wogendes Feld

Floods Of Spring *Op.14,No.11
[Eng] med-high solo,pno CLASSV 1178
(R13)
[Eng] high solo,pno CLASSV 0419
(R14)
[Russ/Ger] med-high solo,pno CLASSV
2154   (R15)

He Took All From Me *Op.26,No.2
[Russ/Ger] high solo,pno CLASSV
2161   (R16)

How? My Heart Aches! *Op.21,No.12
med solo,pno CLASSV 2018   (R17)

I Came To Her *Op.14,No.4
[Russ/Ger] high solo,pno CLASSV
2153   (R18)

In The Silence Of The Night *Op.4,
No.3
[Eng] med solo,pno CLASSV 2150
(R19)
[Russ/Eng] low solo,pno CLASSV 1329
(R20)
[Russ] med solo,pno CLASSV 0551
(R21)
[Russ/Ger] high solo,pno CLASSV
1328   (R22)

In The Soul Of Each Of Us *Op.34,
No.2
[Russ/Fr] high solo,pno CLASSV 2168
(R23)
It Is Time *Op.14,No.12
[Russ] med-high solo,pno CLASSV
2155   (R24)

Like Blossom Dew *Op.8,No.2
[Russ/Ger] high solo,pno CLASSV
2151   (R25)

Lilacs *Op.21,No.5
[Eng/Ger] high solo,pno CLASSV 0428
(R26)
[Eng/Russ] high solo,pno CLASSV
1521   (R27)
[Eng/Ger] low solo,pno CLASSV 2157
(R28)
Loneliness *Op.21,No.6
"Oh! Heart Of Mine" [Russ] med
solo,pno CLASSV 2158   (R29)

No Prophet I *Op.21,No.11
[Russ] med solo,pno CLASSV 2159
(R30)
O, Du Wogendes Feld *Op.4,No.5
"Field Beloved" [Ger/Eng] low solo
RECITAL 2226   (R31)

RACHMANINOFF, SERGEY VASSILIEVICH
(cont'd.)
O Thou Billowy Harvest
[Eng] high solo,pno CLASSV 0552
(R32)
Oh! Heart Of Mine
see Loneliness

Oh Stay *Op.4,No.1
[Russ/Ger] high solo,pno (E min,
higher than original key) CLASSV
2149   (R33)

Soldier's Wife *Op.8,No.4
[Russ/Ger] S solo,pno CLASSV 2152
(R34)
Sorrow In Springtime *Op.21,No.12
[Russ/Ger] med-high solo,pno CLASSV
2160   (R35)

Through The Silent Night
[Eng] high solo,pno CLASSV 0443
(R36)
To The Children *Op.26,No.7
[Eng] high solo,pno CLASSV 2163
(R37)
Vocalise *Op.34,No.14
high solo,pno CLASSV 1354   (R38)

When Yesterday We Met *Op.26,No.13
[Russ/Ger] high solo,pno CLASSV
2166   (R39)

RACINE FRICKER, PETER
see FRICKER, PETER RACINE

RADIANTE AMERICA see Krieger, Armando

RADULESCU, HORATIO (1942-   )
Colonne D'alba
S solo,vla,alto fl,pno 4-hands,
perc,elec gtr EDI-PAN EP 7471
(R40)
RADULESCU, MICHAEL (1943-   )
Poeta, De
"Wessobrunner Gebet, Das" S solo,
org DOBLINGER 08 878   (R41)

Versi
S solo,org DOBLINGER 08 877   (R42)

Wessobrunner Gebet, Das
see Poeta, De

RÅE BERGVEGGEN see Evensen, Bernt
Kasberg

RAFF, JOSEPH JOACHIM (1822-1882)
Maria Stuart, Op. 172 *song cycle
[Ger] MezTBar soli RECITAL 379
(R43)
RAGNARSSON, HJALMAR H. (1952-   )
Astarljod Mitt
S solo,pno ICELAND 030-035   (R44)

By The River
S solo,pno ICELAND 030-040   (R45)

Embla
S solo,pno ICELAND 030-029   (R46)

Falling Leaves
Bar/A solo,pno/org [3'15"] ICELAND
030-016   (R47)

Four Songs To Icelandic Poems
solo voice,fl,vcl,pno ICELAND
030-032   (R48)

Hatidasongur
S solo,pno (text by H. Ibsen)
ICELAND 030-038   (R49)

Sei Canti
A solo,3inst ZERBONI 9109   (R50)

Songur Solveigar
S solo,pno (text by H. Ibsen)
ICELAND 030-037   (R51)

Thrir Söngvar Ur Petri Gaut
S solo,pno (text by H. Ibsen)
ICELAND 030-036   (R52)

Vögguvisa Solveigar
S solo,pno (text by H. Ibsen)
ICELAND 030-039   (R53)

RAGOSSNIG, K.
O Sanctissima: 10 Christmas Songs
From Italy, England, Spain And
France *CC10U,Xmas
solo voice,gtr PLUCKED STR ZM 1719
$6.00   (R54)

RAGS OF TIME, THE see Emmer, Huib

RAGWITZ, ERHARD (1933-   )
Fünf Liebeslieder *Op.60
A solo,pno DEUTSCHER DV 9049 (R55)

Lachende Herz, Das *Op.40, song
cycle
med solo,pno DEUTSCHER DV 9040
(R56)

RAGY see Zahradník, Zdenek

RAICHL, MIROSLAV (1930-   )
   Elegie Na Odchodnou
     S solo,2.2.2.2. 2.2.0.0. perc,harp,
     pno,strings [16'] CESKY HUD.
                           (R57)

   Letela Tudy Labute *song cycle
     S solo,pno PANTON 147   (R58)

RAIN see Masseus, Jan see Mourant,
   Walter

RAIN IN MAY see Asgeirsson, Jon

RAIN, RAIN: FIVE SONGS see Stallcop,
   Glenn

RAINING IN FEBRUARY see Walker, Gwyneth

RAKKI see Johannsson, Magnus Bl.

RAKOWSKI
   Songs On Poems Of Louise Bogan
     S solo,pno PETERS 67381   (R59)

RAM OF TIDES see Apollyon, Nicolay

RAMEAU, JEAN-PHILIPPE (1683-1764)
   Amants Trahis, Les *cant
     TBar soli,pno CLASSV 1112   (R60)

   Aquilon Et Orithie *cant
     Bar solo,pno CLASSV 1111   (R61)

   Dardanus: Monstre Affreux
     B solo,pno CLASSV 1547   (R62)
     Bar solo,pno CLASSV 1116   (R63)

   Hippolyte Et Aricie: Rossignols
     Amoureux
     [Fr] high solo,pno CLASSV 1792
                           (R64)

   Indes Galantes, Les: Brillant Soleil
     Bar solo,pno CLASSV 1113   (R65)

   Musette, La *cant
     Bar solo,pno CLASSV 1114   (R66)

   Thétis *cant
     Bar solo,pno CLASSV 1115   (R67)

RAMILLETE DE CANCIONES ESPANOLAS *CCU
   (Yanagi, Sadako) ONGAKU 523610 f.s.
                           (R68)

RAMMO, PEETER
   Four Songs To Poems By Claes Gill
     *Op.7, CC4U
     solo voice,pno NORGE f.s.   (R69)

RAMP, DE see Beyerman-Walraven, Jeanne

RANAS see Revueltas, Silvestre

RANGSTRÖM, TURE (1884-1947)
   Enda Stunden, Den
     med solo,pno CLASSV 2020   (R70)
     "Idyll" solo voice,pno EGTVED 432
       from AKSEL SCHIOETZ ANTHOLOGY OF
       NORDIC SOLO SONGS, THE, VOL. 2
                           (R71)

   Hafvets Sommar (10 Sange)
     [Swed/Ger] high solo (not available
       outside U.S.A.) RECITAL 380 (R72)

   Idyll
     see Enda Stunden, Den

   Vattnet Rörs Och Vinden Spelar
     med solo,pno CLASSV 2019   (R73)

RANTZEN, TORSTEN
   Romanser Och Sånger I Urval
     solo voice,pno GEHRMANS 6729 (R74)

RAPHLING, SAM (1910-1988)
   Dream Keeper, The
     solo voice BELWIN CAM0035 $7.95
                           (R75)

RASTLOSE LIEBE see Schubert, Franz
   (Peter)

RASTRELLI, JOSEPH
   Vier Gesänge
     T/S solo,pno SCIEN 1327   (R76)

RATAPLAN, THE see Donizetti, Gaetano

RATTENFÄNGER see Schubert, Franz
   (Peter)

RATTENFANGER, DER see Wolf, Hugo

RAUB DER EUROPA, DER see Terzakis,
   Dimitri

RÄUBER UND SEIN KNECHT, DER see Eisler,
   Hanns

RAUCH, DER see Marx, Joseph

RAUCHSCHRIFT see Koetsier, Jan

RAUSCH, CARLOS
   Cancion De Cuna
     med solo,pno [3'] sc AM.COMP.AL.
     $3.10   (R77)

   Chaconne
     S solo,pno [6'] APNM sc $4.75, set
     $9.25   (R78)

   Manos Amigas
     med solo,pno [3'] sc AM.COMP.AL.
     $2.35   (R79)

   Ojos Nunca Tan Amados
     med solo,pno [3'] sc AM.COMP.AL.
     $1.95   (R80)

   Song Cycle *song cycle
     S solo,pno [15'] APNM sc $7.25, set
     $14.00   (R81)

   Three Songs From Long Island *CC3U
     S solo,horn,trp,trom APNM sc $3.75,
     set $7.25   (R82)

   Variations On The Folk Song Of
     Ukranian Hero Sava Chalij
     S solo,pno,vln,vcl [12']
     AM.COMP.AL.   (R83)

RAVEL, MAURICE (1875-1937)
   Adieu Cellule
     see Heure Espagnole, L': Gonzalve's
     Aria

   Alyssa *cant
     STBar soli,pno/orch pno red
     SALABERT 50481198   (R84)

   Grands Vents Venus D'Outremer, Les
     med solo,pno CLASSV 0640   (R85)

   Heure Espagnole, L': Gonzalve's Aria
     "Adieu Cellule" T solo,pno CLASSV
     0980   (R86)

   Heure Espagnole, L': Oh! La Pitoyable
     Aventure!
     [Fr] S solo,pno CLASSV 1515   (R87)

   Melodies Posthumes
     (CC6U) SALABERT 50480879   (R88)

   Pièce En Forme De Habanera
     "Vocalise" high solo,pno CLASSV
     1122   (R89)
     "Vocalise" med solo,pno CLASSV 0849
                           (R90)
     "Vocalise" low solo,pno CLASSV 0850
                           (R91)

   Shéhérazade: L'Indifférent
     "Tes Yeux Sont Doux" med solo,pno
     CLASSV 1102   (R92)

   Tes Yeux Sont Doux
     see Shéhérazade: L'Indifférent

   Vocalise
     see Pièce En Forme De Habanera

RAWSTHORNE, ALAN (1905-1971)
   Medieval Diptych
     Bar solo,3.2.3.2. 4.3.3.1. timp,
     perc,harp,strings without vln,vla
     [12'] OXFORD   (R93)

   Pastoral Symphony, A (Symphony No. 2)
     S solo,2.2.2.2. 4.2.3.0. timp,
     2perc,harp,strings [22'] OXFORD
                           (R94)

   Symphony No. 2
     see Pastoral Symphony, A

RAXACH, ENRIQUE (1932-   )
   Grand Duo Concertant
     S solo,db [9'] DONEMUS   (R95)

RAZZI, FAUSTO (1932-   )
   Che Nulla Sia Dissolto
     solo voice,pno EDI-PAN EP 7628
                           (R96)

   Colori
     2 female soli, 54 strings EDI-PAN
     EP 7558   (R97)

   Elogium
     S solo,alto fl,3vla,3vcl EDI-PAN
     EP 7828   (R98)

   Frammento
     S solo,vcl EDI-PAN EP 7234   (R99)

   Frammento 2
     solo voice,gtr EDI-PAN EP 7629
                           (R100)

RE PASTORE, IL: L'AMERÒ see Mozart,
   Wolfgang Amadeus

READ MY HEART see Brown

REALITES see Globokar, Vinko

REALITY IS AN ACTIVITY OF THE MOST
   AUGUST IMAGINATION see Bell, Larry

REALITY SANDWICHES see Little, David

REBEL, MEEUWIS (1957-   )
   Corinthians I: 13
     "Eerste Corinthe: 13" S solo,fl,ob,
     clar,bsn,pno,vln,vla,vcl [10']
     DONEMUS   (R101)

   Eerste Corinthe: 13
     see Corinthians I: 13

   Pomes Penyeach *CC13L
     solo voice,pno DONEMUS f.s. [45'],
     texts by James Joyce   (R102)

REBEL, MIJN HART see Flothuis, Marius

REBER, NAPOLEON-HENRI (1807-1880)
   Mélodies, Vol. 2
     solo voice,pno CLASSV C060   (R103)

RECEPT see Orthel, Leon

RECITAL see Blank, Allan

RÉCITATIF ET AIR DU MESSIE see Handel,
   George Frideric

RECITATION see Shut, Wasyl

RECKMANN, J.
   Nach Hause Geh'n Wir Nicht
     solo voice,pno (easy) SCHAUR (R104)

RECOLLECTIONS (SIX SONGS FOR SOPRANO
   AND ORCHESTRA) see Maxym, R.

RECOLLECTIONS (SIX SONGS FOR SOPRANO
   AND PIANO) see Maxym, R.

RECONTRE see Faure, Gabriel-Urbain

RECORDARE III see Pezzati, Romano

RECUEIL D'AIRS DIVERS DE LULLY see
   Lully, Jean-Baptiste (Lulli)

RECUEIL DE MÉLODIES VOL. 1 see
   Schlesinger, S.

RECUEIL DE MÉLODIES VOL. 2 see
   Schlesinger, S.

RECUEILLEMENT see Debussy, Claude

RECUERDO see Meschwitz, Frieder

RECURRING THOUGHTS OF A HAUNTED
   TRAVELLER see Marez Oyens, Tera de

RECYCLING see Ehlen, Margriet

RED, RED ROSE, A see Walker, George
   Theophilus

RED, ROSEY BUSH see Four Traditional
   American Songs

RED SARAFAN, THE see Varlamov,
   Alexander

RÉDEMPTION, 1ER AIR DE L'ARCHANGE see
   Franck, Cesar

RÉDEMPTION, 2E AIR DE L'ARCHANGE see
   Franck, Cesar

REED PIPE, THE see Tal, Marjo

REFLECTIONS see Constantinides, Dinos
   Demetrios see Nilsson, Anders see
   Tillis, Frederick C.

REFLECTIONS: THREE SONGS see Nilsson,
   Anders

REFLEKS see Kverndokk, Gisle

REFRAIN see Arashino, Hideo

REGAMÜNDUNG see Koetsier, Jan

REGATA VENEZIANA, LA see Rossini,
   Gioacchino

REGATA VENEZIANA, LA: VOGA, O TONIO see
   Rossini, Gioacchino

REGEN see Marx, Joseph

REGEN SPINT ZIJN DUNNE DRADEN, DE see
   Regt, Hendrik de

REGENTAG AM STRAND see Koetsier, Jan

REGER, MAX (1873-1916)
   Fünf Neue Kinderlieder
     high solo,pno PETERS 3991A   (R105)

   Fünf Neue Kinderlieder *Op.142, CC5U
     low solo,pno PETERS f.s.   (R106)

   Two Cradle Songs, Op. 76 *CC2U
     BOTE med solo BB2A f.s.; high solo
     BB18270 f.s.   (R107)

REGIMENTER GEHN see Eisler, Hanns

REGINA COELI see Biechteler, B. see
Cernohorsky, Bohuslav Matěj see
Galuppi, Baldassare see Lully,
Jean-Baptiste (Lulli) see Mouret,
Jean Joseph

REGINELLA: BELLA DEL TUO SORRISO see
Braga, Gaetano

REGLE DU JEU, LA (REQUIEM) see Ager,
Klaus

REGN I DEMRING see Madsen, Trygve

REGN UM NOTT see Kaldalóns, Sigvaldi S.

REGRETS see Delibes, Léo

REGT, HENDRIK DE (1950-   )
A Une Dame Creole
see Trois Chansons De Baudelaire,
Op. 70

Belle Esclave De Maure, La
Bar solo,pno [3'] DONEMUS f.s. from
TROIS CHANSONS, OP. 71   (R108)

Canzoni E Scherzi, Op. 30
S solo,fl,harp DONEMUS f.s. [20'-
25']
contains: Getrooste Dood, De;
Licht Van Binnen; Melopee;
Overtocht, De; Regen Spint Zijn
Dunne Draden, De   (R109)

Chat, Le
see Trois Chansons De Baudelaire,
Op. 70

Getrooste Dood, De
see Canzoni E Scherzi, Op. 30

Il Pleut Doucement Sur La Ville
Bar solo,pno [3'] DONEMUS f.s. from
TROIS CHANSONS, OP. 71A   (R110)

Licht Van Binnen
see Canzoni E Scherzi, Op. 30

Lune Offensee, La
see Trois Chansons De Baudelaire,
Op. 70

Melopee
see Canzoni E Scherzi, Op. 30

Mort D'Hercule, La
Bar solo,pno [2'] DONEMUS f.s. from
TROIS CHANSONS, OP. 71B   (R111)

Overtocht, De
see Canzoni E Scherzi, Op. 30

Regen Spint Zijn Dunne Draden, De
see Canzoni E Scherzi, Op. 30

Trois Chansons De Baudelaire, Op. 70
Bar solo,ob,gtr DONEMUS f.s. [9']
contains: A Une Dame Creole;
Chat, Le; Lune Offensee, La
(R112)

Trois Chansons, Op. 71
see Belle Esclave De Maure, La

Trois Chansons, Op. 71a
see Il Pleut Doucement Sur La Ville

Trois Chansons, Op. 71b
see Mort D'Hercule, La

REGTEREN ALTENA, LUCAS VAN (1924-   )
Des Levres Nocturnes
see Poeme Discontinu

Figurine
see Poeme Discontinu

Poeme Discontinu
S solo,fl,pno,vln,vcl DONEMUS f.s.
[16']
contains: Des Levres Nocturnes;
Figurine   (R113)

REHNQVIST, KARIN (1957-   )
Andrum
2 female soli,trom,2perc REIMERS
101204   (R114)

Davids Nimm
SSMez soli SUECIA 351A   (R115)

Puksånger - Lockrop
female solo&female solo,perc [23']
sc REIMERS 101174   (R116)

REHOR, BOHUSLAV (1938-   )
Symphony No. 4
B solo,2.2.3.2. 4.3.3.1. timp,perc,
vibra,strings [24'] CESKY HUD.
(R117)

REI VAN BRABANTSE VROUWEN see Bremer,
Jetse

REIBEL, GUY (1936-   )
Chohina 2
S solo,synthesizer [8'] SALABERT
EAS18443 f.s.   (R118)

REICH UND ARM see Borodin, Alexander
Porfirievich

REIF, PAUL (1910-1978)
Artist, The
AB soli,chamber group SEESAW f.s.
(R119)

Circus, The
S solo,pno SEESAW f.s.   (R120)

Fishes And Poet's Hands
solo voice,pno SEESAW f.s.   (R121)

German For Americans
solo voice,pno SEESAW f.s.   (R122)

O You Who Often
S solo,pno SEESAW f.s.   (R123)

Richard Cory
S solo,pno SEESAW f.s.   (R124)

White Roses
S solo,pno SEESAW f.s.   (R125)

REIJINSO see Nakada, Yoshinao

REIKULT ER ROTLAUST THANGID see
Isolfsson, Pall

REILLY, DADEE
Place For Mary To Lie, A   *Xmas
AMSI V-17   (R126)

REIMANN, ARIBERT (1936-   )
Impression IV
solo voice,pno SCHOTTS ED 7683
(R127)

Kinderlieder
S solo,pno SCHOTT ED 7682   (R128)

REINDEER RIDE, THE see Fladmoe, Arvid,
Bukkerittet

REINE DE CHYPRE: LE GONDOLIER DANS SA
PAUVRE NACELLE see Halévy, Jacques

REINE DE SABA: INSPIREZ-MOI see Gounod,
Charles François

REINE DE SABA: PLUS GRAND DANS SON
OBSCURITÉ see Gounod, Charles
François

REINE DE SABA: SOUS LES PIEDS D'UNE
FEMME see Gounod, Charles François

REINECKE, CARL (1824-1910)
Acht Lieder, Op. 81
[Ger] high solo RECITAL 285 (R129)

REINER, KAREL (1910-1979)
"A" Strummings
med solo,pno [7'] CESKY HUD. (R130)

Out Of "Tame Xenias"
low solo,pno [10'] CESKY HUD.
(R131)

Songs To Ancient Chinese Poetry
ABar soli,orch [24'] CESKY HUD.
(R132)

Three Songs To Words By F. T. Csokor
med solo,pno [10'] DOBLINGER (R133)

REINHARDT, BRUNO (1929-   )
Who Knows?
Bar solo,pno OR-TAV   (R134)

REINICK, ROBERT
Lieder Eines Malers Mit
Randzeichnungen Seiner Freunde
SCIEN 1336   (R135)

REISE, JAY (1950-   )
Alice At The End
S solo,ob,clar,vln,pno,2perc [15']
APNM sc $16.25, pts rent (R136)

REISE MED BÅT UTEN BÅT see Bibalo,
Antonio

REISELIED see Mendelssohn-Bartholdy,
Felix

REIZENSTEIN, FRANZ (1911-1968)
Five Sonnets, Op. 36
T solo,pno BARDIC BE0233   (R137)

REJCHA, ANTONIN (1770-1836)
Arie Dell'opere Perdite
T/S solo,2.2.2.2. 2.0.0.0. strings
[3'] CESKY HUD.   (R138)

Aure Amiche, Ah Non Spirate
"Ma Lasko Vzacna" S solo,2ob,2horn,
strings [13'] CESKY HUD. (R139)

Basta! Ti Credo
"Staci! Ja Verim" T solo,2ob,2horn,
strings [9'] CESKY HUD.   (R140)
see Italian Arias For High Voice

REJCHA, ANTONIN (cont'd.)

And Orchestra

Donne, Donne, Chi Vi Crede
"Zeny, Zeny, Kdo Vam Veri" S/T
solo,2ob,2horn,strings [3'] CESKY
HUD.   (R141)
see Italian Arias For High Voice
And Orchestra

Italian Arias For High Voice And
Orchestra
high solo,2ob,2horn,strings CESKY
HUD. f.s.
contains: Basta! Ti Credo!;
Donne, Donne, Chi Vi Crede
(R142)

Lyre, Fidele O Mon Amie (from Sappho)
"Lyro, Ty Lasko, Ma Druzko Stala" S
solo,2.2.2.2. 2.0.0.0. harp,
strings [3'] CESKY HUD.   (R143)

Lyro, Ty Lasko, Ma Druzko Stala
see Lyre, Fidele O Mon Amie

Ma Lasko Vzacna
see Aure Amiche, Ah Non Spirate

Staci! Ja Verim
see Basta! Ti Credo

Zeny, Zeny, Kdo Vam Veri
see Donne, Donne, Chi Vi Crede

REJSEMINDER FRA FJELD OG FJORD see
Grieg, Edvard Hagerup

RELAZIONI FRAGILI see Cerha, Friedrich

RELIEF IV see Krzanowski, Andrzej

RELIGIEUSE PORTUGAISE, LA see Duclos,
Pierre

RELIGION see Zumsteeg, Emilie

REMEMBER see Lyne, Peter

REMEMBRANCE see Fisher, Alfred, Zakhor
see Kirkwood, Antoinette

REMEMBRANCE NOISE see Kurtag, György

REMUNERATION, THE see Davidsson, Elias

RENDINE, SERGIO
Denique Apertos Baccus Amat Colles
S solo,clar,vln,pno 4-hands EDI-PAN
EP 7543   (R144)

RENKA I see Hosokawa, Toshio

RENN AVSTED see Backer-Lunde, Johan,
Hie Away

RENNA, ENRICO
Canzoni Eleatiche
solo voice EDI-PAN EP 7547   (R145)

RENOSTO, PAOLO (1935-1988)
Preludium
S/Mez solo,electronic tape SEESAW
(R146)

RENOUNCING OF LOVE, A see Kuiper, Klaus

RENOVATIONES see Welin, Karl-Erik

REQUIEM see Whitehead, Gillian

REQUIEM AUF HIROSHIMA see Behrend,
Siegfried

REQUIEM "FROM UNDERWOODS" see Homer,
Sidney

REQUIEM IM PARK see Pütz, Eduard

REQUIEM: INGEMISCO see Verdi, Giuseppe

REQUIEM POUR UNE MAREE NOIRE see
Rabinowitch, Alexandre

RESIST NOT, OH MAIDEN see Reuland,
Jacques

RESOLUTION see Eisler, Hanns

RESPIGHI, OTTORINO (1879-1936)
Au Milieu Du Jardin
[Fr] med-high solo,pno CLASSV 2021
(R147)

Laud To The Nativity
[Eng] RICORDI-IT 133002   (R148)

Musiche Vocali Italiane De Camera:
Respighi
(Bertagnolio, L.; Fujisaki, I.)
(CCU) ONGAKU 523805   (R149)

Nebbie
high solo,pno CLASSV 0360   (R150)

Nevicata
high solo,pno CLASSV 1145   (R151)

RESPIGHI, OTTORINO (cont'd.)

Stornellatrice
med solo,pno CLASSV 1029   (R152)

RESPONSE see Walker, George Theophilus

REST IN THE FOREST see Kjerulf,
Halfdan, Hvile I Skoven

REST SWEET NIMPHS see Shifrin, Seymour
J.

RESTORATION DUETS *CCU
(Timothy) 2 solo voices STAINER
3.3142 $5.95   (R153)

RESURGAM see Telfer, Nancy

RETROSPEKT see Killengreen, Christian

RETTER, DER see Müller, Adolf

RETURN OF THE LOFOTEN PEOPLE, THE see
Eggen, Arne, Ho Mor Faer
Lofotfolket Sitt Heim

RETURN TO THE SOUTH, A see Permont,
Haim

RETURNING THE SCROLL TO THE ARK see
Karlins, M. William

RETZEL, FRANK (1948-)
Amber Glass
MezA soli,clar/bass clar,vln,pno
[21'] APNM sc $11.75, set $22.00
  (R154)
One
S solo,vla,hpsd [12'] APNM sc
$5.75, set $16.50   (R155)

REULAND, JACQUES (1918-)
Five Lyrics
Mez solo,pno DONEMUS f.s.
contains: Natura Creatrix; Oh,
God Come Down; Resist Not, Oh
Maiden; Silver Bells; You
Breathing Wonder   (R156)

Handsome Nell
see Songs

Here's To Thy Health
see Songs

Natura Creatrix
see Five Lyrics

Oh, God Come Down
see Five Lyrics

Ploughman's Life, The
see Songs

Resist Not, Oh Maiden
see Five Lyrics

Silver Bells
see Five Lyrics

Songs
S solo,pno DONEMUS f.s.
contains: Handsome Nell; Here's
To Thy Health; Ploughman's
Life, The   (R157)

You Breathing Wonder
see Five Lyrics

REVE see Orland, Henry

RÊVE, UN see Balakirev, Mily
Alexeyevich

REVE SUR LE SABLE, LE see Ropartz,
Joseph Guy (Marie)

REVELATION see Weigl, [Mrs.] Vally

REVELATION IS NOT SEALED see Clarke,
Henry Leland

RÊVERIE see Hahn, Reynaldo see
Thwaites, Penelope

RÉVERSIBILITÉ see Aliprandi, Paul

REVES ET REALITES see Petit, Jean
Armand

REVIENS, REVIENS see Bizet, Georges,
Absence

REVUELTAS, SILVESTRE (1899-1940)
Bullfrogs
see Ranas

Duet For A Duck And A Canary
see Duo Para Pato Y Canario

Duo Para Pato Y Canario
"Duet For A Duck And A Canary" S
solo,1+pic.1.1.1. 0.1.1.0. perc,
pno [4'0"] PEER   (R158)

REVUELTAS, SILVESTRE (cont'd.)

I Don't Know What You Are Thinking
see No Se Por Que Piensas Tu

No Se Por Que Piensas Tu
"I Don't Know What You Are
Thinking" Bar solo,0.0.1(clar in
E flat,bass clar).1. 0.2.2.0.
banjo,4vln,db [10'0"] PEER (R159)

Owl, The
see Tecolote, El

Ranas
"Bullfrogs" S solo,2.1.0.1.
1.1.0.0. perc,2vln,vcl [3'0"]
PEER   (R160)

Seven Songs
see Siete Canciones

Siete Canciones
"Seven Songs" med solo,1.0.3.1.
1.2.1.1. tamb,strings [10'0"]
PEER   (R161)

Tecolote, El
"Owl, The" S solo,1.2.0.1. 1.0.0.0.
pno,vln,vcl [3'0"] PEER   (R162)

REY DE THULE, EL see Schubert, Franz
(Peter)

REY DEL ABEDUL, EL see Schubert, Franz
(Peter)

REYER, LOUIS ÉTIENNE ERNEST (1823-1909)
Madeleine Au Désert, La
med-high solo,pno CLASSV 2023
  (R163)
Maître Wolfram: Les Larmes
Bar solo,pno CLASSV 1471   (R164)

Sigurd: Esprits, Gardiens De Ces
Lieux Vénérés
T solo,pno CLASSV 2022   (R165)
Sigurd: Et, Toi Freia
[Fr] Bar solo,pno CLASSV 1506
  (R166)
Vieilles Chansons Of 17-18c, 40
solo voice,pno CLASSV C061   (R167)

Vingt Mélodies, Vol. 2
med solo,pno CLASSV C062   (R168)

REYNOLDS
Blind Men
solo voice,instrumental ensemble
PETERS 6826   (R169)

REZITATIV UND ARIE DER ERMINIA see
Scarlatti, Alessandro

RHAPSODIE see Campbell-Tipton, Louis
see Keussler, Gerhard von

RHEINISCHE LIEDER (VIER LIEDER) see
Cornelius, Peter

RHENE-BATON (RENÉ BATON) (1879-1940)
Cinq Melodies, Op. 16
[Fr] med solo RECITAL 286   (R170)

RHODES, PHILLIP (1940-)
Five Songs On Children's Poems *CC5U
S solo,pno sc AM.COMP.AL. $5.40
  (R171)
Three Scenes
med solo,pno [9'] sc AM.COMP.AL.
$10.70   (R172)

RHYMES (STUDIES IN IMITATION) VOL. 1
see Hughes, Herbert

RICCARDI, RICCARDO
Bruna Sei Tu Ma Bella
Bar solo,strings,perc EDI-PAN
EP 7687   (R173)

RICCI, PAOLO
Lettera A Rainer Maria Rilke
S solo,fl,harp,vla,db EDI-PAN
EP 7801   (R174)

Tre Liriche Di Kavafis
S solo,clar,gtr ZERBONI 9604 (R175)

RICE, THOMAS N. (1933-)
Corona
T solo,fl,clar,trom,perc,strings
SEESAW f.s.   (R176)

Fully Clothed
SB soli,vln,vcl SEESAW f.s.   (R177)

Musician's Prayer
B solo,pno SEESAW   (R178)

RICH, RICHARD J.
And A Record Shall Be Kept
solo voice,pno PIONEER PMP9002
$1.75   (R179)

RICHARD COEUR DE LION: O RICHARD, Ô MON
ROI! see Grétry, André Ernest
Modeste

RICHARD CORY see Reif, Paul

RICHARDS, STEPHEN (1935-)
Hin'ni
high solo,kbd TRANSCON. 991240
  (R180)
med solo,kbd TRANSCON. 991241
  (R181)
R'tzei
high solo,kbd, opt SATB cor
TRANSCON. 991261   (R182)
med solo,kbd, opt SATB cor
TRANSCON. 991263   (R183)

RICHTER, NICO (1915-1945)
Lied
high solo,pno DONEMUS   (R184)

RICORDO, UN see Brogi, Renato

RIDE BÅTKVELVET see Fladmoe, Arvid

RIDING ON WIND see Marez Oyens, Tera de

RIDUM, RIDUM see Runolfsson, Karl Otto

RIE, MUJER, RIE see Camprubi, J.

RIEDEL, AUGUSTE
Gesänge *Op.8,No.1-6, CC6U
solo voice KISTNER f.s.   (R185)

Gesänge *Op.11,No.1-4, CC4U
solo voice KISTNER f.s.   (R186)

RIEDEL, HERMANN
Drei Lieder, Op. 3
solo voice,pno SCIEN 1349 f.s.
contains: Du Fragst, Warum Ich
Liebe?; Einen Augenblick Sich
Finden; Im Dorfe Die Gasse
Entlang   (R187)

Du Fragst, Warum Ich Liebe?
see Drei Lieder, Op. 3

Einen Augenblick Sich Finden
see Drei Lieder, Op. 3

Im Dorfe Die Gasse Entlang
see Drei Lieder, Op. 3

RIEDLBAUCH, VACLAV (1947-)
Touzenec Pisni
T solo,pno PANTON 148   (R188)

RIEDSTRA, TOM (1957-)
Wisecracks
S solo,3clar,bass clar [16']
DONEMUS   (R189)

RIENZI: ALMÄCHTIGER VATER see Wagner,
Richard

RIENZI: GERECHTER GOTT see Wagner,
Richard

RIGHINI
Twelve Ariettas (composed with
Penhorwood, Edwin)
SOUTHERN B471   (R190)

RIGHINI, VINCENZO (1756-1812)
Enea Nel Lazio: Deh! Se In Ozio
S solo,pno CLASSV 0866   (R191)

Selva Incantata, La: Al Nome Tuo
Temuto
B solo,pno CLASSV 1578   (R192)

RIGOLETTO: CARO NOME see Verdi,
Giuseppe

RIGOLETTO: CORTIGIANI, VIL RAZZA see
Verdi, Giuseppe

RIGOLETTO: LA DONNA È MOBILE see Verdi,
Giuseppe

RIGOLETTO: PARI SIAMO see Verdi,
Giuseppe

RIGOLETTO: QUESTA O QUELLA see Verdi,
Giuseppe

RIJCK GOD, WIEN SAL ICK CLAGHEN see
Badings, Henk

RIKADLA see Hübner, Jaroslav

RILEY
Summer Music
solo voice,fl,gtr PETERS 67057
  (R193)

RILEY, DENNIS (1943-)
Clouds: Five Songs *CC5U
S solo,pno sc AM.COMP.AL. $3.85
  (R194)

Wedding Canticle *Op.11b
[Lat] Bar solo,vla [3'] sc
AM.COMP.AL. $4.60   (R195)

RILKE see Blumenfeld, Harold

RILKE-LIEDER see Hundsnes, Svein see Norby, Erik see Voortman, Roland see Voortman, Roland

RILKE LIEDER II see Voortman, Roland

RIMARIUM: TIO TONSATTA TANKAR see Sund, Robert

RIMED WOOD see Tveitt, Geirr, Rimet Skog

RIMET SKOG see Tveitt, Geirr

RIMMER, JOHN
Composition 9
S solo,electronic equipment WAI-TE-ATA 115 (R196)

RIMPROVERO, IL see Rossini, Gioacchino

RIMSKY-KORSAKOV, NIKOLAI (1844-1908)
Aria Of Levko
see May Night: Sleep, My Dear

Chanson Hebraique *Op.7
BELAIEFF 299 (R197)

Coq D'Or, Le: Hymn To The Sun
[Eng/Fr] high solo,pno CLASSV 0425 (R198)

Dragonflies, Op. 53
see Two Vocal Works

Four Romances, Op. 2
[Eng/Russ] KALMUS K 05268 f.s.
contains also: Four Romances, Op. 3; Four Romances, Op. 4; Four Romances, Op. 7 (R199)

Four Romances, Op. 3
see Four Romances, Op. 2

Four Romances, Op. 4
see Four Romances, Op. 2

Four Romances, Op. 7
see Four Romances, Op. 2

Four Romances, Op. 26
see Six Romances, Op. 8

Four Romances, Op. 27
[Eng/Russ] KALMUS K 05270 f.s.
contains also: Four Romances, Op. 39; Four Romances, Op. 40 (R200)

Four Romances, Op. 39
see Four Romances, Op. 27

Four Romances, Op. 40
see Four Romances, Op. 27

Four Romances, Op. 41
[Eng/Russ] KALMUS K 05271 f.s.
contains also: Four Romances, Op. 42; In Spring - Four Romances, Op. 43 (R201)

Four Romances, Op. 42
see Four Romances, Op. 41

Four Romances, Op. 55
[Eng/Russ] KALMUS K 05274 f.s.
contains also: Two Romances, Op. 56 (R202)

I Have Come To Greet You *Op.42,No.2
[Russ] high solo,pno CLASSV 2169 (R203)

In Spring - Four Romances, Op. 43
see Four Romances, Op. 41

May Night: Sleep, My Dear
"Aria Of Levko" [Russ/Ger/Fr] T solo,pno CLASSV 1060 (R204)

On Georgian Hills *Op.3,No.4
[Russ] med-high solo,pno CLASSV 2170 (R205)

Rose Enslaves The Nightingale
[Eng/Fr] high solo,pno CLASSV 0451 (R206)
[Russ] high solo,pno CLASSV 0829 (R207)

Russian Folksongs, 100, Op. 24
KALMUS K 05284 (R208)

Sadko: Berceuse or Wiegenlied
[Russ/Fr/Ger] S solo,pno CLASSV 1356 (R209)

Sadko: Song Of India
[Eng/Fr] high solo,pno CLASSV 0519 (R210)
[Russ/Fr/Ger] high solo,pno CLASSV 1123 (R211)

Sadko: Song Of The Viking Guest
[Russ/Fr] B solo,pno CLASSV 1270 (R212)

RIMSKY-KORSAKOV, NIKOLAI (cont'd.)

Six Romances, Op. 8
[Eng/Russ] KALMUS K 05269 f.s.
contains also: Two Romances, Op. 25; Four Romances, Op. 26 (R213)

Snegurochka (Snow Maiden): Snow-Flake's Arietta
[Eng] high solo,pno CLASSV 2171 (R214)

Songs To Texts Of Pushkin Vol. 1
[Russ] solo voice,pno CLASSV 2172 (R215)

Songs To Texts Of Pushkin Vol. 2
[Russ] solo voice,pno CLASSV 2173 (R216)

Two Duet, Op. 52
see Two Vocal Works

Two Romances, Op. 25
see Six Romances, Op. 8

Two Romances, Op. 56
see Four Romances, Op. 55

Two Vocal Works
[Eng/Russ] KALMUS K 05276 f.s.
contains: Dragonflies, Op. 53 (female solo&female solo&female solo); Two Duet, Op. 52 (SMez/TBar soli) (R217)

RINEHART, JOHN (1937-)
Passages
S solo,3.2.2.2. 4.2.3.1. timp,perc, harp,pno,strings,electronic tape [10'] sc AM.COMP.AL. $20.55 (R218)

Three Songs From Chamber Music *CC3U
S solo,pno sc AM.COMP.AL. $5.75 (R219)

RING, THE see Haxton, Kenneth

RINGELNATZ-CAPR. see Wolter, Detlef

RINGS OF SATURN, THE see Evensen, Kristian

RINGS SCHALLEN SCHON TROMPETEN see Handel, George Frideric

RIONDY, LUCIEN (1919-)
Jeanne D'Arc
Mez solo,3.2.2.2. 4.3.3.1. 2perc, timp,strings [20'] pno red,sc,pts BILLAUDOT (R220)

RIPPENTROP, DENICE
Christmas Angels
S solo,pno BEAUT BSP-115 (R221)

RISURREZIONE: PIANGI, SI, PIANGI see Alfano, Franco

RITRATTI see Sampaoli, Luciano

RITUAL see Nielsen, Tage

RIVER, THE see Sevriens, Jean

RIVER-MERCHANT'S WIFE, THE see Willingham, Lawrence

RIVIER ONDER DE GROND see Dekker, Dirk

RIVIÈRE, LA see Massenet, Jules

RIVIERES RIAIENT, LES see Bunge, Sas

RIVULET, THE see Backer-Lunde, Johan

ROA ROA RAMBINN see Tomasson, Jonas

ROARING FLAME see Dillon

ROBBE, W. DE V.
Songs On Poems By Emily Dickinson *song cycle
solo voice,pno [8'] SODEN (R222)

ROBBER BRIDEGROOM (SELECTIONS) see Waldman, Robert

ROBBER'S CHRISTMAS EVE, THE see Stolarczyk, Willy, Røverens Juleaften

ROBERT BRUCE: QUE TON ÂME SE NOBLE see Rossini, Gioacchino

ROBERT LE DIABLE: NONNES QUI REPOSEZ (INVOCATION) see Meyerbeer, Giacomo

ROBERT LE DIABLE: ROBERT, TOI QUE see Meyerbeer, Giacomo

ROBERTS, TIMOTHY
O Tuneful Voice
high solo,pno OXFORD 60.017 (R223)

ROBERTSSON, KARL-OLOF (1918-)
Ur Tobits Lovsång
S/T solo,org NOTERIA 1875 (R224)

ROBIN AND MARIAN MOTETS, VOL. 2
(Thomas, Wyndham) 3 solo voices
ANTICO AE25 (R225)

ROBIN AND MARIAN MOTETS, VOL. 3
(Thomas, Wyndham) 2 solo voices
ANTICO AE29 (R226)

ROBIN AND MARION MOTETS, VOL. 1
(Thomas, Wyndham) 3 solo voices
ANTICO AE22 (R227)

ROBIN GRAY see Franck, Cesar

ROCHBERG, A. GEORGE (1918-)
Seven Early Love Songs *song cycle
solo voice,pno (med diff) PRESSER 411-41093 (R228)

String Quartet No. 7
Bar solo,string quar PRESSER pno red 111-40113C, pts 111-40113P, sc 111-40113F (R229)

ROCKMAKER, JODY
Two Songs *CC2U
T solo,vla APNM sc $3.25, set $6.25 (R230)

RODD VOLVU see Helgason, Hallgrimur

RODGERS, LOU
Color Scheme
med solo,clar,vcl,pno [20']
AM.COMP.AL. (R231)

Warrior Saint, The
S solo,fl,trp,vcl,pno [30']
AM.COMP.AL. (R232)

RODRIGO, JOAQUÍN (1902-)
Canciones
solo voice,pno SCHOTTS ED 7598 (R233)

Duermete, Nino *Xmas
SBar soli,chamber orch pno red SCHOTT ST07596 (R234)
SBar soli,chamber orch SCHOTT ED 7596 (R235)

Four Catalonian Songs
solo voice,orch pno red SCHOTT ST07591 (R236)

Rosaliana
S solo,orch/pno red SCHOTT ST07719 (R237)
(Ludwig, Claus-Dieter) solo voice, pno SCHOTT ED 7719 (R238)

Villancicos *Xmas
solo voice,pno SCHOTTS ED 12406 (R239)

Villancicos, For Voice And Piano *CCU
EUR.AM.MUS. ST12406 f.s. (R240)

RODRIGUEZ PERIS, MARTIN JOSE (1949-)
Canciones Infantiles
solo voice,pno EMEC f.s.
contains: Cómo Dibujar Un Niño; Cómo Dibujar Una Bruja; Cucu; Pajarito, El; Sapito Feo, El (R241)

Cómo Dibujar Un Niño
see Canciones Infantiles

Cómo Dibujar Una Bruja
see Canciones Infantiles

Cucu
see Canciones Infantiles

Pajarito, El
see Canciones Infantiles

Sapito Feo, El
see Canciones Infantiles

ROE, BETTY (1930-)
Compliments Of The Season
med solo (med) NOVELLO (R242)
med solo (med) THAMES (R243)

ROELLI, H.
Lieder, 101
solo voice,gtr/pno KUNZEL GM 1014 (R244)

ROETHKE-LIEDER, BOOK 1 see Hodkinson, Sydney P.

ROETHKE LIEDER, BOOK 2 see Hodkinson, Sydney P.

ROETHKE LIEDER, BOOK 3 see Hodkinson, Sydney P.

ROFF, JOSEPH (1910-)
Entreat Me Not To Leave You
FITZSIMONS F0115 (R245)

ROGERS, BERNARD (1893-1968)
Let God Arise
see Psalm No. 68

ROGERS, BERNARD (cont'd.)

Psalm No. 68
"Let God Arise" Bar solo,
3.2.2.2(contrabsn). 4.3.3.1.
timp,perc,strings [13'0"] PEER
(R246)

ROGERS, JAMES HENDERSON (1852-1933)
Five Quatrains From The Rubáiyât Of
Omar Khayyam
high solo,pno CLASSV 2024   (R247)

ROGERS, PATSY (1938-   )
Sonja, A Song Cycle, For Soprano And
Piano
HILD 09202   (R248)

ROHR, HEINRICH
Leidensgeschichte Nach Johannes
3 solo voices CHRIS 50714 f.s.
(R249)

Leidensgeschichte Nach Lukas
3 solo voices CHRIS 50713 f.s.
(R250)

ROI A FAIT BATTRE TAMBOUR, LE see
Arrieu, Claude

ROI DE LAHORE, LE: J'AI FUI LA CHAMBRE
NUPTIALE! see Massenet, Jules

ROI DE LAHORE, LE: QUE LES DOULEURS DE
LA TERRE see Massenet, Jules

ROI DE LAHORE: FERME LES YEUX see
Massenet, Jules

ROI DE LAHORE: PROMESSE DE MON AVENIR
see Massenet, Jules

ROI D'YS, LE: VAINEMENT see Lalo,
Edouard

ROI ET LE FERMIER, LE: I REGARDAIT MON
BOUQUET see Monsigny, Pierre-
Alexandre

ROI L'A DIT, LE: AH! QUELLE OFFENSE see
Delibes, Léo

ROI L'A DIT, LE: DE JA LES HIRONDELLES
see Delibes, Léo

ROIS MAGES, LES see Brenet, Therese

ROISIN DUBH (2 VERSIONS) see Tal, Marjo

RÖKKURLJOD see Björnsson, Arni

RÖKKURLJOD THEODORU see Halldorsson,
Skuli

ROLAND HAYES BEATEN (GEORGIA 1942) see
Flothuis, Marius

ROLLIN, ROBERT LEON (1947-   )
Song Of Deborah
S solo,chamber group SEESAW f.s.
(R251)

ROLLING DOWN TO RIO see German, [Sir]
Edward (Edward German Jones)

ROMANCE see Debussy, Claude

ROMANCE DE LA ROSE see Flotow,
Friedrich von

ROMANCE DE MIGNON see Duparc, Henri

ROMANCE DE NADIR see Bizet, Georges

ROMANCE DE NINA: LE BAL MASQUÉ see
Glazunov, Alexander Konstantinovich

ROMANCE, OP. 44 see Rubinstein, Anton

ROMANCES, OP. 121 (ON TEXTS FROM
"KROKODIL" see Shostakovich, Dmitri

ROMANSA see Blaustein, Susan

ROMANSER OCH SÅNGER I URVAL see
Rantzen, Torsten

ROMANZE see Herold, Louis-Joseph-
Ferdinand

ROMANZEN UND BALLADEN, OP. 49 see
Schumann, Robert (Alexander)

ROMANZEN UND BALLADEN, PART 1, OP. 45
see Schumann, Robert (Alexander)

ROMANZEN UND BALLADEN, PART 2, OP. 49
see Schumann, Robert (Alexander)

ROMANZEN UND BALLADEN, PART 3, OP. 53
see Schumann, Robert (Alexander)

ROMANZEN UND BALLADEN, PART 4, OP. 64
see Schumann, Robert (Alexander)

ROMANZEN UND MONOLOGE NACH PUSCHKIN see
Shostakovich, Dmitri

ROMEO ET JULIETTE: AH, JE VEUX VIVRE
see Gounod, Charles François

ROMEO ET JULIETTE: AH! LÈVETOI, SOLEIL!
see Gounod, Charles François

RONDE see Lekeu, Guillaume

RONDE AUTOUR DU MONDE, LA see Hubeau,
Jean

RONDEAU see Hall, Pauline see Orthel,
Leon

RONDEAU A LA MORT see Franken, Wim

RONDEEL VOOR HET LIEFSTE KIND see
Röntgen, Johannes

RONDEEL VOOR RODE ROZEN see Röntgen,
Johannes

RONDEL see Escher, Rudolf George see
Flothuis, Marius

RONDEL DE F. VILLON see Jolivet, Andre

RONDEL DE LA BELLE AU BOIS see
Massenet, Jules

RONDELS (1ER SÉRIE) see Koechlin,
Charles

RONDELS (2E SÉRIE) see Koechlin,
Charles

RONDELS, VOL.1 see Hahn, Reynaldo

RONDELS, VOL.2 see Hahn, Reynaldo

RONDINE, LA: CHI IL BEL SOGNO see
Puccini, Giacomo

RONDINE, LA: DIMMI CHE VUOI SEGUIRMI
see Puccini, Giacomo

RONDINE, LA: TWO ARIAS see Puccini,
Giacomo

RONSHEIM, JOHN RICHARD (1927-   )
Bitter-Sweet
S/Mez solo,vibra [3'] APNM sc
$2.50, set $4.75   (R252)

Easter-Wings
S solo,vibra [6'] APNM sc $2.50,
set $4.75   (R253)

Prayer
S solo,pno [3'] APNM sc $3.00, set
$5.75   (R254)

Sailing Homeward
S solo,vibra [4'] APNM sc $3.00,
set $5.75   (R255)

Words From Shakespeare
S solo,vibra,harp,pno [6'] APNM sc
$3.50, set $13.50   (R256)

RÖNTGEN, JOHANNES (1898-1969)
Laatste Woord, Het
see Vier Rondelen, Uit "Stilte Voor
Het Hart"

Rondeel Voor Het Liefste Kind
see Vier Rondelen, Uit "Stilte Voor
Het Hart"

Rondeel Voor Rode Rozen
see Vier Rondelen, Uit "Stilte Voor
Het Hart"

Speels Rondeel
see Vier Rondelen, Uit "Stilte Voor
Het Hart"

Vier Rondelen, Uit "Stilte Voor Het
Hart"
S solo,pno DONEMUS f.s.
contains: Laatste Woord, Het;
Rondeel Voor Het Liefste Kind;
Rondeel Voor Rode Rozen; Speels
Rondeel   (R257)

ROO, PAUL DE (1957-   )
Although The Moon
see Tanka I

Behold
see Tanka I

Tanka I
S solo,pno,vln DONEMUS f.s. [7']
contains: Although The Moon;
Behold; Though Going And Coming
(R258)

Though Going And Coming
see Tanka I

ROOM 231: SOMETHING BLACK see
Bortolotti, Mauro

ROOS, ROBERT DE (1907-1976)
Abenddämmerung
see Drei Romantische Lieder

Asra, Der
see Drei Romantische Lieder

Bergstimme
see Drei Romantische Lieder

Drei Romantische Lieder
S solo,pno DONEMUS f.s.
contains: Abenddämmerung; Asra,
Der; Bergstimme   (R259)

ROOSENDAEL, JAN ROKUS VAN (1960-   )
Eerste Lentedag
see Facetten

Facetten
S solo,pic&fl,fl,clar,bass clar,
pno,2vln,vla,vcl DONEMUS f.s.
[15']
contains: Eerste Lentedag; Leven
En Dood; November   (R260)

Fancy
see Harp Of Fire, The

Harp, The
see Harp Of Fire, The

Harp Of Fire, The
S solo,alto fl&pic,clar,2perc,harp,
pno DONEMUS f.s. [13']
contains: Fancy; Harp, The; Harp
Of Fire, The; His Road; Song Of
The Boat   (R261)

Harp Of Fire, The
see Harp Of Fire, The

His Road
see Harp Of Fire, The

Leven En Dood
see Facetten

November
see Facetten

Song Of The Boat
see Harp Of Fire, The

ROOSEVELT, [JOSEPH] WILLARD (1918-   )
American Sampler, An
S solo,horn,pno [14'] sc
AM.COMP.AL. $10.70   (R262)

Aria
high solo,pno [4'] sc AM.COMP.AL.
$4.60   (R263)

Four Songs [1] *CC4U
S solo,clar sc AM.COMP.AL. $4.60
(R264)

Four Songs [2] *CC4U
S solo,vla sc AM.COMP.AL. $5.00
(R265)

Human Fly, The
med solo,pno [2'] sc AM.COMP.AL.
$1.60   (R266)

May Song It Flourish
SMezBar soli,1.1.1.1. 2.1.1.0.
2perc,strings [14'] sc
AM.COMP.AL. $18.25   (R267)

Three Songs From Poe *CC3U
S solo,clar,pno AM.COMP.AL. sc
$10.70, pts $1.95   (R268)

To E E
med solo,pno [1'] sc AM.COMP.AL.
$1.60   (R269)

Two Songs [1] *CC2U
S solo,pno sc AM.COMP.AL. $1.95
(R270)

Two Songs [2] *CC2U
S solo,pno sc AM.COMP.AL. $4.60
(R271)

ROOTH, ANNA-GRETA
All Den Stjärnsådd
solo voice,pno STIM f.s.   (R272)

Blåklocka Och Klöver
solo voice,pno STIM f.s.   (R273)

Brinner En Eld, Det
solo voice,pno STIM f.s.   (R274)

Fyra Sånger Till Dikter Av Gabriela
Mistral *CC4U
solo voice,pno/org STIM f.s. (R275)

Kvinnan Och Sommaren
solo voice,pno/org STIM f.s. (R276)

Lyssna
solo voice,pno/org STIM f.s. (R277)

Överge Mig Aldrig
solo voice,pno/org STIM f.s. (R278)

ROOTH, ANNA-GRETA (cont'd.)

Var Inte Rädd För Mörkret
solo voice,pno/org STIM f.s. (R279)

ROPARTZ, JOSEPH GUY (MARIE) (1864-1955)
Quatre Poèmes D'après L'Intermezzo De
Henri Heine
[Fr] B solo,pno CLASSV 1222 (R280)

Reve Sur Le Sable, Le
[Fr] (5 poems by Charles Guerin)
RÉCITAL 331 (R281)

RORATE see Hovland, Egil

ROREM, NED (1923-)
Schuyler Songs
BOOSEY VAB0264 (R282)

Six Irish Poems
S/med solo,2.2.2.2. 2.0.0.0. harp,
perc,strings [18'0"] PEER (R283)

Song Album, Vol. 3
(CCU) BOOSEY VAB0259 f.s. (R284)

Three Calamus Poems
BOOSEY VAB0231 (R285)

ROSA see Ludt, Finn

ROSA DEL ESPINO see Schubert, Franz
(Peter)

ROSALES, ANTONIO (ca. 1740-1801)
Canción Contra Las Madamitas
Gorgoritadoras
see Galvan, Ventura, Seguidilla Del
Oficial Cortejante

ROSALÍA see Massana, A.

ROSALIANA see Rodrigo, Joaquín

ROSALIE see Dittersdorf, Karl Ditters
von

ROSALINDA: MECO VERRAI see Veracini,
Francesco Maria

ROSAURA, LA: NON DAR PIÙ PENE, O CARO
see Scarlatti, Alessandro

ROSAURA, LA: UN COR DA VOI FERITO see
Scarlatti, Alessandro

ROSE, THE see Medtner, Nikolai
Karlovich

ROSE AND THE GARDENER, THE see Foote,
Arthur

ROSE, COMME EN PEU D'ESPACE, LA see
Tsujii, Eisei

ROSE DES ABENDLANDES see Lothar, Mark

ROSE ENSLAVES THE NIGHTINGALE see
Rimsky-Korsakov, Nikolai

ROSE SAUVAGE see Schubert, Franz
(Peter), Heidenröslein

ROSEMAN, RONALD
Three Psalms *CC3U
S solo,fl/pic,clar/bass clar,vla,
vcl AM.COMP.AL. sc $14.50, pts
$9.90 (R286)

Two Religious Songs *CC2U
S solo,fl,ob,vcl,hpsd AM.COMP.AL.
sc $12.95, pts $29.65 (R287)

ROSEN see Evensen, Bernt Kasberg

ROSEN, JEROME (1921-)
Serenade
S solo,alto sax [8'] sc AM.COMP.AL.
$7.70 (R288)

ROSENDUFT...DUNKLER PARK see Borodin,
Alexander Porfirievich

ROSENKAVALIER, DER: DI RIGORI ARMATO
see Strauss, Richard

ROSENMAN, LEONARD (1924-)
Chamber Music No. 2
S solo,alto fl,English horn,clar,
bass clar,alto sax,harp,pno,vln,
vla,vcl,db,electronic tape
[22'0"] PEER (R289)

Looking Back At Faded Chandeliers
S solo,fl,clar,vln,vcl,pno [13'0"]
PEER (R290)

Prelude And Four Scenes
S solo,fl&pic&alto fl,ob&English
horn,clar&bass clar,trp,2perc,
harp,pno/cel,vln,vcl,db [30'0"]
PEER (R291)

ROSENMAN, LEONARD (cont'd.)

Your Childhood In Menton: Chamber
Music No. 2
S solo,instrumental ensemble PEER
60159-221 sc $30.00, set rent
(R292)

ROSENMÜLLER, JOHANN (ca. 1620-1684)
O Dives
A solo,2vla,vcl KING'S ROS3 (R293)

ROSENSTADEN see Jensen, Ludwig Irgens

ROSENWEIG, WILHELM
Ob Ich Dich Liebe
low solo,pno SCIEN 1368 (R294)

ROSES DE MAIG see Mestres, Apeles

ROSES DU MIDI see Strauss, Johann,
[Jr.]

ROSES FROM THE SOUTH see Strauss,
Johann, [Jr.], Roses Du Midi

ROSES OF PICARDY see Wood, Haydn

ROSS, COLIN ARCHIBALD CAMPBELL
(1911-)
Four Songs To Words By Madeline Chase
S solo CHILTERN (R295)

Lorna's Song
S solo CHILTERN (R296)

ROSSI, D.
Ditirambo
T solo,pno BOIL B.0968 (R297)

Serenata Italiana
solo voice,pno BOIL B.0824 (R298)

ROSSIGNOL, LE see Glazunov, Alexander
Konstantinovich

ROSSIGNOL, LE: ARIETTE see Delibes, Léo

ROSSIGNOL DES LILAS, LE see Hahn,
Reynaldo

ROSSIGNOLET DU BOIS, ROSSIGNOLET
SAUVAGE see Nigg, Serge

ROSSINI, GIOACCHINO (1792-1868)
Ariette À L'Ancienne
[It] med solo,pno CLASSV 1410
(R299)

Assisa A Piè D'un Salice
see Othello: Willow Song

Au Chevet D'un Mourant
"Élégie" [Fr] S solo,pno CLASSV
1670 (R300)

Ave Maria
med solo,pno CLASSV 1672 (R301)

Barber Of Seville, The: Ecco Ridente
T solo,pno CLASSV 0491 (R302)

Barber Of Seville, The: La Calunnia
B solo,pno (C maj, lower) CLASSV
0504 (R303)
B solo,pno (D maj, original key)
CLASSV 0497 (R304)

Barber Of Seville, The: Largo Al
Factotum
Bar solo,pno (B flat maj) CLASSV
0516 (R305)
Bar solo,pno (original key) CLASSV
0496 (R306)
"Hey! For The Factotum" Bar solo
RICORDI-IT LD115232 (R307)

Barber Of Seville, The: Una Voce Poco
Fà
Mez solo,pno (E maj, original key)
CLASSV 1208 (R308)
S solo,pno (F maj) CLASSV 1204
(R309)

Barbieri Di Siviglia, Il: Cavatina Di
Figaro
Bar solo,pno BOIL B.1611 (R310)

Barbieri Di Siviglia, Il: La Calunnia
B solo,pno BOIL B.1612 (R311)

Barbieri Di Siviglia, Il: Una Voce
Poco Fa
Mez solo,pno BOIL B.1610 (R312)

Beltà Crudele (Santo-Mango)
[It] med solo,pno CLASSV 1407
(R313)

Bianca E Falliero: Della Rosa Il Bel
Vermiglio
S solo,pno CLASSV 1470 (R314)

Canzonetta
"Nizza, Je Puis Sans Peine" [Fr]
Mez solo,pno CLASSV 1412 (R315)

Canzonetta Spagnuola
[Span] Mez solo,pno CLASSV 1408
(R316)

ROSSINI, GIOACCHINO (cont'd.)

Cenerentola, La: Nacqui All'
Affanno...Non Più Mesta
Mez solo,pno CLASSV 0818 (R317)

Cenerentola: Un Segreto D'Importanze
BB soli,pno SCIEN 1372 (R318)

Chanson Du Bébé, La
Mez solo,pno CLASSV 1673 (R319)

Comte Ory: En Proie À La Tristesse
[Fr] S solo,pno CLASSV 1683 (R320)

Comte Ory: Que Les Destins Prospères
[Fr] T solo,pno CLASSV 1682 (R321)

Comte Ory: Veiller Sans Cesse
[Fr] B solo,pno CLASSV 1230 (R322)

Danza, La
"Tarantella Napoletana" [It/Fr]
high solo,pno CLASSV 1087 (R323)
"Tarantella Napoletana" [It/Fr] med
solo,pno CLASSV 2025 (R324)

Élégie
see Au Chevet D'un Mourant

Gazza Ladra, La: Di Piacer Mi Balza
Il Cor
[It] S solo,pno CLASSV 1246 (R325)

Gita In Gondola, La
[It/Fr] med-high solo,pno CLASSV
1086 (R326)

Gorgheggi E Solfeggi (Vocalises)
solo voice,pno CLASSV 1088 (R327)

Guglielmo Tell: O Muto Asil Del
Pianto
T solo,pno CLASSV 0932 (R328)

Guglielmo Tell: Resta Immobile
[It] Bar solo,pno CLASSV 0534
(R329)

Guglielmo Tell: Selva Opaca
S solo,pno CLASSV 0982 (R330)

Guillaume Tell: Sois Immobile
[Fr] Bar solo,pno CLASSV 1636
(R331)

Hey! For The Factotum
see Barber Of Seville, The: Largo
Al Factotum

Invito, L'
[It/Fr] high solo,pno CLASSV 1084
(R332)

Italiana In Algeri, L': Cruda Sorte!
Amor Tiranno!
A solo,pno CLASSV 0896 (R333)

Maometto: "Sorgete": In Sì Bel
Giorno. Duce Di Tanti Eroi
B solo,pno CLASSV 0930 (R334)

Melodie Italiane Per Canto E
Pianoforte
solo voice,pno ZEN-ON 714790 (R335)

Nizza, Je Puis Sans Peine
see Canzonetta

Notturno A Due Voci
see Regata Veneziana, La: Voga, O
Tonio

Orgia, L'
[It/Fr] high solo,pno CLASSV 1083
(R336)

Orpheline Du Tyrol, L'
[Fr] Mez solo,pno CLASSV 1411
(R337)

Othello: Willow Song
"Assisa A Piè D'un Salice" [It] S
solo,pno CLASSV 0366 (R338)

Partenza, La
[It/Fr] med-high solo,pno CLASSV
1082 (R339)

Pastorella, La: Odia La
[It] Mez solo,pno CLASSV 1413
(R340)

Pastorella Delle Alpi, La
[It/Fr] med-high solo,pno CLASSV
1085 (R341)

Promessa, La
[It/Fr] high solo,pno CLASSV 1080
(R342)

Regata Veneziana, La
high solo,pno CLASSV 1079 (R343)

Regata Veneziana, La: Voga, O Tonio
"Notturno A Due Voci" SS soli,pno
CLASSV 1089 (R344)

Rimprovero, Il
[It/Fr] med-high solo,pno CLASSV
1081 (R345)

ROSSINI, GIOACCHINO (cont'd.)

Robert Bruce: Que Ton Âme Se Noble
    B solo,pno CLASSV 1575   (R346)

Semiramide: In Sì Barbara
    Mez solo,pno CLASSV 1604   (R347)

Semiramide: No, Non Ti Lascio
    SA soli,pno CLASSV 2027   (R348)

Separazione, La
    [It] med-high solo,pno CLASSV 1409
                                   (R349)
    [It/Eng] med solo,pno CLASSV 1163
                                   (R350)

Siège De Corinthe: La Gloire Et La
      Fortune
    Bar solo,pno CLASSV 1649   (R351)

Soirees Musicales, Vol. 1 *CC8U
    [It/Fr] high solo,pno KALMUS
      K 06855 f.s.   (R352)

Soirees Musicales, Vol. 2 *CC4U,duet
    [It/Fr] KALMUS K 06856 f.s. (R353)

Stabat Mater: Inflammatus
    [Lat/Eng] S solo,pno CLASSV 2026
                                   (R354)

Stabat Mater: Pro Peccatis
    [Lat/Eng] B solo,pno CLASSV 1268
                                   (R355)

Tancredi: Di Tanti Palpiti
    Mez solo,pno CLASSV 1605   (R356)

Tancredi: Fühlst Du Bei Vatertränen
    AT soli,pno SCIEN 1371   (R357)

Tarantella Napoletana
    see Danza, La

Ultimo Ricordo, L'
    Bar solo,pno CLASSV 1671   (R358)

Varianten Zur Cavatine Der Rosina
      ("Una Voce Poco Fa") (from The
      Barber Of Seville)
    KUNZEL GM 108   (R359)

Vocalises Et Solfeges *CCU
    solo voice FRANG $5.95   (R360)

ROSSINYOL, EL see Mestres, Apeles

ROTFÄRBUNG DES FLUSSES see Meijering,
  Cord

ROTOLI
    Mia Sposa Sarà La Mia Bandiera
    med-high solo,pno CLASSV 0518
                                   (R361)
    [It] high solo,pno CLASSV 1371
                                   (R362)

ROTREGLA see Albertsen, Per Hjort

ROTTENBERG, LUDWIG (1864-1932)
    Zwölf Lieder
    [Ger] (texts by Heinrich Heine)
      RECITAL 382   (R363)

ROUNDELAY see Rowland, David

ROUSE, CHRISTOPHER (1949-   )
    Aphrodite Cantos
    Mez solo,clar,perc,pno,vla,vcl,
      conductor [30'] AM.COMP.AL. sc
      $19.90, pts $36.00   (R364)

    Dream Of Christophene, The
    S solo,alto fl,bsn,horn,perc,vln,
      vcl,db, conductor [18']
      AM.COMP.AL. sc $21.30, pts $48.30
                                   (R365)

    First Stratum Of Empyrean
    S solo,fl,2perc,pno,2vln,vla,vcl
      [12'] AM.COMP.AL. sc $16.10, pts
      $44.40   (R366)

    Gacela Del Amor Imprevisto
    SS soli,ob d'amore,vla,pno,2perc
      [18'] AM.COMP.AL. sc $13.70, pts
      $26.60   (R367)

    Mitternachtlieder
    B solo,ob/English horn,clar,trp,
      pno/cel,2perc,vln,vla,vcl,db
      [17'] AM.COMP.AL. sc $21.45, pts
      $56.60   (R368)

ROUSSEL, ALBERT (CHARLES PAUL)
      (1869-1937)
    Douze Melodies
    [Fr] (CC12U) SALABERT 50488446
                                   (R369)

ROVENSTRUNCK, BERNHARD
    Lautende Stille - Larmender Tag
    solo voice,gtr PLUCKED STR T 0605
      $12.50   (R370)

RØVERENS JULEAFTEN see Stolarczyk,
  Willy

ROVICS, HOWARD (1936-   )
    All We Need
    S solo,pno [3'] sc AM.COMP.AL.
      $2.35   (R371)

    Guest, The
    female solo/male solo,gong [3'] sc
      AM.COMP.AL. $4.25   (R372)

    Inside This Clay Jug
    S solo,pno 4-hands,vcl [2']
      AM.COMP.AL. sc $4.60, pts $.80
                                   (R373)

    Klallam Song
    S solo,pno [2'] sc AM.COMP.AL.
      $1.60   (R374)

    Six Songs On Chinese Poetry *CC6U
    med solo,pno sc AM.COMP.AL. $10.70
                                   (R375)

    Songs For The Harvester Of Dreams
    S solo,clar/vln,2pno [12'] sc
      AM.COMP.AL. $16.50   (R376)

    Songs On Chinese Poetry *CCU
    S solo,fl/pic,clar/bass clar,vln,
      vcl,pno,perc AM.COMP.AL. sc
      $14.50, pts $11.45   (R377)

ROWLAND, DAVID (1939-   )
    Adieu, Farewell Earth's Bliss
    see Nashe Songs

    And Then He Flew On Her
    see Roundelay

    Fair Summer Droops
    see Roundelay

    I Saw A Summer Banqueting House
    see Nashe Songs

    Nashe Songs
    S solo,pno DONEMUS f.s. [12']
      contains: Adieu, Farewell Earth's
      Bliss; I Saw A Summer
      Banqueting House; Strength
      Stoops Unto The Grave; Thy Lips
      On Mine; Would I Could Bark The
      Sun   (R378)

    Roundelay
    S solo,fl,clar,perc,pno,vln,vla,vcl
      DONEMUS f.s. [20']
      contains: And Then He Flew On
      Her; Fair Summer Droops; Stars
      Fall; To The Execution Place
                                   (R379)

    Stars Fall
    see Roundelay

    Strength Stoops Unto The Grave
    see Nashe Songs

    Thy Lips On Mine
    see Nashe Songs

    To The Execution Place
    see Roundelay

    Would I Could Bark The Sun
    see Nashe Songs

ROZTOMILY SLAVICKU see Ryba, Jan Jakub
  Simon

R'TZEI see Richards, Stephen

RUBAIYAT FRAGMENTS see Leichtling, Alan

RUBAIYAT SONG CYCLE see Garlick, Antony

RUBINSTEIN, ANTON (1829-1894)
    Demon
    [Russ] Bar/B solo,pno (4 arias: 2
      baritone, 2 bass) CLASSV 1158
                                   (R380)

    Desire *Op.8,No.5
    "Sehnsucht" [Eng] high solo,pno
      CLASSV 2175   (R381)

    Klinge, Klinge, Mein Pandero
    med solo,pno CLASSV 0685   (R382)

    Melodie
    KAHNT 4136   (R383)

    Mélodies Persanes
    see Twelve Persian Songs, Op. 34

    Nerone: O Lumière Du Jour
    [Fr/Russ] T solo,pno CLASSV 2028
                                   (R384)

    Romance, Op. 44
    KAHNT 3716   (R385)

    Sehnsucht
    see Desire

    Twelve Persian Songs, Op. 34
    [Eng/Ger] high solo,pno CLASSV 0660
                                   (R386)
    "Mélodies Persanes" [Fr] high solo,
      pno CLASSV 0659   (R387)

RUDBECK, OLOF (1630-1702)
    Funeral Song And Lament
    see Sorg- Och Klagesång

    Sorg- Och Klagesång
    (Moberg, Carl-Allan; Ruden, Jan-
      Olof) "Funeral Song And Lament"
      [Swed] high solo&high solo,cont
      (vol. also includes "Veni Sancte
      Spiritus" by Düben and "Lamentum"
      by Dijkman) sc,pts REIMERS 107011
                                   (R388)

RUDD-MOORE, DOROTHY (1940-   )
    Sonnets On Love, Rosebuds And Death
    S solo,vln,pno [22'] sc AM.COMP.AL.
      $13.80   (R389)

RUDHYAR, DANE (DANIEL CHENNEVIÈRE)
      (1895-   )
    Trois Chansons De Bilitis *CC3U
    low female solo,1.1.1.1. 1.1.1.0.
      pno,harp,cel,vibra,2vln,vla,vcl,
      db AM.COMP.AL. sc $13.70, pts
      $21.45   (R390)

    Trois Poemes Tragiques *CC3U
    A solo,vln,pno sc AM.COMP.AL. $7.60
                                   (R391)

RUGGED YANK, THE see Dawson, William
  Levi

RUGIADOSE, ODOROSE see Scarlatti,
  Alessandro, Violette, Le

RUHE, MEINE SEELE! see Strauss, Richard

RUIKT NAAR BIER, HET see Delden, Lex
  van

RUIN, THE see Cohen, Edward

RUITER, WIM DE (1943-   )
    Answer July
    see Five Songs (Emily Dickinson)

    As Imperceptibly As Grief
    see Five Songs (Emily Dickinson)
    see Four Songs

    Biezen Mandje
    see Zes Liederen

    Door De Bomen Staart
    see Ossuarium

    Five Songs (Emily Dickinson)
    S solo,woodwind quin,pic,pno,vln,
      vla,vcl,db DONEMUS f.s. [25']
      contains: Answer July; As
      Imperceptibly As Grief; In
      Winter In My Room; There Are
      Two Mays   (R392)

    Four Songs *CC4U
    S solo,pno DONEMUS f.s.   (R393)

    Four Songs
    S solo,pno DONEMUS f.s. [20'],
      texts by Emily Dickinson
      contains: As Imperceptibly As
      Grief; In Winter In My Room;
      There Are Two Mays; Winter
      Under Cultivation   (R394)

    Gehoord Gedicht
    see Zes Liederen

    Heerser
    see Ossuarium

    In Winter In My Room
    see Five Songs (Emily Dickinson)
    see Four Songs

    Kazematten, De
    see Ossuarium

    Kooitje
    see Zes Liederen

    Lucht, Een
    see Ossuarium

    Ook Vandaag Weer
    see Zes Liederen

    Ossuarium
    Bar solo,pno DONEMUS f.s. [20']
      contains: Door De Bomen Staart;
      Heerser; Kazematten, De; Lucht,
      Een; Soms; Wat Nog Splijten Kon
                                   (R395)

    Soms
    see Ossuarium

    Stap, Stap
    see Zes Liederen

    There Are Two Mays
    see Five Songs (Emily Dickinson)
    see Four Songs

    Tien Vocale Minuten
    MezBar/MezB soli [10'] DONEMUS
                                   (R396)

RUITER, WIM DE (cont'd.)

Wat Nog Splijten Kon
see Ossuarium

Winter Under Cultivation
see Four Songs

Zeer Vrij Naar Het Chinees
see Zes Liederen

Zes Liederen
high solo&med solo,pno DONEMUS f.s.
[14']
contains: Biezen Mandje; Gehoord
Gedicht; Kooitje; Ook Vandaag
Weer; Stap, Stap; Zeer Vrij
Naar Het Chinees   (R397)

RULE, BRITANNIA see Arne, Thomas
Augustine

RUNDE ERDE see Geelen, Mathieu

RUNOLFSSON, KARL OTTO (1900-1970)
Alfamaerin
solo voice,pno ICELAND 016-058
(R398)
Den Farende Svend
solo voice,pno [2'2"] ICELAND
016-023   (R399)
Enn Syngur Vornottin
solo voice,pno ICELAND 016-053
(R400)
Fjogur Songlog
solo voice,pno ICELAND 016-025
(R401)
Forkeikur Ad "Skugga-Sveini"
solo voice,pno ICELAND 016-012
(R402)
Heimthra
solo voice,pno ICELAND 016-062
(R403)
Hja Lygnri Modu
solo voice,pno ICELAND 016-050
(R404)
Ingalo
solo voice,pno ICELAND 016-061
(R405)
Japanskt Ljod
solo voice,pno ICELAND 016-047
(R406)
Last Dance
solo voice,pno ICELAND 016-059
(R407)
Oraefi
solo voice,pno ICELAND 016-046
(R408)
Ridum, Ridum
solo voice,pno (Icelandic folk
song) ICELAND 016-051   (R409)
Segdu Mer Sögu
solo voice,pno ICELAND 016-040
(R410)
Songlog
solo voice,pno ICELAND 016-032
(R411)
Söngur Idnadarmanna
solo voice,pno ICELAND 016-044
(R412)
Sunset
solo voice,pno ICELAND 016-060
(R413)
Thrju Sönglög
solo voice,pno ICELAND 016-024
(R414)
Tveir Fuglar Flugu Af Björgum
solo voice,pno ICELAND 016-048
(R415)
Tvö Islensk Thjodlög
solo voice,pno ICELAND 016-052
(R416)
Vidtal Vid Spoa
solo voice,pno [1'0"] ICELAND
016-007   (R417)
Vikingsvalsinn
solo voice,pno ICELAND 016-043
(R418)
Vorljod
TBar soli,pno ICELAND 016-042
(R419)

RUNSWICK, DARYL (1946-   )
Lady Lazarus
FABER 51202 X   (R420)

RUPES, G.
Vingt Mélodies, Vol. 1
solo voice,pno CLASSV C052   (R421)

RURAL SONGS see Kelly, Robert T.

RUSALKA: ARIE DES WASSERMANNS see
Dvorák, Antonín

RUSALKA: CAVATINA ACT III see
Dargomyzhsky, Alexander Sergeyevich

RUSALKA'S SONG TO THE MOON see Dvorák,
Antonín

RUSAVA see Schneeweiss, Jan

RUSLAN AND LUDMILLA: CAVATINA OF
LUDMILLA see Glinka, Mikhail
Ivanovich

RUSSEL, HENRY
Dandy Jim Of Caroline
SCIEN 1397   (R422)
Will Nobody Marry Me
SCIEN 1398   (R423)
Woodman, Spare That Tree!
SCIEN 1399   (R424)

RUSSELL, ARMAND KING (1932-   )
Ballad With Epitaphs
2 solo voices,perc SEESAW f.s.
(R425)

RUSSIAN FOLKSONGS, 100, OP. 24 see
Rimsky-Korsakov, Nikolai

RUSSIAN SONGS, BAND 1 see Tcherepnin,
Alexander

RUSSIAN SONGS, BAND 2 see Tcherepnin,
Alexander

RUSSIAN SONGS, BAND 3 see Tcherepnin,
Alexander

RUSSIAN SONGS, BAND 4 see Tcherepnin,
Alexander

RUSSISCHE ROMANZE see Louis Ferdinand,
Prince Of Prussia

RUSSISCHES VOLKSLIED see Louis
Ferdinand, Prince Of Prussia

RUYNEMAN, DANIEL (1886-1963)
Diwan
see Drei Persische Lieder

Drei Persische Lieder
high solo,pno DONEMUS f.s.
contains: Diwan; O Komm,
Geliebte; Was Kann Das Leben
Uns Denn Nun Noch Weiter
Frommen   (R426)

O Komm, Geliebte
see Drei Persische Lieder

Was Kann Das Leben Uns Denn Nun Noch
Weiter Frommen
see Drei Persische Lieder

RUZICKA, PETER (1948-   )
...Der Die Gesänge Zerschlug
Bar solo,chamber group sc SIKORSKI
1803   (R427)

Vier Gesänge Nach Fragmenten Von
Nietzsche
Mez solo,pno SIKORSKI 802   (R428)

RYBA, JAN JAKUB SIMON (1765-1815)
Duet In E-Flat
see Duetto In Mi-Flat

Duetto In Mi-Flat
"Duet In E-Flat" [Lat] SA soli,
2vln,db [2'] CESKY HUD.   (R429)

Jak Mile, Rozkosne
A solo,2horn,org,strings [4'] CESKY
HUD.   (R430)

Libou Pisnicku Svemu Jezisku
see Sest Chvalozpevu

Mili Synackove, Pojd'te K Betlemu
see Sest Chvalozpevu

O, Jak Plesa Ve Mne Srdicko
see Sest Chvalozpevu

Roztomily Slavicku
A solo,2horn,org,strings,vln solo
[5'] CESKY HUD.   (R431)
see Sest Chvalozpevu

S Pastyri Budu Muzikovat
see Sest Chvalozpevu

Sest Chvalozpevu
SA soli,1.0.2.1. 2.1.0.0. strings,
org CESKY HUD. f.s.
contains: Libou Pisnicku Svemu
Jezisku; Mili Synackove,
Pojd'te K Betlemu; O, Jak Plesa
Ve Mne Srdicko; Roztomily
Slavicku; S Pastyri Budu
Muzikovat; Spi, Spi Nevinatko
(R432)
Spi, Spi Nevinatko
SA soli,2horn,org,strings [3']
CESKY HUD.   (R433)
see Sest Chvalozpevu

Usni, Male Poupatko
solo voice,2horn,org,strings [3']
CESKY HUD.   (R434)

RYDBERG, BO
Innocence In Iron
[Eng] S solo,bass clar,pno TONOS
(R435)
RYOANJI see Cage, John

RYOANJI TEMPLE see Marez Oyens, Tera de

RYPDAL, TERJE (1947-   )
Spegling
Mez solo,2.2.1.1. 2.1.1.0. timp,
perc,kbd,strings [18'] NORGE f.s.
(R436)

S

'S BESTI PARL see Baumann, Alexander

S(C)ENSHU, JIRO (1934-   )
　　Prajuna-Paramita
　　　T solo,pno [20'] JAPAN　　　　(S1)

'S DEANDERL ÁM BACH see Suppe, Franz
　　von

'S DIERNDL ALS CONCERT-SÄNGERIN see
　　Suppe, Franz von

S.F., THREE SONGS see MacBride, David
　　Huston

'S GHAIMNISS see Stelzhammer

'S HOCHZEIT GSANGL see Baumann,
　　Alexander

'S IS ANDERSCHT see Baumann, Alexander

'S MEISTERWERK see Suppe, Franz von

S PASTYRI BUDU MUZIKOVAT see Ryba, Jan
　　Jakub Simon

SÅ ER DU FRI see Baden, Conrad

SÅ ER MIN HÅND IGJEN BLITT TOM see
　　Volle, Bjarne, Liten Vise, En

SÅ FINT ATT DIN HAND see Strandsjö,
　　Göte

SÅ HØY EN HIMMEL see Groven, Eivind

SAA TAG MIT HJERTE see Alfvén, Hugo

SAARIAHO, KAIJA (1952-   )
　　Il Pleut
　　　S solo,pno JASE　　　　　　(S2)

SACCHINI, ANTONIO (MARIA GASPARO
　　GIOACCHINO) (1730-1786)
　　Amavit Eum: Offertorium
　　　(Voxman, Himie) solo voice,ob,pno
　　　NOVA NM259 f.s.　　　　　(S3)

　　Dardanus: Jours Heureux
　　　T solo,pno CLASSV 1525　　　(S4)

　　O Quam Carae Et Quam Beatae Silvae
　　　S solo,string orch,cont KUNZEL
　　　GM 1280　　　　　　　　　(S5)

SACRE, GUY
　　Cartes Postales
　　　solo voice,pno DURAND　　　(S6)

　　Clair-Obscur
　　　Bar solo,pno (med diff) DURAND (S7)

　　Six Poemes De "Vocabulaire" *song
　　　cycle
　　　solo voice,pno (diff) DURAND　(S8)

SACRED AND SECULAR SONGS see Haydn,
　　[Franz] Joseph

SACRED CLASSICS
　　high solo,pno (CC10L) LEONARD-US
　　　00747013 accomp tape available (S9)
　　low solo,pno (CC10L) LEONARD-US
　　　00747014 accomp tape available
　　　　　　　　　　　　　　　(S10)

SACRED DUETS see Schütz, Heinrich

SACRED SONGS
　　("World's Favorite Series") ASHLEY
　　143　　　　　　　　　　　　(S11)

SACRI MUSICALI AFFETTI, OP. 5 see
　　Strozzi, Barbara

SACRILEGE OF A. KENT see Hutchison, W.

SÅDAN KÄRLEK see Blomberg, Erik

SADKO: BERCEUSE OR WIEGENLIED see
　　Rimsky-Korsakov, Nikolai

SADKO: SONG OF INDIA see Rimsky-
　　Korsakov, Nikolai

SADKO: SONG OF THE VIKING GUEST see
　　Rimsky-Korsakov, Nikolai

SAELASTE PÅ JORD, DET see Hovland, Egil

SAELE see Olsen, Sparre

SAEUNN AND THE POET see Halldorsson,
　　Skuli

SAEVERUD, TORMOD
　　Der Viddevinden Bur
　　　[Norw] solo voice,pno MUSIKK (S12)

SAEVIT MARE SURGUNT VENTI see Senkyr,
　　Augustin

SÅG DU MITT LAND see Olsen, Sparre

SAGVIK, STELLAN (1952-   )
　　Vokalis
　　　S solo,org TONOS　　　　　(S13)

SAILING HOMEWARD see Ronsheim, John
　　Richard

SAINT-GEORGES, CHEVALIER DE
　　see SAINT-GEORGES, JOSEPH BOULOGNE DE

SAINT-GEORGES, JOSEPH BOULOGNE DE
　　(1739-1799)
　　Clemengis La Douloureuse Image, De
　　　see Duo From "Ernestine"

　　Duo From "Ernestine"
　　　"Clemengis La Douloureuse Image,
　　　De" SS soli,2ob,2bsn,2horn,
　　　strings [5'0"] PEER　　　(S14)

　　Scena From "Ernestine"
　　　S solo,2ob,2bsn,2horn,strings
　　　[7'0"] PEER　　　　　　　(S15)

SAINT PAUL: BUT THE LORD IS MINDFUL OF
　　HIS OWN see Mendelssohn-Bartholdy,
　　Felix

SAINT PAUL: O GOD, HAVE MERCY see
　　Mendelssohn-Bartholdy, Felix

SAINT-SAËNS, CAMILLE (1835-1921)
　　Attente, L'
　　　med-high solo,pno CLASSV 2035 (S16)

　　Bonheur Est Chose Légère, Le
　　　high solo,pno CLASSV 0826　(S17)
　　　high solo,pno,vln CLASSV 0522 (S18)

　　Cendre Rouge, La
　　　[Fr] (10 poems by Georges Docquois)
　　　RÉCITAL 332　　　　　　　(S19)

　　Chanson À Boire Du Vieux Temps
　　　"Philosophes Rêveurs" med solo,pno
　　　CLASSV 2030　　　　　　　(S20)

　　Chant De Ceux Qui S'en Vont Sur Mer
　　　high solo,pno CLASSV 1522　(S21)

　　Cloche, La: Seule En Ta Sombre Tour
　　　high solo,pno CLASSV 2033　(S22)
　　　med solo,pno CLASSV 1205　(S23)
　　　low solo,pno CLASSV 0697　(S24)

　　Dans Les Coins Bleus
　　　med solo,pno CLASSV 2031　(S25)

　　Déjanire: Epithalame
　　　"Vien, Ô Toi" [Fr] T solo,pno
　　　CLASSV 1187　　　　　　　(S26)

　　Desdichado, El
　　　SS/SMez/ST soli,pno CLASSV 0616
　　　　　　　　　　　　　　　(S27)

　　Dix Mélodies
　　　solo voice,pno CLASSV C056　(S28)

　　Étienne Marcel: O Beaux Rêves
　　　Évanouis
　　　S solo,pno CLASSV 1611　　(S29)

　　Guitares Et Mandolines
　　　med solo,pno CLASSV 2032　(S30)
　　　[Fr] high solo,pno CLASSV 1494 (S31)

　　Henry VIII: Qui Donc Commande Quand
　　　Il Aime
　　　B solo,pno CLASSV 1638　　(S32)

　　Ici Les Tendres Oiseaux
　　　see Pastorale

　　Lola, Op. 116 *scena
　　　[Fr] 2 solo voices,pno (not
　　　available outside U.S.A.) RECITAL
　　　385　　　　　　　　　　　(S33)

　　Mélodies Persanes
　　　[Fr] med-high solo,pno CLASSV 1415
　　　　　　　　　　　　　　　(S34)

　　Mort D'Ophélie, La
　　　med-high solo,pno CLASSV 2034 (S35)

　　Nightingale And The Rose
　　　S solo,pno CLASSV 0338　　(S36)

　　Nuit Persanes
　　　[Fr] voc sc CLASSV 1507　(S37)

　　Pas D'Armes Du Roi Jean, Le
　　　B solo,pno CLASSV 2029　　(S38)
　　　Bar solo,pno CLASSV 1207　(S39)

　　Pastorale
　　　"Ici Les Tendres Oiseaux" SBar
　　　soli,pno CLASSV 1206　　　(S40)

SAINT-SAËNS, CAMILLE (cont'd.)

　　Philosophes Rêveurs
　　　see Chanson À Boire Du Vieux Temps

　　Pourquoi Rester Seulette
　　　[Fr/Eng] coloratura sop,pno CLASSV
　　　1186　　　　　　　　　　(S41)

　　Samson Et Delilah: Amour! Viens Aider
　　　Mez solo,pno CLASSV 1601　(S42)

　　Samson Et Delilah: Mon Coeur S'ouvre
　　　À Ta Voix
　　　Mez solo,pno CLASSV 1602　(S43)

　　Samson Et Delilah: Printemps Qui
　　　Commence
　　　Mez solo,pno CLASSV 0511　(S44)

　　Soirée En Mer: Près Du Pêcheur
　　　high solo,pno CLASSV 2036　(S45)

　　Vien, Ô Toi
　　　see Déjanire: Epithalame

　　Viens
　　　SBar soli,pno CLASSV 1185　(S46)

　　Vingt Mélodies Et Duos Vol. 2
　　　solo voice,pno CLASSV C057　(S47)

　　Vingt Mélodies Vol. 1
　　　solo voice,pno CLASSV C055　(S48)

SAINT-YVES, BAX
　　Agnus Dei
　　　Mez/B solo,org LEDUC f.s.　(S49)

　　Ave Maria
　　　solo voice LEDUC f.s.　　(S50)

SAIS-TU, LE see Massenet, Jules

SAISONS DU COEUR, LES see Pfister

SAITO, TAKANOBU
　　Avalanche In Spring: Song Album *CCU
　　　S/T solo,pno ONGAKU f.s. [115']
　　　　　　　　　　　　　　　(S51)
　　Yearn For Native Land: Six Songs
　　　T/S solo,pno [25'] JAPAN　(S52)

SAKURA DENSETSU see Yuyama, Akira

SAKURA TSUKIYO see Arima, Reiko

SAKURASO see Hirai, Takeichiro

SAKYAMUNI COMING OUT FROM THE MOUNTAIN
　　see Little, David

SALAS, JUAN ORREGO
　　see ORREGO-SALAS, JUAN

SALIGE ER DE DØDE see Kverno, Trond

SALINA
　　Ojos Negros
　　　solo voice,pno BOIL B.1124　(S53)

SALLEY GARDENS, THE see Corigliano,
　　John

SALME see Dorumsgaard, Arne see
　　Evensen, Bernt Kasberg see
　　Kielland, Olav see Torjussen,
　　Trygve

SALME 40, OP.6 see Haegeland, Eilert M.

SALME FOR DAGEN, EN see Karlsen, Kjell
　　Mørk

SALME FOR DAGEN-HERRE, DET STORMER I
　　MITT SINN, EN see Karlsen, Kjell
　　Mørk

SALME OM KUNSTEN see Ørbeck, Anne Marie

SALMO QUARANTESIMOSECUNDO see Marcello,
　　Benedetto

SALMO QUARANTESIMOSESTO see Marcello,
　　Benedetto

SALMO VIGESIMOPRIMO see Marcello,
　　Benedetto

SALMUR see Isolfsson, Pall see
　　Stefansson, Finnur Torfi

SALTER, MARY TURNER (1856-1938)
　　From Old Japan *song cycle
　　　[Eng] high solo RECITAL 287　(S54)

SALTERIO POPOLARE I see De Grandis,
　　Renato

SALTERIO POPOLARE II see De Grandis,
　　Renato

SALVADOR, MATILDE
Cançons Per A Veu I Piano *CCU
solo voice,pno PILES 1212-V f.s.
(S55)

SALVADORI, LUCA
Luoghi Da Ares
solo voice,fl EDI-PAN EP 7817 (S56)

SALVATOR ROSA: FORMA SUBLIME, ETEREA
see Gomes, Antônio Carlos

SALVATOR ROSA: MIA PICCIRELLA see
Gomes, Antônio Carlos

SALVE REGINA see Biechteler, B.

SAMAMA, LEO (1951-)
Changement De Decor
see Wit, Op. 33

Ik Word Zo Donker
see Wit, Op. 33

Sneeuw
see Wit, Op. 33

Sneeuw Ligt In Den Morgen Vroeg, Een
see Wit, Op. 33

Westelijk
see Wit, Op. 33

Winter
see Wit, Op. 33

Wit, Op. 33
S solo,harp DONEMUS f.s. [13']
contains: Changement De Decor; Ik
Word Zo Donker; Sneeuw; Sneeuw
Ligt In Den Morgen Vroeg, Een;
Westelijk; Winter (S57)

SAME THING, THE see Bolcom, William
Elden

SAMEN see Dirriwachter, Wim

SAMIRA'S ARIA see Corigliano, John

SAMKENND see Thordarson, Hilmar

SAMLA INTE SKATTER PÅ JORDEN see Sköld,
Bengt-Göran

SAMMARTINI, GIOVANNI BATTISTA
(1701-1775)
Pianto Delle Pie Donne, Il
(Marley, Marie) 3 solo voices,2ob,
2vln,vla,db,cont. horns A-R ED
ISBN 0-89579-244-3 (S58)

SÄMMTLICHE COMPOSITIONEN see Schubert,
Franz (Peter)

SÄMMTLICHE LIEDER see Zelter, Carl
Friedrich

SAMPAOLI, LUCIANO
Banda, La
S solo,sax,pno EDI-PAN EP 7841
(S59)

Briciole, Le
S solo,clar,bsn,harmonium EDI-PAN
EP 7390 (S60)

Canto III
S solo,fl,pno EDI-PAN EP 7491 (S61)

Logorato Il Tempo
Mez solo,fl,bsn EDI-PAN EP 7489
(S62)

Ritratti
S solo,clar,bsn,harmonium EDI-PAN
EP 7494 (S63)

Tempo Futuro, Il
S solo,harmonium EDI-PAN EP 7350
(S64)

SAMSON ET DELILAH: AMOUR! VIENS AIDER
see Saint-Saëns, Camille

SAMSON ET DELILAH: MON COEUR S'OUVRE À
TA VOIX see Saint-Saëns, Camille

SAMSON ET DELILAH: PRINTEMPS QUI
COMMENCE see Saint-Saëns, Camille

SAMSON: LET THE BRIGHT SERAPHIM see
Handel, George Frideric

SÄMTLICHE LIEDER see Mendelssohn-
Bartholdy, Felix

SÄMTLICHE LIEDER, ORIGINALTONARTEN see
Wagner, Richard

SÄMTLICHE LIEDER UND GESÄNGE MIT
KLAVIER, BAND 1 see Beethoven,
Ludwig van

SÄMTLICHE LIEDER UND GESÄNGE MIT
KLAVIER, BAND 2 see Beethoven,
Ludwig van

SAMUEL, GERHARD (1924-)
Dying, Dying In The Night!
see This Heart That Broke So
Long... Three Songs On Poems By
Emily Dickinson

This Heart That Broke
see This Heart That Broke So
Long... Three Songs On Poems By
Emily Dickinson

This Heart That Broke So Long...
Three Songs On Poems By Emily
Dickinson
high solo,pno MMB X814012 f.s.
contains: Dying, Dying In The
Night!; This Heart That Broke;
You Love Me - You Are Sure
(S65)

VAPP
S solo, pitch pipe MMB X810001
(S66)

You Love Me - You Are Sure
see This Heart That Broke So
Long... Three Songs On Poems By
Emily Dickinson

SAN BASILIO see Pizzetti, Ildebrando

SANCHO MARRACO
Album De Cancons
solo voice,pno BOIL B.0591 (S67)

SANCTUS-AGNUS DEI see Eftestol, Sverre

SANDERS, NOEL
Four Poems From Aftonland
S solo,pno WAI-TE-ATA 123 (S68)

Goethe Nightsongs
solo voice,pno WAI-TE-ATA 124 (S69)

SANDSTRÖM, JAN (1954-)
Fågeldröm, En
see Tvä Sonnevi-Sonetter

Små Klanger; En Röst
[Swed] A&speaking voice,3.3.3.3.
4.3.3.1. strings,cel,pno STIM
(S70)

Smärtans Vinge
see Tvä Sonnevi-Sonetter

Tvä Sonnevi-Sonetter
S solo,fl REIMERS 101143 f.s.
contains: Fågeldröm, En; Smärtans
Vinge (S71)

SANDSTRÖM, SVEN-DAVID (1942-)
Sånger Om Kärlek
S solo,2.2.2.2. 2.2.2.0. strings
TONOS (S72)

SANDVOLD, ARILD (1895-)
Bønn
solo voice,pno NOTON (S73)

SÅNG FÖR RÖST OCH ORGEL see Larson,
Martin

SANG I SKUMRING see Knutsen, Torbjorn

SANG PÅ ELVA see Baden, Conrad

SÅNG TILL JESUS see Strandsjö, Göte

SANG VOM SACHSENKRIEG, DER see
Gundlach, Wilhelm

SÄNGE EINES FAHRENDEN SPIELMANNS see
Colaço Osorio-Swaab, Reine

SANGE ER VÅBEN see Dahl, Vivian

SANGE, OP. 5 see Jordan, Sverre

SANGE TIL ÅRSTIDERNE see Dahl, Vivian

SANGE, VOL. 1 see Alnaes, Eyvind

SANGE, VOL. 2 see Alnaes, Eyvind

SANGEN OM ET SLOTT see Madsen, Trygve

SANGEN OM IVER HUITFELDT see Halvorsen,
Johan

SÄNGER see Wolf, Hugo

SÄNGER AM RHEIN, DER see Lachner, Franz

SANGER AV EICHENDORFF see Kielland,
Olav

SANGER AV OBSTFELDER see Kielland, Olav

SANGER FOR EN MELLOMSTEMME PIANO see
Jordan, Sverre

SÅNGER OCH VISOR VID PIANOFORTE see
Lindblad, Adolf Fredrik

SANGER OM DØDEN see Fladmoe, Arvid

SÅNGER OM FÖRTRÖSTAN, OP. 3 see Gefors,
Hans

SÅNGER OM GLÄDJE see Gefors, Hans

SÅNGER OM KÄRLEK see Sandström, Sven-
David

SANGER, OP. 2 see Albertsen, Per Hjort

SANGER, OP. 18 see Albertsen, Per Hjort

SANGER, OP. 25 see Albertsen, Per Hjort

SANGER, OP. 36 see Albertsen, Per Hjort

SANGER TIL DIKT AV ARNULF ØVERLAND see
Tveitt, Geirr

SANGER TIL DIKT AV HERMAN WILDENVEY see
Taubo, Lillian Gulowna

SANGER TIL DIKT AV JOHAN FALKBERGERT
see Tveitt, Geirr

SANGER TIL DIKT AV KNUT HORVEI see
Tveitt, Geirr

SANGER TIL DIKT AV LIV HOLTSKOG see
Kverndokk, Gisle

SANGER TIL DIKT AV OLAV H. HAUGE see
Tveitt, Geirr

SANGER TIL DIKT AV TARJEI VESAAS see
Tveitt, Geirr

SANGER TIL TEKSTER FRA HANS E. KINCKS
DRAMA "DRIFTEKAREN" see Groven,
Eivind

SÄNGERS MORGENLIED, D. 163, SETTING #1
see Schubert, Franz (Peter)

SÄNGERS MORGENLIED, D. 163, SETTING #2
see Schubert, Franz (Peter)

SANGSVANEN see Kaldalóns, Sigvaldi S.

SANKA see Uchikawa, Hiroyuki

SANKTA MARIA see Marx, Joseph

SANTA LUCIA
med solo,pno CLASSV 2037 (S74)
see Arona, C.

SANTA LUCIA (COLORATURA ARR.) see
Braga, Gaetano

SANTOLIQUIDO, FRANCESCO (1883-1971)
Canti Della Sera, I
med-high solo,pno CLASSV 0899 (S75)

Petits Poëmes Japonais
med solo,pno CLASSV 2038 (S76)

SANTORSOLA, GUIDO (1904-)
Agonia
"Agony" med solo,pno sc PEER
60018-203 $2.50 (S77)

Agony
see Agonia

SANTY ISN'T SANTA CLAUS see Heilner,
Irwin

SAPER VORREI SE M'AMI see Haydn,
[Franz] Joseph

SAPHO: AH! QU'IL EST LOIN MON PAYS see
Massenet, Jules

SAPHO: HÉRO, SUR LA TOUR SOLITAIRE see
Gounod, Charles François

SAPHO: JE T'AI TENUE ENTRE MES BRAS see
Massenet, Jules

SAPHO: O JOURS HEUREUX see Gounod,
Charles François

SAPHO: O MA LYRE IMMORTELLE see Gounod,
Charles François

SAPITO FEO, EL see Rodriguez Peris,
Martin Jose

SAPP, GARY J. (1944-)
Shimo
S solo,fl,pno SEESAW f.s. (S78)

SAPPHO FRAGMENTE see Terzakis, Dimitri

SAPPHO FRAGMENTS see Stucky, Steven
Edward

SARACEN SONGS (7 SONGS) see Burleigh,
Henry Thacker

SARAH BROWN see Boldemann, Laci

SARAH'S ENCORES
(Walker, Sarah; Vignoles, Roger) solo
voice,pno (CCU) NOVELLO (S79)

SARAI CONTENTA UN DI see Handel, George
Frideric

SARDANA HIROBA see Nakamura, Yukitake

SARDANAPALE: LE FRONT DANS LA POUSSIÈRE
see Joncieres, Victorin de

SARGON
Jump Back
solo voice,pno SOUTHERN V086 (S80)

SARRI, DOMENICO (1679-1744)
Didone Abbandonata: Non Ha Ragione,
Ingrato
BOIL B.1762 (S81)

SARTI, GIUSEPPE (1729-1802)
Lungi Dal Caro Bene
med solo,pno CLASSV 0545 (S82)
high solo,pno CLASSV 0485 (S83)

SASAKI, SHIGERU (1945-)
Itsuka Yuhi No
S solo,pno [4'] ONGAKU (S84)

Shiroi Bohyo
Mez solo,pno [4'] ONGAKU (S85)

SATEREN, LELAND BERNHARD (1913-)
This Glad Day
med solo AUG-FOR 11-8470 $4.50
(S86)

We Three Are One *Marriage
med solo AMSI V-13 (S87)

SATIE, ERIK (1866-1925)
Genevieve De Brabant
(Volta, Ornella) solo voice,pno
UNIVER. UE 19131 (S88)

Melodies Et Chansons
solo voice,pno (CC23U) SALABERT
50480766 (S89)

Tendrement
med-high solo,pno CLASSV 1031 (S90)

SATIRES (PICTURES OF THE PAST) OP. 109
see Shostakovich, Dmitri

SATISFIED see Warren, Betsy

SATOH, SHIN (1938-)
Five Songs
S solo,pno [12'] JAPAN (S91)

SAUD THID HANA SYSTUR MINA see
Isolfsson, Pall see Thorarinsson,
Leifur

SAUDEK, VOJTECH (1951-)
Characters From Shakespeare
Mez solo,pno [16'] CZECH RADIO
(S92)

Dve Pisne
S solo,3.2.3.2. 4.3.3.1. timp,perc,
harp,cel,strings [12'] CESKY HUD.
(S93)

Outing To The Mountains
Mez solo,11inst [15'] (text by
Kafka) CZECH (S94)

Vylet Do Hor
Mez&speaking voice,1.1.1.1.
1.0.0.0. pno,strings [11'] CESKY
HUD. (S95)

What Does Not Pass
S solo,orch [22'] (text by
Shakespeare) CESKY HUD. (S96)

SAUGUET, HENRI (1901-1989)
Chevrefeuille, La *song cycle
Bar solo,pno ESCHIG 8793 (S97)

Polymetres: Six Lieder Sur Des Poèmes
De Jean-Paul
solo voice,pno ESCHIG 8792 (S98)

Visions Infernales
med solo LEDUC HE 31285 (S99)

SAVINA, CARLO (1919-)
Lontananza
solo voice,pno CURCI 10498 (S100)

SAVOUREEN DEELISH see Tal, Marjo

SAXE, SERGE
Wedded Souls
S solo,2.1(English horn).2.2.
4.2.3.1. timp,perc,harp,strings
[6'30"] PEER (S101)

SAYGUN, AHMED ADNAN (1907-1991)
Seven Songs
B solo,2.2.2.2. 4.3.3.0. timp,perc,
harp,strings [21'25"] PEER (S102)

SAYONARA, A JAPANESE ROMANCE, OP. 49
see Cadman, Charles Wakefield

SAYONARA DAKKO see Itoh, Ohsuke

SAZANKA IN A GARDEN see Minemura,
Sumiko

SCALI
Bourricotin
SCHOTT-FRER 9155 (S103)

SCARLATTI, ALESSANDRO (1660-1725)
Ardo È Ver Per Te D'Amore *cant
S solo,fl,cont ZANIBON 6304 (S104)
S solo,fl,cont KUNZEL GM 736 (S105)

Cantata Pastorale
S solo,strings,cont sc,set KING'S
(S106)

Chi Vuole Innamorarsi
high solo,pno CLASSV 1706 (S107)

Five Short Arias *CC5U
solo voice,pno FRANG $6.95 (S108)

O Cessate Di Piagarmi
low solo,pno CLASSV 0882 (S109)
high solo,pno CLASSV 0883 (S110)
solo voice,pno BOIL B.1721 (S111)

Rezitativ Und Arie Der Erminia
(Meylan, R.) S solo,strings,cont
PETERS 8012 (S112)

Rosaura, La: Non Dar Più Pene, O Caro
[It/Ger] S solo,pno,vln CLASSV 2039
(S113)

Rosaura, La: Un Cor Da Voi Ferito
[It/Ger] A solo,pno CLASSV 2040
(S114)

Rugiadose, Odorose
see Violette, Le

Violette, Le
"Rugiadose, Odorose" [It] high
solo,pno CLASSV 1105 (S115)
"Rugiadose, Odorose" [It] med solo,
pno CLASSV 1104 (S116)

SCAT 2 see Bond, Victoria

SCELSI, GIACINTO (1905-1988)
Il Est Grand Temps
T solo SALABERT EAS18440 f.s.
(S117)

Meme Si Je Voyais
T solo SALABERT EAS18440 f.s.
(S118)

SCENA DI UNA SEDUZIONE see Giani
Luporini, Gaetano

SCENA FROM "ERNESTINE" see Saint-
Georges, Joseph Boulogne de

SCENE AUS FAUST: ACH NEIGE, DU
SCHMERZENREICHE see Loewe, Carl
Gottfried

SCÈNE DE LA LETTRE see Tchaikovsky,
Piotr Ilyich

SCENES FROM A NOVEL see Kurtag, György

SCHAATHUN, ASBJØRN
Dualis: Liederbuch Nach Texten Von
Pablo Neruda Und Fernando Pessao
[Span] Mez solo,pno [11'] NORGE
(S119)

SCHAFER, M.
see SCHAFER, R. MURRAY

SCHAFER, R. MURRAY (1933-)
Beauty And The Beast
solo voice,string quar [28'] sc
ARCANA (S120)

Brébeuf *cant
Bar solo,3.3.3.3. 4.3.3.1. pno,
harp,cel,perc,strings [30'] sc
ARCANA (S121)

Garden Of The Heart, The
Mez solo,3.2.2.2. 4.2.1.1. 2perc,
strings [24'] sc ARCANA (S122)

Gitanjali
S solo,2.2.2.2. 2.2.0.0. perc,
strings [23'] sc ARCANA (S123)

Minnelieder
Mez solo,3.3.3.2. 4.2.2.0. harp,
perc,strings [30'] sc ARCANA
(S124)

Testa D'Adriane, La
S solo,acord [14'] ARCANA (S125)

SCHÄFER UND DER REITER, DER see
Schubert, Franz (Peter)

SCHAIK, JOHAN ANT. STEPHANUS VAN
Op Een Priesterfeest
Mez/Bar solo ZENGERINK R.114 (S126)

SCHAT, PETER (1935-)
For Lenny, At 70 *Op.35
T solo,pno [8'] DONEMUS (S127)

Kind En Kraai *Op.26, song cycle
"Kind Noch Kegel" S solo,pno [35']
DONEMUS (S128)

SCHAT, PETER (cont'd.)
Kind Noch Kegel
see Kind En Kraai

Trein, De (from Symposion)
TBarBarBarB soli,3.3.4.3.3sax.
4.3.3.2. 2marimba,perc,2harp,
strings [45'] DONEMUS f.s. (S129)

SCHATTEN DER ROSE see Einem, Gottfried
von

SCHATZGRÄBER see Schubert, Franz
(Peter)

SCHEINPFLUG, PAUL (1875-1937)
Worpswede *Op.5
med solo,vln,English horn/vla,pno
MCGIN-MARX (S130)

SCHELB, JOSEF (1894-1977)
Drei Sonette Michelangelos, Op. 5
med solo,pno CLASSV 2041 (S131)

SCHELLE, MICHAEL (1950-)
Daydream
S&speaking voice,fl/pic,bsn/ob,
horn,trom/synthesizer,perc [12']
AM.COMP.AL. (S132)

Misadventures Of Struwwelpeter, The
high solo,pno (six tales of naughty
children) MMB X814011 (S133)

Swanwhite
S solo,pno [17'] sc AM.COMP.AL.
$10.30 (S134)

SCHELM VON BERGEN, DER: BALDUIN-MARSCH
see Oelschlegel, Alfred

SCHERZO see Mesritz van Velthuysen,
Anny

SCHERZO OF SEASONS, OP.7 see Grondahl,
Sissel Margrethe

SCHI-KING see Beekhuis, Hanna

SCHIAVO, LO: QUANDO NASCESTI TU see
Gomes, Antônio Carlos

SCHIBLER, ARMIN (1920-)
Stille Des Herbstes *song cycle
low solo,pno voc sc KUNZEL GM 975
(S135)

Streichquartett No.4, Op.66
high solo,string quar KUNZEL GM 976
(S136)

Weil Alles Erneut Sich Begibt
low solo,vla,pno KUNZEL GM 974
(S137)

SCHICKELE, PETER (1935-)
see also "BACH, P.D.Q."

see "BACH, P.D.Q."

SCHIDLOWSKY, LEON (1931-)
An Anna Blume: Szene Für Sopran, Alt
Und Bariton
[10'-12'] ARIAD 80019 (S138)

Verra La Morte
S solo [8'] ARIAD 80017 (S139)

SCHIFFBRÜCHIGE, DER see Kirkwood,
Antoinette

SCHIFFLEIN, DAS see Mendelssohn-
Bartholdy, Felix

SCHILD, TH. F.
Das Sind Triumpfe Unsrer Zeit
solo voice,pno SCIEN 1418 (S140)

Herz Voller Lieb, Das
solo voice,pno SCIEN 1421 (S141)

Schönste Krone Österreichs, Das Ist
Mein Goldnes Wien, Die
solo voice,pno SCIEN 1423 (S142)

SCHILFLIED see Mendelssohn-Bartholdy,
Felix

SCHILLER, BENJIE ELLEN
All The World
see V'ye-Etayu

V'ye-Etayu
*All The World" [Heb/Eng] solo
voice,kbd, opt cong TRANSCON.
991627 (S143)

Zeh Dodi *Marriage
solo voice,kbd TRANSCON. 992032
(S144)

SCHILLINGS, MAX VON (1868-1933)
Herbstlied
KAHNT 4827 (S145)

SCHIPPER, DIRK (1912-   )
  Kvin Kantoj
    high solo,pno DONEMUS f.s.
    contains: La Kapelo; Mi Amas La
    Rozojn; Pluvo; Tre Ofte; Vin Mi
    Memoras   (S146)

  La Kapelo
    see Kvin Kantoj

  Mi Amas La Rozojn
    see Kvin Kantoj

  Pluvo
    see Kvin Kantoj

  Tre Ofte
    see Kvin Kantoj

  Vin Mi Memoras
    see Kvin Kantoj

SCHIRMER'S SINGER'S LIBRARY: ARIAS FOR
    BARITONE, VOL.1
    (Adler) (CC17L) SCHIRM.G ED3096
                                     (S147)
SCHIRMER'S SINGER'S LIBRARY: ARIAS FOR
    BARITONE, VOL.2
    (CC19L) SCHIRM.G ED3097   (S148)

SCHIRMER'S SINGER'S LIBRARY: ARIAS FOR
    BASS, VOL.1
    (CC18L) SCHIRM.G ED3098   (S149)

SCHIRMER'S SINGER'S LIBRARY: ARIAS FOR
    BASS, VOL.2
    (CC19L) SCHIRM.G ED3099   (S150)

SCHIRMER'S SINGER'S LIBRARY: ARIAS FOR
    MEZZO SOPRANO (ALTO), VOL.1
    (Adler) (CC20L) SCHIRM.G ED3092
                                     (S151)
SCHIRMER'S SINGER'S LIBRARY: ARIAS FOR
    MEZZO SOPRANO (ALTO), VOL.2
    (Adler) (CC20L) SCHIRM.G ED3093
                                     (S152)
SCHIRMER'S SINGER'S LIBRARY: ARIAS FOR
    SOPRANO, VOL.1
    (Adler) (CC22L) SCHIRM.G ED3090
                                     (S153)
SCHIRMER'S SINGER'S LIBRARY: ARIAS FOR
    SOPRANO, VOL.2
    (Adler) (CC21L) SCHIRM.G ED3091
                                     (S154)
SCHIRMER'S SINGER'S LIBRARY: ARIAS FOR
    TENOR, VOL.1
    (Adler) (CC21L) SCHIRM.G ED3094
                                     (S155)
SCHIRMER'S SINGER'S LIBRARY: ARIAS FOR
    TENOR, VOL.2
    (Adler) (CC21L) SCHIRM.G ED3095
                                     (S156)

SCHLAFEND TRÄGT MAN MICH IN MEIN
    HEIMATLAND see Marx, Joseph

SCHLANGENBESCHWÖRUNG see Orthel, Leon

SCHLEE, THOMAS DANIEL
  Dicite: Pusillanimes Confortamini,
    Op. 17
    S solo,2vln,vcl,opt fl,opt org
    LEMOINE   (S157)

SCHLEMM, GUSTAV ADOLF (1902-   )
  Drei Lieder
    T solo,pno SEESAW   (S158)
    solo voice,pno SEESAW   (S159)

  Vier Fabeln
    B solo,pno SEESAW   (S160)

SCHLESINGER, S.
  Recueil De Mélodies Vol. 1 *CC25U
    solo voice,pno CLASSV C053 f.s.
                                     (S161)
  Recueil De Mélodies Vol. 2 *CC34U
    solo voice,pno CLASSV C054 f.s.
                                     (S162)

SCHLICHTE LIEDER see Koenig, Franz

SCHLICK, E.
  Drei Lieder, Op. 10
    solo voice,pno SCIEN 1430 f.s.
    contains: Glöcklein, Das; Jäger
    Und Seine Mutter, Der; Vedette,
    Die   (S163)

  Glöcklein, Das
    see Drei Lieder, Op. 10

  Jäger Und Seine Mutter, Der
    see Drei Lieder, Op. 10

  Vedette, Die
    see Drei Lieder, Op. 10

SCHLUNZ, ANNETTE
  Tout Est Rever
    S solo,clar/bass clar,perc BOTE
                                     (S164)
SCHMIDT, CHRISTFRIED (1932-   )
  Des Himmels Dunklerer Bruder *cant
    Bar solo,ob,English horn,trom,perc,
    pno,vla,vcl,db DEUTSCHER (S165)

SCHMIDT, CHRISTFRIED (cont'd.)

  Ed E Subito Sera...
    "Kammermusik II" A solo,ob,vln,vla,
    vcl DEUTSCHER   (S166)

  Kammermusik II
    see Ed E Subito Sera...

  Zeit Und Die Zeit Danach, Die
    Bar solo,fl,ob,clar,bsn,pno
    DEUTSCHER   (S167)

SCHMIDT, LORENZ
  Duft Von Licht, Ein
    solo voice,gtr VOGT VF 405A   (S168)

SCHMIDT, SHARON YVONNE DAVIS
    (1937-   )
  Birthday, A
    med-high solo,pno WESTERN AV259
                                     (S169)
  Merrie English Love Songs
    female solo,trom (no. 4 with
    percussion) WESTERN AV272   (S170)

  Prodigal Planet
    T solo,bass trom,pno WESTERN AV256
                                     (S171)
  Six Songs On Poems Of William Pillin
    *CC6U
    high solo,pno (gr. IV) WESTERN
    AV242 $8.00   (S172)

  Though Men Call Us Free
    S solo,clar,pno (gr. IV) WESTERN
    AV207 $10.00   (S173)

  Three Fables Of Stephen Crane
    high solo,pno WESTERN AV260   (S174)

  Three Moods Of Emily Dickinson
    S solo,vln,vcl,pno (gr. V) WESTERN
    AV209 $15.00   (S175)

  Three Poems Of William Blake *CC3U
    S solo,alto clar in E flat,bass
    clar,contrabass clar,bass clar
    solo (gr. IV) WESTERN AV220 $7.00
                                     (S176)
SCHMIDT, WILLIAM JOSEPH (1926-   )
  Afro-American Suite
    Bar solo,5brass WESTERN AV275
                                     (S177)
SCHMITT, FLORENT (1870-1958)
  Ils Ont Tué Trois Petites Filles
    S solo,pno CLASSV 1039   (S178)

  O Triste Était Mon Ame
    med-high solo,pno CLASSV 1034
                                     (S179)
  Tristesse Au Jardin
    med solo,pno CLASSV 1033   (S180)

SCHMITZ, MANFRED
  Chanson-Boutique, Band 2 *CCU
    DEUTSCHER DV 31059 f.s.   (S181)

SCHNABEL, ARTUR (1882-1951)
  Notturno
    A/T solo,pno APNM sc $6.50, set
    $13.00   (S182)

SCHNEE ODER ASCHE see Ehlen, Margriet

SCHNEEFLÖCKCHEN see Gretchaninov,
    Alexander Tikhonovich

SCHNEEMUSIK see Stucky, Steven Edward

SCHNEEWEISS, JAN (1904-   )
  Rusava
    solo voice,pno PANTON 942   (S183)

SCHNEIDER, GARY M.
  Night, You Aren't Here
    high solo,pno [5'] sc AM.COMP.AL.
    $1.60   (S184)

  Tell-Tale Heart, The *cant
    B solo,clar,bsn,perc,vln,vcl,
    conductor [15'] AM.COMP.AL. sc
    $11.45, pts $21.45   (S185)

SCHNEIDER VON ULM, DER see Delnooz,
    Henri

SCHNELLE TAG IST HIN, DER see Gerlach,
    Günter

SCHOBER, BRIAN (1951-   )
  Sunflower Splendor
    S solo,3+pic.3.4.3. 4.4.3.1. 4perc,
    2pno,2harp,elec gtr [15']
    AM.COMP.AL. sc $32.20, pts
    $116.25   (S186)

  Three Dreams
    female solo,pno [6'] AM.COMP.AL.
                                     (S187)
SCHOECK, OTHMAR (1886-1957)
  Spielmannsweisen *Op.56
    high solo,harp/pno UNIVER. UE 11693
    f.s.   (S188)

SCHOENBERG, ARNOLD (1874-1951)
  Gurrelieder: Nun Sag Ich
    S solo,pno CLASSV 0635   (S189)

  Gurrelieder: So Tanzen
    T solo,pno CLASSV 0636   (S190)

  Seven Early Songs
    FABER 50932 0   (S191)
    (CC7U) FABER 50489246   (S192)

SCHOFIELD, JOE
  He Is My Redeemer
    (Jackson, Greg) 1-2 solo voices
    JACKMAN $1.75   (S193)

SCHON LACHT DER HOLDE FRÜHLING see
    Mozart, Wolfgang Amadeus

SCHON SCHWAND DER TAG see Arensky,
    Anton Stepanovich

SCHÖNE MÜLLERIN, DIE see Bredemeyer,
    Reiner see Schubert, Franz (Peter)

SCHÖNE STERN, DER see Zimmerman, S.A.

SCHÖNHEIT see Marx, Joseph

SCHÖNSTE KRONE ÖSTERREICHS, DAS IST
    MEIN GOLDNES WIEN, DIE see Schild,
    Th. F.

SCHÖNSTEN AUGEN, DIE see Stigelli,
    Giorgio

SCHÖNZELER, HANS HUBERT
  Tristesse *song cycle
    solo voice,pno KUNZEL GM 1145
                                     (S194)
    solo voice,strings (texts by Paul
    Verlaine) KUNZEL GM 1145   (S195)

SCHOON LIEVEKEN see Maessen, Antoon

SCHOONENBEEK, KEES (1947-   )
  Peace
    see Three Wintersongs

  Song, A
    see Three Wintersongs

  Three Wintersongs
    S solo,org DONEMUS f.s. [8']
    contains: Peace; Song, A;
    Winternight, A   (S196)

  Winternight, A
    see Three Wintersongs

SCHOP, JOHANN (? -1665)
  Himmlische Lieder
    OLMS   (S197)

SCHOSTAKOWITSCH, DMITRI
    see SHOSTAKOVICH, DMITRI

SCHOUWMAN, HANS (1902-1967)
  Avondster
    see Notturno, Op. 59

  Maanlicht
    see Notturno, Op. 59

  Notturno, Op. 59
    Mez solo,pno,vcl DONEMUS f.s.
    contains: Avondster; Maanlicht;
    Teleurgesteld Wachten   (S198)

  Teleurgesteld Wachten
    see Notturno, Op. 59

SCHRAMOWSKI, HEBERT
  Fünf Dialoge
    med solo,pno DEUTSCHER DV 9059
                                     (S199)

SCHRECKENBERGER see Wolf, Hugo

SCHREIBER, JOSEF (1900-   )
  Lidova Nokturna
    solo voice,fl,harp/pno PANTON 943
                                     (S200)
SCHREITEN GOTTES WIRD ZUM STURM, DAS
    see Badings, Henk

SCHREKER, FRANZ (1878-1934)
  Fünf Lieder, Op. 4
    high solo,pno CLASSV 1138   (S201)

SCHRIJVERS, JEAN (1889-1978)
  Ave Maria, Op.13
    Mez/Bar solo ZENGERINK S.13   (S202)

  Ave Maria, Op.29
    Mez/Bar solo ZENGERINK S.29   (S203)

  Inviolata
    solo voice,kbd ZENGERINK S.19
                                     (S204)
  Jesu Dulcis Memoria
    Mez/Bar solo ZENGERINK S.28   (S205)

  Memorare
    Mez/Bar solo ZENGERINK S.16   (S206)

SCHRIJVERS, JEAN (cont'd.)

Tota Pulchra Es
    ZENGERINK S.18   (S207)

SCHRITTE, DIE see Lothar, Mark

SCHUBACK, THOMAS
    Snett Och Runt
        solo voice,pno GEHRMANS 6694 (S208)

SCHUBERT, FRANZ (PETER) (1797-1828)
    Al Torrente
        solo voice,pno BOIL B.1149   (S209)

    Alborada
        solo voice,pno BOIL B.1139   (S210)

    Almighty, The
        [Eng/Ger] high solo,pno ROBERTON
        491-00355 $1.50   (S211)

    Alpenjäger, Der
        see Schäfer Und Der Reiter, Der

    Amor Sin Descanso
        solo voice,pno BOIL B.1134   (S212)

    An Den Schlaf *D.447
        "Komm, Und Senke Die Umflorten"
        high solo,pno CLASSV 0801   (S213)

    An Die Freunde
        see Mädchen, Das

    An Schwanger Kronos
        see Four Songs

    Anhelo
        solo voice,pno BOIL B.1147   (S214)

    Auf Dem Strom, Op. 110
        [Ger] high solo,horn,pno KALMUS
        K 06426   (S215)

    Auf Dem Wasser *Op.72
        "Barcarole" solo voice,pno,fl/vln
        SCHUBERTH,J   (S216)

    Auf Dem Wasser Zu Singen *D.774
        high solo,pno CLASSV 0415   (S217)
        med solo,pno CLASSV 0416   (S218)
        solo voice,pno SCIEN 1454   (S219)

    Aus Heliopolis
        see Lied Eines Schiffers An Die
        Dioskuren

    Ausgewählte Lieder Aus Band 4-7, 52
        low solo,pno PETERS 3505   (S220)

    Ave Maria
        Mez solo,pno LEDUC f.s.   (S221)
        [Lat] T solo SCHOTT-FRER 8613
                                      (S222)
        [Lat] Bar solo SCHOTT-FRER 8614
                                      (S223)
        high solo,pno CLASSV 0476   (S224)
        [Ger/Eng/Lat] high solo,pno,vln/fl/
        vcl CLASSV 0830   (S225)
        low solo,pno CLASSV 0479   (S226)
        solo voice,pno BOIL B.1067   (S227)
        see Hymne An Die Jungfrau

    Barcarole
        see Auf Dem Wasser

    Bella Molinera, La
        see Impaciencia Del Ciclo De
        Canciones

    Berthas Lied In Die Nacht
        see Mädchen, Das

    Blinde Knabe, Der
        solo voice,pno SCIEN 1455   (S228)
        see Vier Lieder

    Caminante, El
        solo voice,pno BOIL B.1137   (S229)

    Canconer Selecte Vol. 2 (25 Cancons
        Selectes)
        solo voice,pno BOIL B.2180   (S230)

    Canto Della Quaglia, Il
        see Wachtelschlag, Der

    Cerca Del Amado
        solo voice,pno BOIL B.1135   (S231)

    Dass Sie Hür Gewesen
        see Vier Gedichte Von Rückert Und
        Platen In Musik Gesetzt

    Drei Schubert-Lieder (Nach Gedichten
        Von Goethe)
        solo voice,pno SCIEN 1460 f.s.
            contains: Heidenröslein;
            Rattenfänger; Schatzgräber
                                      (S232)
    Du Bist Die Ruh
        see Vier Gedichte Von Rückert Und
        Platen In Musik Gesetzt

SCHUBERT, FRANZ (PETER) (cont'd.)

    Du Liebst Mich Nicht
        see Vier Gedichte Von Rückert Und
        Platen In Musik Gesetzt

    Ellens Zweiter Gesang
        solo voice,pno SCIEN 1481 from
        SIEBEN GESÄNGE AUS WALTER SCOTTS
        FRÄULEIN VOM SEE   (S233)

    En La Tumba De Anselmo
        solo voice,pno BOIL B.1142   (S234)

    Entsühnte Orest, Der
        see Nachgelassene Musikalische
        Dichtungen

    Erlkönig
        [Ger/Eng] low solo,pno CLASSV 1664
                                      (S235)
        solo voice,pno SCIEN 1463   (S236)

    Erster Verlust
        see Rastlose Liebe

    Favorite Songs, 24
        [Eng/Ger] low solo KALMUS K 09871
                                      (S237)
        [Eng/Ger] high solo KALMUS K 09872
                                      (S238)
    Fischer, Der
        see Rastlose Liebe

    Four Songs
        solo voice,2.2.2.2+contrabsn.
        4.2.3.0. timp,strings OXFORD perf
        mat rent
            contains: An Schwanger Kronos;
            Geheimnes; Gruppe Aus Dem
            Tarturus; Memnon   (S239)

    Freywilliges Versinken
        see Nachgelassene Musikalische
        Dichtungen

    Fünf Lieder *CC5UL
        (Ragossnig) S/T solo,gtr HEINRICH.
        2299 f.s.   (S240)

    Geheimnes
        see Four Songs

    Gesänge Aus Wilhelm Meister Von Göthe
        solo voice,pno SCIEN 1464   (S241)

    Gretchens Bitte
        see Stimme Der Liebe

    Gruppe Aus Dem Tarturus
        see Four Songs

    Heidenröslein
        "Rose Sauvage" (original key)
        SCHOTT-FRER 8808   (S242)
        see Drei Schubert-Lieder (Nach
        Gedichten Von Goethe)

    Hirt Auf Dem Felsen, Der *Op.129
        "Shepherd On The Rock, The" [Eng/
        Ger] high solo,clar,pno KALMUS
        K 06936   (S243)

    Hymne An Die Jungfrau
        "Ave Maria" T solo SCHOTT-FRER 8589
                                      (S244)
    Im Frühling
        see Vier Lieder

    Impaciencia Del Ciclo De Canciones
        "Bella Molinera, La" solo voice,pno
        BOIL B.1517   (S245)

    Impatience
        see Ungeduld

    Joven En El Tozal, El
        solo voice,pno BOIL B.1151   (S246)

    Komm, Und Senke Die Umflorten
        see An Den Schlaf

    König Von Thule, Der
        see Rastlose Liebe

    Lachen Und Weinen
        see Vier Gedichte Von Rückert Und
        Platen In Musik Gesetzt

    Lago Erlaf, El
        solo voice,pno BOIL B.1150   (S247)

    Lamentación Del Pastor
        solo voice,pno BOIL B.1145   (S248)

    Leise Flehen
        see Serenade

    Lied Eines Schiffers An Die Dioskuren
        solo voice,pno SCIEN 1487 f.s.
            contains also: Wanderer, Der; Aus
            Heliopolis   (S249)

    Lieder Nach Texten Von Rellstab,
        Heine Und Seidl *CC15L
        HENLE high solo,pno 516 f.s.; med

SCHUBERT, FRANZ (PETER) (cont'd.)

        solo,pno 517 f.s.   (S250)

    Lieder (Neuausgabe), Band 1
        (Fischer-Dieskau, Dietrich) PETERS
        f.s. high solo,pno; med solo,pno;
        low solo,pno
            contains: Schöne Müllerin, Die;
            Schwanengesang; Winterreise
                                      (S251)
    Lieder (Neuausgabe), Band 2
        (Fischer-Dieskau) low solo,pno
        PETERS 8304C   (S252)
        (Fischer-Dieskau) high solo,pno
        PETERS 8304A   (S253)
        (Fischer-Dieskau) med solo,pno
        PETERS 8304B   (S254)
    Lieder (Neuausgabe), Band 3
        (Fischer-Dieskau) high solo,pno
        PETERS 8305A   (S255)
        (Fischer-Dieskau) med solo,pno
        PETERS 8305B   (S256)
        (Fischer-Dieskau) low solo,pno
        PETERS 8305C   (S257)
    Lieder (Neuausgabe), Band 4
        (Fischer-Dieskau) low solo,pno
        PETERS 8306C   (S258)
        (Fischer-Dieskau) high solo,pno
        PETERS 8306A   (S259)
        (Fischer-Dieskau) med solo,pno
        PETERS 8306B   (S260)

    Lindenbaum
        "Tilleul, Le" (original key)
        SCHOTT-FRER 8816   (S261)

    Lob Der Thränen
        see Schäfer Und Der Reiter, Der

    Mädchen, Das
        SCIEN 1468 f.s. contains also:
        Berthas Lied In Die Nacht; An Die
        Freunde   (S262)

    Männerlieder
        PETERS 3963   (S263)

    Mar En Calma - Primer Desengaño
        solo voice,pno BOIL B.1144   (S264)

    Margarita En La Rueca
        solo voice,pno BOIL B.1133   (S265)

    Memnon
        solo voice,pno BOIL B.1141   (S266)

    Memnon
        see Four Songs

    Misterio
        solo voice,pno BOIL B.1143   (S267)

    Mondnacht, Die *D.238
        "Siehe, Wie Die Mondesstrahlen"
        high solo,pno CLASSV 0799   (S268)

    Morgenlied
        see Wanderer, Der

    Muerte Y La Doncella, La
        solo voice,pno BOIL B.1146   (S269)

    Mutter Erde, Die
        see Stimme Der Liebe

    Nachgelassene Musikalische Dichtungen
        solo voice,pno SCIEN 1471 f.s.
            contains: Entsühnte Orest, Der;
            Freywilliges Versinken; Orest
            Auf Tauris; Philoctet   (S270)

    Nacht, Die
        (Fuessl, Karl Heinz) solo voice,pno
        pno red UNIVER. UE19326   (S271)

    Nacht Und Träume
        solo voice,pno SCIEN 1474   (S272)

    Nachtigall Singt Überall, Die
        see Seufzer

    Nähe Des Geliebten
        see Rastlose Liebe

    Nocturno Del Cazador
        solo voice,pno BOIL B.1136   (S273)

    Orest Auf Tauris
        see Nachgelassene Musikalische
        Dichtungen

    Pastorella, La *D.528
        "Pastorella Al Prato, La" [It/Ger]
        high solo,pno CLASSV 0800   (S274)

    Pastorella Al Prato, La
        see Pastorella, La

    Pescador, El
        solo voice,pno BOIL B.1148   (S275)

SCHUBERT, FRANZ (PETER) (cont'd.)

Philoctet
see Nachgelassene Musikalische
Dichtungen

Pilgrim Und Der Alpenjäger, Der
solo voice,pno SCIEN 1476 (S276)

Rastlose Liebe
solo voice,pno SCIEN 1477 f.s.
contains also: Nähe Des
Geliebten; Fischer, Der; Erster
Verlust; König Von Thule, Der
(S277)

Rattenfänger
see Drei Schubert-Lieder (Nach
Gedichten Von Goethe)

Rey De Thule, El
solo voice,pno BOIL B.1138 (S278)

Rey Del Abedul, El
solo voice,pno BOIL B.1131 (S279)

Rosa Del Espino
solo voice,pno BOIL B.1132 (S280)

Rose Sauvage
see Heidenröslein

Salve Regina for Solo Voice and
Strings, Op. 153, in A
S solo,strings KUNZEL EKB 10P (S281)

Sämmtliche Compositionen
(Winkler, L.; Sattler, H.) solo
voice,pno (in 6 volumes: heft 6,
12, 31, 102, 105, 112) SCIEN 1450
(S282)

Sängers Morgenlied, D. 163, Setting
#1
"Süsses Licht" high solo,pno CLASSV
0797 (S283)

Sängers Morgenlied, D. 163, Setting
#2
"Süsses Licht" high solo,pno CLASSV
0798 (S284)

Schäfer Und Der Reiter, Der
solo voice,pno SCIEN 1478 f.s.
contains also: Lob Der Thränen;
Alpenjäger, Der (S285)

Schatzgräber
see Drei Schubert-Lieder (Nach
Gedichten Von Goethe)

Schone Mullerin, Die *Op.25
(Friedlaender, M.) [Ger] solo
voice,pno POLSKIE (S286)
see Lieder (Neuausgabe), Band 1

Schubert Album 1 *CCU
low solo ONGAKU 520040 f.s. (S287)

Schwanengesang
solo voice,pno SCIEN 1479 (S288)
(Friedlaender, M.) [Ger] solo
voice,pno POLSKIE (S289)
see Lieder (Neuausgabe), Band 1

Sehnsucht, Die
solo voice,pno SCIEN 1480 (S290)

Serenade
"Leise Flehen" [Ger] high solo,pno
CLASSV 0408 (S291)
(Rondinella, P.) [Eng/Ger/It] high
solo&med solo,pno CLASSV 2043
(S292)
see Ständchen

Serenata
solo voice,pno BOIL B.1096 (S293)

Seufzer *D.198
"Nachtigall Singt Überall, Die"
high solo,pno CLASSV 0795 (S294)

Shepherd On The Rock, The
see Hirt Auf Dem Felsen, Der

Sieben Gesänge Aus Walter Scotts
Fräulein Vom See
see Ellens Zweiter Gesang

Siehe, Wie Die Mondesstrahlen
see Mondnacht, Die

Sixteen Songs
(Heck, Thomas F.) solo voice,gtr
TECLA TE013 (S295)

Songs For Voice And Piano, Vol. 1
solo voice,pno (includes "Die
Schöne Müllerin" and
"Schwanengesang") LEA 23 (S296)

Songs For Voice And Piano, Vol. 2
solo voice,pno (includes "Die
Winterreise") LEA 24 (S297)

SCHUBERT, FRANZ (PETER) (cont'd.)

Songs For Voice And Piano, Vol. 3
solo voice,pno LEA 112 (S298)

Songs For Voice And Piano, Vol. 4
solo voice,pno LEA 113 (S299)

Songs For Voice And Piano, Vol. 5
solo voice,pno LEA 114 (S300)

Songs For Voice And Piano, Vol. 6
solo voice,pno LEA 115 (S301)

Songs For Voice And Piano, Vol. 7
solo voice,pno LEA 116 (S302)

Songs, Vol. 3
[Eng/Ger] high solo KALMUS K 06425
(S303)

Ständchen
"Sérénade" Bar solo SCHOTT-FRER
8289 (S304)
"Sérénade" T solo SCHOTT-FRER 8288
(S305)

Sterne, Die *D.176
"Was Funkelt Ihr So Mild" high
solo,pno CLASSV 0796 (S306)

Stimme Der Liebe
solo voice,pno SCIEN 1482 f.s.
contains also: Mutter Erde, Die;
Gretchens Bitte (S307)

Süsses Licht
see Sängers Morgenlied, D. 163,
Setting #1
see Sängers Morgenlied, D. 163,
Setting #2

Tilleul, Le
see Lindenbaum

Tilo Sin Flor, El
solo voice,pno BOIL B.1140 (S308)

Trost Im Liede
see Vier Lieder

Trucha, La
solo voice,pno BOIL B.1516 (S309)

Ungeduld
"Impatience" (original key) SCHOTT-
FRER 8809 (S310)

Vier Gedichte Von Rückert Und Platen
In Musik Gesetzt
solo voice,pno SCIEN 1483 f.s.
contains: Dass Sie Hür Gewesen;
Du Bist Die Ruh; Du Liebst Mich
Nicht; Lachen Und Weinen (S311)

Vier Lieder
solo voice,pno SCIEN 1484 f.s.
contains: Blinde Knabe, Der; Im
Frühling; Trost Im Liede;
Wanderers Nachtlied: Über Allen
Gipfeln Ist Ruh (S312)

Wachtelschlag, Der
"Canto Della Quaglia, Il" solo
voice,pno SCIEN 1485 (S313)

Waldesnacht
SCIEN 1472 (S314)

Wanderer, Der
solo voice,pno SCIEN 1486 f.s.
contains also: Morgenlied;
Wanderers Nachtlied (S315)
see Lied Eines Schiffers An Die
Dioskuren

Wanderers Nachtlied
see Wanderer, Der

Wanderers Nachtlied: Über Allen
Gipfeln Ist Ruh
see Vier Lieder

Was Funkelt Ihr So Mild
see Sterne, Die

Winter Journey
see Winterreise

Winterabend, Der
SCIEN 1473 (S316)

Winterreise *Op.89, song cycle
[Ger/Fr] solo voice,pno SCIEN 1488
(S317)
"Winter Journey" [Eng/Ger] high
solo KALMUS K 09865 (S318)
"Winter Journey" [Eng/Ger] low solo
KALMUS K 09866 (S319)
"Winter Journey" [Eng/Ger] low solo
oct KALMUS K 06429 (S320)
(Friedlaender, M.) [Ger] solo
voice,pno POLSKIE (S321)
see Lieder (Neuausgabe), Band 1

SCHUBERT, MANFRED (1937-)
Canzoni Amorosi
Bar solo,3.2.3.3. 4.3.3.1. timp,
3perc,harp,cel,strings [25'] sc,
solo pt DEUTSCHER DV 1091 (S322)

Nachtgesänge
med solo,alto fl,English horn,harp,
2tam-tam,string quin sc DEUTSCHER
DV 1147 (S323)

SCHUBERT ALBUM 1 see Schubert, Franz
(Peter)

SCHUDEL, THOMAS (1937-)
Edging Out
S solo,pno/fl&vibra SEESAW (S324)

Queer Cornered Cap
Mez solo,fl,marimba SEESAW (S325)

SCHUETZ, HEINRICH
see SCHÜTZ, HEINRICH

SCHULTHEISS, ULRICH (1956-)
Liebeslieder
PETERS 8617 (S326)

SCHUMANN, CLARA (WIECK) (1819-1896)
Canciones De Infancia, Tomo 1
solo voice,pno BOIL B.2693 (S327)

Canciones Infantiles, Tomo 2
solo voice,pno BOIL B.2719 (S328)

Cantemos Vol. 1
solo voice,pno BOIL B.2695 (S329)

Como Nace El Amor
solo voice,pno BOIL B.2641 (S330)

Complete Songs, Vol. 1 *CCU
solo voice,pno BREITKOPF-W EB 8558
f.s. (S331)

Complete Songs, Vol. 2 *CCU
solo voice,pno BREITKOPF-W EB 8559
f.s. (S332)

Niñez, La, Vol. 2
solo voice,pno BOIL B.2696 (S333)

Nuestras Canciones Vol. 1
solo voice,pno BOIL B.2692 (S334)

Nuestras Canciones Vol. 2
solo voice,pno BOIL B.2694 (S335)

Nueva Colección De Canciones
Infantiles Vol. 1
solo voice,pno BOIL B.2682 (S336)

Nueva Collección De Canciones
Infantiles Vol. 2
solo voice,pno BOIL B.2691 (S337)

Seven Lieder
high solo,pno (texts by Heine,
Rückert, Serre and Goethe) HILD
09102 (S338)

SCHUMANN, ROBERT (ALEXANDER)
(1810-1856)
Abendlied *Op.85,No.12
Mez solo,vln/vcl/horn,pno
SCHUBERTH,J (S339)

Ausgewählte Lieder, 30
(Friedlaender) high solo,pno PETERS
8160A (S340)
(Friedlaender) med solo,pno PETERS
8160B (S341)
(Friedlaender) low solo,pno PETERS
8160C (S342)

Balsatzar, Op. 57
[Ger] low solo KALMUS K 06795 f.s.
contains also: Romanzen Und
Balladen, Part 4, Op. 64 (med
solo,pno); Lieder Und Gesänge,
Part 3, Op. 77 (high solo,pno);
Lieder Album Für Die Jugend, Op.
79 (high solo,pno) (S343)

Beiden Grenadiere, Die
[Ger/Eng] solo voice,pno SCIEN 1524
from ROMANZEN UND BALLADEN, OP.
49 (S344)

Campana Que Camina, La
see [Canciones] Cuaderno 1, Op. 79

[Canciones] Cuaderno 1, Op. 79
solo voice,pno BOIL B.0702 f.s.
contains: Campana Que Camina, La;
Es Ella!; Estrella Del
Anochecer, La; Mariposa (S345)

[Canciones] Cuaderno 2: Vida Amorosa
De Una Mujer, Op. 42 *CC8L
solo voice,pno BOIL B.1638 f.s.
(S346)

[Canciones] Cuaderno 3
solo voice,pno BOIL B.1244 f.s.
contains: Noche De Luna; Noche De
Primavera; Visión (S347)

SCHUMANN, ROBERT (ALEXANDER) (cont'd.)

[Canciones] Cuaderno 4
  solo voice,pno BOIL B.1245 f.s.
    contains: Cerca De Ti;
    Dedicatoria; Secreto, El   (S348)

[Canciones] Cuaderno 5: El Amor De Un
  Poeta, Op. 48 *CCU
  solo voice,pno BOIL B.1779 f.s.
                                 (S349)

Canconer Selecte Vol. 3
  solo voice,pno BOIL B.2667   (S350)

Cerca De Ti
  see [Canciones] Cuaderno 4

Dedicatoria
  see [Canciones] Cuaderno 4

Dichterliebe, Op. 48
  (Köhler) high solo,pno PETERS 9537
                                 (S351)
  see Romanzen Und Balladen, Part 1,
    Op. 45

Es Ella!
  see [Canciones] Cuaderno 1, Op. 79

Estrella Del Anochecer, La
  see [Canciones] Cuaderno 1, Op. 79

Fensterscheibe, Die
  see Sechs Gesänge, Op. 107

Fifty-Five Songs
  [Ger/Eng] low solo,pno KALMUS
    K 09867   (S352)
  [Ger/Eng] high solo,pno KALMUS
    K 09868   (S353)

Frauenliebe Und Leben *Op.42
  "Woman's Life And Love" [Ger/Eng]
    high solo,pno KALMUS K 09862 (S354)
  "Woman's Life And Love" [Ger/Eng]
    low solo,pno KALMUS K 09861 (S355)

Frauenliebe Und Leben, Op. 42
  see Zwolf Gedichte, Op. 37

Frühlingsglocken
  (Reinecke, C.) SS soli,pno
    SCHUBERTH,J f.s. contains also:
    Lotosblume, Die   (S356)

Fünf Gedichte Der Königin Maria
  Stuart *Op.135
  [Ger] med solo,pno CLASSV 1369
                                 (S357)

Fünf Lieder, Op. 40
  see Zwolf Gedichte, Op. 37

Gärtner, Der
  see Sechs Gesänge, Op. 107

Herzeleid
  see Sechs Gesänge, Op. 107

Hidalgo, Der *Op.30,No.3
  high solo,pno CLASSV 0618   (S358)

Lieder Album Für Die Jugend, Op. 79
  see Balsatzar, Op. 57

Lieder Und Gesange, Part 2, Op. 51
  see Romanzen Und Balladen, Part 1,
    Op. 45

Lieder Und Gesänge, Part 3, Op. 77
  see Balsatzar, Op. 57

Liederkreis, Op. 39
  (Köhler) high solo,pno PETERS 9535
                                 (S359)
  see Zwolf Gedichte, Op. 37

Lotosblume, Die
  [Ger/Eng] med solo,pno (D maj)
    CLASSV 2044   (S360)
  [Ger/Eng] low solo,pno (D flat maj)
    CLASSV 2052   (S361)
  [Ger/Eng] med solo,pno (E flat maj)
    CLASSV 2053   (S362)
  see Frühlingsglocken

Mariposa
  see [Canciones] Cuaderno 1, Op. 79

Meine Rose *Op.90,No.2
  high solo,pno CLASSV 0619   (S363)

Mythen, Op. 25 *song cycle
  solo voice,pno SCIEN 1519   (S364)

Noche De Luna
  see [Canciones] Cuaderno 3

Noche De Primavera
  see [Canciones] Cuaderno 3

Romanzen Und Balladen, Op. 49
  see Beiden Grenadiere, Die

SCHUMANN, ROBERT (ALEXANDER) (cont'd.)

Romanzen Und Balladen, Part 1, Op. 45
  [Ger] low solo/med solo,pno KALMUS
    K 06794 f.s. contains also:
    Dichterliebe, Op. 48 (med solo,
    pno); Romanzen Und Balladen, Part
    2, Op. 49 (med solo,pno); Lieder
    Und Gesange, Part 2, Op. 51 (med
    solo/high solo,pno); Romanzen Und
    Balladen, Part 3, Op. 53 (med
    solo,pno)   (S365)

Romanzen Und Balladen, Part 2, Op. 49
  see Romanzen Und Balladen, Part 1,
    Op. 45

Romanzen Und Balladen, Part 3, Op. 53
  see Romanzen Und Balladen, Part 1,
    Op. 45

Romanzen Und Balladen, Part 4, Op. 64
  see Balsatzar, Op. 57

Schumann Duette Pieces *CCU
  (Adachi, Masaru) 2 solo voices,pno
    ONGAKU 523020 f.s.   (S366)

Sechs Gesänge, Op. 107
  solo voice,pno SCIEN 1525 f.s.
    contains: Fensterscheibe, Die;
    Gärtner, Der; Herzeleid   (S367)

Secreto, El
  see [Canciones] Cuaderno 4

Songs For Voice And Piano, Vol. 1
  solo voice,pno (includes
    "Dichterliebe"; "Frauenliebe und
    Leben"; "Liederkreis, Opp. 24 &
    39") LEA 25   (S368)

Songs For Voice And Piano, Vol. 2
  solo voice,pno LEA 117   (S369)

Songs For Voice And Piano, Vol. 3
  solo voice,pno LEA 118   (S370)

Spanische Liebes-Lieder, Op. 138
  SATB soli,pno 4-hands CLASSV 1816
                                 (S371)

Visión
  see [Canciones] Cuaderno 3

Widmung
  high solo,pno CLASSV 0492   (S372)

Woman's Life And Love
  see Frauenliebe Und Leben

Zwolf Gedichte, Op. 37
  [Ger] high solo,pno KALMUS K 06793
    f.s. contains also: Liederkreis,
    Op. 39 (med solo,pno); Fünf
    Lieder, Op. 40 (med solo,pno);
    Frauenliebe Und Leben, Op. 42
    (med solo,pno)   (S373)

SCHUMANN DUETTE PIECES see Schumann,
  Robert (Alexander)

SCHUTSLUIS, DE see King, Harold C.

SCHÜTZ, HEINRICH (1585-1672)
  Buccinate In Neomania Tuba
    solo voice,cornetto,bsn, trombetta
    sc,set KING'S f.s. contains also:
    Jubilate Deo   (S374)

Concertos Sacred
  PETERS 66030   (S375)

Drei Kleine Geistliche Konzerte
  solo voice,org PETERS 4174   (S376)

Herzlich Lieb Hab Ich Dich
  [Ger] A solo,2vln,org/hpsd KALMUS
    K 06858   (S377)

Jubilate Deo
  see Buccinate In Neomania Tuba

O Jesu Nomen Dulce
  see Two Sacred Songs

O Misericordissime Jesu
  see Two Sacred Songs

Sacred Duets
  (Dittberner) [Ger] 2 med soli,org/
    pno PETERS FK46   (S378)

Two Sacred Songs
  solo voice,gtr PLUCKED STR ZM 1718
    $4.50
    contains: O Jesu Nomen Dulce; O
    Misericordissime Jesu   (S379)

SCHÜTZT DIESE WELT
  PETERS 9109   (S380)

SCHUYLER SONGS see Rorem, Ned

SCHUYLER'S "SONG" see Park, James

SCHWAB, SIGI
  Children Of Love
    solo voice,pno SCHOTTS MM 107
                                 (S381)

  My Love Is A Tango
    solo voice,pno SCHOTTS MM 105
                                 (S382)

SCHWÄCHER see Straesser, Joep

SCHWAEN, KURT (1909-   )
  Mädchenlieder
    PETERS 5199   (S383)

SCHWAN, DER see Franken, Wim

SCHWANENGESANG see Schubert, Franz
  (Peter)

SCHWANTNER, JOSEPH (1943-   )
  Magabunda
    S solo,orch EUR.AM.MUS. EA00516
    $35.00   (S384)

  New Morning For The World (Daybreak
    Of Freedom)
    speaking voice,orch study sc
    EUR.AM.MUS. EA 484 $25.00   (S385)

SCHWARTZ
  Children Of Eden Theme Song
    FABER 51232 1   (S386)

SCHWARTZ, FRANCIS (1940-   )
  My Eyebrows Are Not Bushy
    solo voice,acap sc PEER 60821-201
    $2.50   (S387)

SCHWEHR, CORNELIUS (1953-   )
  Vom Himmel
    A solo,bsn,pno,2vln,vla perf sc
    BREITKOPF-W KM 2201 f.s.   (S388)

SCHWENDINGER, LAURA (1962-   )
  sky a silver dissonance, the
    Bar solo,pno (text by e.e.
    cummings) FREEPUB FP19   (S389)

SCHWERTSIK, KURT (1935-   )
  Da Uhu Schaud Me So Draurech Au
    solo voice,pno ARIAD 78030A (S390)

SCIOSTAKOVIC, DMITRI
  see SHOSTAKOVICH, DMITRI

SCOGNA, FLAVIO EMILIO
  Canto Primo
    S solo,pno EDI-PAN EP 7227   (S391)

  Canto Secondo
    Mez solo,pno EDI-PAN EP 7228 (S392)

  Canto Terzo
    Bar solo,pno EDI-PAN EP 7229 (S393)

SCOTT, ALICIA ANN
  see SCOTT, [LADY] JOHN

SCOTT, [LADY] JOHN (ALICIA ANN)
  (1810-1900)
  Annie Laurie
    "Maxwelton Braes Are Bonny" low
    solo,pno CLASSV 1713   (S394)
    "Maxwelton Braes Are Bonny" med-
    high solo,pno CLASSV 0966   (S395)

  Jasmine Door, The
    med solo,pno CLASSV 2047   (S396)
    med-high solo,pno CLASSV 2046
                                 (S397)
    high solo,pno CLASSV 2045   (S398)

  Maxwelton Braes Are Bonny
    see Annie Laurie

SCOTTISH BALLAD "EDWARD", OP. 46, NO. 2
  see Tchaikovsky, Piotr Ilyich

SCOTTISH CRADLE SONG see Beach, [Mrs.]
  H.H.A. (Amy Marcy Cheney)

SCOTTISH MELODIES, 24
  (Holst, M.) solo voice,gtr TECLA
    TE046   (S399)

SCRIVENER, JOSEPH
  Psalm No. 139
    med solo,pno CORMORANT 5-101-3
    $2.75   (S400)

SCROLL see Silsbee, Ann

SCULTHORPE, PETER [JOSHUA] (1929-   )
  Song Of Tailitnama
    FABER sc 50697 6, pts 50698 4
                                 (S401)

SE see Denza, Luigi

SE PER FATAL DESTINO see Handel, George
  Frideric

SE SOLENS SKJONNE PRAKT see Nystedt,
  Knut

SE TU M'AMI see Parisotti see
  Pergolesi, Giovanni Battista

SEA, THE see Borodin, Alexander Porfirievich see MacDowell, Edward Alexander

SEA AND THE HONEYCOMB, THE see Le Baron, Anne

SEA-BIRD, THE see Fischer, Irwin

SEA-CHANGES see Eckert, Michael

SEA FEVER see Andrews, Mark see Ireland, John

SEA ROSE see Pieper, Rene

SEA WRACK see Stanford, Charles Villiers

SEAFARER, THE see Lundborg, (Charles) Erik

SEAL LULLABY see Weigl, [Mrs.] Vally

SEAL-WOMAN, THE see Flothuis, Marius

SEASCAPES: FOUR SONGS see Alwyn, William

SEASON OF VIOLET see Nakada, Yoshinao

SEASONAL see Erickson, Robert

SEASONS IN TIME, VOL. 1: SOLO SONGS FOR THE JEWISH FAMILY LIFE CYCLE see Isaacson, Michael Neil

SEASONS IN TIME, VOL. 2: DUETS FOR HOLIDAY AND LIFE CYCLE see Isaacson, Michael Neil

SECCHI, A. (1761-1833)
 Lungi Dal Caro Bene
  med-high solo,pno CLASSV 1040
                                    (S402)
  med solo,pno CLASSV 2048   (S403)

SECHS FRÜHE LIEDER see Mahler, Gustav

SECHS GEDICHTE, OP. 14 see Dohnányi, Ernst von

SECHS GEDICHTE VON GOETHE, OP. 18 see Medtner, Nikolai Karlovich

SECHS GESÄNGE, OP. 34 see Mendelssohn-Bartholdy, Felix

SECHS GESÄNGE, OP. 86 see Mendelssohn-Bartholdy, Felix

SECHS GESÄNGE, OP. 99 see Mendelssohn-Bartholdy, Felix

SECHS GESÄNGE, OP. 107 see Schumann, Robert (Alexander)

SECHS GESÄNGE, OP. 154 see Spohr, Ludwig (Louis)

SECHS HERBSTLIEDER see Norby, Erik

SECHS KAVATINEN, OP. 39 see Giuliani, Mauro

SECHS LIEDER see Blumenthal, Jacob (Jacques)

SECHS LIEDER see Mendelssohn-Bartholdy, Felix

SECHS LIEDER see Badings, Henk

SECHS LIEDER see Hartmann, Ludwig

SECHS LIEDER see Fischer, A.

SECHS LIEDER NACH GEDICHTEN VON HERMANN HESSE see Hummel, Bertold

SECHS LIEDER, OP. 4 see Zumsteeg, Emilie

SECHS LIEDER, OP. 10 see Zemlinsky, Alexander von

SECHS LIEDER, OP. 12 see Goetz, Hermann

SECHS LIEDER, OP. 13 see Zemlinsky, Alexander von

SECHS LIEDER, OP. 46 see Kaun, Hugo see Novak, Vitezslav

SECHS LIEDER, OP. 50 see Sibelius, Jean

SECHS LIEDER, OP. 57 see Mendelssohn-Bartholdy, Felix

SECHS LIEDER, OP. 71 see Mendelssohn-Bartholdy, Felix

SECHS ROMANZEN, OP. 44 see Arensky, Anton Stepanovich

SECHS SCHOTTISCHE NATIONALLIEDER see Mendelssohn-Bartholdy, Felix

SECHS WASSERLIEDER see Geelen, Mathieu

SECHS ZWEISTIMMIGE LIEDER, OP. 63 see Mendelssohn-Bartholdy, Felix

SECOND BALLAD ALBUM *CCU
 BOOSEY VAB0292 f.s.   (S404)

SECOND BOOK OF SONGS see Jeffreys, John

SECRET AVEU see Aubert, Louis-Francois-Marie

SECRETO, EL see Schumann, Robert (Alexander)

SECULAR SONGS AND ARIAS FROM SCHEMELLI'S SONGBOOK *CCU
 solo voice,pno BREITKOPF-W EB 8476 f.s.   (S405)

SEDLÁCEK, BOHUSLAV (1928-)
 Vonicka Z Kviti Milostneho
  solo voice,pno PANTON 938   (S406)

SEDM PISNI see Sommer, Vladimír

SEDMIKVITEK see Stedron, Milos

SEE THE CHARIOT AT HAND see Vaughan Williams, Ralph

SEEGER
 American Folk Songs For Children *CCU
  solo voice DOVER BKDD 00013C $15.95
                                    (S407)
 Five Songs
  A solo,pno PETERS 67207   (S408)

SEEING YOU LEAVE see Johnson, A. Paul

SEEK THOU THIS SOUL OF MINE see Franck

SEEMEEU see Badings, Henk

SEFARDIC SONGS AND BALLADS see Milner, Ch.

SEGDU MER SÖGU see Runolfsson, Karl Otto

SEGUIDILLA see Bizet, Georges, Carmen: Près Des Remparts De Séville

SEGUIDILLA DEL OFICIAL CORTEJANTE see Galvan, Ventura

SEGUIDILLA DOLOROSA DE UNA ENAMORADA see Muson, L.

SEGUIDILLAS see Sor, Fernando

SEGUIDILLAS MAJAS see Laserna, Blas de

SEGUIDILLAS RELIGIOSAS see Pla, M.

SÉGUIDILLE see Falla, Manuel de

SEHET, WIR GEH'N HINAUF NACH JERUSALEM see Bach, Johann Sebastian

SEHNSUCHT see Krebs, Karl August see Rubinstein, Anton, Desire

SEHNSUCHT, DIE see Schubert, Franz (Peter)

SEHNSUCHT NACH GOTT see Kuntz, Michael

SEI CANTATE PROFANE see Vivaldi, Antonio

SEI CANTI see Ragnarsson, Hjalmar H.

SEI CANZONETTE see Ferrari

SEI DIR ENDLICH DES LENZTRUGS BEWUSST see Glière, Reinhold Moritzovich

SEI UNS GEGRÜSST, DU WEIHNACHTSBAUM see Eisler, Hanns

SEIDEL, JAN (1908-)
 Me Pisne
  PANTON 940   (S409)

SEIDSTICKER, CARL
 Ausgewählte Deutsche Lieder Mit Begleitung Der Guitarre, 60
  SCIEN 1543   (S410)

SEKLES, BERNHARD (1872-1934)
 Aus Dem Schi-King, Op. 15, Vol.I: 1-9
  [Ger] high solo RECITAL 388   (S411)
 Aus Dem Schi-King, Op. 15, Vol.II: 10-18
  [Ger] high solo RECITAL 389   (S412)

SEKS BARNERIM FRA GUDBRANDSDALEN see Karlsen, Kjell Mørk

SEKS MUTASJONER see Alterhaug, Bjorn

SEKS NORSKE DIKT, OP. 40 see Lunde, Ivar

SEKS POESIER, OP. 18 see Jordan, Sverre

SEKS SALMETONER see Nystedt, Knut

SEKS SALMETONER, OP. 5, NO. 2 see Karlsen, Kjell Mørk see Karlsen, Kjell Mørk

SEKS SALMETONER TIL TEKSTER AV ERLING DITTMANN, OP.5, NO.2 see Karlsen, Kjell Mørk

SEKS SANGE see Bjerg, Jens

SEKS SANGE, OP. 21 see Jordan, Sverre

SEKS SANGE TIL KLAVER, OP. 23 see Jordan, Sverre

SEKS SANGER, OP. 3 see Karlsen, Kjell Mørk

SEKS SANGER, OP. 9 see Johnsen, Hallvard

SEKS SANGER, OP. 149, NOS. 1-6 see Fongaard, Bjørn

SEKS SANGER TIL TEKST AV JOHAN HERMAN WESSEL, OP. 3 see Karlsen, Kjell Mørk

SEKS SIVLE-SONGAR see Kielland, Olav

SEKS SONETTER, OP. 38 see Nystedt, Knut

SELECTED ARIAS FOR BASS, TRUMPET AND PIANO see Bach, Johann Sebastian

SELECTED LIEDER, VOL. 6 see Wolffs, Felix

SELECTED LIEDER, VOL. 7 see Wolffs, Felix

SELECTED LIEDER, VOL. 8 see Wolffs, Felix

SELECTED LIEDER, VOL. 9 see Wolffs, Felix

SELECTED LIEDER, VOL. 10 see Wolffs, Felix

SELECTED SONGS see Lang, Josephine

SELECTED SONGS BY AUSTRALIAN COMPOSERS
 solo voice,pno (med, contains 23 songs) ALLANS   (S413)

SELECTED SONGS FOR HIGH VOICE see Grieg, Edvard Hagerup

SELECTED SONGS FOR LOW VOICE see Grieg, Edvard Hagerup

SELECTED SONGS FROM SCHEMELLI'S SONGBOOK see Bach, Johann Sebastian

SELECTED SONGS, VOL. 2 see Hensel, Fanny Mendelssohn

SELECTION OF ITALIAN ARIAS (1600-1800), A, VOL.1 *CC21L
 (Lewis, Anthony) ABRSM f.s. high solo,kbd 1 85472 239 5; low solo, kbd 1 85472 240 9   (S414)

SELECTION OF JAPANESE SONGS, VOL. 1 *CCU
 (Maki No Kai) solo voice ONGAKU 522500 f.s.   (S415)

SELECTION OF JAPANESE SONGS, VOL. 2 *CCU
 (Maki No Kai) solo voice ONGAKU 522510 f.s.   (S416)

SELECTIONS FROM DER ROSENKAVALIER, A MASTER CLASS WITH EVELYN LEAR see Strauss, Richard

SELEN, REINHOLD
 Abfahrt In Dämmernder Stille *song cycle
  Bar/B solo,pno [20'] DONEMUS   (S417)

SELFDEPENDENCE see Lund, Signe

SELIG IST DER MANN see Bach, Johann Sebastian

SELIGE NACHT see Marx, Joseph

SELIGKEIT DER LIEBE, DIE see Haydn, [Johann] Michael

S'ELLA VUOL RENDERSI see Benda, Georg Anton (Jiří Antonín)

SELMER, JOHAN PETER (1844-1910)
Do Not Let Me Die
see La Meg Ei Dø

Fishergirl In Despair, The
see Fiskerjenten Fortvilet

Fiskerjenten Fortvilet *Op.34,No.1
"Fishergirl In Despair, The" solo
voice,2.2.2.2. 2.2.3.0. timp,
perc,strings NORGE f.s.   (S418)

Greece
see Grekenland

Grekenland *Op.43,No.1
"Greece" Bar solo,2.2.2.2. 4.2.3.1.
perc,strings HANSEN-DEN f.s.
                                     (S419)

I Choose April
see Jeg Velger Meg April

Jeg Velger Meg April *Op.34,No.2
"I Choose April" S solo,2.2.2.2.
2.2.3.0. timp,perc,strings
HANSEN-DEN f.s.   (S420)

Knife, The
see Tollekniven

La Meg Ei Dø *Op.43,No.2
"Do Not Let Me Die" Mez/Bar solo,
2(pic).2.2.2. 4.2.3.1. perc,
strings HANSEN-DEN f.s.   (S421)

Lament Of Tasso
see Tassos Klage

Philosophie Der Liebe *Op.13,No.3
[Ger] Bar solo,2(pic).2.2.2.
4.2.3.0. timp,perc,strings NORGE
f.s.   (S422)

Tassos Klage *Op.13,No.1
"Lament Of Tasso" [Ger] T solo,
2(pic).2.2.2. 4.2.3.0. timp,perc,
strings NORGE f.s.   (S423)

Tollekniven *Op.24,No.10
"Knife, The" solo voice,2.2.2.2.
4.1.3.1. strings [3'] NORGE f.s.
                                     (S424)

Wanderer Der Welt, Die *Op.13,No.2
Bar solo,2(pic).2.2.2. 4.2.3.1.
timp,perc,strings NORGE f.s.
                                     (S425)

SELVA INCANTATA, LA: AL NOME TUO TEMUTO
see Righini, Vincenzo

SEM DROPI TINDRANDI see Speight, John
A.

SEMELE: HENCE, HENCE, IRIS, HENCE AWAY
see Handel, George Frideric

SEMELE: WHERE'ER YOU WALK see Handel,
George Frideric

SEMENOFF, IVAN (1917-1972)
Contagion, La
SBar soli,2.2.2.2. 2.2.2.0. 2perc,
timp,harp,strings [33'] sc,pts,
pno red BILLAUDOT   (S426)

SEMIOLOGY FOR JOHN DOWLAND see
Matsudaira, Yori-Aki

SEMIRAMIDE: IN SÌ BARBARA see Rossini,
Gioacchino

SEMIRAMIDE: NO, NON TI LASCIO see
Rossini, Gioacchino

SEMIRAMIDE RICONOSCIUTA: VIENI, CHE POI
SERENO see Gluck, Christoph
Willibald, Ritter von

SEND ME A LEAF see Sveinsson, Atli
Heimir

SENIDYL see Colding-Jorgensen, Henrik

SENKYR, AUGUSTIN (1736-1796)
Aria De Quovis Festo
see Saevit Mare Surgunt Venti

Aria Pastoritia
see Huc, Huc, Pastorculi

Huc, Huc, Pastorculi
(Marusan, Frantisek) "Aria
Pastoritia" S solo,org,strings
without vcl [9'] CESKY HUD.
                                     (S427)

Saevit Mare Surgunt Venti
(Marusan, Frantisek) "Aria De
Quovis Festo" [Lat] B solo,2horn,
org,strings without vcl [7']
CESKY HUD.   (S428)

Salve Regina
(Marusan, Frantisek) [Lat] SS soli,
2horn,org,strings without vcl
[5'] CESKY HUD.   (S429)

SENN see Helgason, Hallgrimur

SENTENCE ONCE BEGUN, A see Bottje, Will
Gay

SENTIMENT DE SOLITUDE see Tal, Marjo

SENZA NISCIUNO see Curtis, Ernesto de

SENZA TESTO see Mandanici, Marcella

SEPARATION see Dring, Madeleine

SEPARAZIONE, LA see Rossini, Gioacchino

SEPT CHANSONS DE BRETAGNE see Hure,
Jean

SEPT CHANSONS DE CLÉMENT MAROT, OP.15
see Enesco, Georges (Enescu)

SEPT CHANSONS DE TROUBADOURS DES 12E ET
13E SIECLES
(Ravier, Charles) S/countertenor,rec,
harmonium,lute,harp, viol, hurdy-
gurdy, psaltery [12'] BILLAUDOT
                                     (S430)

SEPT CHANSONS POPULAIRES DE BURGOS see
Collet, Henri

SEPT POEMES see Manneke, Daan

SEPT RONDELS, SERIES 2 see Koechlin,
Charles

SEPTEMBERMOND 1-2 see Freudenthal, Otto

SEPTEMBERMORGEN see Marx, Joseph

SEQUENTIA: LABYRINTISCHE FORM NACH
TEXTEN VON ISOLDE LOOCK see Hegdal,
Magne

SERA JETTE see Tiritomba

SEREBRIER, JOSE (1938-   )
Orpheus Times Light
S solo,2(pic).1.0.0. 2.2.1.1. timp,
perc,harp,pno/cel,strings PEER
                                     (S431)

SERENADE see Basart, Robert see Duparc,
Henri see Gounod, Charles François
see Gudmundsson, Björgvin see
Karlsen, Kjell Mørk see Kunieda,
Harue see Leoncavallo, Ruggiero,
Pagliacci: O Columbina see
Schubert, Franz (Peter) see
Schubert, Franz (Peter), Ständchen

SERENADE AV "VENETIANERNE" see Groven,
Eivind

SERENADE D'AUTREFOIS see Silvestri,
Constantin

SERENADE DE ZANETTO see Massenet,
Jules, Sérénade Du Passant

SÉRÉNADE DU PASSANT see Massenet, Jules

SERENADE FOR ORCHESTRA AND BARITONE see
Bliss, [Sir] Arthur (Drummond)

SÉRÉNADE FRANCAISE see Leoncavallo,
Ruggiero

SERENADE II see Mamiya, Michio

SÉRÉNADE INUTILE see Brahms, Johannes,
Vergebliches Ständchen

SÉRÉNADE NAPOLITAIN see Leoncavallo,
Ruggiero

SERENATA see Brahms, Johannes see
Galante, Carlo see Handel, George
Frideric see Marx, Joseph see
Schubert, Franz (Peter) see Tosti,
Francesco Paolo see Zandonai,
Riccardo

SERENATA, LA see Zandonai, Riccardo

SERENATA AMOROSA see Worsley, C.

SERENATA: COME COL CAPO SOTTO L'ALA
BIANCA see Mascagni, Pietro

SERENATA DI LORENZO STECCHETTI see
Mascagni, Pietro

SERENATA III see Bosco, Gilberto

SERENATA ITALIANA see Rossi, D.

SERENATELLA see Medina, Emilio

SERPENT, THE see Hoiby, Lee

SERRES CHAUDES, OP. 24 see Chausson,
Ernest

SERSE: OMBRA MAI FU see Handel, George
Frideric

SERSE: OMBRA MAI FU (LARGO) see Handel,
George Frideric

SERVENTA BONICA, LA see Morera, Enrique

SES MELODIES OEUVRES COMPLETES 1 see
Faure, Gabriel-Urbain

SEST CHVALOZPEVU see Ryba, Jan Jakub
Simon

SEST' PESEN (SIX SONGS) see Tal, Marjo

SESTINA: ALTAFORTE see Gerber, Steven
R.

SETERSUITE see Storbekken, Egil

SETROM-SONGAR, OP. 12 see Nystedt, Knut

SETTINGS FROM PIERROT LUNAIRE see
Kraft, William

SEUFZER see Schubert, Franz (Peter)

SEVEN, THE see Bertelsen, Michael

SEVEN (A CYCLE OF SEVEN EMILY DICKINSON
POEMS) see Brown, Francis James

SEVEN EARLY LOVE SONGS see Rochberg, A.
George

SEVEN EARLY SONGS see Schoenberg,
Arnold

SEVEN ELIZABETHAN LYRICS, OP. 12 see
Quilter, Roger

SEVEN EPITAPHS see Thompson, Bruce A.

SEVEN EXCERPTS FROM WASHINGTON'S
FAREWELL ADDRESS see Warren, Betsy

SEVEN HOUSMAN SONGS see Hoekman,
Timothy

SEVEN LIEDER see Schumann, Clara
(Wieck)

SEVEN LYRIC MELODIES, OP. 21 see
Ferrata, Giuseppe

SEVEN MASS SONGS FOR VOICE AND PIANO,
OP. 79 see Prokofiev, Serge

SEVEN MASS SONGS FOR VOICE AND PIANO,
OP. 89, NO. 2 see Prokofiev, Serge

SEVEN POEMS BY E.E. CUMMINGS see
Harper, Edward James

SEVEN POEMS OF PUSHKIN, OP. 29 see
Medtner, Nikolai Karlovich

SEVEN SANCTUARY SONGS see Zaninelli

SEVEN SELECTED SONGS see Hopkins,
Franklin

SEVEN SILLY SONGS see Frandsen, John

SEVEN SONGS see Halldorsson, Skuli see
Revueltas, Silvestre, Siete
Canciones see Saygun, Ahmed Adnan
see Sveinbjörnsson, Sveinbjörn

SEVEN SONGS see Liptak, David

SEVEN SONGS see Weigl, Karl

SEVEN SONGS see Thomas, Andrew

SEVEN SONGS see Griffes, Charles
Tomlinson

SEVEN SONGS, OP. 28 see Medtner,
Nikolai Karlovich

SEVEN SONGS, OP. 47 see Tchaikovsky,
Piotr Ilyich

SEVEN SONGS, OP. 70 see Parker, Horatio
William

SEVEN SONGS TO POEMS BY INGE KROKANN
see Olsen, Sparre, Sju Krokann-
Songar

SEVEN SPANISH FOLKSONGS see Falla,
Manuel de

SEVEN TEXTURAL SETTINGS OF JAPANESE
POETRY see Udow, Michael William

SEVENTEEN LYRICS FROM SING-SONG, BOOK 1
see Homer, Sidney

SEVENTEEN LYRICS FROM SING-SONG, BOOK 2
see Homer, Sidney

1776 VOCAL SELECTIONS see Edwards,
Sherman

SEVILLANA see Massenet, Jules

SEVRIENS, JEAN
Coda (The Wind)
see Songs From Diana

Dernier Rendez-Vous, Le
S solo,pno [7'] DONEMUS (S432)

Oak, The
see Songs From Diana

River, The
see Songs From Diana

Songs From Diana
high solo,gtr DONEMUS f.s. [12']
contains: Coda (The Wind); Oak,
The; River, The; Twilight
(S433)

Twilight
see Songs From Diana

SEX LÖG see Sveinbjörnsson, Sveinbjörn

SEX SÅNGER TILL TEXTER AV EMIL HAGSTRÖM
see Lindgren, Olof

SEX SONGLOG see Halldorsson, Sigfus

SEXTET see Fongaard, Bjørn

SEXTET III, SONGS FROM THE TAO TE KING
see Badings, Henk

SEXTIU OG SEX EINSÖNGSLÖG see
Gudmundsson, Björgvin

SGAMBATI, GIOVANNI (1841-1914)
Quattro Melodie, Op. 35
[It] med-high solo RECITAL 288
(S434)

SHA'AR, LEVI
Two Songs By Rachel
solo voice,pno OR-TAV (S435)

SHACHAR AVAKESHCHA see Gottlieb, Jack
S.

SHADOW see Nakada, Yoshinao

SHADOW OF A PRAYER see Marez Oyens,
Tera de

SHADOW OF THE BLUES: FOUR POEMS BY
LANGSTON HUGHES see Meschwitz,
Frieder

SHADOWES THAT IN DARKNESSE DWELL see
Lindgren, Pär

SHADOWS see Hutcheson, Jere T.

SHADOWS OF AN ORANGE-LEAF see Zonn,
Paul

SHADOWSONG see Meyerbeer, Giacomo,
Dinorah (Pardon De Ploërmel): Ombre
Légère

SHAKESPEARE SONGS I (H), PNO see
Thomson, Virgil Garnett

SHAKESPEARE SONNET CXXVIII see Zallman,
Arlene (Proctor)

SHAKESPEARE SONNET XVIII see Zallman,
Arlene (Proctor)

SHAKUKEI see Hirai, Kozaburoy

SHANTY LAD, THE see Haufrecht, Herbert

SHAPERO, HAROLD SAMUEL (1920-   )
Three Hebrew Songs
T solo,pno,string orch [21'0"] PEER
(S436)

SHAPEY, RALPH (1921-   )
Songs Of Joy
S solo,pno PRESSER 111-40114 (S437)

String Quartet No. 5
solo voice,pno pno red PRESSER
111-40120 (S438)

This Day
female solo,pno PRESSER 111-40121
(S439)

Walking Upright
female solo,vln PRESSER 111-40122
(S440)

SHARLIN, WILLIAM (1920-   )
V'shamru
[Heb] med solo,kbd TRANSCON.
991219
(S441)

SHATIN, JUDITH (1949-   )
Three Summer's Heat
Mez solo,electronic tape [20']
AM.COMP.AL. (S442)

SHATTER ME MUSIC see Speight, John A.

SHE MOVED THROUGH THE FAIR see
Corigliano, John

SHE NEVER TOLD HER LOVE see Haydn,
[Franz] Joseph

SHE WEEPS OVER RAHOON see Gideon,
Miriam

SHE WROTE see Anderson, Beth

SHEARER, ALLEN
Five Poems Of Wallace Stevens
Bar solo,pno [11'] FALLEN LEAF 33
(S443)

SHEEP AND LAMBS see Homer, Sidney

SHEEP IN FOG see Altena, Maarten

SHÉHÉRAZADE: L'INDIFFÉRENT see Ravel,
Maurice

SHEHERAZADE, TEIL 1 see Koechlin,
Charles

SHEHERAZADE, TEIL 2 see Koechlin,
Charles

SHEPHERD ON THE ROCK, THE see Schubert,
Franz (Peter), Hirt Auf Dem Felsen,
Der

SHEPHERD ON THE ROCKS, WITH A TWIST (S.
12 TO 1) see "Bach, P.D.Q." (Peter
Schickele)

SHEPHERD! THY DEMEANOUR VARY see Brown,
Thomas

SHIBATA, MINAO (1916-   )
Collection Of Songs, A *CCU
solo voice ONGAKU 524780 f.s.
(S444)

Poem Recited In The Night
S solo,chamber group ONGAKU 491342
f.s. (S445)

SHIBUYA, TAKUCHO (1930-   )
Asu Ga Arukara
S/T solo [4'] ONGAKU (S446)

Ki No Yoni
S/T solo [3'] ONGAKU (S447)

SHIELD, WILLIAM (1748-1829)
Flaxen Headed Cow Boy, A (from The
Farmer)
T solo,2vln,vcl,fl,kbd sc KING'S
(S448)

SHIELDS, ALICE (1943-   )
Black Lake, The (from Shaman)
T solo,vcl,electronic tape [10'] sc
AM.COMP.AL. $6.15 (S449)

SHIFRIN, SEYMOUR J. (1926-1979)
Birthday Greeting, A
S solo,gtr [1'] APNM sc $2.50, set
$4.75 (S450)

Five Songs *CC5U
S solo,pno APNM sc $6.50, set
$12.50 (S451)

Five Songs *CC5U
S solo,orch APNM sc $15.00, pts
rent (S452)

Rest Sweet Nimphs
S solo,clar [2'] APNM sc $2.50, set
$4.75 (S453)

Three Songs *CC3U
S solo,pno APNM sc $4.75, set $9.25
(S454)

SHIGON'BO see Sugiura, Masayoshi

SHILFLIED see Bacon, Ernst L.

SHIMAZU, TAKEHITO (1949-   )
Diagonal Line
Mez solo, jushichi-gen, shakuhachi
[15'] JAPAN (S455)

SHIMIZU, OSAMU
Lieder, Vol. 1 *CCU
solo voice ONGAKU 524800 f.s.
(S456)

Lieder, Vol. 2 *CCU
solo voice ONGAKU 524802 f.s.
(S457)

SHIMO see Sapp, Gary J.

SHIMOYAMA, HIFUMI (1930-   )
Catalysis No.3
S solo,tuba [9'] JAPAN (S458)

SHIO GA HIKU YOUNI see Kosuge, Yasuo

SHIPWRECK AND LOVE SCENE FROM BYRON'S
"DON JUAN" see Thomson, Virgil
Garnett

SHIROI BOHYO see Sasaki, Shigeru

SHIROI MANJUSHAGE see Nakajima, Hal

SHOCHNEI BATEI CHOMER see Suben, Joel
Eric

SHOGEH V'CHEIK see Suben, Joel Eric

SHORE, CLARE
Four Vocalises
S solo,mel inst NL NLP 001 (S459)

SHOSTAKOVICH, DMITRI (1906-1975)
Ass And The Nightingale, The
see Two Krylov Fables, Op. 4

Aus Jiddischer Volkspoesie *Op.79a
[Russ/Ger] SAT soli,pno SIKORSKI
2346 (S460)

Dragonfly And The Ant, The
see Two Krylov Fables, Op. 4

Five Romances
see Satires (Pictures Of The Past)
Op. 109

Foreword To My Works, Op. 123
see Romances, Op. 121 (On Texts
From "Krokodil"

Gedichte
PETERS 5784 (S461)

Romances, Op. 121 (On Texts From
"Krokodil"
B solo SIKORSKI 2277 f.s. contains
also: Foreword To My Works, Op.
123 (S462)

Romanzen Und Monologe Nach Puschkin
low solo,pno PETERS 4793 (S463)

Satires (Pictures Of The Past) Op.
109
"Five Romances" [Russ/Ger] S solo
SIKORSKI 2317 (S464)

Spanish Songs, Op. 100
[Russ] Mez solo SIKORSKI SIK6765
(S465)

Suite For Verses Of Michelangelo
Buonarroti *Op.145
SCHIRM.G ED3426 (S466)

Suite On Verses Of Michelangelo
Buonarroti, Op. 145
SIKORSKI SIK2282 (S467)

Two Krylov Fables, Op. 4
[Russ/Ger] SIKORSKI SIK2322 f.s.
contains: Ass And The
Nightingale, The; Dragonfly And
The Ant, The (S468)

SHOTO see Doi, Yoshiyuki

SHOULD I ENVY THE GODS? see Straesser,
Joep

SHOULD LANTERNS SHINE see Ford, Ronald

SHROPSHIRE LAD, A see Manney, Charles
Fonteyn see Somervell, Arthur

SHROUD OF TURIN, THE see Franco, Johan

SHULE AGRA see Tal, Marjo

SHUT, WASYL (1899-1982)
Before It Dies
see Zaky Umre

Chansonette
see Two Songs

Doshchyk
see Narodni Pisni (Folk Songs)

Dream, The
see Son

Duma Pro Savu Tchaloho
see Narodni Pisni (Folk Songs)

Great You Are
see Velyka Ty

I Did Not Break The Flower
see Ne Lamala Tsvitu

I Will Return
see Ja Pryjidu

If You Only Knew
see Jakby Ty Znav

Ja Pryjidu
"I Will Return" [Ukranian] med
solo,pno DUMA (S469)

Jaka Krasa Vidrodzhennia Krainy
see Two Songs On Texts By
Oleksander Oles

Jakby Ty Znav
"If You Only Knew" [Ukranian] solo
voice,pno DUMA (S470)

Lito
"Summer" [Ukranian] S/T solo,pno
DUMA (S471)

SHUT, WASYL (cont'd.)

Lyst
    see Three Songs

Mami
    "To Mother" [Ukranian] solo voice,
        pno DUMA   (S472)

Muza
    see Three Romances

Napyshit' Khto Nebud'
    see Three Romances

Narodni Pisni (Folk Songs)
    [Ukranian] solo voice,pno DUMA f.s.
    contains: Doshchyk, "Rain, The";
        Duma Pro Savu Tchaloho, "Ballad
        Of Sava Tchalyj, The"; Oy, Na
        Hori Zhyto, "Wheat Up Above"
                                        (S473)

Ne Lamala Tsvitu
    "I Did Not Break The Flower"
    [Ukranian] S solo,pno DUMA (S474)

O, Jak Bahato
    see Three Romances

Ot Idu Ja Slobodoiu
    see Two Songs

Oy, Na Hori Zhyto
    see Narodni Pisni (Folk Songs)

Pisnia
    see Three Songs

Pisnia Pro Poltavu
    see Three Romances

Pryjshla
    see Three Songs

Recitation
    [Ukranian] solo voice,pno DUMA
                                        (S475)

Skarb
    "Treasure, The" [Ukranian] med
        solo,pno DUMA   (S476)

Snih
    see Three Romances

Soldier, Don't Be Sad
    see Usususe Ne Sumuj

Son
    "Dream, The" [Ukranian] ST soli,pno
        DUMA   (S477)

Spit' Skalitcheni
    see Two Songs On Texts By
        Oleksander Oles

Student Serenade
    see Studentska Serenada

Studentska Serenada
    "Student Serenade" [Ukranian] high
        solo,pno DUMA   (S478)

Summer
    see Lito

Tetche Voda Z Pid Javora
    "Water Flows From Under The
        Sycamore" [Ukranian] med solo,pno
        DUMA   (S479)

Three Romances
    [Ukranian] S/T solo,pno DUMA f.s.
    contains: Napyshit' Khto Nebud',
        "Please Write, Someone"; Pisnia
        Pro Poltavu, "Song Of Poltava";
        Snih, "Snow"   (S480)

Three Romances
    [Ukranian] solo voice,pno DUMA f.s.
    contains: Muza, "Muse, The"; O,
        Jak Bahato, "Oh, How Many";
        Zatykh Vzhe Hrim, "Thunder Has
        Subsided, The"   (S481)

Three Songs
    [Ukranian] solo voice,pno DUMA f.s.
    contains: Lyst, "Letter, The";
        Pisnia, "Song, A"; Pryjshla,
        "She Came"   (S482)

To Mother
    see Mami

Treasure, The
    see Skarb

Trio
    [Ukranian] SABar soli,pno,vln DUMA
                                        (S483)

Two Songs
    [Ukranian] S/T solo,pno DUMA f.s.
    contains: Chansonette; Ot Idu Ja
        Slobodoiu, "I Go Through The
        Village"   (S484)

SHUT, WASYL (cont'd.)

Two Songs On Texts By Oleksander Oles
    [Ukranian] S/T solo,pno DUMA f.s.
    contains: Jaka Krasa
        Vidrodzhennia Krainy, "What
        Beauty, The Rebirth Of A
        Nation"; Spit' Skalitcheni,
        "Sleep, Injured Ones"   (S485)

Usususe Ne Sumuj
    "Soldier, Don't Be Sad" [Ukranian]
        med solo,pno DUMA   (S486)

Velyka Ty
    "Great You Are" [Ukranian] S/T
        solo,pno DUMA   (S487)

Water Flows From Under The Sycamore
    see Tetche Voda Z Pid Javora

Zaky Umre
    "Before It Dies" [Ukranian] solo
        voice,pno DUMA   (S488)

Zatykh Vzhe Hrim
    see Three Romances

SI J'ÉTAIS see Duparc, Henri, Sérénade

SI MES VERS AVAIENT DES AILES see Hahn,
    Reynaldo

SI-SCHY see Brandse, Wim

SI TIL SIONS DATTER see Maehlum, Svein

SI TU M'AIMAIS! see Denza, Luigi

SI TU VEUX, MIGNONNE see Massenet,
    Jules

SI VES UN MONTE DE ESPUMAS see Nin-
    Culmell, Joaquin

SI VOUS L'AVIEZ COMPRIS! see Denza,
    Luigi

SI YO ROBARA AL RUISEÑOR see Massana,
    A., Sijo Tingués Del Rossinyol

SIBELIUS, JEAN (1865-1957)
    Acht Lieder, Op. 57
        [Ger/Eng/Swed] high solo (not
            available outside U.S.A.) RECITAL
            394   (S489)
        [Ger/Eng/Swed] low solo (not
            available outside U.S.A.) RECITAL
            395   (S490)

    Acht Lieder, Op. 61
        [Ger/Eng/Swed] high solo (not
            available outside U.S.A.) RECITAL
            396   (S491)

    Early On One Wintry Cool Day: Arioso
        S/T solo,string orch PEER sc
        60064-221 $6.00, pts 60063-222
        $25.00   (S492)

    First Kiss
        see Första Kyssen, Den

    Första Kyssen, Den
        "First Kiss" [Swed/Ger] high solo
            RECITAL 2242   (S493)

    Sechs Lieder, Op. 50
        [Ger/Eng/Swed/Finn] high solo (not
            available outside U.S.A.) RECITAL
            392   (S494)
        [Ger/Eng/Swed/Finn] low solo (not
            available outside U.S.A.) RECITAL
            393   (S495)

    Songs, Op. 17, Nos. 4:7
        high solo,pno CLASSV 1929   (S496)

    Songs, Op. 35, Nos. 1:2
        high solo,pno CLASSV 1930   (S497)

    Songs, Op. 36, Nos. 1:6
        high solo,pno CLASSV 1931   (S498)

    Songs, Op. 37, Nos. 1:5
        high solo,pno CLASSV 1932   (S499)

    Songs, Op. 38, Nos. 1:5
        high solo,pno CLASSV 1933   (S500)

    Songs, Op. 60, Nos. 1:2
        med solo,pno CLASSV 1934   (S501)

    Songs, Op. 72, Nos. 3:6
        med-high solo,pno CLASSV 1935
                                    (S502)

    Songs, Op. 90, Nos. 1:6
        med-high solo,pno CLASSV 1936
                                    (S503)

    Svarta Rosor
        [Swed] low solo,pno CLASSV 1264
                                    (S504)
        [Swed/Ger] med solo,pno CLASSV 0525
                                    (S505)

SIBERIA: ORRIDE STEPPE! see Giordano,
    Umberto

SICILIANA see Pergolesi, Giovanni
    Battista

SICK ROSE, THE see Haxton, Kenneth see
    Homer, Sidney

SIDASTI VALSINN see Halldorsson, Skuli

SIE SCHWEBT' MIR NOCH KÜRZLICH see
    Arensky, Anton Stepanovich

SIE WAREN SO SCHÖN UND HERRLICH see
    Clostre, Adrienne

SIEBEL'S ARIA see Gounod, Charles
    François, Faust: Faites Lui

SIEBEN GESÄNGE AUS WALTER SCOTTS
    FRÄULEIN VOM SEE see Schubert,
    Franz (Peter)

SIEBEN KLEINE KIRCHENKOMPOSITIONEN see
    Jommelli, Niccolo

SIEBEN LEHMANNLIEDER see Pasatieri,
    Thomas

SIEBEN LIEDER see Blumenthal, Jacob
    (Jacques)

SIEBEN LIEDER see Mahler, Gustav

SIEBEN LIEDER, OP. 1 see Ast, Max

SIEBEN LIEDER, OP. 28 see Albert,
    Eugène Francis Charles d'

SIEBEN LIEDER VON ROBERT BURNS see
    Jensen, Adolf

SIEBEN SCHWESTERN see Dessau, Paul

SIEBERT, F.
    Kleine Geschichte
        S solo,orch pno red KUNZEL EES 440
                                    (S506)

SIECZYNSKI, RUDOLF
    Wien, Du Stadt Meiner Träume
        [Ger] high solo,pno CLASSV 1690
                                    (S507)
        [Ger] med solo,pno CLASSV 1691
                                    (S508)

SIÈGE DE CORINTHE: LA GLOIRE ET LA
    FORTUNE see Rossini, Gioacchino

SIEH, DA STEHT DAS ERHOLUNGSHEIM see
    Eisler, Hanns, Wohltätigkeit

SIEH, DEN HERBST see Pieper, Rene

SIEHE, WIE DIE MONDESSTRAHLEN see
    Schubert, Franz (Peter), Mondnacht,
    Die

SIEM, KARE (1914-1986)
    Til Deg
        LYCHE 44   (S509)
        [Norw] solo voice,pno (text by T.
            Stadskleiv) LYCHE   (S510)

SIESTA see Sveinsson, Atli Heimir

SIETE CANCIONES see Garcia Morante,
    Manuel see Revueltas, Silvestre

SIETE CANCIONES see Fernandez, Luis
    Sanchez

SIETE CANCIONES POPULARES DE BURGOS see
    Collet, Henri, Sept Chansons
    Populaires De Burgos

SIFONIA, FIRMINO (1917-   )
    Cantus
        S solo,fl,ob,clar,bsn,trp in C,
            trom,pno EDI-PAN EP 7249 (S511)
        S solo,pno,11strings EDI-PAN
            EP 7250   (S512)

    Lines
        S solo,pno EDI-PAN EP 7680 (S513)

    Prologo
        SMez soli,horn EDI-PAN EP 7671
                                    (S514)

SIGARAMI see Hachimura, Yoshio

SIGFUSSON, STEINGRIMUR (1919-1976)
    Beautiful World
        solo voice,pno ICELAND 042-006
                                    (S515)

    Good Night
        solo voice,pno ICELAND 042-004
                                    (S516)

    Party Is Over, The
        solo voice,pno ICELAND 042-008
                                    (S517)

    Private Matter
        solo voice,pno ICELAND 042-007
                                    (S518)

    Three Songs
        solo voice,pno ICELAND 042-003
                                    (S519)

SIGFUSSON, STEINGRIMUR (cont'd.)

Ver Treystum Thvi
Bar solo,pno/org ICELAND 042-009
(S520)

Your Gentle Smile
solo voice,pno ICELAND 042-005
(S521)

SIGLUM A SAEINN see Helgason,
Hallgrimur

SIGNAAL, HET see Guichelaar, Jan

SIGNPOST SINGS, THE see Kjerulf,
Halfdan, Veiviseren Synger

SIGURBJORNSSON, HRODMAR INGI
(1958-   )
Naeturlag
solo voice,pno ICELAND 052-022
(S522)

Nocturne
solo voice,pno [50"] ICELAND
052-017
(S523)

Um Glokoll Og Sumartunglid
solo voice,pno ICELAND 052-021
(S524)

SIGURBJÖRNSSON, THORKELL (1938-   )
David 112
Mez solo,org [8'0"] ICELAND 022-147
(S525)

Four Christmas Songs
T solo,fl [5'30"] ICELAND 022-131
(S526)

Four Songs
S solo,pno [8'0"] ICELAND 022-089
(S527)

I Am So Big
Bar solo,clar,pno [8'0"] ICELAND
022-164
(S528)

Lilja
Bar solo,pno [3'8"] ICELAND 022-062
(S529)

Mater Dolorosa
S solo,pno [2'0"] ICELAND 022-060
(S530)

Musik
S solo,gtr [3'30"] (text by Rainer
Maria Rilke) ICELAND 022-161
(S531)

Nine Songs
S solo,pno [16'55"] ICELAND 022-055
(S532)

Old Poem, An
Bar solo,pno [2'30"] ICELAND
022-120
(S533)

Songs For Small People
S solo,pno [6'0"] ICELAND 022-003
(S534)

Tune From "Atomstodin", A
solo voice,pno [1'5"] ICELAND
022-044
(S535)

Twelve Folk Songs
S solo,pno [6'0"] ICELAND 022-018
(S536)

Vocalise
S solo,org [6'0"] ICELAND 022-102
(S537)

SIGURD: ESPRITS, GARDIENS DE CES LIEUX
VÉNÉRÉS see Reyer, Louis Étienne
Ernest

SIGURD: ET, TOI FREIA see Reyer, Louis
Étienne Ernest

SIGURD JORSALAFAR see Danielsson, Harry

SIJO TINGUÉS DEL ROSSINYOL see Massana,
A.

S'IL EST UN CHARMANT GAZON (1ST
VERSION) see Liszt, Franz

S'IL EST UN CHARMANT GAZON (2ND
VERSION) see Liszt, Franz

SILCHER, FRIEDRICH (1789-1860)
Loreley
[Eng/Ger] med-high solo,pno CLASSV
2049
(S538)

SILENCE see Horvit, Michael M. see
Manneke, Daan see Telfer, Nancy

SILENT BOUGHS see Kraft, William

SILENT LOVE see Beach, [Mrs.] H.H.A.
(Amy Marcy Cheney)

SILENT NOON see Vaughan Williams, Ralph

SILENT, SILENT NIGHT see Engle, David,
Night Song see Luening, Otto

SILENT SPRING see Brown, James

SILENTIUM see Blumenfeld, Harold

SILENZIO see Oppo, Frank

SILETE VENTI see Handel, George
Frideric

SILHOUETTEN see King, Harold C.

SILHOUETTES, LES see Carpenter, John
Alden

SILSBEE, ANN (1930-   )
De Amore Et Morte: Seven Songs *CC7U
[Lat] S solo,clar,vln,vcl,2perc,pno
AM.COMP.AL. sc $19.15, pts $68.90
(S539)

Leavings
S solo, prepared pno [7'] sc
AM.COMP.AL. $5.40
(S540)

Mirages
B solo,vcl,hpsd [9'] sc AM.COMP.AL.
$7.70
(S541)

Only The Cold Bare Moon
S solo,fl,pno [22'] sc AM.COMP.AL.
$21.45
(S542)

Scroll
S solo,fl/alto fl,trp,perc,vln,db,
pno [9'] AM.COMP.AL. sc $9.15,
pts $5.40
(S543)

SILVANO: S'È SPENTO IL SOL see
Mascagni, Pietro

SILVER BELLS see Reuland, Jacques

SILVERMAN, FAYE-ELLEN (1947-   )
In Shadow
S solo,clar,gtr SEESAW f.s. (S544)

Journey Toward Oblivion
ST soli,fl,English horn,vla,vcl,db,
perc SEESAW
(S545)

SILVESTRI, CONSTANTIN (1913-   )
Serenade D'Autrefois
[It/Eng] high solo,pno CLASSV 1314
(S546)

ŠIMAI, PAVOL (1930-   )
Mitt Fröding-Diarium Värmland 25 Juli
- 6 Augusti 1972
solo voice,pno SUECIA 363   (S547)

SIMENI KACHOTAM AL LIBBECHA see
Wallach, Joelle

SIMON
Kinderliederfolge
PETERS 5022
(S548)

SIMON, HERMANN (1896-1948)
Drei Laub Auf Einer Linden
solo voice,pno KISTNER f.s. (S549)

SIMON BOCCANEGRA: IL LACERATO SPIRITO
see Verdi, Giuseppe

SIMONS, NETTY (1923-   )
Songs For Jenny
solo voice,pno,db PRESSER 141-40023
(S550)

SIMONSEN, MELVIN
Dronningens Klage Og Bønn
[Norw] solo voice,pno NORGE (S551)

SIMPLE SONG see Bernstein, Leonard

SIMPLE SONGS see Wiemann, Beth

SIMPLES see Dembski, Stephen

SIMPLICITY see Steinberg, Eitan

SIMS, EZRA (1928-   )
Aeneas On The Saxophone
SMezTB soli,clar,bass clar,horn,
trom,vla,db [2'] sc AM.COMP.AL.
$7.60
(S552)

Air From Cunegonde, The
high solo,pno [2'] sc AM.COMP.AL.
$1.60
(S553)
high solo&high solo,pno [2'] sc
AM.COMP.AL. $1.90
(S554)

Brief Glimpses...
TTTT soli,pno [8'] sc AM.COMP.AL.
$5.35
(S555)

Celebration Of Dead Ladies
med solo,alto fl,bass clar,vla,vcl,
perc [12'] sc AM.COMP.AL. $30.60
(S556)

Chamber Cantata On Chinese Poems
T solo,fl,bass clar,hpsd/pno,vla,
vcl [8'45"] AM.COMP.AL.   (S557)

Come Away: Five Songs *CC5U
Mez solo,clar,vla,alto fl,horn,
trom,db sc AM.COMP.AL. $11.10
(S558)

Elegie - Nach Rilke
S solo,fl,clar,vln,vla,vcl [14']
AM.COMP.AL. sc $21.45, pts $21.85
(S559)

SIMS, EZRA (cont'd.)

Five Songs *CC5U
A solo,vla sc AM.COMP.AL. $11.10
(S560)

Lullaby In Come Away, The
S solo,vla/vln [3'] sc AM.COMP.AL.
$1.95
(S561)

Solfeges, A System Of Moveable "Do"
solo voice [1'] sc AM.COMP.AL. $.80
(S562)

Song
Mez solo,clar,vla [5'] AM.COMP.AL.
sc $4.60, pts $3.10
(S563)

Three Cradle Songs *CC3U,cradle
Mez solo,2clar,gtr sc AM.COMP.AL.
$1.95
(S564)

When The Angels Blow Their Trumpets
3 actor-singers, acap [1'] sc
AM.COMP.AL. $1.95
(S565)

SINCE I LEFT YOU see Ketting, Piet

SINDING, CHRISTIAN (1856-1941)
Eg Tarv Ikkje Ljose Å Kvejkje
*Op.40,No.14
[Norw/Ger] solo voice,clar,strings
NORGE f.s.
(S566)

Evening, The
see Kvelden

Heaviest Sorrow And Grief, The
see Tyngste Sorg Og Møda, Den

Jane Grey *Op.109,No.3
[Eng/Ger] Mez/Bar solo,1.1.2.2.
2.0.0.0. timp,strings BREITKOPF-W
f.s.
(S567)

Jung Diethelm *Op.109,No.4
[Eng/Ger] Mez/Bar solo,
3(pic).2.2.2. 4.2.3.1. timp,perc,
harp,strings BREITKOPF-W f.s.
(S568)

Kvelden
"Evening, The" solo voice,1.2.1.2.
2.0.0.0. strings NORGE f.s.
(S569)

New Year In Norway
see Nyttår I Norge

Nyttår I Norge *Op.38,No.6
"New Year In Norway" T solo,
1.1.1.0. 1.1.1.0. perc,pno,cel,
strings [3'] NORGE f.s.   (S570)

Sylvelin *Op.55
[Norw/Dan] solo voice,fl,clar,trp,
trom,perc,pno,strings [2'] NORGE
f.s.
(S571)

Tyngste Sorg Og Møda, Den *Op.55,
No.8
"Heaviest Sorrow And Grief, The"
[Norw/Dan/Ger] solo voice,ob,
clar,bsn,horn,strings NORGE f.s.
(S572)

SINFONIA see Suben, Joel Eric

SING ME A SONG OF A LAD THAT IS GONE
see Homer, Sidney

SING MY CHORDS see Jordan, Sverre, Syng
Mine Strengjer

SING SOLO: BARITONE
(Case, John Carol) (CCU) OXFORD
68.404
(S573)

SING SOLO BARITONE *CC11L
(Case) OXFORD 345777-6 $7.75 contains
works by: Boyce, Britten, Handel,
Mozart, Tate, Warlock and others
(S574)

SING SOLO: CHRISTMAS
(Case, John Carol) high solo,pno
OXFORD 68.405
(S575)
(Case, John Carol) low solo,pno
OXFORD 68.406
(S576)

SING SOLO: CONTRALTO
(Shacklock, Constance) (CCU) OXFORD
68.402
(S577)

SING SOLO CONTRALTO *CC10L
(Shacklock) OXFORD 345779-2 $7.75
contains works by: Brahms, Delius,
Giordano, Grieg, Mendelssohn,
Purcell and others
(S578)

SING SOLO: SOPRANO
(Allister, Jean) (CCU) OXFORD 68.401
(S579)

SING SOLO SOPRANO *CC10L
(Allister) OXFORD 345780-6 $7.75
contains works by: Boyce, Catalani,
Fauré, Handel, Mozart and others
(S580)

SING SOLO: TENOR
(Tear, Robert) (CCU) OXFORD 68.403
(S581)

SING SOLO TENOR *CC10L
(Tear) OXFORD 345778-4 $7.75 contains
works by: Bach, Donizetti, Haydn,
Sullivan, Warlock and others (S582)

SING TO THE LORD
(2 book set) SHAWNEE 5097   (S583)

SING WITH THE KIDS GUITARBOOK see
Stratfod, Elaine

SINGER, THE see Medtner, Nikolai
Karlovich

SINGER BY THE YELLOW RIVER see Walker,
R.

SINGER'S COLLECTION, THE, BOOK 1: HIGH
VOICE *CC16L
(Ridout, Alan) high solo,pno MAYHEW
3611008 f.s. contains songs by:
Butterworth, Warlock, Bridge,
Gurney, Holst, and others   (S584)

SINGER'S COLLECTION, THE, BOOK 2: HIGH
VOICE *CC16L
(Ridout, Alan) high solo,pno MAYHEW
3611009 f.s. contains songs by:
Butterworth, Warlock, Gurney,
Holst, and others   (S585)

SINGING see Masseus, Jan see Mourant,
Walter

SINGING LESSON, THE see Squire, William
Henry

SINGLE GIRL see Four Traditional
American Songs

SINGLE TONE see Tipei, Sever

SINGS HARRY see Lilburn, Douglas

SINIGAGLIA, LEONE (1868-1944)
Tre Canti, Op. 37
[It/Ger] med-high solo RECITAL 289
(S586)

SINITE LAGRIMARI see Stradella,
Alessandro, De Immaculata
Conceptione

SINKT SIE see Geelen, Mathieu

SINN see Baden, Conrad

SIRATO see Maros, Rudolf

SIS CANCONS see Carreras, F.

SIS CANÇONS ITALIANES see Martín Y
Soler, Vicent

SISTE HILSEN see Taubo, Lillian Gulowna

SISTE ULTRICEM DEXTERAM see Kopriva,
Karel Blazej

SIX AUDEN SONGS see Speight, John A.

SIX AUSTRALIAN BUSH SONGS see James,
William G.

SIX BRIEF VERSES see Pleskow, Raoul

SIX CANTATAS see Arne, Thomas Augustine

SIX CANTATES
(Blanchard, R.) solo voice,cont CURCI
10357 f.s.
contains: Bassani, Giovanni
Battista, Ti Lascio Eurilla;
Bononcini, Giovanni, O Frondoso
Arboscello; Carissimi, Giacomo, E
Bello L'ardire; Cesti, Marc'
Antonio, Amanti Io Vi Disfido;
Rossi, Luigi, M'uccidete Begli
Occhi; Scarlatti, Alessandro,
Rosignuolo, Il   (S587)

SIX CANZONETTE, OP. 4 see Bach, Johann
Christian

SIX CHANSONS DE BRIGITTE SOURISSE see
Sourisse, Brigitte

SIX DUETS see Vogrich, Max

SIX ELEGIAC SONGS, OP.59 see Grieg,
Edvard Hagerup

SIX FABLES DE LA FONTAINE see Moreau,
H.

SIX FAMOUS CLASSICAL SONGS
(CC6U) LYCHE 67   (S588)

SIX FRAGMENTS OF GERTRUDE STEIN see
Kernis, Aaron Jay

SIX FRENCH SONGS, OP. 65 see
Tchaikovsky, Piotr Ilyich

SIX INSTANTS POÉTIQUES see Vercken,
François

SIX IRISH POEMS see Rorem, Ned

SIX JAPANESE SONGS, FOR SOPRANO,
CLARINET AND PIANO see Garwood,
Margaret

SIX KOREAN FOLKSONGS see Bavicchi, John
Alexander

SIX LOVE SONGS, OP. 40 see MacDowell,
Edward Alexander

SIX MELODIES see Dubois, Theodore see
Hüe, Georges-Adolphe see Mazellier,
Jules see Pessard, Emile-Louis-
Fortune

SIX MELODIES ITALIENNES, OP. NOS. 32 &
35 see Widor, Charles-Marie

SIX OCCASIONAL SONGS see Orland, Henry

SIX POEMES DE "VOCABULAIRE" see Sacre,
Guy

SIX POÈMES LYRIQUES DU VIEUX JAPON see
Thiriet, Maurice

SIX POEMS BY AMY LOWELL see Cresswell,
Lyell

SIX POEMS FROM THE JAPANESE see
Eiriksdottir, Karolina

SIX POEMS OF EMILY DICKINSON see
Warren, Betsy

SIX POESIES D'ARMAND SILVESTRE see
Castillon, Alexis de

SIX ROMANCES, OP. 8 see Rimsky-
Korsakov, Nikolai

SIX RONDELS see Dutacq, Amedee

SIX SEPHARDIC SONGS *CC6U
(Charkey, Stanley) med solo,gtr sc
PEER 61611-203 f.s.   (S589)

SIX SONGS see Bacon, Ernst L. see
Hopkinson, Francis see Kaldalóns,
Sigvaldi S. see Mascagni, Pietro
see Pfautsch, Lloyd Alvin see
Vidar, Jorunn

SIX SONGS see Perlongo, Daniel James

SIX SONGS see Griffes, Charles
Tomlinson

SIX SONGS see Zemlinsky, Alexander von

SIX SONGS see Norholm, Ib

SIX SONGS BASED ON UNKNOWN TEXTS see
Howe, Hubert S.

SIX SONGS FOR MEDIUM VOICE AND PIANO
see Bridge, Frank

SIX SONGS FROM "ORPHEUS BRITTANICUS"
see Purcell, Henry

SIX SONGS OF WOMEN see Farquhar, David

SIX SONGS ON CHINESE POETRY see Rovics,
Howard

SIX SONGS ON POEMS BY SPIKE MILLIGAN
see Larson, Martin

SIX SONGS ON POEMS OF WILLIAM PILLIN
see Schmidt, Sharon Yvonne Davis

SIX SONGS ON POEMS OF WILLIAM STAFFORD
see Winslow, Walter

SIX SONGS, OP. 1 see Karlowicz,
Mieczyslaw

SIX SONGS, OP. 3 see Medtner, Nikolai
Karlovich

SIX SONGS, OP. 6 see Tchaikovsky, Piotr
Ilyich

SIX SONGS, OP. 16 see Tchaikovsky,
Piotr Ilyich

SIX SONGS, OP. 24 see Haegeland, Eilert
M.

SIX SONGS, OP.25 see Grieg, Edvard
Hagerup see Tchaikovsky, Piotr
Ilyich

SIX SONGS, OP. 27 see Tchaikovsky,
Piotr Ilyich

SIX SONGS, OP. 28 see Tchaikovsky,
Piotr Ilyich

SIX SONGS, OP. 33 see Gaathaug, Morten,
Vinden Ser Aldri På Veiviseren

SIX SONGS, OP. 38 see Tchaikovsky,
Piotr Ilyich

SIX SONGS, OP.39 see Grieg, Edvard
Hagerup

SIX SONGS, OP. 57 see Tchaikovsky,
Piotr Ilyich

SIX SONGS, OP.60 see Glazunov,
Alexander Konstantinovich

SIX SONGS, OP. 63 see Tchaikovsky,
Piotr Ilyich

SIX SONGS, OP. 73 see Tchaikovsky,
Piotr Ilyich

SIX WELSH FOLK SONGS *CC6U
(Hoddinott, Alun) high solo OXFORD
345860-8 $9.75   (S590)

SIXTEEN CHILDREN'S SONGS, OP. 54, VOL.
1 see Tchaikovsky, Piotr Ilyich

SIXTEEN CHILDREN'S SONGS, OP. 54, VOL.
2 see Tchaikovsky, Piotr Ilyich

SIXTEEN SELECTED SONGS see Mendelssohn-
Bartholdy, Felix

SIXTEEN SONGS see Delius, Frederick see
Schubert, Franz (Peter)

SIXTH PROGRAMME see Krzanowski,
Andrzej, Audycja VI

SJÅ GUD see Thoresen, Lasse

SJÅ LYSET ER TENT see Coates, Robert

SJÄLEN ÄR BLIND [1] see Blomberg, Erik

SJÄLEN ÄR BLIND [2] see Blomberg, Erik

SJETTE DAG, DEN see Evensen, Bernt
Kasberg

SJO EINSONGSLOG see Thordarson,
Sigurdur

SJO SONGLOG see Halldorsson, Sigfus see
Isolfsson, Pall

SJOBERG, C. (1873-1935)
Tonerna
high solo,pno CLASSV 0967   (S591)

SJÖBLOM, HEIMER (1910-   )
Bröllopssång
solo voice,pno STIM f.s. contains
also: Vid Ett Ungt Pars Bröllop
(S592)
Jag Önskar Jag Ägde Rosor *Op.4,No.1
solo voice,pno STIM f.s.   (S593)

Jobs Klagan
solo voice,pno/org STIM f.s. (S594)

Vårbud
solo voice,pno STIM f.s.   (S595)

Vid Ett Ungt Pars Bröllop
see Bröllopssång

SJØEN see Tveitt, Geirr

SJU DIKTER see Alfvén, Hugo

SJU KROKANN-SONGAR see Olsen, Sparre

SJU VISER see Sønstevold, Gunnar

SKALDID ER THAGNAD see Björnsson, Arni

SKALL STENARNA ROPA see Forsberg,
Roland

SKARB see Shut, Wasyl

SKARGA STWORU see Lason, Aleksander

SKARVE ENGEL I BRUTALIAS LAND, EN see
Germeten, Gunnar

SKILNADUR see Halldorsson, Skuli

SKIN see Søderlind, Ragnar

SKINNVENGBREV see Lie, Harald

SKIP DANCE see Itoh, Ohsuke

SKIRMISH see Kverndokk, Gisle

SKJAERGAARDSØ see Sommerfeldt, Öistein
see Tveitt, Geirr

SKJAERGÅRDSØ see Sommerfeldt, Öistein

SKJOTT HEFUR SOL BRUGDID SUMRI see
Halldorsson, Sigfus

SKLENICKA, KAREL (1933-   )
Quattuor Dialogi
[Lat] SB soli,1.2.2.2. 2.0.0.0. pno
[22'] CESKY HUD.   (S596)

SKÖLD, BENGT-GÖRAN (1936-   )
Lova Herren Min Själ
A solo,horn,pno NOTERIA 1865 (S597)

När Jag Skall Lämna Världen
solo voice,pno/org NOTERIA 1871
                              (S598)

Samla Inte Skatter På Jorden
solo voice,org/pno NOTERIA 1872
                              (S599)

Triptyk, Op. 23
S solo,ob,timp,strings NOTERIA 1876
                              (S600)

SKÖNASTE JAG VET ÄR DIN VIDÖPPNA FAMN,
DET see Leijon, Jerker

SKRINET MED DET RARE I see Evensen,
Bernt Kasberg

SKRIVANEK see Broz, František

SKROUP, FRANTIŠEK (1801-1862)
Kde Domov Muj?
T solo,bsn,horn,strings,vln solo
[7'] CESKY HUD.   (S601)

Na Rozloucenou
solo voice,pno CESKY HUD.   (S602)

SKUMRING see Fongaard, Bjørn

SKY see Hayashi, Hikaru

SKY A SILVER DISSONANCE, THE see
Schwendinger, Laura

SLANGEN, JOHN (1951-   )
Deur In Lood, Een
see Twee Liederen

Twee Liederen
high solo,woodwind quin,pno,2vln,
vla,vcl,db DONEMUS f.s. [16']
contains: Deur In Lood, Een; Uit
Zee Gestoken   (S603)

Uit Zee Gestoken
see Twee Liederen

SLATTUVISA see Stefansson, Finnur Torfi
see Thordarson, Sigurdur

SLEEP LITTLE CHILD JESUS see Eggen,
Arne, Sov Barn Jesus Lille

SLEEP, MY ANGEL, SLUMBER MILD see
Glinka, Mikhail Ivanovich

SLEEP NOW see Barber, Samuel see Perera

SLEEPING PRINCESS, THE see Borodin,
Alexander Porfirievich

SLEEPY CHIPMUNK, A see Nakada,
Kazutsugu

SLEETH, NATALIE WAKELEY (1930-1992)
How Will They Know?
solo voice SONOS S082 $2.50 (S604)

SLEZAK, PAVEL (1941-   )
Chvalozpevy Miru
T solo,2.0.2.1. 2.1.1.1. perc,pno,
strings [19'] CESKY HUD. (S605)

SLONIMSKY, NICOLAS (1894-   )
And Then Her Doctor Told Her...
see Five Advertising Songs

Children Cry For Castoria!
see Five Advertising Songs

Five Advertising Songs
solo voice,pno CAMBRIA CP202 f.s.
contains: And Then Her Doctor
Told Her...; Children Cry For
Castoria!; Make This A Day Of
Pepsodent!; No More Shiny
Nose!; Snowy White   (S606)

Gravestones At Hancock, N.H.
solo voice,pno CAMBRIA CP203 f.s.
contains: Here Peacefully Lies
The Once Happy Father; Lovely
Rose, In Memphis, Tennessee, A;
Lydia; Stop, My Friends, As You
Pass By; Vain World   (S607)

Here Peacefully Lies The Once Happy
Father
see Gravestones At Hancock, N.H.

Lovely Rose, In Memphis, Tennessee, A
see Gravestones At Hancock, N.H.

Lydia
see Gravestones At Hancock, N.H.

Make This A Day Of Pepsodent!
see Five Advertising Songs

SLONIMSKY, NICOLAS (cont'd.)

No More Shiny Nose!
see Five Advertising Songs

Snowy White
see Five Advertising Songs

Stop, My Friends, As You Pass By
see Gravestones At Hancock, N.H.

Vain World
see Gravestones At Hancock, N.H.

Very Great Musician, A
solo voice,pno CAMBRIA CP204 (S608)

SLOPIEWNIE, OP. 47 see Szymanowski,
Karol

SLOTHOUWER, JOCHEM (1938-   )
Oroyson Nostre-Dame, L'
Mez solo,fl,harp,vln,vla,vcl [10']
DONEMUS   (S609)

Pole Star
Bar/B solo,pno [10'] DONEMUS (S610)

SLOTLIED see Frid, Geza

SLOVA see Kubik, Ladislav

SLOVACKE PISNE see Klusak, Vladimir

SLOW LAMENT see Brief, Todd

SLOWISIEN see Szymanowski, Karol

SLOWLY IT ALL COMES BACK see Walton,
[Sir] William (Turner)

SLUKA, LUBOŠ (1928-   )
Kvetomluva *song cycle
[Czech/Ger] solo voice,pno PANTON
945   (S611)

Vyznani
B solo,string orch [11'] CESKY HUD.
                              (S612)

SLUMBER SONG see Gretchaninov,
Alexander Tikhonovich see
MacDowell, Edward Alexander see
Quilter, Roger

SMÅ KLANGER; EN RÖST see Sandström, Jan

SMALASTULKAN see Helgason, Hallgrimur

SMALL SONG see Pollock, Robert Emil

SMÄRTANS VINGE see Sandström, Jan

SMEDEN OG BAGEREN see Arnestad, Finn

SMEETS, LEO
Pie Jesu
T/S solo ZENGERINK R.559   (S613)

SMIDURINN see Isolfsson, Pall

SMILE see Sveinsson, Atli Heimir

SMIT SIBINGA, THEO H. (1899-1958)
Enfants-Poetes
DONEMUS Mez solo,pno f.s.; S solo,
pno f.s.
contains: Lune Est Venue, La;
Petit Garcon, Le; Petit Poisson
Rouge, Un; Petite Fleur, La
                              (S614)

Lune Est Venue, La
see Enfants-Poetes

Petit Garcon, Le
see Enfants-Poetes

Petit Poisson Rouge, Un
see Enfants-Poetes

Petite Fleur, La
see Enfants-Poetes

SMITH, HALE (1925-   )
Three Patterson Lyrics *CC3U
S solo,pno (diff) MERION 441-41019
$10.00   (S615)

SMITH, LARRY
Infant Crying, An *Suite
T/S solo,gtr [22'] (med diff)
MERION 141-40017 $12.00   (S616)

SMOLANOFF, MICHAEL LOUIS (1942-   )
Day Of Calm Sea
S solo,chamber group SEESAW f.s.
                              (S617)

Four Haiku Songs *CC4U
S solo,pno SEESAW f.s.   (S618)

From The Orient
S solo,fl,harp,electronic tape
SEESAW f.s.   (S619)

Heralds
A solo,4fl,English horn,harp,timp,
perc SEESAW f.s.   (S620)

SMOLANOFF, MICHAEL LOUIS (cont'd.)

Psalm: For A Feastday
narrator,org SEESAW f.s.   (S621)

World, The
S solo,winds,brass,perc SEESAW f.s.
                              (S622)

SMOLKA, MARTIN (1959-   )
Sinfonietta
S solo,4.0.3.0.sax. 2.2.2.0. perc,
xylo,2harp,prepared pno,
electronic tape,strings [30']
CESKY HUD.   (S623)

SMÖRBLOMSTER see Tveitt, Geirr

SNARE, THE see Haxton, Kenneth

SNART see Madsen, Trygve

SNATI OG OLI see Isolfsson, Pall

SNE see Ørbeck, Anne Marie

SNEEUW see Samama, Leo

SNEEUW LIGT IN DEN MORGEN VROEG, EEN
see Samama, Leo

SNEEUW OF AS see Ehlen, Margriet

SNEEUWGANG see Broekman, Hans

SNEGUROCHKA (SNOW MAIDEN): SNOW-FLAKE'S
ARIETTA see Rimsky-Korsakov,
Nikolai

SNETT OCH RUNT see Schuback, Thomas

SNIH see Shut, Wasyl

SNJO see Eggen, Arne

SNO (I. OF IMPRESSIONS) see Harris,
Matthew

SNØSTORM see Tveitt, Geirr

SNOW see Eggen, Arne, Snjo

SNOW GREW OUT OF THE SKY LAST NIGHT,
THE see Fennimore, Joseph William

SNOWFLAKE see Kirkwood, Antoinette

SNOWMAN, THE see Blake, Howard

SNOWSTORM see Tveitt, Geirr, Snøstorm

SNOWY WHITE see Slonimsky, Nicolas

SO CHE PUGNANDO see Benda, Georg Anton
(Jirí Antonín)

SO FRÜH? see Solbiati, Alessandro

SO ICH TRAURIG BIN see Colaço Osorio-
Swaab, Reine

SO LANG EI TID see Olsen, Sparre

SO PRETTY see Bernstein, Leonard

SO PROUD SHE WAS TO DIE see Haxton,
Kenneth

SO RO GODT BARN see Sommerfeldt,
Oistein

SO RO RULL: EIN REISE-RONDO see
Haugland, Glenn Erik

SO RODDE DEI FJORDAN see Ørbeck, Anne
Marie

SO RUHIG GEH' ICH MEINEN PFAD see Uhl,
Alfred

SO, SIR PAGE see Mozart, Wolfgang
Amadeus, Nozze Di Figaro, Le: Non
Più Andrai

SO VOLL FRÖHLICHKEIT see Strauss,
Johann, [Jr.], Zigeunerbaron, Der:
Walzerlied

SO WE'LL GO NO MORE A-ROVING see
Karpman, Laura see Walker, George
Theophilus

SODE NURURU see Matsudaira, Yori-Tsune

SØDERLIND, RAGNAR (1945-   )
Eg Hev Funne Min Fløyne Lokkar Att I
Mitt Svarmrus, Op. 35b
[Norw] S solo,pno [9'] NORGE (S624)

Eg Hev Funne Min Fløysne Lokkar Att I
Mitt Svarmerus *Op.35c
"I Have Found My Handsome Lover
Back" S solo,2(pic).2.2.2.
4.2.3.1. timp,perc,harp,strings
[10'] NORGE f.s.   (S625)

SØDERLIND, RAGNAR (cont'd.)

Er Den Draumen, Det
see Fire Songar, Op. 29

Fire Songar, Op. 29
[Norw] solo voice,pno NORGE f.s.
contains: Er Den Draumen, Det; No
Er Min Hug Still; Skin; Stundom
Gjeng Straumen I Ring   (S626)

Gong, Ein
see Tre Songar Til Tekstar Av Åse
Marie Nesse

I Have Found My Handsome Lover Back
see Eg Hev Funne Min Fløysne Lokkar
Att I Mitt Svarmerus

Körsbärsblommor: 5 Korta Japanska
Kärleksdikt *Op.9
[Swed] Bar solo,fl,English horn,
vcl,2perc [6'] NORGE   (S627)

Legg Ikkje Ditt Liv I Mi Hand
see Tre Songar Til Tekstar Av Åse
Marie Nesse

Musikk For Stjerner, Op. 51
[Norw] solo voice,fl,vln,vcl,pno
NORGE   (S628)
[Norw] solo voice,fl,vln,vcl,pno
NORGE   (S629)

No Er Min Hug Still
see Fire Songar, Op. 29

På Botnen Av Alt
see Tre Songar Til Tekstar Av Åse
Marie Nesse

Pietá *Op.5
[Swed] Mez solo,strings [6'] NORGE
f.s.   (S630)

Skin
see Fire Songar, Op. 29

Stundom Gjeng Straumen I Ring
see Fire Songar, Op. 29

Tranströmer-Svit *Op.52
[Swed] solo voice,2pno,2perc [25']
NORGE   (S631)
[Swed] solo voice,pno,2perc,strings
[25'] NORGE   (S632)

Tranströmer-Svit, Op.52
[Swed] solo voice,2pno,2perc [25']
NORGE   (S633)

Tre Songar Til Tekstar Av Åse Marie
Nesse *Op.39a
[Norw] solo voice,pno NORGE f.s.
contains: Gong, Ein; Legg Ikkje
Ditt Liv I Mi Hand; På Botnen
Av Alt   (S634)

SÖDERMAN, [JOHAN] AUGUST (1832-1876)
Flyg Ej Undan
solo voice,pno EGTVED 432 from
AKSEL SCHIOETZ ANTHOLOGY OF
NORDIC SOLO SONGS, THE, VOL. 2
(S635)
Mitt Älskade Lilla Sockerskrin
solo voice,pno EGTVED 432 from
AKSEL SCHIOETZ ANTHOLOGY OF
NORDIC SOLO SONGS, THE, VOL. 2
(S636)

SOFDU, UNGA ASTIN MIN see Kaldalóns,
Sigvaldi S.

SOFNAR LOA see Einarsson, Sigfus

SOFT AND PURE, LIKE A DREAM see Flotow,
Friedrich von, Marta: M'appari
Tutt'amor

SOGUGABB see Sveinsson, Atli Heimir

SOHAL, NARESH (1939-   )
From Gitanjali
Bar solo,orch NOVELLO f.s.   (S637)

SOIR see Gretchaninov, Alexander
Tikhonovich

SOIR DE RÊVE see Massenet, Jules

SOIR PAÏEN: LA LUNE GLISSE SOUS LES
BOIS see Hüe, Georges-Adolphe

SOIRÉE EN MER: PRÈS DU PÊCHEUR see
Saint-Saëns, Camille

SOIREE, IL TOMBE DE LA NEIGE see
Maruyama, Kazunori

SOIREES MUSICALES, VOL. 1 see Rossini,
Gioacchino

SOIREES MUSICALES, VOL. 2 see Rossini,
Gioacchino

SOJOURN OF THE SPIRIT, A see Verrall,
John Weedon

SØK HERREN see Baden, Conrad

SOKNUDUR see Halldorsson, Skuli see
Isolfsson, Pall

SOL DE PIEDRA see Ansink, Caroline

SOLARDAGUR see Kaldalóns, Sigvaldi S.

SÓLARLJÓÐ: SOLSANGER FRA NORRØN
MIDDELALDER see Plagge, Wolfgang

SÓLARLJÓÖ see Plagge, Wolfgang

SOLBIATI, ALESSANDRO
Lied
S solo,3inst ZERBONI 9513   (S638)
...Piu Sopra Le Stelle...
S solo,orch ZERBONI 9335   (S639)
So Früh?
S solo,8inst ZERBONI 9452   (S640)

SOLDAG I FJELLET see Nystedt, Knut

SOLDIER, DON'T BE SAD see Shut, Wasyl,
Usususe Ne Sumuj

SOLDIER TIR'D OF WAR'S ALARMS see Arne,
Thomas Augustine

SOLDIER TIRED OF WAR'S ALARMS see Arne,
Thomas Augustine

SOLDIER'S BRIDAL, THE see Mori, Frank

SOLDIER'S WIFE see Rachmaninoff, Sergey
Vassilievich

SOLE, LL. MA.
Parla L'avi, Cancó
solo voice,pno BOIL B.2655   (S641)

SOLEFALDSSANG see Olsen, Otto

SOLEIL COUCHANT see Massenet, Jules

SOLEIL NI LA MORT, LE see Clarke, Henry
Leland

SØLEKAKESANG see Sommerfeldt, Öistein

SOLER
Ave Maria
solo voice,vln,org DOBLINGER 08 875
(S642)
SOLER, J.
Ich Bin Die Seel' Im All
S solo,vibra,gtr PLUCKED STR
ZM 2221 $9.00   (S643)
Stunden Buch, Das
SS soli,pno BOIL B.2658   (S644)

SOLER, JOSEP (1935-   )
Passio Jesu Christi
SBar soli,vla,vcl,hpsd,org [32']
MOECK 5064   (S645)

SOLER, VICENT MARTÍN Y
see MARTÍN Y SOLER, VICENT

SOLFAGER see Eggen, Arne

SOLFEGES, A SYSTEM OF MOVEABLE "DO" see
Sims, Ezra

SOLFEGGI see Mozart, Wolfgang Amadeus

SOLFEGGIO see Gillet, Bruno

SOLI HEV SITT SAME LAG see Johnsen,
Hallvard

SOLILOQUY OF A SILHOUETTE see Dillard,
Donald E.

SOLITUDES, 15 see Hillemacher, Paul

SOLLBERGER, HARVEY (1938-   )
Life Study
S solo,fl/alto fl/pic,harp [20'] sc
AM.COMP.AL. $16.90   (S646)

SOLO BOOK, THE *CCU
low solo GOODLIFE L04022L $8.95
(S647)
SOLO SINGER *CCU
(Tkach, P.) solo voice,pno KJOS V33
f.s.   (S648)

SOLOKANTATE NO. 1 see Kvandal, Johan

SOLOLIEDER see Tubin, Eduard,
Soololaule

SOLOLIEDER (1926-1944) see Tubin,
Eduard, Soololaule

SOLOMON SONGS see Thornton

SOLOMON SONGS, BOOK see Dydo, J.
Stephen

SOLOMOTETT FOR ALLEHELGENSDAG see
Maehlum, Svein, Deretter Så Jeg

SOLOMOTETT, OP. 3, NO. 4 see Holter,
Stig Wernø, Folk Som Vandrer I
Mørket, Det

SOLOS FOR THE CHURCH SOLOIST see
Pfautsch, Lloyd Alvin

SOLRODIN SKY see Björnsson, Arni

SOLSANGER FRA NORRØN MIDDELALDER see
Plagge, Wolfgang, Sólarljóö

SOLSETURSLJOD see Halldorsson, Skuli

SOLVEJG'S CRADLE SONG see Grieg, Edvard
Hagerup

SOLVEJG'S SONG see Grieg, Edvard
Hagerup

SOM EIT RUGKORN see Støyva, Njål Gunnar

SOM HELD UT VIL ALLTID FINNE, DEN see
Sønstevold, Gunnar

SOM HJORTEN SKRIGER EFTER RINDENDE
VAND, OP.68 see Koppel, Herman
David, David's 42. Psalm

SOM SANG, EN see Haugland, Glenn Erik

SOM VIND PÅ HEIDI see Olsen, Sparre

SOME NIGHTMARE MUSIC see Moland, Eirik

SOME OF THE COLOURS YOU LIKE see
Minciacchi, Diego

SOME PEOPLE see Man, Roderik De

SOMERS, HARRY STEWART (1925-   )
Owl And The Pussycat
SAT soli OXFORD 02.210   (S649)

SOMERS-COCKS, JOHN
Eager Spring
high solo,pno BARDIC BE0289   (S650)
Echo
high solo,pno BARDIC BE0291   (S651)
Every One Sang
high solo,pno BARDIC BE0290   (S652)
New Year's Eve, 1913
high solo,pno BARDIC BE0288   (S653)
Song
"When I Am Dead, My Dearest" solo
voice,pno BARDIC BE0292   (S654)
When I Am Dead, My Dearest
see Song

SOMERVELL, ARTHUR (1863-1937)
Cycle Of Songs From Tennyson's Maud
low solo,pno CLASSV 2050   (S655)
Kingdom By The Sea, A
high solo,pno CLASSV 1659   (S656)
Maud *song cycle
[Eng] low solo (poetry of Alfred
Lord Tennyson) RECITAL 291   (S657)
Shropshire Lad, A *song cycle
[Eng] low solo (texts by A.E.
Housman) RECITAL 290   (S658)

SOMETHING RICH AND STRANGE see Hold,
Trevor

SOMETHING'S COMING see Bernstein,
Leonard

SOMETIMES TASTE SOUR see Meyers,
Randall

SOMEWHERE see Bernstein, Leonard

SOMEWHERE A VOICE IS CALLING see Tate,
Arthur

SOMEWHERE I HAVE NEVER TRAVELED see
Johnston, Benjamin Burwell (Ben)

SOMEWHERE INSIDE ME... see Moss,
Lawrence Kenneth

SOMMER, VLADIMÍR (1921-   )
Sedm Pisni
Mez solo,pno PANTON 149   (S659)

SOMMERDAGEN see Taubo, Lillian Gulowna

SOMMERFELDT, ÖISTEIN (1919-   )
About Love *Op.46
[Norw] Mez solo,vcl [6'] NORSK
(S660)

SOMMERFELDT, ÖISTEIN (cont'd.)

Anne-Karin
[Norw] solo voice,pno (text by M.
Takvam) NORGE (S661)

Bansull
see To Sanger

Bestemors-Rokken
[Norw] solo voice,pno (text by M.
Takvam) NORGE (S662)

Bias Vise
[Norw] solo voice,pno NORGE (S663)

Even Kjerringdalt
see Tre Muntre Viser

Fattig Er Mitt Liv
see To Sanger

Fløitestubb
see To Hamsun-Sanger, Op. 26

From Kathleen Raine's Poetry, Op. 55
[Eng] solo voice,pno NORSK (S664)

From William Blake's Poetry *Op.53
[Eng] S/T solo,rec,gtr,pno NORSK (S665)

Hafrsfjord *Op.30
narrator,3.2.2.2. 4.3.3.1. perc,
pno,cel,strings [15'] NORGE f.s.
(S666)

Hildring I Speil, Op. 48
[Norw] S solo,fl,pno [8'] NORSK (S667)

Katten Og Månen
[Norw] solo voice,pno NORGE (S668)

Kjell
see Tre Muntre Viser

Kvelding-Seter
see Tri Lyriske Bilder

Kvitsymre
see Tre Lyriske Sanger, Op. 6

Løvetann
[Norw] solo voice,pno NORGE (S669)

Metamorfose
see Tvo Stein Mehrensanger

Midtsommersang
[Norw] solo voice,pno NORGE (S670)

Morn, Morn
[Norw] solo voice,pno NORGE (S671)

Mot En Verden Av Lys: To Stein
Mehren-Sanger, Op. 34a
solo voice,pno [7'] NORSK (S672)

Skjaergaardsø
see Tri Lyriske Bilder

Skjaergårdsø
see To Hamsun-Sanger, Op. 26

So Ro Godt Barn
see Tre Lyriske Sanger, Op. 6

Sølekakesang
[Norw] solo voice,pno NORGE (S673)

Stjerneregn
see Tvo Stein Mehrensanger

Storvegen No. 9: Ekko-Vise
[Norw] solo voice,pno NORGE (S674)

Sudlands-Brur
see Tre Lyriske Sanger, Op. 6
see Tri Lyriske Bilder

To Hamsun-Sanger, Op. 26
[Norw] solo voice,pno NORSK f.s.
contains: Fløitestubb;
Skjaergårdsø (S675)

To Sanger
solo voice,pno LYCHE 220 f.s.
contains: Bansull; Fattig Er Mitt
Liv (S676)

Tre Lyriske Sanger, Op. 6
LYCHE 547 f.s.
contains: Kvitsymre; So Ro Godt
Barn; Sudlands-Brur (S677)

Tre Muntre Viser
LYCHE 444 f.s.
contains: Even Kjerringdalt;
Kjell; Vent Ikkje Pa Brev
(S678)

Tre Naturstemninger, Op. 16
[Norw] solo voice,pno NORSK (S679)

Treet I Gata
[Norw] solo voice,pno NORGE (S680)

SOMMERFELDT, ÖISTEIN (cont'd.)

Trekløver, Op.72
[Norw] S solo,acord NORGE (S681)

Tri Lyriske Bilder *Op.33b
S/T solo,2.2.2.2. 4.3.0.0. timp,
perc,pno,strings NORSK f.s.
contains: Kvelding-Seter;
Skjaergaardsø; Sudlands-Brur
(S682)

Trollet Kan
[Norw] solo voice,pno NORGE (S683)

Tvo Stein Mehrensanger *Op.34b
solo voice,3.2.2.2. 3.2.3.0. perc,
harp,pno/cel,strings NORSK f.s.
contains: Metamorfose;
Stjerneregn (S684)

Vent Ikkje Pa Brev
see Tre Muntre Viser

Vet Du At...
[Norw] solo voice,pno NORGE (S685)

Vill-Kirsebaer, Op.71
[Norw] S solo,acord NORGE (S686)

Visa Om Tatjana
[Norw] solo voice,pno NORGE (S687)

SOMMERFUGLEN see Groven, Eivind

SOMMERFUGLER see Backer-Lunde, Johan,
Butterflies

SOMMERGÅTE see Ørbeck, Anne Marie

SOMMERGEDENKEN see Ágústsson, Herbert
Hriberschek

SOMMERLICHE FREUDEN AUF DEM LANDE see
Hekster, Walter

SOMMERLIED see Marx, Joseph

SOMS see Ruiter, Wim de

SON see Shut, Wasyl

SON-SONETA, LA see Mestres, Apeles

SONÁMBULA, LA: AH! NON CREDE A MIRARTI
see Bellini, Vincenzo

SONÁMBULA, LA: CARE COMPAGNI. COME PER
ME SERENO see Bellini, Vincenzo

SONATA DI SPAZZATURA see Lerstad, Terje
B.

SONATA FOR VARIOUS INSTRUMENTS see
Lerstad, Terje B., Sonata Di
Spazzatura

SONATA LIRICA see Boháč, Josef

SONATE see Broekman, Hans

SONATE FOR DIVERSE INSTRUMENTER see
Lerstad, Terje B., Sonata Di
Spazzatura

SONETTI DELLE FATE, I: 6 LIRICHE see
Malipiero, Gian Francesco

SONETY O PRAZE see Bartoš, Jan Zdenek

SONEVYTSKY, IHOR (1926-)
Withered Leaves *song cycle
[Ukranian] Bar solo,pno DUMA (S688)

SONG see Pollock, Robert Emil see Sims,
Ezra see Somers-Cocks, John

SONG, A see Schoonenbeek, Kees

SONG ALBUM see Walton, [Sir] William
(Turner)

SONG ALBUM (15 SONGS) see Chadwick,
George Whitefield

SONG ALBUM (17 SONGS) see Chadwick,
George Whitefield

SONG ALBUM see Miyahara, Teiji

SONG ALBUM see Kusagawa, Kei

SONG ALBUM see Koyama, Kiyoshige

SONG ALBUM see Moriwaki, Kenzo

SONG ALBUM (ACHT LIEDER) see Lassen,
Eduard

SONG ALBUM II see Nevin, Ethelbert
Woodbridge

SONG ALBUM, VOL. 1 see Head, Michael
(Dewar)

SONG ALBUM, VOL. 1 see Vaughan
Williams, Ralph

SONG ALBUM, VOL. 2 see Vaughan
Williams, Ralph

SONG ALBUM, VOL. 2: ROMA see Head,
Michael (Dewar)

SONG ALBUM, VOL. 3 see Head, Michael
(Dewar) see Rorem, Ned

SONG BOOK, THE see Hutcheson, Jere T.

SONG BY THE SUNSET see Olsen, Otto,
Solefaldssang

SONG CYCLE see Lauer, Elizabeth see
Pollock, Robert Emil see Rausch,
Carlos

SONG FOR NUPTIALS see Taylor, Clifford
Oliver

SONG IN A WINTER NIGHT see Phillips,
Burrill

SONG IN THE TWILIGHT see Knutsen,
Torbjorn, Sang I Skumring

SONG IN THE TWILIGHT, THE see Bax,
[Sir] Arnold

SONG OF BATTLE see Stanford, Charles
Villiers

SONG OF DEBORAH see Rollin, Robert Leon

SONG OF DEIRDRE see Kauder, Hugo

SONG OF FREEDOM see Stanford, Charles
Villiers see Torphicen, Pamela

SONG OF GEORGIA, A see Balakirev, Mily
Alexeyevich

SONG OF HOPE see Stanford, Charles
Villiers

SONG OF IVER HUITFELDT, THE see
Halvorsen, Johan, Sangen Om Iver
Huitfeldt

SONG OF KAARE, THE see Nordraak,
Rikard, Kaares Sang

SONG OF LOVE see Breimo, Bjørn

SONG OF PEACE see Stanford, Charles
Villiers

SONG OF RUTH see Gounod, Charles
François

SONG OF SONGS see Blaustein, Susan see
Moya, H.

SONG OF SONGS, THE see Hovland, Egil

SONG OF TAILITNAMA see Sculthorpe,
Peter [Joshua]

SONG OF THE BOAT see Roosendael, Jan
Rokus van

SONG OF THE DAGGER see Griffes, Charles
Tomlinson

SONG OF THE DARK FOREST see Borodin,
Alexander Porfirievich

SONG OF THE FISH see Arensky, Anton
Stepanovich

SONG OF THE FISHERMAN OF CACRU see
Kirkwood, Antoinette

SONG OF THE FLEA see Mussorgsky, Modest
Petrovich

SONG OF THE FORGE see Foote, Arthur

SONG OF THE REGIMENT, THE see
Donizetti, Gaetano

SONG OF THE SEA see Backer-Lunde,
Johan, Kvat Havbåra Syng

SONG OF TRUST see Stanford, Charles
Villiers

SONG OF WISDOM see Stanford, Charles
Villiers

SONG OFFERINGS see Harvey

SONG PICTURES - FIVE SONGS BASED ON
NATIVE AMERICAN POETRY see Karpman,
Laura

SONG "THE HOPE", A see Kobayashi, Arata

SONG TO MY HEART see Stutschevsky,
Joachim

SONG VON ANGEBOT UND NACHFRAGE see
   Eisler, Hanns

SONG WITHIN, THE see Pluister, Simon

SONG WITHOUT WORDS see Stutschevsky,
   Joachim

SONGBOOK 1 (from The Songbook Series)
   CC16L,educ
   solo voice,kbd (very easy) HARRIS
   f.s.   (S689)

SONGBOOK 2 (from The Songbook Series)
   CC17L,educ
   solo voice,kbd (easy) HARRIS f.s.
                                  (S690)

SONGBOOK 3 (from The Songbook Series)
   CC16L,educ
   solo voice,kbd (med easy) HARRIS f.s.
                                  (S691)

SONGBOOK 4 (from The Songbook Series)
   CC15L,educ
   solo voice,kbd (med) HARRIS f.s.
                                  (S692)

SONGBOOK 5 (from The Songbook Series)
   CC18L,educ
   solo voice,kbd (med) HARRIS f.s.
                                  (S693)

SONGBOOK 6 (from The Songbook Series)
   CC16L,educ
   solo voice,kbd (med diff) HARRIS f.s.
                                  (S694)

SONGEN OM VESLE MAGNI see Åm, Magnar

SONGEN TIL HAN SOM ER KOMEN IGJENOM see
   Barth, Frode

SÖNGLISTIN see Björnsson, Arni

SONGLJOD I see Isolfsson, Pall

SONGLOG see Halldorsson, Skuli see
   Runolfsson, Karl Otto

SÖNGLÖG, 10 see Björnsson, Arni

SONGS see Bacewicz, Grazyna, Piesni see
   Blass, Noah see Halldorsson, Sigfus
   see Halldorsson, Skuli see
   Kristinsson, Sigursveinn D. see
   Mozart, Wolfgang Amadeus see
   Szymanowski, Karol, Piesni

SONGS, 22 see Einarsson, Sigfus

SONGS, 23 see Beach, [Mrs.] H.H.A. (Amy
   Marcy Cheney)

SONGS, 25; 3 MICHELANGELO LIEDER see
   Wolf, Hugo

SONGS, 26 see Kristjánsson, Oddgeir

SONGS, 33 see Chausson, Ernest

SONGS, 50 see Bacon, Ernst L.

SONGS, 50 see Takata, Saburo

SONGS, 79 see Mendelssohn-Bartholdy,
   Felix

SONGS II TO FRENCH TEXTS
   (Poirier, Lucien) "Chansons II Sur
   Textes Français" CAN.MUS.HER.
                                  (S695)
SONGS III TO FRENCH TEXTS
   (Poirier, Lucien) "Chansons III Sur
   Textes Français" CAN.MUS.HER.
                                  (S696)
SONGS IV TO ENGLISH TEXTS
   (Hall, Frederick A.) "Chansons IV Sur
   Textes Anglais" CAN.MUS.HER. (S697)

SONGS see Reuland, Jacques

SONGS see Beethoven, Ludwig van

SONGS (1909-1922) see Boulanger, Nadia

SONGS AMERICA VOTED BY
   (Silber, Irwin) solo voice,gtr
   PRESSER   (S698)

SONGS AND CANTATAS see Handel, George
   Frideric

SONGS AND DANCES OF DEATH see
   Mussorgsky, Modest Petrovich

SONGS AND EPITAPHS see Gabel, Gerald L.

SONGS ARE WEAPON see Dahl, Vivian,
   Sange Er Våben

SONGS AT PARTING see Bacon, Ernst L.

SONGS BY ARTHUR FOOTE, OP.26 see Foote,
   Arthur

SONGS BY LACHNER see Lachner

SONGS (COMPLETE) see Beethoven, Ludwig
   van

SONGS FOR BARITONE AND GUITAR see
   Walker, Gwyneth

SONGS FOR CHILDREN
   ("World's Favorite Series") ASHLEY
   096-4   (S699)
   see Sveinsson, Atli Heimir

SONGS FOR COUNTERTENORS, VOL. 1
   (Hodgson) (CCU) THAMES   (S700)

SONGS FOR JENNY see Simons, Netty

SONGS FOR LEONTYNE see Hoiby, Lee

SONGS FOR LOVING MYSELF see Fukushima,
   Yujiro

SONGS "FOR PEOPLE WHO ARE CHILDREN AT
   HEART" see Mori, Konate

SONGS FOR SINGING AND PLAYING
   ("World's Favorite Series") ASHLEY
   033-6   (S701)

SONGS FOR SMALL PEOPLE see
   Sigurbjörnsson, Thorkell

SONGS FOR SOPRANO AND 3 CHAMBER
   ENSEMBLES see Holm, Mogens Winkel,
   Syster, Min Syster

SONGS FOR THE FOUR PARTS OF THE NIGHT
   see Van de Vate, Nancy Hayes

SONGS FOR THE HARVESTER OF DREAMS see
   Rovics, Howard

SONGS FOR THE HOLIDAY SEASON see Wayne

SONGS FOR THE TURNING see Medema

SONGS FOR VOICE AND PIANO see Lalo,
   Edouard see Mozart, Wolfgang
   Amadeus see Puccini, Giacomo

SONGS FOR VOICE AND PIANO see Glantz,
   Yehuda Leib

SONGS FOR VOICE AND PIANO, VOL. 1 see
   Schubert, Franz (Peter) see
   Schumann, Robert (Alexander)

SONGS FOR VOICE AND PIANO, VOL. 2 see
   Schubert, Franz (Peter) see
   Schumann, Robert (Alexander)

SONGS FOR VOICE AND PIANO, VOL. 3 see
   Schubert, Franz (Peter) see
   Schumann, Robert (Alexander)

SONGS FOR VOICE AND PIANO, VOL. 4 see
   Schubert, Franz (Peter)

SONGS FOR VOICE AND PIANO, VOL. 5 see
   Schubert, Franz (Peter)

SONGS FOR VOICE AND PIANO, VOL. 6 see
   Schubert, Franz (Peter)

SONGS FOR VOICE AND PIANO, VOL. 7 see
   Schubert, Franz (Peter)

SONGS FOR YOUTHFUL TENORS OF ALL AGES
   *CCU
   (Van Camp, Leonard) T solo,pno LAUDA
   LAQ129B accomp tape available
                                  (S702)
SONGS FROM CONNACHT see Hughes, Herbert

SONGS FROM DIANA see Sevriens, Jean

SONGS FROM HERMANN HESSE see
   Willingham, Lawrence

SONGS FROM QUASIMODO (THREE ITALIAN
   SONGS) see Zallman, Arlene
   (Proctor)

SONGS FROM QUEEN'S ROAD see White

SONGS FROM SCANDINAVIA
   (Roe) solo voice,pno KJOS PV80 (S703)

SONGS FROM SPOON RIVER see Downes,
   Andrew

SONGS FROM THE JAPANESE see Hekster,
   Walter

SONGS FROM THE PAGE OF SWORDS see Asia,
   Daniel

SONGS FROM THE SOMERSET HILLS see
   Weigl, [Mrs.] Vally

SONGS FROM "THE WILD SWANS AT COOLE"
   see Gerber, Steven R.

SONGS FROM WALT WHITMAN see Peyton,
   Malcolm C.

SONGS FROM WATER AND STONE see Biggs,
   Hayes

SONGS I see Halldorsson, Skuli

SONGS I SAID see Lieberman, Glenn

SONGS IN THE TEMPEST, THE (C.1746) see
   Fesch, Willem de

SONGS IN WINTER see Leichtling, Alan

SONGS NEWLY SEEN IN THE DUSK see Weigl,
   [Mrs.] Vally

SONGS 1918-1919 see Heseltine, Philip
   ("Peter Warlock")

SONGS 1911-1917 see Heseltine, Philip
   ("Peter Warlock")

SONGS 1920-1922 see Heseltine, Philip
   ("Peter Warlock")

SONGS 1922-1923 see Heseltine, Philip
   ("Peter Warlock")

SONGS OF A NATURE see Bon, Willem
   Frederik

SONGS OF ALL SEASONS see Hekster,
   Walter

SONGS OF AWAKENING LOVE see Berkeley,
   Michael

SONGS OF CHARLES GRIFFES, VOL. 1 see
   Griffes, Charles Tomlinson

SONGS OF CHARLES GRIFFES, VOL. 2 see
   Griffes, Charles Tomlinson

SONGS OF CONCERN see Weigl, [Mrs.]
   Vally

SONGS OF DEATH AND BLUELIGHT DANCING
   see Drew, James M.

SONGS OF ENGLAND *CCU
   (Jones) BOOSEY VAB0296 f.s.   (S704)

SONGS OF ERIN, 50 *Op.76
   (Stanford, C. Villiers) solo voice,
   pno CLASSV 2200   (S705)

SONGS OF ERNEST CHARLES see Charles,
   Ernest

SONGS OF EVE, OP. 102 see Woollen,
   Russell

SONGS OF FRANCESCO PAOLO TOSTI, THE see
   Tosti, Francesco Paolo

SONGS OF GOOD COUNSEL, OP. 73 see
   Cruft, Adrian

SONGS OF ILLUMINATION see Anderson,
   T.J.

SONGS OF INNOCENCE see Bois, Rob du see
   Frandsen, John see Galante, Carlo

SONGS OF INNOCENCE AND EXPERIENCE see
   Willingham, Lawrence

SONGS OF IRELAND *CCU
   (Jones) BOOSEY VAB0299 f.s.   (S706)

SONGS OF JOHN DUKE see Duke, John Woods

SONGS OF JOHN JACOB NILES, THE see
   Niles, John Jacob

SONGS OF JOHN KEATS see Karchin, Louis
   S.

SONGS OF JOHN KEATS see Karchin, Louis
   S.

SONGS OF JOSEPH MARX [1] see Marx,
   Joseph

SONGS OF JOSEPH MARX [2] see Marx,
   Joseph

SONGS OF JOY see Shapey, Ralph

SONGS OF LAUGHTER, LOVE AND TEARS see
   Biggs, John

SONGS OF LIFE AND LOVE see Beckler,
   Stanworth R.

SONGS OF LONELINESS see Gottlieb, Jack
   S.

SONGS OF LOVE AND AFFECTION *CCU
   BOOSEY VAB0230 f.s.   (S707)

SONGS OF LOVE AND LEAVING [1] see
   Weigl, [Mrs.] Vally

SONGS OF LOVE AND LEAVING [2] see
   Weigl, [Mrs.] Vally

SONGS OF LOVE AND SITE see Steinberg,
   Eitan

SOROCHINTSY FAIR: PARASHA'S REVERY AND DANCE see Mussorgsky, Modest Petrovich

SORROW IN SPRINGTIME see Rachmaninoff, Sergey Vassilievich

SORTNAR THU SKY see Halldorsson, Skuli

SOSPIRS see Massana, A.

SOTA L'OMBRETA see Massana, A.

SOUND AND SMOKE ("SCHALL AND RAUCH") *CCU
    solo voice SCHOTT ST 07147 $12.95
                                        (S735)

SOUND AND THE FURY, THE see Haxton, Kenneth

SOUND IN THE VALLEY, THE see Stutschevsky, Joachim, Hatslil Bagai

SOUND THE TRUMPET see Purcell, Henry

SOUPER, HET see Broekman, Hans

SOUPIRS see Badings, Henk

SOURCE TOMBAIT DU ROCHER, LA see Bilt, Willem van der

SOURDRE see Lovano, Maguy

SOURIS, ANDRE (1899-1970)
    Petit Jeu
        child solo,pno SCHOTT-FRER 9179
                                        (S736)

SOURISSE, BRIGITTE
    Coquillages
        see Six Chansons De Brigitte Sourisse

    Koala
        see Six Chansons De Brigitte Sourisse

    Nuages, Les
        see Six Chansons De Brigitte Sourisse

    Pauvre Pierrot
        see Six Chansons De Brigitte Sourisse

    Pêcheur De Crevettes
        see Six Chansons De Brigitte Sourisse

    Pommiers, Les
        see Six Chansons De Brigitte Sourisse

    Six Chansons De Brigitte Sourisse
        (Lesage, Jean-Marc) solo voice,pno
        A CŒUR JOIE f.s.
            contains: Coquillages; Koala;
            Nuages, Les; Pauvre Pierrot;
            Pêcheur De Crevettes; Pommiers,
            Les   (S737)

SOUS LE DÔME ÉPAIS see Delibes, Léo

SOUTHERN MAMMY SINGS see Heilner, Irwin

SOUVENANCE see Franck, Cesar

SOUVENIR DE SALZBRUNN ET WARMBRUNN see Muller, C.F.

SOUVENIRS DU VOYAGE see Powers, Anthony

SOV BARN JESUS LILLE see Eggen, Arne

SØVNEN see Jordan, Sverre

SOWERBY, LEO (1895-1968)
    Little Jesus, Sweetly Sleep
    FITZSIMONS F0102   (S738)

SØYLE I CHARTRES, EN see Madsen, Trygve

SPAGNOLA, LA
    (Di Chiara) med-high solo,pno CLASSV
    1309   (S739)

SPANISCHE LIEBES-LIEDER, OP. 138 see Schumann, Robert (Alexander)

SPANISCHES LIEDERBUCH AUSWAHL, BAND 1: GEISTLICHE LIEDER see Wolf, Hugo

SPANISCHES LIEDERBUCH AUSWAHL, BAND 2: WELTLICHE LIEDER see Wolf, Hugo

SPANISCHES LIEDERBUCH, VOL. 2 see Wolf, Hugo

SPANISCHES LIEDERBUCH, VOL. 3 see Wolf, Hugo

SPANISCHES LIEDERBUCH, WELTLICHE LIEDER, HEFT 1 see Wolf, Hugo

SPANISCHES LIEDERBUCH, WELTLICHE LIEDER, HEFT 2 see Wolf, Hugo

SPANISCHES LIEDERBUCH, WELTLICHE LIEDER, HEFT 3 see Wolf, Hugo

SPANISH FOLK-SONG see Steinberg, Eitan

SPANISH SERENADE see Backer-Lunde, Johan

SPANISH SONGS see Greenburg, Laura

SPANISH SONGS, OP. 100 see Shostakovich, Dmitri

SPARROW, THE see Eggen, Arne, Sporven

SPAZIERGÄNGE, DIE see Eisler, Hanns

SPEAK SOFTLY see Blickhan, Charles Timothy

SPEAKS, OLEY (1874-1948)
    On The Road To Mandalay
        B solo,pno CLASSV 1349   (S740)
        Bar solo,pno CLASSV 0517   (S741)
        T solo,pno CLASSV 1350   (S742)

    Sylvia
        low solo,pno CLASSV 1339   (S743)
        med-low solo,pno CLASSV 1338   (S744)
        med solo,pno CLASSV 1337   (S745)
        high solo,pno CLASSV 1336   (S746)

SPECKS OF LIGHT see Levy, Frank Ezra

SPEELS RONDEEL see Röntgen, Johannes

SPEGLAR ME OSS AV see Kverndokk, Gisle

SPEGLING see Rypdal, Terje

SPEIGHT, JOHN A. (1945-   )
    Jasper Terrace, The
        S/T solo,pno ICELAND 011-004 (S747)

    Sem Dropi Tindrandi
        solo voice,pno ICELAND 011-048
                                        (S748)

    Shatter Me Music
        S/T solo,pno (text by R.M. Rilke)
        ICELAND 011-007   (S749)

    Six Auden Songs
        high solo,pno ICELAND 011-053
                                        (S750)

    Three Shakespeare Songs
        countertenor,hpsd ICELAND 011-037
                                        (S751)

    Three Shakespeare Songs (Version 2)
        Mez/A/countertenor,pno ICELAND
        011-046   (S752)

    Three Songs
        S solo,pno [5'0"] ICELAND 011-011
                                        (S753)

SPEKTRUM 89: LIEDER UND ZYKLEN *CCU
    DEUTSCHER DV 9060 f.s. contains works
    by: Berthold, Bredemeyer, Franke,
    Freiheit, and others   (S754)

SPES ULTIMA see Mascagni, Pietro

SPHÄRENMUSIK see Karg-Elert, Sigfrid

SPI, SPI NEVINATKO see Ryba, Jan Jakub Simon

SPIELMANNSWEISEN see Schoeck, Othmar

SPIEWNIK DOMOWY, ANTOLOGIA PIESNI see Moniuszko, Stanislaw

SPINNERIN, DIE see Pijper, Willem

SPIRIT FLOWER, A see Campbell-Tipton, Louis

SPIRIT OF DELIGHT see Hamilton, Iain

SPIRITUAL CYCLE see Tillis, Frederick C.

SPIRITUALS *CC7U
    (McIntyre, Phillip) FITZSIMONS F0114
    f.s.   (S755)

SPIT' SKALITCHENI see Shut, Wasyl

SPLEEN see Poldowski, [Lady] Dean Paul

SPLEEN POUR RIRE see Kef, Kees

SPLENDID TEAR, A see Arco, Paolo

SPOHR, LUDWIG (LOUIS) (1784-1859)
    Azor And Zemira: Rose Softly Blooming
        [Ger/Eng] high solo,pno CLASSV 0478
                                        (S756)

    Sechs Gesänge, Op. 154
        med solo,pno,vln CLASSV 0592 (S757)

SPORCK, GEORGES
    Cinq Melodies
        [Fr] med-high solo (not available
        outside U.S.A.) RECITAL 397
                                        (S758)

    Sur La Route Ardente
        [Fr] med solo (not available
        outside U.S.A.) RECITAL 398
                                        (S759)

SPØRSMÅL, EIT see Taubo, Lillian Gulowna

SPORVEN see Eggen, Arne

SPRACHSYMBOLE see Mamangakis, Nikos

SPRING see Beach, [Mrs.] H.H.A. (Amy Marcy Cheney)

SPRING AND FALL see Lundborg, (Charles) Erik

SPRING IN THE HARBOR see Kraft, Leo Abraham

SPRING MORNING, A see Wilson, Henry Lane

SPRING NIGHT see Killengreen, Christian, Vårkveld

SPRING ONIONS see Man, Roderik De

SPRING RAIN (FRÜHLINGSREGEN) see Bax, [Sir] Arnold

SPRING SONG see Jordan, Sverre, Vårvisa

SPRING TIDE see Eggen, Arne, No Sprette Lauvet

SPRING VOICES see Strauss, Johann, [Jr.] see Strauss, Johann, [Jr.], Frühlingsstimmen

SPRINGTIME OF LOVE see Moszkowski, Moritz

SPRUCH: WENN WIR ALLE LIEBTEN UNS HIENIEDEN see Strauss-König, Richard

SPURVEN see Hovland, Egil

SQUIRE, WILLIAM HENRY (1871-1963)
    Singing Lesson, The
        ABar soli,pno CLASSV 1258   (S760)

STAAT VAN EENDRACHT, DE see Veldhuis, Jacob ter

STABAT MATER
    (Pais, Aldo) S solo,2vln,vla,vcl,db
    ZANIBON sc 6098 f.s., pts 6099
    f.s., pno red 6100 f.s.   (S761)

STABAT MATER: INFLAMMATUS see Rossini, Gioacchino

STABAT MATER: PRO PECCATIS see Rossini, Gioacchino

STACCATO see Dresden, Sem

STACHOWSKI, MAREK (1936-   )
    Madrigali Dell' Estate
        [It] solo voice, string trio [10']
        sc POLSKIE   (S762)

STACI! JA VERIM see Rejcha, Antonin, Basta! Ti Credo

STACKARS see Blomdahl, Karl-Birger

STAHMER, KLAUS H. (1941-   )
    Tre Paesagi
        solo voice,gtr,perc,electronic tape
        (tape - $18.75) PLUCKED STR
        ZM 1986 $15.00   (S763)

STALLCOP, GLENN
    Rain, Rain: Five Songs *CC5U
        S solo,pno sc AM.COMP.AL. $11.45
                                        (S764)

STAMBOGSRIM see Grieg, Edvard Hagerup

STAMP MUSIC I see Lidholm, Ingvar

STAND see Bailey, Bob

STÄNDCHEN see Schubert, Franz (Peter)

STÄNDCHEN FÜR EINEN VERLEGER: "HO, MICH TRÄGT DIE WELLE" see Miller, Franz R.

STANFORD, CHARLES VILLIERS (1852-1924)
    Bible Songs: A Song Of Freedom (Psalm No. 126) Op.113,No.1
        med-high solo,pno CLASSV 1518
                                        (S765)

    Bible Songs: A Song Of Peace *Op.113,No.4
        med-high solo,pno CLASSV 1519
                                        (S766)

STANFORD, CHARLES VILLIERS (cont'd.)

Bible Songs, Op.113
high solo/low solo,org CHILTERN
f.s.
contains: Song Of Battle; Song Of
Freedom; Song Of Hope; Song Of
Peace; Song Of Trust; Song Of
Wisdom (S767)

Crossing The Bar
high solo CHILTERN (S768)

Cushendall, Op. 118 *song cycle
[Eng] low solo (7 poems of John
Stevenson) RECITAL 292 (S769)

Father O'Flynn
med-high solo,pno CLASSV 1183
(S770)

I'd Rock My Own Sweet Childie
see Irish Lullaby, An

Irish Idyll, An *song cycle
[Eng] high solo (poems by Moira
O'Neill) RECITAL 293 (S771)
[Eng] low solo (poems by Moira
O'Neill) RECITAL 294 (S772)

Irish Lullaby, An
"I'd Rock My Own Sweet Childie"
CLASSV (S773)

Molly Brannigan
med solo,pno CLASSV 1357 (S774)

My Love's An Arbutus (from Coola
Shore)
med solo,pno CLASSV 1910 (S775)

Psalm No. 126
see Bible Songs: A Song Of Freedom

Sea Wrack
high solo CHILTERN (S776)

Song Of Battle
see Bible Songs, Op.113

Song Of Freedom
see Bible Songs, Op.113

Song Of Hope
see Bible Songs, Op.113

Song Of Peace
see Bible Songs, Op.113

Song Of Trust
see Bible Songs, Op.113

Song Of Wisdom
see Bible Songs, Op.113

Songs Of The Fleet *Op.117
[Eng] Bar solo,pno CLASSV 1363
(S777)

Songs Of The Sea *Op.91
[Eng] Bar solo,pno CLASSV 1365
(S778)

STANISLAW MONIUSZKO - SELECTED SONGS
AND ARIAS, FRYDERYK CHOPIN -
SELECTED SONGS FROM OPUS 74 see
Moniuszko, Stanislaw, Antologia
Piesni I Arii Stanislawa Moniuszki
Oraz Piesni Fryderyka Chopina

STANZAS FOR MUSIC see Amerongen, Jan
van see Karpman, Laura see Karpman,
Laura

STAP, STAP see Ruiter, Wim de

STAR MOSS see Ames, William T.

STAR OF BETHLEHEM see Adams, S.

STAR VICINO see Anonymous

STARER, ROBERT (1924-   )
Two Sacred Songs
high solo,fl,ob,hpsd,vln,vla,vcl
[7'30"] PEER (S779)

STARESONG see Ørbeck, Anne Marie

STARKE, DEN see Hallin, Margareta

STARS FALL see Rowland, David

STARS HAVE NOT DEALT ME THE WORST THEY
COULD, THE see Heilner, Irwin

STARS HILL VALLEY see Lessard, John
Ayres

STATUE AT CZARSKOE-SELO, THE see Cui,
César Antonovich

STATUE OF LIBERTY, THE see Enloe, Neil

STEARNS, PETER PINDAR (1931-   )
Cathedral Of The Incarnation
S solo,vln [7'] sc AM.COMP.AL.
$3.85 (S780)

STEDRON, MILOS (1942-   )
Sedmikvitek
med solo,2.2.2.2. 4.3.3.1. timp,
perc,harp,cel,cimbalom,strings
[13'] CESKY HUD. (S781)

STEFANI, GIOVANNI
Affetti Amorosi *CC32U
solo voice,gtr,db FORNI 5370 f.s.
(S782)

STEFANSSON, FINNUR TORFI (1947-   )
Dark Lady, The
Mez solo,pno (text by Shakespeare)
ICELAND 057-007 (S783)

Homesickness
solo voice,pno ICELAND 057-032
(S784)

Kissed By Sun
solo voice,pno ICELAND 057-031
(S785)

Morning
countertenor,gtr ICELAND 057-023
(S786)

Salmur
solo voice,pno ICELAND 057-035
(S787)

Slattuvisa
solo voice,pno ICELAND 057-030
(S788)

Til Söngsins
solo voice,pno ICELAND 057-026
(S789)

STEFANSSON, FJÖLNIR (1930-   )
Endurfundir
solo voice,pno ICELAND 004-011
(S790)

Five Songs
solo voice,pno ICELAND 004-002
(S791)

STEIN, LEON (1910-   )
Kaddish
T solo,string orch [5'] sc
AM.COMP.AL. $5.75 (S792)

STEINBERG, BEN (1930-   )
Esa Einai
[Heb] med solo,kbd TRANSCON. 991113
(S793)

Wedding Blessings And Seven
Benedictions, The
solo voice,org,opt string quar
TRANSCON. 991298 (S794)

STEINBERG, EITAN (1955-   )
Arabic Folk-Song
see Simplicity

Benakik Nistar
see Songs Of Love And Site

Bulgarian Folk-Song
see Simplicity

Capre, La
see Songs Of Love And Site

Interlude
see Simplicity

Na Protigenim
see Songs Of Love And Site

Simplicity
solo voice,soprano sax,acord,gtr
ISR.MUS.INST. perf mat rent
contains: Arabic Folk-Song;
Bulgarian Folk-Song; Interlude;
Interlude; Spanish Folk-Song
(S795)

Songs Of Love And Site
solo voice,tamb,vla ISR.MUS.INST.
6919R perf mat rent
contains: Benakik Nistar, "In A
Hidden Cleft"; Capre, La,
"Goat, The"; Na Protigenim,
"Unique Days"; Taraiatil
Manazilu Bil Katibi, "Winds Of
The Desert"; Tarara, La,
"Peasant Girl, The"; Zoniked
Veig, "Sun's Route, The" (S796)

Spanish Folk-Song
see Simplicity

Taraiatil Manazilu Bil Katibi
see Songs Of Love And Site

Tarara, La
see Songs Of Love And Site

Zoniked Veig
see Songs Of Love And Site

STEINER, GITTA HANA (1932-   )
Concert Piece 1
S solo,chamber group SEESAW f.s.
(S797)

Concert Piece 2
S solo,chamber group SEESAW f.s.
(S798)

Dream Dialogue
S solo,perc SEESAW f.s. (S799)

STEINER, GITTA HANA (cont'd.)

Four Songs *CC4U
med solo,vibra SEESAW f.s. (S800)

Interlude
S solo,vibra SEESAW f.s. (S801)

New Poems
solo voice,vibra SEESAW f.s. (S802)

Pages From A Summer Journal
S solo,pno SEESAW f.s. (S803)

Three Poems *CC3U
med solo,2perc SEESAW f.s. (S804)

Three Songs *CC3U
med solo,pno SEESAW f.s. (S805)

Trio
med solo,pno,perc SEESAW f.s.
(S806)

Two Songs *CC2U
S solo,pno SEESAW f.s. (S807)

STEINKE, GREG A. (1942-   )
Three Sonnets *CC3U
S solo,fl,strings SEESAW f.s.
(S808)

STELLA POLARE see Porto, Nino

STELLDICHEIN, EIN see Weigl, Karl

STELLE CHIARE see Cimara, Pietro

STELZHAMMER
'S Ghaimniss
SCIEN 1582 from STELZHAMMER'S
LIEDER IN OBDERENNS'SCHER MUNDART
(S809)

Stelzhammer's Lieder In
Obderenns'scher Mundart
see 'S Ghaimniss

STELZHAMMER'S LIEDER IN OBDERENNS'SCHER
MUNDART see Stelzhammer

STENHAMMAR, WILHELM (1871-1927)
Folk, Ett, Op. 22
(Hedwall, Lennart) [Swed] solo
voice,2wind quin,db TONOS (S810)

STEPHEN FOSTER SONGBOOK see Foster,
Stephen Collins

STEPKA, KAREL VACLAV (1909-   )
Jihoceske Leto
Bar solo,pno PANTON 101 (S811)

STER SPRONG OP, EEN see Maessen, Antoon

STERBENDE HELD, DER see Beekhuis, Hanna

STERN, ROBERT LEWIS (1934-   )
Al Tifg'i Vi
see Two Hebrew Art Songs

Numi, Numi
see Two Hebrew Art Songs

Two Hebrew Art Songs
S solo,pno TRANSCON. 991308 f.s.
contains: Al Tifg'i Vi; Numi,
Numi (S812)

STERNBILD DER GRENZE see Globokar,
Vinko

STERNE, DIE see Schubert, Franz (Peter)

STERNE SCHAU'N IN STILLER NACHT, DIE
see Mendelssohn-Bartholdy, Felix

STERNENHIMMEL, DER see Zumsteeg, Emilie

STERVENDE, DE see Broekman, Hans

STEUERMANN, EDWARD (1892-1964)
Drei Lieder
B solo,pno sc BOELKE-BOM (S813)

Four Songs *CC4U
S solo,pno APNM sc $3.75, set $7.25
(S814)

STEV see Albertsen, Per Hjort

STEVENS, BERNARD GEORGE (1916-1983)
Two Beddoes Songs
T solo,pno BARDIC BE0331 (S815)

STEVENS, HALSEY (1908-1989)
Sonnet
low solo,pno [3'] sc AM.COMP.AL.
$1.95 (S816)

STEVENSON, JOHN
Fallen Is Thy Throne, Oh Israel
SCIEN 1585 (S817)

Farewell! But, Whenever You Welcome
The Hour
SCIEN 1586 (S818)

STRAESSER, JOEP (cont'd.)

Zynische Lieder
Bar solo,pno DONEMUS f.s. [14']
contains: Erste Hilfe; Fragen
Eines Engagierten Dichters;
Fragen Und Die Antworten, Die;
Gezieltes Spielzeug; Schwächer;
Unbekümmerte Künstlernatur
(S852)

STRAND, RAGNVALD (1910-   )
Earth
see Jord

Hymn
see Hymne

Hymne
"Hymn" Bar solo,1.1.2.1. 2.2.1.0.
pno,strings NORGE f.s.   (S853)

Jord
"Earth" narrator,1.1.2.1. 2.2.1.0.
pno,strings NORGE f.s.   (S854)

STRAND, TOR
Julesang
SA soli,pno/org NOTON N-9016 (S855)

STRANDSJÖ, GÖTE (1916-   )
Är Människor En Börda
see Varför Vara Rädd För Natten!,
Vol. 1

Guds Idag
see Varför Vara Rädd För Natten!,
Vol. 1

Hemma
see Varför Vara Rädd För Natten!,
Vol. 2

Så Fint Att Din Hand
see Varför Vara Rädd För Natten!,
Vol. 1

Sång Till Jesus
see Varför Vara Rädd För Natten!,
Vol. 2

Stora Är Barnens Ögon
see Varför Vara Rädd För Natten!,
Vol. 2

Tre Kyrkovisor
solo voice SVERIG PROP 7933 (S856)

Varför Vara Rädd För Natten
see Varför Vara Rädd För Natten!,
Vol. 1

Varför Vara Rädd För Natten 1
SVERIG PROP 7943   (S857)

Varför Vara Rädd För Natten 2
SVERIG PROP 7944   (S858)

Varför Vara Rädd För Natten!, Vol. 1
solo voice,kbd PROPRIUS 7943 f.s.
contains: Är Människor En Börda;
Guds Idag; Så Fint Att Din
Hand; Varför Vara Rädd För
Natten   (S859)

Varför Vara Rädd För Natten!, Vol. 2
solo voice,kbd PROPRIUS 7944 f.s.
contains: Hemma; Sång Till Jesus;
Stora Är Barnens Ögon (S860)

STRANGE HARMONY see Puccini, Giacomo,
Tosca: Recondita Armonia

STRANGER, THE see Johnson, A. Paul

STRASSE IN TREPTOW AN DER REGA see
Koetsier, Jan

STRATFOD, ELAINE
Sing With The Kids Guitarbook
solo voice,gtr UNIVERSE   (S861)

STRAUS, OSCAR (1870-1954)
Chocolate Soldier: My Hero
[Eng] high solo RECITAL 2228 (S862)
"Come! I Love You Only" S solo,pno
CLASSV 1490   (S863)

Come! I Love You Only
see Chocolate Soldier: My Hero

STRAUSS, JOHANN, [JR.] (1825-1899)
Adele's Laughing Song
see Fledermaus, Die: Mein Herr
Marquis
see Mein Herr Marquis

Beautiful Blue Danube
(Weckerlin) Mez solo,pno CLASSV
0973   (S864)
(Weckerlin) high solo,pno CLASSV
0974   (S865)

Fledermaus, Die: Mein Herr Marquis
"Adele's Laughing Song" [Ger] S
solo,pno CLASSV 1236   (S866)

STRAUSS, JOHANN, [JR.] (cont'd.)

Frühlingsstimmen
"Spring Voices" [Ger] S solo,pno
CLASSV 2055   (S867)

Mein Herr Marquis (from Die
Fledermaus)
"Adele's Laughing Song" [Ger/Eng]
SCHIRM.G ST38033   (S868)

Roses Du Midi
"Roses From The South" [Fr] solo
voice,pno CLASSV 2054   (S869)

Roses From The South
see Roses Du Midi

So Voll Fröhlichkeit
see Zigeunerbaron, Der: Walzerlied

Spring Voices
"Voci Di Primavera" [It/Eng] S
solo,pno CLASSV 0531   (S870)
"Voci Di Primavera" [It/Eng] Mez
solo,pno CLASSV 0975   (S871)
"Voci Di Primavera" [It/Eng] A
solo,pno CLASSV 0976   (S872)
see Frühlingsstimmen

Voci Di Primavera
see Spring Voices

Zigeunerbaron, Der: Walzerlied
"So Voll Fröhlichkeit" [Ger] high
solo,pno CLASSV 1235   (S873)

Zigeunerbaron, Der: Wer Hat Euch Denn
Getraut?
[Ger] ST soli,pno CLASSV 1266
(S874)

STRAUSS, RICHARD (1864-1949)
Allerseelen
high solo,pno CLASSV 0376   (S875)

Ariadne Auf Naxos: Lieben
Bar solo,pno CLASSV 0541   (S876)

Ariadne Auf Naxos: Zerbinetta, 1st
Edition Version
coloratura sop,pno CLASSV 0542
(S877)

Befreit
low solo,pno CLASSV 0437   (S878)

Einsame, Der
see Zwei Basslieder, Op. 51

Lob Des Leidens *Op.15,No.3
med solo,pno CLASSV 1520   (S879)

Malven
med solo BOOSEY SGB2709   (S880)

Morgen
high solo,pno CLASSV 0377   (S881)
med solo,pno CLASSV 0389   (S882)
high solo,pno,vln,vcl CLASSV 1678
(S883)

Nachlese
BOOSEY VAB0243   (S884)

Rosenkavalier, Der: Di Rigori Armato
T solo,pno (semi-tone lower) CLASSV
1261   (S885)
T solo,pno (original key) CLASSV
1696   (S886)

Ruhe, Meine Seele!
high solo,pno CLASSV 0444   (S887)
low solo,pno CLASSV 0442   (S888)

Selections From Der Rosenkavalier, A
Master Class With Evelyn Lear
SCHIRM.G 50488456   (S889)

Thal, Das
see Zwei Basslieder, Op. 51

Traum Durch Die Dammerung
high solo,pno CLASSV 0378   (S890)

Zwei Basslieder, Op. 51
B solo,pno CLASSV 0573 f.s.
contains: Einsame, Der; Thal, Das
(S891)

STRAUSS-KÖNIG, RICHARD (1930-   )
Spruch: Wenn Wir Alle Liebten Uns
Hienieden
med solo,horn,pno BOHM f.s.   (S892)

STRAVINSKY, IGOR (1882-1971)
Berceuse Du Chat
solo voice,pno pno red MMB X800003
(S893)

Deux Poésies De K. Balmont
[Russ/Ger/Fr/Eng] S solo,pno CLASSV
1401   (S894)

Pastorale (Vocalise)
med-high solo,pno CLASSV 2056
(S895)

Trois Poésies De La Lyrique Japonaise
[Russ/Fr/Eng] S solo,pno CLASSV
1400   (S896)

STREICHER, THEODORE (1874-1940)
Hafis-Lieder
[Ger/Eng] (contains 25 lieder on
Daumer's translations of poems of
Hafiz) RECITAL 400   (S897)

Lieder Aus Des Knaben Wunderhorn, 30,
Vol. 1, Nos. 1-10
[Eng/Ger] RECITAL 295   (S898)

Lieder Aus Des Knaben Wunderhorn, 30,
Vol. 2, Nos. 11-20
[Eng/Ger] RECITAL 296   (S899)

Lieder Aus Des Knaben Wunderhorn, 30,
Vol. 3, Nos. 21-30
[Eng/Ger] RECITAL 297   (S900)

STREICHQUARTETT NO.4, OP.66 see
Schibler, Armin

STRENGTH STOOPS UNTO THE GRAVE see
Rowland, David

STRIDSMAND see Islandsmoen, Sigurd

STRINDBERG, HENRIK (1954-   )
First Lay Of Gudrun, The
see Första Kvädet Om Gudrun, Det

Första Kvädet Om Gudrun, Det
Mez solo,gtr REIMERS 101144 (S901)
"First Lay Of Gudrun, The" S solo,
gtr [19'] REIMERS 101144   (S902)

STRING QUARTET 2 see Koch, Frederick

STRING QUARTET NO. 4 see Turok, Paul
Harris

STRING QUARTET NO. 5 see Shapey, Ralph

STRING QUARTET NO. 7 see Rochberg, A.
George

STROHBACH, SIEGFRIED (1929-   )
Bruder Liederlich *CC4U
Bar solo,pno BREITKOPF-W EB 6458
f.s.   (S903)

Vier Kleine Weihnachtslieder *CC4U,
Xmas
solo voice,pno BREITKOPF-W EB 5987
f.s.   (S904)

STROHL, RITA
Dix Poesies
[Fr] med-high solo (not available
outside U.S.A.) RECITAL 401
(S905)

STRÖMHOLM, FOLKE (1941-   )
Fragmenter, Op. 13
[Norw] solo voice,pno NORGE (S906)

Glede
[Norw] solo voice,pno NORGE (S907)

Syntaks *Op.14
"Syntax" B solo,2.2.2.2. 4.3.3.1.
timp,perc,harp,strings [18']
NORGE f.s.   (S908)

Syntax
see Syntaks

STROZZI, BARBARA (fl. ca. 1650)
Sacri Musicali Affetti, Op. 5
DA CAPO ISBN 0-306-76195-5 (S909)

STRUGGLE WITH THE ANGEL see Bodorova,
Sylvie

STRUGNELL'S HAIKU see Matthews, Colin

STUCK, JEAN BAPTISTE (1680-1755)
Aurore Et Cephale, L' *cant
S solo,fl,2vln,vla,vcl,hpsd [18']
BILLAUDOT   (S910)

STUCKY, STEVEN EDWARD (1949-   )
Sappho Fragments
Mez solo,fl,clar,perc,pno,vln,vcl,
conductor [12'] AM.COMP.AL. sc
$19.15, pts $37.50   (S911)

Schneemusik
S solo,pno/perc [11'] sc
AM.COMP.AL. $9.15   (S912)

Two Holy Sonnets Of John Donne *CC2U
Mez solo,ob,pno AM.COMP.AL. sc
$9.15, pts $2.70   (S913)

STUDENT SERENADE see Shut, Wasyl,
Studentska Serenada

STUDENTSKA SERENADE see Shut, Wasyl

STUNDEN BUCH, DAS see Soler, J.

STUNDOM GJENG STRAUMEN I RING see
Søderlind, Ragnar

STUNDOM INGEN UM ELSKEN VEIT see
Kielland, Olav

STUPPNER, HUBERT (1944-)
De La Soiree Passee
S solo,fl,perc,vln [12'] MODERN
1854   (S914)

STUTSCHEVSKY, JOACHIM (1891-1982)
Four Songs
OR-TAV   (S915)

Hatslil Bagai
"Sound In The Valley, The" SMez
soli,pno OR-TAV   (S916)

In Sleepless Nights
OR-TAV f.s. from NINE SONGS FOR
VOICE AND PIANO   (S917)

Invocation
solo voice,pno,opt vcl OR-TAV f.s.
from NINE SONGS FOR VOICE AND
PIANO   (S918)

Jumping Raindrop, The
OR-TAV f.s. from NINE SONGS FOR
VOICE AND PIANO   (S919)

Love Song
OR-TAV f.s. from NINE SONGS FOR
VOICE AND PIANO   (S920)

Lullaby
OR-TAV f.s. from NINE SONGS FOR
VOICE AND PIANO   (S921)

Nine Songs For Voice And Piano
see In Sleepless Nights
see Invocation
see Jumping Raindrop, The
see Love Song
see Lullaby
see Pair Of Sandals, A
see Promise, The
see Song To My Heart
see Song Without Words

Pair Of Sandals, A
OR-TAV f.s. from NINE SONGS FOR
VOICE AND PIANO   (S922)

Promise, The
OR-TAV f.s. from NINE SONGS FOR
VOICE AND PIANO   (S923)

Song To My Heart
OR-TAV f.s. from NINE SONGS FOR
VOICE AND PIANO   (S924)

Song Without Words
OR-TAV f.s. from NINE SONGS FOR
VOICE AND PIANO   (S925)

Sound In The Valley, The
see Hatslil Bagai

Two Songs On Poems By H. Rabinson
OR-TAV   (S926)

Zemer Am (Five Jewish Folksongs In
Yiddish And Hebrew)
OR-TAV   (S927)

STUTTERING LOVERS, THE see Hughes,
Herbert

SU PER L'ARGTENTEO CIEL LA LUNA VOLA
see Zandonai, Riccardo, Serenata

SUBEN, JOEL ERIC (1946-)
Adonai Ma Adam
[Heb] med solo,pno/org [2'] sc
AM.COMP.AL. $2.35   (S928)

Five Goethe Songs *CC5U
Bar solo,gtr,vcl APNM sc $5.00, set
$13.50   (S929)

Five Negro Spirituals *CC5U,spir
med solo,1.0.2.alto sax.1. 1.1.0.1.
harp,pno,strings pno red
AM.COMP.AL. $6.85   (S930)

Fremde Oign *cant
T solo,2vln,vla,vcl [3'] APNM from
HA-AZINU sc $3.50, set $15.50
    (S931)

Ha-Azinu
see Fremde Oign
see Shochnei Batei Chomer
see Shogeh V'cheik
see Sinfonia

Ochila La-El
[Heb] high solo,vln [2'] sc
AM.COMP.AL. $1.20   (S932)

Shochnei Batei Chomer *cant
T solo,vln [3'] APNM from HA-AZINU
sc $2.50, set $4.75   (S933)

Shogeh V'cheik *cant
T solo,vla [2'] APNM from HA-AZINU
sc $2.50, set $4.75   (S934)

Sinfonia *cant
T solo,2vln,vla,vcl [3'] APNM from
HA-AZINU sc $4.00, set $17.00

SUBEN, JOEL ERIC (cont'd.)
    (S935)
Three Songs *CC3U
S solo,pno sc AM.COMP.AL. $5.40
    (S936)

SUBLIME AND THE BEAUTIFUL, THE see
Kraft, William

SUCCESS see Lunde, Ivar

SUCH A LONG TIME see Olsen, Sparre, So
Lang Ei Tid

SUDLANDS-BRUR see Sommerfeldt, Öistein

SUDRAENI BLAER, HINN see Halldorsson,
Skuli

SUENOS GRISES see Aleman, Eduardo A.

SUGIURA, MASAYOSHI (1921-)
Asukabutsu
Mez solo,pno [5'] ONGAKU   (S937)

Enchu
Mez solo,pno [5'] ONGAKU   (S938)

Shigon'bo
solo voice, ko-tsuzumi JAPAN 9110
    (S939)
Mez solo, ko-tsuzumi [12'] JAPAN
    (S940)

SUITCHO see Itoh, Ohsuke

SUITE AUX TROUBADOURS see Bond,
Victoria

SUITE DI FRAMMENTI DA "IL CAVALIER
SELVATICO" see Molino, Francesco

SUITE FOR VERSES OF MICHELANGELO
BUONARROTI see Shostakovich, Dmitri

SUITE ON VERSES OF MICHELANGELO
BUONARROTI, OP. 145 see
Shostakovich, Dmitri

SULAMITH: ROMANTISCHE SZENE see Glaser,
Werner Wolf

SULEIKA see Mendelssohn-Bartholdy,
Felix

SULEIKA UND HATEM see Mendelssohn-
Bartholdy, Felix

SULLE, SULLE LABBRA see Arditi, Luigi,
Bacio, Il

SULLIVAN
Psalm No. 23 (composed with Joncas,
Michael)
med-high solo,kbd (easy) GIA G-2853
$2.50   (S941)

SULLIVAN, [SIR] ARTHUR SEYMOUR
(1842-1900)
Arthur Sullivan Songs, Book 1 *CC6U
(Borthwick, Alan; Wilson, Robin)
med solo,pno GALAXY 3.3224 $8.50
    (S942)

Lost Chord
low solo,pno CLASSV 2058   (S943)
med solo,pno CLASSV 2057   (S944)

Orpheus With His Lute
high solo,pno CLASSV 1189   (S945)
low solo,pno CLASSV 1188   (S946)

Pirates Of Penzance
solo voice voc sc BELWIN HANE8496
$7.95   (S947)

Pirates Of Penzance: Poor Wandering
One
S solo,pno CLASSV 2219   (S948)

SUMAR see Isolfsson, Pall

SUMARAUKI see Halldorsson, Sigfus

SUMARKVEDJA TIL ISLENZKRA BARNA see
Halldorsson, Sigfus

SUMARNOTT see Sveinsson, Atli Heimir

SUMMER see Shut, Wasyl, Lito

SUMMER FRAGMENTS see Svoboda, Tomas

SUMMER IMAGES AND REFLECTIONS see
Ogdon, Wilbur L.

SUMMER IS AWAY see Nowak, Lionel

SUMMER LANDSCAPE see Delius, Frederick

SUMMER MUSIC see Riley

SUMMER SONG see Dydo, J. Stephen

SUMMER VILLANELLE see Man, Roderik De

SUMMERMAIE see Hess, W.

SUN DIAL, THE see Branscombe, Gena

SUND, ROBERT (1942-)
Rimarium: Tio Tonsatta Tankar
solo voice,pno GEHRMANS 6312 (S949)

SUNFAIR see Eggen, Arne, Solfager

SUNFLOWER SPLENDOR see Schober, Brian

SUNNI SYNG see Olsen, Sparre

SUNNY DAY IN THE MOUNTAIANS see
Nystedt, Knut, Soldag I Fjellet

SUNRISE see Ives, Charles

SUNSET see Runolfsson, Karl Otto

SUPPE, FRANZ VON (1819-1895)
Ariette Der Röserl (from 'S Alraunl)
solo voice,pno SCIEN 1699   (S950)

Gefangen
solo voice,vcl,vln/fl,horn SCIEN
1704   (S951)

Iberisches Ständchen
"Lausche Meinen Tönen" [Ger] high
solo,pno CLASSV 2059   (S952)

Ländlich - Sittlich
solo voice,pno SCIEN 1705   (S953)

Lausche Meinen Tönen
see Iberisches Ständchen

'S Deanderl Ám Bach
see Zwei Gedichte In Österr.
Volksmundart

'S Dierndl Als Concert-Sängerin
solo voice,pno SCIEN 1701   (S954)

'S Meisterwerk
solo voice,pno SCIEN 1706   (S955)

Vergissmeinnicht, Das
solo voice,pno SCIEN 1710   (S956)

Was Is Á Wundá
see Zwei Gedichte In Österr.
Volksmundart

Zwei Gedichte In Österr. Volksmundart
solo voice,pno SCIEN 1700 f.s.
contains: 'S Deanderl Ám Bach;
Was Is Á Wundá   (S957)

SUPPLE SUITOR..., THE see Barkin,
Elaine R.

SUPRA ROSA see Anderson, Allen

SUR LA ROUTE ARDENTE see Sporck,
Georges

SUR LA VILLE SOLITAIRE see Tosti,
Francesco Paolo, Aubade (2nd
Mattinata)

SUR LE QUI-VIVE see Pousseur, Henri

SUR UNE TOMBE see Lekeu, Guillaume

SURCAR VEMOS see Pablo, Luis de

SURENNE, I.T.
Araby Maid, The
SCIEN 1712   (S958)

SURINACH, CARLOS (1915-)
Three Songs Of Spain
S solo,1.1.1.1. 1.1.1.1. timp,perc,
strings [3'0"] PEER   (S959)

SURROUNDINGS see Cory, Eleanor

SUSPIROS see Massana, A., Sospirs

SÜSSES LICHT see Schubert, Franz
(Peter), Sängers Morgenlied, D.
163, Setting #1 see Schubert, Franz
(Peter), Sängers Morgenlied, D.
163, Setting #2

SUZETTE ET SUZON see Lecocq, Charles

SUZUKI, HIDEAKI (1938-)
Oto, Hana
S/T solo,pno [4'] JAPAN   (S960)

SUZUKI, SATOSHI (1941-)
Three Songs For Children, From
Shigeko Miyata's Poem
S solo,pno [8'] JAPAN   (S961)

SUZUKI, TERUAKI (1958-)
Motet D' Adonis
S solo,sax,perc,pno [10'] JAPAN
    (S962)

SVALORNA see Wallgren, Jan

SVANA ELD see Fladmoe, Arvid

SVANA ELD FRA "PÅ KANNARHAUGENË see Fladmoe, Arvid

SVART LYS see Aagaard-Nilsen, Torstein

SVARTA ROSOR see Sibelius, Jean

SVARTE KROSSAR see Tveitt, Geirr

SVATOS, VLADIMIR (1928-   )
Zapadaj Slniecko
female solo,pno PANTON 948   (S963)

SVEINBJÖRNSSON, SVEINBJÖRN (1847-1927)
Faninn
solo voice,pno ICELAND 038-021
(S964)
Gallop, The
solo voice,pno ICELAND 038-026
(S965)
Gold And Green
solo voice,pno ICELAND 038-023
(S966)
Hugsad Heim
solo voice,pno ICELAND 038-031
(S967)
Iceland
solo voice,pno ICELAND 038-016
(S968)
Icelandic Folk Songs
solo voice,pno ICELAND 038-014
(S969)
In Vernalis Temporis
solo voice,pno ICELAND 038-027
(S970)
King Sverre
solo voice,pno ICELAND 038-017
(S971)
Like A Lilac
solo voice,pno ICELAND 038-025
(S972)
Lover's Lament, The
solo voice,pno ICELAND 038-015
(S973)
Now Is The Month Of Maying
2 solo voices,pno ICELAND 038-022
(S974)
O, Gud Vors Lands
solo voice,pno ICELAND 038-006
(S975)
Seven Songs
solo voice,pno ICELAND 038-029
(S976)
Sex Lög
solo voice,pno ICELAND 038-004
(S977)
Troubadour, The
solo voice,pno (text by Sir Walter
Scott) ICELAND 038-019   (S978)
Trysting
solo voice,pno ICELAND 038-018
(S979)
Up In The North
solo voice,pno ICELAND 038-020
(S980)
Valagilsa
solo voice,pno ICELAND 038-028
(S981)
Winter
solo voice,pno ICELAND 038-024
(S982)

SVEINSSON, ATLI HEIMIR (1938-   )
Afi Gamli
solo voice,pno ICELAND 002-126
(S983)
Bradum Kemur Betri Tid
solo voice,pno ICELAND 002-131
(S984)
December
solo voice,pno ICELAND 002-135
(S985)
Eftirmali Aevintyris (Finale)
solo voice,pno ICELAND 002-146
(S986)
Eg Er Gull Og Gersemi
solo voice,pno ICELAND 002-062
(S987)
Eg Vil Kenna Ther Oskarad
solo voice,pno ICELAND 002-129
(S988)
Eignir Karls
solo voice,pno ICELAND 002-144
(S989)
Enn A Kuldaskom
solo voice,pno ICELAND 002-150
(S990)
Erlustef
solo voice,pno ICELAND 002-141
(S991)
Fina Kisa
solo voice,pno ICELAND 002-123
(S992)
Fingramal
solo voice,pno ICELAND 002-143
(S993)
Fiskirodur
solo voice,pno ICELAND 002-121
(S994)
Gakktu Haegt
solo voice,pno ICELAND 002-127
(S995)

SVEINSSON, ATLI HEIMIR (cont'd.)
Gibba
solo voice,pno ICELAND 002-120
(S996)
Grimseyjarkarlinn
solo voice,pno ICELAND 002-124
(S997)
Haust
solo voice,pno ICELAND 002-136
(S998)
Hugsjon
solo voice,pno ICELAND 002-139
(S999)
Karins Mansdotters Lullaby For King
Eric XIV
solo voice,fl,alto sax,gtr,perc
[12'0"] ICELAND 002-045   (S1000)
Kisa Min
solo voice,pno ICELAND 002-140
(S1001)
Komdu
solo voice,pno ICELAND 002-134
(S1002)
Krotad I Sand
solo voice,pno ICELAND 002-137
(S1003)
Ljodakorn
solo voice,pno (29 songs) ICELAND
002-032   (S1004)
Ofvitinn
solo voice,pno ICELAND 002-084
(S1005)
Öll Börn Sofa
solo voice,pno ICELAND 002-125
(S1006)
Plant A Tree
solo voice,pno ICELAND 002-026
(S1007)
Poem
solo voice,pno ICELAND 002-133
(S1008)
Prayer
countertenor,gtr (text by Sören
Kierkegaard) ICELAND 002-096
(S1009)
Send Me A Leaf
solo voice,pno ICELAND 002-100
(S1010)
Siesta
solo voice,pno ICELAND 002-149
(S1011)
Smile
T solo,pno ICELAND 002-091   (S1012)
Sogugabb
solo voice,pno ICELAND 002-145
(S1013)
Songs For Children
solo voice,pno [7'0"] ICELAND
002-048   (S1014)
Sumarnott
solo voice,pno ICELAND 002-132
(S1015)
Tengdamaedurnar
solo voice,pno ICELAND 002-142
(S1016)
Three Songs
solo voice,ob,pno ICELAND 002-158
(S1017)
solo voice,pno ICELAND 002-104
(S1018)
Tilvonandi Reidhross
solo voice,pno ICELAND 002-122
(S1019)
Ur Dimbilvoku
solo voice,pno ICELAND 002-138
(S1020)
Ur Pislargrati
solo voice ICELAND 002-105   (S1021)
Vid Stokkinn
solo voice,pno ICELAND 002-119
(S1022)
Vorid Goda
solo voice,pno ICELAND 002-147
(S1023)
Vorvisur Ur Barnabok
solo voice,pno ICELAND 002-148
(S1024)

SVEINSSON, GUNNAR REYNIR (1933-   )
Brefid Hennar Stinu
solo voice,pno ICELAND 005-081
(S1025)
Cantata
solo voice,org ICELAND 005-028
(S1026)
Eg Er Myrkrid
ABar soli,pno ICELAND 005-080
(S1027)
Fimm Numer I Islenskum Thjodbuningum
solo voice,pno ICELAND 005-050
(S1028)
Fimm Postludiur
solo voice,org [21'0"] ICELAND
005-020   (S1029)
I Kirkjugardi
T solo,org [10'15"] ICELAND 005-052
(S1030)
Madur Hefur Nu
solo voice,pno ICELAND 005-079
(S1031)

SVEINSSON, GUNNAR REYNIR (cont'd.)
Nottin Er Til Thess Ad Grata I
solo voice,pno ICELAND 005-043
(S1032)
Til Mariu
Mez/Bar solo,org ICELAND 005-069
(S1033)
Undanhald Samkvaemt Aaetlun
S solo,pno [20'10"] ICELAND 005-008
(S1034)

SVEND HERLUFSENS ORD see Hall, Pauline

SVEND HERULFSENS ORD see Johansen,
David Monrad

SVENSK ROMANSSÅNG, DEL A: FÖR SOPRAN
ELLER TENOR *CC19L
SVERIG SK 485 f.s.   (S1035)

SVENSK ROMANSSÅNG, DEL B: FÖR ALT ELLER
BAS *CC20L
SVERIG SK 486 f.s.   (S1036)

SVIK see Olsen, Sparre

SVOBODA, JIRÍ (1897-1970)
Manon, Op. 21
[Czech/Ger] Mez solo,pno PANTON 949
(S1037)
SVOBODA, TOMAS (1939-   )
Summer Fragments *Op.139
S solo,pno STANGLAND   (S1038)

SVORT ER EG... see Isolfsson, Pall

SWAN, A see Grieg, Edvard Hagerup

SWANWHITE see Schelle, Michael

SWATCHES see Anderson, Beth

SWAYNE, GILES (1946-   )
god-song
Mez solo,instrumental ensemble
NOVELLO f.s.   (S1039)

SWEEDEN, HANS VAN
Dead Pigeons Are Falling Around Me
see Dode Duiven Vallen Om Mij Heen

Dode Duiven Vallen Om Mij Heen
"Dead Pigeons Are Falling Around
Me" S/Mez solo,pno DONEMUS
(S1040)

SWEET CORK see Barry, Gerald

SWEET, LET ME GO see Walker, George
Theophilus

SWEET PASTORALE see Lyell, Margaret

SWEET WAS THE SONG THE VIRGIN SANG see
Anonymous

SWEETHEARTS see Meneely-Kyder, Sarah

SWIETY FRANCISZEK see Szymanowski,
Karol

SWING, THE see Menotti, Gian Carlo see
Mourant, Walter

SWING LOW, SWEET CHARIOT see Gospel
Favourites

SWISS GIRL, THE see Linley, George

SYDEMAN, WILLIAM J. (1928-   )
Full Circle
SAB soli,chamber group SEESAW f.s.
(S1041)
Malediction
T solo,string quar,electronic tape
SEESAW f.s.   (S1042)

SYLPHE, LE see Franck, Cesar see
Haxton, Kenneth

SYLVELIN see Sinding, Christian

SYLVIA see Speaks, Oley

SYMFONICKY DIPTYCH see Zamecnik, Evzen

SYMFONIE see Felix, Václav

SYMPHONIC REVELATION see Ishiketa,
Mareo

SYMPHONISCH GEDICHT (DE LEGENDE VAN HET
SOLSCHE GAT see Delft, Marc van

SYNERGO see Kruse, Bjørn Howard

SYNG see Albertsen, Per Hjort

SYNG, DET see Grieg, Edvard Hagerup

SYNG EN LITEN SANG see Sønstevold, Maj

SYNG FRJALSA LAND see Björnsson, Arni

SYNG MINE STRENGJER see Jordan, Sverre

SYNTAKS see Strömholm, Folke

SYNTAX see Strömholm, Folke, Syntaks

SYNTHIAS REVELLS: THREE SONGS see
     Parris, Robert

SYSTER, MIN SYSTER see Holm, Mogens
     Winkel

SYSTURNAR GODU see Helgason, Hallgrimur

SYV SANGER, OP. 3 see Kjeldaas, Arnljot

SYV SANGER, OP. 4 see Kvandal, Johan

SYV SANGER, OP. 18 see Kjeldaas,
     Arnljot

SYV WILDENVEY SANGER, OP. 24 see
     Kjeldaas, Arnljot

SZALONEK, WITOLD (1927-   )
     Herbstlied
        [Polish/Ger] Bar solo,harp,string
        orch [22'] MOECK 5417   (S1043)

SZULC, JOSEF ZYGMUNT (1875-1956)
     Dansons La Gigue *Op.83,No.6
        Bar solo,pno (text by Verlaine)
        CLASSV 1242   (S1044)

     En Sourdine *Op.83,No.9
        high solo,pno (text by Verlaine)
        CLASSV 1244   (S1045)

     Hantise D'Amour
        [Fr] high solo,pno CLASSV 1259
                                     (S1046)

     J'ai Peur D'un Baiser *Op.83,No.4
        high solo,pno (text by Verlaine)
        CLASSV 1241   (S1047)

     Lune Blanche, La *Op.83,No.8
        high solo,pno (text by Verlaine)
        CLASSV 1243   (S1048)

     Mandoline *Op.83,No.10
        S solo,pno (text by Verlaine)
        CLASSV 1245   (S1049)

SZYMANOWSKI, KAROL (1882-1937)
     Des Hafis Liebeslieder, Op. 24
        [Ger/Czech] high solo (not
        available outside U.S.A.) RECITAL
        403   (S1050)

     Kalinowe Dwory
        see Slopiewnie, Op. 47

     Piesni
        (Neuer, A.) "Songs" [Polish/Fr/Ger]
        solo voice,pno (contains: Op. 24,
        31, 32, 41, 42, 46bis, 48, 49,
        54, 58 and posth.) POLSKIE C11
                                     (S1051)

     Slopiewnie, Op. 47
        (Chylinska, T.) [Polish/Fr] solo
        voice,pno fac ed POLSKIE f.s.
        contains: Kalinowe Dwory,
        "Cranberry Manors"; Slowisien,
        "Wordseeds"; Swiety Franciszek,
        "St. Francis"; Wanda; Zielone
        Slowa, "Green Words"   (S1052)

     Slowisien
        see Slopiewnie, Op. 47

     Songs
        see Piesni

     Swiety Franciszek
        see Slopiewnie, Op. 47

     Wanda
        see Slopiewnie, Op. 47

     Zielone Slowa
        see Slopiewnie, Op. 47

     Zwölf Lieder, Op. 17
        [Ger/Czech] high solo (not
        available outside U.S.A.) RECITAL
        402   (S1053)

T

TAAIE WINTER, EEN see Bank, Jacques

TAAIE WINTER, EEN, NR. 2 see Bank,
     Jacques

TABLET OF 'ABDU'L-BAHAI see Thoresen,
     Lasse

TAESCH, R.
     I'll Tell You How The Sun Rose
        solo voice,2gtr (available in high,
        medium, or low voice) JELLO
        TGV102   (T1)

TAG MIT SEINEM LICHTE, DER see Gerlach,
     Günter

TAGAL FUGL see Volle, Bjarne see Volle,
     Bjarne

TAGELIED see Hall, Pauline

TAILLEFERRE, GERMAINE (1892-1983)
     Autre Jour En M'y Promenant, L'
        solo voice,fl,clar,vln,vla,vcl
        BILLAUDOT from CHANSONS DU
        FOLKLORE DE FRANCE   (T2)

     En Revenant De Nantes
        solo voice,fl,ob,clar,bsn,harp
        BILLAUDOT from CHANSONS DU
        FOLKLORE DE FRANCE   (T3)

     Jean De La Réole
        solo voice,fl,ob,clar,bsn,horn
        BILLAUDOT from CHANSONS DU
        FOLKLORE DE FRANCE   (T4)

     Mon Père Toujours Me Crie
        solo voice,fl,ob,clar,bsn,harp
        BILLAUDOT from CHANSONS DU
        FOLKLORE DE FRANCE   (T5)

     Nocture-Fox
        2Bar,1.0.0.1.soprano sax.alto sax.
        0.1.1.1. perc,harp,pno,cel,db
        [5'] BILLAUDOT from CHANSONS DU
        FOLKLORE DE FRANCE   (T6)

     Pernette Se Lève, La
        solo voice,fl,ob,clar,vln,vla,vcl
        BILLAUDOT from CHANSONS DU
        FOLKLORE DE FRANCE   (T7)

TAKAMI, TOSHIO (1916-   )
     Itsumademo
        B solo,pno [8'] JAPAN   (T8)

     Mizuiro No Beru
        S solo,pno [6'] JAPAN   (T9)

TAKATA, SABURO (1913-   )
     Songs, 50 *CCU
        solo voice ONGAKU 525020 f.s. (T10)

TAKE see Hayakawa, Kuzuko

TAKE AWAY MY HEART see Tchaikovsky,
     Piotr Ilyich

TAKE CARE OF THIS HOUSE see Bernstein,
     Leonard

TAKE ME, JESUS, TO THY BREAST see
     Macmillan, Alan

TAKE ME OUT TO THE BALL GAME, AND OTHER
     FAVORITE SONG HITS: 1906 - 1908
     *CC23U
        (Levy, Lester S.) solo voice BELWIN
        BKD002049 $5.95   (T11)

TAKE MNOU ZIJE AMERIKA! see Dvorácek,
     Jiri

TAKI, RENTARO
     Complete Album *CCU
        (Kocho, Hisako) solo voice ONGAKU
        525000 f.s.   (T12)

TAKK FOR DEN HEILAGE ANDE see Baden,
     Conrad

TAL, JOSEPH (1910-   )
     Bitter Line
        Bar solo,clar,bsn,horn,2vln,vcl,db
        [13'] ISR.MUS.INST. sc 6900, pno
        red 6900B   (T13)

     Wars Swept Through Here
        Bar solo,fl/pic,English horn,clar,
        tenor sax,horn,trp,trom,tuba,
        perc,pno,vla,vcl [10']
        ISR.MUS.INST. sc 6885, pno red
        6885B   (T14)

TAL, MARJO (1915-   )
     Acht Engelman-Liederen *CC8L
        med solo,pno DONEMUS f.s. [20']
                                     (T15)

     After Depriving Me
        see Sest' Pesen (Six Songs)

     Canciones Espanolas *CC7L
        med solo,pno DONEMUS f.s.   (T16)

     Cest Anelet Qui J'ai Ou Doy
        see Deux Rondeaux, Pris Dans Le
        Recueil "Tendre Et Dangereux"

     Chansons Les Plus Courtes..., Les
        see En Sourdine

     Coda
        see Tendre Et Dangereux

     Dear Friend
        see Sest' Pesen (Six Songs)

     Dear Friend, Don't You See
        see Sest' Pesen (Six Songs)

     Deux Rondeaux, Pris Dans Le Recueil
        "Tendre Et Dangereux"
        S solo,pno DONEMUS f.s. [5']
        contains: Cest Anelet Qui J'ai Ou
        Doy; Il Me Tarde Que Lundi
        Viengne   (T17)

     En Sourdine
        S solo,fl DONEMUS f.s. [12']
        contains: Chansons Les Plus
        Courtes..., Les; Hotels; Il
        Faut Travailler...; Pas Vu Ca;
        Sentiment De Solitude   (T18)

     Four Settings Of Irish Country Songs
        solo voice,fl/A rec,pno/hpsd,vcl/
        vla da gamba DONEMUS f.s. [14']
        contains: Gallows Tree, The;
        Roisin Dubh (2 Versions),
        "Little Black Rose (2
        Versions)"; Savoureen Deelish;
        Shule Agra   (T19)

     Four Songs
        see Tendre Et Dangereux

     Gallows Tree, The
        see Four Settings Of Irish Country
        Songs

     Hommage A Jacques Prevert
        see Tendre Et Dangereux

     Hotels
        see En Sourdine

     Il Faut Travailler...
        see En Sourdine

     Il Me Tarde Que Lundi Viengne
        see Deux Rondeaux, Pris Dans Le
        Recueil "Tendre Et Dangereux"

     Kindness To Horses
        see Sest' Pesen (Six Songs)

     Miniaturen, Cahier 4 (Solfeggio)
        *CCU
        solo voice,pno/inst DONEMUS f.s.
                                     (T20)

     Miniaturen, Cahier IV *CCU
        solo voice/ solo voices,pno/inst
        DONEMUS f.s.   (T21)

     Pas Vu Ca
        see En Sourdine

     Poet, The
        see Sest' Pesen (Six Songs)

     Reed Pipe, The
        see Sest' Pesen (Six Songs)

     Roisin Dubh (2 Versions)
        see Four Settings Of Irish Country
        Songs

     Savoureen Deelish
        see Four Settings Of Irish Country
        Songs

     Sentiment De Solitude
        see En Sourdine

     Sest' Pesen (Six Songs)
        low solo,pno DONEMUS f.s.
        contains: After Depriving Me;
        Dear Friend; Dear Friend, Don't
        You See; Kindness To Horses;
        Poet, The; Reed Pipe, The (T22)

     Shule Agra
        see Four Settings Of Irish Country
        Songs

     Tendre Et Dangereux
        med solo,pno DONEMUS f.s. [25']
        contains: Coda; Four Songs;
        Hommage A Jacques Prevert (T23)

TCHAIKOVSKY, PIOTR ILYICH (cont'd.)

Pourquoi?
  [Fr/Eng/Ger] high solo,pno CLASSV
  0441   (T87)

Scène De La Lettre (from Eugene
  Onegin)
  solo voice,1.1.1.1. 4.1.3.0. timp,
  harp pts,voc sc BOIS   (T88)

Scottish Ballad "Edward", Op. 46, No.
  2
  [Russ] SBar soli,pno CLASSV 1949
                                          (T89)

Seven Songs, Op. 47
  [Russ] solo voice,pno CLASSV 1954
                                          (T90)

  see Six Songs, Op. 28

Six French Songs, Op. 65
  [Fr/Russ] med solo,pno CLASSV 1693
                                          (T91)

Six Songs, Op. 6
  [Russ] solo voice,pno CLASSV 1938
                                          (T92)

Six Songs, Op. 16
  [Russ] solo voice,pno CLASSV 1940
                                          (T93)

Six Songs, Op. 25
  [Russ] solo voice,pno CLASSV 1943
                                          (T94)

Six Songs, Op. 27
  [Russ] solo voice,pno CLASSV 1944
                                          (T95)

Six Songs, Op. 28
  med solo,pno KALMUS K 06762 f.s.
  contains also: Six Songs, Op. 38;
  Seven Songs, Op. 47   (T96)
  [Russ] solo voice,pno CLASSV 1946
                                          (T97)

Six Songs, Op. 38
  [Russ] solo voice,pno CLASSV 1947
                                          (T98)

  see Six Songs, Op. 28

Six Songs, Op. 57
  [Russ] solo voice,pno CLASSV 1957
                                          (T99)

Six Songs, Op. 63
  [Russ] solo voice,pno CLASSV 1960
                                         (T100)

Six Songs, Op. 73
  [Russ] high solo,pno CLASSV 1961
                                         (T101)

Sixteen Children's Songs, Op. 54,
  Vol. 1
  [Russ] solo voice,pno CLASSV 1955
                                         (T102)

Sixteen Children's Songs, Op. 54,
  Vol. 2
  [Russ] solo voice,pno CLASSV 1956
                                         (T103)

Take Away My Heart
  [Russ] med solo,pno CLASSV 1941
                                         (T104)

Tears, Op. 46, No. 3
  [Russ] SMez soli,pno CLASSV 1950
                                         (T105)

Three Early Songs
  solo voice,pno CLASSV 1937 f.s.
  contains: Mezza Notte; My Genius;
  Zemphira's Song   (T106)

To Forget So Soon
  [Russ] med-high solo,pno CLASSV
  1939   (T107)

Twelve Songs, Op. 60, Vol. 1
  [Russ] solo voice,pno CLASSV 1958
                                         (T108)

Twelve Songs, Op. 60, Vol. 2
  [Russ] solo voice,pno CLASSV 1959
                                         (T109)

We Have Not Far To Walk
  [Russ] med-high solo,pno CLASSV
  1945   (T110)

Zemphira's Song
  see Three Early Songs

TCHEREPNIN, ALEXANDER (1899-1977)
  Russian Songs, Band 1
  PETERS 66155A   (T111)

  Russian Songs, Band 2
  PETERS 66155B   (T112)

  Russian Songs, Band 3
  PETERS 66155C   (T113)

  Russian Songs, Band 4
  PETERS 66155D   (T114)

TCIMPIDIS, DAVID
  Cycle Of Four Religious Songs, A
  S solo,pno WILLIS 11117 f.s. text
  adapted from "Divine Poems" of
  John Donne
  contains: Deliver Us; Hear Us,
  Lord; This Is My Play's Last
  Scene; Thou Hast Made Me (T115)

  Deliver Us
  see Cycle Of Four Religious Songs,
  A

TCIMPIDIS, DAVID (cont'd.)

  Hear Us, Lord
  see Cycle Of Four Religious Songs,
  A

  This Is My Play's Last Scene
  see Cycle Of Four Religious Songs,
  A

  Thou Hast Made Me
  see Cycle Of Four Religious Songs,
  A

TE KJAERASTEN MIN see Kielland, Olav

TE SOUVIENS-TU see Godard, Benjamin
  Louis Paul

TE VOGLIO BENE ASSIJE
  med-high solo,pno CLASSV 1912 (T116)

TEARDROP MILLIONAIRE, THE see Heilner,
  Irwin

TEARS AT THE HAPPY HOUR see Bolcom,
  William Elden

TEARS OF THE NIGHTINGALE see Gürsching,
  Albrecht, Nachtigallentränen

TEARS, OP. 46, NO. 3 see Tchaikovsky,
  Piotr Ilyich

TECOLOTE, EL see Revueltas, Silvestre

TEED, ROY (1928-   )
  Holy Thursday
  solo voice,pno ROBERTON   (T117)

TEFILOT SHEVA see Gottlieb, Jack S.

TEIRLINCK, GEO (1922-   )
  Viva Musica
  SCHOTT-FRER 9063   (T118)

TELEFONO, LO see Denza, Luigi

TELEMANN, GEORG PHILIPP (1681-1767)
  Evangelisches-Musikalisches Lieder-
  Buch
  OLMS   (T119)

  Moralische Kantaten *CCU
  [Ger/Eng] solo voice,cont DEUTSCHER
  DV 9508 f.s.   (T120)

  Zwo Geistliche Cantaten, So In
  Hamburg Als Daselbst Das Grosse
  Jubel-Fest
  2 solo voices,2vln,vla,vcl,hpsd
  SCHUBERTH,J   (T121)

TELEMARKIN see Tveitt, Geirr

TELEURGESTELD WACHTEN see Schouwman,
  Hans

TELFER, NANCY
  Jesus My Love My Joy
  S solo LESLIE f.s.
  contains: Resurgam; Silence;
  Virgin Mary To Christ On The
  Cross   (T122)

  Resurgam
  see Jesus My Love My Joy

  Silence
  see Jesus My Love My Joy

  Virgin Mary To Christ On The Cross
  see Jesus My Love My Joy

TELL ALL THE TRUTH see Haxton, Kenneth

TELL-TALE HEART, THE see Schneider,
  Gary M.

TEMPO DI MENUETTO see Broekman, Hans

TEMPO FUTURO, IL see Sampaoli, Luciano

TEMPORA NOCTIS see Nordheim, Arne

TEMPRO LA CETRA see Monteverdi, Claudio

TEN FAVORITE SONGS FROM THE OPERA
  T solo (CC10U) LYCHE 60   (T123)

TEN SOLO CANTATAS, VOL. 1 see Handel,
  George Frideric

TEN SOLO CANTATAS, VOL. 2 see Handel,
  George Frideric

TEN SONGS see Björnsson, Arni see
  Fairchild, Blair see Gibbs, Cecil
  Armstrong

TEN SONGS see Bizet, Georges

TEN SONGS FROM THE OPERETTA "I ALÖGUM"
  see Thordarson, Sigurdur

TEN STRINGS see Lewkovitch, Bernhard

TEN ZEN SONGS see Alkema, Henk

TENDRE ET DANGEREUX see Tal, Marjo

TENDREMENT see Satie, Erik

TENDRIL see Carlsen, Philip

TENEBRAE FACTAE SUNT see Nystedt, Knut

TENGDAMAEDURNAR see Sveinsson, Atli
  Heimir

TENNEY, JAMES C. (1934-   )
  Listen...!
  3A,pno SMITH PUB   (T124)

  Thirteen Ways Of Looking At A
  Blackbird
  B solo,alto fl,ob,vla,vcl,db SMITH
  PUB   (T125)

  Voice(S): Version 2
  solo voice/ solo voices,
  instrumental ensemble,electronic
  equipment SMITH PUB   (T126)

  Voices
  female solo,electronic equipment
  SMITH PUB   (T127)

TENNEY, MRS. JOHN FERGUSON
  see BRANSCOMBE, GENA

TENOR-ALBUM AUS DEM REPERTOIRE VON
  JULIUS PATZAK *CC16L
  (Werba, E.) DOBLINGER 08 502 f.s.
                                 (T128)

TENOR AND BARITONE see Wilson, Henry
  Lane

TENOR VOICE see Frissell

TEPPICHWEBER VON KUJAN-BULAK, DIE see
  Eisler, Hanns

TER VELDHUIS, JACOB
  see VELDHUIS, JACOB TER

TERASHIMA, NAOHIKO (1930-   )
  Monochrome
  S solo,pno [4'] JAPAN   (T129)

TERJE VIGEN see Guttormsen, Guttorm

TERZAKIS, DIMITRI (1938-   )
  Erotikon
  S solo,vln,clar,vcl [10']
  BREITKOPF-W f.s.   (T130)

  Ethos Gamma I
  Mez/Bar solo [2'] BREITKOPF-W
  BG 1185 f.s.   (T131)

  Ethos Gamma II
  low solo,fl,pno [6'] BREITKOPF-W
  BG 1277 f.s.   (T132)

  Raub Der Europa, Der
  S solo,1.1.1.1. 1.0.0.0. vibra,
  strings [15'] BREITKOPF-W f.s.
                                 (T133)

  Sappho Fragmente
  high solo,pno BREITKOPF-W BG 1349
  f.s.   (T134)

TERZETTE see Jadassohn, Solomon see
  Koch

TERZETTE FÜR 2 TENÖRE, BASS UND KLAVIER
  see Mozart, Wolfgang Amadeus

TES YEUX SONT DOUX see Ravel, Maurice,
  Shéhérazade: L'Indifférent

TESTA D'ADRIANE, LA see Schafer, R.
  Murray

TESTIMONIALS TO LIBERTY see Ployhar,
  James D., Editor

TESTIMONY see Dillard, Donald E.

TETCHE VODA Z PID JAVORA see Shut,
  Wasyl

TETRAPTIEK see Weegenhuise, Johan

TETT BAK DIN FOT see Madsen, Trygve

T'FILAH see Piket, Frederick

THAD ER LEIKUR AD LAERA see
  Halldorsson, Skuli

THAD KOM SONGFUGL AD SUNNAN see
  Halldorsson, Skuli

THAD VEX EITT BLOM FYRIR VESTAN see
  Thorarinsson, Jón

THAÏS: AH! JE SUIS FATIGUÉ...DIS-MOI
  QUE JE SUIS BELLE see Massenet,
  Jules

THAÏS: DUO DE L'OASIS see Massenet, Jules

THAL, DAS see Strauss, Richard

THAT WHICH IS see Fischer, Irwin

THAW see Nystedt, Knut, Isgangsvaer

THÉ, LE see Koechlin, Charles

[THE]MET AL POND see Larson, Martin

THEGAR THEIR JORDUDU JONGEIR see Halldorsson, Skuli

THEIR FUNDU HANN see Halldorsson, Skuli

THEME CELEBRE AVEC VARIATION see Proch, Heinrich

THEN THEY ROWED ON THE FJORD see Ørbeck, Anne Marie, So Rodde Dei Fjordan

THEODORA see Halldorsson, Skuli

THEODORAKIS, MIKIS (1925-   )
  Amour Et La Mort, L'
    [Fr/Greek] solo voice,strings sc
    DEUTSCHER DV 1143   (T135)

THERE ARE FAIRES AT THE BOTTOM OF OUR GARDEN see Lehmann, Liza

THERE ARE NO BIRDS SINGING see Jordan, Sverre, Der Synger Ingen Fugle

THERE ARE TWO MAYS see Ruiter, Wim de

THERE IN BLISSFUL SHADE: SERENATA see Handel, George Frideric

THERE IN BLISSFUL SHADES see Handel, George Frideric, Serenata

THERE IS A BALM IN GILEAD see Dawson, William Levi

THERE IS A GARDEN IN HER FACE see Herbert-Caesari, Edgard

THERE IS A GREEN HILL FAR AWAY see Gounod, Charles François

THERE IS A PLACE I RECOGNIZE see Bollen, Jan-Bas

THERE IS NO ROSE see Davies, Eiluned

THERE LIES A COUNTRY see Nordraak, Rikard, Der Ligger Et Land

THERE SHALL BE NO SORROW see Fischer, Irwin

THERE'S A REASON see Foster, Dan

THERE'S MUSIC see Vea, Ketil

THÉTIS see Rameau, Jean-Philippe

THEY ARE ALWAYS WITH ME see Corigliano, John

THEY CALL ME MIMI see Puccini, Giacomo, Mi Chiamano Mimi

THEY WISH THEY COULD KILL ME see Corigliano, John

THID SJAIST ALDREI FRAMAR see Isolfsson, Pall

THIELE, SIEGFRIED (1934-   )
  Nachtgesänge
    Bar solo,2vcl DEUTSCHER   (T136)

THIRD AND LAST BOOK OF SONGS see Jeffreys, John

THIRIET, MAURICE (1906-1972)
  Six Poèmes Lyriques Du Vieux Japon
    S solo,2.2.2.2. 2.0.0.0. timp,cel,
    harp,strings [12'45"] pno red,sc,
    pts BILLAUDOT   (T137)

THIRTEEN FOLKSONGS see Grainger, Percy Aldridge

THIRTEEN FOLKSONGS, VOL.1 see Grainger, Percy Aldridge

THIRTEEN FOLKSONGS, VOL.2 see Grainger, Percy Aldridge

THIRTEEN SONGS see Hoiby, Lee

THIRTEEN SONGS, VOL. 1 see Elgar, [Sir] Edward (William)

THIRTEEN SONGS, VOL. 2 see Elgar, [Sir] Edward (William)

THIRTEEN WAYS OF LOOKING AT A BLACKBIRD see Tenney, James C.

THIRTEEN YEARS see Jordan, Sverre, Tretton År

THIS BOOK OF HOURS see Griffes, Charles Tomlinson

THIS CITY MAKES ME WEEP see Carl, Robert

THIS DAY see Shapey, Ralph

THIS GLAD DAY see Sateren, Leland Bernhard

THIS HEART THAT BROKE see Samuel, Gerhard

THIS HEART THAT BROKE SO LONG... THREE SONGS ON POEMS BY EMILY DICKINSON see Samuel, Gerhard

THIS IS MY GOD see Piket, Frederick

THIS IS MY PLAYE'S LAST SCENE
  B solo,horn,trom/bass trom,vla,vcl,db
  [6'] (parts for each are for rent)
  sc APNM $4.00 from SONNETS FROM
  JOHN DONNE   (T138)

THIS IS MY PLAY'S LAST SCENE see Tcimpidis, David

THIS IS THE GARDEN see Bennett

THIS LAND OF WATER see Bisley, Brigid

THIS LITTLE PIG see Jeffreys, John

THIS MEMORY WHIRLS TOWARDS ME see Bollen, Jan-Bas

THIS MUCH I KNOW see Levi, Paul Alan

THIS PARTRIDGE see Clarke, Henry Leland

THIS WAY TO WINTER see Mourant, Walter

THISTLE, YARROW, CLOVER see Weigl, [Mrs.] Vally

THOMAS, AMBROISE (1811-1896)
  Caid, Le: Tambour Major
    B solo,pno CLASSV 0373   (T139)

  Comme Une Pâle Fleur
    see Hamlet: Arioso

  Hamlet: Arioso
    "Comme Une Pâle Fleur" [Fr] Bar
    solo,pno CLASSV 0363   (T140)

  Hamlet: Drinking Song
    "O Vin, Dissipe La Tristesse" Bar
    solo,pno CLASSV 0361   (T141)

  Hamlet: Ophelia's Mad Scene
    S solo,pno CLASSV 0374   (T142)

  I Am Titania (from Mignon)
    [Fr/Eng] S/Mez solo,pno UNITED MUS
    f.s.   (T143)

  Knowest Thou (from Mignon)
    [Fr/Eng] S/Mez/A solo,pno UNITED
    MUS f.s.   (T144)

  Me Voici Dans
    see Mignon: Frederick's Gavotte

  Mignon: Connais-Tu Le Pays?
    A solo,pno CLASSV 0629   (T145)
    Mez solo,pno CLASSV 0410   (T146)
    S solo,pno CLASSV 1276   (T147)

  Mignon: De Son Coeur J'ai Calmé La
    Fièvre
    B solo,pno CLASSV 1567   (T148)

  Mignon: Elle Ne Croyait Pas
    T solo,pno CLASSV 1536   (T149)

  Mignon: Frederick's Gavotte
    "Me Voici Dans" A solo,pno CLASSV
    0420   (T150)

  Mignon: Je Suis Titania
    S solo,pno CLASSV 0356   (T151)

  Mignon: Légères Hirondelles
    MezBar soli,pno CLASSV 0453 (T152)

  Mignon: Romanze
    Mez solo,pno SCIEN 1727   (T153)

  O Vin, Dissipe La Tristesse
    see Hamlet: Drinking Song

THOMAS, ANDREW (1939-   )
  Four
    Mez solo,pno [10'] sc AM.COMP.AL.
    $15.30   (T154)

THOMAS, ANDREW (cont'd.)

  From The Bat Poet
    S solo, sax quartet [10'] sc
    AM.COMP.AL. $20.30   (T155)

  Seven Songs *CC7U
    Mez solo,perc,vln,pno sc
    AM.COMP.AL. $24.45   (T156)

  Twelve Points Of The Modified
    Mercalli Scale, The
    S solo,2.2.2.2. 2.2.2.0. pno,harp,
    3perc,strings,electronic tape
    [20'] sc AM.COMP.AL. $55.05
                             (T157)

THOMAS CESUS see Anonymous, Thomas Gemma Cantuarie

THOMAS GEMMA CANTUARIE see Anonymous

THOME, DIANE
  Lucent Flowers
    S solo,1.1.1.1. 1.1.1.0. timp,harp,
    string quar [15'] AM.COMP.AL.
                             (T158)

THOMMESSEN, OLAV ANTON (1946-   )
  Echo Of An Echo
    Mez solo,fl,pno,perc [13'] NORGE
                             (T159)

  Gnostic Fragments: A Musical
    Reconstruction
    Mez solo,fl,vln,vcl,pno NORGE f.s.
                             (T160)

  Gratias Agimus: A Song For Peace
    S solo,pno NORGE   (T161)

  Vaevet Af Staengler: A Symphonic Song
    [Norw] S solo,strings [23'] NORGE
                             (T162)

THOMMESSEN, REIDAR (1889-1986)
  Fille Aux Fleurs, La
    [Fr] solo voice,pno MUSIKK (T163)

  Midsummer Night
    solo voice,pno NORSK NMO 9609 f.s.
                             (T164)

  Min Verden
    [Norw] solo voice,pno MUSIKK (T165)

  Når Stjernene Tennes
    [Norw/Eng] solo voice,pno NORSK
                             (T166)

THOMPSON, BRUCE A.
  Seven Epitaphs
    med solo,horn,vcl,pno THOM ED MB1
                             (T167)

THOMPSON-LIEDEREN see Amerongen, Jan van

THOMSON, VIRGIL GARNETT (1896-1989)
  Collected Poems
    SBar soli,chamber orch PEER
    60201-210 pno red $6.00, set rent
                             (T168)
    SBar soli,1.1.1.1. 0.0.1.0. perc,
    pno,strings [7'0"] PEER   (T169)

  Courtship Of The Yongly Bongly Bo
    SCHIRM.G ST47522   (T170)

  Five Songs From William Blake
    Bar solo,2(pic).2.2.2. 4.2.3.1.
    timp,perc,harp,strings [17'0"]
    PEER   (T171)
    Bar solo,2.2.2.2. 2.1.1.0. timp,
    perc,harp,strings [17'0"] PEER
                             (T172)

  Five Tenor Solos From The Opera "Lord
    Byron"
    T solo,2.2.2.2. 4.2.3.1. timp,perc,
    strings [7'30"] PEER   (T173)

  Shakespeare Songs I (H), Pno *CCU
    sc PEER 61103-212 $5.00   (T174)

  Shipwreck And Love Scene From Byron's
    "Don Juan"
    T solo,4(pic).4(English
    horn).4(bass clar).4. 4.4.4.1.
    2perc,harp,pno,strings [14'0"]
    PEER   (T175)

THORA see Adams, S.

THORARINSSON, JÓN (1917-   )
  Minni Prentlistarinnar
    solo voice,pno ICELAND 013-025
                             (T176)

  Of Love And Death
    Bar solo,pno (text by C.G.
    Rossetti) ICELAND 013-009 (T177)

  Thad Vex Eitt Blom Fyrir Vestan
    solo voice,pno [2'10"] ICELAND
    013-018   (T178)

  Three Songs
    solo voice,1.1.1.1. 1.1.0.0. cel,
    timp,perc,strings ICELAND 013-900
                             (T179)

  Two Songs
    S solo,pno [4'50"] ICELAND 013-017
                             (T180)
    solo voice,pno ICELAND 013-020
                             (T181)

THORARINSSON, JÓN (cont'd.)

S solo,pno [4'7"] ICELAND 013-003
(T182)

Vögguvisa
solo voice,pno ICELAND 013-022 (T183)

Vorvisa
solo voice,pno ICELAND 013-023
(T184)

When I Am Dead
solo voice,pno (text by C.G.
Rossetti) ICELAND 013-024 (T185)

THORARINSSON, LEIFUR (1934-   )
Dalvisur
solo voice,pno ICELAND 017-058 (T186)

Kastrup Lufthavn
T solo,pno ICELAND 017-062 (T187)
solo voice,pno ICELAND 017-019
(T188)

1993
solo voice,pno [5'0"] ICELAND
017-061 (T189)

Old Song
solo voice,pno [7'0"] ICELAND
017-060 (T190)

Saud Thid Hana Systur Mina
solo voice,pno ICELAND 017-057
(T191)

Two Songs
solo voice,pno [3'0"] ICELAND
017-023 (T192)
B solo,pno [6'0"] ICELAND 017-059
(T193)

Two Songs From "Leggur Og Skel"
solo voice,pno ICELAND 017-900 (T194)

THORDARSON, HILMAR (1960-   )
Samkennd
S solo,pno ICELAND 067-010 (T195)

THORDARSON, SIGURDUR (1895-1969)
Berceuse
solo voice,pno ICELAND 026-019 (T196)

Fimm Sönglög
solo voice,pno ICELAND 026-007
(T197)

I Lundi Ljods Og Hljoma
solo voice,pno ICELAND 026-025 (T198)

Lour I Akri
solo voice,pno ICELAND 026-020 (T199)

Nordur
solo voice,pno ICELAND 026-027
(T200)

Sjo Einsongslog
solo voice,pno ICELAND 026-009
(T201)

Slattuvisa
solo voice,pno ICELAND 026-029
(T202)

Ten Songs From The Operetta "I
Alögum"
solo voice,pno ICELAND 026-010
(T203)

Three Songs
solo voice,pno ICELAND 026-018
(T204)

Vogguljod
solo voice,pno ICELAND 026-011
(T205)

THORESEN, LASSE (1949-   )
Guds Port
[Norw] solo voice,pno NORGE (T206)

O, Du Som Er Vårt Liv Og Lys
solo voice NORGE (T207)

Sjå Gud
[Norw] solo voice,pno NORGE (T208)

Tablet Of 'Abdu'l-Bahai
[Eng] solo voice NORGE (T209)

To Danser
S solo,clar,vln,vibra,marimba [14']
NORGE (T210)

Vår
[Norw] solo voice,pno NORGE (T211)

THORKELSDOTTIR, MIST (1960-   )
Dance
solo voice,gtr [13'0"] ICELAND
048-002 (T212)

THORN, A see Grahn, Ulf

THORNE, FRANCIS BURRITT (1922-   )
Nature Studies
Mez solo,fl,harp [16'] AM.COMP.AL.
sc $10.30, pts $12.25 (T213)

THORNTON
Solomon Songs
solo voice,pno SOUTHERN V082 (T214)

THORODDSEN, EMIL (1898-   )
Abschied
solo voice,pno ICELAND 024-010
(T215)

Hatidasongvar Sjomannadagsins
solo voice,pno ICELAND 024-005
(T216)

Voggukvaedi
solo voice,pno ICELAND 024-006
(T217)
(Thorarinsson, Jon) solo voice,
1.1.1.1. 0.0.0.0. strings ICELAND
024-013 (T218)

Wiegenlied
solo voice,pno ICELAND 024-011
(T219)

THOU ART AS TYRANNOUS, SO AS THOU ART
see Andriessen, Jurriaan

THOU HAST MADE ME see Tcimpidis, David

THOU MAY'ST LOVE see Price, Marion
James

THOU SOFT FLOWING AVON see Arne, Thomas
Augustine

THOU WHO WITH ICE see Puccini, Giacomo,
Turandot: Tu Che Di Gel

THOUGH GOING AND COMING see Roo, Paul
de

THOUGH LOVE BE A DAY see Walker,
Gwyneth

THOUGH MEN CALL US FREE see Schmidt,
Sharon Yvonne Davis

...THOUGH WHAT MADE IT HAS GONE... see
Wallin, Rolf

THOUSAND VOICES IN THOUSAND HEARTS see
Ishiketa, Mareo

THRATEFLI see Helgason, Hallgrimur

THREE ANCIENT SONGS see Leifs, Jon

THREE ANGEL POEMS see Brown, Francis
James

THREE ARIAS see Wright, Maurice

THREE BILLY-GOATS GRUSE, THE see
Mowinckel, Johan Ludvig, Tre
Bukkene Bruse, De

THREE BYRON SONGS see White

THREE CALAMUS POEMS see Rorem, Ned

THREE CELEBRATED WALTZES
[Eng/Fr] solo voice,pno SCIEN 1730
f.s.
contains: Hungarian Air; Lieber
Augustin; Tyrolian Air (T220)

THREE CHILDREN'S SONGS see Prokofiev,
Serge

THREE CHILDREN'S SONGS, OP. 68 see
Prokofiev, Serge

THREE CHRISTMAS PSALMS see Kvandal,
Johan

THREE CHRISTMAS SONGS see Humperdinck,
Engelbert, Drei Weihnachtslieder

THREE CILLA MCQUEEN SONGS see Farquhar,
David

THREE CONTRALTO SONGS see Erickson,
Robert

THREE CRADLE SONGS see Sims, Ezra

THREE DEVOTIONAL MINIATURES see Fink

THREE DICKINSON SONGS see Lindenfeld,
Harris Nelson

THREE DONALD HALL SONGS see Bolcom,
William Elden

THREE DREAMS see Schober, Brian

THREE EARLY SONGS see Pleskow, Raoul
see Tchaikovsky, Piotr Ilyich

THREE EASY ROUNDS (3:4VOCI), ACAP see
Weigl, [Mrs.] Vally

THREE EDDA SONGS see Leifs, Jon

THREE EMILY DICKINSON SONGS see Butler,
Martin

THREE EMILY DICKINSON SONGS see
Langert, Jules

THREE ENGLISH FOLK-SONGS see Brown,
Francis James

THREE FABLES OF STEPHEN CRANE see
Schmidt, Sharon Yvonne Davis

THREE FACES OF LOVE see Horvit, Michael
M.

THREE FOR EMILY see Cohen, Fred

THREE FRENCH SONGS FROM THE LATE
FOURTEENTH CENTURY
(Wilkins, Nigel) 2-4 solo voices,opt
inst ANTICO AE7 (T221)

THREE GERMAN FOLKSONGS see Grahn, Ulf

THREE HEBREW PSALMS see Flender,
Reinhard David, Pirkei Tehillim

THREE HEBREW SONGS see Shapero, Harold
Samuel

THREE HOPKINS SONGS see Edwards, George

THREE IMPROVISATIONS see Tipei, Sever

THREE INDIAN SONGS, OP.32 see Farwell,
Arthur

THREE IRISH FOLKSONG SETTINGS see
Corigliano, John

THREE IRISH SONGS see Bolcom, William
Elden

THREE KNOTS see Pollock, Robert Emil

THREE LITTLE FAIRY SONGS see Besly,
Maurice

THREE LOVE SONGS see Palsson, Pall P.

THREE LOVE SONGS see Parris, Robert

THREE LULLABIES see Field, Corey

THREE LULLABIES see Plante, Daniel

THREE MADRIGALS see Bartolino da Padova
see Jacopo da Bologna

THREE METIS SONGS see Forsyth,
Josephine

THREE MOODS OF EMILY DICKINSON see
Schmidt, Sharon Yvonne Davis

THREE MOTETS IN HONOUR OF GASTON FEBUS
(Lefferts, Peter) 3-4 solo voices
ANTICO AE23 (T222)

THREE MYSTICAL SONGS see Tremain,
Ronald

THREE NONSENSE SONGS see Drakeford,
Richard

THREE NUMBERS FROM THE EARLY TWENTIES
see Clarke, Henry Leland

THREE ODEN see Weigl, Karl

THREE ORKNEY SONGS see Wilson, Thomas

THREE ORNAMENTED ARIAS see Handel,
George Frideric

THREE PATTERSON LYRICS see Smith, Hale

THREE PIECE SONG CYCLE see Warren,
Betsy

THREE POEMS see Butterworth, Neil see
Chance, Nancy Laird see Hattori,
Kazuhiko

THREE POEMS see Steiner, Gitta Hana

THREE POEMS BY BASHO see Evensen,
Kristian

THREE POEMS BY CZESLAW MILOSZ see
Palester, Roman, Trzy Wiersze
Czeslawa Milosza

THREE POEMS BY STEPHEN CRANE see
Greeson

THREE POEMS IN FRENCH see Kim, Earl

THREE POEMS OF AI QING see MacBride,
David Huston

THREE POEMS OF EMILY DICKINSON see
Eckert, Michael

THREE POEMS OF KENNETH REXROTH see
Olan, David

THREE POEMS OF OSIP MANDELSTAM see
Firsova, Elena

THREE POEMS OF WILLIAM BLAKE see
Schmidt, Sharon Yvonne Davis

THREE PSALM FRAGMENTS see Stokes, Harvey J.

THREE PSALMS see Roseman, Ronald

THREE PSALMS (34, 140, 238) see Honegger, Arthur

THREE RILKE SONGS see Moss, Lawrence Kenneth

THREE ROMANCES see Shut, Wasyl

THREE ROMANCES see Shut, Wasyl

THREE ROMANCES, OP. 73 see Prokofiev, Serge

THREE SACRED SONGS see Primosch, James

THREE SACRED SONGS see Warren, Betsy

THREE SAGA SONGS see Leifs, Jon

THREE SAMPLERS FROM THE NEWARK MUSEUM see Brown, Francis James

THREE SCENES see Rhodes, Phillip

THREE SCOTTISH NURSERY RHYMES see Young, Douglas

THREE SELECTED POEMS, OP. 79 see Hemberg, Eskil

THREE SERIOUS SONGS see Willingham, Lawrence

THREE SHAKESPEARE SONGS see Speight, John A. see Vaughan Williams, Ralph

THREE SHAKESPEARE SONGS (VERSION 2) see Speight, John A.

THREE SHAKESPEARE SONNETS see Kleiberg, Ståle see Norby, Erik

THREE SOLO CANTATAS see Kvandal, Johan

THREE SONGS see Bax, [Sir] Arnold see Bridge, Frank see Canning, Thomas see Halldorsson, Skuli see Hardarson, Arni see Hawley, Charles Beach see Kaldalóns, Sigvaldi S. see Leifs, Jon see Lilburn, Douglas see McDonald, Harl see Marks, James see Niikura, Ken see Sigfusson, Steingrimur see Speight, John A. see Stewart, Robert see Sveinsson, Atli Heimir see Thorarinsson, Jón see Thordarson, Sigurdur see Tillis, Frederick C. see Turok, Paul Harris see Vaughan

THREE SONGS [1] see Cohen, Edward

THREE SONGS [2] see Cohen, Edward

THREE SONGS see Bailey, Marshall

THREE SONGS see Brown, Francis James

THREE SONGS see Suben, Joel Eric

THREE SONGS see Golub, Peter

THREE SONGS see Pisk, Paul Amadeus

THREE SONGS see Winslow, Walter

THREE SONGS see Altena, Maarten

THREE SONGS see Herbert-Caesari, Edgard

THREE SONGS see Turok, Paul Harris

THREE SONGS see Bialosky, Marshall H.

THREE SONGS see Steiner, Gitta Hana

THREE SONGS see Ogdon, Wilbur L.

THREE SONGS see Shifrin, Seymour J.

THREE SONGS see Weiss, Herman

THREE SONGS see Zahler, Noel Barry

THREE SONGS see Fladmoe, Arvid

THREE SONGS see Fabricius, Jacob

THREE SONGS see Shut, Wasyl

THREE SONGS AFTER RILKE see Lindenfeld, Harris Nelson

THREE SONGS BY STEPHEN FOSTER see Foster, Stephen Collins

THREE SONGS FOR CHILDREN, FROM SHIGEKO MIYATA'S POEM see Suzuki, Satoshi

THREE SONGS FOR HIGH VOICE see Duke

THREE SONGS FOR ST. CECILIA'S DAY see Lessard, John Ayres

THREE SONGS FOR SOPRANO AND SMALL ORCHESTRA see Luening, Otto

THREE SONGS FOR SOPRANO AND STRINGS see Weber, Ben Brian

THREE SONGS FOR TENOR see Duke

THREE SONGS FOR TRES VOCES see Walker, Gwyneth

THREE SONGS FROM ANTIGONE see Merryman, Marjorie

THREE SONGS FROM CHAMBER MUSIC see Rinehart, John

THREE SONGS FROM EL BARRIO see Ortiz, William

THREE SONGS FROM LONG ISLAND see Rausch, Carlos

THREE SONGS FROM MEDIEVAL JAPAN see Massumoto, Kikuko

THREE SONGS FROM OP. 18 (TO WINE & BEAUTY) see Quilter, Roger

THREE SONGS FROM PEER GYNT, OP.23 see Grieg, Edvard Hagerup

THREE SONGS FROM POE see Roosevelt, [Joseph] Willard

THREE SONGS FROM THE CHINESE see Eckert, Michael

THREE SONGS FROM THE GHETTO see Kingsley, Gershon Gary

THREE SONGS OF CHRIST
[Span/Eng] med solo,org (med easy) UNIVERSE (T223)
(Busch, Douglas E.) [Eng/Span] med solo,org (CC3U) UNIVERSE (T224)
(Busch, Douglas E.) med solo,org (med easy) UNIVERSE 491-00392 (T225)

THREE SONGS OF DEATH see Chapiro, Fania

THREE SONGS OF ELLEN, OP. 106 see Koetsier, Jan

THREE SONGS OF EMILY DICKINSON see Leichtling, Alan

THREE SONGS OF SLEEP AND LOVE see Veeneman, Curt

THREE SONGS OF SPAIN see Surinach, Carlos

THREE SONGS OF THE KING see Orbon, Julian, Tres Cantigas Del Rey

THREE SONGS OF THE SEA, OP. 1 see Quilter, Roger

THREE SONGS OF WILLIAM BLAKE, OP. 20 see Quilter, Roger

THREE SONGS ON POEMS OF ELINOR WYLIE see Woollen, Russell

THREE SONGS ON TEXTS BY ALICE VERY see Bevelander, Brian

THREE SONGS ON TEXTS BY HILDA MORLEY see Bevelander, Brian

THREE SONGS, OP. 28 see Kopylov, Alexander Alexandrovich

THREE SONGS, OP. 45 see Barber, Samuel

THREE SONGS, OP. 54 see Norholm, Ib

THREE SONGS, OP. 63 see Lunde, Ivar

THREE SONGS, OP. 75 see Norholm, Ib

THREE SONGS TO POEMS BY PAAL BREKKE see Mortensen, Finn, Greners Tyngde

THREE SONGS TO RADNOTI POEMS see Soproni, Jozsef

THREE SONGS TO WORDS BY F. T. CSOKOR see Reiner, Karel

THREE SONNETS see Ketting, Piet

THREE SONNETS see Steinke, Greg A.

THREE SONNETS FROM THE PORTUGUESE see Pasatieri, Thomas

THREE SONNETS OF WILLIAM SHAKESPEARE see Horvit, Michael M.

THREE SPANISH SONGS see Wallach, Joelle

THREE SUMMER'S HEAT see Shatin, Judith

THREE SYMPHONIC SPIRITUALS see Tillis, Frederick C.

THREE TREES see Hilliard, John

THREE VARIATIONS see Gerschefski, Edwin

THREE VILLENALLES see Nadelson, Andrew

THREE VOICES: LIGHTNING, PEACE, GRASS see O'Leary, Jane

THREE WHITMAN SONGS see Vaughan Williams, Ralph see Wallach, Joelle

THREE WINTERSONGS see Schoonenbeek, Kees

THRIR SÖNGVAR UR PETRI GAUT see Ragnarsson, Hjalmar H.

THRIR VALSAR see Halldorsson, Skuli

THRJU SONGLOG see Björnsson, Arni see Runolfsson, Karl Otto

THROUGH THE CENTURIES see Dring, Madeleine

THROUGH THE EDGE see Mygatt, Louise

THROUGH THE LOOKING GLASS see Veyvoda, Gerald Joseph

...THROUGH THE SILENCE see Pope, Conrad

THROUGH THE SILENT NIGHT see Rachmaninoff, Sergey Vassilievich

THU BLAFJALLA GEIMUR see Helgason, Hallgrimur

THU EINA HJARTANS YNDID MITT see Kaldalóns, Sigvaldi S.

THU HRYGGIR MIG, GLEDI see Björnsson, Arni

THUILLE, LUDWIG (WILHELM ANDREAS MARIA) (1861-1907)
Drei Frauenlieder, Op. 5 see Fünf Lieder, Op. 4

Fünf Lieder, Op. 4
[Ger] RECITAL 406 f.s. contains also: Drei Frauenlieder, Op. 5 (T226)
Von Lieb Und Leid, Op. 7 *song cycle [Ger] high solo (poems by Karl Stieler) RECITAL 298 (T227)

THWAITES, PENELOPE
Forestry
med solo,pno BARDIC BE0158 (T228)

Reverie
med solo,pno BARDIC BE0159 (T229)

THY BEAMING EYES see MacDowell, Edward Alexander

THY BEAUTY see Beach, [Mrs.] H.H.A. (Amy Marcy Cheney)

THY BLACK IS FAIREST (3 SHAKESPEARE SONNETS) see Andriessen, Jurriaan

THY LIPS ON MINE see Rowland, David

TI FOLKETONER *CC10L,folk song (Kjellsby, Erling) LYCHE 440 f.s. (T230)

TI SALMER, OP.78 see Johnsen, Hallvard

TI SALMETONER, OP.5, NO.1 see Karlsen, Kjell Mørk

TI SONGAR (TEN SONGS) see Grieg, Edvard Hagerup

TICHE PISNE see Fischer, Eduard

TIDEN OCH EN FLICKA see Forsell, Jonas

TIEFE KÄMMERLEIN, DAS see Backer-Lunde, Johan

TIEN VOCALE MINUTEN see Ruiter, Wim de

TIERLIEDER OP. 39 see Dressel, Erwin

TIERRA QUE ERA MIA, LA see Bianchini, Riccardo

TIGER, THE see Brown, Francis James

TIGIDA PIPA see Montague, Stephen

TIL BERGMANNEN see Olsen, Sparre

TIL DEG see Siem, Kare see Volle, Bjarne

TIL DEN LILLE FUGL see Fongaard, Bjørn

TIL ELISE MERETE see Lerstad, Terje B.

TIL ELSKUNNAR see Halldorsson, Skuli

TIL EN GAMMEL KIRKE see Eggen, Arne

TIL ET BARN see Jordan, Sverre

TIL KONGEN see Egge, Klaus see Jensen, Ludwig Irgens

TIL MARIU see Sveinsson, Gunnar Reynir

TIL MIN GYLLENLAKK see Groven, Eivind see Olsen, Sparre

TIL MINDE see Akerwall, Martin

TIL NAETURINNAR see Kaldalóns, Sigvaldi S.

TIL NORGE see Grieg, Edvard Hagerup

TIL ROSARINNAR see Halldorsson, Skuli

TIL SÖNGSINS see Stefansson, Finnur Torfi

TIL TELEMORK see Kielland, Olav

TILFELLET JANICE: FRA EN SYKEJOURNAL see Germeten, Gunnar

TILGI, MEG JESUS see Karlsen, Kjell Mørk

TILL NÅGON SOM ÄR MYCKET UNG see Wallgren, Jan

TILLEUL, LE see Schubert, Franz (Peter), Lindenbaum

TILLIS, FREDERICK C. (1930-   )
  Four Songs *CC4U
    S solo,pno sc AM.COMP.AL. $6.55
                                    (T231)

  Music For An Experimental Lab
      Ensemble, No. 2
    med solo,fl,2trp.pno [2'] sc
    AM.COMP.AL. $5.00   (T232)

  Reflections
    S/T solo,pno [7'] sc AM.COMP.AL.
    $9.15   (T233)

  Spiritual Cycle *song cycle
    S solo,2.2.2.2. 4.3.3.1. timp,
    2perc,strings [15'] sc
    AM.COMP.AL. $32.20   (T234)

  Three Songs (from "Shadows And
      Distance Nowhere")
    [6'] AM.COMP.AL.   (T235)

  Three Symphonic Spirituals *CC3U
    med solo,2.2.2.2. 2.2.2.1. cel,
    timp,perc,strings sc AM.COMP.AL.
    $18.40   (T236)

  Two Songs [1] *CC2U
    Bar/med solo,pno sc AM.COMP.AL.
    $9.15   (T237)

  Two Songs [2] *CC2U
    S solo,pno sc AM.COMP.AL. $7.70
                                    (T238)

TILO SIN FLOR, EL see Schubert, Franz (Peter)

TILVONANDI REIDHROSS see Sveinsson, Atli Heimir

TIME see Even-Or, Mary

TIME EXCURSIONS see Fox, Frederick Alfred (Fred)

TIME LAG ZERO see Dillon

TIME, STAY AWHILE see Osawa, Kazuko

TIME TO RISE see Mourant, Walter

TIMES ARE NIGHTFALL, THE see Haxton, Kenneth

TINC ENVEJA DEL MATÍ see Fluvia, A.

TIO JAPANSKA ROMANSER see Karkoff, Maurice

TIO NAIVA SÅNGER see Linde, Bo

TIO SMÅ ANDLIGA SÅNGER see Janácek, Bedrich

TIPEI, SEVER (1943-   )
  Ezra Pound's Canto CXVI
    Bar solo,pno [12'] sc AM.COMP.AL.
    $6.15   (T239)

TIPEI, SEVER (cont'd.)

  Melopoeia
    S solo [14'] sc AM.COMP.AL. $6.85
                                    (T240)

  Single Tone
    any 5 voices and-or instruments
    [5'] sc AM.COMP.AL. $1.90   (T241)

  Three Improvisations *CC3U
    2-6voices and-or instruments incl.
    sop., perc sc AM.COMP.AL. $11.80
                                    (T242)

  Undulating Michigamme
    S solo,3.3.3.3. 4.3.3.2. pipe,
    2harp,4perc,2pno,strings [28'] sc
    AM.COMP.AL. $38.00   (T243)

TIPPETT, [SIR] MICHAEL (1905-   )
  Boyhood's End
    (Tillett, Michael) Bar solo,pno
    SCHOTT ED 12331   (T244)

TIPSY SONG see Offenbach, Jacques, Périchole, La: Ah! Quel Diner

TIRINDELLI, PIER ADOLFO (1858-1937)
  Di Te!...
    T solo,pno CLASSV 0841   (T245)

  Mistica
    med-high solo,pno,vln/vcl CLASSV
    0802   (T246)

  O Primavera
    high solo,pno CLASSV 0351   (T247)

TIRITOMBA
  "Sera Jette" high solo,pno CLASSV
  1505   (T248)

'TIS SAD TO PART see Herz, Henri

TISE see Kalach, Jiri

TISNE, ANTOINE (1932-   )
  Passage
    S solo,string orch [18'] BILLAUDOT
                                    (T249)
    S solo,string orch BILLAUDOT perf
    mat rent   (T250)

TITL, ANTON EMIL (1809-1882)
  Brunnengeplätscher, Op. 34
    solo voice,pno SCIEN 1731   (T251)

TIU LÖG see Franzson, Björn

TIU SONGLOG see Halldorsson, Sigfus

TJERE WAS A CROOKED MAN see Jeffreys, John

TO A CHILD DANCING IN THE WIND see Cacioppo, Curt see Haxton, Kenneth

TO ADVENTSALMER see Nyhus, Rolf

TO AN OLD CHURCH see Eggen, Arne, Til En Gammel Kirke

TO BED, TO BED see Jeffreys, John

TO BIBELSKE SANGE see Koppel, Herman David

TO BIBELSKE SANGER see Nyhus, Rolf

TO BIBELSKE SANGER, OP. 104 see Baden, Conrad

TO BLOSSOMS see Foote, Arthur

TO DANSER see Thoresen, Lasse

TO DIKT see Brustad, Karsten

TO E E see Roosevelt, [Joseph] Willard

TO ELECTRA see Torphicen, Pamela see Willan, Healey

TO FABLER see Jensen, Ludwig Irgens

TO FAIR FIDELE'S GRASSY TOMB see Arne, Thomas Augustine

TO FORGET SO SOON see Tchaikovsky, Piotr Ilyich

TO FRÖDING-SANGER: MIN STJÄRNAS SONGER see Kvandal, Johan

TO FRÖDING-SANGER, OP.96 see Baden, Conrad

TO HAMSUN-SANGER, OP. 26 see Sommerfeldt, Öistein

TO HIS IMAGINARY MISTRESS see Adolphe, Bruce

TO HIS WIFE see Heilner, Irwin

TO JOHANNA: ASLEEP AFTER OUR BATTLE FOR YOU see Evensen, Bernt Kasberg

TO JULIA see Quilter, Roger

TO JULIA (SIX LYRICS OF R. HERRICK) see Quilter, Roger

TO MARGARITA DEBAYLE see Lockwood, Normand

TO MOTETTER see Nystedt, Knut

TO MOTHER see Shut, Wasyl, Mami

TO MUSIQUE, TO BECALME HIS FEVER see Douw, Andre

TO ONE UNKNOWN see Carpenter, John Alden

TO PLAY TO DAY see Christiansen, Henning

TO RELIGIØSE FOLKETONER see Tøsse, Eilert

TO RELIGIØSE SANGER see Kvandal, Johan

TO RILKE SANGE see Norby, Erik

TO ROBERT GRAVES see Larson, Martin

TO SALMER see Okkenhaug, Ingrid Buran

TO SALMER, OP. 6 see Kielland, Olav

TO SANGER see Nyhus, Rolf

TO SANGER see Olsen, Sparre

TO SANGER see Sommerfeldt, Öistein

TO SANGER see Ørbeck, Anne Marie

TO SANGER see Nyhus, Rolf

TO SANGER, OP. 4 see Hall, Pauline

TO SANGER, OP. 9 see Kjeldaas, Arnljot

TO SANGER, OP. 30 see Kjeldaas, Arnljot

TO SOLOMOTETTER see Karlsen, Kjell Mørk

TO STEV see Baden, Conrad

TO TEKSTER FRA SPÅRVAGNSLEKTYR AV JOHANNA SCHWARZ see Mostad, Jon

TO THE CHILDREN see Rachmaninoff, Sergey Vassilievich

TO THE DISTANT BELOVED see Beethoven, Ludwig van, An Die Ferne Geliebte

TO THE EAST AND TO THE WEST see Van de Vate, Nancy Hayes

TO THE EXECUTION PLACE see Rowland, David

TO THE FABLED PRINCESS see Morita, Shin-Ichi

TO THE GUITARISTS see Heilner, Irwin

TO THE LIGHTHOUSE see Bavicchi, John Alexander

TO THE MOON see Wiemann, Beth

TO THE RIVER see Adolphe, Bruce

TO..., THREE SONGS see MacBride, David Huston

TO TORMOD-STEV (TWO NORWEGIAN FOLK SONGS) see Okkenhaug, Paul

TO UNGE ELSKENDE see Hall, Pauline

TOBER-VOGT, ELKE
  Prosit Bei Tag Und Nacht
    solo voice,plucked insts VOGT
    VF 1068A   (T252)

TOBIN, JOHN
  It's Wonderful To Be An American
    (Kessel) low solo WILLIS 10902 $.75
                                    (T253)

TOC D'ORACIÓ see Mestres, Apeles

TOD, DER see Straesser, Joep

TOD DES VERRÄTHERS, DER see Cornelius, Peter

TODAY'S NEWS: FROM A NEWSPAPER 1979 see Kvam, Oddvar S.

TODESLIED DER BOJAREN see Mendelssohn-Bartholdy, Felix

TOEBOSCH, LOUIS (1916-   )
    Maria *Op.73c (from Kerstcantate)
        S solo,pno [8'] DONEMUS   (T254)
        Mez/A solo,org [8'] DONEMUS (T255)

TOEKOMST see Mengelberg, Karel

TOGNI see Knutsen, Torbjorn

TOGNI, CAMILLO (1922-   )
    Ghirlande De Blois, La
        solo voice,pno ZERBONI 8458 (T256)

TOLLEKNIVEN see Selmer, Johan Peter

TOLV BARNERIM FRA JAEREN see Karlsen,
    Kjell Mørk

TOLV SONGAR AV ASLAUG LÅSTAD LYGRE, OP.
    246 see Tveitt, Geirr

TOM THE PIPER'S SON see Jeffreys, John

TOMASSON, JONAS (1946-   )
    Easter
        S solo,pno ICELAND 014-055 (T257)

    Hviti Trudurinn
        S solo,pno [5'0"] ICELAND 014-053
                                    (T258)
    Roa Roa Rambinn
        S/T solo,pno [1'30"] ICELAND
        014-051   (T259)

TOMBEAU DE JEAN COCTEAU, UN see Ogdon,
    Wilbur L.

TOMBEAU DE JEAN COCTEAU III, UN see
    Ogdon, Wilbur L.

TOMBEAU DE RAINER MARIA RILKE, LE see
    Bailly, Jean Guy

TOMBELLE, FERDINAND DE LA
    see LA TOMBELLE, FERNAND DE

TON, DER see Marx, Joseph

TON, EIN see Cornelius, Peter

TON COEUR EST D'OR PUR see Paderewski,
    Ignace Jan

TONADAS QUE CANTO, LAS see Beethoven,
    Ludwig van

TONDELEYO see Halldorsson, Sigfus

TONEN see Albertsen, Per Hjort see
    Nordraak, Rikard see Tveitt, Geirr

TONERNA see Sjoberg, C.

TONERNAS RIKE see Österberg, Sven

TONHENDUR 1. HEFTI see Gudmundsson,
    Björgvin

TONHENDUR, NYTT SAFN 1. HEFTI see
    Gudmundsson, Björgvin

TONHENDUR, NYTT SAFN 2. HEFTI see
    Gudmundsson, Björgvin

TONIGHT see Bernstein, Leonard

TONOS HUMANOS DEL SIGLO XVII see
    Querol, Miguel

TOO-LATE BORN, THE see Gideon, Miriam

TØR JEG see Fongaard, Bjørn

TORD FOLESON see Tveitt, Geirr

TOREADOR SONG see Bizet, Georges,
    Carmen: Votre Toast

TORELLI, GIUSEPPE (1658-1709)
    Cantata Per Il Venerdi Santo
        "Karfreitagskantate" [It] A solo,
        org,cont KUNZEL GM 765   (T260)

    Karfreitagskantate
        see Cantata Per Il Venerdi Santo

TORERO PIECE see Anderson, Beth

TORII see Evensen, Bernt Kasberg

TORJUSSEN, TRYGVE (1885-1977)
    Forlatt
        "Left Behind" solo voice,1.1.1.1.
        2.0.0.0. strings [2'] NORGE f.s.
                                    (T261)
    Great Spring, A
        see Veldig Forår, Et

    Left Behind
        see Forlatt

    Nirvana
        solo voice,1.1.1.1. 2.2.2.0. timp,
        perc,harp,strings [5'] NORGE f.s.
                                    (T262)

TORJUSSEN, TRYGVE (cont'd.)

    Psalm
        see Salme

    Salme
        "Psalm" solo voice,1.1.1.1.
        2.0.0.0. strings [4'] NORGE f.s.
                                    (T263)
    Veldig Forår, Et
        "Great Spring, A" solo voice,
        1.1.1.1. 2.2.2.0. timp,perc,
        strings NORGE f.s.   (T264)

TORNA! see Denza, Luigi

TORNA A SURRIENTO see Curtis, Ernesto
    de

TORNA AMORE see Buzzi-Peccia, Arturo

TORNAN LE STELLE see Cimara, Pietro

TORNQUIST, PETER (1963-   )
    Täuschung
        [Ger] Bar solo,string quar NORGE
                                    (T265)

TORPHICEN, PAMELA
    Awakening, The
        med solo,pno BARDIC BE0298 (T266)

    Isle, The
        high solo,pno (text by P.B.
        Shelley) BARDIC BE0299   (T267)

    Not Yet
        med solo,pno BARDIC BE0373 (T268)

    Song Of Freedom
        med solo,pno BARDIC BE0296 (T269)

    To Electra
        med solo,pno (text by Robert
        Herrick) BARDIC BE0297   (T270)

TORREK see Leifs, Jon

TORSTENSSON, KLAS (1951-   )
    Ack Värmeland Du Sköna
        (Jonsson, Josef) [Swed] solo voice,
        pno EGTVED   (T271)

    Aksel Schioetz Anthology Of Nordic
    Solo Songs, The
        (Schioetz, Gerd) solo voice,pno
        EGTVED   (T272)

    Urban Solo
        S solo,perc [18'] (2 songs for a
        sop. playing 1 bowed crotale and
        2 maracas, and who stamps her
        feet, snaps her fingers and turns
        around her own axis) DONEMUS
                                    (T273)
    Urban Songs
        S solo,synthesizer,orch DONEMUS
                                    (T274)

TORTOISE AND THE HARE, THE see Kavasch,
    Deborah

TOSCA: E LUCEVAN LE STELLE see Puccini,
    Giacomo

TOSCA: NON LA SOSPIRI see Puccini,
    Giacomo

TOSCA: RECONDITA ARMONIA see Puccini,
    Giacomo

TOSCA: VISSI D'ARTE see Puccini,
    Giacomo

TOSCA'S LOVE IDYLL see Puccini,
    Giacomo, Tosca: Non La Sospiri

TOSKANISCHER FRÜHLING see Marx, Joseph

TØSSE, EILERT (1954-   )
    Boka Med Sju Segl
        [Norw] solo voice,org NORGE (T275)

    Fire Folketoner Om Det Kristne Håp
        [Norw] S solo,org NORGE   (T276)

    Langt Inn På Ville Hei
        see To Religiøse Folketoner

    O Salighet Stor
        see To Religiøse Folketoner

    Stabat Mater
        [Lat] Mez solo,vcl NORGE   (T277)

    To Religiøse Folketoner
        [Norw] S solo,fl,org NORGE f.s.
        contains: Langt Inn På Ville Hei;
        O Salighet Stor   (T278)

TOSTI, FRANCESCO PAOLO (1846-1916)
    A Vucchella
        high solo,pno CLASSV 0414   (T279)
        med solo,pno CLASSV 1281   (T280)

    Abbassa Gli Occhi
        solo voice,pno (med) BERBEN (T281)

TOSTI, FRANCESCO PAOLO (cont'd.)

    Addio
        [It] high solo,pno CLASSV 0434
                                    (T282)
    Adieux À Suzon
        [Fr/It] high solo,pno CLASSV 1273
                                    (T283)
    Alba Separà Dalla Luce L'Ombra, L'
        high solo,pno CLASSV 0614   (T284)
        med solo,pno CLASSV 0613   (T285)

    Altro È Parlar Di Morte
        med solo,pno CLASSV 0605   (T286)

    Amour! Amour!
        [Fr/Eng] med solo,pno CLASSV 0604
                                    (T287)
    Aprile
        low solo,pno CLASSV 0606   (T288)
        med solo,pno CLASSV 1680   (T289)

    Aubade (2nd Mattinata)
        "Sur La Ville Solitaire" [Fr] med
        solo,pno CLASSV 2061   (T290)

    Canta!
        med solo,pno CLASSV 0611   (T291)

    Canzone Veneziana
        [It] med solo,pno CLASSV 1171
                                    (T292)
    Carmela
        med solo,pno CLASSV 0609   (T293)

    Chanson De L'Adieu
        [Eng/Fr] high solo,pno,vln CLASSV
                                    (T294)
    Complete Songs Vol. 1
        high solo,pno (CC34UL) RICORDI-IT
        R134844   (T295)

    Composizioni Da Camera Per Canto E
    Pianoforte 2
        solo voice,pno ZEN-ON   (T296)

    E Morto Pulcinella!
        med solo,pno CLASSV 0610   (T297)

    Goodbye
        high solo,pno CLASSV 0510   (T298)
        med solo,pno CLASSV 0430   (T299)

    Ha Da Venir!
        med solo,pno CLASSV 0612   (T300)

    Ideale
        high solo,pno CLASSV 0379   (T301)
        med solo,pno CLASSV 0607   (T302)

    Invano!
        [Eng] high solo,pno CLASSV 1161
                                    (T303)
    Io Voglio Amarti!
        med solo,pno CLASSV 0608   (T304)

    Luna D'Estate
        med solo,pno CLASSV 0897   (T305)

    Marechiare
        "Quando Sorge La Luna" high solo,
        pno CLASSV 0362   (T306)
        "Quando Sorge La Luna" med-low
        solo,pno CLASSV 1289   (T307)

    Musiche Vocali Italiane De Camera:
    Tosti 1
        (Bertagnolio, L.; Fujisaki, I.)
        (CCU) ONGAKU 523803   (T308)

    Musiche Vocali Italiane De Camera:
    Tosti 2
        (Bertagnolio, L.; Fujisaki, I.)
        (CCU) ONGAKU 523804   (T309)

    Parla! "Non Mi Guardar Cosí"
        [It] med-high solo,pno CLASSV 2062
                                    (T310)
    Pour Un Baiser!
        [Fr] high solo,pno CLASSV 0988
                                    (T311)
        [Fr] med solo,pno CLASSV 0989
                                    (T312)
    Quando Sorge La Luna
        see Marechiare

    Serenata
        low solo,pno CLASSV 1679   (T313)
        med solo,pno CLASSV 1286   (T314)
        high solo,pno CLASSV 0424   (T315)

    Songs Of Francesco Paolo Tosti, The
        high solo,pno HLH f.s.   (T316)
        low solo,pno HLH f.s.   (T317)

    Sur La Ville Solitaire
        see Aubade (2nd Mattinata)

    Ultima Canzone, L'
        med solo,pno CLASSV 0831   (T318)
        high solo,pno CLASSV 0350   (T319)

    Ultimo Bacio, L'
        high solo,pno CLASSV 0435   (T320)

TRI MARIA-KVEDE, OP. 29 see Madsen, Trygve

TRI PISNE see Horky, Karel

TRI SANGER TIL DIKT AV SIGBJØRN OBSTFELDER, OP. 4 see Evensen, Bernt Kasberg

TRI SPEWY see Metsk, Juro, Drei Lieder

TRI VISUR I VÅ OG VON, OP. 29 see Kielland, Olav

TRI ZPEVY DOMOVA see Jirák, Karel Boleslav

TRIAL AND DEATH see Leichtling, Alan

TRIBUTARIES see Bacon, Ernst L.

TRIESTE see Keulen, Geert van

TRIO see Shut, Wasyl

TRIO OF PRAISE see Koch, Frederick

TRIONFO DI CECILIA, IL: AH RITORNA ETÁ DEL ORO see Gluck, Christoph Willibald, Ritter von

TRIOSONATE see Aufschnaiter, Benedikt Anton

TRIPTICO CELESTE see Prado, Ameida

TRIPTIEK see Weegenhuise, Johan

TRIPTYCH see Chasalow, Eric see Koch, Friedrich E.

TRIPTYK, OP. 23 see Sköld, Bengt-Göran

TRIPTYQUE MACONNIQUE, OP. 57 see Masseus, Jan

TRISTAN UND ISOLDE: ISOLDE'S LIEBESTOD see Wagner, Richard

TRISTE EST LE STEPPE see Gretchaninov, Alexander Tikhonovich

TRISTESSE see Chopin, Frédéric see Schönzeler, Hans Hubert

TRISTESSE AU JARDIN see Schmitt, Florent

TRISTEZA NO CEU see Hartke, Stephen Paul

TRITT AUF DIE GLAUBENSBAHN see Bach, Johann Sebastian

TRITT MEIN LIEBCHEN IN DEM GARTEN see Abt, Franz

TRITTICO DELL' IMMAGINARIO see Lanza, Sergio

TROILUS AND CRESSIDA: THREE ARIAS see Walton, [Sir] William (Turner)

TROIS BALLADES DE FRANCOIS VILLON see Debussy, Claude

TROIS CHANSONS see Weill

TROIS CHANSONS, AUS "STRATEGEN DER LIEBE" see Koetsier, Jan

TROIS CHANSONS D'AMOUR ET UNE EPIGRAMME see King, Harold C.

TROIS CHANSONS DE BAUDELAIRE, OP. 70 see Regt, Hendrik de

TROIS CHANSONS DE BILITIS see Rudhyar, Dane (Daniel Chennevière)

TROIS CHANSONS DE BILITIS see Debussy, Claude

TROIS CHANSONS DE SHEHERAZADE see Lazzari, Silvio

TROIS CHANSONS NEGRES see Beers, Jacques

TROIS CHANSONS, OP. 71 see Regt, Hendrik de

TROIS CHANSONS, OP. 71A see Regt, Hendrik de

TROIS CHANSONS, OP. 71B see Regt, Hendrik de

TROIS CHANTS DES HOMMES see Jolivet, Andre

TROIS DUOS see Francaix, Jean

TROIS JOLIS TAMBOURS see Arrieu, Claude

TROIS LIEDER, OP.27 see Chausson, Ernest

TROIS MELODIES see Grovlez, Gabriel (Marie) see Landormy, Paul (Charles-Rene) see Paray, Paul

TROIS MÉLODIES see Falla, Manuel de

TROIS MÉLODIES SUR DES POÈMES DE JEAN DOMINIQUE see Grovlez, Gabriel (Marie)

TROIS POEMES see Jolivet, Andre

TROIS POÈMES see Lekeu, Guillaume

TROIS POÈMES CHASTES see Massenet, Jules

TROIS POEMES DE RONSARD see Bunge, Sas

TROIS POEMES DE TRISTAN CORBIERE see Escher, Rudolf George

TROIS POEMES DE VERLAINE, OP. 10 see Bon, Willem Frederik

TROIS POEMES TRAGIQUES see Rudhyar, Dane (Daniel Chennevière)

TROIS POÉSIES DE LA LYRIQUE JAPONAISE see Stravinsky, Igor

TROIS RONDES ET CHANSONS see Busser, Henri-Paul

TROIS SALUTATIONS A NOTRE-DAME see Vermeulen, Matthijs

TROIS SONNETS SPIRITUELS see Andriessen, Hendrik

TROIS VOEUZ RUSTIQUES see Koumans, Rudolf

TROLDMANDEN I BAKKEBY see Gislinge, Frederik

TROLLDOM see Lunde, Ivar

TROLLET KAN see Sommerfeldt, Öistein

TROMBONCINO, BARTOLOMEO
    Frottole Alla Corte Mantovana *CCU
    (Rizzoli, F.) solo voice,gtr CURCI
    10362 f.s.   (T331)

TROMBONE see Tveitt, Geirr, Basun

TROMPETER VON SÄKKINGEN: ES HAT NICHT SOLLEN SEIN see Nessler, Victor E.

TROOST VOOR GESCHOKTE CONCERTBEZOEKERS see Braal, Andries de

TROPHY, A see Warfield, Gerald Alexander

TROST I TAKLAMPA see Sønstevold, Maj

TROST IM LIEDE see Schubert, Franz (Peter)

TRÖSTUNG see Mendelssohn-Bartholdy, Felix

TROUBADOUR, THE see Sveinbjörnsson, Sveinbjörn

TROUBLED WOMAN see Flothuis, Marius

TROVAS see Nobre, Marlos

TROVATORE, IL: AH SI, BEN MIO see Verdi, Giuseppe

TROVATORE, IL: D'AMOR SULL' ALI ROSEE see Verdi, Giuseppe

TROVATORE, IL: DI QUELLA PIRA see Verdi, Giuseppe

TROVATORE, IL: IL BALEN DEL SUO SORRISO see Verdi, Giuseppe

TROVATORE, IL: STRIDE LA VAMPA! see Verdi, Giuseppe

TROVATORE, IL: TACEA LA NOTTE PLACIDA see Verdi, Giuseppe

TROYENS, LES: JE VAIS MOURIR! see Berlioz, Hector (Louis)

TRU OG SAELEDRUST see Nystedt, Knut

TRÜBESLIED see Hekster, Walter

TRUCHA, LA see Schubert, Franz (Peter)

TRUHLAR, JAN (1928-   )
    Cuba Si (composed with Urban, J.)
    [Czech/Span] solo voice,gtr PANTON
    954   (T332)

TRUMPET OF PALE-BLUE COLOR see Kurokami, Yoshimitsu

TRUST HER NOT see Balfe, Michael William

TRUSTING LIGHTNESS see Biscardi, Chester

TRUTH, THE see Levi, Paul Alan

TRYSTING see Sveinbjörnsson, Sveinbjörn

TRZY PIESNI DO SLOW KAZIMIERY ILLAKOWICZOWNY see Lason, Aleksander

TRZY WIERSZE CZESLAWA MILOSZA see Palester, Roman

TSCHAIKOWSKY, PJOTR ILJITSCH see TCHAIKOVSKY, PIOTR ILYICH

TSONTAKIS, GEORGE
    Galway Kinnell Songs
    Mez solo,string quar,pno PRESSER
    pts 141-40031P, sc 141-40031S
                                    (T333)

TSUJII, EISEI
    A La Complainte D'Automne
    S solo,fl,clar,vln,db,perc,pno
    [15'] JAPAN   (T334)

    Rose, Comme En Peu D'Espace, La
    solo voice,fl,clar,vln,vibra,perc,
    pno [10'] JAPAN   (T335)

TSUKATANI, AKIHIRO (1919-   )
    Creature
    S solo,pno [5'] ZEN-ON   (T336)

    Dream Island
    Bar solo,pno [5'] ZEN-ON   (T337)

TSUKI NO KASA see Arashino, Hideo

TU! see Denza, Luigi

TU AVRAI DELLE STELLE COME NESSUNO HA see Alandia, Edgar

TU, CA NUN CHIAGNE! see Curtis, Ernesto de

TU SCENDI DALLE STELLE see Tre Celebri Canti Di Natale

TU VEDRAI (BELLINI) see Four Italian Melodies

TUBIN, EDUARD (1905-1982)
    Sololieder
    see Soololaule

    Sololieder (1926-1944)
    see Soololaule

    Soololaule
    (Rumessen, Vardo) "Sololieder" solo
    voice,pno NORDISKA   (T338)
    (Rumessen, Vardo) "Sololieder
    (1926-1944)" solo voice,pno
    NORDISKA 10631   (T339)

TUE BENTSONS SONGS see Jordan, Sverre, Av "Tue Bentsons Viser"

TUL, TUL see Nieland, Henk

TUMBLING HAIR see Pollock, Robert Emil

TUNE, THE see Nordraak, Rikard, Tonen see Tveitt, Geirr, Tonen

TUNE FROM "ATOMSTODIN", A see Sigurbjörnsson, Thorkell

TURANDOT: NESSUN DORMA see Puccini, Giacomo

TURANDOT: NON PIANGERE, LIU see Puccini, Giacomo

TURANDOT: SIGNORE, ASCOLTA see Puccini, Giacomo

TURANDOT: TU CHE DI GEL see Puccini, Giacomo

TURKAT, MICHAEL (1957-   )
    Hommage A Johann Sebastian Bach
    S solo,clar,org ERES 2651   (T340)

TURKEY BUZZARD, THE see Beers, Jacques

TURNING see Biscardi, Chester

TUROK, PAUL HARRIS (1929-   )
    Lanier Songs
    S solo,fl,English horn,trp,bass
    clar,vcl,pno SEESAW   (T341)
    S solo,pno SEESAW   (T342)

    String Quartet No. 4
    Mez solo,string quar SEESAW   (T343)

TUROK, PAUL HARRIS (cont'd.)

Three Songs
  S solo,fl SEESAW   (T344)

Three Songs *CC3U
  S solo,fl SEESAW f.s.   (T345)

Two Songs
  S solo,clar,pno SEESAW   (T346)

TURULL, XAVIER (1922-   )
  Amor Incert, L'
    solo voice,pno EMEC   (T347)

TUS OJOS see Llovera, J.

TUSSCHEN GOD EN DE MENSCHEN see Delden,
  Lex van

TUSSEN BOMEN see Heppener, Robert

TUTINO, MARCO
  Due Arie
    solo voice,pno ZERBONI 9949 (T348)

  Due Canti Antichi
    solo voice,pno ZERBONI 9981 (T349)

  Tutti Li Miei Penser
    S solo,6inst ZERBONI 8917   (T350)

TUTTI LI MIEI PENSER see Tutino, Marco

TVÅ FOLKLIGA SÅNGER see Freudenthal,
  Otto

TVÅ KYRKOVISOR see Bäck, Sven-Erik

TVÅ MALUNGSMELODIER see Koch, Erland
  von

TVÅ SÅNGER see Lundin, Dag

TVÅ SÅNGER see Alinder, Hakan

TVA SANGER, OP. 54 see Jordan, Sverre

TVÅ SONNEVI-SONETTER see Sandström, Jan

TVEIR FUGLAR FLUGU AF BJÖRGUM see
  Runolfsson, Karl Otto

TVEITT, GEIRR (1908-1981)
  At The Overturned Bottom
    see Paa Hvelvet

  Atomkjernen
    see Sanger Til Dikt Av Tarjei
      Vesaas

  Basun
    "Trombone" solo voice,
      3(pic).3(English horn).3(bass
      clar).3(contrabsn). 4.3.3.1.
      timp,perc,pno,strings [11'] NORGE
      f.s.   (T351)

  Buttercup
    see Smørblomster

  Byrdi Betri
    see Håvamål

  Dellings Durum
    see Håvamål

  Des Iles
    [Fr] T solo,1.1.1.1. 1.0.1.0. harp,
      strings [6'] NORGE f.s.   (T352)

  Deyr Fe, Deyr Frendar
    see Håvamål

  Eg Hev Tvetta Haoret Mjukt
    [Norw] solo voice,pno NORGE (T353)

  Eli Sjursdotter Syng Åt Frieren
    [Norw] [1'] NORGE   (T354)

  Fortrolla Skog
    see Sanger Til Dikt Av Olav H.
      Hauge

  Gammel Bergstue, En
    see Sanger Til Dikt Av Johan
      Falkbergert

  Gattir Adlar
    see Håvamål

  Gøym Meg Mor *Op.166,No.5
    "Hide Me Mother" Bar solo,2clar,
      2horn,trom,bass trom,pno,strings
      NORGE f.s.   (T355)

  Gudelunder I Portaasskogen
    solo voice,1.1.2.2. 2.2.2.0. pno,
      strings NORGE f.s.   (T356)

  Gullgravervise Frå Strilelandet
    solo voice,2.1.2.1. 2.0.1.0. pno,
      strings NORGE f.s.   (T357)

TVEITT, GEIRR (cont'd.)

  Håvamål
    solo voice,ob,horn,gtr,strings
      NORGE f.s.
      contains: Byrdi Betri; Dellings
        Durum; Deyr Fe, Deyr Frendar;
        Gattir Adlar; Hjardir Dat Vitu
                                 (T358)

  Hide Me Mother
    see Gøym Meg Mor

  Hjardir Dat Vitu
    see Håvamål

  Høst Ved Rugelsjøen
    see Sanger Til Dikt Av Johan
      Falkbergert

  I Bjørkeskogen Klokken Fire Morgen
    see Sanger Til Dikt Av Johan
      Falkbergert

  I Istida
    see Sanger Til Dikt Av Tarjei
      Vesaas

  Island In The Skerries
    see Skjaergaardsø

  Jeu De La Solstice
    see Jonsokspel

  Jonsoknatt
    "Mid-Summer Night" STBar&narrator,
      fl,clar,pno,strings [45'] NORGE
      f.s.   (T359)

  Jonsokspel
    "Jeu De La Solstice" [Norw/Fr] solo
      voice,pno NORGE   (T360)

  Ketil
    see Sanger Til Dikt Av Tarjei
      Vesaas

  Kina-Reis
    "Travel To China, The" solo voice,
      2.1.2.1. 2.3.2.0. perc,pno,
      strings NORGE f.s.   (T361)

  Langeleiken
    see Sanger Til Dikt Av Olav H.
      Hauge

  Lullaby
    see Voggesong

  Mid-Summer Night
    see Jonsoknatt

  Mørke Natt Forgangen Er, Den
    see Sanger Til Dikt Av Johan
      Falkbergert

  Natta, Gunnar Og Bjørka
    see Sanger Til Dikt Av Tarjei
      Vesaas

  Olav Kyrre *Op.166,No.1
    S solo,2.0.2.1. 3.1.1(bass trom).0.
      pno,strings NORGE f.s.   (T362)

  På Haukeli Alle Inne
    see Sanger Til Dikt Av Tarjei
      Vesaas

  Paa Hvaelvet
    "At The Overturned Bottom" solo
      voice,3(pic).3(English
      horn).3(bass clar).3(contrabsn).
      4.3.3.1. timp,strings [4'] NORGE
      f.s.   (T363)

  Rimed Wood
    see Rimet Skog

  Rimet Skog
    "Rimed Wood" solo voice,2.2.2.2.
      4.2.3.1. timp,strings [7'] NORGE
      f.s.   (T364)

  Sanger Til Dikt Av Arnulf Øverland
    *CC10L
    T solo,2.1.2.1. 2.2.2.0. timp,perc,
      pno,strings NORGE f.s.   (T365)

  Sanger Til Dikt Av Johan Falkbergert
    S/T solo,orch NORGE f.s.
      contains: Gammel Bergstue, En;
        Høst Ved Rugelsjøen; I
        Bjørkeskogen Klokken Fire
        Morgen; Mørke Natt Forgangen
        Er, Den; Sjøen   (T366)

  Sanger Til Dikt Av Knut Horvei
    *Op.249, CC8L
    Bar solo,2.1.2.1. 2.2.2.0. timp,
      perc,pno,strings NORGE f.s.
                                 (T367)

  Sanger Til Dikt Av Olav H. Hauge
    *Op.243
    solo voice,orch NORGE f.s.
      contains: Fortrolla Skog;
        Langeleiken; Svarte Krossar
                                 (T368)

TVEITT, GEIRR (cont'd.)

  Sanger Til Dikt Av Tarjei Vesaas
    solo voice,strings NORGE f.s.
      contains: Atomkjernen; I Istida;
        Ketil; Natta, Gunnar Og Bjørka;
        På Haukeli Alle Inne   (T369)

  Sjøen
    see Sanger Til Dikt Av Johan
      Falkbergert

  Skjaergaardsø
    "Island In The Skerries" B solo,
      3(pic).3(English
      horn).3.3(contrabsn). 4.0.3.1.
      timp,perc,strings [5'] NORGE f.s.
                                 (T370)

  Smørblomster
    "Buttercup" S/T solo,2fl,2clar,
      4horn,harp,strings NORGE f.s.
                                 (T371)
    "Buttercup" S/T solo,2.1.2.1.
      2.1.2.0. strings NORGE f.s.
                                 (T372)

  Snøstorm
    "Snowstorm" Bar solo,2.1.2.1.
      2.2.2.0. timp,pno,strings NORGE
      f.s.   (T373)

  Snowstorm
    see Snøstorm

  Svarte Krossar
    see Sanger Til Dikt Av Olav H.
      Hauge

  Telemarkin
    Mez&narrator,2.2.2.2. 4.3.3.0.
      perc,strings, hardanger fiddle
      [45'] NORGE f.s.   (T374)

  Tolv Songar Av Aslaug Låstad Lygre,
    Op. 246
    [Norw] solo voice,pno NORGE (T375)

  Tonen
    "Tune, The" solo voice,
      1.1.2.3(contrabsn). 4.1.1.0.
      perc,strings [3'] NORGE f.s.
                                 (T376)

  Tord Foleson *Op.166,No.2
    Bar solo,2.0.2.1. 3.1.1(bass
      trom).0. pno,strings NORGE f.s.
                                 (T377)

  Travel To China, The
    see Kina-Reis

  Trombone
    see Basun

  Tune, The
    see Tonen

  Vårherre Han Vild' Ikkje Ha Meg
    [Norw] solo voice,pno NORGE (T378)

  Voggesong
    "Lullaby" B solo,2(pic).2(English
      horn).2.2(contrabsn). 3.3.3.0.
      timp,perc,pno,strings [5'] NORGE
      f.s.   (T379)

TVO EDDA KVAD see Olsen, Sparre

TVÖ ISLENSK THJODLÖG see Runolfsson,
  Karl Otto

TVO KRISTELIGE SANGER see Grinde, Nils

TVO SANGE (TWO SONGS) see Lie, Sigurd

TVO SONGAR see Groven, Eivind

TVO STEIN MEHRENSANGER see Sommerfeldt,
  Oistein

TVO VISNALOG see Halldorsson, Sigfus

TWAALF VOCALISES see Veldhuis, Jacob
  ter

TWAALF VOCALISES *CC12U
  (Vlijmen, Jan Van) solo voice,
    variable accomp. DONEMUS f.s.
                                 (T380)

TWAALF VOCALISES *CC12U
  (Vlijmen, Jan Van) solo voice,pno,
    perc,vcl DONEMUS f.s.   (T381)

TWANG see Lindwall, Christer

TWEE KWATRIJNEN see Beekhuis, Hanna

TWEE LIEDEREN see Beekhuis, Hanna

TWEE LIEDEREN see Brandse, Wim

TWEE LIEDEREN see Slangen, John

TWEE LIEDEREN, OP. 15 see Flothuis,
  Marius

TWEE LIEDEREN, OP. 53 see Orthel, Leon

TWEE LIEDEREN, OP. 54 see Orthel, Leon

TWEE LIEDEREN, OP. 56 see Orthel, Leon

TWEE LIEDEREN ("SCULPTUREN") see Bijvanck, Henk

TWEE LIEDEREN VOOR BARITON see Bijvanck, Henk

TWEE MIDDELEEUWSE KERSTLIEDEREN see Weegenhuise, Johan

TWEE PSALMEN (121 EN 133) see Klerk, Albert de

TWEE SONNETTEN, OP. 10 see Flothuis, Marius

TWEE SPAANSE GEDICHTEN see Bilt, Willem van der

TWEE TANTUM ERGO see Andriessen, Hendrik

TWEE TRANEN see Braal, Andries de

TWELVE ARIETTAS see Righini

TWELVE ELEGANT BALLADS (1750) see Pleyel, Ignace Joseph

TWELVE ENGLISH SONGS (1750) see Pasquali

TWELVE ENGLISH SONGS (C.1744) see Chilcot, Thomas

TWELVE FOLK SONGS see Sigurbjörnsson, Thorkell

TWELVE FOLKSONG ARRANGEMENTS *CC12U (Nestor) BOOSEY VAB0222 f.s.   (T382)

TWELVE MOTHER GOOSE SONGS see Lessard, John Ayres

TWELVE MOTHER GOOSE SONGS see Lessard, John Ayres

TWELVE PERSIAN SONGS, OP. 34 see Rubinstein, Anton

TWELVE POINTS OF THE MODIFIED MERCALLI SCALE, THE see Thomas, Andrew

TWELVE SONGS, OP. 60, VOL. 1 see Tchaikovsky, Piotr Ilyich

TWELVE SONGS, OP. 60, VOL. 2 see Tchaikovsky, Piotr Ilyich

TWENTIETH CENTURY see Clarke, Henry Leland

TWENTY-FOUR ITALIAN SONGS AND ARIAS [Eng/It] med-high solo KALMUS K 09874   (T383)

TWENTY-FOUR YEARS see Ford, Ronald

TWENTY HUNGARIAN FOLKSONGS, VOL. 1 see Bartók, Béla

TWENTY HUNGARIAN FOLKSONGS, VOL. 2 see Bartók, Béla

TWENTY HUNGARIAN FOLKSONGS, VOL. 3 see Bartók, Béla

TWENTY HUNGARIAN FOLKSONGS, VOL. 4 see Bartók, Béla

TWENTY MELODIES see Bizet, Georges

TWENTY-ONE SONGS see Mozart, Wolfgang Amadeus

TWENTY-SEVEN SONGS, VOL. 1 see Kilpinen, Yrjö

TWENTY-SEVEN SONGS, VOL. 2 see Kilpinen, Yrjö

TWENTY-SEVEN SONGS, VOL. 3 see Kilpinen, Yrjö

TWENTY-SEVEN SONGS, VOL. 4 see Kilpinen, Yrjö

TWENTY-SEVEN SONGS, VOL. 5 see Kilpinen, Yrjö

TWILIGHT see Ames, William T. see Sevriens, Jean

TWILIGHT FANCIES see Delius, Frederick

TWILIGHT PEOPLE see Vaughan Williams, Ralph

TWILIGHT SERENADE see Glinsky, Albert

TWILIGHT SONGS see Zuckerman, Mark

TWILIGHT STOOD, THE see Kirchner, Leon

TWO ARIAS FROM LA RONDINE see Puccini, Giacomo, Rondine, La: Two Arias

TWO BALLADS see Orland, Henry

TWO BEDDOES SONGS see Stevens, Bernard George

TWO BEGGARS, THE see Wilson, Henry Lane

TWO BLUES FOR FEMALE AND CLARINET see Gottlieb, Jack S.

TWO CANADIAN POEMS, OP. 56 see Cruft, Adrian

TWO CRADLE SONGS, OP. 76 see Reger, Max

TWO DANCES FROM WILLIAM CARLOS WILLIAMS see Mackey, Steven

TWO DREAMS see Kitzke, Jerome P.

TWO DUET, OP. 52 see Rimsky-Korsakov, Nikolai

TWO EARLY SONGS see Johnson, A. Paul

TWO EARLY SONGS see Walton, [Sir] William (Turner)

TWO FOLK-SONGS OF LITTLE RUSSIA (Zimbalist, Efrem) [Eng] high solo, pno CLASSV 2089   (T384)

TWO FOR JAN see Wernick, Richard F.

TWO FOURTEENTH-CENTURY MOTETS IN PRAISE OF MUSIC (Bent, Margaret) 2 solo voices,opt inst ANTICO AE15   (T385)

TWO HEBREW ART SONGS see Stern, Robert Lewis

TWO HOLY SONNETS BY JOHN DONNE see Blank, Allan

TWO HOLY SONNETS OF JOHN DONNE see Stucky, Steven Edward

TWO INTERMEZZI see Bibalo, Antonio

TWO KETCHWA SONGS see Ogdon, Wilbur L.

TWO KRYLOV FABLES, OP. 4 see Shostakovich, Dmitri

TWO LAST WORDS see Fisher, Alfred

TWO LITTLE WHOS see Carlsen, Philip

TWO LYRICS see Gerber, Steven R.

TWO MELODIES, OP.27 see Glazunov, Alexander Konstantinovich

TWO NIGHT PIECES FROM "FINNEGAN'S WAKE" see Buller, John

TWO NOCTURNES ON POEMS BY SHELLEY see Korn, Peter Jona

TWO NURSERY RHYMES, OP. 23 see Cruft, Adrian

TWO OLD SONGS, OP. 9 see MacDowell, Edward Alexander

TWO-PART AMERICAN SONGS, BOOK 2 see Williams

TWO PIECES ON THE FANTASY IN AN OLD CAPITAL see Oyama, Junko

TWO POEMS see Kahrs, Sven Lyder

TWO POEMS BY APRIL BERNARD see Wiemann, Beth

TWO POEMS BY MONTALE see Kleiberg, Ståle

TWO POEMS OF DEPARTURE see Becker, John

TWO POEMS OF ROBERT HEDIN see Lindenfeld, Harris Nelson

TWO PRAYERS see Ghezzo, Dinu Dumitru

TWO PROVERBS see Leichtling, Alan

TWO PSALMS OF DAVID see Christensen, Bernhard

TWO RELIGIOUS FOLK TUNES *CC2U (Tøsse, Eilert) S solo,fl,org NORGE f.s.   (T386)

TWO RELIGIOUS SONGS see Roseman, Ronald

TWO RILKE SONGS see Perle, George

TWO ROMANCES, OP. 25 see Rimsky-Korsakov, Nikolai

TWO ROMANCES, OP. 56 see Rimsky-Korsakov, Nikolai

TWO RONDELS, OP.4 see Griffes, Charles Tomlinson

TWO SABBATH SONGS see Zur, Menachem

TWO SACRED SONGS see Starer, Robert

TWO SACRED SONGS see Schütz, Heinrich

TWO SANGE MED ORKESTER see Jordan, Sverre

TWO SHAKESPEARE SONGS see Benton, Daniel Joseph

TWO SHAKESPEARE SONGS see Walker, G.

TWO SOLO MOTETS FOR SOPRANO AND ORGAN, OP. 19, NOS. 1&2 see Karlsen, Kjell Mørk

TWO SONGS see Canning, Thomas see Garlick, Antony see Gudmundsson, Björgvin see Ikebe, Shin-Ichiro see Leifs, Jon see Thorarinsson, Jón see Thorarinsson, Leifur see Turok, Paul Harris

TWO SONGS [1] see Roosevelt, [Joseph] Willard

TWO SONGS [1] see Tillis, Frederick C.

TWO SONGS [2] see Roosevelt, [Joseph] Willard

TWO SONGS [2] see Tillis, Frederick C.

TWO SONGS see Mourant, Walter

TWO SONGS see Violette, Andrew

TWO SONGS see Steiner, Gitta Hana

TWO SONGS see Kauder, Hugo

TWO SONGS see Erickson, Robert

TWO SONGS see Plante, Daniel

TWO SONGS see Rockmaker, Jody

TWO SONGS see Willan, Healey

TWO SONGS see Shut, Wasyl

TWO SONGS BY KEATS see Colding-Jorgensen, Henrik

TWO SONGS BY RACHEL see Sha'ar, Levi

TWO SONGS FOR BARITONE see Duke

TWO SONGS FOR BARITONE AND PIANO see Fricker, Peter Racine

TWO SONGS FROM EDDA, OP. 18 see Baden, Conrad

TWO SONGS FROM "LEGGUR OG SKEL" see Thorarinsson, Leifur

TWO SONGS FROM THE OPERA NAIMA see Loevendie, Theo

TWO SONGS, FROM THE OPERA NAIMA see Loevendie, Theo

TWO SONGS OF ARIEL 1957 see Stout, Alan

TWO SONGS OF QUIET, OP. 12 see Cruft, Adrian

TWO SONGS ON POEMS BY H. RABINSON see Stutschevsky, Joachim

TWO SONGS ON TEXTS BY OLEKSANDER OLES see Shut, Wasyl

TWO SONGS, OP. 13 see Medtner, Nikolai Karlovich

TWO SONGS, OP.22 see Grieg, Edvard Hagerup

TWO SONGS, OP. 45 see Jensen, Walther G.

TWO STEVIE SMITH SONGS see Bush, Geoffrey

TWO TOGETHER see Amato, Bruno

TWO VISIONS see Carl, Robert

TWO VOCAL WORKS see Rimsky-Korsakov, Nikolai

TWO VOCALISES see Gabus, Monique

TWO WEDDING AIRS see Godfrey, Daniel

TWO WHITMAN SONGS see Goldberg, William

TWO WYATT SONGS see Kuiper, Klaus

TYNGSTE SORG OG MØDA, DEN see Sinding, Christian

TYROLIAN AIR see Three Celebrated Waltzes

TYST MITT HJÄRTA see Karkoff, Maurice

U

U.S.A. see Yavelow, Christopher Johnson

UÅR see Jordan, Sverre

ÜBER DEN STERNEN IST RUH see Abt, Franz

ÜBERGÄNGE 1. FOLGE see Focke, Fré

ÜBERGÄNGE 2. FOLGE see Focke, Fré

ÜBERGÄNGE 3. FOLGE see Focke, Fré

ÜBERGÄNGE, 11 LIEDER NACH JAPANISCHEN GEDICHTE see Focke, Fré

ÜBERGLÜCKLICHE, DER see Jonsson, Thorarinn

UBUNG see Baggiani, Guido

UCHIKAWA, HIROYUKI (1947-   )
    Sanka
        S solo,pno, shakuhachi [9'] JAPAN
                                          (U1)

UDOW, MICHAEL WILLIAM (1949-   )
    Eight American Indian Children's
        Poems *CC8U
        S solo,ob/English horn,bsn,pno
        AM.COMP.AL. sc $11.45, pts $9.95
                                          (U2)

    Electric Silence
        B solo,fl/pic,bass clar,bsn,trom,
        2perc,pno,vln,vcl,db [8']
        AM.COMP.AL. sc $7.70, pts $6.90,
        pno red $3.85   (U3)

    Seven Textural Settings Of Japanese
        Poetry *CC7U
        female solo,4vcl,2fl,bass clar,
        2perc,6vln,2trp AM.COMP.AL. sc
        $10.70, pts $24.45   (U4)

    White Dwarf
        Mez solo,pno [12'] sc AM.COMP.AL.
        $6.15   (U5)
        Mez solo,pno,opt tuba, backstage
        sound effects [12'] sc
        AM.COMP.AL. $6.15   (U6)

UDSIGT FRA FLØIEN see Nielsen, Thorvald

UDSIGTER FRA ULRIKKEN
    (Volle, Bjarne) solo voice,pno NOTON
    N-9141-A   (U7)

UGLAND, JOHAN VAREN (1946-   )
    Fem Johannes-Sanger
        [Norw] A solo,org/pno NOTON   (U8)
        A solo,org NOTON N-9271   (U9)
        A solo,org NOTON N-9271   (U10)

UGOLETTI, PAOLO (1956-   )
    Ariette
        S/T solo,pno ZERBONI 9645   (U11)

    Grand' Aria Di Scena
        Bar solo,orch ZERBONI 8704   (U12)
        B solo,pno,vln,vcl,orch ZERBONI
        8704   (U13)

    Notturni
        solo voice,pno ZERBONI 9644   (U14)

UHL, ALFRED (1909-1992)
    So Ruhig Geh' Ich Meinen Pfad
        DOBLINGER 08 625   (U15)

UIT see Andriessen, Jurriaan

UIT ZEE GESTOKEN see Slangen, John

ULLMANN, JAKOB (1958-   )
    Voice, Books And Fire
        solo voice [70'] ARIAD 91054   (U16)

ULTAN, LLOYD (1929-   )
    Epithalamium Brevis
        S/T solo,vln,vla,vcl [3'30"]
        AM.COMP.AL.   (U17)

    I Will Give You Shepherds
        T solo,org/pno [5'] sc AM.COMP.AL.
        $4.25   (U18)

    Pitchipoi, The Childen Of Drancy
        MezBar soli,2.2.2.2. 2.2.0.0. timp/
        bass drum,pno,strings,vla solo
        [35'] AM.COMP.AL. sc $39.55, pno
        red $16.75   (U19)

    Wedding Song
        S/T solo [3'] AM.COMP.AL.   (U20)

ULTIMA CANZONE, L' see Tosti, Francesco Paolo

ULTIMO BACIO, L' see Tosti, Francesco Paolo

ULTIMO RICORDO, L' see Rossini, Gioacchino

UM GLOKOLL OG SUMARTUNGLID see Sigurbjornsson, Hrodmar Ingi

UM KVÖLD see Björnsson, Arni

UNA DE ESTAS MANANAS see Zuidam, Rob

UNBEKÜMMERTE KÜNSTLERNATUR see Straesser, Joep

UNCLE see Glinka, Mikhail Ivanovich

UND ES FÄLLT DER REGEN see Badings, Henk

UND GESTERN HAT ER MIR ROSEN GEBRACHT see Marx, Joseph

...UND NAHM GESTALT AN see Linke, Norbert

UND SO SINK' ICH LEISE IN MICH SELBST HINEIN see Bischof, Rainer

UNDANHALD SAMKVAEMT AAETLUN see Sveinsson, Gunnar Reynir

UNDER HAENDER, ET see Jordan, Sverre

UNDER THE TREES see Wood, Kevin Joseph

UNDER THE WISTERIA TRELLIS see Itoh, Mikio

UNDULATING MICHIGAMME see Tipei, Sever

UNENDLICHKEIT see Lothar, Mark

UNFORGOTTEN, THE see Homer, Sidney

UNFORTUNATE COINCIDENCE see Horder, Mervyn

UNG AASLAUG see Jordan, Sverre

UNG ASLAUG see Jordan, Sverre

UNGE PIKES VALS, DEN see Backer-Lunde, Johan

UNGEDULD see Schubert, Franz (Peter)

UNIUN see Flothuis, Marius

UNKNOWN GROUND see Finnissy, Michael

UNKNOWN PUCCINI, THE see Puccini, Giacomo

UNLOVED TO HIS BELOVED, THE see Haxton, Kenneth

UNRUHE see Warren, Betsy

UNS IST EIN KIND GEBOREN see Kortkamp, Johann

UNSCHULD, KLEINOD REINER SEELEN see Bach, Johann Sebastian

UNTER DER BLANKEN HACKE DES MONDES see Burt, Francis

UNVERGAENGLICHKEIT see Korngold, Erich Wolfgang

UNVERGÄNGLICHKEIT see Korngold, Erich Wolfgang

UNZEITIGE GSOASS, DER see Baumann, Alexander

UOCCHIE CELESTE see De Crescenzo

UP-COUNTRY FISHING: FOUR SONGS see Stock, David Frederick

UP IN THE NORTH see Sveinbjörnsson, Sveinbjörn

UPON JULIA'S VOICE see Carlsen, Philip

UPON MY JULIA'S CLOTHES see Adolphe, Bruce

UPON SILENCE see Benjamin

UPON THE TROUBLESOME TIMES see Douw, Andre

UR DIMBILVOKU see Sveinsson, Atli Heimir

UR FRIDOLINS VISOR see Peterson-Berger, (Olof) Wilhelm

UR MIN PORTFÖLJ see Jacobsson, John

UR PISLARGRATI see Sveinsson, Atli Heimir

UR TOBITS LOVSÅNG see Robertsson, Karl-Olof

UR UTSAE RISA ISLANDSFJOLL see Isolfsson, Pall

URANAKU MO see Matsudaira, Yori-Tsune

URBAN SOLO see Torstensson, Klas

URBAN SONGS see Torstensson, Klas

UROCZNICA see Lason, Aleksander

USIGNUOLO, L' see Alabiev, Alexander Nicholaevich, Nightingale

USNI, MALE POUPATKO see Ryba, Jan Jakub Šimon

USUSUSE NE SUMUJ see Shut, Wasyl

UT see Palsson, Pall P.

UT, JA UT, DET VAR NORDMANNS TRAA see Eggen, Arne

UT MOT UDDEN see Larsson, Lars-Erik

UT QUEANT LAXIS see Monteverdi, Claudio

UTA NO KAGE YORI see Minami, Satoshi

UTAIMASHO see Fujiwara, Michiyo

UTE FRA VERDEN DEN VIDE see Knutsen, Torbjorn

UTROLIG see Sønstevold, Maj

UTSYN: FEM TABLEAUER FRA ARNE GARBORG see Marcussen, Kjell

UW HANDEN see Mulder, Herman

UW JONGE MELODIEEN-VOLLE VINGEREN see Beekhuis, Hanna

UZAKI, KOICHI (1935-   )
   Four Lyric Songs
      S solo [12'] JAPAN   (U21)

V

V.B.NIMBLE, V.B.QUICK see Blank, Allan

V KRAJINE VZPOMINANI see Kvech, Otomar

VAAGE, KNUT (1961-   )
   Centenium
      [Norw] Mez&speaking voice,fl/pic,
         pno,vcl NORGE   (V1)

   Eg Strøyer Mine Songar Ut
      [Norw] S solo,pno,fl/pic/clar/bass
         clar/soprano sax NORGE   (V2)
      [Norw] S solo,pno,fl/pic/clar/bass
         clar/soprano sax NORGE   (V3)

   For Havet
      [Norw] A&speaking voice,fl,vln,
         horn,electronic tape,combo NORGE
                                     (V4)

VAAREN, OP. 30 see Kielland, Olav

VACCAI, NICOLA (1790-1848)
   Giulietta Et Romeo: Ah! Se Tu Dormi
      Mez solo,pno CLASSV 1591   (V5)

VACEK, MILOŠ (1928-   )
   Hledam Te, Kraso *song cycle
      solo voice,pno PANTON 955   (V6)

   Vecny Duel
      B solo,string orch [15'] CESKY HUD.
                                     (V7)

VACKÁR, DALIBOR CYRIL (1906-1984)
   Pisnicky K Siti
      female solo,pno PANTON 956   (V8)

VACKAR, TOMAS (1945-1963)
   Tri Dopisy Divkam
      med solo,1.1.3.1. 1.1.2.1. perc,
         vibra,harp,pno,db [13'] CESKY
         HUD.   (V9)

VADA see Guerrero, Francisco

VADO SE TU LO AMI see Benda, Georg Anton (Jirí Antonín)

VAEVET AF STAENGLER: A SYMPHONIC SONG see Thommessen, Olav Anton

VAGA LUNA CHE INARGENTI see Bellini, Vincenzo

VAGANTVISER see Brevik, Tor

VAGEBOND, DE see Broekman, Hans see Orthel, Leon

VAGGSONG see Ørbeck, Anne Marie

VAGGVISA see Danielsson, Harry

VAGHE LUCI È TROPPO CRUDO see Caldara, Antonio

VAIN SUIT, THE see Brahms, Johannes, Vergebliches Ständchen

VAIN WORLD see Slonimsky, Nicolas

VAKRASTE BLOMEN, DEN see Elgarøy, Jan

VAKRESTE ROSEN, DEN see Hovland, Egil

VALAGILSA see Sveinbjörnsson, Sveinbjörn

VALD see Kaldalóns, Sigvaldi S.

VÁLEK, JIRÍ (1923-   )
   Hudebnich Bajek, 7
      solo voice,pno PANTON 958   (V10)

VALEN, FARTEIN (1887-1952)
   Anakreons Grab
      see Zwei Lieder, Op. 31

   Darest Thou Now O Soul *Op.9
      [Eng] S solo,2.2.2.2. 1.0.0.0.
         strings [3'] LYCHE f.s.   (V11)

   Denk Es, O Seele
      see Zwei Lieder, Op. 39

   Dunkle Nach Der Seele, Die
      see Noche Oscura Del Alme, La

   Gedichte Von Goethe, Op. 6
      S solo,pno NORGE   (V12)

   Gruppe Aus Dem Tartarus
      see Zwei Lieder, Op. 31

   Mignon *Op.7
      [Ger] S solo,2.2.2.2. 4.1.0.0.
         timp,harp,strings [10'] NORSK
         f.s.   (V13)

VALEN, FARTEIN (cont'd.)

   Noche Oscura Del Alme, La *Op.32
      "Dunkle Nach Der Seele, Die" [Span/
         Ger] S solo,2.2.2.2. 2.1.0.0.
         strings [6'] LYCHE f.s.   (V14)

   Tretet Leise
      see Zwei Lieder, Op. 39

   Zwei Chinesische Gedichte *Op.8,
      CC2U
      [Ger] solo voice,2.2.2.2. 1.1.3.0.
         timp,strings LYCHE f.s.   (V15)

   Zwei Lieder, Op. 31
      S solo,pno LYCHE 841 f.s.
         contains: Anakreons Grab; Gruppe
         Aus Dem Tartarus   (V16)

   Zwei Lieder, Op. 39
      S solo,pno LYCHE 271 f.s.
         contains: Denk Es, O Seele;
         Tretet Leise   (V17)

VALENTE
   Manella Mia!
      T solo,pno CLASSV 1056   (V18)

VALENTINI, GIOVANNI (1582-1649)
   Hodie Christus Natus Est
      (Fürlinger, Wolfgang) A/B solo,
         2vln,cont (Coppenraths Kleine
         Reihe, Heft 6) COPPENRATH   (V19)

VALLEDOR, JACINTO
   Canción Timida
      (Subira, Jose) solo voice,pno BOIL
         B.1175 f.s. contains also: Pla,
         M., Seguidillas Religiosas;
         Bustos, M., Canción Contra Las
         Violetistas   (V20)

VALORI, ANGELO
   Tre Pezzi
      S solo,clar,soprano clar in E flat,
         glock EDI-PAN EP 7239   (V21)

VALSEN FRÅN FÖRR see Danielsson, Harry

VALVERDE, JOAQUIN (1846-1910)
   Clavelitos
      [Span/Eng] high solo,pno CLASSV
         2076   (V22)
      [Span/Eng] med solo,pno CLASSV 0968
                                     (V23)

VAN DE VATE, NANCY HAYES (1930-   )
   Cradlesong *cradle
      S solo,pno [3'] sc AM.COMP.AL.
         $1.20   (V24)

   Earth Is So Lovely, The
      med solo,pno [3'] sc AM.COMP.AL.
         $3.10   (V25)

   Four Somber Songs *CC4U
      Mez solo,pno sc AM.COMP.AL. $7.70
                                     (V26)

   Letter To A Friend's Loneliness
      S solo,string quar [10']
         AM.COMP.AL. sc $11.45, pts $8.80
                                     (V27)

   Night In The Royal Ontario Museum, A
      S solo,electronic tape [12'] sc
         AM.COMP.AL. $5.75   (V28)

   Songs For The Four Parts Of The Night
      med solo,pno [8'] sc AM.COMP.AL.
         $7.70   (V29)

   To The East And To The West
      S solo,pno [3'] sc AM.COMP.AL.
         $3.10   (V30)

   Youthful Age
      high solo,pno [1'] sc AM.COMP.AL.
         $1.20   (V31)

VAN DELDEN, LEX
   see DELDEN, LEX VAN

VAN GROTE EN KLEINE VOGELS see
   Veldhuis, Jacob ter see Veldhuis,
   Jacob ter

VAN LIER, BERTUS
   see LIÉR, BERTUS VAN

VAN NOSTRAND, BURR (1945-   )
   Earth Manual - 1976
      S solo,fl/pic,clar,bass clar,vln,
         vcl,prepared pno,perc [20'] sc
         AM.COMP.AL. $19.90   (V32)

   Lunar Possession Manual - 1973, A
      Winter Ceremonial
      S solo,fl/pic,clar,vln,vcl,db,pno,
         perc, opt dancers [19'] sc
         AM.COMP.AL. $19.90   (V33)

VAN ROOSENDAEL, JAN ROKUS
   see ROOSENDAEL, JAN ROKUS VAN

VANDERSTUCKEN, FRANK (1858-1929)
Fünf Liebeslieder, Op. 16
[Ger] (5 poems by Friedrich
Rückert) RECITAL 333   (V34)

Lieder Und Gesänge, Vol. 1
(contains 8 lieder from op. 29, 30
& 31. Not available outside
U.S.A.) RECITAL 408   (V35)

Lieder Und Gesänge, Vol. 2
(contains 8 lieder from op. 33 &
34. Not available outside U.S.A.)
RECITAL 409   (V36)

VANDOR, IVAN (1932-   )
From The Book Of Songs
female solo&countertenor,vla da
gamba/vcl,hpsd,perc EDI-PAN
EP 7668   (V37)

VANDROVALI HUDCI see Kostel, Arnost

VAPP see Samuel, Gerhard

VÅR see Thoresen, Lasse

VAR EG see Volle, Bjarne

VAR INTE RÄDD FÖR MÖRKRET see
Dorumsgaard, Arne see Rooth, Anna-
Greta

VAR JEG SOM DUGG see Backer-Lunde,
Johan, Were I A Cloudlet

VAR STILLA, HJÄRTA see Dorumsgaard,
Arne

VÅRBEKKEN see Jensen, Ludwig Irgens

VÅRBLÅ HIMMEL I MARS see Olsen, Sparre

VÅRBUD see Sjöblom, Heimer

VÅRDAG see Johnsen, Hallvard

VÅREN see Grieg, Edvard Hagerup

VÅREN KOMMER see Groven, Eivind

VÅRFÄSTMÖ, EN see Baden, Conrad

VARFÖR VARA RÄDD FÖR NATTEN see
Strandsjö, Göte

VARFÖR VARA RÄDD FÖR NATTEN 1 see
Strandsjö, Göte

VARFÖR VARA RÄDD FÖR NATTEN 2 see
Strandsjö, Göte

VARFÖR VARA RÄDD FÖR NATTEN!, VOL. 1
see Strandsjö, Göte

VARFÖR VARA RÄDD FÖR NATTEN!, VOL. 2
see Strandsjö, Göte

VÅRHERRE HAN VILD' IKKJE HA MEG see
Tveitt, Geirr

VARIANTEN ZUR CAVATINE DER ROSINA ("UNA
VOCE POCO FA") see Rossini,
Gioacchino

VARIATIONS ON GREEK THEMES see Lewin,
Frank

VARIATIONS ON THE FOLK SONG OF UKRANIAN
HERO SAVA CHALIJ see Rausch, Carlos

VÅRKVELD see Killengreen, Christian

VARLAMOV, ALEXANDER (1801-1848)
Red Sarafan, The
(Allen, F. De Lisle) solo voice,gtr
LENGNICK 437A   (V38)

VÅRT ANSVAR see Elgaröy, Jan

VÅRT FEDRELAND see Albertsen, Per Hjort

VÅRVISA see Jordan, Sverre see Lilja,
Bernhard

VÅRVISE see Albertsen, Per Hjort see
Grov, Magne see Ludt, Finn

VASE BRISÉ, LE see Franck, Cesar

VASE FOR LAMENTATION see Konishi,
Nagako

VASLAV'S SONG see Bolcom, William Elden

VATER UNSER see Cornelius, Peter see
Krall, Johann see Krall, Johann,
Pater Noster

VATERUNSER see Lichey, Reinhold

VATTNET RÖRS OCH VINDEN SPELAR see
Rangström, Ture

VAUCORBEIL, AUGUSTE-EMMANUEL
(1821-1884)
Mélodies, 22
solo voice,pno CLASSV C058   (V39)

VAUDEVILLE see Badings, Henk

VAUGHAN
Three Songs
S solo,tuba WIMBLEDN W1013   (V40)

VAUGHAN WILLIAMS, RALPH (1872-1958)
Collected Songs Of R. Vaughan
Williams Vol. 1
OXFORD 60.018 f.s.
contains: Four Last Songs;
Greensleeves; Three Shakespeare
Songs; Three Whitman Songs
(V41)
Collected Songs Of R. Vaughan
Williams Vol. 2
OXFORD 60.019 f.s.
contains: Four Poems Of Shove;
How Can The Tree But Wither?;
In The Spring; See The Chariot
At Hand; Twilight People (V42)

Collected Songs Of R. Vaughan
Williams Vol. 3 *CC7U
OXFORD 60.020 f.s. contains 7 songs
from "Pilgrim's Progress"   (V43)

Five Mystical Songs *CC5U
Bar solo,2.2.2.2. 4.2.3.1. timp,
harp,strings KALMUS A6124 voc sc
$4.00, sc $27.00, pts $60.00 (V44)
Four Last Songs
see Collected Songs Of R. Vaughan
Williams Vol. 1

Four Poems Of Shove
see Collected Songs Of R. Vaughan
Williams Vol. 2

Greensleeves
see Collected Songs Of R. Vaughan
Williams Vol. 1

How Can The Tree But Wither?
see Collected Songs Of R. Vaughan
Williams Vol. 2

In The Spring
see Collected Songs Of R. Vaughan
Williams Vol. 2

Linden Lea
high solo,pno CLASSV 0954   (V45)
low solo,pno CLASSV 0952   (V46)
med solo,pno CLASSV 0953   (V47)

Orpheus With His Lute
med solo,pno CLASSV 1044   (V48)
high solo,pno CLASSV 1045   (V49)

See The Chariot At Hand
see Collected Songs Of R. Vaughan
Williams Vol. 2

Silent Noon
low solo,pno CLASSV 0972   (V50)
med-high solo,pno CLASSV 0530 (V51)
high solo,pno CLASSV 0923   (V52)

Song Album, Vol. 1 *CCU
BOOSEY VAB0225 f.s.   (V53)

Song Album, Vol. 2 *CCU
BOOSEY VAB0265 f.s.   (V54)

Three Shakespeare Songs
see Collected Songs Of R. Vaughan
Williams Vol. 1

Three Whitman Songs
see Collected Songs Of R. Vaughan
Williams Vol. 1

Twilight People
see Collected Songs Of R. Vaughan
Williams Vol. 2

VE-AHAVTA see Gottlieb, Jack S.

VEA, KETIL (1932-   )
Är Vackrast, Det
[Swed] NORSK   (V55)

Elegy
SBar soli,clar,vln,vcl,pno NORGE
f.s.   (V56)

Før Det Sner
[Norw] solo voice,pno NORSK   (V57)

Hjärtat
[Swed] solo voice,pno NORGE   (V58)

Jiedna
S solo,3(pic).2.3.2. 4.3.3.1. timp,
perc,strings NORSK f.s.   (V59)

Konsert For Fløyte Solo, Resitasjon
Og Kammerorkester
[Norw/Eng] narrator,1(pic).2.2.2.

VEA, KETIL (cont'd.)
2.1.1.0. timp,perc,pno,strings,fl
solo [20'] NORSK f.s.   (V60)

Nordlandet
[Norw] S&narrator,2(pic).2.2(bass
clar).2. 4.2.2.0. timp,perc,pno,
strings [32'] NORGE   (V61)

Pinnochio
[Norw] Mez solo,pno NORGE   (V62)

There's Music
[Eng] Bar solo,fl,clar,horn,vln,
vla,vcl,pno NORGE   (V63)

VECCHIA DEL SONNO, LA see Hinohara,
Hidehiko

VECERNI PISNE, OP. 31 see Dvorák,
Antonín

VECHT, DE see King, Harold C.

VECNY DUEL see Vacek, Miloš

VECTORS see Waring, Rob

VED HAVET see Jordan, Sverre

VED NÅDENS BRØNN see Elgaröy, Jan

VED NÅDENS BRØNN: 9 SANGER TIL TEKST AV
SVERRE THERKELDSEN see Elgaröy, Jan

VED NATT see Backer-Lunde, Johan, Into
The Night

VED OSCARSHALL see Bergh, Sverre

VED RONDANE see Grieg, Edvard Hagerup

VED SØBREDDEN see Jordan, Sverre

VEDETTE, DIE see Schlick, E.

VEDRAI CARINO see Lyric Soprano Arias:
A Master Class With Evelyn Lear,
Vol. 1

VEDURVISUR see Halldorsson, Skuli

VEENEMAN, CURT
Among Thy Green Braes
solo voice,fl&alto fl&pic,clar&bass
clar,horn,harp,4perc,vln,vcl
[30'] AM.COMP.AL.   (V64)

Sonnet
med solo,vla,pno [6'] AM.COMP.AL.
(V65)
Three Songs Of Sleep And Love
S/T solo,clar,pno [17'] AM.COMP.AL.
(V66)

VEGIR LIGGJA TIL ALLRA ATTA & LITILL
FUGL see Halldorsson, Sigfus

VEILCHEN, DAS see Mozart, Wolfgang
Amadeus

VEIVISEREN SYNGER see Kjerulf, Halfdan

VEIZLUSÖNGUR ROTARY see Isolfsson, Pall

VELDHUIS, JACOB TER (1951-   )
Doodlopende Weg
see Van Grote En Kleine Vogels

Insonnia, Op. 34
S solo,bass clar,perc,acord [11']
DONEMUS   (V67)

Staat Van Eendracht, De
see Van Grote En Kleine Vogels

Twaalf Vocalises *CC12U
solo voice DONEMUS f.s.   (V68)

Van Grote En Kleine Vogels *Op.35
S solo,opt electronic tape DONEMUS
f.s.
contains: Doodlopende Weg; Staat
Van Eendracht, De; Van Grote En
Kleine Vogels   (V69)

Van Grote En Kleine Vogels
see Van Grote En Kleine Vogels

VELDIG FORÅR, ET see Torjussen, Trygve

VELLA, LA see Mestres, Apeles

VELYKA TY see Shut, Wasyl

VENDANGES see Kapr, Jan

VENEDIG, OP. 83 see Frid, Geza

VENETIAN SERENADE see Drigo, Riccardo

VENETIANISCHES GONDELLIED see
Mendelssohn-Bartholdy, Felix

VENETIANISCHES WIEGENLIED see Marx,
Joseph

VENEVIL see Kjerulf, Halfdan

VENEXIANA I see Powers, Anthony

VENEZIA see Hahn, Reynaldo see Voorn,
Joop

VENEZIANE see Cambissa, Giorgio

VENEZIANISCHES GONDELLIED see
Mendelssohn-Bartholdy, Felix

VENI CREATOR SPIRITUS see Galuppi,
Baldassare

VENI SANCTE see Leroux, Philippe

VENICE SANKA see Okiyama, Chikako

VENILIA see Luening, Otto

VENITE EXULTEMUS see Mouret, Jean
Joseph

VENITE FILI... see Zecca, Giannino

VENSTERLIEDEKEN see Weegenhuise, Johan

VENT IKKJE PA BREV see Sommerfeldt,
Öistein

VENTANA ABIERTA see Aponte-Ledee,
Rafael

VENUS AND ADONIS see Bush

VER BISTU MENTSH? see Hans, Edith

VER TREYSTUM THVI see Sigfusson,
Steingrimur

VERACINI, FRANCESCO MARIA (1690-1768)
Rosalinda: Meco Verrai
[Eng/It] med solo,pno CLASSV 0581
(V70)
[Eng/It] high solo,pno CLASSV 0580
(V71)

V'ERASTICH LI L'OLAM see Wallach,
Joelle

VERBA MEA AURIBUS see Beers, Jacques

VERBORGENHEIT see Wolf, Hugo

VERCKEN, FRANÇOIS (1928-   )
Six Instants Poétiques *CC6U
4 solo voices DURAND f.s.   (V72)

Versets
S solo,fl,clar,string quin [10']
BILLAUDOT   (V73)

VERCOE, ELIZABETH (1941-   )
Herstory I *song cycle
S solo,vibra,pno [20'] sc
AM.COMP.AL. $12.25   (V74)

Herstory III: Jehanne De Lorraine
Mez solo,pno [25'] ARSIS   (V75)

VERDELOT, PHILLIPPE (? -ca. 1550)
Tre Madrigali *CC3U
(Rossi, F.) solo voice,gtr CURCI
10339   (V76)

VERDI, GIUSEPPE (1813-1901)
Aida: Celeste Aida
[It/Eng] T solo,pno CLASSV 1196
(V77)
T solo,pno BOIL B.2627   (V78)
"Heavenly Aida" T solo RICORDI-IT
LD114340   (V79)

Aida: O Cieli Azzuri
[Eng/It] S solo,pno CLASSV 2077
(V80)

Aida: Ritorna Vincitor
[It] S solo,pno CLASSV 1195   (V81)
"May Laurels Crown Thy Brow" S solo
RICORDI-IT LD114299   (V82)

Art Of Joan Sutherland, The, Vol. 7:
Verdi Arias
(Bonynge, Richard; Sutherland,
Joan) WEINBERGER f.s.
contains: Attila: Oh! Nel
Fuggente Nuvolo; Attila: Santo
Di Patria; Masnadieri, I: Tu
Del Mio Carlo; Rigoletto: Caro
Nome; Traviata, La: Ah! Fors' E
Lui; Sempre Libera; Trovatore,
Il: D'amor Sull' Ali Rosee
(V83)

Attila: Dagli Immortali Vertici
Bar solo,pno CLASSV 1628   (V84)

Attila: Ella In Poter Del Barbaro
T solo,pno CLASSV 0928   (V85)

Attila: Oh Dolore
(Spada) T solo,orch pno red ZERBONI
8324   (V86)

VERDI, GIUSEPPE (cont'd.)

Attila: Oh! Nel Fuggente Nuvolo
see Art Of Joan Sutherland, The,
Vol. 7: Verdi Arias

Attila: Santo Di Patria
see Art Of Joan Sutherland, The,
Vol. 7: Verdi Arias

Ballo In Maschera, Un: Eri Tu
Bar solo,pno (D maj, lower) CLASSV
0523   (V87)
Bar solo,pno (F maj) CLASSV 0666
(V88)

Ballo In Maschera, Un: Eri Tu Che
Macchiavi
"It Was Thou The Destroyer" Bar
solo RICORDI-IT LD485   (V89)

Ballo In Maschera, Un: Morrò Ma Prima
In Grazia
S solo,pno CLASSV 1209   (V90)

Corsaro: Medora's Aria
"Egli Non...Non So Le Tetre" S
solo,pno CLASSV 1288   (V91)

Dearest Name
see Rigoletto: Caro Nome

Don Carlo: Dormirò Sol Nel Manto Mio
Regal
B solo,pno CLASSV 1548   (V92)

Don Carlo: Fontainebleau!
T solo,pno CLASSV 1658   (V93)

Don Carlo: O Don Fatale
A solo,pno CLASSV 0493   (V94)
Mez solo,pno CLASSV 0411   (V95)
"O Fatal Gift" Mez solo (in 2 keys:
A flat maj (LD49261); F maj
(LD114339)) RICORDI-IT   (V96)

Don Carlo: Per Me Giunto
Bar solo,pno CLASSV 1631   (V97)

Drinking Song
see Traviata, La: Brindisi (Libiam
Ne Lieti)

Due Foscari, I: Cabaletta Di Jacopo
(Spada) T solo,orch pno red ZERBONI
8324   (V98)

Due Foscari: Dal Più Remoto Esilio
T solo,pno CLASSV 1526   (V99)

E La Vita
(Spada) S solo,pno BSE   (V100)

Egli Non...Non So Le Tetre
see Corsaro: Medora's Aria

Ernani: Ernani Involami
S solo,pno CLASSV 0560   (V101)

Ernani: Infelice... E Tuo Credevi
B solo,pno CLASSV 0834   (V102)
B solo,pno BOIL B.1609   (V103)

Fair Provence
see Traviata, La: Di Provenza

Falstaff: E Sogno? O Realtà?
"Ford's Monologue" [It] Bar solo,
pno CLASSV 1177   (V104)

Falstaff: Quand' Ero Paggio
Bar solo,pno CLASSV 0902   (V105)

Falstaff: Sul Fil D'un Soffio Etesio
S solo,pno CLASSV 0901   (V106)

Father Of Heaven
see Forza Del Destino, La: Pace,
Pace Mio Dio

Fierce Flames Are Raging
see Trovatore, Il: Stride La Vampa!

Ford's Monologue
see Falstaff: E Sogno? O Realtà?

Forza Del Destino, La: Madre, Pietosa
Vergine
S solo,pno CLASSV 1615   (V107)

Forza Del Destino, La: Pace, Pace
S solo,pno CLASSV 0462   (V108)

Forza Del Destino, La: Pace, Pace Mio
Dio
"Father Of Heaven" S solo RICORDI-
IT LD410   (V109)

Heavenly Aida
see Aida: Celeste Aida

Inediti Per Tenore
(Spada) solo voice,pno ZERBONI 8324
(V110)

Io La Vidi
(Spada) TT soli,orch ZERBONI 8324
(V111)

VERDI, GIUSEPPE (cont'd.)

It Was Thou The Destroyer
see Ballo In Maschera, Un: Eri Tu
Che Macchiavi

Lombardi, I: La Mia Letizia Infondere
[It] T solo,pno CLASSV 2078   (V112)

Lombardi, I: Salve Maria
[It] S solo,pno CLASSV 2079   (V113)

Macbeth: Ah, La Paterna Mano
T solo,pno CLASSV 1533   (V114)

Macbeth: Come Dal Ciel Precipita
B solo,pno CLASSV 1561   (V115)

Macbeth: Pietà, Rispetto, Onore
Bar solo,pno CLASSV 1641   (V116)

Masnadieri, I: Tu Del Mio Carlo
see Art Of Joan Sutherland, The,
Vol. 7: Verdi Arias

May Laurels Crown Thy Brow
see Aida: Ritorna Vincitor

Mine Is A Cruel God
see Otello: Credo In Un Dio Crudel

Nabucco: Preghiera Di Fenena
(Spada) S solo,orch pno red ZERBONI
8417   (V117)

Nabucco: Tu Sul Labbro De Veggenti
B solo,pno CLASSV 1568   (V118)

O Fatal Gift
see Don Carlo: O Don Fatale

Otello: Ave Maria
S solo RICORDI-IT LD118146   (V119)

Otello: Credo In Un Dio Crudel
"Mine Is A Cruel God" Bar solo
RICORDI-IT LD118147   (V120)

Otello: Salce
"Willow Song" S solo RICORDI-IT
LD118145   (V121)

Requiem: Ingemisco
T solo,pno CLASSV 0388   (V122)

Rigoletto: Caro Nome
S solo,pno BOIL B.1613   (V123)
"Dearest Name" S solo RICORDI-IT
LD114724   (V124)
see Art Of Joan Sutherland, The,
Vol. 7: Verdi Arias

Rigoletto: Cortigiani, Vil Razza
Bar solo,pno CLASSV 1647   (V125)

Rigoletto: La Donna È Mobile
T solo,pno BOIL B.1614   (V126)
"Woman's A Fickle Jade" T solo (in
2 keys: B maj (LD114729); A flat
maj (LD178A)) RICORDI-IT   (V127)

Rigoletto: Pari Siamo
Bar solo,pno BOIL B.1615   (V128)

Rigoletto: Questa O Quella
T solo,pno CLASSV 0550   (V129)
"When A Charmer" T solo RICORDI-IT
LD115242   (V130)

Simon Boccanegra: Il Lacerato Spirito
B solo,pno CLASSV 0937   (V131)
"Weary And Worn With Suffering" B
solo RICORDI-IT LD385   (V132)

Tantum Ergo
(Spada) T solo,orch pno red ZERBONI
8324   (V133)

Traviata, La: Addio, Del Passato
S solo,pno CLASSV 0452   (V134)

Traviata, La: Ah! Fors' E Lui; Sempre
Libera
see Art Of Joan Sutherland, The,
Vol. 7: Verdi Arias

Traviata, La: Aria Di Violetta
S solo,pno BOIL B.1624   (V135)

Traviata, La: Brindisi (Libiam Ne
Lieti)
"Drinking Song" T solo RICORDI-IT
LD248   (V136)

Traviata, La: De' Miei Bollenti
Spiriti
[It] T solo,pno CLASSV 2080   (V137)

Traviata, La: Di Provenza
"Fair Provence" Bar solo RICORDI-IT
LD310   (V138)

Traviata, La: Di Provenza Il Mar
B solo,pno CLASSV 1219   (V139)
Bar solo,pno BOIL B.1625   (V140)

VERDI, GIUSEPPE (cont'd.)

  Trovatore, Il: Ah Si, Ben Mio
    [It] T solo,pno CLASSV 1233   (V141)

  Trovatore, Il: D'amor Sull' Ali Rosee
    see Art Of Joan Sutherland, The,
    Vol. 7: Verdi Arias

  Trovatore, Il: Di Quella Pira
    T solo,pno BOIL B.1695   (V142)

  Trovatore, Il: Il Balen Del Suo
    Sorriso
    Bar solo,pno CLASSV 1652   (V143)

  Trovatore, Il: Stride La Vampa!
    [It/Eng] Mez solo RECITAL 2238
                       (V144)
    A solo,pno BOIL B.1608   (V145)
    "Fierce Flames Are Raging" Mez solo
    RICORDI-IT LD487   (V146)

  Trovatore, Il: Tacea La Notte Placida
    [It] S solo,pno CLASSV 2081 (V147)

  Verdi Arias For Soprano
    (CC7U, INCLUDES RECORDED PIANO
    ACCOMPANIMENTS) RICORDI-IT
    R134623   (V148)

  Vespri Siciliani, I: Mercè, Dilette
    Amiche
    S solo,pno CLASSV 0911   (V149)

  Vespri Siciliani, I: Nouvelle Romance
    (Spada) T solo,orch pno red ZERBONI
    8324   (V150)

  Vespri Siciliani, I: O Tu, Palermo
    [It] B solo,pno CLASSV 1197 (V151)

  Weary And Worn With Suffering
    see Simon Boccanegra: Il Lacerato
    Spirito

  When A Charmer
    see Rigoletto: Questa O Quella

  Willow Song
    see Otello: Salce

  Woman's A Fickle Jade
    see Rigoletto: La Donna È Mobile

VERDI, RALPH C. (1944-)
  Wedding Song
    med solo,kbd (med) GIA G-2945 $2.50
                       (V152)
    med solo,kbd GIA G-2945   (V153)

VERDI ARIAS FOR SOPRANO see Verdi,
  Giuseppe

VEREWIGT GLÜHT HIER HERZ UND SINN see
  Mozart, Wolfgang Amadeus

VERGÄNGLICHKEIT, DIE see Haydn,
  [Johann] Michael

VERGEBLICHES STÄNDCHEN see Brahms,
  Johannes

VERGERS VII see King, Harold C.

VERGERS VIII see King, Harold C.

VERGERS IX see King, Harold C.

VERGERS XII see King, Harold C.

VERGERS XVI see King, Harold C.

VERGERS XVIII see King, Harold C.

VERGERS XXIV see King, Harold C.

VERGERS XXVII see King, Harold C.

VERGERS XXVIII (LA DEESSE) see King,
  Harold C.

VERGERS XXXII see King, Harold C.

VERGERS XXXIII see King, Harold C.

VERGERS XXXVI see King, Harold C.

VERGERS XL see King, Harold C.

VERGERS LVI (LA DORMEUSE) see King,
  Harold C.

VERGERS, VOL. 1 see King, Harold C.

VERGERS, VOL. 2 see King, Harold C.

VERGERS, VOL. 3 see King, Harold C.

VERGERS, VOL. 4 see King, Harold C.

VERGESSEN see Marx, Joseph

VERGIFTET SIND MEINE LIEDER see Gideon,
  Miriam

VERGISSMEINNICHT, DAS see Suppe, Franz
  von

VERGNUGTE RUH, BELIEBTE SEELENLUST see
  Bach, Johann Sebastian

VERHAAR, ARY (1900-)
  Drei Chinesische Lieder
    see Lieder Aus Asien, Op. 11

  Drei Geisha Lieder
    see Lieder Aus Asien, Op. 11

  Drei Vaganten Lieder
    see Lieder Aus Asien, Op. 11

  Feueranbeter, Der
    see Lieder Aus Asien, Op. 11

  Lieder Aus Asien, Op. 11
    DONEMUS f.s. [34']
      contains: Drei Chinesische Lieder
      (S solo,pno); Drei Geisha
      Lieder (A solo,pno); Drei
      Vaganten Lieder (B solo,pno);
      Feueranbeter, Der (T solo,pno)
                       (V154)

VERKÜNDIGUNG see Meima, Herman

VERKÜNDIGUNG, MONUMENTUM VEIT STOSS see
  Lechner, Konrad

VERLANGEN see Zagwijn, Henri

VERLASSENE MUTTER AM STROME, DIE see
  Haydn, [Johann] Michael

VERLASSENEN MÄGDLEIN see Wolf, Hugo

VERLIEBTE SCHÄFERIN SCAPINE, DIE see
  Loewe, Carl Gottfried

VERLOREN see Hekster, Walter

VERMEULEN, MATTHIJS (1888-1967)
  De L'Aube
    see Trois Salutations A Notre-Dame

  De Midi
    see Trois Salutations A Notre-Dame

  Du Soir
    see Trois Salutations A Notre-Dame

  Filles Du Roi D'Espagne, Les
    med solo,pno [9'] DONEMUS (V155)

  On Ne Passe Pas
    high solo,pno [2'] DONEMUS (V156)

  Trois Salutations A Notre-Dame
    high solo,pno DONEMUS f.s. [9']
      contains: De L'Aube; De Midi; Du
      Soir   (V157)

VERNAL EQUINOX see Heilner, Irwin

VERONICAS BØN see Groven, Eivind

VERRA LA MORTE see Schidlowsky, Leon

VERRA LA MORTE E AVRA I TUOI OCCHI see
  Mannucci, Andrea

VERRALL, JOHN WEEDON (1908-)
  Colonial Heritage
    high solo/low solo,pno [11'] sc
    AM.COMP.AL. $6.15   (V158)

  Sojourn Of The Spirit, A
    med solo,pno [3'] sc AM.COMP.AL.
    $1.60   (V159)

  Songs Of Nature
    med solo,pno [14'] sc AM.COMP.AL.
    $6.15   (V160)

VERS BÉTHLÉEM see Massenet, Jules

VERSCHWIEGENE LIEBE see Wolf, Hugo

VERSES see Crotty, Gerard

VERSES FROM SONG OF SONGS see Inwood,
  Mary

VERSES IN MEMORIAM DAVID MUNROW see
  Crosse, Gordon

VERSETS see Vercken, François

VERSI see Radulescu, Michael

VERSTOSS'NE, DER see Baumann, Alexander

VERSUCH FÜR ALLE see Karkoschka, Erhard

VERSUCHUNG, DIE see Orthel, Leon

VERTO see Berstad, Ragnhild

VERY BAD CHARACTER, A see Bank, Jacques

VERY GREAT MUSICIAN, A see Slonimsky,
  Nicolas

VESAAS-SANGER, OP. 35B see Plagge,
  Wolfgang

VESCOVO, ITALO
  Piccolo Omaggio A Dallapiccola
    S solo,fl,clar,harp,pno,vla,vcl
    EDI-PAN EP 7345   (V161)

VESLE BLÅ BUKKEN see Karlsen, Kjell
  Mørk

VESPRI SICILIANI, I: MERCÈ, DILETTE
  AMICHE see Verdi, Giuseppe

VESPRI SICILIANI, I: NOUVELLE ROMANCE
  see Verdi, Giuseppe

VESPRI SICILIANI, I: O TU, PALERMO see
  Verdi, Giuseppe

VET DU AT... see Sommerfeldt, Öistein

VETRARSOLHVORF see Helgason, Hallgrimur

VEVEN see Baden, Conrad

VEYVODA, GERALD JOSEPH (1948-)
  Through The Looking Glass
    A solo,woodwind quin,electronic
    tape SEESAW f.s.   (V162)

VI HILSER DEG HAMAR see Bergh, Sverre

VI MØTER ORKESTRET see Brevik, Tor

VI STÅR MED TOMME HENDER see Okkenhaug,
  Ingrid Buran

VI VENDER OSS TIL HERREN see Coates,
  Robert

VIANANT, EL see Mestres, Apeles

VIARDOT-GARCIA, PAULINE (1821-1910)
  Au Jardin De Mon Père
    med solo,pno CLASSV 1032 (V163)

  Chanson De L'Infante
    [Fr/Span] med solo,pno CLASSV 1399
                       (V164)
  Grands Oiseaux Blancs
    [Fr] high solo,pno CLASSV 1381
                       (V165)

VICAR, JAN (1949-)
  Japonsky Rok *song cycle
    S solo,fl,pno PANTON 959 (V166)

VID DAGSETUR see Björnsson, Arni

VID ETT UNGT PARS BRÖLLOP see Sjöblom,
  Heimer

VID HAVET see Eyser, Eberhard

VID STOKKINN see Sveinsson, Atli Heimir

VID SUNDID see Kaldalóns, Sigvaldi S.

VID SVALA LIND see Halldorsson, Skuli

VIDA BREVE, LA: AIR DE SALUD see Falla,
  Manuel de

VIDAR, JORUNN (1918-)
  Icelandic Folk Songs
    solo voice,pno ICELAND 015-005
                       (V167)

  Im Kahn
    solo voice,pno [2'45"] ICELAND
    015-010   (V168)

  In Memory Of A Failed Virtuoso
    solo voice,pno [2'40"] ICELAND
    015-011   (V169)

  Old Christmas Song, An
    solo voice,pno [1'40"] ICELAND
    015-006   (V170)

  Six Songs
    solo voice,pno [12'0"] ICELAND
    015-004   (V171)

VIDTAL VID SPOA see Runolfsson, Karl
  Otto

VIDUITÉ see Paderewski, Ignace Jan

VIE DU SIEUR DE DALIBRAY, LA see
  Escher, Rudolf George

VIE EST UNE FLEUR ESPINEUSE, LA see
  Andriessen, Hendrik

VIEILLE CHANSON ESPAGNOLE see Aubert,
  Louis-Francois-Marie

VIEILLES CHANSONS OF 17-18C, 40 see
  Reyer, Louis Étienne Ernest

VIEILLES CHANTERIES see La Tombelle,
  Fernand de

VIEL EENS HEMELS DOUWE, HET see
  Badings, Henk

"VIELLEICHT"-LIED, DAS see Eisler, Hanns

VIEN, Ô TOI see Saint-Saëns, Camille, Déjanire: Epithalame

VIENI! see Denza, Luigi

VIENI SUL MAR!
med-high solo,pno CLASSV 1319   (V172)

VIENNA, CITY OF MY DREAMS *CCU
high solo,pno WEINBERGER f.s.   (V173)

VIENS see King, Harold C. see Saint-Saëns, Camille

VIENS PRÈS DE MOI see Balakirev, Mily Alexeyevich, O Come To Me

VIENS! UNE FLÛTE INVISIBLE see Caplet, André see Delibes, Léo, Églogue see Godard, Benjamin Louis Paul

VIER A. ROLAND HOLST-LIEDEREN see Broekman, Hans

VIER ACHTERBERG LIEDEREN see Hekster, Walter

VIER BERÜHMTE AVE MARIA
S/T solo,pno (contains settings by: Cherubini, Schubert, Franck, and Gounod) SCHOTT SF 9419   (V174)

VIER BOUTENS-LIEDEREN see Weegenhuise, Johan

VIER DUETTE, OP. 20 see Dvořák, Antonín

VIER DUETTE, OP. 38 see Dvořák, Antonín

VIER DWAZE LIEDEREN see Braal, Andries de

VIER ERNSTE GESÄNGE see Brahms, Johannes

VIER FABELN see Schlemm, Gustav Adolf

VIER GEDICHTE VON FRIEDRICH HÖLDERLIN see Bernert, Helmut

VIER GEDICHTE VON RÜCKERT UND PLATEN IN MUSIK GESETZT see Schubert, Franz (Peter)

VIER GEDICHTEN VAN REVIUS see Andriessen, Jurriaan

VIER GEDICHTEN VAN REVIUS see Andriessen, Jurriaan

VIER GEISTLICHE STÜCKE FÜR EINZELSTIMME UND ORGEL see Dvořák, Antonín

VIER GESÄNGE see Rastrelli, Joseph

VIER GESÄNGE see Becker, Günther

VIER GESÄNGE NACH AFRO-AMERIKANISCHER NEGERLYRIK see Bresgen, Cesar

VIER GESÄNGE NACH FRAGMENTEN VON NIETZSCHE see Ruzicka, Peter

VIER GESÄNGE, OP. 44 see Eröd, I.

VIER HERBSTLIEDER see Dragstra, Willem

VIER KINDERLIEDJES see Geraedts, Jaap

VIER KLEINE WEIHNACHTSLIEDER see Strohbach, Siegfried

VIER LIEDER see Vogel, E.

VIER LIEDER see Dittrich, Paul-Heinz

VIER LIEDER see Haydn, [Johann] Michael

VIER LIEDER see Schubert, Franz (Peter)

VIER LIEDER see Zimmerman, S.A.

VIER LIEDER FÜR SOPRAN UND KLAVIER see Gibson, Robert

VIER LIEDER NACH CHINESISCHER POESIE see Haas, Pavel

VIER LIEDER NACH GEDICHTEN VON EVA STRITTMATTER see Wolschina, Reinhard

VIER LIEDER, OP. 2 see Dvořák, Antonín
see Farwell, Arthur, Mädchenlieder see Grieg, Edvard Hagerup

VIER LIEDER, OP. 3 see Dvořák, Antonín

VIER LIEDER, OP. 6 see Dvořák, Antonín

VIER LIEDER, OP. 7 see Dvořák, Antonín

VIER LIEDER, OP. 8 see Zemlinsky, Alexander von

VIER LIEDER, OP. 9 see Dvořák, Antonín

VIER LIEDER, OP. 12 see Zilcher, Hermann

VIER LIEDER, OP. 73 see Dvořák, Antonín

VIER LIEDER, OP. 82 see Dvořák, Antonín

VIER LIEDER, OP. 216, HEFT 1 see Abt, Franz

VIER LIEDER, OP. A-10 see Manen, Joan

VIER LIEDEREN see Beekhuis, Hanna

VIER LIEDEREN see Bijvanck, Henk

VIER LIEDEREN, OP. 64 see Orthel, Leon

VIER LIEDEREN, OP. 86 see Orthel, Leon

VIER LIEDEREN UIT 1912-'13 see Pijper, Willem

VIER LIEDEREN UIT KAF, OP. 5B see Delden, Lex van

VIER LIEDJES, OP. 75 see Orthel, Leon

VIER LIEDJIES VAN WEEMOED, OP SUID-AFRIKAANSE TEKSTE see Badings, Henk

VIER MARIANSCHE ANTIPHONEN see Biechteler, B.

VIER MORGENSTERN LIEDEREN, OP. 3 see Flothuis, Marius

VIER RONDELEN, UIT "STILTE VOOR HET HART" see Röntgen, Johannes

VIER SONETTE, OP. 48 see Cui, César Antonovich

VIER TIERLIEDER see Einem, Gottfried von

VIER TUCHOLSKY CHANSONS see Andriessen, Jurriaan

VIER WINZIGE WUNDERHORNLIEDER OP. 9B see Fromm-Michaels, Ilse

VIERGE, LA: L'EXTASE DE LA VIERGE see Massenet, Jules

VIERGE A MIDI, LA see Andriessen, Hendrik

VIERNE, LOUIS (1870-1937)
Tantum Ergo
S solo,org LEDUC f.s.   (V175)

VIEW FROM AGIOS PETROS, ANDROS, THE see Brown, Francis James

VIGNETTES see Marez Oyens, Tera de

VIJF GEESTELIJKE SONGS OP MELODIEËN VAN NEGRO-SPIRITUALS
(Emmausmis) ZENGERINK R.539   (V176)

VIJF LEOPOLD-LIEDEREN see Broekman, Hans

VIJF LIEDEREN, OP. 94 see Orthel, Leon

VIJF LIEDEREN VOOR SOPRAAN EN PIANO see Bijvanck, Henk

VIJF NAGELDEUNTJES see Andriessen, Jurriaan

VIJF NIJHOFF-LIEDEREN see Broekman, Hans

VIKINGSVALSINN see Runolfsson, Karl Otto

VILIA see Lehar, Franz

VILKET FRÄMMANDE SPEL see Gefors, Hans

VILL-GURI see Olsen, Sparre see Ørbeck, Anne Marie

VILL-KIRSEBAER, OP.71 see Sommerfeldt, Öistein

VILLA-LOBOS, HEITOR (1887-1959)
Bachianas Brasileiras No. 5
[Span/Eng] S solo AMP AMP194547   (V177)
Big Ben
S solo,2.2(English horn).2.2. 2.1.2.1. timp,perc,cel,harp,pno, strings [4'0"] PEER   (V178)

VILLANCICOS see Rodrigo, Joaquín

VILLANCICOS, FOR VOICE AND PIANO see Rodrigo, Joaquín

VILLANELLE see Bolcom, William Elden see Dell'Acqua, Eva see Mul, Jan

VILLANELLE, DIRGE AND SONG see Pleskow, Raoul

VILLI, LE: ANIMA SANTA DELLA FIGLIA MIA see Puccini, Giacomo

VILLI, LE: SE COME VOI PICCINA see Puccini, Giacomo

VILLI, LE: TORNA AI FELICI DÌ see Puccini, Giacomo

VIN DE LA REVANCHE, LE see Diepenbrock, Alphons

VIN MI MEMORAS see Schipper, Dirk

VINDEN SER ALDRI PÅ VEIVISEREN see Gaathaug, Morten

VINGAR I SKYMNINGEN see Degen, Johannes

VINGT CINQ, VOL.2 see David, Félicien-César

VINGT MELODIES see Chausson, Ernest see David, Félicien-César see Massé, Victor see Pessard, Emile-Louis-Fortune

VINGT MÉLODIES ET DUOS VOL. 2 see Saint-Saëns, Camille

VINGT MÉLODIES, VOL. 1 see Cuvillier, Charles see Gounod, Charles François see Hüe, Georges-Adolphe see Massenet, Jules see Rupes, G. see Saint-Saëns, Camille

VINGT MÉLODIES, VOL.2 see Gounod, Charles François see Hillemacher, Paul see Hüe, Georges-Adolphe see Massenet, Jules see Reyer, Louis Étienne Ernest

VINGT MÉLODIES, VOL.3 see Gounod, Charles François see Massenet, Jules

VINGT MÉLODIES VOL. 5 see Massenet, Jules

VINGT MÉLODIES VOL. 6 see Massenet, Jules

VINTERNAT see Backer-Lunde, Johan

VINTERNATT see Gjerstrom, Bjorn G.

VINTERNATT, OP.12 see Fongaard, Bjørn

VINTERVISA see Freudenthal, Otto

VINTERVISA, EN see Baden, Conrad

VIOLETTE, ANDREW
Black Tea, Lament For Viet Nam
S solo,harp,db,perc [9'] sc AM.COMP.AL. $5.40   (V179)

Harmonizations (Luther Chorales)
4 solo voices,4inst,pno/org [150'] sc AM.COMP.AL. $16.75   (V180)

Margarita Debayle, A
med solo,pno [7'] sc AM.COMP.AL. $6.90   (V181)

Mejor Tinta, La
T solo,pno [5'] sc AM.COMP.AL. $1.20   (V182)

Two Songs *CC2U
med solo,pno sc AM.COMP.AL. $1.60   (V183)

VIOLETTE, LE see Scarlatti, Alessandro

VIOLINE, DIE see Marx, Joseph

VIRGIN MARY TO CHRIST ON THE CROSS see Telfer, Nancy

VIRGINAL BOOK, THE see Babbitt, Milton Byron

VISA OM TATJANA see Sommerfeldt, Öistein

VISAN OM KOSSAN OCH FLUGAN see Lilja, Bernhard

VISE see Åm, Magnar

VISHVA RUPA see Newell, Robert M.

VISIÓN see Schumann, Robert (Alexander)

VISION BLURRED, A see Bakke, Ruth

VISIONE! see Tosti, Francesco Paolo

VISIONE VENEZIANA see Brogi, Renato

VISIONS INFERNALES see Sauguet, Henri

VISIONS OF TERROR AND WONDER see
Wernick, Richard F.

VISIONS PROPHÉTIQUES DE CASSANDRE, LES
see Brenet, Therese

VISIT TO THE KILLING FIELDS see
Kirkwood, Antoinette

VISSER, PETER (1939-   )
Die Hardekens
see Drie Kerstliederen

Drie Kerstliederen
S solo,pno/org DONEMUS f.s. [11']
contains: Die Hardekens; Kint Is
Ons Gheboorn, Een; Liedekijn
(V184)

Herbst
see Zes Rilke-Liederen

Ist Einer...
see Zes Rilke-Liederen

Kint Is Ons Gheboorn, Een
see Drie Kerstliederen

Knabe, Der
see Zes Rilke-Liederen

Liedekijn
see Drie Kerstliederen

Nacht Der Frühlingswende, Die
see Zes Rilke-Liederen

Protestsongs *CC9L,song cycle
med solo,pno DONEMUS f.s. [20']
(V185)

Vorgefühl
see Zes Rilke-Liederen

Wolken, Die *CC7L,song cycle
med solo,pno,vla/vcl DONEMUS f.s.
[25'] (V186)

Zes Rilke-Liederen
med solo,pno DONEMUS f.s. [25']
contains: Herbst; Ist Einer...;
Knabe, Der; Nacht Der
Frühlingswende, Die; Vorgefühl;
Zum Einschlafen (V187)

Zum Einschlafen
see Zes Rilke-Liederen

VISST MÅSTE DET VARA NÅ'T SÄRSKILT DÄR
see Leijon, Jerker

VIST ERTU, JESU, KONGUR KLAR see
Isolfsson, Pall

VISTO DE CERCA see Pablo, Luis de

VISUR VATNSENDA-ROSU see Asgeirsson,
Jon

VITA MIA see Dall'Ongaro, Michele

VITASLAGUR see Helgason, Hallgrimur

VIVA MUSICA see Teirlinck, Geo

VIVA SEVILLA see Folklore Andalusia

VIVALDI, ANTONIO (1678-1741)
Alla Caccia
see Sei Cantate Profane

Amor Hai Vinto
see Sei Cantate Profane

Elvira Anima Mia
see Sei Cantate Profane

Farfaletta S'aggira Al Lume, La
see Sei Cantate Profane

Farfalletta S'Aggira Allume Cantata,
La *RV 660
(Degrada) (critical edition)
RICORDI-IT RPR1257 (V188)

Geme L'onda Che Parte Del Fonte
see Sei Cantate Profane

Indarno Cerca La Tortorella
see Sei Cantate Profane

Sei Cantate Profane
(Blanchard) solo voice,cont CURCI
10358 f.s.
contains: Alla Caccia; Amor Hai
Vinto; Elvira Anima Mia;
Farfaletta S'aggira Al Lume,
La; Geme L'onda Che Parte Del
Fonte; Indarno Cerca La
Tortorella (V189)

VLEERMUIS ZWINGT, DE see Mulder, Herman

VLIET, HENK VAN DER (1928-   )
Drie Liederen
low solo,pno DONEMUS f.s. [10']
contains: Pathologie; Sonnet;
Sonnet (V190)

Pathologie
see Drie Liederen

Sonnet
see Drie Liederen

VO CERCANDO FRA LE OMBRE see Astorga,
Emanuele d'

VO SOLCANDO UN MAR CRUDELI see Benda,
Georg Anton (Jirí Antonín)

VOCAL WORKS ON TEXTS BY YAR SLAVUTYCH
[Ukranian] solo voice,pno DUMA (V191)

VOCALISE see Danielsson, Harry see
Florentz, Jean-Louis see Jacobsen,
Odd-Arne see Klerk, Albert de see
Leeuw, Ton de see Nasveld, Robert
see Rachmaninoff, Sergey
Vassilievich see Ravel, Maurice,
Pièce En Forme De Habanera see
Sigurbjörnsson, Thorkell

VOCALISE FOR TWO SOPRANOS AND ENSEMBLE
see Evensen, Kristian

VOCALISES DE L'ÉCOLE ITALIENNE
(Panzera) med solo SCHOTT-FRER 9178
(V192)
(Panzera) high solo SCHOTT-FRER 9177
(V193)

VOCALISES ET SOLFEGES see Rossini,
Gioacchino

VOCALISES I & II see Tremain, Ronald

VOCE 'E NOTTE see Curtis, Ernesto de

VOCI DI PRIMAVERA see Strauss, Johann,
[Jr.], Spring Voices

VOEL JE NIET BRANDEN see Zagwijn, Henri

VOEU D'UNE DAME A VENUS see Keizer,
Henk

VOGEL, E.
Vier Lieder
Mez solo,vln,pno DOBLINGER 08 876
(V194)

VOGEL, ROGER CRAIG (1947-   )
It Is Best Not To Be Born
Bar solo,pno [3'] sc AM.COMP.AL.
$3.85 (V195)

When She Went Alone Into The House
S solo,pno [6'] sc AM.COMP.AL.
$5.00 (V196)

VOGELHÄNDLER, DER: WIE MEIN AHNL
ZWANZIG JAHR see Zeller, Carl

VOGELSCHAU see Hall, Jeffrey

VOGELWEIDE see Castelnuovo-Tedesco,
Mario

VOGGESONG see Brevik, Tor see Tveitt,
Geirr

VOGGESONG TIL SIRI see Hovland, Egil

VOGGSONG see Olsen, Sparre

VOGGUKVAEDI see Thoroddsen, Emil

VOGGULJOD see Thordarson, Sigurdur

VOGGUVISA see Björnsson, Arni see
Fridriksson, Rikhardur H. see
Thorarinsson, Jón

VOGGUVISA HOLLU see Gudmundsson,
Björgvin

VÖGGUVISA SOLVEIGAR see Ragnarsson,
Hjalmar H.

VOGRICH, MAX (1852-1916)
Six Duets
[Ger] ST soli RECITAL 410 (V197)

VOICE AND PERCUSSION see Wiernik, Adam

VOICE, BOOKS AND FIRE see Ullmann,
Jakob

VOICE OF ONE'S HOME, THE see Bazant,
Jaromir

VOICE OF THE SHADES see Fowler,
Jennifer

VOICE(S): VERSION 2 see Tenney, James
C.

VOICEQUINTET see Malipiero, Riccardo

VOICES see Beerman, Burton see Tenney,
James C.

VOICES FROM ELYSIUM see Gideon, Miriam

VOICI NOËL, O DOUCE NUIT see Hamelle

VOIX DE FEMMES see Massenet, Jules

VOIX DE LA MEMOIRE, LES see Gaussin,
Allain

VOIX DU VERSEAU, LES see Goeyvaerts,
Karel

VOIX SUPRÊME see Massenet, Jules

VOKALIS see Sagvik, Stellan

VOKALNI POEMA see Boháč, Josef

VOLKMAR, ANDRAE (1879-1962)
Lieder Album
(contains 10 lieder, selected from
op. 10, 12, 15 & 16. Selections
from op. 16 in Swiss dialect.)
RECITAL 338 (V198)

VOLKONSKY, ANDREI (1933-   )
Psalm No. 148
3 solo voices,org,timp BELAIEFF 511
(V199)

VOLKS-KINDERLIEDER see Herzogenberg,
Elisabeth Von

VOLKSLIED see Mendelssohn-Bartholdy,
Felix

VOLKSLIEDER NEGER see Pankey

VOLKSLIEDER, OP. 11B see Kochan

VOLLE, BJARNE (1943-   )
Alles Øyne
SA soli,pno NOTON N-8903-F (V200)
"Går Du På Gaten En Dag" solo
voice,pno NOTON N-8903-A (V201)

Alles Øyne: 3 Songs
[Norw] solo voice,pno NOTON (V202)
[Norw] solo voice,org NOTON (V203)

Altar
high solo,trp,org NOTON N-9135
(V204)
low solo,fl,org NOTON N-9135L
(V205)

Beethoven På Ringve
solo voice,pno,vln NOTON N-9140
(V206)

Du Ska Itte Trø I Graset
solo voice,pno NOTON N-8905-A
(V207)
SA soli,pno NOTON N-8905-F (V208)

Fødd I Går: Three Songs To Haldis
Moren Vesaas Texts
[Norw] solo voice NORGE (V209)

Går Du På Gaten En Dag
see Alles Øyne

Herren Er Blitt Konge
[Norw] S solo,org NORGE (V210)

Jeg Beiled' En Gang Til En Pige
see Kjaerlighedsvise, En

Kjaerlighedsvise, En
"Jeg Beiled' En Gang Til En Pige"
NOTON N-8907-A (V211)

Liten Vise, En
SA soli,pno NOTON N-8904-F (V212)
"Så Er Min Hånd Igjen Blitt Tom"
solo voice,pno NOTON N-8904-A
(V213)

Så Er Min Hånd Igjen Blitt Tom
see Liten Vise, En

Tagal Fugl
NOTON N-9136 f.s.
contains: Tagal Fugl; Til Deg;
Var Eg (V214)

Tagal Fugl
[Norw] solo voice,pno NOTON (V215)
see Tagal Fugl

Til Deg
see Tagal Fugl

Var Eg
see Tagal Fugl

VOLLMOND: DREI JAPANISCHE HAIKU-
GEDICHTE see Malmlöf-Forssling,
Carin

VOLVANKVAD see Halldorsson, Skuli

VOM HIMMEL see Schwehr, Cornelius

VOM HIMMEL ZUR ERDE (DREI VOLKSTÜMLICHE
LIEDER) *CC3U
(Taubert, Karl Heinz) solo voice,pno,
fl/vln RIES f.s. (V216)

VOM KIND, DAS SICH NICHT WASCHEN WOLLTE
see Delnooz, Henri

VOM SCHMERZ see Mattiesen

VON DER SÜHNE see Keussler, Gerhard von

...VON GOETHE see Jung, Helge

VON LIEB UND LEID, OP. 7 see Thuille,
Ludwig (Wilhelm Andreas Maria)

VON WAELDERN UND ZIGEUNER see Bresgen,
Cesar

VOND DAG see Grieg, Edvard Hagerup

VONICKA Z KVITI MILOSTNEHO see
Sedlácek, Bohuslav

VOOR DE VERRE PRINSES see Franken, Wim
see Orthel, Leon

VOOR TINEKE see Orthel, Leon

VOORMOLEN, ALEXANDER NICOLAS
(1895-1980)
Canzonetta
Bar solo,pno [3'] DONEMUS (V217)

VOORN, JOOP (1932-)
Drie Lucebert Liederen
S solo,pno DONEMUS f.s.
contains: Droom; Herfst Der
Muziek; Maan (V218)

Drie Vroman Liederen
Bar solo,pno DONEMUS f.s.
contains: Venezia; Wandeling;
Zekerheid (V219)

Droom
see Drie Lucebert Liederen

Herfst Der Muziek
see Drie Lucebert Liederen

Maan
see Drie Lucebert Liederen

Venezia
see Drie Vroman Liederen

Wandeling
see Drie Vroman Liederen

Zekerheid
see Drie Vroman Liederen

Zeven Liederen Op Gedichten Van
Christian Morgenstern *CC7L
S solo,glock/pno DONEMUS f.s. [15']
(V220)

VOORPOST, DE see Orthel, Leon

VOORTMAN, ROLAND (1953-)
Ach Aus Eines Engels Fühlung Falle
see Rilke Lieder II

Hebend Die Blicke Vom Buch
see Rilke Lieder

Ist Schmerz, Sobald An Eine Neue
Schicht
see Rilke Lieder II

Nachtstunde, Bin Ich Ohne Angst
see Rilke Lieder

Nun Erst
see Rilke Lieder

Rilke Lieder
A solo,2fl,2ob,clar&bass clar,2bsn,
2horn DONEMUS f.s. [6']
contains: Hebend Die Blicke Vom
Buch; Nachtstunde, Bin Ich Ohne
Angst; Nun Erst (V221)

Rilke Lieder
A solo,2fl,2ob,2clar,2bsn,2horn
[6'] DONEMUS f.s. (V222)

Rilke Lieder II
A solo,2fl,2ob&English horn,2clar&
bass clar,2bsn&contrabsn,2horn
DONEMUS f.s. [8']
contains: Ach Aus Eines Engels
Fühlung Falle; Ist Schmerz,
Sobald An Eine Neue Schicht;
Wie Der Abendwind Durch
Geschulterte Sensen Der
Schnitter (V223)

Wie Der Abendwind Durch Geschulterte
Sensen Der Schnitter
see Rilke Lieder II

VOR see Halldorsson, Skuli

VOR BILDERN LYONEL FEININGERS, 12
LIEDER, HEFT 1 see Koetsier, Jan

VOR BILDERN LYONEL FEININGERS, 12
LIEDER, HEFT 2 see Koetsier, Jan

VOR DEM GESETZ see Govers, Klaas

VOR IHRA HITN see Baumann, Alexander

VORBLAER see Palsson, Helgi

VORDERNBACH, ALMLIED see Baumann,
Alexander

VORFRÜHLING, OP. 15 see Flothuis,
Marius

VORGEFÜHL see Louis Ferdinand, Prince
Of Prussia see Visser, Peter

VORID GODA see Sveinsson, Atli Heimir

VORLJOD see Runolfsson, Karl Otto

VORSINS FRIDUR, VORSINS THRA see
Kaldalóns, Sigvaldi S.

VORST see Kleppe, Joost

VORVINDUR see Kaldalóns, Sigvaldi S.

VORVISA see Thorarinsson, Jón

VORVISUR UR BARNABOK see Sveinsson,
Atli Heimir

VOSTRE RIURE see Fluvia, A.

VOTE FOR NAMES! *CCU
(Sperry, Paul) solo voice,kbd PEER
61655-211 f.s. Peer-Southern's 20th
Century American Songbook (V224)

VOTE FOR NAMES!
(Sperry, Paul) (contains 18 songs by
Bales, Diamond, Duke, Flanagan,
Ives, Riegger, Rorem, Siegmeister,
Thomson, Ward, Hoiby, Lauridsen, &
Walker) PEER (V225)

VOTO DE DONCELLA see Chopin, Frédéric

VOYAGE DANS LA LUNE: MONDE CHARMANT see
Offenbach, Jacques

VRANKEN, ALPH.
Pater Noster
S/T solo ZENGERINK R.167 (V226)

VRIES ROBBE, WILLEM DE (1902-)
Bruid, De
see Drie Liederen

Drie Liederen
med solo,pno DONEMUS f.s. [4']
contains: Bruid, De; Holland;
Landschap (V227)

Herschepping
Mez solo,pno [1'] DONEMUS (V228)

Holland
see Drie Liederen

Landschap
see Drie Liederen

Zwerver En Elven
solo voice,pno [2'] DONEMUS (V229)

VRIJHEID see Lier, Bertus van

V'SHAMRU see Sharlin, William

VSTUPNI ARIE VERUNY see Blodek, Vilem
(Wilhelm)

VUGGESANG see Janson, Alfred see
Knutsen, Torbjorn

VUGGEVISE: OG DRENGEN LIGGER PÅ MODERS
SKJØD see Jordan, Sverre

VUGGEVISE TIL KOTICK see Germeten,
Gunnar

VUILLEMIN, LOUIS
Quatre Rondels Melancoliques
[Fr] (poems by Catulle Mendes)
RECITAL 334 (V230)

VUURSTEEN, FRANS (1945-)
Attristant Et Isolant
Mez/A solo,fl&pic&alto fl,gtr,
acord,vln,vcl [10'] DONEMUS
(V231)

Fin De La Jornee, La
S/Mez solo,fl&alto fl,ob,clar,bsn,
pno,vln,vla,vcl,db [11'] DONEMUS
(V232)

VUURVLIEG, DE see Bunge, Sas

V'YE-ETAYU see Schiller, Benjie Ellen

VYLET DO HOR see Saudek, Vojtech

VYZNANI see Sluka, Luboš

W

W KOSCIELE see Baird, Tadeusz

WAALER, FREDRIKKE (1865-1952)
Hamarsangen
solo voice,pno NOTON N-9329-A (W1)

WAAR ZAL IK WEZEN... see Franken, Wim

WACHTELSCHLAG, DER see Schubert, Franz
(Peter)

WAER IS U LIEF see Andriessen, Jurriaan

WAFFENSCHMIED, DER: ER SCHLÄFT - ER IST
SO GUT see Lortzing, (Gustav)
Albert

WAGEMANS, PETER-JAN (1952-   )
Wie, Op. 27 *song cycle
A solo,2clar,2horn [16'] DONEMUS
(W2)

WAGNER, RICHARD (1813-1883)
Deux Grenadiers, Les
[Fr] med-high solo,pno CLASSV 2082
(W3)

Fliegende Holländer: Traft Ihr Das
Schiff
S solo,pno CLASSV 1614   (W4)

Gebet Des Amfortas
see Parsifal: Mein Vater

Im Treibhaus (from Wesendonk Lieder)
solo voice,pno SCIEN 1766   (W5)

Lohengrin: Elsa's Dream
S solo,pno CLASSV 0384   (W6)

Lohengrin: In Fernem Land
T solo,pno CLASSV 1532   (W7)

Meistersinger Von Nürnberg, Die: Am
Stillen Herd
T solo,pno CLASSV 1534   (W8)

Meistersinger Von Nürnberg, Die:
Morgenlich Leuchtend
T solo,pno CLASSV 2091   (W9)

Meistersinger Von Nürnberg, Die: Nun
Hört Und Versteht
B solo,pno CLASSV 1564   (W10)

Meistersinger Von Nürnberg, Die:
Wahn! Wahn!
B solo,pno CLASSV 1566   (W11)

Meistersinger Von Nürnberg, Die:
Walther's Prize-Song
T solo,pno CLASSV 1535   (W12)

Meistersinger Von Nürnberg, Die: Was
Duftet Doch Der Flieder
B solo,pno CLASSV 1565   (W13)

Melodie Italiane 1 Dall' Ottocento Al
Novecento
ZEN-ON 713226   (W14)

Melodie Italiane 2 Dall' Ottocento Al
Novecento
ZEN-ON   (W15)

O Pure And Tender Star Of Eve
(England) [Eng/Ger] solo voice,pno
ROBERTON 491-00354 $1.50   (W16)

Parsifal: Mein Vater
"Gebet Des Amfortas" Bar solo,pno
CLASSV 1645   (W17)

Rienzi: Almächtiger Vater
T solo,pno CLASSV 0346   (W18)

Rienzi: Gerechter Gott
Mez solo,pno CLASSV 1599   (W19)

Sämtliche Lieder, Originaltonarten
(Sato, S.) ZEN-ON 713920   (W20)

Tannhäuser: Blick' Ich Umher
Bar solo,pno CLASSV 1650   (W21)

Tannhäuser: Dich, Teure Halle
S solo,pno CLASSV 0386   (W22)

Tannhäuser: Elizabeth's Prayer
S solo,pno CLASSV 0385   (W23)

Tannhäuser: O Du Mein Holder
Abendstern
Bar solo,pno CLASSV 0436   (W24)

Tannhäuser: Oh! Vergin Santa
S solo,pno BOIL B.2033   (W25)

Tannhäuser: Salve D'Amor Recinto
Eletto
S solo,pno BOIL B.2030   (W26)

WAGNER, RICHARD (cont'd.)
Tristan Und Isolde: Isolde's
Liebestod
S solo,pno CLASSV 1624   (W27)

Walküre, Die: Leb' Wohl
"Wotan's Farewell" B solo,pno
CLASSV 1580   (W28)

Walküre, Die: Siegmunds Liebeslied
"Winterstürme Wichen" T solo,pno
CLASSV 1544   (W29)

Winterstürme Wichen
see Walküre, Die: Siegmunds
Liebeslied

Wotan's Farewell
see Walküre, Die: Leb' Wohl

WAGNER-REGENY, RUDOLF (1903-1969)
Gesänge Zur Leier
PETERS 5461   (W30)

Hausmusik
PETERS 5050   (W31)

Lieder *CCU
solo voice,pno DEUTSCHER DV 9005
f.s.   (W32)

Lieder Nach Fontane
PETERS 5462   (W33)

WAHLBERG, RUNE (1910-   )
Dingeding-Visan
[Swed] solo voice,pno TONOS (W34)

Morgon Mellan Fjällen
solo voice,org STIM   (W35)

WÄHRENDE, DAS see Louis Ferdinand,
Prince Of Prussia

WAIL see Horder, Mervyn

WAISENKNABE see Bijvanck, Henk

WAIT TILL I PUT ON MY CROWN see McLin,
Lena J.

WAITING BOTH see Blank, Allan

WAITING FOR THE MOON see Wallach,
Joelle

WAKE AGAIN, A see Crosse, Gordon

WALDESNACHT see Schubert, Franz (Peter)

WALDMAN, ROBERT
Robber Bridegroom (selections)
solo voice,pno SCHIRM.G 50251760
(W36)

WALDSELIGKEIT see Marx, Joseph

WALKER, G.
Two Shakespeare Songs *CC2U
high solo,pno NOVA PEM 25 f.s.
(W37)

WALKER, GEORGE THEOPHILUS (1922-   )
Bequest
see Emily Dickinson Songs

Bereaved Maid, The
med solo,pno MMB S814011   (W38)

Emily Dickinson Songs
S solo,pno (diff) PEER f.s.
contains: Bequest; I Have No Life
But This; What If I Say...;
Wild Nights   (W39)

Emily Dickinson Songs *CCU
high solo,pno sc PEER 61616-212
f.s.   (W40)

Ev'ry Time I Feel De Spirit *spir
high solo,pno MMB S814006   (W41)

Hey Nonny No
med solo,pno MMB S814016   (W42)

I Got A Letter From Jesus
med solo,pno MMB S814014   (W43)

I Have No Life But This
see Emily Dickinson Songs

I Went To Heaven
high solo,pno MMB S814018   (W44)

Lament
med solo,pno MMB S814015   (W45)

Mary Wore Three Links Of Chain *spir
med solo,pno MMB S814007   (W46)

Nocturne
high solo,pno sc PEER 61615-202
f.s.   (W47)

Red, Red Rose, A
med solo,pno MMB S814008   (W48)

WALKER, GEORGE THEOPHILUS (cont'd.)
Response
med solo,pno MMB S814012   (W49)

So We'll Go No More A-Roving
med solo,pno MMB S814013   (W50)

Sweet, Let Me Go
high solo,pno MMB S814009   (W51)

What If I Say...
see Emily Dickinson Songs

Wild Nights
see Emily Dickinson Songs

With Rue My Heart Is Laden
low solo,pno MMB S814010   (W52)

WALKER, GWYNETH (1947-   )
Hor d'Oeuvres (composed with Isele,
David Clark) *CC6U
solo voice (med diff) WALKER MUS.
PRO. $10.00   (W53)

I Speak For The Earth
S solo,fl,ob,pno [13'] (med diff)
WALKER MUS. PRO. sc $7.50, pts
$2.00   (W54)

Just A Little Rain
TBar&countertenor,gtr,perc [5']
(diff) sc WALKER MUS. PRO. $1.50
(W55)

Raining In February *CC4U
Bar solo,pno (med diff) WALKER MUS.
PRO. $5.00   (W56)

Songs For Baritone And Guitar *CC3U
Bar solo,gtr WALKER MUS. PRO. $6.00
(W57)

Songs Of The Night Wind *CC5U
S solo,vcl/pno (diff) WALKER MUS.
PRO. $12.00   (W58)

Though Love Be A Day *CC5U
high solo,pno (med diff) WALKER
MUS. PRO. $12.00   (W59)

Three Songs For Tres Voces *CC4U
TBar&countertenor,gtr (diff) WALKER
MUS. PRO. $6.00   (W60)

Wedding Songs *CC6U,Marriage,duet
WALKER MUS. PRO. $8.00 high solo,
pno; med solo,pno   (W61)

WALKER, R.
Singer By The Yellow River
S solo,fl,harp NOVELLO f.s. (W62)

WALKING IN THE AIR see Blake, Howard

WALKING UPRIGHT see Shapey, Ralph

WALKÜRE, DIE: LEB' WOHL see Wagner,
Richard

WALKÜRE, DIE: SIEGMUNDS LIEBESLIED see
Wagner, Richard

WALLACH, JOELLE
Amen
high solo,treb inst [2'] sc
AM.COMP.AL. $1.60   (W63)

Cantares De Los Perdis
solo voice,tuba,timp,perc [13']
AM.COMP.AL.   (W64)

Cords
S solo,2db [8'] AM.COMP.AL. sc
$5.75, pts $1.95   (W65)

Door Standing Open, The
solo voice,pno [15'] AM.COMP.AL.
(W66)

Five-Fold Amen
SA soli,acap [2'] sc AM.COMP.AL.
$1.55   (W67)

Mourning Madrigals
ST soli,fl,harp [12'] AM.COMP.AL.
sc $10.65, pts $1.90   (W68)

Of Honey And Vinegar
Mez solo,2pno [14'] sc AM.COMP.AL.
$14.50   (W69)

Simeni Kachotam Al Libbecha
Mez solo,1.1.1.1. 0.0.0.0. 2perc,
string quin/string orch [17']
AM.COMP.AL.   (W70)

Three Spanish Songs
Mez solo,pno [14'] AM.COMP.AL.
(W71)

Three Whitman Songs
solo voice,horn,vcl,clar [14']
AM.COMP.AL.   (W72)

V'erastich Li L'olam
2 solo voices [4'] AM.COMP.AL.
(W73)

WALLACH, JOELLE (cont'd.)

　Waiting For The Moon
　　solo voice,pno [5'] AM.COMP.AL.
　　　　　　　　　　　　　　　　　　　(W74)

　Youth's Serenade
　　Mez solo,fl,bsn,harmonium,harp
　　[14'] sc AM.COMP.AL. $9.15 (W75)

WALLGREN, JAN
　Aftonbön
　　see Karins Sånger

　I Rörelse
　　see Karins Sånger

　Karins Sånger
　　[Swed] Mez solo,string quar STIM
　　　f.s.
　　　contains: Aftonbön; I Rörelse;
　　　Nattens Djupa Violoncell;
　　　Svalorna; Till Någon Som Är
　　　Mycket Ung　　　　　　　　(W76)

　Nattens Djupa Violoncell
　　see Karins Sånger

　Svalorna
　　see Karins Sånger

　Till Någon Som Är Mycket Ung
　　see Karins Sånger

WALLIN, PETER (1964-　　)
　Dägä Dägä
　　female solo&female solo STIM (W77)
　　[Swed] 2 solo voices TONOS　(W78)

WALLIN, ROLF (1957-　　)
　...Though What Made It Has Gone...
　　[Russ/Eng] Mez solo,pno NORGE (W79)

WALLY, LA: EBBEN? NE ANDRÒ LONTANA see
　Catalani, Alfredo

WALLY, LA: NÈ MA DUNQUE see Catalani,
　Alfredo

WALLY, LA: UN GIORNO SCIOLTE LE SUE
　VELE see Catalani, Alfredo

WALTER, KARL (1862-1929)
　Ave Maria
　　S solo,org,opt vln sc,pts STYRIA
　　5406 f.s.　　　　　　　　　　(W80)

WALTON, [SIR] WILLIAM (TURNER)
　(1902-1983)
　Diomede
　　see Troilus And Cressida: Three
　　Arias

　How Can I Sleep?
　　see Troilus And Cressida: Three
　　Arias

　Slowly It All Comes Back
　　see Troilus And Cressida: Three
　　Arias

　Song Album
　　(Palmer, Christopher) (CCU) OXFORD
　　68.060　　　　　　　　　　　　(W81)

　Troilus And Cressida: Three Arias
　　S solo,3.3.3.3. 4.2.3.1. timp,perc,
　　2harp,strings OXFORD perf mat
　　rent
　　　contains: Diomede; How Can I
　　　Sleep?; Slowly It All Comes
　　　Back　　　　　　　　　　　　(W82)

　Two Early Songs　*CC2U
　　high solo OXFORD 345860-8 $5.00
　　　　　　　　　　　　　　　　　　　(W83)

WALTZ SONG, OP. 34, NO. 1 [ARR.] see
　Moszkowski, Moritz, Springtime Of
　Love

WALZ, ADAM
　I Am Thine, O Lord　*Gen
　　high solo AMSI V-11　　　　　(W84)

WALZER-GESÄNGE, OP. 6 see Zemlinsky,
　Alexander von

WANDA see Szymanowski, Karol

WANDELING see Voorn, Joop

WANDELLIED see Otten, Ludwig

WANDERER, DER see Proch, Heinrich see
　Schubert, Franz (Peter)

WANDERER DER WELT, DIE see Selmer,
　Johan Peter

WANDERER ERWACHT IN DER HERBERGE see
　Bijvanck, Henk

WANDERER SONG CYCLE see Dalby, Martin

WANDERERS NACHTLIED see Marx, Joseph
　see Pope, Conrad see Schubert,
　Franz (Peter)

WANDERERS NACHTLIED: ÜBER ALLEN GIPFELN
　IST RUH see Schubert, Franz (Peter)

WANDERLIED see Mendelssohn-Bartholdy,
　Felix

WANDERLIEDCHEN see Marx, Joseph

WANDRERS NACHTLIED: DER DU VON DEM
　HIMMEL BIST see Loewe, Carl
　Gottfried

WANDRERS NACHTLIED: ÜBER ALLEN GIPFELN
　IST RUH see Loewe, Carl Gottfried

WAR SCHÖNE ALS DER SCHÖNSTE TAG see
　Loewe, Carl Gottfried, Canzonette

WAR SONG OF THE KINGDOM OF STAR, A see
　Morita, Shin-Ichi

WAR SONGS see Marthinsen, Niels

WARABE UTA see Fukui, Tetsuo

WARBLE FOR LILAC-TIME see Carter,
　Elliott Cook, Jr.

WARFIELD, GERALD ALEXANDER (1940-　　)
　Trophy, A
　　S solo,pno [7'] sc AM.COMP.AL.
　　$7.70　　　　　　　　　　　　(W85)
　　S solo,vln,vcl,pno [7'] sc
　　AM.COMP.AL. $9.15　　　　　(W86)

WARING, ROB (1956)
　Har Dommedag Funnet Sted?
　　[Norw] Mez solo,perc,synthesizer
　　[7'] NORGE　　　　　　　　　(W87)
　　[Norw] Mez solo,perc,synthesizer
　　[7'] NORGE　　　　　　　　　(W88)

　Vectors
　　S solo,sax,clar,trp,vcl,db,vibra,
　　pno,2perc [9'] NORGE　　　　(W89)

WARLAMOW, ALEXANDER
　see VARLAMOV, ALEXANDER

WARLOCK, PETER
　see HESELTINE, PHILIP

WARNUNG see Marx, Joseph

WARREN, BETSY
　Asyl
　　TMez soli WISCAS f.s. from THREE
　　PIECE SONG CYCLE　　　　　　(W90)

　Christ My Refuge
　　med solo,pno/org (texts by Mary
　　Baker Eddy) WISCAS f.s. from
　　THREE SACRED SONGS　　　　　(W91)

　Christmas Morn
　　see Four Sacred Songs

　Communion Hymn
　　see Four Sacred Songs

　Dieu Vous Gard'
　　T solo,string quar UNITED MUS f.s.
　　　　　　　　　　　　　　　　　　　(W92)

　Feed My Sheep
　　med solo,pno/org (texts by Mary
　　Baker Eddy) WISCAS f.s. from
　　THREE SACRED SONGS　　　　　(W93)

　Four Sacred Songs
　　WISCAS f.s. texts by Mary Baker
　　Eddy
　　　contains: Christmas Morn;
　　　Communion Hymn; Love; Mother's
　　　Evening Prayer　　　　　　(W94)

　Four Songs For Solo Voice And
　　Woodwind
　　(texts by McCord, Mew, Millay, &
　　Larkin) WISCAS　　　　　　　(W95)

　Jonah　*cant
　　Bar solo,string quar UNITED MUS
　　f.s.　　　　　　　　　　　　(W96)

　Landung, Die
　　Bar solo,clar WISCAS f.s. from
　　THREE PIECE SONG CYCLE　　　(W97)

　Love
　　see Four Sacred Songs

　Mother's Evening Prayer
　　see Four Sacred Songs

　Psalm No. 33
　　see Psalm No. 121

　Psalm No. 121
　　solo voice,rec UNITED MUS f.s.
　　　contains also: Psalm No. 33 (W98)

　Pussy Cat Duets　*duet
　　2 solo voices,pno UNITED MUS f.s.
　　　　　　　　　　　　　　　　　　　(W99)

WARREN, BETSY (cont'd.)

　Satisfied
　　med solo,pno/org (texts by Mary
　　Baker Eddy) WISCAS f.s. from
　　THREE SACRED SONGS　　　　　(W100)

　Seven Excerpts From Washington's
　　Farewell Address
　　narrator, 2 brass choirs UNITED MUS
　　f.s.　　　　　　　　　　　　(W101)

　Six Poems Of Emily Dickinson
　　SSATBarB soli,acap WISCAS　(W102)

　Three Piece Song Cycle
　　see Asyl
　　see Landung, Die
　　see Unruhe

　Three Sacred Songs
　　see Christ My Refuge
　　see Feed My Sheep
　　see Satisfied

　Unruhe
　　S solo WISCAS f.s. from THREE PIECE
　　SONG CYCLE　　　　　　　　　(W103)

WARRIOR SAINT, THE see Rodgers, Lou

WARS SWEPT THROUGH HERE see Tal, Joseph

WAS AUS DIR TÖNT see Badings, Henk

WAS FRAG' ICH NACH DEN MENSCHEN see
　Giltay, Berend

WAS FUNKELT IHR SO MILD see Schubert,
　Franz (Peter), Sterne, Die

WAS HAT UNS DAZU BEWOGEN see Geelen,
　Mathieu

WAS IS Á WUNDÁ see Suppe, Franz von

WAS IT A DREAM? see Herbert-Caesari,
　Edgard

WAS KANN DAS LEBEN UNS DENN NUN NOCH
　WEITER FROMMEN see Ruyneman, Daniel

WAS SCHERZ SEI UND WAS LEIDEN see Bach,
　Johann Sebastian

WAS STERBLICH WAR... see Linke, Norbert

WAS THERE A TIME see Ford, Ronald

WASSERFALL BEI NACHT see Flothuis,
　Marius

WASSERTIEFE see Geelen, Mathieu

WASSERTROPFEN see Geelen, Mathieu

WAT BEWEEGT DAAR SNEL see Koetsier, Jan

WAT NOG SPLIJTEN KON see Ruiter, Wim de

WATANABE, KENJI (1950-　　)
　Machi Ni
　　Mez solo,pno [3'] ZEN-ON　(W104)

WATCHING THE MOON see Nakada, Yoshinao

WATCHING THE NEEDLEBOATS AT SAN SABBA
　see Keulen, Geert van

WATER-COLORS see Carpenter, John Alden

WATER FLOWS FROM UNDER THE SYCAMORE see
　Shut, Wasyl, Tetche Voda Z Pid
　Javora

WATERLEELIE, DE see Orthel, Leon

WAVES...THOUGHTS... see Medtner,
　Nikolai Karlovich

WAYNE
　Songs For The Holiday Season
　　SOUTHERN B485　　　　　　　(W105)

WAYNE, HARRY
　Four Poems (From A Child's Garden Of
　　Verses)
　　med-high solo HHP　　　　　(W106)

WE CAME TO THE SAND see Permont, Haim

WE HAVE NOT FAR TO WALK see
　Tchaikovsky, Piotr Ilyich

WE THREE see Beach, [Mrs.] H.H.A. (Amy
　Marcy Cheney)

WE THREE ARE ONE see Sateren, Leland
　Bernhard

WE WALK THE EARTH TOGETHER see Marez
　Oyens, Tera de

WEARY AND WORN WITH SUFFERING see
　Verdi, Giuseppe, Simon Boccanegra:
　Il Lacerato Spirito

WEIGL, [MRS.] VALLY (cont'd.)

Nightfall In The Mountains
med-high solo,vla/vln,pno [4'] sc
AM.COMP.AL. $1.95   (W159)

Not Earth Alone
med solo,pno [3'] sc AM.COMP.AL.
$1.60   (W160)

Oh Lord Of Mysteries
med solo,pno [14'] sc AM.COMP.AL.
$5.40   (W161)
med solo,vln,vcl [14'] sc
AM.COMP.AL. $5.40   (W162)

Oh, Love Doth Make The Day
med solo/high solo,pno [3'] sc
AM.COMP.AL. $3.85   (W163)
med solo/high solo,pno,marimba/gtr
[3'] sc AM.COMP.AL. $3.85   (W164)

Only The Moon Remembers *Suite
med solo,ob,clar,bsn/vcl [12']
AM.COMP.AL. sc $7.70, pts $4.25
                                 (W165)

Other Hearts
Mez solo,pno [2'] sc AM.COMP.AL.
$1.20   (W166)

Other Summers
Mez/Bar solo,pno [2'] sc
AM.COMP.AL. $1.20   (W167)

Peace, My Heart
med solo,pno [4'] sc AM.COMP.AL.
$1.95   (W168)
med solo,vln,vcl [4'] sc
AM.COMP.AL. $1.95   (W169)

Playthings Of The Wind
BarMez soli,clar/vla,pno [6']
AM.COMP.AL. sc $4.60, pts $.80
                                 (W170)

Revelation
med solo,2vln,vla,vcl [8']
AM.COMP.AL. sc $4.60, pts $1.95
                                 (W171)

Seal Lullaby
Mez solo,pno,rec/ob [2'] sc
AM.COMP.AL. $1.20   (W172)

Songs From The Somerset Hills
Mez solo,pno [9'] sc AM.COMP.AL.
$4.60   (W173)

Songs Newly Seen In The Dusk
Mez solo,vcl sc AM.COMP.AL. $6.15
                                 (W174)

Songs Of Concern *CCU
MezBar soli,fl/vln,pno AM.COMP.AL.
sc $9.15, pts $3.80   (W175)

Songs Of Love And Leaving [1] *CCU
med solo,vln/fl/clar,vla,vcl,gtr
AM.COMP.AL. sc $13.00, pts $6.90
                                 (W176)

Songs Of Love And Leaving [2] *CCU
med solo,vln,alto fl/clar,vla
AM.COMP.AL. sc $13.00, pts $8.45
                                 (W177)

Soon
med solo,fl/vln/clar,pno [3'] sc
AM.COMP.AL. $1.20   (W178)

Still Will Be
SSA soli,acap [1'] sc AM.COMP.AL.
f.s.   (W179)

Thistle, Yarrow, Clover
med solo,pno [3'] sc AM.COMP.AL.
$1.95   (W180)
med solo,fl,clar,bsn [3'] sc
AM.COMP.AL. $1.95   (W181)

Three Easy Rounds (3:4voci), Acap
*CC3U,round
sc AM.COMP.AL. $.80   (W182)

Who Is At My Window?
med solo,pno [3'] sc AM.COMP.AL.
$1.20   (W183)

Year, The
MezBarT soli,pno,timp,2vln,vla,vcl
[9'] AM.COMP.AL. sc $4.60, pts
$3.45   (W184)

WEIHNACHTLICHES KONZERT, 2 BAROCK-ARIEN
see Krieger, Johann

WEIHNACHTSALBUM see Krug

WEIHNACHTSBÄUMLEIN, DAS see Lothar,
Mark

WEIHNACHTSLIED see Eisler, Hanns, Sei
Uns Gegrüsst, Du Weihnachtsbaum see
Koch

WEIL ALLES ERNEUT SICH BEGIBT see
Schibler, Armin

WEIL ALLES UNSAGBAR IST see Primosch,
James

WEILL
Complainte De La Seine
see Trois Chansons

Je Ne T'aime Pas
see Trois Chansons

Trois Chansons
LEDUC HE 33701 f.s.
contains: Complainte De La Seine;
Je Ne T'aime Pas; Youkali
                                 (W185)

Youkali
see Trois Chansons

WEILL, KURT (1900-1950)
Four Walt Whitman Songs
solo voice,pno EUR.AM.MUS. EA00584
                                 (W186)

Frauentanz *Op.10, CC7U
S solo,fl,vla,clar,horn,bsn voc sc
UNIVER. UE 7748 f.s.   (W187)

WEIR, JUDITH (1954-   )
Consolations Of Scholarship, The
Mez solo,chamber group NOVELLO f.s.
                                 (W188)

WEISGALL, HUGO (1912-   )
Lyrical Interval *song cycle
solo voice PRESSER 411-41088 f.s.
                                 (W189)
low solo,pno [55'] (diff) PRESSER
                                 (W190)

WEISS, HERMAN (1946-   )
Cantata No. 1
Mez solo,clar,vln,vla [8'] APNM sc
$4.50, set $17.50   (W191)

Cantata No. 2
Mez solo,clar,vln,pno [6'] APNM sc
$5.00, set $16.50   (W192)

Cantata No. 3
SATB soli,horn,2vcl,db,pno [14']
APNM sc $21.50, pts rent   (W193)

Three Songs *CC3U
S solo,pno APNM sc $6.50, set
$12.50   (W194)

WEISS, MANFRED (1935-   )
Erfüllung Der Zeiten *song cycle
Bar solo,vcl,pno DEUTSCHER DV 9404
                                 (W195)

WEISS SCHLAGEN DIE WELLEN see Focke,
Fré

WEISSE ROSE see Zimmermann, Udo

WELIN, KARL-ERIK (1934-1992)
Renovationes
solo voice,fl,vln,hpsd,perc SEESAW
                                 (W196)

WELLOCK, RICHARD (1917-   )
In Ev'ry Flower
med solo,pno/org (easy) GLOUCHESTER
                                 (W197)

WELT IST ZERBROCHEN, EINE see Badings,
Henk

WEM ICH ZU GEFALLEN SUCHE see Matthus,
Siegfried

WENDUNGEN, 17 GEDICHTE VON W. FOCKE see
Focke, Fré

WENN ALLE BRÜNNLEIN FLIESSEN
(177 german folksongs) PETERS 10300
                                 (W198)

WENN DER BLÜTHEN FRÜHLINGSREGEN see
Loewe, Carl Gottfried

WENN DIE MUTTERLEIN see Mahler, Gustav

WENN DIE STERNE see Hanson, Sten

WENN DIE UHREN SO NAH see Orthel, Leon

WENN ICH AUF DEM LAGER LIEGE see
Mendelssohn-Bartholdy, Felix,
Abendlied

WENN MEIN.SCHATZ HOCHZEIT MACHT see
Mahler, Gustav

WENN SICH ZWEI HERZEN SCHEIDEN see
Mendelssohn-Bartholdy, Felix

WENN WEIHNACHT IST see Herrmann, W.

WENSIECKI, EDMUND
Advent And Christmas Songs *CCU
[Ger] solo voice,gtr PLUCKED STR
ZM 2398 $6.50   (W199)

WERE I A CLOUDLET see Backer-Lunde,
Johan

WERE I BUT LIKE THESE see Puccini,
Giacomo, Villi, Le: Se Come Voi
Piccina

WERE YOU THERE? see Gospel Favourites

WERGELANDS BARNESANGER see Beck, Thomas
Ludvigsen

WERNICK, RICHARD F. (1934-   )
Ball Of Sun
solo voice,pno (med diff) PRESSER
111-40112   (W200)

I Too
solo voice,pno PRESSER 111-40123
                                 (W201)

Oracle II
S solo,ob,pno [12'] (diff) PRESSER
111-40107   (W202)

Poison Tree, A
S solo,chamber group [12'] (diff)
sc PRESSER 416-41112 $15.00, ipr
                                 (W203)

Songs Of Remembrance
Mez solo, shawm+english horn+ob sc
PRESSER 111-40126   (W204)

Two For Jan
SMez soli,ob,bass clar,vcl PRESSER
pts 111-40132P, sc 111-40132S
                                 (W205)

Visions Of Terror And Wonder
S solo,pno pno red PRESSER
111-40106 $15.00   (W206)
Mez solo,pno PRESSER 111-40106
                                 (W207)

WERTHER: J'AURAIS SUR MA POITRINO see
Massenet, Jules

WESSEX GRAVES see Berkeley, Michael

WESSOBRUNNER GEBET, DAS see Radulescu,
Michael, Poeta, De

WEST SIDE STORY SELECTIONS see
Bernstein, Leonard

WESTELIJK see Samama, Leo

WESTWINDS see Antoniou, Theodore

WETZ, RICHARD (1875-1935)
Gesänge *CCU
solo voice,pno KISTNER f.s. (W208)

WETZLER, HERMANN HANS (1870-1943)
Fünf Lieder
[Ger] high solo (not available
outside U.S.A.) RECITAL 411
                                 (W209)

WETZLER, ROBERT
God, Hurrah!
Mez solo,English horn,vcl,pno sc,
pts AMSI V-14   (W210)

Wedding Blessing
med-high solo AMSI V-8   (W211)

WETZLER, ROBERT PAUL (1932-   )
Wedding Blessing
high solo AMSI V-8 $1.25   (W212)

WEYNACHT-ANDACHT see Krieger, Johann

WEYRAUCH, JOHANNES (1897-1977)
Erdengang
PETERS 9269   (W213)

WHAT CHILD IS THIS see Wolff, Ernst
Victor

WHAT COULD SHE SAY? see Yavelow,
Christopher Johnson

WHAT DOES NOT PASS see Saudek, Vojtech

WHAT IF I SAY... see Walker, George
Theophilus

WHAT IS LIFE TO ME? see Gluck,
Christoph Willibald, Ritter von,
Orfeo Ed Euridice: Che Faro Senza
Euridice?

WHEAR, PAUL WILLIAM (1925-   )
Lamb, The
solo voice LUDWIG VS-07 $2.00
                                 (W214)

WHEN A CHARMER see Verdi, Giuseppe,
Rigoletto: Questa O Quella

WHEN I AM DEAD see Thorarinsson, Jón

WHEN I AM DEAD, MY DEAREST see Somers-
Cocks, John, Song

WHEN I WAS YOUNG see Jeffreys, John

WHEN I WAS YOUNG, PART 2 see Jeffreys,
John

WHEN I WAS YOUNG, PART 3 see Jeffreys,
John

WHEN ICICLES HANG BY THE WALL see
Foote, Arthur

WHEN LOVE HAS GONE see Franz, Carl

WHEN LOVE IS KIND see Lehmann

WHEN SHE WENT ALONE INTO THE HOUSE see
  Vogel, Roger Craig

WHEN THE ANGELS BLOW THEIR TRUMPETS see
  Sims, Ezra

WHEN THE FLOWERS SLEEP see Björnsson,
  Arni

WHEN THE HAND OF SPRING see Haxton,
  Kenneth

WHEN THE STARS WERE BRIGHTLY SHINING
  see Puccini, Giacomo, Tosca: E
  Lucevan Le Stelle

WHEN THIRTEEN SOUNDS see Nash, Paul

WHEN WE ARE LOST see Bax, [Sir] Arnold

WHEN WE DEAD AWAKEN see Pütz, Eduard

WHEN YESTERDAY WE MET see Rachmaninoff,
  Sergey Vassilievich

WHERE CORALS LIE see Elgar, [Sir]
  Edward (William)

WHERE GO THE BOATS? see Masseus, Jan
  see Mourant, Walter

WHERE IS THE SONG IN THE FOREST see
  Olsen, Sparre, Kvi Tralar Det Ikkje
  Lenger I Skogen

WHERE POPPIES BLOW! see Harrington,
  Frank J.

WHERE SILENCE REIGNS see Geller,
  Timothy

WHERE THE BEE SUCKS see Arne, Thomas
  Augustine

WHERE THE MOUNTAIN CROSSES see Zupko,
  Ramon

WHERE - WER see Goorissen, Jan

WHISPERING NATURE see Medtner, Nikolai
  Karlovich

WHISPERS FROM HEAVENLY DEATH see Henze,
  Hans Werner

WHISPERS OF HEAVENLY DEATH see Luedeke,
  Raymond

WHISTLING WIND see Korte, Karl

WHITE
  Songs From Queen's Road
    solo voice,fl,pno SOUTHERN V089
                                    (W215)

  Three Byron Songs
    solo voice,pno SOUTHERN V090 (W216)

WHITE AUTUMN, A: SONG CYCLE see Mori,
  Konate

WHITE CAMELLIA see Igarashi, Tadashi

WHITE DWARF see Blank, Allan see Udow,
  Michael William

WHITE ELECTION, THE see Getty, Gordon

WHITE ONES, THE see Flothuis, Marius

WHITE ROSES see Reif, Paul

WHITEHEAD, GILLIAN
  Requiem
    Mez solo,org WAI-TE-ATA 137 (W217)

WHO CAN FIND A VIRTUOUS WOMAN? see
  Diemer, Emma Lou

WHO DO YOU LOVE see Dillon

WHO IS AT MY WINDOW? see Weigl, [Mrs.]
  Vally

WHO KNOWS? see Reinhardt, Bruno

WHOLE SHEET OF SOLITUDE, A see
  MacBride, David Huston

WHOOPEE see Donaldson, Walter

WHY? see Bakke, Ruth see Mourant,
  Walter

WHY ARE WE BY ALL CREATURES WAITED ON
  B solo,horn,trom/bass trom,vla,vcl,db
  [6'] (parts for each are for rent)
  sc APNM $4.00 from SONNETS FROM
  JOHN DONNE   (W218)

WHY, NO ONE TO LOVE? see Foster,
  Stephen Collins

WHY SHOULD I BLUSH TO OWN I LOVE? see
  Mourant, Walter

WHY THE SOUP TASTES LIKE THE DAILY NEWS
  see Heilner, Irwin

WHY THY SORROW, WHY THY WEEPING? see
  Glinka, Mikhail Ivanovich

WICKED AND UNFAITHFUL SONG, THE see
  Austin, John

WIDER VIEW, THE see Adams, Leslie

WIDERSTEHE DOCH DER SUNDE see Bach,
  Johann Sebastian

WIDMUNG see Schumann, Robert
  (Alexander)

WIDOR, CHARLES-MARIE (1844-1937)
  Non Credo
    solo voice,pno LEDUC f.s.   (W219)

  O Salutaris
    A/B solo,org LEDUC f.s.   (W220)

  Six Melodies Italiennes, Op. Nos. 32
  & 35
    [It] high solo RECITAL 300   (W221)

WIDOW'S LAMENT IN SPRINGTIME, THE see
  Haxton, Kenneth

WIE DER ABENDWIND DURCH GESCHULTERTE
  SENSEN DER SCHNITTER see Voortman,
  Roland

WIE DIE KRÄHE see Eisler, Hanns

WIE EINST see Marx, Joseph

WIE IM TRAUM LIEGT DER MORGEN see
  Focke, Fré

WIE MICHS BANGT see Glière, Reinhold
  Moritzovich

WIE, OP. 27 see Wagemans, Peter-Jan

WIE TROSTREICH IST UNS ADAMSKINDERN see
  Haydn, [Johann] Michael

WIE ZAUBERISCH GLÜH'N see Glière,
  Reinhold Moritzovich

WIEGELAND HOOFD see Mulder, Herman

WIEGENLIED see Bijvanck, Henk see
  Brahms, Johannes see Erdlen,
  Hermann see Isolfsson, Pall see
  Louis Ferdinand, Prince Of Prussia
  see Thoroddsen, Emil

WIEGENLIED IM SOMMER see Wolf, Hugo

WIEGENLIEDER DER WELT *CCU
  (Behrend, Siegfried) solo voice,gtr
    PLUCKED STR ZM 1819 $5.25   (W222)

WIEMANN, BETH
  Simple Songs
    S solo,pno [10'] AM.COMP.AL. (W223)

  Songs Without Words
    S solo,ob,bsn,pno,vcl [10']
      AM.COMP.AL.   (W224)

  To The Moon
    S solo,ob,bsn,pno [6'] AM.COMP.AL.
                                    (W225)
  Two Poems By April Bernard
    S solo,pno,db [6'] AM.COMP.AL.
                                    (W226)

WIEN, DU STADT MEINER TRÄUME see
  Sieczynski, Rudolf

WIENER COUPLETS FÜR PIANOFORTE UND
  GESANG see Kriebaum, Franz

WIENERLIEDER see Hanson, Sten

WIENHORST, RICHARD (1920-   )
  Easter: A Song Cycle *Easter
    Mez/A solo,harp/pno sc AM.COMP.AL.
    $9.60   (W227)

  Magnificat
    S solo,org sc AM.COMP.AL. $1.60
                                    (W228)
  Sonnet: No Longer Mourn
    Mez solo,pno sc AM.COMP.AL. $1.95
                                    (W229)

WIERNIK, ADAM (1916-   )
  Inspiration
    solo voice,pno,db SUECIA 366 (W230)

  Voice And Percussion
    solo voice,perc STIM f.s.   (W231)

WIGGLESWORTH, FRANK (1918-   )
  Five Songs Of Robert Frost *CC5U
    med solo,alto fl sc AM.COMP.AL.
    $6.15   (W232)

WIGGLESWORTH, FRANK (cont'd.)
  God, That Madest All Things
    S solo,pno [3'30"] AM.COMP.AL.
                                    (W233)
  More Songs Of Autumn
    S solo,pno [21'] AM.COMP.AL. (W234)

WIJDEVELD, WOLFGANG (1910-   )
  Liederen Op Zuid-Afrikaanse Tekst
    *CC7L
    high solo,pno DONEMUS f.s.   (W235)

WIJFKEN, STAAT OPPE see Ehlen, Margriet

WILBRANDT, JÜRGEN (1922-   )
  Liederzyklus Beppino
    PETERS 5236   (W236)

WILD AIR see Edwards, George

WILD NIGHTS see Walker, George
  Theophilus

WILD SWANS see Duke

WILD WINDS see Berkeley, Michael

WILDBERGER, JACQUES (1922-   )
  Stimme, Die Alte, Schwächer Werdende
  Stimme, Die
    S solo,3(pic).2(English horn).2.2+
    contrabsn. 4.3.4.0. perc,harp,
    cel,elec org,strings,electronic
    tape,vcl solo BREITKOPF-W f.s.
                                    (W237)

WILDE, STEILE BRANDUNG see Focke, Fré

WILDER STURM DURCHBRAUSTE LAND UND
  HEIMAT, EIN see Bunge, Sas

WILHELM HAT EIN SCHLOSS see Eisler,
  Hanns

WILL NOBODY MARRY ME see Russel, Henry

WILLAN, HEALEY (1880-1968)
  O Mistress Mine
    see Two Songs

  To Electra
    see Two Songs

  Two Songs
    med solo,pno CLASSV f.s.
      contains: O Mistress Mine; To
      Electra   (W238)

WILLIAM AND EMELY see Boldemann, Laci

WILLIAMS
  Two-Part American Songs, Book 2
    SOUTHERN B391   (W239)

WILLIAMS, DAVID H. (1946-   )
  Fair Child Of Mine *Xmas
    AMSI V-16   (W240)

  Holiest Vow, The *Marriage
    med solo AMSI V-18   (W241)

WILLIAMS, RALPH VAUGHAN
  see VAUGHAN WILLIAMS, [SIR] RALPH

WILLINGHAM, LAWRENCE
  Carol Of The Thrush *Op.15
    S solo,fl,clar,vln,vla,vcl [39'] sc
    AM.COMP.AL. $49.00   (W242)

  Count Ugolino *Op.12
    Bar solo,ob,2timp,perc,3vla,6vcl,
    conductor [24'] sc AM.COMP.AL.
    $15.30   (W243)

  Lake, The *Op.25
    S solo,clar,vla,perc,pno [5'] sc
    AM.COMP.AL. $9.15   (W244)

  Mad Song *Op.24
    S solo,clar,2perc,2vln,vla,vcl,
    conductor [10'] sc AM.COMP.AL.
    $11.45   (W245)

  River-Merchant's Wife, The *Op.20
    S solo,fl,perc,pno,vcl [13'] sc
    AM.COMP.AL. $15.20   (W246)

  Songs From Hermann Hesse *Op.26, CCU
    med solo,pno sc AM.COMP.AL. $10.30
                                    (W247)
  Songs Of Innocence And Experience
    *Op.17, CCU
    S solo,pno sc AM.COMP.AL. $9.95
                                    (W248)
  Three Serious Songs *Op.9, CC3U
    Bar/T solo sc AM.COMP.AL. $9.15
                                    (W249)

WILLOW, THE see Fomenko, Mykola

WILLOW BRANCHES, THE see Wilson, Thomas

WILLOW BROOK SUITE NO. 2 see Woollen,
  Russell

WILLOW GARLAND, A see Adolphe, Bruce

WILLOW SONG see Verdi, Giuseppe, Otello: Salce

WILLOW TREE, THE see Medtner, Nikolai Karlovich

WILLST DU NOCH LÄNGER see Bois, Rob du

WILSON, HENRY LANE (1871-1915)
Spring Morning, A
high solo,pno CLASSV 1736 (W250)

Tenor And Baritone
TBar soli,pno CLASSV 1169 (W251)

Two Beggars, The
TBar soli,pno CLASSV 1201 (W252)

WILSON, RICHARD (EDWARD) (1941-)
Persuasions
S solo,alto fl,ob&English horn,bsn&
contrabsn,hpsd [20'0"] PEER
(W253)

WILSON, THOMAS (1927-)
Three Orkney Songs
SBar soli,fl,ob,vln,vcl,pno [10']
QUEEN (W254)

Willow Branches, The *song cycle
solo voice,2.2.2.2. 2.0.0.0. harp,
cel,2perc,timp,strings [21']
QUEEN (W255)
solo voice,pno [21'] QUEEN (W256)

WILT THOU FORGIVE see Humfrey, Pelham

WINDMÜHLE see Flothuis, Marius

WINDOW FLOAT IN LAKE see Kurokami, Yoshimitsu

WINDRÄDER see Marx, Joseph

WINDSONGS see Pasatieri, Thomas see Zimmerman

WINDY NIGHTS see Masseus, Jan see Mourant, Walter

WING'D HOUR see Gideon, Miriam

WINHAM, GODFREY (1934-1975)
Habit Of Perfection, The
S solo,2vln,vla,vcl [14'] APNM sc
$5.00, set $18.50 (W257)

WINNIE THE POOH see Knussen, Oliver

WINSLOW, WALTER
Anagrams *song cycle
Bar solo,fl,vcl,elec gtr,pno [12']
sc AM.COMP.AL. $9.15 (W258)

Canzone
S solo,fl,clar,bsn,horn,trp,perc,
pno,strings [18'30"] AM.COMP.AL.
(W259)

Concert Aria
S solo,fl,clar,horn,perc,harp,
strings [20'] sc AM.COMP.AL.
$25.85 (W260)

Evening Star
SSAATTB soli,fl,horn,harp,pno,perc,
2vln,vcl [10'] AM.COMP.AL. sc
$17.50, pts $13.30 (W261)

Nahua Songs *CCU
high solo,pno sc AM.COMP.AL. $15.30
(W262)

Palinurus
T solo,fl,clar,horn,trp,trom,2perc,
pno [20'] sc AM.COMP.AL. $48.25
(W263)

Serenade
S solo,horn,2vln,vla,vcl [13']
AM.COMP.AL. sc $11.45, pts $11.45
(W264)

Six Songs On Poems Of William Stafford
S solo,pno [10'35"] AM.COMP.AL.
(W265)

Three Songs *CC3U
Bar solo,ob,clar,harp,pno
AM.COMP.AL. sc $9.15, pts $6.90
(W266)

WINTER
Fröhliche Weihnacht
KAHNT 6493 (W267)

WINTER see Kleppe, Joost see Kleppe,
Joost see Maxym, R. see Samama, Leo
see Sveinbjörnsson, Sveinbjörn

WINTER, TOMAS (1954-)
Fyra Stagneliussånger *Op.141
Bar solo,pno STIM (W268)

WINTER COME see Lauridsen, Morten Johannes

WINTER IS A COLD THING see Clarke, Henry Leland

WINTER JOURNEY see Schubert, Franz (Peter), Winterreise

WINTER LOVE see Fennimore, Joseph William

WINTER NIGHT see Backer-Lunde, Johan, Vinternat

WINTER SETTINGS see Oliver, Harold

WINTER SONG see Dydo, J. Stephen see Hoiby, Lee

WINTER UNDER CULTIVATION see Ruiter, Wim de

WINTERABEND, DER see Schubert, Franz (Peter)

WINTERNACHT see Lothar, Mark

WINTERNIGHT, A see Schoonenbeek, Kees

WINTERRAST see Helgason, Hallgrimur

WINTERREISE see Schubert, Franz (Peter)

WINTERREISE, DIE see Bredemeyer, Reiner

WINTER'S ROSE, A see Pluister, Simon

WINTERSTÜRME WICHEN see Wagner,
Richard, Walküre, Die: Siegmunds
Liebeslied

WIR BETEN DICH UNENDLICH WESEN see
Haydn, [Johann] Michael

WIR GENESSEN DIE HIMMLISCHEN FREUDEN
see Mahler, Gustav

WIR WANDELTEN see Freudenthal, Otto

WIREN, DAG IVAR (1905-1986)
Ormvisa
solo voice,pno GEHRMANS 6617 (W269)

WISECRACKS see Riedstra, Tom

WISH, THE see Parke, Dorothy

WISSEND WÜRZTE ES DEN ANFANG see Focke,
Fré

WISSMER, PIERRE (1915-)
Et l'Aube Rouvre Le Poing
Bar solo,pno DURAND f.s. (W270)

WIT, OP. 33 see Samama, Leo

WITCHCRAFT BY A PICTURE see Haxton,
Kenneth

WITH A PRIMULA VERIS see Grieg, Edvard
Hagerup, Med En Primula Veris

WITH RUE MY HEART IS LADEN see Walker,
George Theophilus

WITHERED LEAVES see Sonevytsky, Ihor

WITZENMANN, WOLFGANG
Oden I
solo voice,pno EDI-PAN EP 7230
(W271)
Oden III
T solo,pno EDI-PAN EP 7231 (W272)
Oden V
Mez solo,pno EDI-PAN EP 7232 (W273)

WO STILL EIN HERZ VON LIEBE GLÜHT see
Kücken, Friedrich Wilhelm

WO WOHNT DER LIEBE GOTT? see
Goltermann, Georg

WOE IS ME see Avni, Tzvi

WOEDENDE TIENER KEURT HEMD AF see
Braal, Andries de

WOHER ICH KOMME see Louis Ferdinand,
Prince Of Prussia

WOHL DENK ICH OFT see Wolf, Hugo

WOHLTÄTIGKEIT see Eisler, Hanns

WOLF, HUGO (1860-1903)
Alles Endet
low solo,pno PETERS 3155B (W274)

Anakreons Grab
low solo,pno PETERS 3228G (W275)

Auch Kleine Dinge
high solo,pno PETERS 3144A (W276)

Auf Dem Grünen Baum
high solo,pno PETERS 3150E (W277)

Eichendorff-Lieder, Vol. 1 *song
cycle
low solo,pno KALMUS K 05111 (W278)

WOLF, HUGO (cont'd.)
Eichendorff-Lieder, Vol. 2 *song
cycle
low solo,pno KALMUS K 05112 (W279)

Elfenlied
high solo,pno PETERS 3141D (W280)

Epiphanias
med solo,pno PETERS 3227K (W281)

Er Ist's
high solo,pno PETERS 3227B (W282)
low solo,pno PETERS 3228D (W283)

Freund
high solo,pno PETERS 3227D (W284)
low solo,pno PETERS 3228D (W285)

Fühlt Meine Seele
low solo,pno PETERS 3115C (W286)

Fussreise
high solo,pno PETERS 3140K (W287)
low solo,pno PETERS 3140L (W288)

Ganymed
high solo,pno PETERS 3159R (W289)

Gärtner
high solo,pno PETERS 3227I (W290)

Gebet
low solo,pno PETERS 3228C (W291)

Gedichte Von Johann Wolfgang Von
Goethe, Heft 1 *CCU
(Spitzer, L.) low solo DOBLINGER
08 531 f.s. (W292)

Gedichte Von Johann Wolfgang Von
Goethe, Heft 2 *CCU
(Spitzer, L.) low solo DOBLINGER
08 532 f.s. (W293)

Gedichte Von Johann Wolfgang Von
Goethe, Heft 3 *CCU
low solo,pno DOBLINGER 08 533 f.s.
(W294)

Gedichte Von Johann Wolfgang Von
Goethe, Heft 4 *CCU
low solo,pno DOBLINGER 08 534 f.s.
(W295)

Gedichte Von Johann Wolfgang Von
Goethe, Heft 5 *CCU
low solo,pno DOBLINGER 08 535 f.s.
(W296)

Gedichte Von Johann Wolfgang Von
Goethe, Heft 6 *CCU
low solo,pno DOBLINGER 08 536 f.s.
(W297)

Gedichte Von Johann Wolfgang Von
Goethe, Heft 7 *CCU
low solo,pno DOBLINGER 08 537 f.s.
(W298)

Gedichte Von Johann Wolfgang Von
Goethe, Heft 8 *CCU
low solo,pno DOBLINGER 08 538 f.s.
(W299)

Gesang Weylas
high solo,pno PETERS 3143H (W300)

Goethe-Lieder, Vol. 2
KALMUS K 05124 (W301)

Goethe-Lieder, Vol. 3
KALMUS K 05125 (W302)

Heimweh
low solo,pno PETERS 3228A (W303)

In Dem Schatten
high solo,pno PETERS 3150B (W304)

Italian Songbook
see Italienisches Liederbuch

Italienisches Liederbuch
"Italian Songbook" solo voice,pno
LEA 179 (W305)

Italienisches Liederbuch Auswahl
low solo,pno PETERS 3184 (W306)

Italienisches Liederbuch, Vol. 1
*song cycle
KALMUS K 05106 (W307)

Italienisches Liederbuch, Vol. 2
*song cycle
KALMUS K 05107 (W308)

Lieder Aus Der Jugendzeit *song
cycle
[Ger/Eng] KALMUS K 05100 (W309)

Mausfallensprüchlein
high solo,pno PETERS 3153F (W310)

Michelangelo Lieder
B solo,pno CLASSV 1070 (W311)

Mignon (1)
low solo,pno PETERS 3228H (W312)

WOLF, HUGO (cont'd.)

Moerike-Lieder In Two Volumes, Vol. 1
*song cycle
low solo,pno KALMUS K 05130   (W313)

Moerike-Lieder In Two Volumes, Vol. 2
*song cycle
low solo,pno KALMUS K 05131   (W314)

Moerike-Lieder, Vol. 1 *song cycle
high solo,pno KALMUS K 05113   (W315)

Moerike-Lieder, Vol. 2 *song cycle
high solo,pno KALMUS K 05114   (W316)
low solo,pno KALMUS K 05119   (W317)

Moerike-Lieder, Vol. 3 *song cycle
low solo,pno KALMUS K 05120   (W318)
high solo,pno KALMUS K 05115   (W319)

Moerike-Lieder, Vol. 4 *song cycle
high solo,pno KALMUS K 05116   (W320)

Moerike-Lieder, Vol. 5 *song cycle
low solo,pno KALMUS K 05122   (W321)
high solo,pno KALMUS K 05117   (W322)

Musikant
high solo,pno PETERS 3227E   (W323)
low solo,pno PETERS 3228E   (W324)

Nachgelassene Werke, Folge 1: Lieder
Mit Klavierbegleitung
[Ger/Eng] SCIEN 1935   (W325)

Nixe Binsefuss
high solo,pno PETERS 3143K   (W326)

Nun Wandre Maria
high solo,pno PETERS 3149C   (W327)
low solo,pno PETERS 3149D   (W328)

Rattenfanger, Der
T/Bar solo,2+pic.2.2.2. 2.2.0.0.
perc,strings [3'30"] KALMUS A6122
sc $9.00, pts $15.00   (W329)

Sänger
low solo,pno PETERS 3156K   (W330)

Schreckenberger
high solo,pno PETERS 3147K   (W331)

Songs, 25; 3 Michelangelo Lieder
solo voice,pno LEA 180   (W332)

Spanisches Liederbuch Auswahl, Band
1: Geistliche Lieder
low solo,pno PETERS 3185A   (W333)

Spanisches Liederbuch Auswahl, Band
2: Weltliche Lieder
low solo,pno PETERS 3185B   (W334)

Spanisches Liederbuch, Vol. 2 *song
cycle
KALMUS K 05103   (W335)

Spanisches Liederbuch, Vol. 3 *song
cycle
KALMUS K 05104   (W336)

Spanisches Liederbuch, Weltliche
Lieder, Heft 1 *CCU
(Spitzer, L.) low solo DOBLINGER
08 543 f.s.   (W337)

Spanisches Liederbuch, Weltliche
Lieder, Heft 2 *CCU
(Spitzer, L.) low solo DOBLINGER
08 544 f.s.   (W338)

Spanisches Liederbuch, Weltliche
Lieder, Heft 3 *CCU
(Spitzer, L.) low solo DOBLINGER
08 545 f.s.   (W339)

Verborgenheit
high solo,pno PETERS 3140N   (W340)
low solo,pno PETERS 3140M   (W341)

Verlassenen Mägdlein
high solo,pno PETERS 3140P   (W342)

Verschwiegene Liebe
high solo,pno PETERS 3227F   (W343)
low solo,pno PETERS 3228F   (W344)

Wiegenlied Im Sommer
low solo,pno PETERS 3228M   (W345)

Wohl Denk Ich Oft
low solo,pno PETERS 3115A   (W346)

WOLF-FERRARI, ERMANNO (1876-1948)
Aprila
see Jewels Of The Madonna: Serenade

Jewels Of The Madonna: Bacio Di Lama
[It/Eng] Bar solo,pno CLASSV 1173
                               (W347)

Jewels Of The Madonna: E Ndringhete,
Ndranghete
S solo,pno CLASSV 1174   (W348)

WOLF-FERRARI, ERMANNO (cont'd.)

Jewels Of The Madonna: Serenade
"Aprila" Bar solo,pno CLASSV 0890
                               (W349)

Quattro Rispetti, Op. 12
[It/Ger] Mez solo RECITAL 242
                               (W350)

WOLFF, ERNST VICTOR
What Child Is This
SCHIRM.G ST41639   (W351)

WOLFF, JOACHIM
I Dream Of Meadows And Other Songs To
Poems Of Yar Slavutych
(Manevytch, V.) [Ukrainian] med
solo,pno DUMA   (W352)

WOLFFS, FELIX
Selected Lieder, Vol. 6
high solo,pno PRESSER   (W353)

Selected Lieder, Vol. 7
med solo,pno PRESSER   (W354)

Selected Lieder, Vol. 8
solo voice,pno PRESSER   (W355)

Selected Lieder, Vol. 9
high solo,pno PRESSER   (W356)

Selected Lieder, Vol. 10
med solo,pno (diff, contains 13
songs) PRESSER   (W357)

WOLKEN, DIE see Visser, Peter

WOLKENBOOT see Andriessen, Hendrik

WOLPE, STEFAN (1902-1972)
Dance Master, The
see La-Menatzeach Al Ha-Mecholot

Fünf Lieder Nach Friedrich Hölderlin
med solo,kbd PEER 61738-213   (W358)
Mez/A solo,pno (diff) PEER   (W359)

La-Menatzeach Al Ha-Mecholot
"Dance Master, The" solo voice,
clar,pno (text by Chaim Bialik)
MCGIN-MARX   (W360)

Lazy Andy Ant
narrator,2pno SEESAW f.s.   (W361)

Quintet With Voice
B solo,clar,horn,vcl,harp,pno
[22'0"] PEER   (W362)

WOLSCHINA, REINHARD (1952-   )
Kosmische Zeichen
Bar solo,3perc,strings [15']
DEUTSCHER   (W363)

Vier Lieder Nach Gedichten Von Eva
Strittmatter *CC4U
Bar solo,pno DEUTSCHER 9058 f.s.
                               (W364)

WOLTER, DETLEF (1933-   )
Ringelnatz-Capr.
KÄHNT 9169.   (W365)

WOMAN OF VALOR, A see Gideon, Miriam

WOMAN'S A FICKLE JADE see Verdi,
Giuseppe, Rigoletto: La Donna È
Mobile

WOMAN'S LAST WORD, A see Homer, Sidney

WOMAN'S LIFE AND LOVE see Schumann,
Robert (Alexander), Frauenliebe Und
Leben

WOMEN see Kruse, Bjørn Howard

WOMEN USELESSE - AN HYMNE TO LOVE see
Douw, Andre

WOOD, CHARLES (1866-1926)
Ethiopia Saluting The Colors
low solo,pno (text by Walt Whitman)
CLASSV 2087   (W366)

WOOD, HAYDN (1882-1959)
Roses Of Picardy
low solo,pno RECITAL 2230   (W367)
med solo,pno CLASSV 2086   (W368)
high solo,pno CLASSV 2085   (W369)

WOOD, JOSEPH (1915-   )
Four Chinese Love Poems *CC4U
A solo,pno sc AM.COMP.AL. $5.00
                               (W370)

Fragments From Hipponax
S solo,pno [5'] sc AM.COMP.AL.
$4.60   (W371)

WOOD, KEVIN JOSEPH (1947-   )
Under The Trees
med solo,clar,vla,vcl,pno sc,voc sc
UNICORN 2.0042.3 $9.95   (W372)

WOODFORDE-FINDEN, AMY
Four Indian Love Songs
med solo BOOSEY VAB0291   (W373)

WOODMAN, SPARE THAT TREE! see Russel,
Henry

WOOLLEN, RUSSELL (1923-   )
Five Songs *Op.63, CC5U
S solo,pno sc AM.COMP.AL. $11.45
                               (W374)

Songs Of Eve, Op. 102
S solo,pno [14'10"] AM.COMP.AL.
                               (W375)

Three Songs On Poems Of Elinor Wylie
*CC3U
S solo,pno sc AM.COMP.AL. $7.70
                               (W376)

Willow Brook Suite No. 2
med solo,pno [20'] sc AM.COMP.AL.
$18.40   (W377)

WORD CAME FORTH, THE see Franco, Johan

WORDS see Bois, Rob du

WORDS FOR MUSIC PERHAPS see Gerber,
Steven R.

WORDS FROM SHAKESPEARE see Ronsheim,
John Richard

WORDS OF PRAISE see Medema, Kenneth
Peter

WORDS OF SVEND HERULFSEN, THE see
Johansen, David Monrad, Svend
Herulfsens Ord

WORDS OVERHEARD see Birtwistle,
Harrison

WORDSWORTH, WILLIAM (1908-1988)
Come Away Death
solo voice BANKS f.s.   (W378)

Constant Lover, The
solo voice BANKS f.s.   (W379)

WORGAN
Collection Of New Songs And Ballads
Sung At Vauxhall, A
sc KING'S   (W380)

WORKS FOR VOICE AND PIANO, VOL. 3 see
Prokofiev, Serge

WORLD, THE see Smolanoff, Michael Louis

WORLD A HUNTING IS, THE see Manneke,
Daan

WORLD FAMOUS SONGS (from The World
Famous Series) CC42U
solo voice,kbd HARRIS f.s.   (W381)

WORLD INSIDE, A: FIVE SONGS see
Nielson, Lewis

WORLD IS OUR HOME, THE see MacBride,
David Huston

WORLD YOU'RE COMING INTO, THE see
McCartney, [John] Paul

WORLD'S GREATEST SONGBOOK *CCUL
solo voice,pno,gtr ALFRED f.s.
"fakebook" style   (W382)

WORPSWEDE see Scheinpflug, Paul

WORSLEY, C.
Serenata Amorosa
[Span/It/Fr] solo voice,pno BOIL
B.0462   (W383)

WORTE TRÜGEN, WORTE FLIEHEN see Colaço
Osorio-Swaab, Reine

WOTAN'S FAREWELL see Wagner, Richard,
Walküre, Die: Leb' Wohl

WOULD I COULD BARK THE SUN see Rowland,
David

WOULDN'T THAT BE QUEER see Beach,
[Mrs.] H.H.A. (Amy Marcy Cheney)

WREN, THE see Benedict, [Sir] Julius

WRIGHT, MAURICE (1949-   )
Basilio's Lament
S solo,fl,pno [10'] APNM sc $6.75,
set $16.00   (W384)

Four Songs *CC4U
med solo,pno sc AM.COMP.AL. $7.70
                               (W385)

Lament Of The Martyrs, The
S solo,pno [5'] sc AM.COMP.AL.
$4.60   (W386)

Mozartian Constraint
S solo,fl,vln,bsn,gtr [10'] APNM sc
$3.75, set $15.75   (W387)

WRIGHT, MAURICE (cont'd.)

Night Watch *song cycle
S solo,pno [12'] APNM sc $6.50, set
$12.50   (W388)

Sonnet At Trifling Intervals
S solo,fl,clar [5'] APNM sc $3.25,
set $9.00   (W389)

Three Arias *CC3U
S solo,pno sc AM.COMP.AL. $9.15
(W390)

WRITER, THE see Austin, John

WUSTMANN, GUSTAV
Als Der Grossvater Die Grossmutter
Nahm
SCIEN 1946   (W391)

WYNER, YEHUDI (1929-   )
Disillusionment At 10 O'clock
S solo,pno [3'] sc AM.COMP.AL.
$3.85   (W392)

Fragments From Antiquity
S solo,2.2.3.2. 4.2.2.1. 2perc,
marimba,harp,strings [20'] sc
AM.COMP.AL. $35.00   (W393)

Intermedio: Lyric Ballet
S solo,string orch [16'] sc
AM.COMP.AL. $15.40   (W394)

On This Most Voluptuous Night: Five
Songs *CC5U
S solo,fl,horn,pno,2vln,vla,vcl
AM.COMP.AL. sc $26.00, pts $37.50
(W395)

X

XOCHICUICATL see Zumaque, Francisco

Y

Y AVAIT DIX FILLES DANS UN PRÉ see
Arrieu, Claude

YAMA NO KAREHA see Kikuchi, Masaharu

YANNATOS, JAMES D. (1929-   )
Priere Dans l'Arche
S solo,1.1.1.1. 1.1.1.0. 2vln,vla,
vcl,db [9'] AM.COMP.AL. sc
$18.40, pts $20.70   (Y1)

Prieres Dans l'Arche
S solo,pno [9'] sc AM.COMP.AL.
$9.15   (Y2)

YANNAY, YEHUDA (1937-   )
Eros Reminisced: Four Songs *CC4U
med solo,pno sc AM.COMP.AL. $9.95
(Y3)

Five Songs *CC5U
T solo,2.2.2.2. 2.2.2.1. harp,pno,
3perc,strings sc AM.COMP.AL.
$21.45   (Y4)

Noiseless Patient Spider, A
8 women, acap [6'] sc AM.COMP.AL.
$7.60   (Y5)

YASASHISA KAMOSHITE see Arima, Reiko

YAVELOW, CHRISTOPHER JOHNSON
(1950-   )
Four Songs Of Sappho *CC4U
S solo,pno sc AM.COMP.AL. $5.00
(Y6)

U.S.A.
S solo,pno [2'] sc AM.COMP.AL.
$1.60   (Y7)

What Could She Say?
S solo,pno [2'] sc AM.COMP.AL.
$3.85   (Y8)

YE SACRED MUSES see Byrd, William

YE WHO HAVE DULY LEARNT see Mozart,
Wolfgang Amadeus, Nozze Di Figaro,
Le: Voi Che Sapete

YEAR, THE see Weigl, [Mrs.] Vally

YEAR AFTER YEAR see Haxton, Kenneth

YEARN FOR NATIVE LAND: SIX SONGS see
Saito, Takanobu

YEAR'S AT THE SPRING, THE see Beach,
[Mrs.] H.H.A. (Amy Marcy Cheney)

YELLOW LEAVES see Eggen, Arne, Gulnar
Lauvet, Det

YES, IT CERTAINLY HURTS see Kruse,
Bjørn Howard, Ja Visst Gör Det Ont

YES SIR REE see Anderson, Beth

YIHYU L'RATZON see Davidson, Charles
Stuart

YNDIGSTE ROSE, DEN see Nyhus, Rolf

YO M'ENAMORI D'UN AIRE see Four
Sephardi Songs

YOGATARI NI (DIT DU GENJI) see
Matsudaira, Yori-Tsune

YOM GILA see Neumann, Richard J.

YOM KIPPUR AFTERNOON SERVICE see
Horvit, Michael M.

YOU ARE MY HEART'S DELIGHT see Lehar,
Franz

YOU ARE THE CHOSEN OF THE LORD see
Fedak, Alfred V.

YOU ASK ME TO SING see Björnsson, Arni

YOU BREATHING WONDER see Reuland,
Jacques

YOU LOVE ME - YOU ARE SURE see Samuel,
Gerhard

YOUKALI see Weill

YOUNG
Our Love Is Precious
high solo,kbd GIA G-3080   (Y9)

YOUNG, DEREK (1929-   )
Buch Der Bilder, Das *song cycle
B solo,pno [20'] (texts by Rainer
Maria Rilke) LYNWD   (Y10)

YOUNG, DOUGLAS (1947-   )
  Folksongs
    RICORDI-IT LD762   (Y11)

  Lullaby Of The Nativity, A
    solo voice,2inst RICORDI-IT LD697
                              (Y12)

  Three Scottish Nursery Rhymes
    S solo,clar RICORDI-IT LD704 (Y13)

YOUNG AASLAUG see Jordan, Sverre, Ung
  Aaslaug

YOUNG JESUS SWEIT see Phillips, John C.

YOUR CHILDHOOD IN MENTON: CHAMBER MUSIC
  NO. 2 see Rosenman, Leonard

YOUR GENTLE SMILE see Sigfusson,
  Steingrimur

YOUR NATIVE LAND see Borodin, Alexander
  Porfirievich, Dans Ton Pays

YOUR TINY HAND IS FROZEN see Puccini,
  Giacomo, Bohème, La: Che Gelida
  Manina

YOU'RE BRINGING OUT THE VERY BEST IN ME
  see Harris, Ronald S.

YOUTH see Bax, [Sir] Arnold

YOUTHFUL AGE see Van de Vate, Nancy
  Hayes

YOUTH'S SERENADE see Wallach, Joelle

YTTREHUS, ROLV (1926-   )
  Gradus Ad Parnassum
    S solo,1.1.1.1. 1.2.1.0. 2perc,pno,
    vln,vla,vcl,db,electronic tape
    [32'] AM.COMP.AL. sc $59.70, pts
    $108.70   (Y14)

YUKIKEMURI see Hayakawa, Kuzuko

YURIKAMOME see Fujiwara, Michiyo

YUYA see Ikenouchi, Tomojiro

YUYAMA, AKIRA (1932-   )
  Biwa No Hana
    solo voice [3'] JAPAN   (Y15)

  Chiisana Hana
    solo voice [3'] JAPAN   (Y16)

  Kokorotte Fushigi
    solo voice [3'] JAPAN   (Y17)

  Nocturne
    solo voice [4'] JAPAN   (Y18)

  Sakura Densetsu
    solo voice [5'] JAPAN   (Y19)

YUZUTSU O MITE see Hayakawa, Kuzuko

Z

Z GORZKICH ZALOW (PLACZ Z GROBU
  CHRYSTUSA PANA) see Nikodemowicz,
  Andrzej

Z PLANI A PRALESU see Graham, P.

ZAGWIJN, HENRI (1878-1954)
  God, Lief
    see Verlangen

  Ik Droom Van Bergen
    see Verlangen

  Laat Nu Uitslaan M'n Wild Verlangen
    see Verlangen

  O, Altijd Dat Moe-E Verlangen
    see Verlangen

  Verlangen
    Mez solo,pno DONEMUS f.s. [10']
    contains: God, Lief; Ik Droom Van
    Bergen; Laat Nu Uitslaan M'n
    Wild Verlangen; O, Altijd Dat
    Moe-E Verlangen; Voel Je Niet
    Branden   (Z1)

  Voel Je Niet Branden
    see Verlangen

ZAHLER, NOEL BARRY (1951-   )
  All Night
    S solo,clar,vln,vcl,pno [10'] APNM
    sc $6.75, set $24.00   (Z2)

  Four Songs Of Departure *CC4U
    S solo,pno APNM sc $5.00, set $9.50
                              (Z3)

  Three Songs *CC3U
    Mez solo,fl,ob,clar,horn,trp,harp,
    3perc,vln,vla,vcl APNM sc $7.50,
    pts rent   (Z4)

ZAHRADNÍK, ZDENEK (1936-   )
  Monolog Julie
    S solo,2.2.2.2. 2.2.0.0. timp,
    strings [8'] CESKY HUD.   (Z5)

  Monolog Julie II
    S solo,2.2.2.2. 2.2.0.0. timp,perc,
    strings [8'] CESKY HUD.   (Z6)

  Ragy
    S solo,ob/clar,pno PANTON 960 (Z7)

ZAÏDE (BOLÉRO - 1ST VERSION) see
  Berlioz, Hector (Louis)

ZAKHOR see Fisher, Alfred

ZAKY UMRE see Shut, Wasyl

ZALLMAN, ARLENE (PROCTOR) (1934-   )
  Ballata
    T solo,pno [3'] APNM sc $3.00, set
    $5.75   (Z8)

  Shakespeare Sonnet CXXVIII
    Bar solo,pno [4'] APNM sc $3.75,
    set $7.00   (Z9)

  Shakespeare Sonnet XVIII
    S solo,pno [3'] APNM sc $3.25, set
    $6.25   (Z10)

  Songs From Quasimodo (Three Italian
    Songs) *CC3U
    S solo,alto fl,vcl,pno APNM sc
    $4.75, set $14.50   (Z11)

ZALO DIEVCA see Dvorák, Antonín

ZAMECNIK, EVZEN (1939-   )
  Symfonicky Diptych
    Bar solo,2.2.2.2. 4.2.3.0. timp,
    perc,harp,strings [10'] CESKY
    HUD.   (Z12)

ZANDONAI, RICCARDO (1883-1944)
  Assiuolo, L'
    [It] med solo,pno CLASSV 0825 (Z13)

  Cantare, Il Giorno, Ti Sentii:
    Felice?
    see Patria Lontana

  Cose Belle, Le
    see Serenata, La

  Due Tarli, I: Il Tarlo Della Vecchia
    Biblioteca
    [It] med solo,pno CLASSV 1118 (Z14)

  Patria Lontana
    "Cantare, Il Giorno, Ti Sentii:
    Felice?" [It] high solo,pno
    CLASSV 1120   (Z15)

ZANDONAI, RICCARDO (cont'd.)

  Serenata
    "Su Per L'Argtenteo Ciel La Luna
    Vola" [It] high solo,pno CLASSV
    1117   (Z16)

  Serenata, La (from Sei Liriche)
    "Cose Belle, Le" [It] high solo,pno
    CLASSV 1119   (Z17)

  Su Per L'Argtenteo Ciel La Luna Vola
    see Serenata

  Tre Liriche
    solo voice,pno CARISCH 22145 (Z18)

ZANGELMI, PIERO LUIGI
  Costellazione Di Arianna
    S solo,vln,pno EDI-PAN EP 7602
                              (Z19)

ZANGRIG BLAAST EEN KNAAP DE FLUIT see
  Koetsier, Jan

ZANINELLI
  Beginnings
    solo voice,pno SHAWNEE 0080 (Z20)

  Five American Gospel Songs
    solo voice SHAWNEE 5085   (Z21)

  Five American Revival Songs
    med solo,pno SHAWNEE 5094 (Z22)

  Five Folk Songs, Vol. 2
    med solo SHAWNEE 0073   (Z23)

  Seven Sanctuary Songs
    SHAWNEE 5090   (Z24)

ZANINELLI, LUIGI (1932-   )
  Battle Of Vicksburg, The
    S&narrator,pno [25'] SCHIRM.G
    ECK20250   (Z25)

ZANOLINI, BRUNO
  Nunc Est
    S solo,2inst ZERBONI 9640 (Z26)

ZAPADAJ SLNIECKO see Svatos, Vladimir

ZÄRTLICHE ODE, EINE see Hegdal, Magne

ZASADIT STROM see Lukas, Zdenek

ZATYKH VZHE HRIM see Shut, Wasyl

ZAUBERFLÖTE: ACH! ICH FÜHL'S see
  Mozart, Wolfgang Amadeus

ZAUBERFLÖTE: DER HÖLLE RACHE see
  Mozart, Wolfgang Amadeus

ZAUBERFLÖTE: DIES BILDNIS see Mozart,
  Wolfgang Amadeus

ZAUBERFLÖTE: IN DIESEN HEILGEN see
  Mozart, Wolfgang Amadeus

ZAUBERFLÖTE: O ISIS UND OSIRIS see
  Mozart, Wolfgang Amadeus

ZAUBERFLÖTE: O ZITTRE NICHT see Mozart,
  Wolfgang Amadeus

ZAZA: BUONA ZAZÀ see Leoncavallo,
  Ruggiero

ZAZA: NON ODI? see Leoncavallo,
  Ruggiero

ZAZA: O MIO PICCOLO TAVOLO see
  Leoncavallo, Ruggiero

ZAZA: ZAZA PICCOLA ZINGARA see
  Leoncavallo, Ruggiero

ZE ZITTEN NAAST ELKANDER see Beekhuis,
  Hanna

ZECCA, GIANNINO (1911-   )
  Venite Fili... *sac,mot
    S/T solo,org BERBEN 1749 f.s. (Z27)

ZECHLIN, RUTH (1926-   )
  Frühe Kafka-Texte
    solo voice,fl,ob,clar,vcl,perc sc
    LIENAU RL 4004   (Z28)

ZEER VRIJ NAAR HET CHINEES see Ruiter,
  Wim de

ZEFIRO TORNA see Monteverdi, Claudio

ZEH DODI see Schiller, Benjie Ellen

ZEH HAYOM see Aloni, Aminadav

ZEHN BIBLISCHE LIEDER, OP. 99 see
  Dvorák, Antonín

ZEHN EPIGRAMME, OP. 56 see Karg-Elert,
  Sigfrid

ZEHN LIEDER see Adler, Hugo Chaim

ZEHN LIEDER NACH GEDICHTEN VON JOSEPH
VON EICHENDORFF see Kont, Paul

ZEHN LIEDER NACH GEDICHTEN VON THEODOR
STORM see Hummel, Bertold

ZEIT UND DIE ZEIT DANACH, DIE see
Schmidt, Christfried

ZEITRISSE see Pröve, Bernfried

ZEKERHEID see Voorn, Joop

ZELLER, CARL (1842-1898)
Vogelhändler, Der: Wie Mein Ahnl
Zwanzig Jahr
solo voice,pno SCIEN 1948   (Z29)

ZELM, JAN VAN (1959-   )
Ondergang Van Tenochtitlan, De
Bar solo,bass clar,horn,trom,perc,
2vcl [15'] DONEMUS   (Z30)

ZELTER, CARL FRIEDRICH (1758-1832)
Sämmtliche Lieder
OLMS   (Z31)

ZEMER AM (FIVE JEWISH FOLKSONGS IN
YIDDISH AND HEBREW) see
Stutschevsky, Joachim

ZÉMIRE ET AZOR: DU MOMENT QU'ON AIME
see Grétry, André Ernest Modeste

ZÉMIRE ET AZOR: LA FAUVETTE see Grétry,
André Ernest Modeste

ZEMLINSKY, ALEXANDER VON (1871-1942)
Acht Gesänge, Op. 5
[Ger] (not available outside
U.S.A.) RECITAL 414   (Z32)

Dreizehn Lieder, Op. 2
[Ger] RECITAL 413   (Z33)

Fünf Lieder, Op. 7
[Ger] (not available outside
U.S.A.) RECITAL 415 f.s. contains
also: Vier Lieder, Op. 8 (Z34)

Sechs Lieder, Op. 10
[Ger] (not available outside
U.S.A.) RECITAL 416 f.s. contains
also: Sechs Lieder, Op. 13 (Z35)

Sechs Lieder, Op. 13
see Sechs Lieder, Op. 10

Six Songs *Op.13, CC6U
solo voice UNIVER. UE 05540 $8.95
                              (Z36)

Vier Lieder, Op. 8
see Fünf Lieder, Op. 7

Walzer-Gesänge, Op. 6
[Ger/Eng] solo voice,pno (med)
SIMROCK   (Z37)

ZEMPHIRA'S SONG see Tchaikovsky, Piotr
Ilyich

ZEN SONGS FOR GUITAR AND VOICE see
Meyers, Randall

ZENKL, MICHAL (1955-1983)
Noc Pred Krasnym Dnem
solo voice,pno PANTON 961   (Z38)

ZENY, ZENY, KDO VAM VERI see Rejcha,
Antonin, Donne, Donne, Chi Vi Crede

ZERO HOUR see Gondai, Atsuhiko

ZERSTREUTE WEGE see Glaus, D.

ZES LIEDEREN see Guichelaar, Jan

ZES LIEDEREN see Ruiter, Wim de

ZES RILKE-LIEDEREN see Franken, Wim

ZES RILKE-LIEDEREN see Visser, Peter

ZES SLAUERHOFF-LIEDEREN see Franken,
Wim

ZEVEN LIEDEREN OP GEDICHTEN VAN
CHRISTIAN MORGENSTERN see Voorn,
Joop

ZEVEN VOCALISES see Manneke, Daan

ZIANI, MARC ANTONIO (1653-1715)
Tanto Foco
S solo,strings [2'30"] BILLAUDOT
                              (Z39)

ZIELONE SLOWA see Szymanowski, Karol

ZIGEUNER see Marx, Joseph

ZIGEUNERBARON, DER: WALZERLIED see
Strauss, Johann, [Jr.]

ZIGEUNERBARON, DER: WER HAT EUCH DENN
GETRAUT? see Strauss, Johann, [Jr.]

ZIGEUNERKNABE, DER see Zimmerman, S.A.

ZIGEUNERLIEDER, OP. 14 see Novak,
Vitezslav

[SIEBEN] ZIGEUNERMELODIEN, OP. 55 see
Dvorák, Antonín

ZIJ TOT HEM see Andriessen, Jurriaan

ZIJT STIL NU see Beyerman-Walraven,
Jeanne

ZILCHER, HERMANN (1881-1948)
Vier Lieder, Op. 12
[Ger] high solo (not available
outside U.S.A.) RECITAL 417 (Z40)

ZIMMERMAN
Windsongs
solo voice,pno TRANSCON. 991329
                              (Z41)

ZIMMERMAN, S.A.
Drei Lieder
solo voice,pno SCIEN 1964 f.s.
contains: Jäger, Der; Lied; Lied
                              (Z42)

Drey Thraenen, Die
see Vier Lieder

Jäger, Der
see Drei Lieder

Lied
see Drei Lieder

Schöne Stern, Der
see Vier Lieder

Vier Lieder
solo voice,pno SCIEN 1965 f.s.
contains: Drey Thraenen, Die;
Schöne Stern, Der;
Zigeunerknabe, Der; Zweifel
                              (Z43)

Zigeunerknabe, Der
see Vier Lieder

Zweifel
see Vier Lieder

ZIMMERMANN, BERND ALOIS (1918-1970)
Abendglocke
see Drei Geistliche Lieder

Altdeutsches Bild
see Drei Geistliche Lieder

Altkölnischer Meister
see Drei Geistliche Lieder

Drei Geistliche Lieder
med solo,pno SCHOTT ED 7565 f.s.
contains: Abendglocke;
Altdeutsches Bild;
Altkölnischer Meister   (Z44)

ZIMMERMANN, UDO (1943-   )
Gib Licht Meinen Augen
SBar soli,4.3.4.0. 3.3.3.1. timp,
3perc,harp,2pno,strings [40'] sc
DEUTSCHER DV 1148   (Z45)

Weisse Rose
2 solo voices,fl,ob,clar,horn,trp,
trom,bass trom,perc,harp,pno,
string quin DEUTSCHER 6140 f.s.
                              (Z46)

ZING EN SPEEL ME MAAR
(Bouman, S.M.; Van Tertholen) [Dutch]
med solo,pno (contains 68 Dutch
children's songs) ALBERSEN   (Z47)

ZINGARA, LA see Donizetti, Gaetano

ZINGEN see Weegenhuise, Johan

ZINK, MICHEL
Chansons De Toile, Les *CCU
solo voice SLATKINE f.s.   (Z48)

ZIPOLI, DOMENICO (1688-1726)
Dell' Offese A Vendicarmi *cant
(Becheri) solo voice,cont ZANIBON
6135   (Z49)

ZISKA, FRANZ
Oesterreichische Volkslieder Mit
Ihren Singeweisen
SCIEN 1966   (Z50)

ZIVLY see Petrzelka, Vilém

ZONDAGMORGEN see Brandse, Wim

ZONIKED VEIG see Steinberg, Eitan

ZONN, PAUL (1938-   )
I Love My Lady
3 male soli,clar in E flat,clar,
clar in A [6'30"] AM.COMP.AL.
                              (Z51)

Shadows Of An Orange-Leaf
S solo,ob,trom,pno,perc,vcl,db
[17'] sc AM.COMP.AL. $24.35 (Z52)

ZOO STIL see Broekman, Hans

ZORZAL, EL see Ponjee, Ted

ZPEV JANKA see Blodek, Vilem (Wilhelm)

ZPEVY STARE CINY see Buzek, Jan

ZPIVAME ANGLICKY
"Let's Have An English Song" (CC43U)
PANTON 96   (Z53)

ZROZENI CLOVEKA see Kohoutek, Ctirad

ZUCKERMAN, MARK (1948-   )
Twilight Songs
S solo,fl [5'] APNM sc $5.00, set
$9.50   (Z54)

ZUFRIEDENHEIT, DIE see Lohmann, Heinz

ZUIDAM, ROB (1964-   )
General No Es Malo, Es Emocionadito,
El
see Pancho Villa

Pancho Villa
Mez solo,pno DONEMUS f.s. [22']
contains: General No Es Malo, Es
Emocionadito, El; Para Mi La
Guerra Empezo Cuando Naci; Una
De Estas Mananas   (Z55)

Para Mi La Guerra Empezo Cuando Naci
see Pancho Villa

Una De Estas Mananas
see Pancho Villa

ZUM EINSCHLAFEN see Visser, Peter

ZUM EINSCHLAFEN ZU SAGEN see Franken,
Wim

ZUMAQUE, FRANCISCO (1945-   )
Xochicuicatl
S solo,fl,clar,pno&cel,perc,strings
[12'30"] PEER   (Z56)

ZUMPE ZUMPITTE! see Albanese, Guido

ZUMSTEEG, EMILIE
An Meine Zither
see Sechs Lieder, Op. 4

Kapelle, Die
see Sechs Lieder, Op. 4

Lied In Der Ferne
see Sechs Lieder, Op. 4

Morgenfreude
see Sechs Lieder, Op. 4

Religion
see Sechs Lieder, Op. 4

Sechs Lieder, Op. 4
solo voice,pno SCHOTTS ED 7808 f.s.
contains: An Meine Zither;
Kapelle, Die; Lied In Der
Ferne; Morgenfreude; Religion;
Sternenhimmel, Der   (Z57)

Sternenhimmel, Der
see Sechs Lieder, Op. 4

ZUPKO, RAMON (1932-   )
Where The Mountain Crosses
Mez solo,pno PETERS 66966 $17.50
                              (Z58)

ZUR, MENACHEM (1942-   )
Affairs
S solo,fl,clar,trp,trom,vla,pno,
perc SEESAW f.s.   (Z59)

Pygmalion
S solo,pno SEESAW f.s.   (Z60)

Two Sabbath Songs *CC2U
S solo,pno SEESAW f.s.   (Z61)

ZURFLUH, ELIANE
Chantons Noel *Xmas
solo voice,pno/org (15 French
carols) ZURFLUH   (Z62)

ZWANZIG AUSGEWÄHLTE LIEDER see Liszt,
Franz

ZWANZIG DEUTSCHE VOLKSLIEDER see
Brahms, Johannes

ZWEI BASSLIEDER, OP. 51 see Strauss,
Richard

ZWEI BLAUEN AUGEN, DIE see Mahler,
    Gustav

ZWEI CHINESISCHE GEDICHTE see Valen,
    Fartein

ZWEI DEUTSCHE KIRCHENLIEDER, K.343 see
    Mozart, Wolfgang Amadeus

ZWEI DUETTE see Haydn, [Franz] Joseph

ZWEI GEDICHTE IN ÖSTERR. VOLKSMUNDART
    see Suppe, Franz von

ZWEI GEDICHTE VON NIETZSCHE see
    Medtner, Nikolai Karlovich

ZWEI GEISTLICHE GESAENGE see Lachner,
    Franz

ZWEI GEISTLICHE LIEDER see Hanson, Sten

ZWEI GESÄNGE see Mendelssohn-Bartholdy,
    Felix

ZWEI GESÄNGE, OP. 1 see Nyary, Thomas

ZWEI HEINE-LIEDER see Weegenhuise,
    Johan

ZWEI KÖNIGE SASSEN AUF ORKADAL see
    Griffes, Charles Tomlinson

ZWEI LIEDER AUS GOETHES EGMONT, OP.84,
    NOS.1&2 see Beethoven, Ludwig van

ZWEI LIEDER DES MEPHISTO OP. 39 see
    Lothar, Mark

ZWEI LIEDER FÜR SINGSTIMME UND GITARRE
    see Bresgen, Cesar

ZWEI LIEDER, OP. 31 see Valen, Fartein

ZWEI LIEDER, OP. 39 see Valen, Fartein

ZWEI LORCA-LIEDER see Meijering, Cord

ZWEI NACHTLIEDER NACH SHELLEY see Korn,
    Peter Jona, Two Nocturnes On Poems
    By Shelley

ZWEI PASTORELLEN see Haydn, [Franz]
    Joseph

ZWEI VENI SPONSA CHRISTI see Jommelli,
    Niccolo

ZWEI WEIHNACHTSLIEDER see Haydn,
    [Johann] Michael

ZWEIFEL see Zimmerman, S.A.

ZWERVER EN ELVEN see Vries Robbe,
    Willem de

ZWIEGESPRÄCH see Grabner, Hermann

ZWILICH, ELLEN TAAFFE (1939-   )
    Passages
        S solo,chamber group MARGUN MP9001
                                            (Z63)
ZWO GEISTLICHE CANTATEN, SO IN HAMBURG
    ALS DASELBST DAS GROSSE JUBEL-FEST
    see Telemann, Georg Philipp

ZWOLF GEDICHTE, OP. 37 see Schumann,
    Robert (Alexander)

ZWÖLF GESÄNGE, OP. 8 see Mendelssohn-
    Bartholdy, Felix

ZWÖLF GESÄNGE VON PAUL HEYSE see
    Jensen, Adolf

ZWÖLF LIEDER see Rottenberg, Ludwig

ZWÖLF LIEDER, OP. 17 see Szymanowski,
    Karol

ZWÖLF LIEDER VON GOETHE, OP. 15 see
    Medtner, Nikolai Karlovich

ZWÖLF LOTHRINGER VOLKSLIEDER see Pinck,
    Louis

ZWÖLF SONGS NACH ALTEN JIDDISCHEN
    WEISEN see Klein, Richard Rudolf

ZWÖLF TAG- UND NACHTLIEDER, OP. 73 see
    Einem, Gottfried von

ZYNISCHE LIEDER see Straesser, Joep

JACKSON, GREG
Schofield, Joe
He Is My Redeemer

JACKSON, RICHARD
Gottschalk, Louis Moreau
Complete Published Songs Of Louis
Moreau Gottschalk (With A
Selection Of Other Songs On Mid-
Nineteenth Century America)

Popular Songs Of Nineteenth-Century
America

JEFFERY
Songs With Guitar

JOHNSON; JOHNSON
American Negro Spirituals

JONES
Handel, George Frideric
Ten Solo Cantatas, Vol. 1
Ten Solo Cantatas, Vol. 2

Songs Of England

Songs Of Ireland

Songs Of Scotland

Songs Of Wales

JONES, DAVID WYN
Haydn, [Franz] Joseph
Fifteen Scottish, Welsh And Irish
Folksongs

JONSSON, JOSEF
Torstensson, Klas
Ack Värmeland Du Sköna

JOSEPHSON, J.A.
Almquist, Carl Jonas Love
Hjärtats Blomma

Bellman, Carl Michael
Fjäriln Vingad Syns På Haga

KANTHOU, E.
Bresgen, Cesar
Zwei Lieder Für Singstimme Und
Gitarre

KAYE, MICHAEL
Puccini, Giacomo
Songs For Voice And Piano
Unknown Puccini, The

KEESECKER
Hayford
Majesty

KELLY, STEPHEN
Perugia, Niccolo da
Eleven Ballate
Five Madrigals And A Caccia

KESSEL
Tobin, John
It's Wonderful To Be An American

KIRCHBERGER, A.
Gebhard, A.M.
Salve Regina

KIRKPATRICK
Ives, Charles
Sunrise

KJELLBERG, OLLE
Danielsson, Harry
Melodi

KJELLSBY, ERLING
Ti Folketoner

KNAPP, ALEXANDER
Four Sephardi Songs

KOCHAN, GÜNTER
Deutsche Volkslieder

KOCHO, HISAKO
Taki, Rentaro
Complete Album

KÖHLER
Schumann, Robert (Alexander)
Dichterliebe, Op. 48
Liederkreis, Op. 39

LACHEVRE, FRÉDÉRIC
Chouvigny, Claude de
Chansons Libertines De Claude De
Chouvigny, Les

LAMM
Mussorgsky, Modest Petrovich
Boris Godunov: Boris' Monologue
Boris Godunov: Pimen's Tale (Act 4,
Scene 1)

LARSEN, ROBERT L.
G. Schirmer Opera Anthology: Arias
For Baritone

G. Schirmer Opera Anthology: Arias
For Bass

G. Schirmer Opera Anthology: Arias
For Mezzo-Soprano

G. Schirmer Opera Anthology: Arias
For Soprano

G. Schirmer Opera Anthology: Arias
For Tenor

LAUTERBACH
Mozart, Wolfgang Amadeus
Re Pastore, Il: L'Amerò

LE LACHEUR
O Canada

LEFFERTS, PETER
Five Ballades For The House Of Foix

Three Motets In Honour Of Gaston
Febus

LEHRNDORFER, F.
Bernabei, Giuseppe Antonio
Fiera, La

LEISS, K.
Arie Antiche, Vol. 1

Arie Antiche, Vol. 2

LEMETRE
Barathon
Chansons Traditionnelles Des
Provinces De France

LESAGE, JEAN-MARC
Sourisse, Brigitte
Six Chansons De Brigitte Sourisse

LEVY, LESTER S.
Take Me Out To The Ball Game, And
Other Favorite Song Hits: 1906 -
1908

LEWIS, ANTHONY
Selection Of Italian Arias (1600-
1800), A, Vol.1

LINDBERG, NILS
Koch, Erland von
Två Malungsmelodier

LINDER, KERSTIN
Lindblad, Adolf Fredrik
Sånger Och Visor Vid Pianoforte

LUCIA, I.
E Natale Cantiamo Insieme

LUDWIG, CLAUS-DIETER
Rodrigo, Joaquín
Rosaliana

LYON
Especially For Vocalists, Book II

MCINTYRE, PHILLIP
Spirituals

MAKI NO KAI
Selection Of Japanese Songs, Vol. 1

Selection Of Japanese Songs, Vol. 2

MALUKOFF, A.
Fifteen Russian Songs And Romances

MANCUSO, U.
Jachino, Carlo
Carme Secolare, Il

MANEVYTCH, V.
Wolff, Joachim
I Dream Of Meadows And Other Songs
To Poems Of Yar Slavutych

MARLEY, MARIE
Sammartini, Giovanni Battista
Pianto Delle Pie Donne, Il

MARTIENSSEN
Opernduette Für 2 Frauenstimmen, Band
1

Opernduette Für 2 Frauenstimmen, Band
2

MARUSAN, FRANTISEK
Senkyr, Augustin
Huc, Huc, Pastorculi
Saevit Mare Surgunt Venti
Salve Regina

MAUNDER
Mozart, Wolfgang Amadeus
Exultate, Jubilate

MAUNDER, RICHARD
Mozart, Wolfgang Amadeus
Exultate, Jubilate

MAYER, B.
Adeste Fideles

MEYLAN, R.
Scarlatti, Alessandro
Rezitativ Und Arie Der Erminia

MILLIGAN
Hopkinson, Francis
Six Songs

MOBERG, CARL-ALLAN; RUDEN, JAN-OLOF
Rudbeck, Olof
Sorg- Och Klagesång

MOLKENBUR
Liebes- Und Erotische Volkslieder

MOMPELLIO, FEDERICO
India, Sigismondo d'
Musiche De Cantar Solo, Le

MOODY, NELL; MOODY, JOHN
Massenet, Jules
Melodies Vol. 1
Melodies Vol. 2

MOORE, DOROTHY RUDD
Charity

Lullaby

Mendelssohn-Bartholdy, Felix
On Wings Of Song

Purcell, Henry
If Music Be The Food

MOORES, M.
Four Traditional American Songs

MOSER
Alte Meister Des Deutschen Liedes

NAUWELAERS
Choix Et Arrangements Pour 2 Voix Et
Piano De Mélodies Célèbres De
Schumann (Scènes Champêtres)

Choix Et Arrangements Pour 2 Voix Et
Piano De Mélodies Célèbres De
Strauss (Gazouillis De Printemps)

NESTOR
Twelve Folksong Arrangements

NEUER, A.
Szymanowski, Karol
Piesni

NORDHUES, PAUL; WAGNER, ALOIS
Kantorenbuch Zum Gotteslob

NOWACZYK, E.
Moniuszko, Stanislaw
Spiewnik Domowy, Antologia Piesni

O'BRIEN; DOCKER
Irish Magic

OLAV LILJEKRANS
Eggen, Arne
Olavs Monolog Og Arie

OLSEN, C.G.SPARRE
Grieg, Edvard Hagerup
Elsk
Første Møtes Sødme, Det
Jeg Reiste En Deilig Sommerkveld
Killingdans
Syng, Det
Vond Dag

Kjerulf, Halfdan
Hvile I Skoven
Løkkende Toner
På Fjellet
Prinsessen: Aftenstemning
Veiviseren Synger

Nordraak, Rikard
Der Ligger Et Land
Taylors Sang
Tonen

OLSEN, CARL GUSTAV SPARRE
Grieg, Edvard Hagerup
Første Møde, Det

PADRO, J. MA.
Cancionero Escolar Clásico

PAIS
Boccherini, Luigi
Duetto Accademico In Mi Bem.
Maggiore
Quindici Arie Accademiche, Fasc. 5

PAIS, ALDO
Stabat Mater

PALMER, CHRISTOPHER
Walton, [Sir] William (Turner)
Song Album

PANZERA
Cinquantes Mélodies Françaises

Vocalises De L'école Italienne

PARKER, ALICE
Folksong Transformations

PATON
Italian Songs And Arias, 26

Mendelssohn-Bartholdy, Felix
Mendelssohn: 24 Songs

Mozart, Wolfgang Amadeus
Mozart: 12 Songs

PEDRELL, FELIPE
Cancionero Musical Popular Español:
Tomo 1: El Canto En La Vida
Doméstica

Cancionero Musical Popular Español:
Tomo 2: El Canto En La Vida
Pública

Cancionero Musical Popular Español:
Tomo 3: El Canto Popular Y La
Técnica De La Escuela Musical
Española

Cancionero Musical Popular Español:
Tomo 4: El Canto Popular Y La
Técnica De La Escuela Musical
Española (Continuación)

PHILIPP
Chopin, Frédéric
Minute Waltz

PIKE, LIONEL
Philips, Peter
Fifteen Motets For Solo Voice And
Continuo

PILSS, KARL
Mozart, Wolfgang Amadeus
Terzette Für 2 Tenöre, Bass Und
Klavier

POIRIER, LUCIEN
Songs II To French Texts

Songs III To French Texts

PROUT
Handel, George Frideric
Acis And Galatea: O Ruddier Than
The Cherry

RAGOSSNIG
Schubert, Franz (Peter)
Fünf Lieder

RASTALL, RICHARD
Four Religious Songs From C.U.L. Add.
MS 5943

RAVIER, C.
Des Prez, Josquin
Huit Chansons

Dufay, Guillaume
Huit Chansons

RAVIER, CHARLES
Sept Chansons De Troubadours Des 12e
Et 13e Siecles

RAYNER, JOSEPHINE
Abide With Me

REINECKE, C.
Schumann, Robert (Alexander)
Frühlingsglocken

RICHTER, ERNST
Hoffmann Von Fallersleben, Heinrich
August
Neue Kinderlieder, 50

RIDOUT, ALAN
Singer's Collection, The, Book 1:
High Voice

Singer's Collection, The, Book 2:
High Voice

RIEGER, E.
Sopran-Album Aus Dem Repertoire Von
Irmgard Seefried

RIEGER, EVA; WALTER, KÄTE
Frauen Komponieren

RIGHINI; PENHORWOOD
Operatic And Chamber Ensembles

RIST, G.; ZIMBELIUS, L.
Alle Jahre Wieder...

RIZZOLI, F.
Tromboncino, Bartolomeo
Frottole Alla Corte Mantovana

ROBERTS, TREVOR
Five Welsh Folk Songs

ROE
Songs From Scandinavia

ROMA
Canciones Españolas Antiguas Vol. 1

Canciones Españolas Antiguas Vol. 2

ROSENTHAL
Brahms, Johannes
Zwanzig Deutsche Volkslieder

ROSLER, G.
Pergolesi, Giovanni Battista
Stabat Mater

ROSSI, F.
Verdelot, Phillippe
Tre Madrigali

ROVENSTRUNCK, BERNHARD
Katalanisches Liederbuch

RUHLAND, KONRAD
Aufschnaiter, Benedikt Anton
Pastorella
Pastorella: Laufet Ihr Hirten

Crudeli, Matthias
Salve Regina

Esterhazy, [Prince] Pal
Dormi Jesu Dulcissime

Hagerer, Franz Sales Ignaz
Salve Regina

Jungbauer, Coelestin
Hier Liegt Vor Deiner Majestät

Leuttner, Georg Christoph
Alma Redemptoris Mater

Loth, Urban
Drei Geistliche Konzerte Zur
Weihnachtszeit

RUMESSEN, VARDO
Tubin, Eduard
Soololaule

RUSSEL, MYRA TEICHER
Palmer, Geoffrey Molynuex
James Joyce's Chamber Music: The
Lost Song Settings

SACCHETTI
Stradella, Alessandro
De Immaculata Conceptione

SANVOISIN, M.
Lully, Jean-Baptiste (Lulli)
O Dulcissime Domine
Regina Coeli

SARGENT
Brahms, Johannes
Four Serious Songs

SATO, S.
Wagner, Richard
Sämtliche Lieder, Originaltonarten

SCHINDLER
Colomba, La

SCHINDLER, K.
Anonymous
Petite Anne, La

SCHIOETZ, GERD
Torstensson, Klas
Aksel Schioetz Anthology Of Nordic
Solo Songs, The

SCHLETTERER, HANS MICHEL
Hoffmann Von Fallersleben, Heinrich
August
Kinderlieder, 43

SESTAK, ZDENEK
Anonymous
Bella Quando Aurora

Kopriva, Jan Jachym
Benedictus

Lokaj, Jakub
Haec Aurora Gratiosa

SEWELL, GREGG
Contemporary Christian Classics, Vol.
2

SHACKLOCK
Sing Solo Contralto

SHACKLOCK, CONSTANCE
Sing Solo: Contralto

SHARP, C.
Anonymous
Barbara Ellen
Keys Of Canterbury

SHI TO ONGAKU NO KAI
New Japanese Songs

SILBER, IRWIN
Songs America Voted By

SJÖSTEN, LARS
Bjork, Torgny
Horisontlinje: 10 Visor

SKÖLD, SVEN
Peterson-Berger, (Olof) Wilhelm
Marits Visor

SMITH, MICHAEL W.; KAISER, KURT
O Love That Wilt Not Let Me Go

SMOLA, EMMERICH
Offenbach, Jacques
Lieder And Romances

SÖDERLIND, RAGNAR
Grieg, Edvard Hagerup
Ti Songar (Ten Songs)

SPADA
Puccini, Giacomo
Inno A Diana

Verdi, Giuseppe
Attila: Oh Dolore
Due Foscari, I: Cabaletta Di Jacopo
E La Vita
Inediti Per Tenore
Io La Vidi
Nabucco: Preghiera Di Fenena
Tantum Ergo
Vespri Siciliani, I: Nouvelle
Romance

SPERRY, PAUL
Vote For Names!

SPITZER, L.
Wolf, Hugo
Gedichte Von Johann Wolfgang Von
Goethe, Heft 1
Gedichte Von Johann Wolfgang Von
Goethe, Heft 2
Spanisches Liederbuch, Weltliche
Lieder, Heft 1
Spanisches Liederbuch, Weltliche
Lieder, Heft 2
Spanisches Liederbuch, Weltliche
Lieder, Heft 3

STANFORD
Fill The Bumper Fair!

STANFORD, C.V.
Irish Melodies Of T. Moore, Op.60

STANFORD, C. VILLIERS
Irish Songs And Ballads, 30

Songs Of Erin, 50

Songs Of Old Ireland, 50

STATFORD, ELAINE
Christmas Guitar Songbook, The

STEBER, ELEANOR; BEATIE
Mozart, Wolfgang Amadeus
Eight Operatic Arias For The
Soprano Voice

STEPHAN, K.D.
Kunad, Rainer
Klopstock-Ode

STICKLES
Greensleeves

SUBIRA, JOSE
Castell, J.
Canción De La Gitana Habilidosa

Galvan, Ventura
Seguidilla Del Oficial Cortejante

Palomino, J.
Canción Picaresca

Valledor, Jacinto
Canción Timida

SURINACH, CARLOS; SUBIRA, JOSE
Four Tonadillas: By Thge Inn's Gate

Four Tonadillas: Lovers' Quarrels

Four Tonadillas: The Beggars

Four Tonadillas: The Lemon Girl

SUTHERLAND, JOAN; BONYNGE, RICHARD
Art Of Joan Sutherland, The, Vol. I:
Famous Mad Scenes

Art Of Joan Sutherland, The, Vol. II:
Eighteenth Century Arias

Art Of Joan Sutherland, The, Vol.
III: ROMANTIC ITALIAN ARIAS

Art Of Joan Sutherland, The, Vol. IV:
Donizetti Arias

SWAROWSKY, HANS
Mozart, Wolfgang Amadeus
Solfeggi

SZULC
Moszkowski, Moritz
Guitarre

TAPPERT, JOHANNES
Klein, Richard Rudolf
Männlein In Der Gans, Das

TAUBERT, KARL HEINZ
Advents- Und Weihnachtsmusik

Alte Passions- Und Osterlieder Aus
Fünf Jahrhunderten

Vom Himmel Zur Erde (Drei
Volkstümliche Lieder)

TAYLOR
Classic Songs

Contemporary American Songs

TEAR
Sing Solo Tenor

TEAR, ROBERT
Sing Solo: Tenor

THOMAS, WYNDHAM
Robin And Marian Motets, Vol. 2

Robin And Marian Motets, Vol. 3

Robin And Marion Motets, Vol. 1

THORARINSSON, JON
Einarsson, Sigfus
Augun Blau
Draumalandid
Gigjan

Kaldalóns, Sigvaldi S.
Heimir
Three Songs
Thu Eina Hjartans Yndid Mitt
Vid Sundid

Thoroddsen, Emil
Voggukvaedi

TILLETT, MICHAEL
Tippett, [Sir] Michael
Boyhood's End

TIMOTHY
Restoration Duets

TINTORI, G.
Paisiello, Giovanni
Idolo Cinese, L'

TKACH, P.
Solo Singer

TØSSE, EILERT
Fire Folketoner Om Det Kristne Håp

Two Religious Folk Tunes

TURULL, X.
Cant Dels Ocells, El

TVEIT, SIGVALD
Iddane Hermund

TYSON, ALAN
Mozart, Wolfgang Amadeus
Eight Variant Versions From "Le
Nozze Di Figaro"

VAN CAMP, LEONARD
Dozen Duets For Everyone, Everywhere,
A

Songs For Youthful Tenors Of All Ages

VARGA
Favorite Opera Arias

VAUGHAN WILLIAMS, RALPH
I Will Give My Love An Apple

VEA, KETIL
Grieg, Edvard Hagerup
Borte
Lys Nat
Til Norge

VERONA, G. GENTILI
Bononcini, Giovanni
Tre Cantate

VERSCHAEVE; BERSTEL
Lully, Jean-Baptiste (Lulli)
Recueil D'airs Divers De Lully

VIGNOLES, ROGER
Mermaid& Two Other Water Songs, The

VIOLETTE, ANDREW
Danny Boy

VLIJMEN, JAN VAN
Twaalf Vocalises

Twaalf Vocalises

VOLLE, BJARNE
Dale, Sjur
Tre Koraler

Udsigter Fra Ulrikken

VOLTA, ORNELLA
Satie, Erik
Genevieve De Brabant

VOXMAN, HIMIE
Sacchini, Antonio (Maria Gasparo
Gioacchino)
Amavit Eum: Offertorium

WALKER, SARAH; VIGNOLES, ROGER
Sarah's Encores

WALTERS, RICHARD
Classical Carols

Opera American Style: Arias For
Soprano

Popular Ballads For Classical Singers

WALTERS, RICHARD; LARSEN, ROBERT L.
Mozart, Wolfgang Amadeus
Mozart Arias For Baritone & Bass
Mozart Arias For Mezzo-Soprano
Mozart Arias For Soprano
Mozart Arias For Tenor

WARLOCK, PETER
Songs Of The Gardens

WATANABE, K.; MISAWA, T.
Handel, George Frideric
Opera Arias

WATHEY, ANDREW
Berkeley Castle, Select Roll 55:
Motets And Sequences

WECKERLIN
Strauss, Johann, [Jr.]
Beautiful Blue Danube

WERBA, E.
Tenor-Album Aus Dem Repertoire Von
Julius Patzak

WESTPHAL, HARTMUT
Adam, Adolphe-Charles
Bravour Variationen Über Ein Thema
Von Mozart "Ah! Vous Dirai-Je,
Maman

WHEAR
Hopkins
God's Grandeur

WILKINS, NIGEL
Bartolino da Padova
Three Madrigals

Jacopo da Bologna
Three Madrigals

Three French Songs From The Late
Fourteenth Century

WILLAN, HEALEY; BARBEAU, MARIUS
Chansons Canadiennes

WILSON, H. LANE
Monro, George
My Lovely Celia

Storace, Stephen
Pretty Creature, The

WINKLER, L.; SATTLER, H.
Schubert, Franz (Peter)
Sämmtliche Compositionen

WUYTACK, JOS
Choralia

YANAGI, SADAKO
Ramillete De Canciones Espanolas

YOUNG, PERCY M.
Elgar, [Sir] Edward (William)
Five Scenes From "The Spanish Lady"

ZANINELLI
Foster, Stephen Collins
Three Songs By Stephen Foster

Franck
Seek Thou This Soul Of Mine

ZIMBALIST, EFREM
Two Folk-Songs Of Little Russia

ZIMMERMAN
Handel, George Frideric
Serenata
There In Blissful Shade: Serenata

ZIMMERMANN
Meyerbeer, Giacomo
Lieder, Band 1

ZIMMERMANN, REINER
Debussy, Claude
Frühe Lieder
Fünf Lieder Auf Gedichte Von Paul
Bourget
Trois Chansons De Bilitis

BRAHMS
   Schubert, Franz (Peter)
     Drei Lieder
     Ellens II. Gesang
     Greisengesang

BRAMAN, BARRY
   Keep Me Goin', Lord

BREAM
   Seiber, Matyas György
     Four French Folk Songs

BRISCOE, JAMES R.
   Debussy, Claude
     Sept Poèmes De Banville

BRITTEN, BENJAMIN
   Bach, Johann Sebastian
     Geistliche Lieder

   Purcell, Henry
     When Night Her Purple Veil

BRONARSKI, LUDWIK; PADEREWSKI, IGNACY
JAN; TURCZYNSKI, JÓZEF

   Chopin, Frédéric
     Piesni I Piosnki

BROWN, HOWARD MAYER
   Florentine Chansonnier From The Time
     Of Lorenzo The Magnificent, A, 2
     Vols.

BROWN, IRVING
   Alto Arias From Oratorios, Volume 1

   Alto Arias From Oratorios, Volume 2

   Arias For Baritone, Volume 1

   Arias For Baritone, Volume 2

   Arias For Bass, Volume 1

   Arias For Bass, Volume 2

   Arias For Mezzo-Soprano And Alto,
     Volume 1

   Arias For Mezzo-Soprano And Alto,
     Volume 2

   Arias For Soprano, Volume 1

   Arias For Tenor, Volume 1

   Arias For Tenor, Volume 2

   Baritone Arias From Oratorios, Volume
     1

   Baritone Arias From Oratorios, Volume
     2

   Bass Arias From Oratorios, Volume 1

   Bass Arias From Oratorios, Volume 2

   Soprano Arias From Oratorios, Volume
     1

   Soprano Arias From Oratorios, Volume
     2

   Tenor Arias From Oratorios, Volume 1

   Tenor Arias From Oratorios, Volume 2

BROWN, R.
   New Songs Of Faith

BRUCE, ROBERT
   Boyce, William
     Lyra Britannica

BURKHART, F.
   Mozart, Wolfgang Amadeus
     Bandel, Das

   Silcher, Friedrich
     So Nimm Denn Meine Hände

   Von Guter Art

BURROWS, DAVID L.
   Cesti, Marc' Antonio
     Four Chamber Duets

BURTON, A. J.
   Dvořák, Antonín
     New World Prayer, A

BUSH, GEOFFREY; TEMPERLEY, NICHOLAS
   English Songs 1800-1860

   Romantic Songs

   Songs Of The Linleys

   Stanford, Charles Villiers
     Six Songs

CALDWELL
   Celebration Of Melody, A

CANTELOUBE, J.
   Anthologie Des Chants Populaires
     Français, Vol. 1

   Anthologie Des Chants Populaires
     Français, Vol. 2

   Anthologie Des Chants Populaires
     Franco-Canadiens

   Chants De France, Vol. 1

CARDAMONE, DONNA G.
   Pisador, Diego
     Canzone Villanesche Alla Napolitana
     And Villotte

CARLI, A.
   Songs Of The Pyrenees, Book 1

   Songs Of The Pyrenees, Book 2

CAUCHIE, MAURICE
   Quinze Chansons Françaises Du XVI
     Siècle

CHARLES, J.
   Nouveaux Amusements Tendres Et
     Bacchiques, Livre Premier

CHAROSH, PAUL; FREMONT, ROBERT A.
   Song Hits From The Turn Of The
     Century

CHARPENTRAU, SIMONE
   Livre d'Or De La Chanson Française,
     Vol. 1

   Livre d'Or De La Chanson Française,
     Vol. 2

   Livre d'Or De La Chanson Française,
     Vol. 3

CHIESA, RENATO
   Sette Canzoni Veneziane Del XVIII
     Secolo

CHIESA, RUGGERO
   Giuliani, Mauro
     Sechs Lieder

CHILESOTTI, OSCAR
   Vecchi, Orazio (Horatio)
     Arie, Canzonette E Balli

CHRISTY, V.; ZYTOWSKI, C.
   Fifty-Seven Classic Period Songs

CHYBINSKI, A.; SIKORSKI, K.
   Stachowicz, Damian
     Veni Consolator

CLIMENT, JOSÉ
   Cançoner Valencia

COATES
   Amazing Grace

   McGlohon, Loonis
     In His Hands
     Teach Me, Lord

   Nearer, My God To Thee

COCKSHOTT
   Carey, Henry
     Friendly Adviser, The

COCKSHOTT, GERALD
   Somebody Fetch My Flute

COFONE, CHARLES J.F.
   Favorite Christmas Carols

COGNI, G.
   Cogni, A.
     Antologia Lirica

COLLINA, F.S.
   Seidler, G.
     Arte Del Cantare, L'

COSTANZA, P.
   Raccolta Di Canti Folkloristici
     Siciliani

COUSSY, NOË
   Bordogni, Giulio Marco
     Vocalises, 36

COX
   Waters
     Highest Praise, The

CRAIG BELL
   Negro Spirituals

CRAWFORD, RICHARD
   Civil War Songbook, The

CROCKETT
   Cundick, Robert Milton
     When Someone Cares

CURTÍS, GARETH
   Power, Lyonel
     Mass Alma Redemptoris Mater

CURZON
   Schumann, Robert (Alexander)
     Mélodies, 40

CZERNIK, W.
   Trunk, Richard
     In Stiller Dämmerung

DAGNINO, EDOARDO
   Nenna, Pomponio
     Madrigali

DALMAR, A.
   Boleros: Latin-American Popular Song
     Styles

DAMAIS
   Selleron, J.
     Litanies Florales

DANIEL, LADISLAV
   My Little Pipe

DANNER, DAVID
   Seabough, Ed.
     People Of The World, Rejoice

DARVAS
   Pergolesi, Giovanni Battista
     Salve Regina

DAVENET
   Selleron, J.
     Miracle Du Printemps

DAY, CYRUS LAWRENCE
   Urfey, Thomas d'
     Songs Of Thomas d'Urfey, The

DAY, THOMAS
   Lotti, Antonio
     Duetti, Terzetti, E Madrigali A Piu
     Voci

DE BRITO, MANUEL CARLOS
   Five Portuguese Villancicos

DECOU
   Gaither, William James (Bill)
     Bill Gaither Songs For Male Quartet

DEGRADA
   Pergolesi, Giovanni Battista
     Domine Ad Adiuvandum Me Festina

DEGRADA, FRANCESCO
   Vivaldi, Antonio
     Alla Caccia Dell'alme E De' Cori
     All'ombra d'Un Bel Faggio
     Nel Partir Da Te Mio Caro
     Se Ben Vivono Senz'alma
     T'intendo Sì Mio Cor

DEIOSSO, G.; ATZENI, S.
   Sei Canzoni Provenzali

DEL TREDICI
   Thomson
     Two Songs On Poems Of James Joyce

DELIUS, NIKOLAUS
   Schürmann, Georg Caspar
     Arien

DEYRIS, EDITH; DOURSON, PAUL
   Vivre La Musique En Liberté, Vol. 2

DIAZ, ENRIQUE
   Puerto Rican Danzas

DILLE
   Bartók, Béla
     Five Hungarian Folksongs
     Young Bartok, The, Vol. 1: Selected
     Songs

DRECHSLER, OTTO
   Scarlatti, Alessandro
     Endimione E Cintia

DUARTE
   Sing Christmas Carols

   Sing Negro Spirituals

DUNCKER, MIREILLE; PINCHARD, MAX
   Vivre La Musique En Liberté, Vol. 1

DUNHAM, MENEVE
   Vivaldi, Antonio
     Cantatas For Solo Voice

DUPRÉ
   Dowland, John
     Six Songs

HAACKE, WALTER
  Franck, Johann Wolfgang
    Weil, Jesu, Ich In Meinem Sinn

HAAN, ED. DE
  Siebzehn St. Nicolaasliederen En 32
    Kerstliederen

HABETIN, RUDOLF
  Fleischer, Hans
    Sechs Weihnachtslieder

HADER
  Schubart, (Christian Friedrich)
    Daniel
    Vergessene Lieder

HAEUSSLEIN
  Lied I, Das: Ausgewählte Lieder Aus
    Zwei Jahrhunderten

  Lied III, Das: Geistliche Gesänge

HAIK VANTOURA, S.
  Musique De La Bible Révélée, La

HALE, PHILIP
  French Art Songs Of The Nineteenth
    Century

HALFFTER
  Falla, Manuel de
    Seven Popular Spanish Songs

HALLOWELL, EMILY
  Calhoun Plantation Songs

HAMBLEN, SUZY
  Baxter, Dick
    Promises To Keep

HARLEY, J.
  Purcell, Henry
    Selected Songs

HARNED, ALFRED
  Roes, Carol Lasater
    Maui Aloha

HARRIMAN
  Italian Duets Of The 14th Century,
    Vol. 1

  Machaut, Guillaume de
    Guillaume Machaut, Vol. I: Four
      Chansons

HATANAKA, RYOSUKE
  Ausgewählter Deutsche Lieder, Vol. 1:
    Originaltonarten

HATTORI, KOICHI
  Tokoshie No Aki No Uta

HATTORI, RYUTARO
  Japanese Folk Songs

  Traditional Folk Songs Of Japan

HAUPT; STUMMER
  Ungarische Volkslieder

HAUS; MOCKL
  Lied International

HAYES
  Markley
    Undying Love

HAYES, MARK
  Songs Of Inspiration I

  Songs Of Inspiration II

HECK, THOMAS F.
  Giuliani, Mauro
    Sechs Lieder

  Schubert, Franz (Peter)
    Sixteen Songs With Guitar
      Accompaniment

HEDMONDT
  Lütgen
    Kunst Der Kehlfertigkeit, Die, Vol.
      1: 20 Tägliche Übungen
    Kunst Der Kehlfertigkeit, Vol. 2

HEDWALL, LENNART
  Hakånson, Knut Algot
    Fem Frida-Visor

HELLMANN
  Telemann, Georg Philipp
    Kleines Magnificat

HELMER, AXEL
  Söderman, [Johan] August
    Songs

HEMBERG, ESKIL
  Anonymous
    Två Duetter

HENDRIE; DART
  Coperario, Giovanni (John Cooper)
    English Lute Song Series 1, No. 17:
      Funeral Teares; Songs Of
      Mourning; The Masque Of Squires

HENKE
  Bellman, Carl Michael
    Bellman-Brevier Heft 1: Zehn Lieder
      Aus "Fredmans Episteln"
    Bellman-Brevier, Heft 2: Zehn
      Lieder Aus "Fredmans Lieder" Und
      "Bacchi Tempel"

HENKE, MATTHIAS
  Bellman, Carl Michael
    Bellman Brevier, Heft 3: 10 Lieder
      Aus "Fredmans Episteln" Und
      "Fredmans Lieder" (2. Parthie)

HENKEMANS, HANS
  Lier, Bertus van
    Eens

HESS, WILLY
  Beethoven, Ludwig van
    Szene Aus "Vestas Feuer"

HILL
  Gaither, William James (Bill)
    Precious Jesus

HILLER
  Schubert, Franz (Peter)
    Junge Nonne, Die

HIROTA, YURIKO
  Ryutaro Hirota Album, Vol. 1

  Ryutaro Hirota Album, Vol. 2

  Ryutaro Hirota Album, Vol. 3

HITCHCOCK, H. WILEY
  Caccini, Giulio
    Nuove Musiche, Le
    Nuove Musiche E Nuova Maniera Di
      Scriverle (1614)

  Foster, Stephen Collins
    Minstrel Show Songs

HOFFMAN, DON S.; WOOLLEN, RUSSELL
  Porter, Walter
    Since All Things Love

HOFFMANN, HANS
  Schütz, Heinrich
    Herr Ist Mein Licht, Der

HOFMANN, K.
  Telemann, Georg Philipp
    Göttlichs Kind, Lass Mit Entzücken
    Ich Will Den Herrn Loben Allezeit

HOGWOOD, CHRISTOPHER
  Arne, Thomas Augustine
    Lyric Harmony

HOLM, GUNNAR
  Blott En Dag Och Fem Andra Sånger

  Grieg, Edvard Hagerup
    Store Hvide Flok, Den

HOPKINS
  Bach, Johann Sebastian
    Christmas Music By J.S. Bach

  Binchois, Gilles (de Binche)
    Chansons D'Amour, Vol. I
    Chansons D'Amour, Vol. II

  Byrd, William
    Four Sacred Songs

  Cantus Firmus Trios From The
    Renaissance

  Christmas-Cellany, Vol. I

  Dances, Songs And Motets Of
    Renaissance Poland, Vol. I

  Dances, Songs And Motets Of
    Renaissance Poland, Vol. II

  Des Prez, Josquin
    Ars Sacra Et Comica Of Josquin

  Elizabethan Songs, Vol. I

  Elizabethan Songs, Vol. II

  England's Golden Century Of Song

  Four Early Italian Madrigals

  German Tenorlieder, Vol. I

  German Tenorlieder, Vol. II

  Morley, Thomas
    Three Secular Songs

HOPKINS, BERNARD
  Early English Duets

  Lassus, Roland de (Orlandus)
    Bicinia From The Liturgy

  Six Duets From The Renaissance

HORN
  Schein, Johann Hermann
    Also Heilig Ist Der Tag
    O Maria, Gebenedeiet Bist Du
    Siehe, Das Ist Mein Knecht

HORN, PAUL
  Brahms, Johannes
    Regina Coeli

HORTON, JOHN
  Book Of Early Music, A

HOWAT
  Debussy, Claude
    Jane

HUFF
  Gaither, William James (Bill)
    God Save The Song

  Paxton, Gary S.
    Praise The Lord

  Peterson, John W.
    Miracle Goes On, The

HURD, MICHAEL
  Gurney, Ivor
    Fifth Volume Of Ten Songs, A

INGRISCH
  Einem, Gottfried von
    Lieder Vom Anfang Und Ende

ISHII, KAN
  Japanese Folk Songs: Chugoku District

  Japanese Folk Songs: Hokkaido
    District

  Japanese Folk Songs: Kyushu District

  Japanese Folk Songs: Okinawa District

  Japanese Folk Songs: San-In And
    Hokuriku Districts

  Japanese Folk Songs: Shikoku District

ISHIKETA, MAREO
  Kappa Tan

  Kon Kon Tan

JACKMAN, JERRY R.
  Ashton, Myriel
    My Testimony

JACKSON, GREGORY
  Goodrich, Jeff
    I Heard Him Come

  Schofield, Joe
    He Is My Redeemer

JACKSON, GREGORY A.
  I Am A Child Of God

JANCIK, HANS
  Wolf, Hugo
    Kritische Gesamtausgabe, Band I:
      Gedichte Von Eduard Mörike
    Kritische Gesamtausgabe, Band II:
      Gedichte Von Joseph Von
      Eichendorff
    Kritische Gesamtausgabe, Band III-
      1: Gedichte von Johann Wolfgang
      von Goethe
    Kritische Gesamtausgabe, Band III-
      2: Gedichte von Johann Wolfgang
      von Goethe
    Kritische Gesamtausgabe, Band IV:
      Spanisches Liederbuch
    Kritische Gesamtausgabe, Band V:
      Italienisches Liederbuch
    Kritische Gesamtausgabe, Band VI:
      Lieder Nach Verschiedenen
      Dichtern
    Kritische Gesamtausgabe, Band VII-
      1: Nachgelassene Lieder I
    Kritische Gesamtausgabe, Band VII-
      2: Nachgelassene Lieder II
    Kritische Gesamtausgabe, Band VII-
      3: Nachgelassene Lieder III
    Kritische Gesamtausgabe, Vol. 8:
      Lieder Mit Orchesterbegleitung 1
    Kritische Gesamtausgabe, Vol. 9:
      Lieder Mit Orchesterbegleitung 2

JANETZKY, KURT
  Hasse, Johann Adolph
    Zwölf Solfeggi Für Eine Singstimme

  Heinichen, Johann David
    Nisi Dominus Aedificaverit Domum

JEANROY, ALFRED; BRANDIN, LOUIS; AUBRY,
  PIERRE

    Lais Et Descorts Français Du XIIIe
      Siècle

JEFFERY, BRIAN
  Sor, Fernando
    Seguidillas

JEFFERY, BRIAN; RUCKER, MANUEL
  Moretti, Federico
    Doce Canciones

JONES, E.H.
  Lanier, Nicholas
    Six Songs

JUNG; PACHNICKE
  Es Ist Ein Ros Entsprungen:
    Collection

JÜRGEN, JÜRGENS
  Monteverdi, Claudio
    Duo Seraphim
    Nigra Sum
    Pulchra Es

KALCKSTEIN; SOBOTKA; WERBA
  Anleitung Zum Liedgesang

KANAI, KIKUKO
  Songs Of Okinawa

KANTHOU, EUGENIA
  Weihnachtslieder

KELLER, P.
  Unsere Schweizerlieder

KILIAN, DIETRICH
  Buxtehude, Dietrich
    Dein Edles Herz
    Ecce Nunc Benedicite Domino
    Erfreue Dich, Erde
    Jesu, Meines Lebens Leben
    Schlagt, Künstler, Die Pauken

KINGSLEY
  Ten Folk Songs

KIRMSSE, HEIDI
  Spektrum 79: Neue Lieder Und Gesänge

KLEIN, RUDOLF
  Beethoven, Ludwig van
    Sämtliche Kanons: Ausgabe B
    Notentext Allein (Singheft)

KLEMM
  Mahler, Gustav
    Kinder-Totenlieder

KOBAYASHI, ARATA
  Poésie d'Animaux

KOCH, ERLAND
  Koch, Sigurd Christian Erlund von
    Gammalswenska Wijsor

  Melodier Runt Siljan

KOCHO, HISAKO
  Rentaro Taki Complete Album

KÖHLER
  Hammerschmidt, Andreas
    Gelobet Seist Du, Jesu Christ
    Nun Lob, Mein Seel, Den Herren.
    Sonata

KOHLHASE
  Zelenka, Jan Dismas
    Christe Eleison

KOK, JOHN B.
  Accordionette, Vol. 5

KOMMA, KARL MICHAEL
  Brahms, Johannes
    Vier Ernste Gesänge

KRÄMER, W.
  Schubart, (Christian Friedrich)
    Daniel
    Vergessene Lieder

KROEGER
  Herbst
    Three Sacred Songs

KROEGER, KARL
  Pelissier, Victor
    Pelissier's Columbian Melodies:
    Music For The New York And
    Philadelphia Theaters

KUSAKAWA, KEI
  Song Album

KUSH, JOSEPH T.
  Chants For The Readings Of Christmas,
    Easter Triduum And Pentecost

LAMBERT, G.
  Charpentier, Marc-Antoine
    Tenebrae Factae Sunt

LANDON, H.C. ROBBINS
  Haydn, [Franz] Joseph
    Drei Baritonarien
    Sopranarien, Vol. 1
    Sopranarien, Vol. 2
    Vier Tenorarien

LANDON, R.; TRÖTZMÜLLER, K.
  Haydn, [Franz] Joseph
    Salve Regina

LANDSHOFF
  Alte Meister Des Bel Canto

LANG, H.; SIEGL, O.; ZIPP, F.; ZOLL, P.
  Sololied Im Chorkonzert, Vol. 1:
    Volkslieder In Sätzen
    Zeitgenössischer Komponisten

LAURIE, MARGARET
  Purcell, Henry
    Secular Songs For Solo Voice

LAVAGNE, E.
  Beethoven, Ludwig van
    Ehre Gottes Aus Der Natur, Die

LAVENDER, PETER; BINNEY, MALCOLM
  Sullivan, [Sir] Arthur Seymour
    Authentic Gilbert And Sullivan
    Songbook, The

LEAH, SHIRLEY
  Chester Book Of Celebrated Songs,
    The, Book 1

  Chester Book Of Celebrated Songs,
    The, Book 2

  Chester Book Of Celebrated Songs,
    The, Book 3

LEDBETTER, STEVEN J.
  Chadwick, George Whitefield
    Flower Cycle, A, and Told In The
    Gate

LEE, CAROLYN
  Five Villancicos

  Seven Courtly Love-Songs

LEMAIRE, G.
  Fiocco, Joseph-Hector
    Laudate Pueri

LEPPARD, RAYMOND
  Handel, George Frideric
    Lucrezia: O Numi Eterni

  Monteverdi, Claudio
    Five Scherzi Musicali

  Scarlatti, Domenico
    Salve Regina

LERMA, DOMINIQUE-RENE DE
  Saint-Georges, Joseph Boulogne de
    Ernestine: Scena

LEWIS A.
  Selection Of Italian Arias, A, Vol. I

LIANI
  Frescobaldi, Girolamo
    In Te Domine Speravi

LINDEMANN, F.
  Mozart, Wolfgang Amadeus
    Alleluja

LONARDI, M.
  Monteverdi, Claudio
    Scherzi Musicali

LONGHURST, JOHN
  Piccolomini, Marietta
    Link Divine, The

LOSSE
  Schumann, Robert (Alexander)
    Ausgewählte Lieder

  Unterrichtslieder; Neue Folge: Das
    Lied Der Gegenwart

  Unterrichtslieder: Veränderte Auswahl

  Unterrichtslieder, Vol. 1: 60
    Ausgewählte Lieder (Bach Bis
    Reger)

LÜTGE, KARL
  Schütz, Heinrich
    Meine Seele Erhebt Den Herren

LUXON, BENJAMIN; TEAR, ROBERT
  Victorian Songs And Duets

LYON, LAURENCE
  Fox, Luacine Clark
    Love One Another

  Kjar, Marjorie
    Where Love Is

LYON, SHARON
  I Saw The Cross Of Jesus

MACHIDA, HITOSHI
  Lyric Songs

MAEGAARD, JAN
  Schoenberg, Arnold
    Serenade, Op. 24

MALATESTA, G.
  Beethoven, Ludwig van
    An Die Freude

MANN, ALFRED
  Gibbons, Orlando
    Christmas Day

  Handel, George Frideric
    Two Sacred Arias

  Thanksgiving Hymn, The

  Veni Emmanuel

MARIX, JEANNE
  Musiciens De La Cour De Bourgogne Au
    XVe Siècle (1420-1467), Les

MARTIENSSEN
  Duettenkranz: 12 Opern-Duette Für 2
    Frauenstimmen

  Duettenkranz: 14 Weltliche Duette Für
    1 Frauen- Und 1 Männer-Stimme

  Duettenkranz: 15 Opern-Duette Für 1
    Frauen- Und 1 Männer-Stimme

  Duettenkranz: 18 Weltliche Duette Für
    2 Frauenstimmen

MARX, JOSEF; RIKKO, FRITZ
  Krieger, Johann Philipp
    Sing, Oh My Spirit

MATTHEWS, COLIN
  Britten, [Sir] Benjamin
    Quatre Chansons Françaises (Four
    French Songs)

MAXWELL DAVIES, PETER
  Buxtehude, Dietrich
    Also Hat Gott Die Welt Geliebt

MCAFEE, DON
  Schütz, Heinrich
    Herr, Ich Hoffe Darauf
    Ihr Heiligen Lobsinget Dem Herren
    O Hilf, Christe, Gottes Sohn
    Schaffe In Mir, Gott, Ein Reines
    Herz

MCGRADY, RICHARD
  Lawes, Henry
    Dialogue On A Kiss, A

MCGUIRE
  Gaither, William James (Bill)
    My Father's Angels
    We Are Persuaded

MCGUIRE, DONY
  Gaither, William James (Bill)
    Ordinary Baby

MEIMA, HERMAN
  Sint Bij Het Orgel

MENDELSSOHN, A.
  Schütz, Heinrich
    Drei Kleine Geistliche Konzerte

MENKE, WERNER
  Telemann, Georg Philipp
    Alles Redet Jetzt Und Singet

MERCANTINI, L.
  Olivieri, A.
    Inno Di Garibaldi

MEREDITH, HENRY
  Scarlatti, Alessandro
    Con Voce Festiva
    Farò La Vendetta
    In Terra La Guerra
    Mio Tesoro
    Rompe Sprezza
    Sette Arie Con Tromba Sola
    Si Riscaldi Il Tebro
    Si Suoni La Tromba

MEYER, C.F.
  Fleischer, Hans
    Sechs Lieder

MEYER, EVE R.
Carr, Benjamin
Musical Miscellany In Occasional
Numbers
Selected Secular And Sacred Songs

MICHAELIS, RUTH
Church Year In Song, The

MIES, P.
Haydn, [Franz] Joseph
Lieder Für Eine Singstimme Mit
Begleitung Des Klaviers

MIES, P.; HELMS, M.
Haydn, [Franz] Joseph
Lieder

MINCHIN
Brahms, Johannes
Wiegenlied

MIYAHARA, TEIJI
Song Album

MOFFAT, ALFRED
Master Songs Of All Time

Purcell, Henry
Fairest Isle, All Isles Excelling
In A Cottage By The Green
What Shall I Do To Show How Much I
Love Her

MÖLLER, EBERHARD
Schütz, Heinrich
Klaglied Auf Den Tod Seiner Ehefrau
Magdalena Schütz

MOLNÁR; KERN; ADÁM
Daloskert: Songs From Four Centuries

MÖNKEMEYER, HELMUT
Altenburg, Michael
Intraden: Heft 1
Intraden: Heft 2

MONMA, NAOE
Collections Of The World's Folk
Songs: English Album I

Collections Of The World's Folk
Songs: English Album II

Collections Of The World's Folk
Songs: French Album

Collections Of The World's Folk
Songs: German Album

Collections Of The World's Folk
Songs: Italian Album I

Collections Of The World's Folk
Songs: Italian Album II

Collections Of The World's Folk
Songs: Russian Album

Collections Of The World's Folk
Songs: Spanish Album

MONMA, NAOMI
Collections Of The World's Folk
Songs: Central European Album

MONNIOTTE
Marly
Chant Des Partisans, Le

MOORE
New Gaither Vocal Band

MORIWAKI, KENZO
Song Album

MORLAYE, G.
Certon, Pierre
Psaumes De Pierre Certon Réduits
Pour Chant Et Luth

MORONI, G.E.
Natale

MORTARI, V.
Cavalli, (Pietro) Francesco
Tre Frammenti Di Opere

Monteverdi, Claudio
Tempro La Cetra

Vivaldi, Antonio
Ingrata Lidia

MOSÓCZI
Huzella, Elek
Four Love Songs

MUELLER
Galuppi, Baldassare
Et Incarnatus Est

MUGGIA
Bettinelli
Due Liriche

NAGURA, AKIRA
Collected Songs

NAKADA, YOSHINAO
Elegant Songs To Confess Love

NAVAS
Albéniz, Isaac
Cadiz
Granada

NELHYBEL, VACLAV
Bach, Johann Sebastian
Bist Du Bei Mir

Dvořák, Antonín
Hospodin Jest Muj Pastyr

NEUBERT
Böddecker, Philipp Friedrich
Natus Est Jesus

NEUER, A.
Szymanowski, Karol
Piesni (Songs)

NEUER, ADAM
Szymanowski, Karol
Piesni

NEUMANN
Durme, Durme

NEUMANN, RICHARD
Una Matica De Ruda

Yo M'Enamori D'Un Aire

NIGGLI
Lieder Der Heimat

NOLIANI, C.
Canti Del Popolo Americano

NOWACZYK, ERWIN
Moniuszko, Stanislaw
Ballady I Spiewy Dramatyczne

NOWAK, LEOPOLD
Bach, Wilhelm Friedemann
Dies Ist Der Tag: Sinfonie Und
Kantate

OBARA, AKIO
Japanese Lullabys, 50

ODE, JAMES
Handel, George Frideric
Three Arias For D Trumpet And Bass
Voice
Three Arias For D Trumpet And
Soprano Voice

OESER, FRITZ
Weber, Carl Maria von
Wonnig Süsses Hoffnungsträumen:
Rezitativ Und Aria

OGAMI, KAZUHIKO
Song Album "Dokoku"

ØIAN, J.; HARTMANN, CHR.
Øian, Johan
Nøtteliten

O'NEAL, BARRY
American Art Songs; 32 Amerikanische
Kunstlieder Des 20. Jahrhunderts
Von Ives Bis Carter

Wedding Garland, A

OREL, ALFRED
Haydn, [Franz] Joseph
Berenice, Che Fai
Chi Vive Amante

OTTEN JUDITH
Panorama Of American Song, A, Vol. 1:
"The American Baroque" (1600-
1750)

Panorama Of American Song, A, Vol. 2:
"An Era Of Rebellion" (1750-1820)

Panorama Of American Song, A, Vol. 3:
"Between The Wars" (1820-1860)

Panorama Of American Song, A, Vol. 4:
"The Era Of Enlightenment" (1860-
1900)

Panorama Of American Song, A, Vol. 5:
"In Our Time" (1900-)

Panorama Of American Song, A, Vol. 6:
"America's Women" (1700-)

PACHNICKE
All Mein Gedanken: 280 Deutsche
Volkslieder

Deutsche Volkslieder

German Folk Songs

PAGE, CHRISTOPHER
Hildegard Of Bingen
Sequences And Hymns

PALMER
Pepusch, John Christopher
Miranda

PANDER
Mussorgsky, Modest Petrovich
Lieder Und Tänze Des Todes

PANENKA, H.
Weber, Carl Maria von
Einst Traumte Meiner Sel'gen Base

PANKEY
Amerikanische Neger-Volkslider; Neue
Folge

Amerikanische Neger-Volkslieder

PARKER, IAN
Ventadorn, Bernart de
Ab Joi Mou Lo Vers E-L Comens

PATTERSON, WILLIS
Anthology Of Art Songs By Black
American Composers

PAUMGARTNER, BERNHARD
Monteverdi, Claudio
Lettera Amorosa

PAXTON
Gaither, William James (Bill)
Free At Last
Kids Under Construction

PELLINI, GIULIO; CISILINO, SIRO
Sei Missae Dominicales

PELOSI, T.
O Bianco Fiore

PERRY, JANICE KAPP
Glenn, Jamie
Walk Tall You're A Daughter Of God

PETZOLD
Opernarien Russischer Und
Sowjetischer Meister: 19 Arien
Für Bariton

Opernarien Russischer Und
Sowjetischer Meister: 20 Arien
Für Tenor

PFAUTSCH, LLOYD
Solos For The Church Year

PFLÜGER, HANS GEORG
Cornelius, Peter
Drei Kön'ge Wandern Aus Morgenland

PILKINGTON
English Lutesongs, Book 1

English Lutesongs, Book 2

PILKINGTON, MICHAEL
Arne, Thomas Augustine
Twelve Songs, Vol. 1
Twelve Songs, Vol. 2

Early Georgian Songs, Book 1

Early Georgian Songs, Book 2

Eccles, John
Eight Songs

Hook, James
Eight Songs

Storace, Stephen
Seven Songs

PITTION, COLETTE; PINCHARD, MAX
Douze Chants Irlandais Traditionnels
Et Révolutionnaires

PLATT, RICHARD
Eccles, John
Judgment Of Paris, The

POLNAUER, FREDERICK F.
Songs Of The Italian Baroque

POWELL
MacKenzie
That's Him

POWELL, JOHN S.
Charpentier, Marc-Antoine
Vocal Chamber Music

WESTON, PAMELA
  Arne, Thomas Augustine
    When Daisies Pied

  Crusell, Bernhard Henrik
    From Ganges' Beauteous Strands

WHITE, OLIVER
  Gounod, Charles François
    O Divine Redeemer

WIEMER, WOLFGANG
  Bach, Johann Sebastian
    Denket Doch, Ihr Menschenkinder

WIKLUND, A.
  Stenhammar, Wilhelm
    Du Hade Mig Så Kär
    Guld Och Gröna Skogar
    I Lönnens Skymning
    Låt Oss Dö Unga

WILBRUN
  Gaither, William James (Bill)
    It's Beginning To Rain

WILKINS, NIGEL
  Bartolino da Padova
    Three Madrigals

  Jacopo da Bologna
    Three Madrigals

  Three French Songs

WILLAN, HEALEY
  Chansons Canadiennes

  Songs Of The British Isles

WILLE, STEWART
  Tchaikovsky, Piotr Ilyich
    Moskva: Prayer

WILLIAMS
  Two Part American Songs

WILLIAMS, PATRICK
  Christmas Carols

  Well Known Hymns

WISHART; LEHANE
  Purcell, Henry
    Songs, Book 1
    Songs, Book 2
    Songs, Book 3

WISHART, PETER
  Handel, George Frideric
    Messiah, Ornamented

WOJCIECHOWSKI
  Cimarosa, Domenico
    Gloria
    Quoniam Tu Solus Sanctus

WOOD, DALE
  Five Wedding Songs

WYATT
  Parry, Sir Charles Hubert Hastings
    Jerusalem

WYATT, JANET
  Parry, Sir Charles Hubert Hastings
    Jerusalem

YANAGI, TEIKO
  Granados, Enrique
    Granados Song Album

YOUNG, OVID
  Classic Collection, The

  Hale And Wilder Classic Collection Of
    Sacred Duets

YUYAMA, AKIRA
  Kaze No Nakano Kaze No Uta

ZAHNER
  Dietrich, J. Heinrich
    Psalmenmesse V

ZANINELLI
  Five American Folk Songs

ZEPLER, B.
  Mascagni, Pietro
    Cavallo Scalpita, Il
    Intermezzo Sinfonico
    Viva Il Vino Spumeggiante
    Voi Lo Sapete

ZIMMERMAN
  Handel, George Frideric
    There In Blissful Shade

ZIMMERMANN
  Debussy, Claude
    Ariettes Oubliées
    Chansons De Bilitis
    Cinq Poèmes De Baudelaire
    Fêtes Galantes 1 and 2
    Lieder Nach Bourget

ZIMMERMANN (cont'd.)

    Lieder Nach Verschiedenen Dichtern
    Proses Lyriques
    Sechs Lieder Nach Verlaine
    Trois Ballades De Villons
    Trois Chansons De France
    Trois Poèmes De Mallarmé

ZÜGNER
  Haydn, [Franz] Joseph
    Ewiges Lied

ZWISSLER, KARL MARIA
  Wolf, Hugo
    Alles Endet
    Fühlt Meine Seele
    Wohl Denk Ich Oft

A.W.
Äktenskapsfragan

AARTO; SUONIO
Unkarilaisia Kansanlauluja VI

ABLONIZ
Scarlatti, Alessandro
Sento Nel Core

ADAM
Mozart, Wolfgang Amadeus
Ah, Vous Dirai-Je Maman

Schubert, Franz (Peter)
Schubert Album

Tulipan

ADAM, J.
Masters Of Song, Vol. 1

Masters Of Song, Vol. 2

Masters Of Song, Vol. 3

Masters Of Song, Vol. 4

Masters Of Song, Vol. 5

Masters Of Song, Vol. 6

Masters Of Song, Vol. 7: Books A-C

Viragim, Viragim

ADLER
Operatic Anthology, Vol. I

Operatic Anthology, Vol. II

Operatic Anthology, Vol. III

Operatic Anthology, Vol. IV

Operatic Anthology, Vol. V

ADLER, CHARLES
Marcello, Benedetto
Aria Sacra

ADLER, GUIDO; BAGGE, SELMAR; DAVID, F.;
ESPAGNE, F.; MANDYCEWSKI, E.;
NOTTEBOHM, G.; REINECKE, C.;
RICHTER, E.F.; RIETZ, J.

Beethoven, Ludwig van
Complete Works

ADLER, KURT
Duets From The Great Operas I

Duets From The Great Operas II

ADRIO, ADAM
Riccio, Giovanni Battista
Jubilent Omnes

AGAY, DENES
Dearly Beloved

Sing Unto The Lord

AGUILA
Las Canciones Del Pueblo Espanol

Seis Habaneras Tradicionales

ALBONIZ
Durante, Francesco
Danza, Danza, Fanciulla

ALEVIZOS, SUSAN; ALEVIZOS, TED
Folk Songs Of Greece

ALEXANDROV, A.; MIKHALOV, I.;
REGUISTAN, E.

Hymne Sovietique

ALGAZI, L.
Six Folk Songs

AMELN, KONRAD
Rhau, Johannes
Deutsche Zwiegesànge

Weihnachtslieder Fùr Klavier

ANDERSEN, SVEN JORN
Sing Song Folksongs

ANDRE, JULIE
Songs From South Of The Border

ANDRESON, R.
Heller, A.
Lord's Prayer, The

ANDRIEESEN, HENDRIK
Diepenbrock, Alphons
Es War Ein Alter Kònig

ANDRIESSEN, HENDRIK
Diepenbrock, Alphons
En Sourdine
Kann Ich Im Busen Heisse Wùnsche
Tragen?

ANGEL
Villancicos Populares

ANKA, PAUL
Mana-Zucca, Mme.
I Love Life

ANTHONY, G.W.
Carols For Christmas

ANTHONY, JAMES R.; AKMAJIAN, DIRAN
Monteclair, Michel Pignolet de
Cantatas For One And Two Voices,
Book III

ARETZ
Veintedos Canciones Y Danzas
Tradicionales Argentinas

ARGENT
Saint-Saèns, Camille
La Solitaire

ARKWRIGHT
Boyce, William
Song Of Momus To Mars, The

ARMA, PAUL
Chantons Les Vielles Chansons
D'Europe

Cinqundquatre-Vent Berceuses De Tous
Les Peuples

Les Peuples Chantent Noèl

Noèl, Chantons Noèl

ARNE, T.
Songs To The Plays Of Shakespeare,
Vol. I

ARTHUR, DAVE; ARTHUR, TONI
Song Book

ASCENCIO-KAMHI
Rodrigo, Joaquin
Cantos De Amor Y De Guerra

ASLANOFF
Delibes, Leo
Passepied

Grieg, Edvard Hagerup
My Johann

Liadov, Anatol Konstantinovitch
Une Tabatiere A Musique

ASTON, PETER
Jeffries, George
Heu, Me Miseram!

AUBERT, L.
Aubert, Louis-Francois-Marie
Vieille Chanson Espagnole

AUSTIN, F.
Twelve Days Of Christmas

AVENARY, HANOCH
Rossi, Salomone
Il Primo Libro Delle Canzonette A
Tre Voci Di S. Rossi

AXMAN, E.
Russische Volkslieder

AZPAIZU
Falla, Manuel de
Tus Ojillos Negros

Granados, Enrique
Callejeo

AZPIAZU
Anonymous
Tres Morillas Me Enamoran

Bermudo, Fray Juan
Mira Nero De Tarpeya

Chapi, R.
Las Hijas Del Zebedeo

Daza, E.
Enfermo Estaba Antioco

Enriquez de Valderrabano, Enrique
Ay De Mi
Ya Cabalga Calainos

Granados, Enrique
Amor Y Odio
El Majo Discreto
El Majo Timido
El Mirar De La Maja
El Tralala Y El Punteado
La Maja De Goya
La Maja Dolorosa

AZPIAZU (cont'd.)

Las Currutacas Modestas

Luna, P.
El Nino Judio

Milan, Luis
Levaysme Amor D'aquesta Terra

Mille Regretz

Mudarra, Alonso de
Isabel, Perdiste La Tu Faxa
Triste Estaba El Rey David

Narvaez, Luis de
Con Que La Lavare

Pisador, Diego
Guarte, Guarte El Rey Don Sancho
La Manana De San Juan

Tabuyo, I.
La Del Panuelo Rojo

Torroba, F.M.
Petenera De La Marchenera

Turina, Joaquin
Cantares

Valverde, Joaquin
Clavelitos

Vazquez, J.
De Los Alamos Vengo

BABAD, HARRY
Roll Me Over

BACARISSE
Tres Canciones Medievales

BACH, JOHANN SEBASTIAN
Pergolesi, Giovanni Battista
Stabat Mater

BACHMAIR, J.
Stölzel, Gottfried Heinrich
Liebster Jesu, Deine Liebe Findet
Ihresgleichen Nicht

BACON, ERNST
Along Unpaved Roads

BAER, ABRAHAM
Baal T'fillah (Complete Edition)

BAIRD, MARGERY ANTHEA
Manchicourt, Pierre de
Twenty-Nine Chansons

BAKER, SCOTT
My True Love Hath My Heart

BALLIN, ERNST AUGUST
Mozart, Wolfgang Amadeus
Lieder

BALTZELL, W.J.
Something To Sing

BANTOCK
Bach, Johann Sebastian
Aria

Delibes, Leo
Les Filles Des Cadix

God Save The Queen

Greensleeves

Songs Of England, Book I

Songs Of England, Book II

Strauss, Johann
Mein Herr Marquis
Strauss Vocal Waltzes

BANTOCK, G.
On Hundred Songs Of England

Sixty Patroitic Songs Of All Nations

BANTOCK, GRANVILLE
Easter Hymn

Lord Rendal

BARDOS
Gyòngyvirag

Szaszszorszep

BARGIEL, W.; BRAHMS, J.; FRANCHOMME,
A.; LISZT, F.; REINECKE, C.;
RUDORFF, E.

Chopin, Frederic
Frederic Chopin's Works - First
Critical Edition

BARNABY
Clough-Leighter, Henry
O Perfect Love

BARTHOLOMEW
Songs Of Yale

BARTLETT, GENE
All The Way My Savior Leads Me

BARTLEY
Chadwick, George Whitefield
Come Unto Me

BARTOK, B.; KODALY, Z.
Hungarian Folk Songs

Twenty Hungarian Folksongs

BARTOK, BELA
Bornefeld, Helmut
Hirtenlieder

BASHMAKOV
Kohottakaa Riemuhuuto

BAUD-BOVY, SAMUEL
Chansons Populaires De Crete
Occidentale

BAUER, R.
Schriebl, Karl
Schneewalzer

BAUM, RICHARD; GERICKE, HERMANN PETER
Bruder Singer

BAUM, RICHARD; HOFMANN, FRIEDRICH
Klavierchoralbuch

BECKER
Mozart, Wolfgang Amadeus
Alleluia
Arie Scelte (Dalle Opera), Vol. I:
Soprano Leggero
Arie Scelte (Dalle Opera), Vol. II:
Soprano
Arie Scelte (Dalle Opera), Vol.
III: Tenore
Arie Scelte (Dalle Opera), Vol. IV:
Baritono E Basso

BECKWITH, JOHN
Five Songs

BEHREND
Behrend, Siegfried
Songs By Miguel De Cervantes And
Others For Guitar And Voice

Dowland, John
Two Songs

Gretry, Andre Ernest Modeste
Serenade

Handel, George Frideric
Pensieri Notturni Di Filli: Nel
Dolce Dell' Oblio

Paisiello, Giovanni
Rossine's Aria

Volkslieder Aus Aller Welt, Book I:
England

Volkslieder Aus Aller Welt, Book II:
France

Volkslieder Aus Aller Welt, Book III
Spain & Portugal

Volkslieder Aus Aller Welt, Book IV:
Italy

Volkslieder Aus Aller Welt, Book IX:
Poland

Volkslieder Aus Aller Welt, Book VII:
Balkan

Volkslieder Aus Aller Welt, Book
VIII: Russia

Volkslieder Aus Aller Welt, Book X:
Germany

Volkslieder Aus Aller Welt, Book XI:
America

Volkslieder Aus Aller Welt, Book XII:
Indonesia

BEHREND, J.
Foster, Stephen Collins
Unknown Foster, The

BEHREND, SIEGFRIED
Altitalienische Arien

Bergerettes

Bòddecker, Philipp Friedrich
Natus Est Jesus

BEHREND, SIEGFRIED (cont'd.)

Dowland, John
Achtzehn Lieder

Europàische Weihnachtslieder

Fùnf Altjapanische Geishalieder

Handel, George Frideric
No Se Emendera Jamas

Internationale Volklieder, Nol. 3

Internationale Volkslieder, Vol. 2

Internationale Volkslieder, Vol. 4:
Lieder Aus Cambodia, Israel,
Kongo, Philippinen

Internationale Volslieder, Vol 1

Lieder Der Vòlker, Heft 1

Lieder Der Vòlker, Heft 2

Lieder Der Vòlker, Heft 3

Lieder Der Vòlker, Heft 4

Lieder Der Vòlker, Heft 5

Lieder Der Vòlker, Heft 6

Milan, Luis
Pavanen, Fantasien, Romanzen Und
Vilancicos

Monteverdi, Claudio
Scherzi Musicali
Tre Madrigali

Mozart, Wolfgang Amadeus
Lieder Für Singstimme Und Gitarre

Taubert, Karl Heinz
Wiegenlied

Vier Altfranzòsische Volkslieder

Vier Italienische Canzonetten

Wiegenlieder Der Welt

BELL
Roberton, Hugh Stevenson
Oran-A-Chree

BELLINGHAM, BRUCE; EVANS, EDWARD G.,
JR.

Sixteenth-Century Bicinia: A Complete
Edition Of Munich, Bayerische
Staatsbibliothek, Mus. Ms. 260

BELZA, I.
Karlowicz, Mieczyslaw
Songs (Second Edition)

BENEDITO
Canciones Folkloricas Espanolas

Canciones Populares Espanolas, Vol.
IV

Canciones Populares Espanolas, Vol. V

Canciones Populares Populares
Espanolas, Vol. III

Pueblo

Pueblo, Vol. IX

Pueblo, Vol. V

Pueblo, Vol. VII

Pueblo, Vol. VIII

Pueblo, Vol. X

Raza

Seis Villancicos Rusticos Espanoles

Villancicos Populares

BENNETT, RICHARD RODNEY
This Worldes Joie

BENSON
He's Got The Whole World In His Hands

BENTLEY, ERIC; ROBINSON, EARL
Brecht-Eisler Song Book, The

BERBERIAN, ONNIK
Chansons D'Alaghiaz

BERBERICH
Mozart, Wolfgang Amadeus
Dreizehn Arien Aus Mozarts Messen,
Vespern, Motetten Und Kantaten

BERGEN
We Praise Thee, O God

BERGER, DONALD
Folk Songs Of Japan

BERGER, JEAN
Perti, Giacomo Antonio
Laudate Pueri

BERGMANN
Telemann, Georg Philipp
Locke Nur

BERGMANN; HUNT
Handel, George Frideric
Pensieri Notturni Di Filli: Nel
Dolce Dell' Oblio

BERNSTEIN
Rameau, Jean-Philippe
Le Berger Fidele

BEVAN
Arne, Thomas Augustine
Hail! Immortal Bacchus
How Engaging, How Endearing
To All The Sex Deceitful
Why So Pale And Wan, Fond Lover?

Boyce, William
Whether I Grow Old Or No

Howard, John Tasker
Soft Invader Of My Soul

Pepusch, John Christopher
Cupid, Cupid Bend Thy Bow

Stanley, John
Be Pleasant, Be Airy
Cupid's Power I Despise
Sweet Pretty Bird

BEYER
Rossini, Gioacchino
Varianten Zur Cavatine Der Rosina
"Una Voce Poco Fa"

BEYER, FRANK MICHAEL
Pepping, Ernst
Fùnf Lieder Aus Dem Paul-Gerhardt-
Liederbuch

BEZIADE; BELDENT
Douceur De Mon Pays

BEZIADE; VERRIER
Vive L'Anjou

BIANCHI, LINO
Scarlatti, Alessandro
Agar Et Ismaele Esiliati
La Passione Di Nostro Signore Gesu
Cristo

Scarlatti, Domenico
Missa Quatour Vocum
Pur Nel Sonno Al Men Tal'ora

Vivaldi, Antonio
Juditha Triumphans

BIBB
Handel, George Frideric
Aria Di Pollissena
Aria Di Poppea

BILBAO
Albeniz, Isaac
Granada

BINDER
Pioneer Songs Of Israel

BINDER, A.W.
Offenbach, Isaac
Brotherhood

Palestinean Folk Songs, Book I

BIRTNER, HERBERT
Schùtz, Heinrich
Freuet Euch Des Herren, Ihr
Gerechten
Herr, Nun Làssest Du Deinen Diener
Im Friede Fahren
Herr, Unser Herrscher

BISSELL, KEITH
Ten Folk Songs Of Canada

BITTENGER, WERNER
Schùtz, Heinrich
Der Herr Ist Mein Licht
Es Steh Gott Auf
Gib Unsern Fürsten
Herr, Neige Deine Himmel
Iss Dein Brot Mit Freuden
Symphoniae Sacrae II, Heft II
Verleih Uns Frieden
Vom Aufgang Der Sonnen
Zweierlei Bitte Ich, Herr, Von Dir

BITTINGER, WERNER
Schütz, Heinrich
Die So Ihr Den Herren Fùrchtet
Drei Schòne Dinge Seind
Herzlich Lieb Hab Ich Dich, O Herr
Heute Ist Christus, Der Herr,
Geboren
Ich Danke Dir, Herr
Ich Werde Nicht Sterben, Sondern
Leben
Lobet Den Herren, Alle Heiden
Lobet Den Herrn In Seinem Heiligtum
Mein Herz Ist Bereit
Meine Seele Erhebt Den Herren
Singet Dem Herrn Ein Neues Lied
Symphoniae Sacrae II, Heft I
Symphoniae Sacrae II, Heft III
Von Gott Will Ich Nicht Lassen

BJARNEGARD
Roman, Johan Helmich
Sa Ar Nu Intet Fòrdòmligt

BJÒRLIN, ULF
En Sang, Ett Vapen

BLANCHARD, ROGER
Vivaldi, Antonio
La Gloria E Imeneo

BLECH
Strauss, Johann
Liebeswalzer

BLYTON, CAREY
Six Regional Canadian Folksongs

BOALCH
Morley, Thomas
Two-Part Canzonets For Voices And
Recorders (Viols)

BOARDMAN, HARRY; BOARDMAN, LESLEY
Folk Songs And Ballads Of Lancashire

BOATNER
Oh, What A Beautiful City!

Soon I Will Be Done

BOATNER, EDWARD
On Ma Journey

BOCK, F.
Dungan, Olive
Eternal Life

Greenway
Visiting With Jesus

Phieffer, Don
It's A Happy Day

Songs I Sing In Sunday School

BOCK, FRED
Jones, Marjorie
Songs Of Marjorie Jones, Vol. 1
Songs Of Marjorie Jones, Vol. 2

Lyman, Ed.
Poor Little Lost Lamb

BOGGS, FRANK
Low Voice Solos

BOHLÀNDER
Old Folks At Home

BONA
Book Of A Thousand Songs

BOND
Songs Everybody Sings

BONDS, M.
Bonds, [Margaret]
I Got A Home In That Rock

Didn't It Rain'

Ezek'el Saw The Wheel

Go Tell It On The Mountain

He's Got The Whole World In His Hands

Hold On

Joshua Fit De Battle Of Jericho

BONIFAY, F.
Petrov, A.
Je M'balade Dans Moscau
La Petrouille Perdue

BONIN, MARY
Hebrew And Yiddish Folk-Songs

BONNAL, ERMEND
Flaìolet

BORDESE, STEPHEN
Bùsser, Henri-Paul
Revolte

Chaminade, Cecile
Les Trois Baisers

Chansons De Page

Delmet, Paul
Liberte

Dubois, Theodore
Le Vittrail

Duvernoy, Victor-Alphonse
Doux Larcin

Fontenailles, H. de
Legende Des Fleurs

Ganne, Louis Gaston
Lamento

Hahn, Reynaldo
Adieu

Lefebvre, Channing
Aveu

Levade, Charles (Gaston)
Enlevement

Marechal, Henri-Charles
Le Reve

Puget, Paul-Charles-Marie
Le Luth

BORG, KIM
Sibelius, Jean
Die Libelle "Schòne Libelle,
Schwirrtest Mir Herein"
Hallila, Uti Storm Och Regn
Kaiutar
Lastu Lainehilla
Lockung

Wolf, Hugo
Michelangelo-Lieder

BORNEFELD
Brahms, Johannes
Vier Ernste Gesànge

BORNEFELD, HELMUT
Dvorak, Antonin
Psalmen

Monteverdi, Claudio
Marienklage

BORSY; ROSSA
Tiszan Innen, Dunan Tul

BOTSFORD, FLORENCE H.
Botsford Collection Of Folk-Songs,
Vol II

Botsford Collection Of Folk-Songs,
Vol. III

BOUD, RON
Two Part Stylings No. I

BOWRING
Murray
In The Cross Of Christ I Glory

BOYD
Handel, George Frideric
La Solitudine

BOYD, MALCOLM
Handel, George Frideric
La Solitudine

BRAHMS, J.; BRUELL, I.; DOOR, A.;
FUCHS, J.N.; GAENSBACHER, J.;
EPSTEIN J.; HELLMESBERGER, J.;
MANDYCZEWSKI, E.

Schubert, Franz (Peter)
Complete Works

BRAHMS, J.; ESPAGNE, F.; GOLDSCHMIDT,
O.; JOACHIM, J.; RITTER VON
KOECHEL, LUDWIG; NOTTEBOHM, G.;
REINECKE, C.; RUDORFF, E.;
SPITTA, P.; WILDER, V.; WUELLNER,
F.; WALDERSEE, P.

Mozart, Wolfgang Amadeus
Complete Edition

BRAHMS, JOHANNES
German Folk Songs

Handel, George Frideric
Six Italian Chamber Duets

BRANBERGER, J.
Album Des Tschechischen Belcantos

BREACH, WILLIAM
Art-Song Argosy

BREAM
Henze, Hans Werner
Drei Fragmente Nach Hòlderlin Und
Drei Tentos Aus "Kammermusik
1958"

BRECK
Bach, Johann Sebastian
Jesus Bleibet Meine Freude

BREGUET, J.
Canti Di Natale

BREIG, WERNER
Schildt, Melchior
Ach Mein Herzliebes Jesulein

Schütz, Heinrich
Wo Gott Der Herr Nicht Bei Uns Hàlt

BRESGEN
Anonymous
Czechoslovakian Suite

BRESGEN, C.
Der Goldvogel

BRESGEN, CESAR
Vier Gesànge

BRESGEN; ZANOSKAR
Lied- Und Gitarrenspiel, Band I-II

BRITTEN, BENJAMIN
Folksong Arrangements, Vol. 1:
British Isles

Folksong Arrangements, Vol. 2: France

Folksong Arrangements, Vol. 3:
British Isles

Folksong Arrangements, Vol. 4:
Moore's Irish Melodies

Folksong Arrangements, Vol. 5:
British Isles

Folksong Arrangements, Vol. 6:
England

BRITTEN; PEARS
Purcell, Henry
Blessed Virgin's Expostulation
Five Songs
Job's Curse
Man Is For The Woman Made
Queen's Epicedium, The
Saul And The Witch At Endor
Seven Songs
Six Duets
Six Songs
Suite Of Songs
Three Divine Hymns
Two Divine Hymns And Alleluia

Quilter, Roger
Arnold Book Of Old Songs
Five Shakespeare Songs

BROADWOOD, LUCY; MAITLAND, FULLER
English Country Songs

BROCKWAY, HOWARD
Lonesome Tunes

BRODDE, OTTO
Choralsingbuch

Herr, Vor Dein Antlitz Treten Zwei

Wie Kòstlich Ist Der Heiligen Tod

BROGI
Canto Toscano

BROOKS
Peter
Here In These Words
When I Was One And Twenty

BROWN
Songs For Worship

BROWN, AARON
American Country Hymn Book, The

Faye, Linda
Today's Gonna Be A Brighter Day

Gospel From The House Of Cash

Gospel's Best Words And Music, Vol. 1

Gospel's Best Words And Music, Vol. 2

Gospel's Best Words And Music, Vol. 3

Matthew Twenty-Four

BROWN, F. E.
  Purcell, Henry
    Hark! The Echoing Air

BROWN, L.
  Five Negro Songs

BROWN, LAWRENCE
  Spirituals (Five Negro Songs)

BROWN, S.H.
  Children's Songs Of Spain

BRUEGGEN
  Noëls D'autrefois

BRUNI, M.
  Vivaldi, Antonio
    Nisi Dominus

BRYKS, NEGRI
  Dieci Arie Italiane Del Sei E
    Settecento

BUCK
  Gluck, Christoph Willibald Ritter von
    O Saviour, Hear Me

BUCK, D.
  Handel, George Frideric
    Ombra Mai Fu

BUHE
  Gitarren Spielt Auf, Heft I-VII

  Spirituals And Folksongs

BUHRMAN
  Intercollegiate Song Book For Hammond
    Organ

BUNJES
  Lossius, Lukas
    Holy, Holy, Holy

BUNJES, PAUL
  Wedding Blessings (A Collection Of
    Sacred Solos And A Duet)

BURKHART, F.
  Mozart, Wolfgang Amadeus
    Liebes Mandel, Wo Is 'S Bandel

BURKHART, FR.
  Von Guter Art

BURKHART, FR.; SCHEIT, K.
  Gitarrelieder Für Alle

  Volksliederbuch Zur Gitarre, Band 1:
    Kinderlieder

  Volksliederbuch Zur Gitarre, Band 2:
    Wander- Und Abschiedslieder

BURLEIGH
  Negro Spirituals, Vol. I

  Negro Spirituals, Vol. II

BURLEIGH, H. T.
  Balm In Gilead

  By An' By

  Couldn't Hear Nobody Pray

  De Blin' Man Stood On De Road An'
    Cried

  De Gospel Train

  Deep River

  Don't Be Weary Traveler

  Don't You Weep When I'm Gone

  Dry Bones

  Give Me Jesus

  Go Down In The Lonesome Valley

  Go Down Moses

  Go Tell It On De Mountains

  Hard Trials

  Hear De Lambs A-Crying

  Heav'n Heav'n

  He's Got The Whole World In His Hands

  He's Just De Same Today

  I Got A Home In-A-Dat Rock

  I Got A Home In A-Dat Rock

  I Know De Lord's Laid His Hands On Me

  I Stood On De Ribber Ob Jordon

BURLEIGH, H. T. (cont'd.)
  I Want To Be Ready

  I've Been In De Storm So Long

  John's Gone Down On De Island

  Joshua Fit De Battle Ob Jericho

  Let Us Break Bread Together

  Let Us Cheer The Weary Traveler

  Little David Play On Your Harp

  Little Mother Of Mine

  Mammy's Lil' Baby

  My Lord What A Morning

  My Way's Cloudy

  Nobody Knows De Trouble I've Seen

  O Rocks Don't Fall On Me

  Oh Didn't It Rain

  Ride On King Jesus

  Sinner Please Doan Let Dis Harves'
    Pass

  Sometimes I Feel Like A Motherless
    Child

  Stan' Still Jordan

  Steal Away

  Swing Low, Sweet Chariot

  'Tis Me O Lord

  Wade In De Water

  Weepin' Mary

  Were You There

  You May Bury Me In De Eas'

BURLEIGH, HARRY T.
  Album Of Negro Spirituals

BURROUGHS, BOB
  Jesus Said It

  Milham, Richard
    He Is Near

BURROWS
  Rubinstein, Anton
    True Romance

BURROWS, DAVID L.
  Cesti, Marc' Antonio
    Four Chamber Duets

BUSH
  Arne, Thomas Augustine
    Pleasing Tales In Dear Romances
    Should You Ever Find Her Complying

  Dibdin, Charles
    Come, Every Man Now Give His Toast

  Hook, James
    Softly Lulling, Sweetly Thrilling

  Shield, William
    Ere Bright Rosina Met My Eyes

BUTTERWORTH, GEORGE
  Folk Songs From Sussex

BUXO
  Veinte Y Cinco Canciones Populares
    Catalanas Navidenas

CADOW, PAUL
  Salieri, Antonio
    Zwei Kanons

CAFAGNA, MARIA PIA
  Seven Greek Folk Songs

CALI'
  Album Di Duodici Canzoni Popolari
    Siciliane

CANTELOUBE, J.
  Alsace

  Anjou

  Antholgie Des Chants Populaires
    Franco-Canadiens

  Anthologie Des Chants Populaires
    Francais Tome I

  Anthologie Des Chants Populaires
    Francais Tome III

CANTELOUBE, J. (cont'd.)
  Anthologie Des Chants Populaires
    Francais Tome IV

  Artois

  Bailero

  Bearn

  Berry

  Bourbonnais

  Bourgogne

  Bretagne

  Champagne

  Chants De France Vol. I

  Chants De France Vol. II

  Comte De Foix

  Corse

  Flandre

  Franche-Comte

  Gascogne

  Guyenne

  Haut-Dauphine Et Bas-Dauphine

  Ile-De-France

  La Haute Et Basse-Auvergne

  L'Angoumois

  Languedoc

  L'Aunis Et La Saintonge

  Limousin

  Lorraine

  Lyonnais

  Maine

  Marche

  Nivernais

  Normandie

  Orleanais

  Picardie

  Poitou

  Provence

  Roussillon

  Savoie

  Touraine

  Vendee

CANTRELL; TERRY; PAIRAMORE
  Marion County Tradition

CANTU, M.
  Mozart, Wolfgang Amadeus
    Tre Arie

CARAWAN, GUY; CARAWAN, CANDIE
  Freedom Is A Constant Struggle

CARLE, BILL; BOERSMA, JAMES
  Sacred Selections For Low Voice

CARLO, MUSI
  A S Fa Zinquntanov!

  Al Turnara!

  Avrir E Assrar

  Canzunetta Dl'Espusizion

  Canzunetta Pruibe

  Che Bell Nas!

  Chiudi!!

  Ciaccher E Narzisat

  Con Un Occ'

  Corylopsis!

  Da Ql' Altra Part!

  Dai Dal Gess!!

CARLO, MUSI (cont'd.)

Dein, Dan, Don

Dirala D' Se?

Do, Re, Mi, Fa, Sol

Dottrina In Musica

Dreyfus!

E So Pader Li Manda A Dir

El Barbir E La Toca!

El Carnaval

El Cinematogrof

El Dou Torr Dla Mercanzi Artensis E Riccadonna

El Fiaccaresta

El Genasi

El Gnaccher!

El Lonede Di Barbir

El Mester Squass!

El Mi Ritratt

El Mond L'e Fatt Acse!

El Redder

El San Michel, La Ca E La Rata D'affet

El Tango

El Vagabond

I Zalett

I Zever

L' A-J Passaria!

La Mi Premma Mrousa!

La Muntagnola

La Muntura Di Impiega Dla Posta

La Pison!

La Purtinara

La Quadreglia

La Scheccia Angot!

La Scuffiareina

La "Sonambula"

La Tassa Souvra Ai Tlon!

La Zeinta Daziaria

L'accademia De "La Lira"

L'Acquedott

L'era Fasol!

Mo Che, Pickmann?!

Oh! Ch'al Scusa!

Oh! Che Miraquel!

Oh! Che Zucca

Piron El Furnar

Pr' Un Lavativ!

Pst! Pst! Pst!

San Martein

Sulfanein E Luster!

Sussezza, Cudghein E Zampon

Ta-Ta

Trei Mnester

Tripoli Se, Tripoli No

Turnand Indri Da Paderen!

Un' Avventura A Veglion!

Una Bona Medseina

Very Smart!

CARMICHAEL
Here And Now, I Believe

CARMICHAEL, RALPH
Amazing Grace Duets And Solos

As We Come To Thee In Prayer

Ashton, Bob
Songs Of Living Faith
Songs Of Living Hope

Back To Love

Ballard, Ann
Oh, What A Sunrise

Be Still My Soul

Beyond All Time

Bright New World

Brother, Let Me Take Your Hand

Church Is Finally Over

Closer Than A Brother

Collegian's Prayer

Consider Now The Lily

Cross And The Switchblade, The

DeSylva
Chapel Bells
Take Me Home

Flame Of God's Redeeming Love, The

God Can See Us

God Loves You

God Of Miracles, The

Great Music From Billy Graham Films

Heart Is A Rebel, The

He'll Never Let You Fall

He's There Waiting

His Land

His Land

How Wonderful

I Believe God Is Real

I Cannot Hide From God

I Expect A Miracle

I Found What I Wanted

I Looked For Love

I'm Living In His Love

Is There Not A Cause

It Seems I've Always Loved You

It's Our World

Joy Is The Center Of His Will

Land Without Tears

Life Worth Living, A

Like A Lamb Who Needs The Shepherd

Looking For The Man Named Jesus

Love

Man, The

Miracle Of Faith, The

Miracle Of Grace, The

My Father's Favorite Songs

My Father's Table

My Little World

My Master

Natural High

New Mind, A

New Twenty-Third, The

New Wine

No Greater Love

Not With A Sword

CARMICHAEL, RALPH (cont'd.)

Now I Only Know In Part

Numbers Song, The

Oh Great God

Oh Great God

One Hundred Songs You Love To Sing

Our Front Porch

Over In Bethlehem

Pearl Of Great Price

Quiet Place, A

Restless Ones, The (Theme Song)

Return

Right Now

Savior Is Waiting, The

Searching Questions

Searching Questions

Season Of The Long Rains

Seed And The Sower, The

Something Good Is Going To Happen To You

Symbols And Tokens

Tell It Like Is Is

There Is More To Life

Thy Will Be Done

Tower Of Strength, A

We Are More Than Conquerors

We Love You, Call Collect

When I Think Of The Cross

You Can Touch Him If You Try

CASELLA, A.
Vivaldi, Antonio
Chiare Onde
Stabat Mater

CASH, JOHNNY
Over The Next Hill We'll Be Home

CASS-BEGGS, MICHAEL; CASS-BEGGS, BARBARA

Folk Lullabies

CASSLER, G. WINSTON
Christmas Carols For Solo Voice

Nativity Carols

Sacred Duets For Equal Voices

Three Wedding Solos

CASTLETON, G.
Opera Repertoire For Soprano

Opera Repertoire For Tenor

CAVICCHI, ADRIANO
Luzzaschi, Luzzasco
Madrigali Per Cantare E Sonare

CELAN
Erbse, Heimo
Der Uns Die Stunden Zàhlte

CELLIER, ALEXANDRE
Bach, Johann Sebastian
Mer Hahn En Neue Oberkeet

CHAILLEY, A.
Bernier, Nicolas
Accurite

CHAILLY
Tre Liriche Vietnamite

CHALIAPINE
Koeneman, T.
Chant Des Bateliers Du Volga

CHAMBERS
Adam, Adolphe-Charles
Cantique De Noel

CHAMPAGNE
Marier
Christmas Is Here

DETT, R. NATHANIEL
  I'm Goin' To Thank God

DEVRIVIS, LOUIS
  Mendelssohn-Bartholdy, Felix
    Belle Jeunesse
    Frühlingslied
    O Nuit Tranquille
    Sur Les Ailes Des Songes

DEWS
  Firestone, Idabelle
    In My Garden

DIACK, J. M.
  Ae Fond Kiss

  Captain Mackintosh And Colonel Anne

  I Lo'e Na A Laddie But Ane

  Lass O' Gowrie, The

DIACK, J. MICHAEL
  Scottish Orpheus, Vol. I, The

  Scottish Orpheus, Vol. II, The

  Scottish Orpheus, Vol. III, The

  Scottish Song Albums

DIAMOND, DAVID
  Hebrew Melodies

DICKINSON
  Bach, Johann Sebastian
    God, My Shepherd

  Saint-Saëns, Camille
    Prayer, A

DICKINSON; ALWARDT
  Buxtehude, Dietrich
    My Jesus Is My Lasting Joy

DICKINSON, C.
  In A Stable Mean And Lowly

  Jesu! Thou Dear Babe Divine

  Puccini, Giacomo
    Neighbors Of Bethlehem, The

DIETRICH, FRITZ
  Laterne, Laterne, Sonne, Mond Und
    Sterne

  Volksliedbüchlein Für Klavier

  Weihnachtslieder Zum Singen Und
    Spielen Am Klavier

DIEWALD, J.; LOHMANN, A.; THURMAIR, G.
  Kirchenlied Teil I

  Kirchenlied Teil II

DILLE
  Young Bartok, The, Vol. 1

DILLER, ANGELA; PAGE, KATE STEARNS
  Diller-Page Carolbook, The

DINO
  Folk Musical Themes

  My Tribute

DITON, CARL
  Schirmer's American Folk-Song Series,
    Set XII (36 South Carolina
    Spirituals)

DOERFFEL
  Choralbuch

DOLMETSCH
  Have You Seen But A Whyte Lillie
    Grow?

DOLMETSCH, A.
  Select English Songs And Dialogues Of
    The Sixteenth And Seventeenth
    Centuries

  Select French Songs From The Twelfth
    To The Eighteenth Centuries

DOMANDL
  Brahms, Johannes
    Ausgewählte Lieder, Volumes I And
      II
    Selected Songs, Vol. I
    Selected Songs, Vol. II

  Schubert, Franz (Peter)
    Lieder

DOMOKOS
  Rezeda

DONALDSON
  Cardillo
    Core' Ngrato

DONAUDY
  Trentesei Arie Nello Stile Antico,
    Vol. I

  Trentesei Arie Nello Stile Antico,
    Vol. II

  Trentesei Arie Nello Stile Antico,
    Vol. III

DOORMANN, LUDWIG
  Schein, Johann Hermann
    Drei Choralkonzerte
    Sechs Choralkonzerte

DORSEY
  They Led My Lord Away

DOWNING, K.
  O'Hara, Geoffrey
    Prayer Of Thanksgiving

  Prayer Of Thanksgiving

DOYEN, ALB.
  Chant Des Haleurs De La Volga

DRATHS
  O Wunder, Was Will Das Bedeuten

  St. Martins-Lieder

DRATHS; LECHNER
  Der Volksmusikant

DRATHS; LUTZ
  Der Singaut

DREJAC, J.
  Ostrovski, A.
    Du Soleil Pour Tout Le Monde

DUARTE, J.W.
  Schubert, Franz (Peter)
    Songs By Schubert

DUCAMP, M.
  Godard, Benjamin Louis Paul
    Printemps

DUCLOUX
  Puccini, Giacomo
    Donna Non Vidi Mai
    In Quelle Trine Morbide

  Verdi, Giuseppe
    O Cieli Azzurri

DUMAS
  Strauss, Johann
    An Der Schönen Blauen Donau

DUNCAN, STUART
  My True Love Hath My Heart

DUNGAN
  Bush
    New Day

DUNHILL
  Purcell, Henry
    Myrtle Shade, The

DUNHILL, THOMAS F.
  John Peel

DÜRR, ALFRED
  Bach, Johann Sebastian
    Schafe Können Sicher Weiden
    Virga Jesse Floruit

  Telemann, Georg Philipp
    Gesegnet Ist Die Zuversicht

DÜRR, WALTHER
  Schubert, Franz (Peter)
    Ausgewählte Lieder
    Lieder, Band 6
    Lieder, Band 7
    Lieder, Band I, Teil A
    Lieder, Band I, Teil A Und B
    Lieder, Band I, Teil B

EASSON, J.; MERCHANT, D.
  Opera Airs For Girls' Classes

EBY, MARGARETTE
  Dilliger, Johann
    Eighteen Vocal Concertos

ECKERBERG, S.
  Stenhammar, Wilhelm
    Gammal Nederländare

EDDY
  Handel, George Frideric
    Ombra Mai Fu

EDEKER
  Whittle
    Do You Know Jesus?

EHMANN, WILHELM
  Schütz, Heinrich
    Ich Hab Mein Sach Gott Heimgestellt
    Jubilate Deo
    Kleine Geistliche Konzerte Heft VI
    Kleine Geistliche Konzerte Heft VII
    Kleine Geistliche Konzerte Heft
      VIII
    Kleine Geistliche Konzerte Heft IX
    Kleine Geistliche Konzerte Heft XI
    Kleine Geistliche Konzerte Heft XII
    Kleine Geistliche Konzerte Heft XIV
    Kleine Geistliche Konzerte Heft XV
    Kleine Geistliche Konzerte Heft
      XVII
    Kleine Geistliche Konzerte Heft XIX

EHRENBERG, CARL
  Trunk, Richard
    Sieben Weihnachtslieder

EKLUND, HARRY
  Friesen, Dick
    Straw Carol, The

ELZEVIER, K.
  Mahaut, Antonio
    Maendelyks Musikaels Tydverdryf,
      Vol. 1: October
    Maendelyks Musikaels Tydverdryf,
      Vol. 2: November
    Maendelyks Musikaels Tydverdryf,
      Vol. 3: December
    Maendelyks Musikaels Tydverdryf,
      Vol. 4: Januari
    Maendelyks Musikaels Tydverdryf,
      Vol. 5: Februari
    Maendelyks Musikaels Tydverdryf,
      Vol. 6: Maert
    Maendelyks Musikaels Tydverdryf,
      Vol. 7: April
    Maendelyks Musikaels Tydverdryf,
      Vol. 8: Mey
    Maendelyks Musikaels Tydverdryf,
      Vol. 9: Juny

EMMERECHTS; JOULAIN, EMILE
  C'est Le Vent

  Printemps D'Anjou

EMMERESHTS; BELDENT
  Fille D'Anjou

  La Parapluie De Ma Grand'mere

  Ronde Du Vin Doux

  Valse Des Blancs Jupons

ENDICOTT
  Arne, Thomas Augustine
    Air

ENGEL, HANS
  Vierdanck, Johann
    Ich Verkündige Euch Grosse Freude
    Siehe, Wie Fein Und Lieblich Ist's

ENGELBRECHT, CHRISTIANE
  Schütz, Heinrich
    Ich Hab Mein Sach Gott Heimgestellt

EPHIRIKIAN
  Vivaldi, Antonio
    Laudate Pueri

EPHRIKIAN
  Vivaldi, Antonio
    Salve Regina

EPHRIKIAN, ANGELO
  Vivaldi, Antonio
    Salve Regina

ERDLEN, HERMANN
  Schulz, Joh. Abraham Peter
    Stille Welt

ERDMANN, HANS
  Vierdanck, Johann
    Lobe Den Herren
    Mein Herz Ist Bereit

ERK; FRIEDLÄNDER
  Deutscher Liederschatz

ERMELER, ROLF
  Telemann, Georg Philipp
    Kleine Kantate Von Wald Und Au
    Tod Und Moder Dringt Herein

ESTELLA, JOSEPH M.
  Jewish Song Hits Book

EWERHART, RUDOLF
  Anerio, Giovanni Francesco
    Drei Geistliche Konzerte

  Anonymous
    Intonuit De Coelo

HEADY (cont'd.)

I'm On The Highway Home
Lord, Don't Let Me Fail You
They Call His Name Jesus
Till He Wipes Away My Tears
When I Wait Before His Throne

HECKER, W.; PIKET, F.
Gerovitsch, Eliezer
Songs Of Prayer

HEENAN, ASHLEY
Lowdown, Lonesome Low

HELFMAN, MAX
Ad Or Ha-Boker

Al Tira

Am Yisrael Chai

Anu Nosim Lapidim

Ashrey Ha-Ish

B'er Ba-Sadeh

Eyn Ki-Y'rushalayim

Ha-Kotzrim

Ki Mi-Tziyon

Ma Tovu

Matai Yavo Ha-Mashiach

Rappaport, Eda
Harhorey Laila

Rikud Ha-Goren

Sadot She-Ba-Emek

Shir Ha-Avoda

Shir Ha-Emek

Shir Ha-Mered

Shir La-Moledat

Tz'ena Ur'ena

Ush'avtem Mayim

Zemer Chag

Zot Artzenu

HELLMAN, I.
Eklöf, Einar
Morgon

HELLMANN
Des Lasst Uns Alle Fröhlich Sein

HELLMANN, DIETHARD
Bach, Johann Sebastian
Ich Habe Genug

HELLMANN, IVAR
Sibelius, Jean
Den Första Kyssen
Illalle
Såv, Såv Susa
Svarta Rosor

HELLMUNDT
Shostakovich, Dmitri
Sechs Romanzen

HENDERSON
Music Of Hawaii

HENDERSON, W.J.
Sacred Songs

HENKING, BERNHARD
Schütz, Heinrich
Was Betrübst Du Dich

HERBAGE, JULIAN
Dies Alla

HERBERT, G.; SUMMERS, JOSEPH
Newlin, Dika
Quidditie, The

HERLE J.
Fibich, Zdenko
Modlitba

HERNANDEZ
Flores De Espana

HESS
Beethoven, Ludwig van
Gesänge Mit Orchester, Vol. II
Nei Giorni Tuoi Felici

HESS, WILLY
Beethoven, Ludwig van
No, Non Turbati

HESSEN BERG, K.
Der Tag, Der Ist So Freundenreich

HILL, HARRY
Franck, Cesar
Panis Angelicus

HILL, HOWARD
Ten Sacred Songs For Baritone

Ten Sacred Songs For Contralto

Ten Sacred Songs For Soprano

Ten Sacred Songs For Tenor

HILLE, WALDEMAR
People's Songbook, The

HINNENTHAL, JOHANN PHILIPP
Bernier, Nicolas
Le Cafe

Sweelinck, Jan Pieterszoon
Rimes Francoises Et Italiennes

HITCHCOCK, H. WILEY
Caccini, Giulio
Le Nuove Musiche
Nuove Musiche E Nuova Maniera Di
Scriverle

Civil War Songs

HITZEL
Eli, Eli

HJERTAAS, ELLA
Songs For Christmas

HOBOHM; BERNSTEIN
Telemann, Georg Philipp
Ha, Ha! Wo Will Wi Hüt Noch Danzen

HOFFMANN
Schütz, Heinrich
Vier Hirtinnen

HOFFMANN, HANS
Schütz, Heinrich
Frohlocket Mit Händen
Hütet Euch
Kleine Geistliche Konzerte Heft I
Kleine Geistliche Konzerte Heft II
Kleine Geistliche Konzerte Heft III
Kleine Geistliche Konzerte Heft IV
Kleine Geistliche Konzerte Heft V
Vier Hirtinnen
Wohl Dem, Der Nicht Wandelt Im Rate
Der Gottlosen

HOHMANN, EDMUND
Schütz, Heinrich
Was Betrübst Du Dich, Meine Seele

HOLFORD, FRANZ
I Have A Bonnet Trimmed With Blue

Keel Row

HOLM, GUNNAR
Blott En Dag Ett Ögonblick I Sänder

HOLST, IMOGEN
Folklore Ecossais

HOPKINS, A.
Five French Folk Songs

Two French Folk Songs

HORN
Roberton, Hugh Stevenson
Cherry Ripe

HOWE
Grant
Crimond

Handel, George Frideric
Ingratitude's The Queen Of Crimes
That God Is Great
Thou Didst Blow With The Wind
What's Sweeter Than A New Blown
Rose

Haydn, (Franz) Joseph
She Never Told Her Love

Mozart, Wolfgang Amadeus
An Chloe

Mussorgsky, Modest
Song Of The Flea

Parry, Charles Hubert Hastings
Jerusalem

Purcell, Henry
I Attempt From Love's Sickness To
Fly
If Music Be The Food Of Love

HOWE (cont'd.)

Music For Awhile
What Shall I Do To Show How Much I
Love Her
When I Am Laid In Earth

Rowley, Alec
Spring Joy

Schubert, Franz (Peter)
Die Forelle
Hark, Hark, The Lark
Im Abendroth

Schumann, Robert (Alexander)
Since I First Beheld Him

Softly Rest

HOWE; SIMON
Steffe, William
Battle Hymn Of The Republic

HOWLAND, ALICE; ZEITLIN, POLDI
Art Song, The

HUBER; PAUL
Altbayerisches Liederbuch

HUFSTADER
Arne, Thomas Augustine
Delia
Morning, The

HUGHES, H.
Irish Country Songs, Vols. 1-4

HUHN
Sarti, Giuseppe
Lungi Dal Caro Bene

HUMPHREYS
Songs For Christian Science Services

HUNTER, G.; PALISCA, C.
Monteverdi, Claudio
Five Songs

HYMAN, JOY; RICE, JENNIFER
Singaround Folksongs, Bk. 1

Singaround Folksongs, Bk. 2

IGNATIEFF, MICHAIL; IGNATIEFF, NADIA
Neue Sammlung Russischer Volkslieder

Tschastuschki

IGNATIEFF, MIKAIL
Zwölf Beliebte Russische
Zigeunerromanzen Und Lieder

INSPIRATIONS
We Shall Arise

IPHIGENIE EN TAURIDE
Gluck, Christoph Willibald Ritter von
Von Jugend Auf Im Treusten Bunde

ISENBERG, KARL
Geistliche Sololieder Des Barock Heft
I

Geistliche Sololieder Des Barock Heft
III

JACKSON, RICHARD
Popular Songs Of The Nineteenth
Century America

JACOB
Boyce, William
Rail No More, Ye Learned Asses

JACOBSEN
Rubinstein, Anton
Dream Of Delight

JACOBSON
Dunhill, Thomas Frederick
How Soft Upon The Ev'ning Air

Handel, George Frideric
La Speranza E Giunta

Mozart, Wolfgang Amadeus
Ridente La Calma

JAFFE, BEN; KAMMEN, JACK
Israeli And Jewish Song Hits

JALAS, JUSSI
Sibelius, Jean
Die Libelle "Schöne Libelle,
Schwirrtest Mir Herein"
Hundra Vågar
Illalle
Kaiutar
Lastu Lainehilla
Märzschnee
Romeo
Under Strandens Graver
Var Det En Dröm?

JAMESON
Wake And Sing

JANCIK, HANS
Wolf, Hugo
Italienisches Liederbuch
Lieder Nach Gedichten Von E. Mòrike
Lieder Nach Gedichten Von
Eichendorff
Mòrike-Lieder
Nachgelassene Lieder II
Spanisches Liederbuch
Spanisches Liederbuch

JANETZKY; STOLZENBACH
Heinichen, Johann David
Nisi Dominus Aedificaverit Domum

JARRETT
Just A Closer Walk With Thee

JENNINGS
Turn Back, My Child

JESSETT, M.
Nine Traditional Songs

JESSETT, MICHAEL
Musgrave, Thea
Five Love Songs

JESSON, ROY
Lawes, William
Dialogues For Two Voices And
Continuo

Vier Dialoge

JOHNER
Neun Alte Weihnachtsgesànge

JOHNSON
Green Pastures

JOHNSON, DAVID N.
Lone, Wild Bird, The

Sweet Was The Song The Virgin Sang

When Jesus Left His Father's Throne

JOHNSON, HALL
Thirty Negro Spirituals

JOHNSON, J. ROSAMOND
Negro Spirituals

Negro Spirituals

Nobody Knows De Trouble I See

JOHNSON, M.; JOHNSON, T.
Early American Songs

JOHNSON; MCCORKLE
Three Sacred Songs For Soprano

JOHNSON, T. ROSAMOND
Give Me Jesus

JOHNSTON
Redden, Finvola
Boat Song

JOHNSTON; VINCI
Scarlatti, Alessandro
Sento Nel Core
So Venite A Consiglio

JOHNSTONE, H. DIACK
Croft, William
My Heart Is Ev'ry Beauty's Prey

JONES
Men Of Eureka And Other Songs

JONSSON, DEHNOW
Treintatres Aires Escandinavos

JOSEPH, NATHAN; WINTER, ERIC
New English Broadsides

JOULAIN, EMILE
Chanson Des Joueux De Boule

JUST, HERBERT
Purcell, Henry
Die Nacht
How Pleasant Is This Flowery Plain
And Ground

KAGEN, SERGIUS
Brahms, Johannes
Seventy Songs

Chausson, Ernest
Twenty Songs

Debussy, Claude
Forty-Three Songs

Duparc, Henri
Songs

KAGEN, SERGIUS (cont'd.)

Faure, Gabriel-Urbain
Thirty Songs

Forty French Songs, Vol. I

Forty French Songs, Vol. II

Hahn, Reynaldo
Twelve Songs

Handel, George Frideric
Forty-Five Arias From Operas And
Oratorios, Vol. I
Forty-Five Arias From Operas And
Oratorios, Vol. II
Forty-Five Arias From Operas And
Oratorios, Vol. III

Mozart, Wolfgang Amadeus
Arias From Operas For Bass
Arias From Operas For Bass Or
Baritone, Vol. I
Arias From Operas For Bass Or
Baritone, Vol. II
Arias From Operas For Coloratura
Soprano
Arias From Operas For Contralto
Arias From Operas For Mezzo-Soprano
Arias From Operas For Soprano, Vol.
I
Arias From Operas For Soprano, Vol.
II
Arias From Operas For Soprano, Vol.
III
Arias From Operas For Soprano, Vol.
IV
Arias From Operas For Tenor
Exsultate, Jubilate

Mussorgsky, Modest
Nursery, The

Purcell, Henry
Four Sacred Songs
Six Songs For Bass

Schubert, Franz (Peter)
Die Schòne Mùllerin
Die Winterreise
Two Hundred Songs, Vol. I (Contains
All The Cycles Plus 42 Selected
Songs)
Two Hundred Songs, Vol. II
Two Hundred Songs, Vol. III

Schumann, Robert (Alexander)
Dichterliebe
Eighty-Five Songs
Frauenliebe Und Leben
Liederkreis
Ninety Songs

Strauss, Richard
Thirty Songs

Wolf, Hugo
Five Arias
Sixty-Five Songs
Two Arias

KAISER
Ackley, A.H.
If Your Heart Keeps Right

KAISER, KURT
Abide With Me

Ackley, Bentley D.
When I Kneel Down To Pray

KAMPP, EJNAR
Diguedondaine

KAMPP, EJNAR; BRO RASMUSSEN, HENNING
Songs And Ballads, Vol. I

KANE
Rose Of Tralee, The

KAPRALOVA
Martinu, Bohuslav
Koleda Milostna

KARL; TAUBERT, HEINZ
Europàische Weihnachtslieder

KARPELES, MAUD
Folk Songs Of Europe

KATCHKO, A.
Thesaurus Of Cantorial Liturgy (Part
I)

KATZ
Four Fifteenth-Century Chansons

Four Italian Villanellas

KELLER
Bach, Johann Sebastian
Anna Magdalena Bach's Music Book

KELLER, HERMANN
Arien Und Kanzonetten

Bach, Johann Sebastian
Bereite Dich, Zion, Mit Zartlichen
Trieben
Seufzer, Trànen, Kummer, Not

KELLY
Folk Music Festival In Hawaii

KENNEDY-FRASER, M.; MACLEOD, K.
Eriskay Love Lilt

Island Sheiling Song

Kishmul's Galley

Land Of Heart's Desire

Road To The Isles

Songs Of The Hebrides, Vols. 1-3

To People Who Have Gardens

KERENYI
Nursery Rhymes

KERR
Stiffler, Georgia
Healer Of Broken Hearts

KEVESS, ARTHUR
German Folk Songs

KEY, FRANCIS SCOTT; SMITH, STAFFORD
Star Spangled Banner, The

KHOKHLOV, YU.
Schubert, Franz (Peter)
Selected Songs, Vol. II: Songs To
Words By Schiller And Mayrhofer

KINES, TOM
Songs From Shakespeare's Plays And
Popular Songs Of Shakespeare's
Time

KING
Chiapanecas

KING FAMILY
Love At Home

KIRBY, WALTER
Noel-Noel

Seventeen Sacred Songs

KIRCHBERGER, A.
Haydn, (Johann) Michael
Wir Bitten Dich Unendlich Wesen

KIRCHNER, GERHARD
Schütz, Heinrich
Attendite Popule Meus Legem Meam
Benedicam Dominum
Domine, Labia Mea Aperies
Exquisivi Dominum
In Lectulo Per Noctes
Invenerunt Me Custodes
Veni, Dilecte Mi

KIRKPATRICK
Ives, Charles
Eleven Songs And Two Harmonizations

KIRMSSE, H.
Spektrum 69, Heft I

Spektrum 69, Heft II

KISS
Rozmaring

Wedding Songs

KITTEL
Schütz, Heinrich
O Sùsser Jesu Christ

KLEIN, HERMAN; KREUZ, EMIL
Brahms, Johannes
Metzler's Masterpieces Vol. 9:
Brahms Lieder For Soprano
Metzler's Masterpieces Vol. 10:
Brahms Lieder For Contralto Or
Mezzo-Soprano
Metzler's Masterpieces Vol. 11:
Brahms Lieder For Tenor
Metzler's Masterpieces Vol. 12:
Brahms Lieder For Baritone Or
Bass

Metzler's Masterpieces Vol. 13: Six
Songs For Soprano

Metzler's Masterpieces Vol. 14: Six
Songs For Mezzo-Soprano Or
Contralto

Metzler's Masterpieces Vol. 15: Six
Songs For Tenor

Metzler's Masterpieces Vol. 16: Six

PIDOUX, PIERRE (cont'd.)

  Hammerschmidt, Andreas
    Es Danken Dir, Gott, Die Völker

PIJPER, W.
  Sekstende Arhundrede Marialied

PILLNEY, KARL HERMANN
  In Dulci Jubilo

PIMIÀ
  Kuusisto, Taneli
    Armahin Muisto

PINGOUD, ERNEST
  Sibelius, Jean
    Bollspelet Vid Trianon
    Flickan Kom Ifran Sin Älsklings
      Mote
    Jubal
    Lastu Lainehilla
    Lockung
    Men Nin Fagel Märks Dock Inte
    Schlaf Ein "Mein Bleicher Liebling
      Soll Giessen"

PINKHAM
  Purcell, Henry
    Man Is For The Woman Made

PISADOR
  Anonymous
    Madonna Mia Fa

PITCHER; MCBRADD
  Long Wharf Songs

PITTION, COLETTE PAUL
  Wolf, Hugo
    Quinze Lieder, Cahier I
    Quinze Lieder, Cahier II

PLATH, WOLFGANG
  Mozart, Wolfgang Amadeus
    Cara, Se Le Mie Pene

PLETKA; RYSAVY; URBAN
  Sovetske Pisne Obrany A Prace

POHL; BUSCHBAUM
  Kinder Spielen Zur Weihnacht

POHL, LOTTA; BUSCHBAUM, RAINER-GLEN
  Kinder Spielen Zur Weihnacht

PORRET, J.
  Shostakovich, Dmitri
    Au Devant De La Vie

PORRET, J; PHILIPPE-GERARD
  Blanter, M.
    Katioucha

PÒSCHL; WINKLER; MOISSL
  Wer Will, Wer Mag?

POSTON
  Boyce, William
    Tell Me, Lovely Shepherd

  Defesch, William
    Colin's Success

POTTER
  Reliquary Of English Song, Vol. I
    (1250- 1700)

PRATELLA, G.B.
  Dodici Cante Romagnole

PRESLEY, ELVIS
  Rader
    Only Believe

PRUEFER, ARTHUR
  Schein, Johann Hermann
    Collected Works

PRUSOVA; JANZUROVA
  S Pisnikou U Klaviru

PUJOL
  Anonymous
    Dindirindin
    En Avila Mis Ojos

  Attaignant, Pierre
    Tant Que Vivrai

  Besard, Jean-Baptiste
    Belles Deesses
    Cruelle Departie
    Moy, Pauvre Fille

  Broqua, Alfonso
    El Nido
    El Tango
    Tres Cantos Uruguayos
    Vidalita

  Cara, M.
    Io Non Compro

PUJOL (cont'd.)

  Dowland, John
    Come Again, Sweet Love

  Flecha, Mateo
    La Girigonza

  Le Jeune, H.
    Chanson

  Le Roy, A.
    J'ai Le Rebours
    Je Ne Suis Moins Aimable
    Laissez La Verte Couleur
    Mes Peines Et Ennuis

  Mudarra, Alonso de
    Triste Estaba El Rey David

  Pisador, Diego
    Si Te Vas A Banar Juanica

  Secular Spanish Songs Of The
    Seventeenth Century, Vol. I

  Secular Spanish Songs Of The
    Seventeenth Century, Vol. II

  Vasquez, Juan
    En La Fuente Del Rosel
    Vos Me Matastes

  Vecchi, H.
    Non Vuo Pregare

PUTTERMAN; KOSAKOFF
  Marcello, Benedetto
    B'rochos Shel Chanukoh

QUEROL
  Music In Cervantes Works

RAGOSSNIG, K.
  O Sanctissima

  Schütz, Heinrich
    Zwei Geistliche Gesänge

RANDEGGER
  Mozart, Wolfgang Amadeus
    Das Veilchen

RANKI
  Jaj, De Szepen Muzsikalnak

RANTA, SULHO
  Kansansàvelmà

RAPHAEL, G.
  Bach, Johann Sebastian
    Ich Habe Genug
    Jauchzet Gott In Allen Landen
    Tritt Auf Die Glaubensbahn
    Vergnùgte Ruh, Beliebte Seelenlust
    Widerstehe Doch Der Sùnde

  Hoffmann, Georg Melchoir
    Schlage Doch, Gewùnschte Stunde

RAPHAEL, GUNTER
  Brahms, Johannes
    Vier Ernste Gesänge

  Wolf, Hugo
    Anakreons Grab
    Der Freund
    Der Gàrtner
    Der Tambour
    Elfenlied
    Er Ist's
    Fussreise
    Gebet
    Heimweh
    In Der Frùhe
    Schlafendes Jesuskind
    Verborgenheit
    Zum Neuen Jahr

RASHEED, BAHEEGA SIDKY
  Egyptian Folk Songs

RAVIZE, A.
  Dix Noèls Bourguignons

RAYMER, ELWYN
  Broadman Solo Collection

REBE, LOUISE C.
  Six Polish Christmas Carols

RECUERDO
  Memories Of Latin-America

REDL
  Strauss, Johann
    Kùnsterleben

REDMOND FRIEL
  Paterson Irish Song Book, The

REGER
  Wolf, Hugo
    Der Freund
    Fourteen Sacred Songs
    Stàndchen

REGER (cont'd.)

    Sterb Ich, So Hùllt In Blumen Meine
      Glieder
    Und Willst Du Deinen Liebsten
      Sterben Sehn

REGER, MAX
  Adam, Adolphe-Charles
    Mes Amis Ecoutez L'histoire

  Schubert, Franz (Peter)
    An Die Musik
    Dem Unendlichen
    Du Bist Die Ruh
    Greisengesang
    Im Abendrot
    Litanei
    Memnon
    Nacht Und Tràume

  Weber, Carl Maria von
    Unbefangenheit

REICHERT
  Lieder Salzburger Komponisten

  Mozart, Wolfgang Amadeus
    Lieder Und Gesànge

REICHERT, E.
  Klingende Lyrik

REICHERT, ERNST
  Bach, Johann Christian
    Sechs Italienische Duettinen

  Mozart, Wolfgang Amadeus
    In Te Spero, O Sposo Amato

REID
  Owens
    Nurny Song, The

REIN; LANG
  Der Wundergarten

REINECKE, CARL
  Gluck, Christoph Willibald Ritter von
    Berenice, Ove Sei?

REINHART
  Bach, Johann Sebastian
    Twelve Sacred Duets From Cantatas,
      Vol. I
    Twelve Sacred Duets From Cantatas,
      Vol. II
    Twelve Sacred Duets From Cantatas,
      Vol. III
    Twelve Sacred Duets From Cantatas,
      Vol. IV

RESPIGHI, O.
  Bach, Johann Sebastian
    Pieta Ti Prenda Mio Dio

REUTTER, HERMANN
  Das Zeitgenòssische Lied, Band I

  Das Zeitgenòssische Lied, Band II

  Das Zeitgenòssische Lied, Band III

  Das Zeitgenòssische Lied, Band IV

REYNOLDS
  Dibdin, Charles
    Ye Gloomy Thoughts

REYNOLDS, WILLIAM J.
  Gospel Singer, The

RHAU, GÙNTER
  Dittersdorf, Karl Ditters von
    Drei Italienische Konzertarien

RICCI
  Paisiello, Giovanni
    Nel Cor Piu Non Me Sento
      (Variaciones Sobre El Tema)

RICH, MARTIN
  Art Songs And Their Interpretation

RIDOUT, GODFREY
  Folk Songs Of Eastern Canada

  Greensleeves

RIETZ, JULIUS
  Mendelssohn-Bartholdy, Felix
    Collected Edition

RILEY
  Stenson, E.J.
    Prayer Perfect, The

RIMSKY-KORSAKOV
  Mussorgsky, Modest
    Song And Dances Of Death
    Sunless

RIMSKY-KORSAKOV; LJABUNOW; LABINSKY
Mussorgsky, Modest
Der Feldherr
Ständchen
Trepak
Wiegenlied

RIMSKY-KORSAKOV, N.
Mussorgsky, Modest
Höret Mich An, Geheime Mächte

RIMSKY-KORSAKOV, NICOLAI
Cento Canti Nazionali Russi, Vol. 1

Cento Canti Nazionali Russi, Vol. 2

Cento Canti Nazionali Russi, Vol. 3

RIMSKY-KORSAKOV; STRAVINSKY
Mussorgsky, Modest
Song Of The Flea

RITCHIE
Garland Of Mountain Song, A

RITCHIE, JEAN
Folk Songs Of The Southern
Appalachians

Singing Family Of The Cumberlands

RIVENBURG
Oh Lord, What Then

ROBERTON, H.S.
I Got A Robe

Little David, Play On Your Harp

ROBERTON, HUGH S.
Celtic Lullaby, A

Charlie Is My Darling

Dance To Your Daddy

De Battle Ob Jericho

Deep River

Fidgety Bairn, The

Glenlyon Lament

Health And Joy Be With You

Hebridean Shanty

Highland Cradle Song

Ho-Ree, Ho-Ro, My Little Wee Girl!

Holy Night

Hush-A-Ba Birdie

I'll Bid My Heart Be Still

Island Spinning Song

Joy Of My Heart

Lewis Boat Song

Lewis Bridal Song

Mingulay Boat Song

Morag's Cradle Song

Nobody Knows De Trouble I See

None So Sweet

Oh, By An' By

Oh, Peter, Go Ring Dem Bells

Queen's Marys, The

Rise And Follow Love

Rising Of The Lark, The

Sing At The Wheel

Songs Of The Isles

Steal Away To Jesus

Sweet Nightingale

Swing Low, Sweet Chariot

Uist Tramping Song

Were You There?

Westering Home

When De Stars Begin To Fall

Windjammer, The

ROBERTSON
Hymns From The Crossroads

RODEMANN, ALBERT
Böddecker, Philipp Friedrich
Natus Est Jesus

ROE, GLORIA
Pearson, Albie
Yes, I Love Him

Rader
Only Believe

ROFF, J.
Bach, Johann Sebastian
One In Heart And One In Mind

ROGNONI
Sinigaglia, Leone
Ventiquatro Vecchie Canzoni
Populari Del Piemonte

ROKSETH, YVONNE
Anonymous
Lamentation De La Vierge Au Pied De
La Croix

ROLFE
Deep River

God Be With You Till We Meet Again

Londonderry Air

ROMA
God Shall Wipe Away All Tears

ROMERO
Coleccion De Cantos Y Bailes
Populares Espanoles, Vol. I

Coleccion De Cantos Y Bailes
Populares Espanoles, Vol. II

RONDEGGER
Handel, George Frideric
Twelve Songs

ROPARTZ, GUY
Bach, Johann Sebastian
Ich Will Den Kreuzstab Gerne Tragen

ROSENBERG
Roman, Johan Helmich
Vieni Prode Federico

ROSKIN
Bimkom Ha-Eretz

Birnbaum
Hashkivenu

Do Thine Eyes In Wonderment

Dos Gebet

Viglid

ROSSINI
La Danza

La Pastorella Delle Alpi

ROTH, H.
Handel, George Frideric
Neun Deutsche Arien
Patenza

ROTHENBERG, F.S.; THURMAIR, G.
Singe, Christenheit!

ROW
Practical Library Of Sacred Songs,
Book 1

Practical Library Of Sacred Songs,
Book 2

Young Singer

RUBIN, RUTH
Jewish Folk Songs

RÜCKAUF
Schubert, Franz (Peter)
Schubert Lieder Band I

RUFOLD, EDUARD
Tchaikovsky, Piotr Ilyitch
Romance

RUHRMANN
All Mein Gedanken

Reutter, Hermann
Alte Weihnachtslieder

RUNGE
Drei Arien Aus Dem Seibzehnten
Jahrhundert

RUST, W.; RIETZ, J.; HAUPTMANN, M.;
BECKER, C.F.; KROLL, F.;
DOERFFEL, A.; NAUMANN, E.; VON
WALDERSEE; KRETZCHMAR, H.

Bach, Johann Sebastian
Complete Works. Bach Gesellschaft
Edition

RYBRANT, S.
Stenhammar, Wilhelm
Stajärnöga

RYDBERG
Sibelius, Jean
Pa Verandan Vid Havet

SAFFE, FERDINAND
Weiland, Johannes Julius
Jauchzet Gott, Alle Lande

SAINT-SAENS, CAMILLE; MALHERBE, CH.;
EMMANUEL, M.; TENEO, M.

Rameau, Jean-Philippe
Complete Works

SALZMANN
Der Zupfgeigenhansl

SAMAZEUILH
Chabrier, Emmanuel
A La Musique

SAMINSKY, L.
Song Treasury Of Old Israel, A

SAMMARTINO
Foster, Stephen Collins
Diez Canciones Populares
Norteamericanas

SAMPSON; HARRIS
Seven Seas Shanty Book

SANCHEZ
Vent Chants De France Et D'ailleurs

SANDBERG, SVEN
Sibelius, Jean
Hundra Vågar

SANDOVAL, MIGUEL
Twenty-Five Favorite Latin-American
Songs

SARGENT
Brahms, Johannes
Vier Ernste Gesänge (Four Serious
Songs)

SARLIN, ANNA
Joululauluja III

Joululauluja VI

Joululauluja VIII

SATOW, KARL
Kistenmacher, Arthur
Trinklied

SAUNDERS, M.
Hallowed A-Be Thy Name

SAUNDERS, M.; EVANS, H.
Edric Connor Collection Of West
Indian Spirituals And Folk Tunes

SAVILLE, EUGENIA
Italian Vocal Duets From The Early
Eighteenth Century

SCHALLER
Lieder Um Ostern

Lieder Um Weihnacht

SCHALLER, E.
Handel, George Frideric
Pensieri Notturni Di Filli: Nel
Dolce Dell'oblio

SCHANZLIN, HANS PETER
Gletle, Johann Melchoir
Geistliche Gesänge I
Geistliche Gesänge II

SCHEIT, K.
Bach, Johann Sebastian
Betrachte, Meine Seel, Mit
Angstlichem Vergnügen

Dowland, John
Sieben Lieder Aus Der
Lautentabulatur

Handel, George Frideric
Zwei Gesänge Aus Den "Deutschen
Arien"

Haydn, (Franz) Joseph
Drei Lieder

TAYLOR, B.
German Art Songs

TAYLOR, BERNARD
Bach, Johann Sebastian
Bach Arias For Soprano

Wedding Bouquet

TAYLOR, DEEMS
May Day Carol

Twenty, Eighteen

Waters Ripple And Flow

TENKKU
Seimen Äärellä

TERRELL, BEVERLY
Beverly Terrell's Favorite Gospel
Solos

TERRY, R.R.
Shenandoah

TESCHEMACHER
d'Hardelot, Guy
Because

THE CARPENTERS
Carmichael, Ralph
Love Is Surrender

THIRIET
Quince Canciones De Las Provincias De
Francia

THOMAS
Cryes Of Olde London, Book I

Cryes Of Olde London, Book II

THOMAS, D.
Riegger, Wallingford
Dying Of The Light, The

THOMAS, PAUL
Third Morning Star Choir Book, A

THOMSON, VIRGIL
My Shepherd Will Supply My Need

TIERSOT, JULIEN
Vingt Noèls Francais

TIERSOT, JULINE
Forty-Four French Folk-Songs And
Variants From Canada, Normandy,
And Brittany

TILLETT, BEVERLY
Climb Ev'ry Mountain - The
Inspirational Songbook

TILLMAN MERRITT, A.; LESURE, FRANCOIS
Jannequin, Clement
Chansons Polyphoniques

TINGLEY, GERTRUDE
Sunday Solo: Eighteen Sacred Songs
From The Classics, The

TINTORI
Scarlatti, Alessandro
Quatro Cantate

TODT, B.
Bach, Johann Sebastian
Ich Bin In Mir Vergnügt
O Holder Tag, Erwünschte Zeit
Schweigt Stille, Plaudert Nicht
Weichet Nur, Betrübte Schatten

TOLDRA
Doce Canciones Populares Espanolas

Nueve Canciones Populares Catalanas

TOMC, MATIJA
Osem Narodnih Pesmi

TOMELLERI, LUCIANO
Belcanto

Rossini, Gioacchino
Petite Messe Solunnelle

TONI, A.
Monteverdi, Claudio
Combattimento Di Tancredi E
Clorinda

TORCHI, LUIGI
L'Arte Musicale In Italia

TORLIND
Sju Svenska Folkvisor, Heft 1-2

TRAVENET
Vieille Chanson De Mezieres

TREDE, HILMAR
Monteverdi, Claudio
Canzonetten Heft I
Canzonetten Heft II
Scherzi Musicali, Heft I
Scherzi Musicali, Heft II

TRENNER, FRANZ
Strauss, Richard
Lieder Of Richard Strauss, Vol. 1:
Op. 10 To Op. 41
Lieder Of Richard Strauss, Vol. 2:
Op. 43 To Op. 68
Lieder Of Richard Strauss, Vol. 3:
Op. 69 To Op. 88
Lieder Of Richard Strauss, Vol. 4

TREVINE, OWEN
Deep Sea Shanties

TREW
Bain
Brother James's Air

TRÖTSCHEL, HEINRICH R.
Schein, Johann Hermann
Uns Ist Ein Kind Geboren

TRUILLET-SOYER, M.
Rameau, Jean-Philippe
Tambourin

TURCHI, GUIDO
Vivaldi, Antonio
Four Arias

TURUNEN
Ollos Huoleton, Poikas Valveill' On

TUVYA, OVADIA
Mala'ib El Nur

UNGARETTI, G.
Procaccini, T.
Dannazione E Preghiera

UPHAUS, DWIGHT
Songs For A Chosen Generation

UPPLING
Eighteen Songs

Ny Samling Sangduetter, Heft 1

Ny Samling Sangduetter, Heft 2

Tolv Duetter Fòr Flickskolornas Hògre
Sangklasser

URBAN; HRONEK
Pisne Narodu SSSR

Sovetske Pisne Pro Mladez

URBAN, J.; HRONEK, M.
Slavne Sovetske Historicke A Vezenske
A Revolucni Pisne

VARGAS
Famous Opera Arias, Vol. 1

Famous Opera Arias, Vol. 2

Famous Opera Duets, Vol. 1

Famous Opera Duets, Vol. 2

VATELLI, F.
Anonimi Vari Dei Secoli XVII e XVIII,
Part I

Anonimi Vari Dei Secoli XVII e XVIII,
Part II

Autori Romani Del '600, Vol. I

Autori Romani Del '600, Vol. II

VAUGHN WILLIAMS
Purcell, Henry
Evening Hymn

VECSEY; SOMFAI
Serate D'Opere Di Eszterhaza, Vol. 1

Serate D'Opere Di Eszterhaza, Vol. 2

Serate D'Opere Di Eszterhaza, Vol. 3

VEHANEN, KOSTI
Little Finnish Folk Song

VENE
Catholic Wedding Folio

VIEUXBLE, R.
Chabrier, Emmanuel
Espana

VILBAC
Mendelssohn-Bartholdy, Felix
Frühlingslied

VOGEL
Chòmed Chinde, Mir Wänd Singe

VOGEL; DOST
Myrten Und Rosen, Band I

VOGEL, J.
Lidove Pisne Z Tesinka, Ses. 1-2

VOLKMANN
Komponisten Auf Abwegen Heft I:
Lieder

Komponisten Auf Abwegen Heft II:
Arien

VOLKMANN, JOACHIM
Komponisten Auf Abwegen Oder Die
Seltsamen Verwandlungen Von
"Hänschen Klein", Heft I & II

VRIES, L. DE
Italiaanse Volksliederen

VUILLERMOZ, EMILE
Popular French And Canadian Songs

WAGHALTER, IGNATZ
R'itiha

WAGNER, LAVERN J.
Turnhout, Gerard de
Sacred And Secular Songs For Three
Voices

WAILES
Pepusch, John Christopher
Corydon

WALCHA
Deutsche Liebeslieder

WALKE; WALTERS
Folksongs Of Trinidad And Tobago

WALLIS
Pestalozza, Heinrich
Ciribiribin

WALTER
Kramer, A. Walter
Great Awakening, The

WALTER, G.A.
Bach, Johann Christian
Zwei Weltliche Arien

Bach, Johann Christoph Friedrich
Die Amerikanerin

Bach, Karl Philipp Emanuel
Phyllis Und Thirsis

Jauchzet Dem Herrn Alle Welt

WALTER, GEORG
Schütz, Heinrich
Lobet Den Herrn In Seinem Heiligtum

WALTER, GEORG A.
Bruhns, Nicholaus
Jauchzet Dem Herrn Alle Welt

WARD
Singing Road, Vol. 1

Singing Road, Vol. 2

Singing Road, Vol. 3

WARING
Didn't My Lord D'liver Daniel?

Steal Away

WARLOCK; WILSON
Danyel, John
Chromatic Tunes

WARMING, PER; BENGTSSON, GUSTAV
Folkelige Morgensange

WARRACK
Arne, Thomas Augustine
O Peace, Thou Fairest Child Of
Heaven

WARRENRATH, R.
Modern Scandinavian Songs, Vol. II:
Lange-Muller To Winge

WASHINGTON, B.T.
Were You There?

WASNER
Steffani, Agostino
Quanto, Quanto
Vieni O Cara, Amata Sposa

WATKINSON, G.
Christujenna

Einhundertelf Kinderlieder Zur Bibel

9 X 11 Neue Kinderlieder Zur Bibel

WEATHERLY
  Adams, Stephen
    Holy City, The

WECKERLIN
  Bergerettes

  Ranskalaisia Paimenlauluja

WECKERLIN, J. B.
  Bergerettes

WECKERLIN, JEAN BAPTISTE
  Arrigo, Girolamo
    Episodi

  Bergerettes

  Pastourelles

WECKSELL
  Sibelius, Jean
    Demanten Pa Marssnon

WEINER, L.
  Five Jewish Art Songs

WEIS, K.
  Lidove Pisne

WEISMANN
  Franz, Robert
    Fifty Selected Songs

  Haydn, (Franz) Joseph
    Three-Part Songs

WEISS; ANDREAE
  Een Alleen Is Maar Verdrietig

WEISS, G.; KLEIN, TH.
  Ariosti, Attilio
    La Rosa
    L'Olmo

WEKERLIN, J.B.
  Bergerettes

  Lassus, Roland de (Orlandus)
    Mon Coeur Se Recommande A Vous

WELLESZ
  Ventadorn, Bernart de
    Six Songs In Provencal

WERBA
  Baritone-Bass Album From The
    Repertory Of Hans Hotter

WERBA, E.
  Bariton-Bass Album

WERBE
  Schubert, Franz (Peter)
    Lieder Der Liebe, Landschaft,
     Geselligkeit

WETZLER, ROBERT
  Bless Us, God Of Loving

WHEELER
  Bach, Johann Sebastian
    Lord All Holy, All Merciful

WHITEHEAD
  Bach, Johann Sebastian
    Bist Du Bei Mir

WHITMAN
  Harrison, Lou
    Fragment From Calamus

WHITSETT, ELEANOR
  Christmas Carol Ensembles

WHITTAKER
  Water Ot Tyne

WHITTAKER, W.G.
  Blow The Wind Southerly

WHITTIER
  Ives, Charles
    Serenity

WHITWORTH
  Bailey
    He Will Pilot Me

  Henson
    Keep A Happy Heart

WICK
  Kiecker
    Bless Our Vows

WIDDICOMBE
  Gospel Train, The

  I Got A Robe

  Little David, Play On Your Harp

  Swing Low, Sweet Chariot

WIDDICOMBE, TREVOR
  Crystal Fountain, The

WIER
  Sullivan, Sir Arthur Seymour
    Gilbert And Sullivan At Home

WILD
  Cruickshank, R.
    He Is There
    Little People's Prayer

  Liddell, R.
    Cross Was Hewn From A Tree, A
    Dawn Of Creation
    It Costs So Little
    Life's Journey

WILHOUSKY
  Boyce
    I Love America

  Carol Of The Bells

WILKINS, MARIE; WILKINS, JOSEPH
  Great Duets From The Masters, Vol. I

  Great Duets From The Masters, Vol. II

  Great Duets From The Masters, Vol. IV

WILLAN, HEALEY
  Ten Songs

WILLCOXON, LARRY
  O'Brien, Bill
    Disciple's Prayer, A

WILLIAMS
  Rosenmüller, Johann
    Dream Of Olwen, The

WILLIAMS, JOHN
  Seventeenth Century English Songs

WILLIAMS, W.S. GWYNN
  Suo-Gan

WILMANS, W.
  Choice Sacred Songs

WILSON
  Solo Singer, Vol. 1

WILSON, H.L.
  Come Let's Be Merry

  My Lovely Celia

  Shepherd, Thy Demeanor Vary

  When Dull Care

  Wilson, Harry [Robert]
    I Kneel To Pray

WILSON, H. LANE
  Old English Melodies

WINLAW, MAURICE
  Comin' Thro' The Rye

  In Cellar Cool

WINSCHERMANN
  Graun, Karl Heinrich
    Sokrates

WINTER
  Campra, Andre
    Les Femmes

  Petz (Pez), Johann Christoph
    Mentre Fra Mille Fiori

  Pohle, David
    Wie Der Hirsch Schreyet

WISEMAN, HERBERT
  Children's Songs Of Russia

WITHER
  Hovhaness, Alan
    As On The Night

WITT, THEODOR DE; RAUCH, J.N.;ESPAGNE,
    FR.;COMMER, FR.; HABERL, FR.X.

  Palestrina, Giovanni
    First Critical Edition Of The Works
     Of Palestrina

WOBERSIN, W.
  Koschat, Thomas
    Album, Band II
    Album, Band III

WOLF, H.; RAPHAEL, G.
  Wolf, Hugo
    Sechzehn Lieder Heft I
    Sechzehn Lieder Heft II

WOLFE
  De Glory Road

  G'wine To Hebbn'

WOLFES, FELIX
  Selected Songs, Vol. 1

  Selected Songs, Vol. 2

  Selected Songs, Vol. 3

  Selected Songs, Vol. 4

  Selected Songs, Vol. 5

WOLFF
  Handel, George Frideric
    Fifteen Arias For High Voice

WOLFF, E.
  Granados, Enrique
    Danza Espanola, No. 5

WOLFF, ERNST V.
  Greensleeves

WOLKI
  Dimmler, L.
    Meine Kleinen Lieder

WOLPERT, FRANZ ALFONS
  Aria Di Giovanni: "Willst Du Dein
    Herz Mir Schenken"

WORK, BERTRAM G.
  Work, Henry Clay
    Henry Clay Work Songs

WYRTZEN, DON
  Times And The Seasons, The

ZAGWIJN, HENRI
  Suite Negre

ZANON
  Bach, Johann Sebastian
    Arie Scelte Dalle Cantate, Vol. I
    Arie Scelte Dalle Cantate, Vol. II
    Arie Scelte Dalle Cantate, Vol. III
    Arie Scelte Dalle Cantate, Vol. IV

  Duodieci Arie Italiane Dei Secoli
    XVII e XVIII

ZANON; DUNN, G.
  Trentesei Arie Italiane Di Diversi
    Autori Dei Secoli XVII e XVIII

ZELAND; STERNVALL
  Visfynd I-II

ZENCK, HERMANN
  Handel, George Frideric
    Crudel Tiranno, Amor
    Cuopre Tal Volta Il Cielo
    Dalla Guerra Amorosa
    Tra Le Fiamme
    Tu Fedel, Tu Costante?

ZILCHER
  Brahms, Johannes
    Deutsche Volkslieder, Vol. I
    Deutsche Volkslieder, Vol. II

ZILCHER, H.
  Mozart, Wolfgang Amadeus
    Nehmt Meinen Dank, Ihr Holden
     Gönner

ZOLI, UDO
  Nielsen, Riccardo
    Due Poesie Di Apollinaire

ZSCHIESCHE
  Das Klampfenlied

  Klingende Fahrt

  Querfeldein

ZSCIESCHE
  Sing Mir, Morena!

Publisher Directory

The list of publishers which follows contains the code assigned for each publisher, the name and address of the publisher, and U.S. agents who distribute the publications. This is the master list for the Music-In-Print series and represents all publishers who have submitted information for inclusion in the series. Therefore, all of the publishers do not necessarily occur in the present volume.

Code	Publisher	U.S. Agent
A COEUR JOIE	Éditions A Coeur Joie Les Passerelles, BP 9151 24 avenue Joannès Masset F-69263 Lyon cédex 09 France	
A MOLL DUR	A Moll Dur Publishing House	
A-R ED	A-R Editions, Inc. 801 Deming Way Madison, WI 53717	
AAP	Edition AAP (Audio Attic Productions) Aas-Wangsvei 8 N-1600 Fredrikstad Norway	
ABC	ABC Music Co.	BOURNE
ABER.GRP.	The Aberbach Group 988 Madison Avenue New York, NY 10021	
ABERDEEN	Aberdeen Music, Inc. 170 N.E. 33rd Street Fort Lauderdale, FL 33334	PLYMOUTH
ABINGDON	Abingdon Press P.O. Box 801 Nashville, TN 37202	
ABRSM	Associated Board of the Royal Schools of Music 14 Bedford Square London WC1B 3JG England	PRESSER
ACADEM	Academia Music Ltd. 16-5, Hongo 3-Chome Bunkyo-ku Tokyo, 113 Japan	KALMUS,A
ACCURA	Accura Music P.O. Box 4260 Athens, OH 45701-4260	
ACORD	Edizioni Accordo	CURCI
ACSB	Antigua Casa Sherry-Brener, Ltd. of Madrid 3145 West 63rd Street Chicago, IL 60629	
ADAM	D. Adams Music P.O. Box 8371 Asheville, NC 28814	
ADD.PRESS	Addington Press	ROYAL
ADD.-WESLEY	Addison-Wesley Publishing Co., Inc. 2725 Sand Hill Road Menlo Park, CA 94025	
AEOLUS	Aeolus Publishing Co. 60 Park Terrace West New York, NY 10034	
AGAPE	Agape	HOPE
AHLINS	Ahlins Musikförlag Box 26072 S-100 41 Stockholm Sweden	

Code	Publisher	U.S. Agent
AHN	Ahn & Simrock Sonnenstraße 19 D-8 München Germany	
AKADDV	Akademische Druck- und Verlagsanstalt Schönaugasse 6 A-8010 Graz Austria	
AKADEM	Akademiska Musikförlaget Sirkkalagatan 7 B 41 SF-20500 Abo 50 Finland	
ALBERSEN	Muziekhandel Albersen & Co. Groot Hertoginnelaan 182 NL-2517 EV Den Haag Netherlands	DONEMUS
ALBERT	J. Albert & Son Pty. Ltd. 139 King Street Sydney, N.S.W. Australia 2000	
ALBERT	J. Albert & Son - U.S.A. 1619 Broadway New York, NY 10019	
ALCOVE	Alcove Music	WESTERN
ALEX.HSE.	Alexandria House 211 Whitsett Road Nashville, TN 37210	
ALFRED	Alfred Publishing Co. 16380 Roscoe Blvd. P.O. Box 10003 Van Nuys, CA 91410	
ALKOR	Alkor Edition	FOR.MUS.DIST.
ALLANS	Allans Music Australia Ltd. P.O. Box 4072 Richmond East Victoria 3121 Australia	PRESSER
ALLOWAY	Alloway Publications P.O. Box 25 Santa Monica, CA 90406	
ALMITRA	Almitra	KENDOR
ALMO	Almo Publications	CPP-BEL
ALPEG	Alpeg	PETERS
ALPHENAAR	W. Alphenaar Kruisweg 47-49 NL-2011 LA Haarlem Netherlands	
ALPUERTO	Editorial Alpuerto Caños del Peral 7 28013 Madrid Spain	
ALSBACH	G. Alsbach & Co. P.O. Box 338 NL-1400 AH Bussum Netherlands	
ALSBACH&D	Alsbach & Doyer	

Code	Publisher	U.S. Agent
AM.COMP.ALL.	American Composers Alliance 170 West 74th Street New York, NY 10023	
AM. GEHR	American Guild of English Handbell Ringers, Inc.	LORENZ
AM.INST.MUS.	American Institute of Musicology	FOSTER
AM.MUS.ED.	American Music Edition 263 East Seventh Street New York, NY 10009	PRESSER (partial)
AMADEUS	Amadeus Verlag Bernhard Päuler Am Iberghang 16 CH-8405 Winterthur Switzerland	FOR.MUS.DIST
	American String Teachers Association see ASTA	
AMICI	Gli Amici della Musica da Camera Via Bocca di Leone 25 Roma Italy	
AMP	Associated Music Publishers 225 Park Avenue South New York, NY 10003	LEONARD-US (sales) SCHIRM.G (rental)
AMPHION	Éditions Amphion 12, rue Rougement F-75009 Paris France	
AMS PRESS	AMS Press, Inc. 56 East 13th Street New York, NY 10003	
AMSCO	AMSCO Music Publishing Co.	MUSIC
AMSI	Art Masters Studios, Inc. 2710 Nicollet Avenue Minneapolis, MN 55408	
ANDEL	Edition Andel Madeliefjeslaan, 26 B-8400 Oostende Belgium	
ANDERSONS	Anderssons Musikförlag Sodra Forstadsgatan 6 Box 17018 S-200 10 Malmö Sweden	
ANDPR	Andrea Press 75 Travis Road Holliston, MA 01746	
ANDRE	Johann André Musikverlag Frankfurterstraβe 28 Postfach 141 D-6050 Offenbach-am-Main Germany	
	Andrea Press see ANDPR	
ANDREU	Andreu Marc Publications 611 Broadway, Suite 615 New York, NY 10012	MUSIC SC.
ANERCA	Anerca Music 35 St. Andrew's Garden Toronto, Ontario M4W 2C9 Canada	
ANFOR	Anfor Music Publishers (Div. of Terminal Music Supply) 1619 East Third Street Brooklyn, NY 11230	MAGNA D

Code	Publisher	U.S. Agent
ANGLO	Anglo-American Music Publishers 4 Kendall Avenue Sanderstead Surrey, CR2 0NH England	
ANTARA	Antara Music Group 468 McNally Drive Nashville, TN 37211	
ANTICO	Antico Edition P.O. Box 1, Moretonhampstead Newton Abbot Devon TQ13 8UA England	BOSTON EMC
APM	Artist Production & Management	VIERT
APNM	Association for Promotion of New Music 2002 Central Avenue Ship Bottom, NJ 08008	
APOGEE	Apogee Press	WORLD
APOLLO	Apollo-Verlag Paul Lincke Weihergarten 5 6500 Mainz Germany	
ARCADIA	Arcadia Music Publishing Co., Ltd. P.O. Box 1 Rickmansworth Herts WD3 3AZ England	
ARCANA	Arcana Editions Indian River Ontario K0L 2B0 Canada	
ARCO	Arco Music Publishers	WESTERN
ARGM	Editorial Argentina de Musica & Editorial Saraceno Beunos Aires, Argentina	PEER
ARIAD	Ariadne Buch- und Musikverlag Schottenfeldgasse 45 A-1070 Wien Austria	
ARION	Coleccion Arion	MEXICANAS
ARION PUB	Arion Publications, Inc. 4964 Kathleen Avenue Castro Valley, CA 94546	
ARISTA	Arista Music Co. 8370 Wilshire Blvd. Beverly Hills, CA 90211	CPP-BEL
ARNOLD	Edward Arnold Series	NOVELLO
ARS NOVA	Ars Nova Publications 121 Washington San Diego, CA 92103	PRESSER
ARS POLONA	Ars Polona Krakowskie Przedmieś cie 7 Skrytka pocztowa 1001 PL-00-950 Warszawa Poland	
ARS VIVA	Ars Viva Verlag Weihergarten D-6500 Mainz 1 Germany	EUR.AM.MUS.
ARSIS	Arsis Press 1719 Bay Street SE Washington, DC 20003	PLYMOUTH
ARTHUR	J. Arthur Music The University Music House 4290 North High Street Columbus, OH 43214	

Code	Publisher	U.S. Agent
ARTIA	Artia Prag Ve Smečkkách 30 Praha 2 Czech Republic	
	Artist Production & Management see APM	
ARTRANSA	Artransa Music	WESTERN
ASCHERBERG	Ascherberg, Hopwood & Crew Ltd. 50 New Bond Street London W1A 2BR England	
ASHBOURN	Ashbourne Publications 425 Ashbourne Road Elkins Park, PA 19117	
ASHDOWN	Edwin Ashdown Ltd.	BRODT
ASHLEY	Ashley Publications, Inc. P.O. Box 337 Hasbrouck Heights, NJ 07604	
ASPEN	Aspen Grove Music P.O. Box 977 North Hollywood, CA 91603	
ASSMANN	Hermann Assmann, Musikverlag Franz-Werfel-Straße 36 D-6000 Frankfurt 50 Germany	
	Associated Board of the Royal Schools of Music see ABRSM	
	Associated Music Publishers see AMP	
	Association for Promotion of New Music see APNM	
ASTA	American String Teachers Association 2740 Spicewood Lane Bloomington, IN 47401	PRESSER
ATV	ATV Music Publications 6255 Sunset Boulevard Hollywood, CA 90028	CHERRY
	Audio Attic Productions see AAP	
AUG-FOR	Augsburg Fortress Publishers 426 South Fifth Street P.O. Box 1209 Minneapolis, MN 55440	
AULOS	Aulos Music Publishers P.O. Box 54 Montgomery, NY 12549	
AUTOGR	Autographus Musicus Ardalavägen 158 S-124 32 Bandhagen Sweden	
AUTRY	Gene Autry's Publishing Companies	CPP-BEL
AVANT	Avant Music	WESTERN
BAGGE	Jacob Bagge	STIM
BANK	Annie Bank Muziek P.O. Box 347 1180 AH Amstelveen Netherlands	
BANKS	Banks Music Publications The Old Forge Sand Hutton York YO4 1LB England	INTRADA

Code	Publisher	U.S. Agent
BARDIC	Bardic Edition 6 Fairfax Crescent, Aylesbury Buckhamshire, HP20 2ES England	PRESSER
BÄREN.	Bärenreiter Verlag Heinrich Schütz Allee 31-37 Postfach 100329 D-3500 Kassel-Wilhelmshöhe Germany	FOR.MUS.DIST.
BARNHS	C.L. Barnhouse 205 Cowan Avenue West P.O. Box 680 Oskaloosa, IA 52577	
BARON,M	M. Baron Co. P.O. Box 149 Oyster Bay, NY 11771	
BARRY-ARG	Barry & Cia Talcahuano 860, Bajo B Buenos Aires 1013-Cap. Federal Argentina	BOOSEY
BARTA	Barta Music Company	JERONA
BASART	Les Éditions Internationales Basart	GENERAL
BASEL	Musik-Akademie der Stadt Basel Leonhardsstraße 6 CH-4051 Basel Switzerland	
BAUER	Georg Bauer Musikverlag Luisenstraße 47-49 Postfach 1467 D-7500 Karlsruhe Germany	
BAVTON	Bavariaton-Verlag München Germany	ORLANDO
	Mel Bay Publications see MEL BAY	
BEACON HILL	Beacon Hill Music	LILLENAS
BEAUDN	Stuart D. Beaudoin 629 Queen Street Newmarket, Ontario Canada L3Y 2J1	
BEAUT	Beautiful Star Publishing, Inc. 3 Thrush Lane St. Paul, MN 55127-2613	
BECKEN	Beckenhorst Press P.O. Box 14273 Columbus, OH 43214	
BEECHWD	Beechwood Music Corporation 1750 Vine Street Hollywood, CA 90028	WARNER
BEEK	Beekman Music, Inc.	PRESSER
BEIAARD	Beiaardschool Belgium	
BELAIEFF	M.P. Belaieff Kennedyallee 101 D-6000 Frankfurt-am-Main 70 Germany	PETERS
	Centre Belge de Documentation Musicale see CBDM	
BELLA	Bella Roma Music 1442A Walnut Street Suite 197 Berkeley, CA 94709	
BELMONT	Belmont Music Publishers P.O. Box 231 Pacific Palisades, CA 90272	

Code	Publisher	U.S. Agent
BELWIN	Belwin-Mills Publishing Corp. 15800 N.W. 48th Avenue P.O. Box 4340 Miami, FL 33014	CPP-BEL PRESSER (rental)
BENJ	Anton J. Benjamin Werderstraße 44 Postfach 2561 D-2000 Hamburg 13 Germany	PRESSER
BENNY	Claude Benny Press 1401½ State Street Emporia, KS 66801	
BENSON	John T. Benson P.O. Box 107 Nashville, TN 37202-0107	
BERANDOL	Berandol Music Ltd. 110A Sackville Street Toronto, Ontario M5A 3E7 Canada	
BERBEN	Edizioni Musicali Berben Via Redipuglia 65 I-60100 Ancona Italy	PRESSER
BERGMANS	W. Bergmans	BANK
BERKLEE	Berklee Press Publications	LEONARD-US
BERLIN	Irving Berlin Music Corp. 29 W. 46 Street New York, NY 10036	
BERNOUILLI	Ed. Bernouilli	DONEMUS
BESSEL	Éditions Bessel & Cie	BREITKOPF-W
BEUSCH	Éditions Paul Beuscher Arpège 27, Boulevard Beaumarchais F-75004 Paris France	
BEZIGE BIJ	De Bezige Bij	DONEMUS
BIELER	Edmund Bieler Musikverlag Thürmchenswall 72 D-5000 Köln 1 Germany	
BIG BELL	Big Bells, Inc. 33 Hovey Avenue Trenton, NJ 08610	
BIG3	Big Three Music Corp.	CPP-BEL
BILLAUDOT	Éditions Billaudot 14, rue de l'Echiquier F-75010 Paris France	PRESSER
BIRCH	Robert Fairfax Birch	PRESSER
BIRNBACH	Richard Birnbach Musikverlag Aubinger Straße 9 D-8032 Lochheim bei München Germany	
BIZET	Bizet Productions and Publications	PRESSER
BMI	Broadcast Music, Inc. 320 West 57th Street New York, NY 10019	
	Boccaccini and Spada Editori see BSE	
BOCK	Fred Bock Music Co. P.O. Box 333 Tarzana, CA 91356	ANTARA
BODEN	Bodensee-Edition Gewerbestr. 12 D-78345 Moos am Bodensee Germany	

Code	Publisher	U.S. Agent
BODENS	Edition Ernst Fr. W. Bodensohn Dr. Rumpfweg 1 D-7570 Baden-Baden 21 Germany see also ERST	
BOEIJENGA	Boeijenga Muziekhandel Kleinzand 89 NL-8601 BG Sneek Netherlands	
BOELKE-BOM	Boelke-Bomart Music Publications Hillsdale, NY 12529	JERONA
BOETHIUS	Boethius Press 3 The Science Park Aberystinyth Dyfed SY23 3AH Wales	
BOHM	Anton Böhm & Sohn Postfach 110369 Lange Gasse 26 D-8900 Augsburg 11 Germany	
BOIL	Casa Editorial de Musica Boileau Provenza, 287 08037 Barcelona Spain	
BOIS	Bureau De Musique Mario Bois 17 Rue Richer F-75009 Paris France	
BOMART	Bomart Music Publications	BOELKE-BOM
BONART	Bonart Publications	CAN.MUS.CENT.
BONGIOVANI	Casa Musicale Francesco Bongiovani Via Rizzoli 28 E I-40125 Bologna Italy	
BOONIN	Joseph Boonin, Inc.	EUR.AM.MUS.
BOOSEY	Boosey & Hawkes Inc. 24 East 21st Street New York, NY 10010 Boosey & Hawkes Rental Library 52 Cooper Square New York, NY 10003-7102	
BOOSEY-CAN	Boosey & Hawkes Ltd. 279 Yorkland Boulevard Willowdale, Ontario M2J 1S7 Canada	BOOSEY
BOOSEY-ENG	Boosey & Hawkes Music Publishers Ltd. 295 Regent Street London W1 R 8JH England	BOOSEY
BORNEMANN	Éditions Bornemann 15 rue de Tournon F-75006 Paris France	KING,R PRESSER
BOSSE	Gustav Bosse Verlag Von der Tann Straße 38 Postfach 417 D-8400 Regensburg 1 Germany	EUR.AM.MUS.
BOSTON	Boston Music Co. 9 Airport Drive Hopedale, MA 01747	
BOSTON EMC	Boston Early Music Center see Early Music Shop of New England	
BOSWORTH	Bosworth & Company, Ltd. 14-18 Heddon Street, Regent Street London W1 R 8DP England	BRODT

Code	Publisher	U.S. Agent
BOTE	Bote & Bock Hardenbergstraβe 9A D-10623 Berlin Germany	PRESSER
BOURNE	Bourne Co. 5 W. 37th Street New York, NY 10018-6232	
BOWDOIN	Bowdoin College Music Press Department of Music Bowdoin College Brunswick, ME 04011	
BOWM	Bowmaster Productions 3351 Thornwood Road Sarasota, FL 33581	
BRCONT.MUS.	British And Continental Music Agencies Ltd.	EMI
BRADLEY	Bradley Publications 80 8th Avenue New York, NY 10011	CPP-BEL
BRANCH	Harold Branch Publishing, Inc. 95 Eads Street West Babylon, NY 11704	
BRANDEN	Branden Press, Inc. 17 Station Street P.O. Box 843 Brookline Village, MA 02147	
BRASS PRESS	The Brass Press 136 8th Avenue North Nashville, TN 37203-3798	
BRATFISCH	Musikverlag Georg Bratfisch Hans-Herold-Str. 23 D-95326 Kulmbach Germany	PRESSER
BRAUER	Les Éditions Musicales Herman Brauer 30, rue St. Christophe B-1000 Bruxelles Belgium	
BRAUN-PER	St. A. Braun-Peretti Hahnchenpassage D-53 Bonn Germany	
BRAVE	Brave New Music	SON-KEY
BREITKOPF-L	Breitkopf & Härtel (Leipzig)	
BREITKOPF-LN	Breitkopf & Härtel	
BREITKOPF-W	Breitkopf & Härtel Walkmühlstraβe 52 Postfach 1707 D-6200 Wiesbaden 1 Germany	SCHIRM.G (rental)
BRENNAN	John Brennan Music Publisher Positif Press Ltd. 130 Southfield Road Oxford OX4 1PA England	ORGAN LIT
BRENT	Michael Brent Publications, Inc. P.O. Box 1186 Port Chester, NY 10573	CHERRY
BRENTWOOD	Brentwood Publishing Group Inc. P.O. Box 19001 Brentwood, TN 37027	
BRIDGE	Bridge Music Publishing Co. 1350 Villa Street Mountain View, CA 94042	
BRIGHT STAR	Bright Star Music Publications	WESTERN
	British and Continental Music Agencies Ltd. see BR.CONT.MUS.	

Code	Publisher	U.S. Agent
	Broadcast Music, Inc. see BMI	
BROADMAN	Broadman Press 127 Ninth Avenue, North Nashville, TN 37234	
BRODT	Brodt Music Co. P.O. Box 9345 Charlotte, NC 28299-9345	
BROEKMANS	Broekmans & Van Poppel B.V. van Baerlestraat 92-94 NL-1071 BB Amsterdam Netherlands	
BROGNEAUX	Éditions Musicales Brogneaux 73, Avenue Paul Janson B-1070 Bruxelles Belgium	
BROOK	Brook Publishing Co. 3602 Cedarbrook Road Cleveland Heights, OH 44118	
BROUDE,A	Alexander Broude, Inc.	PLYMOUTH
BROUDE BR.	Broude Brothers Ltd. 141 White Oaks Road Williamstown, MA 01267	
	Broude Brothers Ltd.-Rental Dept. 170 Varick St. New York, NY 10013	
BROWN	Brown University Choral Series	BOOSEY
BROWN,R	Rayner Brown 2423 Panorama Terrace Los Angeles, CA 90039	WESTERN COMP.LIB
BROWN,WC	William C. Brown Co. 2460 Kerper Boulevard Dubuque, IA 52001	
BRUCK	Musikverlag M. Bruckbauer "Biblioteca de la Guitarra" Postfach 18 D-7953 Bad Schussenried Germany	
BRUCKNER	Bruckner Verlag Austria	PETERS (rental)
BRUZZI	Aldo Bruzzichelli, Editore Borgo S. Frediano, 8 I-50124 Firenze Italy	MARGUN
BSE	Boccaccini and Spada Editori Via Francesco Duodo, 10 I-00136 Roma Italy	PRESSER
BUBONIC	Bubonic Publishing Co. 706 Lincoln Avenue St. Paul, MN 55105	
BUDAPEST	Editio Musica Budapest (Kultura) P.O.B. 322 H-1370 Budapest Hungary see also EMB	BOOSEY PRESSER (partial)
BUDDE	Rolf Budde Musikverlag Hohenzollerndamm 54A D-1000 Berlin 33 Germany	
BUGZY	Bugzy Bros. Vocal Athletics P.O. Box 900 Orem, UT 84057	MUSICART
BUSCH	Hans Busch Musikförlag Stubbstigen 3 S-18147 Lidingö Sweden	

Code	Publisher	U.S. Agent
BUSCH,E	Ernst Busch Verlag Schlossstrasse 43 D-7531 Neulingen-Bauschlott Germany	
BUTZ	Dr. J. Butz Musikverlag Postfach 3008 5205 Sankt Augustin 3 Germany	
CAILLARD	Edition Philippe Caillard 5 bis rue du Château-Fondu 78200 Fontenay-Mauvoisin France	
CAILLET	Lucien Caillet	SOUTHERN
CAMBIATA	Cambiata Press P.O. Box 1151 Conway, AR 72032	
CAMBRIA	Cambria Records & Publishing P.O. Box 374 Lomita, CA 90717	
CAMBRIDGE	Cambridge University Press The Edinburgh Building Shaftesbury Road Cambridge CB2 2RU England	
CAMERICA	Camerica Music 535 Fifth Avenue, Penthouse New York, NY 10017	CPP-BEL
CAMPUS	Campus Publishers 713 Ellsworth Road West Ann Arbor, MI 48104	
CAN.MUS.CENT.	Canadian Music Centre 20 St. Joseph Street Toronto, Ontario M4Y 1J9 Canada	
CAN.MUS.HER.	Canadian Musical Heritage Society Patrimoine Musical Canadien P.O. Box 262, Station A Ottawa, Ontario K1N 8V2 Canada	
CANAAN	Canaanland Publications	WORD
CANT DO	Cantate Domino Editions de musique Rue du Sapin 2a C.P. 156 2114 Fleurier Switzerland	
CANTANDO	Cantando Forlag Bj. Bjφrnsonsgt. 2 D N-4021 Stavanger Norway	
CANTORIS	Cantoris Music P.O. Box 162004 Sacramento, CA 95816	
CANYON	Canyon Press, Inc. P.O. Box 447 Islamorada, FL 33036	KERBY
CAPELLA	Capella Music, Inc.	BOURNE
CAPPR	Capital Press	PODIUM
CARABO	Carabo-Cone Method Foundation 1 Sherbrooke Road Scarsdale, NY 10583	
CARISCH	Carisch S.p.A. see Nuova Carisch	
CARLAN	Carlanita Music Co.	LEONARD-US (sales) SCHIRM.G (rental)

Code	Publisher	U.S. Agent
CARLIN	Carlin Publications P.O. Box 2289 Oakhurst, CA 93644	
CARLTON	Carlton Musickverlag	BREITKOPF-W
CARUS	Carus-Verlag	FOSTER
CATHEDRAL	Cathedral Music Maudlin House Westhampnett Chichester West Sussex PO18 0PB, England	
	Catholic Conference see U.S.CATH	
CAVATA	Cavata Music Publishers, Inc.	PRESSER
CAVELIGHT	Cavelight Music P.O. Box 85 Oxford, NJ 07863	
CBC	Cundey Bettoney Co.	FISCHER,C
CBDM	CeBeDeM Centre Belge de Documentation Musicale rue d'Arlon 75-77 B-1040 Bruxelles Belgium	
CCMP	Colorado College Music Press 14 E. Cache La Poudre Colorado Springs, CO 80903	
CEL	Celesta Publishing Co. P.O. Box 560603, Kendall Branch Miami, FL 33156	
	Centre Belge de Documentation Musicale see CBDM	
	Éditions du Centre Nationale de la Recherche Scientifique see CNRS	
CENTO	Centorino Productions P.O. Box 4478 West Hills, CA 91308	
CENTURY	Century Music Publishing Co. 263 Veterans Boulevard Carlstadt, NJ 07072	ASHLEY
CENTURY PR	Century Press Publishers	
CESKY HUD.	Cesky Hudebni Fond Parizska 13 CS-110 00 Praha 1 Czech Republic	BOOSEY (rental) NEW W
CHANT	Éditions Le Chant du Monde 23, rue Royale F-75008 Paris France	
CHANTERL	Éditions Chanterelle S.A. Postfach 103909 D-69 Heidelberg Germany	BÄREN.
CHANTRY	Chantry Music Press, Inc. Wittenberg University P.O. Box 1101 Springfield, OH 45501	AUG-FOR
CHAPLET	Chaplet Music Corp.	PARAGON
CHAPPELL	Chappell & Co., Inc. 1290 Avenue of the Americas New York, NY 10019	LEONARD-US
CHAPPELL-CAN	Chappell Music Canada Ltd 85 Scarsdale Road, Unit 101 Don Mills, Ontario M3B 2R2 Canada	LEONARD-US

Code	Publisher	U.S. Agent
CHAPPELL-ENG	Chappell & Co. Ltd. Printed Music Division 60-70 Roden Street Ilford, Essex IG1 2AQ England	LEONARD-US
CHAPPELL-FR	Chappell S.A. 25, rue d'Hauterville F-75010 Paris France	LEONARD-US
CHAR CROS	Charing Cross Music, Inc. 1619 Broadway, Suite 500 New York, NY 10019	
CHARTER	Charter Publications, Inc. P.O. Box 850 Valley Forge, PA 19482	PEPPER
CHENANGO	Chenango Valley Music Press P.O. Box 251 Hamilton, NY 13346	
CHERITH	Cherith Publishing Co.	INTRADA
CHERRY	Cherry Lane Music Co. 110 Midland Avenue Port Chester, NY 10573	CPP-BEL
CHESTER	Chester Music 8-9 Frith Street London W1V 5TZ England	SCHIRM.G
CHILTERN	Chiltern Music see Cathedral Music	
CHOIR	Choir Publishing Co. 564 Columbus Street Salt Lake City, UT 84103	
CHORAG	Choragus Box 1197 S-581 11 Linköping Sweden	
CHORISTERS	Choristers Guild 2834 West Kingsley Road Garland, TX 75041	LORENZ
CHOUDENS	Édition Choudens 38, rue Jean Mermoz F-75008 Paris France	PRESSER
CHRI	Christopher Music Co. 380 South Main Place Carol Stream, IL 60188	PRESSER
CHRIS	Christophorus-Verlag Herder Hermann-Herder-Straße 4 D-7800 Freiburg Breisgau Germany	
CHURCH	John Church Co.	PRESSER
CJC	Creative Jazz Composers, Inc. 1240 Annapolis Road Odenton, MD 21113	
CLARION	Clarion Call Music	SON-KEY
CLARK	Clark and Cruickshank Music Publishers	BERANDOL
CLASSV	Classical Vocal Reprints P.O. Box 20263 Columbus Circle Station New York, NY 10023	
CLIVIS	Clivis Publicacions C-Còrsega, 619 Baixos Barcelona 25 Spain	

Code	Publisher	U.S. Agent
CMP	CMP Library Service MENC Historical Center/SCIM Music Library/Hornbake University of Maryland College Park, MD 20742	
CNRS	CNRS Editions 20-22 rue Saint-Amand F-75015 Paris France	SMPF
CO OP	Co-op Press RD2 Box 150A Wrightsville, PA 17368	
COBURN	Coburn Press	PRESSER
CODERG	Coderg-U.C.P. sàrl 42 bis, rue Boursault F-75017 Paris France	
COLE	M.M. Cole Publishing Co. 919 North Michigan Avenue Chicago, IL 60611	
COLEMAN	Dave Coleman Music, Inc. P.O. Box 230 Montesano, WA 98563	
COLFRANC	Colfranc Music Publishing Corp.	KERBY
COLIN	Charles Colin 315 West 53rd Street New York, NY 10019	
COLOMBO	Franco Colombo Publications	CPP-BEL PRESSER (rental)
	Colorado College Music Press see CCMP	
COLUM UNIV	Columbia University Music Press 562 West 113th Street New York, NY 10025	SCHIRM.EC
COLUMBIA	Columbia Music Co.	PRESSER
COLUMBIA PIC.	Columbia Pictures Publications see CPP	
COMBRE	Consortium Musical, Marcel Combre Editeur 24, Boulevard Poissonnière F-75009 Paris France	PRESSER
COMP.FAC.	Composers Facsimile Edition	AM.COMP.AL.
COMP.LIB.	Composer's Library Editions	PRESSER
COMP-PERF	Composer/Performer Edition 2101 22nd Street Sacramento, CA 95818	
COMP.PR.	The Composers Press, Inc.	OPUS
COMPOSER'S GR	Composer's Graphics 5702 North Avenue Carmichael, CA 95608	
CONCERT	Concert Music Publishing Co. c/o Studio P-R, Inc. 16333 N.W. 54th Avenue Hialeah, FL 33014	CPP-BEL
CONCERT W	Concert Works Unlimited	SHAWNEE
CONCORD	Concord Music Publishing Co.	ELKAN,H
CONCORDIA	Concordia Publishing House 3558 South Jefferson Avenue St. Louis, MO 63118-3968	
CONGRESS	Congress Music Publications 100 Biscayne Boulevard Miami, FL 33132	

Code	Publisher	U.S. Agent
CONSOL	Consolidated Music Publishers, Inc. 33 West 60th Street New York, NY 10023	
CONSORT	Consort Music, Inc. (Division of Magnamusic Distributors) Sharon, CT 06069	
CONSORT PR	Consort Press P.O. Box 50413 Santa Barbara, CA 93150-0413	
CONSORTIUM	Consortium Musical	PRESSER
	Consortium Musical, Marcel Combre Editeur see COMBRE	
CONTINUO	Continuo Music Press, Inc.	PLYMOUTH
	Editorial Cooperativa Inter-Americana de Compositores see ECOAM	
COPPENRATH	Musikverlag Alfred Coppenrath Postfach 11 58 D-84495 Altötting Germany	
COR PUB	Cor Publishing Co. 67 Bell Place Massapequa, NY 11758	
CORMORANT	Cormorant Press P.O. Box 169 Hallowell, ME 04347	PLYMOUTH
CORONA	Edition Corona-Rolf Budde Hohenzollerndamm 54A D-1 Berlin 33 Germany	
CORONET	Coronet Press	PRESSER
COROZINE	Vince Corozine Music Publishing Co. 6 Gabriel Drive Peekskill, NY 10566	
COSTALL	Éditions Costallat 60 rue de la'Chaussée d'Antin F-75441 Paris Cedex 09 France	PRESSER
COVENANT	Covenant Press 3200 West Foster Avenue Chicago, IL 60625	
COVENANT MUS	Covenant Music 1640 East Big Thompson Avenue Estes Park, CO 80517	
CPP	Columbia Pictures Publications 15800 N.W. 48th Avenue Miami, FL 33014	CPP-BEL
CPP-BEL	CPP-Belwin Music 15800 N.W. 48th Avenue Miami, FL 33014	
CRAMER	J.B. Cramer & Co., Ltd. 23 Garrick Street London WC2E 9AX England	CPP-BEL
CRANZ	Éditions Cranz 30, rue St.-Christophe B-1000 Bruxelles Belgium	
	Creative Jazz Composers see CJC	
CRES.-NETH	Uitgeverij Crescendo	DONEMUS
CRESCENDO	Crescendo Music Sales Co. P.O. Box 395 Naperville, IL 60540	FEMA

Code	Publisher	U.S. Agent
CRESPUB	Crescendo Publications, Inc. 6311 North O'Connor Road #112 Irving, TX 75039-3112	
CRITERION	Criterion Music Corp. P.O. Box 660 Lynbrook, NY 11563	
CROATICA	Croatian Music Institute	DRUS.HRVAT.SKLAD.
CRON	Edition Cron Luzern Zinggentorstraße 5 CH-6006 Luzern Switzerland	
CROWN	Crown Music Press 4119 North Pittsburgh Chicago, IL 60634	BRASS PRESS (partial)
	Cundey Bettoney Co. see CBC	
CURCI	Edizioni Curci Galleria del Corso 4 I-20122 Milano Italy	
CURTIS	Curtis Music Press	KJOS
CURWEN	J. Curwen & Sons	LEONARD-US SCHIRM.G (rental)
CZECH	Czechoslovak Music Information Centre Besedni 3 CS-118 00 Praha 1 Czech Republic	BOOSEY (rental)
DA CAPO	Da Capo Press, Inc. 233 Spring Street New York, NY 10013	
	Samfundet til udgivelse at Dansk Musik see SAMFUNDET	
DANE	Dane Publications 1657 The Fairway, Suite 133 Jenkintown, PA 19046	
DANTALIAN	Dantalian, Inc. Eleven Pembroke Street Newton, MA 02158	
DAVIMAR	Davimar Music M. Productions 159 West 53rd Street New York, NY 10019	
DAYBRK	Daybreak Productions	ALEX.HSE.
DE MONTE	De Monte Music F-82240 Septfonds France	
DE SANTIS	Edizioni de Santis Viale Mazzini, 6 I-00195 Roma Italy	
DEAN	Roger Dean Publishing Co. 345 West Jackson Street, #B Macomb, IL 61455-2112	LORENZ
DEIRO	Pietro Deiro Publications 133 Seventh Avenue South New York, NY 10014	
DELRIEU	Georges Delrieu & Cie Palais Bellecour B 14, rue Trachel F-06000 Nice France	SCHIRM.EC

Code	Publisher	U.S. Agent	Code	Publisher	U.S. Agent
DENNER	Erster Bayerischer Musikverlag Joh. Dennerlein KG Beethovenstraβe 7 D-8032 Lochham Germany		DOUBLDAY	Doubleday & Co., Inc. 501 Franklin Avenue Garden City, NY 11530	
DESC	Descant Publications	INTRADA	DOUGLAS,B	Byron Douglas	CPP-BEL
DESERET	Deseret Music Publishers P.O. Box 900 Orem, UT 84057	MUSICART	DOVEHOUSE	Dovehouse Editions 32 Glen Avenue Ottawa, Ontario K1S 2Z7 Canada	
DESHON	Deshon Music, Inc.	CPP-BEL PRESSER (rental)	DOVER	Dover Publications, Inc. 31 East 2nd Street Mineola, NY 11501	ALFRED
DESSAIN	Éditions Dessain Belgium		DOXO	Doxology Music P.O. Box M Aiken, SC 29802	ANTARA
DEUTSCHER	Deutscher Verlag für Musik Walkmühlstr. 52 D-6200 Wiesbaden 1 Germany	BREITKOPF-W	DP	Dilia Prag	BÄREN.
DEWOLF	DeWolfe Ltd. 80/88 Wardour Street London W1V 3LF England	DONEMUS	DRAGON	Dragon Music Co. 28908 Grayfox Street Malibu, CA 90265	
DIAPASON	The Diapason Press Dr. Rudolf A. Rasch P.O. Box 2376 NL-3500 GJ Utrecht Netherlands		DREIK	Dreiklang-Dreimasken Bühnenund Musikverlag D-8000 München Germany	ORLANDO
DIESTERWEG	Verlag Moritz Diesterweg Hochstraβe 31 D-6000 Frankfurt-am-Main Germany		DRK	DRK Music Co. 111 Lake Wind Rd. New Canaan, CT 06840	
	Dilia Prag see DP		DRUS.HRVAT. SKLAD.	Društvo Hrvatskih Skladatelja Berislavićeva 9 Zagreb Croatia	
DIP PROV	Diputacion Provincal de Barcelona Servicio de Bibliotecas Carmen 47 Barcelona 1 Spain		DRUSTVA	Edicije Drustva Slovenskih Skladateljev Trg Francoske Revolucije 6 Ljubljana Slovenia	NEW W
DITSON	Oliver Ditson Co.	PRESSER	DRZAVNA	Drzavna Zalozba Slovenije	DRUSTVA
DOBER	Les Éditions Doberman-Yppan C.P. 2021 St. Nicholas, Quebec G0S 3L0 Canada	BOOSEY	DUCHESS	Duchess Music Corp.	MCA PRESSER (rental)
DOBLINGER	Ludwig Doblinger Verlag Dorotheergasse 10 A-1011 Wien I Austria	FOR.MUS.DIST.	DUCKWORTH	Gerald Duckworth & Co., Ltd. 43 Gloucester Crescent London, NW1 England	
DOMINIS	Dominis Music Ltd. Box 11307, Station H Ottawa Ontario K2H 7V1 Canada		DUMA	Duma Music Inc. 580 Alden Street Woodbridge, NJ 07095	
DONEMUS	Donemus Foundation Paulus Potterstraat 14 NL-1071 CZ Amsterdam Netherlands	PRESSER	DUN	Dunstan House P.O. Box 1355 Stafford, VA 22555	ANTARA
DOORWAY	Doorway Music 2509 Buchanan Street Nashville, TN 37208		DUNV	Dunvagen Music Publishers, Inc.	SCHIRM.G
DORABET	Dorabet Music Co. 170 N.E. 33rd Street Ft. Lauderdale, FL 33334	PLYMOUTH	DURAND	Durand & Cie 215, rue du Faubourg St.-Honoré F-75008 Paris France	PRESSER
DORING	G.F. Döring Musikverlag Hasenplatz 5-6 D-7033 Herrenburg 1 Germany		DUTTON	E.P. Dutton & Co., Inc. 201 Park Avenue South New York, NY 10003	
DORN	Dorn Publications, Inc. P.O. Box 206 Medfield, MA 02052		DUX	Edition Dux Arthur Turk Beethovenstraβe 7 D-8032 Lochham Germany	DENNER
			DVM	DVM Productions P.O. Box 399 Thorofare, NJ 08086	
			EAR.MUS.FAC.	Early Music Facsimiles P.O. Box 711 Columbus, OH 43216	

Code	Publisher	U.S. Agent
	Early Music Shop of New England 65 Boylston Street Brookline, MA 02146	
	East West Publications see WP	
EARTHSNG	Earthsongs 220 N.W. 29th Corvallis, OR 97330	
EASTMAN	Eastman School of Music	FISCHER,C
EBLE	Eble Music Co. P.O. Box 2570 Iowa City, IA 52244	
ECK	Van Eck & Zn.	DONEMUS
ECOAM	Editorial Cooperativa Inter-Americana de Compositores Casilla de Correa No. 540 Montevideo Uruguay	PEER
EDI-PAN	Edi-Pan	DE SANTIS
EDUTAIN	Edu-tainment Publications (Div. of the Evolve Music Group) P.O. Box 20767 New York, NY 10023	
EERSTE	De Eerste Muziekcentrale Flevolaan 41 NL-1411 KC Naarden Netherlands	
EGTVED	Edition EGTVED P.O. Box 20 DK-6040 Egtved Denmark	FOSTER
EHRLING	Thore Ehrling Musik AB Linnegatan 9-11 Box 5268 S-102 45 Stockholm Sweden	
EIGEN UITGAVE	Eigen Uitgave van de Componist (Composer's Own Publication)	DONEMUS
ELITE	Elite Edition	SCHAUR
ELKAN,H	Henri Elkan Music Publisher P.O. Box 279 Hastings On Hudson, NY 10706	
ELKAN&SCH	Elkan & Schildknecht Vastmannagatan 95 S-113 43 Stockholm Sweden	
ELKAN-V	Elkan-Vogel, Inc. Presser Place Bryn Mawr, PA 19010	
ELKIN	Elkin & Co., Ltd	PRESSER
EMB	Editio Musica Budapest P.O.B. 322 H-1370 Budapest Hungary see also BUDAPEST	BOOSEY PRESSER
EMEC	Editorial de Musica Española Contemporanea Ediciones Quiroga Alcalá, 70 Madrid 9 Spain	
EMERSON	Emerson Edition Windmill Farm Ampleforth York YO6 4HF England	EBLE GROVE KING,R WOODWIND PRESSER

Code	Publisher	U.S. Agent
EMI	EMI Music Publishing Ltd. 127 Charing Cross Road London WC2H 0EA England	INTER.MUS.P.
ENGELS	Musikverlag Carl Engels Nachf. Auf dem Brand 3 D-5000 Köln 50 (Rodenkirchen) Germany	
ENGSTROEM	Engstroem & Soedering Palaegade 6 DK-1261 København K Denmark	PETERS
ENOCH	Enoch & Cie 193 Boulevard Pereire F-75017 Paris France	PRESSER SCHIRM.G (rental-partial)
ENSEMB	Ensemble Publications P.O. Box 98, Bidwell Station Buffalo, NY 14222	
ENSEMB PR	Ensemble Music Press	FISCHER,C
EPHROS	Gershon Ephros Cantorial Anthology Foundation, Inc	TRANSCON.
ERDMANN	Rudolf Erdmann, Musikverlag Adolfsallee 34 D-62 Wiosbaden Germany	
ERES	Edition Eres Horst Schubert Hauptstrasse 35 Postfach 1220 D-2804 Lilienthal/Bremen Germany	
ERICKSON	E.J. Erickson Music Co. 606 North Fourth Street P.O. Box 97 St. Peter, MN 56082	
ERIKS	Eriks Musikhandel & Förlag AB Karlavägen 40 S-114 49 Stockholm Sweden	
ERST	Erstausgaben Bodensohn see also BODENS	
ESCHENB	Eschenbach Editions 28 Dalrymple Crescent Edinburgh, EH9 2NX Scotland	PRESSER
ESCHIG	Éditions Max Eschig 215 rue du Faubourg Saint-Honoré F-75008 Paris France	PRESSER

	Editorial de Musica Española
	  Contemporanea
	  see EMEC	

	Union Musical Española see UNION ESP	
ESSEX	Clifford Essex Music	MUSIC-ENG
ESSO	Van Esso & Co.	DONEMUS
ETLING,F	Forest R. Etling see HIGHLAND	
ETOILE	Etoile Music, Inc. Publications Division Shell Lake, WI 54871	MMB
EUGANEA	Euganea Editoriale Comunicazioni Via Roma 82 I-35122 Padova Italy	
EULENBURG	Edition Eulenburg	EUR.AM.MUS. (miniature scores)

Code	Publisher	U.S. Agent
EUR.AM.MUS.	European American Music Corp. P.O. Box 850 Valley Forge, PA 19482	
EWP	East West Publications	MUSIC
EXC.MH	Excellent Music Holland Postbus 347 1180 AH Amstelveen Netherlands	
EXCELSIOR	Excelsior Music Publishing Co.	PRESSER
EXPO PR	Exposition Press 325 Kings Highway Smithtown, NY 11787	
FABER	Faber Music Ltd. 3 Queen Square London WC1N 3AU England	LEONARD-US (sales) SCHIRM.G (rental)
FAIR	Fairfield Publishing, Ltd.	PRESSER
FAITH	Faith Music	LILLENAS
FALLEN LEAF	Fallen Leaf Press PO 10034-N Berkeley, CA 94709	
FAR WEST	Far West Music	WESTERN
FARRELL	The Wes Farrell Organization	LEONARD-US
FAZER	Musik Fazer P.O. Box 169 SF-02101 Espoo Finland	PRESSER
FEEDBACK	Feedback Studio Verlag Gentner Strasse 23 D-5 Köln 1 Germany	BÄREN.
FEIST	Leo Feist, Inc.	PRESSER
FELDMAN,B	B. Feldman & Co., Ltd	EMI
FEMA	Fema Music Publications P.O. Box 395 Naperville, IL 60566	
FENETTE	Fenette Music Ltd.	BROUDE,A
FENTONE	Fentone Music Ltd. Fleming Road, Earlstrees Corby, Northants NN17 2SN England	PRESSER
FEREOL	Fereol Publications Route 8, Box 510C Gainesville, GA 30501	
FEUCHT	Feuchtinger & Gleichauf Niedermünstergasse 2 D-8400 Regensburg 11 Germany	
FIDDLE	Fiddle & Bow 7 Landview Drive Dix Hills, NY 11746	HHP
FIDELIO	Fidelio Music Publishing Co. 39 Danbury Avenue Westport, CT 06880-6822	
FIDULA	Fidula-Verlag Johannes Holzmeister Ahornweg, Postfach 250 D-5407 Boppard/Rhein Germany	HARGAIL
FILLMH	Fillmore Music House	FISCHER,C
FINE ARTS	Fine Arts Press 2712 W. 104th Terrace Leawood, KS 66206	ALEX.HSE.

Code	Publisher	U.S. Agent
FINN MUS	Finnish Music Information Center Runeberginkatu 15 A SF-00100 Helsinki 10 Finland	
FISCHER,C	Carl Fischer, Inc. 62 Cooper Square New York, NY 10003	
FISCHER,J	J. Fischer & Bro.	BELWIN PRESSER (rental)
FISHER	Fisher Music Co.	PLYMOUTH
FITZSIMONS	H.T. FitzSimons Co., Inc. 18345 Ventura Boulevard P.O. Box 333, Suite 212 Tarzana, CA 91356	ANTARA
FLAMMER	Harold Flammer, Inc.	SHAWNEE
FMA	Florilegium Musicae Antiquae	HÄNSSLER
FOETISCH	Foetisch Frères Rue de Bourg 6 CH-1002 Lausanne Switzerland	SCHIRM.EC
FOG	Dan Fog Musikforlag Grabrodretorv 7 DK-1154 København K Denmark	
FOLEY,CH	Charles Foley, Inc.	FISCHER,C PRESSER (rental)
FORBERG	Rob. Forberg-P. Jurgenson, Musikverlag Mirbachstraße 9 D-5300 Bonn-Bad Godesberg Germany	PETERS
FOR.MUS.DIST.	Foreign Music Distributors 13 Elkay Drive Chester, NY 10918	
FORLIVESI	A. Forlivesi & C. Via Roma 4 50123 Firenze Italy	
FORNI	Arnaldo Forni Editore Via Gramsci 164 I-40010 Sala Bolognese Italy	OMI
FORSTER	Forster Music Publisher, Inc. 216 South Wabash Avenue Chicago, IL 60604	
FORSYTH	Forsyth Brothers Ltd. 126 Deansgate Manchester M3 2GR England	
FORTEA	Biblioteca Fortea Fucar 10 Madrid 14 Spain	
FORTISSIMO	Fortissimo Musikverlag Margaretenplatz 4 A-1050 Wien Austria	
	Fortress Press	AUG-FOR
FOSTER	Mark Foster Music Co. 28 East Springfield Avenue P.O. Box 4012 Champaign, IL 61820-1312	
	Foundation for New American Music see NEWAM	
FOUR ST	Four Star Publishing Co.	CPP-BEL

Code	Publisher	U.S. Agent
FOXS	Sam Fox Publishing Co. 5276 Hollister Avenue Suite 251 Santa Barbara, CA 93111	PLYMOUTH (sales) PRESSER (rental)
FRANCAIS	Éditions Françaises de Musique	PRESSER
FRANCE	France Music	AMP
FRANCIS	Francis, Day & Hunter Ltd.	CPP-BEL
FRANG	Frangipani Press	ALFRED
FRANK	Frank Music Corp.	LEONARD-US SCHIRM.G (rental-partial)
FRANTON	Franton Music 4620 Sea Isle Memphis, TN 38117	
FREDONIA	Fredonia Press 3947 Fredonia Drive Hollywood, CA 90068	SIFLER
FREEMAN	H. Freeman & Co., Ltd.	EMI
FROHLICH	Friedrich Wilhelm Fröhlich Musikverlag Ansbacher Straβe 52 D-1000 Berlin 30 Germany	
FUJIHARA	Fujihara	
FURORE	Furore Verlag Johannesstrasse 3 3500 Kassel Germany	TONGER
FURST	Fürstner Ltd.	BOOSEY
GAF	G.A.F. and Associates 1626 E. Williams Street Tempe, AZ 85281	
GAITHER	Gaither Music Company	ALEX.HSE.
GALAXY	Galaxy Music Corp.	SCHIRM.EC
GALLEON	Galleon Press 17 West 60th St. New York, NY 10023	BOSTON
GALLERIA	Galleria Press 170 N.E. 33rd Street Fort Lauderdale, FL 33334	PLYMOUTH
GALLIARD	Galliard Ltd. Queen Anne's Road Southtown, Gt. Yarmouth Norfolk England	GALAXY
GARLAND	Garland Publishing, Inc. 717 5th Avenue, #2500 New York, NY 10022-8101	
GARZON	Éditions J. Garzon 13 rue de l'Échiquier F-75010 Paris France	
GEHRMANS	Carl Gehrmans Musikförlag Odengatan 84 Box 6005 S-102 31 Stockholm Sweden	BOOSEY
GEMINI	Gemini Press Music Div. of the Pilgrim Press Box 390 Otis, MA 01253	PRESSER
GENERAL	General Music Publishing Co., Inc. 145 Palisade Street Dobbs Ferry, NY 10522	BOSTON
GENERAL WDS	General Words and Music Co.	KJOS
GENESIS	Genesis	PLYMOUTH

Code	Publisher	U.S. Agent
GENTRY	Gentry Publications P.O. Box 570567 Tarzana, CA 91356	ANTARA
GERIG	Musikverlage Hans Gerig Drususgasse 7-11 (Am Museum) D-5000 Köln 1 Germany	BREITKOPF-W
GIA	GIA Publications 7404 South Mason Avenue Chicago, IL 60638	
GILBERT	Gilbert Publications 4209 Manitou Way Madison, WI 53711	
GILLMAN	Gillman Publications P.O. Box 155 San Clemente, CA 92672	
GILPIN	Gilpin-McPheeters Publishing	INTRADA
GLOCKEN	Glocken Verlag Ltd. 12-14 Mortimer Street London W1N 8EL England	EUR.AM.MUS.
GLORY	Glory Sound Delaware Water Gap, PA 18327	SHAWNEE
GLOUCHESTER	Glouchester Press P.O. Box 1044 Fairmont, WV 26554	HEILMAN
GM	G & M International Music Dealers 1225 Candlewood Hill Road Box 2098 Northbrook, IL 60062	
GOLDEN	Golden Music Publishing Co. P.O. Box 383 Golden, CO 80402-0383	
GOODLIFE	Goodlife Publications	CPP-BEL
GOODMAN	Goodman Group (formerly Regent, Arc & Goodman)	WARNER LEONARD-US (choral)
GOODWIN	Goodwin & Tabb Publishing, Ltd.	PRESSER
GORDON	Gordon Music Co. Box 2250 Canoga Park, CA 91306	
GORNSTON	David Gornston	FOX,S
GOSPEL	Gospel Publishing House 1445 Boonville Avenue Springfield, MO 65802	
GRAHL	Grahl & Nicklas Braubachstraβe 24 D-6 Frankfurt-am-Main Germany	
GRANCINO	Grancino Editions 15020 Burwood Dr. Lake Mathews, CA 92370	
	Grancino Editions 2 Bishopswood Road London N6 4PR England	
	Grancino Editions Schirmerweg 12 D-8 München 60 Germany	
GRAS	Éditions Gras 36 rue Pape-Carpentier F-72200 La Flèche (Sarthe) France	SOUTHERN
GRAY	H.W. Gray Co., Inc.	CPP-BEL PRESSER (rental)

Code	Publisher	U.S. Agent
GREENE ST.	Greene Street Music 354 Van Duzer Street Stapleton, NY 10304	
GREENWOOD	Greenwood Press, Inc. 88 Post Road West P.O. Box 5007 Westport, CT 06881	WORLD
GREGG	Gregg International Publishers, Ltd. 1 Westmead, Farnborough Hants GU14 7RU England	
GREGGMS	Gregg Music Sources P.O. Box 868 Novato, CA 94947	
	Gregorian Institute of America see GIA	
GROEN	Muziekuitgeverij Saul B. Groen Ferdinand Bolstraat 6 NL-1072 LJ Amsterdam Netherlands	
GROSCH	Edition Grosch Phillip Grosch Bahnhofstrasse 94a D-8032 Gräfelfing Germany	THOMI
GROVEN	Eivind Grovens Institutt for Reinstemming Ekebergveien 59 N-1181 Oslo 11 Norway	
GUARANI	Ediciones Musicals Mundo Guarani Sarmiento 444 Buenos Aires Argentina	
GUILYS	Edition Guilys Case Postale 90 CH-1702 Fribourg 2 Switzerland	
GUNMAR	Gunmar Music, Inc. see Margun/Gunmar Music, Inc.	JERONA
HA MA R	Ha Ma R Percussion Publications, Inc. 333 Spring Road Huntington, NY 11743	BOOSEY
HAMBLEN	Stuart Hamblen Music Co. 26101 Ravenhill Road Canyon Country, CA 91351	
HAMELLE	Hamelle & Cie 175 rue Saint-Honoré F-75040 Paris Cedex 01 France	KING,R PRESSER SOUTHERN
HAMPE	Adolf Hampe Musikverlag Hohenzollerndamm 54A D-1000 Berlin 33 Germany	BUDDE
HAMPTON	Hampton Edition	MARKS
HANSEN-DEN	Wilhelm Hansen Musikforlag Bornholmsgade 1,1 1266 Copenhagen K Denmark	SCHIRM.G
HANSEN-ENG	Hansen, London see CHESTER	
HANSEN-FIN	Edition Wilhelm Hansen, Helsinki	SCHIRM.G
HANSEN-GER	Edition Wilhelm Hansen, Frankfurt	SCHIRM.G
HANSEN-NY	Edition Wilhelm Hansen-Chester Music New York Inc. New York, NY	SCHIRM.G

Code	Publisher	U.S. Agent
HANSEN-SWED	Edition Wilhelm Hansen see NORDISKA	SCHIRM.G
HANSEN-US	Hansen House Publications, Inc. 1824 West Avenue Miami Beach, FL 33139-9913	
HÄNSSLER	Hänssler-Verlag Röntgenstrasse 15 Postfach 1230 D-7312 Kirchheim/Teck Germany	ANTARA
HARGAIL	Hargail Music Press P.O. Box 118 Saugerties, NY 12477	CPP-BEL
HARMONIA	Harmonia-Uitgave P.O. Box 210 NL-1230 AE Loosdrecht Netherlands	FOR.MUS.DIST.
HARMS,TB	T.B. Harms	WARNER
HARMUSE	Harmuse Publications 529 Speers Road Oakville, Ontario L6K 2G4 Canada	
HARP PUB	Harp Publications 3437-2 Tice Creek Drive Walnut Creek, CA 94595	
HARRIS	Frederick Harris Music Co., Ltd. 529 Speers Road Oakville, Ontario L6K 2G4 Canada	HARRIS-US
HARRIS-US	Frederick Harris Company, Ltd. 340 Nagel Drive Buffalo, NY 14225-4731	
HARRIS,R	Ron Harris Publications 22643 Paul Revere Drive Woodland Hills, CA 91364	ALEX.HSE.
HART	F. Pitman Hart & Co., Ltd.	BRODT
HARTH	Harth Musikverlag Karl-Liebknecht-Straße 12 D-701 Leipzig Germany	PRO MUSICA
HASLINGER	Verlag Carl Haslinger Tuchlauben 11 A-1010 Wien Austria	FOR.MUS.DIST.
HASTINGS	Hastings Music Corp.	CPP-BEL
HATCH	Earl Hatch Publications 5008 Aukland Ave. Hollywood, CA 91601	
HATIKVAH	Hatikvah Publications	TRANSCON.
HAWK	Hawk Music Press 668 Fairmont Avenue Oakland, CA 94611	
HAYMOZ	Haydn-Mozart Presse	EUR.AM.MUS.
	Hebrew Union College Sacred Music Press see SAC.MUS.PR.	
HEER	Joh. de Heer & Zn. B.V. Muziek-Uitgeverij en Groothandel Rozenlaan 113, Postbus 3089 NL-3003 AB Rotterdam Netherlands	
HEIDELBERGER	Heidelberger	BÄREN.
HEILMAN	Heilman Music P.O. Box 1044 Fairmont, WV 26554	

Code	Publisher	U.S. Agent
HEINN	Heilmann Publications P.O. Box 18180 Pittsburgh, PA 15236	
HEINRICH.	Heinrichshofen's Verlag Liebigstraβe 16 Postfach 620 D-26354 Wilhelmshaven Germany	PETERS
HELBING	Edition Helbling Kaplanstraβe 9 A-6021 Neu-Rum b. Innsbruck Austria	
HELBS	Helbling Edition Pffäfikerstraβe 6 CH-8604 Voketswil-Zürich Switzerland	
HELICON	Helicon Music Corp.	EUR.AM.MUS.
HELIOS	Editio Helios	FOSTER
HENDON	Hendon Music	BOOSEY
HENKLE	Ted Henkle 5415 Reynolds Street Savannah, GA 31405	
HENLE	G. Henle Verlag Forstenrieder Allee 122 Postfach 71 04 66 D-81454 München Germany G. Henle USA, Inc. P.O. Box 1753 2446 Centerline Industrial Drive St. Louis, MO 63043	
HENMAR	Henmar Press	PETERS
HENN	Editions Henn 8 rue de Hesse Genève Switzerland	
HENREES	Henrees Music Ltd.	EMI
HERALD	Herald Press 616 Walnut Avenue Scottdale, PA 15683	
HERITAGE	Heritage Music Press	LORENZ
HERITAGE PUB	Heritage Music Publishing Co.	CENTURY
HEUGEL	Heugel & Cie 175 rue Saint-Honoré F-75040 Paris Cedex 01 France	KING,R PRESSER SOUTHERN
HEUWEKE.	Edition Heuwekemeijer & Zoon Postbus 289 NL-1740 AG Schagen Netherlands	PRESSER
HHP	Hollow Hills Press 7 Landview Drive Dix Hills, NY 11746	
HIEBER	Musikverlag Max Hieber KG Postfach 330429 D-80064 München Germany	
HIGH GR	Higher Ground Music Publishing	ALEX.HSE.
HIGHGATE	Highgate Press	SCHIRM.EC
HIGHLAND	Highland/Etling Music Co. 1344 Newport Avenue Long Beach, CA 90804	
HILD	Hildegard Publishing Co. Box 332 Bryn Mawr, PA 19010	
HINRICHSEN	Hinrichsen Edition, Ltd.	PETERS

Code	Publisher	U.S. Agent
HINSHAW	Hinshaw Music, Inc. P.O. Box 470 Chapel Hill, NC 27514	
HINZ	Hinz Fabrik Verlag Lankwitzerstraβe 17-18 D-1000 Berlin 42 Germany	
HIRSCHS	Abr. Hirschs Forlag Box 505 S-101 26 Stockholm Sweden	GEHRMANS
HISPAVOX	Ediciones Musicales Hispavox Cuesta Je Santo Domingo 11 Madrid Spain	
HLH	HLH Music Publications 611 Broadway, Suite 615 New York, NY 10012	MUSIC SC.
HOA	HOA Music Publisher 756 S. Third Street Dekalb, IL 60115	
HOFFMAN,R	Raymond A. Hoffman Co. c/o Fred Bock Music Co. P.O. Box 333 Tarzana, CA 91356	ANTARA
HOFMEISTER	VEB Friedrich Hofmeister, Musikverlag, Leipzig Karlstraβ 10 D-701 Leipzig Germany	
HOFMEISTER-W	Friedrich Hofmeister Musikverlag, Taunus Ubierstraβe 20 D-6238 Hofheim am Taunus Germany	
HOHLER	Heinrich Hohler Verlag	SCHNEIDER,H
	Hollow Hills Press see HHP	
HOLLY-PIX	Holly-Pix Music Publishing Co.	WESTERN
HONG KONG	Hong Kong Music Media Publishing Co., Ltd. Kai It Building, 9th Floor 58 Pak Tai Street Tokwawan, Kowloon Hong Kong	
HONOUR	Honour Publications	WESTERN
HOPE	Hope Publishing Co. 380 South Main Place Carol Stream, IL 60188	
HORNPIPE	Hornpipe Music Publishing Co. 400 Commonwealth Avenue P.O. Box CY577 Boston, MA 02215	
HUEBER	Hueber-Holzmann Pädagogischer Verlag Krausstraβe 30 D-8045 Ismaning, München Germany	
HUG	Hug & Co. Flughofstrasse 61 CH-Glattbrugg Switzerland	EUR.AM.MUS
HUGUENIN	Charles Huguenin & Pro-Arte Rue du Sapin 2a CH-2114 Fleurier Switzerland	
HUHN	W. Huhn Musikalien-Verlag Jahnstraβe 9 D-5880 Lüdenshied Germany	

Code	Publisher	U.S. Agent
HULST	De Hulst Kruisdagenlaan 75 B-1040 Bruxelles Belgium	
HUNTZINGER	R.L. Huntzinger Publications	WILLIS
HURON	Huron Press P.O. Box 2121 London, Ontario N6A 4C5 Canada	
ICELAND	Íslenzk Tónverkamidstöd Iceland Music Information Centre Sidumuli 34 108 Reykjavik Iceland	
IISM	Istituto Italiano per la Storia della Musica Academia Nazionale di Santa Cecilia Via Vittoria, 6 I-00187 Roma Italy	
IMB	Internationale Musikbibliothek	BÄREN.
IMC	Indiana Music Center 322 South Swain P.O. Box 582 Bloomington, IN 47401	
IMPERO	Impero-Verlag Liebigstraβe 16 D-2940 Wilhelmshavn Germany	PRESSER (partial)
INDEPENDENT	Independent Publications P.O. Box 162 Park Station Paterson, NJ 07513	
INDIANA	Indiana University Press 601 N. Morton Street Bloomington, IN 47404-3797	
INST ANT	Instrumenta Antiqua, Inc. 2530 California Street San Francisco, CA 94115	
INST.CO.	The Instrumentalist 200 Northfield Road Northfield, IL 60093-3390	
	Institue Of Stringed Instruments Guitar & Lute see ISI	
	Editorial Cooperativa Inter-Americana de Compositores see ECOAM	
INTERLOCH	Interlochen Press	CRESCENDO
INTERNAT.	International Music Co. 5 W. 37th Street New York, NY 10018	
INTER.MUS.P.	International Music Publications Woodford Trading Estate Southend Road Woodford Green, Essex IG8 8HN England	
	Internationale Musikbibliothek see IMB	
INTERNAT.S.	International Music Service P.O. Box 66, Ansonia Station New York, NY 10023	
INTRADA	Intrada Music Group P.O. Box 1240 Anderson, IN 46015	
IONA	Iona Music Publishing Service P.O. Box 8131 San Marino, CA 91108	

Code	Publisher	U.S. Agent
IONE	Ione Press	SCHIRM.EC
IRIS	Iris Verlag Hernerstraβe 64A Postfach 100.851 D-4350 Recklinghausen Germany	
IROQUOIS PR	Iroquois Press P.O. Box 2121 London, Ontario N6A 4C5 Canada	
	Íslenzk Tónverkamidstöd see ICELAND	
ISI	Institute of Stringed Instruments, Guitar & Lute Poststraβe 30 4 Düsseldorf Germany	SANDVOSS
	Aux Presses d'Isle-de-France see PRESSES	
ISR.MUS.INST.	Israel Music Institute P.O. Box 3004 61030 Tel Aviv Israel	PRESSER
ISR.PUB.AG.	Israel Publishers Agency 7, Arlosoroff Street Tel-Aviv Israel	
ISRAELI	Israeli Music Publications, Ltd. 25 Keren Hayesod Jerusalem 94188 Israel	PRESSER
	Istituto Italiano per la Storia della Musica see IISM	
J.B.PUB	J.B. Publications 404 Holmes Circle Memphis, TN 38111	
J.C.A.	Japan Composers Association 3-7-15, Akasaka Minato-Ku Tokyo Japan	
JACKMAN	Jackman Music Corp. P.O. Box 900 Orem, UT 84057	MUSICART
JAPAN	Japan Federation of Composers Shinanomachi Building 602 33 Shinanomachi Shinjuku-Ku Tokyo Japan	
JAREN	Jaren Music Co. 9691 Brynmar Drive Villa Park, CA 92667	
JASE	Jasemusiikki Ky Box 136 SF-13101 Hàmeenlinna 10 Finland	
JAZZ ED	Jazz Education Publications P.O. Box 802 Manhattan, KS 66502	
JEANNETTE	Ed. Jeannette	DONEMUS
JEHLE	Jehle	HÄNSSLER
JENSON	Jenson Publications, Inc. 7777 W. Bluemound Road Milwaukee, WI 53213	LEONARD-US
JERONA	Jerona Music Corp. P.O. Box 5010 Hackensack, NJ 07606-4210	

Code	Publisher	U.S. Agent
JOAD	Joad Press 4 Meredyth Road London SW13 0DY England	FISCHER,C (rental-partial)
JOBERT	Editions Jean Jobert 76, rue Quincampoix F-75003 Paris France	PRESSER
JOED	Joed Music Publications 234 Stanley Park Road Carshalton Beeches Surrey, SM5 3JP England	
JOHNSON	Johnson Reprint Corp. 757 3rd Avenue New York, NY 10017	
JOHNSON,P	Paul Johnson Productions P.O. Box 2001 Irving, TX 75061	
JOSHUA	Joshua Corp.	SCHIRM.G
JOY	Joy Music Press	INTRADA
JRB	JRB Music Education Materials Distributor	PRESSER
JUNNE	Otto Junne GmbH Sendlinger-Tor-Platz 10 D-8000 München Germany	
JUS-AUTOR	Jus-Autor Sofia, Bulgaria	BREITKOPF-W
JUSKO	Jusko Publications	WILLIS
KAHNT	C.F. Kahnt, Musikverlag Kennedyallee 101 6000 Frankfurt 70 Germany	PETERS
KALLISTI	Kallisti Music Press 810 South Saint Bernard Street Philadelphia, PA 19143-3309	
KALMUS	Edwin F. Kalmus P.O. Box 5011 Boca Raton, FL 33431	CPP-BEL (string and miniature scores)
KALMUS,A	Alfred A. Kalmus Ltd. 38 Eldon Way, Paddock Wood Tonbridge, Kent TN12 6BE England	EUR.AM.MUS.
KAMMEN	J. & J. Kammen Music Co.	CENTURY
KAPLAN	Ida R. Kaplan 1308 Olivia Avenue Ann Arbor, MI 48104	
KARTHAUSE	Karthause Verlag Panzermacherstrasse 5 D-5860 Iserlohn Germany	
KAWAI	Kawai Gafuku	JAPAN
KAWE	Edition KaWe Brederodestraat 90 NL-1054 VC Amsterdam 13 Netherlands	KING,R
KAY PR	Kay Press 612 Vicennes Court Cincinnati, OH 45231	
KELTON	Kelton Publications 1343 Amalfi Drive Pacific Palisades, CA 90272	
KENDALE	Kendale Company 6595 S. Dayton Street Englewood, CO 80111	

Code	Publisher	U.S. Agent
KENDOR	Kendor Music Inc. Main & Grove Streets P.O. Box 278 Delevan, NY 14042	
KENSING.	Kensington Music Service P.O. Box 471 Tenafly, NJ 07670	
KENYON	Kenyon Publications	LEONARD-US
KERBY	E.C. Kerby Ltd. 198 Davenport Road Toronto, Ontario M5R IJ2 Canada	LEONARD-US BOOSEY (rental)
KIMM	Kimmel Publications, Inc. P.O. Box 1472 Decatur, IL 62522	HOPE
KINDRED	Kindred Press	HERALD
KING,R	Robert King Sales, Inc. Shovel Shop Square 28 Main Street, Bldg. 15 North Easton, MA 02356	
KING'S	King's Music Redcroft, Bank's End Wyton, Huntingdon Cambridgeshire PE17 2AA England	
KIRK	Kirkland House	LORENZ
KISTNER	Fr. Kistner & C.F.W. Siegel & Co. Adrian-Kiels-Straße 2 D-5000 Köln 90 Germany	CONCORDIA
KJOS	Neil A. Kjos Music Co. 4382 Jutland Drive Box 178270 San Diego, CA 92117-0894	
KLIMENT	Musikverlag Johann Kliment Kolingasse 15 A-1090 Wien 9 Austria	
KNEUSSLIN	Edition Kneusslin Amselstraße 43 CH-4059 Basel Switzerland	FOR.MUS.DIST.
KNOPF	Alfred A. Knopf 201 East 50th Street New York, NY 10022	
KNUF	Frits Knuf Uitgeverij Rodeheldenstraat 13 P.O. Box 720 NL-4116 ZJ Buren Netherlands	PENDRGN
KODALY	Kodaly Center of America, Inc. 1326 Washington Street West Newton, MA 02165	SUPPORT
KON BOND	Kon. Bond van Chr. Zang- en Oratoriumverenigingen	DONEMUS
KONINKLIJK	Koninklijk Nederlands Zangersverbond	DONEMUS
KOPER	Musikverlag Karl-Heinz Köper Schneekoppenweg 12 D-3001 Isernhagen NB/Hannover Germany	
KRENN	Ludwig Krenn Verlag Neulerchenfelderstr. 3-7 A-1160 Wien Austria	
KROMPHOLZ	Krompholz & Co Spitalgasse 28 CH-3001 Bern Switzerland	

Code	Publisher	U.S. Agent
KRUSEMAN	Ed. Philip Kruseman	DONEMUS
KUNZEL	Edition Kunzelmann Grutstrasse 28 CH-8134 Adliswil Switzerland	FOR.MUS.DIST.
KYSAR	Michael Kysar 1250 South 211th Place Seattle, WA 98148	
LAB	Editions Labatiaz Case Postale 112 CH-1890 St. Maurice Switzerland	
LAKES	Lake State Publishers P.O. Box 1593 Grand Rapids, MI 49501	
LAMP	Latin-American Music Pub. Co. Ltd. 8 Denmark Street London England	
LAND	A. Land & Zn. Muziekuitgevers	DONEMUS
LANDES	Landesverband Evangelischer Kirchenchöre in Bayern	HÄNSSLER
LANG	Lang Music Publications P.O. Box 11021 Indianapolis, IN 46201	
LANSMAN	Länsmansgarden PL-7012 S-762 00 Rimbo Sweden	
	Latin-American Music Pub. Co. Ltd. see LAMP	
LARK	Lark Publishing	INTRADA
LATINL	The Latin American Literary Review Press 2300 Palmer St. Pittsburgh, PA 15218	
LAUDA	Laudamus Press	INTRADA
LAUDINELLA	Laudinella Reihe	FOSTER
LAUMANN	Laumann Verlag Alter Gartenweg 14 Postfach 1360 D-4408 Dülmen Germany	
LAUREL	Laurel Press	LORENZ
LAURN	Laurendale Associates 15035 Wyandotte Street Van Nuys, CA 91405	
LAVENDER	Lavender Publications, Ltd. Borough Green Sevenoaks, Kent TN15 8DT England	
LAWSON	Lawson-Gould Music Publishers, Inc. 250 W. 57th St., Suite 932 New York, NY 10107	ALFRED
LEA	Lea Pocket Scores P.O. Box 138, Audubon Station New York, NY 10032	EUR.AM.MUS.
LEAWOOD	Leawood Music Press	ANTARA
LEDUC	Alphonse Leduc 175 rue Saint-Honoré F-75040 Paris Cedex 01 France	KING,R PRESSER (rental)
LEE	Norman Lee Publishing, Inc. Box 528 Oskaloosa, IA 52577	BARNHS

Code	Publisher	U.S. Agent
LEEDS	Leeds Music Ltd. MCA Building 2450 Victoria Park Avenue Willowdale, Ontario M2J 4A2 Canada	MCA PRESSER (rental)
LEMOINE	Henry Lemoine & Cie 17, rue Pigalle F-75009 Paris France	PRESSER
LENGNICK	Alfred Lengnick & Co., Ltd. Purley Oaks Studios 421a Brighton Road South Croydon, Surrey CR2 6YR England	
LEONARD-ENG	Leonard, Gould & Bolttler 60-62 Clerkenwell Road London EC1M 5PY England	
LEONARD-US	Hal Leonard Music 7777 West Bluemound Road Milwaukee, WI 53213	
LESLIE	Leslie Music Supply P.O. Box 471 Oakville, Ontario L6J 5A8 Canada	BRODT
LEUCKART	F.E.C. Leuckart Nibelungenstraβe 48 D-8000 München 19 Germany	
LEXICON	Lexicon Music P.O. Box 2222 Newbury Park, CA 91320	ALEX.HSE.
LIBEN	Liben Music Publications 1191 Eversole Road Cincinnati, OH 45230	
LIBER	Svenska Utbildningsförlaget Liber AB Utbildningsförlaget, Centrallagret S-136 01 Handen Stockholm Sweden	
LICHTENAUER	W.F. Lichtenauer	DONEMUS
LIED	VEB Lied der Zeit Musikverlag Rosa-Luxemburg-Straβe 41 D-102 Berlin Germany	
LIENAU	Robert Lienau, Musikverlag Hildegardstr. 16 D-10715 Berlin Germany	
LIGA	Liga de Compositores de Musica de Concierto de Mexico, A.C. Mayorazgo No. 129 Col. Xoco 03330, Mexico, D.F. Mexico	
LIGHT	Light of the World Music	INTRADA
LILLENAS	Lillenas Publishing Co. P.O. Box 419527 Kansas City, MO 64141	
LINDSAY	Lindsay Music 23 Hitchin Street Biggleswade, Beds SG18 8AX England	PRESSER
LINDSBORG	Lindsborg Press P.O. Box 737 State Road 9 South Alexandria, VA 46001	ANTARA

Code	Publisher	U.S. Agent
LINGUA	Lingua Press % 1st Ntl Bk 310 S. Hamel Road Los Angeles, CA 90048-3844	
LISTER	Mosie Lister	LILLENAS
LITOLFF,H	Henry Litolff's Verlag Kennedy Allee 101 Postfach 700906 D-6000 Frankfurt 70 Germany	PETERS
LITURGICAL	Liturgical Music Press St. Johns Abbey Collegeville, MN 56321	
LLUQUET	Guillermo Lluquet Almacen General de Musica Avendida del Oeste 43 Valencia Spain	
	London Pro Musica Edition see LPME	
LONG ISLE	Long Island Music Publishers	BRANCH
LOOP	Loop Music Co.	KJOS
LORENZ	Lorenz Corporation 501 East Third Street P.O. Box 802 Dayton, OH 45401-9969	
LPME	The London Pro Musica Edition 15 Rock Street Brighton BN2 1NF England	MAGNA D
LUCKS	Luck's Music Library P.O. Box 71397 Madison Heights, MI 48071	
LUDWIG	Ludwig Music Publishing Co. 557-67 East 140th Street Cleveland, OH 44110-1999	
LUNDEN	Edition Lundén Bromsvagen 25 S-125 30 Alvsjö Sweden	
LUNDMARK	Lundmark Publications 811 Bayliss Drive Marietta, GA 30067	SUPPORT
LUNDQUIST	Abr. Lundquist Musikförlag AB Katarina Bangata 17 S-116 25 Stockholm Sweden	
LYCHE	Harald Lyche Postboks 2171 Stromso N-3003 Drammen Norway	WALTON (partial)
LYDIAN ORCH	Lydian Orchestrations 31000 Ruth Hill Road Orange Cove, CA 93646	SHAWNEE
LYNWD	Lynwood Music Photo Editions 2 Church St. West Hagley West Midlands DY9 0NA England	
LYRA	Lyra Music Co. 133 West 69th Street New York, NY 10023	
MAA	Music Associates of America 224 King Street Englewood, NJ 07631	
MACNUTT	Richard Macnutt Ltd. Hamm Farm House Withyham, Hartfield Sussex TN7 4BJ England	

Code	Publisher	U.S. Agent
	Mac Murray Publications see MMP	
MAGNA D	Magnamusic Distributors Route 49 Sharon, CT 06069	
MALCOLM	Malcolm Music Ltd.	SHAWNEE
MANNA	Manna Music, Inc. 22510 Stanford Avenue Suite 101 Valencia, CA 91355	
MANNHEIM	Mannheimer Musikverlag Kunigundestraβe 4 D-5300 Bonn 2 Germany	
MANU. PUB	Manuscript Publications 120 Maple Street Wrightsville, PA 17368	
MAPA MUNDI	Mapa Mundi—Music Publishers 72 Brewery Road London N7 9NE England	SCHIRM.EC
MARBOT	Edition Marbot GmbH Mühlenkamp 43 D-2000 Hamburg 60 Germany	PEER
MARCHAND	Marchand, Paap en Strooker	DONEMUS
MARGUN	Margun/Gunmar Music, Inc. 167 Dudley Road Newton Centre, MA 02159	JERONA
MARI	E. & O. Mari, Inc. 38-01 23rd Avenue Long Island City, NY 11105	
MARK	Mark Publications	CRESPUB
MARKS	Edward B. Marks Music Corp. 1619 Broadway New York, NY 10019	LEONARD-US (sales) PRESSER (rental)
MARSEG	Marseg, Ltd. 18 Farmstead Road Willowdale, Ontario M2L 2G2 Canada	
MARTIN	Editions Robert Martin 106, Grande rue de la Coupée F-71009 Charnay-les-Macon France	PRESSER
MASTER	Master Music	CRESPUB
MASTERS	Masters Music Publications P.O. Box 810157 Boca Raton, FL 33481-0157	
MAURER	J. Maurer Avenue du Verseau 7 B-1020 Brussel Belgium	
MAURRI	Edizioni Musicali Ditta R. Maurri Via del Corso 1 (17R.) Firenze Italy	
MAYHEW	Kevin Mayhew LTD. Rattlesden Bury St. Edmunds Suffolk IP30 0SZ England	BRODT
MCA	MCA and Mills/MCA Joint Venture Editions 1755 Broadway, 8th Floor New York, NY 10019	LEONARD-US (sales) PRESSER (rental)
MCAFEE	McAfee Music Corp.	CPP-BEL

Code	Publisher	U.S. Agent
MCGIN-MARX	McGinnis & Marx 236 West 26th Street, #11S New York, NY 10001	
MDV	Mitteldeutscher Verlag Thalmannplatz 2, Postfach 295 D-4010 Halle — Saale Germany	PETERS
MEDIA	Media Press P.O. Box 250 Elwyn, PA 19063	
MEDICI	Medici Music Press 5017 Veach Road Owensboro, KY 42301-9643	
MEDIT	Mediterranean	GALAXY
MEL BAY	Mel Bay Publications, Inc. P.O. Box 66 Pacific, MO 63069	
MELE LOKE	Mele Loke Publishing Co. Box 7142 Honolulu, Hawaii 96821	HIGHLAND (continental U.S.A)
MELODI	Casa Editrice Melodi S.A. Galleria Del Corso 4 Milano Italy	
MENC	Music Educators National Conference Publications Division 1902 Association Drive Reston, VA 22091	
MERCATOR	Mercator Verlag & Wohlfahrt (Gert) Verlag Köhnenstraβe 5-11 Postfach 100609 D-4100 Duisberg 1 Germany	
MERCURY	Mercury Music Corp.	PRESSER
MERIDIAN	Les Nouvelles Éditions Meridian 5, rue Lincoln F-75008 Paris 8 France	
MERION	Merion Music, Inc.	PRESSER
MERRYMOUNT	Merrymount Music, Inc.	PRESSER
MERSEBURGER	Merseburger Verlag Motzstraβe 13 D-3500 Kassel Germany	
METRO	Metro Muziek Uilenweg 38 Postbus 70 NL-6000 AB Weert Netherlands	
METROPOLIS	Editions Metropolis Van Ertbornstraat, 5 B-2108 Antwerpen Belgium	
MEULEMANS	Arthur Meulemans Fonds Charles de Costerlaan, 6 2050 Antwerpen Belgium	
MEXICANAS	Ediciones Mexicanas de Musica Avenida Juarez 18 Mexico City Mexico	PEER
MEZ KNIGA	Mezhdunarodnaya Kniga 39, Dimitrov St. Moscow 113095 Russia	
MIDDLE	Middle Eight Music	CPP-BEL
MILLER	Miller Music Corp.	CPP-BEL
MILLS MUSIC	Mills Music Jewish Catalogue	TRANSCON. PRESSER (rental)
MINKOFF	Minkoff Reprints 8 rue Eynard CH-1211 Genève 12 Switzerland	OMI
MIRA	Mira Music Associates 199 Mountain Road Wilton, CT 06897	
	Mitteldeutscher Verlag see MDV	
MJQ	M.J.Q. Music, Inc. 1697 Broadway #1100 New York, NY 10019	FOX,S
MMB	MMB Music, Inc. Contemporary Arts Building 3526 Washington Avenue St. Louis, MO 63103-1019	
MMP	Mac Murray Publications	MUS.SAC.PRO.
MMS	Monumenta Musica Svecicae	STIM
MOBART	Mobart Music Publications	JERONA
MOD ART	Modern Art Music	SON-KEY
MODERN	Edition Modern Rhodter Strasse 26 D-76185 Karlsruhe Germany	
MOECK	Hermann Moeck Verlag Postfach 143 D-3100 Celle 1 Germany	EUR.AM.MUS.
MOLENAAR	Molenaar's Muziekcentrale Industrieweg 23 Postbus 19 NL-1520 AA Wormerveer Netherlands	GM
MONDIAL	Mondial-Verlag KG 8 rue de Hesse Genève Switzerland	
MONTEVERDI	Fondazione Claudio Monteverdi Via Ugolani Dati, 4 1-26100 Cremona Italy	
MORAVIAN	Moravian Music Foundation	CPP-BEL BOOSEY BRODT PETERS
MORN.ST.	Morning Star Music Publishers 2117 59th St. St. Louis, MO 63110-2800	
MOSAIC	Mosaic Music Corporation	BOSTON
MÖSELER	Karl Heinrich Möseler Verlag Hoffman-von-Fallersleben-Straβe 8-10 Postfach 1661 D-3340 Wolfenbüttel Germany	
MOSER	Verlag G. Moser Kirschweg 8 CH-4144 Arlesheim Switzerland	
MOWBRAY	Mowbray Music Publications Saint Thomas House Becket Street Oxford OX1 1SJ England	PRESSER
MSM	MSM Music Publishers	BRODT

Code	Publisher	U.S. Agent
MT.SALUS	Mt. Salus Music 709 East Leake Street Clinton, MS 39056	
MT.TAHO	Mt. Tahoma	BROUDE,A
MÜLLER	Willy Müller, Süddeutscher Musikverlag Marzgasse 5 D-6900 Heidelberg Germany	
MUNSTER	Van Munster Editie	DONEMUS
MURPHY	Spud Murphy Publications	WESTERN
MUS.ANT.BOH.	Musica Antiqua Bohemica	SUPRAPHON
MUS.ART	Music Art Publications P.O. Box 1744 Chula Vista, CA 92010	
	Music Associates of America see MAA	
MUS.PERC.	Music For Percussion, Inc. 170 N.E. 33rd Street Fort Lauderdale, FL 33334	
MUS.RARA	Musica Rara Le Traversier Chemin de la Buire F-84170 Monteux France	
	Musica Russica see RUSSICA	
MUS.SAC.PRO	Musica Sacra et Profana P.O. Box 7248 Berkeley, CA 94707	
MUS.SB	Music Service Bureau 1645 Harvard St. NW Washington, D.C. 20009-3702	
MUS.SUR	Musica del Sur Apartado 5219 Barcelona Spain	
MUS.VERA	Musica Vera Graphics & Publishers 350 Richmond Terrace 4-M Staten Island, NY 10301	ARISTA
MUS.VIVA	Musica Viva 262 King's Drive Eastbourne Sussex, BN21 2XD England	
MUS.VIVA.HIST.	Musica Viva Historica	SUPRAPHON
MUSIA	Musia	PETERS
MUSIC	Music Sales Corp. Executive Offices 225 Park Avenue South New York, NY 10003 Music Sales Corp. (Rental) 5 Bellvale Road Chester, NY 10918	
MUSIC BOX	Music Box Dancer Publications Ltd.	PRESSER
	Music Educators National Conference see MENC	
MUSIC-ENG	Music Sales Ltd. Newmarket Road Bury St. Edmunds Suffolk IP33 3YB England	MUSIC
	Musica Russica see RUSSICA	
MUSIC INFO	Muzicki Informativni Centar—ZAMP Ulica 8 Maja 37 P.O. Box 959 Zagreb Croatia	BREITKOPF-W

Code	Publisher	U.S. Agent
MUSIC SC.	Musical Score Distributors 611 Broadway, Suite 615 New York, NY 10012	
MUSIC SEV.	Music 70, Music Publishers 170 N.E. 33rd Street Fort Lauderdale, FL 33334	
	Société d'Éditions Musicales Internationales see SEMI	PLYMOUTH
MUSICART	Musicart West P.O. Box 1900 Orem, UT 84059	
MUSICIANS PUB	Musicians Publications P.O. Box 7160 West Trenton, NJ 08628	
MUSICO	Musico Muziekuitgeverij	DONEMUS
MUSICPRINT	Musicprint Corporation P.O. Box 20767 New York, NY 10023	
MUSICUS	Edition Musicus P.O. Box 1341 Stamford, CT 06904	
MUSIKAL.	Musikaliska Konstföreningen Aarstryck, Sweden	WALTON
MUSIKHOJ	Musikhojskolens Forlag ApS	EUR.AM.MUS
MUSIKINST	Verlag das Musikinstrument Klüberstraße 9 D-6000 Frankfurt-am-Main Germany	
MUSIKK	Musikk-Huset A-S P.O. Box 822 Sentrum 0104 Oslo 1 Norway	
MUSIKWISS.	Musikwissenschaftlicher Verlag Wien Dorotheergasse 10 A-1010 Wien 1 Austria	FOR.MUS.DIST (Bruckner & Wolf)
	Muzicki Informativni Centar-Zamp see MUSIC INFO	
	Eerste Muziekcentrale see EERSTE	
MUZYKA	Muzyka Publishers 14 Neglinnaya Street 103031 Moscow Russia	
MYRRH	Myrrh Music	WORD
MYRTLE	Myrtle Monroe Music 2600 Tenth Street Berkeley, CA 94710	
NAGELS	Nagels Verlag	
NATIONAL	National Music Publishers 16605 Townhouse Tustin, CA 91680	ANTARA
NEUE	Verlag Neue Musik An der Kolonnade 15 Postfach 1306 D-1080 Berlin Germany	FOR.MUS.DIST
NEW HORIZON	New Horizon Publications	TRANSCON.
	New Music Edition see NME	
NEW MUSIC WEST	New Music West P.O. Box 7434 Van Nuys, CA 91409	

Code	Publisher	U.S. Agent
NEW VALLEY	New Valley Music Press of Smith College Sage Hall 49 Northampton, MA 01063	
NEW W	New World Enterprises of Montrose, Inc. 2 Marisa Court Montrose, NY 10548	
NEWAM	Foundation for New American Music	LUCKS
NGLANI	Edition Nglani Box 871 Merrifield, VA 22116-2871	
NIEUWE	De Nieuwe Muziekhandel	DONEMUS
NIPPON	Nippon Hosu	PRESSER
NL	NL Productions Inc.	PLUCKED ST
N.LIGHT	Northlight Music Inc.	SCHIRM.G
NME	New Music Edition	PRESSER
NO.AM.LIT.	North American Liturgy Resources Choral Music Department 10802 North 23rd Avenue Phoenix, AZ 85029	
NOBILE	Nobile Verlag Aixheimer Straβe 26 D-7000 Stuttgart 75 Germany	
NOETZEL	Noetzel Musikverlag Liebigstraβe 16 Postfach 620 D-2940 Wilhelmshavn Germany	PETERS
NOMOS	Edition Nomos	BREITKOPF-W
NOORDHOFF	P. Noordhoff	DONEMUS
NORDISKA	AB Nordiska Musikförlaget Nybrogatan 3 S-114 34 Stockholm Sweden see also HANSEN-SWEDEN	
NORGE	Norsk Musikkinformasjon Toftesgatan 69 N-0552 Olso 5 Norway	
NORK	Norske Komponisters Forlag Gjernesvegen 24 N-5700 Voss Norway	
NORRUTH	Norruth Music Publishers	MMB
NORSK	Norsk Musikforlag AS Karl Johansgaten 39 P.O. Box 1499 Vika N-0116 Oslo 1 Norway	
	Norske Komponisters Forlag see NORK	
	North American Liturgy Resources see NO.AM.LIT.	
	Northlight Music Inc. see N. LIGHT	
NORTHRIDGE	Northridge Music, Inc. 7317 Greenback Lane Citrus Heights, CA 95621	CPP-BEL
NORTON	W.W. Norton & Co., Inc. 500 Fifth Avenue New York, NY 10003	
	Norwegian Music Information Center see NORGE	

Code	Publisher	U.S. Agent
NOSKE	A.A. Noske	DONEMUS
NOTERIA	Noteria S-590 30 Borensberg Sweden	STIM
NOTON	Noton Kolltjernvn. 11 P.O. Box 1014 N-2301 Hamar Norway	
NOVA	Nova Music Ltd. Goldsmid Mews 15a Farm Road Hove Sussex BN3 1FB England	SCHIRM.EC
NOVELLO	Novello & Co., Ltd. Newmarket Road Bury St. Edmunds Suffolk IP33 3YB England	SHAWNEE MUSIC (rental)
NOW VIEW	Now View	PLYMOUTH
	Nuova Carisch s.r.l. Via M.F. Quintiliano, 40 20138 Milano Italy	
NYMPHEN	Edition Nymphenburg Unterföhring, Germany	PETERS
OAK	Oak Publications	MUSIC
OCTAVA	Octava Music Co. Ltd.	WEINBERGER
OECUM	Oecumuse 52a Broad St. Ely, CB7 4AH England	CANTORIS
OISEAU	Éditions de L'Oiseau-Lyre Les Remparts Boite Postale 515 MC-98015 Monaco Cedex	MAGNA D OMI
OJEDA	Raymond J. Ojeda 98 Briar Road Kentfield, CA 94904	
OKRA	Okra Music Corp.	SEESAW
OLIVIAN	Olivian Press	ARCADIA
OLMS	G. Olms Verlag Hagentorwall 7 D-3200 Hildesheim Germany	
OMI	OMI — Old Manuscripts & Incunabula P.O. Box 6019, FDR Station New York, NY 10150	
ONGAKU	Ongaku-No-Tomo Sha Co. Ltd. Kagurazaka 6-30, Shinjuku-ku Tokyo 162 Japan	PRESSER
OPUS	Opus Music Publishers, Inc. 1318 Chicago Avenue Evanston, IL 60201	
OPUS-CZ	Opus Ceskoslavenske Hudobne Vydaratelstro Mlynske nivy 73 827 99 Bratislava Slovakia	BOOSEY (rental)
OR-TAV	Or-Tav Music Publications Israel Composers League P.O. Box 3200 113, Allenby Street Tel-Aviv Israel	

Code	Publisher	U.S. Agent
ORGAN	Organ Music Co.	WESTERN
ORGAN LIT	Organ Literature Foundation 45 Norfolk Road Braintree, MA 02184	
ORGMS	Organmaster Music Series 282 Stepstone Hill Guilford, CT 06437	
ORION MUS	Orion Music Press P.O. Box 145, University Station Barrien Springs, MI 49104	OPUS
ORLANDO	Orlando Musikverlag Kaprunerstraβe 11 D-8000 München 21 Germany	
ORPHEUM	Orpheum Music 10th & Parker Berkeley, CA 94710	
OSTARA	Ostara Press, Inc.	WESTERN
ÖSTER	Österreichischer Bundesverlag Schwarzenberg Platz 5 A-1010 Wien Austria	
OSTIGUY	Editions Jacques Ostiguy Inc. 12790 Rue Yamaska St. Hyacinthe, Quebec Canada J2T 1B3	
OSTNOR	Φstnorsk Musikkforlag Nordre Langgate 1 B N-9950 Vardφ Norway	
OTOS	Otos Edizioni Musicali Via Marsillo Ficino, 10 I-50132 Firenze Italy	
OUVRIERES	Les Éditions Ouvrières 12, Avenue Soeur-Rosalie F-75621 Paris Cedex 13, France	KING,R
OXFORD	Oxford University Press 7-8 Hatherly Street London SW1P 2QT England	
OXFORD	Oxford University Press 200 Madison Avenue New York, NY 10016	
PACIF	Pacific Publications	INTRADA
PAGANI	O. Pagani & Bro., Inc. c/o P. Deiro Music 289 Bleeker Street New York, NY 10014	
PAGANINI PUB	Paganiniana Publications, Inc. 1 T.F.H. Plaza 3rd & Union Avenue Neptune City, NJ 07753	
PAIDEIA	Paideia Editrice	BÄREN.
PALLMA	Pallma Music Co.	KJOS
PAN	Editions Pan Schaffhauserstraβe 280 Postfach 176 CH-8057 Zürich Switzerland	PRESSER
PAN AM	Pan American Union	PEER
PAN F	Edition Pan of Finland Vihertie 56C 01620 Vantaa Finland	

Code	Publisher	U.S. Agent
PANTONH	Panton Radlická 99 CS-150 00 Praha 5 Czech Republic	NEW W
PARACLETE	Paraclete Press P.O. Box 1568 Hilltop Plaza, Route 6A Orleans, MA 02653	
PARAGON	Paragon Music Publishers	CENTURY
PARAGON ASS.	Paragon Associates	ALEX.HSE.
PARIS	Uitgeverij H.J. Paris	DONEMUS
PARKS	Parks Music Corp.	KJOS
PASTORALE	Pastorale Music Company 235 Sharon Drive San Antonio, TX 78216	
PASTORINI	Musikhaus Pastorini AG Kasinostraβe 25 CH-5000 Aarau Switzerland	
PATERSON	Paterson's Publications, Ltd. 8-10 Lower James Street London W1R 3PL England	MUSIC
	Patrimoine Musical Canadien see CAN.MUS.HER.	
PAVAN	Pavane Publishing P.O. Box 2931 San Anselmo, CA 94979	INTRADA
PAXTON	Paxton Publications Sevenoaks, Kent, England	PRESSER
PECK	Pecktackular Music 3605 Brandywine Drive Greensboro, NC 27410	
PEER	Peer Southern Concert Music 810 Seventh Avenue New York, NY 10019	PRESSER
PEER MUSIK	Peer Musikverlag GmbH Muhlenkamp 43 Postfach 602129 D-2000 Hamburg Germany	PEER
PEG	Pegasus Musikverlag Liebig Straβe 16 Postfach 620 D-2940 Wilhelmshaven Germany	PETERS
PELIC.C	Pelican Cay Publications	PLYMOUTH
PELIKAN	Musikverlag Pelikan	EUR.AM.MUS.
PEMBROKE	Pembroke Music Co., Inc.	FISCHER,C
PENADES	José Penadés En Sanz 12 Valencia Spain	
PENDRGN	Pendragon Press R.R. 1, Box 159 Stuyvesant, NY 12173-9720	
PENGUIN	Penguin Books 120 Woodbine Street Bergenfield, NJ 07621	
PENN STATE	Penn State Press The Pennsylvania State University Barbara Building, Suite C University Park, PA 16802-1003	
PENOLL	Penoll Goteberg, Sweden	STIM

Code	Publisher	U.S. Agent
PEPPER	J.W. Pepper And Son, Inc. P.O. Box 850 Valley Forge, PA 19482	
PERF.ED.	Performers' Editions	BROUDE BR.
PERFORM	Perform Our Music Leuven, Belgium	PEER
PERMUS	Permus Publications P.O. Box 02033 Columbus, OH 43202	
PETERER	Edition Melodie Anton Peterer Brunnwiesenstraße 26 Postfach 260 CH-8409 Zürich Switzerland	
PETERS	Edition Peters C.F. Peters Corp. 373 Park Avenue South New York, NY 10016	
	Edition Peters Postfach 746 D-7010 Leipzig Germany	
	C.F. Peters Musikverlag Postfach 700851 Kennedyallee 101 D-6000 Frankfurt 70 Germany	
	Peters Edition Ltd. Bach House 10-12 Baches Street London N1 6DN England	
PETERS,K	Kermit Peters 1515 90th Street Omaha, NE 68124	
PETERS,M	Mitchell Peters 3231 Benda Place Los Angeles, CA 90068	
PFAUEN	Pfauen Verlag Adolfsallee 34 Postfach 471 D-6200 Wiesbaden Germany	
PHILH	Philharmonia	EUR.AM.MUS. (miniature scores)
PHILIPPO	Editions Philippo	ELKAN-V
PHOEBUS	Phoebus Apollo Music Publishers 1126 Huston Drive West Mifflin, PA 15122	
PIEDMONT	Piedmont Music Co.	PRESSER (rental)
PILES	Piles Editorial de Musica Archena 33y Yatova, 4 Apartado 8.012 E-46080 Valencia Spain	
PILLIN	Pillin Music	WESTERN
PILLON	Pillon Press	THOMAS
PIONEER	Pioneer Music Press	MUSICART
PIPER	Piper Music Co. P.O. Box 1713 Cincinnati, OH 45201	LIBEN
PLAINSONG	Plainsong & Medieval Music Society Catherine Harbor, Hon. Sec. c/o Turner 72 Brewery Road London N7 9NE England	

Code	Publisher	U.S. Agent
PLAYER	Player Press 139-22 Caney Lane Rosedale, NY 11422	
PLENUM	Plenum Publishing Corp. 233 Spring Street New York, NY 10013	DA CAPO
PLESNICAR	Don Plesnicar P.O. Box 4880 Albuquerque, NM 87106	
PLOUGH	Plough Publishing House Rifton, NY 12471	
PLUCKED ST	Plucked String P.O. Box 11125 Arlington, VA 22210	
PLYMOUTH	Plymouth Music Co., Inc. 170 N.E. 33rd Street P.O. Box 24330 Fort Lauderdale, FL 33334	
PODIUM	Podium Music, Inc. 360 Port Washington Boulevard Port Washington, NY 11050	
POLSKIE	Polskie Wydawnictwo Muzyczne Al. Krasinskiego 11a PL31-111 Krakow Poland	PRESSER
POLYPH MUS	Polyphone Music Co.	ARCADIA
POLYPHON	Polyphon Musikverlag	BREITKOPF-W
PORT.MUS.	Portugaliae Musicae Fundaçao Calouste Gulbenkian Avenida de Berna 45 P-1093 Lisboa Codex Portugal	
	Postif Press Ltd. see BRENNAN	
POST	Posthorn Press	INTRADA
POWER	Power and Glory Music Co. 6595 S. Dayton St. Englewood, CO 80111	SON-KEY
PRAEGER	Praeger Publications 383 Madison Avenue New York, NY 10017	
PRB	PRB Productions 963 Peralta Avenue Albany, CA 94706-2144	
PREISSLER	Musikverlag Josef Preissler Postfach 521 Bräuhausstraße 8 D-8000 München 2 Germany	
PRELUDE	Prelude Publications 150 Wheeler Street Glouchester, MA 01930	
PRENTICE	Prentice-Hall, Inc. Englewood Cliffs, NJ 07632	
PRESSER	Theodore Presser Co. Presser Place Bryn Mawr, PA 19010	
PRESSES	Aux Presses d'Isle-de-France 12, rue de la Chaise F-75007 Paris France	
PRICE,P	Paul Price Publications 470 Kipp Street Teaneck, NJ 07666	
PRIMAVERA	Editions Primavera	GENERAL

Code	Publisher	U.S. Agent	Code	Publisher	U.S. Agent
PRINCE	Prince Publications 1125 Francisco Street San Francisco, CA 94109		RARITIES	Rarities For Strings Publications 11300 Juniper Drive University Circle Cleveland, OH 44106	
PRO ART	Pro Art Publications, Inc.	CPP-BEL	RAVEN	Raven Press 1185 Avenue of the Americas New York, NY 10036	
PRO MUSICA	Pro Musica Verlag Karl-Liebknecht-Straβe 12 Postfach 467 D-7010 Leipzig Germany		REAL	Real Musical Carlos III, no. 1 28013 Madrid, Spain	
PRO MUSICA INTL	Pro Musica International 130 Bylor P.O. Box 1687 Pueblo, CO 81002		RECITAL	Recital Publications, Ltd. P.O. Box 1697 Huntsville, TX 77342-1697	
PROCLAM	Proclamation Productions, Inc. Orange Square Port Jervis, NY 12771			Regent, Arc & Goodman see GOODMAN	
PROGRESS	Progress Press P.O. Box 12 Winnetka, IL 60093		REGENT	Regent Music Corp. 488 Madison Avenue 5th Floor New York, NY 10022	LEONARD-US
PROPRIUS	Proprius Musik AB Vartavagen 35 S-115 29 Stockholm Sweden		REGINA	Regina Verlag Schumannstraβe 35 Postfach 6148 D-6200 Wiesbaden 1 Germany	
PROSVETNI	Prosvetni Servis	DRUSTVO	REGUS	Regus Publisher 10 Birchwood Lane White Bear Lake, MN 55110	
PROVIDENCE	Providence Music Press 251 Weybosset St. Providence, RI 02903		REIMERS	Edition Reimers AB Box 15030 S-16115 Bromma Sweden	PRESSER
PROVINCTWN	Provincetown Bookshop Editions 246 Commercial Street Provincetown, MA 02657		REINHARDT	Friedrich Reinhardt Verlag Missionsstraβe 36 CH-4055 Basel Switzerland	
PROWSE	Keith Prowse Music Publishing Co. 138-140 Charing Cross Road London, WC2H 0LD England	INTER.MUS.P	REN	Les Editions Renaissantes	EUR.AM.MUS.
PRUETT	Pruett Publishing Co. 2928 Pearl Boulder, CO 80301-9989		RENK	Musikverlag Renk "Varia Edition" Herzog-Heinrich-Straβe 21 D-8000 München 2 Germany	
PSALTERY	Psaltery Music Publications P.O. Box 11325 Dallas, TX 75223	KENDALE	RESEARCH	Research Publications, Inc. Lunar Drive Woodbridge, CT 06525	
PSI	PSI Press P.O. Box 2320 Boulder, CO 80306		RESTOR	Restoration Press	THOMAS
PURIFOY	Purifoy Publishing P.O. Box 30157 Knoxville, TN 37930	JENSON	REUTER	Reuter & Reuter Förlags AB Box 26072 S-100 41 Stockholm Sweden	
PUSTET	Verlag Friedrich Pustet Gutenbergstraβe 8 Postfach 339 D-8400 Regensburg 11 Germany		RHODES,R	Roger Rhodes Music, Ltd. P.O. Box 1550, Radio City Station New York, NY 10101	
PYRAMINX	Pyraminx Publications	ACCURA	RICHMOND	Richmond Music Press, Inc. P.O. Box 465 Richmond, IN 47374	
QUEEN	Queensgate Music 120 Dowanhill Street Glasgow G12 9DN Scotland		RICHMOND ORG.	The Richmond Organization 11 W. 19th St., Suite 711 New York, NY 10011 see also TRO	PLYMOUTH
QUIROGA	Ediciones Quiroga Alcalá, 70 28009 Madrid Spain	PRESSER	RICORDI-ARG	Ricordi Americana S.A. Cangallo, 1558 1037 Buenos Aires Argentina	LEONARD-US BOOSEY (rental)
RAHTER	D. Rahter Werderstraβe 44 D-2000 Hamburg 13 Germany	PRESSER	RICORDI-BR	Ricordi Brasileira S.A. R. Conselheiro Nebias 773 1 S-10-12 Sao Paolo Brazil	LEONARD-US BOOSEY (rental)
RAMSEY	Basil Ramsey Publisher of Music	INTRADA			

Code	Publisher	U.S. Agent
RICORDI-CAN	G. Ricordi & Co. Toronto Canada	LEONARD-US BOOSEY (rental)
RICORDI-ENG	G. Ricordi & Co. Ltd. The Bury, Church Street Chesham, Bucks HP5 1JG England	LEONARD-US BOOSEY (rental)
RICORDI-FR	Société Anonyme des Éditions Ricordi	LEONARD-US BOOSEY (rental)
RICORDI-GER	G. Ricordi & Co. Gewürzmühlstraβe 5 D-8000 München 22 Germany	LEONARD-US BOOSEY (rental)
RICORDI-IT	G. Ricordi & Co. Via Salomone 77 I-20138 Milano Italy	LEONARD-US BOOSEY (rental)
RIDEAU	Les Éditions Rideau Rouge 24, rue de Longchamp F-75116 Paris France	PRESSER SCHIRM.G
RIES	Ries & Erler Charlottenbrunner Straβe 42 D-1000 Berlin 33 (Grunewald) Germany	
RILEY	Dr. Maurice W. Riley Eastern Michigan University 512 Roosevelt Boulevard Ypsilanti, MI 48197	
ROBBINS	Robbins Music Corp.	CPP-BEL PRESSER (rental)
ROBERTON	Roberton Publications The Windmill, Wendover Aylesbury, Bucks, HP22 6JJ England	PRESSER
ROBERTS,L	Lee Roberts Music Publications, Inc. P.O. Box 225 Katonah, NY 10536	
ROBITSCHEK	Adolf Robitschek Musikverlag Graben 14 (Bräunerstraβe 2) Postfach 42 A-1011 Wien Austria	
ROCHESTER	Rochester Music Publishers, Inc. 358 Aldrich Road Fairport, NY 14450	ACCURA
RODEHEAVER	Rodeheaver Publications	WORD
ROLLAND	Rolland String Research Associates 404 E. Oregon Urbana, IL 61801	BOOSEY
RONCORP	Roncorp, Inc. P.O. Box 724 Cherry Hill, NJ 08003	
RONGWEN	Rongwen Music, Inc.	BROUDE BR.
ROSSUM	Wed. J.R. van Rossum	ZENGERINK
ROUART	Rouart-Lerolle & Cie	SCHIRM.G
ROW	R.D. Row Music Co.	FISCHER,C
ROYAL	Royal School of Church Music Addington Palace Croydon, Surrey CR9 5AD England	
	Associated Board of the Royal Schools of Music see ABRSM	
ROYAL,TAP.	Royal Tapestry 50 Music Square West Suite 500A Nashville, TN 37203	ALEX.HSE.
ROZSAVÖ.	Rozsavölgi & Co.	BUDAPEST
RUBANK	Rubank, Inc. 16215 N.W. 15th Avenue Miami, FL 33169	LEONARD-US
RUBATO	Rubato Musikverlag Hollandstraβe 18 A-1020 Wien Austria	DONEMUS
RUH,E	Emil Ruh Musikverlag Zürichstraβe 33 CH-8134 Adliswil - Zürich Switzerland	
RUMAN.COMP.	Uniunea Compozitorilor din R.S. Românîa (Union of Rumanian Composers) Str. C. Escarcu No. 2 Bucureşti, Sector 1 Rumania	
RUSSICA	Musica Russica 27 Willow Lane Madison, CT 06443	
RUTGERS	Rutgers University Editions	JERONA
RYDET	Rydet Music Publishers P.O. Box 477 Purchase, NY 10577	
SAC.MUS.PR.	Sacred Music Press of Hebrew Union College One West Fourth Street New York, NY 10012	TRANSCON.
SACRED	Sacred Music Press	LORENZ
SACRED SNGS	Sacred Songs, Inc.	WORD
SALABERT	Francis Salabert Éditions 22 rue Chauchat F-75009 Paris France	LEONARD-US (sales) SCHIRM.G (rental)
SAMFUNDET	Samfundet til udgivelse af Dansk Musik Valkendorfsgade 3 DK-1151 Kobenhavn Denmark	PETERS
SAN ANDREAS	San Andreas Press 3732 Laguna Avenue Palo Alto, CA 94306	
SANJO	Sanjo Music Co. P.O. Box 7000-104 Palos Verdes Peninsula, CA 90274	
SAUL AVE	Saul Avenue Publishing Co. 4172 Fox Hollow Drive Cincinnati, OH 45241-2939	
SANTA	Santa Barbara Music Publishing P.O. Box 41003 Santa Barbara, CA 93140	
SAVGOS	Savgos Music Inc. P.O. Box 279 Elizabeth, NJ 07207	
SCARECROW	The Scarecorw Press, Inc. 52 Liberty Street P.O. Box 656 Metuchen, NJ 08840	
SCHAUM	Schaum Publications, Inc. 2018 East North Avenue Milwaukee, WI 53202	

Code	Publisher	U.S. Agent	Code	Publisher	U.S. Agent
SCHAUR	Richard Schauer, Music Publishers 67 Belsize Lane, Hampstead London NW3 5AX England	PRESSER	SCHWEIZER.	Schweizerischer Kirchengesangbund Markusstrasse 6 CH-2544 Bettlach Switzerland	FOSTER
SCHEIDT	Altonaer Scheidt-Ausgabe	HÄNSSLER	SCOTT	G. Scott Music Publishing Co.	WESTERN
SCHERZANDO	Muziekuitgeverij Scherzando Lovelingstraat 20-22 B-2000 Antwerpen Belgium		SCOTT MUSIC	Scott Music Publications	ALFRED
			SCOTUS	Scotus Music Publications, Ltd. see Eschenbach	ESCHENB
SCHIRM.EC	E.C. Schirmer Music Co. 138 Ipswich Street Boston, MA 02215-3534		SCREEN	Screen Gems Columbia Pictures	WARNER
SCHIRM.G	G. Schirmer, Inc. (Executive Offices) 257 Park Avenue South, 20th Floor New York, NY 10010	LEONARD-US (sales)	SDG PR	SDG Press 170 N.E. 33rd Street Ft. Lauderdale, FL 33334	PLYMOUTH
	G. Schirmer Rental Performance Dept. P.O. Box 572 5 Bellvale Road Chester, NY 10918		SEAMONT	Seamont International	INTRADA
SCHMIDT,H	Musikverlag Hermann Schmidt Berliner Straße 26 D-6000 Frankfurt-am-Main 1 Germany		SEESAW	Seesaw Music Corp. 2067 Broadway New York, NY 10023	
SCHMITT	Schmitt Music Editions	CPP-BEL	SELMER	Selmer Éditions 18, rue de la Fontaine-au-Roi F-75011 Paris France	
SCHNEIDER,H	Musikverlag Hans Schneider Mozartstraße 6 D-8132 Tutzing Germany		SEMI	Société d'Editions Musicales Internationales	PEER
SCHOLA	Editions Musicales de la Schola Cantorum Rue du Sapin 2A CH-2114 Fleurier Switzerland		SENART	Ed. Maurice Senart 22 rue Chauchat F-75009 Paris France	SCHIRM.G
SCHOTT	Schott & Co. Ltd. Brunswick Road Ashford, Kent TN23 1DX England	EUR.AM.MUS.	SEPT	September Music Corp. 250 W. 57th Street New York, NY 10019	
SCHOTT-FRER	Schott Frères 30 rue Saint-Jean B-1000 Bruxelles Belgium	EUR.AM.MUS.	SERENUS	Serenus Corp. 145 Palisade Street Dobbs Ferry, NY 10522	
SCHOTT,J	Schott & Co. Kasuga Bldg., 2-9-3 Iidabashi, Chiyoda-ku Tokyo 102 Japan	EUR.AM.MUS.	SERVANT	Servant Publications P.O. Box 8617 840 Airport Boulevard Ann Arbor, MI 48107	
SCHOTTS	B. Schotts Söhne Weihergarten 5 Postfach 3640 D-6500 Mainz Germany	EUR.AM.MUS.	SESAC	Sesac, Inc. 10 Columbus Circle New York, NY 10019	
			SHALL-U-MO	Shall-U-Mo Publications P.O. Box 2824 Rochester, NY 14626	
SCHROTH	Edition Schroth Kommandatenstrasse 5A D-1 Berlin 45 Germany	BÄREN.	SHAPIRO	Shapiro, Bernstein & Co., Inc. 10 East 53 Street New York, NY 10022	PLYMOUTH
SCHUBERTH	Edward Schuberth & Co., Inc.	CENTURY	SHATTINGER	Shattinger Music Co. 1810 S. Broadway St. Louis, MO 63104	
SCHUBERTH,J	J. Schuberth & Co. Rothenbaumchaussee 1 D-2000 Hamburg 13 Germany		SHAWNEE	Shawnee Press, Inc. 49 Waring Drive Delaware Water Gap, PA 18327-1099	MUSIC
SCHUL	Carl L. Schultheiß Denzenbergstraße 35 D-7400 Tübingen Germany		SHEPPARD	John Sheppard Music Press	EUR.AM.MUS.
				Antigua Casa Sherry-Brener, Ltd. see ACSB	
SCHULZ.FR	Blasmusikverlag Fritz Schulz Am Märzengraben 6 D-7800 Freiburg-Tiengen Germany		SIDEMTON	Sidemton Verlag	BREITKOPF-W
			SIFLER	Paul J. Sifler 3947 Fredonia Drive Hollywood, CA 90068	
SCHWANN	Musikverlag Schwann	PETERS	SIGHT & SOUND	Sight & Sound International 3200 South 166th Street Box 27 New Berlin, WI 53151	

Code	Publisher	U.S. Agent
SIJN	D. van Sijn & Zonen Banorstraat 1 Rotterdam Netherlands	
SIKORSKI	Hans Sikorski Verlag Johnsallee 23 Postfach 132001 D-2000 Hamburg 13 Germany	LEONARD-US
SIMROCK	Nicholas Simrock Lyra House 37 Belsize Lane London NW3 5AX England	PRESSER
SINGSPIR	Singspiration Music The Zondervan Corp. 1415 Lake Drive S.E. Grand Rapids, MI 49506	
SIRIUS	Sirius-Verlag	PETERS
SKAND.	Skandinavisk Musikforlag Gothersgade 9-11 DK-1123 Kφbenhavn K. Denmark	
SLATKINE	Slatkine Reprints 5 rue des Chaudronniers Case 765 CH-1211 Genève 3 Switzerland	
SLOV.AKA.	Slovenska Akademija Znanosti in Umetnosti Trg Francoske Revolucije 6 Ljubljana Slovenia	DRUSTVO
SLOV.HUD.FOND.	Slovenský Hudobný Fond Fucikova 29 811 02 Bratislava Slovakia	BOOSEY (rental)
SLOV.MAT	Slovenska Matica	DRUSTVO
SMITH PUB	Smith Publications-Sonic Art Editions 2617 Gwynndale Avenue Baltimore, MD 21207	
SMPF	SMPF, Inc. 16 E. 34th St., 7th Floor New York, NY 10016	
SOC.FR.MUS.	Société Française de Music	TRANSAT.
	Society for the Preservation & Encouragement of Barber Shop Quartet Singing in America see SPEBSQSA	
SOC.PUB.AM.	Society for the Publication of American Music	PRESSER
	Société d'Éditions Musicales Internationales see SEMI	
	Society of Finnish Composers see SUOMEN	
SOLAR	The Solar Studio 178 Cowles Road Woodbury, CT 06798	
SOLID	Solid Foundation Music	SON-KEY
SOMERSET	Somerset Press	HOPE
SON-KEY	Son-Key, Inc. P.O. Box 31757 Aurora, CO 80041	
SONANTE	Sonante Publications P.O. Box 74, Station F Toronto, Ontario M4Y 2L4 Canada	

Code	Publisher	U.S. Agent
SONOS	Sonos Music Resources, Inc. P.O. Box 1510 Orem, UT 84057	
SONSHINE	Sonshine Productions	LORENZ
SONZOGNO	Casa Musicale Sonzogno Via Bigli 11 I-20121 Milano Italy	PRESSER
SOUTHERN	Southern Music Co. 1100 Broadway P.O. Box 329 San Antonio, TX 78292	
SOUTHERN PUB	Southern Music Publishing Co., Pty. Ltd. Sydney, Australia	PEER
SOUTHWEST	Southwest Music Publications Box 4552 Santa Fe, NM 87501	
SPAN.MUS.CTR.	Spanish Music Center, Inc. 4 Division Street P.O. Box 132 Farmingville, NY 11738	
SPEBSQSA	Society for the Preservation & Encouragement of Barber Shop Quartet Singing in America, Inc. 6315 Third Avenue Kenosha, WI 53143-5199	
SPIRE	Spire Editions	FISCHER,C WORLD
SPRATT	Spratt Music Publishers 17 West 60th Street, 8th Fl. New York, NY 10023	PLYMOUTH
ST.GREG.	St. Gregory Publishing Co. 64 Pineheath Road High Kelling, Holt Norfolk, NR25 6RH England	ROYAL
ST. MARTIN	St. Martin Music Co., Inc.	ROYAL
STAFF	Staff Music Publishing Co., Inc. 170 N.E. 33rd St. Ft. Lauderdale, FL 33334	PLYMOUTH
STAINER	Stainer & Bell Ltd. P.O. Box 110, Victoria House 23 Gruneisen Road London N3 1DZ England	SCHIRM.EC
STAMON	Nick Stamon Press 4280 Middlesex Drive San Diego, CA 92116	
STAMPS	Stamps-Baxter Music Publications Box 4007 Dallas, TX 75208	SINGSPIR
STANDARD	Standard Music Publishing, Inc.	
STANGLAND	Thomas C. Stangland Co. P.O. Box 19263 Portland, OR 97280	
STEIN	Edition Steingräber Auf der Reiswiese 9 D-6050 Offenbach/M. Germany	
STILL	William Grant Still Music 22 S. San Francisco Street Suite 422 Flagstaff, AZ 86001-5737	
STIM	STIMs Informationcentral för Svensk Musik Sandhamnsgatan 79 Box 27327 S-102 54 Stockholm Sweden	

Code	Publisher	U.S. Agent
STOCKHAUS	Stockhausen-Verlag Kettenberg 15 D-5067 Kürten Germany	
	Stockhausen-Verlag, U.S. 2832 Maple Lane Fairfax, VA 22030	
STOCKTON	Fred Stockton P.O. Box 814 Grass Valley, CA 95945	
STRONG	Stronghold Publications	ALEX.HSE.
STUD	Studio 224	STUDIO
STUDIO	Studio P/R, Inc.	CPP-BEL
STYRIA	Verlag Styria Schönaugasse 64 Postfach 435 A-8011 Graz Austria	
SUECIA	Edition Suecia	STIM
SUISEISHA	Suiseisha Editions	ONGAKU
SUMMIT	Summit Music Ltd. 38 North Row London W1R 1DH England	
SUMMY	Summy-Birchard Co. 265 Secaucus Road Secaucus, NJ 07096-2037	LEONARD-US
SUOMEN	Suomen Säveltäjät ry (Society of Finnish Composers) Runeberginkatu 15 A SF-00100 Helsinki 10 Finland	
SUPPORT	Support Services 79 South Street P.O. Box 478 Natick, MA 01760	
SUPRAPHON	Supraphon Palackeho 1 CS-112 99 Praha1 Czech Republic	FOR.MUS.DIST. (rental) NEW W
	Svenska Utbildningsförlaget Liber AB see LIBER	
SVERIG	Sveriges Körförbund Box 38014 S-100 64 Stockholm, Sweden	
SWAN	Swan & Co. P.O. Box 1 Rickmansworth, Herts WD3 3AZ England	ARCADIA
SWAND	Swand Publications 120 North Longcross Road Linthicum Heights, MD 21090	
	Swedish Music Information Center see STIM	
SYMPHON	Symphonia Verlag	CPP-BEL
TAUNUS	Taunus	HOFMEISTER-W
TCAPUB	TCA Publications Teacher-Composer Alliance P.O. Box 6428 Evanston, IL 60204	
TECLA	Tecla Editions Soar Chapel Penderyn South Wales CF 44 9JY United Kingdom	

Code	Publisher	U.S. Agent
TEESELING	Muziekuitgeverij van Teeseling Buurmansweg 29B NL-6525 RV Nijmegen Netherlands	
TEMPLETN	Templeton Publishing Co., Inc.	SHAWNEE
TEMPO	Tempo Music Publications 3773 W. 95th Street Leawood, KS 66206	ALEX.HSE.
TEN TIMES	Ten Times A Day P.O. Box 230 Deer Park, L.I., NY 11729	
TENUTO	Tenuto Publications see also TRI-TEN	PRESSER
TETRA	Tetra Music Corp.	PLYMOUTH WESL (rental)
TFS	Things For Strings Publishing Co. P.O. Box 9263 Alexandria, VA 22304	
THAMES	Thames Publishing 14 Barlby Road London W10 6AR England	
THOMAS	Thomas House Publications P.O. Box 1423 San Carlos, CA 94070	INTRADA
THOMI	E. Thomi-Berg Musikverlag Bahnhofstraβe 94A D-8032 Gräfelfing Germany	
THOMP.	Thompson Music House P.O. Box 12463 Nashville, TN 37212	
THOMPS.G	Gordon V. Thompson Music 85 Scarsdale Rd., Ste 104 Don Mills, Ontario M3B 2R2 Canada	OXFORD
TIEROLFF	Tierolff Muziek Centrale P.O. Box 18 NL-4700 AA Roosendaal Netherlands	
TISCHER	Tischer und Jagenberg Musikverlag Nibelungenstraβe 48 D-8000 München 19 Germany	
TOA	Toa Editions	ONGAKU
TONGER	P.J. Tonger, Musikverlag Auf dem Brand 3 Postfach 501865 D-5000 Köln-Rodenkirchen 50 Germany	
TONOS	Editions Tonos Ahastraβe 9 D-6100 Damstadt Germany	SEESAW
TOORTS	Muziekuitgeverij De Toorts Nijverheidsweg 1 Postbus 576 NL-2003 RN Haarlem Netherlands	
TRANSAT.	Éditions Musicales Transatlantiques 151, avenue Jean-Jaures F-75019 Paris France	PRESSER
TRANSCON.	Transcontinental Music Publications 838 Fifth Avenue New York, NY 10021	

Code	Publisher	U.S. Agent
TREKEL	Joachim-Trekel-Verlag Postfach 620428 D-2000 Hamburg 62 Germany	
TRI-TEN	Tritone Press and Tenuto Publications P.O. Box 5081, Southern Station Hattiesburg, MS 39401	PRESSER
TRIGON	Trigon Music Inc.	LORENZ
TRINITY	Trinity House Publishing	CRESPUB
TRIUNE	Triune Music, Inc.	LORENZ
TRN	TRN Music Publishers 111 Torreon Loop P.O. Box 1076 Ruidoso, NM 88345	
TRO	TRO Songways Service, Inc. 11 W. 19th St., Suite 711 New York, NY 10011 see also RICHMOND ORG.	PLYMOUTH
TROY	Troy State University Library Troy, AL 36081	
TUSKEGEE	Tuskegee Institute Music Press	KJOS
U.S.CATH	United States Catholic Conference Publications Office 1312 Massachusetts Avenue N.W. Washington, D.C. 20005	
UBER,D	David Uber Music Department Trenton State College Trenton, NJ 08625	
UFATON	Ufaton-Verlag	ORLANDO
UNICORN	Unicorn Music Company, Inc.	BOSTON
UNION ESP.	Union Musical Ediciones Carrera de San Jeronimo 26 Madrid 14 Spain	SCHIRM.G
UNISONG	Unisong Publishers	PRESSER
UNITED ART	United Artists Group	CPP-BEL PRESSER (rental)
UNITED MUS.	United Music Publishers Ltd. 42 Rivington Street London EC2A 3BN England	PRESSER
UNIV. ALA	University of Alabama Press Box 870380 Tuscaloosa, AL 35487-0380	
UNIV.CAL	University of California Press 2120 Berkeley Way Berkeley, CA 94720	
UNIV.CH	University of Chicago Press 5801 South Ellis Avenue Chicago, IL 60637	
UNIV.CR.	University College - Cardiff Press P.O. Box 78 Cardiff CF1 1XL, Wales United Kingdom	
UNIV.EVAN	University of Evansville Press P.O. Box 329 Evansville, IN 47702	
UNIV.IOWA	University of Iowa Press Iowa City, IA 52242	
UNIV.MIAMI	University of Miami Music Publications P.O. Box 8163 Coral Gables, FL 33124	PLYMOUTH

Code	Publisher	U.S. Agent
UNIV.MICRO	University Microfilms 300 North Zeeb Road Ann Arbor, MI 48106	
UNIV.MINN	University of Minnesota Press 2037 University Avenue S.E. Minneapolis, MN 55455	
UNIV.MUS.ED.	University Music Editions P.O. Box 192-Ft. George Station New York, NY 10040	
UNIV.NC	University of North Carolina Press P.O. Box 2288 Chapel Hill, NC 27514	
UNIV.OTAGO	University of Otago Press P.O. Box 56 Dunedin New Zealand	
UNIV.TEXAS	University of Texas Press P.O. Box 7819 Austin, TX 78712	
UNIV.UTAH	University of Utah Press Salt Lake City, UT 84112	
UNIV.WASH	University of Washington Press Seattle, WA 98105	
UNIVER.	Universal Edition Bösendorfer Straße 12 Postfach 130 A-1015 Wien Austria	EUR.AM.MUS.
	Universal Edition (London) Ltd. 2/3 Fareham Street, Dean Street London W1V 4DU England	EUR.AM.MUS.
UNIVERH	Universal Songs Holland Postbus 305 1200 AH Hilversum Netherlands	GM
UNIVERSE	Universe Publishers 733 East 840 North Circle Orem, UT 84057	PRESSER
UP WITH	Up With People 3103 North Campbell Avenue Tucson, AZ 85719	LORENZ
VAAP	VAAP 6a, Bolshaya Bronnaya St. Moscow 103670,GSP Russia	SCHIRM.G
VALANDO	Valando Music, Inc.	PLYMOUTH
VAMO	Musikverlag Vamö Leebgasse 52-25 Wien 10 Austria	
VAN NESS	Van Ness Press, inc.	BROADMAN
VANDEN-RUP	Vandenhoeck & Ruprecht Theaterstrasse 13 Postfach 3753 D-3400 Göttingen Germany	
VANDERSALL	Vandersall Editions	EUR.AM.MUS.
VANGUARD	Vanguard Music Corp. 357 W. 55th Street New York, NY 10019	
VER.HUIS.	Vereniging voor Huismuziek Utrechtsestraat 77 Postbus 350 NL-3041 CT Ijsselstein Netherlands	

Code	Publisher	U.S. Agent
VER.NED.MUS.	Vereniging voor Nederlandse Muziekgeschiedenis Postbus 1514 NL-3500 BM Utrecht Netherlands	
VEST-NORSK	Vest-Norsk Musikkforslag Postboks 4016, Dreggen N-5023 Bergen Norway	
VIERT	Viertmann Verlag Lübecker Straβe 2 D-5000 Köln 1 Germany	
VIEWEG	Chr. Friedrich Vieweg, Musikverlag Nibelungenstraβe 48 D-8000 München 19 Germany	LEONARD-US SCHIRM.G (rental)
VIKING	Viking Press, Inc. P.O. Box 4030 Church Street Station New York, NY 10261-4030	
VIOLA	Viola World Publications 14 Fenwood Road Huntington Station, NY 11746	
VOGGEN	Voggenrieter Verlag Viktoriastraβe 25 D-5300 Bonn Germany	
VOGT	Musikverlag Vogt & Fritz Friedrich-Stein-Straβe 10 D-8720 Schweinfurt Germany	
VOLK	Arno Volk Verlag	BREITKOPF-W
VOLKWEIN	Volkwein Brothers, Inc.	CPP-BEL
WADSWORTH	Wadsworth Publishing Co. 10 Davis Street Belmont, CA 94002	
WAGENAAR	J.A.H. Wagenaar Oude Gracht 109 NL-3511 AG Utrecht Netherlands	ELKAN,H
WAI-TE-ATA	Wai-te-ata Press Dept. of Music Victoria Univ. of Wellington P.O. Box 600 Wellington, New Zealand	
WALKER	Walker Publications P.O. Box 61 Arnold, MD 21012	
WALKER MUS.PRO.	Walker Music Productions 643 Oenoke Ridge New Canaan, CT 06840	
WALTON	Walton Music Corp.	PLYMOUTH
WARNER	Warner Brothers Publications, Inc. 265 Secaucus Road Secaucus, NJ 07096	CPP-BEL
	Warner-Chappell Music 810 Seventh Avenue New York, NY 10119	
WATERLOO	Waterloo Music Co. Ltd. 3 Regina Street North Waterloo, Ontario N2J 4A5 Canada	
WEHMAN BR.	Wehman Brothers, Inc. Ridgedale Avenue Morris County Mall Cedar Knolls, NJ 07927	

Code	Publisher	U.S. Agent
WEINBERGER	Josef Weinberger Ltd. 12-14 Mortimer Street London W1N 7RD England	BOOSEY CANTORIS BOCK
	Josef Weinberger Neulerchenfelderstrasse 3-7 A-1160 Wien Austria	
WEINTRAUB	Weintraub Music Co.	SCHIRM.G (rental)
WELT	Welt Musik Josef Hochmuth Verlage Hegergasse 21 A-1160 Wien Austria	
WESL	Wesleyan Music Press P.O. Box 1072 Fort George Station New York, NY 10040	
WESSMAN	Wessmans Musikforlag S-620 30 Slite Sweden	STIM
WESTEND	Westend	PETERS
WESTERN	Western International Music, Inc. 3707 65th Avenue Greeley, CO 80634	
WESTMINSTER	The Westminster Press 925 Chestnut Street Philadelphia, PA 19107	
WESTWOOD	Westwood Press, Inc. 3759 Willow Road Schiller Park, IL 60176	WORLD
WHITE HARV.	White Harvest Music Publications P.O. Box 1144 Independence, MO 64051	
WIDE WORLD	Wide World Music, Inc. Box B Delaware Water Gap, PA 18327	
WIEN BOH.	Wiener Boheme Verlag GmbH Sonnenstraβe 19 D-8000 München 2 Germany	
WIENER	Wiener Urtext Edition	EUR.AM.MUS.
WILDER	Wilder	MARGUN
WILHELM	Wilhelmiana Musikverlag see HANSEN-GER	
	William Grant Still Music see STILL	
	Williams School of Church Music see WSCM	
WILLIAMSN	Williamson Music, Inc.	LEONARD-US
WILLIS	Willis Music Co. 7380 Industrial Road Florence, KY 41042	
WILLSHIRE	Willshire Press Music Foundation, Inc.	WESTERN
WILSHORN	Wilshorn	HOPE
WILSON	Wilson Editions 13 Bank Square Wilmslow SK9 1AN England	
WIMBLEDN	Wimbledon Music Inc. 1888 Century Park East Suite 10 Century City, CA 90067	

Code	Publisher	U.S. Agent
WIND MUS	Wind Music, Inc. 153 Highland Parkway Rochester, NY 14620	KALMUS,A
WINGERT	Wingert-Jones Music, Inc. 2026 Broadway P.O. Box 419878 Kansas City, MO 64141	
WISCAS	Wiscasset Music Publishing Company Box 810 Cambridge, MA 02138	
WOITSCHACH	Paul Woitschach Radio-Musikverlag Grosse Friedberger Strasse 23-27 D-6000 Frankfurt Germany	
WOLF	Wolf-Mills Music	WESTERN
WOLLENWEBER	Verlag Walter Wollenweber Schiffmannstrasse 4 Postfach 1165 D-8032 Gräfelfing vor München Germany	FOR.MUS.DIST
WOODBURY	Woodbury Music Co. 33 Grassy Hill Road P.O. Box 447 Woodbury, CT 06798	PRESSER (rental-partial)
WOODWARD	Ralph Woodward, Jr. 1033 East 300 South Salt Lake City, UT 84102	
WOODWIND	Woodwind Editions P.O. Box 457, Station K Toronto, Ontario Canada M4P 2G9	
WORD	Word, Incorporated 3319 West End Avenue Suite 200 Nashville, TN 37203	
WORD GOD	The Word of God Music	SERVANT
WORLD	World Library Publications, Inc. 3815 Willow Road P.O. Box 2701 Schiller Park, IL 60176	
WORLDWIDE	Worldwide Music Services P.O. Box 995, Ansonia Station New York, NY 10023	
WSCM	Williams School of Church Music The Bourne Harpenden England	
WYE	WYE Music Publications	EMERSON
WYNN	Wynn/Music Publications P.O. Box 739 Orinda, CA 94563	
XYZ	Muziekuitgeverij XYZ P.O. Box 338 NL-1400 AH Bussum Netherlands	
YAHRES	Yahres Publications 1315 Vance Avenue Coraopolis, PA 15108	
YBARRA	Ybarra Music P.O. Box Box 665 Lemon Grove, CA 92045	
YORKE	Yorke Editions 31 Thornhill Square London N1 1BQ England	SCHIRM.EC
YOUNG WORLD	Young World Publications 10485 Glennon Drive Lakewood, CO 80226	

Code	Publisher	U.S. Agent
	Yugoslavian Music Information Center see MUSIC INFO	
ZALO	Zalo Publications & Services P.O. Box 913 Bloomington, IN 47402	FRANG
ZANIBON	G. Zanibon Edition Piazza dei Signori, 44 I-35100 Padova Italy	
ZEN-ON	Zen-On Music Co., Ltd. 3-14 Higashi Gokencho Shinjuku-ku Tokyo 162 Japan	EUR.AM.MUS MAGNA D
ZENEM.	Zenemukiado Vallalat	BOOSEY GENERAL
ZENGERINK	Herman Zengerink, Urlusstraat 24 NL-3533 SN Utrecht Netherlands	
ZERBONI	Edizioni Suvini Zerboni Via Quintiliano 40 I-20138 Milano Italy	BOOSEY (rental)
ZIMMER.	Musikverlag Zimmermann Gaugrafenstraβe 19-23 Postfach 940183 D-6000 Frankfurt-am-Main Germany	
ZIMMER.PUBS.	Oscar Zimmerman Publications 4671 State Park Highway Interlochen, MI 49643-9527	
ZINNEB	Zinneberg Musikverlag	LEUCKART
	The Zondervan Corp. see SINGSPIR	
ZURFLUH	Éditions Zurfluh 73, Boulevard Raspail F-75006 Paris France	PRESSER

Advertisements

Index to Advertisers

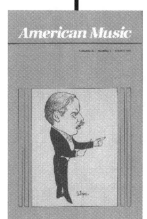
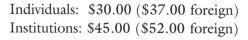

New and Forthcoming Books From The Music Library Association

MLA INDEX SERIES

No. 25: **Analyses of Nineteenth- and Twentieth-Century Music, 1940-85,** compiled by Arthur B. Wenk, 1987. ISBN 0-914954-36-9; $29.00

No. 26: **Opera Performances in Video Format: A Checklist of Commercially Released Performances,** by Charles Croissant, 1992. ISBN 0-914954-43-1; $15.00

No. 27: **The Works of Robert Valentine: A Thematic Catalog,** compiled by J. Bradford Young. (to be published in early 1993).

MLA TECHNICAL REPORTS SERIES

No. 16: **Authority Control in Music Libraries: Proceedings of the Music Library Association Preconference, March 5, 1985,** edited by Ruth Tucker, 1989. ISBN 0-914954-22-3; $22.00

No. 17: **Planning and Caring for Library Audio Facilities,** edited and with a preface by James P. Cassaro, 1989. ISBN 0-914954-38-5; $20.00

No. 18: **Careers in Music Librarianship,** compiled by Carol Tatian, 1990. ISBN 0-914954-41-5; $19.00.

No. 19: **In Celebration of Revised 780: Music in the Dewey Decimal Classification, Edition 20,** compiled by Richard Wursten, 1990. ISBN 0-914954-42-3; $20.00

No. 20: **Space Utilization in Music Libraries,** compiled by James P. Cassaro, 1992. ISBN 0-914954-44-X; $30.00

No. 21: **Archival Information Processing for Sound Recordings,** by David H. Thomas, 1992. ISBN 0-914954-45-8; $33.00.

SPECIAL PUBLICATIONS

Cumulative Five-Year Index to the MUSIC CATALOGING BULLETIN. (to be issued in late 1992).

Music Cataloging Decisions, As Issued by the Music Section, Special Materials Cataloging Division, Library of Congress in the MUSIC CATALOGING BULLETIN through December 1991, indexed and edited by Betsy Gamble, 1992. ISBN 0-914954-39-3; $24.00.

Music Librarianship in America; Papers of a Symposium Held October 5-7, 1989, to Honor the Establishment of the Richard F. French Chair in Music Librarianship at Harvard University, edited by Michael Ochs, 1991. $22.00 (available exclusively through the Music Library Association).

Available from library booksellers or from
The Music Library Association, P.O. Box 487D, Canton, MA 02021.
Membership information is also available from the same address.
MLA members receive a 10% discount on all publications.
Institutions requesting billing will be charged for handling.